The Legal Environment of Business

MICHAEL BIXBY Boise State University
CARYN BECK-DUDLEY Utah State University
PATRICK CIHON Syracuse University

Upper Saddle River, New Jersey 07458

Senior Editor: Linda Schreiber
Assistant Editor: Jennifer Surich
Media Project Manager: Michele Faranda
Senior Marketing Manager: Debbie Clare
Managing Editor (Production): Judy Leale
Production Editor: Lynda P. Hansler
Production Assistant: Keri Jean
Production Manager: Arnold Vila
Associate Director, Manufacturing: Vincent Scelta
Designer: Steve Frim
Design Manager: Patricia Smythe
Interior Design: Robin Hoffman
Cover Design: Donna Wickes
Cover Art: Jennifer Hewitson/SIS, Inc.
Associate Director, Multimedia Production: Karen Goldsmith
Manager, Multimedia Production: Christy Mahon
Composition: Elm Street Publishing Services, Inc.

Library of Congress Cataloging-in-Publication Data

Bixby, Michael B.
The legal environment of business/Michael Bixby, Caryn Beck-Dudley, Patrick Cihon.—1st ed.
p. cm.
Includes index.
ISBN 0-13-019492-1
1. Business enterprises—Law and legislation—United States. 2. Business law—United States. I. Beck-Dudley, Caryn, 1958– II. Cihon, Patrick J. III. Title

KF1355.B59 2001
346.7307—dc21 00-039137

10 9 8 7 6 5 4 3 2 1
ISBN 0-13-019492-1

I would like to dedicate this book to my students and my family. My students continually keep me alert and "on my toes" with their thoughts, comments, and ideas, many of which have become part of the book. The support and encouragement of my family—my wife, Sharon, our sons, Daniel and Matthew, my sister, Norah, and my father, Meredith Bixby, have provided me with the energy and persistence needed to complete this book.

MICHAEL BIXBY

This book is dedicated to my husband, Lynn, my children, Michael and Stacia, and my parents, Malcolm and Sharon Beck.

CARYN BECK-DUDLEY

In appreciation of my co-authors, other friends and colleagues, my family, and dedicated to the memory of my father, John E. Cihon.

PATRICK J. CIHON

ABOUT THE AUTHORS

MICHAEL B. BIXBY is a Professor of Legal Studies in Business at Boise State University, where he has been honored twice in the past six years as "Outstanding Teacher of the Year" in the College of Business. Before joining the Boise State faculty, Professor Bixby practiced law for 11 years. Since then, in addition to writing and presenting more than 25 papers at academic conferences, he has authored 11 articles concerning various legal issues in business for *The Oregon Law Review*, *Willamette Law Review*, *American Business Law Journal*, *Idaho Law Review*, and the *Journal of Public Policy and Marketing*. Professor Bixby is the past president of the Pacific Northwest Business Law Association of Legal Studies in Business. Bixby's undergraduate and law degrees are from the University of Michigan.

CARYN L. BECK-DUDLEY is a Professor of Legal Studies in Business at Utah State University. She has also been a Visiting Professor at the University of Michigan School of Business and the Terry College of Business at the University of Georgia. Professor Beck-Dudley is a past president of the Academy of Legal Studies in Business and is currently chair of the Academy of Legal Studies in Business Task Force on Assessment. She has articles in the *American Business Law Journal*, *Journal of Business Ethics*, *Employee Rights and Responsibilities*, *Journal of Public Policy and Marketing*, *Journal of Energy Law and Policy*, as well as several others. She is a recipient of the Holmes/Cardozo award and Ralph C. Hoeber Award from the Academy of Legal Studies in Business for her research. She was named the College of Business Professor of the Year in 1988.

PATRICK J. CIHON is an Associate Professor of Law and Public Policy at Syracuse University School of Management. He was with the Ontario Ministry of Labour before joining the Syracuse faculty. He received a BA from Pennsylvania State University, an LL.B. from Osgoode Hall Law School of York University in Toronto, and an LL.M. from Yale Law School. He was voted Outstanding Faculty Member by the Syracuse University Association of Graduate Business Students and by the Syracuse Chapter of Beta Gamma Sigma undergraduate honor society. His research interests are in the areas of employment law, labor relations, and employment discrimination law, and he has authored or co-authored a number of books and articles in those fields.

BRIEF CONTENTS

CONTENTS

PREFACE

Welcome to the study of legal issues in business. Just as business students must learn the basic principles of accounting, marketing, economics, finance, management, statistics, and information, so must they master the fundamental knowledge of critical legal and regulatory issues affecting business. As a result of the authors' combined 60 years of experience in teaching and practicing law, *The Legal Environment of Business* presents both practical and academic insight into the primary legal issues that businesspeople need to understand. We believe this text is one that students will read, understand, remember, enjoy, and most importantly, use in their present or future careers.

The Legal Environment of Business will not create lawyers, nor should it. Rather, it will help prepare businesspeople to recognize and avoid legal problems. If each student can avoid one legal problem in the future because of something learned here, this book will have made a worthwhile contribution to the student and to society. Our text will help students address legal problems when they arise, know when to call a lawyer and what to discuss, and know how to participate in the solutions to legal problems.

TARGET AUDIENCE

This textbook is primarily designed for business students who are beginning their study of law. Every aspect of this book has been developed to maximize the "real world" nature of the various legal principles presented. We have tried to take complex material and break it down into bite-sized chunks that can be easily digested. We are attempting to speak directly to the non-law student in a common-sense, practical manner. The coverage of important legal topics, while current and comprehensive, is clear and readable.

CONTENT COVERAGE AND ORGANIZATION

The Legal Environment of Business contains comprehensive coverage of private and public law topics. When possible, we have grouped subjects together in a manner that emulates their evolution as legal principles. For example, our discussion of contracts is followed by the discussion of laws of sales, warranties, and product liability, which represent modern adaptations and expansions of the earlier theories.

This practical approach allows us to demonstrate how and why topics in the law change over time. By doing this we better prepare students to become businesspeople who, by virtue of their understanding of legal evolution, are better prepared to anticipate and plan for future changes.

Among the key topics we address are the following:

- Judicial and alternative forms of dispute resolution (Chapters 2 and 3)
- The Constitution and business (Chapter 4), including recent court decisions that address the "Federalism" cases
- International Law (Chapter 6), including detailed discussions of the European Union, NAFTA, and WTO
- Business ethics (Chapter 7)
- Agency and business organizations (Chapters 8 and 9), including treatment of limited liability partnerships and limited liability companies
- Business torts and business crimes (Chapter 11)
- Real, personal, and intellectual property (Chapter 14), including Internet and cyberspace legal issues
- Environmental law (Chapter 15)
- Employment law (Chapters 19, 20, 21, and 22), including extensive coverage of contemporary legal issues in employment, equal opportunity in employment, and labor management law and regulations.

STUDENT-ORIENTED FEATURES

The Legal Environment of Business contains the following features to help students better understand and retain the material:

Learning Objectives and Outlines begin each chapter and help students organize the chapter content and highlight key content.

Key Terms are defined in the margin as they are introduced in the text and are included in the glossary at the end of the book.

Social/Ethical Issues boxes appear throughout the chapters and raise questions concerning current social and ethical controversies in the legal environment of business. These questions require critical thinking and analysis and are good vehicles for class discussion.

"*A Memo from Your Lawyer*" boxes offer practical advice concerning legal subjects covered in the chapters.

"*In Consultation*" features appear periodically throughout the text and offer students an opportunity to put themselves in business situations dealing with realistic legal issues.

Readings and Cartoons from *The Wall Street Journal*, *U. S. News and World Report*, *EPA Journal*, and other sources help to explain the law and demonstrate its relevance to the business world.

Cases were chosen and edited for each chapter (three and four per chapter) on the basis of relevance, interest, and when possible, currency. While some cases are very recent, others represent classic cases. Each case is one to two pages long and has a Facts/Decision/Case Questions format. The case questions raise several legal and ethical questions designed to assist students in analyzing the case. Unlike in some legal textbooks, the language used in the court cases (while often the court's own) is edited to ensure it includes only words and phrases explained elsewhere in the chapter.

End-of-Chapter Problems raise both legal and ethical issues. Questions often arise from actual court cases, and in those cases the citations are included for optional reference.

Practical Exercises offer a unique learning tool. One of these exercises appears at the end of each chapter and allows students to either independently or collaboratively analyze a hypothetical situation based on the material presented in the chapter. Use in our own classrooms has shown that these "learning-by-doing" exercises can significantly aid students' retention of the material.

Web sites of interest are listed at the end of each chapter, providing students with resources for additional exploration and study.

AACSB STANDARDS

The 1992 revision of the American Assembly of Collegiate Schools of Business (AACSB) standards state that the undergraduate and MBA curricula of all business colleges should provide the following:

> A(n) understanding of perspectives that form the context for business. Coverage should include
> - Ethical and global issues
> - The influence of political, social, legal and regulatory, environmental, and technological issues
> - The impact of demographic diversity on organizations

How does *The Legal Environment of Business* address these issues? First, we thoroughly cover ethical and global issues in law. Chapter 6, *International Law*, discusses the intricacies of doing business beyond the borders of the United States. Chapter 7 is dedicated to ethical theories and their relevance to corporate decision making. This chapter is practical in nature and shows students how to analyze and apply ethical principles to real business situations. Furthermore, both international and ethical issues are addressed in boxed features and cases within the chapters, as well as exercises at the end of each chapter.

Second, political, social, legal and regulatory, environmental, and technological issues are all discussed within relevant chapters. The use of an "evolution of legal topics" organization uniquely demonstrates the interrelationship of law and these other societal influences.

Finally, our emphasis on the practical application of law to the "real world" along with a complete examination of equal opportunity laws sensitizes students to issues involving diversity within organizations. In addition to coverage within the text narrative, issues involving diversity are presented in readings, feature boxes, and cases.

ACKNOWLEDGMENTS

The authors would like to express their appreciation to their families, first and foremost, without whose support, this text would not have been possible. In addition, we received wonderful support from Prentice Hall. Our thanks to Linda Schreiber, our editor, for shepherding us through the process, to Lynda Hansler (Prentice Hall) and Staci Schnurr (Elm Street Publishing Services), our production editors, for their superb handling of all of the production details, to Marilyn Stone, our copyeditor, for her obsessive attention to detail, and to Debbie Clare, our marketing manager, for her dedication to this project.

We would also like to thank our reviewers who have helped to make this book what it is. They are Elizabeth Cameron, Alma College; William McDevitt, St. Joseph's University; and Daphyne Saunders Thomas, James Madison University.

Michael Bixby
Caryn Beck-Dudley
Patrick Cihon

PART 1:

THE GLOBAL, LEGAL, REGULATORY, POLITICAL, AND SOCIAL ENVIRONMENT OF BUSINESS

CHAPTER 1

INTRODUCTION TO LAW

LEARNING OBJECTIVES

After you have read this chapter, you should be able to:

1. Identify several theories of jurisprudence and describe how they affect our understanding of the law.
2. Classify the different types of law.
3. Discuss the sources of law and distinguish between statutory and common law.
4. Read and understand legal cases and answer questions about them.

CHAPTER OUTLINE

At the end of every chapter in this book there will be a "Practical Exercise." These brief scenarios will ask you to discuss and use, in a "real life" situation, some of the terms and concepts explained in the chapter. The situation at the end of this chapter involves a person who has had a difficult day, with many unfortunate happenings. You are asked to analyze some of the legal issues she may face.

WHY STUDY LEGAL ISSUES?

This book examines the most important legal issues affecting business—in other words, the "legal environment" in which American business firms operate. Laws, legal theories, and court decisions affect nearly every aspect of business. Suppose, for example, that Dan, Dorothy, and Matt decide to start a computer repair business during their third year in business school. One of their first decisions will be to select the form of business entity they want to use—a partnership, corporation, or some other form. They then must secure space for their business by purchase or lease, obtain financing through a loan, from investors, or from their own funds, and acquire the equipment they need through loan, purchase, or lease. Of course, they will then have to perform the service (computer repair) that is the function of their business. The three owners may decide to hire employees to perform some services as well. Each of these business functions involves numerous legal issues.

As the business grows, many additional legal issues will arise. These include product liability concerns, occupational safety and environmental requirements, labor and employment laws, interactions with creditors and debtors, collection of debts and bankruptcy, and consumer protection and antitrust laws, to name just a few.

Laws and legal issues are, and likely will always be, a major factor in business decisions. Many of us might wish that there were fewer laws, cases, and administrative regulations influencing business. But since the court system is the arena in which many traditional American doctrines and values have always been enforced, a high volume of cases and a steady outgrowth of new laws and regulations seem inevitable. American society has long valued individual rights, promoted individual responsibility, and steadfastly guaranteed such concepts as "due process of law," "enforcement of promises," and "equal justice for all." The continued development and fine-tuning of these theories through the legal system is unlikely to change in the future.

In addition, the United States Constitution sets forth the basic structure of our government, carefully carving out roles for the executive, legislative, and judicial branches through the concept of the "separation of powers." Generally, the legislative branch enacts laws, the executive branch enforces them, and the judicial branch interprets the laws when there are disputes. This basic structure has remained consistent for more than 200 years, and although we continue to improve its efficiency and to streamline some procedures, the general rules outlined in this book will almost certainly continue for many years to come.

Businesspeople all at some point must deal with the three branches of government. They will almost surely interact with an administrative agency, and perhaps with a local senator concerning some actual or proposed legislation. And, at some point, most businesses must deal with the court system. Throughout the operation of the business, the owner should carefully monitor laws and regulations in order to *avoid* legal problems before they arise. As a businessperson you can throw up your hands and say, "There are too many laws, I just can't stand it!" Or instead you can attempt to gain a better understanding of how the legal system affects business and use this knowledge in a positive and proactive way for the benefit of the individual and the business. It is our hope that after you finish your study of these materials, you will adopt the latter approach.

This book will introduce you to the most critical legal issues and concepts that affect business, so that as businessmen and women you will be better able to:

1. Avoid legal problems.
2. Know when to engage the services of a lawyer.
3. Converse intelligently with an attorney and actively participate in legal decisions that need to be made.

The material examined in this course will also assist you in dealing with important legal issues in other relationships—those between managers and employees within the business; those with other private business firms including suppliers, creditors, and competitors; and interactions with government officials. Much like the introductory courses in accounting, statistics, economics, finance, marketing, and management, this course will not make you an expert in the subject but will provide basic information and education regarding fundamental elements of the topic. With this knowledge, you will be able to make better business decisions today and in the future.

The following cartoon is what this book intends *not* to do.

In order to offer broad coverage of the most important regulations and legal issues that influence business operations, this book has been divided into 22 chapters, grouped according to subject matter. This is a broad course, covering many subjects in fairly quick succession. Although each topic could certainly be explored more deeply (and, in fact, each chapter of this book comprises at least one full semester course in law school), our goal with this textbook is to provide you with significant information regarding a wide range of fundamental and important concepts comprising the "legal environment of business" while leaving the detail work to future classes.

Throughout this textbook, our emphasis is on practical knowledge. We attempt to explain important legal concepts in a clear, understandable fashion. We want students to be able to use this information tomorrow and the next day, in their personal and business dealings. This textbook follows what we call

"Your first responsibility is to prevent people from understanding the law."

From *The Wall Street Journal*, January 25, 1995. Reprinted with permission of Cartoon Features Syndicate.

an "organic" approach. In other words, we attempt to organize the topics in a way that emulates their evolution as legal principles. The early part of the book looks at the origins and sources of law, including a discussion of the various legal systems in the United States and around the world, an examination of the law established by administrative agencies, and the role played by ethics and moral thought in creating and shaping law. In subsequent chapters we will scrutinize a variety of specific legal topics, such as contracts, torts, environmental law, labor and employment law, and many others. But first, an analysis of this thing we call "law" is in order. What is it? Why do we have law? What exactly comprises "the law"?

WHAT IS LAW?

Every society has established rules to govern the conduct of its members. Sometimes these rules are informally developed and passed along verbally by elders to younger persons. In the United States our system of rules is quite formally established, based upon our Constitution, federal and state statutes, administrative regulations, and several hundred years of court decisions that form the basis of much of our law (known as *common law*). Of course, our families, religious training, organizations, and peers also contribute to our beliefs concerning the proper boundaries of conduct. However, American society leans heavily on law to establish and enforce the formal standards of acceptable conduct and to establish a minimum level of behavior expected of its members.

JURISPRUDENCE

jurisprudence: The philosophy of the law.

What is jurisprudence? *Black's Law Dictionary* defines **jurisprudence** as the "science of the law" or the "philosophy of the law." It has often been described as "the study of the philosophies of law." Jurisprudence helps lawyers and judges make decisions in complicated cases.

There are competing jurisprudences in the United States. Occasionally the disagreements among jurisprudences are played out in the popular press, usually when a proposed Supreme Court Justice is testifying in Senate confirmation hearings. Most of the time, however, jurisprudence is not explicitly discussed but must be delineated from court opinions and lawyers' arguments.

positivism: The theory that law is the set of rules adopted by the lawful authority which governs that nation.

By most standards, the predominant jurisprudence in the United States is **positivism** or *legal formalism*. Positivism is organized around the concepts of power, position, and hierarchy, and it refers to laws properly enacted by the appropriate authority in that nation, whether that be a king or a legislature. Positivism is rule and authority based. Moreover, positivism seeks to use something similar to the scientific method to resolve disputes. Therefore, a positivist will look to the exact wording of a statute or past court cases for the authority to determine what the law should be. Citation to previous legal authority is very important for positivist jurisprudence. Citing several cases decided by higher courts or citing the actual language of a statute is common when a judge or lawyer wants to make a positivist argument. Competing jurisprudences are *legal realism*, *law and economics*, *feminist jurisprudence*, *natural law*, *sociological jurisprudence*, *historical jurisprudence*, and *critical legal studies movement*.

Legal realists argue that positivism merely reflects the biases of judges rather than any scientific method. They assert that any set of facts can be manipulated in such a way that a particular judge will not be bound by past authority. The great jurist Oliver Wendell Holmes was a proponent of legal realism. He argued that what was important was an understanding of the background and personality of judges, since in the final analysis the law reflected the bias of the judge who uttered it. He stated, "The prophecies of what the courts will do in fact, and nothing more pretentious, are what I mean by the law."

legal realists: Those who hold that law is simply the body of rules enforced by the courts and society.

Many proponents of the **law and economics movement** are associated with the University of Chicago Law School, and it is therefore often referred to as the Chicago school. This area of jurisprudence focuses on applying free enterprise economics to most areas of the law. One of the first categories in which this occurred was with antitrust law.[1] Antitrust generally has to do with preventing anticompetitive agreements and various other practices by business firms that decrease competition. Almost all antitrust cases are now resolved by looking at an economic analysis of the consequences of proceeding with a particular action. Law and economics proponents have also made inroads in property law. The "greatest good" in law and economics jurisprudence is efficiency, and proponents argue that where moral concepts and efficiency conflict, the case should be resolved in favor of efficiency.

law and economics movement: The theory that law is the set of rules which express the choices of people in a free market system.

Natural law was the predominant jurisprudence in the United States until it lost its hold to positivism around the turn of the century. It is based on the belief that law should reflect morality. Traditional natural law proponents grounded their theories in the belief that a supreme being establishes the law and positivist laws must be judged against this "higher authority." Philosophers such as Aristotle, Plato, Socrates, and Thomas Aquinas have also contributed to the development of natural law theory through analysis of laws and actions as "right or wrong." Many current natural law proponents do not base their system of jurisprudence on a supreme being but on what is in the "common good" without regard to its efficiency. They rely heavily on morality and ethics to make these determinations.

natural law: The theory that law is the basic system of moral principles developed through the power of reasoning, analysis, religion, and philosophy.

Feminist jurisprudence criticizes positivism as perpetuating male domination. It focuses on power, knowledge, morality, and self. The theory maintains that the experiences of men are not necessarily the experiences of women, and therefore when the law views what is reasonable, it may only be asking what is reasonable to men. Feminist jurisprudence questions which underlying assumptions or descriptions of experience are made by the law. How does this affect women both practically and ideologically? In one sexual harassment case, *Ellison v. Brady*, 924 F.2d 872 (9th Cir. 1991), the court held "[w]e adopt the perspective of a reasonable woman primarily because we believe that a gender-blind reasonable person standard tends to be male-biased and tends to systematically ignore the experiences of women." This language is very much reflective of feminist jurisprudence.

feminist jurisprudence: The theory that law has been dominated by males and needs to adjust to more accurately include female views and experiences.

Sociological jurisprudence seeks to understand the law from the basis of its impact on society and how the influence and needs of different groups

sociological jurisprudence: The theory that law is the product of social forces and social movements involving different segments of the population.

[1] This topic will be discussed more fully in Chapter 16.

historical jurisprudence: The theory that law is produced and shaped by important historical facts and developments.

affect the development of law. **Historical jurisprudence** draws upon historical events to explain the law and its place. Both types, however, draw upon social science research to help courts make legal decisions. For example, in *Brown v. Board of Education*, the famous 1954 school desegregation case, the U.S. Supreme Court, when striking down racially segregated schools, relied heavily upon sociological research, which suggested that segregation promoted a feeling of "second-class" status among black children.

SOME IMPORTANT THEORIES OF JURISPRUDENCE

Positivism—Law is the set of rules adopted by the lawful authority that governs the country or jurisdiction.
Legal Realism—The law is merely that body of rules enforced by the courts and by society.
Law and Economics—Law is the set of rules that expresses the choices of people in a free market system.
Natural Law—Law is the basic system of moral principles developed through the power of reasoning and analysis, which may or may not coincide with the laws established by the government.
Sociological—Law is the product of social forces and social movements involving different segments of the population.
Historical—Law is produced and shaped by important historical factors and developments, such as the industrial revolution and the civil rights movement.
Feminism—Law has been largely made and shaped by males, and needs to adjust to more accurately include female views and experiences.
Critical Legal Studies—Laws, particularly those that represent positivist views, are rules established by people currently in positions of power and who seek to maintain their place in society.

Critical Legal Studies Movement: The theory that laws, particularly those which represent a positivist view, are rules established by those who are currently in power.

The **Critical Legal Studies (CLS) Movement** may not refer to itself as a jurisprudence at all. It does, however, see positivism as responsible for maintaining those who are currently in power. Proponents of CLS rely heavily on disciplines such as sociology and anthropology for their studies of power, position, and wealth. Its advocates are highly critical of the status quo and seek to expose legal doctrines reinforcing the current power structure. Many of the leading CLS proponents are professors at major American law schools who have raised serious issues and generated much discussion concerning traditional forms of legal education in recent years.

When reading this text and the cases that are excerpted, pay particular attention to the type of jurisprudence that is actually being used. For example, an opinion may well appear to reflect positivism when in fact it is making a natural law argument.

CLASSIFICATIONS OF LAW

While jurisprudence takes an in-depth look at the underlying basis and philosophy of law, it is also possible to classify types of law and legal issues according to different aspects of their development and function.

CIVIL AND CRIMINAL LAW

The law can usually be classified as either criminal law or civil law. **Criminal law** concerns violations of the rules established by society that set the minimum acceptable standards for behavior. Criminal laws are all statutory—the elements of a crime must be precisely stated by the legislature, and the law must provide a penalty, or a range of penalties, for violations. Since criminal laws are meant to enforce society's standards, violation of such a law results in punishment of the criminal—generally by time in jail and/or a fine—but not necessarily compensation to the victim. In a legal sense, the victim is just one of the witnesses called at the trial to testify that the defendant broke a federal, state, or local criminal law.

criminal law: Violation of a specific statute, enacted by the legislature to protect society, which carries penalties such as a fine or imprisonment.

Criminal cases are always brought by a governmental prosecutor, not an individual, and the decision whether to bring a case, to drop the case, or to settle the case (called plea bargaining in criminal matters) is made by the prosecutor. The case heading is titled something like *The People of the State of California v. Jones* or *The People of the United States of America v. Smith* to indicate that the prosecutor is actually representing the state, rather than any one individual. The chief county prosecutor—often called the District Attorney or County Prosecutor—is normally elected and therefore must be responsive to the general population. Although the top prosecutors always stay in touch with the "victims" of the crime, it should be clearly understood that the criminal law process is designed to enforce society's rules against a lawbreaker, and not primarily to compensate the victim of crime.

Civil cases, on the other hand, are brought by one individual or firm against another. Civil cases can be concerned with contracts, torts (any wrongful action that causes injury to another), labor or employment issues, divorce and family matters, and many other topics. Since they are not criminal, no one will go to jail regardless of the result of the case. Society is not represented by a prosecutor. Instead, the two parties both argue their case, citing previous cases and relevant statutes to support their legal position. Cases are brought by **plaintiffs**, not prosecutors. If the plaintiff wins the civil case, the result may be an award of money damages, or an injunction or some other court order directing the **defendant** to stop doing something.

civil law: The body of law that allows one person or firm to sue a second person or firm for physical or economic damages caused by the second party.

plaintiff: The person who files a civil lawsuit against another.

defendant: The person against whom a civil or criminal lawsuit is brought.

SOCIAL/ETHICAL ISSUES

Do you think that a county or state prosecutor should owe primary duty to the victim of crime? What if there are many victims? What if it is a so-called victimless crime? (Prostitution, gambling, and speeding are examples.) In several states, there are victims' rights movements underway, which aim to increase the crime victim's role in criminal cases and to make it mandatory that victims receive adequate compensation as part of the criminal sentence. As will be discussed in the next section, civil cases can be filed by an injured person to gain compensation from one who has caused the injury. Should criminal actions get more involved in the compensation issue? What might be the positive and negative effects of such a development?

Usually no connection or relation exists between a civil case and a criminal case—a legal action is one type or the other. However, one event sometimes results in *both* civil and criminal cases. For example, suppose that Tom drinks four beers and then drives his car negligently in a way that strikes Julie's car. Following an investigation by the police, or a complaint by Julie, the prosecutor may decide to charge Tom with the crime of Driving Under the Influence of Alcohol (DUI). In order to prevail in a criminal case, the prosecutor must convince the judge or jury that all the elements of the crime (as specified in the statute) have been met **beyond all reasonable doubt**. If any member of the jury has any reasonable doubt about whether Tom committed any element of the crime, Tom should be found *not guilty*. If Tom is convicted at a criminal trial, he may be sent to jail or ordered to pay a fine to the state or both. Sometimes the defendant is ordered, as part of the sentence, to pay some sort of costs and/or expenses (called *restitution*) to the victim, but this amount is usually far less than full compensation.

beyond all reasonable doubt: The standard of proof in a criminal case, which requires the prosecutor to prove each essential element to the point where no member of the jury has any reasonable doubt as to its existence.

If Julie wants to receive complete compensation for her injuries, medical expenses, lost wages, or damage to her car, she must file a separate civil case against Tom. This case will not be connected with the criminal case at all. It will be heard at a different time, in a different court, and the decision will hinge on principles of negligence law (which have developed through common law) and not on whether a criminal statute of the state was broken. To win this case, Julie will merely need to prove that Tom was negligent by a **preponderance of the evidence**—that is, by more than 50 percent of the evidence—a much lower standard than is necessary in a criminal case. If Julie wins the case, Tom will be ordered to pay her money damages, as determined by the judge or jury. He will not be sent to jail, however, no matter how the civil case results.

preponderance of the evidence: Evidence which is of greater weight or more convincing than the evidence which is offered in opposition to it; the standard of proof in a civil case.

SUBSTANTIVE AND PROCEDURAL LAW

Another way to categorize law is to divide it into *substantive* and *procedural* parts. We will be studying primarily **substantive law** in this textbook—the key legal principles that govern a variety of different subject areas affecting business. For example, this book will examine the three main legal theories by which a manufacturer can be held liable for defective products and the essential features of each. The text will also analyze the legal requirements of the five or six most important environmental laws, the major labor laws, the main provisions of the laws regulating the sale of securities, and so on. These are substantive legal issues.

substantive law: The legal principles that define one's rights in specific subject areas.

In actual cases, however, **procedural law** issues play a prominent part. For example, it is often critical whether a case is filed in the proper court and whether the complaint and answer were filed within the appropriate time period. When the case goes to trial, the result may be affected by the calling of witnesses, rulings of the judge concerning direct and cross-examination, and the objections of the attorneys to certain questions and introduction of evidence. Procedural legal issues such as these are absolutely involved in most cases, but they are more properly dealt with by the lawyers in the case. So although Chapter 3 outlines the typical court system and provides some general information about legal procedures, this textbook is written for business

procedural law: The legal rules governing court processes and procedures.

students, and our primary focus is on substantive legal issues of importance to business, rather than procedural "rules of the game."

ACTIONS "AT LAW" AND "IN EQUITY"

When a business becomes involved in a legal dispute with another business firm or an individual, most often the result sought is an award of money damages as compensation for the loss suffered due to the actions of the other. In fact, the early English Courts of Law only had the power to award money damages as a remedy. The legal actions filed were called **actions at law**.

actions at law: Civil cases in which the plaintiff seeks money damages.

However, in some cases the aggrieved party wanted or needed something other than money. For example, suppose that Harold enters into a contract with June in which her business agrees to purchase a 12,000-acre commercial site. However, June later decides she does not want to go through with the agreement. It may well be that what Harold most wants is not money damages for breach of the contract, but that June be ordered to fulfill the terms of the contract to which she agreed. When the early English Law Courts could not provide such relief, the king began to refer such matters to his important advisor, the chancellor. Thus, another court system was created in order to provide such equitable relief. For hundreds of years the Courts of Law and the Chancery courts remained separate in England.

Today the powers of **equity**—to order a defendant to take or not to take some action—are a regular feature of most U.S. courts. In other words, most U.S. courts have both law and equity powers. In the preceding example, Harold may file a court action against June, and if he proves the existence of a valid contract, he can ask the court for a decree of **Specific Performance**, an equitable order directing the defendant to fulfill the terms of a contract.

actions in equity: Civil cases in which the plaintiff seeks to have the court order the defendant to do something or to not do something.

Probably the most commonly sought equitable order is the *injunction*, which is an order issued by a court directing a party *not* to do something. It is sought by a plaintiff who wants the court to prevent another party from taking some particular action before it occurs. For example, if the highway department plans to cut down a row of trees in front of your house, you might rather have the court order the department not to cut down the trees instead of awarding you damages after they are taken out. Other equitable orders include the *temporary restraining order* (a short-term injunction, used to preserve the status quo until the court can schedule a full hearing) and **rescission** (a court order canceling a contract).

specific performance: A court order which requires a party to perform a contract as agreed.

rescission: A court order cancelling a contract.

To receive an equitable order, however, the plaintiff must specifically request such relief when the case is filed, or soon thereafter. In general, courts prefer to award money damages, and equitable relief will only be given if the court is convinced that money damages are "inadequate" to fully compensate the plaintiff. Equity courts were designed to de-emphasize legal technicalities and promote fairness. The chancellor was given considerable flexibility to fashion the relief necessary in order to produce a fair result. In furtherance of this goal, various doctrines previously developed by the English Chancery courts still govern use of the equitable powers. For example, a plaintiff seeking equity must "come into equity with clean hands," and "he who desires equity must do equity." That is, the person seeking the equitable order (injunction, for example) must not use the court to take advantage of someone or to perpetuate a wrong. There are no juries in cases seeking equitable orders, and thus all decisions are made by the judge.

SOURCES OF LAW

THE U.S. CONSTITUTION

In the United States, our hierarchy of legal authority begins with the U.S. Constitution. This amazing document, written in the summer of 1787, established the powers and duties of our federal government, divided them into three branches, and also set out, in general terms, the roles of the federal and state governments. Four years later, largely in response to concerns raised during the debate for ratification of the Constitution, the first 10 amendments, known as the Bill of Rights, were added. These amendments set forth certain basic individual rights with which the government may not interfere (freedom of speech, freedom of press, freedom of religion, the right to be protected against unreasonable searches and seizures, and others). We will explore all of these issues in more depth in Chapter 4 of this book. At this early point in the book, our analysis will only examine how the Constitution, federal statutes, common law, administrative regulations, and court interpretations of all these legal sources produce law.

HOW TO READ AND UNDERSTAND LEGAL CASES

In each chapter of this book there will be a few actual legal cases interspersed with the discussion of legal principles in the text. For example, when we study contract law, there will be cases in the chapter in which courts have ruled on a contract dispute between two parties. The cases you will read have been edited by the authors of this book to make them easier to read than the original decision rendered by the court. Although much of the language of the judge will be retained, a significant amount has been deleted, since court decisions use many words and concepts not explained in this textbook.

Each case included in this textbook has been carefully selected by the authors to help explain a particular point of law addressed in the chapter. Not surprisingly, an excerpted case dealing with a particular legal issue usually follows directly after the text discussion of that issue. The purpose of including cases is to give you a better understanding of how the precise legal point being examined applies in a factual situation as you read and analyze each case.

Each case in this textbook will begin with a statement of "Facts." This section provides the history of the actions of each party that led up to the lawsuit. For example, the facts might include the analysis and determination of such issues as whether Arthur dumped hazardous waste onto Hillary's lawn or whether Sandra rode her bicycle without any brakes when she ran into Thomas. These are factual issues, which will play an important role in the outcome after being combined with appropriate legal principles. Almost all of the cases in this book are decisions of *appellate* courts, which are reviewing the result of a trial held in a lower court. The "Facts" section will conclude with a description of what type of lawsuit was filed and the decision of the lower court.

The second section of each excerpted case is called the "Decision." This portion describes the legal issues that were considered by the appellate court, the arguments of the parties, the decision made by the court, and most importantly, the rationale for the decision—in other words, the legal principles upon which it was based. As you read the cases, it is very important to ascertain and analyze the reasons for the decision. In this way, you will see how legal principles apply to actual cases, so that you can be better prepared to predict the results of future legal controversies—some of which may involve you!

Finally, every case will end with a few questions, called "Case Questions," to help you focus on and analyze key issues in the case, and to provide a starting point for class discussion.

The heading of each case (called the **citation**) gives the name of the parties, an abbreviation indicating the court which is making the decision reported here, and the year in which the decision was made. Each citation also contains the volume number of the set of books containing the case and the page of the volume on which the case begins. For example, the citation *Smith v. Jones*, 5 Ill. 234 (1954) indicates that the case *Smith v. Jones* was decided by the Illinois Supreme Court in 1954 and can be found in Volume 5 of the Illinois Reports on page 234.

case citation: The heading of a court case, which contains the name of the parties, the volume and page of the set of books where it can be found, the court, and year of the decision.

In many cases there are several plaintiffs (those who are bringing the case) and defendants (those against whom the case is brought), but the citation only uses the names of the first plaintiff and first defendant. The citation "U.S." means the case was decided by the U.S. Supreme Court. The citation with "F.2d" or "F.3d" in the middle means that the case was decided by a federal (F) appeals court.

STATUTORY LAW AND STATUTORY INTERPRETATION

One of the primary functions of the court system is to interpret the meaning of laws enacted by Congress and the states. The Constitution, our most fundamental source of law, sets forth in graceful and timeless language the relationship between U.S. citizens and their government and establishes certain fundamental rights of individuals. The phrases used are general, yet they establish clear boundaries on government intrusion into individual rights. For example, part of the Fifth Amendment contains this language:

> *No person shall be deprived of life, liberty, or property, without due process of law; nor shall private property be taken for public use, without just compensation.*

Although this language spells out certain basic rights of U.S. citizens, it obviously is too broad to indicate the precise result in any one case. Therefore, Congress and the state legislatures have enacted thousands of laws to specify in greater detail the legal rights and obligations of the citizens and the government.

statute: A law enacted by the U.S. Congress or by a state legislature.

Laws that are enacted by a legislature are called **statutes**. On the federal level, enacting laws is the primary function of Congress, and of course each state has its own legislature. These bodies meet regularly (some people think they meet much too regularly!) and, after hearing ideas and requests from their constituents, introduce bills that are then studied and debated and may be enacted into law. These statutes may later be amended or repealed completely by the legislative body that enacted them. Cities and towns also have the power to enact statutory laws governing their jurisdictions, and these laws are usually called **ordinances**.

ordinance: A law enacted by a city or town council.

statutory interpretation: The power of courts to interpret laws enacted by legislatures.

Although Congress or a state legislature may have thought it had plainly stated what was intended when a statute was enacted, very often the exact meaning of a law will not be perfectly clear when it is applied to a difficult factual situation. Therefore, one of the main roles courts perform is **statutory interpretation**.

Although statutes are more definite than Constitutional provisions, the exact meaning of such laws is often not clear until the courts have ruled on cases raising particular issues. One of the most important roles played by courts is interpreting how a statute passed by Congress or a state legislature should apply to a specific fact situation. The following case illustrates how a federal appellate court interpreted a federal law dealing with one of the many important "cyberlaw" issues currently being raised.

ZERAN V. AMERICA ONLINE

129 F. 3d 327 4th Cir. (1997)

FACTS

A short time after the bombing of the federal building in Oklahoma City in April 1995, a message was posted anonymously on an America Online (AOL) bulletin board advertising "Naughty Oklahoma T-Shirts." The posting advertised the sale of shirts featuring offensive and tasteless slogans celebrating the tragic bomb blast, which killed 168 persons. The ad stated that interested buyers should call "Ken" at a phone number in Seattle. The phone number given was the actual number of Mr. Kenneth Zeran, who had nothing to do with the posting and most definitely had no such T-shirts for sale.

During the following few weeks, Mr. Zeran received hundreds of phone calls and voice mail messages, almost all expressing extreme anger and outrage over his alleged actions. These calls caused him a great deal of distress. He notified AOL by telephone, letters, and e-mail about the bogus posting and harassment and asked AOL to immediately remove it and issue a public retraction. Although AOL did remove the original posting (the parties dispute how soon this occurred), soon thereafter, the unknown prankster posted another message advertising new T-shirts with more offensive slogans related to the Oklahoma City bombing, again giving Mr. Zeran's number and also stating, "Please call back if busy."

For the next few days, Mr. Zeran's phone rang almost every two minutes with irate messages. Meanwhile the perpetrator of the hoax continued to post new messages on AOL, advertising several new distasteful items (fictitious) such as bumper stickers and key chains celebrating the Oklahoma City massacre and again giving Mr. Zeran's phone number. An Oklahoma City radio station read the messages on the air and encouraged listeners to call Mr. Zeran to express their outrage. During the ensuing days, Zeran was deluged with even more calls, including several death threats. Finally an Oklahoma City newspaper ran an article exposing the T-shirt ads as a hoax, and the radio station issued an apology. The number of calls to Mr. Zeran's home then decreased to about 15 per day.

Mr. Zeran, a 51-year-old entrepreneur who worked out of his home, was the victim of a terrible trick. "Someone pulled a sick joke," he later stated. "It was incredible. One minute I and the entire nation were grieving over the bombing, and the next thing you know, I was associated with it." In 1996, Mr. Zeran sued AOL, alleging that the Internet service provider (ISP) had been negligent in its slowness in removing the series of harmful postings after he had repeatedly notified it that the messages were a hoax. The federal district court later dismissed the suit, holding that the federal Communications Decency Act (CDA) barred the suit. Mr. Zeran then appealed to the Fourth Circuit Court of Appeals.

DECISION

In considering Mr. Zeran's argument that the ISP should be held liable for negligence, the Court of Appeals had to consider the meaning and interpretation of Section 230 of the CDA. This section states, "No provider or user of an interactive computer service shall be treated as the publisher or speaker of any information provided by another information content provider."

Mr. Zeran argued that this section of the CDA was not intended to provide blanket immunity to ISPs but to apply only when an ISP acts in good faith to block material that causes harm. "Unless you can hold them [ISPs] accountable through civil liability . . . there is no way to induce them to carry out their responsibilities in blocking defamatory messages," said Zeran's attorney. [*Defamation* is a legal theory—to be discussed fully in Chapter 11—that imposes liability on someone who makes or repeats false and damaging statements publicly about another person. The two primary types of defamation are libel (written) and slander (oral).]

The plaintiff further argued that the immunity granted by Congress in Section 230 was only intended to apply to "publishers" and that AOL was a cyberspace "distributor," similar to a vendor or bookseller that deals in magazines and books created by others. Although news distributors cannot generally be held liable for defamatory statements in the materials they sell, a distributor can be held liable when it has notice that it is distributing statements that are false and harmful, and does not take appropriate action, as Mr. Zeran had alleged in this case.

The Fourth Circuit Court of Appeals, however, rejected Mr. Zeran's arguments. Chief Judge Wilkinson wrote that the "plain language" of Section 230 created "a federal immunity to any cause of action that would make service providers liable for information originating with a third party user of the service." The court stated that Section 230 precluded courts from entertaining claims that would place a computer service provider in a publisher's role. "Thus, lawsuits seeking to hold a service provider liable for its exercise of a publisher's traditional editorial functions—such as deciding whether to publish, withdraw, postpone or alter content—are barred," wrote Judge Wilkinson. The court noted:

The purpose of this statutory immunity is not difficult to discern. Congress recognized the threat that tort-based lawsuits pose to freedom of speech in the new and burgeoning internet medium. The imposition of tort liability on service providers for the communications of others represented, for Congress, simply another form of intrusive government regulation of speech. Section 230 was enacted, in part, to maintain the robust nature of internet communication and, accordingly, to keep government interference in the medium to a minimum.

The appellate court also rejected Zeran's argument that AOL should be treated as a "distributor" rather than a publisher, finding that such liability was a "subset" of publisher liability. Once AOL received notice from Zeran about the false nature of the posting, it was put into the role of a publisher since AOL then had to decide whether to publish, edit, or withdraw the posted notices. AOL had argued in the case that it had 10 million subscribers creating millions of messages on its bulletin boards every day. Unlike a newspaper, it would be impossible for a service provider such as AOL to check all of its third-party ads and postings for accuracy. Moreover, AOL stated in its court briefs that if the company were subject to liability under Mr. Zeran's theory, it might be forced to get out of the bulletin board business altogether.

For the reasons stated, the Fourth Circuit Court of Appeals affirmed the dismissal of Mr. Zeran's case. He asked the U.S. Supreme Court to accept the case, but his request was denied.

CASE QUESTIONS

1. What federal statute was involved here?
2. Why did Congress provide immunity from lawsuits to ISPs?
3. What reasons did Mr. Zeran give to support his argument that AOL should be treated as a "distributor"?
4. Why did the appellate court rule that AOL should be treated as a "publisher"?
5. Do you agree with the decision's main point—that an ISP should not be responsible for postings made on its service?

Another important part of the Constitution, the Commerce Clause (Art. I, Sect. 8, cl. 3) provides that "[t]he Congress shall have Power . . . to regulate Commerce . . . among the several States." Although this statement contains an express grant of a specific power to the federal government, it has long been understood to have a negative aspect as well. Although states have the power to enact binding laws within their jurisdictions in order to promote the health and welfare of their citizens, numerous cases have held that, by implication, the Commerce Clause acts to prohibit the states from enacting laws that "discriminate against" or "unduly burden" the interstate flow of articles of commerce. The courts deciding these cases reason that the power to regulate such commerce resides with the federal government. Thus, courts often have to decide if a statute passed by a state legislature is unconstitutional because it restricts interstate commerce. In doing so, the court must interpret the meaning and effect of the state statute.

One recent U.S. Supreme Court case decided whether an Oregon law regarding the fees charged for disposal of solid waste conflicted with the provisions of the Commerce Clause. It is instructive to see how the Supreme Court considered and interpreted the Constitution, the Oregon statute, and previous court decisions in rendering its opinion in the next case.

OREGON WASTE SYSTEMS, INC. V. STATE OF OREGON

511 U.S. 93, 114 S. Ct. 1345 (1994)

FACTS

The state of Oregon enacted a comprehensive statute regulating the disposal of solid wastes within its borders, which is administered by the Oregon Department of Environmental Quality. To assist in funding this agency, Oregon imposes a wide range of fees on landfill operators. In 1989 the Oregon Legislature passed a law adding a "surcharge" on "every person who disposes of solid waste generated out-of-state in a disposal site." The surcharge was set at $2.25 per ton by the administrative agency, which meant that waste from the state of Washington was charged $3.10 per ton by the landfill operator, while that from Oregon was charged $0.85 per ton.

The law was challenged by an Oregon landfill operator (Oregon Waste Systems, Inc.) and a company that transports waste by barge from one county in Washington to the Oregon landfill owned by Waste Systems. They argued that the law and the fee impermissibly discriminated against interstate commerce in violation of the Commerce Clause. The Oregon Court of Appeals and the Oregon Supreme Court upheld the law on the basis that the surcharge was justified as a "compensatory cost." The case was then appealed to the U.S. Supreme Court.

DECISION

In an opinion written by Justice Clarence Thomas, the Supreme Court reversed the decision of the Oregon Supreme Court and held that the state imposition of a larger tax on solid waste from out of Oregon was a violation of the "negative aspect" of the Commerce Clause of the U.S. Constitution.

The Supreme Court looked back to the writing of the Constitution and the purposes of the Interstate Commerce Clause, which gave the power to regulate such commerce to the federal government. "The Framers granted Congress plenary authority over interstate commerce in the conviction that in order to succeed, the new Union would have to avoid the tendencies toward economic Balkanization[2] that had plagued relations among the Colonies and later among the States under the Articles of Confederation." The Court quoted language from a 1949 Supreme Court case, which stated that "This principle that our economic unit is the Nation, which alone has the gamut of powers necessary to control the economy . . . has as its corollary that the states are not separable economic units." Justice Thomas even cited Federalist Paper No. 42, written by James Madison, at one point in the opinion.

By a 7-2 majority, the Supreme Court found that the Oregon law imposing the surcharge only on out-of-state solid waste was clearly discriminatory against interstate commerce. "As we use the term here," Justice Thomas stated, "discrimination . . . simply means differential treatment of in-state and out-of-state economic interests that benefits the former and burdens the latter." The court noted that it was "obvious" that the fee was discriminatory, since waste from other states was charged approximately three times more than in-state waste.

The only possible justification for such a discriminatory fee would be that it "advances a legitimate local purpose that cannot be adequately served by reasonable nondiscriminatory alternatives." Although such justifications are sometimes allowed, they will be looked at with the "strictest scrutiny," said the court. Extra fees might have been justified if, for example, (1) the out-of-state waste actually caused higher costs for Oregon than in-state waste or (2) if there were particular health and safety concerns posed by out-of-state waste. Such arguments were not made in this case, however.

Instead, the state of Oregon argued that the additional fees for out-of-state solid waste were necessary as a "compensatory tax" so that shippers of such waste paid their "fair share" of the costs imposed on Oregon. Several previous case decided by the Supreme Court recognized that interstate commerce should "pay its own way" and pay its "just share" of state tax burdens. However, other cases stated that this principle did not allow states to exact "more than a just share" from interstate commerce. In a 1981 case the Supreme Court had allowed a tax on interstate commerce that was roughly approximate to a "substantially similar" tax on intrastate commerce in order to equalize the situation. However, there was no such tax in

[2] To "Balkanize" means to break up into small hostile states, as the Balkan states did during the Balkan wars (1912–13).

the Oregon case to justify the "compensatory tax." Thus, the tax was illegal and invalid under the Commerce Clause.

DISSENTING OPINION

Chief Justice Rehnquist, joined by Justice Blackmun (an unusual alliance of the most conservative and most liberal justices), dissented from the majority opinion.[3]

In this case, the dissenters argued that the Supreme Court opinion ignored the fact that landfill space is evaporating as solid waste accumulates. Justice Rehnquist pointed out that Americans had generated nearly 196 million tons of municipal solid waste in 1990, which was expected to increase to 222 million tons by the year 2000. Finding environmentally safe disposal sites is a serious problem, which is getting worse. Rehnquist termed the majority opinion "myopic" in that it did not recognize that the state of Oregon had suffered a loss and had incurred additional costs when it accepted other states' waste. He argued that the purposes of the Commerce Clause were not met by striking down the additional tax here, since the states were not competing to get waste into their states. Rehnquist asserted that states that did not have adequate landfill space would use this decision to avoid the significant costs of developing, regulating, and cleaning up such sites, while their companies disposed of waste in neighboring states.

[3] In the Supreme Court and all U.S. appellate courts, decisions do not need to be unanimous but are made by majority vote. Often those judges or justices on the losing side decide to set out their reasons for not joining the court opinion in what is called a "dissenting opinion."

CASE QUESTIONS

1. What are the main purposes of the Interstate Commerce Clause in the U.S. Constitution?
2. How did the Supreme Court integrate the language of the Constitution and its purpose, the Oregon law and its purpose, previous case precedents, and logic to reach its conclusion?
3. What are *interstate commerce* and *intrastate commerce*? Why do you think the framers of the Constitution gave Congress (the federal government) the power to regulate interstate commerce?
4. What is the main argument of the dissenting justices? Do you agree? Why do justices write dissenting opinions?

ADMINISTRATIVE RULES AND REGULATIONS

Just as statutes are more specifically drawn than constitutions, so are administrative regulations more precise than statutes. For example, when Congress enacts a law concerning regulation of pollution in rivers and lakes, the statute will probably provide that the discharge of hazardous substances into waterways is illegal. But the statute will not normally state exactly what types of substances will violate the law, nor the exact amounts and over what period of time. Instead, Congress will typically put a clause right in the statute, delegating the power to make detailed regulations covering these matters to an administrative agency. In this case, the agency will likely be the Environmental Protection Agency (EPA), which has a large staff with expertise in various environmental and pollution matters.[4] The EPA will then develop precise rules and regulations concerning the specific actions that are to be prohibited, and those standards, once they are properly issued, will have the force of law.

[4] A detailed discussion of environmental laws is contained in Chapter 15 of this book, and a closer look at the powers and functions of administrative agencies is contained in Chapter 5.

COMMON LAW

Despite the hundreds of statutes passed every year by the Congress and state legislatures and the thousands already "on the books," there are major areas of the law that are not controlled by statutes. For historical reasons, based upon our English legal heritage, a large portion of the legal principles that govern business and personal affairs has developed not from statutes, but from court decisions in individual cases. This body of law is called the **common law**.

common law: Legal theories that arise from precedents established by court decisions, not legislative statutes.

The name *common* came about when English judges in the 13th century began to move from one court to another and to look to the rulings of other jurisdictions in making their decisions, so that the law became more common (similar) across the land. When the Founding Fathers of the United States established our legal system, they followed the English model that permits much of the law to develop solely through court decisions. In fact, not only did we borrow the system of common law development, but most of the major substantive principles that regulate the law of contracts, torts, and agency law today (all of which will be examined in detail later in this book) are primarily based upon English common law doctrines, as modified by more than 200 years of U.S. court decisions.

How does common law actually work? For example, look at contract law, clearly a very important part of the "legal environment" for any business. The principles of law governing contracts have essentially been created by hundreds of court decisions involving individuals where there was a dispute as to whether a valid contract had been created and, if so, whether it had been properly fulfilled. As the courts ruled upon these cases, they wrote about what legal elements were necessary to constitute a valid contract offer or acceptance, or what factors were essential to make a contract binding, or what defenses to a contract action were available to the defendant. The court then applied the rules to the facts of the case at hand and rendered a decision.

Later, other courts facing contract questions used the principles developed in the earlier cases. Each case in this chain expounds upon and modifies the theories further and thus clarifies the law. **Precedents** established in earlier cases are very important in deciding later cases within the same jurisdiction. The principle of ***stare decisis***, "let the decision stand," means that decisions establishing legal principles made by higher courts in one jurisdiction must be followed and respected in subsequent decisions by lower courts within that jurisdiction. For example, if the Supreme Court of New Jersey rules in a contract case that the law of the state requires that both parties to a contract must promise to do something they were not previously required to do in order for the contract to be enforceable, this principle must be followed in subsequent cases by all lower courts in New Jersey. The entire body of U.S. contract, tort, and agency law, and other subjects as well, has developed in this way through common law evolution.

precedents: Judicial decisions used to establish standards for subsequent similar cases.

***stare decisis*:** The legal principle that decisions of a higher court in previous cases establishing legal theories must be followed by lower courts in that jurisdiction.

SUMMARY

The law is a dynamic subject, consisting of many components from many origins, which greatly affects business and personal actions. The law includes constitutions, statutes, administrative regulations, and common law principles. It is shaped by moral, ethical, historical, sociological, and other forces. It represents society's rules of conduct and provides both tools of control for the powerful and rays of hope and the creation of rights for the less fortunate.

The system of law in the United States has been heavily influenced by the English model, from which we borrowed both structure and legal principles. These precepts have been augmented by the addition of American theories, beginning with the U.S. Constitution, and followed by hundreds of federal, state, and local statutes, administrative regulations, and court interpretations over more than 200 years of this country's history. In addition much of our law comes from the common law, which is based solely on decisions of courts, as each decision adds to principles established in earlier cases.

CHAPTER QUESTIONS

1. In 1989, the oil tanker *Exxon Valdez* ran aground in Prince William Sound, Alaska. A leak in the hull then allowed the discharge of nearly 11 million gallons of crude oil into the pristine bay. Some 14,000 fishing professionals, Alaskan natives, and other businesses sued Exxon, claiming they had lost significant amounts of money and their way of life was changed due to Exxon's negligence. They sought several billion dollars in damages. The U.S. EPA and the state of Alaska also filed criminal charges against Exxon claiming violations of federal and state laws. The ship captain, Joseph Hazelwood, was also charged with operating a ship while under the influence of alcohol. What will be the remedy if the fishing professionals and other businesses win their lawsuit? Is it civil or criminal? What might be the result of the EPA action? the action against Mr. Hazelwood? Are these civil or criminal cases?
2. In the Exxon case, the judge made a ruling prior to the trial that while the fishing professionals could sue for damages for their lost fish harvests, they could not sue for the diminished value of their charter permits, or boats. The judge cited a 67-year-old maritime law and an even older court ruling by Justice Oliver Wendell Holmes for support. In that case Justice Holmes had limited the claims of a steamboat charterer who sued because a ship he had chartered (hired or rented) was damaged while in dry dock. Holmes ruled that the claimant could not sue for economic losses while the boat was laid up because the ship was not his. What type of jurisprudence is at work here? Apply the theories discussed in the chapter to these facts. What would Justice Holmes be likely to say if he were alive today?
3. In 1990 Congress passed a law called the Safe Medical Devices Act, which required health care providers like hospitals and doctors to disclose malfunctions of medical equipment to the Food and Drug Administration (FDA). However, a 1994 Congressional report indicated that since the FDA had not issued any regulations specifically stating exactly who must report what, it appeared that the law was largely being ignored. What type of jurisprudence is involved here? Why do you suppose the administrative agency has not issued regulations? Why does Congress not enforce the law itself?

4. Under the federal law known as the Resource Conservation and Recovery Act, the EPA is authorized to regulate all those who treat, store, or dispose of hazardous waste. Does this law apply to the ash generated by a municipal waste facility that incinerates household waste? [*Chicago, Ill. v. Environmental Defense Fund*, 114 S. Ct. 1588 (1994)] What function is the court performing here?
5. What type of jurisprudence is behind the establishment of laws against murder, rape, and theft? How about the Civil Rights Act of 1964? the Clean Air Act and Clean Water Act? the federal laws prohibiting discrimination in employment on the basis of age and disability?
6. When selecting members of a jury (the process called *voir dire*) the lawyers and the judge ask the potential jury members various questions to determine if they are unbiased or have any preconceived opinions about the case. Those who have a bias or some particular relationship to the case are excused. In addition, since the early days of common law, each side has the right to excuse, for no reason, a certain number of jurors—under what are called "peremptory challenges." In recent years, the Supreme Court held that use of peremptory challenges to remove all black jurors in one case [*Batson v. Kentucky*, 476 U.S. 79 (1986)] and all male jurors in another case [*J.E.B. v. Alabama*, 114 S. Ct. 1419 (1994)] was barred by the Constitution. Does this decision relate to procedural or substantive law? Do you think a jury might actually reach a different conclusion in a certain type of case if there were no minorities on the jury panel or if it were an all-male or all-female jury?
7. If the environmental action group Greenpeace files a lawsuit attempting to prevent an oil company from building an oil rig in the ocean off the California coast, what sort of remedy will it probably seek? Is this an action at law or in equity? What standard of proof will the plaintiffs need to establish in order to convince the judge to grant their request?
8. What is the purpose of the Commerce Clause of the U.S. Constitution? In what situations may a state regulate interstate commerce? Do any situations exist in which a state can impose an additional charge on out-of-state companies (as Oregon was not allowed to do in the *Oregon Waste Systems* case)?
9. What is the citation of the *Zeran* case? What court made the decision? What exactly does each number mean? What is the citation of the *Oregon Waste Systems* case? What do these numbers mean?
10. What is the difference between legal principles that are developed through common law and those that are established through statutes? Which type provides more stability and predictability? more flexibility? Why?

PRACTICAL EXERCISE

[*Note to students*: Each chapter will end with a practical exercise designed to enhance learning through the preparation of a written product, based on the material in the chapter. We hope that the exercises are interesting for you to do as well.]

Mary leaves her dormitory room to go shopping at the mall. While she waits for the bus, she gets into an argument with Kevin and shoves him just before getting on the bus. Kevin's head hits a tree and she can see blood coming from his nose as the bus pulls away. She shouts, "Have a nice day!" as the bus pulls away.

While shopping at the mall, she puts a pair of diamond earrings into her pocket in a store because her hands are full. She forgets them and, after paying for other merchandise, leaves the store. Shortly thereafter, Mary is apprehended by a store security guard who accuses her of shoplifting. She is taken to a back room in the store, where she produces the earrings and attempts to explain that it was just an honest mistake. The store personnel keep her in this room for over three hours, shouting at her in a loud voice and threatening to hit her if she does not "tell the truth." Her requests to make a phone call are refused, despite the fact that there is a state law requiring stores that apprehend people for shoplifting to allow them to make two phone calls and to hold them no longer than two hours. Eventually, a police officer arrives and charges her with shoplifting.

Prior to her problems at the mall, Mary went to Linda's Dress Shop and ordered a dress for a price of $300 to be specially made for her to wear to the college formal. Linda promised to have the dress ready in one week. However, after she got home, Mary had second thoughts about the dress, and two days later she called Linda to cancel the order. Linda said she had started on the dress, and the deal could not be canceled.

Mary has clearly had, in the words of a famous children's book by Judith Viorst, a "very bad, no good day." As Mary's friend, you decide to provide her with a written list of the various legal problems she may have encountered. Please list them, and discuss whether they are criminal or civil, whether they involve common law or a statutory law, and whether they may call for "in equity" or "at law" remedies.

FURTHER INFORMATION

www.findlaw.com
A large Web site devoted to law and legal issues.

www.law.cornell.edu
Another very large legal site with links to many others.

www.uncle-sam.com
Great American Web Site helps the user understand U.S. government information.

CHAPTER 2

THE LEGAL SYSTEM IN THE UNITED STATES

LEARNING OBJECTIVES

After you have read this chapter, you should be able to:

1. Describe the organization of the state and federal court systems.
2. Discuss the factors involved in deciding which court may hear and decide a case, including jurisdiction, venue, standing, and preemption.
3. List situations requiring professional legal advice.
4. Outline the issues to consider when choosing a lawyer, including the size of the firm, fees, and ethical issues.
5. Identify several methods of alternate dispute resolution.

CHAPTER OUTLINE

I. State Court Systems
II. The Federal Court System
III. Jurisdiction and Venue
IV. Federalism and Preemption
V. Lawyers and Business
VI. Alternate Dispute Resolution

At the end of Chapter 1, the "Practical Exercise" looked at some legal issues raised in "Mary's Very Bad Day." What type of lawyer could help Mary? What sort of fee arrangement should she make with a lawyer? In what court might she file a case?

INTRODUCTION

The United States has been called "a nation of laws rather than of men" by some, and "a nation overrun with lawyers" by others. Both statements contain elements of truth. We do have a large number of lawyers in this country—Americans have always placed great emphasis upon laws and courts as a way of resolving disputes, and as a means of protecting individual citizens from imperious government officials. Our system of government, starting with the Constitution, has stressed concepts like "due process" and "equal protection." These principles guarantee each citizen the right to a fair hearing before an unbiased tribunal if that person believes that he or she is being treated unjustly. Equally important is the role law has played in this country in facilitating and regulating business and commercial practices.

In the past 30 years there has been a tremendous increase in the number of students attending and graduating from law schools. The number of lawyers in the United States has therefore increased dramatically—to more than 1 million today. Our "free market" system allows people to choose whatever occupation they want, and it is apparent that many Americans want to practice law as a profession. Many of our most popular books, television shows, and movies deal with lawyers, justice, and the court system. Clearly, law and the legal system are major factors in our culture.

Americans, more so than people of many other cultures, tend to believe that when someone suffers a loss due to the wrongful conduct of another person, there should be a remedy. Similarly, a business firm that enters into a contract with another company to furnish a certain amount of materials for its manufacturing process has the right to, and does expect, full performance of the contract at the time and place agreed upon. These basic American social, political, and legal expectations are unlikely to change in the near future, and it is thus important for businesspeople to understand the organization and nature of our court system.

STATE COURT SYSTEMS

Each state (and the District of Columbia) has developed its own court system, independent of all other states. No one state can dictate to another what type of courts it should have, nor what the functions of each should be. Therefore, although this book will make some general observations about state courts, you should study your own state's court system to ascertain how it differs from the model.

Every state has at least one level of courts called "trial courts." Cases are started and trials are held at this level. These are the courts in which witnesses testify to the various facts that are relevant to the case, attorneys "object" to certain types of questions or evidence that they believe to be irrelevant to that particular case, and the witnesses and parties must deal with rulings from the trial judge. This is the level of the court system where there is a jury, if either party has asked for one. The trial courts often carry names such as District Court, Circuit Court, County Court, or Superior Court. (Different names are used in different states.)

In addition, several other specialized trial courts exist to handle specific functions. Many states have Juvenile Courts, which deal with adolescent crime and family matters; Traffic Courts, which deal with a wide variety of motor vehicle infractions; Probate Courts, which deal mainly with inheritance questions; and Small Claims Courts, which deal with disputes over a modest amount of money (and function much like the "People's Court" seen on television). The jurisdiction of small claims courts typically is limited to cases involving no more than $3,000 or $4,000—and the parties usually handle the cases themselves. In some states lawyers are not permitted to appear in small claims courts.

Each state also has at least one appellate court, which hears appeals from decisions of the trial courts. Most states have two levels of appellate courts—most often called the Court of Appeals and the Supreme Court. These courts typically hear no trials and see no witnesses or evidence. The appellate courts hear arguments from the parties (through their attorneys) regarding a case that has been decided in a trial court. One side, called the **appellant**, attempts to convince the appellate court that something was done incorrectly in the trial court, causing that party to lose the case or to receive an inadequate award. The other side, called the **appellee**, then seeks to persuade the court that the trial court did not make any errors, or if there were any that they were of minor importance. These arguments are made first in written documents, called "briefs" (although they are never very brief). Once each side has had the chance to respond to the other's written arguments, the court usually schedules an *oral argument* before a panel of appellate judges (usually three, five, or seven judges). The judges actively question the attorneys during the oral argument and then debate the matter among themselves and issue a written decision a few months later.

appellant: The party who appeals a case to a higher court, after a trial court decision.

appellee: The party who is defending the lower court decision in an appellate court.

The majority of states have intermediate courts of appeal, as pictured in Figure 2.1. The losing party in the trial court always has the right to have at least one appellate court review the trial court decision. Once the court of appeals has ruled on the case, the losing party may ask the state supreme court to hear a further appeal, but the supreme court generally has the option of declining the case. In states where there is no intermediate appellate court, the state supreme court must hear an appeal from a trial court decision if one of the parties so requests.

THE FEDERAL COURT SYSTEM

The federal court system is a national system of courts with branches in every state. Like the typical state court arrangement, there are trial courts (properly called United States District Courts, or more commonly federal district

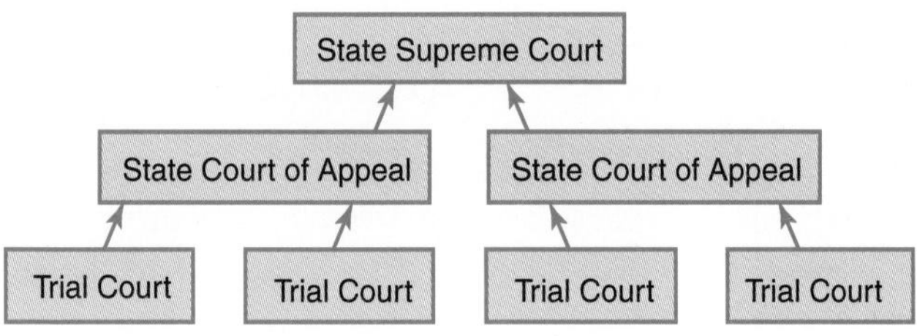

Figure 2.1
Chart of Typical State Court System

courts), appellate courts (called United States Courts of Appeals), and the ultimate appellate court, the U.S. Supreme Court. Cases are normally filed in the U.S. District Courts, although there are some specialized federal trial courts (as there are in state court systems), like U.S. Bankruptcy Court, U.S. Claims Court, or U.S. Tax Court.

Following the decision of the trial court, there is a right to appeal at least once to the appropriate U.S. Court of Appeals (there are 13 such courts). Eleven of these appellate courts hear appeals from federal District Courts within their geographic region. For example, the Court of Appeals for the 7th Circuit hears appeals from federal district court decisions in the states of Wisconsin, Illinois, and Indiana, and the 9th Circuit Court of Appeals hears appeals from district court decisions in nine western states and Guam. In addition, one of the Courts of Appeals is located in the District of Columbia, where it hears numerous appeals concerning actions taken by the federal government, as well as other cases. The final federal Court of Appeals (called the Court of Appeals for the Federal Circuit) hears primarily cases involving intellectual property issues—that is, patent, trademark, and copyright matters, as well as some cases involving international trade law. Figure 2.2 illustrates the 13 federal judicial circuits.

In each U.S. Court of Appeals, there are many judges who usually hear appeals in panels of three. Following a decision of one of the federal Courts of Appeals, either party may request that the U.S. Supreme Court hear the case, which is usually done by filing a *Petition for Writ of Certiorari* with the Supreme Court. The nine justices of the Supreme Court decide which cases the court will hear (four of the justices must vote to accept a case), generally choosing cases of the most significance or cases where two of the Courts of Appeal have reached different conclusions as to the meaning of a particular law. In recent years, the U.S. Supreme Court has usually decided to hear only about 1 percent of the cases on which ***certiorari*** is requested, and the number of

***certiorari*:** The request to the U.S. Supreme Court to hear a particular case.

Figure 2.2
Diagram of Federal Circuit Court System

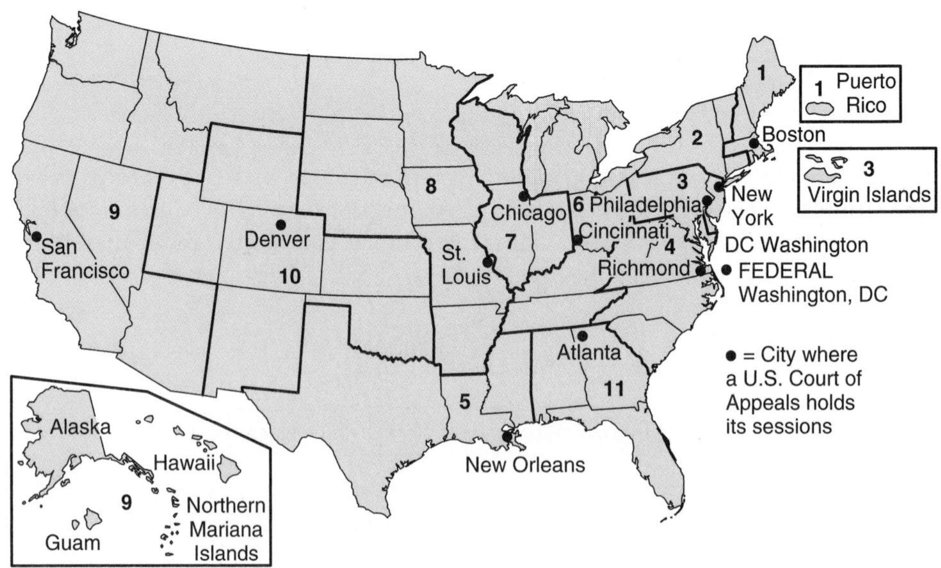

cases heard by the Supreme Court has been declining in the past few years. Recently, the Supreme Court has granted *certiorari* in only about 75–100 cases per year, out of 7500 requests.

There are a few categories where the Supreme Court must accept the case. For example, if a U.S. Court of Appeals has decided that a state statute is in violation of the Constitution or federal law, then there is a right to appeal. Also, a few cases per year may be appealed from the highest court of a state to the U.S. Supreme Court. This right arises if the state supreme court has found a federal statute invalid or has held a state statute unconstitutional or in violation of federal law. Otherwise, once a case is filed in a state court, it almost always stays in the state appellate system, while cases filed in federal court stay in the federal appellate system. One party cannot appeal a state trial court decision to a federal court of appeals.

JURISDICTION AND VENUE

The power of a court to hear and decide a case is called **jurisdiction**. In order for a court to properly hear a case it must have both *subject matter jurisdiction* and *personal jurisdiction*. Certain courts have been given power over specific subjects (e.g., juvenile courts or probate courts) and they may not hear cases that do not involve that particular subject. Also, trial courts are often given power to hear cases involving only a certain amount of money (e.g., less than $10,000) or particular types of criminal charges, with another court having jurisdiction of cases dealing with larger amounts of money or more serious criminal charges. Each court, therefore, only has the power to hear certain types of cases within its *subject matter jurisdiction*.

jurisdiction: The power of a particular court to hear and decide a case.

The power of the court over the parties is termed *personal jurisdiction*. Generally courts located in one state (whether state or federal courts) have power only over those individuals whose home is in that state. So if John Jones, who lives in Michigan, wants to sue Susan Smith, who lives in Utah, he must normally file the lawsuit in either the state or federal court in Utah, so that the court that will be hearing the case will have personal jurisdiction over the defendant.

However, most states have enacted laws, commonly called **long-arm statutes**, that allow a court to acquire personal jurisdiction over nonresident defendants where that person has had some sort of "*minimum contact*" with the forum state. For example, the court system in the state of Michigan might have jurisdiction over Susan Smith, if she had been involved in a business operation in Michigan or had entered into contracts to supply goods and services in Michigan or had driven a car negligently in Michigan (even though she lived in Utah). In these cases, Mr. Jones can probably sue her in a Michigan court, using the *long-arm statute*, and she will have to come to Michigan, or at least hire a Michigan lawyer to appear in court and defend the case.

long-arm statute: A law giving the courts of one state jurisdiction over a non-resident defendant.

One interesting issue being argued in many courts today concerns the question of whether a company that maintains an interactive Web site is therefore subject to jurisdiction in any state where the site is accessed. Courts have reached different results, depending on the level of activity with the state asserting jurisdiction and the "commercial nature" of such activity by the out-of-state firm.

venue: The particular court location within a specific court system, where a case should be heard.

Venue refers to the particular location of a specific court, within a given jurisdiction, which is the appropriate place to hear the case. In other words, once it has been decided that the trial court for the state of Texas has jurisdiction of a particular matter, the specific county where the case should be heard is a *venue* question. Each state has laws concerning venue, usually based on where the defendant lives or where the accident or crime occurred. Determining the appropriate venue is usually a practical matter involving such questions as: Where are the parties? Where is most of the evidence? Where is it possible to get an unbiased jury? It is not unusual for the defendant to be unhappy with the place the case has been filed by the plaintiff and to ask the court for a *change of venue*.

FEDERAL JURISDICTION

The federal courts have limited jurisdiction. In order to file a case in federal district court, not only must there be personal jurisdiction over the defendant, but certain other requirements must be met as well. The two primary bases of federal jurisdiction are *federal question jurisdiction* and *diversity jurisdiction*. Unless the plaintiff (the party who has filed the case) can show that one of these tests is met, the federal courts will refuse to hear the case, although there are a few other laws that specifically grant federal jurisdiction.

federal question jurisdiction: Federal jurisdiction based on the fact that the case involves an issue of federal law.

Federal question jurisdiction exists if the plaintiff's case involves a claim "arising under" any federal law or the U.S. Constitution. For example, if Angela is claiming that her rights under the federal Truth-in-Lending Act were violated, she can file the case in federal district court. (She may also file the case in an appropriate state court.) Determining which one of the hundreds of federal courts around the United States is the appropriate one for her case is a venue question.

As far back as the writing of the Constitution, lawmakers were concerned that there was the potential for bias if out-of-state plaintiffs were always required to sue defendants in the local state courts of their home counties. Local judges, who typically stand for election every few years, and local juries might tend to favor a local individual defending a lawsuit brought by a person or business from another state.

diversity jurisdiction: Federal jurisdiction based on the fact that the parties live in different states, and the case involves $75,000 or more.

Therefore, **diversity jurisdiction** allows a person to file suit against a defendant in the federal court, rather than the state court, when the two parties are residents of different states. In order to take advantage of this provision, however, the lawsuit must involve at least $75,000. Federal judges are appointed for life, do not face any elections, and therefore, theoretically at least, are less subject to local community pressures than state trial court judges. Also, federal court juries are typically drawn from a wider area of the state than local state court juries, which are typically composed of residents of a particular county.

If Alexa, a resident of California, wants to sue Adam, a resident of Florida, concerning a contract problem that had caused her $90,000 in damages, she can clearly choose to file the case in the federal district court in Florida or the appropriate state trial court in Florida. She might also be able to file the case in federal or state court in California, if the appropriate facts existed. If, for example, the contract had been signed and/or performed in California, she probably can file the suit there, using the long arm rules.

When both the state and federal courts have jurisdiction over a case, it is called **concurrent jurisdiction**, and it is initially the plaintiff's choice where to file. If the plaintiff files a case in a state court, and the defendant decides he or she would rather be in federal court, and there is either diversity or federal question jurisdiction, a petition for *removal* may be filed with the federal court. If there is an appropriate jurisdictional basis, the case will be moved to the federal court. A defendant who wishes to remove a case to federal court, however, must institute procedures promptly after the case is filed. Once proceedings get underway in a court, the case will stay in that court system (state or federal) throughout.

concurrent jurisdiction: A type of case in which either the state or federal courts would have jurisdiction.

THE CASE OR CONTROVERSY REQUIREMENT

American courts are limited by the Constitution to deciding actual "cases or controversies." This phrase means that courts will not give advisory opinions to a legislator or public official on whether a law is constitutional or not. The concept is based on the premise that the primary role of the courts is to decide disputes between parties, not to legislate. When two parties have truly adverse interests, they are more likely to thoroughly present the legal arguments and issues on both sides, allowing the court to make the decision. For example, a recent law passed by one state allowed police officers to use roadblocks to stop cars at random to look for drunk drivers. Although many people believed the law was unconstitutional (violation of the "search and seizure" rule of the Fourth Amendment), the courts could not rule on the question until someone was detained by the use of this technique and later challenged the legality of the arrest in court.

STANDING

The concept of **standing** is somewhat similar to the case or controversy requirement in that it also limits the number of disputes that courts can hear. The rule essentially holds that only those persons or businesses who have suffered some loss as the result of another's action or have a personal stake in the outcome of the dispute may sue. Only those persons directly affected have standing to argue the legal issues before the court. If Sally hires Joe's Painting Service to paint her house, and Joe does a really poor job, some of Sally's neighbors might like to sue Joe because Sally's house is now unattractive enough to decrease the property values in the neighborhood. However, a court would probably rule that only Sally had standing to sue Joe for his breach of contract with her. The following case is a recent Supreme Court decision involving "standing."

standing: The requirement that one or more of the plaintiffs in a case show that they have actually suffered some direct effect or loss due to the defendant's actions.

STEEL CO. V. CITIZENS FOR A BETTER ENVIRONMENT

523 U.S. 83 (1998)

FACTS

Citizens for a Better Environment is a group interested in environmental protection. The organization sued Steel Co., a small manufacturing company in Chicago, for past violations of the Emergency Planning and Community Right-to-Know Act of 1986 (EPCRA). This federal law established a framework of state, regional, and local agencies that were to inform the public about the presence of hazardous and toxic chemicals, and to provide for emergency response when necessary.

The law (EPCRA) required users of specified toxic and hazardous chemicals to file annual reports containing much information about the company, the facility, the name and quantity of chemicals used, the waste disposal method employed, and more information. The law stated that it could be enforced against violators by the Environmental Protection Agency (EPA), or state and local governments, or even private citizens, when the EPA declined to act.

Citizens for a Better Environment sent a notice to the EPA and to local and regional governments in 1995, claiming (correctly) that Steel Co. failed to file the required reports every year since the law went into effect (1988). After the notices were received, Steel Co. was notified and then did file all the necessary overdue forms, and the EPA decided not to bring legal action. At that point, Citizens filed this lawsuit in federal district court. The district court dismissed the case, but that decision was later reversed by the Court of Appeals, which held that a citizens group could sue under the EPCRA for past violations. The case was then appealed to the U.S. Supreme Court, which decided that before reaching the substantive legal issues concerning the EPCRA, it must decide whether the plaintiffs had standing to bring the case.

DECISION

In an opinion written by Justice Antonin Scalia, the Supreme Court determined that the plaintiffs did not have standing. The court started its discussion of standing by noting that "Article III, Section 2 of the Constitution extends the 'Judicial Power' of the United States only to 'Cases' and 'Controversies.'" Justice Scalia said, "We have always taken this to mean cases and controversies of the sort traditionally . . . resolved by the court process."

The constitutional minimum of standing contains three elements. First and foremost, there must be alleged (and ultimately proved) an "injury in fact"—a harm suffered by the plaintiff that is "concrete" and "actual or imminent, not conjectural or hypothetical." Second, there must be causation—a fairly traceable connection between the plaintiff's injury and the conduct of the defendant. "And third, there must be redressability—a likelihood that the requested relief will redress the alleged injury."

Turning to the particular allegations of the plaintiffs' complaint in this case, the court found that the plaintiff states it is "an organization that seeks, uses, and acquires data reported under the EPCRA" and reports information to its members concerning storage and releases of toxic chemicals into the environment. The organization also prepares reports to its members and "advocates for changes in public policy to better protect the environment." It states that its members, who live in the area near the Steel Co. facility, will use the EPCRA information to learn about chemical releases and the use of hazardous substances in their communities to attempt to reduce the toxic chemicals in their area. The members' "safety, health, recreational, economic, aesthetic, and environmental interests" in the information "have been, are being, and will be adversely affected" by Steel Co.'s failure to file timely reports under the EPCRA, stated the group.

The Supreme Court then looked at the relief requested by the plaintiff organization, to determine whether any of the measures requested would redress the harm claimed. First, the request for a declaratory judgment, after the reports had been filed, was termed "worthless." Next, the plaintiffs' request for civil penalties (fines) would perhaps help redress the injuries, except that, by law, they are payable to the U.S. Treasury. The gratification that the plaintiffs might feel if the defendant were punished is not redress of the harm. Justice Scalia stated:

By the mere bringing of his suit, every plaintiff demonstrates his belief that a favorable judgment will make him happier. But although a suitor may derive great comfort and joy from the fact that the United States Treasury is not cheated, that a wrongdoer gets his just deserts, or that the Nation's laws are faithfully enforced, that psychic satisfaction is not an acceptable Article III [standing] remedy because it does not redress an Article III injury.

The court then examined the other remedies sought by the plaintiffs and found that none of them would redress the harms allegedly suffered. Even the request for an injunction ordering Steel Co. to provide copies of all EPA reports would not remedy any past wrong but looked to the future. Justice Scalia hinted that if the complaint by the Citizens group had alleged that the violations were continuing and were imminent in the future, perhaps the injunctive remedy would qualify as necessary redress, but no such allegation was in the complaint. Therefore, because the relief sought by the plaintiffs would not redress or compensate them for the harm they claimed, the case was dismissed for lack of standing.

CASE QUESTIONS

1. What is the purpose of the "standing" rule? How is it related to the constitutional requirement that courts only hear "cases and controversies"?
2. Why did Justice Scalia focus on the "redress" issue? How does this tie in with the standing requirement?
3. What did the Supreme Court find lacking in the plaintiff's requests here?
4. Translate the point being made by the Court in the paragraph set out in italics into your own words. What is the point?

CLASS ACTIONS

Sometimes a great number of persons are injured by another's actions or conduct. Suppose that 1 million people have been adversely affected by a nuclear accident at one company or that 100,000 people have purchased tires that were slightly defective from one company. According to the rules mentioned previously, each person may bring a separate lawsuit against the one defendant (because each one has suffered an injury). This would cause tremendous problems for the court system. On the other hand, perhaps the injury to each person is so small ($50 for each tire) that no one will file a lawsuit, and the company will escape any penalty.

For these reasons, the **class action** lawsuit was developed. In such a case, a few individuals file a suit stating that they are representing "all others similarly situated." These individuals, through their attorneys, must convince the court that (1) the number of people involved is very large, (2) that the plaintiffs will adequately present the claims of the larger group, (3) that there are "common questions of law and fact" involved, and (4) that the plaintiffs' claims are typical of the rest of the class.

class action: A type of lawsuit in which a few plaintiffs act to represent a much larger group, who have suffered the same type of injury.

Obviously, when the claims of all the possible injured persons are added up, the damages sought become quite great. In the tire example, even though each consumer's damages were only $50, the aggregated claims involve at least $5 million in damages. Businesses sometimes argue that these cases are the creation of lawyers more interested in their fees (often 1/3 of the total recovery) than in helping injured persons. Consumer advocates, on the other hand, contend that businesses that make defective products must somehow be held accountable for the damage they cause.

The controversy has caused courts to closely supervise class actions. In most federal court actions, the burden of notifying all of the members of the potential class about the lawsuit is put on the plaintiff. This requirement stops many class actions before they start, since the cost of mailing letters to thousands of people is quite significant. Sometimes in very large cases, the court will approve notices in a series of newspapers or some other method, but these instances are becoming less frequent and are vigorously opposed by the business defendants.

Once a person is notified that a class action has been approved by the court and is underway, he or she will be bound by the result unless the court is notified that the individual has chosen to "opt out" and pursue his or her own remedies. If the plaintiffs win the class action case, the award (after payment of costs and attorney fees) must be shared by all the class members, or at least as many as can be found. Those who have "opted out" are not bound by the decision and may pursue their own lawsuits or settlements.

SOCIAL/ETHICAL ISSUES

Do you think it is fair to allow one or two persons, through their lawyers, to say they represent hundreds or thousands of people, each of whom may have a relatively small monetary loss? Then, after starting a lawsuit, the plaintiffs attempt to notify all of these people to see if they want to join in, at no cost. When the claims are aggregated, the total may be several million dollars for which the firm that manufactured the product may be liable.

On the other hand, in the absence of the class action procedure, how many of these people would ever have sued on their own? If the manufacturer has made a product that has caused $25 or $30 of damage to 100,000 people, should it totally escape any financial liability?

FEDERALISM AND PREEMPTION

federalism: The sharing of power between the federal and state governments.

Supremacy Clause: The clause in the U.S. Constitution that establishes the Constitution as the final authority in the land, superior to conflicting state laws.

As we discussed in the section on jurisdiction, it is usually the plaintiff's choice whether to file a case in federal court or state court, although there are some limitations on the types of cases a federal court will hear. Additional federal/state interactions can arise, however, when the legal issue concerns a federal law and a state law that may be inconsistent with each other. The U.S. Constitution establishes a system of government based upon **federalism**, under which certain powers are given to the federal government while others are reserved to the states.

The **Supremacy Clause** of the Constitution states that "The Constitution, and the Laws of the United States which shall be made in Pursuance thereof; and all Treaties made . . . shall be the Supreme Law of the Land; and the Judges of every state shall be bound thereby . . . ." This clause has been interpreted in many cases over the past 210 years, and one important theory has developed that is known as the *preemption doctrine*.

The preemption doctrine holds that when the federal government acts to regulate an area in which it has been given power under the Constitution, its laws and regulations preempt (that is, displace or cancel) any state laws or actions that infringe directly or indirectly on the federal power. This doctrine only operates where (1) the federal government, usually through Congress, is acting in a substantive field as authorized by the Constitution and (2) the state law or action in question conflicts and infringes on the federal power.

The preemption doctrine does not apply if the state law merely supplements the federal law, rather than conflicts with it. For example, the federal government is specifically given the power to set up post offices and establish a copyright system by the Constitution. If a state were to pass a law establishing such a system, the law would be invalid on the basis of *preemption*. The issues become much more difficult and complex when the law regulates business and commerce, involving the Commerce Clause, as will be discussed in Chapter 4.

LAWYERS AND BUSINESS

This book is designed to help business students become more knowledgeable about the many legal issues that affect business. Rather than becoming lawyers, you will someday need to interact with attorneys in your own firm, if it is a large business, or deal with lawyers representing another company. Perhaps you will need to hire a lawyer to assist your own business. The aim of this book is to help you *avoid* legal problems before they become serious, to prepare you to choose an attorney wisely, and to be a more intelligent consumer of legal services—that is, to communicate better with the attorney chosen and to understand and participate more fully in each decision which must be made. So the next section will examine how one becomes a lawyer and will look more closely at the different types of lawyers.

WHAT IS A LAWYER?

There is an endless number of humorous answers to this question—there are probably more "lawyer jokes" (some of us call them "anti-lawyer jokes") making the rounds than any other category—but let us be serious for now. First of all, in the United States the terms *lawyer* and *attorney* mean the same thing—there is no real difference. In England, on the other hand, there is an important difference between the terms *barrister* and *solicitor*. Only barristers argue cases in court, while solicitors handle many other legal matters out of court. In other countries, lawyers are sometimes termed *advocates*, or known by other titles, and each category may limit what one can do. In the United States any lawyer can assist people with the full range of legal concerns and appear in court in jurisdictions where that lawyer is licensed.

Licensing of American lawyers is done primarily on the state level, by the state **bar association** (the organization of lawyers in that state). There is no federal or national licensing of attorneys. You may have heard of the American Bar Association (ABA), a national organization with approximately 350,000 attorney members in January 2000, which often speaks for the legal profession. The ABA is a voluntary organization, however, and lawyers are free to belong or not. It is necessary, however, to apply for admission to the bar association in the state where a lawyer wishes to practice law. A lawyer must be licensed in each state in which he or she wants to practice.

bar association: An organization of attorneys—may be a local, statewide, or national group.

The first step in becoming a lawyer is attending law school, which is normally a three-year course of study following graduation from undergraduate school. The person's undergraduate major is not important—people from a wide variety of bachelors' degrees enroll in law school. After graduation from law school, a candidate must apply to take the "bar exam" in the state where he or she wishes to practice law before becoming an attorney. The exam is a difficult two- or three-day test in most states, and the "pass" rate varies considerably, from around 50 percent in some states up to 75 percent or 80 percent in other states. An unsuccessful applicant can usually attempt the test again at a future time.

If the law school graduate passes the test and his or her "character and fitness" investigation by the state bar association is positive, the applicant is then a "lawyer" and can begin to practice law in that state. Canada and many other nations require a period of apprenticeship with a practicing attorney before the new lawyer can practice alone. This procedure is not normally required in the United States.

A small number of American lawyers—probably only a few hundred—have never graduated from law school. Seven states have procedures allowing persons to sit for the bar exam after a period of "reading law" in a structured program supervised by a licensed attorney. In order to become licensed to practice, the applicant must pass the state's bar exam, like law school graduates.

Since licensing is controlled at the state level, if a lawyer licensed in one state wants to practice law in another state, he or she must seek formal permission from that state. Some states have "reciprocity" laws that allow lawyers practicing in other states to become members of that state's bar association simply by payment of the appropriate fees, as long as the background check does not disclose any previous problems (such as crimes or suspension from that state's bar association). However, many states, particularly in the West, have no reciprocity, so that if a lawyer who has been practicing law for 20 years in Florida wishes to open a practice in Washington state, he or she must sit for the bar exam just like a recent law school graduate. Not only is the initial licensing of lawyers carried out at the state level, but disciplinary actions including sanctions, suspensions, and ultimately "disbarment" of lawyers for misconduct is also done by the state bar associations.

WHEN YOU SHOULD RETAIN A LAWYER

Obviously, if you are sued for money damages or are formally charged with a crime, you need to consult a lawyer. But in many other circumstances, you are wise and financially smart to seek legal assistance long before a lawsuit is filed. It is a good idea for a businessperson to visit an attorney every year or so to review personal and business matters even if there are no immediate legal threats. Often people put off going to a lawyer for advice because they do not want to incur the cost. However, legal problems are much easier to avoid and head off—and much less expensive—if caught early.

Personal Legal Issues It is advisable to have a will. Although this subject will be more thoroughly discussed in Chapter 14, you should know that when a person dies without a will, that person's property will be distributed according to the laws of his or her state—usually to the closest heirs, such as children and parents. The property does not go to the state if one dies without a will—as some people think—unless there are essentially no relatives at all. One's property will be distributed to the closest heirs, such as uncles or cousins. But by preparing a will, a person can specify exactly to whom any or all assets will go and in what amount. A will can also establish a trust fund for children or specify that a certain amount be left to a church, the Humane Society, or other entity.

One reason many people with young children execute a will is to specify who will be named as guardian of their children if both parents should die. If there is no will, a court hearing will need to be held to determine, in the judge's view, who is the best person to care for the children. Sometimes these proceedings cause bitter family squabbles. However, if someone is named guardian of the children in a will and that person agrees to serve, courts will almost always follow these wishes.

Other family matters that often require the services of a lawyer include a divorce and adoption. Although it is possible to "do your own" divorce, if there are children or significant assets or debts involved, an attorney's help will be cost-effective in the long run. There may be complex legal issues involved in divorce that the untrained individual who just wants to "get out of this rotten marriage" may not perceive but which might cause problems later. Similarly, an adoption is an important legal event with substantial consequences for the child and the natural and adoptive parents.

Business Matters For the person involved in business, many situations exist when one should seek legal assistance. As we mentioned at the beginning of this chapter, when starting a business, several pivotal legal decisions need to be made in which a lawyer's advice can be very valuable. Similarly, one should seek legal assistance when buying or selling an existing business. Hiring and firing employees, purchasing or renting property, entering into contracts, and solving tax issues are examples of occasions when an attorney's advice should definitely be sought.

HOW TO CHOOSE A LAWYER

When you have decided that a lawyer's advice is needed, how should you go about choosing one? First, get recommendations from friends you trust and whose opinion you value. In addition, business associates, supervisors, doctors, ministers, and perhaps accountants and bankers with whom your firm has dealt may be able to recommend an attorney. Obviously, recommendations from people who actually have worked with or used the services of the lawyer being considered are much more valuable than those who have just "heard something" about the person.

Most local bar associations (organized lawyer groups) have "referral services." These programs ask lawyers to sign up if they want to receive referrals and to list areas of legal work they engage in. Then, if an individual calls the bar association seeking a lawyer, the service may give out the name and number of an attorney from the list. The referral service does not vouch for the expertise of the lawyer; rather, the service indicates that the lawyer has experience in a particular area. The individual needs to ask questions of the lawyer at the first meeting to make sure that he or she has the appropriate experience.

Lawyer advertising is now a regular feature of the telephone book and even the newspaper, radio, and television—especially in larger cities, where there is a large number of attorneys. While many lawyers have big, fancy offices, leather chairs, and long lists of corporate clients, there are numerous others making a modest living at best. Some of these attorneys are actively seeking new clients and new business and use advertising to publicize their image and their rates. Like other types of businesses, some lawyers feature low cost in their ads, while others stress their experience or expertise in particular matters.

Large, prestigious law firms generally do not advertise a great deal. These distinguished firms often oppose lawyer advertising, arguing that mass advertising lowers the public image of the legal profession. Also, these firms already have numerous clients and obtain most of their new business from referrals.

After two young lawyers in Arizona were disciplined by the bar association in 1977 for advertising in violation of the state rules, the U.S. Supreme Court decided that the "Freedom of Speech" clause in the Constitution prohibited an outright ban on lawyer advertising. [See *Bates v. State Bar of Arizona*, 433 U.S. 350 (1977)]. The Court did allow states to enact regulations to protect the public against false or misleading advertising but not to ban attorney advertising totally. All the states have passed some kind of regulatory measures—some quite general and some very specific—but the regulations cannot prohibit informative, nondeceptive advertising. Consumers should keep in mind, however, that advertising is only that lawyer's own assertion as to his or her qualifications. The more informed the consumer, the better able he or she is to select and benefit from a lawyer's services.

LARGE FIRM OR SMALL FIRM?

Traditionally, the most sought-after jobs for law school graduates have been with large law firms in big cities. In general, these firms, often with hundreds of lawyers and several offices, pay the highest salaries, hire the top law school graduates, and have the most prestige in the law profession. Lawyers in large firms tend to specialize in one or two areas over the years, and such a firm will have experts in taxation, corporate and securities law, environmental law, antitrust law, employment law, and other fields. Large firms demand a lot from their lawyers and generally produce high-quality work.

SUPREME COURT COMEDY CONCERNING LAWYERS

Sometimes even Supreme Court Justices make jokes about the legal profession's image problem. During argument in a case concerning Florida's rule banning lawyers from contacting accident victims in writing for 30 days after a mishap, Chief Justice William Rehnquist wondered whether Florida could limit the perception of a bar filled with "greedy lawyers" with its rule.

Justice John Paul Stevens then commented that Florida could "pass a statute that you can't say un-nice things about lawyers." Justice Ruth Bader Ginsburg proposed a statute that you can't "read Dickens or Shakespeare," whose works contain some nasty references to lawyers. Courtroom titters grew to guffaws. "I'm certainly glad I never passed through the stage of being a lawyer," said Justice Antonin Scalia. "It might have helped you, actually," noted Justice Stephen Breyer, and that brought down the house.

Source: *The Wall Street Journal*, Jan. 12, 1995, B4.

Because of their size, staff, and technical needs, large firms tend to charge higher rates than smaller firms, although there certainly are exceptions. They often pay higher salaries, have more secretaries and **paralegals** (nonlawyers working for a law firm under the supervision of a lawyer), and have higher library expenses. Your legal matter may be handled by a senior partner (at rates exceeding $200 per hour), or it may be given to an **associate** (a lawyer who is a salaried member of the firm but not yet a partner) at a lower hourly rate.

paralegals: Nonlawyers who work for a law firm under the supervision of a lawyer.

associate: A lawyer who is a salaried member of the firm but not yet a partner.

John Grisham's books, *The Firm*, *The Client*, and *The Street Lawyer* and their movie adaptations have dramatically depicted the stress felt by young lawyers who join a large firm. His books clearly portray the tremendous pressure new associates in a large firm face to work long hours, produce a high number of "billable hours" (those that can be directly charged to clients), and please the supervising senior partner in order to "make partner" in six or seven years. Lawyers in large firms work long hours, generally produce excellent work, and earn the highest compensation in the legal field.

Smaller firms may not have experts in all types of legal problems, although they may be very proficient in certain specialties. They may not have an attorney who has previously handled exactly the same type of case as yours. Some small firms do concentrate on one particular area of the law, such as patent law or criminal law. In some cases, the services of a smaller firm will be more personalized, and the number of lawyers and size of the office less overwhelming. The client may get to know one lawyer well, rather than dealing with several different lawyers and paralegals. Regardless of the type of firm selected, it is important for the client to discuss early on the previous experience the particular attorney has with respect to the category of legal issue in question.

The *sole practitioner* is a lawyer who practices by him- or herself. Sometimes clients feel that they receive more personal attention from this attorney than from a large- or medium-sized firm. On the other hand, the law is becoming more complex every day, and the sole practitioner cannot possibly maintain expertise in all the areas of law that a larger firm can offer. The sole practitioner can be compared to the family doctor. Each one has a wide basic knowledge of many areas but may not be a specialist in any one. Some sole practitioners, however, do focus their energies on a few specific subject areas.

INTERNATIONAL LAW AND ACCOUNTING FIRM MERGERS

Recently there has been a trend toward mergers among law firms, not only in the United States but also in Europe. The opening up of a unified European market and the removal of barriers to trade and to services across national borders has opened the door for combinations of law firms from different countries. In addition mergers are taking place between European law firms and giant U.S. accounting firms.

The huge British law firm Clifford Chance now has more than 1,800 lawyers at 24 offices worldwide. "We're going to see more changes in the next two or three years than we've seen in the last 50," predicts one of the managing partners. Clifford Chance now has many teams of local lawyers in many European countries, as corporate clients demand global service.

Competition among accounting and auditing firms has reduced the number of huge firms from 12 in 1990 to a "Big Five" today. These global firms are now seeking mergers with international law firms. While such mergers (called multidisciplinary partnerships) are not allowed by American bar associations at this time, they are permitted in many, but not all, European nations. The power of the Big Five accounting firms, which have legal divisions, makes them an attractive partner for a law firm with international clientele.

While many large U.S. law firms have international offices around the world, the first real merger between an American law firm based in New York and a European law firm with offices in Paris, London, and Moscow occurred in 1998. The firm will have to merge different business cultures and compensation systems, but each partner has many international business clients.

Sources: "Europe's Law Firms Enter Merger Epoch," *The Wall Street Journal* (July 22, 1998), A11; and "Law Firm Merger of New York's Christy and Europe's Salans May Signal Trend," *The Wall Street Journal* (Sept. 18, 1998), B6.

FEES AND COSTS

There are three primary ways that attorneys charge for their services—by the hour, by a set fee or flat fee for a particular service, and by a "contingent fee." The attorney and the client should discuss fees at the very first meeting and should agree on which type of fee will be used for this matter. The client should leave the office knowing how much he or she will be charged for the lawyer's time; paralegal time; and expenses and costs such as photocopying, court costs, and telephone charges; and if the fees depend on whether the case is won or lost.

The American rule: Each party in a lawsuit normally pays his or her own lawyer, whether the case is won or lost.

hourly fee: Where the lawyer charges the client a specified rate for each hour spent on the client's legal matters.

The general rule in the United States is that both parties in a case pay their own lawyer fees, regardless of who wins the case. In many other countries, the rule is different—the winner normally is awarded compensation from the loser for his or her attorney fees, in addition to the other damages awarded. There are an increasing number of U.S. statutes that adopt this principle and allow the judge to assess attorney fees as part of the judgment in particular types of cases, but these are exceptions to the general **American rule**. The statutes where this principle has been adopted are usually those in which Congress has felt a need to encourage citizen enforcement actions such as civil rights, consumer protection, and environmental laws.

The most common way attorneys charge is **by the hour**. Each attorney sets his or her hourly rate—sometimes it is different for out-of-court time or

"You're a partner now, Simpson. You shouldn't be drinking juice from a box."

From *National Law Journal*, 12/19/94. Cartoon © Mike Shapiro.

in-court time. Attorneys' hourly rates vary considerably, and the client is wise to shop around, make calls, check references, and interview several attorneys before committing to a lawyer. Once the attorney begins to work for an individual, he or she will keep close account of all time spent working on that person's legal matter and will charge accordingly. This includes phone calls with the client and other attorneys or witnesses, as well as time spent on legal research, investigation, negotiation, and any other work on that case. It may not be wise to choose the attorney with the lowest hourly rate, but at least the client should be informed of the hourly fee right at the beginning, although the final cost will not be known at that time.

Sometimes at the beginning of the attorney–client relationship, the attorney will ask for a **retainer**. This is a payment in advance of services being performed. This safeguards the attorney against doing a considerable amount of work and then having the client refuse to pay. However, there have been instances when attorneys have abused this type of fee arrangement, as the following case demonstrates.

retainer: An advance payment to secure the services of a lawyer.

MATTER OF COOPERMAN

611 N.Y.S.2d 465 (Ct.App. 1994)

FACTS

A New York attorney, Edward Cooperman, demanded that a number of his clients sign "nonrefundable retainer fee agreements." At the time Mr. Cooperman accepted a criminal case, he had the client sign a statement as follows: "My minimum fee for appearing for you in this matter is Fifteen Thousand Dollars ($15,000). This fee is not refundable for any reason whatsoever once I file a notice of appearance on your behalf." One month after signing this agreement, a client discharged

Mr. Cooperman, but the lawyer refused to refund any portion of the fee. In another criminal case, the client signed a similar agreement (with a nonrefundable fee of $10,000) and then discharged the lawyer two days later, but Mr. Cooperman refused to refund any of the retainer fee.

In connection with accepting representation of a client in a probate proceeding, Mr. Cooperman required a client to sign the following statement: "For the MINIMAL FEE and NONREFUNDABLE amount of Five Thousand Dollars ($5,000), I will act as your counsel." Later in the agreement, this clause appeared: "This is the minimum fee no matter how much or how little work I do in this investigatory stage . . . and will remain the minimum fee and not refundable even if you decide prior to my completion of the investigation that you wish to discontinue the use of my services for any reason whatsoever." The client later discharged Mr. Cooperman, who refused to refund any portion of the retainer fee.

Several of these clients complained to the New York State Bar Association about Mr. Cooperman's practices. Mr. Cooperman had previously received a Letter of Caution from the Bar Association warning him not to use nonrefundable retainer agreements, but he had continued the procedure. The Grievance Committee of one district of the New York Bar Association brought formal charges against him, seeking his suspension or disbarment. The lower court, finding that his practices clearly violated the Code of Professional Responsibility governing lawyers in New York, suspended him from the practice of law for two years. Mr. Cooperman appealed to the New York Court of Appeals, New York's highest court.

DECISION

The Court of Appeals, in a decision authored by Justice Bellacosa, upheld the lower court decision. Beginning with a quote from Sir Francis Bacon that the "greatest trust between people is the trust of giving counsel," the court emphasized the unique fiduciary relationship created when clients hire attorneys to represent them. The court stated that this relationship is "imbued with ultimate trust and confidence." The attorney's obligations transcend those prevailing in the commercial marketplace.

Justice Bellacosa wrote that "the duty to deal fairly, honestly and with undivided loyalty superimposes onto the attorney–client relationship a set of special and unique duties, including maintaining confidentiality, avoiding conflicts of interest, operating competently, safeguarding client property and honoring the client's interests over the lawyer's."

Obviously, the matter of the fee is of significant importance to clients. Therefore, the Code of Professional Responsibility specifically states that an attorney "shall not enter into an agreement for, charge, or collect an illegal or excessive fee" (Rule 2-106A), and upon withdrawal from employment, the attorney shall "refund promptly any part of a fee paid in advance that has not been earned" (Rule 2-110A). Obviously, the "nonrefundable fee," where the entire amount of money paid by the client is retained by the lawyer regardless of the services performed, violates that section of the Rule.

The Court took note of the strong public policy recognizing a client's right to terminate the attorney–client relationship *at any time with or without cause*. This policy has long been enforced because of the special fiduciary relationship of lawyer and client, despite the usual legal principle that parties are bound by the terms of contracts they sign. The court stated, "Special nonrefundable retainer fee agreements diminish the core of the fiduciary relationship by substantially altering and economically chilling the client's unbridled prerogative to walk away from the lawyer."

If the court were to uphold nonrefundable retainers, clients would be "relegated to hostage status in an unwanted fiduciary relationship—an utter anomaly." Such circumstance would impose a penalty on a client for daring to invoke a hollow right to discharge. Interestingly, Mr. Cooperman even acknowledged that the essential purpose of the contract clause was to prevent clients from firing him as their lawyer. This purpose, stated the court, "directly contravenes the Code [of Professional Responsibility] and this State's settled public policy in this regard." Clients may therefore discharge their lawyers at any time without penalty.

The court pointed out that lawyers who are fired by their clients do have remedies available. Under traditional legal theories, supported by many court decisions, the discharged attorney is entitled to recover the reasonable value of services rendered. So Mr. Cooperman would have been entitled to keep whatever portion of the retainer fee he had earned at the time of the discharge, based on the efforts he expended, but the nonrefundable fee agreements were clearly illegal.

Mr. Cooperman's final argument was that he did not deserve to be suspended because he had acted "in good faith," based upon the "limited legal precedents at the time." The court was not persuaded, however, noting that "the conduct of attorneys is not measured by how close to the edge of thin ice they skate." The test instead is "whether the reasonable attorney, familiar with the Code and its ethical strictures," would have notice of what conduct is allowed. Given Mr. Cooperman's level of knowledge, as well as the previous warnings given him, his conduct did not measure up to the requirements. The Court of Appeals concluded that "Cooperman's case, therefore, constitutes a daring test of ethical principles, not good faith. He failed the test."

CASE QUESTIONS

1. What was Mr. Cooperman's reason for having his clients sign nonrefundable retainer fee agreements?
2. Does this case mean that, from now on, all retainer fee agreements are illegal in New York? If not, how do we discern which agreements are legal?
3. If there had been no previous case in New York directly concerning nonrefundable retainer fees, is not Mr. Cooperman correct when he said he was "acting in good faith, based on limited precedent"?
4. Do you think the penalty is too harsh? too lenient?

Sometimes lawyers advertise a **set fee** for a service. Lawyer ads often state such services as "Uncontested Divorce—$200" or "Individual Bankruptcy—$300." If the client really does have a routine legal matter, these arrangements may be a good deal, since they can be performed efficiently by a lawyer who does many of them. If the case becomes more complicated, however, the set fee will not apply. Hopefully, the attorney and the client will have discussed the hourly rate that will be charged in addition to the set fee, should the matter become more involved.

> **set fee:** When a lawyer charges a fixed fee for a specific service.

In cases where the client wants to sue someone for personal injuries, often the **contingent fee** is used. In these cases, there is a strong likelihood that some money will be recovered, either by settlement or at trial. The attorney can offer the client the choice of being charged by the hour (regardless of whether the case is won or lost) or of using a contingent fee. In this arrangement, the client pays no hourly fees at all to the lawyer, but instead agrees that the lawyer's fee will be a certain percentage of whatever judgment or settlement is received. Often the lawyer's fee is in the range of 25 percent to 35 percent of the money recovered. This way, if the case is lost and the client gets nothing, the lawyer also gets no fee. If the client wins $1 million, and the agreed contingent fee is 30 percent, the attorney will receive $300,000. Whether the case is won or lost, the client normally is expected to pay for

> **contingent fee:** When the lawyer's fee is a certain percentage of the total money obtained by the client, at trial or by settlement.

Figure 2.3
Lawyer Salaries and Hourly Rates

	Private Practice	Corporate	Government Attorneys
New York	$93,000	$66,000	$40,000
Washington, D.C.	82,000	50,000	40,000
Philadelphia	72,000	53,000	34,900

Source: *The Legal Intelligencer* (August 4, 1999) [cited at www.lawnewsnetwork.com/stories/A4067—1999Aug3.html]

The median hourly billing rate for lawyers nationwide, as of January 1999, was:

- Equity partner $205/hour
- Nonequity partner 195/hour
- Associate lawyer 140/hour
- Staff lawyer 145/hour

Source: *ABA Journal* (September 1999), page 24.

However, top lawyers at large firms in big cities bill considerably more than those average figures. In Los Angeles, partners at Gibson, Dunn & Crutcher are charging $350 to $500 per hour, and senior partners at Latham & Watkins are now commanding $350 to $450 or more. Meanwhile, partners at the third and fourth largest firms in Los Angeles charge between $200 and $400 per hour.

Source: "L.A. Firms' Dirty Little Secret: Hourly Rates," *California Law Week / Cal Law* (September 13, 1999). [www.lawnewsnetwork.com/stories/A5671-1999Sep14.html]

actual costs, such as court fees, transcripts prepared by court reporters, and so on.

The contingent fee is sometimes controversial. Obviously, lawyers do not offer contingent fee contracts to clients unless they believe the case will be won or a good settlement reached, with money recovered. Some say that this encourages lawyers to file more cases and request more damages than they would if they were charging by the hour. On the other hand, many injured persons simply would not have the money to pursue a lawsuit against someone who had injured them, if they had to pay attorney fees of $100 or $200/hour during the time the case was pending, win or lose. If lawsuits were not filed by injured persons, those individuals or firms who caused the injuries would then escape liability for the harm they caused.

CORPORATE LEGAL DEPARTMENTS

corporate counsel or "in-house" counsel: Lawyers who work full-time, at a salary, for a corporation.

About 10 percent of all American attorneys are employed full-time by corporations. These lawyers, called **in-house counsel** or **corporate counsel**, are regular salaried employees of the company, just like members of the corporate personnel or accounting department. They devote their full energies to the company's legal issues and normally do not have a private practice on the side. Many U.S. corporations increased the size of their in-house legal staff during the past 15 years as a cost-saving measure (rather than hiring private law firms for each legal issue or lawsuit as it arose). There are indications in the past few years, however, that this trend is over, due to cost-saving cutbacks in all staffing levels at many large businesses and lower, more competitive bids from law firms.

Much legal work, of course, by both private law firms and corporate legal departments, does not involve court cases at all, but involves business planning, negotiating contracts, advising company officials and employees regarding compliance with governmental regulations, addressing tax issues, and assisting in other commercial legal matters. However, because of the lawyer certification rules explained previously, when a company does need to file a lawsuit against a defendant in another state, an attorney licensed in that state must be hired to institute the lawsuit.

The following chart indicates, with respect to certain substantive areas of law, how much corporate legal work is done "in house" and how much is done by outside law firms. As can be seen, much of the time when large businesses are involved in court cases (litigation) or bankruptcy, they hire private law firms.

ETHICAL ISSUES FOR ATTORNEYS

A longstanding rule of law is that the client's communications with his or her lawyer are confidential—that is, the lawyer may not disclose anything told to him or her by the client during the time the client was represented by the lawyer, unless the client gives permission for the disclosure. For example, if

WHO DOES THE WORK? IN-HOUSE OR OUTSIDE COUNSEL?

Practice Area	Corporate Law Department	Outside Counsel
Antitrust	56%	35%
Bankruptcy	53	42
Benefits/ERISA	63	31
Contracts	98	1
Environmental	60	31
General Corporate	95	3
International	49	30
Labor (EEOC)	78	19
Litigation*	24	76
Mergers & Acquisitions	60	30
Patent	40	33
Regulatory*	85	11
Securities/Finance	67	24
Tax	42	30
Trademark	52	38

*Excluding environmental

Source: Price Waterhouse 1994 Law Department Spending Survey of 240 companies.

Ben tells his lawyer Teresa that he had slept only two hours the night before his auto accident, Teresa may not repeat this information to anyone else without Ben's authorization. This rule is called the **attorney–client privilege**.

attorney–client privilege: An attorney may not disclose to anyone confidential statements made to him or her by the client.

Although Teresa cannot repeat Ben's comment made to her as his attorney, that does not mean that she should assist Ben in lying, either in or out of court. Teresa should not tell the other attorney or the court what Ben told her, but if Ben is asked questions in court under oath, he will have to tell the truth. As we saw earlier in this chapter with the *Cooperman* case in New York, each state has an ethical code of conduct that governs the professional behavior and conduct of attorneys licensed to practice in that state. These codes require that lawyers be "zealous" in representing their clients but prohibit attorneys from assisting the client in lying to the court. If a client insists on telling falsehoods in court, the attorney should ask the judge to be released from representing the client, in a private conference.

In a case decided in 1998, the U.S. Supreme Court held that the attorney–client privilege continues to exist after the client dies. The case received much publicity because the client who died was Vince Foster, a close friend and legal assistant to President Clinton. Mr. Foster died, apparently by suicide, in 1993. Nine days earlier he had consulted with his lawyer and may have discussed issues concerning the White House. Some years later, Independent Counsel Ken Starr (who was investigating President and Mrs. Clinton) tried to obtain notes taken by the lawyer during his conversation with Mr. Foster. The Supreme Court refused the request, finding that it has "been generally accepted for well over a century, that the attorney–client privilege survives the death of the client."

The public purpose for the attorney–client privilege is that the justice system works best when clients feel free to fully inform their lawyers of all facts they know, whether favorable or unfavorable to their case. Even if some of what the attorney knows is harmful to the client's cause, the attorney can better represent the individual if he or she knows both the strong and weak parts of the case. The American "adversary" system is designed to function so that when each side to a case is vigorously represented, the truth will emerge.

In addition to guarding the confidential communications of clients as discussed previously, most codes state that the attorney must avoid any **conflict of interest**. Obviously, at the least, this means that the lawyer may not represent both the plaintiff and defendant in a case. Also an attorney should avoid any situation in which it appears that he or she may have obtained confidential information from one party that now he or she may attempt to use to benefit the other side.

conflict of interest: A situation that occurs when an attorney attempts to act for both his client and for one whose interest is adverse to that of his client.

Determining whether there is a conflict becomes more difficult when the lawyer represents a business or several businesses. In connection with doing legal work for a corporate client, the lawyer will likely have many private discussions with employees and officers of the corporation. As long as the interests of the corporation and the individuals are exactly the same, there is no problem, but the conflict-of-interest issue becomes sticky when those interests begin to diverge.

Suppose, for example, that the corporation fires the president and he wants to sue the company. Or when the audit is done, there is evidence of mismanagement of money by the controller. Or a member of the Board of Directors asks the attorney for some information that was given to the attorney by the company president. In each case the attorney must determine whether there is any conflict between the representation of the client (the company, in this example) and another party who desires legal advice (such as the board member or the president). The wise attorney declines to become involved in any situation in which there is a potential conflict of interest. She might clearly state that she is representing the company or the individual and recommend that the other party obtain legal counsel of their own.

Attorneys are also considered *officers of the court*. Generally, this means that when licensed to practice law in a jurisdiction, an attorney not only owes allegiance to his clients but has an obligation to the legal system to behave in a way that promotes public confidence in justice. This responsibility involves obeying the court rules and ethical codes governing lawyers in that state and also requires that lawyers not take actions that jeopardize the public's faith in the fairness of the legal system. Attorneys have been disciplined not only for various forms of excessive and misleading advertising, but for various other actions, such as unduly harsh public criticism of a particular judge, which may cause the general public to question the fairness of the system.

ALTERNATE DISPUTE RESOLUTION

In the past decade there has been a significant increase in the number of cases filed in court. The next chapter of this book will discuss litigation—that is, the process of a case moving through the court system. Many jurisdictions have a large backlog of cases to be tried. The resulting delays and the increasing legal costs associated with complex and lengthy litigation, as well as the substantial amount of time that management officials must devote to complicated lawsuits, have caused a great deal of interest in finding ways to resolve civil disputes other than "going to court."

An advantage of alternate dispute resolution (ADR) is that the hearings and paperwork are private. In general, court proceedings and files are open to the press and the public, and anyone can attend trials and hearings. This is not true with ADR proceedings. Some of the more important means of ADR are arbitration, mediation, minitrials, and the so-called rent-a-judge program.

ARBITRATION

Perhaps the best-known of the ADR techniques is **arbitration**, in which the parties refer the dispute to an impartial third party, called the *arbitrator*, who listens to each side and then renders a decision, which is binding on both parties. Arbitration may arise because the parties have agreed earlier (in their contract) to arbitration of all disputes that may arise, or they may decide to arbitrate a dispute after it has arisen.

arbitration: Using a neutral party to hear arguments from the two disputing parties. The arbitrator then makes a decision in the matter.

Arbitration is generally quicker and less expensive than a court trial. Arbitrators can be selected who have specific expertise in the subject area in dispute (for example, an architect can arbitrate a disagreement about the construction of a house). The parties can agree on a specific person they want to be the arbitrator, or the parties can use the services of the American Arbitration Association, a national organization of people who perform arbitration, which has its own set of procedural rules.

FROM THE DESK OF
Laura Lawyer

To: Students
From: Your Lawyer

1. When you decide to engage the services of an attorney, ask friends and business associates, bankers, accountants, and doctors for names of lawyers they can recommend. There is much competition in the legal arena today. You are the consumer and may shop around, ask for references, or ask questions about each attorney's experience with this type of case. You should do this before selecting an attorney.
2. Many attorneys will offer one free consultation to discuss a prospective case. Make sure you know before you go into the office if there will be a fee for the first meeting. This is a good chance to see if you feel comfortable with the attorney and if the attorney seems sharp and listens to you.
3. The best attorneys know a lot about the law but usually are not confident that they have all the answers until they do some research. Every case is somewhat different. If an attorney tells you, "I know all about this; don't worry about a thing," it may be wise to get another opinion.
4. Discuss fee arrangements at the first meeting, and if you decide to retain (hire) the attorney, have the agreement put into writing. Make sure you understand what costs and other expenses you will be expected to pay and how much they will likely be. Find out how often you will be billed, and ask for a detailed billing statement.
5. Discuss who in the law firm will actually handle the case. Will it be this attorney or another or several? Will paralegals (nonlawyers who have studied law and assist the

lawyer) be involved? Paralegals are often very knowledgeable and efficient, but you should know ahead of time if they will assist the attorney.

6. If the lawyer wants a retainer (an "up-front" payment), clarify whether it will be refunded if the time needed is much less than expected and whether it counts against the first few hourly billings.
7. If you are thinking of suing someone, discuss at the first meeting with the lawyer whether it will be possible to collect a judgment from the person being sued. It makes little sense to sue someone who has few assets and no regular job. Courts do not award a "pound of flesh." Even if you are totally right and the other person is wrong, if the defendant has no money or assets and no insurance, you may win the case but never receive any monetary recovery. This is a very frustrating experience for both the lawyer and the client.

In most cases, arbitration is a shorter process than court litigation. The arbitrator probably will not have a backlog of cases like a court and can hear the case sooner; the presentations of the parties are often limited to an hour or a few hours each; and the rules of evidence are much more relaxed than in a court. These factors result in the expenditure of less management and attorney time. The disadvantage is that the parties are generally bound by the decision, and even if they disagree with the result, by agreeing to binding arbitration, they have given up their right to appeal the decision in court. In most cases like the following one, courts have refused to hear an appeal from an arbitration.

SHEARSON/AMERICAN EXPRESS, INC. V. MCMAHON

107 Sup. Ct. 2332 (1987)

FACTS

From 1980 to 1982, Eugene and Julia McMahon were customers of Shearson/American Express, a large national brokerage firm registered with the Securities and Exchange Commission. In October 1984, the McMahons had become quite unhappy with the actions of Shearson broker Mary Ann McNulty and filed this lawsuit against her and Shearson in federal court in New York. The McMahons alleged that Ms. McNulty, with Shearson's knowledge, had engaged in fraudulent practices, had made false statements, and conducted excessive trading on McMahon's accounts, all in violation of the federal Securities Exchange Act of 1934.

When first becoming a client of Shearson, Julia McMahon had signed certain agreements, one of which included the following provision:

"Unless unenforceable due to federal or state law, any controversy arising out of or relating to my accounts . . . shall be settled by arbitration in accordance with the rules, then in effect, of the National Association of Securities Dealers, Inc. or the Board of Directors of the New York Stock Exchange, Inc., and/or the American Stock Exchange, Inc., as I may elect."

Upon receiving notice of the McMahon's lawsuit, Shearson asked the court to dismiss the case and order the McMahons to use arbitration procedures, citing the previous paragraph of the contract they had signed. The federal district court agreed with Shearson, but the McMahons appealed, and the Second Circuit Court of Appeals reversed the decision, finding that a 1953 Supreme Court case, *Wilko v. Swan*, had held that the Securities Exchange Act did not allow a customer to waive his or her right to have a dispute heard in court.

DECISION

The U.S. Supreme Court, in an opinion written by Justice Sandra O'Connor, analyzed the *Wilko* case and several other cases dealing with arbitration, as well as the application of the Federal Arbitration Act. The purpose of this federal law, stated Justice O'Connor, was to "reverse centuries of hostility to arbitration agreements" and to "place arbitration upon the same footing as other contracts." The Act provides that arbitration agreements "shall be valid, irrevocable, and enforceable, save upon such grounds as exist at law or in equity for the revocation of any contract." This federal law thus establishes, said the Court, "a federal policy favoring arbitration" and authorizes a court to order a party to arbitrate "if there has been a refusal or failure to comply with an arbitration agreement," which is exactly what Shearson was contending in this case.

In order to defeat this clear language of the Arbitration Act, Mr. and Mrs. McMahon needed to convince the Court that the Securities Exchange Act intended to exempt disputes with securities brokers from the law. One section of the Exchange Act did state that "the district courts of the United States . . . shall have exclusive jurisdiction of violations of this Act." The McMahons argued that this sentence meant that any contract which took away their rights to go to federal court was invalid.

The Supreme Court, however, found that this sentence must be read in connection with another section of the Securities Exchange Act that prohibited contracts waiving "compliance with any provision" of the law. Justice O'Connor stated that what Congress was concerned about was a contract between a client and a broker by which the customer gave up some substantive right (e.g., the amount of the commission, the duty of the broker to disclose all material facts). Such an agreement would be void, she said, whether it was voluntarily signed or not, but the arbitration agreement in this case did not waive "compliance with the provisions" of the Securities Exchange Act and was legal and binding.

In its conclusion, the Supreme Court discussed some of the concerns that caused the 1953 decision in the *Wilko* case. At that time, arbitration was not nearly as widely accepted as it is now, and many persons were not sure about the ability of arbitrators to handle complex cases. Also, some commentators questioned whether the streamlined procedures used in arbitration deprived some persons of due process of law. Justice O'Connor wrote that "most of the reasons given in *Wilko* have been rejected subsequently" and that numerous significant matters are regularly dealt with through arbitration, without "any consequential restriction on substantive rights."

The Supreme Court therefore reversed the Court of Appeals decision and ordered that the dispute be submitted to arbitration, based on the contract signed by the parties.

CASE QUESTIONS

1. What key factors persuaded the court to order the dispute to arbitration?
2. What were the main arguments of the customers that they should be allowed to file a case in federal court?
3. Why do you suppose the McMahons wanted to have the case heard in court? Why did Shearson want the case heard by an arbitrator?
4. What effect will this case have on future arbitration agreements?

The type of contract between the broker and the customer that was at issue in the *Shearson* case (requiring arbitration of any disputes) is common in the securities business and other financial fields. Controversy has arisen because most arbitrators used in such cases have previously worked as brokers or financial advisors. Studies have shown that brokers have won most of the arbitration cases filed by customers. Stock brokerage and securities associations are now studying possible reforms to make their arbitration procedures more customer-oriented.

Another interesting sidelight to the increasing use of alternate dispute resolution is that many professional arbitrators are developing financial dependency upon certain large companies that regularly use their services to arbitrate disputes with their customers. There is some pressure on these arbitrators to render decisions that do not seriously anger the companies in order to keep their business. Other issues related to arbitration are discussed in the following article.

Escape from Arbitration

Sticking Points in Adhesion Contracts Ruled 'Unfair'

In 1994, Hooters restaurants gave its employees an ultimatum of sorts. If they wanted to be eligible for raises, transfers and promotions, they had to accept binding arbitration of workplace disputes. Annette Phillips, a bartender at a franchise in Myrtle Beach, S.C., signed on the dotted line.

Two years later, she claimed a company official sexually harassed her by grabbing and slapping her buttocks. After complaining to her manager, who advised her to "Let it go," Phillips quit and threatened to sue under Title VII of the 1964 Civil Rights Act.

Instead, Hooters went to court, seeking an order compelling Phillips to arbitrate her claim. The company wanted to enforce the contract, which gave it control over the choice of arbitrators and allowed the company to change the arbitration rules at any time.

No Backing for 'One-sided' Rules

But according to an April 8 decision of the 4th U.S. Circuit Court of Appeals, the company's binding arbitration program was not really binding. The Richmond, Va.-based appeals court refused to enforce the agreement because the arbitration rules were "so one-sided as to undermine the neutrality of the proceeding." *Hooters of America v. Phillips*, No. 98-1459.

Phillips' case is one of several recent decisions in which claimants have been allowed to walk away from the arbitration table because of unfair contract provisions.

In particular, courts are closely scrutinizing arbitration provisions in contracts that must be signed as a condition to employment or other employee benefits, such as raises, promotions or transfers. Courts generally agree that although these are adhesion contracts, public policy dictates they should be honored if they are fair.

"Courts are still in broad scheme very pro-arbitration," says Thomas Stipanowich, chair of the ABA Dispute Resolution Section's Arbitration Committee. "But I do think that with increasing frequency, courts are beginning to look at the guts of arbitration agreements in standardized adhesion contracts, and that's good."

The Hooters agreement did not hold up under such scrutiny, according to Phillips' attorney, Sandra McCallion of Debevoise & Plimpton in New York City. The contract was "egregiously problematic," she says. "The rules didn't provide a level playing field."

Hidden Rules

The rules weren't even communicated to an employee with an age and sex discrimination claim in another case, *Rosenberg v. Merrill Lynch, Pierce, Fenner & Smith Inc.*, 170 F.3d 1 (Feb. 24). As a result, the 1st U.S. Circuit Court of Appeals refused to compel arbitration.

The employee, Susan Rosenberg, signed a form agreeing to arbitrate claims after being hired by Merrill Lynch as a financial consultant. Rather than specifying the kinds of complaints she would have to submit to arbitration, the agreement said Rosenberg must abide by the arbitration rules of various industrial organizations, including the New York Stock Exchange.

Rosenberg sued after being fired, saying her work was better than that of four or more men in the same position who remained on the job.

Merrill Lynch admitted it had agreed to inform Rosenberg of the industry arbitration rules, but "it did not keep its side of the bargain," the 1st Circuit Court said.

The court specified that if the company had made a "modest effort" to make the information available to the employee, she would have been compelled to arbitrate.

When ruling on the enforceability of arbitration contracts, courts look to *Gilmer v. Interstate/Johnson Lane Corp.*, 500 U.S. 20. The 1991 U.S. Supreme Court decision blocked stockbroker Robert Gilmer from suing his employer for age discrimination. The suit was barred because he had signed the security industry's standard form agreeing to arbitrate job claims.

The High Court said the agreement did not interfere with Gilmer's substantive rights under the age discrimination statute; it merely required that they be settled by arbitration rather than the courts.

Of the circuit courts that have considered the issue, all but one have interpreted *Gilmer* to require enforcement of predispute arbitration agreements, so long as they are fair and provide the employees with a forum to vindicate their rights.

The decisions include *Koveleskie v. SBC Markets Inc.*, 167 F.3d 361 (7th Cir. 1999); and *Seus v. Nuveen*, 146 F.3d 175 (3rd Cir. 1998).

On a Track to Arbitrate

The pro-arbitration decisions are gaining momentum, says Marc Greenbaum, a law professor at Suffolk University in Boston. Most appeals courts "view *Gilmer* as the leading engine on this big freight train to arbitrate, arbitrate, arbitrate, and keep the cases out of court," he says. "It's like the little choo-choo train that could."

But the 9th U.S. Circuit Court of Appeals based in San Francisco has attempted a derailment. In *Duffield v. Robertson Stephens & Co.*, 144 F.3d 1182 (1998), the court found that plaintiffs cannot be compelled to arbitrate if a Title VII claim is alleged.

The plaintiff, Tonyja Duffield, had signed an agreement to arbitrate any employment-related disputes as a condition of her employment as a broker-dealer in the securities industry. In refusing to enforce the contract, the 9th Circuit found that Congress intended to preclude compulsory arbitration of Title VII and other statutory discrimination disputes in enacting the Civil Rights Act of 1991.

The Equal Employment Opportunities Commission had filed an amicus brief in the Hooters case urging a similar result. It contended that employees cannot waive their rights to take a statutory discrimination claim to court before a dispute arises.

"In *Gilmer*, the Supreme Court seemed to adopt the distinction between waiving substantive rights and simply waiving the judicial forum," says Robert Gregory, an EEOC senior attorney. "But because we feel that statutory rights are so important, we don't buy that distinction."

The 9th Circuit *Duffield* case remains the exception. In fact, courts seem so willing to encourage arbitration that at least one effectively rewrote an arbitration agreement so it would be fair enough to compel the employees to arbitrate their claims.

In that case, *Armendariz v. Foundation Health Psychcare Services Inc.*, 80 Cal. Rptr. 2d 255 (1998), the California Court of Appeals had found that the company's arbitration agreement unfairly limited the claimants' remedies to back wages from the date of discharge to the date of the arbitration award. Instead of throwing out the entire agreement, however, the court simply severed the remedies provision and ordered the claimants to arbitrate.

Writing Class

Companies writing their own arbitration agreements can look to the published cases for lessons in what not to do. Giving the company control over the choice of arbitrators and allowing it to change the arbitration rules can be fatal to the contract. Failing to inform the employee of the arbitration rules seems to be another deal breaker. So is limiting remedies.

Safeguards to help ensure fairness include having a system for choosing an independent arbitrator and putting an independent administrator in charge of the arbitration system, say experts. In addition, due process protocols should be followed. Claimants must be able to vindicate themselves as fully as if they were before a judge and jury.

Even when the contract is fair, some experts believe that mandatory arbitration for workplace disputes should not be allowed.

"I have a lot of discomfort with the idea that an employer can effectively condition a job on an individual's agreement to waive a judicial forum," says Greenbaum. "I have less of a problem if it is optional."

However, the ABA's Stipanowich believes these agreements can serve a valid purpose. "If properly constructed, various out-of-court processes can offer substantial benefits for consumers and employees as well as corporations," he says.

One point on which the experts do agree: Concerns about arbitration agreements deemed adhesion contracts should not be cited to discourage or ban arbitration agreements made by parties on a level playing field.

"Whatever we do," says Stipanowich, "we don't want to throw the baby out with the bath water. We need to be very careful that in our zeal to address legitimate concerns . . . that we don't undercut the principles of flexibility and autonomy that animate the broader fields of arbitration between business-persons."

"Escape from Arbitration" by Alexander Varney McDonald, *ABA Journal*, August 1999, pp. 32–33. Copyright American Bar Association. Reprinted by permission of the *ABA Journal*.

MEDIATION

mediation: Use of a neutral party to help the two sides reach an agreement.

The process of **mediation** is different from arbitration in that the independent third party who is called upon to assist the two disputing parties does not render a decision, but merely attempts to aid them in reaching a settlement. The Federal Mediation and Conciliation Service has been used successfully to resolve certain well-publicized labor management disputes in recent years.

Many localities have also employed mediation to settle neighborhood disputes without resorting to the court system. Several manufacturers and business associations, like the Better Business Bureau, have utilized mediation as well in their attempts to handle consumer complaints.

There is also a process called *med-arb*, in which the neutral party tries to mediate the dispute first, but later may serve as an arbitrator.

MINITRIALS

minitrial: An out-of-court hearing before a neutral advisor, attended by key officers of each side.

One of the most recent additions to alternate dispute resolution techniques is the **minitrial**. In the 1980s, many corporations and government agencies began to settle disputes using this procedure. In a minitrial, the parties select a "neutral advisor" (who need not be a lawyer) who holds a short hearing—maybe one or two days—at which time the attorneys for each side present their best case. One of the key features of this process is that each side must have a top management official present for the minitrial, and the two managers meet immediately after the minitrial to attempt to settle the dispute.

Minitrials have proven quite successful. When the top managers fully hear both their side and the other side of the dispute, they are better able to ascertain the strengths and weaknesses of each. The process is quick, and the information is kept from public view. Minitrials use a businesslike decision-making procedure, reducing complicated issues down to the essential points of disagreement and then allowing the problem-solving and negotiation skills of top managers to find a solution to the dispute. Many complex business disputes that have dragged on for years have been settled quickly with a minitrial.

RENT-A-JUDGE

"rent-a-judge" process: The parties employ a retired judge to hear the dispute in private.

The **"rent-a-judge" process** taps into the expertise of the many retired judges in our country. The parties make arrangements to employ and pay a judge they select to hear a particular dispute. The process will typically move much faster than if the case were in the regular court system, and the proceedings will normally be kept secret. The judge will make a decision that is normally binding on the parties.

IN CONSULTATION

Marvin Manager has a problem. One of his employees is accusing his company, ABC, Inc., of disability discrimination under the Americans with Disabilities Act. The employee, Edwin, signed a contract when he was hired. Included in the contract is a clause that states:

> I understand that as a condition of employment and continued employment, I agree to submit any complaints to arbitration and to abide by and accept the final decision of the arbitration panel as the ultimate resolution of my complaint(s) for any and all events that arise out of my employment and/or termination of my employment.

Several months after joining ABC and signing this contract, Edwin filed his disability complaints with the Equal Employment Opportunity Commission (EEOC). Marvin was shocked by both the complaint and, more importantly, Edwin's EEOC filing. Marvin assumed that if any of his employees had employment complaints, they would pursue arbitration.

Edwin told Marvin that he did not consider himself bound by the arbitration clause in the contract. He alleged that he did not understand what he was signing away and he also did not feel that he had any power to negotiate because his job was on the line. He intended to pursue all of his rights under the Americans with Disabilities Act, including a jury trial.

Marvin approached his company's in-house corporate counsel, Laura Lawyer. He asked Laura whether Edwin could evade the mandatory arbitration clause. Here is their conversation:

Marvin:	Laura:
(1) Isn't an employment contract binding on both the employees and the employer?	(1) Most employment contracts are binding so long as they are legal, signed by competent parties, and not contrary to public policy.
(2) Then should we be able to force Edwin to go to arbitration?	(2) Not necessarily. Mandatory arbitration clauses are controversial, and some assert they are against public policy.
(3) What about Edwin's allegation that he did not understand what he was signing and that he felt he had no bargaining power?	(3) The court may take Edwin's allegations seriously. Mandatory arbitration clauses are closely scrutinized by the courts because they are often a condition of employment. **Let me research the applicable law to see whether Edwin is bound by the arbitration clause in our contract. I'll get back to you.**

FROM THE DESK OF
Laura Lawyer

To: Marvin Manager

RE: Enforceability of mandatory arbitration clauses in employment contracts

Dear Marvin:

The presence of mandatory arbitration clauses has grown dramatically in recent years. Employers favor them because of the great reduction in costs they offer by providing a rapid solution to disputes without the expense of discovery and a trial. Courts, however, consider mandatory arbitration clauses in employment contracts suspect for several reasons. First, employment disputes often involve civil rights, which are strongly protected by statute and the Constitution. Courts are disinclined to allow employers to force employees to waive their full ability to protect their civil and statutory rights. Second, some courts assume that employees do not understand what they are waiving when they sign a contract containing an arbitration clause. Many employees apparently do not realize that arbitration is binding and that by agreeing to arbitration, they are giving up all access to the regular court system. Finally, courts are wary of employers who take advantage of their significant bargaining power with new hires and force people who need their job to sign away rights. Some courts find this practice oppressive for new employees who may not feel they have the ability to disagree with any clauses in their contract. The EEOC agrees and has stated that it considers mandatory arbitration clauses unenforceable. Nonetheless, the courts are split on whether mandatory arbitration clauses in employment contracts are enforceable.

There is some agreement among the courts, however, as to what must be present in order to enforce a compulsory arbitration clause in an employment contract. Employees cannot be forced to waive substantive rights, so courts require that employees know what they are waiving. It would be very helpful if we could have more information about the circumstances under which Edwin signed his agreement. If we cannot establish that we explained the clause to him or even gave him the opportunity to ask questions, then we may not be able to enforce the arbitration provision. It would also assist our case if we could even establish that Edwin read the clause before signing the contract. Only if we can prove that Edwin knowingly and expressly waived his rights can we enforce our arbitration clause.

With regard to mandatory arbitration clauses in employment contracts, we should consider the following questions:

1. What are the arguments in support of mandatory arbitration in employment disputes?
2. What could Marvin and ABC have done differently to avoid the risk that the company's arbitration clause is unenforceable?
3. Why do you think the courts more closely scrutinize arbitration clauses in employment contracts as compared with other commercial agreements? Do you agree with the courts' concerns over fairness to employees and protection of employees' rights?

SUMMARY

The American legal system contains substantial state and federal components. Within each system there are trial courts, usually intermediate appellate courts, and a supreme court. In order for a court to hear and decide a case, it must have both personal and subject-matter jurisdiction. In addition, there must be an actual dispute between the parties, and the person bringing the case must have standing to make the arguments.

Persons in business will undoubtedly have occasion to employ the services of a lawyer at some time and should do so carefully and in an informed manner. This chapter has examined the process of becoming a lawyer and some of the differences between types of lawyers and large and small law firms. There are primarily three types of fee arrangements clients make with attorneys—hourly, contingent, and set fees. Many large companies have increased the size of their in-house legal staff and are relying less on outside counsel than in the past.

Over the past 20 years various types of ADR techniques have developed as an option to court litigation. The most popular types of ADR are arbitration, mediation, minitrials, and "renting" a judge. These methods are an attempt to reduce the high costs of litigation and resolve business disputes in a quick and private manner.

CHAPTER QUESTIONS

1. Describe the court system in your state. What are the names of the trial courts, and what type of jurisdiction does each have? Is there a small claims court, and what is its jurisdiction? What appellate courts are there?
2. Where is the nearest federal court? How many federal judges are there at that court? List their names and how long each one has been a judge. What federal appellate circuit are you in? Where would an appeal from a decision made by your local federal district court be heard?
3. What are the main differences between arbitration, mediation, minitrials, and the rent-a-judge program?
4. What is the difference between a lawyer in a private practice and one who is "in-house counsel" to a corporation? Are the ethical duties or the application of the lawyer–client privilege or conflict-of-interest rules any different depending on which type of lawyer the person is?
5. International Shoe Co. manufactures and sells shoes and other footwear. It is incorporated in Delaware and has its principal place of business in Missouri. For several years International Shoe had about 12 salespeople in the state of Washington who were compensated by commissions. The company had no offices and no inventory of shoes in Washington, although the salespeople occasionally rented space and rooms to show the shoes, for which they were reimbursed. The salespeople were given some samples, and after they showed the shoes, they solicited orders, which were sent to St. Louis for acceptance. If the contracts were accepted by International Shoe, the shoes were shipped directly from Missouri to the purchasers. The state of Washington decided that the salespeople were "employees" and sued International Shoe in state court in Washington to collect unpaid unemployment compensation contributions. The company argued that the state of Washington had no jurisdiction over it. How would you decide this case? Why? [See *International Shoe Co. v. Washington*, 326 U.S. 310 (1945).]

6. The Funtime Corporation announced plans to develop a major amusement park in a marshy area of central Wisconsin. The park would feature "badger races," roller coasters, and other attractions and would create 500 new jobs. Some citizens were not thrilled, however. The local Sierra Club filed suit to block the development, claiming that the park would destroy the habitat for 30 species of migratory waterfowl and cause other damage to wildlife. In addition, George King, a local resident, complained that he has hiked and camped in that area for 30 years and does not want the project to be built. Does the club have standing to raise these issues? Does George? What are the issues? Please explain your answers.

7. The Federal Arbitration Act establishes the validity of arbitration agreements in all "contracts evidencing a transaction involving commerce." An Alabama state law states that arbitration clauses are not valid to deprive a person of their right to sue in court. An Alabama customer signed a contract with a termite inspection company that contained a clause requiring all disputes to be settled by arbitration. When the customer filed a lawsuit, arising from the inspection, the termite company claimed that the federal law preempted the state law and that the dispute must go to arbitration. How would you decide this case? Why? [*Allied-Bruce Terminex Companies, Inc. v. Dobson*, 513 U.S., 265 (1995)]

8. William, a resident of Massachusetts, was the president and major shareholder of a Massachusetts corporation, which was developing some real estate in New Hampshire. He made certain false statements to purchasers regarding some of the lots his company sold. Some of the unhappy buyers sued him in the New Hampshire state court. He claimed that the New Hampshire courts did not have jurisdiction over him. How would you decide this case? Why? What factors would lead you to change your answer?

9. A lawyer in Los Angeles reportedly called one federal judge "an anti-Semite," "drunk on the bench," and "one of the worst judges on the federal bench." If the attorney did make the remarks, may he be sanctioned by the Bar Association, or are his words protected by the First Amendment?

10. A lawyer placed the following entry in the yellow pages of the telephone book under the heading "Attorneys" in Winter Haven, Florida: "Ibanez, Silvia, S., CPA, CTX1, se habla español." Ms. Ibanez was in fact licensed as a CPA (certified public accountant) and CTX1 (certified financial planner) and apparently did speak Spanish. Nevertheless, she was accused of "false, deceptive and misleading" advertising by the state Board of Accountancy, in part because she was not actively practicing public accounting. She challenged the action of the Board on "freedom of speech" grounds, claiming her ads were legal as a protected form of speech. How would you decide this case? Why? [*Ibanez v. Florida Department of Business and Professional Regulation*, 512 U.S., 114 S.Ct. 2084 (1994)]

PRACTICAL EXERCISE

Using the factual situation outlined at the end of Chapter 1 (Mary's very bad day), prepare a memo indicating (1) what type of fee arrangement Mary might make with a lawyer concerning each of her legal problems; (2) what type of law firm she might seek out to assist her, and why she should make this choice; and (3) what courts, in your state, would have jurisdiction over the various legal disputes in Mary's situation.

FURTHER INFORMATION

www.abanet.org
Official site of American Bar Association.
www.lawnewsnetwork.com
Site containing daily reports on interesting legal issues.
www.uscourts.gov
Home page of the federal court system.
www.adr.org
American Arbitration Association site.

CHAPTER 3

LITIGATION—GOING TO COURT

LEARNING OBJECTIVES

After you have read this chapter, you should be able to:

1. Outline the steps involved in taking a case to court.
2. Describe the procedures of jury selection, including *voir dire* and the types of juror challenges.
3. Identify the stages of a trial and the appellate process.
4. Summarize the different types of judgments and how courts enforce them.

CHAPTER OUTLINE

I. Progress of a Case from Filing to the Trial
II. Jury Procedures
III. The Trial
IV. The Appellate Process
V. Types of Judgments; Enforcing and Collecting Judgments

If a competitor ran advertisements making or implying false statements about your business, how would you respond in court? What allegations would you make in your complaint to effectively present your case?

"Get you off? You'll be lucky if I can defend you with a straight face!"

Source: From *The Wall Street Journal*, January 18, 1995. Reprinted with permission of Cartoon Features Syndicate.

INTRODUCTION

In the previous chapter we learned how the American legal system is structured, what types of cases should be filed in certain courts, and what powers and restrictions govern court jurisdiction. We also discussed the educational process required to become an attorney, the different types of lawyers and what their duties and responsibilities are, and the relationship between lawyers and business. Chapter 2 also examined several types of alternate dispute resolutions (ADR), which are methods of resolving disputes without actually going to court. This chapter continues the explanation of the American legal system by examining the procedures used when a matter does arrive at the courthouse. As before, our goal is not to turn you into an amateur lawyer but to provide you with more information on how the system works. With this knowledge, you will be a more informed consumer of legal services and will be able to participate more fully and more intelligently in business decisions involving legal issues.

THE PROGRESS OF A CASE FROM FILING TO THE TRIAL

COMPLAINT AND ANSWER

Once one of the parties to a dispute decides that he or she wishes to have a court make a decision in the matter, the proper court must be selected, as we have discussed in the previous chapter. The next step, usually taken with the assistance of a lawyer, is to prepare a **complaint**. This is the first document filed in the case; it sets forth, in numbered paragraphs, the arguments and factual assertions made by the **plaintiff** (the one filing the case). A sample complaint appears in Figure 3.1. The complaint must state enough facts so that the court can determine if it has jurisdiction of the case and also so the defen-

complaint: The plaintiff's version of the events that led to the suit, and request for damages or other relief.

plaintiff: The person who files a civil lawsuit against another.

Figure 3.1
Complaint

State of Washington
In The District Court for King County

John Jackson, Plaintiff
v.
Paul Brown, Defendant

COMPLAINT

1. The plaintiff, John Jackson, is a resident of King County in the state of Washington.
2. The defendant, Paul Brown, is a resident of the city of Seattle, King County, in the state of Washington.
3. On May 2, 2000, plaintiff was driving his 1992 Chevrolet automobile in a lawful manner on Pike Street in the city of Seattle, King County, Washington.
4. On the same date, defendant Paul Brown was driving his 1987 Ford pickup on Pike Street in Seattle.
5. At approximately 3:00 p.m. defendant Brown's vehicle was following behind the plaintiff's vehicle, when plaintiff applied his brakes to avoid hitting a dog which had run into the street.
6. Defendant brought his vehicle to a stop directly behind the plaintiff's car.
7. After stopping his truck, the defendant jumped out and ran toward plaintiff's car shouting angry obscenities at the plaintiff because he had stopped.
8. Plaintiff got out of his car to attempt to talk to the defendant, but before he could say anything, the defendant, still shouting, grabbed the plaintiff's shoulders and pushed him against the car.
9. Defendant acted intentionally, and his wrongful battery against plaintiff caused physical injury to him from which he still suffers and will continue to suffer in the future.
10. As the direct result of defendant's actions, plaintiff has suffered considerable pain and suffering, has incurred significant medical expenses, and has lost earnings due to his inability to work for several weeks after the battery by the defendant.

WHEREFORE, plaintiff requests that this Honorable Court award him damages from the defendant in the amount of $500,000 plus his attorney's fees.

____
John Jackson
Plaintiff

summons: A document issued by the court when a civil case is filed. It notifies the defendant of the suit and tells him/her when an answer must be filed.

dant (the person or persons against whom the case is filed) can understand and answer the claims made against him.

SUMMONS AND SERVICE OF PROCESS

In most states the complaint must be signed by the plaintiff; then, the original is taken to the appropriate court and filed with the clerk. At the same time, a **summons** is issued. This document technically comes from the court (although it is usually typed ahead of time by the plaintiff's attorney and then signed by the court clerk) and is directed to the defendant. It tells the defendant what court the case is in, what judge the case is assigned to (which is determined in some random method at the court when the case is filed), and how long the defendant has to respond.

The next stage in the process is **service of process**. Fairness requires that if John is going to sue Paul, he needs to inform him about the lawsuit, not just file the papers at the courthouse. Generally, service of process requires that a copy of the complaint and summons be personally delivered to the defendant—this is called "personal service." If the defendant is not served within a certain time, the case can be dismissed. In some cases, where the defendant's whereabouts are unknown, or the defendant is deliberately evading service, the law will allow some type of "substitute service," such as mailing the notice to him, posting the papers on the defendant's door, or publicizing it in a newspaper. You will recall our discussion from the previous chapter concerning the need for personal jurisdiction over the defendant.

service of process: Delivery of the complaint and summons to the defendant.

After the defendant (Paul) receives the papers, he has a limited time (many state laws allow 20 days) to file an **answer** or take some other action. If Paul files an answer, it must contain a response, either admitting or denying each of the paragraphs of the complaint. A sample answer appears in Figure 3.2. Often, rather than filing an answer, the defendant will file a **motion to dismiss** (a request that the court terminate the case right then) or some other motion within the 20 days. Until the court rules on the motion, the defendant does not have to file an answer.

answer: The defendant's point by point response to the complaint.

motion to dismiss: A request by the defendant that the case be dismissed because no valid legal claim has been made.

MOTIONS

The *motion to dismiss* requests that the court dismiss the case because the plaintiff has failed to properly state a valid legal claim. Most of the time these motions are denied; the court rules that the plaintiff has alleged a valid case and should be given the chance to prove it at trial. The defendant is then ordered to file an answer within a certain time. Occasionally, however, the plaintiff has failed to properly state a recognized legal claim, and the case is dismissed. For example, if Sharon files a lawsuit against Steve alleging a breach of contract, and she fails to state in her complaint sufficient facts to show that there ever was a valid contract existing between the two of them, her complaint would probably be dismissed.

If, after receiving service of process, the defendant fails to answer or bring some type of motion, the plaintiff will be entitled to take a *default* at the end of the time period. If the defendant is so angry upon being served with court papers (as many people are) that he or she tears them up or burns them, thinking that the case will go away, the defendant is badly mistaken. Every competent lawyer keeps track of the day when papers are served in each case and the date when answers are due and will ask the court for a **default judgment** in favor of the client soon after the time period for answers has passed.

default judgment: The court enters judgment for the plaintiff when the defendant fails to answer the complaint.

As the case moves along there may be many other kinds of motions filed by the parties. Most courts will not schedule a trial for at least a year or two (or longer), so if either side wants some action taken by the court before then, the party must schedule a hearing to request a court order. For example, if one

Figure 3.2
Answer

State of Washington
In The District Court for King County

John Jackson, Plaintiff
v.
Paul Brown, Defendant

ANSWER

1. Defendant neither admits nor denies paragraph one of the complaint for lack of information, but leaves plaintiff to his proofs.
2. Defendant admits the allegations of paragraph two.
3. Defendant admits that plaintiff was driving his vehicle on the day in question, but denies that it was in a lawful manner.
4. Defendant admits the allegations of paragraph four.
5. Defendant admits that plaintiff suddenly and abruptly stopped his car in the middle of the street, but denies the remainder of paragraph five.
6. Defendant admits that he had to suddenly stop his vehicle in order to avoid hitting the plaintiff.
7. Defendant admits that he stepped out of his car and criticized plaintiff's driving, but denies the balance of paragraph seven.
8. Defendant denies the allegations of paragraph eight and leaves plaintiff to his proofs.
9. Defendant denies the allegations of paragraph nine and leaves plaintiff to his proofs.
10. Defendant denies the allegations of paragraph ten and leaves plaintiff to his proofs.

WHEREFORE, Defendant requests that the Court dismiss this complaint so wrongfully filed and award attorney fees and costs to defendant.

____
Paul Brown
Defendant

party believes the trial should be held elsewhere (a change of venue, as discussed in Chapter 2), wants a temporary restraining order preventing the other side from selling the property that is the subject of the lawsuit, or desires a list of all doctors the plaintiff has seen, that party must file a motion for relief, and the court will set a date for a hearing on that motion.

counterclaim: The defendant in a civil case files a counter action, alleging that the plaintiff has caused some injury to the defendant.

COUNTERCLAIMS

In some cases, not only does the defendant assert that she did not do what the plaintiff has charged, but that the plaintiff has actually injured her. In this situation the defendant may file a **counterclaim**, which is in effect a complaint by the defendant against the plaintiff, to which the plaintiff will have to file an answer (usually called a "response"). When this is done, the court will eventually have to decide the two cases, one brought by the plaintiff and one by the defendant.

For example, in our mythical *Jackson v. Brown* case, if Mr. Brown not only denies hurting Mr. Jackson, but in fact asserts that it was Mr. Jackson who hit him, he (Brown) might not only file an *answer* as in our example, but might also file a *counterclaim,* seeking damages from Jackson.

While the decision of whether to file a counterclaim is usually an option for the defendant, sometimes the defendant *must* file a counterclaim or lose his or her legal right to file it later. The Federal Rules of Civil Procedure control federal court practice. Rule 13(a) states that if the defendant has any type of counterclaim arising out of the same transaction that is the subject of the plaintiff's complaint and he or she does not assert it at the time of responding to the complaint, he or she will lose the chance to make it at a later date. The legal phrase *res judicata* ("the thing has been decided") means that once a court has decided an issue between two parties in one case, it will not hear and decide that issue in another case. This rule may even apply to issues that *should have been* raised in the previous case, as the next case illustrates.

MARTINO V. MCDONALD'S SYSTEM, INC.

598 F. 2d 1079 (7th Cir. 1979)

FACTS

Louis Martino and his three brothers entered into a franchise agreement with McDonald's in 1962. They organized McDonald's Drive-in of Ottumwa, Iowa, Inc. and operated the business. The contract the Martinos signed with McDonald's provided that neither Martino nor any member of his immediate family would acquire a financial interest in a competing self-service food business without the written consent of McDonald's.

In 1968, however, Martino's son purchased a Burger Chef franchise in Pittsburgh, Kansas, with Martino providing the financing. McDonald's sued Martino and his brothers for this violation of their agreement, and the lawsuit ended with the parties reaching a consent judgment (settlement). The court entered the judgment on the record and included its findings of fact (one of which was that Martino had breached the contract). As part of the settlement, Martino sold the franchise back to McDonald's.

A few years later Martino brought this lawsuit against McDonald's, charging, among other things, that the franchise agreement violated the Sherman Antitrust Act as an illegal restraint on trade. McDonald's brought a motion to dismiss, based on the argument that Martino's claim should have been brought in the first case, because it was a compulsory counterclaim under Federal Rule 13(a). The lower court agreed and dismissed the case.

DECISION

Judge Pell wrote the opinion of the Court of Appeals:

Rule 13(a) says "a *pleading* shall state as a counterclaim any claim which at the time of serving the *pleading* the pleader has against the opposing party...." However, in the earlier action, Martino filed no pleadings, as the word is defined in the federal rules. "Rule 13(a) is in some ways a harsh rule. It forces parties to raise certain claims at the time and place chosen by their opponents or to lose them. The rule, however, is the result of a balancing between competing interests. The convenience of the party with a compulsory counterclaim is sacrificed in the interest of judicial economy."

The drafters of Rule 13(a) did not choose the term "pleading" unadvisedly. It no doubt marks, although somewhat arbitrarily, the point at which "the judicial burden of the earlier lawsuit outweighs the opposing party's interest in bringing an action when and where it is most convenient."

Since the earlier action was concluded by a consent judgment before Martino filed an answer, Rule 13(a) does not apply here. McDonald's argues that the *time for an answer* had expired (even though no answer was filed), but there are other sanctions in the court rules to apply to that problem (i.e., a default judgment). Therefore, the antitrust claim is not barred by Rule 13(a).

There is another theory, however, that bars Martino's claim. The principles of *res judicata* establish a narrowly defined class of "common law compulsory counterclaims." Judge Pell stated that "a judgment on the merits of a case operates as an absolute bar to relitigation between the parties of every matter offered and received to sustain or defeat the claim or demand and every matter *which might have been received* for that purpose." Since the court in the earlier case had included judicial conclusions of law and fact (Martino's breach of contract), he should have, and could have, raised the antitrust claims then and cannot do so now. The judgment of dismissal entered by the district court was affirmed.

CASE QUESTIONS

1. What is the purpose of the compulsory counterclaim rule? Why does Judge Pell describe it as "in some ways a harsh rule"? What does he mean by the "interest of judicial economy"?
2. What pleadings were filed in the earlier case? By whom?
3. What is the *res judicata* rule? What is the purpose of this rule, which causes the court to rule in the end in favor of McDonald's? Where does the common law compulsory counterclaim rule come from?

AFFIRMATIVE DEFENSES

Another defensive document sometimes filed by he defendant is an *affirmative defense,* which claims that even if the plaintiff were to prove all he or she has alleged, there is some legal reason why he or she should lose the case. One example of a valid affirmative defense is the **statute of limitations**, which is a law that specifies how long after an event occurs the plaintiff has to file a lawsuit. In most states, for negligence or tort claims, the statute of limitations is two or three years. If the plaintiff waits too long, the suit will be dismissed even if he or she has a strong case.

statute of limitations: A law that specifies how many years after an event a person has in which to bring a lawsuit.

DISCOVERY

The next phase of the case is the *discovery* stage. This is the time when each side is entitled to learn about the other party's case—the names and addresses of the witnesses who will be called at trial, what they will say, what evidence the other side plans to introduce, and what medical records, bank records, charts, and other physical evidence support each side's claim. Some of the more important types of discovery procedures are set forth in the following sections.

deposition: An out-of-court procedure where the attorney for one side can ask direct questions of the opposing party.

Depositions Each party is allowed to schedule the other for a **deposition**, a sort of minitrial or cross-examination. A deposition is held out of court, generally in one of the attorney's offices, or sometimes in the client's own office, but with a court reporter taking down and later typing up all that is said. The court reporter administers the oath ("Do you swear to tell the truth..."), and then the person is questioned by the opposing attorney.

This proceeding gives each lawyer the opportunity to ask the opposing party any and all questions they may have about any issues that may pertain to the case. The deposition is the only chance for one side's attorney to directly ask the other side's key person a wide-ranging array of questions. Sometimes the questioning gets pretty far off the subject of the case. The party's own attorney is there, of course, to object to certain questions, but the judge is not present, so there is no ruling on the objections. On occasion, the atmosphere gets quite lively, which can make for some interesting reading when the court reporter prepares the transcript of the deposition.

If an attorney really believes that the question is clearly improper, the attorney may tell the client, "I instruct you not to answer." The question may be presented later to the judge, who may or may not issue an order compelling an answer to the question.

Interrogatories Another widely used discovery tool is called **interrogatories**. These are sets of written questions sent by one side to the other, requesting information about the factual basis of the party's claim. These questions are often quite detailed, such as, "Interrogatory 1: Please list all bank accounts you have ever maintained with name and address of bank, date each account was opened and closed, and average balance." While parties must answer all relevant interrogatories, they do so in writing at a later date and after much consultation with their attorneys. The answers, therefore, tend to be the bare minimum required and often are as evasive as possible. Interrogatories are useful for getting at hard facts: names of witnesses, dates, and definite information of one kind or another.

interrogatories: A set of written questions sent by one side to the opposing party.

Request for Production of Documents If there are some important, relevant documents in the possession of one party that the other wants to see, a request for production of documents may be used. Often this request seeks copies of medical reports on the plaintiff's condition, prepared by his or her doctor. In addition, in cases where the plaintiff is alleging physical injury, the defendant is entitled to request the plaintiff to see a doctor of the defendant's choosing, in order to provide another opinion of the plaintiff's condition.

The reason all these discovery tools were developed is that the more each side knows about the other's case, the greater the likelihood that the case will be settled without the necessity of a full trial, thus saving considerable time and money. The discovery rules represent an attempt to move away from the "trial by surprise," which is likened to the Perry Mason scenario in which a previously unknown witness shows up late in the trial and offers dramatic and unexpected testimony. In real court cases, each side is required to provide, long before the trial, a list of witnesses who will be called at trial so the other side can adequately prepare for that testimony and perhaps interview or "depose" them. Every case is different, however, and problems sometimes occur that force the judge to make difficult decisions. The following case concerns a situation where the plaintiff's attorney did not comply with the discovery rules, causing the judge to dismiss the case.

DENNIE V. METROPOLITAN MEDICAL CENTER

387 N.W. 2d 401 (Minnesota Supreme Court, 1986)

FACTS

Mr. Francis Dennie entered Metropolitan Medical Center because of numbness in his right hand. Dr. Harold Nolan examined him and diagnosed carpal tunnel syndrome as well as other nerve diseases and difficulties. Surgery was performed on his hand to correct the carpal tunnel syndrome, and later that day a nurse gave Mr. Dennie a shot in the left buttock to relieve the pain.

In a few hours, however, he began to feel extreme pain in his entire left leg. Mr. Dennie, who was to have been discharged the next day, ended up staying in the hospital for 14 days and was bedridden for three months due to problems in his left leg. He has continued to experience pain in the leg.

About two years later, Mr. Dennie filed suit against the hospital, alleging that the nurse who gave him the shot did so negligently, causing permanent damage to the sciatic nerve in his leg. The hospital denied liability and was going to argue at trial that plaintiff's injury was caused either by an unavoidable accident or by his nerve problems.

Shortly after the case was filed in 1981, the defendant hospital served a set of interrogatories on the plaintiff. When no reply was received, the defendant asked the court for relief, and the Hennepin County District Court ordered the plaintiff to answer within 15 days. The plaintiff then answered that Dr. Nolan would appear as the expert witness at trial and would testify that the injection was given negligently. However, when his deposition was taken a few months later, in April 1982, Dr. Nolan stated that he did not believe that the injection was given negligently. In August 1982 the defendant filed a statement with the court indicating it was ready for trial, but the plaintiff did not respond. Under a court rule, no further discovery could be done thereafter without court permission.

In early 1983 the attorney who had been representing plaintiff left the law firm and another lawyer took over. She made some efforts at reopening discovery but was unsuccessful. At the pre-trial conference she listed her witnesses as "Dr. Nolan, Steven Laven (the nurse), and a neurologist yet to be named." On May 3, 1984, the court scheduled the trial for June 18, 1984. Shortly thereafter, Dr. John Tulloch agreed to testify as the plaintiff's expert witness, and on June 11, the attorney so notified the court and defendant.

When the case was called for trial, defense counsel moved to suppress (prohibit) the testimony of both Dr. Tulloch and Mr. Laven because their identity had not been disclosed in advance, in violation of court rules, and there had been no opportunity for any discovery regarding what their testimony would be. The court denied the motion but instead ordered that their depositions be taken that afternoon, with the trial to start the following day.

Unfortunately, problems developed at the depositions. The plaintiff's attorney refused to let the defense counsel see the medical records reviewed by Mr. Laven. (Because she had put markings on them, she considered them part of the attorney's "work product.") Nor would she allow access to an opinion letter regarding the plaintiff prepared by Dr. Tulloch for the same reason.

The next morning in the court, the defendant's lawyer again asked that the court suppress the testimony of plaintiff's experts, and this time the motion was granted. Plaintiff's attorney asked the court to conduct its own review of the materials in dispute (called an *in camera inspection*), but the judge refused. After determining that the plaintiff had no expert testimony to present on the issue of negligence, the court dismissed the case with prejudice (which means "you cannot file it again—you are done"). On appeal to the Minnesota Court of Appeals, the dismissal was reversed. The court found that the remedy applied by the lower court was too harsh for the circumstances and was "an abuse of discretion" by the trial judge. The hospital then appealed the case to the Minnesota Supreme Court.

DECISION

Chief Justice Amdahl wrote the following opinion of the Supreme Court, affirming the Court of Appeals. "An order of dismissal on procedural grounds runs counter to the primary objective of the law to dispose of cases on the merits . . . . A dismissal with prejudice is the most punitive sanction that can be imposed for noncompliance with court rules. It therefore should be granted only under exceptional circumstances."

The Court noted that in this case the trial court had the difficult task of considering several problems that arose in the course of discovery. The general rule in Minnesota is that expert testimony should be suppressed for failure to make a timely disclosure of the expert's identity "only where the counsel's dereliction [in failing to make the disclosure] is inexcusable and results in disadvantage to the opponent." There are other sanctions available for violation of court rules, including assessing costs and attorneys' fees against the party at fault, which are much less prejudicial to the plaintiff.

After reviewing the problems that occurred in this case, the court decided that the trial court abused its discretion in suppressing both experts' testimony. Plaintiff's counsel had a reasonable legal basis for refusing defendant's attempt to discover the documents objected to at the deposition, and should at least have conducted an *in camera* inspection of the documents. The trial court should have considered the difficulty in preparing a case of this nature (getting doctors to testify against each other) and the limited time the plaintiff's attorney had been working on the case. Then, if the plaintiff's actions were held improper, court costs, fees, and other sanctions short of dismissing the case (such as postponing the trial but limiting the scope of the expert's testimony so as not to prejudice the defendant) should have been assessed. The decision of the Court of Appeals is affirmed.

CASE QUESTIONS

1. What was the trial judge's reason for dismissing the case? What is the public policy behind the reason?
2. Why were the plaintiff's lawyers constantly late in answering interrogatories, providing discovery, and preparing for trial? Was it a weak or difficult case? Poor lawyer preparation?
3. Is it right that an individual (i.e., Mr. Dennie) should lose his case because his lawyers messed up? If not, is it right that a business (i.e., the hospital) should continue to be dragged into court month after month on a case without knowing what the basis of the plaintiff's case is or who the experts are who are going to testify? Where is the proper balance between ensuring everyone his or her "day in court" and at the same time imposing some penalties on those who do not follow the rules?

In recent years, for the reasons brought out in the previous case and the case questions, a movement has begun to put some limitations on the length of time of discovery. In fact, the Minnesota court rule that led to the dismissal of the case was undoubtedly designed to put firm time limits on discovery. While every lawyer would always like to know as much about the case as possible—no lawyer wants to go into a big trial less prepared than the other side—both clients are paying for each hour of attorney time used in the process, and the costs of discovery can be enormous. A significant business case can involve taking 20 or more depositions and sending several sets of interrogatories. Meanwhile, "the meter is running," that is, the attorneys for both sides are charging for each minute spent on the case—perhaps at $200 or $300 per hour. More and more judges and courts are limiting the number of months or years allowed for discovery, as well as the number of depositions each side may take and the number and length of interrogatories. The following reading looks at some proposed changes in discovery rules for federal court actions.

New Limit on Depositions? Maybe

Is everyone ready for the seven-hour deposition limit?

The U.S. Supreme Court now has before it proposed amendments to the Federal Rules of Civil Procedure that include some significant changes in discovery rules. The idea is to decrease costs and increase efficiency.

The Judicial Conference of the United States, the policymaking arm of the federal judiciary, launched a discovery study project in the fall of 1996, after many years of complaints from the bar and the public about the costs associated with discovery.

In the course of its study, the rules committee of the conference learned that in almost 40% of federal cases, discovery is not used at all. But in suits in which it is used, it represents 50% of litigation costs in the average case and up to 90% of litigation costs in cases in which it is used particularly exhaustively.

The conference recently approved and sent to the high court proposed changes that would affect the early disclosure of pretrial information, the scope of discovery and depositions.

As it stands, Rule 26(a)(1) provides for the early, automatic exchange of pretrial information, although it does permit courts to opt out of the requirement. The proposed amendment would eliminate the opt-out provision. An amendment to Rule 26(b)(1) would give judges more authority to control contentious discovery: If the information sought goes beyond what is "relevant to the claim or defense" and the subject matter in general, an attorney would have to obtain a judge's order to proceed.

An amendment to Rule 30 would adopt a presumption that no deposition should last longer than one seven-hour day, unless a longer time is approved by the court.

The time-limit proposal generated considerable public comment by bar groups and attorneys before it was adopted by the Judicial Conference.

The National Association of Consumer Advocates and Trial Lawyers for Public Justice, for example, view the limit positively, noting that time spent in depositions is the single greatest cost of almost any civil lawsuit and that counsel compensated by hourly rates often have incentives to conduct unnecessarily lengthy depositions.

But the New York State Bar Association's federal litigation section said that the limit would be unnecessary in normal cases and unworkable in complex cases. Public Citizen Litigation Group warned that an arbitrary time limit would be likely to increase the need for judicial intervention.

The Supreme Court usually transmits proposed rule changes to Congress by May 1, and Congress has a statutory period of at least seven months to act on the proposals.

IN CONSULTATION

Marvin Manager has a problem. His company, ABC, Inc., is involved in litigation with a direct competitor called Othercorp. Othercorp filed suit against Marvin's company over who has an exclusive contract with a supplier they both use. Shortly after Othercorp filed its complaint, its lawyers sent Marvin several discovery requests. In addition to inquiring about the contract with the supplier, they also sent interrogatories and requests for the production of documents seeking the following information:

1. ABC's earnings for the past five years,
2. ABC's client list,
3. ABC's marketing strategy for the next two years,
4. ABC's financing arrangements with investors and banks, and
5. ABC's research and development plan for the next two years.

Marvin approached his company's in-house corporate counsel, Laura Lawyer. He asked Laura whether he has to produce this information. Here is their conversation:

Marvin:

1. The list of information that Othercorp seeks doesn't have anything to do with our supplier contract. Othercorp should not be able to obtain the information because it is irrelevant.
2. The materials sought by Othercorp are extensive, covering multiple years and several departments within the company. It will take weeks to compile everything and a forklift to deliver it. Isn't that an excessive burden?
3. The list contains proprietary commercial information that would cause a significant competitive disadvantage if it were to fall into Othercorp's hands. It is a direct competitor. Why should we hand them the nuts and bolts of our competitive edge when it has nothing to do with our supplier contracts?

Laura:

1. Information obtainable during discovery is broader than evidence that may ultimately be presented at trial. Irrelevance may not be enough of a reason to prevent Othercorp from obtaining the information they seek.
2. Not necessarily. The court must strike a balance between the seeking party's need for the information and our need to avoid undue burden and expense.
3. The court has the discretion to protect certain commercial information. **I will review the applicable law to see if the items sought by Othercorp qualify for such protection. I will get back to you as soon as I have completed my research.**

FROM THE DESK OF

Laura Lawyer

To: Marvin Manager

Re: Scope of Discovery

Dear Marvin:

The initial answer to any question about information sought during discovery is that a party may obtain information regarding anything relevant to the lawsuit. Relevance is a broad standard that covers more than the specific issue in dispute. The purpose of discovery is to prevent "trial by surprise" and allow each party to adequately prepare all possible issues in the case. Discovery, therefore, requires a much wider scope than simply information that will be admissible at trial. It is often impossible to know whether information is relevant until after you have produced it, so courts are disinclined to prevent discovery unless the irrelevance of the information is so obvious that it could not possibly have any relationship at all to the issues in dispute.

In this case, for example, Othercorp's lawyers could argue that they need ABC's client list so they could find witnesses who have knowledge about ABC's production process. They could argue that they need marketing strategies so they can obtain evidence about the amount of supplies ABC will need. Othercorp may want research and development plans for similar evidence concerning future needs for supplies, demonstrating that information that may appear irrelevant may still be discovered.

Unfortunately, discovery is one of the biggest burdens of the entire litigation process. Complicated commercial litigation often involves substantial discovery with multiple documents, interrogatories, and depositions that inevitably consume hours of company time. Discovery, by definition, is disruptive and expensive. The only way to use that disruption and expense to claim that the discovery is inappropriate would be to prove that Othercorp is abusing the discovery process to harass ABC. Courts are disinclined to make a finding that a party is abusing the discovery process because of the court's keen interest in a full exchange of information with resulting trial preparedness.

In your third question, you mentioned that the materials sought are proprietary commercial information. This fact may offer ABC its best opportunity to avoid producing the items requested. We can file a document called a Motion for Protective Order, in which we will ask the court to protect ABC from being forced to produce the listed items. In order for our motion to prevail, we must be able to prove that the items are trade secrets that will harm our competitive edge if placed in the wrong hands. Trade secrets are broadly defined as information that has economic value, creates a competitive advantage, and is subject to efforts to maintain its secrecy. Othercorp wants to know about our earnings, client list, marketing strategy, financing arrangements, and research and development plans. If those materials give ABC a competitive edge and if we put programs in place to maintain their secrecy, the court may grant a Protective Order and prevent Othercorp from obtaining the information.

With regard to the discovery process trade secrets, we should consider the following questions:

1. Describe the advantages and disadvantages of the broad standards for discovery. Explain whether you think trial preparedness is a sufficient justification for requiring parties to release such an extensive amount of information.
2. What could Marvin do to prepare the company for the burdens of the discovery process?
3. Recommend a trade secret program for ABC to ensure that its earnings, client list, marketing strategy, financing arrangements, research and development plans, and any other proprietary information are kept secret and protected from discovery.

SUMMARY JUDGMENT

At any time before the case goes to trial, but usually after quite a bit of discovery has been done, one side or both may bring a motion for **summary judgment**. This request basically asks the court to enter a summary (quick) judgment in favor of one side rather than proceeding to trial. In order to succeed on this motion, the moving party must convince the judge that there are no "genuine issues of material fact" in dispute—that the parties basically agree on the facts—and that therefore the only remaining issues are legal questions.

summary judgment: The court enters a judgment in favor of one side, without a trial, when there are no "fact issues" in dispute, only legal questions.

Since legal issues are basically decided by the judge, it makes sense to avoid the time and costs of trial (and a possible erroneous decision by a jury) by having the judge decide the case now and entering a judgment for one party. Most of the time there *are* significant differences between the parties regarding factual issues—for example, one party thinks the accident was caused by a red car going 30 mph, and the other thinks it was an orange car going 50 mph. Therefore, these motions are usually denied, and the case is scheduled for trial. However, occasionally the important facts are not really in dispute, and the judge then decides the critical legal issues without a trial and enters a summary judgment in favor of one party.

PRE-TRIAL CONFERENCE

When the time for discovery has expired, the court will schedule a **pre-trial conference**. At this time the judge will meet privately with the attorneys for both sides, discuss what the issues in the case are, and which ones can be agreed upon, where the major differences lie, whether there is a chance of settlement, how many witnesses each side wants to call, and how long the trial may last. Some judges are very aggressive in attempting to get a settlement at the pre-trial conference, asking questions like "What will you take to settle this case? What will you offer? That's all? Can't you go a little higher?"

pre-trial conference: A meeting between the judge and the lawyers, prior to the trial, to discuss the issues in the case and set the date for the trial.

In one case handled by one of this book's authors, the judge said at the pre-trial conference, "Go out and tell your client that I've heard 30 cases like this, and never has the plaintiff received more than $5,000. Now I'm not prejudging the case, of course, and maybe he will be the first one to win $15,000, but the chances are small. The defendant is offering to settle for $4,000, and that seems like a good offer to me." Since both clients are usually required to show up for the pre-trial (but do not get to go back in the judge's office with the lawyers to discuss the case), if a settlement is reached, everyone can go into the courtroom and put the agreement "on the record" by publicly stating it to the judge and having it taken down by the court reporter.

All judges are different. While some really push for settlement at the pre-trial conference, others simply ask what the real issues are in the case, how long each side wants to present its witnesses at trial, whether the attorneys have discussed settlement, and if they believe settlement is possible. At the close of the conference, the judge sets a date for the trial.

SOCIAL/ETHICAL ISSUES

Do you think a judge should aggressively push the parties toward a settlement? Is this a proper role for a judicial officer? Many believe the court should remain neutral and just make decisions as required. On the other hand, trials cost the state and the parties a considerable amount of money. Most court systems are seriously overloaded and backlogged. If the judge can help some parties reach a settlement, others can go to trial sooner. What is the proper amount of pressure a judge should place on the parties to settle?

JURY PROCEDURES

If the case is not settled, it will eventually come to trial. The first decision to make is whether it will be a jury or nonjury trial. In a civil case if either party makes a formal request for a jury at the appropriate time (generally no later than the pre-trial conference), there will be a jury. If neither side requests a jury, the judge will hear the case without one. Sometimes in a complex or technical case, neither side wants to take the risk that the jury will become bored or antagonistic with the case, and the parties are happy to let the judge—who has heard lots of similar cases—decide the matter alone.

JURY SELECTION

If it is to be a jury trial, the selection of the members of the jury is an important step. In order to obtain a cross-section of the community, many persons are asked to come to the courthouse to serve as jurors. Some counties use voter registration lists or drivers license records and other means to make up their lists. Groups are then sent to the various courtrooms where trials are to take place. Before being chosen as a juror in a case, a person must answer a series of questions designed to indicate whether he or she has any bias for or against any of the parties to the case; knows any of the parties, witnesses, or attorneys involved; or has strong opinions about the issues involved in the case. This process is called ***voir dire,*** which means "to see and to say." (In Old French *voir* meant "truth"—that is, medieval jurors were actually witnesses.)

voir dire: The process of asking questions to potential jurors, to make sure they can be fair and impartial.

challenge for cause: One attorney asks the judge to remove a juror from the jury because of some possible bias. The judge decides.

peremptory challenge: Each side in a case is allowed to excuse a few potential jurors without giving a reason.

Voir dire is intended to produce jurors who can hear the evidence without bias. For example, if Bill is suing Michelle, he probably does not want her brother, her best friend, or her minister on the jury. Similarly, if Michelle is a newspaper reporter who has written something about Bill that he believes is false, he probably will prefer that no other newspaper reporters, or perhaps news media workers of any kind, sit on the jury. The judge will ask each prospective juror a series of questions designed to indicate if the person can view the case with an open mind, and often the attorneys ask questions as well.

As the questioning proceeds, one of the attorneys may ask the judge to remove a juror **for cause**, if he or she believes that the juror cannot be totally impartial, and the judge will rule on the request. The number of challenges for cause is not limited. In addition, each side has a certain number of **peremptory challenges**, which can be used to remove a juror without giving any reason and without any decision by the judge. The number of peremptory challenges is limited, and each side has the same number. For example, in Bill and Michelle's case, perhaps there is a prospective jury member who was a classmate of Bill's in high school but has not seen him in a number of years. When challenged for cause by Michelle's lawyer, he tells the court, "I'll be fair and view the case with an open mind." Michelle and her lawyer may decide they would just as soon not test his good faith and use one of their peremptories to "thank and excuse" him from the jury. The following case concerns whether a judge should have dismissed a juror for cause.

STATE V. SHIELDS

709 S.W. 2d 556 (Missouri Court of Appeals, 1986)

FACTS

In this criminal case, the defendant had been convicted of felonious restraint, burglary, and assault after a jury trial. The felonious restraint charges were filed after the defendant broke into his ex-wife's house and forced her and their two children to get dressed and go with him. He then drove them around in the car for five hours before releasing them.

About one month later, the defendant (Mr. Shields) again broke into his ex-wife's house and this time hit her several times with a stick. He also hit her mother across the back. Mr. Shields dragged his ex-wife outside and pushed her over a fence. A neighbor intervened to help the victim and chased Mr. Shields back to his truck where he got a gun and fired a shot at the neighbor. These actions led to the burglary and assault charges. Mr. Shields appealed his conviction, claiming that the judge should have dismissed one of the jurors.

DECISION

Judge Crist wrote the opinion of the court:

The defendant claims that the trial court erred by overruling his challenge for cause to one of the female jurors. It appears that some 17 years earlier the former wife of this woman's husband had forced her way into their home and had attacked her. The woman juror had not seen this person for some ten years, and she consistently told the court that she could give both sides in the case a fair trial under the evidence presented in court and would follow the instructions given by the court. When questioned by the defendant's attorney, she said her former experience "has nothing to do with what's going on here today."

While a defendant is entitled to a full panel of qualified jurors from which to make his peremptory challenges, "decisions concerning a juror's qualifications are consigned to the trial court's discretion and will be reversed only for a clear abuse of discretion," stated the Missouri Court of Appeals. The juror did not equivocate or waiver in her answers to the questions propounded on voir dire. *"She insisted the experience would not affect her, and this insistence was reinforced by the amount of time which had passed between her experience and the trial. We can find no abuse of discretion." Judgment affirmed.*

CASE QUESTIONS

1. Do you think the juror can judge the defendant fairly in this case? Why?
2. We all have experiences that shape the way we feel about the world. These experiences affect how we view such things as crime, drugs, marital violence, discrimination, and politics. How can we tell what prior events will influence a person's judgment in a given case? Try to fashion a rule that you would like applied to potential jurors in a case involving you.
3. Why did the defendant's attorney not use a peremptory challenge to bump the juror from the case after the challenge for cause was denied?

To help with jury selection in important cases, an entire industry of "jury selection consultants" has come into existence. Experts with sociological, psychological, and statistical backgrounds advise attorneys (for a substantial fee, of course) on what types of persons are supposedly more or less sympathetic to various kinds of people and arguments. In the fall of 1994, for example, some six weeks were consumed solely with the selection of the jury for the O.J. Simpson murder trial. Each side retained experts to assist it in jury selection and questioning and used mock juries to assess different people's reactions to various types of evidence.

While we take pride that our justice system accords an individual a trial before an "impartial jury of peers," what each side *really* wants is a jury that will decide in its favor. The attorneys, after all, are representing clients who want to win the case. It is important that judges stay closely involved in the jury selection process to ensure that juries do represent the community and that minorities are not systematically excluded from jury service. In fact, there have been a few U.S. Supreme Court decisions in recent years that have banned the use of peremptory challenges where they were used to exclude all minorities or women from the jury panel hearing a case.

FROM THE DESK OF

Laura Lawyer

To: Students

From: Your Lawyer

Often, when called for jury duty, our first thought is how to "get out of" jury service. True, it is usually inconvenient to find the time to serve. The success of the jury system, however, requires that when called for jury service, employed persons and students try to find a way to serve rather than attempt to avoid serving. Otherwise, juries will not represent the entire community but will be composed of only retired or unemployed persons or others who have "all the time in the world" to serve on juries.

THE TRIAL

THE OPENING STATEMENT

Once the parties, judge, and jury are ready to begin, the first stage of the trial is the **opening statement** of the attorney for each side. At this time the attorney tries to "tell a story" to the jury—specifically the version of events that caused the lawsuit according to her client. The attorney describes in general what the key witnesses are expected to testify—being careful not to be too specific, because witnesses rarely tell the exact story to the court that they told the lawyer back in the office. This is probably the first time the jury has heard anything about the case, and the attorneys want to create interest and build sympathy for their clients. The plaintiff's attorney presents first, and the defendant's attorney either follows directly or waits until the plaintiff's witnesses have all testified to make the opening statement.

opening statement: At the beginning of a trial, each lawyer has an opportunity to tell the jury what the case is about.

PRESENTATION OF EVIDENCE

After the opening statements, the plaintiff begins to present his case through the testimony of witnesses and introduction of evidence. This part of the trial is no doubt familiar to many of you through movies and television. "The plaintiff will call as his first witness, Dr. Samantha Jones," states the plaintiff's attorney, who will then ask Dr. Jones a series of questions pertinent to the case. This type of testimony, offered by "your witnesses," is called **direct examination**.

direct examination: The series of questions asked by an attorney of a witness called by that attorney.

If the case concerns whether the plaintiff has suffered injuries and to what degree of severity and permanence, and Dr. Jones has treated the plaintiff, she will be asked to describe the injuries, the treatment, and her opinion of the severity and permanence. No leading questions are allowed on direct examination. The attorney uses "how," "when," and "where" questions to let the witness describe the events she observed.

The testimony must relate to the facts of the case at hand, however. If the plaintiff's attorney asked Dr. Jones about some other patient or some other medical problem of the plaintiff, the defendant's attorney might stand up and object to the question because it was "Irrelevant, your Honor." The standard of *relevance* means that only evidence that has some direct bearing on one of the issues in this case can be introduced in court. The judge's decision on the objection will depend on whether, in the judge's opinion, the question deals with an issue relevant to the case.

After the plaintiff's attorney has finished questioning Dr. Jones, the defendant's lawyer is given the opportunity to **cross-examine** the witness. While the questions from the plaintiff's attorney were probably friendly and open-ended ("Tell us about the injuries you saw, Dr. Jones"), the questions from the opposing attorney are likely to be hostile, tricky, and closed-ended ("Isn't it true, Dr. Jones, that you first treated the plaintiff while you were at a party?"). The purpose of cross-examination is to test the truth of the nice, neat version of events the witness described on direct examination.

cross-examination: Questions asked by an attorney of a witness called by the opposing side.

The American court system is called *adversarial* because it is expected that the truth will emerge through the examination and cross-examination of witnesses by the opposing attorneys under the general supervision of the judge. In some other countries the judge serves as more of an accuser and asks many questions. But in the United States the judge acts mostly as a referee to ensure fairness, although he or she can sometimes ask questions of witnesses, and all judges do so on occasion.

As the plaintiff's attorney calls one witness after another, there will be physical and documentary evidence that he or she will want to introduce (officially put before the court and jury for their consideration). Generally, each piece of evidence must be described and verified by a witness unless the parties have stipulated (agreed) to its admission. In other words, if the plaintiff's attorney wants to introduce the plaintiff's medical records, he or she must ask Dr. Jones or some other medical professional who is familiar with the records if these in fact are the plaintiff's records and if they have been maintained by the hospital in its regular manner. If the plaintiff's attorney wants to introduce a photograph of the plaintiff's wrecked car, either the person who took the picture or someone else who can testify that this is in fact an accurate depiction of the plaintiff's car right after the accident will have to be called as a witness. Otherwise, it is possible that some photo of another horribly wrecked car might be put before the jury.

MOTIONS FOR DIRECTED VERDICT AND CLOSING ARGUMENTS

directed verdict: When the judge enters a verdict, after the evidence has been presented, because one side has failed to prove some essential element of the case.

After the plaintiff has called all her witnesses, and they have been cross-examined, the plaintiff "rests," which means "That's all I have." In other words, the plaintiff's side has presented all the witnesses and evidence it has chosen to offer. Often, at this point, the defendant will move for a **directed verdict**, which is a request to the judge to enter a decision in his or her favor because the plaintiff failed to prove his or her case or left out some essential element. Most of the time these motions are denied, and the case moves on, but once in a while the judge will grant the motion, and the case is over. If the motion is denied, then the defendant will begin calling witnesses, with each one being cross-examined by the plaintiff's attorney.

After both sides have completed the testimony of witnesses and introduction of evidence, each attorney will make a *closing argument* to the court. This is the time when the oratory of the experienced trial attorney reaches full flower. The attorneys can now refer to specific statements made by witnesses and highlight various items that have been introduced into evidence (e.g., waving the bloody shirt for the jury), without fear that a witness will change his or her story or be contradicted by another witness. Some attorneys are accomplished public speakers and make dramatic appeals to the jury's sense of justice and fairness. Others merely present factual, low-key recapitulations of the evidence favorable to their client's position.

jury instructions: The judge gives the jury instructions on legal issues they must decide and rules they should apply to the case before them.

JURY INSTRUCTIONS, DELIBERATIONS, AND VERDICT

After both sides have presented all their evidence and given their closing arguments, the judge will give **instructions to the jury**. Each side will have previously given the judge a list of proposed instructions, which tell the jury about the burden of proof the plaintiff must meet, the definition of various legal terms relevant to the case, and how the jury should apply the law to the facts of the case. The judge will probably use some of the instructions suggested by the attorneys and may write some of his or her own. There are also standard lists of instructions on all legal topics developed by bar association committees in most states. The judge will have to decide which ones are most appropriate in this case.

After the instructions are given, the jury is excused and taken to a separate room to "deliberate," that is, to reach a decision. Traditionally, juries were composed of 12 persons, and their verdict was required to be unanimous, and this is still true in many cases—certainly in all major criminal cases. However, in recent years many courts in order to save time and money have used six-member juries and non-unanimous verdicts in certain types of cases. The jury is considered the *finder of facts,* that is, the jury decides who did what to whom, how fast the car was going, and so on. In almost all cases, different witnesses will give vastly different accounts of what happened, and the jury's duty will be to determine whom to believe. Most of the time the jury will be asked to deliver a *general verdict,* which is one that decides who should win and how much the damages are. In some cases, a *special verdict* will be requested, which requires the jury to reach an answer to a series of particular questions.

POST-TRIAL MOTIONS

After the jury renders its verdict, the losing side may bring a *motion for new trial* or a *motion for judgment notwithstanding the verdict* (which in Latin is "Non Obstante Veredicto," and often therefore called "**Judgment N.O.V.**"). The motion for new trial asks that the court order a new trial in the case because of some serious and prejudicial error that has occurred or because of the discovery

Judgment N.O.V.: The judge enters a judgment different from the jury verdict.

"Before announcing the verdict we would like to recommend that Harrison Ford play the defendant."

of some important new evidence that was not available at the first trial. The motion for Judgment N.O.V. asks the court to enter a judgment opposite of the jury's decision because the jury's verdict is against the great weight of the evidence (i.e., "If the jury had followed your instructions, it could not possibly have reached the decision it did"). Most of these motions are denied, but every once in awhile, one is granted. Therefore, it often makes sense for the losing attorney to bring them. If nothing else, the denial of such a motion provides another legal basis for appeal of the trial court decision. After the post-trial motions have been argued, the judge will enter the final judgment in the case.

THE APPELLATE PROCESS

Once the trial court judge has entered a judgment in the case, and any post-trial motions have been denied, the losing party's only recourse is to file an appeal. As we have discussed, there is at least one and often two levels of appellate courts in all states, which hear appeals from lower court decisions. The basis for the appeal must be that some serious legal error, made by the trial court judge, affected the outcome of the case and led to an unfair or unlawful result. The trial court judge may have made hundreds of rulings during the trial—whether to admit certain evidence, rulings on various objections to questions, instructions to the jury, and rulings on motions made by the parties—so that the losing side can generally find some issues on which to base an appeal.

The party desiring to appeal (the *appellant*) files a notice with the appropriate appellate court, indicating that he or she is appealing a lower court decision. At some specific time thereafter, the appellant must file a **brief** with the court, which will be a statement (but never very "brief"!) of the party's arguments concerning the errors made during the trial and citing past court decisions and laws supporting the appellant's position. Then, some 30–50 days later (whatever time period is specified by the law in that state), the other side (called the *appellee*) will file a brief in response, arguing that there was no significant error in the lower court and that the decision should stand. The appellee will also cite various supporting cases and statutes.

brief: A written document containing the party's legal arguments.

After both briefs have been filed, the appellate court will, in most cases, schedule a date for *oral argument.* At this time, the attorneys for both parties will appear before the appellate court (remember, there will be several judges on the panel) and attempt to convince the court of the strength of their arguments. Each lawyer will be given a short time—perhaps 30 minutes—to present his or her case, and the judges will interrupt and question the attorney whenever they choose to probe into various aspects of the case. There are no witnesses heard and no evidence presented to the appellate court. The focus is on the legal principles relevant to the case at hand and whether those principles were followed in the lower court. The discussion and debate over the proper legal principles to apply is doubly important because the decision will not only affect the parties to the case at issue, but will also affect all subsequent cases in that jurisdiction, raising similar issues through the rules of precedent and *stare decisis,* as discussed next.

PRECEDENT

The American legal system is very much a *common law* structure. One meaning of the term *common law* is that much of our law is not founded in the statutes passed by legislatures, but in the decisions of the courts. As part of the effort to make the principles of law predictable and stable, lower courts in one jurisdiction must follow the legal principles set out in decisions of higher (appellate) courts in their jurisdiction when they occur in similar situations. For example, if the Supreme Court of Montana has ruled in a 1976 case that driving an automobile while blindfolded was "negligence," and there is now a case being tried in Beaverhead County, Montana, involving similar facts, the trial court will be bound to follow the legal precedent of the 1976 case and find the driver negligent, if the jury decides that he was driving while blindfolded. This rule is called *stare decisis* ("Let the decision stand") and is premised on the idea that the law should be similar ("common") in all parts of a particular jurisdiction.

The rule of precedent or *stare decisis* only applies within the particular jurisdiction over which the higher court presides. Therefore, the decisions of the Montana Supreme Court on the interpretation of certain legal principles must be followed by trial and appellate courts in Montana, but need not be followed in Georgia, Vermont, or any other state. While a court in Georgia might be interested in the reasoning and language of a Montana Supreme Court decision concerning some legal principle, and might decide to adopt the same interpretation because the rationale made a lot of sense, the Georgia court has no obligation to do so. That court will have to follow principles established in earlier Georgia Supreme Court decisions, however.

Although lower courts within a jurisdiction are normally bound to follow the precedents set by earlier cases because of the *stare decisis* rule, sometimes the appellate courts decide that a rule of law has outlived its usefulness. The court that created the rule of law in the first place (the Montana Supreme Court in our earlier example) might decide that after several years of experience with the "driving blindfolded is negligent" rule, there are strong reasons for changing it. While the U.S. Supreme Court and the state supreme courts are reluctant to disregard *stare decisis* and change a longstanding rule, sometimes changes in society have made the old rule obsolete and out of place.

For example, most states used to have a rule that a patient could not sue a nonprofit hospital for damages even if the patient was injured while in the hospital. This rule arose when most nonprofit hospitals were owned by religious or charitable groups, run largely be volunteers, and provided care at no charge to patients. That situation has changed considerably over the years. While there are still many nonprofit hospitals, they are often huge, powerful, and sophisticated businesses that employ large paid staffs and charge for services. In response to this change, most state supreme courts have, in appropriate cases, overruled the old "charitable immunity" rule and held that nonprofit hospitals can be sued for negligence.

On the federal level, the decisions of the U.S. Supreme Court, regarding interpretations of the federal Constitution and federal statutes, are binding on *all* other courts in the nation. Decisions of the U.S. Supreme Courts of Appeal are binding on all lower federal courts within their geographical jurisdiction (see chart in Chapter 2). In diversity cases, the federal district court must follow the decisions on relevant legal principles (e.g., the definition of *negligence*) made by the highest court of the state where the incident took place.

APPELLATE COURT DECISIONS

After reading the briefs and hearing the oral arguments of the parties, the appellate court will likely do one of three things. It may **affirm** (uphold) the decision of the lower court; it may **reverse** the decision—that is, direct that the opposite party should win; or, more commonly, if the appellate court finds that some error occurred at the trial, it will reverse and **remand** the case to the lower court (send it back) with instructions for a new trial, or direct that some further proceedings are necessary. In each case, the appellate court will generally write a lengthy opinion, discussing the facts and legal issues involved in the case and carefully setting out its reasoning and explaining its view of the appropriate legal principles. This opinion will then become precedent to be used in all later cases raising similar issues.

affirm: When an appellate court upholds a lower court decision.

reverse: The appellate court changes the ruling of the lower court.

remand: The appellate court sends the case back to the lower court for more hearings or a new trial.

Similarly, appellate court decisions often involve the interpretation of a statute (*"statutory interpretation,"* as was discussed in Chapter 1). When an appellate court, for example, the Supreme Court of Ohio, issues a decision in a case that involves the interpretation of an Ohio law, that precedent will be binding on all lower courts in Ohio through the doctrine of *stare decisis.* Most of the cases in this textbook will be appellate court decisions, either interpreting a statute or the Constitution or examining a common law legal principle.

TYPES OF JUDGMENTS; ENFORCING AND COLLECTING JUDGMENTS

In Chapter 1, we discussed the difference between "legal" (actions at law) and equitable (actions in equity) remedies. In general, legal remedies are those that require the losing party to pay the winning party a certain sum of money, while "equitable" remedies involve a court order to the defendant to do or not to do a specific action. Equitable remedies can only be obtained where the party convinces the court that money damages will be inadequate compensation. In most cases, courts prefer to award monetary damages to the prevailing party, as described in the next section.

MONEY JUDGMENTS (ACTIONS AT LAW)

The majority of civil actions are brought by people who want another to pay damages for something that the second one has done that injured the first person—actions at law. If the court finds for the plaintiff, it may award several types of money damages.

Compensatory Damages Compensatory damages are the most common type of damages and are designed to compensate the plaintiff for the actual direct costs of the harm caused by the defendant. For example, if the defendant broke a contract he had made to pave the plaintiff's driveway, and the plaintiff had to pay someone else $1,500 more than the original contract to do the job, she would probably be entitled to $1,500 in compensatory damages from the defendant.

Consequential Damages In some cases, the plaintiff alleges that in addition to the cost of the substitute performance, she has suffered further damages as a consequence of the defendant's actions. For example, in the situation just discussed, suppose that the plaintiff was the owner of a convenience store, and the defendant's failure to pave the driveway made it impossible for customers to reach the store until the other paving company did the job one week later. The store owner might want to ask for *consequential damages* to cover the additional losses resulting from the defendant's breach of contract. Such damages are sometimes awarded when the consequences are *foreseeable*—that is, both parties understood what the damages would be if one or the other did not perform.

Other Types of Money Damages Courts sometimes award other money damages called *nominal* and *punitive.* **Nominal damages** are very small sums (perhaps $1) awarded when the plaintiff has won the case but has not established any monetary injury. **Punitive damages** may be awarded when the judge or jury finds that the defendant has acted maliciously or intentionally to harm the plaintiff. These damages may be very large, as they are intended to "make an example" of the defendant (indeed, such damages are often called "exemplary damages"), and go to the plaintiff in addition to whatever damages are awarded.

nominal damages: Very small damages ("in name only") to a winning plaintiff.

punitive damages: A large award of damages, in addition to compensatory damages, to "punish" the defendant for wilful or deliberately malicious actions.

There has been much public debate recently about the role and use of punitive damages, including such questions as: (1) Is it right to allow the plaintiff to receive a "windfall" of money over and above what he or she has proved in damages, solely to punish the defendant? (2) Is it appropriate to allow several courts to independently assess multi-million dollar punitive damage awards against a company (which may have made a defective drug, for example) for the same action, if that results in forcing the company into bankruptcy, thus making it impossible for other injured parties to collect anything? (3) Are punitive damages constitutional? Defendants against whom punitive damages have been awarded have argued that allowing a jury to assess any amount it chooses violates their right to due process of law.

So far, the U.S. Supreme Court has agreed with this argument in only one case, although it has decided several punitive damage cases in recent years. In a 1996 decision the court reversed a $2 million punitive damages award against BMW for selling a repainted BMW car as new. Finding the 500-to-1 ratio between punitive and compensatory damages ($4,000) as "grossly excessive," the Court reversed the award. But lower courts are still not clear on what is allowable. This is an important current legal issue for business, which we will discuss further in Chapter 11.

EQUITABLE REMEDIES

Sometimes the plaintiff does not want money compensation for what the defendant has done but wants the defendant ordered *to do* something or ordered *not to do* something. Perhaps, a business tenant in a downtown building hears

injunction: An equitable order from a court directing someone *not* to do something.

temporary restraining order: A short-term injunction used to preserve the status quo until the court can schedule a full hearing.

specific performance: An equitable order from a court directing someone to fully perform their contract obligations.

that the building is going to be torn down to make way for a parking lot. She may file a lawsuit against the owner seeking an **injunction**, an equitable order from the court directing the defendant not to tear down the building. A **temporary restraining order** is a type of short-term injunction, generally lasting only until the court can hold a hearing on the case. Sometimes a plaintiff asks the court for a *preliminary injunction* early in the case, long before the trial, because she needs some immediate relief. Usually a court will grant such an injunction only when it is necessary to preserve the status quo pending the full trial of the case—in other words, where by the end of the case it might no longer be possible to grant the relief the winning party deserves (for example, if the building has been torn down during the time the case was pending).

Another type of equitable relief is the order of **specific performance**, which directs a party to fulfill ("specifically perform") a contract he has agreed to. In order to receive this type of order, the plaintiff must persuade the court that monetary damages are inadequate to fully compensate her for the injury. For example, if Joe has made a contract to sell Tricia his 1933 Rolls Royce and then tries to back out of the deal, Tricia may be able to persuade the court that the item is "unique" and thus obtain an order of specific performance. If the car were a 1989 Ford, however, the court would probably refuse specific performance and award Tricia money damages for her loss due to Joe's breach of contract. The courts have held that each parcel of real estate is unique, however, so specific performance quite commonly is awarded in cases involving the breach of contract to sell houses, land, and real estate.

Although specific performance orders may sometimes be issued to require parties to fulfill certain contract obligations, courts are reluctant to issue them to require people to perform personal services. While it is possible to require a business firm to deliver 1,000 gallons of gasoline as promised, it is problematic to require an artist to paint a picture, or a singer to perform a concert. Courts are more likely to award money damages in such situations where a contract has been breached. Would you want to attend the concert where an opera singer was performing only because of a court order?

ENFORCEMENT OF JUDGMENTS

Suppose Tara wins a $5,000 judgment against Nancy, but she does not pay it. What can Tara do? One quite surprising feature of our legal system is that court judgments are not automatically enforced by the court. Only when the noncompliance is brought to the court's attention by one of the parties (the one who wants to be paid) is action taken.

garnishment: An order from a court to an employer or other party who owes money to a defendant in a case who has not paid a judgment. The order tells the employer to pay part of the wages owed to the court.

If a judgment has been entered ordering Nancy to pay Tara $5,000, but she fails to pay, Tara may petition the court for several types of action. If Tara knows where Nancy works, she may ask the court for a **garnishment**, which is an order to someone who owes Nancy money (her employer or her bank, for example) to pay a certain percentage of the wages due her (federal law limits the amount to 25 percent) to the court for transfer to Tara.

Another remedy, the *writ of execution,* directs the sheriff to take possession of some property which the defendant owns. The property (which may be either real estate or personal property like a car or machinery) is later sold, in accordance with the state law, and the proceeds are paid to the creditor toward satisfaction of the judgment. Until the judgment is paid, the creditor may return to court to continue her efforts to collect. If she does not know where the debtor works or if the debtor has assets, she may obtain a *discovery subpoena,* ordering the debtor to show up in court at a certain date and answer questions under oath about her assets.

In the early days of our country, nonpayment of debts sometimes resulted in a prison term, but this is no longer true. It is not a crime to owe money or even to fail to pay a court-ordered judgment. With the exception of court-ordered child support and alimony payments, the nonpayment of debts will not result in jail time. The creditor must, even after a court decision awarding a specific amount of money to her in a civil case, seek enforcement through the procedures outlined previously if the defendant does not pay. Courts may, however, issue warrants for the arrest of debtors who ignore discovery subpoenas and fail to appear in court to answer questions about their assets.

SUMMARY

The process of litigation in the American legal system is complex and sometimes quite lengthy. The procedures—from choosing a jury, to questioning witnesses, to deciding what evidence is relevant—are designed to ensure that each person has a full and fair hearing before an impartial decision maker. Fundamental features of the system are that it is *adversarial* (the parties and their attorneys make the arguments with the judge serving as a referee) and that "due process" (procedural fairness) is highly stressed. Although the American judicial system is a model for much of the world, there surely are situations where things do not work perfectly. Some cases seem to go on forever and at great cost to all involved. Persons convicted of horrible crimes sometimes do not go to jail or are allowed to appeal over and over. Juries occasionally render money verdicts that appear excessive to the rest of us.

The material in this chapter is designed to assist you in becoming better informed about the procedural workings of the American court system. Although the system works pretty well most of the time, things do not always go perfectly. As business and community leaders in the future, many of you will have the opportunity to participate in the ongoing attempt to improve the court system in your community—to make it work more efficiently while still guaranteeing due process to all.

CHAPTER QUESTIONS

1. A former employee at a Sam's Club (owned by Wal-Mart) in New Mexico brought a sexual harassment lawsuit alleging that a supervisor had made many sexual remarks to her and had inappropriately grabbed and touched her while she was operating a forklift. Wal-Mart tried to introduce photographs of the forklift at the trial, to show that such acts were impossible. However, Wal-Mart had not listed the photographs on the pretrial list of exhibits. Should the company be able to introduce them at the trial? [*Coates v. Wal-Mart Stores, Inc.,* 976 P. 2d 999 (N. Mex. 1999)]

2. Consolidated Aluminum Co. made ladders with polyethylene feet. Several persons were injured when ladders slipped while in use, causing the users to fall. Consolidated did not know that using polyethylene feet made the ladders defective and dangerous. What types of damages may the injured people recover? May they recover punitive damages? [*Sparks v. Consolidated Aluminum Co.,* 679 S.W. 2d 348 (Missouri court of Appeals)]

3. When should a court grant a motion for directed verdict? How about a motion for judgment notwithstanding the verdict (Judgment N.O.V.)? A motion for new trial? Do these motions serve any purpose for the losing party, even if they are denied?

4. Tricia and Jim Smith and their son Nick were sleeping peacefully in their house one evening when one block away (up a steep hill) from their home, two men were loading a "Bobcat" (a small bulldozer/dirtmover) on a trailer hooked to a pickup truck. When the Bobcat was put on the trailer, it caused the front end to rise, which caused the rear wheels of the pickup to lift off the ground (thus releasing the brake). The whole rig then started to roll downhill, out of control, until it smashed into the Smiths' house, taking out much of the garage and narrowly missing the bedrooms. The two workers worked for a local landscaping company, which had a contract to do some work on a house in the neighborhood. They were moving the Bobcat to another location for the next day's work. The truck driver's license had been suspended, there was no insurance on the truck, the trailer, or the Bobcat, and the landscaping company had no insurance. How will Mr. and Mrs. Smith recover their losses? If they sue the workers and/or the landscaping company and win a judgment, what procedures might they use to collect the judgment?

5. Gerald Martin filed a lawsuit in Idaho state court on May 4, 1995, alleging that the negligent driving of the defendant caused damages to him. His attorney initiated a series of telephone calls with the defendant's insurance company to discuss settlement of the case. The attorney told the insurance representative that they were not going to serve the summons and complaint on the defendant "until such time as we are unable to reach an agreement on settlement of this claim." Several letters and phone calls were exchanged over the next several months, without settlement. At the end of October, the plaintiff's attorney finally tried to obtain service on the defendant, but the sheriff reported that the defendant no longer lived at the address given and had apparently moved out of state some months earlier. The attorney then tried to obtain service on the defendant at an address given in the state of Washington, but found that it was only a mailbox address. Thus, at the end of the six-month period, the defendant had never been served with the papers.

   The rule in Idaho was that service of process must be made on the defendant within six months of the date of the filings of the case. The insurance company referred the case to an attorney who filed, on behalf of the defendant, a motion to dismiss for lack of service. The court rule states that if service of process is not made within six months and the plaintiff "cannot show good cause why such service was not made" within the time period, the case should be dismissed. What should the result be? Why? [*Martin v. Hoblit,* 987 P. 2d 284 (Id. 1999)]

6. What is the purpose of the *stare decisis* rule? What public policy reasons favor use of the rule? When should a court overturn a legal rule that has existed for many years? What effect will this have on individuals and businesses who have relied on the rule?
7. In a suit for damages arising from the *Exxon Valdez* oil spill, defendant Exxon requested discovery (depositions and production of documents) from 10 federal employees regarding their knowledge of the extent of damage to Alaska's natural resources. The employees' supervisors ordered them not to submit to depositions, arguing that a federal law allowed them to set regulations for the conduct of employees and the use of records. However, the same federal law also provided that this "does not authorize withholding of information from the public." Are the federal officials subject to discovery? [*Exxon Shipping Co. v. Department of the Interior,* 34 F. 3d 774 (9th Cir. 1994)]
8. A woman of Vietnamese descent applied for a university position but was not hired. Later the applicant sued the university alleging discrimination on the basis of race, sex, and national origin. She alleged that one member of the selection committee had made biased statements about women and Asians, while another had stated that the position should really be filled by a Japanese male. The university produced evidence that it had promoted and hired other Asian women and moved for a summary judgment prior to trial. The motion was granted. Should this decision be upheld on appeal? What is the standard that must be met in order to obtain a summary judgment? [*Lam v. University of Hawaii,* 40 F. 3d 1551 (9th Cir. 1994)]
9. A developer filed a lawsuit against a Delaware county after it refused to issue him a building permit for a shopping mall. He obtained a preliminary injunction from the federal district court prior to trial, ordering the county to issue the permit and restrain the county from "interfering with the construction" of the mall. The county appealed, arguing that this order violated the purpose and rationale for preliminary injunctions. What is the primary purpose of injunctions? What should be the result on appeal? [*Acierno v. New Castle County,* 40 F. 3d 645 (3rd Cir. 1994)]
10. A lawsuit was filed in Indiana in September 1991, concerning an auto accident that had occurred two years earlier. Discovery proceedings commenced in September 1991 and lasted until March 1992. In February 1992 the defendant's attorney learned from medical records that the plaintiff had been receiving counseling for drug and alcohol abuse. Several court hearings were held in the next few weeks regarding discovery of the full medical records for use at trial. On the opening day of the trial on March 30, after the jury had been chosen, the defendant's attorney sought permission to call an expert witness to testify regarding the plaintiff's reduced life expectancy and future earnings due to drug and alcohol use. No mention of any such witness had been made in any of the pre-trial witness lists previously filed by the attorney with the court and the plaintiff. A final exchange of witness and exhibit lists occurred just ten days before trial. The judge denied the request to call the witness, and following the trial, the defendant appealed. What should be the result? [*Mankey v. Bennett,* 38 F. 3d 353 (7th Cir. 1994)]

PRACTICAL EXERCISE

Christina and Carter are owners of competing pizza shops. For more than 10 years Carter has built up an excellent reputation in the community for the quality of his pizza, and his two shops are making a nice profit. Christina opened her business about one year ago and has aggressively marketed her pizza through flyers and television advertising. She is trying to build up her business. Recently she began to run a series of ads in both media, prepared by the local advertising firm "Fast and Slick," in which a customer exclaims "This is great!" while eating a slice of pizza out of a "Christina's" box. At another table, a man says "This tastes like cardboard" while eating a slice of pizza out of a clearly labeled "Carter's Pizza" box. "And you won't get sick after eating this one, either," says the first person.

Right after the ads began to run on television, Carter noticed a decrease in his business. He had received several "best pizza" awards from public polls in the past and has never had a problem with the health department or any complaints about people becoming ill after eating his pizza. Carter calls Christina and demands that she stop running the "false and misleading" ads, but she says "Too bad, this is just fair competition, buddy." Carter knows that you, his friend, are learning about legal issues in business. Prepare a complaint for Carter to file in local court against Christina and anyone else who may have taken action that unfairly damaged his business. The local county court is the Ada County District Court.

FURTHER INFORMATION

www.law.cornell.edu/supct/index/html

Cornell site—this part specializing in U.S. Supreme Court.

www.lawsource.com

The "ALSO" site contains a comprehensive list and links to "all on-line sources of American law."

www.law.emory.edu

Broad legal site, with many topics.

CHAPTER 4

THE CONSTITUTION AND BUSINESS

LEARNING OBJECTIVES

After you have read this chapter, you should be able to:

1. Discuss how the concepts of federalism, separation of powers, and judicial review affect the organization of the federal and state governments.
2. Describe the constitutional basis for the power of the federal government to regulate business.
3. Explain the concept of eminent domain and its applications.
4. List several of the fundamental rights and protections provided by the amendments to the Constitution.

CHAPTER OUTLINE

Many American business firms now conduct drug tests, both prior to hiring and sometimes during employment. Such testing raises various constitutional issues, including the right to privacy and possible illegal search and seizure. The "Practical Exercise" at the end of this chapter is a situation involving these issues.

INTRODUCTION

The U.S. Constitution establishes the structure of our government and legal system. This remarkable document, drafted in 1787, created the three branches of the federal government, set forth the powers and duties of each, and formulated the basic relationship between the federal and state governments. Although there have been dramatic changes in every aspect of American business, culture, and society since 1787, the Constitution continues to be the primary source of guidance for resolving the most important legal issues of the day. In more than 200 years, the Constitution has been amended only 27 times. The first 10 amendments, called the Bill of Rights, were added within a few years after the Constitution was adopted and are practically part of the original document. Two of the other amendments (the prohibition of the sale of liquor and the repeal of that prohibition) cancelled each other out. Thus, there have really been only 15 other amendments added to the Constitution since 1791. It is an amazing document.

This chapter will begin with a discussion of the history of the writing of the Constitution and its ratification and then will look at the system of government it created and the provisions regulating business. Next, we will examine the concept of "eminent domain" by which government can take ownership of private property for public use. Finally, we will discuss a number of important concepts designed to preserve individual rights from being overcome by a powerful federal government—such as freedom of speech, press, and religion and the "due process" and "equal protection of the law" clauses.

HISTORY OF THE CONSTITUTION

Following the Revolutionary War, the American colonies entered into an agreement (ratified in 1781) called the Articles of Confederation. The purpose of this document was primarily to create an association between the former colonies rather than to develop a new central government. The colonists, having just obtained their freedom from a powerful sovereign (the King of England), were not eager to establish a strong federal government. However, within a few

"Do you ever have one of those days when *nothing* seems constitutional?"

From *The Wall Street Journal*. Reprinted with permission of Cartoon Features Syndicate.

years it became apparent that changes were needed in the Articles of Confederation. The federal government had no power to levy taxes, to regulate commerce, or to create a federal court system. The colony-states were taxing or excluding each other's goods, issuing their own currency, and engaging in other forms of rivalry contrary to the best interests of the new nation.

Therefore, the states agreed to select delegates to meet in Philadelphia in the summer of 1787 in order to consider amendments to the Articles of Confederation. The expressed purpose was *not* to write a new Constitution, and if this had been indicated as the reason for the meeting, it is likely that many states would have refused to participate. However, when the delegates arrived, discussion soon turned, at the urging of James Madison, to the need for a completely new governmental structure.

The delegates were quite a group, consisting of 55 of what we might now term "the best and the brightest" men of the new nation, including George Washington, Alexander Hamilton, Roger Sherman, and Benjamin Franklin, as well as Madison. They were all men, and most were prominent landowners and political figures. Meeting all summer in the building now called Independence Hall in Philadelphia (with the windows of the meeting room nailed shut to ensure privacy), the delegates in September 1787 issued the proposed new Constitution.

The ratification process was not easy. The delegates had breached their instructions and had created a new and powerful federal government. Considerable opposition arose in many of the states to a strong central government and to the resulting reduction in freedom and independence for the states. The system of federalism (described in the next section of this chapter) was a new concept to which many of the former colonists were opposed. Patrick Henry was particularly vociferous in his dissent. The arguments for ratification were led by Hamilton, Madison, and John Jay, who wrote a series of articles called *The Federalist Papers*, which were widely distributed (people actually read them—there was no radio or television in those days). During the course of the debates, in order to improve the chances of ratification, particularly in New York, Rhode Island, and Virginia, the proponents of ratification promised to immediately begin work on a series of amendments designed to safeguard and guarantee individual rights, should the Constitution be ratified. The required number of states did ratify the Constitution by 1788, and the first Congress met in 1789. As promised, the first 10 amendments (the Bill of Rights) were added by 1791.

ORGANIZATION OF THE FEDERAL AND STATE GOVERNMENTS

FEDERALISM

One of the major compromises reached in the writing of the Constitution was the division of powers between the federal and state governments. As we have mentioned, the framers of the Constitution and the American citizens were quite apprehensive about an all-powerful federal government. Therefore, the Constitution specifically granted a series of powers to the federal government, which are termed **enumerated powers**, leaving other powers (not given to the federal government) to the states.

enumerated powers: Those powers specifically given to the federal government in the Constitution.

It has long been accepted, in theory at least, that Congress and the federal government may only exercise powers that were specifically granted them in the Constitution, such as "to lay and collect taxes," "to coin money," "to establish post offices and post roads," "to constitute tribunals inferior to the Supreme Court," and "regulate commerce with foreign nations and among the several states." To clarify this point, the 10th Amendment to the Constitution (added with the Bill of Rights) states, "The powers not delegated to the United States by the Constitution . . . are reserved by it to the states respectively, or to the people." This concept of dividing powers up between the federal and state governments is called *federalism*.

But you may be asking—"if the federal government is limited to doing only the things specifically granted to it in the Constitution, how did it ever become as powerful and pervasive as it is today?" The answer lies in the way the Constitution has been interpreted, particularly with reference to two other important clauses of the Constitution itself. Article VI contains the *Supremacy Clause*, which states that the "Constitution and Laws of the United States which shall be made in pursuance thereof . . . shall be the supreme law of the land."

preemption: The doctrine that holds that when a federal law and a state law are in direct conflict, the federal law prevails.

As was mentioned in Chapter 2, this clause has led to the doctrine of **preemption**, which holds that when a federal law and a state law govern the same subject and are conflicting, the federal law "preempts" (controls and displaces) the state law. As society has become more complex, the subjects that the federal government has chosen to regulate (especially under the Commerce Clause, as discussed later) have greatly expanded. Many of those same areas are dealt with in some way by state laws, and therefore, courts have had to determine on numerous occasions whether the state law should be preempted or not.

In addition, Article I, Section 8, of the Constitution grants Congress the right to make "all laws *necessary and proper* for carrying into execution" the enumerated powers. The "necessary and proper clause" has been interpreted hundreds of times by the courts. Often, judicial decisions have allowed Congress to pass laws to accomplish things not specifically authorized by the Constitution, where those actions are deemed necessary to carry out a power that was specifically assigned to the federal government. Actions taken under this theory are called **implied powers**. In 1819 the Supreme Court decided the first important case dealing with this type of power, *McCulloch v. Maryland*.

implied powers: Laws and actions taken by the federal government that are "necessary and proper" to carry out enumerated powers.

MCCULLOCH V. MARYLAND

17 U.S. 316 (1819)

FACTS

Congress had passed a law establishing a national bank in 1816. The Maryland legislature attempted to tax all banks that were not chartered by the state, but the cashier of the national bank located in Baltimore refused to pay the tax. The state prosecutor brought criminal charges against the cashier. A main issue in the case became whether the federal government has the power to set up a bank. The prosecution pointed out that none of the enumerated powers of the federal government authorize the formation of a national bank.

DECISION

Chief Justice Marshall decided that Congress did have the power to create a national bank. He wrote, "Among the enumerated powers, we do not find that of establishing a bank or creating a corporation. But there is no phrase in the instrument which, like the Articles of Confederation, excludes incidental or implied powers."

Much argument focused on the "necessary and proper" clause of the Constitution. The state argued that the word "necessary" meant that Congress could only pass laws which were "indispensable" to the exercise of the enumerated power. Marshall asked if this was the sense in which the word "necessary" was always used and decided that it was not. "We find that it frequently imports no more than that one thing is convenient, or useful, or essential to another. . . ."

Marshall wrote that there was no question but that the powers of the federal government were limited. But the court found that Congress should have some discretion about the means by which the enumerated powers are carried out. "Let the ends be legitimate, let it be within the scope of the constitution, and all means which are appropriate, which are plainly adapted to that end, which are not prohibited, but consistent with the letter and spirit of the constitution, are constitutional."

CASE QUESTIONS

1. Does the phrase "necessary and proper" mean something different than just the word "necessary"? What do you think were the intentions of the authors of the Constitution when they drafted that phrase?
2. Marshall states that if the "ends are legitimate" that the means for reaching the ends are within the discretion of Congress. What is the legitimate end served by the establishment of a national bank? Can you find an enumerated power that is being assisted by the national bank?
3. Think of as many "implied powers" of the federal government as you can. What are some of the things the government does that are not specifically mentioned in the Constitution?

FEDERALISM AND THE 11TH AMENDMENT

On the final day of its 1998–99 term (June 1999) the U.S. Supreme Court issued three significant decisions (all decided by a 5-4 majority) dealing with federalism and the 11th Amendment, which dramatically strengthened states' rights. The 11th Amendment to the Constitution reads:

> "The judicial power of the United States shall not be construed to extend to any suit in law or equity, commenced or prosecuted against one of the United States by citizens of another state, or by citizens of any foreign state."

This "state immunity from lawsuit" clause was passed by Congress in 1794, one year after the Supreme Court decision in *Chisholm v. Georgia*, which had allowed a suit against a state for damages, pursuant to the Judiciary Act of 1789. The 11th Amendment was enacted specifically to overturn the result of the *Chisholm* case, and was quickly ratified by the states. If we recall the debate over ratification of the Constitution (discussed earlier) and specifically the apprehension that many state leaders had about relinquishing sovereignty to a strong federal government, it is possible to understand the angry reaction that followed the *Chisholm* decision, and the quick addition of the 11th Amendment to restore state immunity from certain lawsuits.

For many years there were a few decisions now and then dealing with the scope of the 11th Amendment. In general, while states were held immune from suit by citizens of other states in federal court (which is what the 11th Amendment specifically provides), it was possible for their own citizens to sue them in their own state courts for various violations. However, under the leadership of Chief Justice Rehnquist, things began to change in recent years.

In 1996, the Supreme Court had held in *Seminole Tribe v. Florida* that Congress only has the power to authorize suits against states in federal court pursuant to its authority under Section 5 of the 14th Amendment (which allows Congress to enact laws to enforce the "due process," "equal protection," and other protections given there). And in 1997 in *City of Boerne v. Flores*, the Court struck down the federal Religious Freedom Restoration Act, saying that Congress exceeded its power under Section 5 by redefining rather than enforcing, the guarantees of the 14th Amendment. In what one commentator called "a series of startling decisions" the Supreme Court in 1999 decided three cases severely restricting the power of the federal government by prohibiting nearly all lawsuits against a state for violation of federal law.

In *Alden v. Maine*, the first of the three 1999 decisions, a group of state probation officers sued in state court under the Federal Fair Labor Standards Act to recover overtime pay allegedly owed them by the state of Maine. The officials had first sued in federal court, but the case was dismissed on the basis of the *Seminole Tribe* decision. In the *Alden* case, the Supreme Court, in an opinion by Justice Anthony Kennedy, held that the officers could not sue the state of Maine in state courts, even if the federal wage and hour laws were violated.

After a lengthy review of the Constitution's structure and history (emphasizing the independent sovereignty of the states), and discussing several previous Supreme Court federalism decisions, Justice Kennedy explained that the 11th Amendment actually "confirmed rather than established" states' immunity from suit. State sovereign immunity preceded the Constitution's ratification, he stated, and was "implicit in the Constitutional design." Thus, the *Chisholm* case "deviated from the original understanding," which was "restored" by the 11th Amendment. Furthermore, since the immunity of the states existed prior to the 11th Amendment, it might be even broader than the words of that amendment and could cover suits in a state court by a state's own citizens, as well as suits by citizens of other states in federal court.

In the *Alden* case the Supreme Court, citing authority as far back as the *Federalist Papers*, confirmed that the states always have had and retained a "residuary and inviolable sovereignty." Calling the question of the states' immunity from suit in its own state courts for violations of federal law "a matter of first impression," the Court found that history and prior cases indicated that states retained constitutional immunity from suit in their own courts.

The Supreme Court stated that "[f]ederalism requires that Congress accord States the respect and dignity due them as residuary sovereigns and joint participants in the Nation's governance. Immunity from suit in federal courts is not enough to preserve that dignity, for the indignity of subjecting a nonconsenting State to the coercive process of judicial tribunals at the instance of private parties exists regardless of the forum." In addition, "[p]rivate suits against nonconsenting states may threaten their financial integrity, and the surrender of immunity carries with it substantial costs to the autonomy, decisionmaking ability, and sovereign capacity of the States."

The result of the trio of 1999 cases is that individuals may not generally sue a state government, in either state or federal court, for its violations of federal law, unless the state chooses to give up its immunity. The *Alden* case involved alleged violation of federal wage, hour, and overtime rules, while the other two cases held that neither companies nor individuals could sue nonconsenting states for patent infringement or false advertising in violation of federal law. The only way for the federal government to remove this immunity is through use of the power it has under Section 5 of the 14th Amendment. But in two other cases decided the same day (June 1999) as *Alden*, the Court indicated that it will be applying "strict scrutiny" analysis of any attempts by Congress to remove state immunity under the 14th Amendment.

The three 1999 decisions have generated considerable comment and controversy. One commentator called the cases a return to "antebellum federal/state relations." Another suggested that the Supreme Court had "experienced Y2K problems six months early and has returned to 1900." Others maintain that it is merely "a continuation of a debate that began in the summer of 1787 and has never been fully resolved—the debate between a state-centered view of the American Constitution and a nationalist view." The following article, written by a well-known constitutional law scholar, examines these issues.

Permission to Litigate

Sovereign Immunity Lets States Decide Who Can Sue Them

In a series of startling decisions, the U.S. Supreme Court has dramatically changed basic principles of judicial jurisdiction.

For the last 212 years, Americans have been able to sue state governments for violating federal laws and inflicting injuries. There has always been some judicial forum available for redress.

However, in three final rulings of the term, the Supreme Court held that state governments generally cannot be sued in state or federal court without their consent. The result is that states often can violate federal law with impunity and not be held accountable.

Profiting at Citizens' Expense

The decisions mean a state laboratory can dump toxic wastes in violation of federal laws and those who become ill will have no recourse. A state university can violate copyright laws by making copies of a book and selling it to students for a few dollars less than its usual price, profiting at the expense of the publisher and author. States can ignore patent laws, violating the rights of inventors and patentholders, and no court will be able to grant relief.

Plaintiffs may sue the state officers in federal court for an injunction to stop the offending practices, but no court will have jurisdiction to award any damages, no matter how great the loss.

Each of the three cases was decided by an identical 5-4 margin, with the majority comprised of Chief Justice William H. Rehnquist and Justices Sandra Day O'Connor, Antonin Scalia, Anthony M. Kennedy and Clarence Thomas. At issue was state sovereign immunity.

The cases clarify the meaning of *Seminole Tribe v. Florida*, 517 U.S. 44, a 1996 decision that substantially expanded states' 11th Amendment immunity to suit in federal court. The case held that Congress may authorize suits against states in federal court only when it acts pursuant to its authority under section 5 of the 14th Amendment. The section authorizes Congress to enact laws to enforce the amendment's due process and other protections.

Now, in *Alden v. Maine*, No. 98-436, the Supreme Court has made clear that states can raise sovereign immunity as a bar to suits in state courts as well.

Alden involved a group of probation officers who sued the state of Maine claiming they were owed overtime pay under the federal Fair Labor Standards Act. They initially sued in federal court, but the suit was dismissed based on the 11th Amendment. The employees then filed their claim in state court. The Maine Supreme Judicial Court held that the state had sovereign immunity and could not be sued in state courts without its consent.

The U.S. Supreme Court affirmed June 23. Writing for the Court, Kennedy said Congress does not have the power under Article I of the Constitution to subject the states to private damage suits in their own courts.

He stressed the importance of state sovereign immunity, which "inheres in the system of federalism established by the Constitution."

The Constitution's text is silent concerning the permissibility of suits against state governments in state courts. Moreover, Kennedy admitted that "the historical record gives no instruction as to the founding generation's intent to preserve state immunity from suit in their own courts."

But Kennedy said the framers' silence on the subject was conclusive evidence that they did not intend to allow states to be sued in state court without their consent. The result is that state employees might be owed substantial amounts of overtime pay under federal law, but they cannot sue to recover these funds in any court.

A Way to Save

The other two cases decided by the Supreme Court involved claims by College Savings Bank of Princeton, N.J., which devised a system for students to save money to pay for college tuition. In two lawsuits, College Savings claimed the Florida Prepaid Postsecondary Education Expense Board copied its system.

One claim was for patent infringement, brought under a 1992 amendment to patent laws that expressly allows states to be sued in federal court for violations.

In *Florida Prepaid Postsecondary Education Expense Board v. College Savings Bank*, No. 98-531, the Supreme Court held June 23 that this authorization of suits against states is unconstitutional. States cannot be sued in federal court for patent infringement without their consent, the majority said. Because federal courts have exclusive jurisdiction in patent cases, *College Savings Bank* means that no court can hear patent suits against state governments.

The decision took a narrow view of the scope of Congress' power under section 5 of the 14th Amendment. The ruling is an extension of the Court's stance two years ago in *City of Boerne v. Flores*, 521 U.S. 507, which held that Congress exceeded its power when it enacted the Religious Freedom Restoration Act.

Although patents are property protected under the 14th Amendment's due process clause, the Court rejected the argument that Congress had acted under section 5 to protect patents. "Congress identified no pattern of patent infringement by the states, let alone a pattern of constitutional violations," Rehnquist wrote in his majority opinion.

College Savings brought its other claim under the Lanham Act, alleging the Florida board made false advertising statements. The Trademark Remedy Clarification Act, adopted by Congress in 1992, authorized such suits against state governments.

The Court, in an opinion by Scalia, found that the authorization of suit was unconstitutional. Congress may override the 11th Amendment only pursuant to its section 5 powers, and the trademark clarification law was not adopted under that authority.

Already the Court has three federalism cases on the docket for next term. In *Kimel v. Florida Board of Regents*, No. 98-971, the justices will consider whether a state can be sued in federal court for violating the federal law prohibiting age discrimination in the workplace.

In *Vermont Agency of National Resources v. United States*, No. 98-1828, the Court will decide whether an individual may sue a state to recover money on behalf of the U.S. government in a qui tam action. The 11th Amendment does not preclude the United States from suing a state government. The Court will decide whether it bars a suit when a private person sues in the name of the United States.

Finally, in *Reno v. Condon*, No. 98-1464, the Court will consider the constitutionality of the Driver's Privacy Protection Act. The law prohibits state departments of motor vehicles from disclosing personal information, such as addresses, without consent. The issue is whether this federal prohibition directed at state governments is a violation of the 10th Amendment, which reserves power to the states. [Note: The three cases were pending in the Supreme Court at the time this book went to press.]

Rights Without Remedies

Almost 200 years ago, in *Marbury v. Madison*, Chief Justice John Marshall declared, "The very essence of civil liberty certainly consists of the right of every individual to claim the protection of the laws, whenever he receives an injury."

Yet, the impact of the Supreme Court's recent rulings is that states can infringe rights created by federal laws and no court will be able to award a remedy.

Moreover, the decisions continue a trend of the Rehnquist Court to narrow the powers of the federal government in the name of federalism. The Court's evolving views in this area have produced a double flip-flop in one line of cases.

Two decades ago, in *National League of Cities v. Usery*, 426 U.S. 833 (1976), the Court held that Congress could not constitutionally apply the Fair Labor Standards Act to state governments. This was expressly overruled in *Garcia v. San Antonio Metropolitan Transit Authority*, 469 U.S. 528 (1985).

The effect of *Alden v. Maine* is basically to reinstate *National League of Cities*: States can ignore the Fair Labor Standards Act and not be sued. In fact, while *National League of Cities* held only that Congress could not regulate state governments in areas of traditional state control, *Alden* means that states can ignore all federal laws, except for those enacted under section 5 of the 14th Amendment.

The three June decisions must be viewed together with earlier Court rulings limiting the scope of Congress' commerce power, narrowing its authority under section 5 of the 14th Amendment, using the 10th Amendment as a constraint on Congress' power, and expanding the scope of states' 11th Amendment immunity.

Cumulatively, these federalism rulings are the Rehnquist Court's most dramatic change in constitutional law.

"Permission to Litigate," by Erwin Chemerinsky, *ABA Journal*, August 1999, pp. 42–43. Copyright American Bar Association. Reprinted by permission of the *ABA Journal*.

separation of powers: The division of federal power into three separate branches of the government.

SEPARATION OF POWERS

Not only did the Constitution set forth the general role of the federal and state governments, but it also divided the powers of the federal government into three **separate branches**. Due in part to the fear of excessive federal government power, the framers created the executive branch, the legislative branch, and the judicial branch of the federal government and gave each one different responsibilities. Through a system of *checks and balances*, each branch was given certain ways of preventing the other branches from assuming excessive power.

Article I of the Constitution grants "*all legislative powers*" to Congress, which "shall consist of a Senate and House of Representatives." Article I goes on to prescribe the necessary qualifications for Senator and Representative, the term of office, manner of election, duties of each body, powers of Congress, and various activities Congress and the states are prohibited from doing.

Article II vests the "*executive power*" in the President of the United States and sets forth the procedures for election of the president and vice-president. The president is directed to "take care that the Laws be faithfully executed" and is given the power to be "Commander in Chief of the Army and Navy," to make treaties, appoint ambassadors, judges of the Supreme Court, and other "officers of the United States," convene both houses of Congress, and shall give Congress "Information on the State of the Union" from time to time.

Article III grants the *judicial power* of the United States to "one Supreme Court, and such inferior courts as the Congress may from time to time ordain and establish." This article provides that judges shall have life terms "during good behavior" and establishes the jurisdiction of the federal courts. For example, one sentence in Article III states that "the judicial power shall extend to all Cases, in law and Equity, arising under this Constitution, the Laws of the United States, and Treaties made . . . under their authority. . . ." *Federal question jurisdiction*, as was discussed in Chapter 2, is based on this phrase in the Constitution. Article III also provides for juries in the "trial of all crimes," with the trial to take place in the state where the alleged crime has been committed.

For much of the past 210 years there has been tension among the three branches of government about the scope of the powers granted to each. Often, the president and executive branch officials complain that Congress is intruding on the power to control the armed forces or conduct international affairs. Likewise, many have argued that court decisions made by the judicial branch often do not merely interpret the laws passed by Congress, but change, alter, or add to them. Finally, senators and representatives have often criticized the extent of powers assumed by popular presidents and the growth in the number of agencies and personnel in the executive branch. This tension and tugging among the various branches is probably exactly what the framers hoped would happen when they created the branches and the "checks and balances."

JUDICIAL REVIEW

Although the Constitution divides the federal powers into three parts, it does not specifically state what is to happen if one branch encroaches upon the responsibilities assigned to another or assumes powers not given to it by the Constitution. For example, suppose Congress passes a law that is signed by the President but that conflicts with a provision of the Constitution.

It did not take long after ratification of the Constitution for such an event to occur, and the resulting Supreme Court decision in *Marbury v. Madison* in 1803 is one of the most important legal decisions in United States history. Justice John Marshall's opinion in that case established the principle of **judicial review**, by which the judicial branch has the power to decide if actions of the legislative branch conform to the Constitution. The Court dealt with the question of what should happen if a law passed by Congress did not comply with the Constitution.

judicial review: The power of the judicial branch to review the actions of the executive and legislative branches to determine if their actions are Constitutional.

MARBURY V. MADISON

5 U.S. 137 (1803)

FACTS

In 1800 John Adams was defeated for reelection as President of the United States by Thomas Jefferson. Adams was a Federalist, and a supporter of a strong federal government, while Jefferson was an anti-Federalist who preferred more local government power. Shortly before leaving office, Adams appointed John Marshall, then his Secretary of State, as Chief Justice of the Supreme Court, and he was quickly confirmed. Congress also passed a law creating a number of new judgeships for the District of Columbia, and Adams quickly appointed 42 persons as judges, who were confirmed by the Senate (on Adams' last day in office).

However, four of the official commissions (papers appointing the Judges) were not delivered by the next day when Mr. Jefferson took office, and he stopped them from being delivered. One of the prospective judges, William Marbury, filed suit in the Supreme Court against James Madison, then the Secretary of State, seeking to force delivery of his commission.

Congress had passed a law, called the Judiciary Act of 1789, which authorized the Supreme Court to issue writs of *mandamus* (a court order directing an individual to do something) to government officials "in cases warranted by the principles and usages of law." Marbury argued that this law gave the Supreme Court the power to order Madison to deliver his commission.

DECISION

Chief Justice John Marshall, in a classic opinion, relying heavily on logic, determined that the Court must decide if the law itself was Constitutional. He found that the Constitution, in Article III, had given the Supreme Court "original jurisdiction" (the power to hear trials rather than appeals) only for certain limited cases, such as those involving ambassadors and ministers, and thus Congress's attempt to expand the range of its powers was unconstitutional.

Marshall wrote, "The question, whether an act, repugnant to the Constitution, can become the law of the land, is a question deeply interesting to the United States; but happily, not of an intricacy proportioned to its interest. It seems only necessary to recognize certain principles, supposed to have been long and well established, to decide it. That the people have an original right to establish, for their future government, such principles, as in their opinion, shall most conduce to their own happiness is the basis on which the whole American fabric has been erected . . . . The principles, therefore, so established, are deemed fundamental . . . and are designed to be permanent."

Marshall continued, "This original and supreme will (the Constitution) organizes the government and assigns to different departments their respective powers . . . [with] certain limits not to be transcended by those departments . . . . To what purpose are powers limited, and to what purpose is that limitation committed to writing, if these limits may, at any time, be passed by those intended to be restrained? The distinction between a government with limited and unlimited powers is abolished, if those limits do not confine the persons on whom they are imposed . . . . It is a proposition too plain to be contested, that the Constitution controls any legislative act repugnant to it.

"It is emphatically the province and duty of the judicial department to say what the law is. Those who apply the rule to particular cases must of necessity expound and interpret that rule. If two laws conflict with each other, the courts must decide on the operation of each.

"So if a law be in opposition to the Constitution, if both the law and the Constitution apply to a particular case . . . the court must determine which of these conflicting rules governs the case. This is the very essence of judicial duty. If, then, the courts are to regard the Constitution, and the Constitution is superior to any ordinary act of the legislature, the Constitution, and not such ordinary act, must govern the case to which they both apply.

"Must the courts close their eyes on the Constitution and see only the law? This doctrine would subvert the very foundation of all written constitutions. It would declare that an act which, according to the principles and theory of our government, is entirely void, is yet, in practice, completely obligatory. It would declare that if the legislature shall do what is expressly forbidden, such act, notwithstanding the express prohibition, is in reality effectual . . . . It is prescribing limits, and declaring that those limits may be passed at pleasure."

The Constitution states that "[t]he judicial power is extended to all cases arising under the Constitution." Justice Marshall asked, "Could it be the intention of those who gave this power, to say that in using it the Constitution should not be looked into? That a case arising under the Constitution should be decided without examining the instrument under which it arises? This is too extravagant to be maintained."

In some cases, then, the Constitution must be looked into by the judges. And if they can open it at all, what part of it are they forbidden to read or obey?

Marshall continued, "It is declared that 'no tax or duty shall be laid on articles exported from any state.' Suppose a duty on the export of cotton, of tobacco, or of flour; and a suit instituted to recover it. Ought judgment to be rendered in such a case? Ought the judges to close their eyes on the Constitution, and only see the law?"

The Constitution declares that "no bill of attainder or ex post facto law shall be passed." If however, such a bill should be passed, and a person should be prosecuted under it; must the court condemn to death those victims whom the Constitution endeavors to protect?

The Court further stated that, "[f]rom these, and many other selections which might be made, it is apparent that the Framers of the Constitution contemplated that instrument as a rule for the government of courts, as well as of the legislature. Why otherwise does it direct the judges to take an oath to support it?"

In conclusion, Justice Marshall wrote, "Thus, the particular phraseology of the Constitution of the United States confirms and strengthens the principle, supposed to be essential to all written constitutions, that a law repugnant to the constitution is void; and that courts, as well as other departments, are bound by that instrument." Thus, the Supreme Court could not issue the writ of *mandamus*, because the law allowing it was unconstitutional.

CASE QUESTIONS

1. Did Mr. Marbury win or lose the case? Will he be installed as a judge?
2. Justice Marshall's ruling actually deprived the Supreme Court of a power that Congress had given it. What was that power? What was the basis of that power?
3. Although the *Marbury v. Madison* case technically took away one power given to the Supreme Court by Congress, was the overall effect of the case to decrease or increase the power of the judicial branch? Discuss the implications of this decision. Is it still important today?
4. How do you suppose former President Adams and Secretary of State Madison reacted to the *Marbury* decision made by their Federalist colleague Marshall? What do you imagine to be President Jefferson's response?
5. What was the foundation or basis of Marshall's opinion?

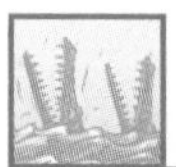

SOCIAL/ETHICAL ISSUES

Do you think it was right for the Supreme Court to give itself the power to review the actions of the other branches of government? As a question of public policy, what would have happened if the Supreme Court did not have this power? What if each branch of the government had the power to decide if its actions were legal and constitutional?

Subsequent cases have established the principle that the judicial system may review not only acts of Congress but also actions of the other branches of government and even state laws to determine if they are in compliance with the Constitution.

THE POWER TO REGULATE BUSINESS ACTIVITIES

THE COMMERCE CLAUSE

Earlier in this chapter we discussed the "necessary and proper" clause, which allows Congress to pass laws necessary to carry out a power specifically given to the federal government (enumerated). Probably the greatest use of this principle has occurred in connection with Congress's power to "regulate commerce with foreign nations, and among the several states," found in Article I, section 8, of the Constitution. Through the **Commerce Clause**, Congress has enacted laws dealing with almost every facet of business enterprise in the United States. In fact, the legal authority for most of the federal laws and regulations discussed in the last half of this textbook, dealing with subjects such

Commerce Clause: The power given to Congress "to regulate commerce with foreign nations and among the several states." It has been interpreted to allow Congress to enact laws in any area that "affects interstate commerce."

as environmental law, securities law, labor–management relations, worker safety, employment discrimination, and consumer law was the federal government's power to regulate "commerce among the several states."

It was not always so. One of the earliest important cases to discuss the Commerce Clause was *Gibbons v. Ogden*, decided by the Supreme Court in 1824. The state of New York wanted to establish a monopoly license system for steamboats on its waters. Justice Marshall wrote the decision striking down the state law because navigation and commerce were interrelated, which meant that the federal government should regulate the matter (and, in fact, a related federal law existed). Marshall stated that the commerce power cannot be used to govern activities that are *wholly intrastate* (within one state), but Congress can regulate those intrastate matters that "affect the states generally" (that is, if they affect matters both within one state and outside that state).

During most of the 1800s, business activity proceeded without much federal regulation. However, by the turn of the century, the industrial revolution had brought tremendous changes to American business, transportation, and communication. The increase in mass production, the expansion of the power and scope of industrial firms, and the emergence of labor organizations created new challenges and problems on a national level. Congress responded by passing new laws, dealing with labor, management, working conditions, and the economy.

From 1900 through the 1930s, the Supreme Court struck down several earlier such laws as being beyond the powers of Congress because they regulated activity that was not actually "in" interstate commerce. For example, a law regulating the hours and conditions of child labor was held unconstitutional as beyond the power of Congress.

But the stock market crash of 1929, the Depression of the 1930s and the election of President Franklin Roosevelt led to major social changes. Roosevelt's New Deal called for greater federal government involvement in solving the country's problems, and the American public generally supported this approach.

By 1937 the mood of the country, as well as Roosevelt's proposal to enlarge the Supreme Court (called the "Court-packing plan"), caused the Court to modify its views and to hold that *any activity that "affected" interstate commerce* was within the power of Congress to regulate. In 1937 the Supreme Court upheld the National Labor Relations Act, which provided substantial rights to employees and unions, and in 1941 the Court upheld a federal law prohibiting manufacturers from shipping goods in interstate commerce unless they complied with federal minimum wage standards.

Since that time, the Supreme Court has almost always upheld the power of Congress to enact laws regulating business, if the activity being regulated somehow "affects" interstate commerce. In the American economy of today, where raw materials, workers, products, costs, and markets are all affected by developments in other states (and around the world), little business activity is so local in character that the federal government cannot regulate it if it chose to.

However, in 1995, for the first time in 60 years, the U.S. Supreme Court declared a federal law unconstitutional on the grounds that the law exceeded the power of Congress under the Interstate Commerce Clause. In *U.S. v. Lopez*, the court faced a challenge to the Gun-Free School Zones Act passed by Congress in 1990, which prohibited possession of a gun within 1,000 feet of a school.

Writing for a 5-4 majority, Chief Justice Rehnquist stated that the law was a "criminal statute that by its terms has nothing to do with commerce, or any sort of economic enterprise." Thus, even though the Commerce Clause has been given an expansive interpretation in modern times, the regulated activity must somehow "substantially affect" interstate commerce in order for the federal law to be constitutional. The majority opinion noted that our dual system (including the federal and state governments) of government requires that federal law not embrace effects upon interstate commerce so "indirect and remote" that it obliterates the distinction between what is local and what is national.

Writing for the four dissenters, Justice Breyer argued that Congress had a rational basis for concluding that the possession of firearms at or near schools was, in fact, having an effect on interstate commerce, and the sale and use of such guns in schools was a national problem. Furthermore, he stated that previous Supreme Court precedents had approved federal regulations with much less significant impact on interstate commerce.

Supporters of the *Lopez* decision hailed the end of the "dominance of the federal government" over the states. Other commentators pointed to language in the majority opinion that hinted that the court was close to allowing states to return to the powerful role they played under the Articles of the Confederation, before the Constitution established a strong federal government. The full ramifications of the *Lopez* decision will be shaped by further Supreme Court and lower court decisions. In a case decided shortly after *Lopez*, and closely watched by commentators, the Supreme Court refused to declare the federal Racketeer Influenced and Corrupt Organization (RICO) law invalid, finding that there was sufficient involvement with interstate commerce to allow for federal regulation.

THE POLICE POWER

The states also have the right to enact laws and regulations concerning business, as long as such regulations are not in conflict with and preempted by federal law, as discussed earlier. States have inherent power to make laws to promote and protect the health, safety, and welfare of their citizens under the so-called **police power**. As long as state laws *do not unduly burden or discriminate* against interstate commerce, the laws are valid and enforceable. For example, one state passed a law requiring trucks traveling through that state to have a different and more expensive type of mud flap ("contour" flaps) than those required by almost all other states ("straight" flaps). The Supreme Court held that this law "unduly burdened" interstate commerce.

police power: The right of states to enact a wide range of laws to protect the health, safety, and welfare of their citizens.

A leading case dealing with "discrimination against" interstate commerce arose when Madison, Wisconsin, enacted an ordinance requiring that all milk sold in the city be processed and bottled within five miles from the center of Madison. The purpose of the law was said to be so that the milk could be inspected locally during processing to ensure the health and safety of residents. However, the court said the law was directly discriminatory against out-of-state businesses (much of the milk sold in Madison at that time came from

Illinois) and there were many other ways to guarantee that the milk sold in Madison was safe and healthful without prohibiting out-of-state milk.

However, in the absence of evidence that the state or local regulation "discriminates against" or "unduly burdens" interstate commerce, the states still do possess the power to enact laws dealing with business, health, safety, education, transportation, communication, and other important topics.

THE TAXING AND SPENDING POWERS

Among the enumerated powers of Congress is the "power to lay and collect taxes," as well as the power "to pay the debts and provide for the common defense and general welfare of the United States" (Article I, Section 8). Clearly, the intent of the framers was to allow the federal government to use taxes to raise revenue. However, the government can use taxation to achieve social or regulatory purposes as well. Some Supreme Court cases in the early 1900s invalidated taxes, which were considered "penalties," the intent of which was to regulate business rather than to raise revenue. However, no case in the past 50 years has followed this pattern, and like the commerce power, the reach of the federal government under the taxing power is considered quite extensive today.

The spending power has not been the subject of many Supreme Court decisions, although it is controversial. Often Congress will make money available to the states and other recipients providing that certain conditions are met. For example, a few years ago, the federal government made substantial highway construction funds available to states on condition that each recipient enact a 55-mph speed limit. All states did pass such laws, but in later years the political mood changed as "states' rights" arguments became more important, and the "mandatory 55-mph limit" was removed.

THE CONTRACT CLAUSE

The Constitution states that "[n]o state shall . . . pass any law impairing the obligation of contracts" (Article I, Section 10). The reason this clause was written into the Constitution was to prevent state legislators from passing laws that release debtors from their financial obligations to creditors. Some states had enacted such legislation prior to the Constitution, and the framers (most of whom were successful businessmen and farmers) wanted to avoid any repetition. While the "contract clause" succeeded in resolving this problem, the issue arose in later years as to how far this constitutional clause should be extended.

Obviously, almost every law adopted by a state has some effect on existing business relationships and contracts. It can be argued that a law (for example, a law requiring cars to have air bags) "impairs" the existing contracts between General Motors and Hertz Car Rental Company. However, in general, courts have taken a restrictive view of the contract clause, finding that if the state has a legitimate reason for the law or regulation, and the law is reasonably related to the purpose, it is not an "impairment" of private contracts just because new duties may be required.

EMINENT DOMAIN

Can the government take your property away from you against your wishes? Surprisingly, the answer is clearly yes. The power of **eminent domain**, which permits the government to take private property in order to build or create something of benefit to the public after payment of fair compensation to the owner, is centuries old. The Constitution recognizes this principle in the last clause of the Fifth Amendment, which states, "*Nor shall private property be taken for public use, without just compensation.*"

eminent domain: The power of government to take title to private property for a "public use," upon payment of just (fair) compensation.

There are thus two essential elements in a lawful eminent domain proceeding: (1) the taking of the property must be for a "public use," and (2) payment of just (fair) compensation must be made to the owner. There have been many cases over the years in which individuals challenged the government's right to acquire their property because it was not for a "public use." When the government wants property for a road, school, or city park, there is little question of the public use. But in the past 30 years or so, local and state governments have used the eminent domain power to acquire private property in order to build low-income housing, to sell parcels to businesses as a "research park," to build a stadium, or to undertake other types of urban redevelopment. As a result, tougher questions have arisen regarding whether the project really is a "public use" or whether it simply is a compelled transfer of property from one private owner to another.

However, the courts have upheld employment of the eminent domain power in most instances, opting to defer to the state legislatures in the determination of what is a public use. Courts have often used the phrase "public purpose" interchangeably with "public use" and ruled that if the legislature has decided that the project serves a "public purpose," then the court should not interfere. The following case carried this theory to its outer limits.

POLETOWN NEIGHBORHOOD COUNCIL V. CITY OF DETROIT

410 Mich. 616 (1981)

FACTS

In the late 1970s and early 1980s the state of Michigan and the city of Detroit in particular were experiencing the most severe economic distress since the Great Depression. The rapid increase in sales of Japanese autos and decline in domestic auto sales was causing severe hardship in the automobile industry, the heart of Michigan's economy. Unemployment in Detroit (the "Motor City") had reached 18 percent, and among Black persons was around 30 percent. Thousands of auto workers had been laid off, which caused a huge ripple effect, affecting most every clothing store, grocery store, shop, supermarket, and community in southeastern Michigan.

Then, in early 1980 General Motors announced that it was going to close two older factories in the Detroit area, which would put another 6,000 employees out of work. The company stated that it was looking for a site to build a new plant, in a cleared "green field" setting, to produce smaller, more fuel-efficient cars. If no such site could be found in Detroit, GM indicated that the new plant would be built in another state.

General Motors issued a 10-page, single-spaced set of "site specifications" detailing what was necessary for a site to qualify, including 465 acres of cleared and prepared land, rail and highway connections, electrical and sewer lines hooked up, and other services. There was obviously no such "green field" site currently in existence within the city of Detroit. Faced with further economic disaster, Mayor Coleman Young and the Detroit City Council used all available tools to quickly create and declare an "industrial redevelopment district" and to condemn all property within its boundaries.

The area chosen, however, was not vacant land but was a section of the city called Poletown, populated predominantly by older persons, many of Polish descent. The project called for the displacement of 3,438 persons and the destruction of 1,176 structures, including many churches and businesses, as well as individual residences. Once title to all property had been obtained by the city, the entire site was to be prepared so as to meet GM's specifications and then was to be sold to GM.

While many residents were happy to sell their property, take the money, and retire in a warm climate, a large and vocal group vigorously resisted the condemnation of the neighborhood where they were born, baptized, married, and had always lived. They sued the city, arguing that the "taking" of their land was not for "public use," but for the "private use" of the General Motors Corporation. The trial court judge upheld the use of eminent domain, and the case moved quickly to the Michigan Supreme Court. (General Motors had set a deadline for acquisition of the property, so time was of the essence.)

DECISION

In what one justice called "an extraordinary case," the Michigan Supreme Court affirmed the lower court and allowed the taking under the power of eminent domain. The court found that the Michigan legislature, in passing a law allowing local municipalities to create Economic Development Corporations (EDCs) and empowering them to use eminent domain, had set forth the "public purpose" necessary for the use of eminent domain.

The court refused to distinguish between the terms "public use" and "public purpose," finding that they had been used interchangeably over the years. Furthermore, the concept of public use "changes with the changing conditions of society," and whether "the public will receive and enjoy the benefit of the use" determines if the use is public or private.

Looking to the facts of this case, the court concluded that the essential public purpose of the project was "to alleviate unemployment and revitalize the economic base of the community" and was therefore within the powers of the city as delegated to it by the state legislature. The fact that a private party (GM) was to receive an "incidental benefit" from the project did not defeat the use of eminent domain, since the primary purpose was to benefit the general public.

CASE QUESTIONS

1. There is an old adage in law that "tough cases make bad law." This was a very difficult situation for all concerned—was the result bad law (as the precedent will be applied in future eminent domain cases)? Put yourself in the shoes of (1) the mayor, (2) General Motors, (3) an elderly resident of Poletown who did not want to move, and (4) a 50-year-old employee of the GM plant that was to be closed down. What would you have done? How would you feel about the use of eminent domain in each situation?
2. In its decision, the Michigan Supreme Court stated, "the determination of what constitutes a public purpose is primarily a legislative function . . . and such determination . . . should not be reversed except in instances where . . . it is palpably and manifestly arbitrary and incorrect." This view reduces the role of the courts and increases the role of the legislature and local governments in deciding when, where, and how the power of condemnation will be used. What are the

positive and negative results from this interpretation?

3. Should "public use" (the phrase used in the Constitution) mean the same thing as "public purpose" or "public benefit"? What are the ramifications for the eminent domain power if the terms are considered to be interchangeable? What if we still required that there be "public use"?

"TAKING" BY INVERSE CONDEMNATION: PRIVATE PROPERTY RIGHTS

Another issue often raised is whether zoning or other government restrictions on the use of one's property can amount to a "*taking*," requiring fair compensation from the government. In most cases, the courts have upheld the use of zoning and other types of land use restrictions under the police power of local governments, and no compensation has been required as long as the land can be used for some purposes. However, in the late 1980s and early 1990s, the Supreme Court issued several decisions that held that in some cases, conditions placed upon the use of private property can be so restrictive that the property has effectively been "taken" or condemned by the government, thus requiring payment of just compensation. When the private property has little value left, because of the government restrictions, courts have sometimes ordered compensation be paid to the owner. This theory is called **inverse condemnation** ("inverse" because it is the individual, not the government, who is claiming that the land has been effectively condemned).

inverse condemnation: When a significant portion of the value of one's private property is "taken" by government-imposed restrictions.

Once a court decides that the power of eminent domain has been properly used, the next issue is the "just compensation," which the owner will receive in order for the government to acquire title to the property. The governmental unit that wants the property (it may be federal, state, or local) assesses the value of the property and offers the landowner a certain sum of money for his or her property. If the owner does not think the offer represents fair market value, he or she is entitled to a hearing before an impartial tribunal to determine what compensation is "just." At the hearing, the owner can introduce evidence as to what his or her real estate experts or appraisers believe the property is worth. The judge or hearing officer will then make a determination as to the appropriate price.

FUNDAMENTAL RIGHTS AND PROTECTIONS

FREEDOM OF SPEECH

The First Amendment is probably the best known and perhaps the most important section of the Constitution. This 45-word sentence captures the essence of the rights and freedoms Americans hold dear and sets boundaries on the role of the government.

THE FIRST AMENDMENT

Congress shall make no law respecting an establishment of religion, or prohibiting the free exercise thereof; or abridging the freedom of speech, or of the press; or the right of the people peaceably to assemble, and to petition the government for a redress of grievances.

During the past 210 years the courts have been called upon to decide hundreds of cases in which a law, regulation, or some other governmental action may violate the First Amendment. Regarding freedom of speech, such recent controversies as laws prohibiting flag burning, censorship of school newspapers, and limitations on cigarette and alcohol advertising have focused on interpretations of the First Amendment.

Although the amendment states that Congress may make "no law . . . abridging the freedom of speech," some possible restrictions on a person's total freedom to say anything he or she wants at any time have been recognized. Justice Oliver Wendell Holmes made a much-quoted statement in a 1919 decision that the First Amendment would not protect the right of a man to falsely shout "Fire!" in a crowded theater. The Supreme Court stated that reasonable time, place, and manner restrictions on speech were sometimes necessary in order to protect a compelling governmental interest. Other public safety concerns have led courts to uphold the necessity of parade permits and other types of licenses for some types of demonstrations. Protection of national security has resulted in cases refusing to allow the publication of Central Intelligence Agency agents' names or defense intelligence secrets.

Copyright and patent laws have also been upheld as allowable legal restrictions upon certain types of speech by those who do not own the rights. In addition, laws prohibiting obscene acts and publications have sometimes been upheld, where there appears to be no artistic content and the matter in question clearly violates "community standards." However, in general, the First Amendment has been read as allowing almost all types of speech, even though the speech may be obnoxious, rude, even false. The "marketplace of ideas" theory holds that if all ideas are put forth, the public will be able to separate the worthy from the unworthy. Even some forms of actions that are done to make a statement about a political issue—such as flag burning—have been protected as "symbolic speech."

Those who have had false statements made about them may use the law of defamation (libel and slander) to recover damages from the perpetrators of the lies, but American courts are very reluctant to enter injunctions preventing the publication of the information ahead of time (**prior restraint**). Particularly with respect to social, political, and economic issues, the Constitution affords almost absolute protection for any of us to say what we want, free from government restrictions.

prior restraint: Court restrictions preventing a person from making a particular statement.

LAW IN CYBERSPACE

Concerned about pornography on the Internet and the ease with which children can access such material, Congress passed the Communications Decency Act (CDA) of 1996. This law [Section 223(a)] makes "knowing transmission of obscene or indecent" messages to any recipient under 18 years of age a federal crime. Another section of the law [Section 223(d)] prohibits the knowing, sending, or displaying to a person under 18 of any message "that, in context, depicts or describes, in terms patently offensive as measured by contemporary community standards, sexual or excretory activities or organs."

The law was immediately challenged as a violation of the Free Speech Clause of the First Amendment by a wide variety of groups, including the American Library Association, American Civil Liberties Union (ACLU), Association of American Publishers, America Online, Apple Computer, Inc., Microsoft Corporation, and many groups promoting freedom of speech. The case was titled *ACLU v. Reno*. (The ACLU was the lead plaintiff, and Attorney General Janet Reno defended the law on behalf of the government.)

A three-judge federal court in Philadelphia heard the case in a thorough trial, including a detailed study of the Internet and World Wide Web, and the availability of sexually explicit material on the Internet. The court made 410 findings of fact and reached the conclusion that large portions of the law were unconstitutional and issued an injunction prohibiting its enforcement. The United State appealed the case to the U.S. Supreme Court.

The Supreme Court began its opinion with a detailed description of the Internet, tracing its beginning to a military program designed to enable computers to communicate with each other. The astounding growth of the system in the civilian sector was reported, with some 9,400,000 host computers today, compared with 300 in 1981. The Court said that at the time of the trial about 40 million people were using the Internet, with the number expected to top 200 million by 1999. It is, said the Court, "a wholly new medium of worldwide human communication."

The Court's opinion, written by Justice John Paul Stevens, considered whether the Internet should be regulated closely, as is the case with broadcasting, or whether it should be accorded a wider range of freedom of speech, as is the case with newspapers and publications. The Court looked to some of the reasons for the extensive regulation of broadcast media—for example, the scarcity of available frequencies and its "invasive" nature. The Court found that there was no problem with access by the public, but rather that the Internet provides "relatively unlimited, low cost capacity for communication of all kinds."

As to the next issue, the court found that the Internet was not as "invasive" as radio or television. As the district court had found, "communications over the internet do not 'invade' an individual's home or appear on one's computer screen unbidden. Users seldom encounter content by accident." Furthermore, "almost all sexually explicit images are preceded by warnings as to the content."

In rejecting the government's argument that the law was valid, the Court noted the vagueness of certain definitions. Specifically, the words "indecent" and "patently offensive" were mentioned as imprecise, and undefined. Since the CDA is a content-based regulation of speech, the regulation raises special First Amendment concerns because of its obvious chilling effect on free speech. Second, the CDA is a criminal statute, threatening violators with up to two years in prison.

Although laws prohibiting "obscene" material have been upheld in the past, never has "indecent" material been legally prohibited. It is unclear what the definition of such material is, but to the extent the law attempts to prohibit legal speech for adults, based on the standard of what is appropriate for children, such a law violates freedom of speech.

The term "patently offensive" had been used before as one of the three prongs set forth in the case *Miller v. California* 413 U.S. 15 (1973), which upheld a law prohibiting the dissemination of "obscene" materials. However, Justice Stevens pointed out that the other two requirements of the *Miller* obscenity test were not found in the CDA. The other two tests—(1) that taken as a whole, the material appeals to the "prurient" interest and (2) that it "lacks serious literary, artistic, political, or scientific value"—critically limited the uncertain sweep of the obscenity definition. The missing clauses significantly weakened the preciseness of the *Miller* rule, which was especially important in freedom of speech matters. The Court opinion noted pointedly that "[j]ust because a definition including three limitations is not vague, it does not follow that one of those limitations, standing by itself, is not vague."

In conclusion, the Supreme Court found that the "breadth of the CDA's coverage was wholly unprecedented." Unlike some earlier laws the CDA is not limited to commercial speech or commercial entities. The general, undefined terms "indecent" and "patently offensive" cover large amounts of nonpornographic material with serious educational or other value. Since there is no effective way of determining the age of a user who is accessing material through e-mail, mail exploders, newsgroups, or chat rooms, the law's breadth would impact and curtail significant amounts of adult conversation on the Internet. Thus, the law must be held unconstitutional.

The Court concluded, "We agree with the District Court's conclusion that the CDA places an unacceptably heavy burden on protected speech, and that the defenses do not constitute the sort of 'narrow tailoring' that will save an otherwise patently invalid unconstitutional provision." Justice Stevens said that in a previous case (in which a law was held to violate freedom of speech), "we remarked that the speech restriction at issue there amounted to 'burning the house to roast the pig.' The CDA, casting a far darker shadow over free speech, threatens to torch a large segment of the Internet community."

SOCIAL/ETHICAL ISSUES

Our laws make it difficult for someone to prevent another person from making a particular statement, even if that statement is false and the speaker knows it is false. Is this right? Is it ethical? Is it morally wrong to make a false statement about someone else ("Joe is a drug addict") that may cause that person significant harm and distress? If it is morally wrong, should our laws and legal system have provisions to stop the statement before it is made rather than force the injured party to sue later and prove damages? Why or why not?

Commercial Speech In the domain called **commercial speech**, however, the decisions have been less clear. For many years advertising and other forms of business speech were not considered to be protected by the First Amendment. But in the mid-1970s the Supreme Court began to recognize commercial speech as a valid exercise of the "freedom of speech" clause, although it was necessary to balance the right against other important government concerns. The Supreme Court held, in several cases, that commercial speech was protected by the Constitution but might be regulated and restricted much more than noncommercial speech. The following case is the leading decision setting forth the tests a court should use in determining that balance.

commercial speech: A type of speech engaged in for business and commercial purposes.

CENTRAL HUDSON GAS AND ELECTRIC CORP. V. PUBLIC SERVICE COMMISSION

447 U.S. 557 (1980)

FACTS

The New York Public Service Commission decided during the "energy crisis" of 1973 that electric utilities should stop all advertising that promoted the use of electricity because the state was running short of fuel supplies to furnish additional electricity. A few years later, when the energy shortage had eased, several utilities wanted the ban lifted, but the Commission refused. Central Hudson, a large utility company, sued the Commission, alleging that its First Amendment rights had been violated. The trial and appellate courts ruled in favor of the Commission, and the plaintiff appealed to the U.S. Supreme Court.

DECISION

The U.S. Supreme Court opinion was written by Justice Powell, who noted that this case involved a "restriction on commercial speech, that is, expression related solely to the economic interests of the speaker and its audience." The First Amendment, he stated, as applied to states by the 14th Amendment, "protects commercial speech from unwarranted government intrusion, but . . . we have rejected the view that government has complete power to suppress or regulate commercial speech. We believe that people will perceive their own best interests if they are well enough informed and the best means to that end is to open the channels of communication, rather than to close them."

The Court stated that its earlier decisions had recognized the "common sense distinction" between speech proposing a commercial transaction, which occurs in an area traditionally subject to government regulation, and other varieties of speech. "The Constitution therefore accords a lesser protection to commercial speech than to other constitutionally guaranteed expression."

Justice Powell stated that in commercial speech cases, a four-part analysis has developed to determine what level of protection is appropriate. First, the message must concern lawful activity and not be misleading. There is no constitutional objection to the suppression of inaccurate commercial speech. Second, the government interest or reason for regulating is "substantial." Then, if both of the first two inquiries yield positive answers, "we must determine whether the regulation directly advances the governmental interest asserted, and whether it is not more extensive than is necessary to serve that interest."

In this case, it was not argued that the advertising was false or related to illegal activity. The Commission has established a connection between the advertising and the important public goal of energy conservation—clearly a substantial state interest, which would be advanced by the order at issue here. However, the Commission's order "reaches all promotional advertising, regardless of the impact of the touted service on overall energy use." The order would prohibit ads promoting electric services that would reduce energy use, such as heat pumps, or through diverting demand from less efficient sources. The Court found that the Commission had not shown that a more limited speech regulation would be ineffective in promoting energy conservation, and the Court could not therefore approve the "complete suppression" of Central Hudson's advertising. Thus, the decision of the lower court was reversed.

CASE QUESTIONS

1. What should the Public Service Commission do now? Is there any type of advertising ban that would be constitutional? If so, how must it be drafted?
2. Describe and discuss each of the four tests the Court says should be applied to a restriction on commercial speech.
3. Do you think that commercial messages should receive the same protection as non-commercial messages? Should a toothpaste ad be treated by the Constitution in the same way as a letter to the editor of the newspaper concerning local politics? Why or why not?
4. The government has banned all cigarette and hard liquor advertising from television. Is this fair? Is it legal? Apply the *Central Hudson* tests to this example.
5. Is a ban on tobacco and liquor advertising ethical? Is it an application of one particular standard of morality to all? There are some religions that prohibit or discourage use of these substances, and others which do not. Is the government remaining neutral or favoring one or more religions?

RELIGION AND THE CONSTITUTION

The First Amendment states that "Congress shall make no law respecting the establishment of religion, nor prohibiting the free exercise thereof." This 16-word sentence contains two key provisions setting forth the legal relationship between church and state in the United States—the so-called **Establishment Clause** and the **Free Exercise Clause**. There have been hundreds of cases decided by courts over the past 200 years in which the central issue involved an interpretation of these few words, as applied to particular circumstances.

The Establishment Clause: The part of the First Amendment that prohibits the government from promoting or "establishing" any religion.

The Free Exercise Clause: The part of the First Amendment which prohibits the government from interfering with a person's right to "exercise" his/her religion.

The establishment cases have concerned situations such as school prayers, or "prayer time" in public schools, Christmas nativity displays in or on the grounds of city halls and other public buildings, and the use of public buildings by religious groups. The central legal issue usually has been whether the activity represented some governmental assistance to or promotion of (i.e., establishment of) religion.

The free exercise cases typically have involved some law or regulation that the members of one religious groups contend they cannot obey because to do so would violate one of the tenets of their religion. For example, members of some religions have refused to receive or allow their children to receive medical care or blood transfusions, to attend public school, to salute the flag, or to work on Saturday or Sunday because of religions principles. These persons have argued that laws that allow them to be penalized for these practices prevent them from "freely exercising" their religion.

SOCIAL/ETHICAL ISSUES

Most of us would probably agree with the broad statements contained in the Establishment and Free Exercise Clauses of the First Amendment. We want to be able to follow our own religion, and we do not want the state or federal government to promote or mandate any religion for us. However, in everyday life, the interrelationship between religion and the law is more difficult. For example, should we have a law prohibiting all abortions because some religions strongly believe that abortion is morally wrong? Should the supervisor of your department store have to rearrange everyone's schedule because one person cannot work on Saturday, because of her religion? Is it morally and legally acceptable for society to allow a child to die from a disease that can be treated by medication or by a blood transfusion because the parents' religion prohibits the taking of medication or the blood transfusion?

Try to think of other issues that have arisen recently in your community or your state that involved an interpretation of the Establishment or Free Exercise Clause. As the examples indicate, these issues tend to generate strong emotion on both sides of the question.

THE CRIMINAL PROCEDURE PROTECTIONS

Search and Seizure The Fourth and Fifth Amendments of the Constitution continue the efforts of the framers to protect the public from excesses of governmental powers and intrusions. The **Fourth Amendment** provides:

> *The right of the people to be secure in their persons, houses, papers, and effects, against unreasonable searches and seizures, shall not be violated, and no Warrants shall issue, but upon probable cause, supported by Oath or affirmation, and particularly describing the place to be searched, and the persons or things to be seized.*

Fourth Amendment: The Amendment to the U.S. Constitution that guarantees people the right to be secure in their homes and property against unreasonable searches and seizures and provides that no warrants shall issue except upon probable cause.

While you may never have studied the actual words of the Fourth Amendment, you have surely watched television shows or read newspaper accounts of cases that revolved around whether a search was "reasonable," whether there was the need for a search warrant, or whether the search warrant was properly prepared and executed.

In general, in order to search a person's home or business, the government must convince a judge, before a search warrant will be issued, that there is "probable cause" that a search will disclose evidence of a crime. This burden can be met by showing the judge certain evidence, by the testimony of police officials or informants, or perhaps the sworn statement of someone who saw the illegal material in the subject's home or knows that it is there. The warrant, when issued, must specify where the search is to be conducted and the items for which the authorities are looking. But what if the police search without a warrant or go into places not covered by the warrant? In order to enforce the Fourth Amendment, courts have devised the so-called **exclusionary rule**, which prevents evidence from being used in court if it was seized in violation of the constitutional requirements.

exclusionary rule: A court-made rule that prohibits evidence which was illegally seized from being used in court by the prosecutor.

Legal thinkers have hotly debated the exclusionary rule, since it does sometimes result in a "guilty" person being acquitted. For example, suppose the police search Rod's house with a warrant and find cocaine, but the warrant was issued for the house next door. Some exceptions to the exclusionary rule exist, but if none apply, the evidence found (the cocaine) cannot be used in a prosecution against Rod. In recent years, the Supreme Court has chipped away somewhat at the exclusionary rule, allowing the "good faith" of police officers to overcome minor errors in a few cases. The basic rule itself, however, is still strictly enforced by courts in most instances as a means of guaranteeing compliance with the Fourth Amendment. The framers of the Constitution were very concerned about preventing the government from conducting general searches of people's homes and businesses whenever an official chose to do so.

Fifth Amendment: The Amendment to the Constitution that provides that no person will be compelled to be a witness against him- or herself; that no person shall be deprived of life, liberty, or property without due process of law; and that property will not be taken for public use without just compensation.

Self-Incrimination The **Fifth Amendment** provides, in part, that:

> *. . . nor shall any person be subject for the same offence to be twice put in jeopardy of life or limb; nor shall be compelled in any criminal case to be a witness against himself, nor be deprived of life, liberty, or property, without due process of law . . . .*

This amendment contains the "*double jeopardy*" clause preventing someone from being tried twice for the same crime, as well as the "due process" clause (about which we will have more to say later). Much attention in recent years has been given to the reach of the "*self-incrimination*" clause contained in the middle of the Fifth Amendment. Many individuals have "taken the Fifth" (that is, refused to answer any questions) when questioned by prosecutors or government officials to avoid discussing incidents that may subject them to possible criminal ramifications. In addition, the Supreme Court decided, in the famous 1966 case, *Miranda v. Arizona*, that in order to really carry out the purpose of the Fifth Amendment, police officers were required to tell a person they had placed in custody that he or she had the right to remain silent (to say nothing), that any statements the person made could be used against him or her, and that he or she had a right to have a lawyer present during questioning. (The Sixth Amendment states that the "accused shall have the assistance of counsel for his defense.") Most years the Supreme Court hears at least one case involving the scope of the *Miranda* case and the so-called "***Miranda* warnings**."

The Miranda rule: The rule, issued in a famous Supreme Court case, that police officers must tell a suspect in custody, of his or her right to remain silent.

For example, in 1990 the Supreme Court was faced with an interesting situation. The police suspected a Mr. Perkins (who was in jail on some other charges) of murder. A police officer posing as an inmate, working with another inmate (the informer), got the defendant to discuss a possible escape. As the conversation progressed, the undercover officer asked the suspect if he had ever "done" anyone, at which point the suspect gave details of the murder under investigation. He was later charged with the murder, and at trial he raised the Fifth Amendment as a defense, claiming that he should have been given his *Miranda* rights before the conversation took place.

The Supreme Court denied his claim, holding that an agent posing as an inmate need not give the warnings before questioning the suspect about a crime he has not been charged with, because of the purposes of the *Miranda* rule. The reason behind the rule, stated the court, was to eliminate the risk of coercion present in an official interrogation of a defendant in custody: "The essential ingredients of a 'police-dominated atmosphere' and compulsion are not present when an incarcerated person speaks freely to someone that he believes to be a fellow inmate," wrote justice Kennedy for the Court [*Illinois v. Perkins*, 496 U.S. 292, 110 S.Ct. 2394 (1990)].

OTHER IMPORTANT CONSTITUTIONAL CONCEPTS

DUE PROCESS OF LAW

One of the most fundamental protections contained in the Bill of Rights is the statement in the Fifth Amendment that "*No person shall . . . be deprived of life, liberty, or property without due process of law.*" While the Fifth Amendment applies literally to the federal government only, the 14th Amendment contains a similar **Due Process Clause** applicable to the states. What this clause means, at its simplest, is that government may indeed take away a person's life, liberty, or property, but only if that person's essential rights are not violated and some fundamentally fair way exists for the person to contest the action. Due process issues may be substantive, procedural, or both.

The Due Process Clause: The constitutional provision that requires some type of fair hearing (process) before the government can take away anyone's life, liberty, or property.

FROM THE DESK OF
Laura Lawyer

To: Students
From: Your Lawyer

The "self-incrimination clause" of the Fifth Amendment only protects individuals, not organizations. Therefore, if an individual person is charged with a crime, he or she cannot be compelled to testify or to reveal evidence that might incriminate them. But a company has no such constitutional privilege, and if charged with a crime, it cannot refuse to provide documents or physical evidence that could lead to a conviction of the firm.

Corporations and other businesses, however, are accorded freedom of speech rights and protection against illegal searches under the First and Fourth Amendments, as we have discussed.

Substantive Due Process Early in the 20th century the doctrine of substantive due process was successfully invoked to invalidate several laws affecting private property and business rights—such as minimum wage laws and maximum hour laws. The rationale was that such laws affected the freedom of the workers and employers to make whatever contracts they wanted. But by the 1930s and 1940s, this doctrine had lost its momentum, at least with respect to economic and social legislation, and the courts will not normally strike down a law on substantive due process grounds unless it alters a fundamental personal right, such as freedom of speech or the right to privacy.

Procedural Due Process This aspect of due process concerns how the government goes about taking away an individual's rights. Did the individual have a fundamentally fair and impartial hearing? Did she have the chance to tell her side of the story? Essentially, the question is, "Was the procedure fair (due)?" This concept will be thoroughly discussed in Chapter 5, "Administrative Law and Regulation," because many government agencies—federal, state, and local—sometimes take away property that individuals want to retain, such as welfare benefits, business licenses, zoning permits, and so on. The "due process" question in each case is whether the government agency used a fair, impartial, just process (due process) in making its decision.

The phrase "procedural due process" merely means that a life, liberty, or property interest is at stake and that some sort of fair process is required. Exactly what type of procedure is necessary to provide "due process" depends on the seriousness of the deprivation. When someone is charged with the crime of murder, courts will demand the full range of possible procedural protections—such as notice of the charges, a full hearing, jury trial, lawyer, witnesses, impartial judge, cross-examination, full opportunity to present one's side of the case, and so on. On the other hand, if the city refuses to issue you a dog license, "due process" is still required, but probably not quite so many procedures are needed in order to afford you a fair opportunity to be heard. So the precise requirements of due process are somewhat flexible, depending on the significance of the deprivation.

Equal Protection of the Law The 14th Amendment to the Constitution, added after the Civil War, says that "*No state shall . . . deny to any person within its jurisdiction the equal protection of the laws.*" But what does this mean? Obviously, there are laws that do not affect all people the same—tax laws, welfare laws, wage and hour regulations, zoning laws, and many more. What causes a law to violate the equal protection clause? The courts have developed two different tests for deciding equal protection cases, the *rational basis* test and the *strict scrutiny* test.

Rational Basis Test In most cases, a law or regulation that charges different rates or imposes different obligations on different people will be upheld if the legislature had a "*rational basis*" for the distinction and the law bears a logical connection to a permissible government interest. In other words, if there is a good reason why some types of businesses are charged higher license fees than others or required to be in a certain area of town by zoning, the law is valid. Courts using this approach allow the legislature to determine what is in the best interests of the population and rarely overturn such a law.

Strict Scrutiny Test When the classification involves what is called a "*suspect class*," or a "fundamental right," however, the courts will apply "*strict scrutiny*" analysis to the law. Such a law will be held unconstitutional unless the state can prove that the classification serves a *compelling state interest*. Suspect classes are those groups of people who have experienced a history of discrimination, often based upon race and national origin. A law treating black persons differently from white persons would be presumed to violate the equal protection clause. Such laws, if subjected to strict scrutiny analysis, are most likely held illegal. Similarly, a law inhibiting a "fundamental right" (such as the freedom of association, the right to vote, and the right to travel) will likely be invalidated unless there is a compelling state interest served by the law.

OTHER BILL OF RIGHTS ISSUES

Many other legal questions involving the Bill of Rights affect individuals and business. One matter of importance is the doctrine of **selective incorporation**. As you have read, the Bill of Rights, by its literal terms, applies to the federal government only. Does that mean that a state government could, for example, pass a law prohibiting the publication of a certain newspaper or the practicing of a particular religion? In a series of cases over the years, the Supreme Court has held that the "due process" clause of the 14th Amendment, which specifically applies to the states, incorporates "fundamental" rights contained in the Bill of Rights. But these cases have dealt with certain rights one at a time, hence the phrase "selective incorporation." Thus, the Supreme Court has held that the important provisions of the First, Fourth, Fifth, Sixth, Eighth, and Ninth amendments *do apply to actions of the states*, but no case has held that *all* the parts of the Bill of Rights apply to the states.

selective incorporation: Although the Bill of Rights technically applies only to the federal government, many of the important protections have been "selectively" applied to state actions by court decisions.

THE RIGHT TO PRIVACY

Another issue of major current importance is the "right to privacy." If you search through the Constitution, you will not find any section specifically establishing such a right. Yet this legal right is at the heart of the controversy involving abortion, birth control information, and other issues. Where did it come from? The Constitution contains the seeds for establishing other rights in the Ninth Amendment, which provides "*The enumeration in the Constitution, of certain rights, shall not be construed to deny or disparage others retained by the people*."

Apparently, the framers of the Constitution were concerned that there may be some other fundamental rights that American people have but that were not specifically mentioned in the Constitution. Until 1965 no other rights were found, but in that year, in the case *Griswold v. Connecticut*, the Supreme Court found a "right to privacy." That case concerned a state law prohibiting anyone from using or providing information to anyone else about birth control devices. The Supreme Court found that the particular guarantees of the Bill of Rights have "penumbras" (fuzzy areas around the edges) that create "zones of privacy."

This zone of privacy was held to be especially important in matters affecting intimate family relations. Provisions of the First Amendment (the right of association), the Third (prohibiting the quartering of soldiers in any house), the Fourth, Fifth, and others were designed to protect "the sanctity of a man's home and the privacies of life" against government intrusion, stated the court in *Griswold*. Later, in 1973, the Supreme Court held in *Roe v. Wade* that the right to privacy "has some extension to activities relating to marriage, procreation, contraception, family relationships, and child rearing and education, and . . . is broad enough to encompass a woman's decision whether or not to terminate her pregnancy"—that is, that the government could not make that decision for her. Thus, the government could not totally prohibit all women from deciding to have an abortion.

Obviously, the *Roe v. Wade* decision has been the subject of much debate and controversy in subsequent years. In later cases, the Supreme Court has upheld some state laws that place certain restriction on abortion decisions, especially later in a woman's pregnancy. But the essential holding of *Roe* and the right to privacy have not been overruled.

NECESSITY FOR "STATE ACTION"

state action: The necessity that there be some governmental action in order to assert the protections of the Bill of Rights.

As we conclude our discussion of the Bill of Rights, it is important to emphasize that the Constitution, and especially the Bill of Rights, protects people from overreaching by *government* and not by other members of the public. Therefore, in order for an action to be declared unconstitutional, the plaintiff in the case must show that there is some significant **state action** involved. Obviously, if the federal government is operating the prison system you claim violates your rights or the state is using the power of eminent domain to take your property or the local city council denies your permit for a rally, there is no problem with proving "state action." But suppose your employer requires a pre-employment drug test, your neighbor puts up a sign attacking your reli-

FROM THE DESK OF
Laura Lawyer

To: Students
From: Your Lawyer
A MEMO FROM YOUR LAWYER

Although the U.S. Constitution does not explicitly contain a "right to privacy," several state constitutions do. Therefore, if your employer or an agency in your state is considering enacting a rule that will affect an employee's intimate personal and family relationships, reference ought to be made to the law of your state to determine if there is a "right to privacy" in the state constitution, and if so, what it covers.

gion, or a country club will not admit you because of your race. In order to claim violation of the Constitution, you must generally show that some branch of the government was involved in the deprivation of your rights. Private action is usually not a violation of the U.S. Constitution, although some states have passed laws making certain private actions illegal in those states.

Actions by state legislatures, courts, executive branch officials, and administrative agencies clearly count as state action. In addition, courts have sometimes held that actions taken by quasi-legislative bodies, like special commissions (e.g., the Governor's Commission on Higher Education), and businesses that are very closely regulated by government or receive the vast majority of their funding from government can be considered state action. Especially with respect to race discrimination, the courts have taken an expansive view of what is state action in order to eliminate instances of racism. For example, in a famous 1948 case, *Shelley v. Kraemer*, the Supreme Court held that a racially restrictive covenant in a deed ("no one but white persons may ever own this property") was unenforceable; since only the court system could enforce it, that would constitute "state action" in violation of the Constitution's equal protection clause.

SUMMARY

The Constitution is the foundation of our form of government and our legal system. This document, written in broad general terms, contains the basic outline of the relationship between the American people and their government, between the state and federal governments (called *federalism*), and between the various branches of the federal government (*separation of powers*). The fact that it has been amended relatively few times in more than 200 years and that we continue to debate on a daily basis "what does that section mean?" attests to the skill of the draftsmen.

The *Commerce Clause* has been broadly interpreted by the courts to permit federal government regulation of any activity that *affects* or is affected by interstate commerce. However, the states continue to have considerable authority to regulate within their boundaries through the *police power*. The taxing and spending powers and the Contract Clause are also important constitutional principles. Under the power of *eminent domain*, federal and state governments may take private property for a public purpose or use, upon payment of just compensation.

The *Bill of Rights* (first 10 amendments) were added to the Constitution to protect American individuals against overreaching by the federal government. The First Amendment protects freedom of speech, religion, and the press, while prohibiting the government from taking actions that "establish" religion. Other important amendments protect against unreasonable search and seizure by governmental authorities and forced self-incrimination of individuals.

The Constitution also requires that all laws and legal procedures provide *due process* of law to those affected by government action and that all persons be given *equal protection of the law*. Each of the many federal and state laws that will be discussed hereafter in this book can be tested (and many have been) to determine if they are constitutional, using the theories set forth in this chapter.

CHAPTER QUESTIONS

1. The City of Chicago passed an ordinance prohibiting "criminal street gang members" from loitering in public places. The law allows a police officer who observes a person he or she "reasonably believes to be a gang member" loitering in a public place with one or more persons, to order them to disperse, with the power to arrest those who refuse the order. The law was challenged as unconstitutionally vague, and also as violating the freedom of assembly clause. What should the result be? On what basis? [*City of Chicago v. Morales*, 119 S.Ct. 1849 (1999)]
2. Patrick Knowles was pulled over for speeding in Newton, Iowa. After the officer gave him a ticket, he searched Knowles and the car's passenger compartment, where marijuana was found. Mr. Knowles was convicted of possession of drugs and sentenced to 90 days in jail. Previous cases have held that officers have the right to "pat down" suspects and look for weapons in a car, in connection with an arrest. On appeal Knowles argued that the issuance of only a traffic citation did not give officers the right to conduct a full search of the car. What is the constitutional issue? What should the result be? [*Knowles v. Iowa*, 119 S.Ct. 484 (1998)]
3. A federal statute was enacted that prohibited radio and television advertising by private gambling casinos. The law was challenged by broadcasters who lived in states where casino gambling was a legal and licensed activity. What will be the legal basis for the challenge? What should the result be? [*Greater New Orleans Broadcasting Association v. United States*, 119 S.Ct. 1923 (1999)]
4. Police in Montana allowed a CNN television camera crew to accompany them and film the search of a ranch where the owner was suspected of poisoning endangered wildlife. In another case, police in Maryland allowed a reporter and photographer from the Washington Post to join them in a search of the home of the parents of a young man who had violated his parole. The officers entered the house at 6:45 A.M., where they surprised the parents in bed. (The suspect was not living there.) The media representatives witnessed an angry confrontation with the boy's father and photographed both parents in their bed clothing. In both cases, the citizens claimed that their constitutional rights were violated by these media "ride-alongs." Was there a constitutional violation? In what way? [*Wilson v. Layne*, 119 S. Ct. 1692 (1999) and *Hanlon v. Berger*, 119 S.Ct. 1706 (1999)]
5. In 1994, Congress enacted a law making the unauthorized recording of live musical performances a crime. The "anti-bootlegging" law, enacted as part of the U.S. ratification of an international treaty, imposes criminal liability for the unauthorized taping of the sounds or images of live musical performances, "knowingly and for purposes of commercial advantage or private financial gain." A person was convicted for violating the law by selling bootleg compact discs featuring live performances by Tori Amos, the Beastie Boys, and other artists. He appealed his conviction, arguing that the law was unconstitutional because Congress lacked power to enact the law under any of its enumerated powers. Are the any clauses that might make this law constitutional? What should the result of these cases be? [*United States v. Moghadam*, 175 F.3d 1269 (11th Cir. 1999)]

6. An Oregon law makes it a crime to use the hallucinogenic drug peyote. A Native American church, however, uses the drug in sacramental ceremonies. An American Indian was charged with a crime after using peyote in such a service. Is the law used in this case unconstitutional? Why? On what basis? What should the decision be? [*Employment Division, Oregon Dept. of Human Resources v. Smith*, 485 U.S. 660 (1990)]
7. In 1989 Congress passed a law making it a felony to burn the American flag. Shortly thereafter, a protester in Seattle burned a flag to test the new law and was arrested. Does the law violate the First Amendment? How so? [*U.S. v. Haggerty*, 496 U.S. 310 (1990)]
8. A Connecticut law allowed the plaintiff in an assault and battery case seeking damages to file an affidavit (sworn statement) that his claim is valid and then to obtain an immediate attachment of the defendant's real estate. The defendant challenged this law in federal court, claiming it violated the Constitution. What part of the Constitution does this case involve? What should the decision be? [*Pinsky v. Duncan*, 898 F.2d 852 (2d Cir. 1990)]
9. Two states enacted laws regarding the acceptance of solid and hazardous waste from out of state. An Alabama law levied an additional fee of $72 per ton for hazardous waste disposed of in Alabama that came from another state. A Michigan law prohibited any landfill from accepting solid waste from another county or state unless specifically authorized by the receiving county. Do these laws discriminate against interstate commerce in violation of the Commerce Clause? [*Fort Gratiot Landfill, Inc. v. Michigan Department of Natural Resources*, 112 S.Ct. 2014 (1992), and *Chemical Waste Management Inc. v. Hunt*, 112 S.Ct. 2009 (1992)]
10. A school district decided to include prayers at a public high school graduation ceremony. The school officials determined the contents of the prayers and selected a rabbi to deliver them. Does such action violate the First Amendment? Why? [*Lee v. Weisman*, 112 S.Ct. 2649 (1992)]

PRACTICAL EXERCISE

The Boston Bean Company is concerned about drug use in society and in its factory. The managers have heard stories about drug use by various employees at work or before coming to work. One of the board members remembers reading a *Time* magazine article stating that 44 percent of those entering the work force had used illegal drugs within the previous year. Robert Bright, Human Resources Director of the company, has proposed to the Board of Directors that Boston Bean initiate a pre-employment urine testing procedure to screen for drugs, as well as a policy to randomly test employees once a month. One of the board members wonders, "Is that legal?" Knowing that you have been studying law, the board asks you to write a memo describing what constitutional issues might be involved in these drug testing programs and whether you think the policy violates the Constitution.

FURTHER INFORMATION

www.law.cornell.edu/topics/constitutional.html
Cornell University.

www.usconstitution.net
Private high-tech site.

www.aclu.org
American Civil Liberties Union site.

http://epic.org
Public interest group concerned with electronic privacy issues.

www.crf-usa.org
Constitutional Rights Foundation, a nonprofit, nonpartisan group that tries to educate young people about the Constitution.

CHAPTER 5

ADMINISTRATIVE LAW AND REGULATION

LEARNING OBJECTIVES

After you have read this chapter, you should be able to:

1. Explain the history of administrative agencies and distinguish between the two types of agencies.
2. Describe the powers and functions of agencies, including rulemaking, enforcement, and adjudication.
3. Outline the steps of an administrative action.
4. Identify the ways in which Congress, the President, and the courts control agencies and describe the legal principles involved in adjudication of administrative cases.
5. List several laws relating to agency practices.
6. Understand how to help shape administrative regulations before they become final.

CHAPTER OUTLINE

Federal administrative agencies such as the Environmental Protection Agency and the Federal Trade Commission (FTC) are well known. However, agencies at the state and local level also play a significant role in the regulation of business. The "Practical Exercise" at the end of this chapter examines a situation where a local developer wants to construct a toxic waste site on vacant land. There are several permits and approvals required, and action is required by both state and federal agencies. You are asked to play the role of the legal advisor to an environmental group that opposes the project and to give advice on a number of administrative legal issues, which are discussed in the chapter.

INTRODUCTION

Much of "the law" concerning business is really the product of administrative agencies. Almost every business is affected by regulations and policies established by government agencies on both the state and federal level. Often called the "fourth branch" of government, administrative agencies are not mentioned in the Constitution, yet their impact on nearly every type of business decision—from the initial hiring interview to the sales and distribution of the end product—is massive. This chapter first discusses some of the history and purposes of administrative agencies and their growth and then explains the two major types of agencies. Next, the chapter delves into the powers and duties of agencies. Lastly, the chapter examines the various controls on administrative agencies and describes certain laws that apply particularly to administrative agencies.

HISTORY AND PURPOSES OF AGENCIES

As we have learned in earlier chapters, the U.S. Constitution distributed federal government power to three distinct branches. However, as American society and business became more complex, the executive branch departments (like the Justice Department, the Treasury Department, and the Labor Department) began to create subdepartments to handle particular issues and programs. For example, the Internal Revenue Service (IRS) is a part of the Treasury Department, and the Federal Housing Administration (FHA) is part of the Department of Housing and Urban Development. Beginning in the late 1800s, the nation began to face more complicated issues that were not being adequately handled by existing governmental structures. In response, Congress enacted laws providing for new rights and responsibilities and sometimes created administrative agencies to interpret, administer, and enforce these laws. The first independent administrative agency was the Interstate Commerce Commission, established in 1887. Today, there are approximately 85 federal regulatory agencies.

As business practices became more sophisticated, additional agencies were created. For example, in the mid-1930s the Securities and Exchange Commission (SEC) was established. This agency saves Congress the job of formulating every rule dealing with the sale and trading of stocks and other securities, approving every sale of securities, and bringing enforcement actions against those who violate the rules. If Congress had to spend this much time simply addressing one issue, imagine the time demands required to formulate detailed regulations concerning air and water pollution, misleading advertising, discrimination in employment, or all the other important issues brought before Congress in the form of legislation.

Congress also establishes agencies for reasons of expertise. How many members of Congress do you suppose really know about the chemical and environmental effects of dioxin or mercury? How many really understand all the federal housing programs and their strengths and weaknesses? Although a few members of Congress are quite knowledgeable about each of these areas, those few will not be very cognizant about many of the other hundreds of topics in which the federal government is involved.

State governments have also established hundreds of agencies, with each one given specific tasks to perform. As we have mentioned, the nature of federalism calls for some tasks to be performed at the federal level, with others left to the states. State and local agencies have taken a leading role in matters dealing with education, highways, health, police, zoning and planning, fish and game regulations, and many other issues. In addition, state agencies work closely with federal agencies in enforcing laws and administrative regulations concerning the environment; the finance, banking, and securities industries; worker safety; wage and hour discrimination; and other matters. Although most of the discussion in this chapter concerns federal agencies, you should remember that state agencies are important to business and function in a generally similar way to federal agencies, although slightly different in each state.

The establishment of administrative agencies allows the government to employ a whole staff of persons who focus on one specific substantive area and thus develop considerable expertise. In theory at least, this should result in better rules and regulations and more speedy resolution of problems. Congress today acts more like a company board of directors, responding to public demands and enacting laws providing general rights, guidance, and policy, while delegating the day-to-day supervision of particular problem areas (air and water pollution, for example) to an administrative agency.

ENABLING LEGISLATION

Since agencies are not mentioned in the Constitution, their powers come from the legislation Congress passes to establish them. These laws are called **enabling acts** for the obvious reason that the law "enables" the agency to come into existence, sets forth the purposes of the agency, and prescribes its functions and responsibilities. An agency only has the power to act within the boundaries of the responsibilities given to it by the enabling act. For example, if the Food and Drug Administration issues a regulation concerning the sale of stock in a company, it will almost certainly be held invalid by a court, as beyond the power of the agency. After an agency is established, later laws will often delegate additional responsibilities to it. Please read carefully the following excerpts from a typical enabling act—the 1972 federal law creating the Consumer Product Safety Commission. The citation at the beginning of each section indicates where this law can be found. For example, "15 U.S.C. Sect. 2051" means the law can be found in Volume 15 of the U.S. Code at Section 2051. The U.S. Code is the set of books containing all federal statutory law.

enabling law: A statute passed by Congress or a state legislature, which creates an administrative agency, or which gives specific powers to an agency.

THE CONSUMER PRODUCT SAFETY COMMISSION

15 U.S.C. Sect. 2051(b). Congressional Declaration of Purpose.
The purposes of this Act are—

(1) to protect the public against unreasonable risks of injury associated with consumer products;

(2) to assist consumers in evaluating the comparative safety of consumer products;

(3) to develop uniform safety standards for consumer products and to minimize conflicting State and local regulations; and

(4) to promote research and investigation into the causes and prevention of product-related deaths, illnesses, and injuries.

15 U.S.C. Sect. 2053(a). Consumer Product Safety Commission
An independent regulatory commission is hereby established, to be known as the Consumer Product Safety Commission, consisting of five Commissioners who shall be appointed by the President, by and with the advice and consent of the Senate. The Chairman shall be appointed by the President, by and with the advice and consent of the Senate, from among the members of the Commission . . . . Any member of the Commission may be removed by the President for neglect of duty or malfeasance in office but for no other cause . . . . Each Commissioner shall be appointed for a term of seven years from the date of the expiration of the term for which his predecessor was appointed.

15 U.S.C. Sect. 2054. Product Safety Information and Research.

(a) The Commission shall—

(1) maintain an Injury Information Clearinghouse to collect, investigate, analyze, and disseminate injury data, and information, relating to the causes and prevention of death, injury, and illness associated with consumer products;

(2) conduct such continuing studies and investigations of deaths, injuries, diseases, other health impairments, and economic losses resulting from accidents involving consumer products as it deems necessary;

(b) The Commission may—

(1) conduct research, studies, and investigations on the safety of consumer products and on improving the safety of such products;

(2) test consumer products and develop product safety test methods and testing devices; and

(3) offer training in product safety investigation and test methods.

15 U.S.C. Sect. 2056(a). Consumer Product Safety Standards.
The commission may promulgate consumer product safety standards . . . . A consumer product safety standard shall consist of one or more of any of the following types of requirements:

(1) Requirements expressed in terms of performance requirements.

(2) Requirements that a consumer product be marked with or accompanied by clear and adequate warnings or instructions, or requirements respecting the form or warnings or instructions.

Any requirement of such a standard shall be reasonably necessary to prevent or reduce an unreasonable risk of injury associated with such product.

15 U.S.C. Sect. 2057. Banned Hazardous Products.
Whenever the Commission finds that—

(1) a consumer product is being, or will be, distributed in commerce and such consumer product presents an unreasonable risk of injury; and

(2) no feasible consumer product safety standard under this Act would adequately protect the public from the unreasonable risk of injury associated with such product,

the Commission may . . . promulgate a rule declaring such product a banned hazardous product.

The paragraphs quoted in the box are only a small part of the statute establishing the Consumer Product Safety Commission, but they will allow you to see how Congress goes about stating the need for and the purposes, functions, and duties of the agency it is creating. The first section quoted (Sect. 2051) indicates clearly the *purposes* for which Congress created the agency. The next section (Sect. 2053) actually *creates* the agency itself ("The Commission") and prescribes the selection of Commissioners. Sections 2054 and 2056 specifically *authorize the Commission to undertake certain activities*—conduct studies and research regarding injuries and deaths caused by consumer products and collect data on these issues, conduct testing of products and training of product investigation techniques, and develop standards for consumer products. The final section quoted, Section 2057, authorizes the Commission to actually ban products that pose an "unreasonable risk of injury."

DELEGATION OF POWER

When Congress creates an agency, it technically transfers some of its power to the new entity. This concept, **delegation of power**, has constitutional ramifications. Article I of the Constitution provides that "All legislative powers . . . shall be vested in a Congress of the United States." A number of cases over the years have focused on the issue of whether the creation of agencies was a "separation of powers" problem on the grounds that Congress's delegation of power to another entity violated its duty to exercise legislative power. In general, however, the Supreme Court has held that Congress may delegate *some* of its power to an agency, if Congress provides some "standards" or "policy guidelines" to measure and control the boundaries of agency action. Congress generally provides, as in the previous example, guidelines as to the scope of the agency's power, and since 1935 no Supreme Court case has held as unconstitutional a delegation of power to an agency.

delegation of power: Congress transfers part of its legislative power to an administrative agency, by giving it the power to enact rules and regulations to implement a statute.

However, in May 1999, the Circuit Court of Appeals for the District of Columbia issued a stunning decision, in overturning certain new air pollution standards issued by the Environmental Protection Agency (EPA). The Court, in *American Trucking Association v. EPA*, 195 F.3d 4 (D.C.Cir. 1999), said, in a 2-1 decision, the regulations were invalid because the Clean Air Act provisions giving the EPA its authority were "an unconstitutional delegation of legislative power" because the law was too nonspecific and open-ended. The dissenting judge accused his two colleagues of "ignoring 64 years of Supreme Court precedents" on delegation of power. This case was being appealed to the U.S. Supreme Court as this book was going to press.

Look back over the Consumer Product Safety Commission Act and notice how carefully Congress set forth its purposes and duties.

TYPES OF AGENCIES

executive branch agencies: Federal agencies which are part of the executive branch of the government, under the control of the President.

On the federal level, there are two basic types of agencies: (1) executive branch agencies and (2) independent regulatory commissions. **Executive branch agencies** are part of the executive branch of the government—that is, under the general control of the President. Most of these agencies are headed by a single person, called an administrator, and are subparts of one of the departments of the President's cabinet. For example, the Occupational Safety and Health Administration (OSHA) is part of the Labor Department. The OSHA administrator's actual title is Assistant Secretary of Labor for Occupational Safety and Health. This person reports to the Secretary of Labor, who is a member of the President's cabinet. Many of the top officials of executive branch agencies are appointed by the President, who may remove them at any time, without any reason being given. These top officials must be confirmed by the Senate, but they are thereafter responsible primarily to the President. They are therefore called "political appointees" and are expected to offer their resignations when a new President is elected. In addition, each agency has hundreds or thousands of "career employees" who continue to work at the agency regardless of the outcome of the Presidential election.

Independent Regulatory Commissions: Agencies established by Congress, which act independently of Congress and the President, to some degree.

The other primary type of agency, the **Independent Regulatory Commission**, is created by Congress to deal with specific problems. The Consumer Product Safety Commission, discussed earlier, is an independent regulatory commission. These agencies often were created by Congress, in part at least, to keep the executive branch from totally controlling an issue. Independent commissions typically are run by a five- or seven-member board, not a single administrator. The Federal Trade Commission, for example, has five commissioners appointed by the President for seven-year terms. The board may have no more than three commissioners from one political party, and although the President appoints them, he cannot remove them, except for very serious misconduct (compare with Section 2053 of the Consumer Product Safety Commission statute). Once they are appointed, the commissioners are not subject to control by the President or the executive branch. They do not resign when the administration changes. Also, the terms of the commissioners are staggered, so that the President will typically only have the chance to appoint one or two members of an independent regulatory commission during his or her four-year term.

POWERS AND FUNCTIONS OF AGENCIES

Although there are some variations among federal agencies, most possess three types of functions: rule making, enforcement, and adjudication. Each of these powers corresponds to the main function of one of the three branches of the federal government—executive, legislative, and judicial.

RULEMAKING

When people think of federal agencies, the first thought that usually comes to mind is "rules and regulations," and that is indeed an important part of the responsibility of most federal agencies. When Congress passes a law, it establishes a series of rights and responsibilities. However, federal statutes are written in broad, general terms, since they must apply to thousands of situations all over the country. In order to provide businesses and the general public with more specific guidance as to what is legal and what is not, many statutes contain a provision authorizing a particular federal agency to write "rules and regulations" indicating more precisely what conduct the law prohibits. Look back to the enabling statute for the Consumer Product Safety Commission and note Section 2056, titled "Consumer Product Safety Standards," which specifically gives the agency power to prescribe "standards" and "requirements" for consumer products. If properly issued, these regulations have the force of law unless they are overturned by a court or withdrawn by the agency. There are two primary methods of adopting regulations.

Formal rulemaking occurs when an agency holds one or more hearings where various witnesses testify for and against a proposed rule or whether there is a need for such a rule. The hearing must be "on the record" (someone is recording the testimony) and allow for the opportunity to cross-examine witnesses and present evidence like a trial. Formal rulemaking is used only if the statute on which the regulation is based requires it. In other words, if Congress wants regulations developed using all possible procedural mechanisms, it can make this requirement part of the law. Since formal rulemaking is costly and lengthy, only a few laws require it.

formal rulemaking: An agency develops and issues regulations after holding at least one public hearing.

Most federal regulations are promulgated using **informal rulemaking**, sometimes called *notice and comment* rulemaking. This process begins when the agency issues a proposed rule. This usually comes after the agency's own investigation has revealed the need for a regulation and after interested parties have been consulted. The rule must be published in the *Federal Register*, a daily federal publication containing all proposed and final rules and regulations of all federal agencies and departments. The actual text of the proposed rule must be published, along with a statement of the authority for the rule, the reasons for the rule, and the name and address of the appropriate person at the agency to contact regarding the rule.

informal rulemaking: An agency develops a proposed federal regulation and then publishes it in the *Federal Register*, so interested persons may offer comments before the regulation is final.

This first notice also will provide a period of time (usually 30–60 days) during which any person may send written comments on the rule to the agency. Every major corporation, trade association, union, and public interest group has someone who reads the *Federal Register* daily. This is so that if a regulation is proposed that affects their business or interest, they can send comments—either supportive or critical—to the agency within the time period. If the proposed regulation is controversial, the agency may receive hundreds of letters commenting on the rule. The agency must consider the comments—but does not need to bend to the majority opinion—and then will usually issue a revised rule at a later date (although sometimes the rule is so heavily criticized that the agency decides to withdraw it completely). In most cases, the agency makes some modifications to the earlier proposal in an attempt to address some of the complaints, and then publishes the "final rule" in the *Federal Register*, again indicating the authority for the rule and the reasons for it. The regulation may become effective on that date or after 30 days.

The following excerpt from the *Federal Register* was published in August 1999 and is an example of the way a federal regulation may develop. This notice states that the Consumer Product Safety Commission is considering whether a regulation should be issued requiring multi-purpose lighters to contain more features to resist operation by children under age 5 years and also how testing of these lighters should be done. The notice asks for public comments on whether a standard should be written requiring that tests should be conducted with the switch in the "on" position.

Consumer Product Safety Commission

16 CFR Part 1212

Multi-Purpose Lighters; Request for Additional Comment

AGENCY: Consumer Product Safety Commission.

ACTION: Supplemental Notice of proposed rulemaking.

SUMMARY: The U.S. Consumer Product Safety Commission ("CPSC" or "Commission") previously proposed a rule that would require multi-purpose lighters to resist operation by children under age 5. 63 FR 52397 (September 30, 1998); *see also* 63 FR at 52394; 63 FR 69030 (December 15, 1998). In that proposal, the degree of child resistance is measured by a test with a panel of children to see how many can operate a multi-purpose lighter that has its on/off switch in the off, or locked, position. In this notice, the Commission proposes that the child-panel tests instead be conducted with the on/off switch in the on, or unlocked, position. This will provide additional protection when the users of the lighters do not return the switch to the off position after use. The Commission solicits written and oral comments on this change. Comments must be limited to issues raised by the changed requirement in this document.

DATES: The Commission must receive any written comments in response to this proposal by October 18, 1999. If the Commission receives a request for oral presentation of comments, the presentation will begin at 10 a.m., September 15, 1999, in Room 420 in the Commission's offices at 4330 East-West Highway, Bethesda, MD 20814.

The Commission must receive requests to present oral comments by September 1, 1999. Persons requesting an oral presentation must file a written text of their presentations no later than September 8, 1999.

ADDRESSES: Written comments, and requests to make oral presentations of comments, should be mailed, preferably in five copies, to the Office of the Secretary, Consumer Product Safety Commission, Washington, D.C. 20207-0001, or delivered to the Office of the Secretary, Consumer Product Safety Commission, Room 502, 4330 East-West Highway, Bethesda, Maryland; telephone (301) 504-0800. Comments also may be filed by telefacsimile to (301) 504-0127 or by email to cpscos@cpsc.gov. Written comments should be captioned "NPR for Multi-Purpose Lighters." Requests to make oral presentations and texts of presentations should be captioned "Oral Comment; NPR for Multi-Purpose Lighters."

FOR FURTHER INFORMATION CONTACT:

Concerning the substance of the proposed rule: Barbara Jacobson, Project Manager, Directorate for Health Sciences, Consumer Product Safety Commission, Washington, D.C. 20207-0001; telephone (301) 504-0477, ext. 1206; email bjacobson@cpsc.gov.

Concerning requests and procedures for oral presentations of comments: Rockelle Hammond, Docket Control and Communications Specialist, Consumer Product Safety Commission, Washington, D.C. 20207; telephone: (301) 504-0800 ext. 1232. Information about this rulemaking proceeding may also be found on the Commission's Web site: www.cpsc.gov.

SUPPLEMENTARY INFORMATION:

A. Discussion

The Commission previously proposed a rule under the Consumer Product Safety Act ("CPSA") that would require multi-purpose lighters to resist operation by children under age 5. 63 FR 52397 (September 30, 1998); see also 63 FR at 52394; 63 FR 69030 (December 15, 1998). As proposed, multi-purpose lighters, which are also known as grill lighters, fireplace lighters, utility lighters, micro-torches, or gas matches, are defined as: hand-held, self-igniting, flame-producing products that operate on fuel and are used by consumers to ignite items such as candles, fuel for fireplaces, charcoal or gas-fired grills, camp fires, camp stoves, lanterns, fuel-fired appliances or devices, or pilot lights, or for uses such as soldering or brazing. See proposed 16 CFR 1212.2(a)(1). The term does not include cigarette lighters (which are subject to the Safety Standard for Cigarette Lighters, 16 CFR 1210.2(c)), devices that contain more than 10 oz. of fuel, and matches, *Id.* The proposal also would require that the child-resistant mechanism automatically return to the child-resistant condition either (1) when or before the user lets go of the lighter or (2), for multi-purpose lighters that remain lit after the users have let go, when or before the user lets go of the lighter after turning off the flame. *Id.* at § 1212.3(b)(3).

In the previous proposal, the degree of child resistance of a multi-purpose lighter is measured by a test with a panel of children to see how many can operate the lighter. That test provides that during testing for child-resistance, multi-purpose lighters with an on/off switch will be tested with the switch in the off, or locked, position. *Id.* at § 1212.4(f)(1).

On/off switches block the operating mechanism of the lighter when in the off, or locked, position. The mechanism is released when the switch is in the on, or unlocked, position. In currently marketed lighters, the switch does not automatically reset to the locked position when the lighter is operated. During testing to determine the baseline child-resistance of currently marketed (non-child-resistant) multi-purpose lighters, the CPSC staff tested four lighters, having on/off switches, with the switch in the locked position. Children who were able to operate the lighters moved the switch to the unlocked position and pulled the trigger. The child-resistance of the lighters so tested ranged from 24 to 41 percent, well below the proposed requirement of 85 percent. The lighter with a child-resistance level of 41 percent was retested with the switch unlocked, and its child-resistance level dropped to 12 percent.

In its December 1998 comments on the proposal, BIC states that many consumers will leave the lighter in the unlocked position. Further, BIC points out that a manufacturer could design a lighter with an on/off switch that is very difficult for a child to unlock, and with a very simple child-resistance mechanism which, in itself, would not meet the 85 percent child-resistance requirement. BIC therefore contends that multi-purpose lighters with on/off switches should be tested with the switch in the unlocked position.

The Commission concurs with BIC's recommended modifications to the test protocol. Testing lighters with the switches in the locked position treats the switch as part of the child-resistance mechanism. On/off switches are not adequate to serve this purpose. First, as the Commission's baseline testing demonstrated, most children in the panel age group (42 to 51 months old) can operate the switches, which are similar to those used on many types of toys. Second, when practical, safety devices should function automatically. When in the locked position, the switch may help delay or deter some proportion of children. This protection, however, is not reliable. To provide this protection, intended users must return the switch to the off position every time the lighter is used. For a variety of reasons, even the most careful adults may fail to return the switch to the off position. Thus, as BIC points out, test results for lighters tested with the switch in the locked position may not reflect the true child-resistance of the product as actually used by consumers. Therefore, the Commission now proposes that the test protocol should require that lighters with on/off switches that do not automatically reset to the off position be tested with the switch in the on, or unlocked, position. This change is consistent with the requirement in the original proposal that the child-resistant mechanism automatically reset to its protective condition after the lighter is used.

B. Preliminary Regulatory Analysis

The CPSA requires the Commission to publish a preliminary regulatory analysis of the proposed rule. This includes a discussion of the likely benefits and costs of the proposed rule and its reasonable alternatives. The Commission's preliminary regulatory analysis was published in the September 30, 1998, proposal. The changed requirement proposed in this notice does not significantly affect the results of that analysis. To the extent that lighters accessible to children are stored in the unlocked position, and thereby reduce the lighters' child resistance, there would be an increase in the expected benefits as a result of this change.

The preliminary regulatory analysis was based on the costs of developing cigarette lighters with child-resistant mechanisms. Generally, cigarette lighters do not have on/off switches separate from the child-resistance mechanism (and thus, under the cigarette lighter standard, are required to reset automatically after each actuation of the lighting mechanism). Accordingly, the Commission's cost estimates in the regulatory analysis did not assume that multi-purpose lighters would have on/off switches separate from the resetting child-resistance feature. Therefore, the change proposed in this notice is in line with the cost estimates the staff already has made.

CPSC baseline testing shows that more children are unable to operate a non-child-resistant multi-purpose lighter if the on/off switch is in the off position than if the switch is in the on position. Thus, it is possible that some models of multi-purpose lighters would fail the certification tests unless the tests were conducted with the on/off switch initially in the off position. Changing the protocol may, therefore, adversely impact manufacturers whose initial child-resistant designs were only marginally effective. However, the preliminary regulatory analysis already considered that some manufacturers may need to revise their designs if their initial attempts to certify their multi-purpose lighters fail. Thus, these costs have already been accounted for in the preliminary regulatory analysis.

C. Regulatory Flexibility Act

The Regulatory Flexibility Act of 1980 requires the Commission to address and give particular attention to the economic effects of the proposed rule on small entities. The original proposal's preliminary regulatory flexibility analysis examined the potential effects of the proposed rule on small entities. As explained above, the change proposed in this notice is likely to have only small changes in the costs and benefits of the final rule. Accordingly, this new requirement does not significantly change the preliminary regulatory flexibility analysis.

D. Preliminary Environmental Assessment

The proposed rule is not expected to have a significant effect on the materials used in the production and packaging of multi-purpose lighters, or in the number of units discarded after the rule becomes effective. Therefore, no significant environmental effects would result from the proposed mandatory rule of multi-purpose lighters.

E. Opportunities for Comment

Written comments limited to the issues raised by the additional requirement proposed in this notice may be submitted until October 18, 1999. There also will be an opportunity for interested parties to present oral comments on these issues on September 15, 1999. See the information under the headings **DATES** and **ADDRESSES** at the beginning of this notice. Any oral comments will be part of the rulemaking records.

Persons presenting oral comments should limit their presentations to approximately 10 minutes, exclusive of any periods of questioning by the Commissioners or the CPSC staff. The Commission reserves the right to further limit the time for any presentation and to impose restrictions to avoid excessive duplication of presentations.

List of Subjects in 16 CFR Part 1212

Consumer protection, Fire prevention, Hazardous materials, Infants and children, Labeling, Packaging and containers, Reporting and recordkeeping requirements.

In the **Federal Register** of September 30, 1998 (63 FR 52397) the Commission proposed to amend Title 16, Chapter II, Subchapter B, of the Code of Federal Regulations. For the reasons set out in the preamble, the Commission proposes the following change to that proposal, as set forth below.

PART 1212—SAFETY STANDARD FOR MULTI-PURPOSE LIGHTERS

1. The authority citation for part 1212 continues to read as follows:

Authority: 15 U.S.C. 2056, 2058, 2079(d).

2. The note in § 1212.4(f)(1) is revised to read as follows:

§ 1212.4 Test protocol.

* * * * *

(F) * * *

(1) * * *

Note: For multi-purpose lighters with an "on/off" switch that does not automatically reset to the "off" position in accordance with § 1212.3(b)(3), the surrogate lighter shall be given to the child with the switch in the "on," or unlocked, position.

* * * * *

Dated: July 28, 1999.

Sadye E. Dunn,

Secretary, Consumer Product Safety Commission.

Another federal publication, the *Code of Federal Regulations (CFR)* is published once a year, and contains all currently effective regulations of each government agency. Once an agency issues a regulation in final form, it will appear in the next annual issue of the *CFR*. Your college library and public library probably have copies of the *Federal Register* and the *CFR*.

promulgating: The correct process for developing and issuing a regulation.

STEPS IN PROMULGATING A REGULATION

1. The statute is passed, giving the agency the power to develop regulations.
2. The agency investigates the problem and studies needs and alternatives.
3. The agency proposes the regulation and publishes it in the *Federal Register*.
4. There is a comment period in which the public and businesses send messages supporting and/or criticizing the proposed regulation.
5. The agency may hold a public hearing at which witnesses testify regarding the proposed regulation. (A hearing is required if formal rulemaking is followed.)
6. The agency staff analyze the comments and may make changes and revisions in the proposed regulation.
7. The agency publishes the final regulation, as amended, in the *Federal Register*.
8. The regulation is then effective and has the force of law.

ENFORCEMENT

Informal Agency Action Administrative agencies carry out many tasks in connection with their responsibilities of enforcing laws and regulations in a particular area. Some of these actions result in bringing formal charges against those who allegedly have violated regulations, as discussed in the next section. But many other activities are more routine—working with businesses to improve their practices and avoid formal charges, issuing licenses for various projects, and developing better administrative techniques for regulating questionable conduct.

The FTC, which has responsibility over deceptive and misleading practices, has recently been faced with a new type of "cyberspace deception" called "pagejacking." The following article describes the FTC's efforts to improve its monitoring of such activity.

FTC Targets Web Fraud

Regulators say they have new tools to fight 'pagejacking'

WASHINGTON (CNNfn)—The Federal Trade Commission Wednesday announced the government has improved its ability to monitor and track "copycat" websites that exploit e-businesses, advertisers and unsuspecting consumers through the process of "pagejacking."

Pagejacking is the practice of illicitly redirecting users from legitimate websites to sites containing pornography and other adult material.

The FTC's Jodie Bernstein, director of the Bureau of Consumer Protection, said the agency has identified three suspects—one located in Portugal, and two others in Australia—who are allegedly behind the practice which at one time or another has affected millions of websites.

Law-enforcement agencies from both nations are cooperating with the FTC's continuing investigation, which has obtained a preliminary injunction to rid the web of the defendants' work pending a legal outcome.

At stake is the credibility of commercial websites and their ability to secure their sites and hang on to advertisers and subscribers in cyberspace. And, there is concern about the seeming ease with which fraudulent website operators can send young viewers to adult sites regardless of filtering systems used by parents.

The case marks the FTC's 100th action targeting Internet scams, and according to Bernstein, "this may be the most pernicious we've seen."

Attorney John Fisher, who specializes in intellectual-property law and represents a U.S. gaming website whose web page was co-opted, said it's "almost impossible" to quantify the financial harm done to burgeoning internet businesses. However, Bernstein notes of the estimated 1 billion websites worldwide, 25 million have been tampered with by the variations of the scam known as "pagejacking and mousetrapping."

In a typical pagejacking scenario, a computer savvy individual with only limited computer code writing ability can attach an illicit site address to the address of a legitimate website. Furthermore, the hacker can disable the ability of the user to back out of or exit the web page. Bernstein said the defendants allegedly "exposed surfers, including children, to the seamiest sort of material, and incapacitated their computers so they couldn't escape."

The FTC has promised to match the growing ingenuity of Internet scam artists, and today unveiled a computer lab, operating independently of the FTC mainframe, that will enable investigators there to monitor the net in search of fraud and abuse. The lab has been operational for six weeks, and work done there is credited with locating the pagejackers named in the FTC's complaint.

Source: CNN fn, September 22, 1999.

The Agency "Prosecutor" Agencies typically not only have the power to make rules and regulations but also to enforce these rules and the federal law itself by bringing actions against firms and individuals who violate the law and regulations. Many agencies have their own legal staff, which can initiate actions seeking civil fines and penalties against violators. These actions are usually brought before an administrative law judge within the agency itself, as discussed in the next section. The agency's attorneys are not really "prosecutors," because they cannot bring criminal actions. If the law itself does contain possible criminal penalties, the agency staff may refer the case to the Justice Department (headed by the Attorney General) if it wants the federal government to pursue criminal action. However, the legal departments of most large federal agencies do have the power to institute civil cases, seeking fines against persons or businesses who violate an agency's rules or regulations.

Agencies bring many types of cases. For example, the Securities and Exchange Commission has instituted actions to recover money made by investors through illegal "insider trading." The FTC has brought administrative cases against companies to prohibit deceptive advertising, and the National Labor Relations Board has filed many administrative cases to penalize firms and unions that have engaged in "unfair labor practices." In each case, the legal staff of the agency files the action.

Search and Seizure In connection with their duties to monitor and enforce rules and regulations, the agencies have inspectors who visit businesses to check on compliance. Even though the violations are almost always civil rather than criminal, the inspectors are still subject to the Constitution. One agency that has often caused controversy is OSHA. Established in 1970 by Congress, this agency is charged with ensuring a "safe working environment for every American man and woman." The OSHA enabling act specifically gave inspectors the power to conduct surprise inspections of businesses, without a search warrant, to determine if OSHA regulations were being followed. However, many businesses were angry about the hundreds of "nit-picking" regulations issued by OSHA during the 1970s and were not happy to see the OSHA inspector appear at their door. Against this backdrop, an OSHA inspector arrived at a business in Pocatello, Idaho, in 1975. The resulting case allowed the U.S. Supreme Court to discuss the application of the Fourth Amendment to administrative searches. The Supreme Court ruling established an important precedent for all administrative agency inspections.

MARSHALL V. BARLOW'S INC.

436 U.S. 307 (1978)

FACTS

On September 11, 1975, an OSHA inspector entered the customer area of Barlow's Inc., a plumbing and electrical installation business in Pocatello, Idaho. The inspector stated that he had come to inspect the working areas of the firm for compliance with OSHA regulations. Bill Barlow, the president and manager of the firm, asked whether there had been any complaints and whether the inspector had a search warrant. The inspector said that there had not been any complaints, but that the business had simply turned up in agency files due for a random inspection. The inspector stated that he did not have a search warrant, but that he did not need one. He showed Mr. Barlow a copy of the federal OSHA statute that provided for warrantless inspections. Mr. Barlow then denied entry to the inspector, pointing to a copy of the Constitution he had hanging on the wall. Indicating the Fourth Amendment, he stated, "Well, I've got a higher law. You need a search warrant." OSHA filed an action in federal district court thereafter to seek an order compelling Barlow to admit the inspector, and Barlow also filed an action in federal court seeking an order that the part of the OSHA law allowing warrantless inspection was unconstitutional. The Idaho federal district court agreed with Mr. Barlow and issued an injunction preventing enforcement of the law, and the case was eventually appealed to the U.S. Supreme Court.

DECISION

The Supreme Court, in an opinion by Justice White, affirmed the decision. The first question in this case, according to the Court, was "whether the Fourth Amendment's protection against unreasonable searches and seizures applies to businesses as well as homes." Justice White wrote that "The Warrant Clause . . . protects commercial buildings as well as private homes. To hold otherwise would belie the origin of the Amendment." The Supreme Court noted that the Bill of Rights was closely modeled after the Virginia Bill of Rights, which specifically prohibited "general warrants" English officers had used prior to the Revolution to conduct searches of suspected places "without evidence of a fact committed." The general warrant was particularly hated by merchants whose premises were often inspected for compliance with British revenue laws. It was clear, then, that the ban on warrantless searches in the Constitution was intended to cover businesses as well as homes.

In previous cases, the Supreme Court had held that warrantless searches without proper consent were generally unreasonable. In two 1967 decisions the Court held that "The businessman, like the occupant of a residence, has a constitutional right to go about his business free from unreasonable official entries upon his private commercial property." That right is placed in jeopardy when an inspector in the field can enter and inspect without "official authority, as evidenced by a warrant." Other cases have held that this rule applies whether the investigation is civil or criminal, because the purpose of the Amendment is to "safeguard the privacy and security of individuals against arbitrary invasions by government officials."

However, later cases have established an exception for "pervasively regulated businesses" and for "closely regulated" industries "long subject to close supervision," such as the sale of liquor and firearms. OSHA sought to extend the rule to cover safety inspections. The Supreme Court, however, stated that the "exceptions" were just that—not the rule. In those specific industries, the proprietors have no reasonable expectation of privacy, given the history of government oversight. To extend that principle to all businesses involved in interstate commerce would make the exception the rule.

Therefore, when the business owner does not consent to the search, the government must obtain a search warrant. However, the Court stated that in order to get a warrant, the government will not have to show probable cause to believe that an OSHA violation has occurred. A warrant will be issued if the government can demonstrate that "reasonable administrative standards" were followed. For example, a showing that "we have set up an impartial random inspection procedure, and your name came up in our computer" ought to be sufficient to obtain a search warrant.

CASE QUESTIONS

1. Why do you think the OSHA law passed by Congress contained a provision allowing the OSHA compliance officers to inspect without a warrant? Does the Barlow case make that purpose impossible to achieve?
2. City health inspectors generally are allowed to do surprise inspections of restaurants in their jurisdiction. Under what authority is this done? Is it legal?
3. Do you think that government agency inspectors should have to meet the same "probable cause" requirements that the police do, in order to get a warrant? Why or why not?

ADJUDICATION

The Administrative Law Judge Once an administrative action is filed, the case is assigned to an **administrative law judge** (ALJ) who hears that type of case. The business or individual charged with violating the law is given a period of time to answer the complaint, much like the process in a regular court case (see Chapter 3). Perhaps even more so than in a court case, generally the agency and the defendant make an effort to settle the case. The firm charged with the violation and its attorneys talk with the agency legal staff to

administrative law judge: An impartial government official who hears and decides administrative cases, involving federal rules and regulations.

determine if both sides can reach an acceptable resolution. Often the case is settled with the company "neither admitting nor denying" the charges but agreeing to make some changes in its procedures and perhaps pay a fine. In return, the agency drops the charges.

If the case is not settled, however, it eventually proceeds to trial before the ALJ. This person is a career appointee who acts as a judge in cases brought by a particular agency or several agencies. The ALJ who hears nothing but labor–management cases becomes quite expert and efficient in labor law issues.

Defendants are understandably concerned, however, that the hearing officer is an ALJ from the same agency. To maintain impartiality, ALJs are hired, and decisions regarding their promotions, wages, and tenure are made by the Civil Service Commission. A federal statute passed in 1946, the Administrative Procedure Act (APA), puts controls on many agency practices to insure impartiality. In particular, the APA requires that the ALJs working in an agency be separate from and not subject to the supervision or control of the investigative or legal staff of the agency. Also, the ALJs are prohibited from having any outside contact with any parties to the case. Thus, although a business charged with violating an agency rule may feel like it's "going into the lion's den," when it faces a trial in front of an agency ALJ, there are important laws in place designed to provide an impartial hearing.

SOCIAL/ETHICAL ISSUES

Do you think it is possible to get a completely fair hearing before an ALJ employed by the federal government when the charges are brought by an attorney employed by a federal agency? Suppose that your company is charged by the EPA with violating regulations issued by the EPA to enforce the Clean Water Act. The ALJ, though not directly employed the EPA, hears many cases involving this agency, has considerable knowledge about EPA rules and procedures, and may have gotten to know agency personnel from earlier hearings. How would you feel if the hearing was held in the EPA building? Can you think of any suggestions for making the process more fair and/or for removing any appearance of unfairness?

The Hearing Process The administrative trial itself is less formal than a court case (e.g., "hearsay" evidence is more likely to be allowed), but has many of the same features, such as attorneys, introduction of evidence, and direct and cross-examination of witnesses. Some time after the hearing, the ALJ will issue a written decision (there is *no jury* in administrative cases) as to whether the defendant violated the regulation and may impose a fine if there was a violation. Remember that this is not a criminal case. In most cases, the ALJ's decision may be appealed either to an appellate body within the agency, or sometimes to the full Commission—that is, the commissioners who actually run the agency. The decision of the commissioners is the final agency decision, which can then be appealed to the federal Circuit Court of Appeals. The procedures applicable to such an appeal are discussed in the next section.

CONTROL OF ADMINISTRATIVE AGENCIES

CONGRESSIONAL CONTROL

As mentioned earlier, agencies have been called the "fourth branch" of the government. However, they must interact with each of the three primary branches in one way or another. With respect to independent regulatory commissions, Congress has created the agency itself and can certainly amend the law to terminate or substantially change the purposes and powers of the agency. Congress sets the budget and appropriates the funding for all agencies. It also regularly holds **oversight hearings**, at which time the relevant committee calls a number of witnesses, both from the agency and outside, to review the performance of the agency. When problems arise concerning an issue within the agency's jurisdiction, the hearings can become quite heated.

oversight hearings: Hearings held by a Congressional Committee to review the performance of an agency.

Within Congress, there are numerous subcommittees, each concerned with a specific substantive area. The chairpersons, members, and committee staff of these subcommittees become quite knowledgeable in, and keep a close watch on, developments in the subject area. They can quickly call a hearing—at which the top agency personnel will be severely grilled—if an issue within the agency's scope of responsibility is not promptly dealt with. Also, the committees must approve key agency appointments and are the first Congressional entities to handle any amendments to laws administered by the agency.

PRESIDENTIAL CONTROL

All federal agencies are affected by the actions of the President. As previously mentioned, the top 10 or 15 officials of executive branch agencies are "political appointees" of the President and resign whenever he or she asks or when he or she leaves office. These people must carry out the policies of the President, or they will be looking for new jobs. The President also appoints the commissioners of independent regulatory commissions but only can do so when a commissioner's term runs out. Hence, a President may only have the chance to appoint one or two commissioners of an agency in a four-year term, and he or she cannot control their actions after appointment.

In the past 20 years or so, the Office of Management and Budget (OMB) has assumed an increasingly significant role in the regulatory process. This agency, part of the executive branch, has been ordered by the President to review all proposed regulations of the executive branch agencies before they are published. OMB is to perform a cost/benefit analysis and make recommendations as to whether a proposed regulation is cost-effective. During the Reagan administration, when there was an effort to decrease agency rulemaking, agencies often had to wait more than a year for OMB to review their proposed regulations. Under the Paperwork Reduction Act, the OMB has certain powers to review the regulations of all agencies. The OMB staff has grown so large that there are now OMB staff experts for each substantive area in which there is an administrative agency (e.g., occupational safety, deceptive advertising, environmental regulations).

JUDICIAL REVIEW OF ADMINISTRATIVE AGENCY ACTIONS

Rulemaking Most agency decisions are reviewable in the courts. Unless Congress has provided specifically in the statute that the agency's decisions are not reviewable, there is the possibility of such review. Rules and regulations promulgated by the agency may be, and often are, challenged by parties adversely affected by them. These cases, usually filed in federal district court, may argue that the agency did not follow the Administrative Procedures Act (APA, as discussed more fully later in this chapter) procedures regarding notice and hearing, that the regulation exceeded the scope of the statute on which it was supposedly based, or that the statute was unconstitutional. If the agency has met these tests, the rule will probably be upheld by the court (which will defer to the expertise of the agency) if there is "*substantial evidence*" to support it, as discussed later. On the other hand, if the agency acted in an "*arbitrary and capricious*" manner in adopting the rule or in making some other determination, the court may overturn the agency decision.

Adjudication After an ALJ has issued a decision in a case charging a violation of a regulation, an appeal may be made to the full governing board of the agency. The agency board (for example, the commissioners of the FTC) will then either affirm or reverse the decision of the ALJ. If a further appeal is taken, it usually goes to a federal Circuit Court of Appeals (although in a few cases Congress has specified that appeals go to the federal district court). Several important legal principles, listed next, affect whether the court will accept the appeal and, if so, how it will review the decisions of the agency.

exhaustion of administrative remedies: A person must use all possible methods of appeal within an administrative agency before a court will hear the case.

1. **Exhaustion of Administrative Remedies**. In order to allow administrative agencies to accomplish their purposes (one of which is to ease the burden on the court system), generally a court will refuse to hear an administrative case until the parties have "exhausted" all administrative remedies available. In other words, a party charged with a regulatory violation cannot take the case to federal court until all possible appellate procedures within the agency have been used. Only after the agency has made a "final decision" can the person appeal to the federal court of appeals. This allows the agency the opportunity to correct any errors without tying up the court system needlessly. If Ace Chemical Co. is charged with illegal sales of company stock by the SEC and is assessed a fine by an ALJ, Ace must appeal to the full five-member SEC and await a decision from that Board before filing an appeal in federal court.

Occasionally, courts will make an exception and allow an individual to appeal to the court system before exhausting all agency appeals if it appears that such action would be "futile." For example, if Ace Chemical Co. is challenging a particular rule of the SEC on constitutional grounds, and the agency commissioners have consistently upheld the validity of the rule, a court might accept the case without requiring Ace to appeal to the full SEC board.

standing: A person must be directly affected by an agency action in order to challenge such action.

2. **Standing**. In general, only persons who have been directly affected or have suffered some legal injury (those who have been "aggrieved by agency action" according to the APA) may challenge agency actions. In a few cases, courts have stretched the doctrine to include those "within the zone of interests protected by the statute" upon which the regulation is based. At any rate, just as in court litigation, a person or group may have very strong feelings about a regulation or a decision of an ALJ, but unless there is some direct

impact on that person or his or her economic interests, he or she probably cannot challenge the regulation or ruling in court.

3. **Ripeness**. Another rule allowing courts to refuse to hear administrative law cases is "**ripeness.**" Just like apples, administrative cases are not ready to be shipped (to the court system) until a certain time (when they are "ripe" for review). That moment does not arise in administrative law until the agency has taken a *final action*, either a final promulgation of a rule or a final adjudication in a contested case by the highest appeal board in the agency. The purpose behind this rule is to allow the agency process to work. The purpose of "notice and comment" rulemaking is defeated if someone can challenge a proposed rule in court when the agency has just published it for the first time and no comments have yet been received. The agency may totally change the rule before it becomes effective, or it may decide to drop the proposed rule completely. To permit an individual to challenge the proposed rule in court would put an unnecessary drain on the court system, as well as interfere with the agency's rulemaking process.

ripeness: A court will not hear a case challenging an agency action until the action or decision is "final."

In the following case, the Supreme Court examines whether two challenges to certain regulations adopted by a federal agency dealing with immigration issues are "ripe" for judicial review.

RENO V. CATHOLIC SOCIAL SERVICES, INC.

113 S.Ct. 2485 (1993)

FACTS

The federal Immigration Reform and Control Act of 1986 established a process by which certain persons living as illegal aliens in the United States can apply first for "temporary resident" status and one year later for "permanent resident" status. The applicant must show that he or she has resided continuously in the United States since January 1, 1982, and also has actually been physically present continuously in the United States since November 6, 1986 (the date the law was enacted).

The Immigration and Naturalization Service (INS), a federal agency, promulgated several regulations to implement the Immigration Reform and Control Act [often just called the Reform Act], which resulted in two lawsuits contesting the rules. One case challenged an INS regulation that stated that any absences from the United States that are more than "brief, casual, and innocent" will disqualify the applicant from a legalization claim. The INS also adopted very strict rules on what type of absences will qualify.

The second case contended that another INS regulation is unlawful. The Reform Act requires illegal aliens who petitioned for legal status under this program to have maintained a "continuous unlawful residence" in the United States prior to their application. The INS regulation states that while certain brief trips abroad might not disqualify the alien from seeking legalization, if the person reenters the United States by presenting "facially valid" documentation (for example, papers stating that the person was a lawful resident of the United States), this action will destroy the "continuous unlawful residence" qualification for the legalization program. This regulation effectively prevents a great number of illegal aliens from obtaining legalization, since many of them must present such documents in order to gain reentry to the United States.

The federal district courts entered injunctions in both cases, preventing enforcement of the regulations on the basis that they are inconsistent with the statute. On appeal, the Ninth Circuit Court of Appeals consolidated the two cases and affirmed the injunctions. The federal government (by Janet Reno, Attorney General of the United States) appealed to the United States Supreme Court.

One argument made on appeal was that the courts should decline to hear the cases, since the administrative regulations were not yet "ripe" for judicial review.

DECISION

Justice David Souter wrote the majority opinion of the Supreme Court. He began by noting that "The Reform Act not only sets the qualifications for obtaining temporary resident status, but provides an exclusive scheme for administrative and judicial review of determinations respecting . . . applications for adjustment of status under the Title II legalization program." The Reform Act did in fact direct the Attorney General to establish an appellate authority providing for a single level of administrative appellate review of legalization determinations.

The Reform Act [at 8 U.S.C. Sect. 1255 a(f) (4) (A)] provides that a denial of adjustment in an alien's status is subject to court review only when an order of deportation has been issued, and then the review is done in the federal Court of Appeals. The law also "closes the circle," according to Justice Souter, by explicitly rendering the scheme exclusive. The statute says, "There shall be no administrative or judicial review of a determination respecting an application for adjustment of status except in accordance with this subsection."

There was clearly federal jurisdiction here, since the issue involved a "federal question" and federal courts are empowered to review federal agency action. However, the plaintiffs still had to meet the "ripeness" requirement, which the Supreme Court found that they had failed to do so.

When applicants seek injunctive and declaratory relief, stated the Supreme Court, such remedies are discretionary, and "courts traditionally have been reluctant to apply them to administrative determinations unless those arise in the context of a controversy 'ripe' for judicial resolution." Justice Souter commented that this meant that in order to be "ripe," the effects of the administrative action challenged must have "been felt in a concrete way by the challenging parties."

In some cases the promulgation of the regulation itself will affect the parties concretely enough to satisfy this requirement, as in *Abbot Laboratories v. Gardner*, 387 U.S. 136 (1967). This case, relied on by the plaintiffs, involved a regulation that forced the parties to choose between compliance and risking serious penalties for violation.

However, other previous Supreme Court cases have held that a controversy concerning a regulation is not ordinarily ripe for review under the APA until the regulation has been applied to the claimant's situation by some concrete action [such as *Lujon v. National Wildlife Federation*, 487 U.S. 871 (1990)]. After looking at the INS regulations at issue in this case, the Court found that "they fall on the latter side of the line."

Justice Souter found that the INS regulations here did not impose any penalties for violating their provisions, but only limited access to a benefit created by the Reform Act. The Act "requires each alien desiring the benefit to take affirmative action . . . and delegates to the INS the task of determining on a case-by-case basis whether the conditions have been met." In such circumstances the promulgation of the challenged regulation did not itself give each member of the plaintiff class a ripe claim. The Court declared that "a class member's claim would ripen only once he took the affirmative steps that he could take before the INS blocked his path by applying the regulation to him."

Ordinarily, the barrier would appear when the INS formally denied the alien's application for legalization. A plaintiff who sought to rely on the denial of his or her application to satisfy the ripeness requirement, however, would still find him- or herself at least temporarily barred by the Reform Act's exclusive review provisions, since he or her would be seeking a "judicial review of a determination respecting an application."

The ripeness doctrine and the Reform Act's jurisdictional provisions would thus, Justice Souter commented, "dovetail neatly, and not necessarily by mere coincidence." Congress may well have assumed that, in the ordinary case, the courts would not hear a challenge to regulations specifying limits to eligibility before those regulations were actually applied to an individual, whose challenge to the denial of an individual application would proceed within the Reform Act's limited scheme.

Thus, the Supreme Court vacated the judgment of the Court of Appeals, lifted the injunctions, and remanded the case to the District Court for further determination regarding whether any claimants had suffered concrete hardships due to denial of legalizations under the INS rules.

CASE QUESTIONS

1. What is the purpose of the "ripeness" doctrine? Will that purpose be achieved by the result in this case?
2. If a person has applied for legal status under the Immigration Reform Act and been denied, when and how can that person challenge this determination in the courts?
3. What effect will this decision have on the powers and role of administrative agencies?
4. Do you think that this interpretation of the Immigration Reform and Control Act is consistent with Congress's intention when enacting the law?

4. **The "Substantial Evidence" Rule**. The three previous rules effectively keep many administrative cases and disputes out of the regular court system. By forcing parties to fully use all the administrative procedures available, many disputes are resolved without involving the courts. In addition, the controversies that are not finally disposed of at the administrative level are much more fully shaped and developed by the time they reach the court system.

The APA allows Congress to enact statutes that prohibit judicial review of agency actions, and a few such laws exist. The vast majority of agency actions, however, may be reviewed by the courts, once the requirements of standing, exhaustion of administrative remedies, and ripeness have been met. When reviewing agency action, the courts follow the **substantial evidence rule**. This doctrine, based on a section of the APA, holds that a court may only set aside findings of fact made by an agency if such findings are "unsupported by substantial evidence." In other words, if there is a good deal of evidence to support the decision made by the agency, the court will support the finding made, even though the court, if it had heard the case first, might have reached a different conclusion. Findings of fact deal with "what happened." For example, an ALJ hearing an OSHA case might determine after hearing many witnesses that the safety guards were removed from 40 machines in a factory, or in an EPA case, an ALJ might rule that one business dumped six gallons of motor oil into the sewer system. These are "factual" matters. If the reviewing court decides that there was "substantial evidence" supporting those factual findings, it will almost always refuse to overturn such conclusions. Whether removal of the safety guards violated the law, on the other hand, is a legal, not a factual question, and the court may well overturn the final decision on legal grounds.

substantial evidence rule: A rule followed by courts in reviewing agency decisions. The court will follow the factual findings made by the ALJ and agency as long as there is "substantial evidence" to support the findings.

The "substantial evidence" theory is much easier to meet than the "preponderance of the evidence" standard used in civil court cases. In that situation, whichever side produces more (a "preponderance" of) credible evidence will win. However, the "substantial evidence" test may lead to an appellate court affirming an agency decision even if it finds less than a majority of factual evidence supporting the opinion. The question on appeal of an agency decision is merely whether there was "substantial" evidence in support.

Like the other rules discussed previously, the substantial evidence rule tends to enhance agency power and *show deference to agency decision making*. As we have said, agency decisions are generally reviewed by one of the federal Circuit Courts of Appeal, and these courts treat agency decisions much like appeals from federal district courts. In both cases there has been a trial held below, and the appellate court is mostly concerned with reviewing whether the law has been appropriately applied in the lower court or agency. The federal Courts of Appeal (the second highest court level in the country) will reverse a case when they find the *law to be interpreted incorrectly*, but they usually will not set aside *findings of fact*, as determined by agencies.

5. **Abuse of Discretion**. Once the Court of Appeals finally gets to the legal question involved in the appeal of an agency decision, there still is consideration given to and *deference* shown toward the agency's expertise. According to the APA, agency decisions—even as to legal matters—will not be set aside unless the agency ruling was "*arbitrary, capricious,* [*or*] *an* ***abuse of discretion***." This means that if the agency has generally followed the requirements of the law, considered all appropriate matters, and operated within the boundaries of the statute in question, its action will usually be upheld. If, on the other hand, the agency made a decision or issued a regulation without considering the factors set out in the statute or based on factors not brought out at hearings or on

abuse of discretion: When an agency has not properly followed the APA rules or has acted in an "arbitrary or capricious" manner.

FROM THE DESK OF

Laura Lawyer

To: Students

From: Your Lawyer

Administrative agencies are here to stay. Regardless of the frequent political rhetoric about reducing the size of the federal and state government, very little reduction has happened in the past few years. For better or worse, business is becoming increasingly complex every day. Competition is now on a global scale for many firms that previously worried only about local issues. Technology is allowing and indeed forcing more and faster decisions than ever before. At the same time, the public is demanding higher standards of business behavior. Neither Congress nor the courts can keep up with the multifaceted, rapidly changing, complicated new issues in business and meet the public expectations. Thus, the work of federal and state administrative and regulatory agencies is continually increasing.

As a businessperson, you will have to deal with agencies on a regular basis—they likely will be your most direct interface with the "legal environment" in which business operates. You might wish to throw up your hands and say, "There are too many agencies, I hate regulation, and I'll fight everything administrators try to do." On the other hand, you can accept administrative agencies as a fact of business life, adopt a proactive approach to work with agencies, and help them see issues from your point of view and understand your type of business.

Get to know the key administrators who prepare regulations for your industry. This can be done face-to-face on the state level, and either directly or by telephone at the federal level. Stay in tune with public discussion of issues that affect your industry, and be prepared to discuss with regulatory personnel any new rules they may decide to propose. Agency personnel must respond to new laws and to demands for action from the public. Sometimes it is possible to see an issue coming and "get ahead of the curve."

Actually, many administrative agency staff—including the top managers—have worked in the private business sector and want input from knowledgeable business officials when they are preparing regulations affecting a segment of an industry. Even career government workers know the logical and political value of receiving suggestions from the "real world" before regulations are issued. Hence, the final regulations almost certainly will better favor your point of view if you participate in the drafting and reviewing process. Also, the contacts made will likely ensure that you will be consulted early when the next regulatory issue appears on the public agenda. And if your firm or trade group later decides to challenge or criticize the regulations in public, you will be in a much stronger position, having tried to work within the system to draft reasonable rules in the first place.

comments from the public, then that action might be held "arbitrary" and be overturned as an "abuse of discretion." This standard particularly applies to regulations issued by an agency pursuant to the informal rulemaking procedures outlined earlier.

DUE PROCESS OF LAW

As discussed in the previous chapter, the Fifth and 14th Amendments of the U.S. Constitution provide that no person may be deprived of "life, liberty or property without due process of law." As we have explained, this constitutional principle applies to all levels of government action. Today, the actions of local, state, and federal administrative agencies affect each individual and business in this country every day. Rules, regulations, and decisions made by administrative agencies affect significantly the air we breathe, the water we drink, the cars we drive, the schools and colleges we attend, our places of employment, the products we purchase, and many other aspects of our lives.

In many situations an individual or a business may believe that an action by a governmental agency has deprived him or her of certain property, liberty, or rights unfairly—that is, without "due process of law." The courts have heard many cases over the years involving individuals who were suspended from school, terminated from some government-sponsored training program or businesses whose operating licenses were revoked, or whose right to bid on a government contract was taken away, thus raising "due process" issues.

As we discussed earlier, *due process* is a flexible term. The first inquiry in an case is whether the concept applies at all—that is, *whether a government agency is taking away someone's life, liberty, or property*. If so, the individual is entitled to due process. The second inquiry concerns the extent of the *specific procedural elements necessary* to afford "due process." The number of elements will vary from case to case, depending on the seriousness of the deprivation. In other words, when a person's life is at stake, the full range of possible procedures—jury trial, attorneys, judge, cross-examination of witnesses, and so on—is required in order to provide due (fair) process. But if a lesser right is being taken away, such as suspension from school for one day, some type of due process is still required by the Constitution but may consist of fewer elements. For example, "due process" here may only require that you be given the chance to state your case to the school principal before your suspension. The following case represents the Supreme Court's most detailed analysis of the due process requirements in connection with an administrative agency's action.

MATHEWS V. ELDRIDGE

424 U.S. 319 (1976)

FACTS

Under the federal Social Security Act, workers who have contributed to social security for a certain length of time are entitled to disability payments if they become disabled and are unable to work. Mr. Eldridge had been injured and had received disability payments for some time, when the Social Security Administration

(SSA)—a part of the federal Department of Health, Education, and Welfare, headed by Mr. Mathews—determined that he was no longer disabled and thus not entitled to further payments. SSA notified him of its decision in a letter and stated that he could submit further medical evidence or information, if he chose to, before a final decision was made. Mr. Eldridge wrote back, protesting the determination, but sending no further information. The agency then notified him that its decision was final, and benefits were cut off. Mr. Eldridge was informed that he had the right to ask for a hearing before an ALJ, to be held at some later date. Instead, he filed suit in federal court, arguing that his rights to "due process of law" were violated by the agency procedures, which deprived him of his benefits without a prior hearing. The lower courts agreed with him, but the U.S. Supreme Court reversed the decision and upheld the agency's procedures.

DECISION

Justice Powell wrote the opinion of the Supreme Court, which began by noting that the Secretary of Health, Education, and Welfare was not contending that the due process clause was inapplicable to terminations of social security benefits. "He does argue, however, that the existing administrative procedures . . . provide all the process that is constitutionally due." Justice Powell pointed out that "The Supreme Court has consistently held that some form of hearing is required before an individual can be finally deprived of a property interest. The fundamental requirement of due process is the opportunity to be heard 'at a meaningful time and in a meaningful manner.'" Both parties in this case acknowledged that there was a right to an impartial hearing in this situation, after benefits are terminated. "This dispute centers on what type of process is due prior to termination of benefits."

"Due process, unlike some legal rules, is not a technical conception with a fixed content unrelated to time, place and circumstances . . . due process is flexible and calls for such procedural protections as the particular situation demands," stated the Court. "Our earlier decisions have established three factors which courts must analyze to determine if a certain procedure meets the requirements of due process." These factors are:

1. The private interest that will be affected by the official action in dispute;
2. The risk of an erroneous deprivation of such interests through the procedures used, and the probable value, if any, of additional procedural safeguards; and
3. The government's interest, including the function involved and the fiscal and administrative burdens that the additional or substitute procedural requirement would entail.

The first test looks at the hardship that will be caused to the individual by the government action. In this case the current SSA rules allow a hearing after the benefits are cut off, at which time the recipient may be awarded full retroactive benefits. However, the hearing will probably not be held for about 10 or 11 months, during which time the individual will not be receiving benefits. Nevertheless, the disabled worker's need is likely to be less than that of a welfare recipient (there was another Supreme Court case a few years earlier that held that welfare recipients were entitled to a hearing prior to the termination of benefits) because there may be more private resources available, and the individual will become eligible for welfare and other benefits after social security is cut off.

As to the second test, the Supreme Court said that the decision to terminate disability benefits will normally turn upon "routine, standard and unbiased" medical reports. Although credibility of the claimant and other witnesses (which could be assessed at a pre-termination hearing) may be a factor in the decision in some cases, this is not usually true in social security disability cases. Therefore, the second test—which asks whether there is much likelihood of error in the procedures used and whether additional procedures (such as a pre-termination hearing) would make a significant difference in the result—was not applicable here.

Regarding the third test, the administrative burden on the government and on fiscal and other societal concerns would certainly be affected by a holding from the U.S. Supreme Court that, as a constitutional right, hearings were required before all disability terminations. Since benefits would continue through the hearing process, this requirement would "assure the exhaustion in most cases of this attractive option." In other words, all claimants would ask for a hearing when they were notified that their benefits were to be terminated. There would be a tremendous increase in hearings—at great cost to the government—as well as a major increase in benefits paid to ineligible recipients (which would be very difficult to recover if the later hearing resulted in a determination that the person was indeed ineligible).

Justice Powell asserted that what really was at issue here involved determining when "judicial-type procedures must be imposed upon administrative action to assure fairness." In the words of former Justice Frankfurter, the differences in the origin and function of administrative agencies "preclude wholesale transplantation of the rules of procedure, trial and review" used by courts. "Judicial procedures are neither necessary nor always the most effective method of decision making in all circumstances." Due process requires that persons facing a loss "be given notice of the case against them and an opportunity to meet it," and procedures should be designed to ensure that they are "given a meaningful opportunity to present their case." Justice Powell concluded by stating that, "Giving weight to the good-faith judgments of the individuals charged by Congress with administering Social Security, we believe the procedures already established assure fair consideration of the claims of individual to benefits."

CASE QUESTIONS

1. Review the three tests set up by the Supreme Court to determine if a given administrative procedure satisfies "due process." Which one was the most important in the *Eldridge* case?
2. What does Justice Powell mean in the last sentence of his opinion, when he speaks of "good-faith judgments of individuals"?
3. What is the procedure for revocation of a driver's license in your state? Test and analyze the procedures established under the three tests required by the *Eldridge* case.

LAWS GOVERNING AGENCY PRACTICES

There are a number of federal laws that control, in some way, the manner in which administrative agencies function.

THE ADMINISTRATIVE PROCEDURES ACT

We have mentioned the APA several times in this chapter. It was enacted in 1946 in order to standardize procedures used by federal agencies in rulemaking and adjudication. The APA is the source of most of the requirements for rulemaking and adjudication procedures described in the previous pages of this chapter. It has been amended several times since 1946. The APA also sets forth practices to be followed by ALJs.

Freedom of Information Act: A federal law allowing members of the public access to information filed with administrative agencies, with some exceptions.

THE FREEDOM OF INFORMATION ACT

The federal government receives thousands of pages of information from individuals and businesses every day. Before the **Freedom of Information Act** (FOIA) was enacted in 1966, it was very difficult for individuals to obtain information held by the government. The FOIA was intended to change this situation, by specifying that most information possessed by the government—including reports, studies, photos, letters, and so on—is available to the public if a proper request is made. The request must provide a reasonable description of what is sought, and the agency then has 10 business days to comply with or reject the request.

The FOIA contains *nine categories of information* that do *not have to be disclosed*. These exceptions are:

1. Foreign policy or national defense matters.
2. Internal personnel practices and rules of an agency.
3. Information covered by another statute that prohibits disclosure.
4. Trade secrets and commercial or financial information that are privileged or confidential.
5. Inter-agency or intra-agency memoranda or letters.
6. Personal or medical files, which would constitute an invasion of privacy if disclosed.
7. Law enforcement investigatory records.
8. Reports of agencies responsible for regulation and supervision of financial institutions.
9. Geological and geophysical information, data, and maps concerning wells.

Although it was expected that members of the public and the press would be the most common users of the FOIA, it has been businesses that have used the law the most over the years. Many firms are interested in obtaining all information possible on their competitors, and they have employed the FOIA to gain access to various reports filed with the government regarding economic factors, environmental concerns, employment practices, health and safety issues, and other facets of competing businesses. In 1987, regulations were issued requiring an agency to notify a firm if "arguably confidential" information about that firm was sought, so that the firm may object to its disclosure. An agency can still release the data, if it believes that the information does not fall under one of the exceptions, by explaining the action in writing.

THE FEDERAL PRIVACY ACT

The **Federal Privacy Act**, a 1974 law, has the opposite objective of the FOIA. The *Privacy Act* states that certain information possessed by the government *may not* be released without the prior written consent of the individual to whom it pertains. Also, the individual's name and address may not be sold to anyone without authorization from the person involved.

Federal Privacy Act: A federal law designed to keep certain information held by agencies private.

The Act does not prevent the agency from using appropriate personal information for agency purposes, although individuals have the right of access to government files on them and can request correction of inaccurate information. Disclosure of information is also allowed for Census Bureau use, for criminal and civil law enforcement, for use by Congress or the General Accounting Office, and for certain other statistical and governmental purposes.

THE GOVERNMENT IN THE SUNSHINE ACT

This law, sometimes called the "open meeting" act, was passed in 1976. Its purpose is to force the independent regulatory commissions to conduct business in open meetings ("in the sunshine"), to the maximum extent possible. There are 10 exemptions (similar to the FOIA exceptions) allowing the meeting to be closed by majority vote of the commission.

SUMMARY

Although administrative agencies are not mentioned in the U.S. Constitution, they are today considered as the "fourth branch" of government and play an important role in the legal environment in which most businesses operate. It is likely that an American firm will have regular interaction with both state and federal agencies in the course of its operations. This chapter has discussed the history and purposes for which agencies were created. The complexities of modern business have indicated the need for the development of governmental expertise in order to regulate particular aspects of business operations and specific types of businesses.

On the federal level there are two main types of agencies—executive branch agencies, which are part of the president's executive branch, and Independent Regulatory Commissions, created by statutes passed by Congress. Each type of agency is controlled in part by the other branches of government. Federal agencies have three main powers—rulemaking, enforcement, and adjudication. Rulemaking is the power to write rules and regulations to more specifically describe the requirements of a law. Once regulations are properly issued, the agencies must see that they are enforced, and they may bring legal actions against individuals and firms who do not comply. These actions are "adjudicated" in administrative courts where an ALJ presides over the case.

After exhausting all possible appeals and remedies within the agency, interested parties may appeal such decisions into the federal court system. Such appeals can only be taken after the agency has completed its actions, and only by parties who have standing to raise the issues. On appeal, the federal courts often show deference to the agency decision because of its expertise in the subject matter. Agency decisions will only be overturned by courts for "abuse of discretion" or "arbitrary and capricious" action by the administrative agency.

The constitutional doctrine "due process of law" requires that agencies follow a fair and impartial procedure when deciding issues that grant or take away rights or licenses, or impose fines and penalties. Finally, the chapter explained several laws regulating agency practices, such as the APA, the FOIA, and the Federal Privacy Act.

CHAPTER QUESTIONS

1. What are the purposes of administrative agencies? Do you think that these purposes have been achieved?

2. We all hear lots of complaints about bureaucracy and administrative "red tape." What would be the likely consequences if all administrative agencies were abolished?
3. Many people would like to obtain information about the activities of the Central Intelligence Agency (CIA). Congress and certain committees have much information on the CIA. Can the public get this information through the FOIA? [*Paisley v. CIA*, 712 F.2d 686 (1983)]
4. OSHA issued what it called a "directive" in which it announced a new program. Under the program, called the Cooperative Compliance Program, certain employers with low rates of workplace injuries would be allowed to participate in a special arrangement, in which OSHA would work with the employer to improve illness and injury rates and would face a reduced chance of a random OSHA inspection. The issuance of the "directive" was challenged by industry groups, because it had been issued by OSHA without any rulemaking—formal or informal—procedures, and no opportunity for "notice and comment." OSHA defended the process, arguing that the directive was a type of policy or procedural rule (which are not subject to the APA rulemaking procedures) rather than a "substantive" rule. What should the result be and why? [*Chamber of Commerce of the United States v. OSHA*, 174 F.3d 206 (D.C. Cir. 1999)]
5. What specific functions has Congress given the Consumer Product Safety Commission the power to perform? Cite the sections of the law that give the Commission each function.
6. When may the Consumer Product Safety Commission actually ban a consumer product? What findings must be made by the Commission? What section of the law gives this power?
7. A public high school in Columbus, Ohio, suspended several students for 10 days for disciplinary reasons, following a period of student unrest and protests. None of the students was given a hearing prior to the suspension. There was a provision in the Ohio law, however, allowing a student or parent to appeal to the local board of education after the suspension had been completed. Have the students been deprived of any constitutional rights? Is the school an administrative "agency"? If so, what sort of procedures are necessary? [*Goss v. Lopez*, 419 U.S. 565, 95 S.Ct.729 (1965)]
8. The U.S. Patent and Trademark Office (PTO) denied an application for a patent on a method for increasing computer security, finding that it was not original. On appeal, the Federal Circuit Court of Appeals reversed, holding that the PTO factfinding was "clearly erroneous." The appellate court did not find the process "arbitrary and capricious" and did not discuss the "substantial evidence" rule. The patent applicant then appealed to the U.S. Supreme Court. Did the appellate court use the appropriate standard for reviewing the agency's action? Why or why not? [*Dickinson v. Zurko*, 119 S.Ct. 1816 (1999)]
9. Two businesses which dispose of nuclear waste were seeking amendments to their licenses from the Nuclear Regulatory Commission (NRC), a federal agency. Another firm, Envirocare, which had been licensed earlier by the NRC to dispose of radioactive waste, sought to intervene in the licensing process of the other two firms, arguing that the NRC was not requiring

those businesses to meet the same standards as it had imposed on it. Envirocare requested a hearing and right to participate in the licensing process. The NRC denied Envirocare's request, for lack of "standing." What should the result be on appeal? What are the rules on standing? [*Envirocare of Utah, Inc. v. Nuclear Regulatory Commission*, 194 F.3d 72 (D.C. Cir. 1999)]

10. The EPA has authority under several statutes to issue administrative orders to persons violating those statutes. These orders take the form of injunctions directing particular persons to do or not to do certain acts. When the EPA issued such an order to a company under the Clean Water Act, the company filed a suit in federal court seeking to set aside the order. The firm argued that since time was critical, it should be allowed to bypass the EPA intra-agency appeal process. What should be the result and why? [*Southern Ohio Coal v. Office of Surface Mining, Reclamation and Enforcement*, 20 F.3d 1418 (1994)]

PRACTICAL EXERCISE

The Lansing, Michigan, city council is considering rezoning a large portion of land from a residential classification to a commercial/industrial designation. The land is vacant—that is, no buildings are constructed on it. The force pushing for the rezoning is Mr. Alex O'Neil, who wants to construct a large landfill/toxic waste dump on the site, for disposal of waste products from other areas of Michigan. Some of the wastes would be incinerated on the site to produce energy. Mr. O'Neil plans to donate part (a small part) of his profits to local youth programs and to build a public school on the site as a public service. The school is to be named "The Earvin Johnson School," after one of Lansing's most famous sons. The slogan for the project is "Turn Waste Into Energy—It's Magic!"

There are several federal and state laws that apply to the situation. For the purposes of this problem, assume that federal law and EPA regulations require that toxic waste facilities be located at least 1/2 mile away from any public school and that no burning of such wastes be done within city limits. Nevertheless, under public pressure, the city zoning commission approves the rezoning, and Mr. O'Neil begins construction, without obtaining EPA approval. (He did file some information about the environmental aspects of the project with EPA, but no action has been taken as yet by the agency.)

At this point, several groups begin to respond. One member of the City Council, which has the power to overturn the Zoning Commission, argues that the Council should do so and take away Mr. O'Neil's permit. The EPA director for central Michigan charges Mr. O'Neil with violation of EPA regulations. The EPA, like other federal agencies, has a two-stage administrative law hearing structure within the agency, providing for a trial before an ALJ and an appeal with an appeal board.

You are the legal advisor to the Stop Lansing Air Pollution organization (SLAP) and are asked to provide the group with information as to a number of issues, including: (1) Can SLAP file a suit in federal court to block the project? (2) Can Mr. O'Neil file a suit in federal court seeking to prevent EPA from enforcing its rules against him? (3) Can SLAP intervene in the EPA administrative hearing against Mr. O'Neil? (4) If the City Council takes away Mr. O'Neil's permit, what issues does this raise? What might he argue, and how successful will he likely be? (5) Can your group obtain all information filed by Mr. O'Neil with the EPA through the FOIA? Please prepare a memo discussing these issues and explaining the basis for your opinion.

FURTHER INFORMATION

www.access.gpo.gov/hara/cfr/index.html
Code of Federal Regulations.

http://thomas.loc.gov/
Federal government's Library of Congress site "in the spirit of Thomas Jefferson."

http://uscode.house.gov/
U.S. Code (federal law) online.

www.cpsc.gov
Consumer Product Safety Commission site.

CHAPTER 6

INTERNATIONAL LEGAL ISSUES IN BUSINESS

LEARNING OBJECTIVES

After you have read this chapter, you should be able to:

1. Examine the legal issues arising in international disputes involving private parties and national governments.
2. List several international organizations and financial agencies playing important roles in international commerce.
3. Describe the history and structure of the European Union.
4. Identify important restrictions and regulations concerning international trade, including U.S. import/export laws.
5. Discuss the issues that arise when domestic laws apply to actions outside the United States.

CHAPTER OUTLINE

I. Types of International Trade and Transactions
II. Resolution of International Business Disputes
III. Jurisdiction of Disputes Involving National Governments
IV. International Organizations
V. International Financial Agencies
VI. The European Union
VII. International Trade: Restrictions, Regulations, and "Free Trade"
VIII. U.S. Laws Controlling Imports and Exports
IX. U.S. Laws That Apply Outside the United States

American businesses now operate in a global arena, with production, marketing, and sales taking place in nations around the world, often including a significant affiliation with local investors and governments. One of the many ramifications of this trend is that legal problems may arise in countries far from the United States. Often it is unclear which nation's laws, and courts should handle the resolution of international business issues. In the practical exercise at the end of this chapter you are asked to analyze certain legal issues that arose from a tragic accident in India in 1984.

INTRODUCTION

The "environment" in which American businesses operate today is clearly a global one. Consider the firms that employ you or your relatives: The chances are good that those companies are directly involved in or indirectly influenced by international methods and business.

During the past quarter century, Japanese auto manufacturers have captured a large share of the American automobile market, and our homes have become filled with electronic products, clothing, and other goods manufactured in Japan, Korea, China, Taiwan, and other Asian countries. The European Union (EU), which began as an effort to coordinate coal and steel policy among six nations in 1952, has now become a powerful economic, social, and political organization, spanning much of Europe. The EU has virtually eliminated tariffs and other nontariff trade barriers on transactions between its 15 member nations. Clearly an economic power, the EU is now moving toward even closer political and monetary cooperation, as it continues to grow. Three more nations joined the Union in 1995, and several of the newly independent nations of Eastern Europe are interested in membership. Even Russia is moving toward capitalism and free enterprise.

The North American Free Trade Agreement (NAFTA) became effective in 1994. NAFTA already has or will eliminate tariffs on most goods traded among

From *The Wall Street Journal*, October 11, 1999. Reprinted with permission of Cartoon Features Syndicate.

Mexico, Canada, and the United States either at once or over several years. NAFTA also opens up the markets of each country to a wide range of service and business firms located in the others. Additional Latin American nations are closely watching how NAFTA develops and may join the free trade association in the coming years. Other regional organizations such as Mercosur are growing in importance and some sort of free trade area may eventually encompass much of the Western Hemisphere.

Large "multinational corporations," with operations located in countries around the world, occupy a significant position in global economic affairs. American businesses must be ready to compete in the international arena, both in the sale of goods and provision of services. Indeed, "global competitiveness" has become an important topic of political debate not only in Washington but even in local governmental decisions regarding business development and expansion. The complexities of international trade and other international business issues involve numerous legal matters. This chapter will raise and discuss some of the most important legal aspects of the global environment in which American businesses now engage.

TYPES OF INTERNATIONAL TRADE AND TRANSACTIONS

INTERNATIONAL SALES CONTRACTS

The most common international business transactions occur when U.S. firms sell goods to buyers in other countries (exports) or when buyers in this country purchase goods from foreign sellers (imports). Such transactions obviously involve legal issues such as contracts, sales law, and warranties, which are discussed in other chapters. This chapter will concentrate on the particular problems and issues that arise when sales cross national borders.

letter of credit: A promise or guarantee of payment by a bank.

One fairly fundamental issue in an international sale is how payment for the goods will be made. The most common method used is the **letter of credit**, a form of payment also used frequently for sales within the United States. The buyer arranges for a letter of credit from a bank, usually located near the buyer. This bank, called the "issuing bank," sends the letter of credit assuring the seller (or the seller's bank in another country) that funds have been set aside to be used as payment for the goods upon satisfactory performance by the seller.

bill of lading: A shipping document that carefully describes the goods shipped and indicates the person who has the right to possession of the goods.

The buyer and seller, as well as the issuing bank, set the terms of the letter of credit. Often the payment will be conditional on the seller producing a **bill of lading**, which is a document issued by the carrier of the goods (such as a ship or airplane), indicating that the goods were delivered to the carrier in good condition and specifying when, where, and how the goods were shipped. The bill of lading is then transferred to the buyer, who, in order to obtain possession of the goods upon arrival, produces that document at the receiving end. Upon receiving a proper bill of lading, the issuing bank pays the seller or perhaps the seller's bank. Sometimes, the contract between the parties requires additional documents to be produced by the seller before payment under a letter of credit, such as invoices, packing lists, certificates of inspection, or necessary import licenses.

INTERPRETATION OF CONTRACTS

If difference or disputes arise in connection with an international contract, it is often important to determine which nation's laws will be applicable. As you may imagine, there are often significant differences in legal rules affecting contract law in different countries. The parties can, and often do, specify in the contract that the laws of a certain nation will be applied to contract interpretation. Such a clause in a contract is called a **choice of law clause**. If the buyer and seller do not so specify, the determination will be made on the basis of a series of legal principles called *conflict of laws*. These theories are complex and not always applied in a uniform fashion under various international law interpretations.

choice of law clause: A provision in a contract specifying which nation's laws will apply in case of contract disputes.

Due to these uncertainties, many countries have entered into an agreement called *The United Nations Convention on Contracts for the International Sale of Goods (CISG)*. This treaty, completed in 1980 after many years of drafting by a group of international business law experts, has now been adopted by more than 40 countries. It was signed by the United States in 1988. The CISG sets out uniform rules that apply to international commercial contracts involving the sale of goods between businesses in countries that have signed the agreement, unless the parties specify otherwise. The CISG does not apply to consumer transactions or to the sale of securities, vessels, aircraft, or certain other matters.

Contracts that span international boundaries require most of the same legal elements in order to be enforceable as contracts within the United States (which we will discuss in Chapter 12), and many of the same defenses are applicable. As in the United States, in order for an agreement to be a "contract," there must be mutual assent by both parties to its terms. Similarly, if one party intentionally deceives the other regarding an important element, the defense of fraud will be successful as it is in a U.S. court.

However, the tremendous differences in language, culture, and customs among the countries of the world have resulted in many different requirements and interpretations of contracts. For example, the CISG, which is an international agreement incorporating principles from many nations, does not require "consideration" (something given in return for the other's promise—necessary in the United States) as an essential element of a contract. Most countries do not have a "statute of frauds" (as do the United States and Great Britain), which requires certain types of contracts to be written.

Americans who negotiate contracts in other parts of the world will soon learn that cultures and custom are dramatically different in each country, and a successful contractual relationship requires understanding, patience, and sensitivity to the language, gestures, and customs of the other party. U.S. businesspeople who think they can easily disregard contracts made in another country because "there is nothing in writing" may be in for an unpleasant surprise.

RESOLUTION OF INTERNATIONAL BUSINESS DISPUTES

When disputes do arise in connection with international contracts, the resolution can be problematic. As we have mentioned, a determination usually needs to be made as to which nation's laws and legal principles will be applied.

Another difficult issue is selecting the proper court to hear the dispute—that is, one which has "jurisdiction" of the parties and the subject matter. Sometimes a court in one country will even apply the laws of another country to the resolution of a dispute, if the contract so requires.

PRIVATE DISPUTE RESOLUTION

Earlier in this book we discussed the concept of jurisdiction with respect to U.S. courts. We learned that in order to render a decision in a case, a particular U.S. court must have jurisdiction of the parties and the subject matter. The same principles have relevance to the resolution of international disputes. It is usually permissible for a plaintiff to initiate a lawsuit in a foreign court in order to sue a company based in that country. For example, if a Mexican company wants to sue a Canadian partnership for breach of a contract between the two firms, it is normally possible for the Mexican company to sue the Canadian firm in a Canadian court. However, in general, a person is not permitted to file a case in his or her home nation and force a foreign company to come there to litigate the matter, unless there is some significant activity (like the "minimum contacts" required for long-arm jurisdiction in the United States discussed earlier) concerning the contract in that country.

Where a legal matter involves more than one nation, there is an international legal principle called ***forum non conveniens,*** which contains a series of tests to determine which nation's court system is the "most convenient" or most appropriate to hear the dispute. This theory is largely based on commonsense factors such as the place of performance of the contract, the location of the majority of witnesses, the principal place of business of the plaintiff and

forum non conveniens: A legal principle that attempts to determine the nation in which the trial would be "most convenient" or appropriate.

FROM THE DESK OF
Laura Lawyer

To: Students
From: Your Lawyer

Since it is not uncommon for a contract to be negotiated in one country, signed in another, and performed in several additional nations, you should anticipate that disputes may arise and specify, in the contract itself, which nation's courts and legal principles will apply to the interpretation of contract disagreements. It might be a better choice to specify that contract disputes would be heard by one of the well-recognized international arbitration centers, as discussed in the next section.

defendant, and the location where the contract was signed, among other factors. For example, the general trial courts of most nations typically have jurisdiction over contract disputes involving agreements made in their particular nation, or over contract disputes in which a major part of the contract performance has taken or will take place in their particular country.

Enforcement and collection of money judgments across national borders can create serious difficulties. Although a court in one nation will sometimes enforce a judgment lawfully entered by a court of another country, this is not always true. In one recent case, a U.S. firm and a Japanese company disagreed about a contract between them that was to be performed in the United States. The U.S. firm sued and won a judgment against the Japanese company in a California court. However, the Japanese business had no assets that could be seized in the United States. Therefore, the U.S. firm had to file another suit in a Japanese court to enforce the U.S. court judgment and to attach certain assets of the defendant in Japan. The Japanese court eventually did recognize and enforce part of the judgment, but it refused to enforce a large portion of the award based on "punitive damages," because Japan does not recognize this legal concept. In other cases, U.S. courts have sometimes refused to enforce foreign judgments when they were based on legal theories not known or employed in the United States.

ARBITRATION

For the reasons set forth previously and others, a large number of international contracts specify that any disputes concerning the contract or performance will be submitted to arbitration. In this way the parties know in advance how and where their differences will be settled, typically in a quicker, more private, and less costly manner than litigation. Also, international arbitration panels may have considerable experience in the subject matter of the dispute, as well as a thorough background in commercial practices.

Several international organizations have developed expertise in commercial arbitration, such as the International Chamber of Commerce in Paris, the American Arbitration Association, the International Center for the Settlement of Investment Disputes, and the U.N. Commission of International Trade Law (UNCITRAL), which has developed rules often used by other arbitrators. In most cases, the parties have agreed that the arbitration decision is final and may be enforced in any nation's courts. However, when this stipulation is not part of the contract, one of the parties may ignore the decision and submit the dispute to a court, or may try to challenge the award for some procedural reason in a national court system.

Sometimes after signing a contract that contains a clause requiring arbitration of any disputes that may arise, one of the parties tries to file a lawsuit in a national court rather than going to arbitration. As is the case with arbitration clauses between parties in the United States, most courts will refuse to entertain the dispute if the arbitration clause appears valid and was voluntarily agreed to, without fraud or deceit of any kind. Unless one of the parties can show that enforcing the arbitration clause will cause severe deprivation of fundamental rights, courts will normally declare that the agreement is binding and order the parties to arbitrate, as they had agreed to do in the contract.

JURISDICTION OF DISPUTES INVOLVING NATIONAL GOVERNMENTS

The previous discussion concerned the jurisdiction of national courts over private parties and companies. Further legal problems exist when the government of a nation is itself involved in commercial activity or where the legal dispute involves the actions of a government.

THE ACT OF STATE DOCTRINE

sovereignty: Each nation's right to decide and determine issues within its borders without interference or control from other nations.

Act of State Doctrine: A principle of law that holds that the courts of one nation will not judge the legality of the actions of other nations' governments.

Every national government develops and implements its own foreign policy and engages in diplomatic efforts to benefit its national interests and those of its own citizens. The **sovereignty** of each nation is a very important principle of international law. The power to conduct foreign policy typically resides in the executive branch of government, both in the United States and in other countries. As a means of allowing foreign governments to establish and develop their own policies and official actions, without being subjected to court review in this country, U.S courts have developed the **Act of State Doctrine**.

This theory holds that the courts of one nation will not examine the validity of an action taken by a foreign government within its own territory. The Act of State Doctrine thus guarantees respect for the sovereignty of foreign nations by prohibiting U.S. courts from asserting jurisdiction over challenges to acts and actions by officials of those states. Therefore, even though an act by a foreign government might violate U.S. laws if committed here, the Act of State Doctrine prevents a U.S. court from deciding whether such an act was legal. The theory can sometimes result in the denial of any legal remedy to an American business for harm caused by the acts of a foreign government.

THE FOREIGN SOVEREIGN IMMUNITIES ACT

Closely related to the Act of State Doctrine is the U.S. federal statute known as the Foreign Sovereign Immunities Act. This law states that "a foreign state shall be immune from the jurisdiction of the courts of the United States and of the states." The act contains several important exceptions, however, indicating situations when the foreign nation *could* be sued in the United States.

The primary exceptions include the following instances:

1. The nation has waived its immunity.
2. The legal action is based on a "commercial activity" carried on in the United States, or even outside the United States if it causes a "direct effect" here.
3. Expropriation of property has taken place, allegedly in violation of international law.
4. The legal action seeks money damages against a foreign state for acts committed by officials or employees of that nation in the United States, which have caused death or injury or damage to property.
5. The legal action seeks to enforce an arbitration agreement or confirm an arbitration award.

6. The suit is brought to enforce a maritime lien against a vessel or cargo of a foreign state based on commercial activity of that state.

The following case examines the requirements of the "commercial activity" exception to a foreign nation's sovereign immunity under the Foreign Sovereign Immunities Act.

ANTARES AIRCRAFT V. FEDERAL REPUBLIC OF NIGERIA

999 F.2d 33 (2nd Cir. 1993)

FACTS

Antares Aircraft is a Delaware limited partnership with its principal place of business in New York. The partnership's sole asset is a DC-8-55 aircraft registered in Nigeria. According to Nigerian authorities, the former lessee of the plane had not paid certain airport landing and parking fees, and the airplane was thus detained at the airport in Lagos, Nigeria. The Nigerian Airports Authority (NAA) refused to release the airplane until all outstanding obligations were paid.

Antares' representatives negotiated with NAA for some time and finally sent roughly $100,000 from a New York bank, which was paid to NAA in Nigerian currency. The plane was then finally released after being held about five months. According to Antares, the plane had suffered physical damage due to exposure to the elements. Antares then filed this lawsuit against NAA and the Federal Republic of Nigeria (FRN) in federal court in New York to recover for conversion (the wrongful taking of another's property) and damages to the plane. The district court granted the defendants' motion to dismiss for lack of jurisdiction over the defendants, and the plaintiff appealed.

DECISION

The Second Circuit Court of Appeals focused its review on whether the activities at issue here fell into one of the exceptions to the Foreign Sovereign Immunities Act (FSIA). There was no dispute that both NAA and FRN were "foreign states" and were thus immune from suit in the United States unless one of the exceptions applied.

The Court then examined the "commercial activity" exception of the FSIA in detail. This exception provides that a foreign state is subject to the jurisdiction of U.S. courts in cases "in which the action is based . . . upon an act outside the territory of the United States in connection with a commercial activity of the foreign state elsewhere and that act causes a direct effect in the United States." 28 U.S.C. Sect. 1605(a)(2). The Court determined that the "act outside the territory of the U.S." was the allegedly wrongful detention of the plane in Nigeria. The court held that the alleged detention and collection of fees were also clearly "in connection with a commercial activity of the foreign state." Therefore, the final point of contention bearing on FSIA jurisdiction was whether the detention of the plane caused "a direct effect in the United States."

In *Republic of Argentina v. Weltover*, decided in 1992, the U.S. Supreme Court decided in another FSIA case that "an effect is direct" if it follows "as an immediate consequence of the defendant's activity." In that case, the government of Argentina had issued $1.3 million in bonds to various parties that were payable in New York in May 1986. When payment became due, Argentina tried to reschedule the due dates, and the other parties sued Argentina in federal court in New York. The government of Argentina asked that the case be dismissed. The Supreme Court found that there was jurisdiction in New York federal court, because the case concerned commercial activity and the "direct effect" of Argentina's rescheduling of the maturity dates would be in the United States, since New York was the contractually designated "place of performance."

However, in this case (*Antares*), the legal cause of action was a tort case rather than a breach of contract action. The Court said that in the contract case, the "legally significant act" was the breach of contract, which occurred in the United States. Reasoning by analogy, the Court analyzed what the legally significant act was in this tort case (in other words what wrongful act had constituted the "tort") and found it to be the detention of the plane, which had occurred in Nigeria.

However, the U.S. federal court might still possess jurisdiction if the tort committed in the foreign country had sufficient contacts with the United States to have a "direct effect" here. The plaintiff argued that there was such a direct effect because the money paid came from a New York bank and also that an American partnership suffered the loss. However, the Court was unpersuaded, finding that the money could have been sent from any bank, and the significant fact was that it had to be *paid* in Nigeria.

Rejecting plaintiff's argument that injury to a U.S. firm should give the court jurisdiction, the Second Circuit Court of Appeals stated that this fact alone could not satisfy the "direct effect" test, or it would basically eliminate the immunity of foreign nations. "Many commercial disputes, like the present one, can be pled [alleged by plaintiffs] as the torts of conversion or fraud and would, if appellant is correct, result in litigation concerning events with no connection to the United States other than the citizenship or place or incorporation of the plaintiff." The Court concluded that the mere fact that an American citizen or firm's wealth is diminished by a foreign tort does not constitute the "direct effect" necessary to eliminate the foreign governmental immunity intended by this statute.

The Court thus affirmed the decision of the lower court.

CASE QUESTIONS

1. The FSIA provides in general that foreign nations may not be sued in U.S. courts, but there are certain exceptions. What principal exceptions to the FSIA are involved in this case?
2. What would it have taken for the plaintiffs to show that the tort allegedly committed in Nigeria had a "direct effect" in the United States? Why is it that even though a U.S. partnership lost $100,000, this did not give the court jurisdiction?
3. Is this result fair to the U.S. partnership and investors? To the Nigerian government?
4. Does the U.S. limited partnership have any other possible course of legal action available?

INTERNATIONAL ORGANIZATIONS

THE UNITED NATIONS

Organized in 1945 following World War II, the United Nations (UN) is the largest and most well-known international organization. Most of the nations in the world now belong to the UN. With headquarters in New York City, the United Nations organization includes the legislative body called the General Assembly (with representatives from all member nations), the Economic and Social Council, which attempts to promote international welfare and progress, and the Security Council, which deals with important issues concerning threats to world peace and stability. There are 15 nations represented on the Security Council—5 "permanent representatives" (the United Kingdom, France, China, the United States, and Russia) and 10 nonpermanent members representing all the other nations, who serve two-year terms each. Each country has one vote, but any of the permanent members may veto measures before the Security Council.

The United Nations has many major subdivisions, which, while they do not receive as much publicity as the Security Council or General Assembly, perform important tasks around the world. For example, the Food and Agricultural Organization (FAO) employs specialists in agriculture, fisheries, and other fields to assist the development of such projects in many countries. The World Health Organization (WHO) attempts to promote health and reduce disease around the world. The United Nations Educational, Scientific, and Cultural Organization (UNESCO) works to improve literacy, education, and science and to promote better understanding of the culture of all nations. The United Nations Commission on International Trade Law (UNCITRAL) has aided in developing uniform rules regarding international contracts, including the United Nations Convention on CISG, discussed earlier in this chapter.

THE WORLD COURT

The International Court of Justice, the principal judicial division of the United Nations, is better known as **the World Court**. This body, located in the Hague (in the Netherlands), adjudicates disputes between nations, applying general principles of international law, custom, and the teachings of experts on international law and interpreting treaties and other international conventions. The World Court does not hear cases involving individuals or businesses, but only sovereign nations. In general, the court can only hear a dispute when the two nations agree that it do so. Although its decisions are expected to be binding, since the court has no power to enforce its judgments, the decisions are only carried out if the nations decide to do so.

The World Court: An international court located in the Netherlands, which hears legal disputes between nations.

The 15 judges on the World Court are elected for nine-year terms by the Security Council and General Assembly, voting separately. No two judges may be from the same country, and decisions are made by majority vote.

INTERNATIONAL FINANCIAL AGENCIES

THE INTERNATIONAL BANK FOR RECONSTRUCTION AND DEVELOPMENT

The International Bank for Reconstruction and Development (IBRD), a financial organization popularly called the "World Bank," was formed in 1945 following a multinational conference in Bretton Woods, New Hampshire, to create a means of making loans to countries when private sources were not readily available. More than 135 nations are now members. The World Bank has made many loans to developing countries for large-scale capital projects and was helpful to the nations of Western Europe in their rebuilding efforts following the end of World War II.

THE INTERNATIONAL MONETARY FUND

The International Monetary Fund (IMF) is associated with the World Bank and the UN. The IMF's primary functions are to stabilize currency and rates of foreign exchange worldwide and to promote a more flexible and fair international monetary system. Intergovernmental loans are available to members from the fund or from other members by using "special drawing rights." Because of demands that its members take strict economic measures, the IMF has often been controversial, especially in developing countries. Actions like price controls and reductions in government spending, taken in order to stabilize the national currency, are not always popular in the country in which they are imposed.

THE EUROPEAN UNION

HISTORY

The organization now called the European Union (EU; known as the European Community until 1994) is actually the combination of three separate entities. Shortly after the end of World War II, many Europeans sought to establish a more peaceful union between the nations of their region, which had been devastated by war twice in a 30-year period. Inspired by the ideas and writings of Frenchman Jean Monnet, Foreign Minister Robert Schuman of France proposed in 1950 that French and German coal and steel production be managed by a common authority through an institution that would be open to other European countries. Shortly thereafter, in 1952, the European Coal and Steel Community (ECSC) began functioning, with France, the Federal Republic of Germany, Italy, Belgium, the Netherlands, and Luxembourg as members.

Treaty of Rome: An important agreement among six nations in 1957 that created the European Economic Community (EEC), which has grown into the European Union.

The foreign ministers of the ECSC members met regularly, and in 1957 the six nations signed the **Treaty of Rome**. This agreement established the European Economic Community (EEC), which created a more integrated economic system among the member nations, and the European Atomic Energy Community (EURATOM), which was intended to develop a common approach to nuclear energy. The three organizations eventually combined efforts and became the European Community (EC). The United Kingdom, Denmark, and Ireland were admitted in 1973, Greece in 1981, and Spain and Portugal in 1986, bringing the EC membership to 12. In 1995 Austria, Sweden, and Finland joined, bringing the membership to 15. The name of the organization officially became the European Union in 1994.

nontariff barriers: Laws and regulations of one nation that tend to restrict the free flow of products into that country from other nations.

The EEC (often called the Common Market) began the elimination of tariffs and duties among member states as early as 1958 and later established a common external tariff—that is, the provision that the same duty would be charged by all member nations on a given import from a nonmember country. As of the mid-1980s, however, so-called **nontariff barriers** (such as safety and health standards, product quality standards, and border controls) still caused considerable restrictions upon the free movement of people and trade among the members.

Single European Act (SEA): An EU treaty that led to the removal of many trade barriers.

EC Commission President Jacques Delors outlined a set of proposals in a 1985 white paper, designed to eliminate the remaining barriers, and create a true "single market." The EC debated and approved nearly 300 of these measures in the next several years. In 1987 the EC members entered into the **Single European Act (SEA)**, which contained important revisions to the earlier treaties, designed to eliminate all barriers to free trade within the EC by the end of 1992. The SEA also set forth new decision-making mechanisms for the EC (providing the Parliament with more power) and gave the Community new responsibilities in the areas of social policy, research and technological development, and protection of the environment.

During the 1990s, the EU and its member nations worked toward **harmonization** of national laws to eliminate nontariff barriers. Each country has undertaken the task of enacting legislation through its own law-making process to bring many of its laws and regulations into harmony with the legislation enacted by the EU. This effort is necessary to achieve the organization's goal of "*free movement of goods, services, people, and capital between the member nations*." For example if the French environmental regulations, worker safety rules, or product standards are significantly different from those in Denmark or Greece, then this will severely hamper the free movement and sale of goods and services across the EU. In theory, at least, goods can be produced much more cheaply in nations with significantly fewer labor or environment rules. Manufacturers in those countries can export heavily to markets in nations with higher standards (where it is assumed that goods cost more to produce), resulting in unfair competition.

harmonization: The process of making the laws of the 15 EU nations more similar to one another.

At the same time that there is an effort to make national laws more similar through harmonization, the member nations want to maintain their own individual sovereignty. When the EU has not legislated in an area, the member states may still enforce their own laws and standards, up to the point where regulation interferes with the "free movement of goods," essential to the single market.

Especially with regard to public health, public security, safety, environmental, welfare, and morality matters, member states are allowed to maintain some individual regulations, where no EU harmonization directive exists. The European Court of Justice (the highest court in the EU, discussed more fully later) has considered many cases in which business firms operating in one nation have argued that a particular law effectively prevented them from competing in another EU country. The government of that nation generally argues that there is a valid, nondiscriminatory reason for the standard. The following case is one of the best-known European Court rulings in this line of decisions.

REWE-ZENTRAL AG V. BUNDESMONOPOLVERWALTUNG FUR BRANNTWEIN [CASSIS DE DIJON]

European Court of Justice (1979)

FACTS

Rewe-Zentral attempted to import a French liqueur, called *Cassis de Dijon*, into West Germany. Rewe was denied permission to import the liqueur by the Bundesmonopolverwaltung (German importing authority). The reason for the refusal was a German law requiring that liqueur have an alcohol content of at least 32 percent. Cassis de Dijon had an alcohol content of only 15 percent to 20 percent.

Rewe-Zentral then filed a suit in Germany seeking to overturn the restriction, arguing that it was an illegal restraint on the free flow of goods within the EC. The German court asked the European Court of Justice for a preliminary ruling as to the validity of the law.

DECISION

At the time of this case, there were no EU regulations or directives dealing with the production and marketing of alcoholic beverages. Thus, EU law allowed the individual states to maintain laws regarding this subject, even if they resulted in some restriction on importation, if these provision related to the protection of public health, fiscal supervision, and the protection of the consumer.

The German government argued that the restrictions here did relate to both the protection of public health and the protection of the consumer against unfair commercial practices. The government asserted that fixing a minimum alcohol content served to protect public health by avoiding the proliferation of low-alcohol beverages on the market, which might more likely induce a tolerance toward alcohol than more highly alcoholic beverages. However, the Court of Justice rejected this contention, noting that the consumer can obtain an extremely wide range of weak or moderate alcohol products already on the market. In addition, many of the high-alcohol products currently sold on the German market "are actually consumed in a diluted form."

The German government also argued that setting the lowest limit of alcohol content at which certain liqueurs could be sold was designed to protect the consumer against unfair practices. This allegation was based on the fact that because of the high rate of taxation on alcohol in Germany, allowing a lower alcohol content beverage would produce an unfair competitive advantage. However, the Court noted that it would be simple to achieve the goal of providing information to the consumer by requiring the display of the amount of alcohol content on the package.

Therefore, the Court of Justice determined that the German law prohibiting lower alcohol liqueurs did not serve a purpose important enough to take precedence over the principle of free movement of goods in the EU. It appears, said the court, that the principle effect of this requirement was to promote German alcoholic beverages having a high alcohol content by excluding products of other member states. This constituted an obstacle to trade, which violated the Treaty of Rome. In the absence of EU legislation, the doctrine of "mutual reciprocity" requires that products lawfully produced and sold in their home nation can generally be marketed in other EU nations.

CASE QUESTIONS

1. What do you think the primary purpose of the German import restriction was—to protect public health, or something else?
2. What sort of national laws will be upheld under the rationale of the Court of Justice? Can you think of an example? What is the test?
3. Should the EU nations be allowed to set their own taxation rates on various products including food and drink? If so, in what circumstances?
4. If the EU enacts a directive regarding the allowable alcohol content of various beverages, will Germany still have the power to regulate alcohol within its borders?

The EU has adopted a number of *directives* regarding internal (within the EU) market matters. Each directive establishes an EU legal standard, which then must be adopted by appropriate implementing legislation in each member country. This process is designed to prevent one country from maintaining or enforcing a particular standard or regulation that effectively prohibits goods made in another country from being sold there (as we saw in the *Cassis de Dijon* case). If this does happen, the EU Commission may bring a legal action against that nation in the EU Court of Justice.

Continuing the move toward a "European Union," the heads of the EC nations signed a treaty in late 1991 at Maastricht, Netherlands, which provided a timetable for moving to a full economic and monetary union over the next six to eight years. The **Maastricht Treaty** also included provisions designed to achieve more unified political ties between the member nations. Closer foreign and defense policies, and coordination of policies regarding education, environmental protection, consumer, and health legislation will be achieved when all member nations finally implement the provisions of the Maastricht Treaty. In fact, changing the name of the organization to the "European Union" was part of the Maastricht Treaty. It took more than two years for all member nations to officially ratify the Treaty, but by 1993, all had done so.

Maastricht Treaty: An important EU treaty signed in 1991 which brought the EU closer to social, economic, and political union.

Perhaps the most noteworthy move resulting from the Maastricht Treaty was the agreement for an EU monetary union. A common monetary unit, the *Euro* came into effect in 1999 for trade among businesses and nations. Actual bills and coins will replace each nation's currency in 2002.

The EU has become the world's largest trading unit, accounting for more than 17.1 percent of world commerce. All EU members are parties to the General Agreement, on Tariffs and Trade (GATT), and members of the World Trade Organization, which will be more fully discussed later in this chapter. The EU has received applications for membership from several countries in Central and Eastern Europe, and is actively considering the "accession" of Estonia, the Czech Republic, Poland, Hungary, and Slovenia.

THE STRUCTURE OF THE EUROPEAN UNION

The governing structure of the European Union is a complex combination of three main bodies handling legislative and executive affairs and one court system settling disputes and interpreting the various treaty provisions. Each will be described in more detail below.

The European Commission The European Commission performs many of the executive functions of the EU. Headquartered in Brussels, Belgium, the Commission is made up of 20 commissioners appointed by common agreement of the 15 governments. Each member country is represented, with the United Kingdom, France, Germany, Spain, and Italy each supplying two commissioners, and the other countries supplying one each. The commissioners act independently of their governments and represent the interest of the community as a whole. Each commissioner serves a five-year term and has responsibility for one or more of the commission's 23 subdivisions, called **Directorates General**.

Directorates General: The 23 cabinet subdivisions of the EU Commission, each one having a particular area of responsibility.

The Directorates actually perform much of the work of the EU. Somewhat similar to the Cabinet agencies in the U.S. government, each Directorate focuses on a substantive area, such as agriculture, telecommunication, economic and financial affairs, or energy. The Directorates each have a full staff, who make recommendations to the Commission for regulations and directives, which the Commission might then formally propose to the Council of Ministers.

The major roles of the Commission include the initial drafting and introduction of all EU legislation, oversight of the implementation of the EU treaties, and the application of community institutional decisions. The Commission can investigate and take legal action against persons, companies, or member nations that violate EU rules. As mentioned previously, the Commission also may initiate EU policy by making proposals to the Council of Ministers.

Another important responsibility of the Commission is the collection and disbursement of EU funds. The Commission may also negotiate trade agreements with nonmember states on behalf of the community as part of its authority to implement Council decisions.

The President of the Commission is appointed by the Council of Ministers to a renewable two-year term. We have mentioned that Mr. Jacques Delors of France served as President from 1985 to the end of 1994. Mr. Delors was the leading spokesman for the EU during that period, as well as the leading advocate of eliminating internal trade barriers. Jacques Santer of Luxembourg served as President from 1995 to 1999. The Commission has a staff of over 17,000 persons, most of whom work for the 23 Directorates-General.

A dramatic series of events occurred in 1999. An independent audit report was released, highly critical of some actions by the Commission, such as entering lucrative contracts with friends, and lax oversight of certain expenditures. Angered by the report, the entire 20-member Commission resigned.

After a few months of intense political maneuvering, the 15 member nations proposed new Commissioners, which were approved by the European Parliament. Former Italian Prime Minister Romano Prodi was chosen as the EU Commission President. He has promised greater accountability and better management of the Commission. Mr. Prodi has a law degree from the Catholic University of Milan, has studied at Stanford and the London School of Economics, and taught at several universities.

NEW EU COMMISSION

A new European Union Commission took office in October 1999 following the resignation of the entire 20 member Commission. The members are an interesting mixture. President Prodi had promised to "clean house," and only four of the former Commissioners were included in the new Commission. Named as vice presidents were Neil Kinnock, a former British Labor Party leader, and Loyola de Palacio of Spain. Among other key appointments were Guenter Verheugen, Germany's deputy foreign minister and a close ally of German Chancellor Gerhard Schroeder, named to lead the EU enlargement program; and Chris Patton, the last British governor of Hong Kong, who will lead the EU foreign affairs department.

In addition to Prodi (the 60-year-old former Italian Prime Minister), the members, nationalities, ages (in late 1999), and areas of primary responsibility (Portfolio) are:

- **Neil Kinnock, vice-president**
  Great Britain, age 57
  Portfolio: Administrative Reform
- **Loyola de Palacio, vice-president**
  Spain, age 49
  Portfolio: Relations with European Parliament
- **Mario Monti**
  Italy, age 56
  Portfolio: Competition policy

- **Franz Fischler**
  Austria, age 53
  Portfolio: Agriculture and Fisheries
- **Viviane Reding**
  Luxembourg, age 48
  Portfolio: Education and Culture
- **Erkki Liikanen**
  Finland, age 49
  Portfolio: Enterprise and Information Society
- **Frits Bolkenstein**
  Netherlands, age 66
  Portfolio: The Internal (within EU) Market
- **Philippe Busquin**
  Belgium, age 58
  Portfolio: Research
- **Pedro Solbes Mira**
  Spain, age 57
  Portfolio: Economic and Monetary Affairs
- **Michaele Schreyer**
  Germany, age 48
  Portfolio: Budget
- **Poul Nielson**
  Denmark, age 56
  Portfolio: Development and Humanitarian Aid
- **Guenter Verheugen**
  Germany, age 55
  Portfolio: EU Enlargement
- **Christopher Patten**
  Great Britain, age 55
  Portfolio: External Relations
- **Pascal Lamy**
  France, age 52
  Portfolio: Trade
- **David Byrne**
  Ireland, age 52
  Portfolio: Health and Consumer Protection
- **Michel Barnier**
  France, age 48
  Portfolio: Regional Policy
- **Margot Wallstrom**
  Sweden, age 45
  Portfolio: Environment
- **Antonio Vitorino**
  Portugal, age 42
  Portfolio: Justice and Home Affairs
- **Anna Diamantopoulou**
  Greece, age 40
  Portfolio: Employment and Social Affairs

The Council of Ministers The Council of Ministers is composed of officials representing the national governments of the member states. It is the primary legislative and decision-making body of the EU. The presidency of the Council rotates among the members, changing every six months. The president presides at meetings and speaks for the Council. The person who actually represents each nation at Council meetings may change from one meeting to the next. While each nation's foreign minister is most often its representative ("Minister") in the Council, at times other government officials, such as the ministers of finance, energy, social affairs, or environmental affairs, might serve as the minister for his or her nation, depending on the issues to be dealt with at that session.

regulations: A type of EU law that is directly effective in all member nations, as though it were a national law.

directive: A type of European Union law that establishes an EU standard but allows each member to enact a law in its own nation to implement the law.

decisions: EU legislation directed at one specific person or nation.

European Council: A meeting, held every six months, attended by the head of state of each EU nation.

The EU has the power to enact various types of legislation. **Regulations** are directly effective in all EU countries and are enforced by the Commission. **Directives** are legislative enactments, which are binding as to the result to be achieved, but require each nation to enact legislation in order to achieve the mandated result. The directive itself is not automatically effective as a law in the member countries, but allows each nation flexibility to adopt its own national legislation to reach the required standard. **Decisions** are orders directed at one specific person or member nation.

Although each nation has one minister at each Council meeting, the voting is not equal. The more heavily populated EU nations have more votes in Council matters than the smaller ones. Germany, France, Italy, and the United Kingdom have 10 votes each while Spain has 8. Belgium, Greece, the Netherlands, and Portugal have 5 votes, Sweden and Austria have 4, while Denmark, Finland, and Ireland have 3 and Luxembourg has 2. The SEA created a system of "*qualified majority*" voting, which allows many (but not all) measures to pass with a total of 62 votes (out of 87). A few important matters require a unanimous vote for approval. The various ministerial groups meet monthly to discuss issues within their area of responsibility.

Twice per year, at the end of each council president's term, the heads of state of each member nation and the Commission president meet as the Council. These meetings are called the **European Council** and have become important political and media events. The leaders may discuss general EU internal policy, as well as political and foreign issues.

The European Parliament The Parliament is a democratically elected body that directly represents European citizens and serves as a public forum to debate issues of importance to the EU. The Commission must always consult the Parliament before proposals are sent to the Council of Ministers for decision. With respect to certain types of legislation, the Parliament also has the right to reject or amend legislation approved by the Council, and may also amend, approve, or reject the budget. The powers of the Parliament have been increasing in recent years. It was an investigation led by the Parliament that caused the entire EU Commission to resign in 1999.

Since 1979 the Parliament has been elected by universal suffrage. There are 626 members, elected to five-year terms and grouped by political party, rather than by country. Many parties are currently represented, including Socialists, Christian Democrats, Liberals, Greens, Conservatives, Communists, and several others.

The Parliament has specialized committees on a number of substantive areas, working toward developing truly European policies on matters such as the internal market, energy, and industrial restructuring. Meeting one week per month in Strasbourg, France, the Parliament also has a staff of some 3,500, which is located in Luxembourg.

The following reading features Nicole Fontaine, the French woman who assumed the Presidency of the 626 member European Parliament in 1999.

Presiding Over Parliament

Fontaine Assumes the Presidency of the European Parliament

Nicole Fontaine, the chic new president of the European Parliament, has a reputation for being deeply religious, modest, a charmer with an ant-like capacity for hard work, and above all, for being a behind-the-scenes consensus builder. The latter trait recently prompted the *Economist* magazine to dub her "a European conciliator-general." It isn't surprising that many of her fellow French citizens do not know what exactly she does.

Today, this fifty-seven-year-old, center-right lawyer who has successfully worked the corridors of the European Parliament and other EU institutions as an MEP since 1984, is not only determined to improve her image and of the EP but is displaying a surprising, combative streak. This side of her personality surfaced, virtually unnoticed by the media, during the state funeral service for King Hassan II of Morocco in early August, which attracted leaders from around the world.

Vacationing with her family in France when she heard of the monarch's death, only four days after her election as EP president on July 20, Fontaine decided to attend the funeral. But not, as surprised Moroccan officials insisted, to sip tea with the wives of President Bill Clinton, President Jacques Chirac, and the other attending heads of state and government. She pressed hard, insisting she was not there as a spouse but as the newly elected president of a parliament representing 400 million Europeans. With the help of a European Commission official in Rabat, palace officials finally allowed her to become the only woman in the funeral procession and then, thanks to a friendly gesture from President Jacques Chirac of France, who likes her, wound up walking alongside the French leader and President Clinton.

Fontaine, whose father was a Normandy doctor, was born in 1942 near the northern port city of Le Havre and attended private Roman Catholic primary and secondary schools there before graduating from a public high school in Le Havre. She then went on to study law in Paris and, as a lawyer, landed her first important job—deputy secretary general of the Catholic Church's national education board, the first layperson to hold the post. Nicknamed Nini, she became increasingly involved—and visible—actively defending government funding of Catholic and other private schools, which the Socialist government in the early 1980s had decided to end. She led massive, public demonstrations against the proposed law, earning the epithet "the Jean d'Arc of Catholic education."

In 1984, the bill abandoned, her reputation established, she decided to run for the European Parliament and won. She was reelected in the 1989 and 1994 elections, always as a member of the centrist UDF party. Elected EP vice-president several times, with experience on the EP's judiciary, culture, education, and women's rights committees, a breakthrough came five years ago when she was backed by her conservative group, the European People's Party, the EPP, to become a member of the Parliament's influential

Conciliation Committee, which is responsible for resolving differences over controversial EU legislation with the Council of Ministers.

In that key job, says Pat Cox, Irish independent MEP, who will replace her as president in two and a half years, she displayed her impressive talents for negotiating compromise agreements under difficult circumstances, backed by reinforced powers provided by the Amsterdam Treaty that went into effect May 1. "She does not come across as a street fighter, eyeballing opponents," says Cox. He adds that long experience in the Parliament as an insider helped her enormously when the EPP, emerging as the Parliament's largest group in the June elections along with Cox's smaller Liberal group, threw their weight behind her for the presidency, defeating the Socialist candidate, Portugal's former president, Mario Soares.

"It was," she says, "one of the most marvelous surprises of my life."

"Presiding Over Parliament" by Axel Krause, *Europe*, October 1999, p. 18. Copyright European Commission 1999. Permission granted by *Europe* magazine, subscriptions available 1-800-627-7961.

European Union Bureaucracy More than 90 percent of the businesses in the EU employ fewer than 200 people. Small and medium-sized enterprises (called SMEs) are given considerable attention by the governing bodies of the EU. The great majority of new jobs created within the EU in recent years are with SMEs.

As in the United States, there is a large bureaucracy that administers most EU programs and projects. Many EU regulations hit small businesses particularly hard. Compliance costs are often higher than for larger businesses, due to many factors. Large firms have departments to deal with health, safety, and environmental regulations, while in small firms, the owners or partners must take the necessary steps to comply, in addition to their many other responsibilities.

Article 118A of the Treaty of Rome recognized these issues long ago, and provided that EU Directives "should avoid imposing administrative, financial and legal constraints in a way which would hold back the creation and development of small and medium-sized undertakings." A few years ago the EU established a "Year of the Small and Medium Sized Enterprises" and created a Directorate General (DG 23) specifically aimed at helping such businesses. Some of the problems that DG 23 has worked on include cash flow difficulties caused by late payments, a lack of management skills and training, and the burdensome effect of EU regulations. The EU continues to devote significant money and energy to improving conditions for SMEs.

The European Court of Justice The highest court within the EU is the **European Court of Justice (ECJ)**. This Court is the final legal authority regarding the interpretation of EU laws, treaties, regulations, and directives. Meeting in Luxembourg, the Court consists of 15 justices—one from each member state plus a president—who are appointed by agreement of all member governments for six-year terms. Decisions are reached by a consensus, with no public disclosure of how each judge voted and no dissenting opinions. The Court has heard nearly 10,000 cases since it was established.

EU Court of Justice (ECJ): The highest court in the European Union, which makes final decisions concerning EU laws and regulations.

The Court hears complaints concerning treaty and rule violations brought by member states or by the Commission. In addition, member nations, EU institutions, and individuals can contest Commission and Council actions in the Court. Following the civil law tradition, the court may call witnesses or hire experts for help with its decisions. There are also six Advocate-Generals, one of whom researches each case and then provides a memorandum and suggested decision to the Court. The decisions of the Court of Justice regarding EU law are supreme and overrule contrary decisions of national courts and inconsistent national laws in the member nations. In addition, the decisions of the Court are binding on all parties and are not subject to appeal. The Court has tended to support and strengthen EU institutions and policies.

Two legal theories employed by the ECJ have greatly enhanced its power as well as the potency of EU laws. The **doctrine of direct effects** holds that when an EU treaty provision, a regulation, or even a directive is clear and concise and establishes unconditional legal norms, it becomes immediately effective in all member nations and supersedes contrary national laws. Using this principle, the ECJ has determined that many treaty provisions, EU regulations, and even some EU directives have "direct effect."

direct effects doctrine: European Court of Justice doctrine that provides that when an EU law or treaty provision is very clear, it becomes immediately effective as law in all EU nations.

Another significant legal procedure was created by the Treaty of Rome (Article 177), which gave the ECJ the authority to issue **preliminary rulings**. This process occurs when a case pending in a national court involves a question of EU law. Such referrals are discretionary with the lower courts but mandatory for the highest court of a member nation. The ECJ then hears and determines the meaning and interpretation of the EU legal issue and sends the case back to the national court. That court must implement the EU ruling as part of its final judgment. The *Cassis de Dijon* case earlier in this chapter was sent to the ECJ for just such a ruling.

preliminary ruling: When a case in a national court of an EU member involves an issue of EU law, the case can be sent to the ECJ for a ruling on the EU law question, and then the case returns to the national court.

In 1987, the SEA established a second court, the *Court of First Instance* (CFI), essentially a lower court. This court has jurisdiction over ECSC matters, as well as matters involving competition, actions involving private companies and individuals, and actions brought by EU officials. The primary motivation behind the creation of this court was to relieve some of the caseload of the Court of Justice. Much employment and noncontractual liability litigation is now handled by the CFI. There is a right of appeal on points of law from the CFI to the Court of Justice.

INTERNATIONAL TRADE: RESTRICTIONS, REGULATIONS, AND "FREE TRADE"

Most of us agree that if a company in Canada or Germany wants to purchase 100 tons of potatoes or 100 automobiles from a U.S. firm, we should do whatever we can to eliminate any barriers hindering such a transaction. The proposition becomes somewhat more difficult, however, if we progress to the next logical step—that a U.S. firm should be able to purchase 100 tons of potatoes or 100 autos from a Japanese or French company anytime it wants to without restrictions. Suppose the Japanese or French firm is in direct competition with a U.S. company or that it receives some sort of subsidies or support from its government. What if a local company would have to eliminate 200 jobs due to a loss of business to the foreign company? What if the product being sold might help develop military power in a nation unfriendly to the United States?

Free and open trade across national boundaries is a desirable goal. But when that broad standard is applied to actual sales of particular products, the forces of competition, the perceived unfairness due to social or economic conditions or government regulations or assistance, and national security questions lead to an extensive series of laws and regulations affecting international trade.

TARIFFS

tariff: A tax assessed on goods as they are imported into a country.

The United States and most other countries have established detailed schedules of **tariffs** and *duties*, which are essentially taxes levied on goods at the time they are imported into a country. The general purpose of such tariffs is to protect domestic industries against lower cost imports. Goods are assessed duties (taxes) upon entry into this country according to the tariff (a percentage of their value, according to the appropriate schedule). The amount of the tariff depends on the type of goods and the country of origin.

TRADE AGREEMENTS

Tariffs and taxes on goods have caused disputes since the early days of our country (remember the Boston Tea Party?). When the United States imposes high tariffs on goods imported from another nation, that country is likely to impose similar duties on U.S. goods shipped there, causing higher prices for consumers and sellers in both nations. Many treaties, both bilateral and multilateral, have been signed as an attempt to lower tariffs on exported goods. A few of them are discussed in the following sections.

NORTH AMERICAN FREE TRADE AGREEMENTS

The United States and Canada maintain the world's largest trading partnership. Canada is both the largest importer of U.S. goods (some 20 percent of all U.S. exports have gone to Canada in recent years) and the largest exporter of goods to the U.S. (about 19 percent of total U.S. imports are from Canada). More than $364.55 billion of trade passed between the nations in 1999. In 1988 the countries signed the *U.S.–Canada Free Trade Agreement*, effective January 1, 1989, which provided for the elimination of all tariffs on trade between the nations over a 10-year period. The agreement also significantly reduced restrictions on foreign investment and trade in services between the two countries.

North American Free Trade Agreement (NAFTA): An agreement between Canada, Mexico, and the United States that will eliminate tariffs on goods traded between the three nations over a 15-year period.

In late 1992, the United States, Canada, and Mexico signed the **North American Free Trade Agreement (NAFTA)**. This trilateral agreement created a huge free-trade area among the three nations, similar in size to the EU. Since the United States and Canada already had entered into the free trade agreement discussed previously, most of the debate about NAFTA concerned Mexico. Mexico is now the second largest trading partner of the U.S., with a total of $196.5 billion in 2-way trade during 1999. NAFTA called for the elimination of all tariffs on imports between the above three nations. Many tariffs were eliminated immediately, and the rest will be abolished over a 15-year period, creating the world's largest free-trade zone.

The debate over ratification of the agreement created considerable political controversy in the United States, and some discussion and debate in Mexico and Canada as well. The major labor unions and businessman/politician H. Ross Perot argued vigorously that the treaty would result in the loss of thousands of U.S. manufacturing jobs. They feared that many businesses would move some operations to Mexico, due to lower labor costs and less stringent environmental and labor regulations there.

The United States negotiated certain "side agreements" to NAFTA with Canada and Mexico during the summer of 1993 in which the nations agreed to create two commissions to hear and decide allegations that one nation had been lax in the enforcement of its labor or environmental laws, thereby affecting NAFTA's free competition and trade provisions. The commissions were given the power to levy fines up to $20 million. If the violations continue, trade sanctions such as tariffs and quotas can be imposed on products of the offending country.

U.S. President Bill Clinton strongly supported the pact (which had been negotiated by former President George Bush during the last year of his administration), asserting that the agreement would enhance the global competitiveness of U.S. firms and would lead to the creation of many new U.S. jobs as companies expanded to serve the needs of all of North America. He also argued that United States exports to Mexico would increase, since the average Mexican tariff assessed on U.S. goods imported into Mexico (before NAFTA) was 10 percent, while U.S. tariffs on Mexican imports only averaged 4 percent. After a vigorous debate over the positive and negative aspects of free trade, the U.S. Congress approved NAFTA, and the agreement became effective on January 1, 1994.

After six years of operation, NAFTA is still controversial. Trade between the three nations has increased sharply—Canada and Mexico are now the first and second leading destination for U.S. exports. Mexican tariffs have been greatly reduced. About two-thirds of U.S. exports enter Mexico tariff-free, and the average remaining tariff is only 2 percent.

However, many unions, employee organizations, and other groups argue that U.S. jobs have been eliminated because of NAFTA. After NAFTA began its existence, the members intended to invite other nations to join, starting with Chile. However, because of the continuing controversy over NAFTA, and because Congress has refused to enact "fast track" legislation (which allows the U.S. president to negotiate treaties without Congress having the power to attach amendments), no further negotiations about expanding NAFTA have occurred. Furthermore, other nations are beginning to take leadership roles concerning the expansion of free trade in the Western Hemisphere.

Mercosur: The "Common Market of the South" is an organization aimed at reducing trade barriers and tariffs. Members are Brazil, Argentina, Paraguay, and Uruguay.

MERCOSUR AND THE FREE TRADE AREA OF THE AMERICAS

Mercosur ("Mercado Comun del Sur" in Spanish, which means "Common Market of the South") is a growing free trade area in South America. Formed in 1991 through the Treaty of Asuncion (Paraguay), the group includes Brazil, Argentina, Uruguay, and Paraguay. Mercosur has a total population of nearly 230 million, and in 1998 had a total gross domestic product (GDP) of $1.2 trillion. Chile and Bolivia are associate members of

Mercosur, and Chile is considering joining the group as a full member in the near future.

The Mercosur agreements call for the elimination of all tariffs on trade between the members, and by 1995 some 80 percent of all products traded among the bloc were duty-free. This elimination of tariffs has led to a dramatic increase in intra-Mercosur trade—from US$4 billion in 1990 to about US$18 billion in 1997—while trade with non-Mercosur nations also increased. Like the EU (but unlike NAFTA) there is a Mercosur headquarters building in Montevideo, Uruguay, with a staff working on various trade issues. There are several bodies already established for governing Mercosur, although nothing comparable to the EU as yet.

The Mercosur nations have established ambitious goals for the organization. Unlike NAFTA, which is strictly a "free trade area" with no central administrative structure or no common external tariff, Mercosur intends to become a *common market* someday, and has already established a *common external tariff (CET)*. A CET means that the members agree to charge the same tariff rate for the same type of goods when imported from outside the organization. For example, if Mercosur agrees to a 10 percent tariff on television sets being imported from Japan, then Brazil, Argentina, and the other Mercosur nations would all have to charge the same rate on television sets coming into their countries from Japan, and all other nations not members of Mercosur.

The economic problems experienced by Brazil in early 1999 caused difficulties in not only Brazil, but nearby countries as well. These events caused some trade tensions among the Mercosur members, which temporarily impeded further harmonization efforts among the member nations. The devaluation of the real, Brazil's currency, caused a sharp drop in imports from Argentina and led to various retaliatory measures. 1999 was a recession year in the Mercosur countries and also in Chile, but by early 2000, some of those differences were being resolved and Mercosur appeared to be moving forward again.

Mercosur is now the third largest regional trading group in the world (after the EU and NAFTA), and is growing in size and importance. It has signed free trade agreements with Mexico, Canada, and other nations, and is negotiating with the EU to remove trade barriers between these two large regional trading organizations. The ties between European nations and their former colonies in Latin America are still strong. Language, as well as cultural and economic factors, bind these two regions.

The EU is already responsible for 43 percent of foreign direct investment in Mercosur, and the EU is Mercosur's largest trading partner. Bilateral trade between those two regions was US$55 billion in 1998. In 1997, some 31 percent of Mercosur exports went to EU countries, and 19 percent went to the United States. Of total Mercosur imports, 33 percent came from EU nations, and 27 percent from the United States.

There is also a free trade agreement among several other South American nations called the *Andean Pact*. Members of this group are Bolivia, Columbia, Ecuador, and Venezuela. The Andean Pact has entered into negotiation with Mercosur and also independently with Brazil and Argentina toward reaching larger free agreements.

In addition, there is considerable activity and movement toward establishing a **Free Trade Area of the Americas (FTAA)**, which would include all 34 democratic nations of the Western Hemisphere (all countries except Cuba). Two summit meetings have been held—in Miami in 1994 and in Santiago, Chile, in 1998, at which all 34 nations pledged to begin talks in order to make "concrete progress" toward reaching such a hemispheric-wide free trade agreement by 2005. There are nine working groups meeting regularly to attempt to reach agreements on such matters as intellectual property and agriculture and to smooth out the difficulties of going forward with the massive undertaking.

Free Trade Area of America (FTAA): A proposed free trade area that would include all 34 democratic nations of South, Central, and North America.

GENERAL AGREEMENT ON TARIFFS AND TRADE (GATT) AND THE WORLD TRADE ORGANIZATION (WTO)

Beginning with a conference in Cuba in 1947 attended by some 50 countries, the GATT has been amended several times and has now been signed by over 130 nations. The GATT has become the primary multilateral treaty aimed at reducing trade barriers among nations all over the world. Since 1947 several "rounds" of GATT negotiations have taken place among nations (one round often lasts several years) to deal with various trade issues. For example, the "Tokyo Round" lasted from 1973 to 1979, and the "Uruguay Round" began in 1986 and was only completed in late 1993. The length of each round has led one commentator to nickname GATT as "The General Agreement to Talk and Talk." At the beginning of 1995, the World Trade Organization (WTO) came into existence and took over all GATT functions and enforcement of the GATT treaties.

The two primary purposes of GATT/WTO are the promotion of free trade and the reduction of trade barriers between nations. One major principle of GATT is called **most favored nation** status (MFN). Under this principle, if one country grants MFN status (preferential treatment regarding tariffs) to another nation, it must do so to all WTO members. In other words, if Spain and the United States negotiate a low tariff rate on television sets imported into Spain from the United States, Spain must use the same tariff rate on television imports from other WTO countries, without each country having to negotiate separately with Spain.

most favored nation (MFN): The term used to describe the rule that if one nation gives a good tariff rate to certain goods from one WTO member, it must give the same rate to all WTO members.

The second major GATT/WTO principle is **national treatment**. This theory prevents imported goods from being treated differently from domestic goods or being subjected to additional taxes, once they have cleared customs. For example, suppose a television set manufactured in Japan has been imported into this country and the importer has paid the required tariff. From then on, the item must not be subjected to any additional requirements not imposed on U.S. goods.

national treatment: The GATT/WTO principle that once goods are legally imported into a nation, they must be treated the same as goods produced in that nation.

In addition to tariffs, there are a number of other obstacles to total free trade, called *nontariff barriers*. National laws and regulations often contain requirements and practices that may intentionally or unintentionally favor domestic industries over foreign firms. Laws setting product safety and labeling requirements and establishing preferences in government procurement programs for domestic products ("Buy American" acts) are but two examples of nontariff barriers.

The Tokyo Round of the GATT negotiations (1973–1979) led to several agreements directed at reducing nontariff barriers by establishing international codes related to product standards, export subsidies, and government procurement. These agreements should have applied to all GATT nations, but many countries—especially the lesser-developed nations—did not sign the agreements. When the nations that had agreed to the new codes decided that MFN status would be given only to those who had signed the agreements, it caused a break in the principle of applying MFN status universally.

Other problems with the GATT/WTO system, including its failure to cover such important issues as intellectual property, agriculture, services, and investment matters, have led to the creation of several regional trading blocs. We have discussed the European Union and the U.S.–Canada–Mexico agreements. Other regions of the world have also established organizations to further trade and cooperation, such as the Economic Community of West African States (ECOWAS), the Caribbean Community (CARICOM), and the Association of Southeast Asian Nations (ASEAN).

In 1994, the United States and European nations reached major agreements that led to the conclusion of the lengthy Uruguay Round of GATT. The 1994 GATT agreements have made a significant difference in the world of international commerce. It is the first global trade agreement containing provisions dealing with subjects such as commercial services, agriculture, and software. The pact allows for easier investment in foreign countries by nonnationals, provides for easier entry into one nation by those who provide commercial services, and creates more international protection for "intellectual property" subjects such as patents, copyrights (including computer software), and trademarks. Lastly, the 1994 agreement established the WTO to carry out the terms of the treaty. The next few years will be crucial in determining whether GATT can meaningfully eliminate barriers and address world trade problems or whether the regional groups will grow and predominate.

The WTO is now the most important world organization concerning international trade. Some 134 countries are members of the WTO, and several more, including China, Taiwan, and Russia, were seeking admission in early 2000. As this book went to press, China was in complex negotiations with the U.S. and the European Union regarding its entry into the WTO. The WTO establishes and enforces the rules for international trade (established by GATT and other treaties) regarding manufactured goods, services (such as banking, insurance, and more), regulations dealing with intellectual property (called T.R.I.P.s), textiles and clothing, and agricultural products.

In carrying out the GATT agreements, the WTO is the primary forum for the expansion of free trade (by removing tariffs and nontariff barriers) and for the settlement of international trade disputes. The primary governing and law making body of the WTO is the *Ministerial Conference*, composed of the top trade officials of all the member nations.

A WTO Ministerial Conference meeting was held in Seattle, Washington (USA), in November and December 1999. This conference scheduled difficult negotiations between nations over trade issues, such as unilateral trade sanctions by nations and the allowable level of government support of local business and agriculture. The conference was overshadowed by major demonstrations and protests from many international groups who oppose further expansion of free trade and "globalization" of business. These groups asserted that the extension of "free trade" laws had enriched the most developed nations and large multinational corporations, while causing significant injury to less developed countries and smaller local business firms. The protestors also argued that unbridled free trade had led to increased unemployment in many parts of the world and also had damaged the environment. The protests and unrest caused the Seattle conference to end without reaching agreement.

WTO Dispute Settlement Procedure One of the major features of the WTO is the establishment of a Dispute Settlement Procedure. The process is intended to resolve conflicts through a neutral arbitration system, rather than have "trade wars" erupt when nations disagree on a trade-related issue and impose unilateral sanctions. The previous GATT dispute resolution system did include a process for arbitration of disputes, but the losing country was able to block the implementation of the decision, if it did not want to comply.

The dispute settlement process has been strengthened under the WTO and one nation can no longer block the WTO panel decisions. The primary role is given to the *WTO Dispute Settlement Body*. The process of dispute resolution includes the following steps:

1. A party who believes another nation is violating a WTO provision can ask for *consultation* to seek a settlement by direct negotiation with the other country.
2. If no settlement is reached, the complaining party can request that a WTO panel be formed to hear the case.
3. A panel of three to five experts will be formed and will hear the arguments of both parties concerning the issue.
4. Other member nations with a *substantial interest* in the case may make written comments before the panel as well.
5. The panel will make and issue an *Objective Assessment* of the case and determine whether the terms of a GATT/WTO agreement have been violated.
6. The decision will be forwarded to the *Dispute Settlement Body*, unless one party files for appeal.
7. If one party appeals, an *Appellate Body* of three people will hear the appeal, and may uphold, modify, or reverse the decision. Its decision is then forwarded to the Dispute Settlement Body.
8. When the *Dispute Settlement Body* receives the case, it can accept the decision or vote by consensus to reject it. If the decision is accepted, the Body can recommend to the offending party some ways that it could come into compliance with the WTO rules, and the party has 30 days to respond.
9. If the offending party does not comply and the trade violation is not removed, the Body may authorize the complaining party to *impose a retaliatory trade sanction* against the offending party. The sanction should be imposed on the same type of goods or industry in question, be temporary, and in an amount equal to the impact of the illegal practices.

The WTO dispute resolution system has sometimes been controversial. It is clearly positive to have an international organization become involved in resolving trade disputes between nations, rather than have each nation resort to sanctions, such as increased tariffs and quotas on imports, when a controversy arises. However, the referral of the dispute to an international body takes away some of the nation's sovereignty in that it deprives the national government of the right to unilaterally impose sanctions when it feels its rights have been violated.

The United States, in particular, has praised the WTO process when it wins a panel decision but has criticized the procedure when a panel has found that a U.S. practice violated a GATT or WTO provision. Although the United States has won far more cases than it has lost, there have been calls to overhaul the WTO panel dispute settlement system after a big case is decided adversely. One case that caused considerable controversy was a 1998 decision by a WTO panel upholding Japan's distribution system for photographic film against U.S. charges that Japan had erected severe "internal barriers" to protect Fuji Film Co. against increased imports of Kodak film.

U.S. LAWS CONTROLLING IMPORTS AND EXPORTS

In opposition to the movement toward reducing trade barriers between nations (exemplified by the WTO and NAFTA) is the strong domestic political pressure governments feel to protect and promote the commercial, manufacturing, and agricultural products of their own countries. To further this objective, many laws have been enacted all over the world, as well as in the United States, that allow a national government to assist domestic companies and/or to impose sanctions against foreign firms in particular circumstances. The overall purpose of such measures is either to attempt to increase domestic exports or to slow certain imports into the country. At the same time, national security concerns may dictate that some governmental controls be placed on the sale and export of sensitive military and high-technology products. A closer look at certain U.S. laws restricting imports and exports is therefore in order.

LAWS REGULATING IMPORTS

A series of U.S. laws allows the federal government to impose quotas on the import of certain foreign goods or to assess duties and tariffs on goods when the exporter has engaged in unfair practices of some kind.

Section 337: A U.S. law which permits sanctions against imports, where unfair trade acts are shown.

Section 337 of the Tariff Act of 1920 provides protection to domestic industries against "*unfair methods of competition*" and other unfair acts in connection with the importation of goods into the United States. The affected domestic industry must file a complaint with the International Trade Commission (ITC), a U.S. federal regulatory agency, which investigates the complaint and issues a decision. The President then reviews the agency's order and may uphold or overturn the ITC's recommendations.

Section 337 has most often been used in connection with violations of a patent and trademark infringement but may apply to a wide variety of unfair trade acts and practices. Sanctions may include cease-and-desist orders and permanent bans on certain products. For years American businesses claimed they were losing billions of dollars due to illegal use of their trademarks and patents and to other violations of intellectual property rights occurring in foreign countries. Congress strengthened the law in 1988 to eliminate the requirement that industries show economic injury due to the infringement and authorized the President to identify and name countries that were not protecting U.S. patents and intellectual property rights.

One portion of the Trade Act of 1974 (called **Section 201**) allows U.S. industries to seek temporary relief when they have been seriously injured by foreign imports, even if no unfair trade practices were used. The claimant must file a Section 201 petition with the ITC, which, if it determines that the domestic industry has suffered an injury, may establish quotas or higher duties on the imported products. The relief usually lasts for no more than five years, and the affected industry must show how the temporary assistance will allow the claimant to better adjust to foreign competition in the long term. The President must review the relief ordered and may affirm or overturn the order, if he finds that such relief would not serve the national economic interest.

Section 201: A U.S. law which allows the temporary imposition of quotas or tariffs on certain imports, where a U.S. producer is seriously harmed.

Dumping The practice called **dumping** occurs when a foreign firm sells its goods in the United States at a price lower than that charged in its home nation or sells the goods at a price below the seller's actual cost of production. Not only the United States but some 40 other countries have antidumping laws. The GATT specifies that this practice is unfair and condemns it "if it causes or threatens material injury to an established industry in the territory of a contracting party or retards the establishment of a domestic industry." The motive for such dumping could be an attempt by a large company with many products to capture a market share for a particular product by selling below cost for a period of time.

dumping: The sale of a product in a foreign country for a lower price than that charged in the home country, or below the cost of production.

In the United States, the complaining party files a petition with the ITC, which holds hearings to determine whether or not illegal dumping has occurred. The ITC may impose a duty on the imported products to raise the price of the imported goods up to the cost of production or to the sales price of the goods in the exporting country.

Countervailing Duty Another section of U.S. trade law is aimed at protecting domestic producers against unfair competition from imports that are substantially subsidized by a foreign government. The governments of most nations undertake programs designed to assist their own manufacturers in order to promote economic growth in their countries. However, subsidies such as grants and extremely low-interest or below-market-rate loans, which are available only to manufacturers of goods being exported, may distort the function of a free, competitive international market. When a U.S. industry can show that such a subsidy from a foreign nation with respect to a particular product is causing injury to a U.S. firm, a **countervailing duty** may be sought. Such a duty or tariff will be added to the cost of the offending goods or to other products of the same firm when they are imported into this country.

countervailing duty: A tax or tariff added to certain imported goods to counteract a subsidy given to the goods by the government of the nation where they were made.

Again, the complainant files a petition with the ITC, which makes a determination whether the U.S. firm is suffering injury. Then, the International Trade Administration, a part of the Department of Commerce, can set the "countervailing duty" or added tariff on the imported products necessary, in order to achieve fair competition. The process for obtaining relief can be lengthy, since the decision is often appealed through several regulatory and legal system tribunals. Because of the many different types of government assistance (such as training programs or incentives to locate plants in certain areas and direct subsidies), making the determination as to whether such a plan is an unfair subsidy or not is often a difficult decision.

LAWS REGULATING EXPORTS

While most nations try to assist their own firms in exporting, certain types of exports are not favored or even allowed by governments. For reasons of national security or in furtherance of its foreign policy objectives, nations may prohibit or restrict sales of certain goods to all countries or just to some countries.

Export Administration Act of 1979: A U.S. law that allows the government to prohibit exports of certain goods from the U.S.

In the United States, the **Export Administration Act of 1979** is the most important law restricting exports. The law allows the federal government to control and limit exports in three situations: (1) where there is a short supply of such goods in the United States, (2) when protecting the U.S. national security by prohibiting the export of goods and technology that "make a significant contribution to the military potential" of other countries, and (3) where necessary to further the foreign policy of the United States.

Every export from the United States requires a license, but in most cases the license is granted without difficulty. However, the Export Administration Act and other laws limiting exports can prevent the export of various items. The "national security" clause has led to a ban on the export of certain technological and chemical products that may have a "dual use"—that is, both military and civilian. The "foreign policy" clause has been employed by the United States to prevent most exports to Cuba, North Korea, and certain other countries as the result of specific events. Both civil and criminal penalties exist for violations of this law.

U.S. LAWS THAT MAY APPLY TO ACTIONS OUTSIDE THE UNITED STATES

In general, laws adopted by one country apply only within the borders of that country. As we have said, one of the difficulties with enforcing principles of international law is that there is no "Federal Statute of the World" enforceable everywhere. Each nation is considered sovereign within its borders. It would certainly restrict the sovereignty of a nation if another country's laws were applicable there. Nevertheless, certain U.S. laws have been applied to actions beyond our borders. The enforcement of these laws, not surprisingly, has created problems at home, as well as antagonism in other countries.

THE FOREIGN CORRUPT PRACTICES ACT

In the mid-1970s U.S. news media reported extensively about a series of incidents in which American companies—including some of our largest and most prestigious—admitted paying bribes to officials of foreign nations. The bribes were paid to secure major contracts with the foreign government. After considerable public outcry against this practice, Congress amended the Securities Act of 1934 by passing the Foreign Corrupt Practices Act (FCPA) in 1977.

This federal statute prohibits the payment of a sum of money to a foreign government or official for the purpose of influencing decisions or obtaining business. Even a payment made to a foreign business or agent will violate the law if the American firm knows that the payment will be used to bribe foreign officials. The FCPA contains severe civil and criminal penalties—individuals can be subject to as many as five years in prison and a $10,000 fine, and corporations can be fined up to $1,000,000.

Another feature of the FCPA requires those American firms who must register under that law to maintain stringent accounting procedures. The FCPA mandates that companies engage in careful record keeping and internal control systems, so that any questionable payments can be identified. Failure to maintain proper records will violate the act, whether or not any bribes are paid.

After complaints from American businesses that such payments were legal and expected in many countries, the law was slightly amended in 1988 to allow so-called "grease payments" to lower-level officials merely to expedite the processing of licenses and permits. Payments to higher-level officials who exercise discretionary powers are still covered by the law, however.

IN CONSULTATION

Marvin Manager has a problem. The Vice President of International Business has asked him to expand ABC, Inc.'s operations in Benswali, a developing country with unstable military leadership. Because Marvin has no contacts in Benswali, he hired an agent to help ABC to form the contacts necessary to enter the Benswali market. Marvin picked an agent that he thought was well connected to powerful people in the government.

The agent recently informed Marvin that in order to secure the necessary licenses and permits to expand ABC's operations in Benswali, certain payments were required. First, the agent said that the Minister of Internal Affairs insisted on a $100,000 commission for any new foreign business within Benswali's borders. The President of Benswali also mandated that any new foreign businesses make a $100,000 investment in the Benswali National Bank, which is fully government owned and run. Marvin told the agent that the payments sounded like bribes. The agent's response was simply that this was how things run in Benswali.

Marvin is afraid that the commission and investment are actually thinly disguised bribes. He approached Laura Lawyer, ABC's in-house counsel, to express his concerns. Here is their conversation:

Marvin:

1. I know bribes are illegal in the United States, but this isn't the United States. When in Rome, can't we do what the proverbial Romans do?
2. Even if the payments look like bribes, why can't we pay a commission and make an investment? Aren't we free to pick which companies to invest in, and if the Minister actually helps us get started, don't we owe him a commission?
3. What if we were to hide the payments on our books and just call them "taxes" or "miscellaneous fees"?

Laura:

1. You are correct that bribing government officials is illegal in the United States. Many of our laws, however, reach our behavior even when we are outside the United States. "When in Rome" isn't a valid legal defense.
2. Not necessarily. It is illegal to offer or make payments to corruptly influence a government official in order to gain business.
3. Hiding bribes in your books is as illegal as the bribes themselves. **Let me review the applicable law to see whether we can make the payments your agent has requested, and I will get back to you.**

FROM THE DESK OF
Laura Lawyer

To: Marvin Manager
Re: Bribery of Foreign Officials in Order to Gain Business

Dear Marvin:
A federal statute directly addresses your concerns about doing business in Benswali. According to the Foreign Corrupt Practices Act (FCPA)[1], the following behavior is illegal:

1. Payments by any company, its employees, or its agents to a foreign government official to improperly influence the government in order to obtain business abroad;
2. Making a payment to an intermediary "while knowing" that the payment is really for a bribe; and
3. Inaccurate record-keeping that disguises either the amount or purpose of a payment (or both) in order to misstate the actual purpose and recipient of the payment.

If we apply the FCPA provisions to your situation with your agent in Benswali, I suspect we would violate the law. The FCPA reaches outside the borders of the United States and prohibits U.S. companies from bribing the officials of other countries. The fact that bribes are an acceptable business practice in Benswali will not relieve ABC, Inc., of liability here. The FCPA does allow so-called grease payments, which are like gratuities or small gifts to expedite routine government functions like telephone installation or mail handling. The payments your agent seeks, however, are likely too large to constitute grease payments. Also, the officials seeking the bribes are too powerful to regulate routine procedures. Although the law allows you to invest where you want and pay commissions to whom you want, you cannot do either if the purpose of the investment or commissions is to corruptly influence a foreign official.

Finally, if you make the payments and then disguise their amount or purpose on the books, you are committing a separate offense under the FCPA with its own penalties. The penalties for FCPA violations are severe. Corporations are liable for $2 million or twice their gain from the offense, along with various other penalties. Individuals are liable for up to $250,000 per offense and subject to up to five years in prison. Accordingly, I highly discourage you from making the payments your agent seeks both to protect the company and yourself from heavy liability.

[1] 15 U.S.C. § 78(a)–(LLL) (1988).

With regard to Marvin's situation, we should consider the following questions:

1. What should Marvin do now that it appears he cannot make the payments the agent says are necessary?
2. What could Marvin's company do to ensure that its employees are not in this predicament in the future?
3. Discuss the advantages and disadvantages of preventing U.S. businesses from bribing foreign officials even if that is customary in the foreign jurisdiction.

U.S. ANTITRUST LAW

As discussed more fully in Chapter 16, the United States has a series of laws dealing with the subject called "Antitrust." In general, these laws are designed to promote competition, to prohibit actions that may lessen competition (price fixing, for example), and to prevent monopolies and mergers that would negatively affect competition. The penalties for violating antitrust laws can be severe. In order to encourage such lawsuits, the U.S. antitrust laws generally allow the winning party to be awarded triple the amount of damages proved to have occurred. Many nations do not have similar laws, however, and some countries actively encourage cartels and agreements between firms in order for them to compete better internationally.

Contrary to the general rules regarding the reach of one nation's laws, U.S. courts have applied the "intended effects doctrine" regarding antitrust law. According to this theory, if an action taken outside the United States is intended to and does affect U.S. commerce, it is subject to U.S. antitrust law. The following case involves a refusal of some firms to participate in a U.S. antitrust case.

IN RE URANIUM ANTITRUST LITIGATION: WESTINGHOUSE ELECTRIC CORP. V. RIO ALGAM LTD.

617 F.2d 1248 (7th Cir. 1980)

FACTS

Westinghouse sued 20 American and 9 foreign uranium producers in U.S. federal court, alleging violations of U.S. antitrust laws and asking for damages. Westinghouse claimed that the 29 companies had conspired to fix the price of uranium in the world market at meetings in France, Australia, South Africa, the Canary Islands, and England, as well as in the state of Illinois. When the 9 foreign defendants refused to answer, Westinghouse obtained default judgments against them. In the following months, the district court entered a series of injunctions prohibiting the defendants and some affiliated companies from transferring money out of the United States. Westinghouse also requested that hearings regarding damages begin against the defaulting defendants. The defendants who had answered opposed this, but the district court denied their motions, and this appeal followed.

On appeal, the governments of Australia, Canada, South Africa, and the United Kingdom filed *amicus curiae* (friend of the court) briefs supporting the defendants and protesting the exercise of jurisdiction over this controversy by the U.S. federal courts. The questions before the appellate court were (1) whether subject matter jurisdiction existed, and (2) if so, whether it should be exercised.

DECISION

The Seventh Circuit Court of Appeals, in an opinion by Judge Campbell, upheld the lower court order. Judge Campbell noted that since the *United States v. Aluminum Co. (Alcoa)* case in 1945 decided by Judge Learned Hand, U.S. courts have exercised jurisdiction over antitrust activity outside the United States where there was an "intended effect" on American commerce. In this case, according to the allegations of the complaint (uncontested as yet by the defendants), some of the meetings took place out of the United States, and some took place within this country. Therefore, the federal court had jurisdiction of this case, which was filed under the Sherman Antitrust Act.

As to whether the jurisdiction *should* have been undertaken, the court noted that the district judge considered three factors: the complexity of the multinational and multiparty litigation, the seriousness of the charges asserted, and the recalcitrant attitude of the defaulters. (One of the defendants tore up the complaint in the presence of the process server!) Although another circuit court of appeals had developed a 10-factor test in deciding whether to hear another extraterritorial antitrust case [*Mannington Mills, Inc. v. Congoleum Corp.*, 595 F.2d 1287, (3rd Cir. 1979)], this court was not bound to follow it, since the decision of one circuit court is not binding on another.

In this case (Westinghouse), the Seventh Circuit court decided that the district judge had made the appropriate decision in entering the default judgment. The court pointedly noted that in the *Mannington* case, the defendants had appeared and contested the matter, while here the alleged conspirators had "contumaciously" refused to come into court and present evidence. The Court of Appeals was "shocked" that the governments of the home countries of the defendants had served as "surrogates" for them and had "subserviently presented their arguments" to the court. There was thus no abuse of discretion by the District Court in entering the default judgments.

CASE QUESTIONS

1. Why was the case filed in federal court? Why does the court have jurisdiction?
2. How does the U.S. court justify its jurisdiction over actions taken outside the United States by non-U.S. parties?
3. Is it fair to force a defendant to litigate a lawsuit in a foreign country, when the defendant has never been to that country? Under what circumstances would it be fair?
4. What does "contumacious" mean?

The *Westinghouse* case in particular, and others like it, have caused considerable resentment and resistance from foreign corporations and governments. Even the members of the EU, which does have laws similar to U.S. antitrust law (called "competition" law in Europe), vigorously opposed the American attempt to apply its laws to conduct outside its jurisdiction. Soon after the Westinghouse decision, eight of the nations involved enacted "blocking" laws that prevented the discovery of documents located in their countries and barred enforcement of American antitrust judgments there. Other countries have laws that prohibit companies from disclosing information to foreign courts if the request is overly intrusive.

Many nations do not have, nor do they want to follow, the "discovery" procedures allowed in American litigation (discussed earlier in this book), which permit parties to obtain substantial documentary internal information on companies and to force the depositions (under oath) of many witnesses. This is an area where substantial disagreement still exists between the United States and other nations, including Great Britain, the United States' closest ally in many legal and business matters.

U.S. CIVIL RIGHTS LAWS

The United States has the most comprehensive legislation in the world prohibiting employment discrimination. As is fully discussed in Chapter 20 of this book, most employees working in this country are protected against discrimination in employment based on race, color, national origin, sex, religion, age, disability, and certain other categories. But is an American worker in another country protected against such discrimination? Normally, as we have seen, the sovereignty of a nation means that only its laws apply within its borders, and most nations do not have employment discrimination laws similar to those in the United States. None are as extensive.

In 1991, in a case titled *Equal Employment Opportunity Commission v. Arabian American Oil Co. (Aramco)*, an American employee working for an American firm in Saudi Arabia claimed that he had been discriminated against in his employment on the basis of his race, religion, and national origin. The U.S. Supreme Court ultimately decided that Title VII of the U.S. Civil Rights Act of 1964 did not apply to his employment in Saudi Arabia, since Congress had not specifically stated that the law should so apply.

Later in 1991, Congress passed major amendments to the Civil Rights Act in an attempt to change the law resulting from the *Aramco* case and other court decisions. Congress expressly extended the application of Title VII to United States citizens working outside of the United States for a firm "*under the control*" *of a U.S. entity*. "Control" depends on the interrelation of operations, the commonality of management, the centralized control of labor relations, and the common ownership of financial control of the employer and the corporation. An exception was allowed (that is, the U.S. law does not apply) if compliance with Title VII would cause the employer to violate the law of the country where the workplace is located.

The United States is a multiracial, multiethnic society, composed of citizens whose ancestors came from hundreds of different nations and cultures. This mixture of backgrounds has led to many exciting developments, as well as serious problems, during our 200-year history—and the struggles are ongoing today. In many other countries, the population is much more homogenous, with respect to race or ethnic or religious background, and anti-discrimination laws have been slow to develop.

The EU, for example, has regulations prohibiting discrimination on the grounds of *nationality* among the members, but not because of race or religion. With some exceptions, EU law prevents one nation from treating nationals of other EU members differently from their own citizens. Also, the EC long ago adopted, in Article 119 of the EEC Treaty, the principle of equal pay for men and women for equal work.

SUMMARY

It is critically important that American students look at business issues today with a global perspective. There are few types of trade, commerce, and services that are not affected in a direct way by developments around the world. The specific principles of international law are more difficult to pin down than national law, because there is no one body of statues that applies all around the world. The "law" applied to international commerce consists of a web of different laws, customs, practices, treaties, agreements, and decisions of national and international courts. Enforcement is also a problem without any one international army or police force. Much of the effectiveness of international law depends on the diplomatic and foreign relations efforts of governmental representatives.

The typical international sales transaction employs a letter of credit and bill of lading to effectively transfer title to goods and effectuate prompt payment. Contract interpretation and dispute settlement can be considerably more complex in international business transactions than domestic sales. Interesting commercial problems arise in connection with the enforcement of national laws, while respecting the sovereignty of national governments. Several important international organizations, such as the UN and the World Bank, play important roles in shaping the rules regarding international commerce. The EU is now the world's largest trading group, and it 15 member nations are rapidly moving toward closer integration of their laws, foreign policy, and monetary systems. The EU has established a complex governing system, featuring three major agencies and its own court system as well. The adoption of the Euro as common currency is moving forward quickly.

The regulation of trade between nations includes many intricate legal issues, including the tariffs and quotas put on imports and various export and import laws and regulations. More and more nations have entered into trade agreements, such as the WTO/GATT, in an effort to remove trade barriers and to promote international trade. Regional free trade agreements, such as NAFTA and Mercosur, are growing in size and importance. The United States has a number of laws regulating exports and imports—such as those that prohibit "dumping" of products. Finally, several U.S. statutes are designed to apply to apply to conduct outside U.S. borders, and the enforcement of these laws has caused political and legal ramifications abroad.

CHAPTER QUESTIONS

1. The primary purpose of the EU structure is to remove barriers to the trading of goods among the member nations. For hundreds of years Germany prohibited the manufacture and sale of "bier" (beer) containing additives (any substitute for malted barley). However, several other members of the EU do not have such a prohibition in their countries, and beer manufacturers in those nations wish to sell their beer in Germany. German officials defended their ban on beer containing additives on public health grounds and also stated that to allow the sale of beer containing additives would be misleading to the German public. In 1987, the Commission brought an action in the ECJ against Germany. What should be the result and why?

Commission of European Communities v. Germany, No. 178/84, March 1987.

2. Mr. Nelson was employed as a systems engineer for a hospital in Saudi Arabia. As part of his job, he reported safety violations at the hospital to the appropriate authorities. Rather than being rewarded, he claimed he was detained and tortured by Saudi government agents in retaliation for his actions. Later, Mr. Nelson sued Saudi Arabia, the hospital where he worked, and a corporation owned by the Saudi government in U.S. federal court. The defendants moved for dismissal on the grounds of lack of jurisdiction under the FSIA. What should be the result and why? *Nelson v. Saudi Arabia*, 923 F.2d 1528 (11th Cir. 1991).

3. Allied Chemical, an American company, entered into a contract to ship chemicals to Banylsa, a Brazilian importer. Allied delivered the goods to Lloyd, a carrier who shipped the goods by sea to Brazil. Allied received a bill of lading, which it sent to a Brazilian bank along with an invoice and with instructions to deliver the documents on payment. However, on arrival, the goods were unloaded and put into a government warehouse. In Brazil, the law allows a buyer to obtain goods from a warehouse either with a bill of lading or with a *carta declaratoria*, a letter from the carrier stating that the import fees had been paid. Using such a letter, Banylsa picked up the goods without paying for them and later became insolvent. Allied sued the carrier in U.S. federal court. What should be the result and why? *Allied Chemical Co. v. Companhia de Navegacao Lloyd Brasileiro*, 775 F.2d 476 (2d Cir. 1985).

4. Zapata, a U.S. oil company, entered into a contract with Unterweser, a German firm, to tow an oil rig from Louisiana across the Atlantic Ocean to a new location near Italy. The contract included a clause stating, "Any dispute arising must be treated before the London Court of Justice." Shortly after the tug "Bremen" began towing the rig to Italy, a severe storm swept into the Gulf of Mexico, causing damage to the oil rig. At Zapata's direction, the rig was towed into port in Tampa, Florida. Zapata then started a lawsuit against Unterweser for damages in U.S. federal court. The towing company argued for dismissal, citing the "choice of forum" clause in the contract and filed a suit against Zapata in the London Court of Justice. Zapata argued that for "public policy" reasons, the U.S. court should not be "ousted" from jurisdiction of a dispute that took place near Tampa, Florida. What should be the result? Why? *M/S Bremen v. Zapata Off-Shore Co.*, 407 U.S. 1 (1972).

5. What are the primary purposes of the GATT agreements? What are the two most important principles? Describe the key parts of the WTO dispute settlement process.

6. Smith-Corona (SC) is currently the only American manufacturer of portable electric typewriters. SC charged that Japanese manufacturers Brother and Silver Seiko had engaged in illegal "dumping" of typewriters in the United States. In determining whether the typewriters were sold in the United States at less than fair value (LTFV), the International Trade Administration had to compute the market value of the typewriters sold by Brother and Silver Seiko in Japan. The ITA allowed for reductions in

that price due to rebates given in Japan (but not in the United States), advertising expenses in Japan, and accessories provided with the typewriters in Japan but not in the United States. These adjustments reduced the "market value" of the typewriters sold in Japan, which thus resulted in a lower "dumping margin" between the price in Japan and the U.S. sales price than Smith Corona believed existed. Were the deductions proper? *Smith-Corona Group v. United States*, 713 F.2d 1568 (Fed. Cir. 1983).

7. A group of American investors lost money after investing in various Lloyds of London entities. The investors, called "names," had signed agreements upon entering into the ventures, by which they agreed to arbitrate any disputes though an organization in England. The "names" tried to file suit in the United States, claiming that the arbitration clauses should not be enforced because they essentially called for the waiver of compliance with U.S. laws regulating the sale of securities and thus violated U.S. "public policy." Will such a suit be successful? Why? *Roby v. Corporations of Lloyds*, 996 F.2d 1353 (2d Cir. 1993).
8. A South Korean factory, which was a subsidiary of a U.S. corporation, closed its doors, putting many employees out of work. The union representing the workers filed suit in the Untied States, claiming that the action was contrary to the labor contract with the employees, thus violating U.S. law dealing with labor–management relations. The labor law cited provided that it applies to "an industry affecting commerce . . . without regard to the citizenship of the parties." The company moved for dismissal of the case due to lack of jurisdiction, but the labor union argued that this clause gave U.S. courts jurisdiction of the matter. What should be the result? Why? *Labor Union of Pico Korea Ltd. v. Pico Products, Inc.*, 968 F.2d 191 (2nd Cir. 1992).
9. The government of Cuba expropriated certain property belonging to an American sugar company in Cuba, which had a contract with an American food broker. After the food broker obtained substitute sugar from Cuban authorities, payment was sent to the original seller. The National Bank of Cuba then sued the broker in a U.S. federal court. The broker defended its actions by alleging that the Cuban government's nationalization was illegal, but the Cuban National Bank urged that the actions of the government could not be challenged in a U.S. court due to the Act of State Doctrine. What should be the result and why? *Banco Nacional de Cuba v. Sabbatino*, 376 U.S. 398 (1964).
10. A Swedish businessman, Mr. Nissen, came to the United States intending secretly to purchase military parts for resale to Iran. U.S. Customs officials had set up a "sting" operation (a false company) that acted as a broker. When Nissen purchased 13 "venturi heaters" for use on Phantom F-4 fighter planes, he listed the designation as Malaysia. However, he transported them through Germany and Sweden to Iran. Later, he attempted to purchase a large airplane and many more parts and was arrested. He was convicted and sentenced to 44 months in prison with his sentence enhanced because he bought "sophisticated weaponry." On appeal, he argued that the sentence was excessive because he just bought a few airplane parts. What law is involved here, and what is the purpose of the law? What result is likely on appeal? *United States v. Nissen*, 928 F.2d 690 (5th Cir. 1991).

PRACTICAL EXERCISE

Early in the morning of December 3, 1984, at a Union Carbide Corporation (UCC) pesticide plant in Bhopal, India, a tragic industrial accident occurred. A large storage tank of methyl isocyanate gas (MIC) malfunctioned, perhaps due to some water entering the gas chamber. When the trouble was noticed, the temperature and the pressure inside the tank were increasing dramatically. The supervisors on duty attempted to turn on the safety devices, and then, seeing a plume of gas rushing out of the stack, ran for their lives. In the next few hours, a huge quantity of gas escaped into the community, where the population was sleeping. The gas drifted silently over the small homes and huts, causing death and permanent injury to thousands. When it was over, more than 3,000 people had been killed, and some 300,000 suffered permanent or temporary injuries.

A large multinational corporation, UCC has plants, facilities, and personnel in many countries. Its headquarters are in Connecticut, and there are significant UCC business operations in New York State. The UCC facility in Bhopal was owned 51 percent by Indians and 49 percent by UCC. It is unclear whether the same safety standards were employed in the Bhopal plant as would be required at a U.S. facility.

The human tragedy led to a complex web of lawsuits and government actions in India and the United States. Within days after the accident, many U.S. lawyers flew to India, signing up victims as clients and forming partnerships with Indian attorneys. The Attorney General of Connecticut (now its U.S. senator), Joseph Lieberman, called it "the greatest ambulance chase in history. It could be the largest and most lucrative civil legal case in the history of the world." Within three months, 40 lawsuits had been filed in U.S. federal courts, 5 in U.S. state courts, and some 1,200 in Indian courts. A federal judicial panel consolidated most of the U.S. federal suits in New York City and assigned them to Judge Keenan.

About one year after the accident, American lawyer Melvin Belli (the so-called "King of Torts") filed a $15 billion class action lawsuit against UCC in a West Virginia court. Early in 1985 the government of India adopted the "Bhopal Act," establishing the authority of the government to file lawsuits representing all Indian citizens for injuries suffered at Bhopal. The government then filed suit asking for damages for all victims in district court in New York, and the case was also assigned to Judge Keenan. There were also criminal charges filed in India against UCC and against its chief executive officer Warren Anderson. Union Carbide brought a motion in the federal court to dismiss the U.S. cases on the grounds of *forum non conveniens*. The company also argued that the Indian courts had no jurisdiction over UCC Chairman Warren Anderson and that the criminal charges should therefore be dismissed.

India has a fully developed legal system, based on the British model. Indian tort law—like that in the United States—has developed primarily through common law, although often wrongs committed by one party against another in India are dealt with by criminal law, rather than tort law. Compensation levels for tort cases in India are generally quite minimal, compared with jury verdicts for similar cases in the United States. Nevertheless, India does recognize tort law and does have a body of common law awarding tort damages to those injured by the actions of others. The concept of "strict liability" has not developed very much in India, however, and Indian courts rarely award "punitive damages." The wages earned in India are much lower than those in the United States, which also tends to keep worker damages at a lower level.

You are a management trainee working at the UCC world headquarters in Connecticut. Since you have a good background in business law, you have been asked to work with the UCC lawyers in dealing with the legal aspects of this tragedy. First, you are to prepare a short (two- or three-page) memorandum for the crisis team dealing with the legal issues involved.

Please discuss: (1) whether the New York federal court has jurisdiction of this matter, (2) whether the Indian courts have jurisdiction of this matter, (3) how the doctrine of *forum non conveniens* should apply to this case, (4) whether Indian law or U.S. law should apply to this case, and (5) whether the Indian courts have jurisdiction over Union Carbide CEO Anderson for the purposes of criminal charges.

FURTHER INFORMATION

www.wto.org
The WTO site.

www.europa.eu.int
The EU site.

www.eurunion.org
European Commission site with many links.

www.sice.oas.org/trade/naftatce.stm
NAFTA information.

www.americasnet.com
Mercosur information.

www.ustr.gov
U.S. trade representative.

CHAPTER 7

BUSINESS ETHICS AND CORPORATE SOCIAL RESPONSIBILITY

LEARNING OBJECTIVES

After you have read this chapter, you should be able to:

1. Explore the relationship between law and ethics and the tension between individual and community ethics.
2. Describe several major ethical theories and differing beliefs about the social responsibility of business.
3. Explain the concept of stakeholder relationships.
4. Apply various ethical theories to contemporary business issues.

CHAPTER OUTLINE

I. Law and Ethics
II. Individualism and Communitarianism
III. Formal Methods of Ethical Reasoning
IV. Business and Its Community
V. Federal Sentencing Guidelines
VI. Contemporary Issues Involving Business Ethics

You are a manager in a large oil company and have been ordered by your boss to destroy certain environmental documents that have been requested by a federal agency. What do you need to know about ethics and social responsibility before deciding whether to comply with this request?

INTRODUCTION

> *Ethics is the name we give to our concern for good behavior. We feel an obligation to consider not only our own personal well-being, but also that of others and of human society as well.*
>
> —ALBERT SCHWEITZER

The majority of this book is concerned with explaining various laws, regulations, and other legal issues affecting business. As you already know, "the law" comes from a number of sources—state and federal constitutions, statutes passed by legislatures, court decisions, regulations issued by government agencies, and other sources. This chapter, however, focuses on whether business or individuals involved in business have any additional obligations—beyond simply obeying the law—due to ethical or moral reasons or to the role business plays in our society.

Throughout the years several major scandals involving unethical business practices have caused the public to question the moral standards of American business. Bribes, kickbacks, insider trading, management buy-outs that seem to benefit only managers, excessive salaries and "perks" for top executives, environmental accidents, the failure of hundreds of savings and loan institutions, and consumer safety cover-ups have made headlines all over the country in the past few years. Often, these incidents involve questions of whether a company or its officials have operated not only legally, but ethically or morally. In response, business ethics has become an integral component of business education. As many as 2,000 corporations have drafted ethical codes for their officers and workers, and numerous universities have established ethics courses.

LAW AND ETHICS

"Thou shall not steal" and "Thou shall not kill" are commands based upon ethical norms common to almost all societies, which have resulted in laws making those actions illegal as well. The "Golden Rule," which states that we should treat others as we wish to be treated, exists in some form in most all major religions of the world. Much of our criminal law is also based on moral and ethical foundations. Clearly, if a person cheats, robs, or assaults another, he or she has violated both the ethical and legal rules.

Similarly, much of our common law is based, at least in theory, on what most people believe is "right." For example, if you make a promise upon which another person relies, it is only right that you should be held to that promise, at least in certain situations. This moral principle is the foundation of contract law. If you carelessly take an action that injures someone else, it is only "fair" that you compensate that person for his or her loss, and that is the basis of negligence law.

Many actions, however, might be ethical but illegal, and others may be legal but unethical. The law provides a floor below which society cannot tolerate certain conduct. Therefore, certain acts that fall below that standard will be punished. Simply because there is a level of conduct required by law, however, does not mean that in a given situation, a person's moral or ethical standards might not require a higher type of behavior. For example, in most states, no legal duty exists to aid a drowning person (unless you have contributed to his or her predicament in some way). But, if you are a strong swimmer and have completed a lengthy Red Cross water safety program, your own ethical, religious, or moral code may require you to rescue the drowning person.

Furthermore, on several occasions in recent years U.S. plants have been closed and the operation moved to an overseas facility where wages are significantly lower and government regulation virtually nonexistent. In the process, hundreds of employees have lost their jobs, and other community businesses have suffered. This is, of course, legal, but some commentators have questioned the ethical consequences of such transactions.

Similarly, there are actions that are illegal, but possibly ethical. A few years ago, while a long and dangerous war raged in parts of Central America, hundreds of people living there attempted to come to the United States in order to keep their families from being killed or injured. The law imposes limits on the number of immigrants from various countries who may enter the United States in one year, and these limits had been reached with respect to El Salvador and Honduras. Nevertheless, many church groups in the United States, believing that they had a moral duty to save the lives of as many Central American citizens as possible, secretly smuggled illegal immigrants into this country in order to provide them sanctuary from the war. These groups who helped the immigrants into this country knew that their actions were illegal, but these groups were willing to take the chance of being prosecuted because they felt that what they were doing was "right." In their eyes, the conduct was ethical, although illegal.

Therefore, while what is legal and what is ethical often overlap, there is not a total correspondence between the two. If the law represents the floor below which conduct is illegal, ethics represents the structures erected above the floor. Persons should strive to operate within these structures and build further on them by behaving in a manner beyond the requirements of the law.

INDIVIDUALISM AND COMMUNITARIANISM

A starting point for any discussion of ethics necessarily concerns a discussion of values. Many students have taken value quizzes where they are asked to prioritize a series of values like love, family, peace, security, or power. Two values important in American society are individualism and communitarianism.

American society has long valued the efforts of the individual. We have celebrated the courage of the Pilgrims, the fortitude of the early settlers, and those who pushed west to populate the frontier. Today, people who have started their own businesses and achieved success are lauded as "entrepreneurs" in books and magazines. Our capitalistic economic system is based, to a large extent, on a concept sometimes called "Social Darwinism"—that is, "survival of the fittest" in business. The economic theory *laissez faire* holds that government should never, or to the minimum extent possible, interfere in economic matters and should leave individuals to succeed or fail on their own. We admire those who courageously stand up for their principles against powerful opposition, and we ardently endorse the Bill of Rights with its protection for individuals against government overreaching. Americans generally believe enthusiastically in the property rights of private individuals. In short, individualism is strongly valued in the United States.

On the other hand, our society has deeply held beliefs in equality, justice, and fairness. These values emphasize the idea that certain actions should not be taken if they would promote the interests of one individual instead of the interests of the community. Much of our Judeo-Christian religious and ethical background rests on "being your brother's keeper." Many other laws and precepts of our society are aimed at promoting conduct that benefits the larger community rather than solely one's own interests. Communitarianism is not simple majoritarianism, but rather focuses on what is good for the community, which often means protecting individual rights. As could be predicted, individualism and communitarianism often conflict.

While some people seem to clearly follow exclusively one value or the other, most of us make an effort to accommodate both values. From time to time, one value or the other becomes more prominent, and then the pendulum swings back. In the 1960s, it seemed that the community value was dominant in the United States. Congress passed more than 20 "consumer protection" laws, designed to thwart behavior that injured others, particularly those less fortunate or less educated. Following the leadership of President John F. Kennedy ("Ask not what your country can do for you, ask what you can do for your country") and Martin Luther King, Jr., a tremendous commitment was made to eliminate, or at least substantially reduce, discrimination based on race, religion, national origin, sex, or poverty. After the untimely deaths of these two leaders, many of the ideas they advocated were implemented by President Lyndon Johnson through his "Great Society" program.

By the mid-1970s, the public mood began to change. More and more focus was placed on self-development (*I'm OK, You're OK* became a very popular book), and less attention was given to the concerns of others. There was growing dissatisfaction in the United States with the expansion and proliferation of government agencies, many of them created or enlarged by legislation passed in the 1960s or early 1970s. The American public became more concerned with the tremendous cost and unclear effectiveness of such programs. By the beginning of the 1980s, many Americans were ready to embrace individualism. Riding this wave of sentiment, Ronald Reagan was elected president, stressing that "It's time to get government off the backs of the American people." Congress and the President responded to the change in mood by cutting back on regulations and lowering the budgets and staff of many agencies.

Neo-classical economics became the preeminent government theory—that is, if each person maximized his or her own welfare, the most efficient firms would succeed, and corresponding benefits would follow for society. Efficiency became another value and television and magazines featured real estate developer Donald Trump and celebrated his conspicuous ambition, lifestyle, and wealth. *Wall Street*, the tale of a ruthless and greedy stockbroker, emerged as a hit movie. Madonna became a music superstar, and one of her biggest hits was a semi-autobiographical song titled "Material Girl."

But by the end of the 1980s, the excesses of selfishness and individual gratification had created dissatisfaction in society. The number and size of corporate mergers and takeovers reached record levels, with many companies closing facilities and, as the result, costing thousands of people their jobs. Ivan Boesky had engineered a scheme to reap enormous individual profits by buying stock of companies after learning secretly about upcoming mergers and takeover bids. It was unclear exactly how much Mr. Boesky made, but after he was caught, he agreed to pay a fine of $100 million (he also went to jail). Michael Milken pioneered the use of "junk bonds" (high-risk, high-yield corporate bonds) through complex transactions that allowed certain investors to make enormous profits (and Milken himself made $1.3 billion over four years). He too, however, was eventually convicted of federal law violations and sentenced to prison. His brokerage firm (Drexel Burnham Lambert) suffered large losses and filed for Chapter 11 Bankruptcy protection. Following the deregulation of the savings and loan industry during the 1980s, hundreds of savings and loans engaged in questionable lending practices and later went bankrupt, costing the taxpayers an estimated $500 billion (through federal insurance for the depositors). Even Donald Trump has struggled to keep his properties and avoid bankruptcy.

As we begin a new century, we see the pendulum swing back to an interest in community duty and a growing emphasis on ethics in business. Thousands of corporations have established codes of ethics. Several leading business schools have set up ethics programs. (Harvard received a $20 million gift to do so.) And most major business and news publications have featured articles on ethics in business and in America. Further, even First Lady Hillary Rodham Clinton wrote a popular book, *It Takes a Village*, calling upon community values for raising the nation's children.

Understanding and identifying these and other values is important, but it is clear that values, in and of themselves, do not necessarily have ethical content. A person is not judged ethical or unethical because he or she prefers individualism over communitarianism or vice versa. For most of us, a person or a decision is either "good" or "bad" depending on our own view of what is right and wrong. Questions of right and wrong are the subject of ethics and formal ethical reasoning (how people should think about right and wrong) is studied by many scholars.

FORMAL METHODS OF ETHICAL REASONING

In general, decisions as to what is right or wrong are made very quickly, informally, and without much thought. When asked, after the fact, why we behaved in a certain way we may give the following reasons: fear of punishment, promise of reward, adhering to a group norm, or obeying the law. For example, if Ann decides not to steal a sweater because she is afraid she will get caught, she is acting ethically only because she fears punishment. If Bobby decides not to hit Jake because his mother has promised him $50 if he does not fight, he is acting ethically only because he will receive a reward. Thirteen-year-old Kay is adhering to a group norm when she tells the truth about her age and pays an adult ticket price at the movie theater. When asked why she tells the truth she says because "in her family we always tell the truth." And when 20-year-old Adam does not drink alcohol at a fraternity party because it is against the law, he is using a legal standard to govern his behavior.

Although there is nothing inherently wrong with using these informal methods of ethical reasoning, there are more formal ways to think about right and wrong conduct. These more formal methods are the subject of ethical reasoning. The three predominant theories we are going to discuss in this text are virtue, utilitarianism, and deontology.

VIRTUE ETHICS

Take a minute to think about these questions. What does it mean to say, "He's a good person"? How do good people behave? What is a good life? What does it mean when you say you want to live a good life or that she lived a good life? What does that life look like? These questions were asked by the Greek philosopher, Aristotle, writing around 350 B.C. The answer is found in Aristotle's *Nichomachean Ethics* and is referred to as virtue ethics. For Aristotle, living a life of virtue was part of living a good life. Virtue does not come easily, however, and Aristotle argued that individuals only become virtuous by acting virtuously. Put another way, a person is not taught to be virtuous. Rather, individuals become virtuous by continually practicing making virtuous decisions.

Well then, just what is a virtue? First, virtues should not be confused with values, even though the popular press uses the terms almost interchangeably. Virtues are individual characteristics that make a person "good" or "bad." So while some values are also considered virtues, like honesty, a value is not a virtue if it does not say anything about a person's character. Second, Aristotle warned that it was difficult to define a virtue in exact terms because virtues can become vices if they are taken to extremes. The "golden mean" or the more modern saying "moderation in all things" is used to identify virtuous behavior. To give you an example of how the "golden mean" is used, let's take the virtue of truthfulness. On one end of the truthfulness spectrum we have lying, which is clearly not a virtue but a vice. On the other end of the spectrum, however, a person might be so truthful that he is vicious. An example would be approaching an overweight person and exclaiming, "You are very fat!" in order to make the person feel bad. This is also a vice. Therefore, the golden mean helps us remember that the virtue of truthfulness falls somewhere in between the two extremes, but it is hard to define exactly where that is without understanding the context of when the "truth" was told.

Aristotle did identify several virtues that he believed a good Athenian should possess: courage, temperance, liberality, magnificence, pride, good temper, friendliness, truthfulness, wittiness, shame, justice, and honor. Several centuries later, St. Thomas Aquinas, in *Summa Theologica*, divided virtue into the religious (theological) virtues of faith, hope, and charity and the principal intellectual virtues of prudence (wisdom), justice, temperance, and fortitude. Robert Solomon, a current philosopher, has written a book titled *Ethics and Excellence*, which is aimed at applying virtue ethics in a contemporary business setting. Solomon argues that the basic virtues applying to business relationships are honesty, fairness, trust, and toughness. He also identifies the virtues of the corporate self as friendliness, loyalty, honor, shame, caring, and compassion. As you can see, there is quite a bit of overlap between Aristotle's list of virtues and Solomon's list of virtues. Many of you probably also identified several of these virtues as you identified what it means to be a good person.

One virtue of particular importance here is justice. Justice was recognized as a virtue by Aristotle, Aquinas, and Solomon, and some have argued that justice is *the* most important virtue. There are basically two types of justice, distributive and commutative. Distributive justice is concerned with what is fair and equitable when goods and services are distributed in a society. Issues of distributive justice are very apparent in the current and continuing debate over affirmative action outlined in Chapter 20. Commutative justice looks at what is fair and equitable among individuals. One aspect of commutative justice is retribution, which deals with punishment. Much of criminal law and tort law, discussed in Chapter 11, concerns commutative justice.

As can be seen, virtue ethicists believe that the "good life" can be explained in objective terms and can be decided upon by the community. Other philosophers, however, disagree. Therefore, the good life and a sense of community are not built into the other philosophical theories we will discuss. These theories can be divided into two groups: **teleology** and **deontology**. In general, the teleologists assess whether an action is ethical by looking not only at the particular act in question, but also at the likely or actual consequences of the act. The following theories are examples of teleological philosophies.

teleology: A group of ethical theories that judge actions by their consequences.

Egoism Egoism is not a difficult theory for most of us to grasp. This doctrine basically holds that each person should decide on a course of action based upon what is best for him or her. Egoism is a form of teleology and thus includes in its ethical analysis the likely results of the contemplated action. Egoists contend that the enlightened pursuit of self-interest will lead to the full realization of each person's potential. An act is therefore "good" if it advances the self-interest of the person.

deontology: A group of ethical theories that examine the nature of the action itself, without regard to its consequences, to determine whether it is ethical.

Utilitarianism Another form of teleological ethics is **utilitarianism**, first articulated in the late 1700s by Jeremy Bentham. This theory holds that an act is good which produces the greatest good for the greatest number of people. An important part of utilitarianism lies in identifying the "good" to be maximized. For Bentham, the good was pleasure and any act that maximized pleasure was ethical. John Stuart Mill argued that happiness was the good to be maximized. Other contemporary philosophers have identified the good as knowledge or life or aesthetic beauty or liberty. Once the good is agreed on, utilitarians look at the social benefit of the action and the social harm of the action. This form of ethical analysis, with considerable modifications, constitutes the basis of the contemporary technique for assessing certain decisions called *cost-benefit analysis*, which attempts to weigh and compare the costs and savings resulting from a particular government or business decision. The good being maximized is either profit or efficiency.

utilitariansim: The theory that an act is good which produces the greatest good for the greatest number of people.

Our capitalistic economic system owes much to utilitarian principles as refined by Adam Smith, the 18th century Scottish philosopher and political economist. Smith's work *The Wealth of Nations* (1776) advocated that the enlightened pursuit of self-interest by merchants and producers, through the free market, results in the most benefits for all of society (that is, "the greatest good for the greatest number"). As if by an "invisible hand," money and resources are allocated by means of free market competition to businesses that produce goods the public wants.

DEONTOLOGY

Other philosophical and religious scholars have developed deontological theories, which insist that the ethical nature of an act must be determined by examining only the act itself, without regard to its consequences. The following theories are examples of this category.

Universalization One of the most well-known moral philosophers of all time was Immanuel Kant, a German who lived from 1724 to 1804. Kant argued that humans had duties and that those duties always had to be acted upon regardless of the consequences. These duties can be identified by using *universal law*. Put anther way, rules and actions are not ethical unless they can be made **universal**—that is, applicable to everyone. Kant argued that to test the ethical correctness of an action, one should assume that the action or decision will become a general law binding on everyone. For example, if Susan is deciding whether or not to tell a lie, she should ask whether it would be morally correct for everyone to tell lies. Kant would conclude that it is not a good moral result for everyone to tell lies, so the principle (it is all right to lie) cannot be universalized.

universal: Applicable to everyone.

Kant also asserted that it is unethical to use people as means to an end. He urged that human beings are too unique to be used as means to achieve some other goal, and instead must be treated as ends in themselves.

Judeo-Christian Principles Although all Americans do not subscribe to any one religion and many are not religious at all, undoubtedly the most prevalent ethical force in the United States is the Judeo-Christian heritage shared by the majority of citizens. Many of the central tenets of the Jewish and Christian religions command individuals to take care of and assist one another. The ethical portions of these religions contain a strong deontological basis—that is, many actions are condemned regardless of their consequences.

The Bible, the sacred writings of Judaism and Christianity, contains a series of books accepted as scripture by both religions. The Old Testament, written by Hebrews over a period of more than a thousand years, contains 39 books and is the Jewish Bible. The Old Testament has three main sections, call the Law (the first five books, called the Torah by Jews), the Prophets, and the Writings. Christians generally accept the Old Testament, but add a second part, called the New Testament, containing 27 more books (the first four are called the Gospels), telling of Jesus Christ and other Christian leaders. The Roman Catholic and Eastern Orthodox Bibles have 73 books—46 in the Old Testament and 27 in the New. While they share much in common, each church uses the Bible somewhat differently.

Perhaps the core of the ethical teachings of the Judeo-Christian religious heritage is the Ten Commandments, which according to Exodus 20:2–17 of the Old Testament were received by Moses from God on Mt. Sinai. Whereas the first four commandments deal with man's relationship with God, the final six contain the following interpersonal duties and prohibition:

- Honor thy father and mother.
- Thou shalt not kill.
- Thou shalt not commit adultery.
- Thou shalt not steal.

- Thou shalt not bear false witness against thy neighbor.
- Thou shalt not covet. (Some versions add "thy neighbor's wife" and "thy neighbor's house.")

These Commandments set forth absolute ethical duties and prohibit acts, irrespective of their consequences (a deontological standard), in a manner familiar to most Americans. These six statements urge people to respect the lives, marital partners, and property of their fellow citizens, as well as their own parents, and provide an expectation of honesty and humbleness in one's actions toward others. Regardless of their religion or lack thereof, most Americans would agree that these statements provide a very basic minimum standard of ethical behavior.

SOCIAL/ETHICAL ISSUES

By most accounts the Olympic Games have been tarnished by recent scandals. It started with allegations that the Salt Lake City Organizing Committee (SLOC) spent perhaps millions of dollars on gifts, services, trips, tuition, health care, and cash payments to the International Olympic Committee (IOC) members and their relatives during the site selection bidding for the 2002 Winter Olympics. Salt Lake City was finally selected. It had lost to Nagano, Japan, for the 1998 Winter Olympics. The United States Organizing Committee asked former U.S. Sen. George Mitchell to investigate the allegations. According to newspaper accounts, "the Mitchell Commission concluded Salt Lake's 'gift creep' was not unique, noting that the receipt of valuables by IOC members has become 'widespread, notorious, continuous, unchecked and ingrained in the way Olympic business is done.'" In fact, it was revealed that the Atlanta Organizing Committee had also engaged in similar practices when bidding for the 1996 Summer Olympic games. The Atlanta Organizing Committee had compiled extensive dossiers on each IOC member detailing the person's particular proclivities, including the types of gifts or inducements the member was likely to prefer. Some have argued the SLOC and Atlanta's activities were necessary in the multinational environment where gift giving and personal relationships are part of the culture. Others have argued that the activities violated the IOC's written rules and were blatantly unethical.

Analyze the situation. What are the ethical issues? How does the multinational environment complicate the issues? Examine these issues using virtue ethics, utilitarianism, and deontology. What would you have done if you were a member of SLOC? Why?

BUSINESS AND ITS COMMUNITY

Did you ever expect a corporation to have a conscience, when it has no soul to be damned, and no body to be kicked?

—THE LORD CHANCELLOR OF ENGLAND, EDWARD FIRST BARON THURLOW

We have set out some of the principal ethical theories by which individuals make decisions. But what about organizations—specifically business firms?

Do companies have ethical standards, duties, and beliefs? Can they? Should they? And if businesses do have such responsibilities, to whom are they owed?

Much has been written in the past 30 years concerning whether businesses do or ought to have ethical or moral duties. Noted economist Milton Friedman effectively advocated the negative position in a 1970 *New York Times* article titled "The Social Responsibility of Business Is to Increase Its Profits." Friedman maintained that the business manager's primary moral obligation was to serve the interests of the shareholders (an argument based in part on agency theory). The shareholders, Friedman said, were interested in return on investment, and therefore, although corporations should follow "the law and ethical custom," businesses and their managers should otherwise focus on increasing their profits.

In an earlier book, Friedman expressed his views on corporate social responsibility as follows:

> Few trends could so thoroughly undermine the very foundations of our free society as the acceptance by corporate officials of a social responsibility other than to make as much money for their stockholders as possible. This is a fundamentally subversive doctrine. If businessmen do have a social responsibility other than making maximum profits for stockholders, how are they to know what it is? Can self-selected private individuals decide what the social interest is? Can they decide how great a burden they are justified in placing on themselves or their stockholders to serve that social interest?[1]

One of the most forceful advocates for greater corporate social and ethical responsibilities is Professor Christopher Stone. His 1975 book *Where the Law Ends* asserts that law alone is inadequate to keep corporations "within socially desirable bounds" because of several factors. First, there is the "time-lag problem"—that is, laws are often passed "after the fact," or after some environmental or workplace tragedy has occurred. The responsible corporate officials may have had some previous knowledge or warning of the dangers inherent in the product or procedure but were not required by the law do anything more at that time. Therefore, preventive actions were not taken, and the unfortunate results occurred.

Second, Stone contends that a number of limitations connected with the making of law inhibit its usefulness. Such factors include the following: (1) Corporations take an active role in shaping the law, (2) A general lack of consensus exists as to the causes and effects of various actions, and (3) Many statutes are vague. (It is often necessary to modify or "water down" a proposed law in order to gain passage.) Furthermore, Stone argued, there are limitations associated with implementing the law as well. First, there are difficulties in fashioning a remedy in complex cases when, under our legal system, one party must win and the other lose. Second, there is the inconsistency of administrative agency enforcement due to vague and over-general statutes and the considerable influence regulated businesses exert on the very agencies set up to regulate these businesses.

[1] M. Friedman, *Capitalism and Freedom*, University of Chicago, 1962, p. 134.

Stone suggests that rather than force society to react to corporate actions after the fact and punish firms or individuals for violations of law, businesses should make fundamental changes in the way they receive and process information and make decisions. Stone proposes the following:

> The society shall have to locate certain specific and critical organizational variables and, where feasible, reach into the corporation to arrange them as it itself deems appropriate. In other words, if we can first clarify what ideal internal configurations of authority and information flow would best ameliorate the problem of, say, corporate pollution . . . the society might then consider programs aimed at mandating such ideal internal configurations directly.
>
> Thus, what I have in mind is a legal system that, in dealing with corporations, moves toward an increasingly direct focus on the *process of corporate decision making*, at least as a supplement to the traditional strategies that largely await upon the corporate acts. Instead of treating the corporation's inner process as a "black box," to be influenced only indirectly through threats laid about its environment like traps, we need more straightforward "intrusions" into the corporation's decision structure and process than society has yet undertaken.[2]

If these changes are adopted, Stone believes that companies will more likely make decisions based not only on the profit motive (the "bottom line"), but also on the effect decisions have on the community and society.

STAKEHOLDER THEORY

One method of assessing and analyzing the potential responsibilities and duties of a business is to apply the concept of **stakeholders**. In recent years, several influential business analysts have argued that each business firm has many groups or individuals, called stakeholders, who can affect or are affected by the actions of the business. This framework obviously considers a set of business relationships more encompassing than merely that between the firm and its owners—the word *stakeholder* is much broader than *shareholder*. Figure 7.1 depicts one example of the firm and the possible relationships of its stakeholders.

stakeholder: Groups or individuals who can affect or are affected by the actions of a business.

If a company accepts the stakeholder theory, it needs to devote considerable thought and energy to managing these stakeholder relationships in the most beneficial way possible. As Figure 7.1 shows, many of the stakeholders do not actually participate in the profits and losses of the business, but affect and are affected by the business in other ways. Therefore, stakeholder analysis necessarily involves consideration of corporate social and ethical duties, as well as political, competitive, and economic factors.

Stakeholder theory has found its way into law by those states that enacted Corporate Constituency Statutes. These statutes have been adopted by over one-half of the states. They require corporate decision makers to take into account the impact their decisions have on nonshareholder constituents.

[2] C. Stone, *Where the Law Ends*, Harper and Row, 1975, pp. 120–121.

Figure 7.1 *Model of Stakeholder Relationships*

Source: Based on the work of E. R. Freeman, M. E. Porter, G. Steiner, J. Steiner, and others.

SOCIAL CONTRACT THEORY

Somewhat related to stakeholder theory is social contract theory. The idea of a social contract is originally found in the works of Thomas Hobbes, the British philosopher, writing in the 17th century. Hobbes argued that morality does not depend on human nature; rather it is a practical solution for selfish individuals who want to live in a peaceful, social order. Hobbes looked at a fictitious "state of nature" or a time before humans were organized into communities. If individuals were taken back to this time, what would life be like? For Hobbes, the answer was not hopeful, and he states in *Leviathon* that in a state of nature "the life of man [is] solitary, poor, nasty, brutish, and short." Hobbes went on to argue that because of this state of nature individuals would agree to a powerful government, with laws and police. John Locke was also a social contract theorist. Using the same method, Locke arrived at a different conclusion. For Locke, humans were benevolent and kind. He believed the state of nature to be one of "perfect freedom to order their actions and dispose of their possessions and persons as they think fit, within the bounds of the law of nature, without asking leave or depending on the will of any other man." Locke, of course, argued for a limited government. Whereas these writers were concerned with the legitimacy of government, modern social contract theorists, Thomas Dunfee and Thomas Donaldson, have taken social contract theory into the business ethics arena.

Dunfee and Donaldson argue that a social contract between society and business does exist in the United States and in much of the industrialized world. That social contract, though unwritten and unspoken, requires that management recognize stakeholder interests. Donaldson has applied social contract theory to international business and argues that part of this social contract requires managers to "show concern for [their] employee's interests and undertake only actions that respect the bounds of rights and justice, for this is how society frames the legitimacy of the organization [they manage]." Under this theory, the international firm has three obligations: (1) to enhance the long term welfare of employees and consumers; (2) to minimize the drawbacks of industrialization; and (3) to operate in a way that acknowledges minimum standards of justice and human rights. Further, as the following article indicates, some jurors are using the legal system to enforce the unwritten social contract.

Jurors Vent Outrage at Industry

Verdicts Against Tobacco, Gun Firms Stake Out New Legal Territory

Tony Vaccaro thought it was time for "the little people" to send a message—the "average citizens," as he put it, "who usually don't have a voice."

The message was this: Tobacco companies have spent decades deceiving the public about the effects of their cigarettes, and they should be made to pay for it.

But the message wasn't just from Vaccaro, a 28-year-old financial services worker in San Francisco. It was the verdict of a 12-person jury on which he served in February. Its $51 million judgment against Philip Morris—one of four verdicts against tobacco since last summer—was part of a populist trend of jurors around the country exacting punishment on disfavored industries.

Tobacco hasn't been the only business newly buffeted by this wave of juror outrage. In February, for the first time, a jury decided to hold gun manufacturers responsible for the criminal use of their products. Again, some jurors said the industry had it coming.

Lawsuits condemning cigarettes and guns are nothing new. Advocacy groups have campaigned for years against the tobacco and firearms industries, using the courts as a weapon. What is new is that juries are listening.

These verdicts coincide with a national trend of juries assessing harsher and harsher damages against corporate defendants, such as the $4.9 billion verdict returned last month against General Motors Corp. for six people whose car exploded—and reduced on appeal last week to about $1 billion. But they add a new element.

Jurors in these cases were staking out new territory in American law, asserting their interest in issues broader than the behavior of a single corporate defendant. Unlike past product liability verdicts, such as those against the Ford Pinto or the Dalkon shield, where a single company was targeted, juries are focusing on broad social problems—smoking-related disease, gun violence—that traditionally have been addressed through legislation.

"Jurors are ready to believe that they are the public avengers. Because the governor won't do it, the state legislature won't do it, the jurors are the only ones who will do it," said Victor Schwartz, a liability law expert who opposes the trend.

The recent verdicts are part of a pattern of juror activism across the country that also includes so-called juror nullification, in which juries have let criminal defendants go free, despite the weight of the evidence against them, in protest of particular laws. In the current product liability disputes, jurors say their verdicts are based on the evidence in the case. But, as with nullification, they also appear to be giving freer rein to their own sense of justice.

"There is a lot of anger out there," said Stanford University law professor Robert Rabin, "and it's getting translated into jury verdicts."

This increased willingness to find against the tobacco and gun industries has released a torrent of new litigation and could have wide repercussions for other businesses and people who claim they have been hurt by their products. Smokers and their families have filed hundreds of individual lawsuits across the country; numerous class action efforts are also pending. And since the groundbreaking Brooklyn gun verdict in February, the firearms industry has faced an onslaught of lawsuits. A total of 27 cities and the NAACP are now suing firearms companies.

"All these cases have a snowball effect," Rabin added, "as potential jurors read . . . about an industry that appears to have been involved in some coverup and then gets nailed. They feel empowered to act likewise."

Some lawyers argue that these verdicts poach on the government's role in regulating tobacco and guns, determining, for example, what constitutes deceptive cigarette advertising or the negligent marketing of firearms.

This trend of jury verdicts—in essence, steering national policy on tobacco and guns—raises important questions. Can a single corporate defendant in a court case receive a fair trial if the jury seeks to punish an entire industry? Can a scattered set of verdicts add up to a coherent national policy? And if this tendency continues, what other unpopular industries might feel themselves targeted by jurors: Health maintenance organizations? The entertainment industry? The media?

Expanding Public Scorn

It may have been inevitable that public scorn for cigarette and gun manufacturers ultimately would find its way into the jury box. A new *Washington Post* survey found that 59 percent of Americans think the tobacco industry has not behaved responsibly in selling its products and about half feel that way about gun manufacturers. But at the same time, the public has watched state legislatures and Congress struggle with how to regulate these controversial but legal industries.

Last year a proposed settlement that would have further regulated the sale of cigarettes collapsed in Congress after the tobacco companies withdrew their support and lobbied hard against it. (A subsequent settlement between the states and companies involved smaller sums and little regulation.)

And despite a series of high-profile shootings that have strengthened public support for gun control, Congress remains at an impasse. Competing Senate and House versions of a juvenile justice bill—one with modest gun control measures, one with none—are expected to be debated in conference when Congress returns from its recess.

The legislative vacuum on tobacco and guns is increasingly being filled by litigation brought by individuals, organizations, states, and the federal government. And that litigation is increasingly finding sympathetic juries.

"In the jury room generally, it is now seen as very acceptable to take a stand against an industry," said David S. Davis, senior vice president of the national jury research firm DecisionQuest. "It used to be that jurors who spoke about individual responsibility would get the applause."

The *Post* poll shows that a majority of those questioned—55 percent—are suspicious of jurors' taking on a more important role in punishing companies for their legal but dangerous products.

But a substantial minority—35 percent—believe it's a good thing if juries take the lead against harmful products when legislatures have failed to act.

Experts found this percentage significant, given that juries traditionally have confined themselves to deciding the facts of a single case. They also noted the potential importance of this minority, because one or two forceful opinions on a jury can affect the outcome of a case.

"The growing body of evidence suggests some jurors are turning mass tort litigation into a vehicle for the moral condemnation of corporate behavior thought to be irresponsible or malevolent," said University of Georgia law professor Richard Nagareda.

Jurors' New Confidence

To be sure, some of the recent cigarette and gun liability lawsuits have ended in the industries' favor, including a verdict against the family of a long-time smoker in Baton Rouge, La., last month. But even in cases where the industry ultimately wins, juries are conscious of appearing pro-tobacco. "People said we weren't sending the right message," said Rodney Marchand, foreman of a Memphis jury that returned verdicts for three cigarette companies in May. "They said we are 'letting the tobacco companies off.'"

This attitude on the part of jurors is a recent development. In four decades of litigation by smokers and their survivors against cigarette companies, there were only two verdicts ordering companies to pay damages to smokers before last summer. The earliest victory for a smoker came in 1988, when a divided jury said Liggett Group was responsible for the death of Rose Cipollone, a New Jersey woman who smoked Chesterfields and died of lung cancer in 1984.

But the second thoughts of the Cipollone jurors were revealing. Many of them told reporters at the time that they were worried that they had done the wrong thing. Some cried about having given in to more dominant jurors. Not until 1996 did a jury again decide in favor of a smoker, and this verdict, like the Cipollone case, was overturned.

Today, after years of allegations of the industry manipulating nicotine levels and concealing the health risks associated with smoking, jurors express no such tentativeness. In recent interviews, juror after juror spoke confidently about the desire to punish the industry, citing its alleged history of misbehaviors and its perceived ability to use large profits to beat the system.

"It was the whole lay of the land," said April Dewees, a 30-year old schoolteacher on the Portland, Ore., jury that awarded a record $80 million to the family of a man who used to smoke three packs of Marlboros a day. "All the ways they played down the dangers of it. Someone said to me afterward, 'Well, all businesses lie.' Well, they shouldn't lie. There are repercussions. They profited from their misrepresentations. They did need to be punished."

John Bowman, a 53-year-old businessman who was on a 1998 Jacksonville, Fla., jury that ordered Brown & Williamson to pay $41 million for the death of a Lucky Strike smoker, including the first punitive damages ever in such a case, said that verdict was an indictment of the whole industry: "We felt that all tobacco products are dangerous." Fellow juror Nicole Boyer, 36, a homemaker, said she believed "all the companies were in on it together, trying to get people hooked on nicotine."

Tony Vaccaro, of the San Francisco jury, added, "We thought it was important to send a message because of the stonewalling they had done for all those decades."

Gary Doski, a 49-year-old electronics technician and the foreman on the 1998 Jacksonville jury, summed up the contrast between his jury and the 1988 Cipollone panel: "Afterward, the lawyers were all surprised at how happy all of us seemed."

Discord on Gun Verdict

In contrast, the watershed verdict in February against gun makers was marked by the kind of discord and angst that the Cipollone jurors felt a decade ago. At one point, the Brooklyn jurors sent the judge a note asking for help: "We are all very upset. We are starting to fight. We cannot reach a decision. . . . Please, please give us more direction!"

One juror expressed some reservations, saying a verdict against the gun manufacturers would "open the floodgate of lawsuits across the country." Other jurors wept. At one point, a note pleaded, "One of the jurors doesn't feel well. Is there any way we can get some Pepto Bismol?'

The Brooklyn jury's discomfort reflected a broader public ambivalence. The *Post* poll found that 70 percent of those questioned said they disapproved of holding gun manufacturers responsible for shooting deaths and other illegal uses of their weapons. But the respondents were evenly divided—46 percent to 45 percent—on the question of whether gun manufacturers have behaved irresponsibly or responsibly in advertising and selling their products.

Even this ambivalence represents a change in the social and legal contest of firearms violence. Shooting victims have been suing gun manufacturers for putting the weapons on the streets for years. But no such lawsuit had ever reached trial until last year when a jury decided, also in a Brooklyn case, in favor of a gun company after about six hours of deliberation.

This year's Brooklyn jury deliberated for six days before ultimately deciding to hold 15 manufacturers responsible for the negligent marketing of handguns in three of the seven shootings covered by the lawsuits. But they awarded damages only in one of the cases, to 19-year-old Steven Fox of Queens, who survived a bullet to the brain.

"The Rubicon has been crossed," said Elisa Barnes, a lawyer for the victims.

A Corrective or Bad Policy?

Some legal experts argue that juries' increased willingness to take on controversial industries is a necessary, democratic corrective to unchecked corporate power.

"What is happening now is that jurors are more angry and aware," said John Banzhaf, a George Washington University law professor active in anti-tobacco litigation. "For years, tobacco companies could say addiction and deaths weren't their responsibility. But the social climate has changed. And this is why we have juries."

"Jurors feel empowered within the system and against an industry that has flagrantly not done the right thing," added Stephanie Hartley, a Florida lawyer who represents smokers.

But defense lawyers argue that juries are unsuited to the broader role they are beginning to embrace. They say jurors who are eager to use their position to send a message to an industry may find it hard to render a fair verdict on whether a specific defendant caused a single victim's cancer or other injury.

Critics also point out the uneven policy likely to result from a patchwork of verdicts that inevitably depend on the predilections of the jurors and the quality of the case mounted by each side's attorneys. Unlike legislators, who typically hold hearings on a subject and seek out information from a multitude of competing interests, jurors are told only what the two sides of a case want them to know.

"Juries aren't equipped to decide social policy," said Anne Kimball, a Chicago lawyer who represented gun makers in the recent Brooklyn case.

"To the extent that we give a jury the power to effectively legislate . . . we are doing damage to the underlying principles of our government."

Meanwhile, industry analysts worry that the negative revelations from the recent cases will only produce more lawsuits, and say unpopular industries must change the way they handle litigation. Corporate defense lawyers say they are now warier about letting cases get to trial, more careful in choosing jurors and, if a trial is inevitable, intent on communicating their own message about the limits of a company's responsibility.

And those on both sides of the debate wonder what industries might be next. Some believe they already have seen signs of incipient jury backlash against media excesses in a verdict against the "Jenny Jones Show" in May.

The talk show was on trial over a killing that arose from a 1995 episode called "Secret Same-Sex Crushes." On the program, Scott Amedure told his friend Jonathan Schmitz that he had a crush on him; three days later, Schmitz gunned down Amedure. The victim's family lodged a wrongful death suit against the show for "ambushing" Schmitz with news of the crush. The jury deliberated about six hours before finding against the "Jenny Jones Show" and awarding the Amedure family $25 million in damages.

Geoffrey Fieger, the lawyer for the victim's family, said the jury was sending a message to the talk show industry: "That type of human exploitation needs to be corralled."

"In the future, defendants that make products that create perceived social costs could all be at risk," said lawyer Schwartz, suggesting as possibilities chemical manufacturers, pharmaceutical companies, and liquor producers. "I have never bought the idea that tobacco is unique. I say: No way. This is the beginning."

"Jurors Vent Outrage at Industry; Verdicts Against Tobacco, Gun Firms Stake Out New Legal Territory" by Joan Biskupic, *The Washington Post*, August 30, 1999, p. A01.

MEDIATING INSTITUTIONS

In critiquing both social contract and stakeholder theories, questions have been raised about whether large business institutions are themselves responsible for unethical behavior. Evolutionary psychologists have argued that the human brain is cognitively still primarily a hunter-gatherer brain. This implies that humans have a limited ability to interact in large groups. While these psychologists opine that the optimal size of the groups for effective interaction ranges from 30 to 150, it is clear that most businesses far exceed these numbers. In utilizing some of this research, Tim Fort has argued that businesses need to create mediating institutions if they want their employees to exhibit ethical behavior. He explains,

> mediating institutions are communities which socialize their members. "Mediating" between the individual and society as a whole, they provide a community. They require individuals to grasp their responsibilities to others, at least within their group, so that a person's very identity is developed. Mediating institutions teach individuals that they are not autonomous beings accountable only to their own wants and desires. Instead, a series of relationships comprise personhood and therefore human beings obtain their identity by becoming accountable for their relationships. In short, mediating institutions teach us that we are relational, not autonomous beings. Because we are relational beings, our very "self" is dependent upon ethical responsibilities. In

mediating institutions, we develop bonds of affection that motivate individuals to treat others well.[3]

Stakeholder theory, social contract theory, and mediating institutions theory all revolve around the assumption that business can self-regulate. Recently, there has been a distrust of self-regulation and a move to use the criminal law system to reward and punish those businesses that behave unethically.

FEDERAL SENTENCING GUIDELINES

The U.S. Federal Sentencing Guidelines resulted from public frustration with corporate criminal conduct in the 1980s. There was a belief that corporations were not being adequately punished for the crimes they committed. This belief was borne out when statistics revealed that "[b]etween 1984 and 1987, only 41 publicly-traded firms were prosecuted for federal crimes nationwide. The mean fine imposed on the 288 corporations sentenced by federal courts during this period was only $48,164."[4] Since corporate sentencing was the responsibility of the court system, there was a public consensus that stiffer penalties would reduce corporate crime. Therefore, the drafting of sentencing guidelines for organizations began in 1986 and after several proposals, these guidelines became effective November 1, 1991. The guidelines were amended in 1997. The amendments provided full restitution for victims of corporate crime and the felony assessments increased.

There are four underlying principles to the guidelines. The first is that victims of corporate crime should be "made whole" or totally reimbursed. Second, businesses that are primarily criminal enterprises should be put out of business. Third, the fines for normal businesses should be based on the organization's culpability and high enough to ensure that the corporation does not ultimately profit. Fourth, options should be pursued that ensure continued and future compliance. These objectives are achieved by providing for compulsory sentencing for corporations engaged in illegal activity. Corporations can receive "bonus points," which can offset the penalties, if they have developed an ethics training program. Also, courts can order a company to institute ethics officers or boards. An example of how courts use the federal sentencing guidelines can be found in the next case, *In re Caremark*.

IN RE CAREMARK INTERNATIONAL, INC. DERIVATIVE LITIGATION

698 A.2d 959; 1996 Del. Ch. LEXIS 125

FACTS

Caremark, a large health-care provider, was involved in a series of health-care provider and referral programs. In 1989 the company had issued a "Guide to Contractual Relations" that set out policies governing contracts between the company and physicians and hospitals. All the programs were reviewed and approved by

[3] Timothy L. Fort, "The Corporation as Mediating Institution: An Efficacious Synthesis of Stakeholder Theory and Corporate Constituency Statutes," 73 *Notre Dame Law Review* 173, 175 (1997).
[4] Richard S. Gruner, "Towards an Organizational Jurisprudence: Transforming Corporate Criminal Law Through Federal Sentencing Reform," 36 *Arizona Law Review*, 407, *3, (1994).

both Caremark's attorneys and accountants, although there was evidence that indicated Caremark knew the programs were questionable. In 1991 the federal government began investigating Caremark's practices to determine if they violated the Anti-Referral Payments Law, which prohibits paying physicians and hospitals for referrals of Medicare or Medicaid patients. As a result of the investigation, in 1991, Caremark's predecessor announced that it would no longer pay management fees to physicians and hospitals. It also revised its policies and required a regional president to approve all contracts between Caremark and physicians. In 1993, Caremark's Audit & Ethics Committee compiled a new employee ethics handbook that "expressly prohibit[ed] payments in exchange for referrals and requir[ed] employees to report all illegal conduct to a toll free confidential ethics hotline." Caremark's president also sent out a letter reiterating the policies and employees were required to attend training sessions on the ethics handbook. Even with all this and after an intensive investigation, a federal grand jury issued a 47-page indictment against the company, two officers, a sales employee, and a physician. In the indictment, it was alleged that the doctor received $1.1 million, in the guise of research grants or consulting agreements, to induce him to distribute a human growth hormone drug marketed by Caremark. This allegation and others ultimately resulted in a plea agreement. Caremark agreed "to plead guilty to two counts of mail fraud, . . . pay $29 million in criminal fines, $129.9 million relating to civil claims, $3.5 million for alleged violations of the Controlled Substances Act, and $2 million, in the form of a donation, to a grant program set up by the Ryan White Comprehensive AIDS Resources Emergency Act." The plea agreement also "included several provisions in a 'Corporate Integrity Agreement' designed to enhance future compliance with law."

Several shareholder derivative actions were filed alleging "Caremark's directors breached their duty of care by failing to adequately supervise the conduct of Caremark employees, or institute corrective measures, thereby exposing Caremark to fines and liability." To resolve the consolidated derivative actions, Caremark agreed, among other things, to establish a new Compliance and Corporate Ethics Committee. This committee would contain four directors, two of whom would be non-management directors. The committee would report to the board semiannually and be responsible for monitoring compliance with anti-referral laws.

DECISION

Judge Allen wrote the opinion of the court:

The only question for the court in approving a proposed settlement in a shareholder derivative action is whether the proposal is fair and reasonable. Since the directors in this case were not involved in self-dealing or other breaches of loyalty issues, the good faith rule is applicable. Under general corporate law directors have an obligation to make "a good faith effort to advance corporate interest." Further, in looking at the federal Organizational Sentencing Guidelines, the court notes that the "Guidelines offer powerful incentives for corporations today to have in place compliance programs to detect violations of law, promptly to report violations to appropriate public officials when discovered, and to take prompt, voluntary remedial efforts." Today, a good faith effort requires that the board take into account the development of the federal Organizational Sentencing Guidelines "and the enhanced penalties and the opportunities for reduced sanctions that it offers." This means that directors need to assure "themselves that information and reporting systems exist in the organization that are reasonably designed to provide to senior management and to the board itself timely, accurate information sufficient to allow management and the board, each within its scope, to reach informed judgments concerning both the corporation's compliance with law and its business performance." With this in mind, the court finds the proposed settlement is fair and reasonable and the derivative claims are dismissed.

CASE QUESTIONS

1. What did Caremark do that resulted in such large penalties?
2. How did the court use the criminal Organizational Sentencing Guidelines in this civil action?
3. Do you agree that the settlement was fair and reasonable or should the directors have suffered additional penalties?

Since the enactment of the Federal Sentencing Guidelines, many companies have added ethics and compliance programs. Arthur Andersen's Ethics and Responsible Business Practices Group conducted a two-year study aimed at identifying and measuring the effects that such ethics/compliance management programs have on the ethical behavior of employees. As seen in the following press release, the effect depends very heavily on the employees' perceptions about management's motivation in establishing the program.

STUDY FIRST TO IDENTIFY AND MEASURE THE EFFECT ETHICS/COMPLIANCE MANAGEMENT PROGRAMS HAVE ON ETHICAL BEHAVIOR

Findings show certain ethics/compliance programs can devastate an organization.

A survey of thousands of randomly chosen employees from six Fortune 1000 firms revealed that the firms' ethics/compliance programs may not be creating ethical companies.

The study looked at the overall ethical culture of the firms, at the specific characteristics of the firms' ethics/compliance programs, and at the orientation of the programs. Employees were asked to anonymously respond to a series of questions. The questions included the types of unethical behavior observed, like padding expense accounts, stealing, lying, and giving kickbacks. The study also asked questions about the employees' perceptions of the company's programs, including ethics awareness, likeliness to report violations, and employee commitment to the organization. A successful program was defined as one where the employees were willing to seek advice and report unethical behavior, where employees exhibited greater commitment to the company, and where employees exhibited better decision making.

The study found that firms emphasizing self-interest were associated with unethical behavior while firms emphasizing fair treatment of employees, ethical leadership, open talk about ethics, and a greater willingness of employees to deliver bad news exhibited more ethical behavior.

The study looked at the orientation of the ethics/compliance programs and used the following categorizations: (1) compliance-based, mainly aimed at preventing, identifying, and punishing unethical or illegal behavior; (2) value-based, emphasizing organizational values and increasing employee commitment to ethical goals and conduct; (3) external stakeholder–based, aimed at improving the company's external image; and (4) protecting top management–based, aimed at protecting upper management. The study found that value-based programs were much more likely to result in ethical behavior than the other three orientations. The worst orientation was protecting top management in which the employees believed the compliance programs were simply used by top management to avoid blame for corporate wrongdoing.

In a news release, Barbara Ley Toffler, one of the authors of the study stated, "A company with a culture where leadership is serious about ethics, where employees feel fairly treated, and where the culture values and rewards ethical behavior, is far less likely to encounter ethics/compliance problems than a company whose culture demands unthinking obedience to authority, focuses solely on punishing bad behavior, and whose leadership gives only lip-service to ethics. The worst situation is to have workers believe that ethics guidelines exist primarily to protect management from blame. This breeds cynicism and, our study shows, actually promotes unethical behavior. In fact, it is worse than having no program at all." Toffler adds, "Employees are very quick to note when management practices what they preach and when they do not. In the end, employees' perception of fair treatment emerged as a powerful factor linked to the success of an ethics/compliance program." The authors of the study also suggest that "When employees feel that they are treated unfairly, they may try to 'balance the scales of justice' by engaging in unethical behaviors such as stealing from the organization."

Companies annually spend millions of dollars on their ethics/compliance programs. This does not include the money spent on legal fees associated with responding to accusations of legal and ethical wrongdoing. Many of these companies have adopted ethics/compliance programs because of the US Sentencing Commission requirements. Companies usually design their programs around the US Sentencing Guidelines. These programs often contain written codes of conduct, ethics officers, ethics telephone hotlines, and strict punishment for violators. This study found that these types of programs did not produce ethical behavior.

As the figure below suggests, the most important factor in reducing unethical conduct by employees was consistency between the words found in corporate policies and in observed actual corporate action. This was followed by rewarding ethical behavior, ethical leadership, punishing unethical behavior, open discussion of ethics, formal mechanisims for reporting unethical behavior, and code of conduct familiarity.

In their recommendations for policy makers, the authors of the study argue that the US Sentencing Commission currently places more emphasis on detection and punishment than on rewards, and totally ignores the importance of the fair distribution of rewards. They also note that the Sentencing Commission ignores the importance of top management leadership and involvement. This approach to encouraging ethical organizations does not appear to result in greater ethical behavior among employees. Rather, the entire company culture must incorporate and act upon ethical principles before programs can be judged successful.

Relative importance of factors on reducing unethical conduct

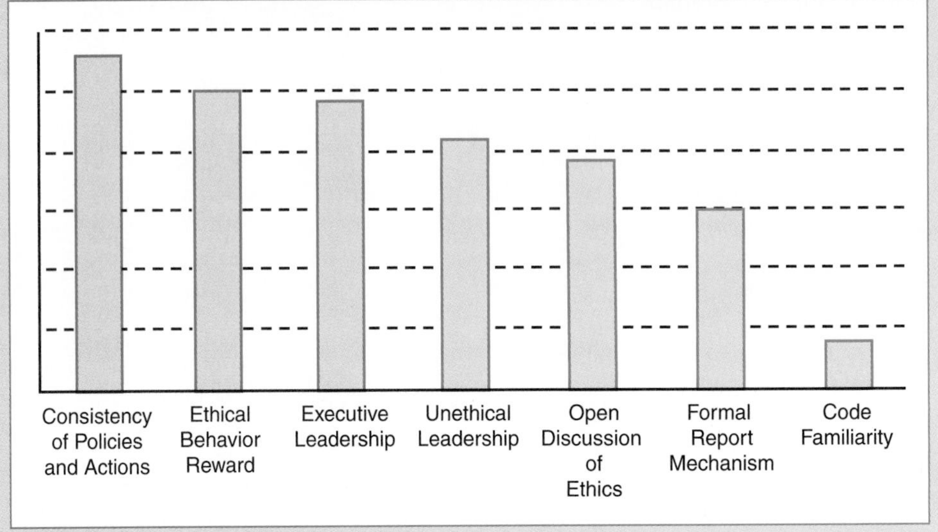

Article compiled using information found in Trevino, L. K., Weaver, G. R., Gibson, D. G. & Toffler, B. L., "Managing Ethics and Legal Compliance: What Works and What Hurts," 41(2) *California Management Review*, 1999, pp. 131–151 and Melissa S. Baucus and Caryn L. Beck-Dudley, "Designing Ethical Organizations," International Association for Business and Society conference, March 2000.

CONTEMPORARY ISSUES INVOLVING BUSINESS ETHICS

WHISTLE-BLOWERS

Shortly before the fateful launch of the Challenger space shuttle mission in 1986, several engineers at Morton Thiokol Co. became concerned about the durability of the O rings that sealed off dangerous hot gases from the oxygen tanks on the rocket propulsion system. These experts worried that if the shuttle was launched when temperatures were below a certain level, the rings could fail and the rockets explode. The engineers expressed their concerns to their supervisors. However, the shuttle program was behind schedule, public support for the high costs of the space program appeared to be waning, and the managers did not want Morton Thiokol to be labeled as the company that slowed down the shuttle program.

Nevertheless, the concerns were passed along to NASA, and certain meetings were convened, but there was tremendous pressure to go ahead with the launch. After all, no shuttle launch had ever resulted in an explosion, and the concerns seemed far-fetched. Unfortunately, the O Rings did fail, the rocket exploded, and the seven-member crew, including the first teacher in space, was killed.

Difficult situations arise on the job—including worker safety, waste disposal, hiring and firing employees, and financial assessment—for which difficult decisions need to be made. In a perfect world, employers would expect all employees who saw something that needed correcting either to take the necessary actions themselves or to bring it to the attention of their supervisors. This course of action would be in the best interests of the corporation, and the employees would be praised and rewarded for such conscientious and ethically proper deeds.

However, in the real world, often the employee who "blows the whistle" concerning some improper or illegal activity (such as reporting a problem to authorities) is penalized rather than praised for the action. When the **whistle-blower** reports that supplies are consistently missing from the stockroom, or that chemicals are being dumped into a nearby river, or that safety equipment has been removed from machines, undoubtedly another employee or manager stands to be reprimanded or fired if the allegations are true. If the problem is serious and pervasive, many people may be involved, some of whom might be receiving significant financial rewards from the scheme. The whistle-blower's credibility will be attacked by many powerful forces, and he or she may end up being fired as the result of performing an ethical act intended to benefit the business.

whistle-blower: One who reveals something covert or informs authorities about some illegal or unethical business actions.

Ernest Fitzgerald, an Air Force employee, discovered billions of dollars in excess charges and overruns billed to the federal government by Lockheed Corporation in 1968. But after he complained, he was fired. George Collier, a regional manager for MCA, noticed that several executives of the entertainment company were ordering big shipments of free records for people not entitled to them. He notified his supervisor three times of this possible kickback scheme, but instead of receiving a reward, he was fired, according to a lawsuit he has filed against the company.

IN CONSULTATION

Marvin Manager has a problem. He recently became the supervising manager for one of ABC's production facilities in Ameritown, a small community. The ABC facility is the primary employer. Almost all Ameritown residents either work for ABC or work for businesses that depend on the presence of ABC. Connie Claimant works at the Ameritown facility on the factory floor. She recently called Marvin, alleging widespread sexual harassment in Ameritown. She described a pyramid of mistreatment of female employees that included everyone from floor supervisors to the highest level managers. Connie told Marvin that if he does not investigate and ultimately fire all of the wrongdoers, she will go to the press.

Marvin's investigation revealed that Connie's complaints were justified. His dilemma, however, is more complicated than it appears. If he fires all of the wrongdoers, he will have to recommend that the Ameritown facility close. If the facility closes, almost everyone in Ameritown will suffer great financial distress, including those who are completely innocent of sexual harassment. If he instead fires Connie, he thinks that the complaint will lose its credibility and that the press will assume that Connie is merely a disgruntled former worker. He is also concerned that by threatening to go to the press, Connie's actual motive is fame and fortune. He thinks that her behavior suggests that she is not loyal to ABC and does not have the best interest of the company as a whole in mind.

Marvin wants to know whether he can fire Connie without creating liability for ABC and/or himself. He contacts Laura Lawyer, in-house counsel, to seek her advice on how he should navigate this dilemma. Here is their conversation.

Marvin:

1. Can I fire Connie to eliminate the threat she presents to ABC and our presence in Ameritown if she "blows the whistle"?
2. Can I fine Connie for exhibiting a lack of loyalty to ABC?
3. Isn't a threat of blowing the whistle on ABC by definition a lack of loyalty?

Laura:

1. It depends. Some federal and state laws prevent employers from firing whistle-blowers. Some types of whistle-blowers receive no protection under state or federal law. The answer lies in the type of behavior that they want to report.
2. On the surface, "lack of loyalty" is a legitimate reason for terminating a employee—so long as that is the true reason.
3. Even if whistle-blowing may reflect mixed loyalties, state and federal law may not allow you as the employer to use her threats as a basis for terminating her employment. **Let me review the applicable law to see which path presents the least liability. I'll get back to you.**

FROM THE DESK OF

Laura Lawyer

To: Marvin Manager

Re: Treatment of Whistle-Blowers

Dear Marvin:

Whistle-blowers are employees who report or threaten to report illegal or unethical company behavior. Some states have statutes that protect employees who blow the whistle on employers that engage in illegal activity. In these states, if an employer fires a whistle-blower, the employee can sue for "wrongful discharge" and recover damages along with reinstatement of his or her employment. Some federal statutes also protect whistle-blowers. For example, if an employee reports a safety violation to the Occupational Safety and Health Agency, the federal statute insulates that employee from any sort of retaliation.[1] Some federal statutes even offer rewards to whistle-blowers who report activity that leads to government recovery of illegally obtained money.[2] The rationale behind whistle-blower protection is to encourage legal compliance.

You asked if you can fire Connie for showing a lack of loyalty. In general, behavior that demonstrates a lack of loyalty is good cause for a termination. If the basis for assuming a lack of loyalty, however, is that the employee is a whistle-blower, the legal analysis changes because whistle-blowers receive the extra protection described previously. Please note that the law does not unilaterally protect all whistle-blowers, because some reports may truly be from disgruntled employees seeking to harass the employer. The courts want to protect legitimate whistle-blowers and yet retain an employer's ability to punish illegitimate whistle-blowers. In order to support a whistle-blower alleging wrongful discharge, the courts are leaning toward requiring a nexus between the whistle-blowing and the employee's termination. The courts try to strike a balance among enforcing the laws, protecting employees, and retaining an employer's right to manage its workforce.

If we try to anticipate how a court would strike that balance in this case, we would have to take into consideration several factors. First, your investigation substantiated Connie's complaint and revealed widespread mistreatment of female employees in Ameritown. On the other hand, Connie seeks to go to the press instead of the appropriate government agency, which may discredit her motives. We need to know more about Connie as an employee and determine if there is any evidence that she was attempting to obtain personal gain from blowing the whistle. If we can find no personal agenda, then terminating her is almost certainly related to her status as a whistle-blower, and we are much more likely to be liable under federal or state law.

I also appreciate your concern that the depth of Connie's allegation may result in closing our Ameritown facility. Although your concern for the people of Ameritown is admirable, the seriousness of the offenses occurring there is actually more likely to result in court protection for Connie—the court will probably want to encourage employees to report such widespread harassment. If the court allowed ABC to fire an employee who brought to light such troubling behavior, then some employees would never report such behavior again.

[1] See 29 U.S.C. § 660(c)(1988).

[2] See 31 U.S.C. §§ 3729–3733(1988).

Consider the following questions with regard to the treatment of whistle-blowers:

1. Studies reveal that even with the growing legal protection for whistle-blowers, many suffer demotions and ill health related to victimization. What can we do to encourage legitimate whistle-blowers to come forward when they face such risks?
2. What sort of policy could ABC put in place to eliminate Marvin's dilemma in the future?
3. Discuss the advantages and disadvantages of removing an employer's managerial discretion to terminate for a lack of loyalty when the lack of loyalty stems from an employee's report of illegal behavior.

EMPLOYEE PRIVACY

In an effort to more closely supervise and evaluate their employees, many companies use sophisticated technology to monitor the activities of their workers. The majority of large U.S. businesses now employ some type of drug-testing program, often before the employee is hired and sometimes on a random basis during employment. Other employers conduct searches of employee lockers or work areas, monitor employee phone calls, and videotape employees at work. One firm even installed special chairs, hooked up to computers to monitor employee wiggling while at their desks, under the belief that "wigglers aren't workers." An increasing number of firms are showing interest in off-the-job activities of workers as well, including smoking, drinking, and sexual and social activities.

In recent years there has been an explosion of the use of electronic mail and the Internet system, by which one can converse instantly with others around the world. Employers are showing concern for and more closely monitoring and controlling the amount of time these services are used by employees, as well as the content and purposes of the communications.

SWEATSHOPS

For many people the "sweatshop" image conjures up photographs taken in the United States in the early 1900s showing children in coal mines and women killed in factory fires because all the doors were locked to prevent them from leaving. As a result, laws were passed aimed at preventing sweatshops. In particular, the Fair Labor Standards Act was passed, which prohibited child labor in the United States and set a federal minimum wage. (This act is discussed in more detail in Chapter 20.) The sweatshop controversy publicly resurfaced in 1996 when it was discovered that clothes bearing the label of television personality Kathie Lee Gifford were made using child labor in overseas factories. Besides child labor, there were also allegations that Thailand makers of athletic shoes received 25 cents an hour for 18-hour days. Workers at a factory in the Dominican Republic claimed to make only 8 cents a hat for baseball caps bearing a Brown University logo.

To try to remedy the child labor problems, Ms. Gifford has established monitoring programs for factories that produce her clothing. Also, several universities, including Brown, Notre Dame, and Duke, have passed codes of conduct aimed at monitoring factories producing college-related merchandise, including apparel. These codes of conduct range from requests that factories comply with local law, to provisions that workers make a living wage, to requirements that the wages match or exceed local prevailing wages or that wages meet the basic needs of workers.

Not everyone agrees that sweatshops are necessarily bad. Some utilitarians argue that sweatshops are essential to move countries to the next level of development. The claim is that sweatshops are always the first step in development and that in many countries children are better off working than being sold into slavery. As the debate rages, it is important to note that the issue is not confined to developing countries. As the U.S. Department of Labor Brochure and "Getta Clue" campaign on pages 216–217 suggests, some U.S. manufacturers are also operating sweatshops.

APPLYING ETHICAL THEORIES

If we apply the ethical theories discussed earlier in the chapter to Connie, the In Consultation whistle-blower's dilemma, probably only the egoist can justify "looking the other way." An egoist would conclude that the personal consequences (which is all the egoist calculates) will likely be negative if the egoist reports improper actions by managers. Of course, a good argument might also be made that whistle-blowing may eventually reap rewards, promotions, and praise for the whistle-blower. In this way, the egoist serves his or her interests by exposing the improper activities.

Virtue ethics would ask whether the whistle-blower was being honest or was exercising integrity. The whistle-blower does not respect fellow employees who are being harassed by staying silent. The utilitarian, on the other hand, must consider whether reporting the violations or not will do the most good for the most people. If the good is happiness, it is possible that the greater good is not served by reporting the incidents since many workers and their families may be hurt. But in any situation involving significant legal liability, the harm to the business firm, other business partners, suppliers, consumers, and society will probably be considerable if the activity continues. Therefore, the greatest good will usually be served by honestly bringing the misconduct to the attention of proper authorities rather than protecting the parties involved.

Under Kant's universalization principle, it is necessary to ask whether the improper actions of certain employees should be the norm for everyone. If employees are harassing some employees for their own pleasure, the application of Kant's logic most likely will conclude that the actions are unethical. In addition, the duty of reporting improper or illegal actions is beneficial to all persons and would thus be morally proper.

Note that in all these scenarios, we have assumed that the whistle-blower, Connie, was correct in the allegations and that the motivation was a sincere and honest attempt to "do the right thing." But in some instances, this is not the case. As Professor Kenneth Walters has observed, "Whistleblowing is done under the guise of serving the public interest ahead of private interest, but while this lofty motive is clearly present in some cases, in other cases the

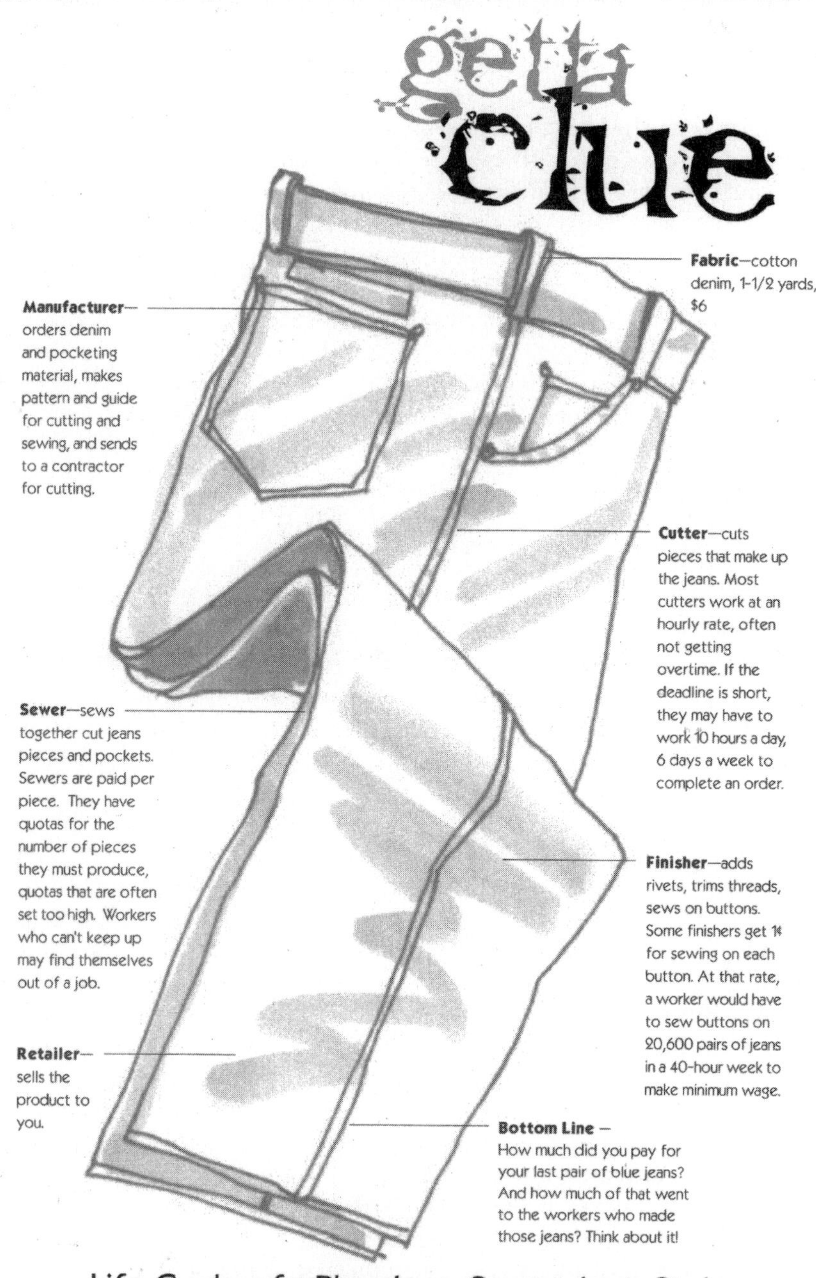

Life Cycle of a Blue Jean, Sweatshop Style

Clearly, not every garment manufacturer or contractor operates a sweatshop. Many follow the law and pay their employees legal wages, and some employers go well beyond the minimum requirements of the law. The situations above are representative of conditions found in a sweatshop. Costs of materials and labor and the production process vary from one manufacturer to the next.

"If I could convince you of one thing, it's that you **can** make a difference in this world. The decisions you make, the actions you take, how you shop can help put an end to sweatshops and make a difference in the lives of so many workers."

Alexis M. Herman
U.S. Secretary of Labor

Working Teen

Many employers in the garment industry want to do the right thing and obey the law, but some don't. Some employers operate sweatshops, where people work in unsafe environments without getting the money they have earned. Sweatshops give a whole new meaning to the phrase, "get a job." Garment workers—some of them younger than you—work to pay rent and put food on the table. They are usually paid for each piece they sew, and they don't always make minimum wage, let alone receive benefits like health insurance. For example, at 15¢ per jeans pocket, you would have to sew at least 275 pockets in 8 hours to make the minimum wage of $5.15 per hour. If you were only able to sew 200 pockets instead of 275, your hourly wage would be $3.75—less than the price of a movie ticket and less than the legal wage.

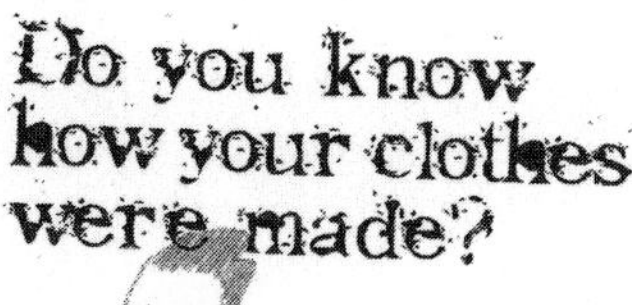

U.S. Department of Labor

Get Involved

Want to make a difference? You can help put sweatshops out of fashion and into the trash heap.

 You can ask questions where you shop about the clothes you are buying.

 You can ask where you shop whether they check on their garment manufacturers to make sure they're following the law.

 You can ask where you shop whether they support "No Sweat" clothing.

Drop into our No Sweat Website at www.dol.gov.

whistleblower is a publicity-seeking egomaniac who masquerades as one possessing superior moral instincts."[5]

Walters points out that in the past 25 years a number of laws have been enacted to give whistle-blowers legal protection from reprisals. Clauses in the Safe Drinking Water Act, the Toxic Substances Control Act, the Occupational Safety and Health Act, and the Clean Air Act contain such protection. In addition, there have been numerous lawsuits in which the employees challenged their terminations on the basis that the discharges violated public policy.

SUMMARY

In dealing with the problem of how to select and retain top quality employees, as well as hundreds of other issues arising every day in business, various ethical and social issues arise. At what point does a company owe its employees loyalty, trust, and responsibility? Is there a difference between what a firm can or should do to test and investigate prospective employees, as opposed to existing employees? Is there any duty to society as well as to the employees? Should a firm adopt an egoist approach (whatever is best for us) or incorporate utilitarianism (greatest good for the greatest number) or attempt to universalize the processes it undertakes? Should a business firm attempt to alter an individual's own beliefs to conform to the views of the management? These are all questions you will need to answer as you face the difficult choices inherent in any business career. The discussions in this chapter may give you some thoughts to consider when the time arrives for making decisions.

CHAPTER QUESTIONS

1. Explain the difference between individualism and communitarianism and give current examples of each.
2. What is the difference between virtues and values?
3. Discuss and compare the most well-known ethical theories, as explained in the text.
4. Compare the arguments of Milton Friedman and Christopher Stone regarding the role and duty of corporations toward society. Which argument is more persuasive to you? Explain.
5. What are some other issues you believe raise ethical dilemmas for business? In your own working experience, have you been put in a situation where you had to decide whether you should do something you did not believe was right? Describe.
6. Shoplifting is a very serious problem for retail store owners, with millions of dollars of merchandise stolen each year. Obviously, some shoplifters put clothing and other items under their clothes and then attempt to leave the store. Video cameras in every bathroom and dressing room would undoubt-

[5] Walters, "The Whistleblower and the Law," in Sethi and Falbe, *Business and Society*, Lexington Books, 1987, pp. 283–284.

edly reduce successful shoplifting. What ethical issues are raised by such action?

7. Have you, or your family or friends, encountered situations where a whistle-blower was, in Professor Walters' words, a "publicity-seeking egomaniac who masquerades as one possessing superior moral instincts." Explain. How often do you think this occurs?
8. Many employees face problems when balancing the demands of their work and their family. Suppose that a single parent works in an office where personal phone calls are prohibited. However, this person's eight-year-old daughter is home alone for three hours every day after school. This employee receives on average two phone calls per day from her daughter as problems arise—some days there are three or four calls, and some days one or none. If you are this person's supervisor and are aware of these calls, what would you do about it? Compare your response using different ethical theories.
9. There have been a number of lawsuits filed by former employees on the basis of libel and slander. These employees had been fired and later applied for another job, only to have their former employer provide unfavorable remarks about their performance. In response to hearing about these lawsuits, some companies refuse to disclose anything other than name and period of employment about former employees. Suppose you are a manager at the Ace Trucking Company, and you have fired a worker because he used drugs while driving and also attempted to pick up young girls for sexual purposes. Is it ethical for you to refrain from giving any of this information to another company who is thinking of hiring this person as a school bus driver? Discuss, applying different theories.
10. Do you agree that corporations are too large? How can a business create a mediating institution?

PRACTICAL EXERCISE

Albert Roberts was manager of environmental affairs for Bigtime Oil Co. The Environmental Protection Agency requires companies like Bigtime to keep various records regarding toxic wastes and discharges from facilities that may cause air and water pollution. Bigtime must also furnish the records to federal and local authorities upon request.

In May, Los Angeles environmental officials seized records from one of Bigtime's facilities. In June, Mr. Roberts' boss ordered him to remove and destroy certain environmental records from a different plant in another California location. Mr. Roberts refused to do so and ordered his staff not to participate in any such removal either. Mr. Roberts was also directed to make changes in certain internal environmental reports before they were given to the company Board of Directors, but he refused to do this as well. In August, Mr. Roberts was laid off, because, according to the company, he had "antagonized his colleagues and become an ineffective manager."

In another state, a year later, a different executive of Bigtime Oil sued the company, alleging that he was fired because he disclosed health and environmental problems associated with Bigtime products. The company denied his claim, stating that he was fired for using company assets to further his own private business.

Assuming that the claims of the fired managers were true, analyze and write a short paper discussing the ethical issues Bigtime is facing. What effect will firing the two managers have on (1) future practices concerning environmental recordkeeping, (2) environmental practices of the company, and (3) the personal ethical practices of all employees who learn of the situation? What would you do if you were now a manager of environmental affairs at a Bigtime facility and you discovered that someone in the company was improperly disposing of toxic waste? Use the ethical theories described in the chapter in reaching your conclusions.

FURTHER INFORMATION

www.ethics.ubc.ca/resources/business/
www.socialinvest.org/
www.dol.gov/dol/esa/public/nosweat/nosweat.htm

PART 2:
LEGAL ISSUES IN BUSINESS ORGANIZATIONS

CHAPTER 8

PRINCIPAL–AGENT RELATIONSHIPS AND PARTNERSHIPS

LEARNING OBJECTIVES

After you have read this chapter, you should be able to:

1. Describe the different types of agency relationships and the duties and liabilities of agents and principals.
2. List the characteristics of the various forms of business organizations.
3. Explain the concepts of personal liability and partnership responsibility for torts and contracts.
4. Detail the special characteristics of partnerships, limited partnerships, and limited liability partnerships.

CHAPTER OUTLINE

I. Creation of Agency Relationships
II. Liabilities of the Principal for Acts of the Agent
III. Sole Proprietorships
IV. Partnerships
V. Limited Partnerships
VI. Limited Liability Partnerships

This is first of two chapters dealing with the formation and operation of various forms of business firms. At the end of this chapter the exercise involves three friends who have decided to form a partnership to engage in the health food business. You are asked to help them put together a partnership agreement, which will reflect their contributions to the business, provide for successful operation, and anticipate changes that may occur as their operations expand.

INTRODUCTION

Although most students have some knowledge of corporations and partnerships, agency relationships may not be so familiar. The concept most people have of an "agent" is likely to be the person who negotiates a contract on behalf of a movie star or a baseball player. While such a person is definitely an agent, the significance of agency relationships is much greater. All partnerships and corporations—from the two-person accounting firm to the multibillion-dollar company—can act *only* through agents. Even corporations with 100,000 shareholders and a 20-member board of directors can only act when some person or group (an employee or the board of directors, for example) takes some action *as its agent* and on its behalf. A large firm's employees and partners will do hundreds of things every day that may or may not legally bind the firm, depending on the laws of agency. A study of the principles of agency law is thus a good place to start our examination of business organizations.

For example, a partner in an accounting firm may agree, on behalf of the firm, to do an audit for the Acme Steel Corporation at the price of $1,000. Such an action is normally within the scope of a partner's authority, and this action will therefore probably create a contract to which the partnership is bound. On the other hand, suppose that a part-time clerk at the accounting firm goes to a bank on his lunch hour and borrows $10,000 "for the firm," without being asked to do so by anyone. It is unlikely that this action will be binding on the accounting firm because of the lack of *authority*. We analyze the concept of an agent's authority thoroughly in the next few pages and then look at other aspects of the agency relationship. Later in the chapter, the legal aspects of the partnership form of business enterprise will be examined in detail.

CREATION OF AGENCY RELATIONSHIPS

agent: One who performs some action on behalf of another person or firm, called the principal.

principal: A person who hires another to act as an agent.

general agent: An agent who has authority to do a wide range of actions for the principal.

special agent: An agent who is hired to do only one task for the principal.

An **agent** is a person who performs some act on behalf of another person called a **principal**. The relationship may be informal, or it may involve a lengthy written contract. One important requirement is that both parties *consent* to the relationship—that is, they both must agree that one will act for and on behalf of the other. As we have mentioned, corporations and partnerships can only operate through the actions certain people (such as agents) take on their behalf. In certain situations the actions of the president of the company or a truck driver for the company may bind the organization, but in others, largely depending on the scope of their authority, the actions of agents will not bind the organization. We begin our study of agency by looking at various types of agents, as well as the duties agents and principals have to each other.

TYPES OF AGENTS

The principal has the right to specify the duties and responsibilities of the agent. The principal also has the right to control the activities of the agent even if such power is not always used. If the agent carries out a wide range of responsibilities for the principal, he or she is termed a **general agent**. If, on the other hand, the agent is hired or asked to do only one task for the principal, he or she is a **special agent**.

For example, Susan, the manager of Sally's Furniture Store, is a general agent. Susan has conversations with the owner of the store, Sally, and Susan has a contract of employment as well. The agreement spells out a series of specific duties, such as the method for purchasing inventory, hiring employees, and the procedure for closing up the store every night.

During the operation of the store, however, issues arise that the owner and the manager have not discussed. In general, the law assumes that owners want managers to take appropriate actions when needs arise, using their own discretion, in the course of managing. If a water pipe bursts, Susan will need to hire someone to immediately fix the pipe and may have to move and store the merchandise somewhere in order to safeguard it. The costs associated with these tasks eventually will be the responsibility of Sally, the owner, because Susan, the agent, had general authority to do them.

Now assume Sally's Furniture Store has employed an attorney to represent the store in a lawsuit against Mr. and Mrs. Johnson, who have refused to pay their furniture bill. In this case, the attorney is a special agent. The lawyer has authority to represent and speak for Sally's Furniture Store in this one particular case. However, the attorney does not have authority to make any commitments for Sally's store in any other legal matters unless so directed by Sally. Unlike the general agent, the special agent does not have the power to make agreements that bind the principal beyond the specific powers for which the agent is retained.

There is a type of special agent called an **independent contractor**. This person is like a special agent in that he or she has been employed by the principal to accomplish one particular task. The independent contractor also operates his or her own business and commonly is hired to do one specific job for the principal. Suppose that Sally has a leaky roof at her house. If she hires Frank from Joe's Roofing Service to come to her house and fix the roof, the carpenter will be an independent contractor. While Frank has the power to climb on the roof, pound nails, and do what is necessary to complete the job, he does not have the right to hire people to build a fence, work on the dishwasher at Sally's house, or to rent her house to someone else. And if Frank drops a hammer and hits the mail carrier, the responsibility to compensate the injured person will be his, not Sally's. The principal is not liable for torts committed by independent contractors. On the other hand, as we will discuss later, principals may be liable for the negligence of a general agent, in some situations.

independent contractor: A type of special agent, hired to do one type of job for the principal. The independent contractor usually is paid by the job, uses his or her own equipment, and often operates his or her own business.

DUTIES OF AGENT TO PRINCIPAL

When someone agrees to act as the agent of another, the law imposes very significant responsibilities—called **fiduciary duties**—on the agent. These duties include the obligations of trust, loyalty, honesty, obedience to the principal's rules and instructions, and due care in performance of the tasks. If the agent is in a position to handle money, he or she must not commingle any personal funds with those of the principal and must account to the principal for every penny spent and earned. If funds get mixed up and a loss occurs, the responsibility must fall to the agent. For example, assume Carl, the agent for a bread company, receives $10,000 from a customer as a deposit toward the purchase of bread, and then invests that $10,000 along with $5,000 of Carl's own money in the stock market. If by the time Carl must account for the money to his

fiduciary duty: The duty owed by the agent to the principal, which includes trust, honesty, loyalty, obedience, and full disclosure of relevant facts.

principal the value of the stock is only $14,000, Carl must give the principal $10,000 and keep only $4,000.

The scope of the fiduciary duties prevents the agent from serving anyone but the principal while performing as agent. The agent cannot indulge in "double-dealing" or make any "side profit" in connection with his or her duties unless this other relationship is fully disclosed and approved by the principal. The agent's sole duty is to serve the interests of the principal and receive compensation from the principal.

For example, suppose the California Wine Co. is looking for a site for its new winemaking facility and hires a real estate agent, Tami, to assist in finding the right property. The company is prepared to spend $200,000 for the property. Tami finds a perfect site that can be purchased for $100,000. Tami buys the property herself and then sells it to the company for $150,000, without disclosing to the company her profit. Even though the company might be happy with the price paid, Tami has clearly violated her fiduciary duty. Tami's job was to find the best property at the best price for the company—she was being trusted and compensated to do so. Tami violated her obligation to the principal by making a personal profit on the deal rather than buying the property for the company at the $100,000 price. If the company learns the true facts and sues Tami, any profit she made will be awarded to the company. In addition, other damages and penalties might be assessed against her.

DUTIES OF PRINCIPAL TO AGENT

In contrast to the strict obligations of the agent set out previously, the principal does not owe the agent nearly the same duties. No fiduciary duty flows from the principal to the agent. Instead, the principal merely has the duty to pay the agent whatever compensation was agreed upon (and many agencies involve no compensation) and to reimburse the agent for expenses reasonably incurred in carrying out the duties of the agency. In other words, if the agent had to spend $50 on gasoline and $75 on repairs while on the road selling the principal's goods, the principal should reimburse the agent for these expenses unless an agreement exists to the contrary. The principal should also refrain from doing anything to hinder the agent's performance of the assigned tasks.

LIABILITIES OF THE PRINCIPAL FOR ACTS OF THE AGENT

LIABILITY FOR TORTS OF THE AGENT

Whenever a person commits a tort (a wrongful act which creates liability), he or she is liable for the consequences of that action. For example, if Harry drives his car negligently and injures Joe, then Harry will be liable. Often the tougher question, however, is whether someone else may also be liable. For example, suppose Harry was not driving his car when he had the accident but was driving a Federal Express van, delivering a package, when the accident occurred. Should Federal Express be liable along with Harry?

The answer to this question depends on several factors. One issue is whether Harry was an *independent contractor* or an *employee*. As we briefly discussed earlier, an independent contractor is a person who is hired or retained to do a particular job, like the carpenter in the example used earlier in the chapter. These persons are usually hired to accomplish a specific result, often have their own business and tools, work for many different people or companies, and are paid by the job. The principal wants them to accomplish particular results and does not directly supervise the physical aspects of their work.

On the other hand, an **employee** (sometimes called a **servant** under older legal terminology) generally is paid by the hour or by the week, uses the tools of the principal, and is under the control of the employer (sometimes called the *master*) regarding the physical performance of his or her job. Thus, while the carpenter who comes to your house for a one-time roof repair would probably be an independent contractor, a carpenter who works for General Motors Corporation (GM) every day for two years, uses GM tools, reports to a specific GM carpentry shop every day for work, and is paid $500/week by GM would probably be considered an employee.

employee or servant: An agent whose actions are under the control of the principal/employer. The employee is usually paid by the hour or week, uses the tools of the employer, is directly supervised by the employer, and may work for several different principals at the same time.

In general, principals are not liable for torts committed by independent contractors. Sally would probably not be liable for the hammer dropped by the carpenter on the mail carrier. However, under the legal theory ***respondeat superior*** (which means "let the master respond"), principals *are liable for torts committed by employees* if the tort was done "while acting within the scope of employment." Therefore, in the Federal Express example, if Harry were driving the company van to deliver packages, the company (in addition to Harry) would likely be liable to the person he injured through his negligent driving. The policy behind the rule is that those who hire employees should bear some responsibility for what they do to others while on the job. Another rationale for the rule is that imposing some liability on employers will encourage them to hire, train, and supervise their employees more carefully. An example of what is sometimes called the "vicarious liability" of principals under *respondeat superior* is shown in the following case.

respondeat superior: The legal theory that holds that an employer/principal can be held liable for torts committed by employees within the scope of employment.

LANGE V. NATIONAL BISCUIT COMPANY

211 N.W. 2d 783 (Minn. 1973)

FACTS

Ronnell Lynch was a cookie salesman for National Biscuit Company (Nabisco). His duties included selling Nabisco's products to grocery stores and actually placing previously delivered merchandise on the shelves of the stores in his area. Mr. Lynch was first assigned his own territory on March 1, 1969, and by the end of his first two months, Nabisco had already received numerous complaints from grocers that he was overly aggressive and was taking the shelf space reserved for competing cookie companies.

On May 1, 1969, Mr. Lynch arrived at the small grocery store managed by Jerome Lange to place previously delivered merchandise on the shelves. An argument developed between the two men concerning Lynch's activities, and Lynch became very angry and started swearing. Lange told Lynch to stop swearing or to leave the store, as children were present. Lynch then became angrier, shouting, "I ought to break your neck!" He went behind the counter and dared Lange to fight. Following Lange's refusal of this offer, Lynch viciously attacked him, threw merchandise around the store, and left. Lange brought a lawsuit against Nabisco, but the trial court entered judgment for the defendant, and Lange appealed to the Minnesota Supreme Court.

DECISION

The court stated that according to the requirements of *respondeat superior*, in order to impose liability on the principal-employer for torts of the agent-employee, the employee must have been acting within the scope of his employment when the actions that caused the lawsuit took place. Some previous Minnesota cases had required that, in addition, the employee's acts must have been motivated by a desire to "further the employer's business."

The Minnesota court refused to follow this theory, finding that the majority of jurisdictions did not agree with it. Justice Todd, writing for the court, quoted an old Mississippi case that had held, "The fallacy of this reasoning was that it made a certain mental condition of the servant the test by which to determine whether he was acting about his master's business or not. It clothed the master with immunity if the act was right, because it was right, and if it was wrong, it clothed him with like immunity because it was wrong." The public might be left totally without redress for intentional injuries inflicted by the agents of a business.

The public policy underlying the theory of *respondeat superior* or vicarious liability is that the employer, knowing that he can be held liable for the torts of his servants, can and should consider this liability as a cost of doing business. He will be more careful in hiring employees and can pass some or all of the cost along to his customers through his prices. "In this way, losses are spread and the shock of the accident is dispersed."

The court stated that the proper rule was "an employer is liable for an assault by his employee when the source of the attack is related to the duties of the employee and the assault occurs within work-related limits of time and place." Applying those factors to this case, the court held that (1) the assault occurred at a work-related place, since it took place in a grocery store where the employee was working; (2) it occurred during normal working hours, so the "time" requirement was met; and (3) the cause of the argument and subsequent assault was a dispute about Lynch's working conduct, that is, where his cookies were to be placed on the shelves. Therefore, the employee was acting within the scope of employment at the time of the aggression, and the employer is liable for his torts under the doctrine of *respondeat superior*. The lower court decision was reversed.

CASE QUESTIONS

1. Assuming that Nabisco had a rule prohibiting its salespeople from slugging store managers while on duty, does it make sense to hold the employer liable for the assault of the salesman here? Is it fair to the company?
2. Is the salesman liable here, too? Why do you think Mr. Lange did not sue him? Could he recover two judgments if he did?
3. What was wrong with the "motivation" test that had been the standard for employer liability in Minnesota until this case?
4. Would the company be liable if the assault had taken place at a bar where the two men were drinking later that evening?

Although the employer will generally be liable for torts committed by the employee "in the scope of employment," as the *National Biscuit* case demonstrates, in some cases the employee's actions are so far from the employment that only the agent-employee is responsible. The courts have developed a theory called *frolic and detour* to analyze situations where the boss should not bear responsibility for an employee's torts. For example, if Heather's job requires her to take a shipment of computers from San Francisco to Dallas, and she decides to visit her sister in Seattle on the way (and has an accident there), it is likely that a court would find her on a "**frolic**" and thus solely responsible, since it was clearly not on the way to Dallas. A "**detour**" is a slight deviation from work duties or rules but which is not so far afield that the employer is released from liability for the tort committed by the employee. For example, an employee driving in the course of employment but exceeding the speed limit in violation of company rules would still be within the general scope of employment if he or she negligently causes an accident.

frolic: When an employee deviates significantly from the scope of employment.

detour: When an employee deviates slightly from the scope of employment. The employer-principal is still liable (along with the employee) for torts committed on a detour.

The law has also developed a "going and coming" to work rule that holds generally that the principal is not responsible for torts committed by employees who are on their way to work or on the way home. However, if the employee is taking care of business while on route or is on call 24 hours a day, and really does get called sometimes, then this rule might be relaxed. Therefore, employers have sometimes been held liable for employee torts committed on the way to and from work in those situations.

LIABILITY FOR CONTRACTS MADE BY THE AGENT

Actual Authority As agents go about representing the interests of the principal, they often do things that create contracts between the principal and someone with whom the agent has dealt, called the **third party**. The key ingredient in determining this contractual liability is whether the agent was acting *within the scope of authority* given by the principal. In many situations, the principal clearly intends that a contract be created. For example, if Jason is a salesman for IBM Corporation, his job is to travel around his region, persuading customers to purchase IBM computers and other products. He and his company (the principal) hope that his efforts will lead to contracts between the customers and IBM.

third party: Someone with whom the agent interacts, on behalf of the principal.

When Jason and a customer reach agreement on the purchase of a computer system, they prepare and sign a written contract containing the details of their agreement. Let us assume that Jason has been given authority from IBM to enter into contracts on behalf of IBM, at specified prices and terms, up to a maximum of $10,000. Therefore, when Jason and the customer sign the contract for the purchase of a computer system for $6,000 (Jason signs as the agent of IBM), the contract is really between the customer and IBM, because Jason has **actual authority** to enter into such a contract on behalf of his principal.

actual authority: An agent's actions that are within the power given by the principal. The principal is bound to contracts made by the agent within the agent's actual authority.

The actual authority of an agent to enter into contracts that bind the principal may be *express* or *implied*. In the preceding example, Jason's authority was express, or clearly spelled out or expressed. However, in the situation we discussed earlier, Susan, the manager of Sally's Furniture Store, had the authority to hire a plumber when a pipe burst in the store although the authority was not expressed. Sally would be bound to pay for the repair because, although Susan was never expressly told to make repairs, such authority can be implied from her role as manager of the store.

disclosed principal: Where the agent clearly informs the third party whom he/she is working for.

partially disclosed principal: Where the agent indicates that he/she is representing a principal, but does not disclose the identity.

undisclosed principal: A type of agency in which neither the existence nor the identity of the agent is disclosed to the third party.

In the IBM example above, suppose that Jason signed the contract with the computer customer as "Jason Hamilton, agent of IBM Corporation." This is an example of what is called a **disclosed principal**. Jason has made perfectly clear the identity of the business he was representing. Therefore, Jason should not be a party to and should not be liable for the contract.

In two other situations the identity of the principal is not made so clear. If Jason had told the customer, "I am representing a large computer company, but I can't tell you which," this is an example of a **partially disclosed principal**. In this situation, the customer can hold Jason responsible on the contract. When the customer (the third party) learns the true identity of the principal, he or she can elect to hold *either* the agent or the principal liable but not both.

Furthermore, if Jason signs the contract "Jason Hamilton" without mentioning that he is working for IBM or anyone else, the principal is **undisclosed**. In this case, Jason is liable on the contract. If and when the identity of the principal is disclosed, however, the customer can elect which party he or she wants to hold responsible.

FROM THE DESK OF
Laura Lawyer

To: Students

From: Your Lawyer

The use of an undisclosed agency occurs frequently when a developer wants to purchase a large tract of land, perhaps for a shopping center. The desired properties may be owned by many people. Often the developer will engage the services of several different agents to purchase various parcels. All agents have agreed to sell all properties purchased to the developer. If the developer went to each property owner individually and disclosed his identity, the price of the real estate would climb sharply after the first few purchases.

In the following case the court examines the question of whether the business firm with whom a consumer dealt was an agent of another company or an independent contractor.

HERMAN V. BONANZA BUILDINGS, INC.

390 N.W. 2d 536 (Neb. 1986)

FACTS

Albert and Mildred Herman wanted to have a building constructed on their property. They had seen an advertisement for "Bonanza Buildings," and Mr. Herman called the long-distance number given in the brochure. The Bonanza representative told Mr. Herman that a dealer in Kearney, Nebraska, would contact him. Shortly thereafter, a salesman from Big Valley Buildings, Inc., of Kearney came to Mr. Herman's house and showed him Bonanza brochures that described different types of buildings and boasted of the "unique engineering of the product." The brochure also contained the following paragraph:

Your new Bonanza Building is designed to be WORRY-FREE . . . . We back it with a Written Warranty and a Local Independent Builder . . . . We think your new Bonanza building is built with a lot of quality and care, so we put it in writing. With every Bonanza building comes a Written Warranty to repair or replace defective material or workmanship . . . . We don't worry about your Bonanza building, and we don't think you should either.

Mr. Herman selected a particular type of building from the brochure, made some modifications, and entered into a contract whereby Big Valley agreed to construct the building for a total price of $9,707.

After the building was completed, Mr. Herman paid Big Valley in full and received a document called "Bonanza Building Warranty," which provided that the "Bonanza Builder named below" (Big Valley) would take care of various problems, including leaks, if they should occur. During the very first rainstorm following completion, the building leaked through the doors, windows, and skylights. Mr. Herman called Big Valley, and during the next few months, a Big Valley worker attempted to make repairs on at least two occasions, but the problems were not corrected.

The next spring, Mr. Herman learned that Big Valley had gone out of business. He contacted Bonanza, which sent two tubes of caulk and arranged for two men to do the caulking. A Bonanza representative told Mr. Herman that Bonanza would take care of the problem. Unfortunately, the leaks—which were apparently the result of faulty construction—were never successfully corrected. Since Big Valley was no longer in business, the Hermans sued Bonanza, arguing that it was liable for their damages, because Big Valley was its agent. The lower court dismissed the case, finding that Big Valley was an independent contractor rather than an agent for Bonanza.

DECISION

The Nebraska Supreme Court affirmed the decision of the district court as to the agency issue (although it stated that Mr. Herman might have a case against Bonanza on the basis of its warranty). The first item considered by the court was the written agreement between Bonanza and Big Valley (which Mr. Herman did not know about at the time the work was done). This agreement provided that Big Valley was an independent contractor and that neither party was an agent for the other. While the court noted this agreement, it was not the primary factor in the court's decision.

In determining whether one party is acting as an independent contractor or an agent of another, the Nebraska Supreme Court listed 10 factors to be considered: (1) the extent of the control the employer may exercise over the details of the work; (2) whether the one employed is engaged in a distinct occupation or business; (3) whether, in this locality, the work in question is usually done by a specialist or under the direction of an employer; (4) the degree of skill required in the particular occupation; (5) who supplied the instrumentalities, tools, and the place of work for the person doing the work; (6) the length of time for which the one employed is engaged; (7) the method of payment, whether by the hour or by the job; (8) whether the work is a part of the regular business of the employer; (9) whether the parties believe they are creating an agency relationship (that was where the written contract between Bonanza and Big Valley came in); and (10) whether or not the employer is in business.

The court stated that although the control or right to control the actions of the party who does the work is the most important factor, all of the listed factors must be considered. In this case, Big Valley was engaged in the distinct business of erecting buildings from components it purchased, "an activity which required special skill." Although Big Valley purchased the components from Bonanza, it was clear that Bonanza "did not exert direction or supervision over the erection of the building." Big Valley negotiated the terms of the contract, signed it in its own name, handled the billing and relations with Mr. Herman, and undertook the modification of the building sold to it by Bonanza. Big Valley had its own business location and used its tools in the construction. Clearly, "Big Valley was an independent contractor and not an agent of Bonanza," wrote the Court.

Evidence introduced at trial that Bonanza referred Big Valley to Mr. Herman, that Big Valley used a brochure prepared by Bonanza, and that Bonanza offered training sessions in construction of Bonanza buildings and "presumably trained Big Valley" did not make Big Valley an agent. The evidence showed that "Big Valley was acting primarily for its own benefit . . . and the agreement out of which this suit arose was between Mr. Herman and Big Valley only." Therefore, the court upheld the portion of the lower court's dismissal based on agency theory. However, the case was remanded to the lower court for further hearings on the question of whether the statements in the warranty had created an express warranty between Bonanza and Mr. Herman.

CASE QUESTIONS

1. Why is it that the agreement between Big Valley and Bonanza, which stated that Big Valley was an independent contractor, did not dispose of Mr. Herman's arguments completely?
2. What factors did the court find particularly important in reaching its decision? What factors tended to indicate that perhaps Big Valley was an agent of Bonanza?
3. Is it fair to Mr. Herman to prohibit him from suing Bonanza? Has justice been done if he has to suffer the damages of an improperly constructed, leaky building after he paid the full price?
4. Who won the case? Is there a chance Mr. Herman might still prevail in his action against Bonanza?

Apparent Authority The previous discussion concerned situations in which the agent had actual authority—either express or implied—to enter into contracts on behalf of the principal. It is sometimes possible, however, for an agent to bind a principal to a contract even when the agent did not have *any* authority to do so. How can this be? In some cases, it would be unfair to the third party to allow the principal to escape responsibility.

Suppose the Chicago Toy Company manufactures this year's hottest new toy—a soft bean bag variation on the G.I. Joe line called "Beanie Commando." Assume that Brenda has been a member of the sales staff at Chicago Toy for 10 years and has represented that company in many dealings with retailers in the Midwest. For 10 years, whenever a store made a contract with Chicago Toy, Brenda did the negotiations and signed the papers. All deposits made to Brenda always reached Chicago Toy. Later, Brenda and Chicago Toy have a disagreement over the ethical implications of the toy. After failing to resolve the dispute, Brenda is fired, effective immediately.

Brenda, however, decides to make one last visit to her five best customers. When visiting these customers, she fails to tell them she has been fired and receives $15,000 in deposits to be applied to orders of Beanie Commando from Chicago Toy. Several months later, after no shipments of the toy have arrived, one of the retailers calls the company and only then learns that Brenda was not employed by the company when the order was taken and the deposit paid.

Chicago Toy states that "she was no longer our agent when she took your money and made the contract." In fact, Chicago Toy never received any money, only a postcard from Brenda in Tahiti saying, "Having a wonderful time; give my regards to Commando." In this situation, the concept of **apparent authority** would probably bind Chicago Toy to the contract. When the *actions of the principal* (not just the agent) lead a third party to the reasonable belief that an agent does have authority to bind the principal, it is possible to hold a principal to a contract even when the agent exceeded his or her authority.

In our scenario, the actions of the principal in accepting all contracts made by Brenda on its behalf for ten years created the reasonable belief that a contract made with her would be honored by the company. The only way for the principal (Chicago Toy) to avoid the liability by apparent authority would have been to give **actual notice** to all its customers that Brenda was no longer with the company. Actual notice means directly telling the other party about the change either by letter or in person. Another type of notice, **constructive notice** (such as putting a notice in the newspaper), would work with retailers and other third parties with whom the agent had not directly dealt before.

apparent authority: A situation where an agent acting without authority can sometimes enter contracts binding on the principal. This theory requires that some action *of the principal* leads the third party to believe that the agent has the authority he or she claims to have.

actual notice: Directly telling the other party about a legal matter either in person or by a letter.

constructive notice: An indirect type of notice, such as putting a notice in the newspaper.

Ratification Sometimes it is even possible for a principal to be bound to contracts made in his or her behalf by an agent who clearly acts without any type of authority. This situation could arise when the principal, although not bound to do so, acts in a way to indicate that he or she feels bound to or wishes to enforce the agreement made by the agent. For example, if the agent is sent to an office supply store to purchase paper and pencils for the business but instead goes to a car dealership and purchases on credit an automobile for the firm, the principal would not be bound to the contract because the agent was acting outside the scope of his authority. But if the principal keeps the car for several weeks, drives it regularly on business matters, and says nothing about returning it, the principal will be bound to the contract with the third party by the doctrine of **ratification**, even though the agent acted without authority.

ratification: When a principal who would not be bound to a contract made by an agent (beyond authority) nevertheless accepts the benefits of the contract, then the principal may be bound to honor it.

TERMINATION OF AGENCY

Since the agency relationship is based on consent, when either the principal or agent decides to end the relationship, the agency is generally terminated. In other words, either party usually has the *power* to terminate the agency at any time. But what if they had a contract? Can the principal still fire the agent? Yes, in almost all situations. Courts have often distinguished between the *power* to terminate the agency and the *right* to do so.

For example, let us look at the baseball career of the late Billy Martin. Over a period of 10 years, Martin was hired approximately seven times to manage the New York Yankees. Each time he was hired, he and the team owner entered into a contract that detailed his salary and the term of his duties. But, on each occasion, he was fired by the principal owner of the team

(George Steinbrenner) before his contract had been completed. When Steinbrenner would call Martin and say, "You're fired," that did in fact terminate the agency relationship. Martin could not put on the uniform, make out the lineup for the game, or sit in the dugout—he was no longer the manager. In this case, the principal had the *power* to terminate the agency. However, because a contract existed, Steinbrenner did not have the *right* to terminate the agency and therefore had to continue to pay Martin on the contract. Similarly, Martin would have had the *power*, but not the *right*, to quit at any time. In other words, Martin could effectively quit when he wanted, but he might have to pay damages if his breach of contract cost the club money.

One type of agency does exist where the principal fails to have the power to terminate the relationship at his or her option, and this is an **agency coupled with an interest**. In this situation, which is fairly rare, the agent has an actual legal interest (part ownership or a mortgage or security interest) in the property that is the subject of the agency, and it would be unfair to allow the principal to cancel the agency without compensation. For example, suppose Leslie takes a ring to a pawnshop and leaves it as collateral for a loan she receives. She gives the shop owner the power, as an agent for her, to sell the ring if she does not pay the loan in a certain time. It is unfair to allow Leslie simply to notify the pawnshop before she had paid back the loan and say, "I'm canceling the agency." Why? The owner will lose his legal interest in the ring. This agency coupled with an interest cannot be terminated without the consent of the agent.

agency coupled with an interest: An unusual type of agency in which the agent has a legal interest in the property of the agency. Such an agent cannot be terminated "at will," unlike a normal agency.

IN CONSULTATION

Marvin Manager has a problem. He recently terminated Andy, one of his account managers, for failure to meet sales goals. Andy was furious and told Marvin that he would steal all of ABC, Inc.'s clients. Despite Andy's threats, Marvin did not insist that Andy give back his company identification, his company cards, or company letterhead. Marvin did not notify any of Andy's accounts that Andy was no longer with ABC—Marvin did not want to embarrass Andy or hinder him from obtaining future employment. He simply reassigned Andy's clients to another account manager.

A month later, Marvin received an angry phone call from one of Andy's former accounts. The client stated he ordered 1,000 widgets from ABC almost three weeks ago and paid a deposit but did not receive his order. Marvin showed no record of the order and asked with whom the client placed his bid. The client replied that he placed his bid with Andy, of course, since Andy is his account manager. Marvin contacted the rest of Andy's former accounts and discovered that many of them had also placed orders and paid deposits to Andy after his termination.

Marvin wants to know whether ABC is responsible for filling the orders and/or refunding the deposits since the orders were placed with Andy after he was terminated. He contacted Laura Lawyer, in-house counsel, for her advice on what ABC's liability is. Here is their conversation:

Marvin:

1. If I fired Andy, how can ABC be responsible for his post-termination actions?
2. Aren't we protected by the fact that we assigned a new account manager to each of Andy's clients?

Laura:

1. Simply firing an employee does not terminate your responsibility for his or her actions. More steps are required to protect third parties that may do business with your agent.
2. Not necessarily. The clients may not have known about the new manager.

3. Even if the clients didn't know, Andy knew he wasn't our employee anymore. Doesn't that make a difference?

3. It makes a difference if we want to sue Andy, but it may not matter for Andy's clients. **Let me review the applicable law to see what our potential liability is, and I will get back to you.**

FROM THE DESK OF

Laura Lawyer

To: Marvin Manager

Re: Liability of Company for Acts of Former Employee

Dear Marvin:

Your scenario raises the issue of company liability for agent's actions and the company's responsibility to its innocent clients. Employees are agents who can create liability for their employer, the principal. Statements, promises, and contracts made by an employee/agent will bind the company that they represent as long as the agent is acting within their authority. *Authority* can mean something as simple as the specific duties delegated to an agent. Authority, however, can be much broader. It may include any power a reasonable third party thinks that agent has. When you terminated Andy, you removed his actual authority to act on behalf of ABC. On the surface, Andy's termination would end any liability ABC may have for Andy's actions.

Unfortunately, terminating Andy was not enough when you dig beneath the surface and explore what Andy's clients were thinking. The law protects innocent third parties who reasonably believe that an agent has authority to act on behalf of a principal. If third parties like Andy's customers reasonably believed that Andy had authority, then the law gives Andy what is known as apparent authority. *Apparent authority* is the authority that is "apparent" from the innocent third party's perspective. When Andy left ABC, he did so with all of the materials that identified him as an ABC employee. You never directly notified his accounts that Andy no longer managed them, nor did you tell Andy's clients that someone new would now handle their orders. Andy's clients were probably reasonable in thinking that Andy had authority to act on behalf of ABC. ABC would, therefore, likely be liable to Andy's customers for the deposits and for fulfilling the orders.

A possible exception to ABC's liability to Andy's former accounts would exist for any customers who had been contacted by the new account manager you assigned. If a customer heard from a new manager, he or she is likely to think that the new manager is the person to whom he or she should direct business, pay deposits, and send orders. Customers who are aware that they have a new manager may have "constructive notice" that Andy is no longer their account manager, and they may not be reasonable in thinking that Andy still had authority to represent ABC.

You are correct that Andy knew he was no longer our agent. ABC, as the principal, can terminate our agency relationship with Andy at any time. By firing Andy, we ended our employment and agency relationship. Without giving notice to third parties, we still have a legal liability to Andy's former accounts. The termination, however, may allow us to seek reimbursement for that liability from Andy. The law will protect the innocent third party—but Andy is not innocent. He represented, either expressly or implicitly, to his former accounts that he had the authority to act on behalf of ABC. He knew he had no authority, which makes him liable to ABC for his behavior.

With regard to Andy's behavior and ABC's resulting liability, consider the following questions:

1. What should Marvin have done differently when he terminated Andy?
2. What sort of policy could ABC put in place to eliminate this type of liability in the future?
3. Discuss why you think the law protects innocent third parties like Andy's accounts but does not protect ABC. Do you think the protection third parties receive is appropriate?

SOLE PROPRIETORSHIPS

Now that we have examined the concepts of agency and analyzed the legal principles governing the common situation where an individual acts on behalf of another person or business firm, it is time to take a closer look at the various legal structures under which businesses are organized. The legal principles of agency have significant impact on all forms of business organizations.

sole proprietorship: A business owned by one person, who has full control and full responsibility.

The simplest and most common type of business formation is the **sole proprietorship**. This type of business is very easy to form—one person simply begins to offer some services or products for sale. No written document, formal organization, or filing of papers with the state are necessary (although, depending on the type of business, a license or permit may be required). The owner has sole power to make decisions and sole liability and responsibility for all business debts. If the business earns a profit, the owner must pay taxes on the income as part of his or her own personal income—there is no separate taxation on the business. Legally, this type of business is not a separate entity from the owner.

partnership: An association of two or more persons, as co-owners, to carry on a business for profit.

PARTNERSHIPS

With a partnership, at least to some extent, a business entity is formed that is separate and different from the owners. A **partnership** is defined as an association of two or more persons, as co-owners, to carry on a business for profit.

This definition is contained in the Uniform Partnership Act (UPA), a model law drafted by a group of businesspeople and legal experts that has been adopted in almost all the states.

FORMATION AND CHARACTERISTICS

A partnership contains several separate requirements, each of which may be important in determining whether a partnership exists. First, there must be at least two people involved. There is no such thing as a "sole partnership." Although many partnerships have two or three partners, some nationwide accounting and law firms have over 1,000 partners. Second, these persons must be co-owners—that is, they must, in some manner, share in the aspects of ownership of a business, as will be discussed subsequently. Finally, the partners must be engaged in a business enterprise in which they are trying to make a profit—simply being co-owners of property is not enough to constitute a partnership.

Every year thousands of small businesses are started—all with high hopes of great success. Some succeed, and the owners have profits to share; others do not, and the owners have substantial losses and debts to pay. In either event, if the business is a partnership, the partners share the profits and losses personally (and equally, if nothing else is agreed upon).

Partnerships are easy to form—so easy, in fact, that people often do not realize they are partners. If Paul and Donna, currently juniors in business school, cut lawns in the summer and remove snow in the winter for 10 businesses, sharing expenses and profits, they probably are partners. No written partnership agreement is required by law. Partnership status does require an agreement, but courts have found that the agreement may be *implied* by the actions of the parties. Since the consequences of being a partner may be very significant, you should *never* begin a business with another person without putting your agreement down in writing. Make sure that if you are a partner, you begin your partnership with an *express agreement*, usually called the **articles of partnership**.

articles of partnership: A written document containing the names of the partnership and the partners, which sets forth the agreements of the partners, including such items as the organizational structure, purposes, ownership percentages, capital contributions, sharing of profits and losses, and other agreements.

What can happen without an express agreement? Suppose that after three years of running the lawn service and snow removal business, Paul and Donna have built a business worth $100,000 and now have 200 clients paying a total of $300,000 per year. After debts, Paul and Donna are finally turning a small profit, with the future prospects bright. At this point, Paul wants to expand the business considerably, while Donna wants to leave the business in order to develop her accounting practice. Paul has put $30,000 into the business—some of it borrowed from his father—and Donna has invested only $5,000 but has worked many more hours on the business. What problems will arise when Donna and Paul attempt to divide the shares of the business and determine and pay the departing partner (Donna) her share?

Partnerships almost always undergo significant changes—people change their minds, they move, they divorce and marry, and their business interests shift. The *only* time it is really feasible to put together a solid partnership agreement is in the very beginning of the enterprise, when the partners are friendly, optimistic, and without substantial assets or debts.

FROM THE DESK OF
Laura Lawyer

To: Students
From: Your Lawyer

As you begin a business enterprise with a friend, if you hear yourself saying, "We don't need a written agreement; a handshake will do," STOP! Instead, say "Let's prepare a simple agreement, so we'll all know where we stand if anything happens or our plans change." The best course of action is to consult a local lawyer to have a partnership agreement drafted that is tailored to your business. The few hundred dollars it will cost is well worth it. If you cannot or will not take that step, draft a simple agreement yourself.

Among other points, you should specify the following:

- Percentage of ownership
- Division of responsibilities and authority
- Salary and distribution of profits
- Buy-in and buy-out provisions
- Death, disability, and retirement contingencies
- Dispute resolution

Many partnership agreement forms can be found in libraries, bookstores, and on the internet. The following is one fairly simple form.

PARTNERSHIP AGREEMENT

This agreement of co-partnership, is made and entered into on this ______ day of ______________, 2000, by and among *John Smith* of *Cleveland, Ohio, Rhonda Jones* of *Provo, Utah*, and *Thomas Anderson* of *Tulsa, Oklahoma*.

WHEREAS, it is the desire of the parties hereto to form a partnership on terms and conditions as set forth below, the parties having mutual confidence in each other, do hereby agree as follows.

1. *PURPOSE*. The parties do hereby form a partnership to conduct a real estate investment and management business, including, but not limited to, the buying, selling, leasing, renting, managing, and otherwise dealing

in real estate of any and all kinds and to engage in all other lawful activities that the partners shall, from time to time, deem appropriate.

2. *NAME AND PRINCIPAL OFFICE*. The partnership shall operate under the name and style of *JRT Associates*. The partnership shall maintain offices for the conduct of partnership affairs at *Cleveland, Ohio*, or at such other place or places as the parties may later agree.
3. *PARTNERSHIP ASSETS*. There have been created, and shall be, three partnership interests, and all partnership assets shall be owned in the following proportions: John—50%, Rhonda—25%, and Thomas—25%.
4. *NET PROFITS AND LOSSES*. All net profits and losses of the partnership will be divided among the partners in accordance with the respective percentage interests set forth in Article 3.
5. *PARTNERSHIP AUTHORITY*. No one of the partners shall, without the consent of one other partner, endorse any notes or act as a surety for any persons. All decisions, other than day-to-day operations, shall be made by a majority vote of the partners. Without such consent, no partner shall, on behalf of the partnership, borrow or lend money, make or accept any commercial paper, execute any mortgage, purchase or contract to purchase or sell any property for or of the partnership.

   No partner shall, except with the advance written consent of all partners, assign, mortgage or sell his/her share in the partnership or its capital assets, or do any acts detrimental to the best interests of the partnership.

   New partners shall only be admitted upon unanimous vote of the partners.
6. *TIME DEVOTED TO PARTNERSHIP*. It is not contemplated that any of the partners will devote full time to the partnership affairs but that John will manage much of the day-to-day business and supervise the Cleveland office. The partners may from time to time allocate additional duties to each partner, as situations may require.
7. *TERM AND TERMINATION*. The partnership shall continue for an indefinite time period during the pleasure of the partners.
   a. *In the event of termination of the partnership because of the mental incapacity or death of a partner*, the remaining partners and the heir or representative of the deceased or incapacitated partner shall jointly determine the market value of the partnership and its assets. In the event they are unable to reach agreement, they will mutually select two appraisers who will attempt to reach an accurate valuation of the partnership. If the two appraisers cannot agree, they will select a third appraiser, whose determination of the value of the partnership will be final.

      After the value determination, the remaining partners will have the right to purchase the former partner's interest by paying to the heirs or representative the departing partner's proportionate share of the valuation. The purchase price shall be paid as follows: 25% within 30 days, and the balance within one year, at 8% interest. If the remaining partners do not choose to purchase the share of the incapacitated or deceased partner, all partnership assets shall be sold, and after payment of debts, the proceeds shall be distributed to the partners and the heirs or representatives of the departing partner.

b. *In the event of termination of the partnership because of the voluntary withdrawal of one of the partners*, the withdrawing partner shall make a written offer to the other partners, indicating the terms and conditions of which he/she is willing to sell his/her interest. The other partners shall have 30 days in which to reach agreement on the purchase of the departing partner's share. If no agreement is reached, the remaining partners may continue the business under the partnership name and initiate the valuation procedure set forth in paragraph 7a, or they may elect to terminate the partnership and distribute the assets according to paragraph 7a.

c. *Termination by sale and/or distribution of assets*. It is agreed that in the event of the sale and/or distribution of all or a majority of the assets of the partnership, then this partnership shall terminate, and each partner shall receive his/her appropriate share of assets and proceeds as set forth previously.

8. *BOOKS AND RECORDS*. The partnership shall maintain full and accurate books of account that shall be kept at the partnership office. Each partner shall cause to be entered in such books all transactions relating to the partnership or its business, and each partner shall at all times have access to and the right to inspect and copy such books and all partnership records.
9. *ACCOUNTING YEAR*. The accounting year of this partnership shall run from January 1 to December 31 of each year, and the books and records shall be maintained on this basis.
10. *PARTNERSHIP ACCOUNTS*. At the end of each year, a full and accurate account shall be made in writing of all of the assets and liabilities of the partnership; all its receipts and disbursements; and the assets, liabilities, and income shall be ascertained; and the accounts of each partner shall be credited or debited accordingly, with his/her share of such net profit or loss. Any partner may demand that the financial statement be audited and certified by a certified public accountant, but in the absence of such a demand, such certification is not required.

IN WITNESS WHEREOF, the parties have executed these documents this ________ day of __________________, 2000, at Cleveland, Ohio.

In the presence of:

______________________________ ______________
John Smith

______________________________ ______________
Rhonda Jones

______________________________ ______________
Thomas Anderson

DOES A PARTNERSHIP EXIST?

a partnership may exist if: (1) The owners share the profits; and (2) also share the right to manage.

The courts often must decide if a partnership exists when a business without a partnership agreement is breaking up, when an owner wants to leave the business or has died, or when the business owes a large liability. The two most important tests are (1) whether there has been a sharing of profits and/or losses and (2) whether there has been a sharing of the right of management and control. The courts also use other tests, such as whether the partners have purchased property together, used funds earned by the business to purchase property, or filed a partnership tax return.

The most significant indication that a partnership exists is if the owners have *shared the profits* earned by the business. Normally, one owner does not split his or her hard-earned profits with someone else without a reason. Courts look closely to determine if such sharing is in the nature of wages for specific jobs performed or payment on a specific debt—which would tend to negate the existence of a partnership. However, if after all debts are paid the owners divide up what is left, that creates the appearance of a partnership. Remember that *profits* are different than *gross income*.

The management/control test examines whether the business owners appear to accept the fact that they all have the right to participate in decision making. When an issue needs to be decided, does one person unilaterally make the decision or do the several owners decide together? If several decide together, this creates the appearance of a partnership.

The following story from *The Wall Street Journal* shows what can happen when the relationship is not made clear.

Dysfunctional Duo Built SAT Prep Firm; Now, They're in Court

Jury Will Have to Choose: (A) The Driven Founder; (B) The 'Creative' Guy

When Adam Robinson and John Katzman formed a business alliance in 1982, they seemed an ideal match—a pair of young Ivy League graduates tutoring Manhattan prep-school kids on how to improve their SAT scores.

The company was called Princeton Review Inc., and the objective was to demystify the test-taking process by training students to think differently. Business was good from the beginning, thanks to positive word-of-mouth, as tutored students' scores increased an average of 150 to 200 points.

But almost instantly, Mr. Katzman, now 39 years old, and Mr. Robinson, 44, began a nearly two-decade cycle of teamwork and feuding, as their business arrangement came to resemble a dysfunctional marriage in which they would break up and make up.

Adam Robinson

After one early split, for instance, Mr. Katzman begged Mr. Robinson to return, urging in a 1985 letter: "I can only promise that I am not a d—. If and when I sell the Review, you and I will walk away both happy and rich." Years later, after another falling out, Mr. Katzman admonished Mr. Robinson for making a stink, and then signed off by writing: "Through adversity and temptation, I have always looked out for you and remained a stalwart ally. I hope we can work things out."

As with so many troubled unions, this one has ended up in court. "Not to emasculate myself here, but I was like a wife who's married to a husband with all the assets in his name," says Mr. Robinson, who is suing Mr. Katzman and Princeton Review, seeking as much as $10 million in compensatory damages.

John Katzman

Mr. Robinson officially left Princeton Review about a decade ago when he took a $200,000 buyout from Mr. Katzman. But the two men have spent the last 10 years squabbling over their share of profits related to Princeton Review books and computer products that Mr. Robinson says are based on his intellectual property. They are set to face off in state court in Manhattan next month.

At the root of the dispute is the definition of "partner." Business partnerships, of course, aren't always about a 50/50 outlay of money and time. Often, they feature decidedly different leadership roles, with one person managing day-to-day operations, while the other has responsibility for the creative, intellectual side.

"It was like being a great chef and someone says, 'Hey, you make great meals, and I'll run the restaurant,'" Mr. Robinson says. His passion, he says, was teaching and developing new techniques, without being distracted by management tasks or balance sheets. Mr. Robinson likens the arrangement to Apple Computer Inc.'s beginnings: "I was Steve Wozniak to Katzman's Steve Jobs."

Mr. Katzman scoffs at such claims for Princeton Review, which has grown to a $75 million-a-year business that coaches more than 75,000 students annually through courses and books. "I set the tone and mission of the company, and I've run it for 20 hours a day, seven days a week for 18 years," he says. "I don't think Adam can point to any 12 months where he was in the office for 30 hours or more a week." (While Mr. Robinson never kept a desk at Princeton Review, he says that was because he spent most of his time "out in the field" either tutoring or training instructors.)

Mr. Katzman maintains that Mr. Robinson was little more than a valuable salaried employee whose titles ranged from head of tutoring to head of research and development. And while Mr. Katzman says he promised Mr. Robinson a significant payout for his work, the two men never had any contractual arrangement.

"It's a stupid lawsuit," Mr. Katzman says. "These are like recovered memories, except in this case it is a lawyer doing this, helping Adam uncover these memories." Mr. Robinson's attorney, Glenn Greenwald, says Adam spent years "building John's company and got nothing for it. It's outrageous that John attempts to blame me for the entire lawsuit."

The dispute has become so bitter that former business associates refer to it as "John and Adam's Vietnam." Refusing an interview request for this article, one such associate, Robert Scheller, wrote: "I pulled my troops out of there many years ago and am not anxious to return soon."

Perhaps not surprisingly, the relationship between Messrs. Robinson and Katzman started as a rivalry. In 1981, Mr. Katzman established Princeton Review, a test-prep service he was running from his parents' New York apartment. He named the business after his alma mater, Princeton University, where he graduated in architecture an admitted "summa cum lousy."

A few months later, Mr. Robinson, a 26-year-old tutor and graduate of the University of Pennsylvania's Wharton School, noticed an ad for Princeton Review's SAT-preparation class. It claimed, "The Best Results of Any Course in NY." He called to challenge Mr. Katzman's claim—and clicked with him almost immediately.

Mr. Robinson showed Mr. Katzman his techniques for identifying potential land mines on the SAT and tips on handling them. Mr. Robinson had invented a hypothetical character named Joe Bloggs, who represented "an earnest but befuddled" SAT taker. Bloggs gets the easy questions right because he always chooses the answer that looks right. But on the hard questions, he uses the same strategy and comes up with the wrong answers. In instructing his students, Mr. Robinson would tell them, when in doubt, pick the answer than seems incorrect.

"These weren't tricks," Mr. Robinson says. "They were ways for students to figure out what to do when they couldn't do anything else. The only reason a hard question is hard is that the answer is made to seem wrong."

So the two men started collaborating. Mr. Robinson, who was still doing private tutoring, started teaching some of the Review's classes, training other instructors and writing some of the course materials.

Impervious to Cramming?

The early 1980s was a time when the Educational Testing Service, the private organization that administers the SAT (formerly called the Scholastic Aptitude Test) was telling the general public that tutoring and coaching couldn't significantly raise a student's score. The SATs, the argument went, were an academic equalizer that measured knowledge acquired over time and were impervious to cramming. But at Princeton Review, the theory held that it helped to know how to take tests.

Early on, the atmosphere was fun. Messrs. Katzman and Robinson would try to take the entire four-hour SAT in 30 minutes. "Other people play gin rummy and we'd take sample SATs for sport," says Fred Bernstein, one of the early Review instructors. Occasional wrestling matches and water-gun fights added to the levity.

To stay on top of new developments in the SAT, Messrs. Katzman and Robinson liked to take actual tests as they were being given. Usually, they were able to take them in New York, but one time the nearest location was in Chicago. After missing the last plane out, they rented a car and sped down to Washington to catch a 5 a.m. flight to Chicago the morning of the test. They arrived late, but talked their way in; afterward, they took some students to lunch to get their impressions of the exam.

Dressing Down

These experiences brought Messrs. Katzman and Robinson closer together. Despite different outside interests—Mr. Katzman runs marathons and is weighing political office, while Mr. Robinson is a chess master and avid reader of science books—Princeton Review "was sort of like a mission," Mr. Katzman says. "Who else loves this test and coaching kids as much as I do? The answer was Adam."

Yet tensions were always present. Once, when Mr. Robinson yelled at a Princeton Review employee over classroom space, Mr. Katzman came in and "just took Adam apart," says the former employee, Matt Rosenthal, who today is a Review franchisee. "You don't yell at my people. These are my people," Mr. Rosenthal recalls Mr. Katzman's saying. "This is my building. You're lucky that I'm even letting you in here."

Mr. Robinson says he can't remember what sparked the disagreement, but that, "It almost came to physical blows." He hastens to add, "We were young and relatively hotheaded and easily working 100 hours a week." Sometimes after these eruptions, the two men wouldn't speak for weeks, even months.

Nonetheless, the pair presented a united front to outsiders. In a Rolling Stone magazine interview in 1985, they talked jointly about how they coached students. In other articles, Mr. Katzman credited Mr. Robinson for many of the Review's test-taking techniques.

Tuning Out

Julia Coopersmith, a literary agent who got the pair their first book deal, initially thought the two men were business "equals."

"They clearly had some kind of arrangement," she says. "They seemed to be consulting about everything." From her vantage point, Mr. Robinson appeared to be the idea guy, while Mr. Katzman was the budding business tycoon.

She also couldn't help but notice the underlying turmoil in the two men's relationship. During one luncheon, she recalls, Mr. Robinson got upset and put on a set of headphones to tune out what Mr. Katzman was saying. "They didn't have a food fight, but it was close," she says.

The book that Ms. Coopersmith helped broker, "Cracking the System," was jointly written by Messrs. Robinson, Katzman and a young journalist named David Owen. The first edition was a huge success, leaping onto national bestseller lists, a bit shocking for a test-preparation book in the mid-1980s.

Messrs. Owen and Robinson immediately started thinking of new titles and spin-off products such as tapes and computer software. But Mr. Katzman was reluctant. "I was afraid of the books cannibalizing the courses," he says. Although the Review proceeded with some projects, Mr. Robinson grew frustrated that Mr. Katzman wasn't expanding the publishing business faster.

Then, in 1989, the question of partnership finally came to a head. "We had been going for years without a formal agreement," Mr. Robinson says. "We'd make fitful and abortive attempts at an ongoing partnership."

Mr. Katzman offered Mr. Robinson a 3% equity stake and double his salary—to $100,000 a year. "I almost reeled," says Mr. Robinson, who expected at least 10%. "Three percent is what I would've given a secretary."

"If I hadn't been a friend, my answer would've been, 'Get lost!'" Mr. Katzman says. "This was a business he walked away from more times than I could count."

The two settled on 4%, which Mr. Robinson then cashed out for $200,000. "I was advised by my attorney just to get out of there. It was like a bad marriage. You want out at all costs," Mr. Robinson says. As part of the buyout, Mr. Robinson waived all claims to an ownership interest in the Review, which at the time had annual revenue of $7.5 million, as well as any share of past revenues. Princeton Review would continue to acknowledge Mr. Robinson as the creator of various of its techniques, including the Joe Bloggs character.

Messrs. Katzman and Robinson remained tethered, however, by the Princeton Review books published by Random House. Messrs. Robinson, Katzman and Owen were each receiving 30% of the book profits while Ms. Coopersmith, the agent, was getting 10%.

A Thinner Slice

In 1991, Mr. Katzman decided that the arrangement needed to be renegotiated if Princeton Review were to fully expand the book-publishing operation, which at the time had six titles. "As the series went on, their involvement lessened a lot," he says, referring to Messrs. Robinson and Owen and Ms. Coopersmith. "I told them if I'm going to do the work, I'm going to own it."

An agreement was hashed out. Essentially, Mr. Owen and Ms. Coopersmith would get a sliding-scale percentage on existing books and nothing on future titles. Mr. Robinson's cut remained at 30% for the existing six books; going forward, he would receive 25.5% royalties on future books and related computer products.

"We didn't want to fight him," Mr. Robinson says, explaining why he agreed to the new profit arrangement. He notes that he and Mr. Owen had no way of taking their ideas to another publisher without the Princeton Review brand name. Ms. Coopersmith says she wasn't representing them on future books so she was "perfectly happy to let go."

The issue of book profits didn't end with the 1991 agreement, however. In 1994, Mr. Katzman offered to pay a lump sum for the rights held by Messrs. Robinson, Owen and Ms. Coopersmith. The impetus: Random House had offered to buy a 20% stake in Princeton Review, and Mr. Katzman was eager to tie up loose ends. Mr. Katzman adds now that the 1991 agreement was "ambiguous."

Mr. Owen and Ms. Coopersmith agreed to sell their rights for a combined $1.8 million, according to Mr. Robinson's attorney. But Mr. Robinson balked at Mr. Katzman's offer of $2 million and demanded to see the accounting records for Princeton Review's publishing arm before agreeing to anything. "John told me that he was being way generous and kept saying 'trust me,'" Mr. Robinson says. The Random House investment went ahead without Mr. Katzman's having to buy out Mr. Robinson's interest.

With the issue of book profits still in limbo, Mr. Robinson retained Mr. Greenwald as his attorney and in 1997 filed suit against Mr. Katzman and the Review, claiming, among other things, breach of contract and unfair competition. Messrs. Katzman and Robinson met with a mediator last summer but were unable to reach a settlement.

Understanding the Anger

Mr. Katzman says he feels sorry for his old chum and says he doesn't understand where the ire is coming from. He notes that in the years after Mr. Robinson left Princeton Review, the two remained good friends and continued to spend time together. When Mr. Katzman got married in 1993, Mr. Robinson was one of the ushers at the wedding. And when Mr. Katzman's wife gave birth to their first child in 1995, Mr. Robinson was among the well-wishers who came to the hospital.

These days, Mr. Robinson lives off his royalty payments, which in the past he says were around $150,000 a year but been declining, as well as assorted educational-training jobs. He says he is working to develop an online education company and is wrapping up his latest book, titled "Welcome to Wonderland: The Art of Unconventional Thinking."

"My cash flow since starting the lawsuit is 50% of what it was before," he says, adding that his lifestyle has been "constrained" by the costs of the legal battle. He stresses that he isn't impoverished, since he can afford to live in a loft in Manhattan's fashionable TriBeCa neighborhood. But he lives more simply than Mr. Katzman, who owns a house in the Hamptons and lives on New York's Upper West Side.

"I'm not belittling Adam's contribution, but the Princeton Review is more than a test-taking technique developed 17 years ago," Mr. Katzman says. "He's smart enough that he could've done something else."

Says Mr. Robinson: "It's not until things get big that you find out that things were just a suggestion, not a commitment." He adds, "There are so many tales here, so many morals."

RELATIONS AMONG PARTNERS

The partnership is a unique form of interdependent business relationship in which a group of individuals join together to create a commercial unit, never totally separate from the individuals. Partners are considered to have high *fiduciary* duties to each other, with all the responsibilities discussed in the preceding section on agency law. They are both agents and principals of each other. The partnership is, for some purposes, a separate **entity** apart from the partners, and for other purposes is merely an **aggregate** of individuals. For example, although the partnership may maintain profit and loss records as an entity, it does not pay income tax. Instead, each partner pays tax on his or her share of the profit. Although the partnership can buy and own property in its own name, in many states the partnership cannot sue or be sued unless each partner is named individually.

entity: A business firm whose existence is separate from its owners.

aggregate: A business firm whose existence is tied in with a certain group of owners.

As we will learn, individual partners can be held personally liable for things other partners do. Therefore, the decision regarding who becomes a partner is critically important and generally must be made by a unanimous vote of the partners. Other partnership decisions addressing normal business matters, however, are made by simple majority vote of the partners. Each partner has one vote, regardless of how much money each put into the business. In many partnerships, the partners will select a "managing partner" to make everyday business decisions, subject to reversal by a majority vote of the other partners. In the absence of such a process, all partners have an equal right in decision making.

Due to their fiduciary relationship, partners have the right to expect complete loyalty, honesty, and good faith from each other. Any partner who acts for personal benefit or profit at the expense of the partnership will be liable to the partnership. Also, each partner has the right to inspect the partnership books and records and to ask for an **accounting**—a detailed statement of all income, expenses, and assets—from the partnership.

accounting: A detailed statement of all income, expenses, and assets of the partnership.

The following case concerns whether a partnership existed, and if so, whether one of the partners breached her fiduciary duty to the others by withdrawing and starting her own business.

BECK V. CLARKSON

387 S.E. 2d 681 (S.C. App.1989)

FACTS

In January 1985 Allen Beck, Sheelah Clarkson, and Gerrye Clegg agreed to form a partnership to be known as CBC Investments. The purpose of the partnership was to build and develop a warehouse in Cherokee County, South Carolina, to be leased to Spring City Knitting Co. Over the next few months the partners (especially Clarkson and Beck) researched the information necessary and made contacts with Spring City. Beck's wife, a real estate agent, procured plats and contacted all property owners near Spring City's plant to ascertain their interest in selling property. The parties obtained building proposals from several contractors and discussed financing. A written proposal was sent to Spring City by Clarkson in March, signed "Sheelah Clarkson, CBC

Investments," listing Beck, Clarkson, and Clegg underneath CBC Investments. A follow-up proposal was sent by Clarkson in June.

In July, however, Clarkson notified Beck that she was withdrawing from the partnership and that she planned to develop the Spring City project with her brothers and sisters. In September, Clarkson, now acting for a family partnership known as "Clarkson Associates" entered into a contract to purchase the land for the warehouse facility and completed the purchase in November. On January 20, 1986, Clarkson Associates entered into a lease agreement with Spring City. The warehouse was built at a cost of about $1,879,000 and leased for $25,800 per month. By the time of the trial, the warehouse was estimated to be worth over $3 million.

Beck sued Clarkson, alleging breach of fiduciary duty, and asking that Clarkson account for all profits from the venture and pay to Beck his rightful share. The trial judge entered a directed verdict in favor of Clarkson, and Beck appealed to the South Carolina Court of Appeals.

DECISION

The court had to decide if Beck, Clarkson, and Clegg formed a partnership. They did not have a written partnership agreement, so the court looked at the events that had occurred. Beck testified that they had agreed to "share profits and losses." Beck's wife testified that Clarkson had told her that Beck, Clarkson, and Clegg were one-third partners. In addition, the parties testified that various documents bore the letterhead "CBC Investments" and the proposals to Spring City had been signed "CBC Investments."

The court cited the UPA definition that "A partnership is an association of two or more persons to carry on as co-owners a business for profit" and pointed out that a partnership does not need to be in writing but may be implied by the conduct of the parties. "If the partners intend to and do enter into such a contract as in the eyes of the law constitutes a partnership, they thereby become partners whether they are designated as such or not . . . ." Here there was ample evidence that the parties did form a partnership known as CBC Investments.

Clarkson then argued that even if there had been a partnership, it was a "partnership at will," which could be terminated by one of the partners whenever he or she wished, as she (Clarkson) had done. The court agreed that since no term was specified by the partners, it probably would have been a partnership at will except for the fact that the partnership was formed for a "definite undertaking" (the building and leasing of a warehouse to Spring City). Given this fact, it was quite possible, said the court, that a jury hearing this case may conclude that the partnership term could not be rightfully terminated by one partner until the completion of the project.

Although the act of one partner in leaving the partnership acts as a dissolution of the partnership, that does not necessarily terminate the fiduciary duties owed by one partner to another. South Carolina law provides that every partner must "account to the partnership for any benefit and hold as trustee for the partnership any profits derived from him" through any transaction connected with the partnership. The court noted with approval the holding of an Oregon court in a similar case:

When a partner wrongfully snatches a seed of opportunity from the granary of his firm, he cannot, thereafter, excuse himself from sharing with his co-partners the fruits of its planting, even though the harvest occurs after they have terminated their association.

A formal disassociation of one partner from the partnership does not allow that partner to exploit a partnership opportunity for his or her own benefit to the exclusion of the copartners.

The court concluded that there was strong evidence that the partnership was not "at will" and that Clarkson had violated her fiduciary duties to her former partners, which should have been decided by the jury. If the jury finds for Beck, "there must be an accounting of any profits" obtained by Clarkson from seizing the "seed of opportunity" connected with the project initiated by CBC Investments. The decision was therefore reversed and remanded back to the lower court for a new trial.

CASE QUESTIONS

1. Why is it that Clarkson could not withdraw from the partnership whenever she wanted to? Why do you suppose she did withdraw?
2. Could a written partnership agreement have made this dispute easier to solve or perhaps prevented it?
3. How long after a partnership terminates do you think a partner should be bound by fiduciary duties owed to copartners?
4. Would a "noncompetition clause" (a contract clause prohibiting one of the business owners from opening a competing business) have prevented this dispute from reaching the courts?

LIABILITIES OF PARTNERS

Personal Liability Partners can be *personally liable* for partnership debts. In other words, the partners' personal bank accounts, cars, homes, and so on can be attached (seized and sold through a judicial process) if the partnership assets are insufficient to pay partnership debts. This potential liability is a very important factor underlying the need to choose partners carefully and draft a partnership agreement before beginning business with someone else.

Liability for Torts As we have discussed earlier, a *tort* is the name for a wide variety of wrongful actions taken by one person which may harm another (such as negligence, battery, or slander). Torts are fully explored in Chapter 11. As we learned earlier in this chapter, employee-agents have the power to create liability on the part of the principal for torts they commit "in the ordinary course of business." Since partners are all agents of the partnership, if they or other agents or employees of the partnership commit torts within the course of business, such actions may bring about liability for the partnership and for the partners as individuals (UPA Section 13). For example, if Kenneth drives negligently and causes someone to be injured while delivering a jade plant from the partnership floral shop, he, the partnership, and the other partners are all liable for the damages caused.

Liability for Contracts As we have learned, according to agency law, the principal is responsible for contracts entered into by an agent on behalf of the principal when the agent is acting within his or her authority. Therefore, the partnership is held to contracts entered into by any partner with a third party when the partner was acting with express, implied, or apparent authority. According to the UPA, partners have implied authority to enter into agreements for the "carrying on of the partnership business in the usual way." This means that if, in the particular business in which the partnership is engaged, it is normal to borrow money, hire employees, or enter into contracts to sell goods and services, one partner has the power to make contracts that are binding on the partnership even if the other partners do not know about or approve such particular contracts.

SOCIAL/ETHICAL ISSUES

Is it fair to impose personal liability on partners for torts committed by other partners or employees of the partnership? This, in effect, allows the personal assets of one partner, such as one's home, bank account, or automobile, to be seized and sold to pay damages for a negligent act by another person. Is this ethical? What about personal responsibility? Even if the person who committed the wrongful act is also liable, does it seem fair to impose joint liability on an innocent partner?

Is it more or less fair or ethical to impose legal contractual liability upon a partner when another partner makes a contract on behalf of the partnership without consulting the partnership? Who is helped and who is hurt by such a principle of law? Does it benefit society?

PARTNERSHIP PROPERTY AND PARTNERSHIP INTERESTS

A partnership is an entity consisting of a distinctive combination of individuals who have chosen to go into business together. Since substantial trust and loyalty (fiduciary duties) are expected of all partners, it is not surprising that all partners have equal rights to use and possess all partnership property. Suppose that the ABC partnership (consisting of Alan, Beth, and Cynthia) owns three vehicles, three desks, and three computers. If Alan always uses the red car, the brown desk, and the Apple computer, and the other two partners always use the other cars, desks, and computers, does Alan have a greater claim on any of the items if the partnership breaks up? No. Can he obtain a personal loan, pledging his interest in the car, desk, and computer as collateral? No. Alan does not have any ownership interest in the items owned by the partnership, called **partnership property**. The partners each have equal rights in all such property.

partnership property: Property owned by the partnership. No partner has exclusive rights to such property.

Partners, however, may have merely loaned or rented certain property to the partnership (such as desks or computers) and retained title in the items themselves. The partnership agreement should specify any such items, and any rental agreements should be put in writing. When a partnership is being dissolved, the partners (and their creditors!) all want their shares to be as large as possible, and memories may be dim about which property was given to the partnership rather than loaned or rented. Although it is probably easy to remember who owns cars and trucks, decisions about other items often become more perplexing.

Suppose two accountants leave successful private practices to join a partnership, each purchasing part of their shares by assigning to the partnership their "accounts receivable" (money owed to the accountant from clients) and their 1/5 interest in a real estate joint venture. If the partnership dissolves 10 years later due to serious disagreements between the partners, it may be difficult to remember, calculate, and allocate each partner's contributions unless they have been carefully documented earlier.

Although partners do not have any ownership interest in specific property owned by the partnership, they each have an interest in the partnership itself, a percentage of ownership of the total net worth of the partnership, called the

partnership interest: Each partner's percentage share of the total net assets of the partnership.

partnership interest. A partner can assign this interest to a creditor or use it as collateral for a loan. When a partner withdraws from the partnership, she (or her heirs if she dies) is entitled to be paid the net value of her partnership interest, as is discussed in the next section. This partnership interest can also be attached by creditors of the individual partner.

TERMINATION OF PARTNERSHIPS

Partnerships only last as long as the partners want them to last. The articles of partnership may specify that the partnership will only exist for a certain period of time or until a certain task is achieved, and its existence will terminate when these events occur. Or the partnership can be ended by what is called "operation of law" if the business of the partnership becomes illegal or a partner dies or goes bankrupt.

The most common way for partnership to end, however, is through the withdrawal of one or more partners. Since partnership is a special relationship among a certain group of individuals, when any one of them dies or withdraws, that causes the **dissolution** of the partnership. The partnership is not finally terminated, however, until all the assets and liabilities are calculated and the partners' shares determined and paid. This process, called the *winding-up*, takes place after dissolution, and when completed, the partnership is said to be *terminated*.

dissolution: The partnership entity comes to an end when one partner dies or withdraws from the partnership.

Many partnership agreements provide for the continuation of the "business" by the remaining partners even if the particular partnership entity is dissolved. For example, suppose that Sheila, Amanda, and Mary have operated SAM's Coffee Shop for 10 years as partners, and now Sheila decides to leave the business. Sheila's withdrawal causes the *dissolution* of the partnership. She is entitled to receive her share of the net assets of the partnership business. The partners will have to make a financial determination of the assets and liabilities of the partnership (winding up) and compute the net worth of the partnership. However, Amanda and Mary may decide to continue the business—the coffee shop—under a new partnership arrangement. Or they all may decide to close down the business and divide the net assets.

Large law and accounting firms have some partners joining and leaving the partnership nearly every year. Their carefully drafted agreements call for an immediate transfer of all assets and liabilities of the business from the old partnership to the new one that beings operations at once. Nevertheless, the old partnership entity does end, and the departing partners or their heirs must be paid the value of their partnership interest within a reasonable time.

During the winding-up period, the assets are sold, and the debts of the partnership paid (if the business is not going to be continued). The partnership can finish projects underway at this time but cannot begin new ones—there is no partnership entity. Regarding the payment of debts, creditors of the partnership have first claim on partnership assets. If these creditors are not fully paid, they may go after the individual assets of the partners, because the partners still have individual liability for partnership debts incurred while they were partners.

In addition, the partners may have considerable individual debts as well. The creditors of the individual partners have first claim on each partner's individual assets. If these individual creditors are not satisfied, they can seek a **charging order**, which is a court order allowing them to attach the partner's partnership interest (his or her share of the partnership).

charging order: A court order allowing creditors of a partner to "attach" and receive the proceeds of the partner's share of a partnership.

LIMITED PARTNERSHIPS

FORMATION AND CHARACTERISTICS

A special type of partnership combines some of the features of partnerships with some of the features of corporations—the limited partnership. This type of business entity cannot be formed by accident—it takes a specific intent to do so. A limited partnership requires a written agreement (often quite long and detailed). The agreement, usually called the articles of limited partnership, must then be filed with and approved by the appropriate official of the state in which the partnership is located. Sometimes a separate certificate must be filed as well. Each state has a law spelling out the requirements for limited partnerships, and the articles of limited partnership must comply with the law in order for the state to certify the creation and existence of the limited partnership.

uniform limited partnership act (ULPA): A model statute setting forth principles governing limited partnerships, which has been adopted by many states.

As is the case with general partnerships, a group of business law experts (the National Conference of Commissioners on Uniform State Laws) has drafted a model law adopted by almost all the states, called the **Uniform Limited Partnership Act (ULPA)**. This law stipulates the primary legal principles applicable to the creation, operation, management, and termination of limited partnerships. The first ULPA was drafted in 1916 and has been updated several times, including a major revision called the Revised Uniform Limited Partnership Act (RULPA) in 1976, which was designed to replace the original ULPA. In 1985, however, the Commissioners wrote a separate new ULPA and later combined its provisions with the RULPA. One of the main stipulations of the revised version was to remove the requirement that the names and addresses of limited partners be listed on the certificate filed with the state. Several states have enacted the newest revisions of the RULPA, often with changes in some provisions, while most states have enacted some form of the older ULPA.

limited liability: When investors, such as limited partners, only risk losing their investment in the business, not their personal assets.

DIFFERENCES FROM GENERAL PARTNERSHIPS

The primary difference between general and limited partnerships is the **limitation on the liability** of the partners—hence the name "limited partnership." In each limited partnership, there must be at least one **general partner**, who has unlimited personal liability, like partners in a regular (general) partnership. The general partner has the duty of managing the business and making almost all business decisions. There must also be at least one **limited partner** (and generally are several) who does not have any personal liability. If the limited partnership incurs a large debt or loss, the limited partners may lose the money they paid to purchase a share of the partnership, but their personal assets will not be at risk for partnership debts.

general partner: The managing partner in a limited partnership who has unlimited personal liability.

limited partner: The partner in a limited partnership who does not have any personal liability for partnership debts.

Investors in various types of business ventures, particularly real estate developments, are often limited partners. They purchase shares with the hope that the value of the business increases, and they can sell their share for a profit later. Equally important is the opportunity to receive various tax benefits, such as taking a share of the depreciation allowance on the real estate, although this benefit has been limited by tax revision legislation.

Management of the business is the responsibility of the general partner or partners. As long as the limited partners do not participate in the management of the enterprise or allow their names to be publicly used in connection with the enterprise, they do not have personal liability for the partnership debt. If the limited partners do get involved in management, however, they may lose their preferred status and find themselves as individual defendants in a lawsuit. The removal (in the latest revision of RULPA) of the requirement that the names and addresses of all limited partners be listed on the certificate filed with the state is intended to confirm that the partnership agreement is the controlling document of a limited partnership. The tax revisions mentioned earlier and the creation of limited liability companies (discussed in the next chapter) have dramatically reduced the value of limited partnerships as a form of business ownership.

TAXATION

One key aspect of both general and limited partnerships is that they are not taxed as an entity. In other words, the partnership does not pay income tax, as a firm, on its profits. Instead, each partner (whether limited or general) pays income tax on his or her share of the profit and can deduct his or her share of the losses as well.

Thus the income tax liability is said to "pass through" the firm, directly to the partners. This tax liability is different from corporations, as we will see in the next chapter. In general, corporations are taxed as an entity, separate from the owners (shareholders). Then, if the corporation distributes some of its profit to shareholders as dividends, those distributions are taxed again as income of the shareholders.

LIMITED LIABILITY PARTNERSHIPS

A new and improved (from the partners' point of view) form of partnership has been created by statutes recently passed in many states, called the **limited liability partnership** (LLP). These organizations have important legal differences from both a general partnership and a limited partnership.

limited liability partnership: A relatively new form of business entity, which permits the partners to take an active role in management, while protecting them from personal liability.

The LLP entity allows all partners to participate fully in the management of the business, but without facing the unlimited personal liability that is characteristic of the general partnership. The LLP laws protect one partner from personal liability for the torts (negligence and other types of wrongful actions) of the other partners. Several of the state LLP laws offer partners limited liability (no personal liability) for other types of partnership debts as well. Partners do remain personally liable for their own torts.

Many law and accounting firms, which have traditionally been formed as general partnerships, are quickly changing to the new LLP form, for obvious reasons (liability). As with other limited liability entities, proper written documents must be filed with the appropriate state officials to formally establish an LLP.

SUMMARY

Many of the important principles controlling the liability of business organizations are based on the law of agency. Organizations can act only through the deeds of people. When one person (principal) asks or hires someone else (an agent) to act for him or her, it creates several significant legal duties and relationships. Agents owe the highest degree of loyalty and trust to their principals—called fiduciary duty. Agents often have the power to make contracts binding on the principal, depending on the scope of their authority. Also, principals sometimes find that they are liable for torts (wrongful actions) committed by employee-agents in the scope of employment.

A sole proprietorship is a business that legally is merely the extension of one owner—who makes all business decisions, is responsible for all debts, and can keep all profits. The business does not have a legal existence separate from the owner. Partnerships are a popular type of business organization, in which the business has an existence somewhat, but not totally, separate from the owners. Partnerships are easy to form, are flexible in structure, and can be used in many categories of ventures. The partners directly control and manage the operation of the business, and partnerships do not pay taxes as an entity—the partners each pay taxes on their shares of the profits. However, partnerships involve significant personal liability risks for the partners. A written partnership agreement and adequate business insurance are extremely important for any partner, in order to protect, as much as possible, his or her personal assets.

Limited partnerships serve as an investment vehicle for persons who do not want to be actively involved in the management of the business or to put their personal assets at risk in a business venture. A new form of business entity, the LLP, is being adopted by many law and accounting firms. All forms of business are significantly affected by the principals of agency law in determining the liabilities of the various members of the business to each other and to outside parties.

CHAPTER QUESTIONS

1. What is the usual rule about the termination of an agency relationship? What must the principal or agent do? What is an "agency coupled with an interest"?
2. Explain the legal theory *respondeat superior*. What is the policy behind such a rule? What effect does this rule have on business organizations?
3. Jane, Edward, and Terry form the JET Partnership to perform accounting and financial planning services. Jane contributes $6,000, Edward $3,000, and Terry $9,000. At the end of the first year, the partnership has a loss of $6,000. How should this be shared? The next year JET makes a profit of $54,000. How should this be allocated?

4. One partner of a law firm (general partnership) signed a contract promising to pay a sum of money annually to a former client, in return for a loan. When the partner did not pay as promised, the client sued the partner, and his other two partners as well. The other partners asked that the case be dismissed, claiming they knew nothing about the contract, and were not liable. What is the key issue here? What should the result be? [*Barnes v. McLendon*, 910 P. 2d 469 (Wash. 1996)]
5. What is the apparent authority theory? What is the reason for and public policy behind this rule?
6. Mr. Roberson, a truck driver, arrived at a Bethlehem Steel Co. loading dock in Burns Harbor, Indiana, to pick up a shipment of steel. After a lengthy wait (while other trucks that had arrived later were serviced), the truck was finally loaded, but the load was not centered properly, making driving hazardous. Roberson complained to the Bethlehem foreman, who told him they would not center the load but would *unload* it. Roberson reluctantly agreed, while expressing his displeasure with this response. After receiving his gate pass so he could leave the steel plant, Roberson and the foreman got into a verbal argument about how Roberson had been treated. As Roberson turned to go, the foreman slugged Roberson violently, breaking his jaw. Roberson sued Bethlehem Steel under the *respondeat superior* theory. At trial, Bethlehem Steel argued that (1) since the foreman had given Roberson his gate pass before the fight began, his tasks relating to Roberson were complete and whatever happened after that was outside the scope of employment; and (2) the foreman's actions were not "in furtherance of the employer's business." How should the court decide this case? [*Roberson v. Bethlehem Steel Corporation*, 912 F.2d 184 (7th Cir. 1990)]
7. The owner of a gas station that also rented Avis cars was sued as the result of a tragic traffic accident. One Sunday afternoon, when the gas station was closed, a 16-year-old boy (Robert Bruno) was on duty for the sole purpose of renting Avis cars. Later that afternoon another young employee arrived to work in his own car. Although the owner had told the employees not to use Avis cars for personal errands, Bruno (with his girlfriend) took an Avis car to get a pizza for lunch for the two young men. On the way back to the station, he negligently collided with another car, killing two people. The families sued the owner of the gas station as well as Bruno. The owner's defense was that Bruno was on a "frolic and detour" at the time of the accident, and he should not be liable. How should the court decide? [*O'Boyle v. Avis Rent-A-Car System, Inc.*, 435 N.Y.S. 2d 296 (1981)]
8. A limited partnership (Winter Park) defaulted on its payment of certain real estate taxes in Colorado. The property was sold at a tax sale after notice had been given by the state to the general partner. Later, after learning of the sale, one of the limited partners tried to redeem (buy back) the property, claiming that no notice had ever been given to the limited partners. However, the time period in which the owners could redeem the property had expired. The partnership was apparently in the process of dissolution, and the general partner had not notified the limited partners of the tax deficiency or sale. Should the time be extended for the limited partners, who did not receive notice? What legal principle applies? [*BMS*

Partnership v. Winter Park Devil's Thumb Inv. Co., 910 P. 2d 61 (Colo. App. 1995)]

9. Metzner and Sellers were officers of Maryland Metals, Inc., for many years. When their request to the primary owner for some equity in the business was refused, they began to plan for organizing their own firm. While they were still employed at Maryland Metals, they formed a corporation and borrowed money and purchased certain necessary equipment for their corporation. They told the primary owner of their intention to form their own company and continued to negotiate beneficial contracts for Maryland Metals right up to the time they left the company. Although the two officers did not fully disclose all their plans to Maryland Metals, there was no evidence that they diverted business to their new firm while employed there, nor was there any evidence of fraud or deception. When their new company began to aggressively compete with Maryland Metals, the owner sued Metzner and Sellers for breach of fiduciary duty. What should be the result in this case? [*Maryland Metals, Inc. v. Metzner*, 282 Md. 31 (1978)]
10. A Virginia partnership made an agreement with a lending institution to borrow $2 million "in installments from time to time" in order to build a new medical office building. All of the partners signed the agreement. Advances were made by the bank to the partnership over the next several years. One year after the loan agreement was signed, a new partner joined the partnership. When the partnership could not repay the loans, the lender sought to collect from the individual assets of the incoming partner for loan advances made after he joined the partnership. Was this partner personally liable? Why or why not? [*Citizens Bank of Massachusetts v. Parham-Woodham Medical Associates*, F. Supp. D.C. Va. 1995, 63 USLW 2461 (2-7-95)]

PRACTICAL EXERCISE

Robert, Kathleen, and Seth are recent graduates of State College. Seth, who has a science and technical background, has been experimenting with ways to use sagebrush as a healthful, high-fiber, dietary food source. Kathleen is a business graduate, well-schooled in the latest management, finance, accounting, marketing, economic, and statistics practices. Robert, a liberal arts graduate, knows a lot about the world and comes from a family of some wealth. These three graduates have decided to embark on a venture together to open a health food store that they hope will expand over the next few years. The project will attempt to develop Seth's sagebrush ideas into a marketable product (perhaps a breakfast cereal called "Sage Loops") and sell a wide variety of other health food items.

Robert has taken a job as a teacher for next year but would be willing to invest $50,000 in the project in return for a substantial share of ownership. Kathleen is excited about the project and would be willing to work full-time on it, at least for a year. Seth can devote part of his time to developing the sagebrush food supplement while he takes some courses in grad school. He can invest $10,000 in the venture and will use various scientific tools and materials of his own in his work (but wants to retain ownership of these items). Kathleen has no money to invest at this point but would like to earn a salary while managing the business.

The three entrepreneurs believe that it will take about $75,000 to start and stock their business for the first year and somewhat less during the second year. They hope to earn a profit by the end of year two. Obviously, if their business expands, they will need substantially more capital. Robert, Kathleen, and Seth have decided to form a general partnership. Prepare a brief (three to five pages) partnership agreement that sets forth the basics of the organizational structure and anticipates and avoids some of the problems they may face later. You may use the form contained in the chapter as a starting point, but it will be necessary to alter it to fit the particular needs of the parties. Some of the provisions will not be necessary.

FURTHER INFORMATION

www.dol.gov
U.S. Department of Labor.

www.sbaonline.sba.gov
Small Business Administration.

www.law.cornell.edu/topics/partnership.html
Cornell Legal Information Institute.

CHAPTER 9

CORPORATIONS

LEARNING OBJECTIVES

After reading this chapter, you should be able to:

1. Understand the steps involved in establishing a corporation.
2. Explain the legal structure of a corporation and the responsibilities and liabilities of the owners.
3. Describe the roles and duties of the various groups governing the corporation, including shareholders, the board of directors, and the corporate officers.
4. Detail the process of capital formation.
5. List the ways in which corporations can be terminated.
6. Describe the characteristics of special types of corporations.
7. Understand the requirements and attributes of a limited liability company.

CHAPTER OUTLINE

The three friends we met at the end of the previous chapter who wanted to start a health food business have now met with some success. They now want to expand their business by opening more stores and selling their cereal nationwide. Therefore, they are now considering changing their business entity to a corporation. You are asked to help them prepare articles of incorporation for their business in the "Practical Exercise" at the end of this chapter.

INTRODUCTION

legal entity: A corporation has an existence separate from, and independent of, any individual shareholder or director.

Corporations are the most important form of business organization in the world today. The legal structure of the corporation is significantly different from partnerships and sole proprietorships. The most important distinction is that the corporation is a completely separate **legal entity** that exists independently from any individual person involved in the business. As we discovered in the last chapter, partnerships are partially separate entities from the owners (for example, they can own property and sue and be sued) but are not totally separate (the partners have personal liability for partnership debts, and the entity dissolves when a partner leaves).

Corporations however, are considered as fully separate *legal persons*. Thus, a corporation can own property in its own name and file and defend lawsuits; however, the corporation must file a tax return and pay income taxes on the profits it earns, much like an individual. Unlike partnerships, though, the owners of the corporation do not normally have personal liability for debts of the business. And when one of the owners (called shareholders) of the corporation dies or wishes to leave the business, that person's shares are just inherited by or sold to someone else, and the corporation continues its existence.

Although the corporation itself has a separate existence, it is an intangible entity and can only act through agents—individuals who perform various services on behalf of the corporation. Thus, the principles of law regarding agency we examined in the preceding chapter are centrally important to determining the liability of corporations for all types of torts and contracts. Large companies have thousands of employees and shareholders as well as many officers and directors, all agents of some type for the corporation. Each group has different tasks and responsibilities—the "scope of authority" or "scope of employment" within which an individual's action may become the action of the corporation. We begin by examining how corporations are formed and then discuss the roles and legal responsibilities of the board of directors and shareholders and other important corporate issues.

ESTABLISHING A CORPORATION

state corporation law: Corporations are formed by following the law of the state where they choose to be incorporated.

Model Business Corporation Act (MBCA): A model state law dealing with corporations, drafted by an organization of business lawyers, which has been enacted by many states.

Unlike general partnerships, a corporation cannot come into existence informally or by accident. Corporations are artificial entities that can be created only through full compliance with the law of the state in which they are incorporated (like limited partnerships). Each state has its own **statutory corporate law** that specifies what must be done to form a corporation, the activities that corporations may undertake, the formalities required of corporations on an annual basis to maintain their status, the capital structure necessary, the manner and requirements for dissolving (terminating) corporations, and other matters.

As with partnerships and limited partnerships, an organization of legal and business experts (The National Commission on Uniform State Laws) has drafted a model law regarding corporations that many states have adopted in whole or in part. This statute, the **Model Business Corporation Act (MBCA)**, sets forth suggested provisions regarding all aspects of corporate formation, operation, and termination. Most of the material reviewed in this chapter is consistent with the principles of the MBCA. The fact that many states have adopted the MBCA promotes uniformity of law from state to state, which is important to the many corporations with operations in several states. Again, we should emphasize that corporations are chartered by states, not the federal government, and each corporation, in order to begin its existence and to operate in a legal manner during its life, must comply with the laws of the state in which it is incorporated.

The powers of corporations are established not only by the relevant state law but also by the corporation's **articles of incorporation**. Every state requires corporations to prepare such a written document, setting forth the name, address, and purposes of the corporation, the key people involved in its creation (the *incorporators*), and its capital structure and internal organization. Often called a **charter**, this document must be filed and approved by the appropriate state official before the corporation can legally exist. In some states, the secretary of state actually issues the charter to the corporation if its paperwork is all in order. In other states, the responsible state official stamps "Approved" on the corporation's articles of incorporation and returns them to the corporation if they are in compliance with the law.

articles of incorporation: A written document prepared by founders (incorporators) of a corporation, which sets out its name, purposes, number of authorized shares, official address, and other information.

charter: Another name for the articles of incorporation, establishing a corporation.

As a practical matter, someone needs to come up with the idea for starting a corporation. That person determines the need or opportunity for the business, raises the necessary funds, obtains commitment from other investors and lenders, finds office space, deals with potential suppliers, obtains any required licenses, and does the other things necessary prior to the beginning of the corporation's legal existence. These persons, called **promoters**, are personally liable for all actions they take before the corporation is formed (since there is no principal at that time). Once the corporation has filed the appropriate documents with the state, and the first board of directors has adopted its articles of incorporation, the promoters will no doubt seek to have the corporation adopt, on its behalf, all contracts and actions the promoters have entered into by that point.

promoters: The people who organize and start the corporation. They may be liable for contracts they make before the corporation is incorporated.

When the corporation accepts responsibility for the contracts, this may relieve the promoter from personal liability, as long as the other party to the contract is willing to substitute the corporation for the promoter. As we said in the previous chapter, when an agent makes a contract on behalf of a partially disclosed principal (for example, a corporation that does not yet fully exist), the contract is between the agent and the third party until the identity of the principal is known. At that time, the third party must choose whether to hold the agent (promoter) or principal (the corporation) liable. The promoters are quite interested, therefore, in seeing that all requirements for incorporation are properly met. When this is accomplished, it is said that a **de jure corporation** (a corporation of law) exists.

de jure corporation: A corporation which has been properly established and has met all incorporation requirements in its state of incorporation.

Once the corporation has established its separate entity, its existence cannot be successfully challenged by the state or creditors. Until the corporation has properly completed all the required steps for incorporation, the promoters will still have primary personal liability for contracts they have made. However, if the promoters have taken almost all necessary steps toward incorporation in good faith but some matter was not completely accomplished, courts may term the corporation a **de facto corporation** (a corporation in fact). For example, one of the promoters may not have signed the articles of incorporation filed with the state. If the corporation is considered *de facto*, the

de facto corporation: A corporation which has been properly established except for minor details, which the incorporators intend to promptly correct.

individual shareholders will not be personally liable as long as they promptly correct the problem. The state may challenge the existence of a *de facto* corporation, but creditors may not. This rule protects the promoters from personal liability. On the other hand, if there is a significant failure to follow state law or if the promoters acted in bad faith, the corporation will not be considered *de facto* or *de jure*, and the promoters (as agents for a nonexistent principal) will be individually liable for any actions taken.

CORPORATE STRUCTURE

There are three important groups of people involved in the legal structure of a corporation—the shareholders, the board of directors, and the officers. One aspect of a corporation that differs from partnerships and sole proprietorships is that often ownership and management of the organization remain separate. The *shareholders* are the owners of the company, and each one has invested money or something else of value in return for a part ownership of the company. The shareholders then elect a group of people called the *board of directors* to manage the business. The number of directors and how they are elected will usually be set forth in the articles of incorporation. Although members of the board are usually shareholders, this is not technically necessary. Some corporations have only one or two directors, while others have 20 or more.

Once elected, the board will often hire certain people to run the day-to-day operations of the company. Called *officers*, these persons (such as the president, vice-president, and treasurer) may or may not be shareholders or directors as well. They are technically employees of the company and carry out the tasks given them by the board of directors. In smaller corporations, the same people may serve as shareholders, directors, and officers; in larger corporations, however, this will not be the case. Thus, in larger companies a real separation exists between control and management of the corporation (by the officers and board of directors) and the ownership (thousands of shareholders, only a few of whom serve as directors).

Many important differences exist between the legal structure of partnerships and corporations and the responsibilities and liabilities of the owners. The next few sections highlight and explain some of these characteristics.

LIMITED LIABILITY

limited liability: Where the investors' liability for business debts is limited to the loss of their investment.

Perhaps the single most significant legal distinction, at least for the business owners, between a partnership and a corporation is that shareholders of a corporation enjoy **limited liability**. These investors purchase an ownership interest in the corporation, and whatever they have contributed to the company (money or property, for example) becomes part of the corporate assets. For example, if George purchases $1,000 worth of shares in the ABC Company and the corporation does not pay a debt it owes, the creditors may be able to attach (seize) the corporate assets, including the capital contributed by George. But in most situations, George cannot be personally sued by the creditors of the corporation for corporate debts. In other words, the liability of George, the shareholder, is *limited* to the loss of his investment in the company and is not extended to his personal assets.

As with many legal concepts, there is an exception to the general rule of limited liability for corporate shareholders. Occasionally, one or two individuals may be held personally liable for a corporate debt, usually when the organization has not acted like a corporation. Courts apply this concept, called **piercing the corporate veil**, to prevent unfairness when it appears that someone is trying to realize the benefits of incorporation (limited liability) without properly conforming with the requirements. This theory allows a court

piercing the corporate veil: The normal rule that shareholders do not have personal liability for debts of the corporation may be overcome where a dominant shareholder has disregarded the corporate form and operated the firm like it was a sole proprietorship, or a mere "alter ego" of that person.

FROM THE DESK OF
Laura Lawyer

To: Students
From: Your Lawyer

Many of you will start businesses or work in small firms. The corporate form offers significant advantages, such as limited liability for shareholders. However, if the business owners want the benefits of the corporate form, they must make sure that the organization behaves like a corporation whether it has two shareholders or 2,000. This means that it must elect a board of directors, hold meetings and keep minutes (in a "corporate book" along with the articles of incorporation, preferably), ensure that the corporate money and financial records are kept separate from any one individual's money, file all necessary state corporate reports, prepare and pay corporate taxes, and perform other acts as a corporation.

Another factor courts consider when "piercing the corporate veil" is whether the corporation is grossly undercapitalized for its own needs. For example, if a manufacturing corporation has only $400 in its treasury and the primary shareholder simply puts money into the corporation as needed, it would appear that the corporate firm is being used merely as a device to avoid personal responsibility by the primary owner. However, it is certainly possible for a corporation with only one or two shareholders to maintain a separate existence and to preserve limited liability if proper procedures are followed.

to overcome the corporate liability shield (i.e., to "pierce" it) and hold a dominant individual shareholder personally responsible to creditors.

Sometimes a person who has gone to the expense and effort of organizing a corporation under the appropriate state law operates it like a sole proprietorship, either intentionally or unintentionally. Suppose Heather has created the HRC Company, of which she is the sole shareholder (this is legal in most states and is allowed by the MBCA), and has properly followed state law in establishing its legal existence. However, Heather makes all decisions by herself, never holds board of director meetings, mixes her own money with corporate funds, and uses the corporate property (cars and computers, for example) for her own purposes whenever she chooses.

Suppose also that Larry has supplied $20,000 worth of office equipment to HRC Corporation. Now HRC Corporation says that it cannot pay Larry and that it has only $500 in assets. Since it is a debt of the corporation, Heather claims that she is not personally liable. If Larry sues Heather, as well as HRC Corporation, the court might decide that she has made the corporation her *alter ego* (merely a manifestation of herself) and allow the creditor (Larry) to pierce the corporate veil.

The following case represents an example of what can happen to an individual who seeks the benefits of the corporate legal structure but does not take the necessary steps to maintain the corporation's separate existence.

CARPENTER PAPER CO. V. LAKIN MEAT PROCESSORS, INC.

231 Neb. 93, 435 N.W. 2d 179 (1989)

FACTS

Lakin Meat Processors, Inc., was incorporated in 1975. Throughout its existence, Charles Lakin was the president and either the sole shareholder or the majority shareholder. Although the corporation's capitalization was stated as $100,000, at no time was more than $75,000 paid. During the course of the operation of the business (purchasing, slicing, packaging, and selling beef livers to retail outlets), Mr. Lakin made personal loans to the corporation on a regular basis. The loan balances reached as high as $1 million at times, and the loans were covered at all times by a security interest in favor of Mr. Lakin in all the tangible and intangible personal property of Lakin Meat, including furniture, machinery and equipment, inventory, accounts receivable, and notes. In other words, Mr. Lakin loaned the corporation considerable money, and the corporation put up as collateral all of its furniture, machinery, and equipment (which could then be seized by Mr. Lakin if the loans were not paid back).

Mr. Lakin was also involved in various other businesses and corporations. He had a checking account in his name at the American National Bank in Omaha that he used as a "sweep account." As checks were received by some of Lakin's various businesses, the checks were deposited into the account. For every business except Lakin Meat Processors, the exact amount of deposited money would then be transferred out of this account into the correct business account within a few days. For Lakin Meat, however, the funds remained in the American National Bank account until someone from Lakin Meat called and requested a transfer to its bank, Emerson State Bank in Emerson, Iowa. The transfers were always made in round numbers, not the exact amounts deposited earlier.

Lakin Meat did have its own place of business, its own employees, and a separate office within the Lakin Building for accounting and bookkeeping work. It also had its own phone, its own letterhead, and used its own invoices. Lakin Meat kept a corporate minutes book, filed its own tax returns, and kept its books and records separate from Lakin's other businesses.

In March 1981, Lakin Meat Processors, Inc., sold substantially all of its assets to Prime Meat Processors, for which Prime Meat paid $450,000 for fixed assets and $196,709 for inventory. At the time of the sale, Lakin Meat owed Mr. Lakin more than $1 million as the result of the loans discussed earlier. Mr. Lakin received the sale proceeds personally, and after the sale, he loaned another $271,000 to Lakin Meat and received loan payments from Lakin Meat of more than $1.2 million, leaving a balance due Mr. Lakin of $37,000.

Carpenter Paper Co. was one of Lakin Meat's creditors and had been a regular supplier for years. However, a dispute had arisen over five invoices in 1979 and 1980 concerning late payments and a shipment of printed liver film by Carpenter that Lakin said was defective. At the time of the sale of the business, the amount in dispute was about $5,900. Carpenter Paper obtained a default judgment against Lakin Meat in July 1982, but there were no assets to attach, so the firm sought to collect from Charles Lakin individually, that is, to pierce the corporate veil. The lower court dismissed the case, and the plaintiff appealed to the Nebraska Supreme Court.

DECISION

The Nebraska Supreme Court started its discussion of the legal issues with the general statement that "When a corporation is or becomes the mere alter ego or business conduit, of a person, it may be disregarded." Looking to the holding of a previous case, the court stated that some of the factors relevant in determining whether to disregard the corporate entity were:

1. Grossly inadequate capitalization;
2. Insolvency of the debtor corporation at the time the debt is incurred;
3. Diversion by the shareholder or shareholders of corporate funds or assets to their own or other improper uses; and
4. The fact that the corporation is a mere facade for the personal dealings of the shareholder and that the operations of the corporation are carried on by the shareholder in disregard of the corporate entity.

The court then applied these tests to the facts of the Lakin Meat case. It found that Lakin Meat had gross receipts of $5 million in 1980 and paid dividends of as much as $200,000 to Lakin in one year, although its capitalization never rose beyond $75,000. Expert witnesses at the trial testified that using various "debt-to-net worth" and other tests, Lakin Meat was "grossly inadequately capitalized," especially since it ran an overdraft of $100,000 in the bank for six years.

Concerning insolvency, Lakin Meat apparently did pay all of its creditors on a regular basis but since it owed Mr. Lakin somewhere between $214,000 to $1 million during most of its operation, its debts greatly outweighed its assets, making it insolvent in the bankruptcy sense at all times. Concerning "diversion of assets for improper uses," there was nothing other than the dividends of over $300,000 paid to Mr. Lakin and the final loan payoff of over $1 million.

The final point was the most telling. The court stated that in spite of the separate bank accounts and bookkeeping, "Lakin Meat was Charles E. Lakin. He controlled the corporation's every move. He ran it as he saw fit." The complicated series of books and accounts did not obscure the fact that "there was a unity of interest as far as Mr. Lakin and Lakin Meat were concerned." The court found that Lakin's manipulations of the business permitted him to, and he did, "terminate the corporation for his own financial well-being to the prejudice of the corporation's creditors." The lower court decision was therefore reversed.

CASE QUESTIONS

1. What was the most important factor the court used in deciding to pierce the corporate veil in this case? What factors supported Mr. Lakin's argument that only the corporation should be liable?
2. What should Mr. Lakin have done differently to avoid personal liability for the debts of the corporation?
3. Does the result in the case seem fair to you? Does it seem that justice was done in this case? Why?

SEPARATE ENTITY

Legally, corporations, much like individuals, are considered separate entities, distinct and apart from one another. Although certain persons play very important roles in every company, the corporation itself is made up of a combination of all the parts—the board, the officers, the shareholders, and, of course, the employees. Even if the sole shareholder dies or the top officers quit, the corporation would continue to exist. The share ownership would transfer after the death of the sole shareholder, and the board would select new officers to replace those who resigned. The corporation itself, however, would neither die nor resign. It is often said that corporations have perpetual existence because they do not depend on any one person, legally at least, for their existence.

TAXATION

Since corporations are considered separate entities, they not only enjoy the benefits of individuals, but they also share certain individual responsibilities—one of which is paying taxes. Unlike partnerships, corporations must pay income taxes on their net profit each year. The tax rates are not the same as those for individuals, but the payment of federal income tax (and generally state income tax, too) is a major corporate responsibility.

In addition, if after the corporation pays its income taxes it still shows a profit for the year, some of that profit will probably be paid to its shareholders as a *dividend*. The individual shareholders then must pay tax on these dividends as income on their own tax returns, a practice that has been called "double taxation."

CORPORATE GOVERNANCE

The actions of shareholders, members of the board of directors, officers, and employees are all important to the proper functioning of corporations. Each group has an important legal position in the process of governing corporate affairs, as discussed in the following sections.

THE ROLE OF THE SHAREHOLDERS

A corporation consists of many different groups of people with different responsibilities—all contributing to the whole. The shareholders are the owners of the corporation, and many corporations consist of only a few shareholders.

These companies, often called **close corporations**, may be owned primarily by family members with no shares being sold to the general public. And, of course, there are multibillion dollar corporations with thousands or millions of shareholders all over the world. In each type of corporation, however, the legal structure is essentially the same. The shareholders—whether there are three or 300,000—are the owners.

close corporations: Corporations with a small number of shareholders, often family members.

Even though they own the company, the shareholders do not manage the business. In a corporate structure, that role falls to the board of directors and the officers. The shareholders' main power is to elect the members of the board. Therefore, when people battle for control of a corporation or an outsider attempts to mount a takeover of a corporation, each side seeks to secure enough votes from the shareholders to elect the people they want to the board.

The shareholders are investors, not managers, and if they become dissatisfied with the way the corporation is going, they can always sell their shares. This is especially true in large companies, where there is a ready market for the shares on either a national stock exchange or the over-the-counter market. Furthermore, the likelihood of one investor being able to have an effect on the corporate policies is small.

The following cartoon is a humorous look at the sometimes contentious relationship between shareholders and managers.

SHAREHOLDER VOTING

Shareholders do have the right to vote on certain matters of great importance to the company, such as a merger or dissolution, amendment of the articles of incorporation, or adoption of measures restricting the free transfer of shares (e.g., a resolution prohibiting the sale of shares to outsiders without first offering the shares to the corporation). But most business decisions are made by the board of directors, not the shareholders.

In voting shares, generally each shareholder has as many votes as shares. Thus, large shareholders have a better chance of electing their choices to the

"There's a shareholder here to see you, sir."

From *The Wall Street Journal*, January 12, 1995. Reprinted with permission of Cartoon Features Syndicate.

cumulative voting: When the shareholders are allowed to vote their shares multiplied by the number of directors to be elected. A shareholder can cast all of these votes for one person.

board. Many corporations, however, have adopted a method of voting called **cumulative voting**, which increases the chance that those owning smaller amounts of shares can elect someone of their choice to the board. In cumulative voting, each shareholder gets as many votes as his or her number of shares multiplied by the number of directors to be elected. If Nancy owns 50 shares and there are five director spots to be filled, she has 250 votes, which she can vote entirely for one person if she chooses. Thus, a shareholder owning 51 percent of the shares in the company cannot be sure of electing *all* the directors—which she could do under regular voting.

In a small company or close corporation, most of the shareholders may also be members of the board and/or officers of the company (and often are employees as well). In this situation, one shareholder may actually be able to change the direction of the company. Also, the shareholder, without a stock market in which to trade, will probably have more difficulty selling his or her shares. But battles for control of small companies do occur. They are often decided by determining whose directors are elected to the board, which is based on share ownership.

In a battle for control of a larger corporation, the two competing sides will attempt to solicit support from the shareholders by mailing them letters explaining the benefits of their position and asking for *proxies* (the right to vote the shareholders' shares) at the meeting. Obviously, access to the shareholder list is critical to this effort, and the management of the corporation is not generally eager to assist its opponents. Although shareholders do have certain rights to obtain a copy of the list of corporate shareholders in order to wage a "proxy battle," that right is not unlimited, as the following case demonstrates.

PILLSBURY V. HONEYWELL, INC.

191 N.W. 2d 406 (Minn. 1971)

FACTS

Mr. Pillsbury was a member of a group of people opposed to American involvement in the Vietnam War. Members of the group learned that Honeywell, Inc., was a major producer of munitions for the Defense Department and embarked on an effort, called the "Honeywell Project," to get Honeywell to stop producing arms, particularly "fragmentation bombs." Pillsbury purchased some Honeywell shares and then requested a copy of the shareholder list and an opportunity to inspect the corporate books and records dealing with weapons and munitions manufacture. The request was denied by Honeywell management, and Pillsbury filed suit. The lower court denied his request, and the case was appealed to the Minnesota Supreme Court.

DECISION

The Court noted that several other courts had agreed with Pillsbury's contention that a shareholder's desire to communicate with other shareholders and to elect directors who shared his views gave him the right to obtain a list of corporate shareholders. However, the court stated, "We believe that a better rule would allow inspections only if the shareholder has a proper purpose for such communication . . . ."

The court took note of the burden that would be placed on large corporations if all shareholders could "roam at will" through the corporate books and records. In addition, it was apparent to the court that Pillsbury had no interest in the affairs of Honeywell other than its production of weapons. He had purchased a very small number of shares and "had made no attempt to determine whether Honeywell was a good investment." In the court's view, he did not have a "proper purpose" for obtaining corporate records.

In determining what was a proper purpose, the court looked primarily at economic factors. "We do not mean to imply that a shareholder with a bona fide investment interest could not bring this suit if motivated by concern with the long- or short-term economic effects on Honeywell resulting from the production of war munitions" (or, noted the court, the economic effects of abstaining from profitable war contracts).

In this case, however, the shareholder's concerns were not for the well-being of Honeywell or for the value of his own investment, but "his sole purpose was to persuade the company to adopt his social and political concerns." While normally an attempt to elect one's slate of directors would be a proper purpose, the court said that "here the purpose was not germane" to either Pillsbury's or Honeywell's economic interests and was therefore not "proper." Therefore, the lower court decision was affirmed.

CASE QUESTIONS

1. How could Pillsbury have rephrased his request so that he would have had the right to look at the corporate records?
2. Do you think that a shareholder should have the right to obtain a list of all shareholders for any and all reasons? Why or why not?
3. What other reasons, other than "economic interest," might qualify as a proper purpose for shareholder access to corporate books and the shareholder list?

THE ROLE OF THE BOARD OF DIRECTORS

Following their election by the shareholders, the **board of directors** has the legal right and duty to manage the regular business affairs of the company. A large number of decisions must be made by the board, as set forth in the following sections.

board of directors: This group of people, elected by the shareholders, has the legal duty of managing the corporation.

Regular Business Decisions Regardless of how many executive officers are hired or how often the board meets, it cannot escape the duties and responsibilities of governing the corporation. The Board is charged, for example, with deciding if the company should open a new plant, manufacture a different product, adopt a certain personnel policy, issue new stock, pay dividends, and many other business decisions. As mentioned previously, only extraordinary matters, such as a merger or dissolution of the corporation, need the approval of the shareholders; all other decisions are for the board to make.

How Board Decisions Are Made One important aspect of the board's role is that the directors may only take action as a board—that is, one or two directors acting independently have no power. A majority action of the board, however, taken at a duly scheduled meeting, upon proper notice, is an act of the corporation. The essence of the legal structure of a corporation is that the shareholders' best interests are served when all the board members meet together, share ideas, debate various courses of action, and then take a majority vote. In many cases courts have overturned board actions when there was no proper notice of the meeting given to all directors, or actions were taken without a meeting. Most states and the MBCA do allow directors to act in some cases without a meeting if they all have agreed to waive prior notice of the meeting. This might occur if there is a need for immediate action and the directors are fully informed of the situation and approve of the action. It will not be upheld if some of the directors decide to hold a meeting without proper notice and do not inform and obtain written consent from all the directors.

Payment of Dividends Not surprisingly, the payment of dividends is a matter of considerable interest to the shareholders. After all, receipt of dividends is one of the reasons why they invested in the company. However, as with most other corporate decisions, determination regarding payment of dividends rests with the board. It may be in the interests of the corporation to retain a larger surplus for some debt or liability contingency or for future construction projects in a particular year rather than to pay most of it out in dividends. As long as the board does not "abuse its discretion" in making the decision (i.e., deciding not to pay dividends for some fraudulent or improper reason), the questions of whether or not to pay dividends or how much of a dividend to pay are strictly for the board. In a very few cases, courts have ordered boards to declare dividends where profits are excessive and no reason exists for refusing to award dividends. The dividends can *only* be paid *out of surplus*, however, and cannot be paid if to do so would render the corporation insolvent.

Corporate Officers The board of directors will, in most cases, appoint certain persons to serve as officers of the corporation. These people, such as the president, vice-president, treasurer, and so on, serve at the pleasure of the board. In other words, they work for the board and can be fired if their performance does not satisfy the board. Some officers do enter into written contracts with the corporation (through the board) and then can be fired only for good cause. In large corporations, the officers are well paid for their services, while in close corporations, they are usually unpaid. Often, certain officers are elected to serve on the board as well. The officers are in charge of the day-to-day operations of the company, making all normal business decisions. Then, every few months, the board meets, listens to reports, and asks questions of the corporate officers. The board still legally has the responsibility for managing the corporation.

WHO REALLY GOVERNS THE CORPORATION?

inside directors: Members of the board of directors who are also officers and/or employees of the corporation.

outside directors: Members of the board who are not officers or employees of the corporation.

Despite the formal legal structure depicted in the preceding section, in which officers answer to the board, which must then answer to the shareholders, for large corporations the actual practice may be just the opposite. A number of commentators have observed that many corporations are actually run by powerful officers who make almost all the decisions. These decisions, then, are later ratified by the board, which may be filled with friends and business associates of the top officers. Directors who are also employees or officers of the corporation are called **inside directors**, and those not so employed are called **outside directors**. The outside directors may be officers of other companies and have only a few hours a month to study the affairs of this corporation. They may rely heavily on information given them by the corporate officers.

Even the election of directors may be actually controlled by the officers through the use of *proxies* (described earlier). In large corporations, relatively few shareholders attend the annual meeting where directors are elected. Along with the notice of the annual meeting, the management typically mails out to the shareholders a request to authorize the top management to vote the shareholder's shares. This form, called a **proxy**, if signed and returned by most of the shareholders (as is common), allows the management to vote large numbers of shares for the slate of directors proposed by the board. Management may vote the shares on any other matters that come before the annual meeting as well. Along with the proxy, the management must send the shareholders a *proxy statement*, which describes the main items of business expected to come up at the annual meeting, as well as the total salaries and compensation paid to the top five corporate officials and other interesting information. The following memo describes some of the information that can be learned from reading proxy statements.

proxy: A written document by which one shareholder authorizes someone else (often management) to vote his or her shares at the annual meeting.

FROM THE DESK OF
Laura Lawyer

To: Students
From: Your Lawyer

WHY YOU SHOULD READ PROXY STATEMENTS

As explained in the text, when management is requesting proxies from its shareholders prior to the annual meeting, it is also required to send "proxy statements." Although the statements are lengthy and filled with numbers and legalistic jargon, there is much useful and interesting information contained in them, which may help shareholders decide on selling or holding their stock.

Proxy statements must explain proposals which will come before the annual meeting, including routine matters such as the appointment of the auditing firm. Proxy statements also contain much more—such as how much the top management is paid, what stock options were granted, lawsuits pending against the company, and any special deals between the corporation and its management and directors.

"They are a soap opera in black and white," noted a vice president of Charles Schwab & Co. "I love to read them. Management has to disclose all the stuff they don't want to." For example, a few years ago, the proxy statement of Circle K Corporation disclosed that the president of one of its suppliers, Steve's Homemade Ice Cream, was serving as an unpaid consultant to Circle K and was helping make such significant decisions as when and where to change Circle K's prices. The proxy statement disclosed that the chairman of Circle K just happened to own 16% of Steve's common stock. The company filed for Chapter 11 bankruptcy protection within a year.

Some of the specific items which must be disclosed in proxy statements, according to the rules of the Securities and Exchange Commission are:

Stock Options. Shareholders can compute how much of the corporation's stock is being given to key management, and what part of their total compensation is in stock options. The shareholders, after all, should have final word on how much of their company they want to give to the management.

Lawsuits. The proxy statement must list and describe all significant lawsuits filed by or against the company, and give a short status report on the litigation. Often a shareholder can detect a disturbing pattern of problems, or a major threat to the company which may not have been clearly explained to shareholders by the management. (Who likes to give out bad news?)

Directors. Proxy statements disclose who the directors are, and who is standing for election this year. Shareholders should look at the background and experience of each person who has been nominated to serve on the board of directors. (The board is nominated by a small sub-committee of existing directors in most cases.) Shareholders should also find out the occupations of the proposed directors and how many of the nominees are "outside" directors. Most shareholder groups believe that having more outside directors (not company management) is good for a company. Too many "good buddies" of the CEO sitting on the board of directors may not be in the best interest of the organization as a whole.

Related Transactions. Many corporate directors have extensive outside business interests. Shareholders should find out if one of the directors is the president of their company's main supplier or customer. Shareholders can learn if their company's officers and directors are benefiting from such "sweetheart" deals between the officers' and directors' other firms and the shareholders' corporation. Does a director own the land or building on which the shareholder's company is located? Does a director own a plane that is leased to the company?

Compensation for Top Management. The proxy statement must list the annual compensation, for the last year, of the five most highly paid executives in the company. It is often interesting and instructive to compare the salary and bonuses and stock benefits paid to the top executives with the overall performance of the corporation—its profit and loss, and the stock price.

Sources: *The Wall Street Journal*, *Business Week*, CNN, and others.

In recent years, under the name of "corporate democracy," several proposals have been made to increase the powers of shareholders and to dilute the power of the incumbent officers and board. Some of the ideas include requiring more outside directors, requiring the selection of board members who represent consumer and environmental organizations, changing the law to allow shareholders to more easily propose resolutions to the annual meeting, and various reforms to the proxy system. While only a few of these proposals have been enacted into law as yet, many corporations have made changes in their procedures in response to public discussion of these issues.

SOCIAL/ETHICAL ISSUES

There has been criticism directed at corporations where the members of the board become "rubber stamps" who approve the policies of the chief executive officer (CEO) and other top officers. As we have discussed, although board members are technically elected by the shareholders, actually they are often chosen by a committee of the board (which may include the CEO or another key inside director). Then the board selects a group of persons who will "run" for election. The management sends out proxies to all shareholders, and most shareholders sign them—only a small percentage actually attend the annual meeting. Therefore, by the beginning of the meeting, the board-nominated group usually has more than enough votes to be elected.

Some changes are occurring. In the mid-1990s, General Motors Corp (GM) established a set of 28 "Guidelines on Corporate Governance." These rules called for the board to select a "lead director" who will call at least three meetings a year of the outside directors; also that the outside directors will make a formal evaluation of the CEO each year; and the outside directors will make decisions regarding corporate governance issues.

What do you think about the need for the board to be independent of management? Should outside directors have more power or different rules than inside directors? What is wrong with having close friends of the CEO on the board?

FIDUCIARY DUTIES OF OFFICERS AND DIRECTORS

The officers and directors of a corporation, like agents and partners, have fiduciary duties to the corporation. The shareholders have put them in a position of considerable trust and responsibility, and they must act accordingly. Two primary legal responsibilities are incumbent upon them: the duty of care and the duty of loyalty.

The Duty of Care Shareholders have the right to expect the directors to exercise their responsibilities thoroughly and carefully. The board, after all, is managing the corporation in which the shareholders have invested their money. The law recognizes and enforces these expectations, and directors are held to the **standard of due care** with respect to their performance.

standard of due care: Board members owe to the shareholders the duty to act with care and to diligently carry out their responsibilities in a non-negligent manner.

The standard of due care is essentially based on *negligence theory*. The legal principle of negligence is based on comparing the actions taken by a person in a particular situation with the level of conduct a reasonably careful person would have used in the same situation. In the corporate setting, if a director carries out the duties of the position in a reasonable and competent manner, he or she will not be liable to the shareholders if the business loses money or encounters trouble. If, on the other hand, a director is negligent in managing the corporation, he or she may be sued by shareholders if the business incurs substantial debts or goes into bankruptcy and the shareholders lose their investment.

The Business Judgment Rule To handle such situations, the legal system has developed a theory called **the business judgment rule**. The rule provides that if the board has made decisions after exercising careful business judgment, the board members will be immune from liability even if the decision turns out to be a bad one for the company. For example, if the board of directors of the Bronco Golf Co. decides to manufacture a line of blue and orange striped golf balls after careful market study, cost analysis, and product testing, the board will probably avoid liability to the shareholders if the project is a failure. However, if the decision was made to go ahead with the project simply and solely because the company president "just loves stripes," then the board might be liable to the shareholders for the project's failure (double bogey).

the business judgment rule: If the directors have made a decision after careful consideration, they will not be liable to the shareholders even if the decision has bad consequences for the company.

In other words, the business judgment rule protects directors by allowing them to make mistakes as long as they go about making the decision in a thorough way. Shareholders cannot expect that the board will never make a bad decision, but they have the right to expect that all decisions will be fully researched and carefully made. Board members of all corporations—big and small—must be prepared to attend meetings regularly, read reports given them by officers, ask questions when something is not clear, and generally act without negligence in order to properly carry out the duties entrusted to them by the shareholders. There is no such thing as a "silent director." If a board member does not have the time or the ability to actively serve as a director, he or she should resign from the board.

During the 1990s, a large number of corporate mergers and takeovers took place. While some were handled in a friendly manner, others were **hostile takeovers** in which an outside investor attempted to purchase all or a majority of stock in the company, against the wishes of the corporate management. This type of bid is called a **tender offer** when it is directed to the shareholders of a company. In the face of an unwanted tender offer from an outsider, generally at a high price, corporate directors were often called on to make difficult decisions, under considerable time pressure, about what was in the best interests of the company and the shareholders. Tender offers will be discussed in more depth in Chapter 10.

A colorful new vocabulary evolved as corporations tried to repel unwanted takeovers. Many companies enacted **poison pill plans**, triggering new shareholder rights whenever a corporate raider acquired a certain percentage of the corporation's stock. Such plans allow the existing shareholders to receive large amounts of stock at a very low price, making the takeover exceedingly expensive for the raider. As the nickname "poison pill" suggests, the corporation's strategy was to tell prospective raiders, "If you swallow our company against our wishes, you will become very ill."

During the battle for control of a company, sometimes the existing management enlists the aid of a third company, with whom a merger would be acceptable, in order to thwart a takeover by an unwanted suitor. This acceptable third company has been termed a *white knight*. One big worry for top company management is that if the company is taken over by another company, after a hostile battle the first thing that the new board of directors will do is fire the former company's management. In response to this concern, a number of company boards adopted **golden parachute** plans, guaranteeing their key executives a handsome severance package if they should be terminated following a takeover.

In the following case, the court interpreted the business judgment rule in a situation in which a corporation's board voted to approve rather than reject a merger.

hostile takeover: A takeover in which an outside investor attempts to purchase all or a majority of stock in a company against the wishes of corporate management.

tender offer: An investor attempts to take control of a corporation by buying a majority of the shares from existing shareholders.

poison pill plan: A defensive tactic used by a company facing an unwanted takeover bid that makes the purchase of its stock very costly.

golden parachute: The nickname for a generous severance package provided to a corporate executive terminated in a takeover.

SMITH V. VAN GORKOM

488 A.2d 858 (Del. 1985)

FACTS

As he approached retirement, the chairman and chief executive officer (CEO) of Trans Union Corporation, Jerome Van Gorkom, concluded that he wanted to sell the company. Mr. Van Gorkom—a lawyer and certified public accountant—had been CEO of the company for 17 years, during which time he had participated in many acquisitions. He analyzed the value of Trans Union on his own (with the aid and knowledge of only one other Trans Union employee) and determined what he considered a fair buyout figure per share.

Mr. Van Gorkom then took his proposal to Jay Pritzker, a well-known takeover specialist and acquaintance of Mr. Van Gorkom's, at Mr. Pritzker's home. At this point Mr. Van Gorkom had not told any Trans Union board members or officers about his idea. Mr. Pritzker was interested, and he and Mr. Van Gorkom then met several times over the next few days (with a few corporate officers present some of the time). Mr. Pritzker decided he wanted to go forward and do a "cash-out merger" (merging Trans Union completely into one of Mr. Pritzker's companies). Mr. Pritzker also demanded that the deal be completed in three days, or he would withdraw his offer.

Trans Union Corp. had, of course, many shareholders and a board of directors. Mr. Van Gorkom hurriedly called an emergency meeting of senior management and a board meeting for the next day without giving the reason for the meetings. After hearing Mr. Van Gorkom's presentation calling for the hasty sale of the company, the top management officials of Trans Union reacted quite negatively. Nevertheless, Mr. Van Gorkom proceeded with the board meeting one hour later. He made a 20-minute presentation, followed by short remarks from the president and chief financial officer (who stated that the proposed share price was "at the low end" of the acceptable range). During this two-hour meeting, the board, at Mr. Van Gorkom's urging, nevertheless approved the merger, despite the absence of any relevant documents, legal opinions, or financial analysis or materials of any kind. Later that evening Mr. Van Gorkom signed a merger agreement at a formal social event he hosted for the Chicago Lyric Opera (attended by Mr. Pritzker). Again, no one else from Trans Union (nor any of its legal or investment advisors) had seen or reviewed the merger document.

Two weeks later, as dissent to the sale mounted within the company, the board met again and heard further details of the agreement and approved some amendments to the merger (although the actual written amendments later put in the contract were not quite the same as Mr. Van Gorkom told the board they would be). The board still did not ask any significant questions or request more time. The board also failed to seek outside advice from any attorneys or the company's investment banker, Salomon Brothers. A few months later the shareholders formally approved the merger. However, several shareholders filed suit against Mr. Van Gorkom and the board of directors, arguing that they had violated their duty of care by approving the sale so quickly. In doing so, they argued, the board had not exercised prudent business judgment. Had the board acted more carefully and thoroughly and considered other buyers, the shareholders argued, they could have gotten considerably more for their shares.

DECISION

The Delaware Supreme Court noted that:

1. The directors based their decision almost entirely on Mr. Van Gorkom's short oral presentation and analysis of the transaction.
2. They did not know that he had actually suggested the price to the buyer.
3. They failed to ask relevant questions about the terms of the merger agreement and approved it in one two-hour meeting.
4. No consultations were made or requested with management or independent advisers (such as the company's investment banker) regarding the "intrinsic value" of the company or the fairness of the transaction.
5. The directors did not request or review copies of any major documents, nor did they seek the advice of their attorneys.

The directors argued that their later meeting, at which further material was provided, along with the subsequent approval of the shareholders, had cured the problems created by the short initial meeting. The Court disagreed, however, finding that the corporation was effectively bound to the agreement after the first meeting, and the shareholder vote was meaningless because the shareholders were not informed fully of the facts behind the board's decision.

The Delaware Supreme Court cited a case it had decided only one year earlier (*Aronson v. Lewis*) concerning the business judgment rule, where the court had written that directors must "inform themselves, prior to making a business decision, of all material information reasonably available to them," in order to come within the protections of the rule. The court held that the directors in *Van Gorkom* had breached their duties of care by approving, in a most hasty manner, the very sale of the corporation—perhaps the most significant decision they would ever be asked to make. The actions of the board members in this instance amounted to "gross negligence" in the performance of their duties.

The case was remanded to the lower court for the purpose of holding hearings on the fair value of the stock of the corporation, with the directors being personally liable for the difference between what was paid for the stock and its fair market value. (The case was later settled, with the individual directors and the company's insurance company paying a large settlement to the shareholders.)

CASE QUESTIONS

1. What should the directors have done differently? Why is it that they did not do more when they had the chance?
2. Why did the directors not have the right to trust and believe the president when he, the CEO of the company, told them the price was fair?
3. Because they want their company to continue as is—with them as directors—a targeted company's board may take action to block a takeover, including the adoption of poison pill resolutions. At what point does this type of activity violate the board members' duty to the shareholders?

SOCIAL/ETHICAL ISSUES

American companies are often criticized by commentators for being composed primarily of white males, who may include friends and business associates of the CEO. Things are changing in the United States, with boards becoming somewhat more diverse and including more outside directors who are not tied to the CEO or top management, due to pressure from shareholder activist groups.

Other nations have different historical and cultural factors that affect the composition and duties of the board of directors. In Germany most companies have two different boards, one of which is largely composed of employee representatives and "public" members. The following reading discusses the historical role of the board in Japanese companies and the changes that are presently underway.

Japanese Corporate Governance: No Country for Old Men

"Damn these old bastards," curses Chiaki Asami, the dashing young politician whose plan to seize power from the geriatrics who run Japan is coming unstuck. The Japanese company men who read about Mr. Asami's unequal struggle in "Sanctuary," one of Japan's most popular *manga* (comic book) series, know just how he feels. Many of them are bursting with fresh ideas—for new products, new markets and new ways of running their

Courtesy of Satoshi Kambayashi.

company. Yet at every turn, it seems, they are blocked by the stubborn old boys on the board.

Japanese boardrooms are packed with antiquities: the average age in the largest firms is 60. Almost all are men; because they are rarely hired from outside the company, most are decidedly inward-looking. But some of these dinosaurs are now on the way out. A rash of recent announcements, including news on April 28th of sweeping changes to the board of Nissan, a car maker, suggests that Japanese firms are at last rethinking how they run their boards, and in whose interests.

At present, directorships in Japan are generally dished out to company managers as rewards for loyalty and long service. As companies grow, so do their boards. The boardroom table of Toyota, a much-admired car maker, seats 56 people. Bank of Tokyo-Mitsubishi, the biggest and strongest lender, has 59 directors. On such big boards, factional politics dominate and any sort of decision becomes tricky. So decisions that matter are taken elsewhere or not at all, leaving the board to rubber-stamp pre-agreed points of little importance.

Even after Sony, a consumer-electronics company, cut its board from 40 to 10 in 1997 (three of these are independent non-executive directors), reform has been patchy. But lately, four well-known firms have said they will shrink their boards: Nissho Iwai, a trading house, Orix, a leasing company, Daiei, a supermarket chain and Nippon Fire & Marine, a non-life insurer. All told, 200 or so listed companies are shedding directors. Nissan's plan is to cut its board from 37 to 10. Remarkably, three of these directors will come from Renault, a French car maker that is buying a 36.8% stake in the company. Nissan says that its new board will be younger, with its directors likely to be in their 40s and 50s.

Companies which reformed their boards last year are already seeing the benefit. For instance, when Toshiba, an electrical conglomerate, cut its board to ten last June, it lost the director responsible for its automated teller-machine business—which has freed the company to spin off this troublesome division.

Smaller boards will allow sharper board oversight of a company's operations and more accountability to shareholders. Together, these could work wonders for profitability in depressed Japan. Yet slimming the board is not the only reform needed to improve corporate governance. Few of the checks and balances that constrain directors elsewhere operate in Japan.

Two other changes in particular would improve matters. The Keizai Doyukai, an association of corporate executives, has said that at least 10% of board directors should come from outside the company. The association's new chairman, Yotaro Kobayashi, might even keep up his reforming zeal: he became president of Fuji Xerox, which makes photocopiers, at the tender age of 44. And the Tokyo Stock Exchange, an unlikely reformer, has ruled that all listed companies must now disclose what they are doing to improve corporate governance when filing their results.

Plenty more change is needed—for instance, in auditing. Under a system borrowed from Germany, Japanese firms must appoint at least three internal auditors to keep an eye on financial management and guard shareholders' interests. But, as Garry Evans of HSBC, a British-based bank, points out, this works badly in practice, because most auditors are company employees, usually retired chairmen. And although companies must hire at least one "independent" auditor, the definition is loose; most are brought in from affiliated companies.

Potentially the most persuasive agents of change ought to be institutional shareholders. Nomura Asset Management recently said it may start voting its shares against management at shareholders meetings. But Nomura is a rarity. The overwhelming majority of institutions still prefer to pre-approve all proposals put before shareholders—and let off steam afterwards with their heads buried in *manga*.

The Duty of Loyalty Shareholders have the right to expect their officers and directors not only to do their best to make good business decisions after careful consideration but also to execute their duties based on what is best for the corporation, not on what is best for them. In many cases, of course, those goals are similar—if the corporation makes a good profit, the directors and officers will benefit as well as the shareholders.

But suppose the corporation is seeking a site to build a new factory and is willing to pay $100,000 for such a piece of property. One of the directors, Art, is involved in real estate and learns of a suitable location. However, before telling the appropriate corporate official about it, Art purchases it himself for $60,000, has the title put in the name of his sister-in-law, and then notifies the company about the land. When the corporation later purchases it for $100,000 (a fair market price), has Art done anything wrong? The answer is definitely yes, because under the **corporate opportunity rule**, officers and directors cannot benefit personally from an opportunity in which the corporation might have been interested. These people are fiduciaries, after all, and they should be thinking about how they can save money or otherwise aid the corporation they have been entrusted to manage.

corporate opportunity rule: If a director learns of a business opportunity that the corporation might want to pursue, he or she must bring the idea to the board for consideration, before taking advantage of it personally.

SOCIAL/ETHICAL ISSUES

Is there really anything ethically wrong with the actions of Art, the director set forth previously? Who was hurt by his action? After all, the corporation got the land it needed at a fair price. Would it have been ethically proper if Art had not put the property in his in-law's name but had told the company that he owned the land? What if he did not disclose that he had just purchased it or the price of the purchase? May a director ever be involved in another business enterprise that does business with the director's corporation?

CORPORATE LAWSUITS

In almost all cases, decisions concerning whether the corporation should initiate a lawsuit against someone or how, when, and in what manner the corporation should defend a lawsuit are board decisions, as part of its responsibility for management of the company. An individual shareholder or a group of shareholders normally has no role in corporate litigation. However, occasionally a shareholder may file what is called a *derivative action*. This type of lawsuit is brought to remedy situations in which the directors or officers have acted outside the scope of their duties, performed in a fraudulent manner or have engaged in self-dealing (creating benefits for themselves through the corporation) in violation of their fiduciary duties.

derivative lawsuit: A lawsuit brought by one or more shareholders on behalf of a corporation, where the board of directors has refused to act.

A **derivative suit** is brought by a shareholder "on behalf of the corporation," and any recovery obtained goes to the corporation, not to the shareholder who brought the suit. Generally, in order to initiate such a suit, the shareholder must have owned stock in the corporation at the time the wrongful act occurred, requested that the board take action, and been turned down. Also, some state laws require the shareholder to post a bond or security to cover the corporate expenses should the lawsuit be decided in favor of the corporation. (The corporation, through its board of directors, will no doubt be on the other side of the case, vigorously opposing the lawsuit.) Sometimes a group of shareholders or a successor (a government body that takes over the corporation) will be given extra time to sue the directors because no suits could be brought while the company was under the "adverse domination" of the old board. Derivative actions serve a useful purpose in allowing shareholders to punish misconduct by directors and officers, but they also offer the possibility for misuse by dissident shareholders. Therefore, they are subject to careful control by the courts and are only available in certain situations in which the directors clearly are not acting in the best interests of the corporation.

CORPORATE COMPLIANCE PROGRAMS

corporate compliance program: A program undertaken by the management of a corporation to ensure that all relevant laws are being followed.

In recent years it has become increasingly important for corporations to implement and maintain **corporate compliance programs**, in order to detect and punish wrongdoing internally. Such programs, instituted by the board of directors and management, started becoming popular about 10 years ago as a way of limiting a company's criminal liability for acts of employees, as well as its civil and regulatory responsibility in a wide range of situations from sexual harassment to workplace safety.

The development of compliance programs is a good example of how the board of directors' duty of care changes and expands with changes in society. The development of the Federal Sentencing Guidelines (as discussed in Chapter 7) gave corporations strong incentive to implement compliance programs (criminal sentences would be reduced). The courts also began to look at a company's internal practices when enforcing criminal law and setting damages in civil cases. Delaware Chancery Judge William Allen wrote, in a case involving Caremark International, "Senior managers and directors must make a good faith effort to ensure that the company has an adequate system to internally detect illegal activity in a timely manner."

So it has now become quite common for large corporations to have a formal plan, involving all job levels and phases of operation, to prevent, detect, and punish illegal actions and other wrongful acts. Corporate counsel and experienced business attorneys argue that large companies cannot afford not to have compliance plans in place before Federal Bureau of Investigation agents or regulatory officials show up. "If the first time you talk to the government about your compliance program is when you're filling out a presentence report (after a conviction) you've got a problem," said the general counsel for International Paper Co.

Companies that find a problem and promptly report it to authorities are much less likely to be charged with criminal violations and, even if convicted, will face lower penalties. However, the firm is expected to cooperate with government inspectors and prosecutors and furnish reports of its internal investigation. In addition to avoiding criminal liability, a compliance program that is vigorously practiced can reduce punitive and other damages in a civil case and may result in lower insurance premiums as well.

Prosecutors and corporate lawyers agree that getting the board of directors and high-level managers on board is key to creating a "compliance culture," which leads to a successful program. The best programs are ones in which the management leads by example. The most effective plans stress company values and positive behavior, rather than focusing only on criminal violations and punishment.

CAPITAL FORMATION

EQUITY AND DEBT SECURITIES

equity securities: Shares of stock representing ownership interests in a corporation.

Corporations are the type of business organization most capable of raising large amounts of capital. When corporations are formed, they normally authorize the sale of corporate shares in the form of stock. No real limitation exists on how many shares of stock a corporation can sell, with each share representing a small percentage of ownership of the company. Over the life of a corporation, there may be only one or two shareholders or several hundred thousand, each owning a number of shares.

When a corporation finds itself needing money for expansion or some other purpose, it can issue new shares, thereby raising money for the corporation and adding many new shareholders. The laws regulating the issuance and trading of shares of stock are an important aspect of the "legal environment of business" and will be thoroughly discussed in the next chapter. Of course, this sale of new shares would dilute the percentage of ownership of each existing shareholder. To deal with this problem, many corporations have adopted a policy called **preemptive rights**. This policy allows existing shareholders the option of purchasing the same percentage of the new shares as their current ownership percentage. For example, if Juanita currently owns 5 percent of the shares in ABC Corporation, she will have the option to purchase 5 percent of any new shares offered. Current shareholders, therefore, will continue to own the same percentage of the corporation.

preemptive rights: The right of shareholders to purchase the same percentage of new shares, as they hold in existing shares.

common stock: The most typical type of equity (stock) ownership by shareholders in a corporation.

Most shares of stock are **common**, which means that when the board of directors of the corporation declares a dividend, all shareholders are paid the same amount per share of ownership. Each shareholder has one vote for each

preferred stock: A type of equity (stock) ownership which provides the owners certain preferences over common stockholders.

debt securities: A loan made to the corporation, such as a bond, that does not carry an ownership interest.

treasury stock: Shares of stock that have been issued and sold by a corporation, and then later repurchased by the corporation.

share of stock owned. Owners of **preferred stock** are generally entitled to receive dividends before the common stockholders do. This stock often specifies dividends of a certain amount and normally does not carry voting rights.

Corporations may also raise money by issuing **debt securities**, such as bonds. These instruments actually represent a type of loan by an individual to the corporation that the company promises to pay back at a certain rate of interest. The bondholders do not become stockholders through the purchase of these debt securities.

One other type of stock is called **treasury stock**. This is stock that a corporation issues and sells, but then repurchases. While owned by the corporation, this stock does not carry voting rights and does not receive dividends. The corporation can use this stock for bonuses to key employees or for other purposes, or it may decide to resell this stock later.

TERMINATION OF CORPORATIONS

MERGER

The 1990s saw the largest mergers in the history of the United States. Some were voluntary, in which two corporations decided to become one (as in *Smith v. Van Gorkom*) and others were hostile takeovers, as discussed earlier. In order for two corporations to legally merge, the action must usually be approved by both companies' shareholders (many states and the MBCA require a two-thirds majority). The resulting corporation acquires all the assets and liabilities of both corporations.

dissent: The right of a shareholder to object to a merger and to be paid the fair market value for the shares owned.

Generally, shareholders of the corporation that has been absorbed are given shares, in a predetermined amount, in the surviving corporation. If some shareholders do not wish to merge or become shareholders in the new company, they can **dissent** in writing from the merger and have the right to be paid the fair market value of their old shares.

DISSOLUTION

dissolution: The termination of the existence of a corporation.

We said earlier that while corporations may have a perpetual existence, sometimes their existence is terminated, which is called **dissolution**. It may be *voluntary* as when a merger occurs or when the articles of incorporation specify a predetermined life span of, say, 10 years. Or the dissolution may be *involuntary*, as when, for example, the corporation has failed to file necessary papers with the state or pay state taxes for several years, or when the corporate charter was obtained by fraud. In these cases, the state has the power to dissolve the corporation. Also, if the shareholders are equally divided and unalterably opposed on every issue, one may seek a court order dissolving the corporation. When the corporation is dissolved, the assets are sold, the creditors paid off, and the balance distributed to the corporate shareholders.

TRANSFER OF A FAMILY BUSINESS

Many small businesses were started by one person who through hard work has built a successful enterprise that now employs many family members. Focused on building their business, these founders typically have not thought about what would happen to the business if they died. The consequences can be disastrous, however, if the primary owner dies and a family feud ensues for control of the business.

A business succession plan can be integrated into an overall plan for the distribution of one's estate. Experts are continually surprised by the number of family business owners who do not have a will that takes into account how the business survives. They advise the creation of a succession plan as the business grows, long before the founder is ready to retire.

The simplest way to transfer business assets is for the founder to make gifts of stock to his or her children—up to $10,000 per child can be given per year tax-free. This plan reduces the owner's taxes and transfers ownership at the same time. Another smart idea is a "buy-sell agreement," by which the corporation or the remaining stockholders are obligated to buy the departing or deceased owner's stock. The value and payment terms of the purchase should be determined in advance. Often the company or each of the major shareholders purchases life insurance covering the key owners, so there is an amount of money available to fund the buyout upon a principal owner's death.

Trusts can also be useful in business succession. Stock can be transferred into a child's trust account, with estate tax savings as described previously. Certain types of trusts can allow the primary owner time to address the issue of who will eventually control the business, especially if the children are young or undecided about joining the business.

OTHER TYPES OF CORPORATIONS AND COMPANIES

The traditional type of corporation we have discussed up to this point is a "for-profit corporation" (called a "C corporation"). Such corporations hope to make a profit and distribute dividends to shareholders as previously discussed. However, there are several other important types of corporations.

S CORPORATIONS

Under a section (Subchapter S) of the Internal Revenue Service Code, it is possible to form a corporation that is taxed like a partnership, thereby avoiding double taxation. So-called **S corporations** cannot have more than 75 shareholders and must obtain 75 percent of their gross revenues from active operations rather than passive sources, like receipt of dividends or investment income. All shareholders must agree to the S corporation status, and there can be only one class of common stock. If an S corporation is successfully created, each shareholder will be treated as receiving (and be taxed on) his or her proportionate share of the corporation's income or loss in a year (whether distributed or not) just as if the organization were a partnership. At the same time, as shareholders of a corporation, the investors enjoy limited liability.

S corporation: A type of corporation in which the shareholders have limited liability.

The chart on the next page compares some of the key features of the different forms of business organizations.

limited liability company: A type of unincorporated business entity which provides limited liability to the owners.

LIMITED LIABILITY COMPANIES

In the past 10 years, the hottest new form of business entity has been the **limited liability company (LLC)**. Starting with the passage of the first LLC

Characteristics of Business Organizations

	Sole Proprietorship	Partnership	Limited Partnership	Corporation	S Corporation	Limited Liability Companies
Ease of formation	Easy—no requirements.	Easy—written articles not required, but strongly recommended.	Written articles required—comply with state law.	Written articles required—comply with state law.	Written article required—comply with state law and IRS rule.	Written articles of organization, filed with state.
Liability of owners	Total personal liability.	Personal liability for partnership debts.	Limited partners have limited liability. General partners have personal liability.	Shareholders have limited liability.	Shareholders have limited liability.	Members have limited liability.
Management	Total control by owner.	Partners control—majority vote.	General partner manages limited partnership.	Shareholders elect board of directors. Board may hire officers.	Shareholders elect board of directors. Board may hire officers.	Members may manage or hire manager .
Transfer of ownership	Owner can sell business.	"Entity" dissolves as a partner leaves—new partners can be admitted by unanimous vote.	Limited partners can sell shares, but it may be difficult to do.	Easy—shareholders can sell shares.	Shareholders can sell shares—may be less market for small corporation shareholders.	Other members must consent to transfer.
Continuity of existence	Difficult—need to find new owner.	Articles can provide for continuation of business—under new partnership—otherwise, may be difficult.	Ends when general partner withdraws.	Continues to exist as shareholders come and go.	Continues to exist as shareholders change—usually less change than C corporation.	Dissolved if member leaves, unless all others decide to continue business.
Taxation	Owner taxed on profit.	Partners each taxed on share of profits.	Partners each taxed on share of profits.	Corporation taxed on profits—shareholders then pay tax on dividends.	Corporation is not taxed. Shareholders are taxed like partners.	LLC is not taxed; members are taxed on their share of income.

law in Wyoming, all states have now enacted laws permitting the formation of LLCs. One recent study indicated that from 1992 to 1996, while the number of new registrations for corporations and limited partnerships increased by 15 percent, the number of new LLC registrations increased 25 times (2500 percent) from 6,118 in 1992 to 148,309 in 1996. Nearly one in every six new business registrations in 1996 was an LLC, and the number has undoubtedly increased since then.

The LLC as a business form combines both the limited liability features of the corporate form, with the "pass-through" tax benefits of a partnership. That is, the investors risk only their investment in the business and are not held personally liable for LLC debts. But the entity is not taxed on profits, and each owner pays tax on his or her proportionate share of LLC income. While these features make an LLC similar to an S corporation, the LLC offers some additional advantages. First, unlike an S corporation, the LLC has no restrictions on the number and type of investors (called *members* in an LLC). Thus, members of an LLC can include an unlimited number of corporations, partnerships, trusts, pension plans, and even charitable organizations.

Second, the LLC offers flexibility in management. Most state laws allow an LLC to choose either (1) management directly by all members or (2) management by one or more managers appointed by the members. Third, LLCs are not subject to the passive income limitations of S corporations. Fourth, S corporations can only have one class of stockholder, whereas LLCs may have different classes of ownership. Fifth, there are certain tax advantages to LLCs. For example, if an LLC member transfers appreciated property (assets that have increased in value) to an LLC, there is no tax paid on the gain, whereas there would be tax assessed on the gain if those assets were transferred to an S corporation by a shareholder. Sixth, an LLC can provide that income, gain, and losses can be allocated to members in percentages different from their shares of ownership, which is generally not true of S Corporations.

LLCs are created by preparing and filing *articles of organization* with the appropriate state office (usually the secretary of state). The articles should include the name of the LLC, its registered address, and the name and address of the manager or one of the members. Then the LLC needs to prepare an *operating agreement*, which sets forth the management structure and governs the rights and duties of the members. Similar to corporate bylaws, such things as allocation of profits and losses of members, restrictions on transfer of membership, and provisions for termination of the LLC are often covered in the operating agreement.

So as not to be taxed as corporations, LLCs do not have perpetual life or free transferability of shares. Typically, the LLC will dissolve upon the expiration of a period fixed in the articles of organization, by the consent of the members, or upon the disassociation of any member through causes such as death, resignation, bankruptcy, or expulsion, unless there is an agreement by all other members to continue the business.

NONPROFIT CORPORATIONS

While most corporations are formed with the hope of earning profits for the investors, an increasingly important category of corporations, called **nonprofit corporations**, or **not-for-profit corporations**, are formed for other reasons. These businesses may be as small and local as your neighborhood Parent-Teacher Association, or they may be as large and powerful as Blue Cross Health Insurance, major union and pension organizations, large hospitals, and educational and religious associations.

nonprofit corporations: Corporations formed under another state law, which are not established to earn a profit, but rather to provide a service. There are no shareholders and no dividends.

Nonprofit corporations have many similarities to for-profit corporations. They have boards of directors and officers; they must file nonprofit articles of incorporation with the state of incorporation, stating their purposes and structure, and make annual reports to the state; they must hold meetings periodically and maintain appropriate corporate books; and perhaps most importantly, they can shield their officers and directors from personal liability for torts and contracts of the corporation.

On the other hand, nonprofit corporations are not in business to make a profit, and if there is an excess of income over expenses at the end of the year, it is not distributed to the members. They have no shareholders, as such, but often have members who must pay a fee to join the organization. It is not illegal for the corporation to have a modest surplus at the end of the year (after all, if there was a deficit for very long, the organization would cease to exist), but the surplus must be retained and used for corporation purposes and not divided up and distributed to members. Nonprofit corporations do not pay income taxes, and some may not have to pay other types of taxes as well.

Board members are selected in a number of ways. Many corporations use a nominating committee to choose certain people to stand for election at a general meeting, similar to the process used by for-profit corporations. Smaller groups may reserve a certain number of spots on the board for persons to be appointed by particular organizations with whom the nonprofit entity works.

For example, one of the authors of this textbook was once the director of a legal services organization with a 15-member board of directors. Ten members were lawyers appointed by the local bar association; five members were representatives of the poor, appointed by certain organized groups of low-income persons; and two were law school professors, appointed by the local law school dean. Although all members were generally in favor of an effective program of legal assistance for poor people, there was sometimes strong disagreement between the local lawyers and the low income representatives about how aggressive the program should be in suing government agencies, landlords, and businesses and about the types of cases that should be accepted and rejected. On the other hand, at times the local attorneys and law school professors were among the most forceful members of the board in insisting on vigorous representation of our clients.

SUMMARY

There is no one "right" legal form of business organization for all purposes. When a person decides to go into business, the choice of form needs to be made as carefully as all other business decisions. Factors such as liability, cost of formation, number of persons involved in the business, management and control of business decisions, the need for raising capital, taxation, continuity, ease of share or ownership transfer, and many other issues should be considered when deciding whether to form a partnership, limited partnership, LLC, corporation or to simply go with a sole proprietorship.

A corporation is a legal entity, separate from any of the owners, that can offer limited personal liability to its shareholders. Certain steps must be carefully taken in order to form a corporation, and there are a number of important legal principles that regulate corporate operation.

In the structure of a corporation, shareholders invest funds in the business but refrain from taking an active role in management. Instead, the shareholders elect a board of directors whose duty it is to make the business decisions necessary to govern the operations of the company. Directors have the legal responsibility to fulfil their duties with care, and they owe fiduciary duties to the shareholders and the corporation as well. The directors hire officers such as a president, treasurer, and others to handle the day-to-day operations of the business.

Other important aspects of corporations are that they have perpetual existence—that is, they do not cease to exist as shareholders come and go—and they have the ability to raise significant amounts of capital for the business. When corporations require funds for business purposes, they can issue and sell more stock to the public, unlike the other forms of organizations, which are more dependent upon the assets and borrowing power of the owners.

Three other special types of companies exist—the S corporation, the LLC, and the nonprofit corporation. A nonprofit corporation has no shareholders/investors, pays no dividends, and is normally formed for some socially beneficial purpose, whereas the S corporation and the LLC are for-profit corporations that offer special taxation and other benefits to shareholders.

CHAPTER QUESTIONS

1. Jack was the president of the Arizona Bicycle Co. (ABC), which manufactures bikes and related equipment. He also owned 75 percent of the stock in the company. Although the company was properly incorporated and there was a board of directors (he, his wife, and a close friend), he made most of the decisions. When he needed money, Jack borrowed it from the company account and then paid it back later. For the past five years Jack has hired all employees of the company, and he has entered into whatever contracts he felt were necessary without interference from the board. In fact, the board has not met at all for the past five years. A consumer who had purchased an ABC bike was injured when the frame of the bike fell apart. The company has few assets at present, and the consumer has now sued Jack personally. Can the consumer prevail against Jack? Under what theory? What will the consumer have to prove? Can the other board members be held liable if the company is insolvent?
2. The board of directors of an Oregon savings and loan (S&L) approved two highly questionable investments in the mid-1980s. Later the S&L was declared insolvent, and the Resolution Trust Corporation, a federal government corporation, took over as receiver. The corporation brought suit against the directors who had approved the improper investments, claiming negligence and breach of fiduciary duty. The directors asked for dismissal of the suit because the two-year statute of limitations on such type of actions had run. The corporation responded by arguing that the statute of limitations should not run while the S&L was under the "adverse domination" of the directors who were acting improperly. This theory holds that the right to sue for negligence and breach of fiduciary duty of corporate officers and directors belongs to the corporation for whom they work, but that it is impossible for such a company to bring the action while it is under the "domination" of the culpable directors. Therefore, the time limit for such suits should be extended. What do you think should be the result?

Why? [*Federal Deposit Insurance Corporation v. Smith*, 328 Or 420, 980 P.2d 141 (1999)]

3. A group of shareholders of Mercury Finance Co. filed suit in Delaware against certain Mercury corporate directors, alleging that over a four-year period the directors had intentionally overstated the company's earnings and financial performance in documents filed with the Securities and Exchange Commission and in communications to shareholders. In subsequent years, as these misrepresentations came to light, the company (and the shareholders) lost essentially all of its former $2 billion value. After they were sued for negligence, lack of care, and breach of fiduciary duty, the directors argued that a cause of action for disclosure violations only exists when the directors are requesting action by the shareholders. What should the result be? Why? [*Malone v. Brincat*, 722 A. 2d 5 (Del. 1998)]

4. What are some of the advantages of a partnership over a corporation as a form of business organization? Why might some people choose to start a partnership rather than a corporation? What are some of the advantages of a corporation over a partnership? Why might some people choose to start a corporation instead of a partnership?

5. Facing an unwanted tender offer, a corporation's board of directors adopted a new form of poison pill takeover defense, called a "dead hand" provision. This resolution would prevent the members of any new board of directors nominated by the hostile bidder from redeeming rights under the company's shareholder rights plan for a six-month period in order to facilitate a merger. Certain shareholders challenged the provision as a violation of Delaware law, which gives a corporation's board of directors the power to manage the company. What should the Delaware Supreme Court decide? Why? [*Quickturn Design Systems, Inc. v. Shapiro*, 721 A. 2d 1281 (Del. 1998)]

6. An Idaho ranch was owned as the only asset of a close corporation consisting of two families. The stock was owned 50 percent by one family and 50 percent by the other. For many years, the arrangement worked well, with duties and profits equally divided. Then, one of the founders died. Several years later, one family has no interest in ranching and wants to sell the land, and the other wants to continue ranching. The votes are evenly split, and no directors have been elected, nor has any business been conducted for the past three years. One family files a court action seeking dissolution of the corporation. What should the court do? [*Gillingham v. Swan Falls Land & Cattle Co.*, 106 Id. 859, 683 P.2d 895 (Ct. App. 1984)]

7. While acting as officers, directors, and shareholders of a company called Bio-Lab Inc., Mr. Morad and Mr. Thomson started and incorporated a competing business in a nearby town called Med-Lab Inc. They believed that Bio-Lab did not have the funds to undertake the project, so Morad and Thomson incorporated Med-Lab on their own. The only other shareholder, Mr. Coupounas, had not been told about this venture. When he found out about it, he filed a derivative lawsuit, on behalf of Bio-Lab, against Morad and Thomson, asking the court to declare that Med-Lab was an asset of

Bio-Lab. What is the issue in this case, and what should be the result? [*Morad v. Coupounas*, 361 So.2d 6 (Ala. 1978)]

8. The board of directors of a California banking corporation made a variety of decisions regarding loans, expenses, and other financial issues, shortly before the bank became insolvent. The directors obtained advice from a number of outside consultants before making their decisions and tried in good faith to do what they believed was in the best interest of the corporation. The directors were later sued for negligence by the federal agency that took over the bank. What will their defense be? Should the directors win the case? [*FDIC v. Castetter*, 184 F.3d 1040 (9th Cir. 1999)]
9. An Oregon corporation was owned by three brothers who were the directors and equal shareholders. The board voted 2-1 to declare a dividend of $12,000 to each shareholder and retain $144,000 to ease the cash flow problems the business was experiencing. The other brother sued, alleging breach of fiduciary duty, since he felt a much larger dividend should have been declared. What should be the result? Why? [*Iwasaki v. Iwasaki Bros. Inc.*, 58 Or. App. 543, 649 P.2d 598 (1982)]
10. A shareholder who owned six shares of stock in a corporation demanded the right to examine the books of the company. This person also happened to be the primary owner of another business that was the first corporation's primary business rival. Did he have the right to inspect the books? Why? [*West Shore Association Ltd. v. American Wilbert Vault Corp.*, Ill. App. (1995), 863 USLW 2475 (2-7-95)]

PRACTICAL EXERCISE

Robert, Kathleen, and Seth have now operated their business as a partnership for three years (recall Chapter 8). Their store is now earning a good, solid profit, and they are ready to open four more stores around the state. In addition, Seth has developed his experimental "Sage Loops" into a great-tasting, crunchy, high fiber cereal that the group wants to market nationwide. Kathleen, remembering what she learned in her legal environment class, has persuaded the other two that they need to form a corporation. Your task is to prepare articles of incorporation for the business. The articles should include paragraphs detailing the following:

1. The purpose of the business;
2. The name of the corporation;
3. The officers and directors;
4. The address and principal place of business;
5. The authorization to issue a certain amount of stock;
6. The provision for amendment of the articles;
7. The provision for duration of the corporation and circumstances that might result in dissolution;
8. Whether cumulative or straight voting by shareholders will be used; and
9. Whether there will be restrictions placed on the shareholders' right to sell their stock to anyone they choose;

Your instructor may ask you to look up the corporation laws in your state to determine if there are other subjects that should be included in order to make the corporation legal.

FURTHER INFORMATION

www.business.gov
Much government information and services for business.

www.lectlaw.com
The " 'Lectric Law Library" at the University of Nevada. A wacky, irreverent, yet informative legal information site. A "must see."

www.ilrg.com
Large legal site with information on many legal issues; also corporate forms and filing information.

CHAPTER 10

SECURITIES LAW AND PROTECTION OF INVESTORS

LEARNING OBJECTIVES

After reading this chapter, you should be able to:

1. Describe a security.
2. Detail the legal consequences of buying and selling securities.
3. Explain the various exemptions.
4. Explain insider trading and the consequences of engaging in insider trading.

CHAPTER OUTLINE

Robert, Kathleen, and Seth want to raise money in order to expand their existing business selling Sage Loops. What do they need to know about securities laws before approaching people to invest?

INTRODUCTION

capital: Accumulated assets (as money) invested or available for investment.

equity: The ownership interests of shareholders in a company.

bondholder: The person or company that holds a certificate of debt issued by a company or government and payable on a specified date.

securities: Term applied to a wide variety of investment vehicles.

blue sky laws: State statutes designed to protect the public from the sale of worthless stocks and bonds.

In Chapters 8 and 9 we learned about the different legal structures people can use to conduct business. Regardless of the structure chosen, all businesses need money to operate. In technical terms, money is referred to as **capital**. Raising capital can be perplexing and frustrating. Business capital can be obtained from a number of sources, including personal funds, family and friends, financial institutions, or unknown persons. If the money comes from personal funds, few laws come into effect. Several laws apply, however, if the money is borrowed from family, friends, or a financial institution, as will be discussed in Chapter 17. The business may also raise capital by selling its **equity** (ownership interest) to investors or by selling its debt to **bondholders**. When a business sells its equity (or a share of its business) to an investor, the business has sold **securities**.

Securities regulation is a highly technical area of the law, and all securities questions should be referred to a competent lawyer. Some lawyers even specialize solely in securities matters. As we will discuss later, violations of the securities laws could lead to stiff financial penalties and jail sentences.

HISTORY AND PURPOSE

England had forms of securities regulation as early as 1285. These early English regulations were primarily aimed at registering those who sold securities. In the United States, however, securities regulation (known as **blue sky laws**) began at the state, rather than federal, level when Kansas adopted a comprehensive licensing statute in 1911. This statute, the first to use the term "blue sky," was aimed at those individuals who would sell worthless investments—in other words, who would try to sell pieces of the "blue sky." Blue sky laws spread rapidly, and virtually every state had adopted them before the stock market crash of 1929. Primarily because of the failure of the stock market, the first federal law, the *1933 Securities Act*, was enacted with two objectives: (1) to provide investors with financial information about an investment and (2) to prohibit misrepresentation, deceit, and fraudulent acts and practices.

The second federal law enacted was the *1934 Securities Exchange Act*, which established the *Securities and Exchange Commission (SEC)*. The SEC, an independent regulatory agency, has five members who are appointed by the President with the advice and consent of the Senate. The SEC is also a bipartisan administrative agency, which means that no more than three of the five members may be from one political party at any one time. Thus, a Democratic president, for example, must appoint a Republican commissioner if three Democratic commissioners already serve, and vice versa. The President does get to select the chair of the commission. Each commissioner's five-year term is staggered so that only one member's term expires each year. The SEC also employs attorneys, accountants, examiners, and analysts.

Recently, the SEC has been faced with numerous challenges brought about by the advent of the Internet. Because of the Internet, individuals can now easily trade stocks without using a stockbroker. The Internet has also made it easier for companies, especially smaller companies, to seek investors using a *direct public offering* (DPO). Further, *electronic communication networks*

(ECNs) have been established to facilitate Internet stock transactions. The SEC is considering changing its traditional structure to help it become more flexible in this new environment. One of the changes being considered is forming a single national **exchange** regulator. There have also arisen problems with "day trading," in which investors trade stocks very quickly. As the following article suggests, there are allegations that day-trading companies loosely comply with federal regulations.

exchange: Any organization, association, or group of persons that constitutes, maintains, or provides a marketplace for facilities for bringing together purchasers and sellers of securities.

SEC probe involves 10 day-trading companies

The Securities and Exchange Commission is investigating 10 day-trading firms after finding signs of misleading advertising, excessive loans to customers and other possible abuses, SEC Chairman Arthur Levitt said Thursday.

"Our preliminary findings indicate that many of these firms have extremely lax compliance practices," Levitt told the Senate Permanent Subcommittee on Investigations.

The SEC investigations, which can lead to possible fines and expulsions from the securities industry, follow its inspections of 30 large day-trading firms. These firms provide facilities for investors to place frequent, rapid-fire electronic trades trying to profit on small changes in stock prices.

Levitt said the commission hadn't found "marked and widespread fraud by these firms." Indications of possible abuses at one-third of the firms inspected, though, is "a very high percentage," he said. The SEC chairman wouldn't identify the firms under investigation.

Regulators' inspections, which eventually will cover 67 day-trading firms, have found possible violations of rules on fair advertising, proper lending, adequate brokerage capital, short-selling of borrowed stock, record-keeping and supervision, Levitt said.

State and federal regulators have focused on day trading, which Levitt likened to gambling. About 5,000 customers pay commissions of 1 or 2 cents a share to make these trades, which account for about 5 percent of U.S. stock volume.

The chairman of one of the largest day-trading firms, All-Tech Investment Group of Montvale, N.J., said very few customers have filed complaints about the firms. "If we're all so terrible, how come no one complains?" All-Tech's Harvey Houtkin said.

All-Tech, which is under SEC scrutiny, requires customers to read and sign a risk disclosure statement, Houtkin said.

Of the 21,030 complaints filed with the SEC in fiscal 1998, 37 involved day trading, SEC spokesman John Heine said.

Day traders have faced scrutiny since July 29, when Atlanta day trader Mark Barton killed 12 people and wounded 12 others before killing himself, leaving a note that cited trading losses.

Most of the killings occurred at branch offices of All-Tech and Momentum Securities.

From "SEC probe involves 10 day-trading companies," the *Atlanta Journal Constitution* (September 17, 1999). Reprinted by permission of Bloomberg News.

WHAT IS A SECURITY?

Usually, *securities* refers to stocks and bonds issued by a corporation. Other financing schemes may also be considered securities, however, if the investor relies on another's efforts to achieve success. For example, assume that Sam gives Dana $100 to invest in Dana's business. Sam does not work for the business, nor is Sam involved in any business decisions. If Dana's business is successful, Sam will receive $150. If the business is unsuccessful, Sam will receive nothing. Because Sam does nothing personally to earn this money, this investment can be considered a security. Sam is relying on Dana's efforts to achieve success. The following case, *SEC v. Koscot Interplanetary*, describes how courts decide if a company is selling securities.

SEC V. KOSCOT INTERPLANETARY, INC.

497 F.2d 473 (5th Cir. 1974)

FACTS

Koscot Interplanetary was engaged in a multilevel network of independent distributors who sold cosmetics. The first level in the network was "beauty advisor." A beauty advisor's sole income came from the retail sale of cosmetics. The second level was "supervisor or retail manager." Supervisors paid Koscot $1,000. In return, supervisors received cosmetics discounted from the retail price. These cosmetics could be sold at retail or directly to the beauty advisor. Furthermore, supervisors bringing others into the supervisor level received $600 out of the $1,000 paid to Koscot. The third level was "distributor." Distributors invested $5,000 with Koscot. This enabled distributors to purchase cosmetics at a greater discount. Furthermore, distributors received $600 for every supervisor and $3,000 for every distributor brought in to the Koscot program.

In order to attract additional investors, current Koscot investors would bring prospects to an "opportunity meeting" or a "go-tour." These events reflected an evangelical atmosphere. Investors read from a preordained script, drove Cadillacs, dressed expensively, and flaunted money. At the end of these events, prospective investors would sign into the network. Koscot had not registered with the SEC.

DECISION

Judge Gewin wrote the opinion of the Court of Appeals. The 1933 and 1934 Acts should be read broadly, since they are designed to protect investors, not to test the creativity of lawyers. The correct test is "whether the efforts made by those other than the investor are the undeniably significant ones, those essential managerial efforts which affect the failure or success of the enterprise." In this case, the luring effect of the opportunity meetings was the critical aspect that determined whether the scheme would succeed. Once the prospects arrived at the meeting, everything else was devised by Koscot. The investor's sole contribution was in "following the script." The promoters had immediate control over all of the scheme's essential management. The investor could not realize any profits without tying it to the promotional scheme. The scheme was not a conventional franchise arrangement. The "solely" requirement set out in the Supreme Court's decision in *SEC v. Howey* is "whether the scheme involves an investment of money in a common enterprise with profits to come solely from the efforts of others." Solely, however, does not necessarily mean solely. The fact that the investor has to expend some efforts to make money does not mean that the securities regulations do not apply. This scheme falls under securities regulation and must be registered with the SEC.

CASE QUESTIONS

1. What distinguishes the Koscot scheme from other multilevel networks?
2. What efforts did the investors expend?
3. Why wasn't the investor's effort enough to take the scheme out of securities regulation?

The courts have held that land sales contracts, limited partnerships, closely held corporations, and other business arrangements can be securities if the person who invests is hoping to profit without expending personal efforts. Businesspeople therefore need to use caution and obtain the advice of a competent attorney when contemplating such transactions. If an investment is held to be a security, then the seller must comply with all SEC regulations, as the Supreme Court discusses in *Landreth Timber Co. v. Landreth et al.*

LANDRETH TIMBER CO. V. LANDRETH ET AL.

471 U.S. 681 (1985)

FACTS

Ivan Landreth and his sons owned a lumber business in the state of Washington. The business operated as a closely held corporation. The Landreths wanted to sell their business and offered their stock for sale. The offers were made both in the state of Washington and through out-of-state brokers. Before any sale occurred, the company's sawmill was heavily damaged during a fire, but the Landreths continued to offer stock in the company. Potential investors were notified about the fire but were told that the mill would be rebuilt and modernized. Samuel Dennis, a Massachusetts tax lawyer, received a letter offering the stock for sale. He eventually found seven other investors. They purchased the stock and then transferred the stock into Landreth Timber, a company they formed to run the business. None of the investors had any experience running a lumber company, and Ivan Landreth agreed to stay on as a consultant to help with the daily operations. The cost of rebuilding the mill turned out to be prohibitive. The mill was eventually sold for a loss, and Landreth Timber declared bankruptcy. The investors sued Landreth for selling the stock without registering it under the Securities Act of 1933. The District Court dismissed the case, holding that the registration requirements did not apply to the sale of 100 percent of the stock of a closely held company. The Ninth Circuit Court of Appeals affirmed. The Supreme Court granted certiorari to resolve the dispute among the Circuit Courts as to whether the federal securities laws apply to the transfer of 100 percent of a business.

DECISION

Justice Powell wrote the opinion of the Court. The Court recognized that its previous decisions on what constituted a "security" were not overly clear. In this case the Landreths had argued that the sale of 100 percent of their closely held corporation fell under the "sale of business" doctrine and exempted them from registering the stock. In looking at its past decisions to determine what constituted a security, the Court held that the Securities Act of 1933 required registration of commonly known instruments like publicly traded stock and bonds. The Act, however, also covered investment contracts as well. In *SEC v. Howey*, the court had held that "offering units of a citrus grove development coupled with a contract for cultivating and marketing fruit and remitting the proceeds to investors" was a security. The so-called Howey test looks at whether "the transaction '[involved] an investment of money in a common enterprise with profits to come solely for the efforts of others.'" The Court held that there was no reason to use the Howey investment contract test, since "'stock' may be viewed as a category by itself for purposes of interpreting the scope of the Acts' definition of 'security.'" The sale of business doctrine does not apply in this case since 100 percent of the stock was sold. The stock should have been registered. The decision of the Court of Appeals was reversed.

CASE QUESTIONS

1. In this case, there were significant negotiations between the buyer and seller before the transfer took place. Are the securities laws meant to apply to these types of transactions?
2. How could the Landreths have structured the sale to stay clear of securities registration requirements?
3. What other types of investments constitute a security?

THE REGISTRATION PROCESS

A major purpose of the SEC is to help investors decide for themselves whether to make a certain investment decision. Therefore, the SEC does not concern itself with whether an investment is good or bad. In order to perform its function, the SEC requires companies to fully disclose material information about securities they wish to issue to the public. The SEC, however, is powerless to rule on the merits of any particular security. The 1933 Act is purely a disclosure statute. It is not meant to guarantee that the security is a safe investment. In fact, some securities are required to disclose that "these securities involve a high degree of risk and substantial dilution. Potential purchasers should not invest in these securities unless they can afford the risk of losing their entire investment." This statement allows the purchaser to decide whether to invest.

The 1933 Act's registration rules only apply to the *original issuance* of securities (when securities are first sold by the issuing company), or the initial public offering (IPO). Traditional IPOs use **underwriters**, **dealers**, and **brokers**, although a DPO on the Internet may not. Once securities are in the hands of an investor, the securities are generally freely transferable in the market, and the 1933 Act does not apply. Most securities offerings must be registered with the SEC. The SEC breaks the registration process into three periods. The first period is the prefiling period, when the securities are being prepared for sale but before the actual registration takes place. During prefiling, the securities cannot be offered for sale or advertised, nor may the promoters or **issuer** try to create excitement or interest in the upcoming offering, a technique called *conditioning* the market. As the next article suggests, false information about stocks also cannot be spread.

underwriter: Purchases or participates in original offering of securities.

dealer: Buys securities from underwriter to resell to general public or for its own account.

broker: Buys securities from underwriter for accounts of others.

issuer: Controlling person, individual, or business offering to sell its own securities.

Big Board Fines Broker for Using Net To Post False Rumors About Stocks

NEW YORK—In what appears to be a first, the New York Stock Exchange has disciplined a former Bear Stearns Cos. broker over Internet postings in which the exchange said he improperly circulated rumors about a stock.

Alan C. Wolman, 47 years old, of Fort Lee, N.J., agreed to pay a $10,000 fine, without admitting or denying any wrongdoing.

The exchange said Mr. Wolman, on three occasions in early 1996 and without Bear Stearns's approval, posted messages to an Internet news group disparaging the short-sell recommendations of some analysts on Diana Corp., in which some of his customers had long positions.

In one posting, Mr. Wolman said that the "strategy [of short selling] will backfire" and that a "painful" short "squeeze" was likely. "[W]e are hearing that several large funds may be initiating long positions over the next few weeks," he said.

The postings, the exchange said, violated a New York Stock Exchange rule that prohibits the circulation of rumors "which might reasonably be expected to affect market conditions" on the New York Stock Exchange. Mr. Wolman also violated an exchange rule requiring a supervisor's pre-approval before a Big Board member distributes any communications to the public, the exchange said.

The New York Stock Exchange said this was the first time it had tackled such a disciplinary case, and used it to issue a warning: Future violations involving such Internet postings will face much more severe penalties.

"Given the heightened sensitivity to the role of the Internet in investing today, a current violation would clearly require a bar or suspension," a Big Board hearing panel said in papers detailing the case.

Mr. Wolman, who now works for Legg Mason Wood Walker Inc., said that "I wasn't doing anything that I thought was illegal or wrong." In his mind, he said, "I was not circulating rumors. I was putting out a posting based on what I believe."

Mr. Wolman also noted that he didn't identify himself as a Bear Stearns broker in his postings. The exchange acknowledged that Mr. Wolman had "a good faith belief in what he said" and that there was no indication Mr. Wolman had engaged in any improper trading in Diana stock.

The next period, the waiting period, starts on the day a registration statement is filed with the SEC and proceeds for the next 20 days. The registration statement must contain the name of the issuer, a balance sheet, year-to-date profit and loss statements, and profit and loss statements for the preceding five years. It also must contain both hard (financial) and soft (e.g., market reports) material information. If the SEC believes that the registration statement does not adequately disclose material information, the issuer will be required to amend the statement, and the 20-day waiting period is extended. During the waiting period, the issuer may provide prospective investors with a preliminary prospectus. A *prospectus* is defined as "a notice, circular, advertisement, letter, or other communication published or transmitted to any person after a registration statement has been filed." The preliminary prospectus must contain the following so-called *red herring* language (set out in red ink in the margin). This language informs potential purchasers that the registration statement may be changed:

> A registration statement relating to these securities has been filed with the Securities and Exchange Commission but has not yet become effective. Information contained herein is subject to completion or amendment. These securities may not be sold nor may offers to buy be accepted prior to the time the registration statement becomes effective. This prospectus shall not constitute an offer to sell or the solicitation of an offer to buy nor shall there be any sale of these securities in any State in which such offer, solicitation or sale would be unlawful; prior to registration or qualification under the securities laws of any such State.

Oral offers for the sale of securities may occur during the waiting period.

Lastly, the post-effective period begins once the SEC approves the registration statement. At this point, the securities may be advertised and sold. The sales contract must be in writing to be enforceable, since the sale of securities falls under the Statute of Frauds. All final sales of securities must be accompanied by a final prospectus.

Securities are advertised using a "tombstone advertisement," so named because it contains a minimum of information and is printed in plain black and white. As can be seen in Figure 10.1, this advertisement identifies the security, states the price and the number of shares offered, and indicates from whom the orders can be executed. These advertisements are found in financial presses like *The Wall Street Journal* and *New York Times*. They are also increasingly being found on the Internet. In some cases companies are choosing to use "virtual road shows" to promote their stock. These road shows take place on the Internet and include the final prospectus and may even have the chief executive officer of the issuer answering questions by e-mail or conducting a chat session.

Because registration statements are prepared by attorneys, accountants, and other professionals, it is very expensive to register securities with the SEC. Therefore, regulations provide that some types of securities are exempt from registration with the SEC, although they may still need to be registered with a state securities commission. The exemptions are mostly designed to allow unregistered securities to be sold to those who have the ability to protect themselves in a securities offering. Exempt securities include intrastate offerings, offerings by businesses whose total sales do not exceed certain specified dollar limits, and private offerings. Exempt securities usually contain restrictions that prohibit their resale for a limited amount of time.

INTRASTATE OFFERINGS

In order to qualify for an intrastate exemption (SEC Rule 147), all shareholders and the business must be residents of the same state. This means that the issuing company either is incorporated in the state or does a substantial amount of its business (at least 80 percent) in the state in which all buyers of the securities are residents. The securities cannot "come to rest" with any nonresident of the state for at least nine months. If any nonresident owns the securities within this time frame, the entire exemption is invalidated. The courts have even held that the offering does not qualify for an intrastate exemption if the proceeds from the offering will be used out of the state.

REGULATION A

SEC Regulation A allows a company to raise up to $5 million in a one-year period with no resale restrictions or limit on the number of investors or investor sophistication requirements. An issuing company is required to make a *low-level registration* with the SEC and provide an offering circular and disclosure document. Since the offering circular and disclosure document closely resemble a preliminary prospectus and therefore contain much of the information required for a full-blown registration, the costs for preparing a Regulation A

This announcement is neither an offer to sell nor a solicitation of offers to buy any of these securities. The offering is made only by the Prospectus, copies of which may be obtained in any State or jurisdiction in which this announcement is circulated only from such of the underwriters as may legally offer these securities in such State or jurisdiction.

NEW ISSUE

February 10, 2000

$92,000,000

Lante

Lante Corporation

4,600,000 Shares
Common Stock

NASDAQ Symbol: "LNTE"

Price $20 Per Share

Prior to the offering there had been no public market for these securities. Lante Corporation is an Internet services company that develops sophisticated technology-based solutions for electronic markets. These markets, which the Company refers to as e-markets, are Internet based networks through which multiple buyers and sellers efficiently conduct business online.

CREDIT SUISSE | FIRST BOSTON

Credit Suisse First Boston

Deutsche Banc Alex. Brown

Thomas Weisel Partners LLC

Friedman Billings Ramsey

Adams, Harkness & Hill, Inc.

Barrington Research Associates, Inc.

Donaldson, Lufkin & Jenrette

E*Offering

First Union Securities, Inc.

Invemed Associates

Lehman Brothers

SG Cowen

Stifel, Nicolaus & Company
Incorporated

TD Securities

Wit SoundView

Figure 10.1
Tombstone Ad

offering are similar to costs required for a full registration. Once the low-level registration document is registered, after a 10-day waiting period the securities can be sold, and there are no restrictions on resale.

REGULATION D

Under SEC Regulation D, rules 504, 505, and 506, securities may be sold without registration to sophisticated investors. Sophisticated investors are divided into two categories: *accredited* and *nonaccredited* investors. Accredited investors (1) have $1 million in net worth; or (2) have incomes exceeding $200,000 over the past two years and reasonably expect a $200,000 income this year; or (3) are directors, executive officers, or general partners of the issuing company; or (4) are institutions, like banks and insurance companies. Nonaccredited investors are those who are "capable alone, or with the assistance of a representative, of evaluating the merits and risks of the investment." Investors fill out signed, witnessed forms indicating how they qualify as accredited investors. These forms are kept by the issuing company. Regulation D does not allow any general advertising of the securities.

Rules 504 and 505 SEC Rule 504 lets a company raise up to $1 million without registration and without any limit on the number of accredited and nonaccredited investors. Resale is not restricted. Under SEC Rule 505, a company can raise up to $5 million, in a 12-month period, without registration. There is a limit of 35 nonaccredited investors but no limit on accredited investors. Under Rule 505, the issuing company must disclose all material information to each investor, including past financial statements and a summary of the business operation. Resale is restricted and can only occur after registration or if the transaction qualifies under another exemption.

Rule 506 SEC Rule 506 allows for a private placement exemption. In order to qualify for a private placement, a company can have no more than 35 nonaccredited investors but any number of accredited investors. Each investor buying in a private placement offering must sign an investment letter stating that the securities are being bought for investment purposes and will not be resold for at least two years.

Rule 144 SEC Rule 144 governs the resale of restricted securities. Restricted securities can be resold after two years if there is adequate public information about the issuer, there is a limited volume of sales, and the SEC is notified. If a person is not affiliated with the issuer, the securities can be resold in three years without restriction.

LIABILITY UNDER THE 1933 ACT

The 1933 Act provides significant civil and criminal penalties for violating its regulations. Under Section 11, investors harmed by the registration statement may, within two years of the effective date of the registration statement, bring a civil lawsuit for the damages suffered. In order to show harm under the 1933 Act, investors must prove only that the registration statement contains material omissions or misstatements. Section 11 creates almost absolute liability. Investors, if they still own the securities, may recover the money paid for securities, plus interest. If the securities have been sold, investors may recover the damages they incurred. In addition, criminal penalties of $10,000 are possible, as well as up to five years in jail, if the violations were willful.

All of the following people can be held liable for any misstatements or misinformation found in the registration statement: those who sign the registration statement, for example, an attorney; those who prepare the certified report, for example, an accountant or engineer; directors or those who were slated to be directors; and underwriters (the company that agreed to sell the stock for the issuer or to buy the shares not sold). Preparers of the registration statement or preparers of portions of the registration statement have a *due diligence defense*; this defense requires a showing that the preparer made a reasonable investigation of the offering and had reasonable grounds to believe, and did believe, that the registration statement was accurate. Experts, like accountants and engineers, are only liable for the portions of the registration statement that they actually prepared. Directors, officers, and underwriters (nonexperts) are liable for any misstatements or omissions contained in the entire registration statement. Nonexperts can prove due diligence as to the portions prepared by experts if they show that they made a reasonable investigation and reasonably believed that the experts' portions were accurate.

In addition to provisions of Section 11, the 1933 Act also allows the SEC, under Section 17, to obtain an injunction prohibiting the sale of *any* security by the following means: (1) any device, scheme, or artifice to defraud; (2) untrue statements or material omissions; or (3) a fraudulent business. Only negligence is required to prove subsections 2 and 3. The courts, however, require *scienter*—the intent to deceive—in proving subsection 1. Scienter is, of course, more difficult to prove than mere negligence.

1934 SECURITIES EXCHANGE ACT

The 1934 Securities Exchange Act covers corporate reporting, proxy solicitation, public tender offers, insider trading, and fraud. All publicly traded corporations with over 500 shareholders and $10 million in assets are required to be registered with the SEC and to file reports. Each company must file with the SEC a form 10-K (the annual report), a form 10-Q (the quarterly report), and a form 8-K (the monthly report) required during the time material events are occurring. These forms become public records and allow interested parties to research publicly traded companies. Also, anyone holding at least 5 percent of a registered company must file a report with the SEC disclosing the amount of stock owned.

PROXY SOLICITATION

As we saw in Chapter 9, *proxies* allow someone other than the shareholder to vote shares of stock. Proxy solicitation is also governed by the 1934 Act. When management is planning to solicit proxies, it must file a preliminary copy of the proposed proxy statement with the SEC. The proxy statement must identify those who are soliciting proxies, the means that will be used (usually the

U.S. mail), those who will pay for the solicitation, the amount that has already been spent on the solicitation, and an estimate of the amounts that will be spent. Detailed information must also appear about those running for the board of directors and their backgrounds. Management almost always solicits its own proxies.

disgruntled shareholders: Those shareholders who disagree with the current management of the company.

beneficial owner: Brokerage firms holding securities in their own name.

Sometimes **disgruntled shareholders** may want to solicit their own proxies and run their own slate of candidates for the board of directors. This is called a *proxy contest*. Anyone may solicit proxies from 10 or fewer persons without complying with the 1934 Act. **Beneficial owners** may also solicit proxies without complying with the federal rules. However, if the disgruntled shareholders want to solicit proxies from more than 10 persons, then they too have to comply with the registration requirements. If management is soliciting proxies, then it must give the disgruntled shareholders either the shareholder list or include the disgruntled shareholders' material with management's material.

Information in the proxy materials is governed by a materiality test. If a misrepresentation or omission of a material fact (one that influences the decision) occurs, then those who prepared the statement can be liable to shareholders.

Proxy contests can be very expensive, and management can be reimbursed for the expenses it incurs in a proxy contest if the expenses were reasonable and the contest occurred because of a difference in corporate policy. Management cannot be reimbursed if officers engaged in the proxy contest in order to keep their jobs with the company. The disgruntled shareholders can be reimbursed if they win, the contest benefited the corporation, and the shareholders ratify the reimbursement.

TENDER OFFERS

tender offer: A public offer to purchase stock at a specified price per share.

A proxy contest is one way to take control of a company. During the 1980s a more popular way was to initiate a **public tender offer**, a public request that shareholders sell their stock to a particular person or company. Before 1968, no federal law specifically regulating tender offers existed. In 1968, the 1934 Act was amended by the Williams Act with the intent of protecting investors from the complexities of tender offers. The Williams Act requires that upon commencement of a tender offer, the *bidder* (in some adverse circumstances, the bidder is called the "raider") must notify the target company's management, all target company shareholders, and the SEC that a public tender offer is taking place. The statement must include the bidder's terms, background, past dealings with the target company, and whether the bidder intends to control the company. A public tender offer must be open to all shareholders, although the bidder may specify that it will only buy a certain percentage of the shares. For example, the bidder may only want to buy 50 percent of the outstanding shares in the belief that 50 percent is enough to exercise control. If more shares are tendered (offered) than the bidder specified, then each tendering shareholder takes pro rata. If there are 1,000 outstanding shares and 800 are tendered, the bidder is only responsible for buying 400, or 50 percent of the total shares tendered. Each shareholder would then sell only 50 percent of her shares to the bidder. Further, all shareholders must be paid the same for each share. If the shares have not been purchased, any stockholder who tenders shares may withdraw them during the first 15 days of the offer or anytime after 60 days. The offer has to remain open for at least 20 days. If the price per share is increased during the offer, then all tendering shareholders receive the benefit of the increased price.

If someone has access to information that suggests a tender offer will take place and that person trades stock based on that information but before the announcement is public, he or she could make a lot of money. The SEC has also enacted Rule 14e-3, which prohibits any person from trading on nonpublic tender offer information.

During the 1980s, so many firms merged that the decade is often referred to as "merger mania." Many of these takeovers were considered hostile. This means the target company's board of directors did not approve of the merger and set out to fight the takeover attempt. Management's attempts to thwart the takeover took on terms like "scorched earth," "poison pill," and "selling the crown jewels." Management's payment to the raider to stop the takeover attempt was known as "greenmail." There was also a "pacman" defense, where management would make a reverse tender offer on the raider's company.

Since the 1980s, many states have passed antitakeover statutes to protect local businesses from out-of-state control. Most of the statutes are specifically aimed at increasing the amount of time it takes to complete a takeover of a corporation. In 1987, the Supreme Court upheld an Indiana antitakeover statute. Since then, a majority of the states have passed some form of antitakeover statute. Most of these statutes require that any merger be postponed for several years unless there was prior approval of the merger by the target company's board of directors.

SOCIAL/ETHICAL ISSUES

Like most issues, the hostile tender offer debate has two sides. The proponents of hostile takeovers claim that most target companies are undervalued and have complacent management in place. The hostile takeover helps set the true economic value of the company and ousts managers who are no longer effective. Opponents claim that the raiders are only seeking to increase their own personal wealth. To raise the capital to pay for the company, raiders will close and/or sell divisions to other companies, showing a lack of concern for the company's employees. Also, attorneys and investment bankers made a fortune in takeover attempts. In fact, it was reported in one case that the investment bankers and lawyers in the Revlon/Pantry Pride contest made over $100 million in the three-month takeover battle. Are hostile takeovers ethical?

SHAREHOLDER RESOLUTION

Sometimes shareholders do not wish to take over the company; rather, they want existing management to change certain policy decisions. One way to get management to change policy is through a shareholder proposal or resolution. A shareholder resolution is voted on by shareholders at the company's annual meeting. If management opposes the resolution, the shareholders may propose a 200-word statement to be voted on by the shareholders. The proposal must be presented if the action requested does not violate the law, relates to the company's business, relates to a business policy issue, does not relate to the payment of a specific amount of dividends, and if no similar proposal has been presented within the past five years and defeated within the past three years.

FRAUD

Section 10(b) of the 1934 Act and the SEC's Rule 10b-5 make it "unlawful and illegal to willfully engage in any practice intending to defraud or to willfully state an untrue material fact in connection with the sale of securities." Unlike Section 12 of the 1933 Act, which only applies to sales, Section 10(b) and Rule 10b-5 apply to both purchasers and sellers as well as to securities that are exempt from registration. As with Section 17 of the 1933 Act, scienter is required to prove a Section 10(b) and Rule 10b-5 violation. In order to violate 10(b) and 10b-5, the statement must be material. Materiality, addressed by the Supreme Court in a 1988 case, *Basic v. Levinson*, is not judged by financial criteria but by whether the reasonable shareholder would consider the information in making an investment decision. Injured parties can bring a civil action demanding an injunction and/or damages under section 10(b). Willful violations can result in criminal penalties of up to $100,000 and up to five years in jail. Section 10(b) has also been used to prevent insider trading.

INSIDER TRADING

Insider trading occurs in two circumstances. The first is when a traditional insider, officer, director, or shareholder owning 10 percent or more of the company's stock trades in the securities of his company. It is assumed that these

FROM THE DESK OF
Laura Lawyer

To: Students
From: Your Lawyer

Violating the antifraud provisions of the securities laws can mean spending time in jail. There are many ways to violate the securities laws. One is to lie about the condition of the investment you are selling. Another way is to buy securities based on information that is not publicly available. Still another way is to give someone else information that is not publicly available and then trade on that information. In any event, competent legal advice is an absolute necessity.

individuals always possess inside information (information that is not public). Therefore, another section of the 1934 Act, section 16(b), prohibits **short swing profits**, which are any profits made by a traditional insider through the purchase and sale of securities in any six-month period. Short swing profits must be returned to the company. For example, if June, the president of AC Corp., bought 20 shares of AC stock for $10 a share on January 1 and then sold 20 shares of AC stock on April 1 for $12 a share, she has made a profit of $40. Under section 16(b) June cannot make a profit on the shares for six months, in this case until July. Under the short swing profit rule, she would have to return her profit to the company. In fact, a television reporter was required to pay her company over $53,000 when, unbeknownst to her, her husband violated the short-swing rule when he tried to sell a few shares of stock only one month after the IPO of the Internet company she started with former U.S. Surgeon General C. Everett Koop.

short swing profits: Profits made by an insider through sale or disposition of the corporate stock within six months after purchase.

Sometimes traditional insiders buy several shares of stock over several different time periods. In determining whether the insider is liable for short swing profits, the courts generally use the *lowest in/highest out* rule. This means that the court matches the number of securities bought and sold. Assume that Carlos, the president of BC Corporation, bought 6 shares on July 1 at $1 per share, 10 shares on July 15 at $2 per share, and 8 shares on July 30 at $3 per share. If Carlos then sells 6 shares on January 14 for $4 per share, the court will rule that all the shares cost $2 per share, because the lowest price in was the July 15 purchase at $2 per share. The July 1 purchase, at $1 per share, has exceeded the six-month time frame. Carlos owes the company $2 per share for 6 shares, or $12. The short swing profit rule is a strict liability rule, meaning that if traditional insiders engage in short swing trading, they are liable.

The other circumstance where inside trading occurs is when someone with access to nonpublic information trades on the information. As the next case shows, a person must disclose material information to the public before trading on the stock.

SEC V. TEXAS GULF SULFUR

401 F.2d 833 (2d Cir. 1968)

FACTS

Texas Gulf Sulfur (TGS) was engaged in mineral exploration in Canada. Its geologists discovered what they believed to be a large copper and minable ore find in Canada. Drilling was halted for about five months while the visual estimates were confirmed through a chemical assay. During these five months TGS's president and vice-president and several geologists executed trades on the company's stock. When drilling resumed, it became clear that a major find existed. Each hole reflected substantial copper mineralization. Several newspapers reported rumors about a "rich strike" in Canada. To combat the rumors, TGS issued a press release indicating that the results of its drilling were "inconclusive." This announcement was false in that TGS had already discovered 6.2 to 8.3 million tons of ore with a value of between $26 to $29 per ton. Three days later, a public announcement was issued stating that TGS had a strike of at least 25 million tons of ore. Some of the defendants also traded shares immediately before the public announcement became widespread.

DECISION

Judge Waterman wrote the opinion of the Court of Appeals. Rule 10b-5 is based on the principle that in the securities market, all investors should have equal access to information. Information can only be kept private if it is used for corporate purposes. The information cannot be kept private and then used for the personal benefit of an individual. Anyone possessing material inside information must either disclose it to the public or abstain from trading and/or recommending the securities to anyone while the information is secret.

In this case, the major mineral discovery was material information. Therefore, all stock transactions in TGS stock by individuals who knew of the drilling results violated Rule 10b-5. Those individuals were not eligible to trade until the official public announcement had been disseminated. Those individuals who traded on the stock in anticipation of the public announcement were responsible for ensuring that the information was available to the investing public. "[A]ll insider activity must await dissemination of the promised official announcement."

CASE QUESTIONS

1. Does the Court's rule extend to secretaries, janitors, and other employees who may have learned of the mineral find?
2. When can individuals with inside information trade on that information?
3. Do you think that the insider trading prohibitions are good or bad for the market? Why?

fiduciary: A relationship that creates a duty to exercise a high degree of care and to not be involved in conflicts of interest. Employees have a fiduciary relationship with their employers.

The rule announced in *Texas Gulf Sulfur* is known as the *disclose or refrain rule*. After *Texas Gulf Sulfur*, several cases have been decided that set limits on who is prohibited from trading on nonpublic information. The first insider trading case to reach the Supreme Court was *Chiarella v. SEC*. Chiarella was a printer and had traded on information he had obtained, through his own efforts as a financial printer, about some public tender offers. The Supreme Court held that he was not guilty of insider trading because he did not have a **fiduciary** relationship to the companies in which he was trading and he did not receive his information from any company insiders. As the next case demonstrates, the U.S. Supreme Court has recently expanded the reach of insider trading laws.

U.S. V. O'HAGAN

521 U.S. 642 (1997)

FACTS

James O'Hagan was a lawyer with a Minneapolis law firm, Dorsey & Whitney. In July 1988, Dorsey & Whitney was asked to represent a London-based company, Grand Metropolitan. Grand Metropolitan was interested in pursuing a public tender offer of Pillsbury Company. Both Grand Metropolitan and Dorsey & Whitney took precautions to keep the tender offer confidential. Dorsey & Whitney withdrew from representing Grand Metropolitan on September 4, 1988. On October 4, 1988 Grand Metropolitan publicly announced that it would buy Pillsbury's stock. O'Hagan did not work on the Grand Metropolitan tender offer but began buying call options on Pillsbury's stock during the time that Dorsey & Whitney represented Grand Metropolitan. [A call option is an options contract giving the holder the right to buy a specified number of shares at a specified price. A call is used when an investor thinks the stock price will rise.] O'Hagan ended up buying 2,500 call options of Pillsbury's stock and another 5,000 shares of Pillsbury's stock. At the time the tender offer was announced, O'Hagan owned more shares of Pillsbury than any other individual investor. When the public tender offer was announced, Pillsbury's stock went up $60 a share. O'Hagan sold his call options and stock and made $4.3 million. The SEC charged him with 20 counts of mail fraud, 17 counts of securities fraud under §10(b) and Rule 10b-5 of the Securities Act of 1934 and 17 counts of fraudulent trading in connection with a tender offer under §14(e) of the Exchange Act and 3 counts of violating federal money laundering statutes. He was found guilty on all counts and sentenced to 41 months in prison. The Court of Appeals for the Eighth Circuit reversed, holding that O'Hagan did not have a fiduciary relationship with Pillsbury and therefore was not liable under the Securities Acts and that all other liability stemmed from the securities violations. The U.S. Supreme Court granted certiorari to resolve a dispute among the Circuit Courts as to whether the misappropriation theory could be used to convict a person of fraud under §10(b) and Rule 10b-5.

DECISION

Justice Ginsburg wrote the opinion for the Court. The Court resolved two questions. The first was whether "misappropriation of material, nonpublic information for securities trading" was actionable and the second was whether the SEC had the power to enact Rule 14e-3(a) prohibiting trading on undisclosed information in connection with a tender offer.

O'Hagan argued that he did not have a fiduciary duty to Pillsbury. Earlier Supreme Court cases, *Dirks v. SEC* and *Chiarella v. United States*, seemed to require that an individual needed a fiduciary relationship with the company in whom stock was traded before there would be criminal liability. The Supreme Court broadens this concept by adopting the misappropriation theory. The Court finds that under the "'misappropriation theory' . . . a person commits fraud 'in connection with' a securities transaction, and thereby violates §10(b) and Rule 10b-5 when he misappropriates confidential information for securities trading purposes, in breach of a duty of loyalty and confidentiality owed to the source of the information. Under this theory a fiduciary's undisclosed, self-serving use of a principal's information to purchase or sell securities, in breach of a duty of loyalty and confidentiality, defrauds the principal of the exclusive use of the information. In lieu of premising liability on a fiduciary relationship between company insider and purchaser or seller of the company's stock, the misappropriation theory premise[s] liability on a fiduciary-turned-trader's deception of those who entrusted him with access to confidential information."

In this case, O'Hagan breached his fiduciary duties (to keep the tender offer information confidential and to not trade on the stock) to Dorsey & Whitney, his employer and Dorsey & Whitney's client, Grand Metropolitan. Since he misappropriated his employer's confidential information and he purchased and sold securities based on the confidential information, he can be found guilty of violating §10(b) and Rule 10b-5. The Court also found that the SEC had the authority to enact Rule 14e-3(a).

O'Hagan also argued that he was not trading on nonpublic information since there had been several news reports in August 1988 that not only reported Grand Metropolitan's interest in Pillsbury but the fact that Grand Metropolitan was selling one of its hotels to raise the needed capital. The Court found that this was a question of sufficiency of evidence which could be addressed on remand. The decision of the Court of Appeals was reversed.

CASE QUESTIONS

1. Why did the court say O'Hagan did not have a fiduciary relationship with Pillsbury?
2. Why did the Court have to adopt a new theory to convict O'Hagan of securities fraud?
3. What is the policy reason for the adoption of the misappropriation theory?

Insider trading was a concern of Congress in the 1980s. The popular press was full of stories of individuals such a Dennis Levine, who reportedly made $12.6 million; Ivan Boesky, who was ordered to disgorge $50 million in profits and pay a $50 million fine; and junk bond guru Michael Milken, who was fined $200 million, sentenced to 10 years in jail and 1800 hours of community service, and forced to disgorge $400 million in profits. In order to try to prevent insider trading, Congress passed legislation aimed at increasing the penalties. In 1984, the Insider Trading Sanctions Act (ITSA) was passed. ITSA provides for criminal penalties of $100,000, civil penalties of three times the profit (treble damages) and a jail term of up to five years for anyone convicted of insider trading in companies engaged in a takeover attempt. The Insider Trading Liability Sanctions Act (ITLSA) was also passed, which penalizes any person who controls a person trading on inside information.

SOCIAL/ETHICAL ISSUES

Insider trading raises questions of fairness. Is it fair for one person to have an advantage over another person when it comes to trading securities on the public stock exchange? While the current law implies that it is not fair, there are those who argue otherwise. Opponents of the current insider trading restrictions claim that it is impossible for everyone to have equal information. Therefore, insider trading should be allowed, since a person without good information can follow the insider's trading activities. When the insider trades, the follower can trade. This would ensure that the follower would at least gain some advantage. These issues raise questions about the purpose of the stock market. Is its purpose to be fair or efficient? What do you think?

TIPPER/TIPPEE LIABILITY

One other type of liability is tipper/tippee liability. In tipper/tippee liability, the court views the *tippee* as stepping into the shoes of the insider who breached his or her fiduciary duty to the company. The tippee ends up with the same liability as the insider. Assume your uncle calls and tells you that his company has just discovered an oil well and that the discovery will be announced tomorrow. Should you buy the company's stock today? If you do, you will be guilty of insider trading. Why? You are a tippee and as such will be required to **disgorge** your profits. If you trade, the *tipper*, your uncle, is also liable.

disgorge: To give up illegally gained profits by court order to prevent unjust enrichment.

STATE BLUE SKY LAWS

Besides complying with the federal securities laws, state blue sky laws are still in effect and apply even when the federal laws do not. State blue sky laws may require companies to register the sale of securities that are exempt from federal registration. Some blue sky laws are patterned after the federal laws and require the filing of extensive registration statements. Others require the payment of a fee and a notification statement that is filed with the state's securities regulatory commission. The notification statement contains basic

FROM THE DESK OF
Laura Lawyer

To: Students
From: Your Lawyer

The best rule to prevent insider trading liability is to avoid trading on any information that is unavailable to the public. This rule should apply regardless of whether you obtain the information from the company you work for, a family member, or friend with a hot tip. Once the information is public, you are, of course, free to trade.

information about the issuer, like name, address, business form, general character, and a description of the type and price of the security.

Most state blue sky laws do not require that a tombstone ad be used. The laws do, however, require that the regulatory commission receive a copy of any advertisement. In 1998, Congress passed the Securities Litigation Uniform Standard Act, which preempts state securities class action suits.

SUMMARY

Securities regulation is a complex area of the law. The primary rules are found in the 1933 Act and the 1934 Act, which aim to provide investors with complete information and to prevent fraud in the securities market. Because of the expense of registration, however, several exemptions exist. More recently, Congress has enacted specific legislation aimed at prohibiting insider trading. States, too, are interested in regulating securities, and state Blue Sky Laws apply to securities that are exempted from federal registration requirements. There has been an explosion of changes due to the advent of the Internet. The states and SEC are still in the process of determining how best to regulate this new approach to raising capital.

CHAPTER QUESTIONS

1. An investment banker passes information concerning pending mergers and acquisitions to a stockbroker. The stockbroker, along with two friends, trades on the information, reaping substantial gains when the takeover information is made public. What should the court do? [*United States v. Newman*, 664 F.2d 12 (2d Cir. 1981)]

2. A football coach innocently overhears two individuals talking about a hot stock tip. The football coach immediately calls his stockbroker and trades on the information. Is he guilty of insider trading? Why or why not? [*SEC v. Switzer*, 590 F. Supp. 756 (W.D. Okla. 1984)]
3. Are all multilevel marketing schemes securities? What determines whether the scheme needs to be registered? [See *In the Matter of Amway Corporation*, 93 F.T.C. 618 (1979).]
4. An accountant is asked to provide financial statements for the prospectus of an issuing company. In the course of her audit, she is only given access to the company's books. She is not allowed to visit the company's office, nor is she allowed to interview company employees other than the officers. What should the accountant do before certifying the financial statements?
5. The Howey Company owned hundreds of acres of land in Florida, cultivated with citrus trees. Customers would purchase a land sales contract, usually for the sale of less than five acres of land, and a service contract. When the land sales contract was paid off, each customer would receive a warranty deed. The service contract lasted for 10 years with no cancellation rights, and the service contract gave the Howey Company total control over cultivating, harvesting and marketing the citrus. The purchasers did not have the right to enter the property without the consent of Howey Company. The purchasers were generally not Florida residents and were business and professional people with little or no experience in citrus farming. Did Howey violate the securities laws? [See *S.E.C. v. W.J. Howey*, 328 U.S. 293 (1946).]
6. Barchris Construction Corporation built bowling alleys. Barchris used a sale and leaseback arrangement by dividing the construction contract into the "interior" of the building and the building itself. When the bowling alley was completed, Barchris would sell the interior to a middleman, James Talcott, Inc., who would pay for the interior and then lease the interior to Barchris' customer or to a Barchris subsidiary, who then leased it to the customer. Barchris had cash flow problems. In order to obtain more capital, Barchris sold "debentures" to the public. A registration statement was filed with the SEC. Barchris filed for bankruptcy and defaulted on the interest payments 18 months later. The investors sued the persons who signed the registration statement, the underwriters, and the auditors. The investors claimed that the registration statement was misleading in that it did not reflect the severe financial condition of the company. The defendants all claimed a due diligence defense. Is it valid? [See *Escott v. Barchris Construction Corporation*, 283 F. Supp. 643 (S.D.N.Y. 1968).]
7. Raymond Dirks provided investment advice, for a fee, to a number of institutions and individual investors. In the course of his work, Dirks was contacted about employee fraud in Equity Funding. During the course of his investigation several Equity employees substantiated the claims. Dirks discussed his findings with several of his clients who then sold their Equity stock and it plunged in value. Did Dirks violate insider trading prohibitions? Why or why not? [See *Dirks v. SEC*, 463 U.S. 646 (1983).]
8. Since the advent of the Internet, several day-trading operations have been established. For a fee, these companies allow individuals to personally buy

and sell stock, without using a securities broker. Many of the individuals are relatively unsophisticated investors. Should day trading be more heavily regulated? Why or why not?

9. ABC Company, a computer software developer, is planning to make a public offering of its stock. While its attorneys and accountants are in the process of preparing the registration statement, ABC takes out full-page advertisements in leading financial publications and on its Web page. The advertisements are colorful and describe the company's new software developments. Have any securities violations occurred?
10. You are a scientist who has discovered that a certain brand of deodorant cures Alzheimer's disease. Is it ethical for you to short the company's stock before making your announcement?

PRACTICAL EXERCISE

Robert, Kathleen, and Seth want to open a new store in an adjoining state (recall Chapter 9). However, they have exhausted the amount of money they can borrow from friends, family, and financial institutions. They now want to get money from rich individuals to open the new store and provide capital to advertise and market "Sage Loops." They currently have a Web page and are thinking about putting a "request for investors" section on the existing page. You are asked to advise Kathleen, Robert, and Seth on their alternatives. Your task is to decide (1) whether they should sell part of the business to several rich individuals, (2) whether bringing in new investors is selling securities, (3) whether they need to file a registration statement with the SEC and/or the state, (4) what types of exemptions are available, (5) the best exemption available for their situation, and (6) whether they can use the Internet to solicit investors. Your instructor may want you to research your own state securities laws to determine what you need to do to comply in your state.

FURTHER INFORMATION

http://securities.stanford.edu/
www.ace-net.org
www.direct-stock-market.com
www.sec.gov/

CHAPTER 11

BUSINESS TORTS AND CRIMES

LEARNING OBJECTIVES:

After reading this chapter, you should be able to:

1. Distinguish between torts and crimes and describe the purpose of tort law.
2. List and describe several types of intentional torts.
3. Explain the elements of negligence.
4. Examine common torts in business situations.
5. Explain the concept of strict liability and examine current attempts at tort reform.
6. Analyze the constitutional protections corporations enjoy, as well as situations in which corporations may be held criminally liable.

CHAPTER OUTLINE

I. Distinguishing Torts and Crimes
II. Purpose of Tort Law
III. Intentional Torts
IV. Negligence—An Unintentional Tort
V. Business Torts
VI. Strict Liability
VII. Tort Reform Statutes
VIII. Criminal Law and Business

This chapter examines business torts (wrongful actions that lead to civil lawsuits) and crimes. The scenario at the end of the chapter takes place outside a health club after a big snowstorm. Various actions by club employees may result in tort liability or criminal charges against the club, where you have just begun work as manager.

INTRODUCTION

In the course of business operations, it is inevitable that operations will not always go perfectly. From time to time in any organization, employees will take actions that are negligent or careless, and they may occasionally commit crimes as well. A worker or manager, for example, may cause damages by driving a vehicle or performing an audit negligently, by making false statements about a competitor, or by cutting corners on workplace safety or environmental protections. As we examined in Chapter 8, such actions by an agent quite frequently create liability not only for the employee but for the business firm as well.

Sometimes, employees, partners, or corporate officers or directors actually engage in work-related criminal activity. In earlier years, business crimes typically involved such financial offenses as embezzlement, forgery, or bribery; however, today, an increasing number of business crimes involve environmental, antitrust, and worker safety violations. Although it is less likely that one employee's conduct will create corporate criminal liability than create civil liability, the number of corporate criminal prosecutions is increasing. This chapter explores the different types of civil and criminal liability encountered by business firms.

DISTINGUISHING TORTS AND CRIMES

Essentially, a **tort** is a wrongful action (or failure to act) that violates a noncontractual duty one person owes another, which action causes injury to a person or property. The many types of torts range from long-established concepts like negligence and battery to newer, still-evolving torts such as infringement of trade secrets, invasion of privacy, and computer tampering. Torts are a "common law" subject in that the applicable legal principles have developed almost entirely from court cases rather than from statutes. Generally, when one person commits a tort that causes some type of physical, economic, or emotional injury or loss to another, the injured person may file a tort lawsuit seeking

tort: A wrongful action done by one person which causes damage or injury to another.

THE WIZARD OF ID — Brant parker and Johnny hart

money damages. New types of torts will be recognized as new forms of wrongful actions, such as those involving computers and the Internet, evolve.

Even though some particular acts will constitute both a tort and a crime, it is important to understand the differences between the two. A criminal action is instituted by a federal, state, or local prosecutor, on behalf of the people of that jurisdiction, to enforce a specific criminal statute. The thrust of a criminal prosecution is to punish an individual who has transgressed the laws of behavior established by society. The penalty upon conviction is generally imprisonment or a fine payable to the appropriate government. Sometimes, as part of the penalty, the defendant is ordered to pay an amount of money as restitution to the victim, but this is secondary in importance to punishing the criminal.

A *tort action* (a civil case), however, does not usually depend on any particular statute. The primary goal is *compensation of the victim* for the consequences of someone else's wrongful (not necessarily criminal) actions. The local, state, and federal prosecutors are not involved. The burden is on the plaintiff to show that the actions of the defendant breached a common law duty to the plaintiff, directly causing some particular harm, and then to show how much money is needed to compensate the injured party.

PURPOSE OF TORT LAW

Criminal law serves the interests of society by setting minimum standards of conduct and providing punishment for those who violate the rules. Tort law, on the other hand, concerns one person's *duty* toward others and involves determining what one's obligations *ought* to be toward one or more specific persons and providing compensation to the injured person when another's conduct falls below the expected level. Most often, no contract exists between the parties, nor is any criminal statute involved. In many cases, like auto accidents, the parties do not even know each other prior to the commission of the tort.

For example, Denise is driving her car and runs into Kim's vehicle at an intersection. Has a tort been committed? This decision depends on whether the judge and jury feel that Denise's actions were those of a "reasonable person," at the moment she took the action she did. In other words, the judge and jury will measure Denise's conduct (in driving her car) against that of a mythical person who would have acted in a careful and prudent manner at the same time in the same situation. If the jury believes that Denise should have been more careful in driving her car then they may find her negligent, which is a tort.

Although there are certain well-known types of torts, such as libel, slander, battery, and negligence, tort law is flexible enough to allow courts to find new torts when someone has acted wrongfully toward another. The most well-known writer on tort law, Dean William Prosser, once stated to this effect:

> Changing social conditions lead constantly to the recognition of new duties. No better general statement can be made than that the courts will find a duty where, in general, reasonable men would recognize and agree that it exists.

In recent years, for example, courts have found torts to be committed through the use of computers, video recorders, and other tools of modern technology, which have been used in ways that interfere with the privacy of, or cause economic damage to, others.

On the other hand, through the passage of time, some actions that were considered torts in the past are no longer deemed appropriate for legal remedies. The following article reports on a case heard before the Georgia Supreme Court concerning the tort of "seduction."

AN OUTDATED TORT

Georgia Seduction Law Overturned

In 1863, the Georgia Legislature passed a law allowing parents to sue men who seduced their unwed daughters. Over the past 131 years, court opinions show only two known instances where the law was used.

But no more. In June 1994, the Georgia Supreme Court declared the law unconstitutional, saying it was outdated and violated the equal protection clause of the state's constitution.

The final attempt to sue under the statute came last year when Nancy Franklin of suburban Atlanta filed a civil claim against her daughter's 11th grade teacher.

Georgia Code 51-1-16 allowed a father to sue for the seduction of his daughter if she was unmarried and living with her parents. If the father was dead, absent or refused to sue, the law permitted the mother to file.

Lawyers for Franklin argued that the law helped protect women from emotional and physical problems, including pregnancy, that result from consensual but nonmarital sex.

Old-Fashioned Notions

The seven justices disagreed. "Rather than seeking to prevent the pregnancy of unwed daughters, the statute was passed to hold men civilly liable for corrupting the morals and compromising the chastity of unmarried women," Justice Norman Fletcher wrote for the unanimous court. He noted that the law was passed at a time when "women and children were the legal property of their husbands and father."

In a concurring opinion, Justice Leah Sears-Collins wrote that the law was "based on outdated legal and societal notions and has a significant history of disuse" and "should be repealed as being obsolete."

Sears-Collins urged the court to set up a standard by which "hopelessly obsolete" statutes could be removed from the books.

In his opinion, Fletcher noted how the issue provoked strong feelings in the mid-1800s. He pointed to a decision written by Georgia's then chief justice, Joseph Henry Lumpkin, in a seduction case that was presented before the court in 1852, 11 years before the state legislature passed the seduction laws.

Lumpkin refused to reduce damages awarded to a father "for the dishonor and disgrace thus cast upon his family; for this atrocious invasion of his household peace. There is nothing like it, since the entrance of Sin and Death into this lower world."

INTENTIONAL TORTS

Some torts are intentional, whereas others are unintentional or accidental. Intentional torts are the result of one or more persons taking some deliberate action that causes personal or economic injury to another. Even though the person taking the action may not have intended the eventual result (for example, a serious injury), if he or she deliberately took the action that caused the injury, the action can be an intentional tort.

ASSAULT AND BATTERY

assault: A condition that occurs when one person's actions put another in fear of bodily harm.

battery: Unauthorized touching of another's body.

Although assault and battery are two torts often combined on television crime shows, each really is a separate act. **Assault** is intentionally putting another person in reasonable apprehension of immediate physical injury. If Alex points a gun at Sebastian and says, "I'm going to shoot you," that would probably constitute an assault. However, if Sebastian knew that the gun was a toy, there would not be the same reasonable apprehension and would likely not be held as an assault. In addition, the victim must know about the threat in order to have the required apprehension. Thus, if Sebastian were asleep when Alex pointed a gun at him, there would not have been an assault.

Battery is the intentional, offensive, unwanted physical touching of another. Some batteries are preceded by an assault, and some are not. Battery often results from one person hitting or beating another, but unwanted caressing, kissing, or touching can also constitute a battery.

FROM THE DESK OF
Laura Lawyer

To: Students

From: Your Lawyer

One increasingly common form of battery lawsuit today results from sexual harassment in the workplace. Persons who are the victims of unwanted touching, pinching, or sexual contact need to file a tort lawsuit (battery) against the wrongdoer to collect damages. If a manager is the offender, or if the employee complains to management but no action is taken to correct the situation, the employer may also be liable. To protect their employees and to reduce their own liability, employers should adopt policies to prevent workplace sexual harassment as well as other types of harassment and should promptly investigate and punish such conduct.

One of the main defenses to the tort of battery is "consent." Defendants often argue that the person who was touched or hit had voluntarily engaged in the fight or invited the overly friendly contact which led to the battery allegation. Another common argument by a defendant is "self-defense"—that is, the person accused of battery was defending against an attack. The law does recognize such a defense but only to the extent necessary to defend against the attack. If Monica and Georgia are having a discussion, and Georgia slaps Monica's face, she cannot shoot Georgia and then claim self-defense from the tort of battery.

The following case involves a tort lawsuit for battery that resulted from a hockey game.

OVERALL V. KADELLA

361 N.W. 2d 352 (Mich. App. 1984)

FACTS

At the conclusion of a hockey game between two amateur teams, a fight broke out between Mr. Kadella and a player from the opposing team. The fight soon became general, with players from both teams "leaving the bench to join the melee." Mr. Overall was a member of the opposing team but remained on the bench during the fight. Nevertheless, during the altercation Kadella skated over to the bench and hit Overall, knocking him unconscious and fracturing the bones around his right eye. Overall sued Kadella for battery. Overall was awarded $21,000 by the trial court for out-of-pocket expenses and pain and suffering and $25,000 as punitive damages because defendant's act had been "intentional and malicious."

DECISION

On appeal Kadella argued that the trial court's findings of fact were erroneous. Kadella pointed out that his three witnesses had testified that although Overall was seated on the bench, he had poked Kadella with his stick before Kadella retaliated. (Overall and his witnesses denied this.) One of the referees at the game also testified that he saw Overall poke Kadella with his stick before Kadella attacked him. The referee also stated that Kadella had been involved in three separate fights after the game and had been given three "game misconduct" penalties (a very serious penalty in hockey). The Appeals Court decided that the trial judge had the right to decide which witnesses to believe and obviously felt that Overall's witnesses had more credibility.

Kadella's other main argument on appeal was that Overall could not sue for battery because of consent—that he was voluntarily participating in a hockey game. This argument is expressed in the phrase *volenti non fit injuria*, or "he who consents cannot receive an injury."

The court noted that participation in a game does involve consent to those bodily contacts that are permitted by the rules of the game. "However, there is general agreement that an intentional act causing injury, which goes beyond what is ordinarily permissible, is an assault and battery for which recovery may be had."

Looking back at a number of decisions from earlier cases, the court particularly mentioned a 1975 Illinois case in which a soccer player had kicked the opposing goalkeeper in the head while he was holding the ball, causing serious injury. The Illinois court had rejected the argument that there was tort immunity for any injury that might occur during the course of a game.

It is our opinion that a player is liable for injury in a tort action if his conduct is such that it is either deliberate, wilful, or with a reckless disregard for the safety of the other player so as to cause injury to that player, the same being a question of fact to be decided by a jury. Nabozny v. Barnhill, *31 Ill. App. 3d 212, 215, 334 N.E. 2d 258, 260 (1975).*

In this case the defendant's own witnesses agreed that the Michigan Amateur Hockey Association rules, in order to stop violence, specifically prohibit fighting. Furthermore, it is even arguable that the battery did not occur during the game at all, but after the game. Whatever consent to physical contact there was during the game did not apply after the game was over. The Appeals Court therefore affirmed the decision of the lower court.

CASE QUESTIONS

1. There was conflicting evidence about whether Overall poked Kadella with his stick before the attack. If you believe the poking did occur, should this change the outcome? What if Overall called Kadella a dirty name?
2. If Overall had skated out and joined the free-for-all on the ice, instead of remaining on the bench, would the result be different?
3. Amateur hockey may be different, but in professional hockey, fighting is quite common even though it is against the rules. How can we fairly determine the point at which the penalty for fighting should be punished by hockey rules (5 or 10 minutes in the penalty box) and when it should be the subject of legal action in the court system? Write out what your standard would be.

DEFAMATION

defamation: The communication of damaging, false information about a person to at least one other person.

libel: Written defamation.

slander: Oral or verbal defamation.

Defamation, the communication of damaging, false information about someone to at least one other person, includes two subparts, *libel* and *slander*. If the statement is published in written form, the tort is called **libel**; if it is published (communicated) in oral form, the tort is called **slander**. The purpose of these torts is to protect one's reputation in the community and to punish those who falsely damage another's character.

To prove defamation it is necessary to establish each element of the tort. The statement must be: (1) untrue, (2) of the type that will cause hurt and injury to the plaintiff or lower others' opinion of the plaintiff, (3) an intentional communication to at least one person other than the plaintiff, and (4) injurious (usually economically) to the plaintiff, in most cases. In other words, Michael can write a news article stating that Lee is a thief, as long as that is true. In addition, he can accuse Lee of theft, in private, even if it is untrue, and there is no defamation. But if he accuses Lee of theft in a staff meeting, and it is untrue, Lee may be able to sue for slander. Since Michael's statement would be false, of the type that would cause harm to Lee, and would be communicated to others, this would probably create a valid tort cause of action.

absolute privilege: Protection from liability for slander or libel given under certain circumstances regardless of the fact that the statements are false or maliciously made.

Certain types of statements can be made without fear of a defamation lawsuit. Statements made during a trial by the judge, attorneys, and witnesses are covered by an **absolute privilege**. This means that someone about whom a slanderous statement was made during the trial would not be able to sue for defamation. The same privilege applies to statements made by legislators during legislative proceedings. Why? Absolute privilege encourages the fullest possible expression of opinion and debate in certain limited circumstances. Within the legislature or the courtroom, a senator or attorney or witness can speak freely without fear of being sued if something said turns out not to be true. If the same statement was made just outside the courthouse or statehouse, however, the individual slandered could sue the attorney or senator for defamation.

In a recent California case, an appellate court refused to dismiss part of a libel action against a judge relating to his comments to a plaintiff in a pending case. Apparently Judge Alexander Williams III became angry at the settlement demands of plaintiff Robert Soliz and screamed at him in a settlement conference in a hallway outside the courtroom. The judge yelled at Mr. Soliz that if he thought there was money in the case, he "had sh.. for brains." Several days later the judge was interviewed by a news reporter and certain comments of his regarding Mr. Soliz were published in the *Los Angeles Daily Journal*.

Mr. Soliz sued Judge Williams for libel, but the lower court dismissed the case, based on the absolute privilege of a judge. The court of appeal upheld the dismissal for Judge Williams' comments in the hallway, finding that he was acting as a judge at that time. However, the appellate court allowed the libel case to go forward as to the comments in the newspaper. "Speaking to a reporter about a pending lawsuit is not a normal judicial function," and thus is not conduct protected by the privilege, ruled the court.

Other types of false or erroneous statements are protected by what is called a **qualified privilege**. This means that the person who made the statement may be protected in some situations but not in others. The usual requirement is that the person must have made the statement in good faith rather than with malice or with knowledge that what he said was false. The most common instance of qualified privilege occurs with regard to defamation suits by *public figures*. These are people who are in the public eye on a regular basis and have to expect that there will be many things said and written about them. In order for politicians, sports stars, and entertainment figures to win defamation suits, they must prove all the regular elements of the case as described previously. They must also show that the defendant published the statement *with malicious intent* or *knew that what was said was false* at the time the statement was made. This rule recognizes the public interest in information (yes, even gossip) about well-known people and makes it more difficult for them to win defamation suits.

qualified privilege: Protection from liability for defamatory statements only if the defendant uttered them without actual malice or had a good reason for doing so.

But sometimes even television stars can win cases where the defamation is particularly outrageous. For example, actress Carol Burnett won a judgment against the *National Enquirer*. The news tabloid had published an article stating that she was drunk and boisterous in a Washington, D.C., restaurant and had engaged in a loud argument with Henry Kissinger. However, she proved that neither of these statements were true. The *Enquirer* never bothered to check the accuracy of a report from a freelance tipster, and in addition editors embellished the report without any factual basis whatsoever. [See *Burnett v. National Enquirer, Inc.*, 144 Cal. App. 3d 991 (1983).]

Defamation cases often arise in business in connection with the giving of job references and recommendations. For example, when Rebecca applies for a job, she will usually be asked for the names of her previous supervisors. Some of her previous employment experiences may not have gone as well as she would have liked (after all, she is looking for a new job!). Suppose that a former boss tells the prospective employer some unfavorable things about Rebecca, perhaps magnifying the actions that caused her dismissal or confusing Rebecca with another employee who left about the same time after failing a drug test. Assuming that Rebecca does not get the new job, what sort of liability for defamation does the former employer have? What defenses does the employer have. The following case explores these issues.

KENNEY V. GILMORE

195 Ga. App. 407 (1990)

FACTS

Ms. Kenney had worked for some time at GIT Travel, Inc. (of which Mr. Gilmore was the head). Ms. Kenney left GIT under "unpleasant" circumstances, following at least one argument with Gilmore and allegations that her mannerisms and performance had caused the travel agency to lose a major client.

Ms. Kenny then applied for a job with United Air Lines, listing GIT as a former employer and signing a card authorizing United to contact the places she had worked. United had a contract with Equifax Co. to screen all its employment applicants, and an Equifax representative called GIT regarding Ms. Kenney. Mr. Gilmore told Equifax that Ms. Kenney was "insubordinate, had caused the agency to lose clients, and would not be rehired should the opportunity arise." Later, a second Equifax employee telephoned GIT to verify the information given and received substantially the same report. United did not hire Ms. Kenney.

When Ms. Kenney learned what had happened, she sued Mr. Gilmore and GIT Travel, Inc. for defamation. She asserted that the defendants had caused her injury by communicating false information to a third party. The trial court granted a summary judgment to the defendants, and Ms. Kenney appealed.

DECISION

In a unanimous opinion, written by Judge Deen of the Court of Appeals of Georgia, the lower court decision was affirmed. The appellate court found that (1) no "publication" had occurred and (2) that even if there was publication, it was covered by a qualified privilege.

The court held that since Ms. Kenney had expressly authorized communication between her former employer and a prospective new employer, the information was only provided to authorized parties, and there had been no "publication" to outside parties. Furthermore, in the circumstances of this case, "the alleged defamation might have been deemed to have been 'invited.'"

In addition, Georgia courts had long recognized that such communication was protected by a privilege. This privilege "shields statements made concerning a current or former employee by a current or former employer to one, such as a prospective employer, who has a legitimate interest in such information." The court noted that the privilege "is a qualified one" and could be overcome by evidence of actual malice. However, the plaintiff has the burden of proof to show the existence of malice, and the record here was "devoid of any evidence of actual malice." Thus, the judgment of the lower court was affirmed.

CASE QUESTIONS

1. Did the plaintiff have a full trial here?
2. Did Ms. Kenney lose the case because she could not prove that the statements made to Equifax were false? Explain.
3. Give an example of the type of evidence Ms. Kenney would have had to offer to prove malice on the part of the defendants.
4. What is the purpose of the policy that allows former employers to make certain false statements about former employees without liability?

FALSE IMPRISONMENT

As one court put it, "false imprisonment is the intentional, unlawful, and unconsented restraint by one person of the physical liberty of another." In order for this tort to occur, the defendant must intentionally restrain the plaintiff, who must realize that his or her freedom has been impaired. Many false imprisonment cases have resulted when retail stores have detained suspected shoplifters. Shoplifting is a major concern, and retail stores have developed various ways to combat this problem, including one-way mirrors, secret cameras, and plain-clothed store security personnel. When a person is suspected of shoplifting, the store will generally try to apprehend the customer, conduct questioning, and examine the questionable items in a private room somewhere on the premises.

This situation—where a person is apprehended and held against his or her will by the store—can obviously lead to a lawsuit for false imprisonment when the accused person is innocent. To avoid some litigation and provide retailers with some latitude in fighting shoplifting, many states have passed statutes giving merchants the legal right to detain suspected individuals for a reasonable time and in a reasonable manner. For example, read the Iowa law set out on page 318.

Therefore, in most states, merchants are allowed to detain suspected shoplifters for a "reasonable period of time" if the detention is handled "in a reasonable manner." Furthermore, there must have been "reasonable grounds to believe" that the person had concealed the item, in order for the later detention to be valid. If the store observes all these "reasonable" precautions, it should not be liable even if the accused person is innocent. The normal process is to question the individual for a short period of time in private and allow him or her to produce a receipt or other indication that the item was not shoplifted. If there is no such proof, the police should be called promptly and charges filed. However, if the merchant's employees treat the shopper roughly, hold the person a long time without calling the police or asking the accused to prove his or her innocence or if they have no good basis for stopping the suspect in the first place, there may be liability for the tort of false imprisonment.

FROM THE DESK OF
Laura Lawyer

To: Students
From: Your Lawyer

Either now or in the future you may work for retail stores. Be sure to examine the policies these employers have regarding shoplifting. Ask the following questions: How does the policy stand up to the rules set forth here? What should you do if you see someone take an item off the shelf and put it in his or her pocket or purse? Does the store follow "reasonable procedures" in deciding whether to apprehend someone, and in how that person is treated while detained?

IOWA CODE ANNOTATED

Section 808.12 Detention and Search in Theft of Library Materials and Shoplifting

1. Persons concealing property . . . may be detained and searched by a peace officer, person employed in a facility containing library materials, merchant, or merchant's employee, provided that the detention is for a reasonable length of time and that the search is conducted in a reasonable manner by a person of the same sex and according to subsection 2 of this section.

2. No search of the person under this section shall be conducted by any person other than someone acting under the direction of a peace officer except where permission of the one to be searched has first been obtained.

3. The detention or search under this section by a peace officer, person employed in a facility containing library materials, merchant, or merchant's employee shall not render such peace officer, library employee, merchant, or merchant's employee liable, in a criminal or civil action, for false arrest or false imprisonment provided the peace officer, library employee, merchant, or merchant's employee had reasonable grounds to believe the person detained or searched had concealed or was attempting to conceal property as set forth in section 714.5 of this code [which defines shoplifting].

NEGLIGENCE—AN UNINTENTIONAL TORT

negligence: The most common type of tort. It involves a person causing injury to another, by doing some action with less than the amount of care expected of a "reasonable person."

Negligence is the most important type of unintentional tort, and it is no doubt the most significant category of tort suit in our court system. Negligence law has had a major effect on business. The legal principles concerning what actions constitute negligent conduct have developed through numerous court decisions, involving every type of situation imaginable. Negligence is the epitome of the common law legal process. The essence of negligence is "fault"—that is, that someone did something without exercising reasonable care or failed to do something that we would have expected a reasonable person to do in that exact situation, with the direct result being an injury to another person.

ELEMENTS OF NEGLIGENCE

Four elements must be present in order to hold a defendant liable for negligence: (1) duty, (2) breach of that duty, (3) actual and proximate cause, and (4) injury to another. *Duty* means that the defendant owed some type of legal obligation to the plaintiff. If the defendant did not meet his or her duty, this is called *breach*. If the failure to meet the standard resulted directly in foreseeable *injury* to someone else, this is *actual and proximate cause* of the injury.

DUTY OF CARE AND BREACH OF DUTY

The legal duty involved in negligence cases need not flow from any previous relationship between the parties (although sometimes that is the case). Hundreds of court decisions have established the general principle that everyone must take reasonable care in all actions so as not to injure another person. Each of us has the duty to act as a jury feels a mythical "reasonable person" would act in any given situation. This is called the *reasonable person* standard. Hence, if Rachel is riding her bicycle across campus, she has the duty (whether she knows it or not) to operate her bike in a reasonably careful manner in order not to injure others. She owes this duty of care to everyone she might encounter on her ride.

If Rachel does not meet this standard—if, for example, she steers with her feet while looking sideways—a court probably will find that she breached (fell below) her duty to operate her bike in a reasonably careful manner in accordance with the standards of the mythical "reasonable person."

PROXIMATE CAUSE AND INJURY

Even though Rachel may have failed to meet the appropriate standard of care, she will not face a negligence suit unless the other two elements are present. Fortunately for all of us, most of the time no one is injured when we are negligent or careless. But when our failure to meet the standard of care of a "reasonable person" does actually and *"proximately"* (directly) cause an *injury* to another person, then all the elements of negligence have been established. The negligence must directly cause the injury. For example, if Rachel's careless bicycle riding caused her to smash into and break the leg of an older business law professor who was slowly walking across campus, she might well be found liable of negligence. Many cases apply the "but for" test to determine proximate cause—that is, whether the injury would have occurred "but for" the negligence of the defendant.

Negligence cases often are won or lost on the determination of **proximate cause** questions. In the preceding example, the proximate cause of the injury was fairly clear. But suppose that Rachel had recently had her bike repaired at a cycle shop and while riding across campus, one of the wheels came off. As she began falling to the ground, the books she was carrying were thrown toward the sidewalk, right in front of Dwayne, who was riding a skateboard. Dwayne swerved to miss the books, running into Tom, who screamed, "Look out!" Some 20 yards away, the professor, startled by the scream, tripped on the steps of the Business Building, breaking his leg. What is the proximate cause of the accident? In resolving such questions, courts often apply a *foreseeability* test—that is, was the injury that occurred within the range of harm that should have been foreseeable to the person who is being charged with negligence?

proximate cause: One of the key elements of a negligence case is that the defendant's lack of care must be the direct cause of the injury to the plaintiff, and that the injury was a "foreseeable" result of such negligence.

Suppose that a negligence suit by the professor against the cycle shop arises from the facts set forth previously. The professor claims that "but for" the shop's failure to tighten the wheel properly after repairing the bike, the accident would not have occurred. The professor argues that the failure to properly tighten the wheel was a breach of the duty of care, since a reasonably careful bicycle shop would have made sure that the wheels were in good order before turning the bike over to Rachel. Furthermore, the professor argues that his injuries were a direct and proximate result of this negligence. It is quite possible, however, that the court will conclude that the series of events were too remote and "unforeseeable" to make the bike shop liable for the professor's injuries—in other words, that its negligence was not the "proximate cause" of the injuries.

Whether Rachel or any of the other players in this drama are liable to the professor depends on a similar analysis—first, whether they were negligent, and then, if so, whether that negligence was an actual, direct, proximate cause of the injuries. Sometimes the owners or managers of property have been sued for negligence due to the criminal acts of third persons. It is not unusual for a landlord to face a negligence suit after a tenant is injured by the assault of a criminal. The general allegation made in these cases is that because of some negligent act that the landlord took or did not take (such as failing to repair broken locks on the building or not replacing lights that had burned out in the entryway or parking lot), the landlord had not met the standard of care expected of a reasonable building owner and was at least partly the direct cause of the injury to the tenant.

Supermarkets and large stores such as K-Mart and Wal-Mart have been sued for negligence as the result of robberies, assaults, and murders that have taken place in their parking lots on occasion. Sometimes the victims win if it is shown that the store management knew or should have known that crimes had taken place in their parking lots earlier, and they had done nothing to try to prevent such crimes from occurring in the future. Most of the time, the stores win, because the courts find that the "proximate cause" of the damages is the criminal act. But the case can turn on the amount of knowledge possessed by the store and whether the actions it took were "reasonable." Two of the questions at the end of the chapter raise similar issues, which have been the subject of recent tort lawsuits.

As we learned in Chapter 8, often business firms are held liable for the actions of their employees. The following article discusses a new type of negligence—use of cell phones.

Crash Course for Business

Companies can be liable for accidents resulting from job-related cell phone use

When Edward Eidelman got a phone call recently from a law student, he figured he was being interviewed for a law review article. The query concerned the $500,000 settlement he got for the family of a young man killed by a driver who claimed he was distracted while using a cell phone.

But it wasn't long before the Allentown, Pa., lawyer realized the caller had another purpose. "He was interning for a big law firm and they asked him to research what their policy should be for using cell phones," Eidelman says.

Costly Conversations

A lot of firms and business concerns likely will be doing the same as cell phone–related car accidents increase, particularly those involving on-the-job calls. In Eidelman's case, the brokerage firm Smith Barney settled for $500,000 in February rather than take a chance on jury sympathy. *Roberts v. Smith Barney*, No 97-2727 (E.D. Pa.).

While the defense believed it could easily defeat scope-of-employment claims, it was faced with facts that could make a jury go with its heart: A stockbroker in a Mercedes on his way to a nice restaurant killed a 24-year-old father of two who was driving his motorcycle to get his family hot dogs for dinner.

"I still say it's not a cell phone case," says Smith Barney's lawyer, Thomas Dinkelacker. "Drivers are distracted when fooling with the radio or looking at maps or handling a cup of coffee. This is just the 1990s version of inattentive driving."

The claim against Smith Barney indeed was tenuous. The firm neither provides cell phones nor requires them for its stockbrokers. And its employee, Robert Tarone, claimed he was making the cold-call sales pitch at 9 p.m. on a Saturday. Further, Tarone's account of the evening's events changed several times, particularly as to whether he had left his office or his home before driving to the restaurant.

Eidelman counters that there was evidence Smith Barney has a policy for its brokers to make calls outside normal business hours to reach some potential customers.

Another company, Domino's Pizza, learned the hard way that employers must pay when workers cause car accidents. The pizza purveyor had promised its customers delivery within 30 minutes or the food is free. When juries started handing out big verdicts in the early 1990s for those killed or injured by speeding delivery drivers, Domino's changed its policy.

Press D for Dangerous

Since 1990, according to personal injury case-tracking Jury Verdict Research, there have been 34 recorded incidents in which cell phone use has contributed to accidents and injuries. The outcomes are as follows: 14 plaintiffs' verdicts, 11 for the defense, six settlements, and three resolved in mediation or arbitration.

In 1997 the *New England Journal of Medicine* reported findings that cell phone use while driving results in a fourfold increase in the likelihood of having an accident.

While attempts to ban cell phone use while driving have failed in several states, New York City recently made the practice illegal for cab drivers. In several other countries, including Australia, Great Britain and Spain, drivers are not allowed to use cell phones.

Earlier this year, the National Traffic Highway Safety Administration agreed that statistics show an increased likelihood for accidents. But it said that not enough data has been collected to differentiate cell phone use from other distractions while driving.

The Smith Barney case probably would not have added much to the growing debate. There was no record of Tarone having made a call at the time of the accident, and he fled the scene and towed his car to another city the next day. He later said he dropped the phone and ran a red light trying to retrieve it.

"I never want to see settlements on these borderline cases," says Victor Schwartz, a leading lobbyist for the tort reform movement. "You're establishing a principle of law where no court has decided it. You're providing a marker that you or someone else will pay if a similar situation occurs again."

But Smith Barney decided it didn't want to go for broke in a trial. "Even though we had a strong case, it was just too dangerous with these facts," Dinkelacker says. "The client had a cut-off point on dollars, and it was met."

"Crash Course for Business" by Terry Carter, *ABA Journal*, August 1999, p. 40.

DEFENSES TO NEGLIGENCE

contributory negligence: A defense to negligence that asserts that the plaintiff was also negligent. If applied, this defense results in dismissal of the case.

Three main legal theories are used to defend against negligence cases. One is called **contributary negligence**. To claim this defense, the party charged with negligence argues that the accident or injury was at least partially caused by the negligence of the plaintiff. In other words, the negligence of the plaintiff "contributed to" the injury. This doctrine developed through the common law during the 1800s and served to protect the interests of businesses against suits by workers and others. Under the strict application of this rule, *any* negligence by the plaintiff (even if small) that contributed to the accident completely barred the plaintiff from recovery against the defendant. This was true even if the defendant was clearly negligent.

For example, suppose Richard is driving down Broadway Avenue in his 1990 Ford. He knows that his brakes are bad but has not had time to get them fixed. In addition, his windshield is covered with ice, but he is in a hurry and has not cleaned it off. After a rolling stop at the corner, Mary Lou, in her 1998 Porsche, pulls out onto Broadway from a side street several hundred feet in front of Richard. He fails to see her at first. When he does, his brakes fail, and he runs into Mary Lou, causing damage to her car. In a lawsuit by Mary Lou against Richard, the jury might find that Richard's negligence was 80 percent of the cause of the accident and Mary Lou's was 20 percent. However, if that state follows the contributory negligence rule, Mary Lou's case will be dismissed, and she will get nothing.

comparative negligence: A defense to negligence that calls for the jury to assess ("compare") the negligence of the plaintiff and the defendant, and adjust the damages to reflect the percentage of negligence of the plaintiff.

Because of the harshness of this rule, during the past 20 or 30 years most states have enacted statutes replacing contributory negligence with a principle called **comparative negligence**. Using this doctrine, a jury compares the negligence of the plaintiff and the defendant and, if the plaintiff's negligence was less, awards the plaintiff a recovery reduced by the amount of his or her negligence. In the previously described situation, for example, if Mary Lou had established damages of $10,000, the jury would award her a judgment of $8,000 under a comparative negligence standard. In other words, the jury would reduce the amount of her recovery by the percentage she was at fault (20 percent in our example).

Most state statutes will allow the plaintiff to recover damages until his or her negligence reaches 50 percent of the cause. When the plaintiff is at least equally at fault with the defendant, most states cut off his right to recover anything. A few states, however, allow the plaintiff to recover damages if the defendant is negligent at all, reduced by the appropriate percentage of the plaintiff's negligence. (E.g., if the defendant was 25 percent negligent and the plaintiff 75 percent, the plaintiff could still recover 25 percent of the damages.)

Often a negligence case involves the question of whether a restaurant or other retail establishment met its "duty of care" to customers who enter the store to shop. There have been thousands of so-called "slip and fall" cases, filed against all type of stores in all states, following a fall by a customer. Sometimes the store wins, and sometimes the customer does, depending on the facts of the case. These are classic negligence cases, with the result turning on the analysis by the court and the jury of the exact duty of the store to its customers, whether the duty was met, and if not, whether the "fault" of the store was the proximate cause of the plaintiff's injuries. Also important is the question of whether the plaintiff was also negligent, and if so, if that negligence contributed to the accident. The following case is an example.

KROGER COMPANY V. BROOKS

500 S.E.2d 391 (Ga. App. 1998)

FACTS

One night in September 1993, Ashley Brooks entered a Kroger grocery store at 11:30 P.M. with a friend to buy some croissants. She headed for the bakery area by going through checkout lane 5, which was not being used at the time. On the way through lane 5 she slipped and fell, injuring her arm and leg, when she stepped on a small, flattened, white paper cup that apparently had mousse both inside and around it. A mousse-smeared streak extended several feet in length from the flattened cup.

A cashier working at lane 7 was the closest person to Ashley and her friend (who did not fall). The cashier quickly came to her aid, and then called for the store manager. The manager testified at trial that "earlier that day" the pastry chef had put out vanilla mousse samples that he had prepared. The chef had departed by the time of the fall, but mousse samples were still out at the bakery counter. The manager testified that the store policy was that the store manager did a walk-through inspection every hour prior to 8 P.M. and at the end of each shift. The store was swept and spot-mopped every hour from 7 A.M. until 7 or 8 P.M., when business dropped off. After that time, cleaning was done only on an "as needed" basis.

Ms. Brooks later filed a negligence suit against Kroger and asked for a jury trial. After all evidence had been introduced, Kroger moved for a directed verdict in its favor, which was denied by the judge. The jury then returned a verdict in favor of Ms. Brooks, based on negligence, and a judgment for money damages was entered by the court. Kroger appealed to the Georgia Court of Appeals.

DECISION

The appellate court said that in order to state a cause of action in a negligence "slip and fall" case, the plaintiff must show that (1) the defendant had actual or constructive knowledge of the foreign substance which caused the fall and (2) the plaintiff was without knowledge of the substance. Furthermore, "constructive knowledge" [that the defendant should have known] of the hazard may be inferred by the jury where there is evidence that an employee of the defendant was "in the immediate vicinity" of the dangerous condition and could have noticed and removed the hazard.

In beginning its analysis of this case, the Court of Appeals stated that there was no evidence at trial that Kroger had "actual knowledge" of the mousse spill. However, the Court noted that Kroger had been giving out samples of the mousse in the evening within 75 feet of where the accident occurred. The fact that there was a trash can placed next to the bakery counter showed Kroger's foreseeability as to the need to carefully dispose of the samples. In fact, the samples were still available until the time of the accident at the bakery counter. The evidence showed that the last time that checkout lane 5 had been swept and mopped was around 8:00 P.M. The night cashier was *supposed* to check the other lanes when she was not waiting on customers, but there was no evidence at trial that she had actually checked on lane 5.

Plaintiff's evidence (the testimony of Ms. Brooks and her friend) showed that the paper cup of mousse had been flattened. The court said that a jury could infer from this evidence that someone else had previously stepped on the cup before Ms. Brooks. The mousse was smeared over several feet of the floor as well. The manager testified that he and the cashier had been on checkout lane 7 most of the evening, although they were supposed to inspect the entire store. The court stated that the jury could certainly infer from this evidence that the manager and cashier had been "in the immediate vicinity" of the spill, and thus had the opportunity to discover the problem. Such a finding would constitute *constructive knowledge*, sufficient to support the verdict in the lower court.

The Court of Appeals stated further that negligence liability based on constructive knowledge could also be established by showing that the owner failed to exercise reasonable care in inspecting the premises over a period of time. Where the evidence raises the inference that the foreign substance was discoverable by a reasonable inspection, a jury may consider whether the store had constructive knowledge of the spill.

Here, there was evidence that the last known sweeping and mopping of checkout lane 5 had occurred at 8 P.M. The manager could not remember when he did his last walk-through inspection of the store, but he was sure he had done one or two during the evening. The paper cup was flattened and the mousse spread over the lane, so the jury could reasonably have come to the conclusion that the spill had been on the floor for some time, from anytime between 8 and 10:30 P.M. It was certainly a jury question then, whether the defendant had exercised ordinary care in its inspection of the store during that period.

Kroger alleged that the plaintiff's own contributory negligence in not seeing the mousse on the floor and avoiding the spill had been part of the cause of the accident. However, the court stated, the customer "is not bound to avoid hazards not usually present on the premises and which she, exercising ordinary care, did not observe." The customer is "not required to look continuously at the floor, without intermission, for defects on the floor." Here, the plaintiff showed that she had been looking where she was going without talking or looking at the displays. Furthermore, the color of the mousse and the floor tiles were similar, and the store manager had also dimmed the lights in the evening to save energy. The court found that no negligence of the plaintiff had contributed to the accident.

Therefore, the Georgia Court of Appeals concluded that "By encouraging others to enter the premises to further the owner's enterprise, the owner makes an implied representation that reasonable care has been exercised to make the place safe for those who come for that purpose . . . An invitee (customer) who responds to this invitation . . . is entitled to expect that the owner/occupier has exercised and will continue to exercise reasonable care to make the premises safe." The Court thus affirmed the jury's verdict in favor of Ms. Brooks.

CASE QUESTIONS

1. Did the store manager or anyone else at Kroger actually know that there was a mousse spill at checkout lane 5? Why did Kroger have "constructive knowledge" of the spilled mousse?
2. What was the "duty of care" that Kroger had to its customers? What exactly did the store do, or not do, that breached its duty?
3. Suppose there had been proof that the spill had only been on the floor for five minutes before Ms. Brooks fell. Would Kroger still have been negligent? Why or why not?
4. Does the legal rule imposing a duty of care on grocery stores and other retail establishments serve a public purpose?

SOCIAL/ETHICAL ISSUES

Which of the two defenses—contributory or comparative negligence—do you think is more socially and ethically correct? Is it fair or just to completely deprive a person of any recovery against a negligent person, just because he or she was a little bit negligent himself? Or is it more fair or just to allow a person to sue and win a damage award against another even if his or her negligence was a 30 percent cause of the accident? Which theory better accommodates business? Which one is better for society?

Another long-recognized defense to a negligence lawsuit is called **assumption of the risk**. This theory holds that if a person voluntarily undertakes an activity knowing exactly what risks are involved, he or she cannot sue later for injuries incurred. This rule was strictly applied in the 1800s, making it very difficult for workers to sue employers for injuries that occurred on the job, since they "assumed the risks" of employment. For example, if Shawna worked in an automobile factory, she would know that there was a chance of getting her arm caught in machinery. If such an accident happened, courts often held that she had "assumed" that risk, and they refused to hold the company liable, even if there was some evidence of negligence. (Perhaps the company had never inspected the machine, for example.)

assumption of the risk: A defense to negligence that asserts that the plaintiff knowingly accepted the risks of the activity causing the injury.

One response to the harsh results of strict application of this rule was the development of workers compensation laws. Workers compensation statutes expressly prohibit the defenses of contributory negligence and assumption of the risk from being raised in connection with a claim for compensation. These statutes also eliminate the so-called *fellow-servant rule*. This defense formerly allowed the employer to escape liability not only if the employee him- or herself was negligent but also if the injury was caused by the negligence of another employee (the fellow servant). Workers compensation is discussed more fully in Chapter 21.

Despite the changes in the law with regard to workers compensation, assumption of the risk is still a viable defense in all regular negligence cases. In order to successfully use the defense, however, the defendant must show that the plaintiff actually knew and understood the risk. When you attend a major league baseball game, for example, you probably assume the risk that a ball may be hit into the stands. However, you do not assume the risk that the walkway leading to your seat will be negligently constructed and maintained and will collapse when stepped on. In some states assumption of the risk is just one of the factors to be considered in allocating the comparative negligence percentages. The following reading discusses liability issues arising from assaults by drunken fans at sports events.

Beer-Battered Fans

Injured ticketholders sue, claiming that alcohol at sporting events fuels violence

Fans who pile into professional football stadiums every fall yearn to witness hard-fought battles and helmet-cracking tackles. But they don't expect to find themselves playing defense.

Yet, incidents of drunken and rowdy behavior have turned sitting in the stands into a contact sport in recent years. In a number of instances, this unsportsmanlike conduct has left spectators with serious, sometimes life-threatening injuries. And when fans start missing games on account of injury, it is only a matter of time before they start looking for someone to blame.

Despite publicity about the problem of alcohol-related violence at sporting events, few cases have actually been brought to determine liability for injuries. But two pending lawsuits involving plaintiffs injured at different pro football games may provide some answers.

Meadowlands Mayhem

In New Jersey, a New York Jets fan is seeking damages from stadium operators for injuries he sustained in a stabbing while leaving the stadium after a game against the New England Patriots in October 1997. Michael McGee, whose lung was punctured in the attack, was assaulted by a 16-year-old who later pleaded guilty to related charges in juvenile court.

The lawsuit, filed in U.S. District Court for the District of New Jersey, charges that the New Jersey Sports and Exposition Authority, which oversees the operation of the stadium, failed to provide sufficient protection to ticketholders. The suit also accuses Aramark Inc., a Philadelphia-based stadium vendor, of serving alcohol to a minor, who was obviously intoxicated. *McGee v. Aramark*, No. 98 Civ. 4387 (S.D.N.J., Jan. 14, 1999).

"We think the concessions operator has a duty to not serve people who are obviously drunk. Absent a breach of that duty, our client wouldn't have been stabbed and nearly killed," says Terence Scheurer, an attorney for McGee.

Neither Aramark nor the New Jersey Sports Authority would comment on the pending litigation. But John Samerjan, vice president of public affairs for the sports authority, says the Meadowlands has one of the more restrictive alcohol policies in the league. Beer sales are cut off after the third quarter of every game. If fans are particularly rowdy, the stadium will end sales even earlier. No alcohol is served at night games, he adds.

In a second case, cardiologist Michael James Covert, 50, filed separate actions against the stadium operator and a security firm after he was assaulted during a Miami Dolphins football game in December 1997 at Pro Player (formerly Joe Robbie) Stadium. *Covert v. South Florida Stadium*, No. 98-07049CA04 and *Covert v. Event Services America*, No. 99-15514CA22.

Covert, a season ticketholder for 15 years, was attacked by three men while sitting in the reserve section. The suits, filed in Dade Country Circuit Court, state that he was punched, kicked and thrown over a row of seats, causing injuries to his head, face, ribs and arms. The assault caused permanent damage to his right arm, and he later was forced to sell his medical practice, he alleges.

"The whole thing is really tragic," says James Nosich, Covert's attorney. Two of the attackers later pleaded guilty to assault-related charges, Nosich says.

In one suit, the complaint alleges that the Contemporary Service Co. failed to provide reasonable security to control and guard against attacks like the one on Covert.

In a separate suit, Covert charges that the South Florida Stadium Corp., the stadium operator, contributed to the beating by promoting alcohol sales and serving it to the perpetrators. In that case, his season ticketholder status is another legal twist.

A circuit court judge dismissed the case against South Florida Stadium Corp. on the ground that Covert, as a season ticketholder, had no right to sue, Nosich says. Season ticketholders sign a liability waiver when they purchase their seats for the year. Nosich is appealing. He says it does not make sense that stadium operators would owe a duty to one portion of spectators but not to another.

Nosich says the underlying problem in most stadium violence cases is alcohol. He adds that suits like his will not, unfortunately, deter stadiums from selling liquor.

"A ban would cure the problem 100 percent, but as long as stadiums make money, they're going to continue to promote it," he says.

PRESUMED NEGLIGENCE

In most cases, negligence must be proved, as set forth previously, by showing that the defendant did not meet the standard of care of the mythical "reasonable person." In a few instances, however, the jury is permitted to presume that the defendant was negligent. One such situation is called **negligence per se**, or "negligence in itself." This might occur if the defendant has violated a statute designed to protect the public, such as a speed limit. If the plaintiff can show that the defendant violated a statute and that the plaintiff was within the class of people the law was designed to protect, the jury may be instructed that the defendant was negligent (but the plaintiff will still have to prove proximate cause and damages to win the case).

negligence per se: A category of negligence in which the defendant has violated a statute intended to protect the public from such conduct.

Another instance in which negligence can be presumed involves the doctrine called ***res ipsa loquitur***, or "the thing speaks for itself." In some cases, the particular accident is so unlikely to happen without negligence, that once the facts are established, the burden of proof shifts to the defendant to show that there was no negligence. For example, if a pedestrian on the sidewalk is hit by a piano falling from a second story window, common sense tells us that someone up there on the second floor was negligent.

res ipsa loquitur: A situation in which the injury-causing incident could not have happened without negligence, and the defendant was in control of the event or premises where the accident occurred.

Two elements are necessary to invoke *res ipsa loquitur*. First, the incident must be one that does not normally occur without negligence. Second, the defendant must have had exclusive control of the precipitating events (he or she occupied or rented the second floor). A case often cited for the principle of *res ipsa loquitur* arose some years ago when a California man sat down on a chair upon his arrival in a cocktail lounge (before he had anything to drink). The chair collapsed, causing injuries to the customer. The court found both elements of the doctrine to be present and upheld a verdict for the plaintiff [*Rose v. Melody Lane of Wilshire*, 247 P. 2d 335 (Cal. Sup. Ct. 1952)].

BUSINESS TORTS

In addition to torts that take place between individuals, and between individuals and businesses, a number of torts normally occur only in business situations. Several of them are related to actions taken by one business that cause injury to a competing business.

DISPARAGEMENT

Disparagement is a type of defamation directed at the product or service of another business, usually a competitor. The same elements necessary to establish defamation—an untrue statement, communicated to at least one other party, relating to a specific business, causing injury—will constitute disparagement. For example, if the Miller Brewing Co. began running ads stating that Budweiser beer was made with contaminated water, that would be considered disparagement, assuming that the statement was untrue.

disparagement: Defamation of a business or product.

INTERFERENCE WITH CONTRACTS

Our market system favors and promotes competition. In order to obtain new contracts for and sales of their products, businesses are encouraged to streamline operations, cut costs, improve services, and try to do a better job than the competition. However, once two firms have entered into a contract, it is considered a tort for a third firm to take actions that interfere with that contract or seek to get either company to breach its contract. Even interference with unsigned contracts has been held as a tort if the parties were reasonably certain to enter into one.

interference with contracts: One person intentionally interferes with a contract between two other people (or businesses).

The elements necessary for this tort are (1) the plaintiff has a contract or a solid business relationship with a third party; (2) the defendant knew about the contract; (3) the defendant intentionally interfered with that contract or did something to prevent performance; and (4) the defendant caused harm to the plaintiff by its actions. The following case, one of the best-known business cases in the past 15 years, involved an **interference with contracts** dispute between two large oil companies, Texaco and Pennzoil.

TEXACO, INC. V. PENNZOIL CO.

729 S.W. 2d 768 (Texas 1987)

FACTS

Late in 1983, Pennzoil Co. was closely watching the growing conflict between the board of directors of Getty Oil Co. and Gordon Getty, a director who controlled (as trustee for the Sarah C. Getty Trust) 40.2 percent of the shares of Getty Oil. In late December, Pennzoil tendered an offer of $100 per share for 43 percent of Getty Oil.

Pennzoil soon contacted Gordon Getty and an agent of the J. Paul Getty Museum (holder of 11.8 percent of the Getty Oil shares) to discuss the offer and possible purchase of Getty Oil. During the first few days of January 1984, intensive discussions between these parties resulted in a memorandum of agreement (an agreement in principle) for the purchase of a majority of Getty Oil (the Trust and Museum shares) at $110 per share plus a $3 per share bonus. The agreement was then submitted to the Getty board, which voted 15-1 to accept Pennzoil's offer if the bonus share was raised to $5.

On January 3, Pennzoil (and the Museum and the Trust) agreed to the modification proposed by the Getty board. Later that day, a press release was drafted by Getty Oil staff and lawyers announcing that an agreement in principle had been reached based on the memorandum of agreement. This press release and a similar one from Pennzoil were issued the next day, January 4. On January 6, *The Wall Street Journal* reported that an agreement had been reached.

While these events were transpiring, Getty Oil's investment banker continued trying to find a better offer for Getty and spoke with Texaco. On January 5, 1984, Texaco's board of directors decided to make an offer of $125 per share for 100 percent of Getty Oil. Texaco representatives met with Gordon Getty that evening to inform him that the Museum had agreed to sell its shares to Texaco. Getty had previously been advised that if Texaco purchased the museum shares and enough public shares to exceed 50 percent ownership of Getty Oil, the Trust could be put in a minority position. Consequently, Gordon Getty accepted Texaco's offer and signed a letter of intent to sell the Trust shares to Texaco.

On January 6, the Getty Oil board met and unanimously decided to "withdraw" its previous agreement or understanding with Pennzoil and to accept Texaco's offer. Immediately, Texaco issued a press release stating that Texaco and Getty Oil would merge [which did occur].

Shortly thereafter, Pennzoil sued Texaco, charging that Texaco had committed the tort of intentional interference with contractual relations. Following trial, the jury found for Pennzoil, and awarded it $7.53 billion in compensatory damages and $3 billion in punitive damages. Texaco appealed to the Texas Supreme Court.

DECISION

Writing for the court, Justice Warren made the following statement: "The main question for our determination is whether the evidence supports the jury's finding that there was a binding contract between the Getty entities and Pennzoil, and that Texaco knowingly induced a breach of such contract."

The first issue addressed was whether Pennzoil had proved that Texaco actually had known that a contract existed between Pennzoil and Getty. According to law it was required that Texaco know "of the existence of contractual right as an element of inducing a breach of the contract." But it was not necessary that Texaco have "full knowledge of all the detailed terms of the contract" in order to be held liable.

Testimony by Texaco's chairman indicated that he was alerted to problems by several facts, including the following: (1) the Museum and the Trust both demanded that Texaco assume any legal liability they had toward Pennzoil, (2) the Getty Museum and Trust both refused to guarantee that the sale to Texaco would not violate the memorandum of agreement, and (3) they required that Pennzoil's offer price be guaranteed even if the sale to Texaco fell through.

The Museum and the Trust refused to sell to Texaco without these conditions being met. Although Texaco presented other testimony that it was informed many times by top executives and representatives of Getty Oil that no binding contract with Pennzoil existed, the fact that the Trust and the Museum made their demands was sufficient evidence to the jury to conclude that Texaco did know of the existence of an obligation to Pennzoil.

Another issue on appeal was whether the evidence was "legally and factually sufficient to show that Texaco actively induced breach of the alleged Pennzoil/Getty contract." In other words, Texaco argued that it was not enough for Pennzoil to show that Texaco knew about the contract and still entered into its own contract with Getty. The burden was on Pennzoil to show that Texaco actively influenced Getty Oil to break its contract with Pennzoil.

Texaco argued that it was merely responding to a "campaign of active solicitation" by representatives of Getty oil who wanted a better offer. However, Texaco was strongly motivated to acquire Getty's oil reserves because of its own dwindling reserves and the high costs of locating new ones. Evidence at trial also indicated that Texaco had held extended meetings and procured expert advice on the best tactics to acquire Getty. These facts contradicted Texaco's claim that it simply accepted terms advanced by Getty Oil, and this supported the jury's verdict.

Therefore, the Texas Supreme Court upheld the compensatory damages award of $7.53 billion. The court found that the punitive damages award of $3 billion was excessive and reduced that figure to $1 billion.

CASE QUESTIONS

1. What should Texaco have done differently? Getty? Pennzoil?
2. What public purpose is served by this type of decision?
3. Do you think that Pennzoil and Getty had a binding agreement at the time Texaco entered the picture?

MISAPPROPRIATION

misappropriation: The wrongful taking of a nonpublic business secret or asset from one firm and its use by another firm.

Trade secrets are business assets such as formulas, devices, customer lists, or other nonpublic information. Such information often becomes the subject of **misappropriation** cases when the material comes into the hands of a competitor. Sometimes a company uses an idea or invention of an author or inventor without compensating the person who thought of it. The required elements of a misappropriation case are the following: (1) the existence of an idea or secret that is not available to the public; (2) information that is novel, concrete, and useful; (3) some type of wrongful taking of that information, such as by theft or by breach of confidentiality; and (4) the use of the information by the second party. For example, a series of cases have been brought against the large automobile manufacturers by a man who claims to have invented the technology for intermittent auto windshield wipers. He claims to have showed them his ideas before the companies went ahead and produced millions of cars with such devices. He received no compensation. As a result, courts have awarded him several million dollars.

SOCIAL/ETHICAL ISSUES

Do the torts of misappropriation, interference with contract, and disparagement have an ethical basis? Is it not good business to try to determine what your competition is planning or to run ads showing how your product is superior to the competition? What is the dividing line between good hard competition and wrongful action?

All of the tort theories discussed so far are based on actions that were either intentionally taken or were taken unintentionally but without the degree of care expected of a reasonable person. The next section of this chapter examines a rapidly growing theory that extends liability to the manufacturers of products and others even though they exercised reasonable care and did not intend to injure anyone.

STRICT LIABILITY

strict liability: Liability without proof of negligence or fault.

The theory of law called **strict liability** originated many years ago in response to situations in which one person created a hazardous condition (without being negligent) that caused injury to another. For example, suppose that Joe is tearing down a building on his property and uses explosives. Although he is as careful as the mythical "reasonable person," several rocks are nevertheless propelled onto Bart's property, breaking windows in his house. Under negligence theory Bart would have to prove the required elements (duty, breach, proximate cause, and damages). In this situation he would lose the lawsuit, since Joe had observed the safety precautions of the normally careful person.

ultrahazardous activity: One which is inherently dangerous.

Such a result (Bart would get nothing) seems unfair; thus the doctrine of strict liability has evolved. It provides that if one person engages in **ultrahazardous activities**, and these actions cause injury to another, the engager should be liable for the injuries whether or not he or she was negligent. Why? Courts and legislatures have begun to believe that public policy was better served by putting the liability on the one who created the risk (even though he or she may not have been negligent) rather than on the innocent person who was injured. If Marlin keeps a lion as a pet and it escapes, or if Martha builds a reservoir on her property to store a toxic liquid and the reservoir breaks, the theory of strict liability would impose the risk of the damage caused by these activities on Marlin and Martha, regardless of whether they were negligent.

In the past 20 or 30 years, the theory of strict liability has come to be widely used as a legal theory allowing recovery of damages by persons injured by defective products. For example, when a machine does not work correctly and someone is injured as a result, public policy in most states now favors placing the liability for the injuries on those who manufacture and sell the products rather than on the innocent consumers. When applied to manufactured products, strict liability is called "product liability." The many aspects and ramifications of this development are more thoroughly discussed in Chapter 13.

TORT REFORM STATUTES

Considerable debate has arisen recently about the need for reform of the tort system. There are many multimillion dollar verdicts against companies every year based on tort and strict liability principles. Business associations have strenuously argued that jury verdicts in tort cases against business have reached "crisis" levels, to the serious detriment of American firms. The legal systems in other countries have generally not been as generous with awards to plaintiffs as have U.S. courts. However, a few years ago the European Union adopted a "strict product liability" standard that is quite similar to the U.S. doctrine, so damage awards against companies in Europe based on strict liability may increase in the future.

Studies have been conducted in the United States in recent years, by organizations allied with business and insurance interests on one side and by attorney and consumer groups on the other, concerning whether there actually has been a major increase in the number and size of verdicts, and if so, whether it is justified. The conclusions on both sides, as one would guess, have been vastly different.

In the past 10 or 15 years, almost all of the states have enacted some type of "tort reform" laws. These statutes typically place monetary limits on *noneconomic damages* (such as "pain and suffering" awards), **punitive damages** (extra damages awarded to punish a defendant for malicious or intentional acts), and *attorney fees*. Also many of these laws establish strict *statutes of limitation* (a time limit within which the plaintiff must sue), and eliminate the concept of *joint and several liability* (by which a winning plaintiff can collect the entire award from any one of several defendants).

punitive damages: Damages, in excess of those required to compensate the plaintiff for the wrong done, that are imposed in order to punish the defendant because of the particularly wanton or willful character of the wrongdoing.

These reform laws passed by state legislatures have been vigorously challenged as unconstitutional in many states. In the summer of 1999, for example, the Supreme Courts in Oregon, Indiana, and Ohio each declared that part or all of their tort reform laws were invalid, as violations of the respective state constitutions.

In Oregon, the court held that the state tort reform law placing a cap of $500,000 on noneconomic damages (pain and suffering) was an infringement on the right to trial by jury, an essential part of the Oregon Constitution enacted in 1857. In the particular case, the Oregon lower court jury had awarded $9.3 million in damages to a man who suffered severe injuries when a nail gun he was using misfired, first kicking the gun's firing end into his face, then causing a nail to be shot into his brain. He suffered permanent paralysis on the left side of his body, and diminished mental and emotional capacity.

The Oregon Supreme Court found that awarding damages in personal injury cases has historically been deemed part of the jury's exclusive fact-finding function, which the State Legislature could not take away by statute.

In Indiana, the Supreme Court refused to apply a two-year statute of limitations that would have barred a malpractice suit by a woman alleging that her doctor had failed to diagnose and treat her breast cancer. The Court did not strike down the entire tort reform law but only held that it was unconstitutional here "as applied" under the Privileges and Immunities clause, since it barred some claims of malpractice that would not be manifested for more than two years. The Ohio Supreme Court struck down a tort reform law that capped punitive and noneconomic damages, which had been passed in 1996 after an earlier version had been held unconstitutional. In Virginia, however, the state Supreme Court upheld a tort reform law that placed a $1 million damage cap on malpractice cases, stating that although the constitution entitles a person to a jury trial, the legislature can limit the outer limits of the jury's functions.

According to Victor Schwartz, counsel to the American Tort Reform Association (the leading organization pushing for tort reform laws) some 90 court decisions around the country in recent years have struck down part or all of state tort reform laws, although a somewhat greater number have upheld such laws. Schwartz admits that the recent trend favors his opponents, however, and 25 state appellate courts have ruled against such laws. He complains that state courts are using obscure constitutional provisions to "guard their own common law powers, and frustrate the policy judgments of the legislative branch."[1]

On the other side of the debate is Robert Peck of the Association of Trial Lawyers of America (ATLA), which opposes tort reform laws, and insists that juries should be free to decide cases without limitations. Mr. Peck argues that it is the state legislatures, urged on by business interests and insurance companies, that are overstepping their bounds. The ATLA also denies that there is a "tort crisis" and that damage awards have increased in recent years.

Those advocating tort reform have also turned to the U.S. Congress. Although in most instances, business organizations favor reducing, not adding more federal laws, several leading business groups (such as the Chamber of Commerce) have been pushing for a federal law limiting tort and product liability. Frustrated by the many different standards, created by common law court decisions in different states, and varying interpretations of liability and tort reform laws, the business lobbies have been behind the introduction of several bills in Congress in recent years that would establish a uniform federal standard for damages and product liability cases.

The measures before Congress would enact many of the same types of reforms that the states have undertaken. One additional idea would require the losing party in tort cases to pay the other side's attorney fees, particularly if the plaintiff had rejected a settlement offer that was more favorable than the eventual verdict. Such "loser pays" legislation would prevent many frivolous lawsuits, according to its sponsors. Opponents argue that it would give a tremendous advantage to big business. Many individual persons with valid cases could not afford to take the chance of suing large corporations if they might end up being forced to pay the huge legal bills of their attorneys. Also,

[1] Much of this information came from "Prying Off Tort Reform Caps," *ABA Journal* (October 1999), 28–29.

they would be forced to accept whatever settlement offers were made by the corporations, so as not to risk being assessed attorney fees later.

So far, despite pressure from those advocating reform and the creation of a federal law dealing with tort and product liability, no such law has been enacted. One measure was passed by both houses of Congress but was vetoed by the President. Many others have been rejected in the legislative process, but efforts continue. It is quite possible that a compromise will be reached, and some sort of federal law will emerge in the future.

Indeed, there is no consensus on whether there is a "tort crisis" at all. Studies by experts for both proponents and opponents of tort reform laws have reached different conclusions on whether damage awards are increasing or decreasing, and whether "punitive damages" are a huge problem or a necessary means to correct the abuses of some powerful corporations. A study by the independent RAND Corporation a few years ago showed that jury verdicts of $1 million or more are reduced by an average of 40 percent on appeal. Although these figures give support to those who argue that this means that excessive jury awards are corrected, others argue that the business defendants in these cases have incurred high costs by defending the case all the way to appellate courts. Furthermore, the publicity of high awards, which may deter bad conduct by some corporations, raises costs for all producers, increases insurance premiums, and stifles innovation and new product development because of fear of liability.

CIVIL TRIAL AND VERDICT RESULTS

A recent report by the U.S. Department of Justice provided a comprehensive look at the results of all civil trials and verdicts in the 75 largest counties in the United States for 1996. The results of this study are particularly informative since they were compiled by a government agency, which is not allied with either side of the tort reform debate.

Among the most significant findings, the Justice Department reported that:

- More than 15,000 civil cases (torts, contracts, and property) were disposed of by trial verdict in 75 counties in 1996.
- 70 percent of the cases were decided by a jury, and 30 percent by a judge.
- Plaintiffs won 52 percent of the cases, and defendants won 48 percent.
- The median award for plaintiffs who won was $33,000.
- About 16 percent of plaintiff winners were awarded over $250,000, and 6 percent were awarded $1 million or more.
- Of the 7,892 trial cases won by plaintiffs, about 5 percent (360 cases) included punitive damages, which totaled $600 million. The median punitive damage amount awarded was $40,000. About 7 percent of the punitive damage awards were over $1 million.
- In 10 percent of the civil cases in which compensatory damages were awarded to the plaintiff, the award was reduced because of contributory or comparative negligence by the plaintiff.
- The average case processing time from the date the case was filed to final verdict or judgment was 25.6 months. Some 59 percent of all trial cases were completed within two years.

- Trials conducted in the nation's 75 largest counties lasted an average of 3.9 days. Jury trials lasted an average of 4.7 days, and bench trials (no jury) averaged 1.9 days.[2]

Although companies must be concerned about facing tort lawsuits related to the products they produce as well as the activities of their employees and other agents, there is another serious type of legal liability that causes concern. In recent years, federal and state prosecutors have increasingly brought criminal charges against U.S. business firms for violations of a wide array of laws.

CRIMINAL LAW AND BUSINESS

Some years ago, a study was done to determine what types of legal issues are most often reported in *The Wall Street Journal*, the nation's leading daily business newspaper.[3] The expectation of the study was that the most-reported issues would concern torts, business contract disputes, or perhaps environmental or toxic waste problems. Surprisingly, more news stories addressed criminal prosecutions of business firms and managers than any other category. A casual look at the news today seems to indicate that this is still true.

Perhaps the results of the survey only prove the old adage that "bad news sells newspapers." While newspapers and television newscasts may give an exaggerated impression as to the number of crimes, arrests, and criminal investigations that occur, one cannot ignore that many leading corporations, as well as hundreds of smaller ones, have been charged with and convicted of serious crimes in recent years. As is discussed more fully subsequently, if a criminal action was somehow authorized or knowingly permitted by managers or other top officials of a business firm, criminal liability may be imposed on the firm as well as the individual. Although a corporation cannot be physically put in prison, it most certainly can be sentenced to pay a high fine, and a criminal conviction may also mean the loss of important business licenses.

Typically, the types of crime most associated with business have been the so-called white collar crimes involving financial misdealings, such as embezzlement, fraud, bribery, and conspiracy. In recent years, however, a sharp upswing in prosecutions for environmental and other nonfinancial workplace crimes has occurred, perhaps reflecting greater public concern with business conduct in these areas. (Chapter 15 describes environmental prosecutions in more detail.)

Another area that has seen an expanding number of criminal charges concerns occupational safety. Across the nation more than 20 criminal cases have been instituted by local prosecutors, following the death or serious injury of a worker. Most often, criminal actions have been brought when a subsequent investigation reveals that key officials in the business knew about an unsafe, dangerous condition posing a serious threat to employees but failed to take action to correct the problem. Sometimes these conditions have even been the

[2] Bureau of Justice Statistics, U.S. Department of Justice, 1999 NCJ 173426.

[3] Bixby, "Coverage of Legal Events in *The Wall Street Journal*," *Journal of Legal Studies in Education* 8 (Fall 1989/Spring 1990), 127.

subject of violation notices from the federal Occupational Safety and Health Administration (OSHA), as discussed in Chapter 21. Although OSHA has the power to refer a case to the Justice Department (headed by the U.S. Attorney General) for criminal charges when a violation of law leads to a worker's death, it has rarely done so, preferring to emphasize civil fines. However, certain local and state prosecutors in a few large cities have brought criminal charges against firms and individuals in recent years—most often for "negligent homicide"—when a known and uncorrected hazardous condition causes the death of a worker.

Although most criminal activities undertaken by employees and managers subject only those individuals to criminal liability, occasionally the employer (the corporation) is also charged with a crime. This situation may occur if the action is authorized by the company board of directors, or by other high managerial personnel, or if those persons have knowledge of the activity and have done nothing to discourage it. For example, if Jason is a truck driver for the Brown Company and he stops to rob a gas station while on duty, he has committed a crime. The Brown Company, however, probably has not committed a crime. On the other hand, if the president or the environmental manager of the Brown Company tells employees to dump toxic chemicals in the river, or knows that they are doing it and does nothing to stop the practice, the criminal charges might be brought not only against the managers but also against the company, since the officials are in a position to act "for the company."

Partly in response to a public perception that business organizations and officials were not being penalized as severely as other defendants convicted of similar crimes, the U.S. Sentencing Commission, an arm of the federal court system, issued a new tough set of Corporate Sentencing Guidelines in late 1991 (as more fully discussed in Chapter 7). These standards called for substantially larger fines for companies and more use of jail time for managers convicted of crime. The guidelines suggest that judges give sentences within a range of penalties for each type of crime, with considerable variance allowed, depending on the corporation's past and present activities.

For example, the normal fine against a company for a criminal environmental violation would increase substantially if, in previous years, the company had failed to take action against those employees or officers responsible for earlier crimes committed, the company had reduced spending for environmental control equipment, or the crimes committed had caused significant harm to the public. Conversely, the penalties would be reduced from the norm if the firm had set up an active program to monitor and prevent corporate criminal actions and had swiftly and firmly disciplined employees found guilty of criminal activity or violation of company policies.

The enactment of a criminal law is a statement by Congress or a state legislature, acting on behalf of society, that a certain type of conduct is so detrimental to the public that those who engage in it must be punished. A criminal case is brought by the government, whose law has allegedly been violated. Criminal cases are often titled with such names as *The People of the United States v. Jones* or *The People of the State of California v. Smith* to indicate that the prosecutor is bringing the case on behalf of all citizens in that jurisdiction. The victim of the crime is not a party to the criminal case. The appropriate prosecutor (federal, state, or local), representing all the people of his or her jurisdiction, decides whether to bring the case, whether to accept a guilty plea

FROM THE DESK OF
Laura Lawyer

To: Students
From: Your Lawyer

It is important for business managers and officers to realize that the public is becoming less tolerant of individual and corporate criminal behavior. Every medium-size or large business firm should have a written policy indicating that the firm will not tolerate criminal actions by employees and that the firm will swiftly punish those who engage in such activities. This policy alone is not enough, however. The company must also follow through on the policy and make sure that it is enforced equally and firmly against employees and managers who violate it. By doing so, the company will not only deter crimes from being committed but also will decrease the chance that the business will be held responsible and, if crimes do occur, lessen any penalties that might be assessed by the courts upon conviction.

or dismiss the case depending on the evidence, whom to call as witnesses, and what sentence to request if the defendant is found guilty.

One fairly recent, but significant addition to the criminal laws affecting business is the **Racketeer Influenced and Corrupt Organization Act (RICO)**. This federal law was enacted with the purpose of penalizing businesses that engaged in organized crime activity. The RICO law provides for both criminal and civil lawsuits against those businesses that have engaged in a "pattern of racketeering activity."

Racketeer Influenced and Corrupt Organization Act (RICO): A federal law allowing a prosecutor to charge a business firm with racketeering if the firm has engaged in two or more prohibited acts within a 10-year period. The law contains very serious penalties and can also be used in civil suits.

In order to constitute a "pattern of racketeering activity," however, it is only necessary for a firm to have engaged in two prohibited acts within a 10-year period. Such "racketeering acts" include gambling, arson, robbery, bribery, pornography, embezzlement, and fraud. It is not unusual for large corporations with thousands of employees to have at least two such convictions in 1 year, much less 10 years, and thus be subject to RICO. Some of the best-known U.S. firms have faced RICO suits, even though they clearly are not involved in organized crime.

In addition to the severe criminal penalties for RICO violations, the law permits prosecutors to freeze the assets of the defendant while the charges are pending. When the Justice Department takes this step, it causes harsh consequences for a business and almost forces a defendant to consider a quick settlement of any RICO charges. In a civil RICO case brought by a competitor, a successful plaintiff may win treble (three times) the actual damages proved, plus court costs and attorney fees. Individuals can be prosecuted for RICO violations as well, if they have allegedly "conducted or participated directly or indirectly in the conduct of such enterprise's affairs through a pattern of racketeering activity." A case decided by the U.S. Supreme Court in 1993 against a large accounting firm held that in order for an individual to be prosecuted for a RICO crime, it must be shown that "he took some part in directing the enterprise's affairs."

Most civil cases have involved allegations of bribery, securities fraud, and mail or wire fraud. Because of the harshness of both civil and criminal RICO penalties, and because the defendants have often been legitimate businesses rather than organized crime organizations, Congress has considered amending the statute. No major changes have been passed as yet, however.

CRIMINAL PROCEDURE

After an event occurs that may constitute a crime, the matter is investigated by the state or local police or sheriff's office, or the FBI, and a recommendation is made to the appropriate prosecutor (often called a "Prosecuting Attorney" or "District Attorney" at the county level and an "Attorney General" at the state level). The prosecutor questions the officers and then makes a decision as to whether a crime has been committed and whether one or more specific people have committed it. If so, charges (somewhat like a complaint in a civil case) are filed in court, and papers are served on the defendant.

Depending on the seriousness of the matter, the defendant may already be in custody or may know nothing about the case. At any rate, the defendant is served with the papers and ordered to appear in court, where the judge will formally announce the crime charged, ask the defendant if he or she understands the charges and wishes to have an attorney, and set the amount of bail. Next, a hearing called an **arraignment** will be held. At this time the defendant, accompanied by an attorney, is asked to plead either guilty or not guilty (legally, there is no such plea as "innocent") to the charges. Depending on the plea, a future date is set either for sentencing or for a **preliminary hearing**.

The preliminary hearing is a procedure designed to protect people from erroneous or wrongful prosecutions. At the preliminary hearing, the prosecutor is required to produce enough evidence to convince the judge that reason exists to believe that the defendant committed the crime charged. The defendant generally does not offer any evidence or call any witnesses but listens to and cross-examines the prosecutor's witnesses. If the prosecutor has a very weak case or is charging the wrong person, the judge will dismiss the case at the preliminary hearing, thus ending the case. But most of the time, sufficient evidence exists to allow the case to go forward and the defendant is "bound over" to stand trial.

Because criminal cases have less discovery than civil cases and the Sixth Amendment to the Constitution guarantees the right to a speedy trial in criminal cases, the proceedings move along fairly quickly to the trial. Most criminal cases (estimates of 85 percent to 90 percent are common) are settled before the date of the trial, usually by the defendant's agreement to plead guilty to a less serious charge in return for dismissal of the pending charge—a process called **plea-bargaining**. This procedure has been controversial, with citizens

arraignment: A court hearing at which the defendant is asked to respond to the criminal charge by stating "guilty" or "not guilty."

preliminary hearing: A court hearing in a criminal case, at which the prosecutor must produce sufficient evidence to show that a crime has been committed and that there is good cause to believe that the defendant committed it.

plea-bargain: The settlement of a criminal case, whereby the prosecutor dismisses one charge if the defendant pleads guilty to another charge.

complaining that defendants are "getting off easy" by pleading to a lesser charge. Prosecutors have countered that plea bargaining does guarantee a conviction, whereas if a trial was held, the defendant could be found not guilty and set free.

The U.S. judicial system, based on the protections afforded by the U.S. Constitution, defends the rights of individuals against the powers of the government. Defendants in criminal cases in U.S. courts carry a "presumption of innocence," which means that although they are accused of a crime, they should not be found guilty until the prosecution has proved *beyond a reasonable doubt* all necessary elements of the crime. In other words, if any members of the jury have doubts about whether all the elements of the crime have been proved with respect to a particular defendant, they must render a finding of not guilty. Since in many cases the defendant has a strong argument that he or she did not commit the crime, was somewhere else at the time, or lacked the intent necessary for conviction, plea bargaining (which does result in a conviction) sometimes makes sense for both the prosecutor and the defendant. The prosecutor must carefully evaluate each case to make sure that society's interests are being protected.

CONSTITUTIONAL PROTECTIONS

As we have mentioned, our justice system carries significant protections for individuals accused of crimes. Hundreds of television shows and movies, along with such books as Scott Turow's *Presumed Innocent* and *The Burden of Proof* and John Grisham's *The Firm*, *Streetlawyer*, and *A Time to Kill*, have brought this point home. We often read in the newspaper that a person accused of a crime has been acquitted on a "technicality." What is not usually spelled out, however, is that the technicality is often based on one of the provisions in the Bill of Rights in the Constitution. It is therefore important to take a closer look at some important constitutional protections.

Freedom From Unreasonable Searches and Seizures The Fourth Amendment provides that "*The right of the people to be secure in their persons, houses, papers, and effects, against unreasonable searches and seizures, shall not be violated*." It further provides that "no warrants shall issue, but upon probable cause . . . particularly describing the place to be searched, and the persons or things to be seized."

This powerful statement of protection from government intrusion has led to hundreds of cases concerning what is "*unreasonable*," what is "*probable cause*," and other like issues. It is clear that in most cases, however, the police need a search warrant to enter someone's house or business unless permission for the search is obtained. Many cases, such as *Marshall v. Barlow's Inc.*, discussed in Chapter 5 (in which OSHA conducted a surprise inspection of a plumbing supply company without a warrant), have reaffirmed that this constitutional protection does apply to businesses as well as to individuals in their homes. Thus, a police officer or other government official generally needs to obtain a warrant to search a business, unless the consent of the business proprietor is obtained.

Certain exceptions have been carved out for various situations, such as when a police officer sees a crime committed, or is in "hot pursuit" of a criminal. But in most cases the Fourth Amendment requires that before a search is conducted, the officer appear before a judge and justify the need for a warrant.

Protection Against Self-Incrimination The Fifth Amendment of the Constitution provides that "*No person . . . shall be compelled in any criminal case to be a witness against himself.*" This important clause has been interpreted broadly and affords criminal defendants the right not only to refuse to testify at their own trial but also to remain silent when questioned by police. The familiar *Miranda* warnings that police are required to give to persons whom they take into custody were formulated by the U.S. Supreme Court in the case *Miranda v. Arizona*, 384 U.S. 436 (1966), to make the Fifth Amendment protection against self-incrimination effective, since many people did not know of their Fifth Amendment rights.

Over the years courts have analyzed a number of law enforcement practices in deciding how to fully enforce the Fifth Amendment. One important fact to note is that the privilege against self-incrimination has been held to apply *only to individuals*. Therefore, while a company treasurer may be able to assert the privilege and refuse to testify or disclose damaging financial records or other information in his own trial, the same rights are not accorded to a corporation if it is charged with a crime.

Right to an Attorney The Sixth Amendment states that "*In all criminal prosecutions, the accused shall have the right . . . to have the assistance of counsel for his defense.*" This provision has been interpreted as requiring not only that a defendant be allowed to have an attorney but that a person accused of any crime that may result in a jail sentence be provided an attorney at public expense if he or she cannot personally afford one.

SUMMARY

A business firm may have one employee or thousands. In either event, the organization acts only through the deeds of people, such as employees, officers, directors, partners, and agents. Sometimes in connection with their duties, these representatives commit torts—intentionally or unintentionally—that cause injury to others. Occasionally business managers or employees even engage in criminal actions. This chapter has examined the legal consequences of several such actions, beginning with intentional torts, in which an action taken deliberately, such as assault, battery, false imprisonment, or defamation, causes economic or physical injury to another person. The most important unintentional tort—negligence—occurs when someone performs an action without using the degree of care expected of a "reasonable person." There are also a series of torts that are normally only committed by businesses, such as disparagement of competition and interference with contract.

An extension of tort theory, called strict liability, sometimes holds liable those who perform very dangerous activities and those who manufacture defective products for injuries caused by their actions and products, without the necessity of proving any intentional or negligent acts. Partly in response to numerous large jury verdicts against companies based on strict liability, there has been a vigorous debate in recent years concerning the need for reforms in the way the U.S. legal system treats tort cases. Many states have enacted tort reform laws.

Finally, situations exist in which corporations and/or their representatives may be held criminally liable for certain actions. Such situations include "white collar" crimes like embezzlement, fraud, bribery, and conspiracy, as well as crimes involving the work place and the environment. The federal RICO law has powerful criminal penalties. The chapter concludes with a short discussion of criminal procedure and the rights of defendants in criminal cases.

CHAPTER QUESTIONS

1. The Environmental Protection Agency (EPA) did an inspection of the Dow Chemical Company's plant at Midland, Michigan, to check for compliance with the Clean Air Act. The EPA then wanted to do a second inspection, but Dow denied permission. The EPA hired a commercial photographer who flew over the site and took many photos of the facility from 3,000 and 1,200 feet up. Dow challenged the action in federal court as a violation of its Fourth Amendment rights. Was this a violation? Why or why not? [*Dow Chemical Co. v. United States*, 471 U.S. 130 (1986)]
2. A law firm made a request to an Ohio hospital for medical records on hundreds of patients, and the hospital did turn over thousands of pages of records and information, without informing the patients. The law firm then called many of the patients and offered to represent them in an attempt to attain Social Security disability benefits. The records included information about many different medical conditions, including diagnoses of alcohol and drug abuse, mental illness, and sexually transmitted diseases, for example. Later, a group of patients filed a class action against the hospital and law firm for damages for the unauthorized disclosure. Was a tort committed? If so, what was it? Should the court recognize a new tort to compensate the plaintiffs in a wrongful action done by someone else? [*Biddle v. Warren General Hospital*, 86 Ohio St. 395, 715 N.E.2d 518 (1999)]
3. Duckworth, Inc., was a real estate agency in Texas. It brought together a potential seller (Chase Manhattan Bank) and a potential buyer (Field) for a prime piece of real estate. Various drafts of sales contracts were prepared (all calling for a commission for Duckworth), but the deal did not go through. Six months later, Field initiated direct contact with Chase, and a contract was signed for the same piece of property (without any commission for Duckworth). After learning of the deal, Duckworth sued Field for interference with contracts and business relations. What should be the result and why? [*Duckworth, Inc. v. Field & Co.*, 516 F.2d 952 (5th Cir. 1975)]
4. A 70-year-old man (Mr. Coblyn) went into a department store in Boston and, after some shopping, purchased a sport coat. After leaving it for alterations, he put back on his hat and topcoat and began to exit the store. At the doorway, he put an ascot around his neck (which he had brought into the store with him) that was in his pocket. Just outside the door he was immediately and roughly stopped by a store employee who demanded to know "Where did you get that scarf?" He was ordered in a loud voice (heard by several other customers) to go back into the store and "See the

manager." On the way to the manager's office, the salesman who had sold Mr. Coblyn the sport coat saw him and assured the other store employee that the ascot belonged to Mr. Coblyn. At that point, Mr. Coblyn experienced chest pains and was hospitalized for a heart attack. He subsequently sued the store for false imprisonment. Will he likely win? Why? [*Coblyn v. Kennedy's, Inc.*, 268 N.E.2d 860 (Mass. 1971)]

5. A company located near Chicago developed a process of recovering silver from used photographic and x-ray film. Most of the employees were Mexican and Polish immigrants, whose English was poor or nonexistent. They cut the film into pieces and dumped them into open vats of sodium cyanide. After the silver separated, the workers removed plates at the bottom of the tanks to which the silver had attached and scraped off the deposits. Many workers experienced dizziness, nausea, and vomiting on a regular basis, but no additional health or safety procedures were taken. The employees' safety equipment consisted of paper masks and cotton gloves. According to one report, "the air was thick with the odor of cyanide and a yellowish haze of cyanide fumes hung inside the plant." The workers were not told much about the hazards of cyanide, and there was some evidence that managers had scraped the "skull and crossbones" symbols off the cyanide containers. Although an antidote for cyanide poisoning was widely available, none was kept at the plant. One day a 61-year-old worker collapsed on the plant floor and died soon thereafter. The company president, safety director, and foreman (all of whom worked in the same building as the workers, but in a different area) were charged with murder. The applicable Illinois law provided that one may be charged with murder where he or she performs certain acts knowing "that such acts create a strong probability of death or great bodily harm," and someone does die from such acts. Should the managers be convicted of this crime? [*People v. Film Recovery Systems, Inc.*, (Cook County Cir. Ct. 1985), rev'd 194 Ill. App. 3d 79, 550 N.E.2d 1090 (1990)]

6. At a Christmas party, employees of an auto dealership discovered that an electric automobile condenser could deliver an electric shock. The company president got into the fun and chased one of the employees around, shocking him several times on the neck. The employee suffered serious headaches later, passed out numerous times in the next few months, and eventually required nerve surgery. He sued the president and the company for damages. The defendants' arguments were (1) it was not a battery but just "horseplay" and (2) if it was battery, workers compensation was the employee's only remedy. What should be the result? Why? [*Caudle v. Betts*, 512 So. 2d 389 (Louisiana 1987)]

7. An anti-smoking advocate appeared as a guest on a radio show. During his interview, the host of the show repeatedly and intentionally blew cigar smoke in the guest's face. The guest filed a battery suit against the host, who moved for dismissal. Was it a battery? Why? [*Leichtman v. WLW Jacor Communications, Inc.*, 634 N.E. 2d 697, 92 Ohio App. 3d 232 (1994)]

8. A gunman walked into a San Francisco law firm in 1993 armed with two TEC-DC9 semiautomatic assault weapons and a semiautomatic pistol and began shooting, eventually killing eight people and wounding six others. Families of those killed and wounded later sued the maker of the weapons

for negligence and strict liability. Evidence was introduced that the gun manufacturer's advertising was "targeted to certain types of persons attracted to or associated with violence," featuring its "military combat style," and that these guns were the "weapons of choice" used in gang shootings and other criminal activities. The case was dismissed by the trial court, but the plaintiffs appealed to the California Court of Appeal. What would the plaintiffs have to show to establish a case (and get to a jury trial) with regard to the elements of negligence, as discussed in this chapter? How could they show "duty," "breach of duty," and "causation"? [*Merrill v. Navegar, Inc.*, 89 Cal. Rptr. 2d 146 (Cal. App. 1999)]

9. The World Trade Center in New York City was damaged by a bomb blast in 1993. Some years later the Port Authority of New York, which owns the Center, filed suit against the manufacturers of the fertilizer used by terrorists to construct the bomb. The suit was brought under both negligence and product liability theories. Does the Port Authority have a negligence case? Discuss the "duty" that might be owed by the manufacturer to a building owner, and the "proximate cause" of the damages which occurred to the building. [*Port Authority of New York and New Jersey v. Arcadian Corp.*, 189 F.3d 305 (3rd Cir. 1999)]
10. An individual was convicted of bribery and conspiracy violations under RICO because of actions he took in connection with his job at a business firm. The judge's instructions to the jury stated that the defendant could be convicted of participating directly or indirectly in the affairs of the business—and thus be guilty of a RICO crime—even if he "played no part in the management and control of the enterprise." Was that a correct statement of the law, or should the conviction be reversed on appeal? Why? [*U.S. v. Viola*, 35 F.3d 37 (2d Cir. 1994)]

PRACTICAL EXERCISE

Pump Iron, Inc., operates 450 fitness centers around the United States, with many types of weight machines, aerobic walkers, stair climbers, and other equipment in each facility. In addition, Pump Iron features racquetball courts, swimming pools, and exercise classes in many of the centers. You have graduated from business school and have just been appointed as the manager of the local Pump Iron club.

One cold day in January, a snowstorm hits town early in the morning. When you arrive at the facility, the walks and driveway are snow-covered and slippery. Shortly after entering your office, the phone rings, and two of your employees call to tell you they cannot get to work. Desperately seeking help, you call Rocky, a part-time employee, who is a football player on the local college team, and he arrives at work about 10 A.M.

You are trying to keep the center open and have not had time to shovel the walk, even though a city ordinance requires that snow be cleared from the sidewalks of all commercial establishments within two hours of any snowstorm. Brenda Smith, a Pump Iron member, comes to work out at 11 A.M. Unfortunately, she slips on some snow and ice and falls on your walkway, breaking her arm. You ask Rocky to take Brenda to the hospital, and he agrees. Unbeknownst to you, his driver's license has been suspended. On the way to the hospital, Rocky negligently runs into another car, causing damage to Jon Summers, the driver, as well as further injuries to Brenda.

While a police officer is investigating the accident, Rocky gets into an argument with him, which ends with Rocky punching the officer and knocking out two of his teeth. Rocky is arrested on criminal battery charges, and Brenda is finally taken to the hospital. The police are considering criminal charges against the club as well.

The Pump Iron regional director, Ms. Patricia Kelly, has asked you to describe, in memo form, the various liability claims the club may face, both criminal and civil, from Ms. Smith, Mr. Summers, and the police as the result of the events described here. Please prepare such a memo, discussing the club's possible responsibility for the torts and crimes committed.

FURTHER INFORMATION

www.rand.org
RAND "think tank" site.

www.aaabiz.com/ATRA
American Tort Reform Association.

www.ATLA.org
American Trial Lawyers Association.

www.findlaw.com/01topics/22tort/sites.html
FindLaw sites with links to tort cases, laws, articles, and Web sites.

PART 3:
COMMON LAW SUBJECTS AND THEIR CONTEMPORARY DIMENSIONS

CHAPTER 12

PRINCIPLES OF CONTRACT LAW

LEARNING OBJECTIVES

After reading this chapter, you should be able to:

1. Explain when you are required to keep your promise.
2. Determine when the Uniform Commercial Code applies to a contract.
3. Identify the remedies available for breaching contracts.
4. Discuss why an understanding of contract law is important for businesspersons.

CHAPTER OUTLINE

I. The Uniform Commercial Code
II. General Contract Terms
III. Elements of a Contract
IV. Contracts in Writing
V. Third-Party Beneficiary and Assignment Contracts
VI. Performance, Discharge, and Breach
VII. Remedies

While surfing the Internet, you found a business that you were interested in buying. What do you need to know about the law of contracts before seizing this "once-in-a-lifetime" opportunity? The "Practical Exercise" at the end of the chapter will explore this issue in more detail.

INTRODUCTION

Almost every transaction a businessperson enters into involves a contract. For example, a contract is made when leasing a building. Hiring employees creates another contract. Obtaining a loan from your bank involves a contract. Ordering merchandise from a manufacturer and then selling it to customers creates two different contracts. As you saw in Chapter 10, even asking a friend to invest in your business creates a contract. Because contracts are such an important part of doing business, it is necessary to discuss in some detail how contracts are formed and enforced.

A contract is a legal document, and as such, the parties to the contract agree to allow a court to enforce the agreement. Note, however, that contracts are not just paper and words: they also involve relationships between people. Contracts can be very formal or very informal. As you will soon discover, most contracts do not even need to be in writing.

The United States has a long history of enforcing the terms of contracts. When you enter into a contract in the United States, you can expect that under most circumstances, you will be required to do exactly what the words in the contract say you will do. In some other countries businesspeople do not view contracts as rigidly. In the heterogeneous culture of the United States, however, contracts are one way to ensure that each party understands exactly what is expected.

THE UNIFORM COMMERCIAL CODE

Historically, all contracts were governed by the common law. As you will remember from Chapter 1, the common law is found in case law and can differ from state to state. The **Restatement of Contracts** sets out what legal scholars believe the common law rules are that govern contracts. But like other areas of common law, judges can modify those rules. Even though the common law of contracts is similar in all states, as business transactions expanded across state boundaries, it became imperative that *commercial law* (the law governing commerce) be uniform, or the same, in all 50 states. The Uniform Commercial Code (UCC) was drafted with this goal in mind. Besides uniformity, the UCC also reflects legal realism jurisprudence, discussed in Chapter 1, in that the UCC attempts to draft laws governing contracts that reflect the way businesspeople really behave.

Restatement of Contracts: One of several volumes produced by American Law Institute and authored by legal scholars that sets forth statements on the law of contracts. It is widely referred to but not binding.

Several legal scholars, initially selected by Professor Karl N. Llewellyn of Columbia Law School, drafted the UCC. Currently, legal scholars make up the Permanent Editorial Board. These scholars are chosen on the basis of their skill and knowledge of commercial law by the American Law Institute and the National Conference of Commissioners on Uniform State Laws. The UCC itself is not law, however, until the state legislature in each state chooses to adopt it. The UCC has several articles on various commercial law aspects. Every state has adopted some form of the UCC. Louisiana, however, has not adopted Article 2, and several states have not adopted Article 2A. So while the UCC's goal is to be uniform, in reality, the state legislatures can change the draft legislation if they want. The UCC continues to be revised to reflect current changes in the way business is conducted. In fact, the Internet has provided many challenges to existing contract law. As the following article reflects, there is no consensus as to how existing law should be modified for electronic commerce transactions.

A U.C.C. for E-commerce Angers Some

Meetings of the venerable but obscure National Conference of Commissioners on Uniform State Laws (NCCUSL) don't often draw picketers. Once, in the early 1980s, objectors showed up when the commissioners debated their Uniform Adoption Act, a subject whose drafting can understandably provoke a heated response.

But a cyber-version of the arid Uniform Commercial Code?

Protesters once again greeted NCCUSL commissioners this July, when the group gathered in Denver to vote on the Uniform Computer Information Transactions Act, (UCITA), which seeks to define and standardize the law of licensing for software and other information-based products, such as databases. What little law regarding the licensing of such products exists is mostly judge-made, which means that it varies from state to state, whereas interstate uniformity is the NCCUSL's raison d'etre.

"I'm sure the UCITA drafting committee regularly broke records for attendance" by outside observers, says outgoing NCCUSL President Gene Lebrun, a name partner at Lynn, Jackson, Schultz & Lebrun P.C., in Rapid City, S.D., and a 22-year commission member.

The commission promulgates proposed statutory packages in areas in which it believes that state-to-state uniformity is valuable. Its 300 members—state delegations of lawyers, law professors, judges and legislators—then fan out to help convince their home legislatures to enact the group's final proposals into law. Its most famous product is the U.C.C.

UCITA was proposed as a companion piece to the U.C.C. The package seeks to facilitate vendor-purchaser transactions in cyberspace. But its controversial nature became apparent in April, when the commission's partner in U.C.C.-related work, the American Law Institute, withdrew its support for UCITA.

"If I'm sitting in an airplane with my laptop open and I complete a contract for computer information, that contract can't be valid in New York but invalid in California—that would create chaos in our national economy," says Carlyle C. Ring Jr., who chaired the UCITA committee and has shepherded three previous NCCUSL acts into law in the overwhelming majority of states.

"Virtually everyone has accepted the proposition that we need uniform rules," states Mr. Ring, of counsel to Washington, D.C.'s Ober, Kaler, Grimes & Shriver.

Virtually, not literally, everyone

But "we strongly endorse the view that uniform rules governing these converging industries are inappropriate at this time," concluded a letter sent to all of the commissioners on July 14 and signed by the most prominent opponents of UCITA—the presidents of the Motion Picture Association of America, the National Association of Broadcasters, the National Cable Television Association, the Newspaper Association of America and the Magazine Publishers of America. The media group believes it is too early to regulate cyberspace and opposes UCITA's goal of bringing all "information transactions" under a single umbrella.

Proponents of the act—primarily such industry groups as the Business Software Alliance, the Software Publishers Association and the Software and

Information Industry Association—argue the virtue of standardization in an area in which the law is murky. Opponents fear the cost of cementing rules in an economic sector whose form is still undefined.

Some opponents, primarily consumer groups, don't object to the concept of UCITA so much as to its details. This segment feels that it tilts significantly in the direction of sellers (a complaint often heard about the U.C.C. as well). One of their major gripes is the provision permitting self-help, which allows licensors to disable their licensees' software if the licensee violates the agreement.

But John M. McCabe, the NCCUSL's legal counsel and legislative director since 1972, says that while cyber-self-help is unusual in that vendors can reach and disable their product over phone lines, it is still analogous to non-judicial repossession, long permitted under the U.C.C.

"Nobody in their right mind would write unlimited self-help into law," Mr. McCabe says. "The issue is whether the remedy ought to be available, and our answer is yes, so long as we can provide some essential due process."

Among the act's nonwaivable requirements: 15 days' notice by the vendor before disabling, during which the licensee can remedy the alleged breach.

The NCCUSL vote on UCITA, with each state delegation casting one ballot, was 43-6—not the dissent-free vote common for final commission proposals, but not an especially large opposition, either.

But higher hurdles await at the state level. "We're going to have a heck of a time with this one," Mr. McCabe says. "We have occasionally passed proposals that have been controversial, but the difference here is the number of well-financed opposition groups we have to deal with."

UCITA wasn't the only proposal on the agenda. The commission passed revisions in other areas, including one on rules of evidence opposing the use of prior sexual-assault allegations against defendants accused of such crimes—a rare break with the Federal Rules of Evidence.

Commissioners also passed a Uniform Disclaimer of Property Interests Act. Often used in estate tax planning, a disclaimer permits an inheritance to pass from beneficiary to heirs as though the beneficiary had predeceased the decedent. The benefit: The property is shielded from creditors, as the debtor is deemed never to have possessed it.

This article, "A U.C.C. for E-Commerce Angers Some" by Harvey Berkman, is reprinted with permission from the August 16, 1999 edition of *The National Law Journal*. © 1999 NLP IP Company.

There are three basic kinds of contracts: (1) contracts for the sale or lease of goods, (2) contracts for service or employment, and (3) contracts for the sale or lease of real property. It is important to distinguish among these types of contracts because the UCC, Article 2, only applies to the sale of goods and Article 2A only applies to the lease of goods. The other types of contracts are governed by the common law, discussed in Chapter 1. In determining what law applies, look at the subject matter of the contract. Goods are tangible, personal property; that is, they can be touched, and they are not land or anything attached to the land. Examples of goods are cars, computers, food (as long as it is not currently growing on the land), books, clothes, and golf clubs.

Sometimes it is hard to distinguish between a contract for the sale of goods, which is governed by Article 2, and a service contract, which is governed by the common law. For example, when you go to the doctor for a flu shot, have you entered into a contract for the sale of goods (the flu vaccine), or have you contracted for the doctor's services (injection of the flu vaccine)? In this type of case, in which you have both a sale and service aspect to the contract, the court looks at the *main purpose* of the contract. If the main purpose of the contract is to buy the goods, then the UCC controls it. If the main purpose is to receive the service, then the common law rules control it. In regard to the flu shot, the main purpose is to receive the service of the doctor, so the UCC does not control it. Assume, however, that the doctor is purchasing the flu vaccine from the manufacturer, who provides a sales representative to explain the research behind the vaccine. Is this a goods contract or a service contract? Because the main purpose of the contract is to buy the vaccine, the doctor has entered into a goods contract with the manufacturer. The information provided by the sales representative is ancillary.

remedy: Money or performance awarded by a court.

Why does it matter whether it is a contract for goods or some other type of contract? The answer lies in the differences between the UCC and the common law of contracts. For example, how a contract can be formed, whether a contract needs to be in writing, the **remedies** available, and how an offer can be accepted all depend on whether the UCC or common law applies. As we proceed to explain contract law, it is important for you to recognize those differences. But as the following case suggests sometimes just determining whether a contract is for goods or services is difficult.

KITTYE MASON V. JODY JACKSON

323 Ark. 252; 914 S.W. 2d 728 (1996)

FACTS

Jody Jackson taught horseback riding lessons to Kittye Mason's daughter, Lydia. Ms. Mason asked Ms. Jackson to find a suitable 10-year-old gelding, trained as a hunter-jumper, for her daughter. Ms. Mason orally agreed to pay Ms. Jackson $500 if Ms. Jackson could find such a horse for $10,000. Ms. Mason heard of an 11-year-old horse, named Norway, for sale in Florida for $11,500. Both Ms. Mason and Ms. Jackson flew to Florida to look at Norway and some other horses. Norway was owned by Coral Hill Farm, and an employee, Carolyn Tanner, told Ms. Mason and Ms. Jackson that Norway was 11 years old. After watching Norway perform at a horse show, Ms. Mason decided to purchase the horse, and the "barn vet" of Coral Hill Farm certified the horse to be 11 years old. Ms. Mason agreed to purchase the horse and have him sent to Arkansas.

When Norway arrived he was ill and suffered from bouts of colic. About two and a half years after his purchase, Ms. Mason asked another veterinarian to examine Norway. This veterinarian determined Norway to be over 20 years old. Ms. Mason brought a lawsuit alleging breach of contract. The trial court found in favor of Ms. Jackson.

DECISION

Judge Newbern wrote the opinion of the court. Ms. Mason appealed the trial court's decision claiming that the UCC should apply. The Supreme Court of Arkansas disagreed, finding that the contract was not a contract for the sale of goods. Rather, the agreement between Ms. Mason and Ms. Jackson was a personal services contract. The only question, then, was whether there was a breach of the oral agreement because the horse was not 11 years old. The trial court had found that the horse met all the other criteria, except age. The trial court had also found that once Ms. Mason agreed to take the barn vet's certification of age, Ms. Jackson was no longer party to the contract. It stated "[i]t is not reasonable to construe that the intent of the parties' agreement was that the Defendant would guarantee that Norway was 11 years old." The Supreme Court held that the trial court's factual conclusions were not clearly erroneous. Judgment for the defendant, Ms. Jackson, was affirmed.

CASE QUESTIONS

1. Why is this a contract for personal services and not a contract for the sale of goods?
2. How might the facts be changed so that a court would determine it was a contract for the sale of goods?
3. Did Ms. Jackson owe Ms. Mason an ethical obligation to ensure that the horse was only 11 years old?

GENERAL CONTRACT TERMS

Creating any contract requires an *offer*, *acceptance*, and **consideration**. The contract also has to be legal, and the parties need to exercise free will and have *legal capacity*. We will consider each of these elements separately. First, it is important to understand some basic contractual terms. When all terms of the contract have been spelled out, the contract is called an *express contract*. Sometimes individuals agree to contract but do not spell out all of the terms. If the intent of the parties can be determined by their conduct, the contract is *implied in fact*. When the parties have not agreed to contract or have not fulfilled the legal requirements necessary to form a contract, the court may still find an **implied in law contract**. Implied in law contracts are not legal contracts; rather, the court implies a contract in order to avoid **unjust enrichment**, or harm to an innocent party. These contracts are referred to as **quasi-contracts**.

One equitable doctrine that is used to enforce a contract even though for some technical reason a contract has not been performed, is **promissory estoppel**.

Promissory estoppel requires that a promise be made with the expectation that it would be relied on, and it is justifiably relied upon to the detriment of the other party. Since one party will be unjustly enriched, the court may say that promissory estoppel applies, and the other party is stopped from denying that a promise was made.

consideration: The promise or performance that the promisor demands as the price of the promise in a contract.

implied in law contract: A contract expressed by conduct or implied or deduced from the facts.

unjust enrichment: A benefit received by chance, mistake or at someone else's expense.

quasi contract: An obligation that is not created by a contract but is imposed by law to prevent unjust enrichment of one party from the acts of another party.

promissory estoppel: A situation in which one party's reliance on a promise prevents the promisor from denying the existence of a contract.

REQUIREMENTS FOR PROMISSORY ESTOPPEL

- Defendant makes a promise
- Plaintiff relies on the promise
- Defendant expected that the promise would be relied on
- Plaintiff suffers detriment
- Defendant is unjustly enriched

As the next case shows, even the doctrine of promissory estoppel still requires a promise.

MACCAFERRI GABIONS, INC. V. DYNATERIA, INC.

91 F.3d 1431; 1996 U.S. App. LEXIS 20893 (11th Cir. 1996)

FACTS

Maccaferri Gabions is a materialman engaged in manufacturing large stone-filled wire mesh baskets called *gabions*. Gabions are used in erosion control. In 1986, Wilkinson & Jenkins Construction (W&J) was awarded an Army Corps of Engineers contract for an erosion control project on Lake Okeechobee in Florida. Ohio Casualty provided the performance bond. W&J subcontracted with Maccaferri to provide the gabions for a test section. This contract was not in dispute. Maccaferri suggested that W&J subcontract some of its remaining work to another firm, Moore & Artis (M&A), and Maccaferri agreed to provide M&A with reduced price gabions. Maccaferri claimed that W&J and M&A agreed to use the Maccaferri gabions for the rest of the work. W&J denied making that promise.

W&J and M&A did enter into a contract, and M&A ordered $574,304.64 worth of gabions from Maccaferri. In anticipation of performing the contract, Maccaferri procured the materials necessary to make the gabions. Because of the large size of the order and questions about M&A's creditworthiness, Maccaferri wanted W&J to guarantee the payment. Instead, W&J and M&A modified their contract to provide that checks written for payment would be in both M&A and Maccaferri's name. Reassured by this change, Maccaferri delivered its first shipment of gabions. Maccaferri only received partial payment for this delivery and sent a collection letter to M&A with a copy to W&J. It turned out that M&A was in serious financial trouble and eventually defaulted on the contract. M&A's surety, Dynateria, promised Maccaferri it would pay the remaining balance and finish the project using only gabions, but Dynateria also eventually defaulted. W&J completed the project using a different material. Maccaferri was never paid the balance of its money, nor were any of the other gabions used in the project. It sued W&J, Ohio Casualty, Dynateria, and M&A. The district court found in favor of Maccaferri, as against W&J under the Miller Act and on the grounds of promissory estoppel.

DECISION

Judge Phillips wrote the opinion of the court. Under the Miller Act, a materialman (someone who does not directly contract with the general contractor) on a government contract has to comply with a strict notice requirement before the general contractor is obligated to pay. Maccaferri did not satisfy these requirements, and W&J was entitled to summary judgment in its favor. The more complicated question for the court was whether the doctrine of promissory estoppel was appropriate in this case. In order to have a claim for promissory estoppel, the court used the *Restatement (Second) of Contracts* definition, which states, "A promise which the promisor should reasonably expect to induce action or forbearance on the part of the promisee or a third person and which does induce such action or forbearance is binding if injustice can be avoided only by enforcing the promise." The court then looked at the following facts to determine whether the first element, a promise, existed. It found that W&J's negotiator did not disclose any promise on which Maccaferri could base its estoppel claim. Further, Maccaferri's negotiator did not mention any promise made by W&J. The court found that "[a]lthough [Maccaferri's negotiator] did testify that 'someone' promised him that the project would be completed entirely with gabions, the only someone named in that portion of his testimony is Dynateria. In the absence of proof that Dynateria was somehow acting as W&J's agent when it made this statement, this promise could not be found made by W&J itself." Finally, the court found that even though "W&J knew the gabions had been delivered, etc. [the documents] are devoid of any reference to a promise by W&J on which Maccaferri could have relied in amassing the materials needed to produce all the gabions."

The judgment of the trial court was reversed and summary judgment was entered for W&J.

CASE QUESTIONS

1. Do the other elements of promissory estoppel exist in this case?
2. What fact(s) is most persuasive in arguing that the Court of Appeals was correct in finding that there was no promise?
3. Do you agree with the Court's decision? Use an ethical analysis to support your position.

MUTUAL ASSENT

Contracts usually require that two parties mutually agree to all the contract's terms. A **bilateral contract** is formed when one party makes an offer and the other party accepts the offer with a promise. For example, Larry offers to sell Ann his car for $1,000. Ann agrees to buy Larry's car for $1,000. When Ann makes the return promise to buy the car, a bilateral contract has been formed. Larry cannot withdraw his offer.

bilateral contract: A contract in which each party makes a promise to the other.

A **unilateral contract** occurs when performance is required to accept the offer. A unilateral contract still has mutual assent even though neither party is bound until performance is complete. For example, Sue agrees to pay Alan $2,000 if Alan paints her house. Alan does not agree to do anything. Sue can withdraw her offer at any time before Alan's performance is completed; however, a unilateral contract is formed when Alan finishes painting Sue's house. In some states, unilateral contracts are accepted by beginning performance.

unilateral contract: A contract in which one party makes a promise offering some benefit if another party performs a specified act (rather than making a return promise).

Other contract terms you should know are *executory*, *partially executed*, and *executed*. When Larry and Ann enter into the car contract it is called an *executory* contract because the contract has been entered into but neither party has performed their obligations under the contract. When Ann pays Larry $1,000, the contract is *partially executed* because one party, Ann, has performed her obligations. When Larry delivers the car to Ann, the contract is considered *executed* since both parties have performed their obligations.

ENFORCEABILITY

Contracts may also be *void*, *voidable*, or *unenforceable*. Neither party to a contract can enforce a void contract (in fact, technically it never was a "contract" to begin with). Void contracts usually are illegal. For example, it is illegal in Utah to enter into any gambling contract. Assume that Joe and Jerry are skiing in Utah in December. On the ski lift Joe bets Jerry $20 that Notre Dame will beat UCLA in that night's bowl game. Notre Dame wins, and Joe tries to collect the $20 from Jerry. Jerry refuses to pay. No Utah court will enforce the contract because the contract was illegal and is therefore *void*.

A **voidable contract** is enforceable by only one party to the contract. As you will soon discover, contracts with a minor are voidable. Jessica, who is 21 years old, agrees to sell her computer to Amy, who is 16, for $400. Amy agrees to buy the computer. Two days later Amy changes her mind and refuses to give Jessica the $400. Jessica will not be able to enforce the contract because Amy is a minor, and minors' contracts are voidable. But if Jessica had been the one to change her mind, Amy would have been able to enforce the contract, since minors' contracts are enforceable at their option.

voidable contract: A contract in which one party has the option to disaffirm the bargain or back out.

unenforceable contract: A contract for which the law gives no court remedy.

An **unenforceable contract** is a contract that the law will no longer allow the courts to enforce. For example, in January 1990, Betty enters into a contract with Bill to pay Bill $700 for his canoe. However, Betty only pays $550 and indicates that she will pay the additional $150 in a month. Betty never pays Bill the remaining amount. Later, in January 1995, Bill hears that Betty won the lottery. Since Bill never received the $150, he decides to sue Betty. However, since the statute of limitations for the sale of goods is four years and expired in 1994, the contract between Bill and Betty is unenforceable.

ELEMENTS OF A CONTRACT

OFFER

Before a contract is formed, one party needs to make an *offer*. The offer must be explicit, set forth the applicable terms, and be communicated to the offeree. Generally, it is clear when an offer is made. As the next article suggests, disputes over what constitutes an offer continue to arise.

Rejected 'Annie' Gets A New Day—in Court

3rd Circuit lets case against Macy's over talent search winner being 'dropped' in Broadway performance go to jury

A jury must decide if Macy's promised the contestants in its national talent search that the winner would get the title role in the Broadway revival of "Annie"—and is therefore liable to the Philadelphia girl who won, but was dumped from the show just prior to opening night—the 3rd U.S. Circuit Court of Appeals has ruled.

The ruling in Pacitti v. Macy's overturns last year's decision by Chief U.S. District Judge James T. Giles that said Joanna Pacitti and her parents, Joseph and Stella Pacitti, had no contract claim against Macy's since they were told that the show's producers always had sole discretion to make casting changes.

Pacitti was 11 when she auditioned in King of Prussia and was chosen from among five finalists. She played the title role of Annie in a national tour that wended its way from Houston, Texas, to Hershey, Pa., with stops in St. Paul, Minn., Chicago, Baltimore and Boston.

But after belting out her role in more than 100 performances, Pacitti claims she was unceremoniously dropped from the cast and replaced by another girl just two weeks before the show opened on Broadway.

The Pacittis' lawyer, Albert C. Oehrle of Norristown, argued that the talent search for "Broadway's new Annie" was a contest and that the Broadway role was the prize. Pacitti won, he said, and was deprived of the prize.

But Giles disagreed, saying "a Broadway role is not comparable to other contest awards."

Joanna Pacitti was always expected to sign a standard Actor's Equity contract with the show's producers, Giles said, which explicitly stated that she could be replaced at any time.

On appeal, the Pacittis hired attorney Alfred W. Putnam Jr. of Drinker Biddle & Reath who argued that Judge Giles had improperly injected his own views into the case.

"The fact is that Macy's said nothing at all about an equity contract, not to mention the specific risk that the producers of the show would ultimately decide against using 'Broadway's New Annie' as 'Annie' once the show made it to Broadway," Putnam wrote.

"Judge Giles simply erred by substituting his own views of the case for the Pacittis' right to present their very different view to a jury," he wrote.

Now the 3rd Circuit has agreed with Putnam, saying Giles erred in finding that the contract Pacitti and her mother signed was unambiguous and made no promise of a Broadway debut.

U.S. Circuit Judge Samuel A. Alito found that "Macy's at no point revealed—either through its printed materials or other means—that the winner of the search would receive only the opportunity to sign a standard actors' equity contract with the producers."

Although Macy's insists it had no power to promise her the role and a Broadway debut, Alito found that the real question was whether Macy's made such a promise and the Pacittis reasonably understood it as a promise.

The only evidence that the producers retained the rights to reject any actor was in documents exchanged between Macy's and the producers—and never seen by the Pacittis—Alito found.

"We do not believe that Macy's role was so 'obvious' that it need not have limited its offer to the public, and we find it telling that Macy's contract with the producers contained qualifications on the prize to be offered," Alito wrote. "Therefore, we conclude that it was reasonable for plaintiffs to believe that Macy's offered the starring role of 'Annie' on Broadway."

The Pacittis file the suit against Macy's and Macy's East Inc., claiming they had explicitly promised a Broadway role to the winner of the nationwide "Annie Off" contest.

The suit against Macy's alleged fraudulent misrepresentation, breach of contract, equitable estoppel and breach of an implied covenant of good faith and fair dealing.

Macy's lawyer, Robert P. Joy of Boston's Morgan Brown & Joy, moved to dismiss the suit, arguing that Pacitti has no claim against the store, which merely agreed to hold a series of auditions.

Although the suit termed the talent search a "contest" in which the winner would be awarded the "prize" of a Broadway role, Joy insisted that the official application and rules made it very clear that the Macy's events were merely "auditions."

Judge Giles agreed with Joy, saying it was legally significant that the talent search papers repeatedly used the term "audition" and that it was therefore unreasonable of the Pacittis to expect that the contest promised a guaranteed Broadway debut.

But Judge Alito, in an opinion joined by U.S. Circuit Judge Morton I. Greenberg and visiting Senior U.S. District Judge William H. Stafford of the Northern District of Florida, found that the Pacittis had a real argument that a Broadway role was promised as the prize in numerous contest papers and advertisements.

As for the use of the word "audition," Alito said Putnam had offered a reasonable alternative interpretation when he argued in his brief that "the word 'audition' refers to the process a contestant must undergo before she can 'win' the prize. . . . It follows, one would think, that the girl selected after the 'final audition' has won something more than an 'audition.'"

Alito found that it was also not unreasonable for the Pacittis to believe that Macy's had the power to offer the winner the starring role since the advertisements described it as "the world's largest store."

The ads, he said, could have been interpreted by some readers as suggesting that the talent search was being conducted as a joint effort of Macy's and the show's producers.

This article, "Rejected 'Annie' Gets a New Day—in Court" by Shannon P. Duffy, is reprinted with permission from the September 3, 1999 edition of *The Legal Intelligencer*.

option contract: A preliminary contract in which value is given to the offeror in exchange for keeping the offer open for a specified time.

An offer typically can be withdrawn at any time before it is accepted. One exception to this is the **option contract**. An option contract is a contract to hold an offer open. Like most other contracts, an option contract needs *consideration* (a mutual exchange of something valuable) to be binding. For example, James is interested in buying Sally's home for $80,000. He is unsure, however, if he can raise the financing. Sally agrees in writing to give James until October 1 to raise the money. James gives Sally $500 to hold the offer open. This is an option contract. Sally cannot sell the home to anyone else until after October 1. If James does not raise the money by October 1, Sally is free to keep the $500 and sell the home to another buyer.

firm offer: An offer that cannot be revoked, withdrawn, or amended for the time stated.

merchant: Person who deals with goods of the kind sold in his or her business.

Under the UCC, §2-205, a written **firm offer** by a **merchant** is enforceable for a reasonable time or for the time period stated, not to exceed three months, if, by its terms, the offer gives the assurance it will be held open. The box, "Enforceable Firm Offers by Merchants," provides an example of a firm offer. A firm offer does not need consideration. For example, Abigail walks into her local car dealership and asks for the price of a new model sports car. Janet, the salesperson, writes down that she will sell Abigail a new model sports car for $20,000 and that the price will be valid for five days. Abigail decides to think about it and leaves the store. Three days later she returns. Can Abigail enforce the offer? Yes, this is a firm offer by a merchant (someone in the business of selling that particular merchandise) and it is in writing. Therefore, it is enforceable even though there was no consideration.

ENFORCEABLE FIRM OFFERS BY MERCHANTS

(U.C.C. §2-205)

- The offer is made by a merchant
- The offer is in writing
- The offer is signed by a merchant
- The offer states it will be held open for a certain or reasonable amount of time
- The offer involves a sale of goods

mirror image rule: A rule that states that in order for an acceptance to exist, the response must be a mirror image of the offer and cannot add new terms.

ACCEPTANCE

Once an offer is made, the offeree can accept the offer, reject the offer, or make a counteroffer. Under the common law, both the offer and acceptance have to be identical or *mirror* each other. This is called the **mirror image rule**. Cathy offers to sell Joe her horse for $800. Joe says that for $800 he also wants Cathy to "throw in" a saddle. So far, there is no contract. Rather, Cathy made an offer, and Joe has made a counteroffer. Cathy tells Joe she will sell the horse and saddle for $850. Joe agrees. Now, the offer and acceptance are the same, and a contract is formed.

An exception to the mirror image rule is found in §2-207 of the UCC. Merchants often exchange forms detailing the particulars of their transactions. After all, merchants are those who are in the business of conducting business. These forms are drafted by each merchant's lawyer and are inevitably different in that they do not mirror each other. For example, one form may say that interest will accumulate at 10 percent per annum on unpaid bills, and another may not mention anything about interest. Section 2-207 says that when merchants are dealing with each other, and there is a written confirmation, additional terms become part of the contract unless the terms materially change the contract or the other party objects within a reasonable time. Many terms are considered "material," including the price or the quantity. A change in these terms reflects that the parties had not reached mutual assent. Other terms, however, may be made part of the contract if a party does not object. The box, "Acceptance and Offer Do Not Need to Mirror Each Other," summarizes the conditions under which an acceptance and an offer need not mirror one another. This means that it is very important for merchants to read their mail and pay attention to the terms found in other merchants' forms.

ACCEPTANCE AND OFFER DO NOT NEED TO MIRROR EACH OTHER

(UCC §2-207)

- The contract is for sale of goods.
- The contract is between merchants.
- The changes in acceptance are minor.
- The response includes a clear expression of acceptance.
- The acceptance is not made conditional on assent by the offeror to different terms.
- Additional terms become part of the contract unless:
  - The offeror limits acceptance to the terms of the offer; or
  - The new terms materially alter the offer; or
  - The offeror notifies the offeree within a reasonable amount of time concerning any objections.

When the parties are not dealing with each other face to face, a problem arises as to when acceptance has occurred. In general, the **mailbox rule** applies here. An offer is accepted at the time the acceptance is placed in the mail. For example, on November 1, Troy sends Tana an offer to sell his computer for $800. On November 5, Tana sends Troy a counteroffer to buy the computer and desk for $800. On November 10, Troy sends his offer to sell the computer and desk for $850. Tana receives the offer on November 12 and mails her acceptance on November 13. Troy calls Tana and *rescinds* (withdraws) the offer on November 14. He receives her acceptance on November 15. Under the mailbox rule, Tana accepted on November 13, and Troy's rescission one day later is ineffective. He is bound to the contract. The person making the offer is master of the

mailbox rule: Making an offer or acceptance valid when it is deposited in the mail.

offer. If Troy wants Tana's acceptance to be effective when he receives it, then he needs to make that term part of the original offer.

Under the common law, if the offeree accepts the offer using an *unauthorized method* (one not specified by the offer), the acceptance is effective only when received. For example, if rather than putting the acceptance in the mail, Ann sends her acceptance with Aunt Betty who is traveling cross-country, then the acceptance is only effective when Aunt Betty delivers it. Accepting the offer by the same means as the offer was received is considered, by the common law, to be an implied authorization. Under the UCC an acceptance can be sent by any reasonable method and is effective when sent, unless the offer itself specifically states otherwise.

Under the common law, silence does not constitute an acceptance—if the other party does not respond, no contract exists. The UCC, however, provides an exception for merchants. Under §2-201(2) of the UCC, if a merchant does not respond to a written confirmation within 10 days, the merchant has accepted the offer. Once again, merchants are responsible for reading and responding to their mail.

Generally, once a contract is accepted the parties must perform. Under §2-608 of the UCC, however, an acceptance of the goods can be revoked under some circumstances. For example, if the goods are *nonconforming* (do not meet the specific terms of the contract) and the nonconformity substantially impairs the value of the contract, then the contract can be revoked. The purchaser must have had to accept the goods unaware of the nonconformity or, if aware, assured that the nonconformity would be *cured* (fixed). **Revocation** must occur within a reasonable time. The following case demonstrates how the law works for these types of contracts.

revocation: Withdrawing an offer before it is accepted or mutual agreement to cancel contract.

DURFEE V. ROD BAXTER IMPORTS, INC.

262 N.W.2d 349 (Minn. 1977)

FACTS

John Durfee purchased a Saab automobile from Rod Baxter Imports. After the purchase, Durfee started to drive home. Within a few blocks several warning lights came on. Durfee returned to the dealership where the warning lights were stopped. Durfee then continued on home; however, on the way, the knob on the shift lever came off, a rattle in the dash began, and another warning light came on. He immediately called the dealership and was told to either bring the car back for repairs or wait until the 1,000-mile inspection. Durfee decided to wait for the 1,000-mile inspection. At the 1,000-mile inspection, Durfee also complained about the windshield-wiper system and air vents. The car was returned to repair the defroster, a continuing rattle, a sticking accelerator, and a brake squeal and choke. The front passenger seat was also removed in an attempt to fix the warning system lights.

At the 6,000-mile inspection, the problems became more pronounced. The car began to stall and was towed several times to the dealer lot. When the car had 6,300 miles on it, Durfee wrote a letter revoking acceptance and canceled the contract. He listed the following as defects: (1) the passenger seat had not been reinstalled; (2) the automobile continued to stall; (3) the seatbelt warning system continued to activate without apparent cause; (4) the "ungodly" rattle persisted; (5) the temperature gauge registered "hot"; and (6) shortly after starting the motor, the heating unit malfunctioned.

The trial court found for Durfee but only awarded him $600 in damages for breach of a warranty. Durfee appealed, claiming that the acceptance should be revoked and the contract should be canceled.

DECISION

The Supreme Court of Minnesota felt that the governing law in this case was §2-608 of the UCC. Section 2-608 allows for revocation when (1) a nonconformity exists that substantially impairs the value of the contract; (2) the nonconformity was not discoverable; and (3) the revocation occurs within a reasonable time. Saab-Scandia, the codefendant, argued that the defects did not substantially impair the contract "because they had already been repaired or were easily repairable." The court found, however, that Durfee "was plagued by a series of annoying difficulties with the Saab (the recurrent rattle and seatbelt buzz among them) as well as difficulty that directly interfered with the Saab's operation (the repeated stalling, which began five months after purchase and which, despite several attempted repairs, was never remedied)." The combination of minor defects and frequent stalling creates substantial impairment. Further, the defendants had numerous opportunities to repair the automobile. The court found revocation appropriate in this case and ordered that Durfee may recover the purchase price and $116.30 in incidental damages.

CASE QUESTIONS

1. Was Durfee justified in revoking his contract?
2. How many times must a consumer have a vehicle repaired before a contract should be allowed to be revoked?
3. Many states have enacted "lemon laws." What is the status of lemon laws in your state?

CONSIDERATION

Besides having an offer and acceptance, a contract must also have legal consideration. The law does not bind people to all promises they make. For example, if Laura promises to love David forever and then later changes her mind, the law will not enforce her promise! *Consideration* means that each party to the contract gave up something that has value. Usually each party will give up money or property. Once in a while, though, an individual will give up a legal right rather than money or property. Imagine that Ned, 21 years old, promises his uncle that he will not drink any alcoholic beverage for five years. In return, his uncle promises that he will pay Ned $10,000 if he successfully lives up to his promise. After five years, Ned is entitled to $10,000 because he gave up his legal right to drink alcoholic beverages. On the other hand, assume Ned's uncle promises to give Ned $10,000 in five years without extracting any promise from him in return. But just before the five years expires, Ned's uncle dies. Is the uncle's estate liable to Ned for $10,000? The answer is no. If Ned's uncle had lived, he would not be legally liable to give Ned the $10,000 because no mutual consideration occurred. Ned did not give up anything of value. In other words, the promise of a gift is not enforceable. A gift is only enforceable when it has actually been delivered.

The promise to perform a new contract without additional consideration is also not sufficient consideration. For example, suppose Randy agrees to build Gary a home for $120,000. Halfway into the construction, Randy decides that it will really cost $150,000 to build the home and demands that Gary pay the higher price. Gary, having just sold his old home and currently living in his car, agrees to pay $150,000 rather than the contract price of $120,000. The new $150,000 contract, however, does not have consideration because Randy did not agree to do any additional work or give up any additional value. Since there was no new consideration, Gary will only have to pay $120,000.

Under the UCC, a *written modification* of an existing contract need not have new consideration to be effective. For example, Randy agrees to sell Gary his sports car for $60,000 and then changes his mind and refuses to sell the car unless Gary pays $70,000. If Gary agrees, in writing, to the $70,000 modification, he will be bound to the contract.

While consideration is very important to contracts, a distinction also exists between mutual consideration and adequacy of consideration. *Mutual consideration* means that consideration underlies the contract and is essential to forming a contract. *Adequacy of consideration* asks whether each party is receiving a fair bargain. The general rule is that courts do not care whether someone entered into a bad bargain. For example, if Zoe sold her $100,000 home to Roe for $5,000, a court would probably not disturb the contract for lack of adequacy. Courts sometimes do look at adequacy, however, to determine whether there was voluntary consent.

liquidated debt: A debt not in dispute.

unliquidated debt: A debt that is disputed.

One type of problem arises when someone pays less than the amount due on a debt and writes on the check *payment in full*. In most circumstances, paying less than the amount owed does not result in a release from paying the full amount. In these circumstances, the parties are satisfying a **liquidated debt**, and the parties do not dispute how much is owed. However, an exception exists for **disputed** or **unliquidated debts**. In these cases, the parties legitimately disagree as to how much is owed, and the question then becomes whether there has been an *accord* and *satisfaction*. An accord and satisfaction occurs when the parties have agreed to a lesser amount on a disputed debt (the accord) and the amount has been paid and accepted (the satisfaction). As the next article discusses, even an accord and satisfaction does not release all contract claims.

Routine Back-of-Check Release Doesn't Prohibit Bad Faith Claim

A federal judge has ruled that an insurance company can still be sued for bad faith even after an insured cashes a check that carried the proviso: "Full & Final Settlement of Any & All Claims."

In his nine-page opinion in *Fleming v. CNA Insurance Co.*, U.S. District Judge J. Curtis Joyner rejected the argument that any plaintiff who endorses such a check is barred from suing by the "doctrine of accord and satisfaction" since the signature effectively gives the check writer a release. And Joyner found that a motion to dismiss on those grounds was especially inappropriate in a bad faith case. "Since claims for bad faith are deemed to be and are adjudicated separately and apart from the contract disputes upon which they are based, we find defendant's argument that its payment of the judgment against it should operate to release it from plaintiff's bad faith claim to border on the frivolous," Joyner wrote. The bad faith suit was filed by attorney Robert E. Slota of Murphy & Slota in Bryn Mawr on behalf of Rita Fleming who sustained serious injuries in a car accident with an underinsured driver in November 1992. In June 1994, Fleming made a demand for benefits under the underinsured motorist provisions of her $300,000 UIM policy. But due to CNA's foot dragging, Fleming claims it took more than three years to get to arbitration and that she was forced to wait even longer for her check to be cut after an arbitrator awarded her $200,000. CNA first denied both her claim and her right to arbitration, the suit says, and then delayed the arbitration. Fleming claims she heard nothing from CNA following the arbitration award and that her lawyer at the time, Bernard DiGiacomo, was forced to write a letter two weeks later requesting prompt payment. The suit says DiGiacomo's letter also advised CNA that Fleming was making a claim for $5,000 in lost wages which the arbitrators had awarded but mistakenly credited CNA for having already paid. The letter also said that Fleming expected CNA to pay interest at the daily rate of $28.33 on the award from the date that it was entered; and that "any check which is forwarded . . . and which does not include appropriate interest . . . and which is submitted as 'full payment' or the equivalent thereof, will be cashed . . . without waiver of legally due interest." When Fleming received the check four days later, she cashed it without any further discussion or complaint about the proviso which appeared in all capital letters. Three months later, Fleming sued CNA for bad faith, alleging that the company failed to respond promptly and to investigate and pay her claim for underinsured motorist benefits. CNA's lawyer, Timothy Costello of Marshall Dennehey Warner Coleman & Goggin argued that Fleming's suit should be dismissed since her endorsement and cashing of the check gave CNA a full release. "We strongly disagree," Joyner wrote. Costello's theory was flawed, Joyner found, since the courts have never applied the doctrine of accord in a case like Fleming's. "An accord and satisfaction is a substitute contract between a debtor and creditor for the settlement of a debt by some alternative performance other than full payment of the debt," Joyner wrote. "Because an accord is a contract, it requires the elements of a contract: offer, acceptance and consideration." To present a proper accord-and-satisfaction defense, Joyner found that a defendant must show three things: a disputed debt; a clear and unequivocal offer of payment in full satisfaction; and acceptance and retention of payment by the offeree. Generally, Joyner said, "the debtor's offer of a full payment check and the creditor's negotiation of that check constitute the offer and acceptance of an accord and satisfaction with the consideration being the resolution of an unliquidated or disputed claim." But another element essential to the defense of accord and satisfaction, he said, is an actual and substantial difference of opinion as to the amount due. "In the absence of such a controversy, the payment of a part of the amount due under a contract, even though accepted by the creditor as in full satisfaction of the debt, does not work a discharge of the entire indebtedness for the reason that there is no consideration for the creditor's agreement that it should so operate," Joyner wrote. Applying that test to Fleming's case, Joyner found that, despite the "Full and Final Settlement of Any and All Claims" proviso, CNA's check was payment for nothing more than the judgment entered in Fleming's favor by the arbitrators. As a result, Joyner said, "there was no disputed debt or unliquidated damages claim which was satisfied and resolved by the tender of the defendants' check." And without that, he said, the contract lacked the required consideration necessary to support an accord and satisfaction defense. Joyner also found that Fleming's lawyer had duly warned CNA that if the check carried a full-payment proviso, it would be cashed without any waiver of rights to seek unpaid interest. By that same logic, Joyner said, Fleming also never waived her right to sue for bad faith. "As a general rule, bad faith claims . . . are initiated based upon behavior of an insurance company occurring subsequent to the negligent or intentional behavior of a third party which spawned the original contractual suit." Joyner wrote. "As was the case with plaintiff's claim for interest and wage loss, such bad faith behavior is temporarily and factually distinct from any behavior that would impact upon the outcome of the damages and liability disposition of the underlying contract claim."

VOLUNTARY CONSENT

As discussed, generally, a valid contract has an offer, acceptance, and consideration. However, what if the person entering the contract was threatened or lied to: Does a contract still exist? The answer is no. Before a valid contract is formed, both parties have to agree freely to be bound. If the contract is not freely entered into, it is usually considered voidable, although sometimes it may be void.

duress: The threat of physical intimidation or coercion aimed at forcing individuals to enter into contracts against their will.

Duress **Duress** is the threat of physical intimidation or coercion aimed at forcing individuals to enter into contracts against their will. The individual has to reasonably believe that the threat can be carried through, and the threat has to be the reason the individual enters into the contract. If he or she would have entered into the contract anyway, the defense of duress is not available. Entering into a contract because of severe financial constraints or the fear of embarrassment is not usually considered duress if the other party did not create the circumstances.

Contracts entered into under duress are voidable. In other words, simply because the one party enters into a contract under duress does not always mean the contract is automatically invalid. Rather, the party may end or void the contract at any time; until he or she does, however, the contract is valid. If, on entering into the contract, the person was subject to physical duress—actually getting beat up—as opposed to the threat of duress, the contract is void.

undue influence: A situation in which a dominant person, or a person in a position of trust and confidence, takes advantage of another person.

Undue Influence **Undue influence** may also invalidate a contract. Undue influence occurs when the parties have a special relationship with each other and one party uses that relationship to influence the other party to enter into a contract. Undue influence is not the same as duress. Undue influence concerns whether one person used a superior position to take unfair advantage of the other person. Typical contracts that raise suspicions are those involving a child and a parent, a physician and patient, a priest and a penitent, a husband and a wife, and an attorney and a client. These types of relationships can result in inequalities and are fraught with emotion. Dominant individuals have the opportunity to use the relationship to entice weaker individuals to enter into unfair contracts. A court looks at whether the parties acted freely and with full knowledge. A party can contract with someone with whom he or she shares a special relationship, but the contract is scrutinized much more carefully.

Fraud A contract can be voided if its formation was based on fraudulent representations. There are two types of fraud: *fraud in the execution* and *fraud in the inducement*. Fraud in the execution occurs when one party does not intend to contract. For example, say Sara approaches her blind grandmother and asks that she sign a piece of paper enabling Sara to rent for her grandmother some novels on tape. In fact, the paper is a contract for the sale of Grandma's new condominium. This is fraud in the execution, and the contract is void. Grandma did not intend to contract.

Fraud in the inducement occurs when one party lies to the other party about a material fact. But for the lie, the contract would not have been formed. Suppose Sara approaches her blind grandmother and asks if she wants to buy Sara's three-bedroom luxury condominium in Florida where Sara has lived the past three years. Her grandmother, tired of the cold winter, agrees to buy the

FROM THE DESK OF

Laura Lawyer

To: Students

From: Your Lawyer

Special relationships can cause legal problems when they come to contract law. If you enter into a contract with a parent or child, especially if you have either emotional or monetary control over his or her life, it is important that an unbiased third party, usually an attorney, be involved. The third party can interview the parent or child to ensure that he or she is acting according to his or her own wishes. The third party may also provide actual legal representation on behalf of the parent or child. This early involvement can prevent later claims that one person was being unduly influenced.

condominium. She discovers later that the condominium does not have three bedrooms, is not luxurious, and is literally falling apart. Under these circumstances, there is fraud in the inducement. Sara intentionally lied to her grandmother about material facts. The grandmother reasonably relied on those misrepresentations, much to her detriment, but she intended to contract. The contract is voidable.

Mistakes Sometimes contracts can be voided because a mistake was made. There are three types of mistakes: *unilateral*, *ambiguous*, and *bilateral*. A unilateral mistake occurs when one party is mistaken under the contract and the other party did not know the party was mistaken. For example, Roger submits a bid to install the lights for a new office building. In compiling his bid, he makes a mathematical error. Roger's bid is accepted. Unless the owners of the office building knew or should have known that Roger made an error, the mistake is unilateral and Roger is bound.

Sometimes terms in the contract are ambiguous, and neither party understands what the other party intended. In the classic example, a contract was formed that stated that goods are to be sent on the ship *Peerless*. The seller believed that the goods would be sent on the *Peerless* that left Bombay, India, in December. The buyer believed that the goods would be sent on a different *Peerless* that left Bombay in October. The court held the term *Peerless* was ambiguous in this situation and that the parties did not have a "meeting of the minds."[1] When the contract was first entered into, both parties believed they

[1] *Raffles v. Wichelhaus*, 159 Eng. Rep. 375 (Court of Exchequer, 1864).

understood its terms. When the contract was to be fulfilled, however, it became clear that neither party had actually understood that each believed *Peerless* to be a different ship. Ambiguous contracts are voidable at either party's option.

The third type of mistake is a mutual, or bilateral, mistake. In this type of case, both parties are mistaken. The question then turns on whether the parties are mistaken as to the subject matter of the contract or if they are mistaken as to the value of the contract. If the mistake is over subject matter, the contract is voidable. The contract is not voidable, however, if the mistake is over value. For example, Ted agrees to buy Tana's Rembrandt painting for $6,000,000. Unknown to either Ted or Tana, the Rembrandt is really a forgery. This is a mutual mistake about the subject matter of the contract and the contract is voidable. On the other hand, assume the Rembrandt is authentic but when Ted tries to resell it, the piece turns out to be worth only $3,000,000. This is a mistake as to the value of the contract, and the contract is not voidable.

CAPACITY

The law presumes that certain individuals, such as minors and incompetents, cannot protect themselves. As a result, the law steps in to protect them when they enter into a contract. These individuals do not have legal *capacity* to enter into contracts.

minor: An individual under the legal age to contract.

disaffirm: A decision not to be bound to a contract.

ratify: To adopt the act even if it was not approved beforehand; to agree to be bound to a contract.

Minors A **minor** is an individual under the legal age to contract. In most states, that age is 18 years. If a contract is entered into with a minor, the contract is voidable, at the minor's option, anytime until the minor reaches majority. When the minor reaches majority, the minor can either **disaffirm** the contract or **ratify** the contract. Minors disaffirming contracts are entitled to be returned to the position in which they began; that is, they get their money back. They are responsible for returning anything they received under the contract, if they still have it. Note that, since the law is aimed at protecting minors from themselves, in most states it makes no difference if minors misrepresent their age—the contract is still voidable.

Incompetency Some people suffer from mental illnesses that might impair their ability to contract. If a court judges a person mentally incompetent, any contract he or she formed is void. If a person is mentally incompetent but not judged so by a court, the question turns on whether the mental illness results in the inability to adequately protect his or her interest. For example, suppose Jan suffers from schizophrenia and believes that demons are following her around town. She stops at Joe's Jewelry Store and insists on buying a large diamond cross necklace costing $5,000 to protect her from the demons. In this case, the mental illness has affected her ability to contract, and the contract is voidable. On the other hand, if Jan stops in the store to buy a gift for her mother's birthday and her mental illness does not affect her ability to understand the contract, she is bound to the contract.

Sometimes intoxication or drug use can impair a person's ability to contract. The question, however, is not merely whether a person had been drinking alcohol (many business contracts could not pass that test!) or under the influence of drugs. Rather, the question is whether there was a *genuineness of assent*. To put it another way, did the individual know that a contract was being formed. If the intoxication or drug use did not impair the ability to understand the contract, incompetency is not a defense.

Necessities Both minors and persons who are found mentally incompetent are still bound to contracts for necessities. Courts reason that incompetent individuals still need the items necessary to sustain life. Necessities are food, clothing, and shelter, not otherwise provided.

LEGALITY

As stated earlier, contracts must be *legal*, which means they cannot violate public policy. Some contracts are illegal because the legislature makes them illegal. In most states, a contract for prostitution is illegal by state statute. Contracts that are not illegal but that violate public policy, however, are more difficult. One such contract is an antenuptial contract, which is a contract entered into before a marriage. Early case law considered these a violation of public policy. That rule is changing and now these contracts are often enforced.

In order to be legal, contracts also have to contain legal subject matter. Therefore, a contract to sell heroin is illegal and illegal contracts are void. However, questions of legality often are not so clear-cut. For example, is a contract between a couple who cannot have children and a woman who agrees to bear a child for the couple legal? The New Jersey Supreme Court, in the so-called Baby M case, ruled that such contracts are illegal and therefore invalid. "While we recognize the depth of yearning of infertile couples to have their own children," wrote Chief Justice Robert Wilentz, "we find the payment of money to a 'surrogate' mother illegal, perhaps criminal, and potentially degrading to women." However, as the next case demonstrates, other states, like California, have enforced **surrogacy** contracts.

surrogacy: An activity in which a woman agrees to give birth to a baby of a mother unable to carry the child.

ANNA JOHNSON V. MARK CALVERT

5 Cal. 4th 84, 851 P.2d 776, 19 Cal. Rptr. 2d 494 (1993)

FACTS

Mark and Crispina Calvert, a married couple, wanted children but were unable to reproduce because Crispina had undergone a hysterectomy. Since Crispina's ovaries were capable of producing eggs, the Calverts were interested in surrogacy. Anna Johnson heard about the Calvert's surrogacy interest and entered into a surrogacy contract with them. The contract provided the following: an embryo created by Mark's sperm and Crispina's egg would be implanted in Anna; the child would be Mark and Crispina's; Anna would relinquish all parental rights; Anna would receive $10,000 and a $200,000 life insurance policy.

The zygote was implanted and Anna was confirmed pregnant. During the pregnancy the relationship between the two parties deteriorated. A month before the baby was born, the Calverts filed a lawsuit seeking a declaratory judgment that the unborn child was legally theirs. Anna filed a lawsuit seeking to be declared the mother. The baby was born and was genetically determined to be the biological child of Mark and Crispina. The trial court found the surrogacy contract valid and terminated Anna's parental rights. The California Appeals Court affirmed.

DECISION

Judge Panelli wrote the opinion of the court. Anna Johnson urged the California Supreme Court to disregard the written contract on the grounds that it violated the following social policies: constituted a prebirth waiver of parental rights which violated the state's adoption laws; violated prohibitions on involuntary servitude contracts; and exploited and dehumanized women. The Supreme Court of California determined that the surrogacy contract did not violate the adoption statutes since the contract was entered into before the child was conceived and any payments made to Anna were for her services during gestation and labor and not because she was giving up her parental rights. The court also dismissed the argument concerning involuntary servitude since there was no evidence that Anna was under duress when she signed the contract. Further, the contract acknowledged Anna's right to abort the pregnancy. Finally, the court was not persuaded that the surrogacy contract demeaned or exploited women. It stated, "[a]lthough common sense suggests that women of lesser means serve as surrogate mothers more often than do wealthy women, there has been no proof that surrogacy contracts exploit them by inducing them to accept lower-paid or otherwise undesirable employment." The court also did not find that Anna had a constitutional right to continued companionship of the child nor was there any violation of due process or equal protection claims.

In its decision the court pointed out that the Calverts were not "mere genetic donors." Instead, "they intended to procreate a child genetically related to them by the only available means." They also noted that Anna was a licensed vocational nurse who had done well in school and had previously had a child. The court found that "[a] woman who enters into a gestational surrogacy arrangement is not exercising her own right to make procreative choices; she is agreeing to provide a necessary and profoundly important service without (by definition) any expectation that she will raise the resulting child as her own." With this in mind, the judgment of the trial court was affirmed.

CASE QUESTIONS

1. Are surrogacy contracts the same as any other contract? Why or why not?
2. What public policy arguments does the court use to uphold the surrogacy contract?
3. Do you agree with the court's decision? Why or why not?

unconscionable contract: A contract so unfair that no reasonable person would enter into it.

adhesion contracts: Standardized contract forms offered to consumers of goods and services on a "take-it-or-leave it" basis.

Sometimes contracts are not illegal but take unfair advantage of a person—usually a poor, disadvantaged consumer. If the contract is so one-sided that a reasonable person would not have agreed to it, a court may find that it is **unconscionable** and refuse to enforce it. Often it is consumers who do not understand the terms of the contract, and the enforcement of those contractual terms puts these consumers at a serious disadvantage. These contracts are signed by consumers and contain technical legal language. **Adhesion contracts** may fall into this category. Adhesion contracts are standardized forms that are offered on a "take-it-or-leave-it" proposition. The consumer lacks "meaningful choice." Unconscionability is rarely found in contracts between businesspeople, because the court generally assumes that businesspeople have equal bargaining power and the ability to protect themselves. An unconscionable contract is voidable.

SOCIAL/ETHICAL ISSUES

Contract law assumes that most individuals can protect themselves when it comes to entering into contracts. It assumes that most of the time everyone has equal bargaining power. Can you think of contracts that you have entered into in which you might not have had equal bargaining power? For example, think about your employment contract, your housing contract, or the warranty contract on your automobile. Did you have equal bargaining power when you entered into those contracts? Should the law continue to assume equal bargaining power?

CONTRACTS IN WRITING

Up until this point we have assumed that contracts can be either oral or in writing. As a practical matter, however, contracts should be in writing because it is more difficult to prove the terms of an oral contract.

STATUTE OF FRAUDS

Some contracts have to be in writing to be enforceable. These contracts fall under the **Statute of Frauds**. All contracts for the sale of real property, for instance, must be in writing, as well as all contracts that cannot possibly be performed within one year. Contracts by executors of estates to personally pay a decedent's debts must be in writing. A contract to guarantee another's debt must also be in writing to be enforced, as does a contract in which marriage is the consideration. Under the UCC, all contracts for the sale of goods over $500 must also be in writing. The UCC rule does exclude contracts in which the goods have been specially manufactured, there has been part performance or part delivery, or the parties admit, in court, that a contract exists.

Statute of Frauds: A state law modeled on the English Statute of Frauds dealing with the enforcement and requirements of agreements in particular circumstances.

CONTRACTS THAT NEED TO BE IN WRITING

- Sale of goods over $500
- Sale of real property
- Cannot possibly be performed in one year
- Executor agreement to personally pay the debt of the deceased
- Guarantee to pay the debt of another
- Marriage is the consideration

PAROL EVIDENCE

Parol evidence is oral testimony in court about the terms of a written contract. Parol evidence only applies to evidence of prior oral agreements, not subsequent ones. Even though most contracts do not have to be in writing to be enforced, it is, of course, very good practice to enter into written contracts. A written contract helps all parties understand exactly what is expected of each.

parol evidence: Oral testimony in court about the terms of a written contract.

integrated: The contract contains all of each party's understanding.

merger clause: A clause in a contract stating that the contract is a complete statement of the agreement and supersedes any prior terms, representations, or agreements whether made orally or in writing.

In order to be enforceable, a written contract needs to be signed by the party who is being sued. If there is a written contract, courts generally do not allow the parties to testify as to what the contract means. The assumption is that the contract contains all the parties' intentions, the contract is **integrated**, and the court can read the contract to determine what it means. This is especially true if the contract contains a **merger clause** that specifically says all previous agreements are merged into the final contract.

Sometimes a contract is said to be *partially integrated*, which means that the parties have not put all of their agreement in writing. For example, if Wayne sells his house to Wanda and includes in the contract a provision for selling his lawn mower and boat, the contract is fully integrated with regard to real and personal property that are to be sold. If Wanda then wants to testify that Wayne also agreed to sell her his lawn furniture, a court probably will not allow the testimony. On the other hand, if the contract did not say anything about the personal property, Wanda can argue that the contract is only partially integrated and that she should be allowed to testify about the sale of personal property. Note that Wanda may only argue this if the amount in question is under $500, since contracts of over $500 for the sale of goods must be in writing—and lawn furniture is a good! Also, if the terms of the contract are ambiguous or a subsequent agreement has taken place, the parties are allowed to testify.

IN CONSULTATION

Marvin Manager has a problem. He is in the process of equipping his sales force with portable phones to ease communications while they travel. He has struck a deal with Airphone Mobile Service, Inc., to provide phones and monthly service for 50 employees. Before Marvin signed the contract, he heard a news report that scientists think there is a connection between portable phones and certain brain cancers. The next day, when he reviews the written contract, he sees that it contains the following clause:

> Airphone Mobile Service, Inc., its subsidiaries, assigns, and heirs bear no liability for any physical, emotional, or other injuries stemming from or related to the use of our portable phones.

Marvin asked his Airphone representative if he could delete the clause because of the recent publicity about possible cancer. The representative said that he did not have the authority to alter the standard terms and conditions of the contract but that Airphone would take responsibility if any of its customers became sick from its phones.

Marvin is afraid to sign the contract with the clause in place. He contacts Laura Lawyer, in-house counsel, for her advice on whether he should sign the contract. Here is their conversation:

Marvin:	Laura:
1. Can Airphone negate all of its liability for injuries from its phone by simply inserting a disclaimer in the contract?	1. The answer is usually yes as long as the clause is clear and the parties bargained competently and in good faith.
2. Aren't we protected by the representative's statements that Airphone will take responsibility?	2. Not necessarily. The timing of his statements is troubling since the conversation occurred prior to any signature of the written contract.

3. Didn't the representative make an oral contract with me when he promised that his company would take responsibility?

3. Promises alone are not contracts. Whether they are written or oral is not the fundamental issue. Instead we must determine whether his oral statements comport with the written agreement. **Let me review the applicable law to see whether you should sign the contract, and I will get back to you.**

FROM THE DESK OF

Laura Lawyer

To: Marvin Manager

Re: Oral Statements Regarding Written Contracts

Dear Marvin:

Your scenario raises questions about statements by agents, oral promises made about written agreements, and oral contracts. In general, statements by an agent will bind the company that he or she represents as long as the agent is acting within the company's authority. Your negotiations with the Airphone representative, however, may be an exception to the rule. Your conversation occurred with specific regard to a written contract. The representative made oral statements that contradict the clear written language prior to either party signing the contract. In order to enforce his statements, you would need to introduce them in court—but a judge is highly unlikely to let you do that. The Parol Evidence Rule says that oral testimony that contradicts the terms of a written agreement is inadmissible. The court must assume that all oral negotiations leading up to a written contract are incorporated into that contract and that the contract contains all of the parties' intentions and agreements. Because the representative's oral promises occurred before you signed the final written contract, they would likely be inadmissible and, therefore, unenforceable. You would be held to the disclaimer that currently exists in the contract, which, as we discussed, is legal so long as it was bargained for competently and in good faith.

If the representative made his promise to take responsibility for any injuries subsequent to the signing of the written agreement, the promise may be a separate oral contract and enforceable on its own terms. His promise, however, is only a contract if it is accompanied by an offer, acceptance, and consideration. If Airphone does not receive something of value in exchange for dropping its disclaimer, the representative's promise may not be enforceable. I would, therefore, recommend that you investigate further the likelihood of illness from using these phones before signing the contract or go higher within Airphone's hierarchy to see if you can change the clause to reflect your concerns prior to signing the agreement. If the representative was telling the truth, Airphone should be willing to back him up with a contract that reflects its position and intent.

With regard to Marvin situation, we should consider the following questions:

1. Why do you think courts prevent parol evidence to contradict written agreements?
2. What could Marvin do to protect his employees while maintaining the relationship he has established with Airphone?
3. Discuss why an oral contract, even if prepared after the written agreement, may not be Marvin's best option if he seeks to hold Airphone responsible if his employees get sick.

INTERPRETING THE CONTRACT

If there is a written contract, the court first looks at the express meaning of the words. If the express meaning does not help in deciding what the contract means, the court next looks at the parties' course of performance (how they dealt with each other on this particular contract). If the court still cannot tell what the contract means, it then looks to course of dealing (how the parties acted on previous contracts). If the court is still undecided, it looks at usage of trade or trade practice (how others in the industry act). If the contract is too ambiguous, the court ultimately may decide that there was no meeting of the minds and, therefore, that the contract does not exist.

FROM THE DESK OF
Laura Lawyer

To: Students

From: Laura Lawyer

If you are responsible for drafting a contract, you need to be aware that a court resolves all disputes about what the contract means against the person who drafted it. Consequently, if a term is ambiguous, a court will decide what the term means by giving the advantageous meaning to the person who did not draft the contract.

third-party beneficiary: A person or entity that is not a party to but has rights under a contract made by two other parties.

incidental beneficiary: A third-party beneficiary to a contract whom the parties to the contract did not intend to benefit.

THIRD-PARTY BENEFICIARY AND ASSIGNMENT CONTRACTS

Once a contract has been formed, the contract is enforceable against either party to the contract. Usually someone who is not a party to the contract cannot sue for its enforcement. However, exceptions do exist for **third-party beneficiary** and *assignment* contracts. In a third-party beneficiary contract, another person (the third party) benefits from the contract. This third party may either be an *intended beneficiary* or an **incidental beneficiary**.

Intended beneficiaries are named in the contract itself. They may be **donee beneficiaries**, which means they received the benefits as a gift. An example is a beneficiary of a life insurance policy. When the policy holder dies, the beneficiary can sue to enforce the policy. Intended beneficiaries may also be **creditor beneficiaries**. A creditor beneficiary is someone who is owed benefits from another contract. For example, suppose Beth owes Al $200. Beth contracts to sell Cass $200 worth of beans, and Cass agrees in the contract to pay the $200 to Al. Al is a creditor beneficiary under the contract and can sue to enforce it.

donee beneficiary: A direct beneficiary whom the party paying for the other party's performance intends to benefit as a gift or donation.

creditor beneficiary: A direct beneficiary whom the party paying for the other party's performance intends to benefit as payment for a debt or obligation.

An incidental beneficiary benefits from a contract (although not named in it) but cannot sue to enforce it. For example, Ellen agrees to pay Dave $5,000 for accounting services. Dave performs the services, but Ellen only pays $1,000. Frank, Dave's 20-year-old son, was planning to receive the $5,000 from his dad to pay for tuition. Although Frank suffers from Ellen's failure to satisfy the contract, Frank is an incidental beneficiary and cannot sue. Only Dave can sue to enforce the contract.

Third parties are also involved when a contract is **assigned**. Contracts have both *rights* and *duties*. A party to a contract may have the right to receive money or the right to receive performance under the contract. Moreover, these rights and duties can be assigned to third parties. For example, Grant has a contract with Harry in which Harry agrees to pay Grant $300 and, in return, Grant agrees to provide Harry with a purebred English springer spaniel. Grant sells his right to receive Harry's $300 to Ingrid for $250. Once Harry receives notice that the contract has been assigned, Harry must pay Ingrid and not Grant. If Harry does not pay Ingrid, Ingrid can sue to enforce the contract. Generally, *rights* can be assigned unless assignment is expressly prohibited in the contract. The right to receive money can always be assigned. Under the UCC, the right to assign damages for breach of contract also can be assigned. A contract cannot prohibit assigning these rights.

assignment: A present transfer of property or rights.

Contractual *duties* may be delegated. If the duty is ministerial (something anyone can do), then the duties are freely delegable. If, however, the duties are unique to that particular person, then they cannot be delegated. For example, Jerry hires Kate to paint his portrait. Kate gets too busy and wants to delegate that duty to her assistant Lee. Since an artist's talents are uniquely personal, Jerry would not have to accept the delegation.

PERFORMANCE, DISCHARGE, AND BREACH

After a contract is formed, it is important that it be performed. Both parties, of course, anticipate that each will fully perform the contract. Otherwise, they would never have entered into the contract in the first place. When a contract is fully performed, each party is **discharged**, which means they have no more obligations under the contract. Discharge can also occur when (1) the contract has a condition that has not been met, (2) the parties agree to discharge, (3) the law allows for a discharge, or (4) one party breaches the contract.

discharge: To release from an obligation.

All contracts are conditional by nature. For example, Harry agrees to buy Paula's car for $5,000, and Paula agrees to sell her car for $5,000. Harry need not pay the $5,000 until he receives the car, and Paula need not give Harry the car until she receives the $5,000. This is referred to as *simultaneous conditions*. As a practical matter, one party will perform before the other, but the conditions

condition precedent: A condition that must be fulfilled before performance under a contract can become due, an estate can vest, or a right can become effective.

condition subsequent: A condition whose fulfillment defeats or modifies an estate or right already in effect or vested or discharges an already existing duty under a contract.

are still considered simultaneous. Another type of condition is a **condition precedent**. This is a condition that has to occur before any party has performance obligations. For example, Harry agrees to buy Paula's car for $5,000 if the interest rate on automobile loans drops to 6 percent in the next month. If automobile loan interest rates do not drop to 6 percent within the month, neither Harry nor Paula is required to perform the contract. The last type of condition is referred to as a **condition subsequent**. This is a rare condition that is imposed after a *breach* (default) has occurred. For example, it is not unusual for insurance companies to require that they be notified of impending lawsuits within one year of when the accident occurred. This is a condition subsequent in that it is a condition that has to be complied with after the insurance company has failed to pay the amount the policy holder believed was due.

Furthermore, the parties can mutually agree to discharge obligations under a contract. A material change in a contract can discharge the nonagreeing party. Bankruptcy (Chapter 17) and the running of the statute of limitations will also discharge the performance obligations. *Impossibility* and *commercial impracticability* may discharge a party. Impossibility occurs when the subject matter of the contract is destroyed and the contract cannot be performed. For example, Bryan contracts to buy Barbara's house for $100,000. The very next day, Barbara's house burns to the ground. The contract is now impossible to perform, since the subject matter has been destroyed (through no fault of either of the parties). Neither party has to perform under the contract. Other incidents that create impossibility include death of one of the parties in a personal service contract and a change in the law that makes performance illegal.

Sometimes courts release individuals from their performance obligations if performance is commercially impracticable or if the *purpose of the contract is frustrated*. Commercial impracticability refers to situations in which, although possible to perform, such performance will be extremely costly. For example, AJ Airways agrees to a contract with JB Petroleum whereby AJ Airways will buy gasoline from JB Petroleum at $1 a gallon for the next year. Within three months of signing the contract, war breaks out in the Middle East, raising gas prices to over $4 a gallon. In this case, since the war was *unforeseeable* and the price per gallon rose *exceedingly high*, some courts would invoke the doctrine of commercial impracticability and release JB Petroleum from its performance obligations. Frustration of purpose occurs when the parties intended one event when the contract was signed and the event did not occur. If the purpose of the contract is frustrated, the parties may not need to perform. Courts are skeptical, however, about invoking either frustration of purpose or commercial impracticability. Therefore, it is only the most extreme circumstances that generally qualify for discharges under these legal doctrines.

SOCIAL/ETHICAL ISSUES

One of the international complaints about U.S. business practices is that contracts are viewed too formally. U.S. businesspeople expect that others will perform a contract even when conditions have changed. Should contracts be more flexible and not so formalistic? Should they be viewed as absolute agreements to perform or should the underlying value of the relationship be more important?

As was stated earlier, each party to the contract can expect full performance from the other party. If full performance does not occur, then the breaching or defaulting party can be sued for damages. The time for performance is generally considered to be a reasonable time. If the parties to a contract want performance to occur at a specific time, they need to include the words "time is of the essence" to ensure that the contract will be performed on a specific day; otherwise, reasonableness is the standard.

Generally, a party is not in breach until performance is due. For example, Sam agrees to deliver a refrigerator to Martha on December 1. Technically, Sam has until December 1 to deliver the goods. If Martha calls Sam on November 15 to make sure that he will be able to deliver the refrigerator and Sam tells Martha that he has sold all of his refrigerators and will not be able to deliver Martha's, Sam has created an immediate breach, referred to as an **anticipatory breach**. If Sam only expressed doubt that he would be able to perform, then under the UCC Martha can demand *adequate assurances* from Sam that he will be able to perform. This is a *written* statement that Sam will be able to deliver the refrigerator on December 1. If Martha does not receive adequate assurances, she can wait until December 1, she can retract her own performance, or she can *cover*, which means she can try to get another person to provide her with a refrigerator. Regardless, Martha is still entitled to damages.

anticipatory breach: The repudiation by a promisor of the contract prior to the time that the performance is required when such repudiation is accepted by the promisee as a breach of the contract.

Under the common law, whether the nonbreaching party has to perform on the contract depends on whether there was *substantial performance*, *partial performance*, or *nonperformance*. Of course, if there is complete performance, then the other party is required to completely perform. Suppose Simpson hires Chancy to build him a house, and as part of the contract, Chancy is to paint Simpson's door brown. Instead of painting the door brown, Simpson paints it white. Clearly the main purpose of the contract has been performed, but it has not been performed completely; therefore, Chancy is in breach. Under this circumstance, the contract has been substantially performed, and Simpson must pay Chancy the agreed-upon price. Simpson is entitled to damages from Chancy, which is the price of having the door repainted. But if Simpson has hired Chancy only to paint the door brown and Chancy painted the door white, Chancy would have only partially performed the contract. The main purpose of the contract is to paint the door brown. Since this purpose was not performed, Simpson is relieved of his performance obligation *under the contract*. This is not the end of the story, however, since Simpson does have a newly painted door. The court will apply the equitable doctrine of ***quantum meruit***. Simpson will not have to pay the contract price, but he will have to pay the reasonable value of Chancy's services minus the damages that he will incur having the door repainted.

quantum meruit: "As much as he deserved."

REMEDIES

When there is not complete performance, the nonbreaching party is entitled to a legal remedy. What that remedy may be depends on the type of contract at issue and what remedy the nonbreaching party wishes to elect. While the nonbreaching party may be able to mix and match forms of relief, there can be only one recovery and the nonbreaching party will be required to elect one of the following remedies.

DAMAGES

Damages are the difference between the contract as promised and the contract as performed. To ask for damages is to ask for a *legal* remedy. For example, Gary promises Dave that he will deliver 500 dogs on March 1, and that time is of the essence. Dave agrees to pay $10 per dog. They also agree that in the event that either party defaults (breaches) the contract, the damage amount will be $50,000. Unknown to Gary, Dave plans to use the dogs in a dog commercial. On March 1, Gary only delivers 250 dogs. Dave calls another supplier, who ships him 250 dogs at a price of $20 per dog. The film crew has to be paid $1,000 for the lost day of filming. The phone calls and shipping prices amount to $200.

incidental damages: Damages recoverable under section 2-715 of the Uniform Commercial Code in breach of contract cases for losses that include expenses incurred in handling and caring for goods which were the subject of the contract, reasonable expenses incurred in obtaining cover, and any other reasonable expenses resulting from the breach that do not fall into any other category.

Gary owes Dave $2,500 for the dogs that were delivered by the other supplier. This is the price difference that Dave was forced to pay at the last minute. Gary was required to try to reduce Dave's liability under a doctrine of *mitigation of damages*. Mitigation requires that the nonbreaching party try to prevent the breaching party's loss. A person does not have to be successful at mitigating the loss; he or she just has to try. All costs incurred as a result of mitigation are recoverable as **incidental damages**. Dave incurred $200 worth of incidental damages, and Gary must pay this amount.

compensatory damages: Actual damages.

Compensatory damages (damages that compensate or make the nonbreaching person whole) are also recoverable and can be calculated in two ways. The first is to figure the difference between what was promised and what was received. For example, Sue agrees with Sally to buy a 1964 Corvair, and Sally delivers a 1968 Corvair. Sue's damage is the difference in price between a 1964 and a 1968 Corvair. In the contract between Gary and Dave, however, Dave had to pay $5,000 in order to receive the additional dogs. Since he owes Gary $2,500 and his total contract price with Gary was $5,000, Dave is entitled to $2,500 in compensatory damages.

consequential or special damages: Damages awarded in an amount deemed to compensate for losses that arise not as a natural result of an injury but because of some particular circumstance of the injured party.

Dave also had to pay the film company $1,000 for the lost day of filming. These are damages that are suffered as a *consequence* of the breach. **Consequential** or **special damages** are only recoverable if they were *foreseeable* to the breaching party. In the previous case, Gary had no idea that the dogs were being used in a dog commercial, so he is not liable for the lost day of filming. If instead of using the dogs in a dog commercial, what if Dave had planned on reselling the dogs for $15 a dog? Dave still could not recover. *Lost profits* are not recoverable because they, too, are considered consequential damages. An exception exists for *volume sellers* (those in the business of reselling goods). If Dave owned a pet shop, he would be a volume seller and could recover his lost profits.

liquidated damages: Damages whose amount is agreed upon by the parties to a contract as adequately compensating for loss in the event of a breach.

The contract between Dave and Gary also had a clause stating that, in the event of a breach, the breaching party would pay the nonbreaching party $50,000. This is called a **liquidated damage clause**. Such a clause agrees to a damage amount before the breach has occurred. A court will not enforce a liquidated damage clause if the amount penalizes rather than compensates the person for breaching the contract. In this case, $50,000 is far in excess of the actual damage suffered and, therefore, is nonenforceable. Courts will enforce liquidate damage clauses if the damages are speculative and hard to calculate after the breach. Failure to complete a construction contract is one such contract. Also, if the amount is close to the actual damage suffered, the clause will be enforced.

Generally, punitive damages are not allowed in breach of contract cases. The following article indicates, however, that breaching contracts with several customers can result in extensive damages, including punitive damages.

Illinois Court Slams Insurer: $600M in Punitive Damages

In a major blow to the nation's largest insurer, an Illinois Circuit Court judge has ruled that State Farm Mutual Automobile Insurance Co. pay $600 million in punitive damages for defrauding millions of policyholders by violating contract terms and using imitation parts to repair their customers' vehicles.

In a ruling issued Friday afternoon, Williamson County Judge John Speroni also ordered the company to pay $130 million in compensatory damages for statutory fraud. It came only four days after a jury ordered State Farm to pay $456 million for breach of contract in the largest jury verdict in a class action on record.

"This is a judgment on the deception of State Farm," said Elizabeth Cabraser, a partner with San Francisco's Lieff, Cabraser, Heimann & Bernstein, who helped certify the suit as a class action and who offered the plaintiffs' 40-minute closing argument about how State Farm violated the Illinois Consumer Fraud and Deceptive Business Practices Act. "The punitive and compensatory damages ought to be enough to get State Farm's attention," she said. "And I think it's a wake-up call to other insurance companies utilizing the same practice."

Cabraser and Lieff, Cabraser partner Morris Ratner were part of a plaintiffs' team assembled from at least four firms around the country to represent more than 4.5 million class members. The firm, which specializes in mounting class actions, was integral in certifying the suit as a class action and arguing to keep it that way when State Farm attorneys brought an emergency writ in the Illinois Supreme Court.

"I'm sure much of my work is still to be done if they in fact choose to appeal," Cabraser said.

In fact, State Farm attorneys are preparing to wage battle in the state's appellate court. Corporate spokesman Phil Supple said in an interview that the entire company was stunned. "Yes, we are going to appeal on the grounds that this constitutes outrageous punitive damages," he said. "We reject the notion that we in any way defrauded our customers. We feel the verdict ignores the evidence presented at the trial and ignores the fact that we comply with the laws and insurance regulations in every state."

The class includes vehicle casualty insurance policyholders, except in Arkansas and Tennessee, who between July 28, 1994, and Feb. 23, 1998, filed a claim for repairs for which State Farm did not use factory-authorized or original equipment manufacturer, or OEM, parts. In California, the class only applies to those who signed up for a policy after Sept. 26, 1996,.

Plaintiffs' attorneys argued that State Farm promised policyholders that the company would repair its vehicles to their original "pre-loss condition" after an accident.

However, the attorneys showed during the eight-week trial that the company consistently breached its contract by not using OEM or factory-authorized parts. Evidence presented during the trial suggested the generic parts consistently ordered by State Farm were of lesser quality.

Boalt Hall School of Law professor Stephen Sugarman, who specializes in automobile insurance and litigation, noted that the judge's ruling on punitive damages is not very large compared to the jury verdict for compensatory damages. He noted it only amounts to roughly 150 percent of what the jury awarded.

"That certainly is not a typical strategy for calculating punitive damages," he said, citing recent class actions in which the punitive damages were considerably higher. Sugarman said it remains to be seen how the ruling will affect other insurers. He noted that generic parts are not necessarily substandard, although evidence apparently was presented in the State Farm case to suggest that the company was using parts of lesser quality.

"I hope [the ruling] doesn't scare off companies from using equitable generic parts, but it will be good if it scares off companies who insist on using shoddy parts," he said.

This article, "Illinois Court Slams Insurer: $600M in Punitive Damages" by Sonia Giordani, is reprinted with permission from the October 11, 1999 edition of *The Recorder*. © 1999 NLP IP Company.

SPECIFIC PERFORMANCE

specific performance: A court order which requires a seller to perform a contract as agreed.

Specific performance is only available for certain types of contracts. In **specific performance** the nonbreaching party asks that the breaching party be required to perform the contract. Specific performance is an *equitable remedy* and is available when damages will not make the nonbreaching person whole. For example, specific performance is available for nonperformance on a contract for the sale of real property. Since real property is *unique*, courts will force a person to sell the property if there is a valid contract. The same is true for contracts to sell *unique* personal property, like the original Mona Lisa. Once again, that exact property cannot be found anywhere else. On the other hand, although a personal service contract is unique, specific performance is not allowed because the 13th Amendment to the U.S. Constitution prohibits involuntary servitude or slavery. For example, Chris, a basketball player, has a seven-year contract to play basketball. After five years, Chris decides he wants to make more money. Chris tells his coach that he will not play unless his contract is renegotiated. However, the coach informs Chris that the team will not renegotiate the contract. The team cannot force Chris to play basketball; however, his seven-year contract probably contained a *negative covenant*, a clause prohibiting Chris from playing basketball for another team. Negative covenants are usually enforced.

FROM THE DESK OF
Laura Lawyer

To: Students
From: Your Lawyer

Obtaining a court order that says you are entitled to receive damages and actually collecting those damages are two very different procedures. Actually collecting damages depends on the opposing party's ability to pay, and the expense of pursuing a collection can be prohibitive. Keep this in mind when you need to sue another party for damages.

RESCISSION

Once in a while, nonbreaching parties want to be put back into the position they were in before the contract was formed. For example, Dane contracted to sell her barren property to Zoe for $50,000. Zoe paid $25,000 but failed to pay the remaining amount. Meanwhile, oil is discovered on Dane's property. Dane does not want damages; rather, Dane wants **rescission** and *restitution*. Restitution means that you give up what you received under the contract. Dane gives Zoe $25,000 back, and Zoe relinquishes the property.

rescind: To take back and make void.

SUMMARY

Because almost all aspects of a business involve contracts, they are very important for businesspeople. Forming a contract requires an offer, acceptance, consideration, legality, free will, and capacity. While contracts should be in writing, most contracts can be oral. The UCC applies to contracts for the sale of goods. Under the UCC, some rules differ from the common law rules of contracts. These differences include the statute of frauds and rules governing when consideration is necessary. If a contract is breached, the nonbreaching party is entitled to damages. Since the damages can be extensive, it is important for individuals to understand what contracts require before they are negotiated.

CHAPTER QUESTIONS

1. DBI, a manufacturer of metal and steel processing equipment, contracted with Wysong for the purchase of two mechanical trimming shears. In September, DBI contacted Wysong concerning the shears. Wysong's sales manager sent DBI's sales manager a price quote and a list of specifications. This quotation was silent on knife length and minimum knife opening. DBI's manager of purchasing faxed back a list of design specifications and asked Wysong to quote a price "most similar to accompanying specifications." DBI's list included the length and minimum knife opening specifications. In response, Wysong faxed to DBI a statement that it could not produce a shear with "kick-out rolls," but the fax was silent as to the other features. Two more faxes concerning the price of the knives changed hands. The price was ultimately agreed upon. On December 9, 1996, in response to Wysong's counterproposal price, Harris sent DBI's purchase order to Wysong for two Wysong Mechanical Trim Shears, price $119,680. The purchase order contained a merger clause. When the shears arrived, DBI discovered the shears were too narrow for the intended purpose and demanded that Wysong ship conforming goods or return the purchase price. Is there a contract? [See *Elta Brands, Inc., v. Wysong & Miles*, 1998 U.S. Dist. LEXIS 14768.]
2. In 1993, the Bernickers approached Mr. Byrne about buying his Chrysler Plymouth dealership. The Bernickers entered into the agreement to buy Byrne's dealership under the impression that in addition to the Chrysler Plymouth dealership that the Bernickers would also be entitled to open a Jeep Eagle dealership. In Pennsylvania, existing franchises within five

miles of a proposed dealership have the right to protest the opening of another franchise. Mr. Byrne assured the Bernickers that he had taken care of the protest and the sale was completed. In 1994 and 1995, the Bernickers were told by the Chrysler Corporation that there was a moratorium on new dealerships in their area. An investigation revealed that Byrne had never cleared the protest. The Bernickers sued Byrne. Are the Bernickers entitled to damages? [See *The Legal Intelligencer* (April 29, 1999), p. 3.]

3. United Airlines contacted Saucy Sisters and invited the company to bid on United's in-flight catering contract. After a series of negotiations United offered Saucy Sisters a three-year catering contract. In order to meet the contract demands, Saucy Sisters spent nearly $1 million to expand its operation. After approximately one year, United Airlines exercised a clause in the contract that gave either party a right to terminate the agreement, at will, with 90 days written notice. After 90 days the agreement was terminated. Saucy Sisters sued United Airlines for wrongful termination of the catering agreement, fraud, and breach of the covenant of good faith and fair dealing What result? [See *United Airlines v. Good Tastes, Inc., d/b/a Saucy Sisters Catering*, 1999 Alas. LEXIS 86.]

4. In 1984, Hileman and Johnsonbaugh entered into an oral agreement with their mother and stepfather, Mr. and Mrs. Eugene P. Kensinger, who were both failing in health. The agreement provided that Johnsonbaugh and Hileman would "provide for" and "take care of" Mr. and Mrs. Kensinger for the rest of their lives. They also agreed that they would not put Mrs. Kensinger in a nursing home. In return, Mr. and Mrs. Kensinger deeded their $70,000 house and lot to Johnsonbaugh and Hileman. Hileman lived in California and Johnsonbaugh lived in Pennsylvania. Johnsonbaugh's son and daughter-in-law entered into an agreement with Hileman where they agreed to move into the house and take care of the Kensingers in exchange for some personal property. Subsequently, the Kensingers died. Mr. Kensinger's sisters were named executrices of his estate and sued Hileman and Johnsonbaugh, claiming the agreement was invalid because of the confidential relationship and in the alternative that the oral agreement was not performed since Hileman and Johnsonbaugh did not personally take care of the Kensingers but rather hired someone else to do it. Do the sisters have a cause of action? [See *Biddle and McConahy v. Johnsonbaugh and Hileman*, 444 Pa. Super. 450; 664 A.2d 159 (1995).]

5. DeNardo opened a long distance telephone calling account with GCI Communication in 1984. DeNardo used the account for several years and then did not use it for over 18 months. After the 18-month inactive period, GCI place the account on inactive status. When DeNardo was unsuccessful in using the card he called a customer service representative, who asked for DeNardo's social security number. DeNardo refused to give his social security number but did give an Employee Identification Number (EIN). Thinking it was a social security number, the GCI representative tried to use it to reopen the account but since it was not the social security number the account remained closed. Two weeks later, DeNardo was contacted and told that he would have to fill out a new application. He refused. During

this time period, GCI ran a promotional where customers were eligible to win prizes and a $1,000,000 grand prize. DeNardo sued GCI for $1,020,000 because he did not have access to GCI's services at the time of the contest. Is GCI liable for damages? [See *Daniel Denardo v. GCI Communication*, 1999 Alas. LEXIS 1111.]

6. Golden Turtle, who had an exclusive licensing agreement with Lucas-Films, offered to sell Dataworks 150,000 "lower-quality" Star Wars calendars. In response, Dataworks submitted a purchase order to Golden Turtle for the purchase of 150,000 Star Wars calendars. Inserted into the purchase order was a 5 percent coop price discount. Golden Turtle argued that the discussions between the parties entailed an understanding that the calendars would not be distributed in areas where the higher quality calendars were already being sold, that is, Wal-Mart and K-Mart. When Golden Turtle discovered that Dataworks was attempting to contract with Wal-Mart to buy the lower quality calendars, Golden Turtle refused to manufacture and deliver the calendars. Dataworks sued for seizure and specific performance under the UCC. What result? [See *Dataworks v. Golden Turtle Press, Inc.*, QDS:22701300, *New York Law Journal* (July 12, 1999), p. 25.]
7. Garner, a general contractor, submitted a bid to the Carrolltown Housing Authority to renovate an apartment complex. It relied on a Georgia Palms written offer to sell its window model S-1100 for the price of $40,027, plus tax. This written offer was open to Garner for 30 days. The model S-1100 window in Georgia Palm's offer was identical to the model S-1100 window submitted to the architect for the Carrolltown Housing Authority for approval. The model did not include a tilt-down sash. After Garner received Georgia Palm's written offer, the parties agreed that, if Garner was awarded the contract, Georgia Palm would furnish and install the windows under Georgia Palm's written offer. After the renovation project was commenced, the housing authority rejected the model S-1100 window because it did not have a tilt-down sash. Georgia Palm refused to furnish a window with a tilt-down sash at the bid price. Garner purchased the window from another supplier. Does the UCC apply? Why does it matter? [See *D.N. Garner Company, Inc. v. Georgia Palm Beach Aluminum Window Corporation*, 233 Ga. App. 252, 504 S.E. 2d 70, 1998 Ga. App. LEXIS 946.]
8. Lee Calan Imports advertised a 1964 Volvo Station Wagon for $1,095. The price was supposed to be $1,795. Christopher O'Brien visited Lee Calan Imports, examined the automobile and indicated that he wished to buy the automobile for $1,095. One of the salespersons initially said that the car would be sold for the lower price. After further consideration, however, the salesperson would not sell the car for $1,095. Is the newspaper advertisement an offer that Mr. O'Brien accepted? [See *O'Keefe v. Lee Calan Imports*, 128 Ill. App.2d 410, 262 N.E.2d 758 (1970).]
9. Debra Hughes, 16 years of age and unmarried, went to Madison General Hospital with her mother. She was 34 weeks pregnant and was in severe labor. She was very ill when she entered the hospital and her mother signed a treatment authorization form. Debra delivered the baby by caesarean section and was released several days later. The hospital attempted to collect from Medicaid but it would only pay for the costs associated with caring for the baby. The hospital then sued Debra. Is Debra liable for the

medical bills? [See *Madison General Hospital v. Haack*, 124 Wis.2d 398, 369 N.W.2d 663 (1985).]

10. Mr. and Mrs. Gross entered into an agreement before they were married (antenuptial agreement) providing that in the event of a divorce the plaintiff would receive $200 a month for ten years. After 14 years of marriage, Mrs. Gross filed for divorce. At the time of the divorce, Mr. Gross' annual income was $250,000 and his net equity was $6,000,000. Is Mrs. Gross bound to the agreement? [See *Gross v. Gross*, 11 Ohio St.3d, 464 N.E.2d 500 (1984).]
11. The law allows people to break their promises if they are willing to financially reimburse those whom they have harmed. Should all promises be performed? Is it ethical to break a promise?
12. The law assumes that people entering into contracts are rational, "equal," and able to protect themselves. This approach has been criticized because it does not take into account human attributes of caring, concern, and trust or that decisions may be made among unequals in intimate relationships and are unchosen. Discuss your opinion on this issue.

PRACTICAL EXERCISE

You have always wanted to own your own business. When surfing the Internet for business opportunities you have discovered that the Castle Health Spa, in your area, is for sale. You e-mail the owner, who tells you that Castle is in its third year of a five-year lease. The spa owns, free and clear, all the exercise equipment. There are currently five employees, two clerks and three instructors. The selling price is $150,000. You have decided to draft your own contract before running it through your attorney.

1. Before buying this business, what other facts do you need to know?
2. Draft a sales contract that includes all the appropriate clauses.
3. What do you need to consider before pursuing a business opportunity found on the Internet?

FURTHER INFORMATION

www.law.cornell.edu/ucc/ucc.table.html
cisgw3.law.pace.edu/
www.cclaw.net/
www.jus.uio.no/lm/eu.contract.principles.part1.1995/index.html

CHAPTER 13

WARRANTY AND LIABILITY ISSUES IN THE SALE OF PRODUCTS

LEARNING OBJECTIVES

After reading this chapter, you should be able to:

1. Describe the different kinds of warranties and distinguish between express and implied warranties.
2. List the provisions of the Magnuson-Moss Warranty Act.
3. Discuss negligence and strict product liability as they apply to the sale of products.
4. Detail the rights and remedies of buyers and sellers.

CHAPTER OUTLINE

I. Warranties
II. Negligence
III. Strict Product Liability
IV. Other Legal Issues in the Sale of Goods

Your friend Larry has purchased several expensive works of art from a gallery after being assured that they were "original lithographs" done by Salvador Dali. Now Larry suspects that the works may not be genuine. The Practical Exercise asks you to consider whether Larry has any legal rights based on express or implied warranties.

INTRODUCTION

In Chapters 11 and 12, we discussed the basic principles of tort and contract law. When two parties voluntarily agree that one will perform some action in return for a promise or payment or performance by the other, a contract may be formed. Also, when one person or business takes some action negligently or intentionally that injures another person, this is likely to be considered a tort. In this chapter we examine how each of these theories has developed with respect to a very common situation—the sale of products.

Remember that sales transactions are governed by Article 2 of the Uniform Commercial Code (UCC), a model law that has been adopted in 49 states. Most of the common law principles of contract law examined in Chapter 12 have been adopted by the UCC and therefore apply to the sale of goods. In this chapter we discuss **warranties**—a subject that originates in contract law but is not part of common law.

warranty: A promise that the goods are of the quality indicated.

WARRANTIES

Most of us are familiar with the word *warranty*. We have all purchased consumer products that include a card or piece of paper with a pretty border around it, titled "Warranty." This warranty usually contains certain statements about the goods and may include promises to repair or replace the item if it does not function properly. Later, we will examine an example of a typical warranty.

Warranties are essentially "promises" regarding the goods sold and create something like a contract. However, warranty issues often involve elements of both contract and tort law. A warranty may be expressly given by the seller or manufacturer of a product, or it may arise automatically because of the type of transaction that has taken place. In contrast to traditional contract principles, in which only the two parties to the contract are bound, the warranty given to the buyer by the seller may (and usually does) extend back to the manufacturer and forward not only to the buyer but also to other members of his or her family and perhaps to subsequent purchasers.

"We had a great Christmas—I just mailed 43 warranty cards."

From *The Wall Street Journal*, February 14, 1995. Reprinted with permission of Cartoon Features Syndicate.

EXPRESS WARRANTIES

Like an express agency, an **express warranty** is one that is clearly stated. Generally, it is written, but it is also possible to create an express warranty in other ways. Section 2-313 of the UCC provides that an express warranty may be created by a seller in three ways: (1) through "an affirmation of fact or a promise" relating to the goods, (2) by a "description of the goods," or (3) by the use of a "sample or model" in connection with the sale of the goods.

express warranty: A warranty that is expressed in written or verbal form, or by use of a sample or model.

Therefore, if the seller provides a written warranty that states, "This product is 100 percent cotton" (affirmation of fact) or "The manufacturer will replace this item if it becomes defective within 90 days" (promise), these are certainly express warranties. But an express warranty is also created if the shoe salesperson demonstrates a pair of cross-training shoes to the buyer and indicates that a different pair of shoes that the buyer is purchasing is "just like these," or a verbal statement is made by the sales clerk that "these shoes will not ever rip or tear."

As explained in our earlier discussion of fraud and misrepresentation, it is important to distinguish between affirmations of fact and **puffing** (mild bragging) or opinion. When the seller states that a wooden table is "made of oak," that statement is an affirmation of fact. This statement is either true or false and will create an express warranty if the sale is completed. But the statement "this is the strongest table you can buy" is likely to be held as puffing and will not create an express warranty that this is in fact the strongest table for sale anywhere. Similarly, the seller's remark "this table is an excellent value at $400" would probably be held as mere opinion, rather than as an express warranty.

puffing: Mild bragging about an item, not specific enough to create a warranty.

An additional requirement for creating an express warranty is that the statement, promise, description, or use of sample must become part of the *basis of the bargain*. In other words, the affirmation, promise, description, or use of model must be important (the UCC uses the word "material") to the buyer—it must be a significant factor in the decision to purchase the item. A statement made in a brochure, advertisement, or the contract itself, or by the sales clerk at the time of sale, may become part of the basis of the bargain, if it is important and relied on by the buyer.

IMPLIED WARRANTIES

When a consumer purchases a new television set from an appliance store, he or she makes certain assumptions about the product regardless of whether the item carries any express warranties. If the television set develops a serious defect within the first few weeks of use, most of us would agree "there ought to be a law" allowing the consumer to take the set back for repairs or replacement. Fortunately for consumers, *there is such a law*. The UCC establishes two types of *implied warranties* that apply to sales of goods in certain situations and give purchasers important rights. The two warranties are the "implied warranty of merchantability" and the "implied warranty of fitness for a particular purpose."

merchantability: The implied warranty given to a purchaser by a merchant—that the item is fit for its ordinary use.

Implied Warranty of Merchantability

The implied warranty of **merchantability**, described in UCC §2-314, provides that if the goods are purchased from a merchant (one who normally sells goods of this type), the goods must (1) be fit for the ordinary purposes for which such goods are used, (2) be adequately contained and packaged, (3) be of "fair average quality," and (4) pass without objection in the trade. There are other factors listed in §2-314 as well, but the thrust of the warranty is that if a consumer buys an item from a manufacturer, a store, or other seller who normally sells such items, the consumer can expect the item to work properly for a reasonable time.

This warranty is "implied," since it arises automatically from the purchase and does not require any specific promises or statements by the seller. Suppose that Katy, a business student, purchases a textbook at the bookstore. When she opens it for the first time, however, the cover falls off. She purchased the book from a merchant and thus may take it back for replacement or a full refund. Clearly, if the cover falls off the first time the book is opened, the book is not "fit for ordinary purposes." If, on the other hand, Katy had purchased the book from a classmate, the implied warranty of merchantability does not apply. Why? The seller was not a merchant. Similarly, if Katy bought a hammer from a hardware store, an implied warranty of merchantability would apply. However, if she bought a used car from the owner of the hardware store (his car), such a warranty would not apply as long as the store did not sell autos.

One case decided in 1989 examined the purchase of a used automobile from a dealer. The consumer was very disappointed by certain information he learned about the car shortly after the sale.

B. J. CURRIER V. ROD SPENCER

772 S.W.2d 309 (Ark. 1989)

FACTS

B. J. Currier placed an advertisement in an Arkansas newspaper in 1986 offering to sell a "one-owner 1984 Datsun 300ZX" for $8,750. Rod Spencer saw the ad and later purchased the car for $8,250 (by giving Currier $5,000 in cash and a $3,250 check). Before his check had cleared, the car began to give Spencer problems. He took it to a repair shop, where he learned that the car had been previously wrecked and the rear one-third of the car had been replaced with the body of another Datsun 300ZX that had been welded onto the front two-thirds of the original auto. The entire car had been repainted.

Spencer stopped payment on the check and tried to return the car, but Currier refused. Spencer stored the vehicle for awhile but was later able to sell it for $6,750. Currier filed suit to recover the balance of the purchase price (the $3,250 check which had not been paid), and Spencer counterclaimed for damages due to breach of express and implied warranties, misrepresentation, and other grounds. The lower court dismissed Currier's claim and instead awarded Spencer $1,500 (the difference between what he had agreed to pay for the car and its true worth). The court then doubled the award because of Currier's misrepresentation and his violation of other laws. Currier appealed.

DECISION

The Arkansas Supreme Court discussed both express and implied warranties under the UCC. "Any affirmation of fact by the seller to the buyer which relates to the goods and becomes part of the basis of the bargain creates an express warranty." Currier had stated that the car was a one-owner 1984 Datsun. The court said, "What Spencer purchased was two-thirds of one car and one-third of another," which clearly violated the warranty given. Obviously, there had been at least two previous owners of this car as it now existed, since it was the combination of two separate cars.

Currier claimed that the implied warranty of merchantability should not apply because he was not a merchant. The Court rejected this argument, noting that since 1985 he had been licensed by the state as a car dealer and had sold 12–15 used cars in the preceding year. Finding that the auto was not "fit for the ordinary purposes for which such goods are used" and could not "pass without objection in the trade" (UCC §2-314), the Court held that the warranty of merchantability had been breached.

Since the standard measure of damages for either breach of warranty or misrepresentation is the difference in value between the product as warranted and its actual value, the Supreme Court of Arkansas affirmed the lower court's decision and award to Mr. Spencer. One justice dissented, arguing that "something is out of whack when the purchaser of a car pays $5,000 for a vehicle, sells it for $6,750 and then collects another $3,000 from the seller."

CASE QUESTIONS

1. What did the seller say (affirmation of fact) that became part of the "basis of the bargain" necessary to create an express warranty?
2. Why did the auto not meet the implied warranty of merchantability? Was the warranty breached simply because Currier did not tell the whole truth?
3. Do you think that Mr. Currier's ethics had a bearing on the court decision? Do you agree with the dissenting justice that the purchaser is getting more of a recovery than he is entitled to? If something is "out of whack" here, what is it?

The warranty of merchantability also applies to "the serving for value of food and drink," whether it is purchased at a restaurant or at a grocery store. People who have had the unpleasant experience of discovering various unexpected objects in their food or drink have brought cases against the producer, seller, or manufacturer. The traditional rule was that the warranty of merchantability was breached by "foreign" objects found in food, such as nails or glass, but not for "natural" objects, such as bones in chicken and pits in olives. Recently, a number of state courts have modified this rule and employed a "*reasonable expectation*" test that considers whether the consumer should reasonably have *expected* the item to be in the food. This test tends to place higher duties on those who sell food and results in more judgments for the consumers.

Implied Warranty of Fitness for a Particular Purpose The other important implied warranty does not require that the seller be a merchant. The implied warranty of **fitness for a particular purpose** is set forth in UCC §2-315, which reads as follows:

> Where the seller at the time of contracting has reason to know any particular purpose for which the goods are required and that the buyer is relying on the seller's skill or judgment to select or furnish suitable goods, there is unless excluded or modified . . . an implied warranty that the goods shall be fit for such purpose.

fitness for a particular purpose: The implied warranty given when the buyer needs the item for some particular (not regular) purpose and relies on the seller to furnish such an item.

This warranty, like merchantability, is *implied*—that is, it arises because of the transaction itself, without any express promise or written document from the seller. The warranty of fitness, however, only exists when the buyer has some *particular purpose* for the goods, and both parties realize that the buyer is relying on the seller's knowledge and experience to provide goods that will work satisfactorily for the exact purpose of the buyer.

For example, if Teresa goes to a furniture store and purchases a chair, she will, by implication, receive a warranty of merchantability that the chair will be suitable for ordinary purposes—that is, a normal amount of being sat upon. Suppose, however, that she actually is buying it for the waiting room of the local bus station, and it falls apart after two months due to heavy use. Since the chair was purchased from a merchant, Teresa received an implied warranty of merchantability. However, the chair was fit for ordinary purposes, so this warranty was not breached. But if Teresa had told the furniture store salesperson about her particular needs and was relying on the salesperson to sell her a heavy-duty chair that would withstand the type of use she had described, the implied warranty of fitness for particular purpose might have been breached when the chair fell apart.

WARRANTY OF TITLE

Another assumption most of us probably make when purchasing goods is that the seller has good title to the items and the right to sell them. This expectation is confirmed by another UCC provision, §2-312, which establishes an implied warranty of title. The warranty also provides that the goods are delivered free of any security interest or lien unless the buyer is informed of it. Although many warranties can be disclaimed (excluded), as we see in the next section, this warranty is difficult to exclude and can be disclaimed only by clear notification to the buyer that the seller does not claim title.

DISCLAIMERS

disclaimer: A statement in a warranty that limits or eliminates implied warranties.

Although the UCC establishes the implied warranties described previously, which are of significant benefit to consumers, it also allows sellers to **disclaim** or cancel such warranties quite easily. UCC §2-316 provides that implied warranties may be eliminated by the use of written statements containing phrases like “as is” or “with all faults.” In addition, the warranty of merchantability may be excluded by specifically mentioning “merchantability” (and if the disclaimer is in writing, it must also be “conspicuous”). The warranty of fitness for particular purpose may be disclaimed by a “conspicuous written statement.” If you look at a warranty you have received with your purchase of a consumer product, you will likely find that some of the implied warranties have been at least partially disclaimed, probably in capital letters (in order to be “conspicuous”).

SOCIAL/ETHICAL ISSUES

Are implied warranties of merchantability and fitness for particular purpose based on ethical principles? Do they appear to conform with what most people would think of as "right" or "fair"? If so, is the rule allowing these warranties to be easily disclaimed (simply using the phrase "as is," for example) an ethical one? Do most consumers really read the text of their product warranties and hence understand that they have no implied warranties?

THE MAGNUSON-MOSS WARRANTY ACT

In the early 1970s, Congress held a number of hearings concerning warranties. The ease with which warranties could be eliminated was just one of the serious problems consumers faced in connection with warranties. At the hearings, numerous individuals testified regarding the great difficulties they had in obtaining warranty service and repairs and determining what parts of their products were covered by warranties. Others were concerned with the high cost of obtaining repairs and the general "illusory" nature of warranties (the warranties the customers thought they had received were disclaimed). As a congressional report stated, "Too often, what the large print giveth, the fine print taketh away."

In 1974, Congress enacted the first federal law dealing with warranties, the **Magnuson-Moss Warranty Act**, effective in 1975. This law *did not require any seller or manufacturer to provide warranties*, but when a seller did choose to give a written warranty, the law imposed several new duties. The Magnuson-Moss Act did not replace the UCC warranty provisions that are part of the law in 49 states but supplemented these provisions by imposing new requirements on all written warranties.

Magnuson-Moss Warranty Act: A federal law that requires certain disclosures and provides certain rights to consumers, where written warranties are provided.

When a written warranty is provided, the Magnuson-Moss Act requires the warrantor to *disclose certain information*. The warranty must state clearly what parts of the product are covered by the warranty, how and where the consumer can obtain repairs covered by the warranty, how long the warranty lasts, and whether the warranty extends to a person other than the first purchaser of the product. The warranty must tell consumers that they may have additional rights under their state laws (such as the UCC implied warranties) and provide other information. The act also provides that the seller must make warranty information available to the buyer prior to the sale, in one of several ways.

The Magnuson-Moss Act states that when a seller gives a written warranty on a consumer product that costs at least $10, the warranty must be entitled either a *"full" or "limited" warranty*. A full warranty means that the seller must repair the product free of charge, replace the product, or refund the purchase price if the product cannot be fixed after reasonable efforts. The act does not specify exactly how many times a consumer must try to have the item repaired before he or she can demand money back. Most states have enacted "lemon laws" that indicate precisely how many attempts to fix the same defect in a new car are required to constitute "reasonable efforts." A limited warranty does not require such relief.

Another important Magnuson-Moss provision concerns *disclaimers*. As we have mentioned, the UCC allows warrantors to disclaim implied warranties fairly easily. However, Magnuson-Moss puts new limitations on such disclaimers. In a *full warranty, there can be no disclaimer of implied warranties*. In other words, if you receive a written warranty titled "full," you will be able to fully enforce any implied warranties of merchantability or fitness for a particular purpose. If the *warranty is limited*, it still may not totally disclaim implied warranties but may *limit them to the duration of the express warranty*. Therefore, many written limited warranties today contain a clause that limits the length of time the implied warranties exist to the same time period as the written express warranty.

One of the most important parts of the Magnuson-Moss Act allows consumers to sue for warranty violations and to collect not only their damages but their attorneys' fees as well. Prior to this enactment, few consumers sued to enforce their UCC rights under express and implied warranties, because the costs of the lawsuit were more than the amount at stake in the warranty claim. Remember that under the so-called American rule, each side of the lawsuit must normally pay its own legal fees, win or lose. However, Magnuson-Moss allows consumers to recover actual attorneys' fees, if they win. Also, both the UCC §2-719(3) and the Magnuson-Moss Act provide that consumers may not be prevented from suing for *consequential damages* due to *personal injuries* caused by defective products. Note, however, that some different interpretations of this section with regard to other types of consequential damages exist in various states. The following box displays an example of a limited warranty. Look closely at the warranty to see how its provisions comply with the Magnuson-Moss Act.

LIMITED 90-DAY WARRANTY—FOR HEWLETT-PACKARD PERSONAL COMPUTER MAINFRAMES AND PERIPHERALS

What We Do

In the U.S.A. and Canada this unit is warranted by Hewlett-Packard against defects in materials and workmanship for 90 days from date of original purchase.* If you transfer ownership, this warranty is automatically transferred to the new owner and remains in effect for the original 90-day period.

During the warranty period we will repair or, at our option, replace at no charge any unit that proves to be defective, provided it is returned, shipping prepaid, to an identified Hewlett-Packard repair facility. You are responsible for all customs duties in connection with the return of the unit.

What Is Not Covered

This warranty does not apply if the product has been damaged by accident or misuse, or as a result of service or modification by other than an authorized HP Repair Facility, or by hardware, software, interfacing or peripherals not provided by Hewlett-Packard. Hewlett-Packard shall have no obligation to modify or update products once manufactured. This warranty does not apply to HP Software Products.

No other expressed warranty is given. The repair or replacement of a product is your exclusive remedy. *Any implied warranty of merchantability or fitness is limited to the 90-day duration of this written warranty.* Some states or provinces do not allow limitations on how long an implied warranty lasts, so the above limitation or exclusion may not apply to you. *In no event shall Hewlett-Packard Company be liable for consequential damages.* Some states or provinces do not allow the exclusion or limitation of incidental or consequential damages, so that above limitation or exclusion may not apply to you.

This warranty gives you specific legal rights, and you may also have other rights which vary from state to state, or from province to province.

This is your warranty. Please retain for your records.

*In other countries, contact your local authorized HP dealer or your local Hewlett-Packard Sales and Service facility to determine warranty terms.

(For addresses, please see the list on the following page or consult your owner's manual.)

How To Obtain Service for Your Equipment

During the warranty period: If after you follow the maintenance procedures outlined in the owner's manual, you determine that a repair is required, you can help assure efficient servicing by following these guidelines:

- Fill in the attached Repair Information Form and include it with your equipment. Return your equipment to your nearest HP Dealer Repair Center or Field Repair Center.
- Provide a copy of you sales invoice or other documentary proof-of-purchase date to establish warranty coverage period.
- If you need to ship your unit, be sure to ship it in a protective package and insure it. We recommend that you save the original shipping materials for this purpose.
- Note: Your warranty will be upgraded from return-to-HP to on-site service free of charge if you purchase a 12-month On-Site Maintenance Agreement within ten days of equipment delivery.
- After the Warranty Period: Maintenance is available at your location, at HP Dealer Repair Centers, or at HP Field Repair Centers. You can purchase service at an annual fixed price or on a per-incident basis.
- Under a Field Repair Center Maintenance Agreement, you ship the product to an HP Field Repair Center, where it is repaired within three working days.
- On-Site Maintenance Agreements are available with various levels of response time and coverage, to allow you to select the level of support that fits your needs.
- If you prefer, service on site or at a Field Repair Center is also available on a per-incident, rather than contract, basis.
- Many authorized HP Dealers offer hardware servicing. To locate your nearest Dealer Repair Center consult your yellow pages or call 800-547-3400. In Oregon, Alaska, or Hawaii, call 503-758-1010. TTY users with hearing or speech impairments, please dial 503-758-5566.

Hewlett-Packard Field Repair Centers

The HP Field Repair Centers listed below provide return-to-HP repair for HP computing equipment—both during and after the warranty period.

If there is no Field Repair Center in your country, contact your authorized HP Series 80 Dealer or your HP Sales and Service Office for shipping instructions.

To find the location of one of the 240 Hewlett-Packard offices serving you worldwide, check your local telephone directory, or contact one of the HP Sales and Service offices listed below.

UNITED STATES
Illinois
Hewlett-Packard Company
5201 Tollview Drive
Rolling Meadows, IL 60008
(312) 255-9800

Texas
Hewlett-Packard Company
930 East Campbell Rd.
Richardson, TX 75081
(214) 231-6101

California
Hewlett-Packard Company
5400 West Rosecrans Avenue
Lawndale, CA 90260
(213) 970-7500

Hewlett-Packard Company
3003 Scott Boulevard
Santa Clara, CA 95050
(408) 988-7000

Georgia
Hewlett-Packard Company
2000 South Park Place
Atlanta, GA 30339
(404) 955-1500

Massachusetts
Hewlett-Packard Company
32 Hartwell Avenue
Lexington, MA 02173
(617) 861-8960

New Jersey
Hewlett-Packard Company
W. 120 Century Road
Paramus, NJ 07652
(201) 265-5000

CANADA
Hewlett-Packard Company
6877 Goreway Dr.
Mississaugua, Ontario LV4 1M8
(415) 678-2350

EUROPE
Hewlett-Packard, S.A.
7 Rue du Bois-du-Lan,
P.O. Box
CH-1217 Meyrin 2
Geneva, Switzerland

OTHER INTERNATIONAL LOCATIONS
Hewlett-Packard Intercontinental
3495 Deer Creek Road
Palo Alto, CA 94304 U.S.A.

FROM THE DESK OF
Laura Lawyer

To: Students
From: Your Lawyer

Most of us have a drawer or shelf at home in which we put all the written warranties that come in the boxes of products we purchase. While you are studying warranties, it might be a good time to take a closer look at the warranties on the more expensive items you own. Do the items carry full or limited warranties? How and where do you obtain warranty service? What parts of the products are covered and for how long? Have the warranties of merchantability and fitness for a particular purpose been limited? In the Hewlett-Packard warranty just shown, can you tell what express warranties were given, and if there were are any implied warranties or disclaimers?

WHO MAY ENFORCE WARRANTIES?

The general rule in contract cases is that only those parties who are *in privity* of contract with each other may enforce the contract. **Privity** means that the parties have a direct contract relationship with each other. In warranty situations, however, the privity rule is not strictly followed. For example, if Adam buys a car manufactured by Ford Motor Co. from Barbara's Auto Sales, he does not have a direct contract with Ford, although he receives a warranty from Ford. Adam is "in privity" of contract with Barbara but not Ford. Despite the lack of privity, Adam will be able to hold Ford to the terms of its warranty, because Ford was expecting (and hoping) that the car would not remain in Barbara's hands but would be sold to a consumer like Adam.

privity: When two parties have contract with each other. This concept is no longer very important in warranty cases.

Another privity problem arises at the other end of the transaction. Adam allows his wife and son to drive his new car. If a defective part causes an accident, injuring Adam's wife, both Ford and Barbara might argue that they have no privity with Adam's wife because they only dealt with Adam. However, the UCC injects a commonsense rule here that states that persons other than the buyer may be covered by the existing warranties. The drafters of the UCC set forth three alternative clauses (A, B, and C) for §2-318, thus allowing each state to decide how far the warranties should be extended at the consumer end of the deal. Alternative A extended the warranty to "any natural person in the family or household of the buyer, or who is a guest in his home." Alternative B extended the warranty even further to "any natural person who may reasonably be expected to use, consume, or be affected by the goods." Alternative C adopts the language of Alternative B but substitutes "any person" for "any natural person," allowing corporations and partnerships to be covered as well as natural persons.

NEGLIGENCE

Chapter 11 discussed the concept of **negligence**. As you recall, the elements necessary to establish a negligence case are the following: (1) the existence of a duty of care by one person toward another, (2) the defendant's breach of this duty, (3) proof that this breach of duty was the proximate cause of an injury to the plaintiff, and (4) damages suffered by the plaintiff.

negligence: The most common type of tort—discussed in Chapter 11—that involves an injury caused by another's lack of due care.

Negligence theory has often formed the basis of personal product injury lawsuits where the injuries were caused by manufactured products. In order to show that the manufacturer had breached its duty of care (was negligent), consumers have alleged such failings as follows: (1) negligent product design; (2) negligent product assembly, manufacture, and packaging; and (3) the failure to warn product users of dangers known to the product manufacturer.

In order to prevail in negligence cases, of course, plaintiffs need to prove the other essential elements as well, such as the defendant was "at fault"—that some action the defendant took or did not take failed to meet the standards expected of the mythical "reasonable" manufacturer. Also, in a "design" case, plaintiffs must show that the product was designed without proper care or in a way that made the product dangerous. For example, a company might have hired designers without experience, failed to follow industry standards, or failed to test the design as sufficiently as a reasonably careful producer should have done. To show negligence in assembly or packaging, plaintiffs must prove that the manner of assembly was not carefully done, did not meet normal industry standards, or that the product was packaged in a way that was hazardous to likely users.

Also, many "failure to warn" negligence cases have been brought against manufacturers and retailers. In these cases, plaintiffs must show that the manufacturer knew or should have known that the product was dangerous to certain potential users and that these users were unlikely to realize the danger, but the manufacturer had not warned them of their peril. The now-familiar warnings seen on many products, from hair dryers to stepladders to skis, are an attempt by manufacturers to limit their liability for negligence because of a failure to warn of product hazards.

Of course, the defenses of contributory negligence, comparative negligence, and assumption of the risk may be raised by the defendant in a product negligence lawsuit, just as in any other type of negligence case. Therefore, even though in many cases plaintiffs can establish that the product manufacturer was negligent, they will lose a negligence case or have the damages reduced if they were personally negligent or knowingly assumed the risk of injury when using the product.

FROM THE DESK OF
Laura Lawyer

To: Students
From: Your Lawyer

Companies and organizations often attempt to limit their liability for negligence through notices printed on the packaging containing a consumer product or through signs warning customers of hazards. These signs and notices do have some legal effect, and it makes good business sense to use them where appropriate. At the very least, they have a deterrent effect—that is, many people may refrain from suing because of a sign on a package or in a store stating, "We are not responsible for any injuries from the use of this product," for example.

However, these warnings are not always binding in court, especially if the result would offend public policy. For example, if the consumer is injured by a defective product while using the item in a relatively normal fashion, no disclaimer of responsibility is likely to be upheld in court.

STRICT PRODUCT LIABILITY

Consumers injured by products have often encountered difficulties in recovering damages from sellers and manufacturers under warranty and negligence theories. As we have seen, warranties are often given only for a limited time period and may be limited or disclaimed fairly easily. In order to win negligence lawsuits, plaintiffs must prove that the manufacturer or seller was "at fault" somehow in the manufacture, design, packaging, or labeling of the product. In addition, defenses of contributory or comparative negligence may prevent or diminish recovery if plaintiffs were at fault in any way.

As our society has become more technologically complex, it also has become more difficult for consumers to prove exactly what a manufacturer did that was negligent in designing or constructing a product, or exactly what part of the product was defective. Most of us do not have a comprehensive understanding of all the parts of an automobile or a piece of machinery, or how each one is manufactured. It is hard for an individual to show, for example, that an auto manufacturer did not meet the standard of a reasonably prudent car builder in the manufacture of one particular part of a complex steering mechanism. Yet, in order to prevail in a negligence suit, if the power steering wheel on an automobile suddenly jerked to the left causing the car to crash, the consumer would have to prove not only that there was a defect and an injury, but also that the manufacturer was "at fault" in some specific way in the manufacture or design of the steering mechanism—that is, that "due care" was lacking.

In response to this problem, many courts in the past thirty years or so have adopted a new theory called **strict product liability**. As discussed in Chapter 11, this theory originally developed to create liability for those who engage in "ultrahazardous" activity, without proof of negligence or fault. For example, if The Jackson Company was performing dynamite operations to clear a site for construction and the blasting caused injury to a neighboring business, Jackson would be liable no matter how much care it exercised.

strict product liability: A legal theory that allows a person injured by a defective product to win a lawsuit against the manufacturer without proving "fault" or lack of due care.

In the past 25 years, the strict liability doctrine has been increasingly applied not only to those engaging in ultrahazardous actions but to all those who manufacture and distribute products. Today, in most states, if a consumer is injured by a defective product that he or she is using in a normal way, the consumer can prevail without proving negligence. The liability is called "strict" because the plaintiff does *not have to show fault* on the part of the defendant.

This doctrine imposes considerably greater duties upon merchants and manufacturers than does negligence theory. Among the justifications set forth in support of the rule are the following:

1. Manufacturers are better able to bear the economic losses caused by defective products than are individual consumers, since they have greater assets and can purchase insurance to protect themselves against liability.

2. Merchants and manufacturers can "pass along" the increased costs to all of society through higher prices rather than forcing an injured consumer to bear the entire cost of an injury.

3. Companies that manufacture and sell products will have an incentive to take preventive measures to design and build safer products if they are held responsible for injuries caused by defects.

Manufacturers, on the other hand, have argued against strict liability because it greatly increases their costs of doing business. Because of the increase in lawsuits and judgments against the makers of products of many types, insurance costs have risen dramatically in some industries. Business groups have asserted that some firms have gone out of business because of lawsuits and insurance costs, and new product innovations have been delayed or canceled because of fears of liability. The much-discussed "liability crisis" of recent years has arisen in large part from the development and ramifications of the strict product liability doctrine.

One of the first cases to explicitly adopt and explain carefully the rationale for the strict liability theory was the California Supreme Court's decision in *Greenman v. Yuba Power Products*, presented next.

GREENMAN V. YUBA POWER PRODUCTS, INC.

377 P.2d 897 (Calif. 1963)

FACTS

Yuba Power Products, Inc., manufactured the Shopsmith, a combination power tool that could be used as a saw, drill, and wood lathe. After seeing the Shopsmith demonstrated and reading a manufacturer's brochure, Mr. Greenman decided he wanted one. His wife purchased a Shopsmith for him for Christmas in 1955. Some two years later he was using the tool as a lathe, when a piece of wood flew out of the machine and struck him on the forehead, causing serious permanent injuries to Mr. Greenman.

Mr. Greenman later sued both the manufacturer and the retailer of the Shopsmith, claiming breach of express and implied warranties and negligence. The lower court judge refused to allow the jury to consider some of the theories, and the jury later entered a verdict against the manufacturer alone for $65,000. It was not clear whether the verdict was based on negligence or on warranty theory. Both Mr. Greenman and Yuba Power Products appealed.

DECISION

The California Supreme Court has often been a trendsetter in the adoption of new legal theories. Justice Roger Traynor, a respected leader of the court for many years, wrote the appellate decision in this case, in which the court upheld the lower court decision but based its decision on the theory of strict product liability.

The defendants argued on appeal that the plaintiff should not have been allowed to pursue his warranty claims because he did not give notice of the product defects to the manufacturer within the appropriate time period specified by a California law. Justice Traynor rejected this allegation, finding that although the notice requirement was "a sound commercial rule" in contract cases between two parties in privity, it was "not an appropriate one" for the court to adopt in actions by injured consumers against manufacturers with whom they have not dealt and thus would simply be "a boobytrap for the unwary."

Mr. Greenman had introduced evidence that his injuries were caused by the Shopsmith's defective design and manufacture. His expert witnesses testified that the set screws used to hold key parts of the machine together were inadequate. The vibration that occurred when the machine operated caused certain parts to loosen, which allowed the piece of wood to fly out. The experts stated that there were alternative ways of designing and constructing the machine that would have prevented the accident.

The California Supreme Court refused to decide the case on the basis of warranty or negligence theory. Instead, the court held that regardless of the existence of an express warranty, "a manufacturer is strictly liable in tort when an article he places on the market, knowing that it is to be used without inspection for defects, proves to have a defect that causes injury to a human being." Justice Traynor wrote that the warranty rules (and notice requirements) previously developed to meet the needs of commercial transactions could not properly be used to limit a manufacturer's liability to consumers for defective products.

The purpose of strict liability, stated the court, was to ensure that the costs of injuries resulting from defective products were borne by the manufacturers that put such products on the market rather than by the injured persons who were powerless to protect themselves. Since this was not a contracts case, the question of whether or not Mr. Greenman carefully read the brochure (as he had done here) should not control the result, nor should the details of the sales agreements between the manufacturer, retailer, and Mrs. Greenman. "The remedies of injured consumers ought not to be made to depend upon the intricacies of the law of sales."

The Supreme Court therefore affirmed the lower court award, basing the decision solely on the doctrine of strict liability.

CASE QUESTIONS

1. In the *Greenman* case, what problems did the plaintiff have in proving his case under warranty theory?
2. What benefits, from a plaintiff's standpoint, does the strict liability theory have over (a) warranty theory and (b) negligence theory?
3. Does the strict liability doctrine reflect a public policy of corporate social responsibility?

Following the Greenman case, many other courts adopted the doctrine of strict liability for cases involving defective products. Probably the clearest statement of the **principles of strict product liability** is contained in the *Restatement of Torts (2d)*, a multivolume treatise on tort law prepared by a group of legal scholars. The Restatement is a summary and compilation of common law principles based on court decisions, published in 1965. It is essentially a statement of what the law is or how it is evolving, concerning various torts. Although it is not a statute and has no binding authority, the Restatement has often been cited by courts in deciding cases involving common law tort cases and the strict liability doctrine spread throughout the country after it was published. Section 402A of the Restatement states the following:

elements of strict liability: 1. Product was defective. 2. Product was unreasonably dangerous. 3. Seller was "in business" of selling these products. 4. Product reached the consumer without alteration in the distribution chain.

1. *One who sells any product in a defective condition unreasonably dangerous to the user or consumer or to his property is subject to liability for physical harm caused to the ultimate consumer or to his property; if*
   a. *the seller is engaged in the business of selling such a product, and*
   b. *it is expected to and does reach the user or consumer without substantial change in the condition in which it is sold.*
2. *The rule stated in Subsection (1) applies although*
   a. *the seller has exercised all possible care in the preparation and sale of his product, and*
   b. *the user or consumer has not bought the product from or entered into any contractual relation with the seller.*

The outline of strict liability contained in the *Restatement* definition shows that certain elements are necessary before a court will impose strict liability on a seller or manufacturer. First, the theory applies only to products sold *in a defective condition*. Thus, in order to recover any damages, the consumer has to establish, by actual or circumstantial evidence, that the item was defective when sold. Although this can prove difficult for purchasers, the standard is much easier to show than the "fault" required in a negligence case. If the brakes on a new car fail, causing an accident, the consumer will likely be able to convince a jury that there was a "defect" (for strict liability purposes) much more easily than to show that the manufacturer's procedure in designing, constructing, or testing the brakes was below the standards of other auto manufacturers (for negligence purposes).

Second, the theory requires that the defect make the product *unreasonably dangerous* to the user. The problem must be such that it creates a danger "beyond that which would be contemplated by the ordinary consumer" who purchases the product with the "ordinary knowledge common to the community as to its characteristics." Certain plaintiffs who are injured by persons using handguns or by drunkards have tried to sue the specific gun or alcohol manufacturer. In most cases, though, the courts have ruled against those claims, finding that the guns and alcohol are not defective in that they contain no mechanical flaws or hidden ingredients not known to the ordinary consumer. However, if in a specific case the alcohol contained a hazardous chemical or the gun had a defective mechanism that caused injury to the shooter and those standing behind him, strict liability might apply. Note that this theory only applies to those *engaged in the business of selling such products*. Much like the warranty of merchantability, discussed earlier, the rationale for this rule is that merchants and manufacturers are better able than consumers to take steps to prevent defects in the first place, to assume the financial risk of defective products, and to pass along the cost of defective products as part of their sales price in the future.

A third requirement of strict liability is that the product *is expected to and does reach the user or consumer without substantial change in the condition in which it is sold*. The manufacturer should not bear the responsibility for products that have been altered or contaminated after leaving the manufacturer. If, for example, a hardware store removes the safety guards on all its lawn mowers in order to display them better, the manufacturer should not be liable for a consumer's injury that the guard would have prevented, although the retailer might be liable. Similarly, the maker of Tylenol was not held liable for the deaths of two people who took Tylenol tablets that had been injected with cyanide while on a grocer's shelf.

The American Law Institute, the group of lawyers and scholars who issued the *Restatement (2d)*, has recently published a new *Restatement of Torts (3d): Product Liability*. In it, the authors attempt to restate the law of strict product liability, after many different definitions of terms such as *defective* and *unreasonably dangerous* had appeared in different state court decisions.

In the new *Restatement*, the experts find that there have been three main ways in which products have been found defective: (1) manufacturing defects, (2) design defects, and (3) defective warnings or instructions. The *Restatement (3d)* describes manufacturing defects as occurring "when the product departs from its intended design, even though all possible care was exercised in the preparation and marketing of the product." This definition is not a significant change from the earlier version.

Probably the most controversial section of the third edition is the definition of *design defects*. Rejecting the view of some courts and consumer advocates, the *Restatement (3d)* does not focus on "consumer expectations" in defining design defects. Instead, the authors have moved in the direction of certain courts, which had adopted a "risk utility" test. This test weighs the utility of the product's design against the risks of the design.

The language of the *Restatement (3d)* states:

> A product is defective in design when the foreseeable risks of harm posed by the product could have been reduced or avoided by the adoption of a reasonable alternative design by the seller . . . and the omission of the alternative design renders the product not reasonably safe.

This standard, if adopted by courts around the country, would require the plaintiff in a product liability case to demonstrate to the court a "reasonable alternative design" in order to get a jury trial on the design defect issue—a considerably tougher standard than now exists in many states.

As to "lack of warning" defects, the *Restatement (3d)* also uses the "risk utility" and "reasonableness" tests. A product is defective because of inadequate warnings when "the foreseeable risks of harm posed by the product could have been reduced or avoided by the provision of reasonable instructions or warnings by the seller." The authors also note that consumers bear some responsibility for preventing harm. They should be expected to read warnings and to observe risks that are obvious or generally known to users.

It remains to be seen if the *Restatement (3d)* will be as widely followed by state courts as the previous version.

THE "CRASHWORTHINESS" DOCTRINE

One controversial variation on strict liability theory is the so-called **crashworthiness** doctrine. Under this rule, a vehicle manufacturer may be liable in negligence or strict liability for injuries suffered in a motor vehicle accident in which the design of the vehicle was not the cause of the accident but nevertheless *enhanced the injuries suffered*. This theory, first recognized in the landmark case *Larsen v. General Motors Corp* [391 F.2d 495 (8th Cir. 1968)], holds that the manufacturer's duty to produce a product reasonably safe for its intended use and not unreasonably dangerous must take into consideration the fact that injury-producing collisions are a regular, foreseeable, and statistically expectable result of such normal use. Therefore, an automobile manufacturer must use reasonable care in designing and manufacturing cars, trucks, and motorcycles, so that its vehicles minimize, rather than increase, the injuries caused when they become involved in collisions.

crashworthiness: The duty of vehicle manufacturers to build cars, trucks, and motorcycles that do not enhance or worsen the injuries of persons when involved in accidents.

In the *Larsen* case, for example, the motorist suffered serious head injuries, not in the initial collision, but when his vehicle rolled over and the roof collapsed on him. As one court noted, the crashworthiness doctrine does not require a manufacturer to provide absolute safety, but it does require the manufacturers to take into account in all phases of the design and manufacturing process the known fact that many vehicles are involved in accidents. The manufacturer must provide some measure of reasonable, cost-effective safety features for the foreseeable use of the product, which includes the very real possibility of collisions and accidents.

DEFENSES TO STRICT LIABILITY

assumption of risk: A common law defense against a personal injury claim that states that when an employee knows an activity is dangerous but continues, he or she cannot collect damages.

While businesses face considerable hurdles in defeating a strict liability claim, certain defenses are available. First, the doctrine of **assumption of risk** is still available. When plaintiffs fully realize the risks of injury in using a product, they cannot sue when one of the known risks causes injury. For example, skiers must realize that, despite purchasing high-class equipment, they may fall and even break bones sometimes while skiing. Susan will not win a lawsuit against the manufacturer of her skis if she takes a tumble while skiing and breaks her leg, unless she can show that some unknown defect in the skis caused her to fall.

On the other hand, where consumers do not realize the hazards inherent in the products they purchase, strict liability can be used against both sellers and manufacturers. In one of the most publicized and controversial cases in recent years, a 79-year-old woman who spilled a cup of coffee purchased from McDonald's was awarded $2.9 million by a jury (later reduced to $640,000 by the judge). She suffered third-degree burns that required considerable medical treatment, including skin grafts and therapy. The woman and her witness apparently convinced the jury that McDonald's coffee was much hotter than most restaurant coffee and therefore was more dangerous than she thought (and thus "unreasonably dangerous").

misuse: When someone uses a product in a way that the manufacturer could not have reasonably foreseen.

Probably the most effective defense manufacturers have to a strict liability lawsuit is **misuse** of the product by the consumer. In order to constitute "misuse," the product must be used in a way that was not foreseeable to the reasonable seller. Suppose that Susan is not using her skis for skiing but instead as a bookshelf. If the one hundred books she has piled on the skis cause them to crack and the books fall down and hit her, breaking her arm, she will not succeed in suing the ski company due to her misuse of the product. The classic example of misuse is the case in which a consumer was using his lawn mower as a hedge trimmer. As a result, the mower jumped and injured his leg. In this situation, the jury denied recovery, finding that the manufacturer had no responsibility for anticipating this type of use or for taking steps to prevent injuries in such an obvious misuse of the product.

The *Van Duzer v. Shoshone Coca-Cola Bottling Co.* case described next discusses the critical elements of strict product liability and the misuse defense.

VAN DUZER V. SHOSHONE COCA-COLA BOTTLING CO.

103 Nev. 383, 741 P.2d 811 (1987)

FACTS

Shelley Van Duzer was working as a cashier at Raley's Supermarket in Reno, Nevada, when a customer wheeled a shopping cart full of groceries into the checkout aisle. As Van Duzer began to remove a bag of potato chips from the cart, a bottle of Canada Dry Seltzer exploded, causing severe injuries to her eye. Her injury required surgery and eventually a cornea transplant. Under strict liability, she sued Owens-Illinois, Inc., the manufacturer of the bottle, and Shoshone Coca-Cola Bottling Co., which bottled the product and placed it on the shelves of the store. The jury rendered a verdict for the defendants, and Van Duzer appealed.

DECISION

The Nevada Supreme Court reiterated that the doctrine of strict liability had long been recognized in Nevada for defects in products that cause injuries. The judge had properly instructed the jury that a "product is defective when it fails to perform in the manner reasonably to be expected in light of its nature and intended function."

The customer had testified at trial that the bottle had exploded while in the shopping cart, without being dropped or mishandled. Van Duzer did not even touch the bottle. The court stated that "a product container that cannot withstand the rigors of normal shopping practices is unreasonably dangerous and, by definition, defective."

The defendants argued that the bottle had shattered after colliding with one of the other glass containers in the cart. They asserted that a "sharp external blow to the bottle" constituted misuse, relieving them of liability. However, the court stated that even if this theory were true, it is of no importance if the external blow happened as the result of normal handling. "Use of a product in a manner which should be reasonably anticipated is not misuse or abuse."

The court found that it was normal for a bottled product to be placed in a shopping cart with other items, some of which may be glass containers. "Some jostling can be anticipated as the items are wheeled around the store." The cart was at a stop at the checkout counter when the accident occurred, and none of the witnesses testified to any unusual impact. As the court stated, "this was not a case where one object was hurled across a speeding cart at another object."

According to the facts of this case (even as stated by the defendants), the bottle shattered because it came into contact with another bottle in the cart. This susceptibility to breakage on impact with other bottles ordinarily found in shopping carts "rendered the bottle dangerous and defective." Because the evidence showed that this defect was inherent in the bottle and present when it left the control of the manufacturer and when it was sold by the distributor, both are liable under the doctrine of strict liability.

Since the jury could only have reached its verdict by disregarding the judge's instructions on strict liability, the decision of the lower court was reversed, and the case was remanded for a new trial.

CASE QUESTIONS

1. Whose fault was it that the bottle exploded? Does it make a difference in the outcome of this case?
2. What did the defendants attempt to establish as a defense? Why did this argument not work to protect them from liability?
3. It is often said that strict product liability represents a public policy decision involving risk allocation. Is it fair to place the risk of injuries from defective products on the sellers and manufacturers of products even if they "exercised all possible care" in the manufacture of the product? Is it ethical?

LIMITATIONS ON THE USE OF STRICT LIABILITY

The theory of strict product liability shifts much of the burden of defective products to the manufacturers and sellers of all types of goods. Not only is there significant liability exposure for those who make defective products, but the cost of insurance for businesses of all kinds has increased in recent years regardless of whether a firm has sold any defective goods. In addition, businesses have had to increase spending for various preventive measures, such as increased research and testing, before a product can be marketed. Many firms and trade groups have argued that the frequent use of the strict liability theory has not only led to an excess of lawsuits against businesses—often for frivolous claims—but has stifled innovation and new product development by manufacturing companies afraid of lawsuits. It is often argued that U.S. manufacturers' competitive position in world markets is hurt by how U.S. courts use strict liability. Ironically, a few years ago the European Union adopted a product safety standard quite similar to the U.S. concept of strict liability.[1]

In the past 20 years business trade groups have pushed for the passage of legislation by state legislatures and Congress to alleviate the so-called tort crisis created by the strict liability doctrine. Almost all of the states have enacted laws that, in one way or another, attempt to put some limits on the manufacturer's potential liability. Also, perhaps in response to the success of companies' and insurance firms' publicity campaign to make the public aware of the excesses of some jury verdicts, it appears that plaintiffs are losing more product liability cases than was true a few years ago. One study of jury verdicts in product defect cases showed that individuals suing companies won 54 percent of the cases in 1987 but won only 41 percent by the mid-1990s.

All states have *statutes of limitation* for various types of legal claims. These laws limit the time period during which a plaintiff may file a case raising a certain argument. Various types of cases call for different time periods. A typical statute of limitation for a product liability claim is four years from the time the defect is discovered, or should have been discovered, by the consumer. For example, the statute of limitations on the exploding sodapop bottle would begin to run the day after the explosion. If the consumer waits longer than the statutory period to sue, the court case will be dismissed.

Sometimes a product user will be injured by a malfunction in a machine or other product that is 20 or 30 years old. The statute of limitations would not bar the suit if the consumer sued within four years after discovering the defect (when the malfunction occurred). Under strict liability (unlike warranties) no automatic expiration of the manufacturer's responsibility exists.

statute of repose: An outer limit on how many years after a product was manufactured that the maker could be held liable for a defect.

To address the problem of a lawsuit being filed twenty years or more after the product was made, a number of states have passed **statutes of repose**. These laws put an outer limit, say 10 or 15 years, on the manufacturer's liability for defects in a product no matter when the problem was discovered by the user or consumer. In 1994 Congress established an 18-year statute of repose for lawsuits against manufacturers of private aircraft. In recent years, Congress has considered bills that would make substantial changes in product liability laws and enact federal standards to preempt many state laws and common law principles. Table 13.1 describes some of the changes proposed in some of the legislation. Such a federal law would put limits on noneconomic damages and would limit punitive damages in cases involving defective products and personal injuries. At the time this book went to press, the proposed federal product liability law had not been enacted.

state of the art defense: A defense to liability recognized in some states, if the product was made using the best methods then available.

Another provision advocated by business groups is the **state of the art defense**. This theory, adopted in several states, allows a manufacturer to successfully defend a product liability lawsuit by proving that at the time the product was made, the company used the best technology, design, and methods then available. Remember that the prevailing law regarding strict liability holds that the manufacturer of a defective product is liable for injuries caused "even though the seller has exercised all possible care in the preparation and sale" of the product. The state of the art defense, then, would bring strict lia-

[1] F. Zollers, S. Hurd, and P. Shears, "Product Safety in the United States and the European Community: A Comparative Approach," 17 Md. *Journal of International Law & Trade* (Fall 1992), 177.

Table 13.1 *Current and Proposed Product Liability Standards*

Subject	Current Law	Proposed Federal Law
Standards for personal injury and product liability lawsuits	No uniform federal laws exist. Variations based on common law from state to state.	Would establish uniform federal laws and standards.
State of the art defense	Some states allow the manufacturer to show that the latest and best technology was used, as a defense to liability.	Would establish a national standard allowing the state of the art defense in product liability cases.
Punitive damages	Plaintiff must prove that manufacturer was "flagrantly indifferent to consumer safety." No national caps on damages, but some states have caps.	Would cap punitive damages at three times compensatory damages. Would require "clear and convincing evidence" of intentional or flagrant action by defendant.
Joint and several liability	Many states provide for this type of liability, which means that the winning plaintiff can collect the whole award from any one of the defendants.	Would require the court or jury to specify the amount of damages for which each defendant is responsible.
Statute of repose	Many states have statutes of repose, no longer than 15 years.	Would establish a federal statute of repose of 18 years for products, with some exceptions.

bility theory back closer to negligence law, with which the plaintiff must show some sort of "fault" to prevail.

Another liability reform measure business backs is the elimination of **joint and several liability**. The general rule in the United States is that if the plaintiff in a liability case proves that two or more defendants each were partially responsible for the plaintiff's injuries, they will be held "jointly and severally" liable. In other words, each defendant is liable for the *whole judgment*—that is, the plaintiff can collect the whole amount awarded from any one defendant. Obviously, this theory allows (indeed encourages) the plaintiff to attempt to collect the entire judgment from the wealthiest defendant, rather than go after a percentage share from each one. This procedure, with the plaintiff looking for the "deep pocket," seems unfair to large companies that were only partly responsible for a consumer's injuries.

joint and several liability: When two or more defendants are found liable, the plaintiff can collect the entire award from any one defendant.

Suppose, for example, that Chrysler Corporation produces and sells a Jeep vehicle to Nick. While driving down a residential street, the accelerator sticks, and Nick crashes into a tree, causing injuries to himself. The accelerator mechanism was actually made by the Ace Machine Co. and supplied to Chrysler, where it was installed in the Jeep. If Nick sues Chrysler and Ace, he might win a judgment with joint and several liability imposed on both defendants, even though Ace was really much more responsible for the defect. Nick would be able to collect the $200,000 judgment from either one or both, in whatever proportion he can; probably, though, Nick will try to collect the whole amount first from Chrysler, the larger and wealthier company. Chrysler could then seek reimbursement from Ace Machine.

Several states have eliminated or modified joint and several liability. In these states, the jury must apportion the percentage of liability of each defendant. Say, for example, the jury decides that Chrysler was 20 percent responsible and Ace was 80 percent responsible for Nick's injuries. Thus, if Nick is awarded $200,000, he can only receive $40,000 from Chrysler, and the remainder, $160,000, will come from Ace. Although this plan appears to be more equitable for manufacturers, consumer advocates and personal injury attorneys generally oppose the elimination of joint and several liability, arguing that it imposes significant additional burdens on the injured consumer. They assert that in many cases, the plaintiff who has been awarded monetary damages by the jury will be unable to collect from the smaller firms and therefore will not actually receive the full amount of damages awarded by the jury.

Strict liability cases are often brought as class actions. As we have discussed earlier, this form of lawsuit allows a few plaintiffs to represent a very large group who have purchased similar items or have suffered similar types of harm due to exposure to harmful or defective products. In recent years, thousands of persons have alleged harm from such products as asbestos, breast implants, the Dalkon Shield, and other products. Numerous class-action lawsuits have been filed in each of these cases as well as hundreds of individual cases.

SOCIAL/ETHICAL ISSUES

The strict liability theory is controversial. Is it ethical for a business firm to be required to pay damages to an individual injured by a defective product when the firm used the latest techniques and best method of design and manufacture in producing its product? If the business is forced to pay damages and carry additional insurance, it may have to lay off some employees as a result. What ethical issues are involved?

On the other hand, if a consumer is injured by a defective product, under negligence theory the manufacturer may escape liability to the individual simply by showing that the firm was careful in designing, making, and packaging the product. Is it fair to place the burden on consumers to inspect complex products and to tell persons who were injured while using the products correctly that they must suffer their own losses without compensation simply because they did not uncover the defect? Who eventually pays for the costs of the injuries? What ethical issues are involved here?

How can we fashion a rule that is fair to all sides? How safe should products be?

The following reading indicates some of the problems and complexities that may occur during the process of a class-action lawsuit involving mass torts.

BREAST IMPLANT CASES

Over the past 10 years, significant court time has been spent on "mass tort" cases. These matters involve products such as asbestos and silicone breast implants, which have allegedly caused harm to thousands, perhaps millions of people. Often the injuries and diseases do not appear for many years. Therefore, it is difficult to determine how many members are in the class (for a class action suit) and what the extent of injuries and total damages are.

Several of the manufacturers of asbestos and breast implants have ended up filing for protection under Chapter 11 of the Bankruptcy Code (discussed in Chapter 17) after being sued hundreds of times and facing more class actions.

In late 1999 a bankruptcy court in Michigan approved a plan by which Dow Corning Corp. would set up a fund of $3.2 billion to settle the claims of up to 170,000 women who claimed health problems related to silicone breast implants. Dow Corning continues to deny that the implants have caused health problems but wants to settle the cases and emerge from bankruptcy court.

Under the settlement, women have up to 15 years to file a disease claim and up to 10 years to request removal of implants. Dow Corning agreed to pay women with ruptured implants at least $20,000, and more depending on medical proof of injury. Most payments are expected to be between $12,000 and $60,000. Women can also reject the plan and file individual lawsuits against the company.

TOBACCO AND GUNS

In the past few years numerous lawsuits have been filed against tobacco and gun manufacturers, based on product liability theories. Many state governments have brought lawsuits against tobacco companies seeking to recover millions of dollars spent by state health agencies to care for persons suffering from lung cancer and other diseases, allegedly caused by tobacco use. Settlements reached between state officials and tobacco companies announced at the time this book went to press already exceeded several billion dollars.

At least 28 cities and counties had filed suit by January 2000 against gun manufacturers, seeking reimbursement for millions of dollars spent on police, medical, and other city services in connection with unintentional shootings, teen suicides, and other criminal activity. Based on product liability theories, the suits center on allegations that gun makers knowingly failed to include safety devices on guns to prevent children and other "unauthorized" users from firing guns. This theory, essentially that guns are "unreasonably dangerous" because of their design, has not worked well in most cases filed by individual victims of gun violence.

The gun manufacturers vigorously defended the suits, arguing that the lack of safety devices was not the cause of injuries from guns. Further, the gun makers deny that they have achieved the development of "personalized weapons" that would only allow the legitimate owner to fire it, as the plaintiffs have claimed. Some of the suits were dismissed by courts, and in others the motions to dismiss were denied, thus beginning the discovery process. Much more will be heard from these lawsuits in coming years.

PREEMPTION

preemption doctrine: The theory that when a federal law and a state law govern the same subject and are conflicting, the federal law may displace or cancel the state law.

One other defense raised by manufacturers is **preemption**. The argument made is that if a product must meet federal standards in order to be sold, the manufacturer should not face product liability lawsuits based on state common law principles.

However, this theory has not always been applied in the courts. The results depend on the exact language used in the federal statute. In a case decided a few years ago, the U.S. Supreme Court refused to apply preemption to block a state lawsuit against the maker of a pacemaker that malfunctioned. Although the medical device had been approved for sale by the Food and Drug Administration (FDA), it had not gone through much regulatory evaluation, and the FDA had not really focused on the safety of that particular device [*Medtronic, Inc. v. Lohr*, 518 U.S. 470 (1996)].

PUNITIVE DAMAGES

As we have discussed briefly in Chapter 11, one of the most controversial issues involved in lawsuits regarding liability for defective products is the awarding of punitive damages. For more than a century, American courts have permitted, in a few cases, the awarding of so-called punitive damages to winning plaintiffs. American and English courts are alone in recognizing this type of damage award. As its name indicates, these monetary damages are intended to punish a defendant for particularly outrageous or malicious or intentional behavior. Sometimes called "*exemplary*" damages, the award is made to "set an example," at the discretion of the jury, but only when the judge rules that the jury may consider such damages.

Although the number of cases in which punitive damages are awarded is relatively small, when such damages are awarded, the amount tends to be large, since the purpose is to punish the defendant. When a company engages in some sort of really reckless conduct, or continues to manufacture and sell a product after it has knowledge that the product is dangerous or harmful to the public, juries occasionally award punitive damages. In order to "send a message" to a large corporation, the amount of money awarded must be substantial, often several million dollars. In Alaska, a jury awarded punitive damages of several billion dollars after the *Exxon Valdez* oil spill.

Among the most controversial aspects of punitive damages are the following: (1) the plaintiff receives the entire punitive damages award in addition to the compensatory and consequential damages based on the actual losses proved by the plaintiff; (2) the jury has complete discretion to determine the amount of damages it finds appropriate to punish the defendant; (3) the manufacturer of one product may be hit with several punitive damage awards in different lawsuits around the country, each one intended to "send a message"; (4) lawyers have incentive to seek punitive damages, since product liability cases are usually taken on a contingency fee, with the lawyers' compensation based on a percentage of the total award; and (5) the jury may base its decision on passion or sympathy, rather than hard evidence.

Consumer groups and plaintiffs' lawyers have argued in support of the continuation of punitive damages. They assert that when a large company deliberately continues to sell a product with known defects, such as the Dalkon Shield or asbestos, a few relatively modest compensatory damage awards can easily be absorbed by the firm as a business expense. The possibility of a large award of punitive damages, assessed by a jury of ordinary citizens, is necessary to focus the attention of some large firms on the effect of their products and actions of the public.

In recent years, businesses have intensified their attempts to have the U.S. Supreme Court review the legality of punitive damages, or at least to define the standards to be used in such awards. The Supreme Court has accepted several cases, but the decisions have not substantially clarified the situation. Since most punitive damages occur in tort and product liability cases, they are based on state laws and state common law decisions, rather than federal standards. Some states have developed much more generous policies than others, based on case decisions. Business firms have argued that the "due process" clause of the U.S. Constitution requires some fair standards be employed in the determination and awarding of punitive damages.

In 1991 the Supreme Court ruled in *Pacific Mutual Life Insurance v. Haslip* that punitive damages were a long-accepted part of the common law and were not, as a matter of law, unconstitutional. However, the Court stated that in a given case such damages might violate the due process clause if there was not sufficient guidance from the trial court to the jury, and some standards provided on which to base the award.

The *Haslip* case concerned a situation in which an insurance agent fraudulently pocketed premiums from clients, which resulted in the lapse of their health insurance policies, causing considerable financial losses. The jury awarded $210,000 in compensatory damages, and $840,000 in punitive damages. In *Haslip* the Supreme Court mentioned seven factors that the Alabama Supreme Court had established regarding the appropriateness of punitive damages in that state. The jury had been instructed on some of the factors and on the nature of such damages (retribution and deterrence). The court held that trial courts should give juries "adequate guidance" and that appellate courts should have the power to review punitive awards based on standards established in their states. Finding that these "general concerns of reasonableness" had been met, the Supreme Court upheld the award in *Haslip*.

Later cases before the Supreme Court and across the country have both affirmed and reversed awards much higher and lower. In 1993, in a case involving a slander of title to a mineral claim, *TXO Production Corp. v. Alliance Resources*, the Supreme Court upheld an award of $10 million punitive damages, where compensatory damages were only $19,000 (a ratio of 526 to 1). But other state and federal courts have reversed high punitive damages awards, where the ratio was much less than 526-1.

In 1994, in *Honda Motor Co. v. Oberg*, the U.S. Supreme Court did reverse a punitive damages award of $5 million entered against Honda as the result of an injury suffered on a three-wheel all-terrain vehicle. However, the basis for the reversal was not the size of the damages, but the fact that the Oregon legal system did not provide for any judicial review of punitive damages, a principle apparently unique to Oregon. Justice Stevens found that the absence of appellate review based on previously established standards did violate the due process clause of the Constitution.

The next opportunity the Supreme Court had to consider punitive damages was in the 1996 case *BMW of North America v. Gore*. In that case, also from Alabama, Dr. Gore had purchased a new BMW automobile. Some time later, he learned that the car had suffered some scratch and paint damage in shipping and a portion of the car had been repainted before its sale as "new" to Dr. Gore. At trial, the court determined compensatory damages were $4,000 but awarded Gore $2 million to "send a message" to BMW that its policy was deceptive. On appeal, the U.S. Supreme Court found the award (a 500-to-1 ratio) "grossly excessive" and reversed the decision [517 U.S. 559 (1996)]. In the years since the *BMW* case, lower courts in various states have interpreted the decision in many different ways, both affirming and reversing punitive damage awards of more and less than a 500-to-1 ratio.

IN CONSULTATION

Marvin Manager has a problem. His team recently designed a cutting-edge new product that has been named the Jetson 2000. The Jetson is the first product of its kind and is expected to sweep the market before ABC, Inc.'s competitors know what hit them. The research and development supporting the Jetson is extensive—ABC has evaluated the Jetson for quality, ease of use, and most importantly, safety. As each group of Jetsons comes off the production line, a safety inspector pulls random samples and runs them through a series of tests. The Jetson has passed every test—except one.

Ivan Inspector recently reported to Marvin that while he conducted the standard tests on one of the Jetsons, he accidentally spilled a little oil and a small fire erupted. Marvin and Ivan agreed that the risk of such a spill occurring again was very small, but they did not want to take any chances. They convened the Jetson's design team to a meeting where they discussed adding a safety shield. The engineers described two possible alternatives. The first shield was permanently welded onto the Jetson and removed any risk of a fire. The second was bolted on but, with enough effort, could be removed, leaving open the risk of burn injuries. The first shield added $25 to the cost of each Jetson, and the second added only $8. The marketing manager adamantly opposed the welded shield because all of the Jetson's market analysis was based on keeping the price low. Ivan Inspector thought either would be fine since the possibility of a spill was small.

Marvin decided that the shield selection should be based on more than market share and guesses as to the likelihood of a spill. He consulted Laura Lawyer, in-house counsel, to see if the two shields presented differing levels of potential liability. Here is their conversation:

Marvin:	Laura:
1. Given how safe the Jetson is, do we have to use a shield in the first place?	1. Probably. It would only take one accident to create significant product liability for ABC.
2. Doesn't the Jetson's safety record at least justify the less-expensive shield?	2. Not necessarily. Our obligation is to make the product as safe as we can. We do not have to make the product perfectly safe at the expense of our market. We do not, however, relish explaining to an injured customer that we could have made the product safer but it was too expensive to do so.

3. What if we use the cheaper shield and add a warning?

3. Adding a warning helps, but it may not be enough. **Let me review the applicable law to see what our obligation and potential liability is. I'll get back to you.**

FROM THE DESK OF
Laura Lawyer

To: Marvin Manager
Re: Product Liability for Jetson 2000

Dear Marvin:

Product liability law is designed to protect consumers. The law is designed to ensure that innocent product users who suffer injuries can recover their loss. We risk liability if any of our products hurt a purchaser, user, or even by-stander. Product liability law allows an injured user to recover if he or she can prove intentional acts, negligence, defective product, or failure to warn of a known danger. If the Jetson causes injury, the court is likely to look at whether we knew the product was unsafe, whether we did everything we could to make it safer, and whether we warned users of potential risks.

Our awareness that there is a risk of fire is the very reason we do safety tests in the first place. Now that we know the Jetson could burn someone, we protect our customers and ourselves from liability if we make the Jetson safer. If we do not use a shield at all, we have knowingly placed a product into the marketplace that is unsafe. That constitutes at least negligence and possibly even an intentional act. Our liability for any injuries would be very high. The question, then, is which shield we should use.

An unsafe product is a defective product. Since defective products create liability, our goal, then, is to make the Jetson as safe as possible. If making a product as safe as possible merely raises costs, then we have a duty to make the product safer. Every manufacturer wants to make its product in as cost-effective a manner as possible—but cost-effectiveness cannot occur at the expense of safety. In this case, we need to balance the cost of the welded shield against the benefits of the safety it brings to the Jetson. We do not want to lose the profit we are likely to make from the Jetson in a lawsuit with an injured user.

In the alternative, we could use the less expensive, removable bolted shield and then provide a warning. Warning users of a product's potential dangers is an effective defense in a product liability suit. Our best defense, however, is to never injure anyone in the first place. From a legal perspective, our safest course of action is to use the welded shield. We then remove the danger of a fire altogether and thereby remove the defect. If this option continues to distress the marketing manager, I will need very detailed information so that I can prove that raising the cost by $25 will make the product virtually impossible to sell. Then ABC can defend against a product liability lawsuit.

Consider the following questions with regard to product liability:

1. Do you agree with Laura Lawyer, or would you have chosen to add the removable shield and place a warning? What are the risks of following this course of action?
2. Do you think manufacturers should have to go to such lengths to make their products safer when it raises the costs of products that will never injure most of us?
3. Can you propose an alternative way for the law to ensure product safety and yet allow manufacturers to bring costs down and continue to place new products in the marketplace?

OTHER LEGAL ISSUES IN THE SALE OF GOODS

Many other important legal issues frequently arise in connection with the sale of products. As goods move in commerce from manufacturers, to wholesalers, to retailers, and finally to consumers, the various parties create numerous contracts and expectations among one another. When a seller and a buyer make a contract for the purchase of some product, whether it is a shipment of one million pounds of potatoes or one airplane, each is expecting the other to fully perform all obligations, and happily, this is often the case. But what if it does not work out that way? Sometimes either the buyer or seller does not fulfill the obligations he or she promised to perform. What are the rights of the buyer and seller?

Each state has enacted laws dealing with the rights of buyers and sellers of goods. In addition to the provisions we have already discussed dealing with warranties and disclaimers, the **UCC** (adopted by all states but Louisiana) also contains many provisions concerning the rights of the parties involved in the sale of products, as will be discussed in the following sections.

uniform commercial code (UCC): A model law dealing with the sale of goods, adopted by 49 states, that specifies contract rights and remedies of buyers and sellers (and other issues).

BUYER'S RIGHTS AND REMEDIES

UCC §2-711 provides that where the seller fails to make delivery or repudiates the contract (states that he or she will not honor the contract), or the buyer rightfully rejects the goods delivered (usually because they do not conform to the contract), the buyer may cancel the contract. The buyer may also do one or more of the following: (1) "cover" (purchase substitute goods), (2) recover damages for nondelivery, (3) recover certain goods still held by the seller, and/or (4) possibly obtain specific performance.

At the time of delivery, the buyer has the right to inspect the goods to determine if they meet the contract specifications. If they do not, the buyer can **reject** the goods. Sometimes the buyer can even *revoke acceptance* of the goods at a later time, even though he or she did not reject them initially (UCC §2-608). For example, a buyer who did not reject the goods upon delivery because of a reasonable assumption that the problem would be cured or because the nonconformity was difficult to discover may revoke acceptance if this assumption proves false. When the buyer later discovers that the goods are nonconforming, the seller must be notified promptly and before "any substantial change in the condition of the goods" has occurred.

rejection: The buyer inspects the goods and says, "These are not the correct items."

When the buyer rejects or revokes acceptance of the goods or the seller simply does not deliver them, quite often this puts the buyer in a real bind. The buyer may need the goods for his or her business or may have a contract to sell the products to someone else. Therefore, the buyer often decides to **cover**, that is, to purchase substitute goods to meet his or her needs (UCC §2-712). In many cases, the substitute goods will cost more than the contract price, and in such situations, the buyer is permitted to recover the difference along with any incidental damages (such as shipping, storage, and other costs) from the seller who has breached the contract.

cover: The buyer's right to purchase substitute goods if the seller fails to deliver the correct goods.

The buyer does not have to cover, however. He or she may have already accepted the goods when the defects become apparent or have decided to keep the goods even though they were not quite right because of an urgent need to use them in a commercial project. In this case the buyer can deduct his or her damages from the price due the seller. The buyer (and perhaps a court eventually) will have to determine how much less the goods as delivered were worth.

Sometimes the buyer does not want money damages but would rather get the actual goods, as promised. The UCC provides for this remedy in §2-716 by allowing a buyer to seek *specific performance* where "the goods are unique or in other proper circumstances." For example, when the buyer really cannot purchase substitute goods anywhere else or when the goods were specifically made to fit the buyer's requirements, the buyer may be able to force the seller to deliver the actual products that were the subject of the contract.

SELLER'S RIGHTS AND REMEDIES

What if the breach of the sales contract is made by the buyer rather than the seller? Suppose that by contract James promises to deliver 100 custom-made leather jackets to Paula on September 1, 1999. James delivers the 100 jackets to Paula on time and on the correct date, but at that time she tells James that she no longer needs the jackets. She refuses to accept or pay for them. What can James do?

The usual and preferred remedy is for James to **resell** the jackets and then sue Paula for any damages he suffers, such as receiving a lower price for the jackets, and any extra costs incurred, such as storage, advertising, or transportation. James must notify Paula of his intention to resell and must sell the goods in good faith and in a "commercially reasonable" manner, according to UCC §2-706.The objective is to put the seller in as good a position as if the contract had been performed. In some cases the seller may claim, under UCC §2-708, the profit he would have made.

resell: If the buyer wrongfully refuses to accept the goods, the seller can sell the goods and then sue the buyer for any loss.

In some situations, the goods may be specially manufactured for the buyer or are for some other reason unusual and unique. If the seller is unable to resell the goods after reasonable efforts, it may be possible to sue for the *full price* of the products. This is an exception, however, and can only be employed when the goods are essentially worthless to the seller or anyone else. Why? It normally would be unfair to allow the seller to keep the products and receive full payment as well. Suppose that James had made 15 leather jackets individually to fit the members of Paula's professional basketball team, with each person's name and team logo on the jacket. Assuming that the players were all quite large people, it might be impossible for James to sell the jackets elsewhere. Thus, if Paula breached the contract without a good reason, James might be able to recover the price in a legal action.

Interestingly, the seller also has the right to **cure** an instance of nonperformance. If the seller has delivered goods that the buyer refuses to accept

cure: The seller who delivers nonconforming goods to the buyer can correct the deficiency if the contract time limit has not expired.

because they do not conform to the contract, the seller, whenever possible, is given the right to "cure" the nonperformance. UCC §2-508 provides that "where any tender or delivery by the seller is rejected because it is nonconforming [it does not meet the contract requirements] and the time for performance has not yet expired, the seller may reasonably notify the buyer of his intention to cure and may then within the contract time make a conforming delivery." Thus, if James has delivered one month before the end of the contract period jackets that are not quite right and Paula rejects them, James can redo the jackets to meet the contract specifications if he does so in time.

James may even have the right to cure nonperformance after the "contract time" if he had reasonable grounds for believing that the performance would be acceptable. In one case, a seller delivered a newer model of a hearing aid ordered previously by a customer, but the customer refused to accept it and attempted to cancel the contract. The seller was permitted to cure by obtaining the exact (older) model ordered and delivering it to the buyer [*Bartus v. Riccardi*, 281 N.Y.S. 2d 222 (N.Y. 1967)].

SUMMARY

The purchase of manufactured products, an everyday occurrence, involves a series of legal issues of importance to business and consumers. Many sellers provide written *express warranties* with their products that guarantee the item will work properly for a certain time and that the seller will repair it during that same time if a problem develops. The sale of products may also carry *implied warranties*, created by provisions in the UCC, which give consumers certain rights based on their probable expectations at the time of the sale. Both the express and implied warranties may be *disclaimed* to some extent, however, by particular language in the written warranty. The federal Magnuson-Moss Warranty Act establishes requirements for all written warranties, restricts the seller's right to completely disclaim implied warranties, and guarantees the right of consumers to sue for warranty violations.

When individuals are injured due to product defects, lawsuits may be brought based on the legal theories of both negligence and *strict liability*. In a negligence action, the plaintiff must show that the manufacturer did not meet the standards expected of a reasonably careful manufacturer in some aspect of the design, production, or sale of the product, and that this negligence was the cause of the injury.

The strict liability theory, which has been increasingly used by the courts in recent years, is based on the philosophy that those who manufacture defective products should bear the costs of resulting injuries, whether or not the manufacturer was negligent. Thus, in a strict liability case, the plaintiff need prove only that the product was *defective*, was unreasonably dangerous, and caused the injury. The increase in number and size of product liability judgments based on strict liability has led many state legislatures to put restrictions on the total freedom of juries to award damages in such cases. Legislation has been introduced in Congress that would establish a uniform set of federal product liability standards and that would make other major changes in the tort liability system.

Other important legal issues arise in connection with the sale of products, such as the rights and responsibilities of buyers and sellers when one side fails or refuses to perform in accordance with the contract. The UCC contains a series of rules for dealing with the breach of sales contracts. The buyer has the *right to reject* goods that do not conform to the contract and may also have the right to *cover* (purchase substitute goods) in the event of improper performance by the seller. On the other hand, if the buyer refuses to pay for the goods, the seller can *resell the goods* and sue the buyer for his or her losses or, in some cases, for the whole price. If the seller delivers goods that do not conform to the contract and there is still some time left before final performance is due, the seller can often *cure* that nonperformance by promptly delivering the proper goods. In most situations, the UCC's remedy is designed to place the parties, as nearly as possible, in the position they would have occupied had the contract been fully performed.

CHAPTER QUESTIONS

1. Johnny was riding his new bicycle when the front wheel came off, and he was injured. His family sued the store where the bike was purchased for violation of the warranty of fitness for a particular purpose, arguing that the store knew that the bike was to be used for pleasure riding by a young boy. What should be the result? Why? [*Crump v. Times Square Stores*, 157 AD 2d 768, 550 NYS 2d 373 (1990)]
2. A customer eating at a Wendy's Restaurant in North Carolina was injured when he chomped on a 1½-inch bone in a hamburger. He sued the company for violation of the implied warranty of merchantability. If North Carolina follows the "reasonable expectation" test, will he win? Explain. [*Goodman v. Wenco Management*, 100 NC App. 108, 394 SE 2d 832 (1990)]
3. A consumer sued a chemical manufacturer claiming that her throat, lungs, and breathing were injured when she opened a container of swimming pool chlorinator tablets. She brought an action under product liability theory for failure to provide adequate directions for opening, closing, and storage of the container. However, the Federal Insecticide, Fungicide, and Rodenticide Act (FIFRA) sets forth standards for labeling such chemical products, and the defendant argued that the federal law should preempt any state law product liability claim over labeling.

   These standards and subsequent EPA regulations were quite specific regarding label content and placement on chemical products. The act also provides that states "shall not impose or continue in effect any requirements for labeling or packaging in addition to or different from those required under the EPA regulations implementing FIFRA." Should the lawsuit be preempted, or allowed to go forward on the product liability claims? Why? [*Hawkins v. Leslie's Pool Mart, Inc.*, 184 F.3d 244 (3d Cir. 1999)]
4. During a July 4 fireworks show at the Western Washington State Fairgrounds in Puyallup, one of the mortars was knocked into a horizontal position. A rocket inside then ignited and flew 500 feet parallel to the ground where it discharged, causing injury to several spectators. The exact

cause of the malfunction could not be determined. The plaintiffs sued under strict liability, arguing that fireworks displays are an "ultrahazardous activity" and the operators of the fireworks show should be strictly liable without a showing of negligence or fault. What should be the result? Why? [*Klein v. Pyrodyne Corp.*, 117 Wash.2d 1, 810 P.2d 917 (1991)]

5. Mr. Laaperi purchased a smoke detector for the family home from Sears, which he then installed. The detector was powered by AC (electrical) current. Less than one year later, the home was destroyed, and Laaperi's three sons were killed by a fire. The smoke detector did not function because the fire started due to a short circuit in the boys' bedroom, which cut off power to the detector. Laaperi sued Sears on the grounds that Sears had negligently failed to warn purchasers that the very same electrical problems that could cause a fire in a home would render this type of smoke detector useless. He stated that if he had understood this risk, he would not have purchased that model detector or, at the very least, would have purchased a battery-powered detector as a backup. What should be the result and why? [*Laaperi v. Sears, Roebuck & Co.*, 787 F.2d 726 (1st Cir. 1986)]
6. Jaime Camacho was operating his two-month-old Honda motorcycle when he collided with an automobile and suffered serious leg injuries. He sued not only the other motorist but also Honda under a strict liability theory, claiming that the motorcycle was defectively designed and therefore unreasonably dangerous. Camacho argued that the motorcycle was not equipped with "crash bars" (steel bars connected to the frame), which would have protected his legs in the event of a collision. The trial court dismissed this claim, and Camacho appealed. What should be the result if Colorado follows the crashworthiness doctrine? [*Camacho v. Honda Motor Co.*, 741 P.2d 1240 (Colo. 1987)]
7. What ethical obligation should a manufacturing firm have toward consumers with respect to its products? Should it have ethical obligations to its wholesalers and retailers? Do these entities have ethical duties to the consumers?
8. In question 9 at the end of Chapter 11, you were asked about the negligence aspects of a recent lawsuit by the Port Authority of New York against the manufacturer of the fertilizer used in the 1993 bombing of the World Trade Center. The Port Authority also included a count in its complaint alleging violation of product liability. The Port Authority argued that the manufacturers should have known for many years that their products were and had been used to make bombs. Furthermore, it was alleged that since 1968 a process has been available to make ammonium nitrate fertilizer nondetonable but was not used by this manufacturer. Should the court dismiss the product liability part of the case or allow it to go forward to the jury? Was the product defective? Unreasonably dangerous? [*Port Authority of New York and New Jersey v. Arcadian Corp.*, 189 F.3d 305 (3d Cir. 1999)]
9. For many years, most state courts have followed a theory called the "learned intermediary doctrine," which provided drug manufacturers with immunity from product liability lawsuits when their products were prescribed by a doctor. A group of women recently filed suit against the maker of Norplant, a contraceptive device implanted under the skin of a woman's upper arm. The plaintiffs alleged that the manufacturer had failed to ade-

quately warn of the product's adverse side effects. Norplant sought dismissal of the suit on the basis of the learned intermediary doctrine.

The plaintiffs urged the New Jersey courts to disregard the doctrine because the circumstances underlying the theory (patients relying on their own doctors to make decisions in their best interests) had changed. They asked the court to hold that the "antiquated premises" of the rule no longer exist today, at least for drugs that are advertised and marketed directly to the public through expensive mass media campaigns. They believed that manufacturers of such drugs should be held to the same product liability standards as manufacturers of other products. Should the court apply the rule or allow the product liability suit to go forward? Why? [*Perez v. Wyeth Laboratories*, 161 N.J. 1, 734 A.2d 1245 (1999)]

10. A helicopter engine was manufactured by General Motors and sold to Bell Helicopter in 1971. Several months later Bell sold the completed helicopter. After 14 years of use, the original purchaser sold the helicopter to a used aircraft dealer, who then sold it to a leasing business. The dealer and leasing business entered into a contract that provided that, among other things, the risk of loss would pass to the purchaser after acceptance of the aircraft, and the helicopter was sold "as is."

    About three years later, the helicopter suffered considerable damage as the result of a power loss, perhaps due to the engine. The leasing company brought suit against General Motors, the manufacturer. What should be the result? Discuss the warranty and strict product liability theories applicable here. [*Bocre Leasing Corp. v. General Motors Corp.*, 621 NYS 2d 497, 645 NE 2d 1195 (1995)]

PRACTICAL EXERCISE

Your friend Larry visited Hawaii several years ago. While there, he and his wife, Lucille, visited an art gallery several times, and eventually purchased two expensive pieces of artwork (original lithographs), supposedly done and hand-signed by the famed surrealist artist Salvador Dali. In the years since, the gallery has solicited Larry and Lucille several times, offering them more Dali works of art, and they have purchased three more lithographs and two wall sculptures. To date, Larry and Lucille have spent more than $35,000 purchasing Dali pieces from this gallery. At the time of each purchase, the gallery assured Larry that the work was done by Dali, and furnished him with a written "Certificate of Authenticity" and an appraisal stating that the piece was of equal or greater value than the purchase price.

Recently Larry and Lucille found out that many complaints had been made against the gallery for selling forged artwork and that the Hawaii Attorney General had filed a complaint against the gallery. Knowing that you are studying law, Larry has asked you to comment on his rights as the purchaser of artwork. "Aren't there some kind of warranty laws that I could use if the art is not genuine?" he asks you. Prepare a memo for Larry and Lucille describing express warranties and implied warranties, the seller's defenses, and the Magnuson-Moss Warranty Act. Also, advise them on their chances of winning a lawsuit using any of these theories. You need to discuss, among other issues, the "basis of the bargain" concept necessary to create an express warranty, as well as the seller's likely defense that UCC §2-313(2) states that "any affirmation merely of the value of the goods or a statement purporting to be merely the seller's opinion" regarding the goods does not create a warranty.

FURTHER INFORMATION

www.cpsc.gov
Consumer Product Safety Commission.

http://productslaw.com
A variety of product liability information.

http://atra.org
American Tort Reform Association site.

http://www.implantclaims.com
Dow Corning Corporation Chapter 11 Breast Implant Claim site.

CHAPTER 14

PROPERTY: REAL, PERSONAL, AND INTELLECTUAL

LEARNING OBJECTIVES

After you have read this chapter, you should be able to:

1. Define real property and describe the different kinds of estates.
2. Discuss the process of acquiring ownership of real property, including financing and recording.
3. List the ways in which laws restrict the use of real property.
4. Define and give examples of personal property.
5. Explain the legal issues involving intellectual property.
6. Discuss how property owners can control the transfer of property through wills and trusts.

CHAPTER OUTLINE

I. Real Property
II. Personal Property
III Intellectual Property
IV. Wills, Probate, and Trusts

As this chapter explains, a copyright protects an author of a book, a musical piece, or a computer program against someone else copying the exact "expression" used by the first author. But suppose someone develops a computer program or software that looks and acts like your copyrighted software, without copying the actual computer code. Is this legal? The "Practical Exercise" at the end of the chapter raises such an issue.

INTRODUCTION

The right to own property and to prevent other persons from using, abusing, or interfering with one's property rights is basic to the free enterprise system. Almost every business will need to rent or own real and personal property of some kind. In this chapter, we examine the different legal concepts pertinent to real property (real estate) and personal property and discuss the methods of acquiring, maintaining, and transferring ownership of each type of property. Next, we examine and compare the various kinds of "intellectual property," an increasingly important form of property in today's business world.

Real property includes land and everything permanently attached to it, as well as the airspace above it and minerals beneath its surface. The legal principles that apply to real property in the United States today are based on common law doctrines, many of which originated in feudal times in Europe. Personal property, on the other hand, generally includes all property that is not real property. Personal property may be tangible (such as chairs, computers, and automobiles) or intangible (such as patents, accounts receivable, and stock). Finally, intellectual property, a type of personal property, includes innovations, inventions, works of literature, art, music, computer programs, trademarks, and "property" that has originated from a person's creative efforts.

REAL PROPERTY

As we have noted, much of the law regarding real property can be traced back to English decisions from the Middle Ages. In medieval England, the ownership of land determined one's position in society. The legal principles that developed protected the lord of the manor and his crops, animals, and houses, and sustained his wealth and his position of power. Over hundreds of years the rules relating to ownership, use, and inheritance of property developed into important common law legal doctrines. The other primary "common law" topics—contracts and torts—began to develop only as offshoots of property-related transactions and problems. Legal theories concerning such matters as contracts for the sale of land and "trespass" and "nuisance" torts affecting the rights of land owners evolved in this way, especially after the industrial revolution as changes occurred to the mercantile society.

The rights of private property owners have always been accorded a very high priority in the United States. The early American legal doctrines were based on the English principles but were modified after reaching this country. Some, but not all, of the numerous detailed rules regarding property were discarded over time. Spanish and French legal theories also had some influence on the development of American common law relating to real property.

freehold estate: An ownership interest lasting at least for one's life.

Historically, an estate (ownership interest) in land could be categorized as "freehold" or "nonfreehold." **Freehold estates** were those that were compatible with a free man, in that they lasted for at least the length of a person's life. Nonfreehold estates, conversely, lasted for a set period of time (whether 30 days or 30 years); hence a tenant acquires not ownership but the legal right to possession.

TYPES OF OWNERSHIP

Fee Simple Absolute The most complete type of ownership possible is called the **fee simple absolute**. The word *fee* denotes an ownership interest. The owner of a fee simple absolute (often just called "fee simple") can use or abuse the land; can sell, lease, or mortgage it; and can leave it to his or her heirs upon death. Because of zoning, environmental issues, and other restrictions to be discussed later, it is not quite accurate to say the owner can do "anything" with the land. However, when you purchase property for your home or business, you will almost certainly want to own it in fee simple.

fee simple absolute: The most complete ownership of real property.

Fee Simple Determinable Let us suppose that Jill is selling some land to Thomas. Sometimes the grantor (the person selling or giving the land) will put a clause in the deed, such as "To Thomas, so long as this property is never used as a tavern." Although Thomas will have a fee simple ownership, if the land is ever used as a tavern, the title *automatically* reverts back to Jill (the grantor) or her heirs. Since Thomas has only those rights to the land, when he sells the land to Teresa, she will be subject to the same condition. If she ever allows the property to be used as a tavern, the title goes back to Jill. This type of deed is often used by those who donate land to cities for parks or schools to guarantee that the land will always be used in that fashion. If a city school district used, for non-school purposes, land given to it under a **fee simple determinable,** the title to the land would automatically revert to the grantor or his or her heirs.

fee simple determinable: A fee simple ownership that may be lost if the property is used in certain ways.

Fee Simple on a Condition Subsequent A fee simple on a condition subsequent is similar to the fee simple determinable, except that the title does not revert automatically. If the deed says, "To Thomas except that if the land is ever used as a tavern, the grantor has the right to retake possession and ownership," it is a fee simple on a condition subsequent. Thomas's title to the land will not be extinguished (even if he operates a tavern) until the grantor (Jill) takes action to repossess the land.

Life Estate The **life estate** is a type of freehold estate that exists for as long as a particular person lives. If the deed states, "To Sarah for life and then to Ryan," Sarah has a life estate. It is a freehold interest in that she has the exclusive right to possess the land, use it, lease it, and maybe even sell it (her life interest). When she dies, however, the land will belong to Ryan. If she sells the land to Verne, his ownership will end when Sarah dies. Sarah has the rights of all other freehold owners, except that she cannot "waste" the property—that is, destroy its value.

life estate: A type of ownership that lasts only for the life of the owner and cannot be extended.

Although Ryan or his heirs will certainly own the land some day, he does not have any legal rights of entry or possession of the property now. Ryan has what is called a **future interest** in the real estate. He has a legal interest in the property; but for now, this interest is not a right to possession or ownership. He can only take legal action if he believes Sarah is wasting the property. Although he may be very concerned with the use of the land and with Sarah's health ("How are you doing? Don't you feel kind of sick?"), he must await her death before he can become the owner.

future interest: A legal right in real property, which will or may become full ownership in the future.

Jill, the grantor in the earlier examples, also has a future interest in the property if it is a fee simple determinable or fee simple on a condition subsequent. Her future interest is "contingent" because Jill may or may not reacquire ownership of the property; she does have, however, a present legal interest in it that may possibly become possessory in the future.

nonfreehold estate: A legal right to possession, but not ownership, of real property, such as a lease.

Nonfreehold Estates The most common type of **nonfreehold estate** is the landlord–tenant relationship. In this case, the fee simple owner makes an agreement to transfer possession (but not ownership) to another person for a period of time. Whether the property is rented for one month or 40 years, the tenant acquires the legal right to possession but does not become the owner.

The landlord (lessor) retains the ownership of the land during the term of the lease. The tenant (lessee) acquires an interest depending on the type of lease. In an *estate for years*, the tenant has the right of possession for a definite period, often one or more years, but it may be for any specific time. In a **periodic tenancy** the property is rented for a certain period, often one month at a time. This type of tenancy can generally be ended when either party gives the other one month's notice. An *estate at will* is not based on any formal rental period but may exist as long as both parties allow it to. This type of tenancy is often created when a tenant "holds over"—holds on to the premises after the lease expires. The landlord can either accept rent and the tenant becomes "at will," or he can begin eviction procedures.

periodic tenancy: A tenancy lasting for a certain time.

Concurrent Ownership At any one time two or more persons may own together any of the various types of real estate interests, except the life estate described previously. The most frequent type of joint ownership is the **tenancy in common**. (Note that even though the word *tenancy* is used, this can either be a freehold or nonfreehold estate.)

tenancy in common: Ownership of property by two or more persons. Each can sell his or her share or leave to heirs. Shares do not have to be equal.

In a tenancy in common, two or more persons own together an "undivided" interest in the property. *Undivided* means that although the persons each own a certain percentage of the total property, no one owns any particular area within the property. The ownership interests do not have to be the same percentage and do not have to arise at the same time. When one co-owner dies, she can leave her percentage of ownership to her heirs. In other words, if Stacey, Bill, and Jessica own a piece of property as tenants in common, it is possible for Stacey to own 50 percent, Bill to own 30 percent, and Jessica 20 percent of the total. No one of them has any greater rights to any particular area within the property, since the ownership is undivided. If the property is sold, each owner will receive his or her proportionate share of the proceeds. If Stacey decides to sell her interest to Bruce, he would then become a tenant in common with Bill and Jessica. If Bill dies, his share of ownership will pass to his heirs.

joint tenancy: Ownership of property by two or more persons. When one dies, his or her share is automatically distributed to the co-owners who **survive**. Joint tenants cannot leave their share to their heirs. Shares must be equal.

In a **joint tenancy**, some aspects of ownership are different. All ownership interests must be equal, no matter how many joint tenants there are. Joint tenancy interests must be created at the same time and carry the right of **survivorship**. Thus, if Stacey, Bill, and Jessica own a property in joint tenancy, they will each own a one-third interest that was created by the same deed to the three of them. If Bill dies, his interest will automatically be redistributed to Stacey and Jessica, not to his heirs. Stacey and Jessica will then be joint tenants, each owning a one-half interest in the property. Even if Bill had drafted a will leaving his share of the property to his sister, she will receive nothing if the property was owned in joint tenancy. Because this is an unusual condition, the courts will rule that a tenancy in common exists if any doubt exists about the type of ownership or any confusion arises about whether a joint tenancy or tenancy in common was intended.

One of the joint tenants can convey his or her portion of the estate to someone else without permission of the others, however. If, for example, Stacey sells her one-third interest to Bruce, he will then have a one-third interest in the property. But he will not be a joint tenant with Bill and Jessica, since he did not acquire his interest at the same time as they did. He will be a tenant in common with the other two, while Bill and Jessica will remain as joint tenants to each other.

Between husband and wife, a special form of joint tenancy exists called the **tenancy by the entireties**. This estate is similar to a joint tenancy, except it only exists for persons married to each other. The law presumes that a married person who buys property with his spouse would want her to automatically become the sole owner in case of his death. If this is not what both spouses want, then they should not purchase property together. Unlike a regular joint tenancy, one spouse cannot convey any interest in property owned in tenancy by the entireties without the signature of the other. Divorce, however, usually converts this tenancy into a tenancy in common; in this case, either party can convey his or her interest. Tenancy by the entireties is used in about one-half of the United States. (The western states, for example, do not use this form of joint tenancy.)

tenancy by the entireties: A type of joint tenancy for married couples.

Property acquired during marriage by married couples in nine states—Arizona, California, Idaho, Louisiana, Nevada, New Mexico, Texas, Washington, and Wisconsin—is owned as **community property**. This concept, originated in Spanish law, means that all property bought or acquired during

community property: A type of property ownership for married couples recognized in nine states.

FROM THE DESK OF
Laura Lawyer

To: Students
From: Your Lawyer

If you desire to purchase property with others as joint tenants, you need to make sure that the deed is drafted properly. The deed must clearly convey the property to "A, B, and C as joint tenants, with rights of survivorship." If there is any ambiguity, the courts will construe the ownership as tenancy in common, since that is a much more typical type of concurrent ownership. In a tenancy in common, of course, when a property owner dies, his or her share is passed on to heirs.

marriage is presumed to be part of the "marital community," owned equally by both spouses. Such property cannot be conveyed without the signature of both spouses. When one spouse dies, the ownership of community property passes to the surviving spouse. It is sometimes possible, although difficult, for one spouse to maintain as "separate property" sole ownership in property owned by him or her prior to marriage or inherited during marriage. Only individual funds can be used to maintain the property, and receipts from and expenses related to the property must not be commingled with the community property of the couple (such as a joint bank account) or the asset will become community property. Many divorce cases in these nine states have been characterized by nasty fights over property that one spouse tried to keep "separate" and out of the marital community.

ACQUIRING OWNERSHIP OF REAL PROPERTY

deed: A written document used to transfer ownership in real property.

Deeds The primary method of transferring ownership in real property is through the sale by one owner to another confirmed by proper execution of a **deed**. A deed is a formally drafted document that conveys ownership from one or more persons to another individual or group. The deed must meet the following requirements:

- It must be written.
- It must name the grantor(s), which is the person or persons giving up ownership, and the grantee(s), which is the person or persons acquiring ownership.
- It needs to be signed by the grantor(s).
- It has to provide the legal description of the property.
- It must contain certain words indicating that the property is being conveyed.
- It must be witnessed by two or three persons (depending on the state law).

warranty deed: A deed that "warrants" that the buyer is receiving good, clear title to the property.

quitclaim deed: A deed that merely conveys what ownership the grantor has without any warranties.

There are several types of deeds. The most common type of deed—and the best form from a purchaser's standpoint—is the **warranty deed**. This instrument contains a "warranty" or promise from the seller to the buyer that he or she is getting good title (a clear title with no defects or problems). Another common type of deed is called a **quitclaim deed**. This document, generally used only to clear up title problems, contains no promises or warranties of any kind. All the seller is stating is that "I am giving you whatever interest I have in this property" (in other words, "I am quitting whatever claim I had to this property"). If you are purchasing real estate for your home or business, you want to make sure you receive a warranty deed for the property.

Inheritance Often the ownership of real estate is acquired by inheritance. In many cases, this happens when an owner of property dies, leaving a will (discussed later in this chapter). The will might state, for example, that "I leave my real property in Washington County called 'Blackacre' to my niece, Heather." After the court concludes the probate process (procedures for disposing of the assets of the deceased person), Heather will be declared the owner of the property in fee simple.

For those who die without a will, any real estate they own will, following the probate process, become the property of their nearest heir as specified by the laws of that state.

Adverse Possession It is also possible for someone to gain ownership of property through the doctrine of "**adverse possession**." In this case, the property is clearly owned by one person, but another person begins to use part of the land without permission. After a certain period of years passes (which may vary from 5 to 20 years, depending on the state), the adverse possessor can become the owner of the property. This doctrine appeared in English common law as far back as the reign of Henry I (1100 A.D.) when land ownership or "seizin" was based upon possession. Possession and title to property were not separated, as they are today (as we discussed in connection with life estates and landlord–tenant matters). When an owner lost possession of land, he (and it was always "he" in those days) lost ownership as well. During the reign of Henry VIII, a statute was passed prohibiting persons from bringing actions to regain possession of land after three score (60) years. Later, while James I was king, the time for these and certain other suits to be filed was changed to 20 years, which became the "common law" rule regarding adverse possession upon the founding of the United States.

adverse possession: One person obtains title to real property by actually "possessing" a portion of the property, for a number of years, without the permission of the owner.

One of the reasons the adverse possession rule survived in the United States was that it forced property owners to look after their land. In order to acquire ownership by adverse possession, the use has to be "*open and notorious*." If the true owner looks at the land, he should readily see that another is using it. The possession must also be "*adverse*," that is, hostile to the owner and without his permission. Quietly sneaking on the land once in a while at night to build a campfire will not work. One court said that the adverse possessor must basically "unfurl his flag" there. The use must also be continuous, with no breaks in usage for the required time period. Some states require the adverse user to "farm it or fence it" to let the true owner know that ownership is being claimed.

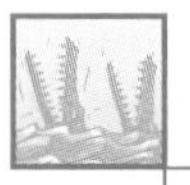

SOCIAL/ETHICAL ISSUES

What do you think of the doctrine of adverse possession? Do you think a legal theory that allows one person to acquire ownership of another's property simply by using it—without permission—makes sense in today's world? Does this encourage responsible property ownership or does it encourage trespassing?

Although some adverse possession cases do occur when one person intentionally begins using land owned by another, others result from fences being improperly placed or rivers changing course. In these situations, if the fence is mistakenly put in the wrong place and the land is actively used by the apparent owner for the required period of time, it is possible that the legal boundary has been changed by the theory of adverse possession. In many western states, for example, the period is only five years, so it behooves owners of property to double-check fence lines, to examine their land "back in the hills" every so often to make sure no one else is using it, and to take action to evict all who are using it.

The following case describes an adverse possession dispute that occurred in rural Alaska.

NOME 2000 V. FAGERSTROM

799 P.2d 304 (Alaska 1990)

FACTS

Charles Fagerstrom recalls that his family used a piece of land overlooking the Nome River in Alaska in the 1940s, while he was still a child, for subsistence and recreation purposes. In 1966 he and his wife brought a small quantity of building materials onto the property. In 1970 or 1971 the Fagerstroms placed four corner-posts on the property to stake off a rectangular portion. They also built a picnic area on one end of the parcel, including a gravel pit, beachwood blocks as chairs, firewood and a 50-gallon barrel for use as a stove. In July 1974 they placed a camper trailer on the north end of the parcel until September, and they repeated this action every summer until 1978. At about the same time, they build an outhouse and a fish rack on the north end of the parcel and planted some spruce trees.

In the summer of 1977 the Fagerstroms built a reindeer shelter on the north end of the parcel, about 8 feet by 8 feet and tall enough for Charles to stand up in it. They also built a pen, about 75 feet in diameter, around the shelter, and housed a reindeer for about six weeks in the summer of 1978. They testified that they were present on the parcel from 1974 through 1978 "every other weekend or so" and "a couple of times during the week if the weather was good." They did, however, allow other people to occasionally come onto the land to pick berries and to fish. In the summer of 1978, the Fagerstroms built a cabin on the property and used the property more extensively after that. However, the record title to the property was held by a firm called Nome 2000. In July 1987, Nome 2000 filed an action to eject the Fagerstroms from the land. Mr. and Mrs. Fagerstrom counterclaimed, arguing that they had acquired title by adverse possession. The trial court, after a jury trial, ruled in favor of the Fagerstroms, and Nome 2000 appealed to the Alaska Supreme Court.

DECISION

Alaska law provides that title to property could be acquired by adverse possession following a 10-year period. Quoting from an older case, the court stated that in order to win, the claimant must show that for the statutory period, "his use of the land was continuous, open and notorious, exclusive and hostile to the true owner." Nome 2000 argued that the Fagerstroms had not met these tests in part because they did not make "significant physical improvements" or show "substantial activity" on the land. Nome admitted that when they constructed the cabin, the Fagerstroms started to be adverse possessors, but that prior to that, their use was insufficient. Nome filed suit in 1987.

The Alaska Supreme Court, in an opinion by Chief Justice Matthews, rejected the arguments of Nome 2000. Stating that nothing in the law requires "significant improvements," the Court ruled that the type of acts necessary for adverse possession depends on the character of the land in question. Where, as here, the land is rural, a lesser degree of dominion and control may be sufficient. With regard to the necessary elements of continuity and exclusivity of possession, the court stated that the question was whether the land was used as an average owner of similar property would use it.

Finding that the disputed parcel was located in a rural area suitable as a seasonal homesite for subsistence and recreational activities, the Court held that this was exactly how the Fagerstroms had used it. Since Nome 2000 admitted the Fagerstroms' adverse possession from 1978 to 1987, the Court focused its inquiry on activities from the summer of 1977 to summer 1978. It found that the Fagerstroms' conduct went well beyond "mere casual and occasional trespasses" and instead "evidenced a purpose to exercise exclusive dominion over the property." Justice Matthews noted that they had placed certain structures such as an outhouse, a fish rack, and a large reindeer pen on the premises for the entire year. During the warmer season the Fagerstroms also placed a camper trailer on blocks on the disputed parcel. The fact that they allowed others to pick berries and fish was consistent with the conduct of "a hospitable landowner" and did nothing to undermine their continuity or exclusivity of ownership.

As to the notoriety requirement, the court found that "a quick investigation of the premises, especially during the season which it was best suited for use, would have been sufficient to place a reasonably diligent landowner on notice that someone may have been exercising dominion and control over at least the northern portion of the property." Further inquiry would have shown that the members of the community regarded the Fagerstroms as the owners. Thus, the notoriety test had been met.

Nome 2000 also argued that the Fagerstroms' adverse possession claim should be denied because they may not have really intended to claim ownership during the time of their possession. An expert witness for Nome 2000 testified that the Fagerstroms' use of the property was consistent with traditional Native American land use, which does not recognize exclusive ownership, but is more in the nature of stewardship. "That is, other members of the claimant's social group may share in the resources of the land without obtaining permission, so long as the resources are not abused or destroyed." However, the Court rejected this argument as well, stating that what the Fagerstroms believed or intended has nothing to do with the legal question of whether their possession was hostile. "Hostility is determined by application of an objective test which simply asks whether the possessor 'acted toward the land as if he owned it,'" stated the Court.

Therefore, the Supreme Court upheld the decision of the trial court that the Fagerstroms had acquired title to the land by adverse possession for the required period of time. The court did, however, only award them title to the northern portion of the property, where the structures were located. The trial court had included the southern portion, where the Fagerstroms had merely used preexisting trails for recreation and had occasionally picked up litter. The Supreme Court held that these actions did not show exercise of dominion and control and thus did not lead to title by adverse. The case was remanded to the lower court for further hearings on the exact boundaries of each portion of the land.

CASE QUESTIONS

1. What were the most important facts supporting the Fagerstroms' case for adverse possession? Do you agree that the Fagerstroms exercised dominion and control over the property?
2. Do you agree with the Court's decision? What purpose is served here by taking the title to the property away from the true record owner? What ethical principles are involved?
3. If this property had been a residential lot within a city, would the Fagerstroms' actions have been enough to acquire title by adverse possession?

Financing of Real Estate Transactions Most of us do not have enough funds in the bank to pay cash when we purchase a house. Therefore, a complex system of financing real estate transactions has arisen. Usually when purchasing a home or other real property, the buyer will arrange for a loan from a bank or other lender for most of the purchase price. The buyer will sign a "mortgage note" that is a written promise to pay the loan back on a specific schedule, often as long as 30 years.

When the lender advances such a substantial sum of money, it wants some security for its loan—in other words, it wants to be a "secured lender." Before making the loan, the lender will almost certainly want to take a security interest in the real property being conveyed. For example, Peter purchases a house.

He pays $10,000 down, and borrows $80,000 in the form of a "mortgage loan" from Friendly Bank to pay the rest. When Peter receives the money (which is then immediately transferred to the seller of the house), he signs a document called a **mortgage**. This legal instrument gives Friendly Bank a **security interest** in the real property. If Peter does not make his loan payments, Friendly Bank can take action to **foreclose** on the mortgage.

mortgage: An agreement to give a lender a legal right in real property owned by another person.

security interest: The legal interest in property owned by another that allows a creditor to repossess and resell collateral and to apply the proceeds to pay off the owner's loan.

foreclosure: The process by which the holder of the mortgage exercises the legal right to force the sale of the property.

redemption period: A period of time during which a foreclosed owner can re-acquire the property.

recording: Filing a deed or mortgage in a public records office to give notice to others of the legal interests in the real property.

Each state has a statute governing foreclosure of mortgages, and there are some differences among the laws. However, in general, a lender must notify the owner that he or she is in "default" on the mortgage loan obligations. If the owner does not quickly comply, the lender can begin the process of foreclosure. This usually involves a certain number of publications in the newspaper (the easy-to-read "Legal Notices" section), followed by a public sale of the property.

Although anyone can attend and bid on the property at the foreclosure sale, often the lender is the only bidder and purchases the property for the amount of the outstanding mortgage. The lender (bank or mortgage company) then resells the property to someone else later. The proceeds are applied to the former owner's loan obligation; if that still does not pay off the balance (after adding the costs of the foreclosure sale) the former owner will still be liable and may be sued for the "deficiency."

As a means of affording compassion to homeowners who lose their property, most state statutes allow the foreclosed owner a **redemption period** after the sale. During this time, which might be as long as six months, the foreclosed owner can redeem the property by paying the entire sale price plus expenses to whomever (usually the lender) purchased the property at the sale. That step is usually only possible if the individual obtains another new mortgage loan or wins the lottery, and this does not occur often. After all, if the homeowner had the money, he or she would have paid the loan in the first place. After the redemption period expires, the buyer can sell the property to someone else.

Recording The proper execution of the mortgage and the mortgage loan documents establish the rights between the lender and the borrower in a real estate transaction. However, in order to safeguard the buyer and lender against other legal interests in the property, the documents should be **recorded**. In each county there is an office, often called the "County Recorder" or "Register of Deeds," that maintains official records of all real estate transactions.

When Peter purchases property from Nina, he will no doubt receive a warranty deed and will probably execute a mortgage in favor of a lender like Friendly Bank. Peter and Friendly will record these documents in the appropriate offices to protect their ownership and security interests, respectively. By filing these documents with the county official, they will be giving *notice of their rights* to anyone who might consider taking a legal interest in that property in the future.

Sometimes through dishonesty or mistake, two parties claim interest in the same real property, and it will be necessary to decide who has the primary claim. These disputes are often settled by deciding who recorded first. For example, suppose Peter purchases a home from Nina on June 10 for $90,000 but does not record his deed. Nina is in urgent need of cash and short on honesty, so on June 20 she sells the home (again) to Lois for $85,000. Lois knows nothing about the sale to Peter. When Peter and Lois both claim ownership of the house, who wins? (By this time, Nina has disappeared and is enjoying life somewhere in the Caribbean.)

In the majority of states, where there are two *bona fide purchasers* (those who buy in good faith, without knowledge of any fraud), the first one to record his or her instrument will have a superior claim. Why? Between two innocent purchasers, the law disfavors the one who could have done something to prevent the harm. In this example, if Peter had recorded his deed, that would have provided notice to the world (including Lois) of his interest, and the problem may not have occurred. In most states, then, if Lois were to record her deed before Peter recorded his, she would be considered the rightful owner of the property. Of course, Peter could sue Nina if he ever can find her; between the two innocent purchasers, however, generally the one who records first has greater rights to ownership of the property.

RESTRICTIONS ON THE USE OF REAL PROPERTY

As we mentioned previously, regardless of the type of ownership one has, usually owners are not permitted to do "anything they want" with their property. Such legal restrictions as zoning laws, land use planning requirements, restrictive covenants, easements, and environmental regulations often put limits on what the landowner can do with the property. First, we will discuss a venerable common law theory that may be used when one person's legal use of his or her property causes problems for the neighbors.

Nuisance The common law principle called **nuisance** holds that there is a right of action for a landowner whose use and enjoyment of his or her property is adversely affected by another's use of his or her property. Most of us would quickly agree with the proposition that "you should be able to use your land in any *legal* way." However, if Jim lives in a nice residential area and his next-door neighbor Brian decides to open a cattle feed lot or a toxic waste dump on his property, Jim might not embrace this theory so completely. Brian's use of his property would no doubt significantly interfere with Jim's backyard barbecues and volleyball games.

nuisance: A common law theory that allows one owner a right to sue a neighbor if that person's use of his or her land interferes with the first owner's use and enjoyment of his or her property.

In hundreds of cases over the years, nuisance theory has been employed to a wide variety of lawful actions, including cattle feed lots; industrial factories that produce smoke, dust, and noise; even churches that have lighted baseball fields on which night games are played. In recent years, many cases have raised issues regarding the right of homeowners to have unrestricted sunlight when neighbors build structures on their land that interfere with such light. Other conflicts have occurred when subdivisions move out into rural areas and encounter common farm land use customs (involving manure, other fertilization practices, and noise) that conflict with suburban homeowner expectations.

Zoning Starting more than 70 years ago, communities began to develop zoning regulations in order to prevent some of these land use conflicts. City planners reasoned that rather than having one neighbor sue another whenever a new use of land was undertaken, it makes better sense to control, in advance, the use of land. As a result, cities and counties began to specify that certain areas of their jurisdiction be reserved for single-family homes, apartments, heavy industrial manufacturing, commercial use, and so on. This practice is

zoning: A plan developed by a city or county that regulates the uses of land in different "zones" of the city or county.

called **zoning**—that is, dividing the city into zones in which different land uses are allowed.

Zoning maps are usually drawn and decisions made—with the assistance of professional staff—by a citizens panel. Once the first zoning plan is established, it must be constantly revised as new areas undergo development and land use patterns change. All over the country, subdivisions are being developed in areas that used to be farmland.

Zoning classifications do restrict what an owner can do with his or her land. For example, if Letitia owns some property that is zoned for single-family residential housing, she will not be able to build a shopping mall there. She may go to the zoning board and attempt to have the classification of her property changed; however, if all the land around her is residential, she will have a difficult time persuading the zoning board to make the change. Still, as the population expands, land use patterns may change, and zoning boards do change classifications from time to time to reflect physical and social changes. In other cases, a landowner can sometimes get the board to allow a **variance**, which basically is a permit allowing one person an exception from the zoning laws for a particularly good reason, without changing the overall zoning classification of the neighborhood.

variance: Permission from a zoning board to use land in a way not allowed by the zoning classification.

Not only do cities and counties have authority to regulate property use under their inherent "police powers" (a subject discussed in Chapter 4), but many other quasi-governmental entities, such as irrigation districts, flood control authorities, and historical preservation authorities, also have the power to enact regulations affecting building and development on the land.

eminent domain: The power of a state, local, or federal government agency to acquire ownership of property from a private owner for some "public use," after paying fair compensation.

taking: When some government action deprives an owner of significant property rights without compensation.

The "Taking" of Property and Eminent Domain As was discussed in Chapter 4, government has the power under the Fifth Amendment to actually take title to private property for some public use through the power of **eminent domain**. However, when this is done, the landowner must be paid the fair market value of the land taken. In recent years property owners have often protested that zoning, building restrictions, and other extensive land use regulations have significantly diminished the value of their property and have thus effectively **taken** away part of their property, for which they should be compensated. In most cases, these arguments are rejected because, since a Supreme Court decision in 1926, the governmental power to regulate land use for the greater benefit of the whole community has been well-recognized. But where the restrictions are particularly extensive, deprive the owner of most of the value of the land, or force the owner to give up part of the land in return for some governmental approval, landowners have sometimes succeeded in forcing compensation from government agencies.

The following case is a recent example of these arguments.

DOLAN V. CITY OF TIGARD

512 U.S. 374 (1994)

FACTS

Florence Dolan owned a 71,500-square-foot lot on Main Street in Tigard, Oregon, on which she operated a retail electrical and plumbing supply store. Pursuant to Oregon law, the city had adopted various land use regulations, including a Community Development Code (CDC) and a Master Drainage Plan (MDP). The CDC established certain landscaping and open space requirements that applied to property in the central business district. These regulations also required new developments to dedicate land for pedestrian/bicycle pathways to help alleviate traffic congestion. The MDP noted that flooding had occurred in several areas in the past and called for certain drainage improvements to particular waterways, including a creek that ran across part of Ms. Dolan's property.

In 1991 Ms. Dolan asked the city for a permit to tear down the store and replace it with a much larger building. The city responded by conditioning the granting of a permit upon Ms. Dolan's giving the city about 7,000 square feet of her property. The City Planning Commission required her to dedicate the portion of her property within the creek floodplain for drainage improvements and an additional 15-foot strip for a pedestrian/bicycle pathway.

The city of Tigard did not propose to pay for the part of the Dolan property it would receive, since it would benefit the entire public. Ms. Dolan claimed that the land transfer would amount to an uncompensated taking of her property, in violation of the Fifth Amendment. Dolan challenged the city's action before the Oregon Land Use Board of Appeals but lost. She then appealed to the Oregon Court of Appeals and the Oregon Supreme Court, without success. Finally, the U.S. Supreme Court agreed to hear the case.

DECISION

In a 5-4 decision, written by Chief Justice Rehnquist, the Supreme Court reversed the lower court decisions. The Supreme Court stated that it was clearly legal, in general, for governments to place various conditions on the granting of permits when the goal is to avoid traffic congestion and other potential problems linked to development. Justice Rehnquist stated that Tigard's goals (flood and traffic control) were legitimate and noted that "cities have long engaged in the commendable task of land use planning, made necessary by increasing urbanization."

However, when the permits are conditioned on the owner giving up ownership of part of her land, the Court held that government planners must produce "specific justifications" that relate to the land in question. Planners had not adequately explained why it was necessary for the 7,000 square feet strip of land to become public property. For example, why not let the owner keep title to the land but be prohibited from building on it? In a key section of the opinion, the Court said that the city, in order to legally impose the conditions it wanted, had to show a "rough proportionality" between the necessity for the owner to give up title to the land and the potential harm of the proposed development.

As to the land in the floodplain, the Court stated that the city must state more clearly why it needed to acquire title to that part of the Dolan property (rather than just an easement) in order to make the drainage project a success. Justice Rehnquist pointed out that the "difference to petitioner (Dolan), of course, is the loss of her ability to exclude others . . . one of the most essential sticks in the bundle of rights that are commonly characterized as property."

Similarly, the majority opinion suggested that Tigard could have offered adequate justification for the pedestrian/bicycle walkway if it had more definitely shown that it would relieve congestion caused by Dolan's larger store. The city had said only that the path "could" offset some of the additional traffic. "No precise mathematical calculation is required, but the city must make some sort of individualized determination that the required dedication is related both in nature and extent to the impact of the proposed development."

In conclusion, while the Court stated that the city's goals for improving the community were laudable, there were "outer limits" on how it could be done. "A strong public desire to improve the public condition [will not] warrant achieving the desire by a shorter cut than the constitutional way of paying for the change."

Thus the decision of the Oregon Supreme Court was reversed.

CASE QUESTIONS

1. If the city of Tigard had only conditioned the granting of the building permit upon Ms. Dolan's giving an easement across her land for a bicycle path, would the result of the case have been the same? Why or why not?
2. What sort of "specific justification" could the city have provided that would have satisfied the Supreme Court's test?
3. What does the Court mean when it says there must be a "rough proportionality" between the need for the owner to give up title to the property and the harm caused by the desired project?
4. Can the city acquire title to the land if it decides to do so, even though Ms. Dolan does not want to sell? If so, how would this work?

restrictive covenant: A restriction on the use of real property, contained in a deed. Such covenants are common in subdivision developments.

Restrictive Covenants An owner's use of land may also be restricted by a **restrictive covenant**. This restriction is not imposed by governments, but by a previous private owner of the property. For example, when a seller of property puts in the deed a clause such as "no fences higher than six feet shall be constructed on this property," that restriction binds the new owner and probably all future owners as well. This type of deed restriction is particularly common in newer housing developments created by one developer. When the lots and houses are sold to individual owners, commonly all the deeds will contain restrictions such as "no basketball hoops may be installed on garages" or "there shall be no television antennas on roofs." These restrictions are intended to enhance the appearance of the neighborhood, and are binding on the homeowners and on future buyers. It is said that they *"run with the land."*

Restrictive covenants are usually stricter than the zoning regulations enacted by the local government. Therefore, a homeowner may be restrained by a covenant from doing something on the property that is perfectly legal under the zoning laws. Often, a neighborhood association may take legal action against a property owner who violates a covenant. If, on the other hand, many owners violate a covenant for several years and the governing body takes no action against them, the court might decide that the covenant is no longer valid and refuse to enforce it.

easement: A legal right to use a portion of real property owned by someone else for a specific purpose.

Easements Although a person might own property in "fee simple," chances are good that there are other individuals and businesses that have some legal rights to the property. We have already mentioned mortgages, in which a lender has a security interest in the property. An **easement** is another type of legal interest held in another's real property. An easement is a legal right one person has to use, for a limited purpose, part of the land owned by another.

Common types of easements are roads, paths, or utility lines over and under one's property. Most residential properties are subject to easements owned by phone, electric, water, and cable television companies, which give them the legal right to place wires or pipes over or under the surface of one's property. These rights (easements) are usually written down in legal documents and recorded in the county office prior to the first sale of the property to a homeowner. Although easements do not give the holder an ownership in any of the land, they do establish the legal right of the holder to use a specific portion of the land for the stated purpose.

FROM THE DESK OF
Laura Lawyer

To: Students
From: Your Lawyer

Most of the planned residential developments in the United States contain restrictive covenants, placed on the property by the developer, that control many aspects of the use of the property. When you purchase residential real estate, you should certainly ask the seller or real estate agent if there are any restrictive covenants on the property. You may be perfectly happy with the covenants, since they are intended to enhance the value of property in the neighborhood. But it is better to know in advance if you cannot build a certain type of fence or install certain types of shrubs, trees, or utility sheds, than to find out later when a dispute arises with the neighborhood association.

PERSONAL PROPERTY

Property that is not real property is *personal property* and may be of two types: *tangible* or *intangible* personal property. **Tangible personal property** has a physical existence, and includes items we can see and touch, like a car, a book, a shirt, or a television set. Intangible personal property may be quite valuable yet have no physical existence, such as a bank account, a shareholder's ownership interest in a corporation, a debt owed to another, or a patent on a product. A patent is an example of an increasingly important type of intangible personal property known as *intellectual property*; it is discussed in more detail later in the next section of this chapter.

tangible personal property: Property, other than real estate, that has a physical existence.

It is possible for personal property to be owned in joint tenancy or tenancy in common, although it is more typical for personal property to be owned by one person or by a married couple. Perhaps when you were younger you were fortunate enough to have a joint bank account with a parent or grandparent. Usually the deposits are made by the grandparent, with the withdrawals made by the grandchild. Upon the death of either (it was expected that the parent or grandparent would pass away first), the entire balance of the account belonged to the survivor if it was owned in joint tenancy with the right of survivorship.

There are various ways in which one may acquire ownership of personal property. The most common way is through a purchase or gift. A deed is only used in connection with real property; instead, when Ted, for example, buys a car or television set, he may receive a bill of sale to provide proof of his ownership.

In order to effectively transfer ownership of personal property through a gift, the person making the gift (the donor) must have the *intent* to make the gift, and the item must actually be *delivered* to the new owner (the donee). Both elements must exist to make the gift valid. For example, when Patty announces that she is going to make a gift to another person but dies or changes her mind before actually delivering the item, the gift is usually not effective, and the donee does not acquire ownership. Sometimes, however, delivery of a symbolic part of the gift (for example, the keys and title to the car but not the car) may be enough to show that the donor intended to part with the item.

Ownership of personal property can also be acquired when the property is *abandoned* by the former owner. In order to be considered abandoned, there must be some indication that the owner really did desire to give up ownership—such as by putting a television set out with the trash by the curb. The first person to take possession of abandoned property becomes the owner, since the former owner intended to give up his or her rights.

When a person finds personal property that has only been *lost* or *mislaid* by the owner, however, the finder does not acquire ownership. If, for example, Miren accidentally drops an expensive fountain pen somewhere in the street, she has not intended to transfer ownership. The finder of the pen (lost property) is entitled to possession of the pen in relation to everyone except the true owner but does not become the owner simply by finding the pen.

Property is considered mislaid if the owner intentionally put it somewhere and then forgot it. For example, if Alvaro stays in a motel, hides $500 under the mattress in the bed, and then leaves the next morning without retrieving the money, it is mislaid property. In this case the owner of the place where the property is found (the motel) has a right to possession of the property that is superior to anyone's right except that of the true owner. Why? Most likely, when Alvaro discovers that his property is missing, he will contact the owner of the premises where the property was left.

INTELLECTUAL PROPERTY

intellectual property: The legal rights covering such topics as patents, copyrights, trademarks, and trade secrets.

In today's business climate, the most important form of property may be neither land nor personal property, but **intellectual property**, a type of personal property created by the efforts of the mind. The work created may be an invention such as a new type of light bulb, a book, a computer program, or a trademark or trade name identifying a particular brand of shoes. Each of these types of intellectual property may have significant value, and the law protects each one in slightly different ways. The tremendous pace of recent technological advances has put pressure on older legal theories; alone, they are no longer effective preservers of the rights of those who create intellectual property. This is a rapidly evolving and very important legal area for businesses today.

PATENTS

A business can gain a competitive edge over its competitors through technological improvement and innovation. Many companies spend millions of dollars on research and development, seeking to develop new and better products and processes. If someone creates a new type of plastic compound, or invents a machine capable of novel functions, the inventor needs to be able to obtain exclusive rights to the invention.

Patent protection is specifically mentioned in the U.S. Constitution, which grants Congress the power to "promote the progress of science and the useful arts, by securing for limited times to . . . authors and inventors . . . the exclusive right to their discoveries." Congress has enacted a number of federal laws regarding patents since that time.

Specifically, a **patent** is a legal right, issued by the U.S. government, pertaining to an *invention, product, or process*. The patent applicant must show that the process or invention is "*novel, useful, and nonobvious*." Upon issuance of the patent, the holder has the exclusive right to make, use, or sell the process, product, or invention in the United States. Even if another person independently develops such a product, he or she will be unable to sell it legally if it is covered by an earlier patent. Other countries also issue patents to control the manufacture, use, and sale of products and inventions within their jurisdictions. Several major treaties exist, signed by the United States and other countries, by which each country agrees to respect patents issued by other member nations.

patent: A legal right of the creator or inventor of a product, process, or invention. The patent holder has the exclusive right to use, develop, and license the subject of the patent for 20 years.

In the United States, patent protection lasts for a period of 20 years from date the application for patent was filed. After that time, any member of the public can use the invention or produce the product. The process of applying for, and obtaining a patent is long and complicated, often taking two to three years. Detailed drawings and descriptions of the invention must be forwarded to the U.S. Patent and Trademark Office (PTO), and the inventor must compare this item or process with similar patented items (called "prior art") and demonstrate how this invention is different. Often the holders of earlier patents on similar devices challenge the issuance of a new patent. As a result, it usually is necessary to retain the services of an attorney specializing in intellectual property to successfully process a patent application. Recently, intellectual property lawyers have begun to be in high demand.

In the past 10 years the PTO has allowed the issuance of patents on software programs if they perform useful and unique functions, and thousands of such patents have been issued to U.S. and foreign companies.

When someone else uses, manufactures, or sells an invention or process that is patented, without permission from the patent holder, this is called **infringement**. The patent holder can bring suit against the alleged infringer and seek damages and/or an injunction prohibiting use of the infringing product. The court will conduct an independent analysis of the validity of the patent. (The PTO's previous determination is only one factor that is considered.) Many patents previously issued by the PTO have been held invalid at trial.

infringement: Unauthorized use of copyrighted or patented material.

One recent lawsuit concerned allegations by Amazon.com that another company had violated its patent on "one click" shopping, as the following article states.

E-commerce companies sue to protect patents

Intellectual rights given legal test

A new front has opened in the battle over intellectual property rights on the internet as an increasing number of companies sue to protect their method of doing e-business.

In the past ten days, two e-commerce companies—Amazon.com, the online bookseller, and Priceline.com, the internet auctioneer—have pioneered a new kind of patent lawsuit, one that defends an internet company's right to a monopoly over a particular way of doing business.

Amazon.com is defending its patent rights over "one click" technology, that allows repeat customers to place new orders with one click of a mouse, rather than forcing them to enter shipping and billing details every time.

Priceline is suing Microsoft for allegedly copying its patented method of "reverse auctions," that allow buyers to name a price and seek a willing seller.

E-commerce companies have been scrambling to obtain such "business methods" patents since a federal circuit court decision last year made it easier to get patent protection for business processes. Applications for such patents have risen 70 per cent this year, according to the US Patent and Trademark Office.

Now companies are preparing to defend their controversial new patents in court. Critics contend that issuing such patents will deter innovation in a fast-moving market.

Patent lawyers predict that the controversy could unleash a flood of litigation.

"Priceline's foray into the legal system is just the beginning," says Daniel Harris, an internet and intellectual property attorney with the Palo Alto, California firm Brobeck, Phleger & Harrison.

"New and existing internet companies will find themselves being targeted by those with legitimate patents based on novel inventions, as well as those seeking to make a quick buck."

Traditionally, patent lawyers had to search a relatively limited database—such as scientific journals and research publications—to determine whether there was "prior art," or evidence of prior invention, in a particular field.

"Now we're dealing with a much broader universe of 'prior art,'" says JT Westermeier, a Washington DC internet attorney with Piper & Marbury, pointing out that many allegedly novel internet business methods may already have been in use at universities or elsewhere.

"Trying to find out if any particular business method was practised before, that will be tricky," says John Daniel, a New York patent attorney with Kramer Levin Naftalis & Frankel.

Tim Berners-Lee, the inventor of the world wide web, maintains that many of these patents merely describe an established business process in software.

Others, he says, "combine well-known techniques in an apparently arbitrary way, like patenting going shopping in a yellow car on a Thursday."

Part of the problem is that doing business on the internet was, in itself, a novel idea just a few years ago.

"The US Patent office is ill-equipped to search for prior art in this new field and seems to have allowed patents by default," says Mr. Berners-Lee.

However, Amazon and Priceline are adamant that their software patents are valid.

Other e-commerce companies will be watching the two cases closely to see whether the patents stand up in court.

"E-Commerce Companies Sue to Protect Patents," by Patti Waldmeier and Louise Kehoe, *Financial Times*, Oct. 25, 1999, p. 16.

COPYRIGHTS

A **copyright** is a legal right that protects the creative output of authors, songwriters, artists, and others who produce original works. Copyright protection is available for "*original works of authorship fixed in a tangible medium of expression*." Such "expression" may be contained in books, journals, movies, sound recordings, computer programs, photographs, or sculptures. Note that copyright covers the "*expression*" of an idea, not the idea itself. In other words, copyright protects against the "*copying*" by another, without permission, *of the actual expression* of the work except in certain circumstances. The ideas embodied in a book or in a work of art can be discussed and debated—and authors and artists hope that they are—but the actual sentences, pages, or replicas usually cannot be photocopied and duplicated without the permission of the author or artist.

copyright: The legal right of an author, composer, or artist to prevent others from copying or reproducing his or her work.

Copyright is a common law legal right that belongs to the author immediately and automatically upon producing the work. The copyright owner has the exclusive right to reproduce, distribute, perform, display, or license his or her work and to produce "derivative" works. There are also complex federal laws specifying the scope of copyright protection and how to create and protect copyrights. One must first *register* the copyright with the U.S. government before a lawsuit for infringement can be filed. Copyright protection in the United States lasts for the life of the author plus an additional 70 years.

The federal "registration" process merely requires authors to send copies of their work to the U.S. Copyright Office (part of the Library of Congress), accompanied by a modest fee and a short form claiming copyright. Unlike patents, the Copyright Office does not check into similar works and does not certify that the owner has the exclusive right to the work. Any author or artist who believes that his or her work has been copied must personally bring a lawsuit against the alleged copier.

Prior to 1989, it was also necessary to place a copyright notice (including the word *Copyright* or ©, along with the date and author's name) on the first page of all copyrightable works, in order to protect the copyright, but this is no longer a requirement. Today, when one creates a work that meets the tests for copyrightability, the copyright exists automatically. However, it is still a good idea to place such a notice on any materials leaving the author's hands; this lets others know that a copyright is claimed and that such works cannot be used without permission.

When one person copies, reproduces, performs, or displays a work that is copyrighted by someone else, that is also called infringement. The copyright owner may bring a lawsuit against the alleged infringer seeking money damages and/or an injunction prohibiting the person from continuing such activities. To be successful, the copyright owner must prove that the infringer "copied" the owner's work. Unlike patents, it is not infringement if one person independently creates a work that just happens to read like, look like, or sound like an existing work. Remember, copyright protects the particular *expression* of the idea, not the idea itself.

For example, a popular book claims that "men are from Mars, women are from Venus." The author undoubtedly hopes that many people discuss whether they believe these allegations are true and what the author really means (i.e., the "idea"). However, no one but the author can legally photocopy, reproduce, or directly copy in any manner more than a very small portion of the exact sentences used in the book. To do otherwise will infringe the copyright of the author (the "expression").

In many recent cases involving popular songs, one person has claimed that the melody or lyrics of a song that became a hit record were copied from his or her already copyrighted song. One key issue in such cases where the first song is not well-known is *access*—that is, whether the second song writer actually had a copy of or a record containing the first song.

SOCIAL/ETHICAL ISSUES

Many college students enjoy popular music, movies, and music videos. The manufacturers of electronic equipment aggressively advertise cassette recorders and players that feature two cassette units, thus making it easy to copy one music tape onto another. The marketing of videotape recorders often stresses the ease of recording from movies or television shows. In Japan, double-cassette video recorders are even sold in stores, although such products are not widely available in the United States. Yet the action of recording popular music and movies may be illegal—it is, in effect, direct copying of the "expression" of a copyrighted work, without the permission of the copyright owner. Such actions do undoubtedly detract from the sales of records, tapes, and CDs by the producers and copyright holders. Should manufacturers be allowed to advertise and sell products that enable and encourage others to violate copyright laws? What about the Internet?

THE "FAIR USE" DOCTRINE

"fair use" doctrine: A legal principle, an exception to a copyright owner's exclusive rights, that allows another to make some limited ("fair") use of the copyrighted work without permission.

The copyright law allows a few exceptions to the exclusive rights of the copyright owner. The most important of these exceptions is the **"fair use" doctrine**. This theory began as common law hundreds of years earlier, and it was made part of the federal law when the Copyright Act was amended in 1976.

The Copyright Act states in §107 [17 U.S.C. 107]:

> Notwithstanding the provisions of Sections 106 and 106A [dealing with the exclusive rights of the copyright owner], the fair use of a copyrighted work, including such use by reproduction in copies or phonorecords or by any other means specified by that section, for purposes such as criticism, comment, news reporting, teaching (including multiple copies for classroom use), scholarship, or research, is not an infringement of copyright. In determining whether the use made of a work in any particular case is a fair use the factors to be considered shall include—
>
> 1. the purpose and character of the use, including whether such use is of a commercial nature or is for nonprofit educational purposes;
> 2. the nature of the copyrighted work;
> 3. the amount and substantiality of the portion used in relation to the copyrighted work as a whole; and
> 4. the effect of the use upon the potential market for or value of the copyrighted work.

Therefore, the fair use doctrine holds that, despite copyright ownership, other persons can use a limited portion of the copyrighted work without the author's permission for certain purposes. As one court said, "the fair use doctrine offers a means of balancing the exclusive rights of copyright holders with the public's interest in dissemination of information affecting areas of universal concern, such as art, science, and industry."

The scope of allowable fair use has been the subject of many court decisions. The four factors set out in the statute had already been used in common law cases. In fact, when Congress enacted this section, the Judiciary Committee report accompanying the bill stated that it "intended to restate the present judicial doctrine of fair use, not to change, narrow or enlarge it in any way." Nevertheless, these four factors have been reinterpreted frequently since the 1976 statute.

In order to help understand how these factors might affect an analysis of fair use, let us assume that Henry has written a 30-page article about zoning laws for an academic journal. At some later time, Jason, without permission from Henry, uses much of the article (including six pages verbatim) in a book he writes. Jason's book is sold by his publisher in bookstores across the nation. The first **fair use factor** considers the *purpose and character of the use* that is being made by the second user. In this case Jason's use is commercial—he hopes to earn some royalties from the sales of his book. If the user had been a nonprofit public school, it would have had somewhat greater rights; however, the court would still have analyzed all the factors before deciding on fair use.

Key Fair Use Factors:

1. The purpose and character of the use.
2. The nature of the copyrighted work.
3. The amount and substantiality of the amount taken.
4. The economic effect of the second use on the copyright owner.

The second factor examines the *nature of the copyrighted work*—in our example, Henry's article. With regard to some scientific, legal, or medical works, courts have generally agreed that, in order to advance science or art, identical words or phrases may be used by later authors. On the other hand, a "student study guide" or some similar work is clearly intended to be sold for profit and does not contain any scientific knowledge that could be used without infringement by other authors in their works. Professors who write for academic journals do not do so for money, and they usually hope that people read their articles. Thus, the "nature of the use" may protect Jason.

The third factor relates to the *amount or substantiality of the copyrighted work that is used* by the second person. Courts have sometimes actually counted words or pages in determining the amount of the original work that was copied. Clearly, if 10–20 percent or more of the original is copied, it is likely to be held infringement. However, even if a fairly small part of the original work is used verbatim, it may still be "substantial" if the part taken is a "key or essential" portion. Jason's use here is fairly large, and if the part taken is important, this test will hurt his fair use argument.

Although each factor is important, the last point, the *economic effect on the copyright holder*—has often been treated as the most critical. The public benefits from the discussion of books, plays, musical compositions, and so on; such discussions, however, do not harm the market and potential economic value of the work—as long as the amount of the original reproduced is fairly small. Indeed, a favorable book review or a description on a news show may well increase the market and the profits for the author. But when the material taken from the copyrighted work begins to cut into the author or artist's potential market, the purposes of the copyright law are violated and fair use will not apply.

The following case involves an analysis of several of the fair use factors.

BASIC BOOKS, INC. V. KINKO'S GRAPHICS CORP.

758 F. Supp. 1522 (N.Y. 1991)

FACTS

Kinko's Graphics Corp., a national chain of photocopy shops, was sued by a group of publishers for copyright infringement. The publishers held copyrights on a number of books from which Kinko's had photocopied portions for "course packets" that were sold to students taking certain classes at New York University. The publishers introduced at the trial five course packets sold by Kinko's in connection with college courses. Each one included several portions of photocopied material from other copyrighted books. In many cases, entire chapters of books were copied, and in one case, three chapters of a book were copied and included in the packet. Kinko's had not sought permission for any of the copying, relying on the fair use doctrine and the clauses in the copyright law about "educational use" and "multiple copies for classroom use."

Kinko's markets its services directly to university students and professors. Several brochures introduced at trial showed that Kinko's openly solicits from professors lists of readings that they plan to use in their courses and then copies excerpts and sells them in bound form to students. Kinko's had net revenue of $42 million in 1988 and $54 million in 1989, with net profits of $300,000 and $3 million, respectively. The publishers sought statutory damages, attorneys' fees, an injunction against further copying without permission, and payment of royalties.

DECISION

Kinko's did not deny that it had photocopied material from copyrighted books and journals; instead, it argued that it was protected by the doctrine of fair use. The federal district court thus was required to carefully analyze the four factors that determine whether a use is "fair."

With regard to the "purpose and character of the use," the court noted that Kinko's was a commercial enterprise and sought to make a profit from its photocopying. Although Kinko's argued that its use was educational, Judge Motley commented that the use of the course packets "in the hands of the students, was no doubt educational." "However," Motley continued, "the use in the hands of Kinko's employees is commercial." In other words, the use of the material by Kinko's was not for commentary, criticism, or other scholarly purpose but for profit.

The second test, "the nature of the copyrighted work," worked in favor of Kinko's. Generally, the scope of fair use is greater with respect to factual than nonfactual works. Fictional works, largely based on an author's subjective impressions, require more protection than biographies, criticism, and commentary. The materials copied here were factual, containing information of public interest, and thus receive somewhat less protection.

The third factor, "the amount and substantiality of the portion used," weighed heavily against Kinko's. Many cases have held that even fairly small amounts of copying can be "substantial" when they are the "heart" of the material. Here, Kinko's copied passages ranging from 14 to 110 pages, representing between 5.2 percent and 25.1 percent of the works. In many instances entire chapters were copied. The court had no trouble finding that the portions copied were both quantitatively substantial and qualitatively significant. Judge Motley pointedly noted that in one case, Kinko's had copied 110 pages of someone's work and sold it to 132 students, a practice "grossly out of line with accepted fair use principles."

The fourth factor, "the effect of the use on potential markets for or value of the copyrighted work," is usually critical, as was true here. Kinko's operates some 200 stores nationwide in close proximity to hundreds of colleges and universities. Thus, stated the court, the potential for widespread copyright infringement is great. The fact that several chapters of other books were copied and included in the packets clearly obviates the need for students to purchase those books, causing loss of income to publishers and authors. The loss is felt even more by authors of out-of-print books, for whom permissions fees constitute a significant source of income. This factor counted heavily against Kinko's.

Kinko's final argument was that a section of the copyright law specifically mentioned that fair use might apply to "multiple copies for classroom use." Part of the legislative history of the 1976 amendments to the Copyright Act included an agreement between groups representing publishers, authors, and educational institutions, titled "Agreement on Guidelines for Classroom Copying in Not-for-Profit Educational Institutions." Although not actually law, this statement has been used in assessing the fairness of certain educational practices. The Guidelines provide a "safe harbor" for classroom use (up to one copy per student) if such copying meets the other fair use tests, if each copy includes a notice of copyright, and if such copying meets the tests of "brevity, spontaneity, and cumulative effect."

In this case, not only did the copying fail the "four factors" tests for fair use, it failed to meet the Guidelines tests as well. First, none of the copies included copyright notices. *Brevity* is defined in the Guidelines to be "an excerpt of not more than 1,000 words or 10% of the work, whichever is less." The copying here vastly exceeded this standard. *Spontaneity* requires that the decision to use the work and the moment of its use be so close that request for permission is unreasonable. The court found this not to be the case here. Finally, *cumulative effect* prohibits any more than nine instances of multiple copying for one course during one term, and to no more than one piece of work per author. Both of these standards were violated here.

In conclusion, the federal court found that Kinko's had clearly violated the Copyright Act and had infringed the copyrights of the various publishers on 12 occasions. Judge Motley issued an injunction prohibiting Kinko's from future "anthologizing" and copying of plaintiffs' works without permission, and assessed statutory damages of $510,000 against Kinko's.

CASE QUESTIONS

1. Does this case mean that it is no longer possible for professors to put together a course packet of readings for use in a course? Does the fair use doctrine still have effect as it applies to education?
2. How much copying from another source can a professor or a copy shop legally do under the fair use doctrine? What must be done to avoid infringement?
3. Would the result have been the same if the copying had been done by the university or the professor? What if the packets had been given, not sold, to the students?

COMPUTER PROGRAMS

Numerous cases filed in recent years have dealt with copyright issues involving computers and computer programs. In the early days of computer programs, some courts refused to accord copyright status to such forms as the software program for a computer game or other software products. Courts were unsure whether a series of symbols was a type of literary or artistic creation that qualified for copyright protection. However, after several important court cases and an amendment to the Copyright Law, it is now clear that computer programs can be copyrighted. Such programs can qualify as a creative work that has been reduced to a "tangible means of expression"—the object code and source code have been expressed in words and symbols in a certain order.

The next wave of computer litigation concerned the so-called **look and feel cases**. This situation arose when one software product became successful, and other developers attempted to produce a similar product. They could not simply

look and feel cases: Where someone has created a computer program or user interface that "looks" and acts ("feels") like another copyrighted program, but the second author did not copy the actual code of the first program.

copy the underlying code of the first program because that would clearly be copyright infringement. Thus, developers would independently devise a new program that looked and acted very much like the first product—that is, one that had the same "look and feel." Although the graphics and the user interface (such things as menu screens, icons, symbols, and key strokes required of the user) would look and feel very much like the earlier copyrighted program, the actual underlying computer code (the "expression") was not the same.

Those who favor strict application of copyright laws argue that it is unfair for developers to reap profits based on their mimicking a program produced through the considerable research effort, time, and expense of someone else. Such experts assert that it is bad public policy to allow software companies to simply "clone" successful products without incurring research expenses, because this discourages innovative and time-consuming efforts.

On the other hand, many software and computer industry veterans argue that public policy should encourage developers to build onto the advances of others, and that standardized icons and menu screens help consumers and the software industry move forward. If basic icons and "looks" are tied up by patents and copyrights, so each program must interface differently with the user, it will make computer use more difficult for the public.

The results of the many "look and feel" cases have varied, depending on a number of factors, including how similar the programs appeared; how original the graphic elements, menu screens, and words used in the first program were; whether the second programmer had "access" to the first program; and whether the second program took earlier ideas and expanded on them or merely misappropriated another's ideas.

Today's advanced computer technology and the Internet and World Wide Web make it possible to browse libraries all over the world and to actually copy (download) onto one's own computer books, articles, photographs, music, artwork, and other forms of creative expression covered by copyright. The problems associated with protection of the copyright owner's rights and potential methods are becoming increasingly complex.

IN CONSULTATION

Marvin Manager has a problem. His company recently began selling sporting goods on-line. To increase the appeal of its Web site, ABC, Inc. developed one-click access so customers could simply key in a user name and immediately begin shopping. The one-click technology only requires customers to fill out registration and shipping forms the first time they visit the site. Repeat customers can buy merchandise by just clicking on a single button. ABC's market research shows that customers are much more likely to buy via a Web site if they do not have to enter a lot of information.

Othercorp, one of ABC's primary competitors, actually began selling on-line first. It also uses one-click access on its Web site. ABC became aware of one-click technology after Othercorp began using it. ABC did not, however, copy Othercorp's actual program. Instead, ABC simply developed its own one-click algorithm.

Othercorp filed suit against ABC, challenging that ABC infringed upon Othercorp's patented one-click software. Othercorp stated in its complaint that not only did ABC copy the technology, but it engaged in unfair competition.

Marvin approached his company's in-house corporate counsel, Laura Lawyer, to determine whether Othercorp's allegations have any chance of succeeding. He asked Laura about ABC's potential liability to Othercorp. Here is their conversation.

Marvin:

1. Just because we came up with software that accomplishes the same one-click access, are we infringing upon Othercorp's patent?
2. What is unfair competition anyway? Isn't all fair in love and war—and business is war?
3. Is the Internet even covered by all of these old laws? I thought that the law did not yet address e-commerce, allowing us to basically do what we want on the Web.

Laura:

1. Patenting software is a new phenomenon. The courts are unsettled as to what sorts of software can be patented and what constitutes infringement.
2. Unfair competitive practices usually include actual violations of the law. The answer to your question depends upon whether ABC infringed as Othercorp alleges.
3. Courts have been challenged by the new technology and the difficulty in applying old law to the Internet. The Internet is, nonetheless, subject to certain rules, including rules that prohibit patent infringement. **Let me research the applicable law to see whether Othercorp's claim is viable, and I'll get back to you.**

FROM THE DESK OF
Laura Lawyer

To: Marvin Manager
Re: Liability for Patent Infringement on the Internet

Dear Marvin:

Protecting software via intellectual property is difficult. Software and computer programs are text, so copyrights were the original protection of choice. Copyrights are limited, however, because if the software designer simply uses different text, he or she can evade another designer's copyright. Not surprisingly, a push toward patents for software has emerged. Patents are a superior form of protection because they allow the patent holder to exclude others from making, using, or selling your invention. A patent holder can increase its profits by licensing its technology in a way a copyright holder cannot.

Patenting software is controversial because not everyone agrees that software is an invention or process. Others assert that software is essentially a machine that performs a function, thereby deserving patent protection. The Patent and Trademark Office recently began issuing patents on software, but many believe that those patents will be challenged in the courts.

The controversy over patenting software affects our case in a couple of ways. First, ABC may be able to prove that Othercorp did not deserve a patent on its one-click software. We would need evidence that either someone else had developed a similar process in the past (i.e., prior art) or that the software is not novel.

Second, even if Othercorp can prove that it deserved a patent, we can defend that we did not infringe on that patent. We developed our own technology that merely accomplishes the same goal as Othercorp's—one-click access. We did not copy Othercorp's code or process and, instead, used our own creative resources to establish one-click access on our Web site. In support of our defense, we can show that many other retailers and wholesalers use some form of one-click access. If it is becoming an industry norm, Othercorp will be hard-pressed to show that the entire sales industry is infringing. If we did not infringe, then we also cannot be accused of unfair competition.

With regard to Othercorp's patent infringement claim, consider the following:

1. Do you think software should be patented? Give arguments against and in support of using patents to protect software development.
2. Do you think Marvin or ABC could have done something differently to prevent Othercorp from having any substance to its claim in the first place?
3. Do you think the United States' current intellectual property system is compatible with the Internet? Describe what you see as the main gaps in the current system and the evolving e-commerce marketplace.

TRADEMARKS

trademark: A word, phrase, or symbol that identifies and distinguishes a product.

Trademarks, like patents and copyrights, can be protected by federal law. A trademark is a word, phrase, symbol, or design that *identifies* and *distinguishes the source* of the goods and services of one party from those of someone else. A trademark may be created either by (1) actual use of the mark or symbol or (2) the filing of an application to register the mark with the PTO, stating that the owner has a bona fide intent to use the mark in commerce. (The owner must then begin to use it within 8 months.) So, as with copyrights, one can acquire a trademark simply by use, but it makes good sense to register the mark with the PTO. Such registration gives notice to others and provides greater rights in any lawsuit.

Unlike patents and copyrights, trademark rights can last for an indefinite time period if the owner continues to use the mark to identify goods or service. Whereas early trademark cases were based on common law protection, most trademark issues today are based upon the Lanham Act, a federal statute enacted in 1946 and amended several times, including 1988. Under this law, federal trademark protection lasts for 10 years but can be continuously renewed.

An individual may file his or her own trademark application with the PTO, with or without an attorney. The application must include a drawing of the mark. When the application is received, an examining attorney with the PTO will compare the mark with other previous registrations and determine if the mark may be registered. If there is a *likelihood of confusion* between the applicant's mark and a registered mark, the applicant will be denied a trademark.

Also, if the term or mark merely describes the goods or services, the trademark request will be refused. Descriptive terms are those that identify a characteristic or quality of the article, such as color, function, or ingredients. Thus, the phrases "blue chair" or "high chair" could not receive trademark protection.

In addition, an attempt to trademark a **generic term** like "table" or "car" will be denied. Generic terms identify a class of products, like "ballpoint pens" or "stereos." However, sometimes a registered trademark term comes, over time, to identify the entire class of similar products and thus becomes generic. The result then is that the owner of the trademark loses the right to exclusive use of the term. Words like *cellophane* and *aspirin* started out as trademarks, but have since become generic. Xerox Corporation, for example, uses a portion of its advertising budget each year to produce ads stating that "Xerox is a registered trademark, so please use the term only when referring to our products, not as a substitute for the noun 'photocopiers' or for the verb 'to photocopy.'"

generic term: A word or phrase that is synonymous with a whole class of products and cannot receive trademark protection.

In a rare case decided a few years ago, the U.S. Supreme Court ruled in a unanimous decision that the particular color of a product may even be protected by trademark. In *Qualitex Co. v. Jacobson Products Co. Inc.*, 514 U.S. 159 (1995), the issue concerned commercial dry cleaning press pads. For more than 30 years Qualitex had manufactured "Sun Glow" press pads, which came in a distinctive greenish-gold color. Qualitex had spent some $1.6 million to promote them. When competitor Jacobson began making press pads of the same color, Qualitex sued for unfair competition and trademark infringement.

The color was a "symbol" of the product and had developed a "secondary meaning" that "identified and distinguished" that particular brand, wrote Justice Stephen Breyer. The Court noted that trademarks had been upheld previously for the shape of a Coca-Cola bottle, the sound of NBC's three chimes, and the scent of plumeria blossoms on sewing thread. "If a descriptive word, and a 'shape,' a sound and a fragrance can act as symbols," ruled Breyer, "why can't a color do the same?" The Court held that there had been a trademark infringement.

Domain Names One significant new type of trademark issue concerns *domain names*, the "URL" set of letters and numbers used to access a site on the World Wide Web. Companies naturally want their domain names to be as close as possible to their corporate name, so consumers can easily access their Web site.

Until recently, one company, Network Solutions, Inc. (NSI), controlled the allocation of all commercial Web sites—those that end with ".com." Not surprisingly, various entrepreneurs saw a business opportunity—they would register a domain name (e.g., "www.mci.com") and then sell the rights to the name to the "real" MCI when it wanted use of the name for its Web site. Such so-called *cybersquatters* caused considerable anger from companies who felt that their trademark registration should cover the domain name issue, and that they should not have to pay a premium just to obtain what should have been theirs—the right to use their name on the Web.

Several cases have been filed by holders of trademarked names against cybersquatters and other businesses that have obtained domain names using symbols, names, and phrases associated with other companies and products. Where it has been shown that the first firm did have a legal trademark and that use of its name by a second firm would cause "dilution" of the trademark's value and likelihood of confusion to consumers, courts have entered injunctions and/or ordered the transfer of the domain name.

One interesting twist on the domain name issue occurred when Lockheed Martin Corp. sued NSI itself. Lockheed stated that it had a trademark on the phrase "Skunk Works," which related to its Southern California aircraft and design laboratory. When it noticed another company using "Skunk Works" as part of a domain name, Lockheed sued NSI arguing that NSI had a duty to ensure that Lockheed's trademark was not infringed, once it was informed by Lockheed.

However, in late 1999, the Ninth Circuit Court of Appeals rejected Lockheed's claim. In an opinion by Judge Stephen Trott, the court held that NSI would only be liable if it intentionally induced a third party to infringe a mark or supplied a product to a third party with "actual or constructive knowledge that the product is being used to infringe the service mark." The appellate court compared NSI to the U.S. Postal Service. "When an Internet user enters a domain name combination, NSI translates it to the registrant's IP address and routes the information or command to the corresponding computer." Judge Trott concluded that "NSI does not supply the domain name combination any more than the Postal Service supplies a street address by performing the routine service of routing mail."

In November 1999 President Clinton signed a new law, The Anticybersquatting Consumer Protection Act, as part of another bill. The new law adds a section to the Lanham Act prohibiting the bad faith registration or use of an Internet domain name that infringes on a trademark or famous mark. This law should prevent cybersquatters from tying up domain names, even if the trademark owner does not immediately object. The law allows proof of actual damages or statutory damages of between $1,000 and $300,000. This provision is important, said one industry lawyer, because "most of these outfits kidnapping domain names are Mom-and-Pop shops or kids sitting in the basement." The first suit to enforce the provisions of the law was filed a few days later by actor Brad Pitt, who sued two California men who had obtained the domain name "bradpitt.com" and then tried to sell it to Mr. Pitt for as much as $50,000.

TRADE SECRETS

The preceding three types of intellectual property—patents, copyrights, and trademarks—all involve "rights" that are granted by (patents) or are registered with (copyrights and trademarks) the federal government. The fourth main type of intellectual property, **trade secrets**, does not share this trait.

trade secrets: Intellectual property assets of a business, such as a formula or a customer list, which are kept secret.

Trade secrets are important assets of a business that are not filed in any government office but instead are kept confidential by the business. For example, the formula for Coca-Cola has never been patented but is carefully maintained as a corporate secret. Only a very few Coca-Cola employees and officers know the formula at one time, and they are strictly bound to secrecy. Other important business secrets may include the strategic plan of a firm, a customer list, or a specific method of doing business. In each case, in order to qualify as a trade secret, the firm must consider the information confidential and must take steps to keep it confidential. Most medium-sized and large businesses today have all their key employees sign confidentiality agreements, by which they promise not to disclose trade secrets or other confidential information.

In addition, many companies require employees to sign **covenants not to compete**, by which the employee promises not to open a competing business within a certain area for a certain period of time after leaving the first employer. These agreements usually include a clause barring use of any confidential information gained from the first employer. Such agreements are generally enforced by courts if they are reasonable in scope and length of time.

covenant not to compete: An agreement by an employee or owner of one business, promising not to open a competing business.

Trade secret legal principles are a common law subject—that is, they are usually developed by case decisions in state courts involving a company and an ex-employee, who have different views about what the former employee should be able to do. Concepts such as "fairness," "equity," "economic injury," and the "terms of the contract" signed by the parties—factors typically involved in common law cases—determine the outcome of cases and development of the law. There is a model statute, The Uniform Trade Secrets Act, which has been adopted in some states.

THE INTERNET AND CYBERSPACE

One of the most dramatic changes in daily life and business practice in the past few years has been the incredible growth of the Internet and World Wide Web. Most of us exchange numerous e-mail messages and visit several "Web sites" every day—a practice unknown a few years ago. Almost every legal issue discussed in this textbook is now being raised in new ways, through cases involving the Internet and the Web—so-called cyberspace. Many other legal issues are arising in new formats or are made more complex by the Internet and the Web. *The New York Times* even has a weekly column on its Web page called "The Cyber Law Journal," published every Friday (www.nytimes.com/library/tech).

For example, there is a question about whether one state court has personal jurisdiction of a defendant because the company had a Web site that was accessible in that state. Several cases have challenged contracts entered into over the Web, when a person using his or her computer clicks a box on the screen with his or her mouse. New forms of torts are created and recognized by courts when one person invades another's privacy, through the use of computer data or searches, or when a software program uses "cookies" to capture information about consumers who visit its Web site and then sell that information. And there are many more such emerging issues. One involves the tort of defamation using the Internet.

Defamation in Cyberspace The very first case reported in Chapter 1, (*Zeran v. America Online*) examined the possible liability of an on-line service provider for libel, due to a nasty, untrue "prank" posting on America Online, stating that T-shirts celebrating the Oklahoma City bombing could be purchased from "Ken" in Seattle and giving Ken's phone number. There was indeed a man named Ken with that phone number, but he had nothing to do with any such T-shirts. In that case, as you recall, the court found the service provider was not liable for the posting, much like the telephone company would not be held liable for slander committed by one person to another in a phone call.

The *Zeran* case was chosen to start the book because it caused the courts to raise an interesting, very contemporary legal issue. But the case also shows that many legal issues take on new dimensions and have new ramifications due to the Internet and Web. For example, in the *Zeran* case, the person who posted the false notice was able to send out his or her message to millions of other people with the click of a mouse. Prior to the Internet, it would have been difficult to send more than a few hundred such fake messages, and there would have been added costs for photocopying, envelopes, postage, and more.

There is a federal law that generally grants immunity to Internet service providers for false postings on their services, unless the provider is aware of or has been involved in creating the posting. This statute was one of the main reasons that America Online won the *Zeran* case. However, there have been other cases in which one person has used the Internet to send messages containing false and hurtful information about someone else. As in non-cyberspace defamation, if the sender can be identified, and the statements are proved false and damaging, there should be liability. Although a lawsuit someday against the perpetrator might somewhat compensate the victim, the speed and scope of the Web allows millions of people to learn of the falsehood in an instant. Most of them will not learn of the later lawsuit or retraction.

Free Speech and Pornography It is often said that sexually explicit sites are among the most visited places on the Web. Parents are obviously concerned that their children will visit sites that are inappropriate and harmful to them, out of error or curiosity. Legislators, in response to the wishes of their constituents, have attempted to regulate sexually oriented Internet sites. In early 1996 Congress passed the *Communications Decency Act* (*CDA*), in an effort to protect children from sexually explicit Web sites.

The CDA banned, and indeed made it a felony criminal offense, to knowingly use a telecommunications device to transmit "obscene or indecent" material knowing that the recipient is under age 18 years. Another key provision outlawed the use of a "computer interactive service"—such as the Internet or a computer bulletin board—to send or display "patently offensive" material. The law was immediately challenged by a wide variety of groups and corporations as a violation of the First Amendment's free speech clause. The case went first to a lower federal court, and then to the U.S. Supreme Court—the very first Internet case to reach the Supreme Court. The Court was faced with balancing the desire of Congress to protect children from certain Web sites with the First Amendment of the Constitution.

On the day the case was argued in the Supreme Court, advocates for both sides of the case braved snow and rain to appear outside the Court, shouting slogans and carrying banners. The demonstrations were civil, however, and the "impromptu debates that inevitably occur around such controversial issues were generally polite," reported one observer. Discussion of the case was one of the first items featured on the national evening news. Both sides viewed the Supreme Court decision in this case as one that would have a major impact on cyberspace. "The future of the Internet is at stake in this case," said the leader of one computer users group which favored broad freedom of speech. Other experts believed that the case could also help shape the rules governing other "information superhighway" areas such as advertising, copyright, trade secrets, libel, and invasion of privacy. Attorney Bruce Ennis, who represented the plaintiffs, said that this case will "set the standard for all future regulation of the Internet." The Supreme Court decision follows.

ACLU V. RENO

117 S. Ct. 2329 (1997)

FACTS

On February 8, 1996, President Clinton signed the CDA, enacted by Congress as part of the major telecommunications reform legislation. A coalition of more than 50 groups, including the American Civil Liberties Union (ACLU), the American Library Association, and several high-technology organizations filed a lawsuit challenging the statute later that same day in the federal district court in Philadelphia. This case was later joined with another suit filed by many business firms, including America Online and Microsoft Corporation.

The sections of the law that were most specifically challenged under the First Amendment were the following:

1. Section 223 (a)(1)(A), which stated that it was an illegal act for "Whoever, in interstate or foreign communications, by means of a telecommunications device, knowingly makes, creates, or solicits, and initiates the transmission of, any comment, request, suggestion, proposal, image, or other communication which is obscene, lewd, lascivious, filthy, or indecent, knowing that the recipient of the communication is under 18 years of age" [47 U.S.C. 223 (a)(1)(A)];
2. Section 223 (d)(1)(A), which established and created a federal crime for anyone who "knowingly uses an interactive service to *send* to a specific person or persons under 18 years of age," any material "that, in context, depicts or describes, in terms patently offensive as measured by contemporary community standards, sexual or excretory activities or organs";
3. Section 223(d)(1)(B), which established and created a federal crime for anyone who "uses any interactive computer service to *display*" any of the material listed previously (using the same language as the previous section); and
4. Section 223 (a)(2) and (d)(2), which established a federal crime for anyone who knowingly "permits the use of a telecommunications device" under such person's control to be used to violate any of the three preceding prohibitions.

Conviction under the law was punishable by a maximum of two years in prison and a fine of up to $250,000.

Under a provision contained in the CDA itself (Congress knew it would be challenged), any lawsuits concerning the law were to be heard by a three-judge panel of federal judges. In March 1996 a panel consisting of Chief Third Circuit Judge Helen Sloviter and District Judges Ronald Buckwalter and Stewart Dalzell began six days of hearings in the case *ACLU v. Reno* in a Philadelphia courtroom.

It was clear from the beginning that all participants viewed it as an extraordinary case. Prior to taking the bench on the first day, Judges Sloviter and Dalzell checked the wiring in the courtroom. When Judge Buckwalter arrived, the court historian took some photographs. "Everyone in the room felt we were involved in making history," said one attorney for the ACLU. On the first day of the trial, the court was treated to a live demonstration of the Internet. Over the next week, the plaintiffs spent considerable time and energy not only arguing about the First Amendment, but educating the judges about cyberspace.

Groups active in the Internet community had felt frustrated when Congress passed the CDA, which they saw as a shocking government intrusion into their once unregulated and freewheeling terrain. Believing that part of the reason for the law was their failure to educate Congress about the Internet, a new strategy was devised for the trial. "We felt if we could just give the court a feeling of how the Internet functions, they could see that these restrictions would cripple the free flow of information," said Daniel Weitzman of the Center for Democracy & Technology.

On June 11, the three-judge panel unanimously struck down the CDA, finding the restrictions in it "profoundly repugnant" to the

First Amendment. Three separate opinions were issued by the court, totaling more than 200 pages. District Judge Dalzell stated that "Any content-based regulation of the Internet, no matter how benign the purpose, could burn the global village to roast the pig."

Borrowing language from an earlier free speech case, Judge Dalzell wrote that "the internet may be fairly regarded as a never-ending world wide conversation. The government may not [through the CDA] interrupt that conversation." Judge Dalzell continued with the strong assertion that "As the most participatory form of mass speech yet developed, the Internet deserves the highest protection from government intrusion."

Another of the opinions noted that "the government . . . implicitly asks us to limit both the amount of speech on the internet and the availability of that speech. This argument is profoundly repugnant to First Amendment principles." Further, the court wrote that "just as the strength of the Internet is chaos, so the strength of our liberty depends upon the chaos and cacophony of the unfettered speech the First Amendment protects."

One of the key issues in the case was whether the Internet should be regulated more like the print media or broadcasters. Opponents of the law argued successfully that the Internet should be classified as print media, to which the courts have granted broad, largely unrestricted powers. The government and supporters of the law argued that since Internet images flow over telecommunications lines, the Internet was a broadcast media. Courts have upheld more restrictions on broadcasters by holding that technology restricts the number of stations, licenses are allocated by government, and images are more accessible to children and come directly into the user's home. The lower court decided that the Internet was more like print media and thus largely free from "prior restraint" on speech by the government.

DECISION

On appeal, the U.S. Supreme Court, in a 7-2 opinion written by Justice John Paul Stevens, agreed that key parts of the CDA were unconstitutional. The Court considered three earlier cases, cited by the government in which the Court had upheld laws or parts of laws controlling certain objectionable sex-related material and conduct. In *Ginsberg v. New York* (1968) the Supreme Court had upheld a New York law barring the sale of "obscene" material to minors. However, in the *Ginsberg* case, the New York law applied only to commercial transactions and clearly defined the word *obscene*, based on previous cases, which had held that *obscene* material did not enjoy First Amendment protection. However in this case (*ACLU v. Reno*), the CDA used the word *indecent*, which was not defined, and the phrase "patently offensive" was defined in a way not consistent with earlier cases. Thus the CDA law was overly vague, compared with the statute upheld in the *Ginsberg* case.

In another earlier case, *Renton v. Playtime Theaters*, the Supreme Court had upheld a zoning law restricting the location of adult theaters. However, the Court noted that the law was primarily aimed at preventing crime and protecting property values, while the CDA's purpose was to protect children from the primary effects of "indecent" and "patently offensive" speech on the Internet and Web. The CDA was clearly a blanket restriction on speech, rather than a zoning or property case—thus raising the "free speech" issues more directly. Especially with the criminal felony provision, it was "overboard" in its prohibition of speech that is legal for adults to read and view. Since there was no realistic way for the one who posts material on the Web or in Internet "chat rooms" to know if minors were receiving the message, the law mandated that the "free speech" rights of adults would be reduced to speech that was appropriate for children.

In the final case considered, *FCC v. Pacifica Foundation*, one of the issues was whether radio broadcasting should be afforded the same level of constitutional protection for speech as print media (which had received broad First Amendment support and freedom from government restriction in earlier cases). Finding that radio messages come easily into the home, and are quite often heard by children, the Court permitted more restrictions on such speech than it had on print media (newspaper, magazines), where the reader had to seek out the message in order to view it. The Court also noted that there was a "scarcity of frequencies" in radio, and that there was thus a greater need for government involvement and control of permissible speech. Neither factor was present in this case (*ACLU v. Reno*), however. Finding that the "broadcast model" did not fit the Internet, the Court decided that allowable restrictions on freedom of speech on the Internet and World Wide Web should be closer to those applicable to print media (quite free of restrictions).

The Court found that the Internet was more like a public square, where freedom of speech is accorded significant protection:

This dynamic, multifaceted category of communication includes not only traditional print and news services, but also audio, video, and still images, as well as interactive, real time dialogue. Through the use of chat rooms, any person with a phone line can become a town crier with a voice that resonates farther than it could from any soap box. Through the use of Web pages, mail exploders, and newsgroups, the same individual can become a pamphleteer. As the lower court found, "the content of the Internet is as diverse as human thought."

Justice Stevens stated that although sexually explicit material on the Internet and Web "is widely available, users seldom encounter such content accidentally." He wrote, "The receipt of information on the Internet requires a series of affirmative steps more deliberate and directed than turning a dial." And since the Internet appeared to offer an infinite number of Web sites, unlike radio frequencies, the government role in supervision should be much less here.

The Court found that the nature of cyberspace made the defenses built into the CDA basically ineffective. That is, restricting access by minors and verifying user ages were, as a practical matter, impossible. Similarly, verification with credit cards was not a workable solution, because many sites were noncommercial and many adults did not own credit cards.

In conclusion, the Supreme Court found that the CDA was overly broad, in that it placed an unacceptably heavy burden on protected speech—such as the broad categories of "indecent" and "patently offensive" material—which adults were constitutionally allowed to view. The Court recognized the government's legitimate interest in protecting children from harmful material but found that the Constitution prohibited "an unnecessarily broad suppression of speech addressed to adults. . . . As we have explained, the Government may not reduce the adult population . . . to . . . only what is fit for children."

CASE QUESTIONS

1. What was the Supreme Court's reason for concluding that the Internet should be treated more like radio than newspapers in terms of free speech? Do you agree?
2. Is there a way for Congress to legally enact a law that would protect children from accessing sexually explicit sites on the Internet? How?
3. The Court found, in another part of its opinion, that because the Web is in fact worldwide, any U.S. law would be ineffective in actually shutting down objectionable sites, because they could move their operations outside the United States. Do you think this would happen? Is there a way the legal system could deal with this problem?
4. The Internet and the Web really do create a "global village" where anyone, anywhere can visit and participate in discussions and get information on almost any topic. Although much information is useful, some of it is "indecent" (as in this case), and some is harmful (as in how to make a bomb). Should we, as a society, be able to place some controls on what is easily accessible on the Web?

Jurisdiction As we learned early in this book, courts in one state generally do not have "personal jurisdiction" over defendants who reside in another state. However, when a company or individual has engaged in "minimum contacts" with the first state (such as engaging in business there, or becoming involved in an auto accident there), the state courts do have jurisdiction over the nonresident defendant.

With the Internet and Web now a factor in daily life, the presence of out-of-state business firms in our homes, via our computers, is a regular part of our day. During the past Christmas shopping season "e-commerce" broke all records. Millions of shoppers and businesses regularly purchase goods from out-of-state firms without leaving their homes. Suppose that something goes wrong, and a lawsuit is needed. Can you sue the out-of-state firm in your home state court system?

Most courts that have heard such cases so far have adopted some form of an "interactive-passive" test. Generally courts have allowed personal jurisdiction in cases in which "interactive" uses of the Internet have taken place within the state. A Web site can be characterized as interactive if business transactions can be conducted over the Internet or if information can be exchanged with users for the purpose of soliciting business.

The greater the commercial nature and level of interactivity associated with the site, the more likely the court will find that it has engaged in personal contacts with the forum state for the purposes of jurisdiction. For example, in *Compuserve, Inc. v. Patterson*, 89 F.3d 1257 (6th Cir. 1996) the court said there was personal jurisdiction where the nonresident defendant sold software over the Internet to 12 people in the forum state.

On the other hand, where an operator maintains a passive Web site that merely makes information available for browsing, courts have been reluctant to allow the owner of the Web site to be sued in any state where someone may access the site. Unlike interactive sites, which foster business transactions, "passive" Web sites merely allow users to gain information about products or services or facts about a firm. In *Cybersell, Inc. v. Cybersell*, 130 F.3d 414 (9th Cir. 1997), the court stated, "No court has ever held that an Internet advertisement alone is sufficient to subject the advertiser to jurisdiction in the plaintiff's home state."

Privacy *Consumer Privacy.* The nature of the Internet and Web, and the fact that we all use computers and on-line services daily, gives rise to the potential loss of privacy. In a report issued in late 1999, the director of the Electronic Privacy Information Center (EPIC; www.epic.com) stated that "online consumers are more at risk today than they ever were." The group researched whether popular on-line stores used profile-based advertising or used "cookies" (a device that tracks user on-line browsing and shopping habits).

The survey found that 18 of the leading shopping sites did not post any privacy policy, while 35 of the sites had profile-based advertisers operating on their pages, and 87 of the leading e-commerce sites used cookies. The president of a private advocacy firm noted "the stated policies of most big shopping sites run the gamut from bad to atrocious. People should have the right to buy without being tracked and without having their personal information sold."

The Federal Trade Commission had held a series of hearings and meetings in 1998 regarding consumer privacy but allowed the industry to show that it could self-regulate before imposing binding rules. The retailers developed a set of "Fair Information Practices," but it appears that such guidelines are not being followed. EPIC has argued that "legally enforceable standards of privacy are necessary to ensure compliance with the Fair Information Practices, and new techniques for anonymity are necessary to protect online privacy."

Privacy in the Workplace. Privacy in the workplace is another issue of increasing importance. As is discussed more fully in Chapter 19, many employers are using technology to monitor the actions of employees. A survey done in 1999 by the American Management Association found that 45 percent of major U.S. firms engage in some electronic monitoring of employee communications, up from 35 percent in 1997. Some 27 percent of companies did some checking of employee e-mail, 11 percent recorded and reviewed telephone conversations, and 6 percent stored and reviewed voice-mail messages. Storage and review of computer files was done by 21 percent of employers, and video recording of job performance was done by 16 percent of major firms.

Employers are concerned not only about the general level of employee performance, but also about such actions as using e-mail to sexually or racially harass other employees, giving away company information, engaging in illegal activities, or conducting personal business on work time. Most employers notify their employees that they will be monitored, and the cases generally support employers who do so against privacy claims of employees, as long as the surveillance is done in a reasonable manner, and private information is not disclosed to others. See Chapter 19 for further information on this topic.

The American Management Association sent an advisory to its 10,000 member companies, urging that policies and practices in electronic monitoring and surveillance should be posted and issued so that "employees are aware that their actions and communications are subject to recording and review." The highest level of electronic monitoring was in the financial services sector, including banking, brokerage, insurance, and real estate industries, with 68 percent, followed by business and professional services, with 51 percent doing monitoring.

European Union Laws. The nations of the European Union (EU) are more concerned about privacy issues than the United States, at least so far. In 1998, the EU enacted a Directive on Data Privacy, which guarantees European citizens absolute control over data concerning them. If a company wants personal information, it must get that person's permission and explain what the information will be used for. It must also promise not to use it for anything else without the citizen's consent. A company would not be allowed to sell its mailing list to another firm that wanted to solicit its customers.

Citizens have the right to know where information about them came from, to demand to see it, to correct it if wrong, and to delete it if objectionable. And they have the right to file suits against any person or company they feel is misusing their data.

Furthermore, Article 29 of the law requires that foreign governments provide data protections as rigorous as Europe's or risk having data flows cut off. This means that the EU Commission has the power to prosecute companies and block Web sites that fail to live up to the EU data privacy standards. As the global leader in on-line business, the United States, with its relative lax rules on privacy, is a particular target of the EU directive.

Europeans hate the American practice of planting cookies that hook into a name, then track the Web sites the person has explored and send back consumer profiles. They are outraged that U.S. governments and firms use the Web to learn facts that people would rather keep to themselves. At the root of the battle is a major philosophical difference. One businessman in Europe says "In Europe, people don't trust companies, they trust government." In the United States, he says, "It's the opposite way around—Americans feel citizens must be protected from actions of the government."

American firms are concerned about the EU data privacy rules, and many discussions are underway to reach agreement. U.S. negotiators have proposed a self-regulation scheme that would involve certifying before a nongovernmental privacy group that they are meeting European standards on data management, much as companies worldwide meet European industrial quality standards with the ISO 9000 certification. Meanwhile software makers and high-technology companies are developing programs to meet privacy needs, while preserving producers' rights to ask questions of consumers.

Europeans have also been slower to embrace the Internet in general, although that is changing. Especially in Southern Europe, in countries like Spain and Italy, e-commerce has been slow to catch on. People like to go out shopping—it is less of a chore and more of a social event. "I want to see what I'm going to buy," said a 41-year-old Spanish man recently. "Even if I had the Internet, I'd still want to go to the store." He enjoys walking around, looking in shop windows, and perhaps finding time for a glass of wine and tapas with friends.

Delivery is also a hassle in many European countries. Unreliable postal service in Italy has made couriers a must, jacking up delivery prices and eliminating one advantage of on-line selling. In Spain, nearly all on-line sellers charge shipping and handling and cannot guarantee delivery dates. Another obstacle is that most of the major online sellers use English as the language of commerce. Nevertheless, new investors are confident that they can develop Web sites that cater to their customers, in their languages, in the near future.

Piracy The whole purpose of intellectual property protection is intended to give the authors, investors, and trademark holders the "exclusive rights" to sell or license others to sell products using the books, songs, computer programs, processes, or goods covered by the intellectual property rights. However, both in the United States and very definitely in other parts of the world, goods are made and sold without permission or approval of the owner of the intellectual property rights. This practice is called **piracy**.

piracy: The manufacture and sale, without permission, of goods copyrighted or trademarked by another firm.

Producers of movies and software have complained loudly in recent years that the vast majority of video tapes and software products sold in China, Brazil, and many other countries are pirated copies, made illegally—which has cost the owners of the intellectual property rights billions of dollars in lost royalties. Many actions have been taken in foreign nations to seek out and close down manufacturers and producers of pirated compact discs and software. However, despite such actions, many consumers around the world and in the United States continue to see copying of copyrighted software, videos, and music as a necessary evil. As one Chinese student told one of the authors of this book recently, "We have to use the [pirated] copies—we can't afford to buy Windows at the prices charged by Microsoft. We can buy the program for $2 in the street, or pay $100 in a store—what would you do?"

The Internet and the Web have made copying copyrighted and trademarked material even easier than before. Much music is now available on the Internet from a number of sites. It is quite possible for users to copy and distribute illegally so-called MP3 audio files. This format has become one of the hottest recent on-line trends, allowing friends to trade songs digitally and music lovers to search the Internet for rare tracks by their favorite artists. But for the musicians and composers holding copyrights, MP3s are a nightmare. Users can easily copy entire company disks and serve them up on the Net for anyone to download free.

The maker of the wildly popular "Beanie Babies," Ty Inc., has been quite aggressive in filing suits against other manufacturers who market similar bean-filled toy dolls that attempt to copy the copyright- and trademark-protected Beanies. In the past four years, Ty has gone after 70 companies for "copycat" designs. The following reading describes the efforts of one company to stop piracy of the popular Pokemon merchandise, made by Nintendo.

In Pursuit of Pokemon Pirates

Nintendo's Top Cop Leads Warehouse Raids, Searches To Catch Counterfeiters

Jodi Daugherty is spearheading the assault on a rash of fake Pokemon products world-wide.

Redmond, Wash.—Ripping up a Pokemon trading card might horrify many a grade-schooler, but Jodi Daugherty does it routinely—to check for counterfeits.

"Hold it up to the light and you can see through it," says Ms. Daugherty, manager of the antipiracy group at Nintendo of America Inc. "That means it's fake. Or you can look at the ink closely, and if it looks like a bunch of dots from a printer, that's a red flag."

To stop piracy of merchandise based on the Pokemon video-game franchise, Ms. Daugherty is leading a small army of private investigators and police world-wide. They are in hot pursuit of counterfeiters trying to foist false "Charmander" and "Pikachu" characters on unsuspecting consumers.

The company has chased video-game pirates for years. But last spring, Nintendo began to see a flood of knock-offs of Pokemon trading cards, figurines, apparel and plush toys. And now it is bracing for another wave of pirated goods as the Christmas holidays approach and Nintendo unveils new Pokemon products and a movie called "Pokemon The Movie: Mewtwo Strikes Back."

Today, the company is expected to announce that more than 8,000 fake Pokemon goods have been seized in raids against 29 New York City retailers. The goods—seized in court-authorized civil actions along with other pirated goods—include fake Pokemon trading cards, stickers and plush toys.

As mastermind of the antipiracy program, Ms. Daugherty hardly fits the stereotype of corporate enforcer. At five-foot-three, the 33-year-old lawyer has an office adorned with photos of her children and big piles of soft and fuzzy Pikachu dolls. Her high-pitched voice could pass for a teenager's. "I walked into a customs office, and the officer said, 'I thought you would be six feet tall and weigh 500 pounds,'" says Ms. Daugherty.

She joined Nintendo six years ago, and, as software piracy grew, so did her importance inside the legal department at the company's U.S. operation here. Last year, the company estimates it lost $725 million to video-game piracy.

After Nintendo launched Pokemon handheld video games in the U.S. last year, Pokemon-merchandise piracy took off as well. The company is convinced the $17 million in fake goods seized by customs agents in the past few months is just the tip of the iceberg.

Over the last 18 months, Pokemon, or "pocket monsters," products have enchanted American children. They play handheld computer games featuring the monsters. And they trade cards with each other in hopes of collecting all 150 creatures. Some cards, such as the "Charizard" character, can sell for well over $50 on the street. Kyoto, Japan-based Nintendo has itself generated an estimated $5 billion in Pokemon revenue over four years.

In May, Ms. Daugherty began hiring lawyers like Tony Stiegler, a partner at outside counsel Cooley Godward LLP in San Diego, to ferret out the pirates through a network of undercover private investigators.

With Ms. Daugherty's approval, Mr. Stiegler and his associates scored big in July with so-called civil-seizure raids at two toy wholesalers in Los Angeles. First, the private investigators secretly videotaped a purchase of what they alleged was fake merchandise. They then secured a court order allowing them to seize the goods. They hired off-duty police officers and, using Los Angeles police as backup, entered the warehouses and confronted the surprised people inside.

No guns were drawn, but investigators found an automatic pistol with ammunition and cash during their search. The operation netted 540,000 fake Pokemon dolls and other goods, all hidden in a labyrinth of boxes on the upper floors of the warehouses. It took one and a half loads of a 18-wheeler to haul away the merchandise. During the search, the lawyers copied data stored on computers in the warehouse, which gave them leads to the wholesaler's international connections, Mr. Stiegler says.

"As we do this, we move on up the distribution chain to the bigger suppliers," Ms. Daugherty adds. "That's how we get back to the manufacturing source."

Nintendo has pending copyright and unfair business practice lawsuits against K-World Trading Co. and Animation Elegant Inc., both Los Angeles-based importers. Both consented to temporary restraining orders allowing the seizure of their goods. The companies declined to comment. Nintendo is pursuing manufacturers overseas, especially in Taiwan, but so far hasn't shut any major operations down.

Nintendo also turned its campaign to retailers, teaching them how to spot counterfeit goods after it found knockoffs at retailers such as Babbages Inc., Wal-Mart Stores Inc. and Electronic Boutique Holdings Corp.

"We did not knowingly sell a product that was fake," says Jeffrey Griffiths, a senior vice president at Electronics Boutique. "Once Nintendo notified us, we pulled it." A spokesman for Wal-Mart said he wasn't aware of the retailer's ever having sold fake Pokemon goods. Babbages declined to comment.

Ms. Daugherty and her team also trained customs agents how to spot fake Pokemon goods—no easy task since Nintendo holds 90 legal licensing agreements. Sometimes purveyors of knockoffs slap a Pokemon logo on a slow-moving toy just to clear inventory, says Thomas Skinner, a U.S. Customs service officer. His group has seized over 1.15 million counterfeit Pokemon goods since June. That doesn't include the Los Angeles bust that resulted in the seizures of goods valued at $5 million.

"I've taken to watching Saturday morning cartoons to get up to speed on Pokemon," says Homer Johnson, senior customs inspector at the Port of Los Angeles. "We've found everything from key chains to basketball hoops—more than 40 different types of goods in all."

Shipments seized in Los Angeles come mainly from Taiwan, China and Hong Kong, Mr. Johnson says. Nintendo says it has also seized $2 million in goods in 25 raids in Canada, and last month it nabbed $1 million in merchandise in three separate raids in Chile. Nintendo has seized so many fakes that the wares are stacked 30 feet high in warehouses.

Once the goods are no longer needed for legal cases, Ms. Daugherty faces another quandary: what to do with it all. She is already searching for an incinerator that can accommodate plastic.

WILLS, PROBATE, AND TRUSTS

Ownership of all types of property—real, personal, and intellectual—can also pass through the death of the property owner. There are several ways for the property owner to control who becomes the owner of property after his or her death; these include wills and trusts.

WILLS

When an individual dies, his or her real and personal property is distributed to others. Who is entitled to the property depends on whether the deceased person (the *decedent*) left a will or not. A **will** is a written document, prepared by a person of "sound mind" (who understands what he or she is doing at the time he or she signs the will), that designates how property is to be distributed following his or her death. Although most states allow handwritten wills (*holographic wills*) in certain cases, the best procedure is for the person making the will (the *testator*) to prepare a typewritten will, with the assistance of an attorney, and

will: A document that states how a person wishes his or her property distributed after death.

sign it in the presence of witnesses (most states require two or three), who then also sign the will.

The original copy of the will should be kept in a safe place, where it will be easily found after the person's death. Until the testator dies, the will has no legal effect and can be changed, amended, or totally canceled by the testator at any time. The people named in someone's will as beneficiaries have absolutely no rights to any of the testator's property until his or her death (the will may be totally changed before then). If the will is amended or material is added (called a **codicil**), or a new will is prepared, the same formalities must be followed as in the original will.

codicil: An amendment to an existing will.

PROBATE COURT

After the testator's death, the will can be filed in the local *probate court*, and the court will take jurisdiction of the distribution of the decedent's assets. Usually the will is filed in court by the **executor**, the person named in the will to represent the testator and carry out the testator's wishes regarding the distribution of his or her estate.

executor: The person named in the will to carry out the decedent's requests and pay bills and expenses.

Sometimes one of the decedent's heirs (who probably has been left little or nothing by the will) challenges the will, and the court has to decide if the person was of sound mind when the will was made. The witnesses may be called to testify about the testator's state of mind on the date he or she signed the will. Also, someone may argue that the will being offered to the probate court is not the last one prepared by the testator. Some people make changes in their wills every few years, and this can cause confusion (as well as anger in those left out or cut out by the later wills—"I hereby leave everything to my kind nurse"). The last valid will made by a testator will be the one certified by the court, and battles often take place about whether the last one found has been prepared correctly or is in fact the most recent one. When preparing a new will, it is a good idea for a person to actually destroy all earlier wills made so that this confusion can be avoided.

If a person dies without leaving a will, he or she is said to have died **intestate**. In this event, every state has a law that specifies how his or her property will be distributed. Although each state law is slightly different from the others, in general the property will be distributed to the person's closest heirs, starting with the spouse and children, then parents, and so on. Only if the decedent dies without any heirs at all will the property go to the state, through the doctrine of *escheat*.

intestate: When a person dies without leaving a will, the property is distributed according to state law.

TRUSTS

A **trust** is a legal mechanism whereby a person (Jerry, for example) transfers ownership of and title to certain property to someone called a **trustee** (First Bank, for example), usually according to a written document that specifies how the trustee is to hold and use the property. The document normally provides that the trustee is to invest or manage the property in a way so that benefits can be paid to someone else (e.g., Jerry's mother), called a **beneficiary**. Trusts have benefits and also facilitate the transfer of property at one's death without the use of a will or the probate court.

trust: A legal mechanism by which one person transfers ownership of property to a **trustee**, who holds, uses, or invests the property for the benefit of another person (the **beneficiary**).

For example, Jerry creates a *testamentary trust* as part of his will. This trust states that on his death, if he is not survived by his wife, all assets will automatically transfer to First Bank. First Bank will hold the assets in trust and invest them in certain ways with the income paid to his two children. Furthermore, Jerry may have provided in the trust document that the trust will terminate when the youngest child reaches 21 years of age, with the entire balance of the trust funds distributed equally to his children at that time. In general, this sort of document ensures that money left by the parents will be safeguarded for the children, that the interest will be used for their benefit, and the balance will be transferred to them in full when they become adults.

SUMMARY

The legal topic of property includes some of the oldest legal principles and some of the newest. Theories regarding real estate ownership, deeds, possession, use, and restrictions date back hundreds of years, and are still important today to large and small businesses. Courts are dealing with newer issues as well, such as eminent domain, "taking" by government action, and restrictive covenants in planned use development. The ownership and transfer of personal property is based on traditional legal principles such as sale, delivery, and intent.

Certainly the most remarkable legal developments in property law are taking place in the intellectual property area. Traditional legal principles such as copyright, patent, trademark, and trade secret law are undergoing rapid and dramatic change with the development of new technology. Copyright law protects the author or composer against someone else using the exact expression in a later work. Where once the cases concerned copying by hand or with a photocopy machine, now computers and the Web allow one to exactly copy a musical or literary work and distribute the work to millions of others with one keystroke or click of a mouse. The same sort of challenges face owners of patents on inventions, products, and processes (including computer software) and the manufacturers of products protected by a trademark.

Many new intellectual property issues are arising, and older legal issues are being reexamined by the possibilities for infringement brought on by the Internet and Web, as well as the globalization of business. The legal issues raised in cyberspace promise to be challenging for all businesses in the next millennium.

CHAPTER QUESTIONS

1. Marion Allaire purchased a residential lot in Kansas in 1966. There was a chicken/hog wire fence dividing her back yard from her neighbor's back yard. Ms. Allaire believed that all the property on her side of the fence was hers, and she acted accordingly. She continuously used and maintained her portion, up to the fence. A woman named Akers purchased the property in 1976. Neither she nor the previous owner did anything to indicate that the fence was not the property line until a survey was done in 1987. It was then discovered that the fence was approximately 10 feet across the true

boundary line with Akers' land. The required time period for adverse possession in Kansas is 15 years. Who owns the 10 feet of land? Why? [*Akers v. Allaire*, 17 Kan. App. 2d 556, 840 P.2d 547 (1992)]

2. A South Carolina man purchased two lots on the ocean in an area called the Isle of Palms near Charleston. He planned to build a house on one and sell the other. After his purchase, in order to protect the beachfront, state and local regulations were enacted barring the construction of any permanent structures on property in the area. He sued, claiming that the government had essentially "taken" his property and that he should be compensated. What should be the result? [*Lucas v. South Carolina Coastal Council*, 112 S. Ct. 2886, 120 L.Ed. 2d 798 (1992)]
3. Since the early 1900s, two Swiss firms, Victorinox Cutlery Co. and Wenger, S.A., have been the sole manufacturers of multifunction pocket knives for the Swiss Armed Forces. Their knives have earned a reputation for durability and quality and have been sold around the world as "Swiss Army" knives. However, the companies have never filed for trademark protection on that phrase. In 1992, an American company began selling in the United States what the court called an "inexpensive and shoddy" pocketknife made in China with the words "Swiss Army" on the side. Can Victorinox obtain protection for the phrase "Swiss Army" on the basis of geographic origin, or has the phrase become generic? [*Forschner Group, Inc. v. Arrow Trading Co.*, 833 F. Supp. 385 (SDNY 1994)]
4. Atlanta, Georgia, enacted a zoning ordinance that required surface parking lots with more than 30 parking spaces to install a certain number of trees, barrier curbs, and other landscaping measures. The city declared the purposes of the law to be the promotion of aesthetic appeal, the improvement of water runoff and other environmental concerns, and the reduction of crime. No owner was required to donate any property to the city, nor could any owner be required to reduce the number of parking spaces by more than 3 percent. Several parking lot owners sued the city, claiming that a "taking" of their property had occurred, relying on *Dolan v. Tigard*. What should be the result and why? [*Parking Association of Georgia v. Atlanta, Ga.*, 450 SE 2d 200 (Ga. 1994), cert. den. 115 S. Ct. 2268 (1995)]
5. A Texaco scientist commonly photocopied articles of interest from various journals, without permission of the copyright owners. He kept copies of the articles for later use. The publisher of one journal (from which the scientist had admitted copying eight articles) sued Texaco for copyright infringement. Texaco argued that the fair use doctrine should protect such photocopying, but its argument was rejected by the New York court. Explain briefly what Texaco's fair use argument was, and what reasons the court might have had for refusing to apply the rule in this case. [*American Geophysical Union v. Texaco, Inc.*, 37 F.3d 881 (2d Cir. 1994)]
6. A group of neighbors who lived near a "drug house" brought a suit against the landlord–owner of the house, claiming that it was a "nuisance." Does such a dwelling meet the definition of a nuisance? [*Lew v. Superior Court of Alameda County*, 25 Cal.Rptr. 2d 42, 20 Cal. 4th 866 (1993)]
7. The *Automobile Red Book*, published eight times a year, lists its editors' estimate of the value of used cars by make, model, and geographic region.

A computerized information firm loaded substantial portions of the *Red Book* onto its database. When sued for copyright infringement, the computer firm argued that the compilation of facts in the Red Book lacked enough originality to be copyrightable. What do you think? Why? [*CCC Information Services Inc. v. Maclean Hunter Market Reports, Inc.*, 44 F.3d 61 (2d Cir. 1994)]

8. Certain freelance authors sold articles to newspapers and magazine publishers for use in collective works (magazines containing a number of different articles). Under the Copyright Law, the authors retained their own articles, while the publisher of the collective work had the copyright to that collective work and "revisions" of that work. When the publisher provided the individual articles to electronic databases such as NEXIS, the authors sued for infringement. What should the result be? Why? [*Tasini v. New York Times Co.*, (2d Cir. 1999) 68 USLW 1180 (10/5/99)]
9. Following the release of its Windows operating system program, Microsoft Corporation was sued by Apple Computer, Inc. for copyright infringement. Apple charged that Windows' use of various desktop "icons" or symbols on its computer screen display and its graphic user interface infringed upon Apple's copyrighted Macintosh graphic user interface. Apple claimed that the Macintosh program structure, sequence and organization, and screen displays were part of the program, which was protected by copyright. Microsoft asserted that the use of certain symbols, arrangement of menus, and design of its "overlapping windows" on the visual display screen were commonly used elements in many programs not copyrightable. Further, Microsoft claimed that the "look and feel" of the Macintosh user interface was not protected by copyright, as long as the computer codes used were not copied. What should the result be? Why? [*Apple Computer, Inc. v. Microsoft Corp.*, 35 F.3d 1435 (9th Cir. 1994)]
10. Over a period of time, including some wet and some dry years, a river changed its course. Essentially, a bend in the river was eliminated, creating several new acres of land on the west bank. The owner of the property adjoining the new land began to allow his animals to graze on the land. He effectively used the land from the former riverbed up to the new river course. After a period of 10 years, the landowner on the east bank (where the river had cut into his land) brought an action seeking to evict the other owner from using his land. Who wins and why?

PRACTICAL EXERCISE

Micro Corporation, based in Portland, Oregon, is a developer of computer software programs. It produces the popular "10-9-8" spreadsheet program. Micro has learned that Paperback Software Co. of Berkeley, California, is selling a program called "Planner" and that Bronco Development Inc. of Denver, Colorado, has developed and is selling a software program called "Graph Paper." Both programs look very much like "10-9-8" and use many of the same commands and user interfaces. "Planner" and "Graph Paper" both sell for about $60, while "10-9-8" is priced at around $300.

Micro has a valid copyright on "10-9-8," and although it does not have any evidence that anyone from Micro gave any secrets to Paperback or Bronco, the two new programs look and operate very much like "10-9-8" and at a much lower price. Micro estimates that sales of the two "clones" have caused it to lose $100,000 so far, and the losses increase each month. Both Paperback and Bronco insist that they developed their programs legally, on their own, without copying anything that Micro could copyright. They believe that the phone calls and letters Micro has sent them are attempts to drive them out of business.

A computer store in Salem, Oregon, "Computers R Us," has sold 70 copies of "Planner" and 50 copies of "Graph Paper," so far, and has more for sale now. Sales representatives from Paperback and Bronco have visited this store and hope to do further business in the future. Among the purchasers of "Planner" is Mr. Edward Breslin, and one of the purchasers of "Graph Paper" (from Computers R Us) is Ms. Norah Meredith. Both Mr. Breslin and Ms. Meredith live in Salem and use the products both at work and at home.

Write a memo describing the legal issues in this situation. What sort of rights do each of the parties have? What laws may have been violated? Which of the various parties may be liable to Micro? What should Micro do to protect its interests?

FURTHER INFORMATION

www.lcweb.loc.gov/copyright
U.S. Copyright Office.
fairuse.stanford.edu
Stanford fair use site.
www.eff.org
Electronic Frontier Foundation, an organization focusing on privacy issues.
www.nolo.com
Nolo Press, publisher of many books about legal issues for nonlawyers.
www.wipo.org
World Intellectual Property Organization.

CHAPTER 15

ENVIRONMENTAL LAW AND REGULATION

LEARNING OBJECTIVES

After reading this chapter, you should be able to:

1. Discuss how the National Environmental Policy Act, including Environmental Impact Statements and the Council on Environmental Quality, affects business.
2. Describe the rulemaking and enforcement responsibilities of the Environmental Protection Agency.
3. Explain the laws designed to prevent and decrease the various forms of pollution.
4. Describe the controversy surrounding the Endangered Species Act.
5. List the statutes enacted to control the use and disposal of hazardous and toxic waste.

CHAPTER OUTLINE

One of your friends was the president of a small company that picked up and disposed of oil waste from various businesses. The disposal site was located on land owned by another person. In the Practical Exercise at the end of this chapter, you are asked to advise your friend and the land owner about their liability if the EPA finds that the tanks holding the oil were leaking.

INTRODUCTION

One of the most significant public policy developments of the last 30 years has been the increase in concern for environmental issues. Some years ago, people carelessly threw soda pop cans and pop tops out of car windows, tossed paper on the ground, and dumped various substances into rivers and lakes. Today these actions are universally condemned. Words and phrases little known in the 1960s—*wetlands*, *acid rain*, *recycling*, *effluents*, *open space*, *global warming*, *toxic waste*—are now commonly used in conversation.

For years, the environment was viewed as a free resource for business. As industry grew and the nature and operations of business became increasingly complex, commercial and industrial activities caused considerable harm to the environment. Today, the public generally accepts that air, water, and other natural resources belong to society, and a business that causes depletion or pollution of these common natural elements should pay for the loss, just as if the firm had cut down a tree on government land. However, whether or not this trend will continue is uncertain. Increasingly, state and federal governments have taken a hard look at some of the more stringent regulations in an effort to assess the costs and benefits of various requirements under all environmental laws. "Will this environmental rule cause the loss of jobs?" is a question being asked more frequently today.

The law often develops in an organic manner. Doctrines that originated hundreds of years ago sometimes generate new theories as the times change, as legal solutions are needed to address new issues. In Chapter 14, we looked at property law and specifically examined several legal theories relating to real property that developed centuries ago. In the past 30 years, the general public has become concerned with the harm caused to the environment by business and industrial activity. Some of the ancient doctrines of property law have engendered new laws and regulations aimed at controlling actions taken by industrial firms that may cause contamination of land, water, and air. This chapter examines a series of federal laws establishing controls on the discharge of various substances into the public air and water, as well as the production, transportation, use, and disposal of chemicals and other hazardous substances on private property. These laws include the Clean Air Act, the Clean Water Act, the National Environmental Policy Act, and the several federal laws dealing with hazardous and toxic waste.

THE NATIONAL ENVIRONMENTAL POLICY ACT

Although individual states had made some efforts to combat pollution in the years prior to 1969—without a great deal of success—major federal involvement in environment regulation began with the passage of the National Environmental Policy Act of 1970 (NEPA). Congress stated the purposes of NEPA to be as follows:

> To declare a national policy which will encourage productive and enjoyable harmony between man and his environment; to promote efforts which will prevent or eliminate damage to the environment and biosphere and stimulate the health and welfare of man; to enrich the understanding of the ecological systems and natural resources important to the Nation; and to establish a Council on Environmental Quality.

NEPA does not require that any particular measures be taken to prevent water, air, or other types of pollution, but responding to considerable public pressure, it established a federal government policy that environmental issues were of the highest concern. This policy was intended to permeate all activities of the federal government. Congress explicitly recognized "the profound impact of man's activity on the interrelations of all components of the natural environment." The act required that the federal government (in cooperation with state governments and other organizations) "use all practicable means and measures" to protect environmental values and to "create and maintain conditions under which man and nature can exist in productive harmony."

The most important actual legal mandate of NEPA was the requirement that an **Environmental Impact Statement (EIS)** be prepared for each "major federal action significantly affecting the quality of the human environment." Another important section of NEPA established the *Council on Environmental Quality*.

Environmental Impact Statement (EIS): A thorough study of the environmental effects that may be caused by a proposed federal project or license, along with alternatives that were considered.

ENVIRONMENTAL IMPACT STATEMENTS

The preparation and filing of an EIS requires substantial time and effort. The NEPA has been interpreted broadly, so that not only does the federal agency actually constructing a project need to prepare an EIS, but also any agency sponsoring, supervising, or perhaps only approving or licensing a project to action that may significantly affect the environment. The statements themselves often are well over 100 pages long. NEPA requires the statement to analyze and describe the following: (1) the environmental impact of the proposed action; (2) any adverse environmental effects of the project that cannot be avoided; (3) alternatives to the proposed action; (4) the relationship between short-term uses of the environment and the maintenance of long-term productivity; and (5) any irreversible and irretrievable commitments of resources that would be involved.

As agencies prepare to embark on a project, a draft EIS is circulated to interested parties and government officials for comment. Once finalized, the EIS is provided to other federal agencies, state agencies, the Council on Environmental Quality, and the public. The EIS is primarily intended to *provide information* to anyone who is interested in the environmental effects of the project and to explain the rationale behind the choices made by the proposing agency. The law does not require that the courts review every EIS, nor are they asked to determine whether the environment will be harmed. Rather, the EIS is intended to inform other agencies and the public about the environmental consequences of a proposed project; with this information, then, any group unhappy with the tentative decisions made by the agency can bring public and internal pressure to force the proposing agency to make changes before the project is begun.

A number of cases, however, have held that a court may review an EIS to determine whether an agency has complied with the requirements of the NEPA. Courts have also held that they can order an agency to prepare a new EIS or issue an injunction to stop a project if the requirements of NEPA have not been met. Some courts have gone even farther and looked into the "substantive" aspects of the agency's decision—that is, whether the agency legally could have made the decision it did if all the aspects of the project had really been evaluated in accordance with NEPA. If the decision proved "arbitrary and capricious," some courts have enjoined the project until a new EIS was done. The following case, decided by the federal district court in Hawaii, shows how the EIS requirement can be applied.

BLUE OCEAN PRESERVATION SOCIETY V. U.S. DEPARTMENT OF ENERGY

767 F.Supp. 1518 (D. Haw. 1991)

FACTS

For several years, the state of Hawaii and the federal government have been working cooperatively on a venture to develop geothermal power as an alternative energy source. The project is called the Hawaii Geothermal Energy Project, and it is located on the slopes of the active volcano Kilauea, on the island of Hawaii. Phases I and II of the project, involving the building of a small plant for research and a study of the feasibility of transporting power to other islands via underground cable, have been completed. (No EIS was prepared.)

Phase III, which involved the drilling of 25 commercial-scale exploration wells throughout the Kilauea East Rift Zone, had started at the time of the lawsuit. If the geothermal resource was "verified" after testing, Phase IV would consist of constructing up to 20 separate geothermal power plants of about 25 megawatts each. The plants would each need 8–10 working wells, and all of the plants would then be connected by roads, plumbing, and power lines. Finally, considerable overland and underwater cable would need to be laid to carry power to the islands of Maui and Oahu.

Although the final project was to be privately built, Congress had contributed $34.7 million to Phases I and II (over 80 percent of the total funding of those phases) and had appropriated $5 million toward Phase III. The Blue Ocean Society, a citizens' group, along with the Sierra Club and other plaintiffs, then filed suit, requesting that all work on the project be halted until an EIS was done.

The Department of Energy (DOE) denied that an EIS was necessary, arguing that this was largely a "research" project, not a "major federal action significantly affecting the human environment." During the course of the lawsuit, the DOE tried unsuccessfully to have the $5 million appropriation "reprogrammed" to another project by Congress. As the lawsuit neared a decision, the DOE finally agreed to prepare an EIS and then argued that the case was "moot"—that is, there was no reason for the court to act. The plaintiffs disagreed, asserting that without a court order, DOE officials could easily change their minds again regarding the EIS and that there were other unresolved issues remaining in the lawsuit.

DECISION

District Judge David Ezra first considered whether the case was moot. Judge Ezra found that it would be quite possible for the government to alter its position on the EIS and denied the DOE claim. The court cited previous cases holding that a lawsuit challenging an action is moot only when it has been "fully and irrevocably carried out." As the judge noted, "This is not a case in which the government has already prepared an EIS, or even commenced such preparation." "Not only is the EIS process not completed here," wrote Judge Ezra, "it has not begun."

In an earlier hearing, the court had ruled that Phases III and IV of the project had to be considered together as part of the same project and that clearly this was a "major federal action," based on the $5 million appropriation and the other federal involvement. Thus, the only remaining question was whether the action was one "significantly affecting the quality of the human environment."

The DOE argued that the project would not significantly affect the environment and that an EIS was thus unnecessary. The DOE claimed that the plaintiffs must prove "significant environmental effects" in order to force the preparation of an EIS. The court, however, noted that the very reason for the EIS requirement is to study and reveal the effects of a project on the environment prior to the time it is undertaken, so the initial decision on whether to do an EIS will always be based on incomplete information. Therefore, stated Judge Ezra, the burden on the plaintiffs is only to "*raise substantial questions*" regarding whether the proposed action *may* have a significant effect upon the human environment. If such questions are raised, "a decision not to prepare an EIS is unreasonable."

The court mentioned that the project contemplated a network of geothermal plants, wells, power lines, roads, and pipes over 26,000 acres in an area that had once been designated as a Natural Area Reserve. A U.S. Fish and Wildlife employee testified in court that the forest was a "unique dynamic ecosystem, valuable for both research on and management of the lowland rain forest habitat on the island of Hawaii," that would be adversely affected by the geothermal development. In addition, three other experts—an ornithologist, a geneticist, and a botanist—submitted affidavits to the court expressing grave concern for the environmental effects of the proposed project. The judge stated that this information "easily raises" the "substantial questions" of possible environmental impact sufficient to require the preparation of an EIS.

Therefore, the court ordered the federal government to commence the preparation of an EIS in compliance with the NEPA, which would address the serious concerns raised regarding the geothermal project. Also, an injunction was issued preventing all defendants from any further participation in the project (other than the funding and preparation of the EIS) until the EIS was completed.

CASE QUESTIONS

1. What is the key legal issue in this case?
2. What standard did the plaintiffs have to meet in order to trigger the preparation of an EIS?
3. In this case, the court was unwilling to defer to the decision of the federal agency that an EIS was unnecessary. Why?

SOCIAL/ETHICAL ISSUES

Regardless of the legal issues in the previous case, is it ethically proper to allow a private company to drill 160 to 200 wells on the slopes of the active Kilauea volcano? How can anyone know for sure what the environmental effects of these actions will be in the future? How would you feel if you lived in a village a short distance below? What if your power rates would be reduced 30 percent as the result?

Like many lawsuits, the controversy over the Hawaiian Geothermal Project involves many more issues than just the interpretation of the meaning of one section of federal law (NEPA). The following reading describes some of the social and cultural issues raised by the project.

THE PELE DEFENSE FUND

Named for Hawaii's volcano goddess and sworn to protect the islands, the Pele Defense Fund is a fiery, grass-roots organization with impact as mighty as its namesake. It has thwarted the Aloha State's effort to tap a live volcano and harness its steam in a $4 billion, federally funded experiment in a rain forest on Hawaii, the largest tropical island in the Pacific.

Pele (pay-lay) is the legendary Hawaiian fire goddess who causes volcanoes to erupt. Despite 170 years of Christianity, many Hawaiians not only believe in Pele's power, they still worship her—and for good reason.

Since January 3, 1983, Madame Pele, as she is known, has thrown up enough hot lava, it is estimated, to build a four-foot wide, four-inch deep sidewalk from Honolulu to New York every two days. The eruptions, still in progress, began soon after the first drills pierced the east rift zone of the 13,679-foot Mauna Loa; one eruption inundated 10,000 acres of the original site with lava. Madame Pele was angry, Hawaiians said.

A dozen outraged islanders first took up Madame Pele's defense in 1982 only to be dismissed as pot-smoking hippies by the local media. "Nobody took us seriously at first," said Ralph Palikapu Dedman, the founding president. Their cause was not immediately understood even in Hawaii, where fewer than 20 percent of the population is Hawaiian, because it recalled arcane Hawaiian religious rites many thought abandoned. "We worship nature gods, like Pele," Dedman said.

This native Hawaiian belief, Dedman claims, has been "ongoing for thousands of years"—much like rites of native American Indians who find spirituality in nature. "The forest is to us like a cathedral to Christians," he said. "To poke holes in Pele is sacrilegious."

In 1988, the Pele Defense Fund brought its cause to national attention in full-page ads in the *San Francisco Chronicle* and the *New York Times*. Claiming Hawaii would become an "industrial slum," the ads stressed the importance of native religious rites and deplored the geothermal plant in the 27,000-acre Wao Kele O Puna rain forest as "Ugly, Toxic, Costly & Sacrilegious." An illustration showed a "new" Hawaii jammed by high rise hotels, its landscape marred by thousands of 10-story electrical towers; a geothermal plant pumps out volcanic steam to chill Waikiki's 50,000 air-conditioned tourist hotel rooms 150 miles away.

Their mouse roar focused media attention on the struggle in the rain forest between native Hawaiians who worship a fire goddess and wildcat drillers from Wyoming trying to plumb the world's most active volcano for steam. "It really changed the awareness," Dedman said. "We are five thousand strong now. People from all over the world support our cause."

Ecology groups like the Sierra Club, Greenpeace, EarthFirst, and the Rainforest Action Network took up the defense of the Wao Kele O Puna (it means "green forest"), which is home to endangered Hawaiian birds, insects, plants—and on occasion humans. "As native Hawaiians, we are part of the ecosystem of these islands," Dedman said. "If we are as important as an endangered tree, environmental groups should chain themselves to us as much as they would a tree." For Pele worshippers the battle was to save what the *New York Times* called "the last big tropical rain forest in the United States. . . ."

An advocate of geothermal for oil-starved Hawaii, the governor lost political face again when his own state health director called geothermal "the stupidest thing we could possibly be doing . . . in the forest." Last summer, a test well exploded and sent people fleeing noxious gases; the hazardous conditions forced the state to shut down operations. It was the latest setback for the haunted geothermal project. Or was it—as Dedman and other native Hawaiians believe—only Madame Pele voicing her displeasure once again?

From *EPA Journal*, March–April, 1992, pp. 49–51.

THE COUNCIL ON ENVIRONMENTAL QUALITY

The NEPA also established the **Council on Environmental Quality (CEQ)**, which calls for a three-member council, appointed by the President and approved by the Senate. The CEQ and its staff advise the President on environmental matters. As well, the CEQ attempts to coordinate programs of the various federal agencies that influence the environment and to mediate disputes between federal agencies over environmental issues. The CEQ receives and comments on EISs filed with it and issues guidelines to agencies concerning the preparation of an EIS. In recent years, the role of the CEQ has diminished somewhat.

CEQ: A three-member agency which advises the President on environmental matters.

THE ENVIRONMENTAL PROTECTION AGENCY

The Environmental Protection Agency (EPA) was created in 1970 through a reorganization of several federal agencies by President Richard Nixon. By combining some 15 departments from five agencies—all of which had some responsibilities for environmental issues—the President created the EPA, which immediately became the primary federal regulatory body addressing environmental issues.

The EPA is an independent agency within the executive branch of government, headed by an administrator appointed by, and serving at the pleasure of, the President. As the scope of environmental issues has grown and the public's interest in environmental issues has increased, the EPA has expanded significantly and is now one of the largest federal agencies. Unlike the CEQ, which has remained a fairly small advisory body, the EPA is a powerful agency with a huge staff. Most of the major environmental laws that Congress has enacted since 1970 have given rulemaking and enforcement responsibilities to the EPA.

We will now turn our attention to the specific federal laws that are designed to prevent and decrease various forms of environmental pollution.

AIR POLLUTION—THE CLEAN AIR ACT

The Clean Air Act is the primary federal statute aimed at preventing air pollution. The Act as we know it today combines more than 10 separate acts of Congress, beginning with the Air Pollution Control Act of 1955. The first version of the Clean Air Act was enacted in 1963, with Congress adding major amendments in 1966, 1967 (the Air Quality Act), 1970, 1977, and 1990. The act requires the EPA to establish standards for certain substances that cause air pollution. These standards, called the **National Ambient Air Quality Standards (NAAQS)**, set forth the maximum allowable amount of each pollutant that the air may legally contain. These pollutants are as follows: particulates, sulfur oxide, carbon monoxide, nitrogen dioxide, ozone, hydrocarbons, and lead. The EPA has established both *primary* standards, which must be met in order

National Ambient Air Quality Standards (NAAQS): Maximum allowable amounts of seven types of pollutants.

to protect human health, and *secondary* standards, which are necessary to protect the "public welfare" (soil, water, vegetation, weather, property, animals, and other aspects of the human environment).

State Implementation Plan (SIP): Each state may develop its own plan for meeting the federal standards.

The structure of the Clean Air Act calls for each state to draft its own **State Implementation Plan (SIP)** to provide for "implementation, maintenance, and enforcement" of the ambient air quality standards in that particular state. This provision furthers the goal of federalism by allowing each state to decide how best to reach the required standards in its own jurisdiction and then to enforce the law and regulations. If state rules or enforcement are lacking, the EPA can require revisions or can impose other sanctions, such as banning new pollution sources (new factories, for example).

As the result of the Clean Air Act, manufacturing, agriculture, and other types of businesses must often spend thousands or millions of dollars to meet the NAAQS. Although expensive, the purchase and installation of complex equipment and procedures may be necessary in order to reduce emissions of certain hazardous substances to allowable levels.

When the Clean Air Act was amended in 1977, Congress placed several requirements on states that had not achieved the national air quality standards established earlier by the EPA. The 1977 amendments required those "*nonattainment*" states to create a permit program regulating new or modified major stationary sources of air pollution. The EPA regulations later issued to implement this statute allowed the states to adopt a plantwide definition of the term *stationary source* (pollution that emanates from one particular fixed point rather than mobile sources, such as automobiles).

bubble policy: An EPA rule that allows a company to expand and emit more pollution from one source of the plant, if it reduces pollution from another source. The plant is said to be under an imaginary "bubble."

These EPA regulations thus allowed businesses some flexibility in complying with the Clean Air Act under what has become known as the **bubble policy**. Under this concept, a large manufacturing plant with several different emission points may treat its facilities as though they are all under an imaginary bubble. Therefore, if the company wants to expand operations in one section of the facility (and thus increase one type of air pollution), it can legally do so as long as it reduces the discharge of that particular type of pollutant somewhere else within its facility (within the 'bubble"). If a company reduces pollution without adding a new source, it receives a "credit" from EPA, which can be used later, sold, or traded to another company that wants to expand its operations in a manner that will increase the emission of that type of substance.

The U.S. Supreme Court considered the legality of the bubble policy in the following case.

CHEVRON V. NATURAL RESOURCES DEFENSE COUNCIL, INC.

467 U.S. 837 (1984)

FACTS

After the EPA adopted its regulation allowing for use of the "bubble" policy in nonattainment areas, the Natural Resources Defense Council (NRDC), an environmental group, challenged the rule. The NRDC argued that this policy was not authorized by the Clean Air Act and in fact would not achieve a reduction in the pollution levels of areas that were already out of compliance with clean air standards. The Court of Appeals agreed and set aside the EPA rule. Chevron had a large industrial plant that was going to be adversely affected if the rule was not upheld, and it appealed to the U.S. Supreme Court.

DECISION

In an opinion by Justice Stevens, the Supreme Court reversed the Court of Appeals and upheld the "bubble rule" issued by the EPA. The Court set forth a two-step procedure for reviewing a regulation of an agency. First, the Court must determine whether Congress has directly spoken with regard to the issue, and if so, the matter ends. If, however, the statute is silent as to the precise point at issue, the Court must ask whether the agency's policy is based on a permissible and reasonable construction of the law.

The 1977 Amendments did not specifically refer to or create a bubble policy. The Amendments did provide that permits were required "for the construction and operation of new or modified major stationary sources" in nonattainment areas. The earlier Clean Air Act defined "stationary source" as "any building, structure, facility, or installation which emits or may emit any air pollutant." Therefore, the real legal question here is whether the term "stationary source" can be interpreted as applying to an entire plant, containing several chimneys and stacks, rather than to each stack separately.

The EPA had articulated several reasons for the bubble policy when it was promulgated. The agency argued that the rule would encourage replacement of "older, dirtier processes and pieces of equipment with new, cleaner ones . . ." and would aid in accommodating the conflict between economic and environmental concerns.

The Supreme Court decided that in interpreting an agency's construction of a statutory provision, the court's role is not to assess the 'wisdom" of the policy but only to assess if it is a reasonable choice within the gap left by Congress. The responsibility of resolving the struggle between competing views of the public interest is a policy decision best left to those in the political arena, who have constituencies.

In this case, the Court found that the administrator's interpretation represented a reasonable accommodation of manifestly competing interests and was entitled to deference, the regulatory scheme was technical and complex, the agency had considered the matter in a detailed and reasoned fashion, and the decision involved reconciling conflicting policies. In conclusion, the Court stated, "We hold that the EPA's definition of the 'source' is a permissible construction of the statute which seeks to accommodate progress in reducing air pollution with economic growth."

CASE QUESTIONS

1. Do you believe the Court's holding here will lead to a reduction in air pollution? Is the ruling good for business?
2. What would the plaintiffs have had to prove to win this case? What was the precise legal issue?
3. Is it ethical or socially responsible for a company to add a new wing to a manufacturing plant (in an area that already is in violation of federal air pollution standards), which will increase the amount of pollution, as long as the company reduces the pollution somewhere else in its facility?

It will probably not surprise you to learn that the largest amount of air pollution from nonstationary sources comes from automobiles. A number of the amendments to the Clean Air Act over the years have concerned emissions of lead, nitrogen oxide, and carbon monoxide pollution from automobile exhaust. The problems are particularly acute in large cities, where auto exhaust combines with other substances in the air to form smog. The amendments to the Clean Air Act have mandated the use, in most instances, of unleaded gasoline, have required catalytic converters in new cars, and have established fuel economy standards that must be met by manufacturers in order to sell new vehicles in the United States.

The 1990 Clean Air Amendments passed by Congress called for substantial reductions in auto tailpipe emissions by 1998, further reduction by 2000, and greater use of alternative fuel vehicles by companies that have fleets of vehicles. Car manufacturers were required to install new pollution control devices to reduce emissions of hydrocarbons and nitrogen oxides, and the equipment will have to last for 10 years (twice as long as previously required). Cleaner blends of gasoline ("reformulated" gasoline), including more use of methanol and ethanol additives, were required by 1995 in the nine smoggiest cities in order to reduce carbon monoxide emissions. A pilot program in California will eventually require auto companies to produce 300,000 clean-fueled vehicles a year. Cars in California will have to get better gas mileage, and some electric cars will be produced as well.

acid rain: Pollution caused by certain gases mixed with rain, which then becomes acidic and causes damage to plants and animals.

Acid rain is a type of pollution caused when sulfur dioxide and nitrogen oxide, emitted largely from coal-burning utility plants, combine with oxygen and moisture at high elevations in the atmosphere to form solutions of nitric and sulfuric acids. When this moisture falls to the ground in the form of rain, drizzle, or snow, it causes serious damage to vegetation, lakes, fish, and other wildlife. Many of the coal-burning utility plants are in the Midwest, where the prevailing winds blow much of the pollution into the Northeastern states and Canada, although many other areas are affected as well.

The production of acid rain can be reduced by using coal with a lower sulfur content and by installing "scrubbers" in the utility plants. Not only are these measures quite expensive to implement, they have political implications as well. Although residents of the Northeast suffer the most from acid rain, corrective measures may mean the loss of industrial jobs in the Midwest and coal-mining jobs in Kentucky and West Virginia (which produce mainly high-sulfur coal). On the other hand, more mining jobs might be created in the West (which has large amounts of low-sulfur coal). In enacting the Clean Air Act of 1990, after many years of negotiations, Congress reached a compromise that requires significant reductions in emissions of nitrogen oxide and sulfur dioxide from electric and manufacturing plants.

EPA REGULATIONS AND ENFORCEMENT

Regulations issued by the EPA in 1992 called for electric utilities to cut sulfur dioxide emissions in half, at a cost to industry estimated at $3 billion per year by the year 2000. These rules also include provisions permitting utilities to choose how to reduce their emissions and creating a market-based trading system that allows utilities to earn *emission allowances and credits* (which can be sold or traded to other companies) for making greater reductions than necessary.

emission allowances: The amount of reduction in emissions of a polluting substance, which results in a "credit" granted by the EPA.

Properly called **emission allowances**, these credits allow companies with "dirty" power plants to either install new equipment to cut emissions or buy the right to exceed federal air-pollution limits from other energy companies that have reduced their emissions below what is required. This innovative concept, included in the Clean Air Act Amendments of 1990, allows market forces to help achieve reductions in pollution, rather than the "command and control" approach of many federal regulations.

Originally the EPA apportioned air pollution allowances among the 445 largest U.S. power plants and some large factories. Then, as the facilities reduced air pollution, they received additional allowances. The allowances are traded by brokerage companies across the nation, and about $1.6 billion of allowances were traded in 1998. Companies that sell allowances often use the proceeds to buy state-of-the-art pollution reducing equipment. A group of brokerage firms specializing in pollution credits has emerged, and even energy companies that do not need pollution allowances have formed trading operations and buy and sell credits to increase their profits.

The program has been quite successful. Electric utilities emitted 25 percent fewer tons of sulfur dioxide in 1999 than in 1980, while 41 percent more electricity was produced. The government's General Accounting Office estimates that the trading program saves utilities $3 billion per year over previous pollution-enforcement approaches. The main criticism of the program is that in some regions of the country, most utilities purchase credits and keep on polluting the air, after buying allowances from energy firms far away that have achieved reductions.

The United States has suggested that the concept be expanded to international trading of emissions credits. An international treaty to reduce global warming was signed in Kyoto, Japan, in 1997 calling for "greenhouse gas" (primarily carbon dioxide) emissions to be cut to below 1990 levels by 2012, using a U.S.-type trading system. Negotiations to implement the program have been difficult, as the topics, industries, national governments, and international issues are much more complicated in a world-wide setting.

The EPA has also issued regulations requiring substantial reductions in nitrogen oxide emissions. The rules are in two parts. The first required coal-fired utilities by the year 2000 to cut emissions at a cost estimated at $300 million per year. The second part of the rule, which took effect in 1995, regulates both utility and nonutility boilers in urban areas with high smog levels and is expected to cost an estimated $500 million a year, although polluters can ask for extensions and exceptions.

The EPA believes that the new rules have cut nitrogen oxide emissions more than 2 million tons per year (from about 19 million tons 10 years ago). Utility and business groups have argued that the rules are overly stringent and will necessitate costly retrofitting in many power plants and industrial boilers used for refining, manufacturing, and processing. In contrast, environmental groups have accused the EPA of being too lenient by failing to require certain technology that would have resulted in deeper cuts in nitrogen oxide (to meet the standards set by Congress) and by setting the stage for the approval of exceptions when the standards are not met.

EPA SUES SEVEN UTILITIES FOR AIR POLLUTION VIOLATIONS

In late 1999, in one of the largest environmental enforcement actions in U.S. history, the EPA sued seven giant electric companies in the Midwest and South, alleging that they had violated the Clean Air Act. Even the federally owned Tennessee Valley Authority, the nation's largest wholesaler of electricity, was targeted for administrative action. The charges involved 32 older power plants, which comprise 30 percent of the nation's capacity of coal-fired plants. If proved, the allegations could result in hundreds of millions of dollars in fines and penalties, the installation of pollution controls costing billions, and higher utility rates for millions of consumers.

The heart of the charges is that the utility companies had made major modifications to their generating plants without modernizing pollution controls as required by the Clean Air Act. The older plants had been "grandfathered" when the 1990 amendments were enacted so they would not have to immediately comply and could make minor improvements without obtaining federal permits and meeting the new standards. However, the law required that if the plants made "major renovations" they must get permits, and install equipment that would bring them into compliance with the new standards.

The EPA's administrator, Carol Browner, in announcing the lawsuits, said that "these are not close calls." She stated that 100 EPA investigators had uncovered many instances in which the utilities had embarked on big capital improvements and tried to call them routine maintenance. "In one plant they spent $60 million for five new furnaces," she said. "That's hardly routine maintenance."

Utility companies vowed to fight the lawsuits vigorously, and were "disappointed" with the EPA action. "We've been working with them over the past 18 months to resolve their concerns on this issue," said one executive. "Our goal has been to cooperate and find a workable solution . . . but they [EPA] have now taken this to another level." Lawyers for the companies argued that even spending millions of dollars to improve a decades-old plant could be considered routine maintenance, if the alternative was to spend several hundred million dollars on a new plant.

The director of one environmental group praised the EPA action, saying that the suit could prevent "thousands of premature deaths, asthma attacks and other pollution-related health problems." New York governor George Pataki welcomed the action. "I hope this is only the first step by the EPA to hold these power plants [all located far from New York] accountable and give New Yorkers the protection we need and deserve from pollution originating in the Midwest and the Southeast."

Sources: "EPA Sues 7 Utilities, Tells TVA to Stop Practices," *Wall Street Journal* (Nov. 4, 1999), B 12; " U.S. Sues 7 Utilities on Air Pollution Charges, Citing 32 Coal-Fired Plants in 10 States," *The New York Times* (Nov. 4, 1999).

Congress has considered legislation that would require a strict cost/benefit analysis of all federal regulations having a significant impact upon business. This legislation would be applied to the Clean Air Act regulations and could produce substantial alterations if it becomes law.

SOCIAL/ETHICAL ISSUES

While the prevention and elimination of pollution is an issue that concerns most U.S. citizens, it is becoming clear that the worst environmental hazards are faced by minorities and the poor. A comprehensive statistical study done by the United Church of Christ's Commission on Racial Justice in 1987 found that communities in which commercial waste facilities were located had about twice the percentage of minorities in their population as those communities without such facilities.

Some 15 studies over the past 25 years have shown that distribution of pollution was unequally concentrated based on race and income. Where the data was analyzed by both income and race, five out of eight studies found that race was more strongly related to high pollution than income. For example, from 1920 to 1970 in the city of Houston, all of the city-owned municipal landfills and six of the eight garbage incinerators were located in African-American neighborhoods. One study in the Detroit area concluded that minority residents in the greater metropolitan area were four times more likely than white residents to live within one mile of a commercial hazardous waste facility.

Other studies have shown that Hispanics, Native Americans, and other minorities have also borne more than their share of toxic waste facilities, polluted air, and other environmental hazards. These findings led to a conference in 1990, sponsored by the University of Michigan, titled, "Race and the Incidence of Environmental Hazards." This conference featured several expert presentations, all of which tended to show that there was indeed such a correlation.

In the years since 1990, many other groups have raised concerns about "environmental justice." The official journal of the EPA once devoted an entire issue to articles dealing with equality in environmental protection, and William Reilly, then EPA administrator, formed an Environmental Equity Workgroup within EPA to more closely examine the issues raised by the Michigan Coalition.

What do you think government and/or business should do about this problem? What can the public do?

WATER POLLUTION — THE CLEAN WATER ACT

The federal government began to take a role in combating water pollution with the enactment of the *Rivers and Harbors Act* in 1899, which banned ships and manufacturing firms from discharging refuse into any navigable waterway or tributary. But significant federal involvement did not occur until 1948 with the *Federal Water Pollution Control Act*, which was substantially amended in 1972 and 1977 (*Clean Water Act*), and by the *Water Quality Act* of 1987. The combined law, as it now stands, is commonly called the *Clean Water Act* (CWA).

One aspect of the Clean Water Act requires the states to designate the uses of significant bodies of water in their jurisdictions and to establish water quality standards to reduce pollution to appropriate levels. Another important feature of the Clean Water Act is the establishment of the **National Pollutant Discharge Elimination System (NPDES)**, which imposes tough standards on the discharge of pollutants from **point sources** into navigable waterways and public sewage systems. A point source is a "discernible, discrete conveyance" such as a pipe, ship, or ditch. Any person or business wishing to make a discharge from a point source must obtain a permit from the EPA. The following case, for example, involved a determination of whether the runoff from a cattle feedlot was a point source.

National Pollutant Discharge Elimination System (NPDES): The system by which those who discharge (from a point source) effluent into streams or lakes are to obtain a state or federal permit.

point source: An identifiable point where liquid waste is discharged.

CARR V. ALTA VERDE INDUSTRIES, INC.

931 F.2d 1055 (5th Cit. 1991)

FACTS

Alta Verde Industries operates a cattle feedlot on 230 acres of land in Texas, generally feeding between 20,000 and 30,000 cattle. Not surprisingly, this feedlot produces considerable waste, primarily cow manure, which drains into a wastewater disposal system of six holding ponds. Alta Verde then uses this water to irrigate and fertilize three adjacent fields.

In the spring of 1987, a series of heavy rains caused the holding ponds to exceed their capacity. In early June, Alta Verde cut a spillway out of the embankment of one pond and discharged wastewater into an unnamed tributary of Rosita Creek. Other discharges may also have resulted at that time. Two citizens filed suit, claiming that Alta Verde did not have a NPDES permit, and therefore the discharges violated the Clean Water Act. The citizens sought damages of $600,000 and an injunction prohibiting Alta Verde from any further discharges in violation of the Act. The federal district court in Texas dismissed the case, and the plaintiffs appealed.

DECISION

The Fifth Circuit Court of Appeals, in an opinion by Circuit Judge King, thoroughly analyzed various sections of the Clean Water Act. The court first addressed Alta Verde's contention that it did not need an NPDES permit for its discharges.

"The Clean Water Act [actually the Federal Water Pollution Control Amendments of 1972] was enacted with the stated purpose of restoring and maintaining the integrity of the nation's waters," wrote the court. "In order for any person lawfully to discharge any pollutant from a point source into navigable waters of the United States, that person must obtain an NPDES permit and comply with its terms." The court explained that, in general, any other discharge would be unlawful.

An NPDES permit must incorporate effluent (discharge) limitations for point sources based on guidelines "promulgated by EPA on an industry-by-industry basis." [33 U.S.C. §1311(b)] requires the EPA to establish effluent limitations guidelines for existing point sources . . . based on the application of the "best available technology economically achievable" (BAT).

Alta Verde claimed, however, that it qualified for an exemption under the EPA regulations dealing with animal feedlots. The Clean Water Act specifically defined *point source* as including "concentrated animal feeding operations" [33 U.S.C. §1362]. An EPA regulation offered more detail:

A concentrated animal feeding operation [exists] if . . . more than 300 slaughter or feeder cattle [are contained] and pollutants are discharged into navigable waters. . . .

Provided, however, that no animal feeding operation is a concentrated feeding operation as defined above if such animal feeding operation discharges only in the event of a 25-year, 24-hour storm event. 40 C.F.R. §122, App. B (1988).

Therefore, if a feeding operation met the tests set forth in the second paragraph of this regulation, it was not treated as a concentrated feeding operation, was not considered a "point source," and did not need an NPDES permit. Alta Verde admitted that it was a feeding operation with more than 300 cattle but argued that it should be exempted under the second paragraph. Why? Its wastewater system could contain effluent pollution except for a 25-year storm, stated Alta Verde.

A "25-year, 24-hour" storm is defined as one that has a probability of occurring only once every 25 years. Experts testified at the trial that in the Eagle Pass area (where Alta Verde was located), such a storm would mean total rainfall of 7.1 inches in 24 hours. However, this level was not reached in the storm that led to the Alta Verde discharge. The lower court determined that the accidental discharge was caused not only by one storm but by the combined rainfall that had occurred during the spring, which exceeded Alta Verde's disposal system capacity.

The district court had found that the Alta Verde facility probably could have met the EPA effluent guidelines at the time of the accident and certainly by the time of the trial. However, the facts as determined by the trial court (there was no jury), showed that the Alta Verde facility *did discharge wastewater*, without the occurrence of a 25-year storm, regardless of the technical capacity of the system. Since an exemption from the permit requirements only applies to operations that discharge "only" in the event of a 25-year, 24-hour storm, clearly Alta Verde did not qualify. Thus, the EPA effluent guidelines quoted previously did not provide an exception to the NPDES requirement, as argued by Alta Verde.

Alta Verde also argued that the plaintiffs lacked "standing" to challenge its operations. According to a recent U.S. Supreme Court decision (*Gwaltney*), in order to bring a citizen suit under the Clean Water Act, the plaintiffs must show that they are seeking to "enjoin or otherwise abate an ongoing violation." To do so, they must make a "good faith allegation of continuous or intermittent violations" by the defendant.

Standing is usually determined at the time the case is filed, and since at that time Alta Verde had no NPDES permit, there was a violation of the law. Because no permit had since been obtained by Alta Verde, there was a "continuing violation" of the act, stated the Court. Although Alta Verde had improved its wastewater disposal system since the discharge, the lower court found that it still might not be sufficient to hold discharges from a "catastrophic or chronic rainfall" (much less a 25-year storm). Therefore, the "trier of fact" (the lower court) could conclude that there was "a likelihood of a recurrence of intermittent or sporadic violations," which would violate the act. The plaintiffs thus had standing to challenge the actions of the defendant Alta Verde. The decision of the lower court was reversed and remanded for further proceedings.

CASE QUESTONS

1. What was the point of discharge in this case? What is the definition of a *point source discharge*?
2. Why did Alta Verde think that an NPDES permit was not needed in this case?
3. When is an NPDES permit required? What is the purpose of such a permit?
4. Alta Verde Industries was a large commercial operation. The owners felt, in 1987, that their wastewater disposal system was sufficient to contain the discharge of cow manure effluent from their operations, even in a 25-year storm. After the accident in 1987, further improvements were made to the system. Is it fair, or just, to subject the company to another trial for damages over the 1987 discharges into the creek? Is society served by this procedure?
5. What is the public policy basis for allowing other private citizens (not just the EPA) to bring legal actions to enforce statutes passed by Congress?

The previous case includes terms such as *effluents* and *BAT*. The EPA has issued increasingly tough standards regarding any substances (called **effluents**) discharged into waterways. In order to obtain permits, industrial sources originally were required to meet standards based on the "**best practicable technology currently available**" (**BPT**). However, as the Alta Verde case demonstrated, new sources of pollution and all other point sources were required to meet higher standards—"**the best available technology economically achievable**" (**BAT**). These standards have been called "*technology-forcing*," because they may require an industrial firm to develop new measures of treating effluent discharges in order to obtain a permit rather than use the technology that is "currently available," as they can under the BPT standards. The BAT standards speak of the "maximum use of technology within the economic capability of the owner or operator," which will result in "reasonable further progress toward eliminating the discharge of all pollutants." Thus, a firm may have to expend the maximum economic resources possible in order to obtain a permit under the BAT standards. Toxic wastes are covered by BAT rules.

effluent: Liquid substances discharged into waterways.

BPT standard: Best practicable control technology currently available; the average of the best existing technology of industrial plants of various sizes.

BAT standard: The best available technology—that is, control and treatment—that now exists or is capable of being achieved.

In a 1980 case, *Environmental Protection Agency v. National Crushed Stone Association*, the U.S. Supreme Court held that, although the law allowed the EPA to grant businesses variances from the tougher BAT guidelines where the firm had spent all that it was economically possible for it to do, no variances were possible under the less-stringent BPT standards. The court stated that the EPA administrator was empowered to make the determination, when a BPT regulation was established, that the benefits of effluent reduction were worth the costs imposed on the industry.

Thus, to grant a variance (exception) to an individual firm because it cannot bear the normal costs of the technological requirements is inconsistent with Congress's intent. Stated the court, "The 1977 limitations were intended to reduce the total pollution produced by an industry, [which] . . . necessarily imposed additional costs on the segment of the industry with the least effective technology." The Supreme Court noted pointedly that "if the statutory goal is to be achieved, these costs must be borne or the point source eliminated," even if that meant some plants must close. As to the tougher, technology-forcing BAT standards, however, the court ruling did permit variances on some occasions.

Another section of the Clean Water Act deals with the perils posed by the transport of petroleum products by oil tankers. Unfortunately, incidents of such oil spills are not uncommon. Perhaps the most publicized accident happened in March 1989, when the tanker *Exxon Valdez* ran aground in Prince William Sound, Alaska, spilling an estimated 11 million gallons of crude oil. The oil spread for 700 miles, causing serious pollution damage to Alaskan waters and shoreline and killing thousands of fish. In addition, more than 36,000 birds died, including at least 100 bald eagles. As the result of that accident, Exxon was charged with two felonies and three misdemeanors by the federal government and was sued by the United States, the state of Alaska, and more than 1,000 other individuals in civil cases. A jury in Alaska ordered Exxon to pay more than $5 billion to these parties. Exxon also spent more than $2 billion on its own in cleanup costs.

WETLANDS

wetlands: Areas saturated or inundated by surface or groundwater.

Areas saturated or inundated by surface or groundwater are considered **wetlands**. It has been recognized in recent years that these areas are an important part of the ecosystem, supporting a wide variety of plant and animal species. The EPA has therefore taken steps to protect such areas as swamps, marshes, and bogs from destruction by developers and others.

In order to make any change in an area designated as a wetland, a permit must be obtained from the Army Corps of Engineers. The EPA may block the issuance of a permit under the Clean Water Act, to prevent environmental damage. Nevertheless, some 10,000 permits are granted each year allowing dredging or filling in wetlands. There have been criminal charges brought, and severe fines and penalties assessed for violating this law.

NON–POINT SOURCES OF POLLUTION

The focus of EPA enforcement efforts under the CWA in the past has been directed at the discharge of effluent from identifiable point sources, as we have discussed. However, in 1999, the EPA issued a series of proposed regulations that would begin to regulate pollution from *non–point sources*, such as the runoff from farms, logging operations, parking lots, mining and other large sites. These operations do not have a readily ascertainable pipe or ditch that carries liquid material, but estimates are that as much as 50 percent of water pollution comes from such sources. The regulations are complex and controversial, so there will likely be several drafts (using the notice and comment process explained in Chapter 5) before a final set of rule emerges.

The proposed EPA regulations would require the states to submit plans within the next 14 years for controlling such pollution and cleaning up waterways that fail to meet water quality standards for fishing, drinking, and swimming, depending on the category in which the waterway is placed. Large hog and poultry farms, cattle feedlots, and dairy operations produce vast amounts of waste, which flows into lakes and streams. Currently less than 2,000 livestock operations are covered by EPA regulations (because of the exceptions discussed in the *Alta Verde* case), and the new regulations would require another 18,000 such operations to obtain permits.

The manure produced on these huge "factory farms," is often used as fertilizer on many other farms as well. The runoffs from thousands of farms and other agricultural facilities after a rainstorm are rich in nutrients like nitrogen and phosphorous, deprive lakes and streams of oxygen essential to maintaining viable fisheries, and may also cause dangerous toxic microorganisms, which have caused fish kills in Maryland and the Carolinas. Loggers would be affected as well and might have to place buffers along streams to control runoff from their operations.

THE ENDANGERED SPECIES ACT

In the past few years, the **Endangered Species Act** has become one of the more controversial environmental laws. This statute, enacted in 1973, requires the Secretary of the Interior to list those animal and plant species that are either "endangered" or "threatened" (slightly less serious) and to define the critical habitat of these species.

Endangered Species Act: A federal law enacted to protect plant and animal species from extinction.

The Act then states that each federal agency shall, in consultation with the Secretary, "insure that any action authorized, funded, or carried out by such agency . . . is not likely to jeopardize the continued existence of any endangered species or threatened species or result in the destruction or adverse modification of habitat of such species. . . ."

Several prominent cases have involved situations in which a business firm was prevented from undertaking some activity, often mining or logging, because such action would cause adverse effects to an endangered species. One much-publicized case concerned the adverse effects that extensive logging in Oregon was having on the northern spotted owl. In the aftermath of that court decision, the Forest Service put into effect substantial restrictions on logging in federal forests. These reductions in the allowable timber harvest caused job losses and layoffs in the timber industry, and numerous protesters argued that "people should be more important than owls."

Recently, Congress has been taking a hard look at modifications to the Endangered Species Act to determine if the benefits of preserving a species and its habitat should always outweigh the adverse economic costs to the surrounding community or if some balancing test should be required. In the

Pacific Northwest, a vigorous debate is taking place over the rapidly decreasing numbers of salmon returning to spawn and whether the removal of several dams on major rivers would help their survival.

HAZARDOUS AND TOXIC WASTE

The disposal of the millions of tons of waste generated by agriculture, business, and individuals is one of our major social problems today. Congress has attempted to control all aspects of the use and disposal of various toxic and hazardous water materials by enacting a series of important statutes in the past 25 years, several of which are discussed in the following sections.

THE RESOURCE CONSERVATION AND RECOVERY ACT

Resource Conservation and Recovery Act (RCRA): A federal law requiring that certain hazardous wastes be documented and tracked from the time they come into existence until proper disposal.

hazardous waste: Solid waste that poses a substantial hazard to human health.

manifest system: A series of documents designed to track hazardous waste.

The **Resource Conservation and Recovery Act (RCRA)** was passed in 1976 as an attempt to control substances defined as **hazardous waste** from the "cradle to the grave." The EPA has defined "hazardous waste" to include any solid waste or combination of solid wastes that, when improperly treated, stored, transported, or disposed of, may pose a substantial hazard to human health or the environment. RCRA instituted a **manifest system** to track and control such wastes from the time they are generated, through their transportation, storage, and use, to their ultimate disposal. A permit must be obtained when the wastes are created and must be updated (and accompany the materials) at each subsequent waste management stage.

The intent of RCRA is to prohibit the previously common practice of simply dumping hazardous materials either on land or in the water. Operators of hazardous waste facilities are now required to obtain permits and to comply with tough standards regarding the construction and operation of their businesses, as well as to maintain a certain level of insurance and provide financial assurances. Although the law exempts municipal resource recovery facilities that receive and burn only household waste, companies and individuals who improperly dispose of hazardous waste or are involved with illegal disposal practices by someone else (e.g., a hazardous waste facility) also have significant liability under RCRA.

In 1984, Congress passed the *Hazardous and Solid Waste Amendments Act*, which added several new programs to RCRA. Regulations were added concerning underground storage tanks, tighter control of small quantity generators, "corrective action" to clean up facilities, and other provisions. The 1984 amendments also required generators of hazardous waste to report to the EPA on their plans for reducing the amount and toxicity of their wastes. This law also added increased penalties for violations, significantly toughened criminal provisions, and authorized private citizens to bring suits when the EPA fails to act.

Toxic Substances Control Act (TSCA): A federal law that requires the notification to, and approval of, the EPA before chemicals can be made or imported.

THE TOXIC SUBSTANCES CONTROL ACT

The **Toxic Substances Control Act (TSCA)**, passed in 1976, requires the EPA to develop a complete inventory of all existing chemicals, along with the characteristics and hazards of each. Americans are now discovering that the thousands of new chemicals developed in recent years to make our lives easier often have long-range negative effects on humans and our environment that were not intended or known when the substances were produced.

In addition to the inventory of existing chemicals, TSCA requires manufacturers to notify the EPA 90 days before manufacturing or importing any new chemicals. The EPA may require testing and analysis of such chemicals before they can be used. The EPA also may prevent use of the substance entirely or require labeling or restrictions on certain uses, and may mandate the reporting of any adverse reactions that occur. The EPA has, for example, totally banned further production of polychlorinated biphenyls (PCBs). Congress did, however, establish a cost/benefit test for TSCA regulations. The law requires that EPA demonstrate a "reasonable basis" for its rules and show that the regulations adopted were the "least burdensome" necessary to achieve a level of "minimum reasonable risk."

THE COMPREHENSIVE ENVIRONMENTAL RESPONSE, COMPENSATION, AND LIABILITY ACT OF 1980 AND THE "SUPERFUND"

The main purpose of the two laws described previously (RCRA and TSCA) is to *prevent* environmental damage from occurring through a detailed series of controls on the production, treatment, handling, and disposal of hazardous substances. In contrast, the **Comprehensive Environmental Response, Compensation, and Liability Act (CERCLA)** is primarily concerned with providing funding and appropriate legal mechanisms for *cleaning up* sites where improper use and disposal of hazardous waste has caused serious environmental damage.

Comprehensive Environmental Response, Compensation, and Liability Act (CERCLA) ("Superfund") Law: A federal law that provides funding for the cleaning up of contaminated areas and imposes strict liability on "owners or operators."

A number of environmental disasters in the 1970s caused Congress to consider how to redress serious environmental contamination after it had occurred. Perhaps the most-publicized incident took place in the Love Canal area in New York state. Here, a canal originally dug to connect Lake Ontario with the Niagara River had been used as a dumpsite for more than 80 deadly chemicals during the 1940s and 1950s. Eventually, a residential subdivision and school were built on the site. In following years, many of the residents experienced serious health problems. As a result, the site was abandoned, and the government purchased all the homes. Legal actions involving Love Canal are still winding their way through the courts.

When Congress enacted CERCLA in 1980, the goal was to provide funds for cleaning up contaminated areas and to impose legal and financial responsibility on those who owned or operated such property, those who transported or arranged for disposal of the waste, and on those who caused the harm. The words *compensation* and *liability* are at the heart of CERCLA but are not found in the other environmental laws. In order to implement the law, the EPA publishes annually a list of the most seriously contaminated sites in the United States. The EPA can then either start cleaning up the site or attempt to require others to do it.

When it enacted CERCLA, Congress set up a huge fund to pay for the cleanup of contaminated sites. Over the years, more than $15 billion has been put into this cleanup fund, which has become known as the "Superfund." When the EPA identifies the Superfund sites that need to be cleaned up, it looks for potentially responsible parties (PRPs) to hold responsible.

Under the CERCLA as amended, PRPs include (1) the current owner or operator of the site; (2) the owner or operator at the time the hazardous wastes were put on the property; (3) any person who arranged for the treatment or disposal of the hazardous substances at the facility; or (4) any person who transported hazardous substances to and/or selected the facility.

The EPA has vigorously enforced CERCLA against various individual and corporate parties who have owned or operated sites where wastes have been deposited, as well as those who actually deposited the wastes. CERCLA is a *strict liability* law, which means that parties may be found liable for cleanup costs, even though they were not "at fault." For example, the current owner of the property, or a previous owner who leased the land to a business tenant, may have had no role in causing the pollution problem but still may be held responsible for the costs of the cleanup. Some estimate the average cost at $25 million. And because the doctrine of joint and several liability is used in CERCLA cases, one of the defendants may end up paying the whole cost of the remediation and then have to try to recover a share by suing other defendants.

Another important issue for business is whether a parent corporation can be held liable under CERCLA for cleanup expenses due to the actions of a subsidiary [a parent corporation owns most or all of the stock of the subsidiary corporation]. Often the parent corporation has considerably more financial assets, and the government or one of the other parties held responsible for CERCLA expenses will be seeking to recover significant costs. Lower court decisions in a number of cases had established different tests for determining when a parent corporation should be held liable for actions of a subsidiary. The U.S. Supreme Court recently considered such an issue and rendered an important decision in the following case.

UNITED STATES V. BESTFOODS

118 S. Ct. 1876 (1998)

FACTS

This case concerned an action by the federal government (EPA) to recover the costs of cleaning up contamination created by a Michigan chemical plant that had been operated by a subsidiary of CPC International, Inc. from 1965 to 1972. [There were several defendants in this case, including Bestfoods, CPC, Cordova Chemical Company (the current owner), and other owners and operators of the property.] The issue on appeal primarily concerned the liability of CPC for the actions of its subsidiary.

During the early 1960s, while the property was owned by a chemical manufacturer, the groundwater under the site became contaminated. Then in 1965 the land was purchased by Ott Chemical Co., a subsidiary of CPC International. Over the next seven years, the disposal of chemical waste in unlined lagoons and overflows of chemicals from a storage basin caused additional pollution of the soil, surface water, and groundwater. The property was later owned by several other parties before the EPA became involved in cleaning up the site in 1981. Later the government sued five former and present owners and operators for liability under CERCLA, and all private owners were held liable by the district court. On appeal, the Sixth Circuit Court of Appeals reversed the liability of CPC, holding that there was no basis for piercing the corporate veil and holding it liable for the actions of its subsidiary, either as an owner or operator. The United States then appealed to the U.S. Supreme Court.

DECISION

The Supreme Court carefully reviewed the language of CERCLA, and the general principle that parent corporations are not liable for the acts of their subsidiaries. Under CERCLA rules liability attaches to (1) the present "owner or operator" of a contaminated facility, and (2) any prior "owner or operator" whose ownership coincided with the contamination of the property. In this instance, since CPC was not the current owner, its only liability would be if it was found to be an "owner or operator" at the time of the disposal of hazardous waste. CPC never did own the property in its own name, and therefore its liability, if any, must be premised on (1) the fact that CPC was an "owner" because of its subsidiary's ownership or (2) the fact that CPC was directly liable as an "operator."

The Supreme Court, in a unanimous opinion written by Justice Souter, vacated and remanded the case for additional evidence. First, the Court looked at CERCLA and determined that the law did not attempt to change the general rule that a corporation is generally not liable for acts of its subsidiaries. However, under fundamental principles of corporate law (as explained in Chapter 9) the corporate veil may be pierced when the corporate form has been misused to accomplish wrongful purposes, most notably fraud of some type. Then, one or more shareholders (in this case, the parent company, which owned most of the stock of the subsidiary) can be held individually liable. The Court called this "derivative" liability.

The district court had held CPC liable largely because CPC had selected Ott's board of directors and filled Ott's executive ranks with CPC officials, and another CPC official had played a significant role in shaping Ott's environmental policy. The Sixth Circuit reversed, finding that whether the parent corporation has derivative liability depends on an analysis of state law principles on piercing the corporate veil, not merely on the fact that the boards of directors of the two companies are quite similar. The Supreme Court agreed with this analysis, and further criticized certain lower court opinions that had imposed vicarious (derivative) liability on corporations because of interlocking boards of directors with the subsidiary.

The Supreme Court stated that a finding of "operator" liability under CERCLA must focus on the parent corporation's relationship with the *facility* at issue, not its relationship with its *subsidiary*. In other words, the parent corporation would only be liable if it actually played a significant part in *operating the facility*, not just having a large role in the management of the subsidiary corporation. The plain language of CERCLA defines *operator* as "any person . . . operating" a facility. Looking further into the meaning of *operator* the Court held that it means:

Manages, directs, or conducts operations specifically related to pollution, that is, operations having to do with the leakage or disposal of hazardous waste, or decisions about compliance with environmental regulations.

Applying this definition to the facts of the case, Justice Souter wrote that activities that are normal for a parent corporation to do in monitoring the activities of its subsidiary, such as reviewing finances, looking at budgetary matters, and setting general policies, do not give rise to liability as an "operator." Nor did interlocking directors (the same people sitting on the boards of the parent and the subsidiary) create operator liability. It is a well-established norm of corporate law for directors and officers of a parent and a subsidiary to hold positions with both.

Finding that CPC did not have derivative liability, the Court turned to the question of whether it had direct liability as an operator. Here, the Supreme Court did not agree with the Sixth Circuit's narrow application of the test for direct liability. Although the existence of interlocking directorates would not be enough for the parent to be held directly liable as an operator, other facts needed to be analyzed. For example, a parent's decision to send an employee of its own to direct disposal and compliance activities of the facility might create direct liability on the part of the parent.

In fact, noted the Court, there was some evidence here that an agent of CPC alone engaged in activities at Ott's plant that were "eccentric" under accepted norms of parental oversight of a subsidiary's facility. Careful examination of the facts of each case is necessary to "distinguish a parental officer's oversight of a subsidiary from his control over the operation of the subsidiary's facility." Here, the District Court's opinion speaks of an agent who played a conspicuous part in dealing with the toxic risks emanating from the plant's operation. This is enough to raise an issue of fact regarding CPC's possible operation of the facility. The case thus must be remanded to the trial court for further hearings and evidence in order to resolve that issue.

CASE QUESTIONS

1. What actions would a parent corporation have to take to be held vicariously liable (on a derivative basis) for the acts of its subsidiary, according to the Court? What actions of a parent are considered "normal" supervision of a subsidiary, and thus do not create liability as an "operator"?
2. When is a parent corporation held liable as an operator of a facility? What actions are considered those of an operator?
3. What advice would you give to managers, officers, and directors of companies, in view of the Bestfoods decision?

innocent landowner: One who carefully researches the history of a property prior to purchase and has no knowledge of any improper disposal of hazardous wastes.

In response to considerable commentary about the unfairness of imposing significant liability on anyone who ever owned the land, Congress has added the **"innocent landowner" defense** to CERCLA. To benefit from this defense, an owner must show that he or she exercised "due diligence" before purchasing the property and that he or she had no knowledge nor any reason to know that hazardous substances were disposed of on the land. To establish such knowledge, the innocent owner must show that it made "all appropriate inquiry into the previous ownership and uses of the property consistent with good commercial or customary practice in an effort to minimize liability."

FROM THE DESK OF
Laura Lawyer

To: Students

From: Your Lawyer

Although the EPA has attempted to clarify and limit the liability of "innocent" parties, the potential consequences of being named a Superfund defendant are enormous. It is foolish for any business to purchase, use, or take a security interest in commercial property, or make any substantial commitment of funds regarding such property, without making a thorough assessment of all environmental issues. All prudent lending institutions now require a detailed "environmental assessment," prepared by scientific consultants, on properties the lenders are considering taking a security interest in, and other businesses should do no less.

In addition to the potential Superfund liability of creditors for the cost of cleaning up environmental contamination, other cases have involved the liability of parent and subsidiary corporations, joint venture partners, and corporate officers and managers, who were somehow involved with the property. A number of company officials have gone to jail as the result of environmental misdeeds.

Any well-run business must have a clear corporate policy, coming from the top, stating that (1) environmental concerns are a high priority, (2) internal compliance efforts must be continuous and serious, (3) problems that do occur are promptly and effectively corrected (not covered up), (4) violators are punished, and (5) continuous improvement in environmental practices of the firm is a top corporate goal and strategy.

In addition, it is important to use care in choosing one's business associates. Why? The law imposes significant liability, and it is not unusual for poorly run firms to improperly dispose of hazardous wastes and have serious financial difficulties and/or go out of business. The result is that society will look for another firm to hold responsible for cleaning up the damage. The joint and several liability allowed by CERCLA often means that a financially sound company will end up paying the full cost of a CERCLA cleanup because the company that dumped the waste is no longer in existence.

LENDER LIABILITY UNDER CERCLA

Lending institutions have had great concern about potential liability under CERCLA as well. Typically, when a bank makes a mortgage loan to enable a person or company to purchase real property, the lender will take a mortgage on the land. But if the land should later show indications of contamination, does the lender want to foreclose the mortgage? Suddenly it is the "owner" of the property, and therefore a potentially responsible party under CERCLA (and a PRP with a lot of money, or so it would seem!).

An appellate case decided in 1990 reinforced the fears of the lending community. In *U.S. v. Fleet Factors Corp*, 901 F.2d 1550 (11th Cir. 1990), the lender's motion to be dismissed from a CERCLA case involving property on which it held a mortgage was denied. The court found that liability was possible if the creditor participated in management to a degree indicating a capacity to influence the corporation's treatment of hazardous waste—that is, if the creditor "could affect hazardous waste disposal decisions if it so chose." This case opened the door for tremendous liability exposure for lenders who become actively involved in trying to assist a struggling business owner with contamination issues.

In 1992, the EPA issued regulations that attempted to clarify that a lender who merely has a security interest and is not involved with the financial or administrative matters of a company is not to be classified as an operator for CERCLA purposes. However, since these were only regulations and not federal law, lenders were still concerned about whether they were completely protected.

Then in 1996, Congress amended the CERCLA law by enacting the Asset Conservation, Lender Liability, and Deposit Insurance Protection Act. This law excluded from the "owner or operator" definition in CERCLA a lender who did not participate in the management of a facility prior to foreclosure. The law defined *participate in management* as "actually participating in the management or operational affairs of the facility." Such a definition should eliminate the possibility of holding the lender liable merely because it had "the capacity" to influence management.

Therefore, lenders today should be exempt from CERCLA liability as owners or operators as long as they stay in their role as creditor and do not become active in managing the facility. Nevertheless, it has become standard, prudent practice in the lending industry to make no loans on real property without doing a careful, thorough "environmental assessment" of the property. Such an assessment should include not only a careful review of the title history (to see who owned the property) but an actual on-site investigation, perhaps taking soil and water samples, if the property has ever been used in an industrial or commercial way.

SOCIAL/ETHICAL ISSUES

In one case decided under CERCLA, the owner of the property, Ashland Oil, was held solely liable for $10 million in order to clean up contamination on property it owned but had leased to another business. Ashland argued that this was unjust and unfair. "We are saddled with liability, just because we are the landlord," said Ashland. The lending institution, Ashland continued, "ought to contribute because it was responsible for the business." Ashland argued that the lender should have looked at to whom they were lending. What do you think? Is it right to make Ashland pay all or part of the cost? Should the financial institution that financed the business share in the cleanup cost?

CIVIL AND CRIMINAL ENFORCEMENT

All of the laws mentioned in this chapter are enforced by the EPA. Most of them also allow one landowner to sue a person or company whose actions cause damage to the landowner's property. Some also allow citizen suits, where an individual (and often an environmental or community organization) is suing to enforce the provisions of an environmental law.

The vast majority of actions brought by the EPA are regulatory in nature. That is, the actions are brought first within the administrative law system as outlined in Chapter 5, and then many go into the federal court system. These actions are seeking civil fines and enforcement orders due to alleged violations of one of the environmental laws examined in this chapter (or one of the many others we did not have space to mention). During 1997, for example, the EPA initiated 3,427 administrative actions for violations of environmental protection laws.

The largest number of actions filed were related to violations of the CWA, with 1,642 cases. Another 391 actions were initiated under the Clean Air Act. RCRA accounted for 423 actions and CERCLA violations led to 305 actions. The level of cases increased somewhat over 1996, due to increased inspections, according to the EPA.

When the EPA feels that a particularly serious or intentional violation has occurred, it refers the case to the Department of Justice, which has the power to initiate criminal charges. (The EPA does not.) During 1997 the EPA and the Justice Department began investigations of 445 cases, more than half of which involved the CWA. Some 211 criminal actions were filed by the Justice Department against individuals and companies, alleging criminal violations of environmental laws. Of the criminal cases completed in 1997, about 85 percent resulted in convictions. Fines were imposed in 64 percent of these cases, with an average fine of $124,000. One defendant, Colonial Pipeline Co., paid a $7 million criminal fine and two civil settlements of more than $6 million resulting from a large oil spill violation.

The EPA has an Enforcement Investigations Center with a staff of more than 200 (including 50 special agents trained as criminal investigators) who work closely with the Justice Department's Environmental Crimes Unit in initiating criminal charges for environmental violations. While a relatively small part of the total enforcement of environmental laws, criminal enforcement is taken seriously. These cases take more time to handle and are typically more complex. Business groups sometimes argue that the EPA should stick to bringing only civil, administrative charges. Environmental groups, however, believe that criminal charges are important. An attorney with one group stated, "I think it is very important to set an example by bringing some criminal charges. There is nothing more chilling than sending someone from the boardroom to the jailhouse."

For example, in November 1999 a federal appellate court upheld the conviction and the 56-month prison sentence of a chemical company salesman from Ohio for illegally transporting hazardous waste from Ohio and disposing of it in Georgia in violation of the RCRA. The salesman was also ordered to pay almost $150,000 in restitution to the owner of the land in Georgia on which he had abandoned 317 tons of hazardous waste (*U.S. v. Cunningham*, (11th Cir.), 30 Env. Rep. 1279 [Nov. 12, 1999]).

Company officials and individuals have also been found criminally responsible for environmental actions under state law. For example, in June 1999 the president of a chemical storage company was sentenced to 14 years in prison for dumping chlorinated solvents onto the water table. Richard Newman, president and chief executive officer (CEO) of Thoro Products of Arvada, Colorado, was convicted of violating Colorado's hazardous waste laws and of committing criminal mischief. Mr. Newman was found to have been directly involved in his firm's "repeated, intentional, and reckless" dumping of hazardous wastes over a 13-year period, which caused a "toxic plume" one-half mile wide and one and one-half miles long.

SUMMARY

Environmental issues are among the most important and controversial public policy issues of our time. We all value clean air and water, open spaces, and wilderness, and we treasure our rich variety of birds, fish, and wildlife. Yet the American public is also concerned about jobs and employment. We want our businesses to be able to continue to grow and prosper, and to be able to expand to meet new global competition. When a manufacturing facility seeks to expand, it often causes a conflict between environmental regulations and the desire for increased employment opportunities. Those of you who will be business managers in the next few years will face many complex decisions in balancing the need for growth with protection of the environment.

The primary federal environmental laws explored in this chapter are the Clean Air Act, which seeks to cut air pollution by establishing federal standards which are enforced and interpreted by the states, and the Clean Water Act, which requires permits be obtained prior to the discharge of effluent material into all navigable waterways in the United States. Regulation of chemical substances and toxic material is the priority of the TSCA and the RCRA. Once an area has been contaminated, the CERCLA allows the EPA to use its "Superfund" to clean up the site and then seek damages from a wide circle of "owners" and "operators" of the property.

These laws have all been enacted within the past 30 years, and will surely undergo some modification in the future. Government will learn to regulate more effectively, businesses will learn how to manufacture with less pollution, to treat their waste more carefully, and to better control the discharge of hazardous substances. We will all learn more about the short- and long-term effects of various air and water pollution, acid rain, and toxic waste material. The challenge of protecting our environment while promoting business growth will continue in the 21st century.

CHAPTER QUESTIONS

1. State transportation officials proposed two highway projects in Texas in order to complete an outer loop (beltway) around a city. Considerable state money had been committed, and state officials had spent significant time working on the projects, but no federal funds were requested or spent. No federal approvals had been given, and federal officials stated that they had no interest in the projects. A community group that feared the environmental consequences of the highway filed a lawsuit seeking to block further action on the project until an environmental impact statement had been prepared. What should be the result? Why? [*Save Barton Creek Association v. Federal Highway Administration*, 957 F.2d 869 (5th Cir. 1992)]
2. A truck manufacturer sought an exemption from the state implementation plan regarding the limits on emissions of volatile organic compounds

released into the air by its manufacturing and assembly plant. What would the company have to show to get an exemption? [*Navistar International Transportation Corp. v. EPA*, 941 F.2d 1339 (6th Cir.1991)]

3. An excavation contractor, working at a Superfund site in California, moved contaminated soils from one place to another on the site. Can the contractor be held liable under CERCLA for a share of the cleanup costs in a cross-claim by one of the other responsible parties who the EPA has sued? [*Kaiser Aluminum & Chemical Corp. v. Cattellus Development Corp.*, 976 F.2d 1338 (9th Cir.1992)]
4. The president and CEO of a chemical blending and distribution company in Washington state was charged with criminal violations of the CWA. The company shipped its products in drums, which were then returned to be cleaned and reused by the company. The cleaning process generated a wastewater regulated by the CWA, but the company never obtained a discharge permit and resorted to various illegal disposal methods. The president did not actually dump any of the wastes himself, but was closely involved and informed about the disposal activities. Can he be held personally responsible in a criminal action? [*U.S. v. Iverson* (9th Cir. 1999), 30 Env. Rep. (BNA) 229 (June 6, 1999)]
5. A cement company that was located in a PSD (prevention of significant deterioration) area converted two older cement kilns to newer, more efficient models. The company then requested exemption from applicable EPA Clean Air Act regulations, since the new kilns were more efficient than the old ones. The new kilns, however, if operated at full capacity, would emit more total pollutants than the older ones, which were only operated at 60 percent of capacity. Should the exemption be granted? Why? [*Puerto Rican Cement Co. v. EPA*, 889 F.2d 292 (1st Cir. 1989)]
6. After finding that asbestos causes cancer and asbestosis, a serious lung disease, the EPA enacted regulations pursuant to the TSCA, which prohibited most present and future commercial uses of asbestos. The EPA estimated that approximately seven lives would be saved by the regulations, which would cost industry some $200–300 million in compliance costs. The EPA did not seriously consider various intermediate methods of regulation, nor did it consider the toxicity of various substitutes for asbestos, which would have to be used instead. A manufacturers' group argued that the regulations were invalid in that they did not meet the requirements of the TSCA. What should be the result? Why? [*Corrosion Proof Fittings v. EPA*, 947 F.2d 1201 (5th Cir. 1991)]
7. A company foreman and a supervisor who directed the discharge of hazardous waste from an industrial firm into a trench, which then emptied into a creek, were charged with a criminal violation of RCRA. The firm did not have an EPA permit for such discharges. The two men argued that the law only contained punishment for "owners and operators" and that, therefore, they could not be held criminally responsible as individuals. What should be the result? Why? [*U.S. v. Johnson & Towers, Inc.*, 741 F.2d 662 (3d Cir. 1984)]
8. A municipal waste facility that incinerates only household waste is exempt from the provisions of the RCRA law. However, an environmental group sued the EPA, seeking a ruling that the post-treatment ash resulting from

incineration is a hazardous waste subject to the requirements of RCRA. What should be the result? [*Environmental Defense Fund, Inc. v. Chicago*, 985 F.2d 303 (7th Cir. 1993)]

9. A photo etching company and its president were convicted of violating RCRA because they improperly stored and disposed of hazardous waste without a permit. The defendants claimed on appeal that they could not be convicted of the crime because they did not know they needed a permit and thus had no "criminal intent." Are they right? Why? [*U.S. v. Wagner*, 29 F.3d 264 (7th Cir. 1994)]

10. The U.S. government contracted with Hercules, Inc. and Vertac Chemical Co. to manufacture the chemical called "Agent Orange," used as a defoliant in the Vietnam War. Some years later the Hercules and Vertac properties were listed as Superfund priority cleanup sites, and the EPA brought an action under CERCLA against Vertac and Hercules as responsible parties. Hercules had chosen to bury hazardous wastes from the production, including dioxin, on its property, without consulting the government.

    Vertac attempted to join the U.S. Defense Department as a co-defendant, arguing that it was liable, too, since the chemical was produced under contract with the Department, and it had the right to control the methods of production at the facility. The Defense Department denied liability, stating that it had not supplied the raw material, nor had any Defense Department officials controlled the production techniques at the plant, and the government was not involved with the improper waste disposal. What should the result be? Why? [*U.S. v. Vertac Chemical Corp.*, 46 F.3d 803 (8th Cir. 1995)]

PRACTICAL EXERCISE

Irene is the president of a small company, Oil Industries Limited (OIL), which collects waste oil products from other firms, hauls it away, and disposes of it. For more than 10 years, she and her company have picked up waste oil from several customers and have taken it to a disposal site on a farm owned by Bruce. Irene (through OIL) leased 10 acres from Bruce for $5000 per year and installed four tanks on the property to hold the waste oil.

After a few years Bruce noticed that one of the tanks was leaking and ordered Irene to pump all the oil out of that tank. He also asked Irene to remove the tanks, but she refused, since her lease still had two years to run. Some six years later, when Irene and OIL were no longer in the oil hauling business, the EPA investigated the site and found that several of the tanks had developed serious leaks, and oil containing PCBs (a very hazardous chemical) had contaminated the ground on the site. The EPA then hired another firm to clean up the site, at a cost in excess of $1 million, and has notified Irene, Bruce, and OIL that they are PRPs. Irene and OIL deny liability, claiming that they never knew that any oil they handled contained PCBs. Bruce denies that he is liable because he was not involved in the business in any way.

Knowing that you are studying "legal stuff," your good friend Irene has asked you to prepare a memo discussing the relevant laws; potential liability of herself, Bruce, and OIL for the contamination; and any defenses that any party might have. Also, she wonders whether Bruce has any rights against her and OIL (which has now been merged into a larger company), in case he has to pay damages. Prepare such a memo discussing these issues thoroughly.

FURTHER INFORMATION

www.epa.gov
U.S. Environmental Protection Agency.
www.doi.gov
U.S. Department of the Interior.
www.usace.army.mil
U.S. Army Corps of Engineers.
www.edf.org
Environmental Defense Fund.
www.nrdc.org
Natural Resources Defense Council.
www.sierraclub.org
Sierra Club.

PART 4:
LEGAL ISSUES INVOLVING CONSUMERS, COMPETITORS, AND SUPPLIERS

CHAPTER 16

ANTITRUST LAW: THE REGULATION OF CORPORATE BEHAVIOR AND STRUCTURE

LEARNING OBJECTIVES

After you have read this chapter, you should be able to:

1. Describe the development of antitrust laws and explain how they are enforced.
2. Contrast the economic, social, and political viewpoints of antitrust policy.
3. Define the rule of reason and the per se rule.
4. Explain the structural provisions of the antitrust laws addressing monopoly, oligopoly, and mergers.
5. Describe the behavioral antitrust provisions dealing with horizontal and vertical restrictions.
6. List the antitrust provisions of the Robinson-Patman Act and Federal Trade Commission Act.

CHAPTER OUTLINE

I. Federal Antitrust Legislation
II. Judicial Analysis
III. Structural and Behavioral Antitrust
IV. Price Discrimination
V. Section 5 of the FTC Act
VI. Exemptions from Antitrust

Can the second-largest firm in the ready-to-eat cereal industry acquire the business of the fifth largest firm? The acquiring firm argues that the purchase will help it compete with the market leader. You, a securities analyst, are asked to analyze the legality of the acquisition. After having studied this chapter, you should be able to determine whether the purchase would violate any antitrust laws.

INTRODUCTION

The competitive behavior and the structure of firms are regulated by antitrust laws. The purpose of antitrust law is to ensure that, by enforcing the rules of the market and eliminating threats to competition, the marketplace in which business operates remains free. Antitrust law in the United States consists of both federal and state statutes. Federal antitrust laws apply to all business activity that qualifies as interstate commerce; in some cases, these laws also apply to wholly intrastate activity that affects interstate commerce. State laws, on the other hand, apply to activity that is wholly intrastate and that does not affect interstate commerce. Because state laws vary, we will focus primarily on federal antitrust law.

FEDERAL ANTITRUST LEGISLATION

The first federal antitrust statute was the *Sherman Act*, passed by Congress in 1890. Section 1 of the Act prohibits any contract, combination, or conspiracy in restraint of trade. Section 2 prescribes monopolizing trade or commerce. The Sherman Act was aimed at eliminating the concentrations of economic power that had developed in the railroads and major industries through the use of cartels and voting trusts and the predatory practices such concentration made possible. A **voting trust** was a device that allowed a few individuals to control all the firms' stock. The term *antitrust* is derived from the law's attack on the voting trusts. The Sherman Act initially was only criminal legislation—it made violations of its provisions criminal offenses and imposed penalties of fines and/or imprisonment.

voting trust: Legal device by which a few persons could control leading firms in an industry through voting rights of the firms' stock.

Despite its intentions, the Sherman Act was not very effective due to several problems with enforcement. Because the act was criminal legislation, penalties were usually imposed after the harm to competition had already occurred; moreover, the criminal penalties did nothing to restore the competition that had been eliminated. The fines that were imposed generally were greatly exceeded by the financial gains resulting from the anticompetitive activity. In addition, several early court decisions held that manufacturing was not "commerce" within the meaning of the Sherman Act, so anticompetitive conduct by manufacturers was beyond the reach of the law. (Those decisions have long since been overruled.)

In response to the problems of enforcing the Sherman Act, Congress passed the *Clayton Act* in 1914. The Clayton Act prohibits specific kinds of conduct that injure competition and provides for civil, rather than criminal, penalties. The Clayton Act also allows for civil remedies under the Sherman Act. The civil nature of the Clayton Act allows for more flexible and effective enforcement—injunctions prohibiting conduct likely to injure competition can be granted by the courts before actual harm to competition occurs. The Clayton Act applies only to activities that are actually in interstate commerce, in contrast to the Sherman Act's coverage of conduct *in or affecting* interstate commerce.

The Clayton Act also allows for private remedies—persons or firms injured as a result of a violation of the act can sue the violator for triple damages (three times the amount of the actual harm suffered). In addition, §4 of the Clayton Act extends the availability of triple damage suits to violations of the

Sherman Act as well. These suits may only be brought by parties directly affected by violations, such as competitors or customers who purchase directly from the violator. Indirect purchasers—those who purchase from the customers of a violator—may not bring triple damage suits, and the federal government is also precluded from bringing such suits against antitrust violators. The Clayton Act has been amended several times: the *Robinson-Patman Act* of 1936 strengthened the §2 prohibitions on price discrimination; the *Celler-Kefauver Act* of 1950 amended the §7 prohibition of mergers that injure competition; and the *Hart-Scott-Rodino Act* of 1976 imposed premerger notification requirements under §7.

The *Federal Trade Commission Act* was also passed in 1914. It created the *Federal Trade Commission* (FTC) to administer and enforce the antitrust laws, in addition to the enforcement efforts of the Justice Department. Congress wanted the FTC to operate as an independent enforcement agency, free from the political pressure that could be brought to bear on the Justice Department.

ENFORCEMENT OF THE ANTITRUST LAWS

Federal antitrust laws are enforced by both the U.S. Justice Department and the FTC. The Antitrust Division of the Justice Department is responsible for the enforcement of the criminal provisions of the Sherman Act, which now provides for fines of up to $10 million for corporations and fines of up to $350,000 and jail terms of up to three years for individuals. The Antitrust Division can file civil or criminal suits in the federal courts; it also enforces the merger provisions of §7 of the Clayton Act. The FTC has no criminal enforcement jurisdiction. It is responsible for enforcement of the Clayton Act and §5 of the Federal Trade Commission Act.

divestiture orders: Court orders requiring firms to separate—to "undo" the merger.

dissolution orders: Court orders requiring a monopolist firm to split up into several firms.

consent decrees or **consent orders:** Settlement agreements allowing firms to cease allegedly anticompetitive conduct without admitting to a violation of the law.

Both the FTC and the Antitrust Division can bring civil enforcement actions. Possible remedies in civil actions include injunctions, **divestiture orders** (court orders requiring merged firms to separate), and **dissolution orders** (court orders requiring single firms to split into separate firms). Other remedies, such as orders to make patents available to competitors or orders prohibiting firms from entering certain fields of business, are also available through civil actions. The FTC can initiate administrative hearings on alleged violations. Both the FTC and the Antitrust Division are making increasing use of pretrial (or prehearing) settlements with firms alleged to have violated the law. These settlements, known as **consent decrees** or **consent orders**, allow a firm to agree to cease challenged conduct without admitting guilt or liability under the laws. These settlements enable the enforcement agencies to stop alleged anticompetitive practices without having to resort to trials, which are both time-consuming and expensive.

In addition to enforcement actions by the government, private antitrust suits by firms or individuals seeking triple damages (under §4 of the Clayton Act) for injuries caused by alleged violations have also become an important enforcement mechanism of the antitrust laws. For example, the price-fixing convictions of manufacturers of electrical equipment in the 1960s resulted in some 2,300 civil suits being filed against the companies involved. The damages awarded in those suits amounted to over $400 million. In recent years, the antitrust enforcement agencies concentrated on concerted activity—price-fixing and collusion by competitors—rather than pursuing merger or monopoly cases. Most of the recent cases involving merger or monopoly claims have involved private suits rather than government enforcement actions.

GOALS OF ANTITRUST POLICY

The basic purpose of antitrust laws is to ensure the free operation of the marketplace. The policies behind the enforcement and interpretation of these laws reflect conflicting interests, however, because antitrust policy is based on a mixture of social, political, and economic theories.

The economic goal of antitrust is to promote efficiency through free competition in the market. When competition is free, though, some firms may compete more effectively than others. According to the economic viewpoint concept (also known as the "Chicago School," after the views of economists associated with the University of Chicago), antitrust law should not penalize firms that become dominant in a market because they have competed successfully; the size of firms should be irrelevant as long as the firms' activities promote efficiency. In contrast, according to the social and political goals of antitrust policy (also known as the "Harvard School," after the views of economists associated with Harvard University), antitrust law should emphasize concern for protecting competing firms as well as promoting competition. From this viewpoint, small individual competitors should be protected to preserve economic freedom of choice; thus antitrust law should strive to avoid the concentration of economic power and political influence in the hands of a few giant firms. This concern for protecting competitors may mean that the size of a firm may determine the legality of its conduct and that protection of competitors should be pursued despite its cost in terms of efficiency. For the Reagan and Bush Administrations, antitrust enforcement was not a priority; with their emphasis on freeing the market from government regulation, they favored the Chicago School's approach. The Clinton Administration reflects more of a balance between the two schools of thought, and antitrust enforcement actions have increased significantly during the years of President Clinton's administration.

Judicial interpretations and government enforcement of the antitrust laws have reflected the tensions between these competing goals of antitrust law. The famous decision in the case of *U.S. v. Aluminum Co. of America*, 148 F.2d 416 (2nd Cir. 1945) and decisions in merger cases in the 1960s emphasized the social and political goals of antitrust. More recent decisions and the enforcement policy of recent administrations reflect an emphasis on the economic goal of antitrust. The courts and enforcement agencies are now more aware of the global character of economic competition and realize that domestic firms should not be unduly hampered in competing against international competitors.

NEW TECHNOLOGY AND NEW THEORIES GIVE ANTITRUST ENFORCERS MORE EFFECTIVE TOOLS

Along with the Clinton administration's renewed interest in antitrust law, technology and new economic theories have supported the enforcement efforts of the Justice Department and the FTC. The development of more powerful computers has allowed economists to develop and analyze increasingly complex models of competitive behavior of firms. Such sophisticated econometric analysis allows antitrust enforcers to predict whether a merger would likely result in higher prices for consumers by reducing competition in the relevant market, rather than simply looking to the increased market share that the merged firm will enjoy. The use of checkout scanner data allows antitrust enforcers to monitor actual price behavior of firms in various geographic markets, and when coupled with the sophisticated econometric analysis, provides support for predictions of a merger's likely effect on prices. For example, in 1997, the office supply retailer Staples sought to merge with its rival, Office Depot. The firms argued that because literally thousands of retail outlets sell office supplies, the merger of the two "superstore" chains would not significantly reduce competition. However, FTC economists, using actual scanner data for all items sold by both chains, discovered that Staples charged lower prices in cities where Office Depot also had a store, but could charge higher prices for the same items in cities where there was no Office Depot store. That evidence provided strong support for the argument that the merger would allow Staples to raise prices and would reduce competition in the office supply market; a federal court for the District of Columbia blocked the merger [*F.T.C. v. Staples, Inc.*, 970 F. Supp. 1066 (D.D.C. 1997)].

In addition to technological improvements, developments in economic theory have also aided antitrust enforcers. The Chicago School economists focused on competitive markets and assumed that the workings of the market would quickly erode any market power a firm might temporarily gain through anticompetitive practices. As a result, Chicago School economists were not overly concerned with predatory conduct. But using more sophisticated economic "game theory" and models of strategic competition, economists can more realistically predict the effects of barriers to entry into markets and of predatory behavior of dominant firms. When two leading aerospace companies, Lockheed-Martin and Northrop Grumman, sought to merge in 1997, the Justice Department argued that the firms' role as leading component suppliers to other aerospace and defense contractors could allow the resulting firm to raise prices to competitors, who would have few other alternative suppliers. After the Justice Department filed suit to stop the merger, the firms abandoned the merger and pledged to compete vigorously in the supply of components to the defense industry.

With the powerful new tools and theories at their disposal, antitrust enforcers can more effectively target firms whose market dominance or predatory practices allow them to exercise power to set prices above the level that would result from competition.

Sources: "The Trustbusters' New Tools," *The Economist* (May 2, 1998); "The Law Is an Ass," *The Economist* (August 29, 1998).

rule of reason: Judicial approach to antitrust law that holds certain conduct illegal only if it unreasonably restricts competition.

per se rule: Judicial approach to antitrust law that holds certain conduct to be illegal regardless of its actual effect on competition.

JUDICIAL ANALYSIS

When the legality of a firm's conduct is challenged under the antitrust laws, a court must consider the impact of that conduct on competition. The courts have developed two different approaches for analyzing that impact—the **rule of reason** and the **per se rule**.

The rule of reason stems from the Supreme Court's decision in *Standard Oil Co. v. U.S.*, 221 U.S. 1 (1911), in which the Court held that some forms of conduct are illegal only if they unreasonably restrict competition. The rule of reason is applied today when the conduct in question has a legitimate business purpose despite its anticompetitive effects. Under the rule of reason, the actual effects of the conduct on competition must be considered; when the effects result in an unreasonable or undue lessening of competition, the court will prohibit the conduct.

The per se rule is derived from the rule of reason; it states that some forms of conduct are considered to be so inherently anticompetitive that they are deemed to be illegal regardless of their actual effects on competition. When the court applies the per se rule, it will refuse to consider any justification for the anticompetitive conduct or any evidence of the impact of the conduct on competition. The per se rule is generally applied to conduct that has no legitimate business justification. An example of such conduct, sometimes called "a naked restraint of trade" by the courts, is price-fixing. The courts have adopted the per se rule in such cases because price-fixing is blatantly anticompetitive; the per se rule eliminates the need to show actual harm to competition from the price-fixing. The per se rule provides a clear standard for predicting the legality of proposed business conduct. (The per se rule will be discussed more fully later in this chapter.)

STRUCTURAL AND BEHAVIORAL ANTITRUST

One way to categorize antitrust law provisions is to decide whether they are structural or behavioral in their focus. Structural provisions are concerned primarily with the competitive structural organization of an industry—monopoly, oligopoly, or workable competition—and with whether such activities as mergers are likely to affect structural organization. Structural antitrust provisions generally involve the application of the rule of reason—particular conduct or activities will be prohibited only if they are likely to have an unreasonable effect on competition in any industry. Behavioral provisions are concerned with anticompetitive practices by firms—price-fixing, group boycotts, price discrimination, or the imposition of restrictive terms as a condition of doing business. Behavioral provisions may involve the application of either the rule of reason or the per se rule: Some behavior, such as price-fixing, may be illegal, regardless of its effect on competition, whereas the legality of other practices, such as price discrimination, may depend on their effects on competition.

STRUCTURAL ANTITRUST PROVISIONS

The legislative provisions involved in structural antitrust policy are §2 of the Sherman Act, which deals with monopolies and oligopolies, and §7 of the Clayton Act, which deals with mergers.

Monopoly From an economic standpoint, the concept of **monopoly** refers to a single firm that is the sole supplier of a unique product—one for which no substitutes exist. Buyers are forced to deal with the monopolist or with no one, and the monopolist has the power to set price and output. The economic harm that results from monopoly is the restriction of output (too little of the product is produced) and the distortion of price (it is higher than it would be if the market were competitive). The social harm resulting from monopoly is the

monopoly: A single firm that is the sole supplier of a product; a firm that has power over price and output.

maldistribution of income—from the customers of the monopoly to its owners or shareholders—and the increasing concentration of economic power in a single firm. Monopoly also creates the potential for undue political influence by the monopolist.

Monopoly and the Sherman Act Monopoly power is the power to set prices or to exclude competitors. Pure "single firm" monopoly is rare, but the possession of some monopoly power by the dominant firm in an industry is a cause for concern. Antitrust policy seeks to prevent any firm from gaining the power to set prices or to exclude competitors. A firm may become dominant in an industry through its superior products, research, and strategy; that may spur other firms to compete more aggressively, which may actually increase competition in the industry. On the other hand, a dominant firm may seek to use its power to prevent other competitors from challenging it, which could lessen competition in the industry. Because of the need to look at the effects upon competition rather than simply consider the existence of monopoly power, the courts use the rule of reason, rather than the per se rule, when considering a charge under §2. The use of monopoly power to destroy or restrict competition may result in the imposition of sanctions under §2 of the Sherman Act, which states:

> Every person who shall monopolize, or attempt to monopolize, or conspire or combine with any other person . . . to monopolize any part of the trade or commerce among the several states . . . shall be deemed guilty of a felony. . . .

Notice that §2 outlaws the act of monopolizing, not the monopoly itself. Any firm that introduces a new product, or that has a patent for such a product, has a monopoly of that product. However, such a monopoly will only be in violation of §2 when the firm uses its power to restrict or to attempt to restrict competition unreasonably.

Judicial Analysis in Monopoly Cases In analyzing a charge of monopolizing under §2, the court must first consider whether the firm charged actually possesses monopoly power. The first step in this process is to identify the product and the geographic market in which the firm operates.

product market: All the reasonably interchangeable products that may be substituted for a particular product.

The courts have defined the **product market** as including all "commodities reasonably interchangeable by consumers for the same purposes." If substitutes for the product in question are available, then the firm producing the product in question may not be able to set the price and determine output independently; consumers will turn to substitutes if the product is too expensive or is unavailable. Thus, the firm producing the product faces competition from the substitutes and therefore does not possess monopoly power. For example, if a firm producing cellophane for food packaging raises its prices, its customers may decide to use foil, kraft paper (brown "butcher paper"), or other wrapping alternatives instead. If the customers seek other packaging materials as substitutes rather than being forced to pay the higher prices for cellophane, then the appropriate product market in which to consider the power of the cellophane firm is the packaging materials market rather than just focusing on cellophane alone.

The definition of the product market is crucial to the determination of whether or not monopoly power exists. The more narrowly the product market is defined, the less likely it is that substitutes will be available and the more likely that the firm producing the product will be held to have monopoly power.

The **geographic market** is that area of the country in which a firm exercises its market power or where the effects of that power are felt. The definition of the geographic market depends upon how far the consumers will go to obtain substitutes. If substitute products are available only at great distances from the consumer, the consumer may choose to deal with the monopolist rather than undergo the difficulty and expense of obtaining the substitutes. If the consumer is willing to go a long way for substitutes, the geographic market with be broadly defined, and the market power of the alleged monopolist is likely to be diminished. Conversely, if the consumer is unwilling to go very far in the search for substitutes, the geographic market will be narrowly defined, and the market power of the alleged monopolist is likely to be enhanced. For example, liquid bleach is a relatively low cost item; the chemical composition of the product is the same regardless of which firm produces it. Because of the product's weight, the cost of transporting it more than a few hundred miles is greater than the value of the product itself. Consumers are likely to purchase bleach produced nearby rather than paying the extra shipping costs for bleach from distant producers. Therefore, the geographic market for considering the market power of a bleach producer would be the geographic area in which its product is marketed rather than the nation as a whole.

geographic market: The area of the country in which a firm exercises market power.

After defining the relevant markets, the court must determine the market share held by the firm charged; that is, the court must consider whether the firm has a dominant position in that market. A dominant firm may be able to set the pricing and production conditions against which the other firms in the industry must compete. The nature of competition in the market must also be considered, because the number and sizes of the other firms in the market will determine the extent to which the alleged monopolist can control pricing and production conditions. If the market is populated by many small firms, a market share of 35 percent may be sufficient to find dominance; in a market populated by a few large firms, dominance requires a much larger market share. If the technology of the industry is rapidly changing, then today's dominant firm may not be so dominant in the future, and its ability to exercise market power may be greatly reduced. For example, IBM was dominant in the computer industry when most computers were large mainframes; the development of the personal computer, however, has greatly reduced the reliance on mainframes, and IBM is no longer dominant in the computer industry as a whole.

Intent to Monopolize If the court finds that a firm possess a substantial share of the relevant market, it must then determine whether the firm has monopolized or attempted to monopolize that market before the firm can be found in violation of §2. The activity of the firm must be examined to determine whether the firm's behavior displays the intent to maintain or to extend its dominant position. According to the decision in *U.S. v. Aluminum Company of America*, (*Alcoa*), 148 F.2d 416 (2nd Cir. 1945), the evidence need only display the firm's general intent to maintain its dominant position; that is, there need not be specific evidence of an intention to exclude competitors or to restrict competition. In *Alcoa*, the court held that apparently normal practices—such as stimulating demand, increasing capacity to meet that anticipated demand, and controlling supplies of raw materials—constituted evidence of general intent to monopolize when engaged in by a dominant firm.

The emphasis on a firm's size in determining the legality of its actions (reflecting the Harvard School's concern about the social and economic power of huge corporations) has been rejected in more recent decisions. Courts (emphasizing the Chicago School approach) now consider whether the activities engaged in by the alleged monopolist are normal business practices available to any firm; only if the activities are "predatory" in intent—that is, only if they are designed to exclude competitors or to restrict competition—will they be considered evidence of an intent to monopolize.

The following case involves the question of whether the refusal by a dominant firm to cooperate with a smaller rival firm in a marketing arrangement constitutes predatory conduct within the meaning of the Sherman Act's prohibition on monopolizing.

ASPEN SKIING CO. V. ASPEN HIGHLANDS SKIING CORP.

472 U.S. 585 (1985)

FACTS

Aspen, Colorado, has four main skiing areas: Ajax, Aspen Highlands, Buttermilk, and Snowmass. Aspen Skiing Co. (Ski Co.) operates Ajax, Buttermilk, and Snowmass. In 1962, the ski areas introduced a six-day, interchangeable, all-Aspen ticket, which allowed visitors the flexibility of skiing all of the ski areas. Use of the ticket was monitored by recording the ticket numbers of persons on the slopes at each ski area. Officials of Highlands met periodically with Ski Co. officials to review usage figures and to distribute revenues based on the usage count for each ski area. The all-Aspen tickets began to outsell Ski Co.'s competing area-specific tickets and, by 1977, accounted for nearly 35 percent of the total skiing in the Aspen area. The use of the all-Aspen ticket was monitored by random sampling; revenues were allocated based on the survey results. Highlands' share of the ticket revenue for the 1973 to 1977 seasons was 17.5 percent, 18.5 percent, 16.8 percent, and 13.2 percent, respectively. Ski Co. officials felt the all-Aspen ticket was siphoning off revenue that they would capture if they discontinued the ticket. For the 1977–78 season, Ski Co. offered to continue participation in the all-Aspen ticket only if Highlands would accept a 13.2 percent fixed share of ticket revenues. Highlands wanted to continue to divide the revenue based on actual usage figures but ultimately agreed to accept a 15 percent fixed share of ticket revenue for that season; no survey of actual usage was conducted. For 1978–79, Ski Co.'s board of directors recommended making Highlands "an offer that it could not accept"; Ski Co. offered Highlands a 12.5 percent share. Highlands suggested a distribution of revenue based on monitoring, electronic counting, or random surveys; it even offered to hire a third-party firm at its own expense to survey usage. Ski Co. refused, insisting on the 12.5 percent fixed share for Highlands; Highlands rejected that alternative. Ski Co. ended its participation in the all-Aspen ticket and substituted a six-day ticket, good only for its three areas; it also embarked on a national advertising campaign that strongly implied that Ajax, Buttermilk, and Snowmass were the only three ski mountains in the Aspen area. Ski Co. also made it difficult for Highlands to market its own multi-area package by refusing to sell Highland any lift tickets for its three areas and refusing to accept vouchers that Highlands tried to use to guarantee the purchase price of lift tickets at Ski Co.'s areas. Because Highlands could not offer any multi-area packages, its share of the total skiing market in Aspen declined steadily after—from 20.5 percent in 1976–77 to 11 percent in 1980–81. Highlands' revenue from ski rentals, ski school, racing events, and restaurant facilities also declined sharply.

Highlands filed suit under §2 of the Sherman Act in 1979, alleging that Ski Co. had monopolized the market for downhill-skiing services in the Aspen area. The trial jury held that Ski Co. violated §2 by willfully acquiring or maintaining monopoly power in the downhill-skiing market in the Aspen area and using that power for anticompetitive or exclusionary purposes. The jury found Highlands' actual damages to be $2.5 million; the court entered judgment, awarding Highlands triple damages of $7.5 million, along with trial costs and attorney's fees. The Court of Appeals affirmed, holding that the all-Aspen ticket was an "essential facility" that Ski Co. had a duty to market jointly with Highlands. Ski Co. appealed to the U.S. Supreme Court, arguing that even a monopolist has no duty to cooperate with a competitor and that none of its conduct could be characterized as exclusionary.

DECISION

The Court stated that Ski Co. elected to make an important change in a pattern of distribution that had originated in a competitive market and had persisted for several years. The all-Aspen ticket originated when independent companies operated all of the ski areas and continued to provide a desirable option for skiers, even when the character of the market was changed by Ski Co.'s acquisition of monopoly power. Such multi-area tickets are used in other multi-mountain ski areas, and such tickets seem to satisfy consumer demand in free competitive markets. Ski Co.'s decision to terminate the all-Aspen ticket was therefore a decision by a monopolist to make an important change in the character of the market. The trial jury was instructed that Ski Co.'s refusal to continue to offer the all-Aspen ticket would not violate §2 if valid business reasons existed for that refusal; however, the jury concluded that there were no valid business reasons for that refusal. The question on appeal is whether there is evidentiary support for that determination.

If a firm attempts to exclude rivals by some basis other than efficiency, that behavior is predatory. The evidence at trial supports the determination that the elimination of the all-Aspen ticket adversely affected consumers; the ticket provided consumers with flexibility and convenience and increased the number of challenging ski runs available to consumers during their week visit to Aspen. The adverse effect of Ski Co.'s actions on Highlands was not disputed; the size of the damage award confirms the substantial character of the effect of Ski Co.'s conduct on Highlands.

Ski Co. was apparently willing to forgo daily ticket sales to skiers who sought to exchange the vouchers from Highlands and to skiers who would have bought lift tickets through Highlands if Ski Co. had permitted Highlands to buy its lift tickets in bulk. The jury could have concluded that Ski Co. was willing to forgo those short-term benefits because it was more interested in reducing competition in the long run by harming its competitor; that conclusion was supported by Ski Co.'s failure to offer any efficiency justification whatsoever for its conduct.

The Court held that "the record in this case comfortably supports an inference that the monopolist made a deliberate effort to discourage its customers from doing business with its rival . . . ," and "the evidence supports an inference that Ski Co. was not motivated by efficiency concerns and . . . was willing to sacrifice short run benefits and consumer goodwill in exchange for a perceived long run impact on its smaller rival." The Court therefore affirmed the decision by the Court of Appeals.

CASE QUESTIONS

1. Is a dominant firm always required to cooperate with its rivals? Explain your answer.
2. What reasons did Ski Co. give for ending the all-Aspen ski pass?
3. How did the trial jury and the Supreme Court characterize Ski Co.'s actions and rationale for refusing to cooperate with Highlands?
4. What is the relevance of the evidence regarding consumers' preferences for the all-Aspen pass?

MICROSOFT HAS A MONOPOLY, BUT HAS IT MONOPOLIZED?

The U.S. Justice Department's suit alleging that Microsoft violated both §1 and §2 of the Sherman Act by attempting to use its dominance in the computer operating systems market (through its Windows products) to force computer manufacturers to include Microsoft's Internet browser [Internet Explorer] rather than browsers from rivals such as Netscape. The Justice Department alleged that operating systems and Internet browsers were two separate product markets, and that Microsoft sought to exploit its market power over operating systems to increase its market share of the browser market by "bundling" Internet Explorer with Windows, and by forcing computer manufacturing firms (OEMs) such as Gateway that "pre-install" Windows products on their computers to include Internet Explorer, thereby restricting user access to rival browsers. Microsoft argued that the operating systems and browsers were a single product, and that by bundling them together, Microsoft was benefiting consumers by offering additional program features at reduced prices.

The trial on the Justice Department's suit began October 19, 1998, and lasted through June 24, 1999. The Justice Department offered extensive evidence to support its charges, including numerous e-mail messages between Microsoft executives and executives of computer manufacturers. The following are two examples of the Justice Department's evidence:

Government Exhibit #295
[Source: http://www.usdoj.gov/atr/cases/ms_exhibits.htm]

Erik Stevenson (LCA)

From: Bill Gates [billg]
Sent: Friday, January 05, 1996 2.18 PM
To: Joachim Kempin
Cc: Brad Silverberg, Brad Chase, John Ludwig, Steve Ballmer, Cameron Myhrvold, Russell Siegelman, Nathan Myhrvold, Pete Higgins, Paul Mantz
Subject: OEMs and the Internet

Winning Internet browser share is a very very important goal for us

Apparently a lot of OEMs are bundling non-Microsoft browsers and coming up with offerings together with Internet Service providers that get displayed on their machines in a FAR more prominent way than MSN or our Internet browser.

I would like to see an analysis of the top OEMs of what they are doing with browsers

I would like to understand what we need to do to convince OEMS to focus on our browser Is our problem proving our technology and its capability? Is our problem that they are getting bounty fees by having Internet service providers pay them a sum or a royalty on the business they get? Is a 3 1 browser a key issue for them?

If their problem is getting an easy way for customers to click and get to their home page we can provide that as a feature of Internet explorer and make it very easy to set up in the OPK.

We really need you to explain to use OEM thinking about browsers and what we need to do Sometime in the next few weeks I would like to see some analysis

Promoting our Internet 2.0 browser to Oems and helping them see our commitment to leadership is very important

Ideally we would also get them to exploit our browser on their web sites Maybe we could incent them by having a page in the Windows95 free that reference licensees home pages if they are enhanced for IE.

MSV 0009445 A
CONFIDENTIAL

GOVERNMENT
EXHIBIT
295

Government Exhibit #308
[Source: http://www.usdoj.gov/atr/cases/ms_exhibits.htm]

CONFIDENTIAL

To: Ted Waitt, Rick Snyder, Jim Von Holle, Jim Collas, Bill Elliott
From: Kathy Skidmore@GW2KUSA
Cc:
Bcc:
Subject: Microsoft / Concerns
Attachment:
Date: 2/28/97 5:30 PM

GATEWAY 2000 CONFIDENTIAL INFORMATION

I just got off the phone with Brian Fujiwara, our new MS account rep. Brian is young and only a 15 month employee with MS. He doesn't "think" before he speaks. The below comments definately crosses the line of "what is legal".

- - -

Brian asked my help in determining if there was any hope for MS that GW change our mind and not use Netscape on our IntraNet.

Brian wanted me to find out what our objects were and make sure that MS has an opportunity to address those objections to their software. They want to know if it was a technical issue or something else.

Brian said that this is a HUGE issue with MS. He said MS want to get back to doing co-marketing and sales campaigns with GW, but they won't if they see GW is anything but pro Microsoft.

He said and I quote, "Dell turned Netscape down because they did not want to hurt their relationship with Microsoft. Therefore, they (Dell) get special things because of it".

Brian is meeting with Joachim on Tuesday, 3/4/96 and wants to let him know where GW stands. He said that this has Ballmer's attention as well.

GOVERNMENT EXHIBIT
308

More than five months after the close of the trial, and after much press speculation about the outcome, U.S. District Judge Thomas Penfield Jackson issued his 207-page findings of fact, *U.S. v. Microsoft* [1999 WL 1001107 (D.D.C. Nov. 5, 1999)]. Judge Jackson defined the relevant product market as the market for "licensing of all Intel-compatible PC operating systems world-wide," and held that Microsoft, with more than 90 percent of that market, is clearly a monopolist and enjoys market power in the relevant market. New entrants to the operating systems market must face high barriers to entry, and PC users lack commercially viable alternatives to Windows. Judge Jackson stated that Microsoft's corporate policy toward firms such as Apple, Netscape, Intel, and Sun Microsystems, whose products (such as Java) might pose a threat to the Windows monopoly, was to pressure those other firms to stop development of software that either competes with Windows or might make it easier for other firms to compete with Microsoft. Microsoft's conduct, especially that regarding Netscape and its browser, Navigator, made sense only when viewed as an attempt to maintain high barriers to entry to the relevant market, and to protect the Windows' entrenched dominance. Microsoft used restrictive licensing agreements, pricing policies, and other tactics to make sure that OEMs installed only Internet Explorer on new personal computers; such restrictions closed off a major channel of distribution from Netscape and forced Netscape to use more expensive, less efficient distribution channels. Microsoft used the enormous profits it made from licensing Windows to OEMs to subsidize the losses from giving away Internet Explorer in order to build market share. Netscape, in order to compete with Microsoft in the browser market, was forced to give away Navigator, but Netscape lacked other sources of profit to make up for the resulting loss of revenue. Microsoft bundled Internet Explorer with Windows 98 in such a way to make it extremely difficult for consumers to use a different browser, or no browser at all. That increased customer support costs for OEMs, and made OEMs much less likely to install browsers other than Internet Explorer.

Judge Jackson specifically concluded that Microsoft had harmed consumers in three ways: (1) Windows 98, while allowing the use of a "default" browser, still requires the use of Internet Explorer in certain situations, causing consumer confusion; (2) consumers who wish to use Windows 98 without a browser are forced to put up with reduced system performance and wasted hard drive space because of the inclusion of Internet Explorer; and (3) for users of Windows 98 with Internet Explorer, a browser "crash" is likely to affect the entire system, and the bundling of Internet Explorer in Windows makes the system more vulnerable to viruses transmitted through Internet Explorer. Judge Jackson held that there was no technical justification for Microsoft's refusal to license Windows 95 and then Windows 98 without including Internet Explorer—"No consumer benefit can be ascribed, however, to Microsoft's refusal to offer a version of Windows 95 or Windows 98 without Internet Explorer, or Microsoft's refusal to provide a method for uninstalling Internet Explorer from Windows 98."

Judge Jackson delayed issuing of his conclusions of law, including whether Microsoft has violated any antitrust laws, to allow the parties time to file additional briefs. Following the release of the findings of fact, Microsoft and the Justice Department entered into negotiations on a possible settlement to the case; Justice Jackson appointed U.S. Court of Appeals Judge Richard Posner, an expert on antitrust law, to act as a mediator in those negotiations. Negotiations for a settlement broke down, and on April 13, 2000, Judge Jackson ruled that Microsoft had illegally used its market power in the operating systems market to attempt to monopolize the Web browser market. An appeal by the losing party is almost certain, and the final resolution of the case may be years away.

Microsoft's antitrust troubles are not limited to the United States. In February 2000, the European Union's Competition Commissioner announced that European Union regulators were investigating whether Microsoft's launch of its Windows 2000 operating system would give Microsoft a dominant position in the software market.

Sources: John T. Aquino, "Microsoft Finding of Fact: What Now," *The Internet Newsletter: Legal & Business Aspects* (November 1999); "Microsoft Is a Monopolist and Has Harmed Consumers, Judge Finds," *Antitrust Litigation Reporter* (November 1999); "Busted," *The Economist* (November 13, 1999); Marcus A. Hamilton, "Power Corrupts: Microsoft Findings Reflect Framers' Fear of Monopoly," *Legal Times* (November 15, 1999); "Microsoft Is a Monopolist and Has Harmed Consumers, Judge Finds: Key Points in Judge Jackson's Findings of Fact," *Computer & Online Industry Litigation Reporter* (November 16, 1999); Neal R. Stoll and Shepard Goldfein, "*U.S. v. Microsoft*: The First Step Toward a Remedy," *New York Law Journal* (November 16, 1999); "The Microsoft Case: The Go Between," *The Economist* (November 27, 1999); "Antitrust on Trial," *The Economist* (November 13, 1999).

Oligopoly The structure of competition in an industry is considered to be an **oligopoly** when a few large firms dominate the industry. When this is the case, the firms are likely to be able to anticipate the reaction of the other firms to any competitive action, and the competitive decisions of the firms are likely to be similar. For example, if Ford announces that it will raise new car prices by an average of 5 percent for the next model year, Chrysler and General Motors may decide to raise their prices a similar amount. Such conduct, where the firms act independently but similarly, is known as **conscious parallelism** and is beyond the reach of the antitrust laws as long as each firm reaches its decisions independently—no agreement or understanding among the firms exists. If, however, the firms act pursuant to a common understanding or agreement, their conduct is in violation of §1 of the Sherman Act, which prohibits **concerted activity** (collective activity among competitors). The existence of

oligopoly: Industry dominated by a few large firms.

conscious parallelism: Firms acting independently, but similarly to their rivals.

concerted activity: Firms acting together, or collectively.

oligopoly may make it easier for the firms to engage in concerted activity or collusion. In the absence of concerted activity, oligopoly itself is legal.

The economic effects of oligopoly may be the same as those of monopoly, as a result of the lack of competition. Nevertheless, oligopoly is not subject to attack under §2 of the Sherman Act because no single firm possesses monopoly power. The legal approach to oligopoly is therefore purely behavioral—did the firms act pursuant to a common arrangement, agreement, or understanding? Behavioral antitrust provisions are discussed in more detail later in this chapter.

Various attempts to pass legislation allowing for a structural attack on oligopoly have been unsuccessful. The FTC at one time attempted to attack oligopolies as "shared monopolies" under §5 of the FTC act, but it subsequently abandoned those efforts. As a result, legal challenges to oligopolies require the courts to search for some sort of concerted behavior—collusion or agreement, either explicit or implicit—among the firms involved. In the absence of an agreement or understanding, even identical behavior by competing firms is legal. For example, Continental Airlines may decide to offer discount rates on popular routes, to try to gain a competitive advantage; if, in response, the other competing airlines offer similar discounts, competition on those routes remains the same. If the airlines each independently decide to offer discounts, their parallel behavior is legal; but if the decision to offer discounts results from an agreement or understanding among the firms, the decision violates the antitrust laws.

Mergers The late 1990s experienced an explosive wave of mergers, dwarfing the merger waves of previous decades: Disney's purchase of ABC, Viacom's acquisition of CBS, Chrysler merging with Daimler-Benz, Ford purchasing Volvo, General Motors acquiring Saab, Exxon merging with Mobil Oil Corp., Time-Warner merging with AOL, and Boeing's merger with McDonnell Douglas are just a few examples. Mergers in 1998 involved firms with assets worth more than one trillion dollars, and the totals for mergers or acquisitions in 1999 are probably greater. Firms in developing industries such as the Internet or telecommunications merge to keep pace with rapidly changing technology that requires innovation and "one stop shopping" (being able to offer consumers complementary products such as cable and Internet service). Firms in "mature" industries such as defense, oil, or automobiles merge in order to compete more efficiently in the global market, and to react more effectively to the changing nature of the market. The increasing globalization of trade means that firms face increasing competition from "foreign" firms, even in their home market; firms may see mergers as the way to counter such threats, or as the key to opening up new markets abroad. A soaring stock market provides firms with enormous amounts of capital to use for such "buying sprees."

Although the legislation dealing with mergers and the general judicial analysis to the legality of mergers have not changed, the attitudes of antitrust enforcement officials have changed. Antitrust enforcers recognize that firms now compete globally and that the nature of competition in industries is changing. They are more willing to allow mergers between huge competitors such as Exxon and Mobil if they result in a large domestic firm able to compete more effectively with foreign "giants" such as Royal Dutch Shell Oil Co. Mergers such as that between Boeing and McDonnell-Douglas will be allowed in order to allow firms to rationalize productive capacity in the dwindling government defense and aerospace industry. Even the changed outlook of the antitrust enforcement officials, however, will not stop them from challenging mergers that create dominant firms with power over prices, or that substantially lessen competition in a given industry.

Section 7 of the Clayton Act prohibits mergers of firms in interstate commerce when the effects of the merger are likely to result in a substantial lessening of competition. Mergers are acquisitions or takeovers of another firm; Section 7 applies to mergers in which one firm purchases either the assets or the stock of another firm. Mergers are only illegal if they are likely to have a detrimental effect on competition; hence, the courts apply the rule of reason in merger cases. The effects of a merger on competition depend on the competitive relationship between the merging firms and the conditions in the industry or industries in which the firms operate. (While most merger cases are brought under §7 of the Clayton Act, mergers can also be challenged under the Sherman Act as an unreasonable restraint of trade or an attempt to monopolize.)

The judicial approach to merger cases under §7 involves the identification of the product market and the geographic market affected by the merger. As in monopoly cases, the product market is defined according to the principles of substitutability; the geographic market is the area or areas of the country likely to be affected by the merger. As in monopoly cases, the definitions of the markets are crucial. The more narrowly the markets are defined, the more likely it is that a merger will substantially affect competition in those markets. After defining the relevant markets, the court must assess the probable effects of the merger on competition in those markets. Note that the court does not have to find any actual lessening of competition—it need only concern itself with the probable results of the merger. If the court finds that the probable result of the merger is a substantial reduction of competition, then the merger is in violation of §7. The court may prohibit the merger or order that it be dissolved.

The assessment of the probable effects of a merger on competition involves consideration of both structural and behavioral factors. The relative importance of those factors depends upon the relationship between the merging firms. Mergers are classified as **horizontal mergers**, involving firms that are competitors; **vertical mergers**, involving firms that are involved in production–supply relationships; or **conglomerate mergers**, involving firms that are neither competitors nor have a production–supply relationship. A merger between large firms may have aspects of all three types of mergers.

horizontal mergers: Mergers among firms that compete with each other.

vertical mergers: Mergers involving firms that are suppliers or customers of each other.

conglomerate mergers: Mergers that are neither horizontal nor vertical.

Horizontal Mergers When the merging firms are competitors in the same market, the merger is a horizontal merger and is likely to have a direct effect upon competition in that market. In this case, the court will consider whether the resulting firm will be dominant in the market. If the merger results in a firm that has a dominant share of a market, in which there are few competitors or in which the competitors are significantly smaller, the merger will probably be held to violate §7. When two small firms merge in order to compete more effectively with a larger rival, the merger is likely to be allowed.

Until the mid-1970s, the courts in most horizontal merger cases placed heavy emphasis upon the size of the resulting firm. When the new firm would have a significant market share in a concentrated industry, the merger would be held to be illegal. As a result, large firms generally avoided acquiring competitors and instead sought to expand through diversification. More recently, the courts have considered the nature of competition in the industry as well as the merged firm's position in that industry. The courts have also been more willing to recognize that competition is now international in character—foreign firms may pose a competitive threat to the merged firm—in determining the probable effects of a merger on competition. As a result, mergers that create firms that are dominant in the domestic market, in order to compete more effectively with international rivals, are more likely to be permitted by the courts today than in the early 1970s.

Vertical Mergers Mergers between firms at different levels of the production chain are called vertical mergers. Examples of such a merger would be the acquisition of a petroleum refining company by a firm that produces petrochemicals or the purchase of a chain of gas stations by a petroleum refining company. In the first example, the acquired firm produces the raw materials for the product of the acquiring firm; in the second example, the acquired firm distributes (or retails) the product of the acquiring firm.

Because the merging firms in a vertical merger do not compete directly with each other, the size of the resulting firm is not significant in determining the probable effects upon competition. The court will consider the size of each firm and its relative position in its market: Does either firm occupy such a significant position in its market that the merger will foreclose a major source of supplies or a major distribution outlet from other competitors? For example, if a chain of gas stations previously carried the products of a number of refiners, the court will consider whether the acquisition of the chain by one refiner will deny the other refiners access to the chain's sales outlets. If so, and if the chain represents a significant share of the retail gasoline sales market, then the acquisition could violate §7 by substantially lessening competition in the distribution and retail sale of gasoline.

In addition to considering the size and relative position of each firm in its own market, the court will determine whether the merger will enable the resulting firm to engage in anticompetitive behavior in either market. When a merger creates significant opportunities for anticompetitive conduct, it can be held to violate §7.

As was the case with horizontal mergers, the courts in the early vertical merger decisions emphasized the relative size of the merging firms in determining the merger's probable effect on competition. The courts also took the position that the size of all of the firms was directly related to the creation of opportunities for predatory conduct; that is, the larger the firms were, the more likely it was that such opportunities would be significant. More recent judicial analysis takes the view that the sizes of the firms are not directly relevant to the creation of opportunities for predatory conduct. Rather, the courts now focus on whether the firm is dominant or possesses monopoly power in its respective market. Much less emphasis is placed on the mere potential for anticompetitive behavior.

Conglomerate Mergers Most recently, corporate mergers have involved conglomerate mergers—in which the merging firms are not competitors and are not involved in a production–supply relationship. Because the firms are not directly related, their sizes are not relevant to the merger's effect on competition. The court must therefore consider whether the combination of the firms will create significant opportunities for anticompetitive behavior.

A court must determine whether the assets of the acquiring firm will enable the acquired firm to engage in predatory pricing or improve an already dominant position. The court must also consider whether the acquiring firm had contemplated entering the market in which the acquired firm operates; if so, the merger precludes that potential entry into the market and prevents an increase in competition in that market. The difficulty in proving that the probable effects of a potential merger will be the creation of significant opportunities for anticompetitive practices makes a legal challenge to a conglomerate merger a formidable task. The antitrust enforcement agencies have not seriously challenged conglomerate mergers in recent years; the last successful government challenge to a conglomerate merger was in the mid 1970s. Conglomerate mergers are no longer as common as they were in the 1970s. Firms have largely abandoned the claims that "synergy" would result from the combination of unrelated businesses; most of the mergers of the 1990s have been horizontal or vertical mergers, as firms focus on core businesses and key products.

The following case involves a private suit challenging a proposed merger of competitors. The case raises the issue of whether the merger provisions of §7 of the Clayton Act protect competitors or competition: What kind of harm to competition must a plaintiff allege in order to challenge a merger successfully?

CARGILL, INC. V. MONFORT OF COLORADO, INC.

479 U.S. 104 (1986)

FACTS

The meatpacking industry is highly competitive, and profit margins of the major beef packers are low. The industry is characterized by two distinct markets—the input market, involving the supply of feed cattle for slaughter, and the output market, involving cut and trimmed beef products ("fabricated beef"). Excel Co., a subsidiary of Cargill, Inc., is the second largest meat packer in the United States; it operates five integrated plants (with both slaughtering and meat fabrication) and one fabrication plant. Cargill, Excel's corporate parent, is a large privately owned corporation with more than 150 subsidiaries in at least 35 countries. Excel agreed to buy Spencer Beef, the third largest meat packer in the United States, which operates two integrated plants and one slaughtering plant.

Monfort is the fifth-largest meat packer in the United States, operating three integrated plants. Monfort's share of the input market was 5.5 percent, and its share of the output market was 5.7 percent. Excel's share of those markets, before the purchase of Spencer, was 13.3 percent and 14.1 percent; after the purchase, Excel's shares would be 20.4 percent and 20.4 percent, respectively. The country's largest meat packer is IBP, Inc.; its market shares are 24.4 percent of the input market and 27.3 percent of the output market.

Monfort filed suit under §7 of the Clayton Act, arguing that the merger of Excel and Spencer would substantially lessen competition and increase concentration of economic power in the input and output markets in the fabricated beef industry. Monfort argued that the increased concentration in the input market would increase the cost of cattle to Monfort and would severely narrow Monfort's profit margin. The trial court held that the merger would cause "antitrust injury" (injury that the antitrust laws were designed to prevent) to Monfort and therefore violated §7 of the Clayton Act; the court issued an injunction prohibiting the merger under §16 of the Act.

Excel appealed, arguing that any harm Monfort would suffer from the merger was simply losses resulting from vigorous competition and was not antitrust injury. The court of appeals affirmed the trial court decision; Excel then appealed to the U.S. Supreme Court. The question before the Supreme Court was whether a private plaintiff seeking to prevent a merger under the Clayton Act must show a threat of antitrust injury to get an injunction under §16 of the Act.

DECISION

The Supreme Court held that a private plaintiff suing under §4 (for triple damages) or §16 (for an injunction) of the Clayton Act must prove that the merger would cause antitrust injury to them. In the case of *Brunswick Corp. v. Pueblo Bowl-O-Mat, Inc.*, 429 U.S. 477 (1977), the Court held that losses due to continuing competition were not antitrust injuries and that the antitrust laws were intended to protect competition, not to protect competitors. Monfort claimed that, after the merger, Excel would be able to lower its prices to a level at, or just slightly above, its cost in order to gain market share. Cargill, Excel's parent, had the financial resources to enable Excel to pursue the price-cutting strategy. Monfort, in response, would have to lower its prices and would suffer a loss in profits as a result. The Supreme Court held that the injury that Monfort would allegedly suffer as a result of the merger was injury resulting from increased competition for market share, which was not antitrust injury. "To hold that the antitrust laws protect competitors from the loss of profits due to such price competition would, in effect, render illegal any decision by a firm to cut prices in order to increase market share." The Court also stated that it "is in the interest of competition to permit dominant firms to engage in vigorous competition, including price competition."

Monfort had only demonstrated that any losses it would suffer because of the proposed merger would result from increased competition; Monfort did not show that the merger threatened the company with antitrust injury. Monfort had failed to prove that the merger would result in harm to competition; therefore, the merger would not violate §7 of the Clayton Act. The judgment of the court of appeals was reversed, and the merger was allowed to proceed.

CASE QUESTIONS

1. What kind of merger is involved here—horizontal, vertical, or conglomerate?
2. What kind of harm does Monfort allege will result from the merger? Who will suffer the alleged harm?
3. Is harm to competitors the same as harm to competition? What kind of harm, according to the Supreme Court, was the antitrust laws intended to prevent?
4. Does this decision emphasize the social or the economic approach to enforcing the antitrust laws?

Premerger Notification Requirements The 1979 amendments to §7 of the Clayton Act, added by the Hart-Scott-Rodino Act, instituted a premerger requirement for mergers involving firms of a certain size. The legislation added §7A, which requires that both the Antitrust Division of the Justice Department and the FTC be notified prior to any merger when the acquiring firm has assets or annual sales of over $100 million and the firm to be acquired has assets or annual sales of over $10 million. The notice must be given at least 15 days prior to the merger if it involves a cash purchase of the acquired firm; for mergers that involve an exchange of securities, the notice period is 30 days.

The purpose of the premerger notification requirement is to give the enforcement authorities an opportunity to analyze the probable effects of the proposed merger before it takes place. The notification requirement does not constitute a formal approval system; the merging firms need not get the permission of the enforcement authorities in order to consummate the merger. In practice, the requirement has allowed the authorities to raise legal concerns prior to some mergers. In most cases in which such concerns have been raised, the firms either abandoned the proposed merger or agreed to sell off operations of the firms that raised competitive concerns.

For example, the FTC approved the Exxon and Mobil merger in 1999 only after the firms agreed to sell off 2,431 gas stations in the Northeast, California, and Texas, where both firms had significant market shares, and Exxon agreed to sell a refinery in California, terminals, and a pipeline.

BOEING FEELS THE LONG ARM OF ANTITRUST LAW

The United States has long taken the position that mergers of foreign firms that have a negative effect on competition within the United States are subject to U.S. antitrust law—even if the merging firms have no offices, plants, or operations in the United States. More recently, the European Union (EU) has argued that its antitrust law and competition policy apply where a merger of U.S. firms has an effect on competition with the EU. Generally, when a merger of U.S. firms is approved by U.S. authorities, the EU competition authorities also grant approval. (The U.S. Justice Department and the FTC executed an agreement with the EU competition authorities on antitrust enforcement in 1991, and a supplemental agreement in 1998.) But when Boeing announced plans to merge with McDonnell Douglas in 1997, the EU insisted upon subjecting the merger to EU law because Boeing accounts for a significant volume of business in Europe. The FTC approved the merger, but the EU's competition commissioner announced that the EU would seek to block the merger because it would significantly reduce competition in Europe.

Under EU competition policy, mergers that "create or strengthen a dominant position . . . shall be declared incompatible with the common market." Boeing, the world's leading manufacturer of civilian aircraft, sought to acquire McDonnell Douglas, the number three manufacturer of civilian aircraft and a leading supplier of military aircraft, primarily as part of a consolidation of the U.S. defense industry. The EU authorities opposed the merger because it would leave European airlines with a choice between Boeing and Airbus, a European firm; the merger would increase Boeing's share of the world market from 64 percent to 70 percent, whereas Airbus has about 30 percent of that market.

Boeing is clearly dominant in the market for large civilian airliners—it has some 70 percent of the market (based on recent aircraft orders) and accounts for about 80 percent of existing airliner fleets. Boeing also had signed exclusive 20-year supply contracts with several airlines—American Airlines, Continental, and Delta (accounting for 11 percent of the world market)—by which the airlines agreed to buy all new airliners from Boeing. The EU commissioner claimed that such contracts would have the effect of shutting out the only other competitor, Airbus, from a large segment of the U.S. market. Lastly, the EU officials were concerned that McDonnell Douglas's research for defense contracts would "spill over" into the civilian airliner market and give Boeing a technological advantage over Airbus. If Boeing and McDonnell Douglas went ahead with the merger, and the EU declared it illegal, the EU could impose fines against Boeing of up to

10 percent of its business turnover, which would amount to almost $4 billion. The EU could also fine any European airline that purchased Boeing aircraft, could impound any new Boeing aircraft landing in Europe, and would effectively cut Boeing off from the European large airliner market, about 26 percent of the world market.

Rather than face such consequences, Boeing ultimately agreed to accept certain conditions imposed by EU authorities in return for EU approval of the merger. Boeing agreed to license to competitors (such as Airbus) any patents that result from its defense work, agreed not to enter into any new exclusive supply contracts for 10 years, and agreed not to enforce its existing exclusive supply contracts. The EU approval then cleared the way for the merger to proceed and also averted a possible "trade war" between the United States and the EU.

Sources: "The Borders of Competition," *The Economist* (July 4, 1998); "Brussels v. Boeing," *The Economist* (July 19, 1997); "Peace in our time: Boeing v. Airbus," *The Economist* (July 26, 1997).

BEHAVIORAL ANTITRUST PROVISIONS

Behavioral antitrust provisions focus on arrangements or agreements among firms and upon firms' pricing policies. Section 1 of the Sherman Act, which prohibits every ". . . contract, combination . . . or conspiracy in restraint of trade or commerce," is the main provision of behavioral antitrust provisions.

In determining the legality of an arrangement, it is usually necessary to determine whether the arrangement is horizontal or vertical. The judicial analysis of the legality of such arrangements generally differs for horizontal and vertical arrangements. It is also important to consider whether the arrangement involves prices or relates only to nonprice matters.

Horizontal Concerted Activity Horizontal arrangements, or concerted activities, involve competing firms. Such arrangements may be pursuant to explicit contracts or to tacit understandings, and they may involve pricing or nonprice competition. Any agreement among competitors is likely to have an adverse effect on competition; therefore, the antitrust laws deal harshly with horizontal arrangements. Any concerted activity among competitors that restricts competition or that is intended to restrict competition is illegal per se. Thus, the conduct is illegal, regardless of its actual effect on competition. (Note that horizontal concerted activity that has little effect on competition rarely ever occurs.)

Per Se Rule The per se rule is the usual judicial approach to horizontal concerted activity. The impact of the per se rule is mainly evidentiary—the court will not consider any justification for the concerted behavior. For example, the fact that an agreement to set prices maintains them at a reasonable level or only specifies a ceiling price is irrelevant to the legality of the agreement. The per se approach, under §1 of the Sherman Act, applies to a variety of horizontal concerted activities. Examples of such activity include territorial market divisions, agreements to restrict output or production, agreements not to deal with certain firms or customers, group boycotts, and agreements not to advertise prices. Because concerted activity intended to restrict competition is illegal per se, it is illegal regardless of the actual effects on competition and regardless of the motives behind the activity. Firms acting independently may choose not to deal with certain customers or in certain areas or to charge certain prices. When such decisions are made in conjunction with competing firms, however, they are illegal. The crucial factor for determining the legality of particular behavior is whether the firms involved are acting jointly or independently.

Because of the per se rule, the judicial approach to cases of alleged horizontal activity involves only the determination of whether the conduct was concerted rather than independent and whether the arrangement was indeed horizontal. If both questions are answered affirmatively, a court will refuse to consider any justification for the activity.

The following case illustrates the application of the per se rule to alleged horizontal concerted activity.

UNITED STATES V. TOPCO ASSOCIATES, INC.

405 U.S. 596 (1972)

FACTS

Topco Associates is a cooperative association of small, regional supermarket chains. Topco's main function is to serve as a purchasing agent for its member chains; it procures and distributes more than 1,000 products that are marketed under the Topco brand name. By 1967, Topco members had combined retail sales of more than $2.3 billion—a figure exceeded only by three national grocery chains. The member supermarket chains operate independently; there is no pooling of profits or advertising efforts, and no grocers do business under the Topco name. The member supermarkets control all of Topco's stock and voting rights, and Topco's board of directors is made up of executives from the various member chains. As a result, the member chains have complete control over Topco's operations.

When a chain applies for membership in Topco, it first has to be approved by the Topco board of directors and then by an affirmative vote of at least 75 percent of the members. However, if the member whose operations are closest to the applicant or members with operations within 100 miles of the applicant vote against the applicant, then an affirmative vote of 85 percent of the members is required for admission. The Topco members generally cooperate in accommodating the wishes of other members, so that in actual practice, the members have a veto against the admission of actual or potential competitors in the territories in which they operate. Following admission, each new member signs an agreement designating the territory in which it may sell Topco brand products; the member may not sell outside the designated territory. Combined with the veto that members have over competitors, the result of the arrangement is effectively to insulate members from competition in Topco brand products.

The grocery industry is very competitive; profit margins from grocery firms of 1 percent to 2 percent are common. The Topco member grocery chains argued that their membership in Topco allows them to compete more effectively with the national grocery chains. Because the members do not face any competition for the Topco brand items within their territories, those items are very profitable; the profits from Topco items allow the members to reduce prices on items to compete with the national grocery chains.

The U.S. government claimed that the arrangement constituted a market division agreement among the supermarket chains (competitors) that operated to prohibit competition in Topco brand products among the retail grocery chains and was in violation of §1 of the

Sherman Act. The trial court held that the arrangement was legal, and the U.S. government appealed directly to the U.S. Supreme Court. Topco argued that restricting competition in Topco brand products actually increased competition by enabling its members to compete successfully against the larger chains.

DECISION

The Supreme Court noted that the evidence indicated that the Topco members were frequently strong competitors in their respective areas, largely due to the success of the Topco brand products. The profits on the Topco brand products were substantial, and their existence had improved the competitive potential of the Topco members against other large grocery chains. But the Court held that the trial court had erred in holding that restricting competition in Topco brand products was legal because it increased competition among grocery chains; the Sherman Act does not grant Topco authority to determine the "respective values of competition in the various sectors of the economy." The Court held that each member chain must decide for itself "whether or not competition with other supermarket chains is more desirable than competition in the sale of Topco-brand products." If any decision to sacrifice competition in one portion of the economy for increased competition in another portion is to be made, stated the Court, it must be made by Congress, and not by private parties or in the courts. In the absence of any congressional directive to the contrary, the arenas in which the Topco members choose to compete must be left to their independent, unfettered choice. The Supreme Court therefore reversed the judgment of the trial court and held that the Topco arrangement was a combination or conspiracy in restraint of trade in violation of §1 of the Sherman Act.

CASE QUESTIONS

1. What was the purpose of Topco's restriction upon the sales areas of its members?
2. What were the effects of Topco's restrictions on competition among large grocery chains? What were the effects on competition among sellers of Topco brand products?
3. Did the trial court characterize the Topco restrictions as horizontal or vertical? Why did the trial court find the restrictions to be legal?
4. Did the Supreme Court characterize the Topco restrictions as horizontal or vertical? Why? Why did the Supreme Court refuse to consider the purpose of the restrictions in considering their legality?
5. If the chains that were members of Topco chose to merge into a single firm in order to compete with the national chains, would their conduct have been held to be illegal?

FROM THE DESK OF
Laura Lawyer

To: Students

From: Your Lawyer

As a business executive, you and your firm may be asked to participate in a trade association or industry promotion council, an organization formed by the firms in a particular industry to promote their interests with the government and consumers. The associations may also collect and publish information about economic and competitive conditions in the industry. Because the member firms of such organizations are competitors, their activities may arouse interest from antitrust enforcement agencies.

Joint lobbying and promotional activities are unlikely to pose legal problems, but collecting and distributing information about industry conditions present the potential for concerted activity based on such information. Therefore, associations and their member firms must exercise great caution in gathering and publishing production and pricing information. Collecting and publishing aggregate information, with no individual firms or customers identified, is legal; however, it is illegal to distribute current prices offered to specific customers when the effect of such information may be to stabilize prices in an industry. Even informal exchanges of current price information, when the firms involved have agreed to adhere to the prices quoted, have been held to violate §1 of the Sherman Act. Groups whose membership is not restricted to the firms of a single industry, such as the Chamber of Commerce or the Business Roundtable, are less likely to pose antitrust problems by their activities.

Horizontal Concerted Activity and the Rule Of Reason Although the courts generally apply the per se rule to horizontal concerted activity, occasional instances arise when the courts may choose to apply the rule of reason. These include situations in which the alleged concerted activity has legitimate justifications or the concerted restrictions are necessary to allow the product to be provided to the public. The case of *N.C.A.A. v. Board of Regents of the University of Oklahoma*, 468 U.S. 85 (1984), involved a challenge to the restrictions placed on college football games involving members of the National Collegiate Athletic Association (NCAA). The restrictions on televising games limited the number of times that a particular team could appear on television in a particular season. Other NCAA restrictions limited the number of athletic scholarships that a school could give, limited the number of games that could be played each season, and ensured that the players remained amateurs. The Supreme Court noted in the following passage that some of the NCAA restrictions were necessary to ensure the availability of college football at all:

> What the NCAA and its member institutions market in this case is competition itself—contests between competing institutions. Of course, this would be completely ineffective if there were no rules on which the competitors agreed to create and define the competition to be marketed. A myriad of

> rules affecting such matters as the size of the field, the number of players on a team, and the extent to which physical violence is to be encouraged or proscribed, all must be agreed upon, and all restrain the manner in which institutions compete. Moreover, the NCAA seeks to market a particular brand of football—college football. The identification of the 'product' with an academic tradition differentiates college football from and makes it more popular than professional sports to which it might otherwise be comparable, such as, for example, minor league baseball. In order to preserve the character and quality of the 'product,' athletes must not be paid, must be required to attend class, and the like. And the integrity of the 'product' cannot be preserved except by mutual agreement; if an institution adopted such restrictions unilaterally, its effectiveness as a competitor on the playing field might soon be destroyed. Thus, the NCAA plays a vital role in enabling college football to preserve its character, and as a result enables a product to be marketed which might otherwise be unavailable. In performing this role, its actions widen consumer choice—not only the choices available to sports fans but also those available to athletes—and hence can be viewed as procompetitive.

The court therefore held that the rule of reason, rather than the per se rule, should be applied to the NCAA restrictions regarding the rules of the game and player eligibility. Those restrictions were held to be legal; however, the restrictions on the televising of games of NCAA members had the effect of restricting output of the product and raising the price that the networks had to pay for the rights to televise them, restricting competition unreasonably, and were therefore illegal under §1 of the Sherman Act.

The following reading involves the application of the rule of reason to other horizontal concerted activity among universities.

M.I.T. IS THE SUBJECT OF AN ANTITRUST LAWSUIT

In 1991, the U.S. government filed an antitrust suit against the Ivy League schools—Brown, Columbia, Cornell, Dartmouth, Harvard, Princeton, Yale, and the University of Pennsylvania—as well as the Massachusetts Institute of Technology (M.I.T.), alleging that the nine schools joined together to fix salaries and establish common levels of financial aid for needy students. This system, called "overlapping," began in the late 1950s in an attempt to avoid the need for each school to spend considerable amounts of time and money outbidding the others for students and faculty.

The Ivy League schools quickly settled with the Justice Department, agreeing to act in accordance with a consent decree that prohibits the schools from meeting to fix salaries and set tuition and scholarship levels. The Justice Department, however, did permit the schools to meet to exchange data on "general principles" governing such aid.

M.I.T. at first refused to settle with the Justice Department, instead choosing to argue its case in federal court. M.I.T. insisted that its actions had not constituted an antitrust violation because the school should be governed by laws concerning charitable organizations rather than those which concern businesses. In particular, M.I.T. argued that the practice had the effect of keeping tuition prices down, thus allowing more poor and minority students to attend the university.

The federal district court refused to accept M.I.T.'s argument; however, the federal court of appeals reversed the lower court's ruling and sent the case back to the district court for a fuller hearing of M.I.T.'s position. Despite this success, M.I.T. agreed a few months later to settle with the Justice Department. In the settlement, M.I.T. agreed to follow the 1991 consent decree that the other Ivy League schools had signed. M.I.T. President Charles M. Vest stated that the settlement offered two particular benefits:

First, the Justice Department will dismiss all claims against M.I.T. Second, the settlement establishes guidelines under which colleges and universities can coordinate their financial aid practices to ensure that their limited financial aid funds are awarded to qualified students solely on the basis of need.

Sources: "Court Gives M.I.T. Another Chance in a Federal Price-Fixing Case," *The New York Times* (18 September 1993), 6; Jackson, Robert L., "MIT Agrees to Settle Antitrust Suit, U.S. Says," *The Los Angeles Times* (23 December 1993), A-14.

Vertical Restrictions Restrictions imposed by a manufacturer or supplier of a product or service upon firms that distribute or retail that product are known as **vertical restrictions**. Such restrictions may involve territorial limits on sales or agreements not to deal with competitors of the supplier. Vertical restrictions are subject to §1 of the Sherman Act or §3 of the Clayton Act. The judicial approach to such restrictions varies with the nature of the restriction. Factors that the courts consider include whether a restriction pertains to pricing or to nonprice issues and whether it is a **tying arrangement** (which requires the purchaser of a product to take other products of the supplier as well) or an **exclusive dealing agreement** (which prohibits a dealer from dealing with other suppliers).

vertical restrictions: Restrictions imposed by a manufacturer or supplier on firms that distribute the product.

tying arrangement: Vertical restriction that conditions the sale of one product upon the sale of a different product.

exclusive dealing arrangement: Agreement prohibiting a firm from dealing with other suppliers of a particular product.

Vertical Price Restrictions Attempts by suppliers or manufacturers to control the price at which their products are sold by a retailer or distributor may be illegal under §1 of the Sherman Act. Although a supplier may set the price for its products by retail outlets that it owns, it may not control the price at which independent outlets resell the product. The supplier is free to choose the retailers with which it will deal and to set the prices at which it will sell products to those retailers. It may even suggest a retail price to the independent retailers or print a suggested retail price on the product, as long as the actual choice of the retail price is left to the retailer.

The supplier may not require the retailer to charge a certain price, nor may the retailer agree with the supplier to charge a certain price. Such required prices or agreements involve concerted action, so they are illegal under §1 of the Sherman Act. An example of such an arrangement occurred in *U.S. v. Parke, Davis & Co.*, 362 U.S. 29 (1960). In that case, a drug manufacturer had required both wholesalers and retailers to adhere to a price list in the resale of drugs. The retailers were also required to agree to refrain from advertising prices for the drugs. The Supreme Court held that the arrangement violated §1 of the Sherman Act. More recently, in the *Monsanto Co. v. Spray-Rite Service Corp.*, 465 U.S. 752 (1984), the Supreme Court said that such vertical price arrangements were illegal when "the manufacturer and others had a conscious commitment to a common scheme designed to achieve an unlawful objective."

Some commentators have questioned the application of the per se rule to vertical price restrictions. Those commentators argue that such restrictions

intrabrand competition: Competition among the dealers of a particular brand of a product—such as all the Starbucks Coffee Shops.

interbrand competition: Competition among all the dealers of a product—such as competition among all the coffee shops.

only affect **intrabrand competition** (competition among the sellers of the supplier's products, such as competition among Toyota dealers) and not **interbrand competition** (competition among the products of various suppliers such as competition among all the auto dealers in an area).

It is clear that vertical price restrictions setting a particular price, or setting a minimum price below which the product cannot be sold, are anticompetitive—they substantially limit or totally eliminate competition on price—and are therefore subject to the per se rule. But should vertical maximum price restrictions be treated the same way? Maximum price restrictions do not prevent price competition, because they allow retailers to sell the product at whatever price they choose, as long as it is below the maximum or ceiling price. Sellers are thus free to compete on price, although there may be a tendency for them to sell at the maximum price. If that is the case, then the ceiling price becomes the set price, the effect of the maximum price restriction becomes the same as an agreement to set a particular price, and price competition is eliminated. In *Albrect v. Herald Co.* [390 U.S. 145 (1968)] the Supreme Court held that vertical maximum price restrictions were subject to the per se rule—that is, they were inherently anticompetitive and were automatically illegal. But in recent years that decision has been questioned by commentators, who argue that vertical maximum price restrictions do not always injure competition. In the following case, the U.S. Supreme Court reconsidered the issue of whether vertical maximum price restrictions should be subject to the per se rule or the rule of reason.

STATE OIL COMPANY V. KHAN

522 U.S. 3 (1997)

FACTS

Barkat Khan leased a gas station from State Oil Company; Khan operated the gas station and an attached convenience store. Under the lease agreement, State Oil supplied gasoline to Khan at a price equal to a suggested retail price minus 3.25 cents per gallon. The lease agreement did not require Khan to sell the gasoline at a particular price, but if he charged more per gallon than the retail price suggested by State Oil, he was required to pay any excess charged over the suggested price to State Oil. If Khan sold the gasoline at a retail price lower than the suggested retail price, his profit margin (the 3.25 cents per gallon) was reduced accordingly. After Khan fell behind in his lease payments, he sued State Oil, alleging that the price provisions in the lease were in violation of §1 of the Sherman Act because they prevented him from raising or lowering the retail price he charged for gasoline. State Oil responded that the lease did not prevent Khan from setting or charging different retail prices for the gasoline. The trial court held that the lease's price provisions were not manifestly anticompetitive and did not have a "pernicious effect" on competition. The trial court granted summary judgment for State Oil. Khan appealed to the U.S. Court of Appeals for the Seventh Circuit. The Court of Appeals held that the lease provisions had the effect of fixing a maximum retail price for gasoline, and therefore were per se illegal according to *Albrecht v. Herald Co.* [390 U.S. 145 (1968)]. Although the Court of Appeals noted that *Albrecht* had been criticized, it felt constrained to follow the precedent. State Oil then appealed to the U.S. Supreme Court.

DECISION

The Supreme Court, in a unanimous opinion written by Justice O'Connor, noted that there was a substantial body of academic studies indicating that vertical maximum price agreements could have procompetitive effects. The Court had earlier held that vertical territorial restrictions and other nonprice restrictions should be subject to the rule of reason rather than the per se rule [*Business Electronics Corp. v. Sharp Electronics Corp.*, 485 U.S. 717 (1988) and *Continental T.V., Inc. v. GTE Sylvania Inc.*, 433 U.S. 36 (1977)]. It is true that vertical maximum price restrictions may interfere with a retailer's freedom to set prices and may have an impact on competition, but they may also prevent dominant or monopolist–dealers from exercising market power to the detriment of competition. In short, there is not a sufficient economic justification for holding that vertical maximum price agreements should be subject to the per se rule. The Court emphasized that it was not saying that all vertical maximum price restrictions were legal, but only that such agreements or restrictions should be analyzed under the rule of reason. In other words, the legality of vertical maximum price restrictions should depend upon their effects on competition—if they unreasonably affect or restrain competition, they will be illegal under the rule of reason.

The Supreme Court therefore overruled *Albrecht v. Herald Co.*, and reversed the decision of the Court of Appeals in this case. It remanded the case to the lower court for reconsideration in light of the Supreme Court decision.

CASE QUESTIONS

1. How does a vertical price restriction or agreement differ from a horizontal price restriction or agreement?
2. How can a vertical maximum price agreement serve to promote competition? How could such an agreement harm competition?
3. What is the rationale for the per se rule? Why should the per se rule be applied to horizontal price agreements?
4. Are all vertical price restrictions subject to the rule of reason or the per se rule? Explain your answer.

Vertical Nonprice Restrictions

Restrictions on Sales Efforts Vertical nonprice restrictions generally pertain to the right of a retailer or distributor to sell in particular areas or to particular customers. These restrictions usually involve the designation of certain retailers as the exclusive supplier of a given product in a particular geographic area. These restrictions benefit the retailer by giving it market power in the particular product market through its status as a sole supplier. The manufacturer or distributor benefits by ensuring that all its retailers will not compete with each other.

Vertical nonprice restrictions affect both interbrand and intrabrand competition. The restrictions generally limit the source of supply for the manufacturer's product in a given area, and they reduce or eliminate intrabrand competition. However, when a number of other firms manufacture and sell similar products, the restrictions may actually enhance interbrand competition. (Recall that this was also the justification for the restrictions on the members in the *Topco* case.) On the other hand, where only one or two firms manufacture and sell the product, any restrictions on intrabrand competition may also reduce interbrand competition.

Because the effects of vertical nonprice restrictions depend on the conditions in the particular industry, a court determining the legality of such restrictions must consider their actual effects on competition in that industry. In *Continental T.V., Inc. v. GTE Sylvania* [433 U.S. 36 (1977)], and *Business Electronics Corp. v. Sharp Electronics Corp.* [485 U.S. 717 (1988)], the Supreme Court ruled that vertical, nonprice restrictions were subject to the rule of reason.

As a result, a court must now consider the actual effects that intrabrand restrictions have upon interbrand competition.

Exclusive Dealing Requirements Vertical nonprice restrictions can also take the form of *exclusive dealing contracts* or *requirements contracts*. These agreements require that a retailer deal only with a certain manufacturer or require a customer to purchase its supply of a particular product from a particular manufacturer or supplier. Exclusive dealing or requirement contracts benefit the retailer by ensuring a stable source of supply of a product; the manufacturer benefits because it has a guaranteed market for its product, and it can be certain that the retailer will devote its efforts to selling the manufacturer's product rather than that of a competitor.

Exclusive dealing or requirement contracts are subject to §1 of the Sherman Act and §3 of the Clayton Act if they involve goods or commodities. When such contracts only involve a service, such as maintenance work or advertising, they are subject only to §1 of the Sherman Act. Section 1 of the Sherman Act prohibits contracts, combinations, or conspiracies in restraint of trade; it applies to any exclusive dealing requirement *in or affecting commerce* when actual harm to competition can be shown. Section 3 of the Clayton Act, on the other hand, applies only to sales, leases, or contracts of sale involving goods or commodities *actually in interstate commerce*. Section 3 also provides that such arrangements are illegal if their effect may be to lessen competition substantially. Thus, a showing of probable harm to competition, as opposed to having to show actual harm, suffices to invalidate such arrangements.

In determining the legality of exclusive dealing or requirements contracts, a court must consider their effect upon competition, requiring a definition of both the relevant product market and the geographic market. The approach is similar to that involving a vertical merger under §7 of the Clayton Act because the degree of control over the customer acquired by the seller through such contracts has an effect on competition similar to that resulting from a vertical merger.

Because the judicial analysis of exclusive dealing or requirements contracts involves consideration of the effect of the arrangement upon competition, courts use the rule of reason approach. Early court decisions based on §3 of the Clayton Act held that such arrangements were illegal when they involved a substantial volume of commerce, regardless of their actual or probable effects on competition. However, in *Tampa Electric v. Nashville Coal* [365 U.S. 320 (1961)], the Supreme Court held that the effect of the arrangement on competition in the relevant market must be considered along with the volume of commerce affected. Today, such arrangements are illegal only if they foreclose competition in a substantial share of the relevant market. For example, if a customer accounting for 30 percent of the purchases of specialized machine tools agreed to use only the products of a leading machine tool manufacturer having 50 percent of the market, other manufacturers would be denied access to a substantial share of the market for machine tools and would be less able to compete with the dominant firm. Because the exclusive dealing arrangement between the customer and the dominant firm substantially reduces competition in the machine tool market, it would likely be illegal.

Tying Arrangements The supplier of a particular product or service may condition the sale of that product upon the purchaser taking a different product as well. For example, the supplier of a fax machine may require that its customers agree to use only its brand of paper in the fax machine. Such agreements "tie" the sale of one product (the fax machine) to the sale of another product (the paper) and, hence, are known as *tying arrangements*. A manufacturer's requirement that customers use only its own products for maintenance and servicing would also be a tying arrangement. The sale of products that are normally sold together or used together, such as the sale of both a left shoe and a right shoe in a pair or the sale of an engine and a set of tires as part of an automobile, are not considered by the courts to be tying arrangements.

Tying arrangements are only practical when one of the supplier's products is highly desirable or when the supplier has some market power with regard to that product. If no one wishes to buy the fax machine, then tying the purchase of paper to the purchase of the fax machine is irrelevant. However, if the supplier of the machine is the sole supplier or the machine is superior to others, then a customer desiring to purchase the fax machine will probably agree to purchase the paper as well, even though the paper may be inferior or overpriced compared with other brands. Tying arrangements often reflect an attempt by the supplier to extend its market power with respect to one product (the *tying product*—the fax machine) to another product in which it does not have such market power (the *tied product*—the paper).

In the *U.S. v. Microsoft* case, the U.S. Justice Department alleged that Microsoft was trying to use its market dominance in operating systems (through its Windows products) to help its Internet browser (Internet Explorer) gain market share against Netscape's Navigator. Microsoft required that personal computer (PC) manufacturers who wished to install Windows on the PCs they sold must also install Internet Explorer and must not feature any other program icon on the same screens as Microsoft Windows and Internet Explorer. Because the PC manufacturers wanted to include Windows, they were forced to take Internet Explorer over Navigator, even if Navigator may have been a superior product. (Recall that Microsoft was charged with violations of §1 and §2 of the Sherman Act—restraining competition and monopolizing.)

Tying arrangements are an attempt to give the tied product an advantage that is unrelated to the qualities of that product itself. A court determining the legality of such an arrangement must consider the effects of the arrangement upon competition in the market for the tied product. Both §1 of the Sherman Act and §3 of the Clayton Act apply when the arrangement involves goods or commodities; however, only §1 of the Sherman Act applies when the arrangement involves services. If the supplier is dominant in the tying product market or possesses a legal monopoly over that product because of a patent or copyright, the use of a tying arrangement could also be challenged under §2 of the Sherman Act as an attempt to extend monopoly power into the tied product market, as in the Microsoft case.

Section 3 of the Clayton Act requires that the tying arrangement involve the sale or lease of goods or commodities involved and that the transaction actually be involved in interstate commerce. Section 1 of the Sherman Act applies to any contract in restraint of trade or affecting interstate commerce. Whereas §1 requires that actual harm to competition result from the restrictive arrangement, §3 only requires the showing of probable substantial lessening of competition. Despite these differences in the statutory provisions, the judicial approach to tying arrangements is similar under either provision.

Court decisions involving tying arrangements have found such arrangements to be illegal per se when the supplier has sufficient power in the tying product market to restrain competition in the tied product market appreciably and the amount of commerce involved is "not insubstantial." However, the application of the per se rule to tying arrangements is not like its application in other situations because it *does* require the court to consider the effects of the arrangement upon competition in the tied product market, Because of this requirement, the judicial approach to tying arrangements really resembles the rule of reason approach, despite its judicial characterization as a per se approach. Tying arrangements are not automatically illegal; they will be held illegal only if they substantially restrict competition in the tied product market.

A court considering the legality of a tying arrangement must first determine whether two separate and distinct products—the tying product and the tied product—are involved. If so, then the court must consider whether the supplier possesses market power in the tying product market. This market power may be due to the supplier's dominance in the market, to the possession of exclusive rights because of a patent or copyright, or to the uniqueness of the product offered. If the supplier is found to have market power in the tying product market, the court must then determine whether linking that market power to the tied product has the effect of substantially lessening or restricting competition in the tied product market. When the effect is to reduce competition substantially, the tying arrangement is illegal if it involves a "not insubstantial" amount of commerce.

Because patents, copyrights, and trademarks create legal monopolies, they confer substantial market power to the firm holding the patent or copyright. Any attempt to tie the sale of a different product to the sale of the patented, copyrighted, or trademarked product in a tying arrangement will likely be illegal because the arrangement will probably substantially lessen competition in the tied product market.

A number of tying arrangement cases have involved franchise agreements. The company granting the franchise—the franchisor—agrees to allow the franchisee to use its particular system of doing business, to market products under the franchisor's well-recognized trademark and to benefit from the franchisor's promotional efforts in return for the payment of a franchise fee. As a condition for being granted the franchise, the franchisee may also be required to purchase supplies from the franchisor. As a general rule, the courts have allowed such arrangements when the supplies tied to the franchise are reasonably related to the identity or the quality of the franchise's characteristic products. For example, a fried chicken company's franchisee may be required to purchase from the franchisor the special blend of "herbs and spices," used in cooking the chicken. By the same token, a Baskin-Robbins ice cream franchisee can be required to purchase its ice cream from Baskin-Robbins. However, when the tied product is not so related, such as paper napkins or drinking straws, then tying the purchase of those items to the sale of the franchise may be illegal.

In the case of *Jefferson Parish Hospital Dist. No. 2 v. Hyde*, 466 U.S. 2 (1984), the Supreme Court considered the legality of a hospital's requirement that patients undergoing surgery at the hospital use a particular group of anesthesiologists. The Court held that the requirement was a tying arrangement. As to its legality under §1 of the Sherman Act, the Court stated:

> Tying arrangements need only be condemned if they restrain competition on the merits by forcing purchases that would not otherwise be made. . . . It is

> safe to assume that every patient undergoing a surgical operation needs the services of an anesthesiologist; at least this record contains no evidence that the hospital "forced" any such services on unwilling patients. . . . Petitioners' [the hospital's] closed policy may raise questions of medical ethics, and may have inconvenienced some patients who would prefer to have their anesthesia administered by someone other than a member of [the required group] . . . , but it does not have the obviously unreasonable impact on purchasers that has characterized the tying arrangements that this court has branded unlawful. There is no evidence that the price, the quality, or the supply or demand for either the "tying product" or the "tied product" involved in this case has been adversely affected . . . by the hospital's requirement

PRICE DISCRIMINATION

price discrimination: Charging different customers different prices for the same product.

Price discrimination is simply the charging of different prices to different customers for the same product. When price discrimination occurs in interstate commerce and its effects are "substantially to lessen competition or tend to create a monopoly . . . or to injure, destroy, or prevent competition," it is illegal under the Robinson-Patman Act. The Robinson-Patman Act is actually §2 of the Clayton Act, although most commentators refer to the prohibitions against price discrimination as the Robinson-Patman Act rather than §2 of the Clayton Act. It was passed in 1936 to strengthen the Clayton Act prohibitions against price discrimination.

The Robinson-Patman Act, passed during the Great Depression, reflects a concern that large retail chains could use the leverage of their purchasing power to extract price concessions from their suppliers. With those price concessions, the chains would have a significant competitive advantage over smaller, independent retailers and could eventually drive them out of business. Congress therefore sought to prohibit sellers from discriminating in price among customers when the effect of such discrimination would be detrimental to competition.

The Robinson-Patman Act reflects a strong emphasis on the social and political concerns of antitrust law rather than on the economic concerns—the act's primary purpose appears to be the protection of competitors rather than the protection of competition. Because the act's focus conflicts with the current emphasis on economic concerns, the antitrust enforcement authorities have not actively enforced the price discrimination provisions since the late 1960s; the courts, reflecting the economic and political climate, have also become less concerned about protecting competitors and have focused more on protecting competition. Most cases brought under the Robinson-Patman Act recently have been private civil actions by competitors of the price discounters. For example, the owners of small, independent pharmacies in Arkansas sued Wal-Mart, alleging that Wal-Mart's high discounts on prescription drugs substantially lessened competition; the trial court upheld their complaint as valid, but it was dismissed on appeal [*Wal-Mart Stores, Inc. v. American Drugs, Inc.*, 319 Ark. 214, 891 S.W.2d 30 (Ark. Sup. Ct. 1995)]. In *Brooke Group Ltd., v. Brown & Williamson Tobacco Corp.* [509 U.S. 209 (1993)], the Supreme Court held that a tobacco company's practice of granting discriminatory price rebates based on volume of purchases of generic brand cigarettes did discriminate against some customers but did not injure competition and therefore did not violate the Robinson-Patman Act.

PRICE DISCRIMINATION UNDER THE ROBINSON-PATMAN ACT

Section 2(a) of the Robinson-Patman Act prohibits:

> discrimination in price between purchasers of commodities of like grade and quality, where either or any purchasers involved in such discrimination are in commerce . . . where the effect of such discrimination may be to substantially lessen competition or tend to create a monopoly in any line of commerce, or to injure, destroy, or prevent competition with any person who either grants or receives the benefit of such discrimination, or with the customers of either. . . .

From the wording of §2(a), we can see that the protection of the act extends not only to firms in competition with the firm granting the discriminatory price (referred to as *primary competitive effects*), but also to firms in competition with customers who receive the discriminatory price (*secondary competitive effects*), and even to firms in competition with the customers of the firms that receive the discriminatory price (*tertiary competitive effects*). For example, if a pharmaceutical manufacturer grants substantial price discounts to a few wholesalers, it may affect competition with other drug manufacturers who do not offer such discounts (primary competition). The drug wholesaler that receives the discounts may have a competitive advantage over other wholesalers that do not receive discounts (secondary competition); and if the wholesaler receiving the discounts passes them along to its pharmacy customers, other pharmacies that compete with those customers may also be at a competitive disadvantage (tertiary competition). When the price discrimination has the effect of substantially lessening any one of these forms of competition, it may be illegal.

Defenses to Price Discrimination Price discrimination may not be illegal if it falls under any of the defenses provided in §2(a) and (b) of the act. When the price differences apply to perishable or obsolete items or when they reflect actual differences in cost due to different methods of manufacture or delivery or because of the volume purchase, they are legal under §2(a). When a discriminatory price is offered by a seller in a good-faith attempt to meet the price of a competitor, it is legal under §2(b). If the price discrimination is only temporary and has no significant effect on competition, it is also legal under the Act.

OTHER PROVISIONS OF THE ROBINSON-PATMAN ACT

Section 2(c), (d), and (e) of the Robinson-Patman Act prohibit other potential abuses by large retail chains. Section 2(c) prohibits granting any allowance or discount as a commission or other compensation for promotional or brokerage services in connection with the sale of a product unless the services are actually performed by the firm receiving the allowance or discount. For example, a small company that manufactures toys may sell its products through a broker, who arranges the sale of the products to retailers and promotes and distributes the product for the manufacturer. In return for these services, the manufacturer pays the broker a commission on sales. If the manufacturer decides to bypass the broker and sell directly to a large retail chain ("eliminate the middleman"), the manufacturer saves the cost of the broker's commission. In this situation, the manufacturer may grant the retail chain a discount reflecting its savings on the broker's commission only if the retail chain performs the distribution and promotion services normally performed by the broker. To grant the retail chain a discount when it does not actually perform those services would violate §2(c)

Sections 2(d) and (e) prohibit paying promotional fees or allowances or furnishing promotional facilities or services only to some customers. Such fees, allowances, facilities, or services must be provided to all customers on proportionately equal terms. For example, if a food processing company pays a large supermarket chain for advertising the processor's products but does not pay for advertising by small, independent grocers, the food processor violates §2(d). Similarly, when a company making sewing patterns provides free display racks and cabinets to large department stores but requires small fabric stores to purchase the equipment, it violates §2(e).

Violations of §§2(c), (d), and (e) are per se offenses, which make the defenses under §§2(a) and (b) unavailable. In other words, when allowances, facilities, or services furnished to some customers are not available to all customers on a proportionate basis, or when allowances are granted for services not actually performed, the Act is violated, and no defenses are available. In contrast, §2(a) can only be violated when the effect of the price discrimination is to lessen competition substantially, which is a rule of reason approach.

Section 2(f) of the Act makes it a violation for a firm to "knowingly induce or receive" a discriminatory price that is prohibited by §2. Unlike the other provisions of the Act, which are directed against the firm engaging in price discrimination, §2(f) is aimed at the customer who receives the discriminatory price. In the case of *Great Atlantic & Pacific Tea Company, Inc. v. Federal Trade Commission* [440 U.S. 69 (1979)], the Supreme Court held that a customer who knowingly receives a discriminatory price that was granted by a supplier who was under the mistaken impression that the price was necessary to meet competition did not violate §2(f). The supplier had a good faith belief that the price was necessary to meet competition, so granting the discriminatory price was protected under §2(b). Because granting the price did not violate §2(a), the customer receiving the price was not in violation of §2(f).

SECTION 5 OF THE FEDERAL TRADE COMMISSION ACT

In addition to the primary antitrust provisions of the Sherman Act and Clayton Act, §5 of the Federal Trade Commission Act has also been used to attack anticompetitive business practices. Section 5 provides that "unfair methods of competition in or affecting commerce and unfair or deceptive acts or practices in or affecting commerce, are hereby declared unlawful." The Federal Trade Commission Act does not define the terms "unfair methods of competition" or "unfair or deceptive acts or practices." Congress wanted to avoid listing specific practices because such a list would have to be updated continually to include new practices as they appeared; Congress therefore empowered the FTC to determine which practices violated §5. The FTC, through its expertise, can adapt §5 to changing business practices.

Given the general wording of §5, its potential reach is very broad. The FTC has generally used §5 to attack deceptive advertising or high-pressure sales practices. The Supreme Court held, in *Federal Trade Commission v. Cement Institute* [333 U.S. 683 (1948)], that §5 could be applied to conduct that the

FTC has determined to be injurious to competition even though the conduct does not violate other antitrust laws.

EXEMPTIONS FROM ANTITRUST

The federal antitrust laws extend to all activities in or affecting interstate commerce; however, several exceptions have been legislatively or judicially created.

Agricultural marketing cooperatives are exempted from the antitrust laws by the *Capper-Volstead Act*, and the *Webb-Pomerene Act* allows U.S. firms to join together for the purpose of export trade. The results of such joint export activity must not, however, restrict trade within the United States or injure U.S. firms that do not join the concerted export activity. The *Foreign Trade Antitrust Improvements Act* grants federal courts jurisdiction over anticompetitive export conduct only when such conduct has a direct, substantial, and reasonably foreseeable effect on trade or commerce within the United States or on import trade or commerce. The *National Cooperative Research Act* of 1984, amended in 1991, provides that contracts among firms to carry out joint research activities are not per se illegal, and in suits involving such contracts, no triple damages can be recovered against the joint research ventures. The *Local Government Antitrust Act* of 1984 provides municipalities with immunity from any antitrust damage liability for "any official action directed by a local government, or official or employee thereof acting in an official capacity."

Bona fide labor union activities are also exempted from antitrust sanctions. Section 6 of the Clayton Act, which states that labor is not an article of commerce, was an early legislative attempt to exempt labor activities from the antitrust laws. It was not until the Supreme Court decision in *U.S. v. Hutcheson* [312 U.S. 219 (1941)], however, that conventional labor activity by a labor organization acting alone was held to be immune from antitrust law. The Supreme Court has held that a union may make agreements with a group of employers as long as the subject matter of the agreement is directly related to terms or conditions of employment and the agreement occurs within the context of a bona fide collective bargaining relationship. On the other hand, if unions join employers' groups in agreements about nonlabor matters, such as prices, or if unions make agreements with one set of employers to demand concessions from a different set of employers, such agreements are not protected by the labor exemption. The Supreme Court has also consistently held that professional baseball is not "commerce" within the meaning of the antitrust laws and is therefore exempted from them (although the recent baseball strike resulted in legislation eliminating baseball's exemption as it applies to labor relations matters); other professional sports do not enjoy baseball's antitrust immunity.

state action doctrine: An exemption from the antitrust laws when government regulation requires the conduct in question.

Perhaps the broadest area of exemption falls under the **state action doctrine**, which deals with the anticompetitive effects of government regulation. Regulatory schemes may require some businesses to engage in conduct that is anticompetitive. For example, agricultural marketing regulations may limit the size of farmers' crops and may set the prices at which those crops can be sold. Such an arrangement, created by the farmers on their own, could violate §1 of the Sherman Act; however, in *Parker v. Brown* [317 U.S. 341 (1943)], the Supreme Court held that such conduct is exempt from the antitrust laws when it is pursuant to a valid government regulatory scheme. Subsequent decisions have narrowed and more clearly defined the state action doctrine exemption: the government (whether state, local, or federal) must play an active role in the regulatory scheme, and the anticompetitive conduct *must* be required by the regulatory scheme in order to be exempt from the antitrust laws.

PATENTS, COPYRIGHTS, AND ANTITRUST

Patents and copyrights are legally granted monopolies for a limited period for the production, reproduction, distribution, or use of the patented or copyrighted item. They give the developing inventors or artists protection from competition, for a limited time, so they can reap the benefits of their efforts. By encouraging invention and artistic creation, patents and copyrights promote the public interest. Therefore, the limited monopoly status that they grant is acceptable even though it may seem inconsistent with the antitrust policy of promoting competition.

Firms or persons that hold patents or copyrights may license others to produce, use, or distribute the protected item. A patent owner may grant a price-restrictive license (which imposes a minimum resale price requirement) only to one other firm; imposing restrictions through licenses on two or more firms creates a concerted price-fixing arrangement and is illegal. Patent licenses may also be used to impose reasonable territorial restrictions upon the licensee's use or distribution of the protected product. However, such restrictions are illegal when their primary purpose is to create a horizontal division of markets among competitors. Firms owning patent rights may not combine their rights or patents with those of competing firms in order to create a "patent pool" cartel, in which the competitors share the patents to the exclusion of all other firms. In addition, tying arrangements that use a patented or copyrighted item as the tying product are illegal.

SUMMARY

Although the antitrust laws are intended to protect and promote competition, the policy behind enforcement efforts has shifted in emphasis from social considerations to economic factors over the years. Courts are less likely to be concerned with protecting competitors and are more likely to analyze the nature of competition in a given industry or market. In monopoly and merger cases, the emphasis on the size of the firms involved (or resulting from the merger) has lessened while the focus on whether they have engaged in, or are likely to engage in, predatory or exclusionary conduct has increased. Horizontal concerted activity such as price fixing, market division, and vertical price restrictions are illegal per se. Vertical, nonprice restrictions, tying arrangements, and price discrimination will be illegal only when they have an unreasonable effect on competition. Recent legislative exemptions to the antitrust laws have allowed firms to act collectively in order to compete more effectively in the international market. Concerted actions affecting competition within the United States are still prohibited.

In addition to government enforcement efforts, firms must also be concerned about the threat of private antitrust actions filed by competitors. It is therefore vital that business managers and executives have an understanding of the antitrust laws and their effect on business.

CHAPTER QUESTIONS

1. Fields Manufacturing Company is the United States' leading producer of machines for manufacturing shoes. A number of different machines are required to complete the various steps of the shoe production process. There are 12 manufacturers of various shoe production machines, but only Fields produces machines for all the steps in the production process. Fields produces almost 70 percent of the machines used by U.S. shoe producers. Its dominant position is due in large part to its engineering and research skills. Fields developed most of the innovations in the manufacturing process. Unlike other manufacturers, Fields will not sell its machines: it leases them to shoe producers instead. The leases are for 10-year periods and cover service and repairs. There are substantial financial penalties for early termination of a lease. The rents charged by Fields for their machines reflect Fields' competitive position—rents are low for machines that are also produced by competitors and high for machines that only Fields produces. Garp Process Company is a small firm attempting to compete with Fields. Garp is having difficulty attracting customers because Fields' leasing system has tied up most of the potential customers. If Garp brings a legal action challenging Fields under §2 of the Sherman Act, who will win the case? If Garp wins, what remedies would it be entitled to? Explain. [*U.S. v. United Shoe Machinery Co.*, 110 F. Supp. 295 (D. Mass) aff'd by 347 U.S. 521 (1954)]
2. The Kansas City Star Publishing Company publishes the only two major daily newspapers in the Kansas City area, the morning *Star* and the afternoon *Times*. The papers are distributed at the retail level by a group of independent distributors to whom Star Publishing awards exclusive distribution routes under one-year contracts. The distributors purchase the papers at wholesale prices from Star Publishing and are free to set their own retail prices. Star Publishing decides to distribute the paper through its own distribution network in order to improve circulation and enhance advertising revenues. Star Publishing announces that it will not renew any distributor contracts when they expire, and it will not sell the papers at wholesale prices anymore. If the distributors, who stand to lose their businesses, file a suit under §2 of the Sherman Act challenging Star Publishing's new policy, who will win the case? Explain. [*Paschall v. Kansas City Star Co.*, 727 F.2d 692 (1984)]
3. Canco is the nation's second largest producer of metal containers, producing 33 percent of all metal containers sold in the United States. The largest can producer has 38 percent of the market, and the third largest producer accounts for 5 percent of the market. The remaining 24 percent of the market is shared among 75 firms. Cans are used for packaging foods, beverages (primarily soda and beer), and other liquids such as motor oil products. Glassco manufactures glass containers and produces 9.6 percent of all the glass containers sold in the United States. It ranks third in the glass container industry. The two largest producers account for 34.2 and 11.6 percent of the market, respectively. Glass containers are used for foods, sauces, baby food, toiletries, and beverages. They have become increasingly popular as nonreturnable packaging for soda and beer. Canco has considered developing its own glass container division, but it decided

to acquire Glassco instead. If the government brings a legal action challenging the Canco–Glassco merger under §7 of the Clayton Act, who will win the case? Explain. [*U.S. v. Continental Can Corp.*, 378 U.S. 441 (1968)]

4. General Motors (GM) is the leading producer of automobiles in the United States. Although there are only three domestic car manufacturers, the auto companies face stiff competition from a number of foreign producers. The U.S. manufacturers dominate the large car market (luxury and full-size models); the foreign producers are superior in the production and sale of compact and subcompact models. Nippon Auto is the largest car producer in Japan. It accounts for the largest segment of the U.S. compact and subcompact car sales. Some Japanese producers are establishing plants in the United States in order to avoid the effects of import quota legislation limiting the importation of foreign cars. Rather than set up its own plant, Nippon agreed with GM to create a jointly owned firm to produce subcompact models in the United States. The newly created firm, General Nippon, Inc., is controlled entirely by the two parent firms, each owning 50 percent of the stock. If the government brings a legal action challenging this joint venture under §7 of the Clayton Act, who will win the case? Explain. [*U.S. v. Penn-Olin Chemical Corp.*, 378 U.S. 158 (1964)]

5. Family Shoe Stores, Inc. is a chain of discount shoe stores that sells low-priced men's, women's, and children's shoes. Family Shoe accounts for 1.2 percent of all shoe sales in the United States, but it is the largest independent chain of shoe stores. Shoes are sold through shoes stores and through shoe departments in department stores. There are approximately 70,000 total retail outlets for shoes, but only 22,000 are classified as shoe stores (which are defined as deriving 50 percent or more of their gross receipts from the sale of shoes). Shoes are produced by almost 970 independent manufacturers. The largest producers account for 24 percent of all shoes produced. These large manufacturers are pursuing a policy of acquiring retail outlets for their shoes. Style-Line Shoe Company is the fourth largest shoe producer, with 4 percent of U.S. shoe production. Style-Line produces high-quality, higher-cost shoes. Style-Line also controls a number of retail shoe outlets, which account for almost 2.7 percent of total shoe sales. Style-Line seeks to acquire Family Shoe Stores, Inc., in order to expand its retail market share. If the government brings a legal action under §7 of the Clayton Act challenging Style-Line's acquisition of Family Shoe Stores, who will win the case? Explain. [*Brown Shoe Co. v. U.S.*, 370 U.S. 294 (1962)]

6. Wilson Corporation is the largest firm selling a general line of sporting goods equipment in the United States. Wilson sells golf clubs; football, basketball, and baseball equipment; sports uniforms; and gym mats. Wilson has annual sales of almost $150 million, and it has 18 percent of the general sporting goods market. Wilson has been seeking to broaden its product line by expanding into other markets such as fishing and gymnastics equipment. Nissen Company is the largest producer of gymnastics equipment in the United States. It has annual sales of $45 million, which account for 26 percent of the gymnastics equipment sold in the United States. There are eight other firms producing gymnastics equipment in the United States, but the top four firms account for 70 percent of all sales. The remaining five firms are small and sell regionally rather than nationally.

Wilson had considered starting its own gymnastics division, but it decides to acquire Nissen instead. If the government brings a legal action challenging the merger, who will win the case? Explain. [*U.S. v. Wilson Sporting Goods Co.*, 288 F. Supp. 543 (1968)]

7. "Holiday" Motels International (HMI) is a firm that grants franchises to persons wishing to operate Holiday Motels. At present, there are four Holiday Motels operating in the Fort Wayne area, but HMI feels that the area could probably support another franchise. After discussing the new franchise with the four existing franchisees, HMI agreed to award it only if none of the existing franchisees objected. They also agreed to give the existing franchisees priority if any of them wished to operate the new franchise. Smith, who is not presently a franchisee, wishes to operate the new franchise. However, one of the existing franchisees has objected, and no franchise has been awarded. If Smith sues under §1 of the Sherman Act, is his suit challenging the refusal to award the franchise likely to be successful? Explain. [*American Motor Inn, Inc. v. Holiday Inns, Inc.*, 521 F.2d 1230 (3rd Cir. 1975)]
8. The *Local Standard* is a daily newspaper published in Syracuse, New York, by Local Publishing Company. The paper is sold by numerous retail outlets and is delivered to homes by paper carriers. The carriers, usually boys and girls, are billed weekly by Local for the papers they deliver. The prices Local charges the carriers are wholesale prices. The carriers charge their customers the "suggested retail price," which is printed on the front page of each paper.
   a. Is the pricing arrangement between Local and the carriers in violation of §1 of the Sherman Act? Why or why not?
   b. Local assigns each carrier a delivery route—a geographic area in which the carrier is the exclusive home-delivery outlet for the *Local Standard*. Is this territorial arrangement legal? Explain your answer.
   c. Local prohibits the carriers from charging a price greater than the suggested retail price, although carriers are free to charge less than the suggested retail price. Carriers who violate this policy have their routes taken away. Is this policy legal under §1? Explain your answer.
9. Local Publishing Company publishes both the *Local Standard*, a morning daily paper, and the *Post Herald*, an afternoon daily. Local requires advertisers wishing to place ads in either paper to purchase advertising space in both. Shaw's Shape-Up, a physical fitness club, wants to advertise in the *Local Standard*, because it reaches a bigger audience than the *Post Herald*. Shaw's feels that ads in the afternoon daily are not cost-effective. Local will only accept Shaw's ad if it appears in both papers. Shaw's files suit challenging Local's advertising policy.
   a. Which provision of the antitrust laws is applicable to the advertising policy? Explain.
   b. What arguments will Local use to support the policy? What arguments will Shaw's use to attack it?
   c. Who will win the case? Explain. [*Times Picayune v. U.S.*, 345 U.S. 594 (1953)]
10. Balkan Burgers, Inc. licenses franchisees to operate Balkan Burger fast-food restaurants. In addition to agreeing to rent the restaurant building from Balkan Burger, Inc., franchisees are required to purchase all kitchen

equipment, paper products, packaging materials, and food products from Balkan Burgers. Balkan Burgers maintains that this requirement is necessary to ensure the quality of the products to preserve Balkan Burgers' reputation and corporate image. Balkan Burgers also prohibits the franchisee from operating any fast-food restaurant other than those licensed by Balkan Burgers. Several franchisees have complained that the prices charged by Balkan Burgers for kitchen equipment and food products are higher than those charged by other suppliers and that Balkan's products are of low quality. These franchises would also like to operate other franchised fast-food restaurants. If they bring a legal action challenging Balkan Burgers' policies, who will win the case? Explain. [*Siegal v. Chicken Delight, Inc.*, 448 F.2d 43 (9th Cir. 1971)]

11. Posner Paving is a small paving contractor that bids on municipal paving jobs in and around Chicago. Its operations are entirely within the state of Illinois. Posner is supplied with asphalt and other paving materials by Bork Products. Bork is a large building materials supply firm that operates throughout the Midwest. Posner has discovered that Bork has been supplying asphalt to the large contractors who work on the interstate highway system in Indiana and Illinois at $250 per truckload while it charges Posner $270 per truckload. Bork sells only in minimum units of at least one truckload, and the costs of delivery per truckload are constant. If Posner brings legal action challenging Bork's pricing policy under the Robinson-Patman Act, is the challenge likely to be successful? Explain. [*Gulf Oil Co. v. Copp Paving Corp.*, 419 U.S. 186 (1974)]
12. The Sullivans desired to purchase a house in Arlington, Virginia. They contacted several lawyers about performing a title search. Each lawyer they contacted informed them that the fee for the search would be the fee set by the minimum-fee schedule of the Virginia State Bar Association. The minimum-fee schedule suggests the minimum fee that Virginia lawyers should charge for various kinds of legal services. Lawyers who wish to practice law in Virginia are required by law to join the Virginia State Bar Association and to abide by the association's Ethical Rules. The Ethical Rules include a prohibition on "habitually charging fees less than those in the minimum-fee schedule." No state laws require adherence to the fee schedule, and the state does not review or approve the fee schedule. The Sullivans have brought a legal action suit against the Virginia State Bar Association, alleging that the minimum fee schedule is illegal under §1 of the Sherman Act. What arguments can each party make to support its case? Who will win? Explain. [*Goldfarb v. Virginia State Bar*, 421 U.S. 773 (1975)]

PRACTICAL EXERCISE

The cold cereal market in the United States is dominated by several large firms. Kellogg, Inc., is the leader, with 35.7 percent of cold cereal sales; General Mills has 26.5 percent, Post Cereal Corp. has 16.4 percent, Quaker Oats has 7.6 percent, Ralcorp (Ralston Purina) has 4.2 percent of sales, private label store brands represent 6.6 percent of sales, and a number of small firms together have 3 percent of sales. Retail prices of cold cereals have been increasing at a rate faster than the cost of living, despite falling prices for the main ingredients of the cereals. Major cereal producers compete vigorously on price through discounts, coupons, and promotions; sales of lower-priced generic and private label cereals have also increased significantly over the past decade. Ralcorp, as the number 5 producer, has had trouble maintaining its profit margin because of increasing price competition with the other major firms. Ralcorp agrees to sell its major cereal brands (Chex, Cookie Crisp, Almond Delight, and the ChexMix snacks) to General Mills; Ralcorp will continue to produce cereals for various stores to sell under private label brands. If the sale goes through, General Mills will have 30.7 percent of the market. General Mills officials claim that they will be able to compete more effectively with Kellogg after the sale. Government officials are concerned that the sale will increase concentration in an already-concentrated market marked by conscious parallelism and steadily increasing retail prices.

You are an industry analyst with a large brokerage firm; you have been asked to consider whether the Justice Department will allow General Mills to purchase Ralcorp's main cereal brands or if it will take action to prevent the sale. Prepare a memo, considering the following questions:

1. How would you characterize the nature of competition that presently exists in the industry?
2. What will be the probable effect of the sale on competition in the industry?
3. How will the sale likely affect consumers?
4. What justifications can be offered for the sale—are there any benefits that will result from it? What potential harm may result?
5. Under which antitrust law(s) could a legal challenge to the sale be filed?
6. What would be the probable result of a legal challenge to the sale—would the Justice Department be able to prevent the sale? Be sure to explain your conclusions and to support them with references to cases and legislation wherever possible.

FURTHER INFORMATION

www.usdoj.gov/atr/
The U.S. Justice Department Antitrust Division.

www.ftc.gov/ftc/antitrust.htm
The Federal Trade Commission Antitrust/Competition Bureau.

www.usdoj.gov/atr/cases/ms_exhibits.htm
The U.S. Department of Justice exhibits in the Microsoft trial.

www.abanet.org/antitrust/home.html
The American Bar Association Antitrust Law Section.

www.europa.eu.int/comm/dg04/index_en.htm
The Directorate on Competition of the Commission of the European Union.

CHAPTER 17

LEGAL RIGHTS OF CONSUMERS, DEBTORS, AND CREDITORS

LEARNING OBJECTIVES

After you have read this chapter, you should be able to:

1. Explain the various laws that protect consumers.
2. Describe how to perfect a security interest.
3. Understand the differences among Chapter 7, Chapter 11, and Chapter 13 bankruptcy.
4. Determine how to collect on a bad debt.

CHAPTER OUTLINE

I. Consumer-Related Issues

II. Disclosing Credit Costs

III. After-Judgment Remedies

IV. Secured Transactions

V. Bankruptcy

Your business sells merchandise on credit and is now having problems collecting the money that is owed. What do you need to know about debtor/creditor law in order to get your money back? The "Practical Exercise" at the end of the chapter will explore this issue in more detail.

INTRODUCTION

Under the common law, consumers were responsible to watch out for their own interests. In general, laws did not protect consumers. The prevailing rule was *caveat emptor*, "let the buyer beware." Why did such a rule exist? This rule originated in an agrarian society in which buyers and sellers knew each other—they were probably neighbors—and products were few and simple. Further, since most products were bought with cash or bartered for, buyers had little need for borrowing money.

The industrial age introduced complex products, processes, and the need for borrowed capital. Manufacturers, far removed from consumers, now build products that wholesalers and retailers sell. Today, it is rare when consumers buy products directly from manufacturers. It is common, moreover, for consumers to borrow money to pay for products.

The stark differences between a commercial transaction in an agrarian society and a commercial transaction in an industrial society gave impetus to the *consumer's movement* in the 1960s. The consumer's movement of the 1960s and 1970s resulted in several pieces of federal legislation aimed at protecting consumers from unscrupulous or unfair business practices. These pieces of legislation were also aimed at giving the consumer enough information to make an informed buying decision.

First, in 1968 Congress passed the *Consumer Credit Protection Act*. This act is very comprehensive and includes the *Equal Credit Opportunity Act*, *Truth in Lending Act*, *Fair Credit Billing Act*, *Fair Debt Collection Practices Act*, *Fair Credit Reporting Act*, and the *Consumer Leasing Act*. Next, in 1972, Congress passed the *Consumer Product Safety Act*, which created the *Consumer Product Safety Commission* (*CPSC*). This commission regulates product safety by recalling unsafe products and banning hazardous products. The CPSC will be discussed in more detail in Chapter 18.

Besides these consumer protection laws, there are also state laws that detail how *collateral* can be used to secure a loan. Collateral is the property that a debtor agrees to give the creditor if the debtor fails to pay the debt in full.

Finally, even the best of intentions can go awry when it comes to debtor/creditor relations. In order to avoid the debtors' prisons of the past, Congress has established federal bankruptcy laws. In order to understand how these laws affect business, it is necessary to look at the rights of consumers as well as the rights of business. This chapter will take the reader through the consumer credit process, starting with applying for credit and ending with bankruptcy.

CONSUMER-RELATED ISSUES

Compiling a credit history is very important. However, as you may know, a typical reason for the denial of credit is the lack of a credit history. Indeed, it is difficult to be able to establish credit for the first time.

Applying for credit (borrowing) usually requires filling out a credit application. Credit applications ask a number of questions about the applicant's financial history, including where you work, how much you earn, what type of property you own, and how much you owe to others. The Equal Credit Opportunity Act (ECOA) prohibits creditors from discriminating based on sex, marital status, race, color, religion, national origin, and age, although these types of questions are sometimes asked on the application form. The ECOA also prohibits discrimination against persons who receive public assistance or those who exercise their rights under ECOA. If a person intends to use a spouse's income to qualify for the loan, the creditor can request the spouse's financial information. As the article "Lender Settles Suit over Loans to Poor" suggests, states can also use the ECOA to curb unscrupulous lending practices.

Lender Settles Suit Over Loans to Poor

The State Law Department and the State Banking Department have worked out their differences over how to rein in the nation's largest home equity lender, which they had both accused of preying on minority neighborhoods, officials of both agencies said yesterday.

The agreement between the two departments over the handling of Delta Funding Corporation of Woodbury, L.I., a company that has annually loaned more than $1 billion a year in 21 states, including New York, allows for a resurrection of a settlement with the State Law Department that was scuttled after Delta negotiated a separate deal with the Banking Department in August.

The new deal doubles from $6 to $12 million the monetary relief provided in the original agreement negotiated, under threat of a lawsuit, by the State Law Department in June. It also stiffens the terms of injunctive relief that were required by the State Banking Department in its August agreement with Delta.

Both agencies had accused Delta of preying upon the poor by using high pressure sales tactics to get residents of minority neighborhoods to purchase high cost loans that gave them little additional benefit and sometimes left them without enough income to live on.

The State Law Department's case was prosecuted by its Civil Rights Bureau, which had claimed that under the federal Equal Credit Opportunity Act, Delta engaged in abusive lending practices in minority neighborhoods in Brooklyn and Queens. The Banking Department, which has regulatory authority over Delta, in contrast, had focused upon alleged violations of the State banking laws and regulations.

Previously, Mr. Spitzer had criticized the Banking Department's August settlement with Delta as "a Swiss cheese agreement." But yesterday, in an interview, Mr. Spitzer said the new deal provided sufficient injunctive protections for Delta's customers.

From the Banking Department's side, its Acting Superintendent Elizabeth McCaul said the Department was "proud to have won $12 million in restitution" for victims of Delta's lending schemes.

Andrew Celli, the head of the Law Department's Civil Rights Bureau, said the agreement contained a number of important injunctive provisions to curb excesses in the way Delta had done business in New York:

- To prevent the refinancing of outstanding loans in a manner that resulted in increased monthly payments that were completely disproportionate to the amount of fresh cash supplied to the borrower, Delta has accepted a mathematical formula that will tie the amount of increase in monthly payments it may charge to the amount of added cash its customers get in their new loan.

- The deal sets a schedule that details how much disposable income families must be left with, depending upon their size, after entering into a loan agreement with Delta.

- The agreement also bars in some instances, and otherwise severely restricts, Delta's past practice of making incentive payments to mortgage brokers who get customers to agree to loans at higher rates than it would normally charge given the customers' financial circumstances.

State officials were not certain how many outstanding loans Delta has in New York, but in 1997 the company made slightly more than 1,000 loans, mostly in Brooklyn and Queens.

Restitution to Be Paid

Those contracts will not be abrogated under the deal, but the $12 million in restitution will be applied as credit to bring down the level of future payments, thus relieving Delta customers of the burden caused by the most onerous provisions of their loans, Mr. Celli said.

In addition, he said, some provisions in existing loans will no longer be enforceable in certain circumstances. For instance, some Delta loans provided that when a borrower missed a payment, the interest rate would escalate to the legal limit, 24 percent. Delta will no longer be able to take that charge where a borrower had to pay more than 8 percent of the loan in fees, Mr. Celli said.

The new agreement settles a suit the State Law Department filed in the Eastern District of New York in August after Delta pulled out of its earlier deal with the Banking Department.

The Law Department also had to give up a provision for a court appointed monitor, which Delta had originally accepted in its June deal. The new agreement, however, gives the Law Department broad access to Delta's financial records and other documents.

After filling out the credit application, a creditor will often do a *credit check*. Instead of personally checking all the public records, the creditor will usually request a credit report from a **credit bureau** or a *credit reporting bureau*. Credit bureaus compile many types of information, often using public documents like bankruptcies, lawsuits, and judgments, to assess a person's *creditworthiness*. The information kept by credit bureaus is generally confined to financial information. A credit reporting bureau prepares reports at the request of individuals like landlords, insurance companies, employers, and, to a lesser extent, creditors. The credit reporting bureau conducts an investigation and talks to family, friends, and acquaintances. If an account has been turned over to a collection agency, it is usually noted on the credit history.

credit bureau: A private business that compiles information on consumers' creditworthiness and provides this information to lenders.

Several problems are associated with credit reports. For example, sometimes they contain inaccurate, misleading, or irrelevant information. Also, people can obtain the report who do not have a legitimate interest in the information.

Before 1971, consumers did not have the right to look at their credit histories. In 1971 the Fair Credit Reporting Act (FCRA) was added to the Consumer Credit Protection Act. The FCRA requires credit bureaus to maintain accurate information. Adverse information can only be used for seven years; after seven years, it must be purged. Bankruptcy information can only remain on the record for 10 years. Investigative reports must purge the information on a person's character, living arrangements, and other personal attributes every three months unless it is reverified. Reports can only be furnished for credit, insurance, employment, the gaining of a government license or benefit, or any legitimate business need. A consumer must be notified, in advance, if an investigative report has been ordered. A creditor is required to furnish the name and address of the credit bureau if a credit report is used in rejecting credit or insurance. In 1997, the FCRA was amended to give consumers better rights when a consumer report was ordered in connection with some type of employment decision. Now, if an employer wants to order a credit report, the employee (or applicant) must receive notice of the request and give permission, in writing. Before pulling the report, the employer must also tell employees that if they are not hired or are terminated based on what is contained in the report, they have a right to see the report. The employer also needs to provide employees with a copy of the Federal Trade Commission's (FTC's) summary of rights under the FCRA. If, because of the report, an adverse decision is made, the employer needs to provide employees with the name and address of the credit bureau providing the report and inform them of their right to dispute information in the report. If the employer does not follow these rules, the employer may be liable for damages.

In other cases, a consumer does not have a right to see his or her actual credit report. However, the consumer is entitled to receive, free of charge and within 30 days of the rejection, a summary of the nature of the report, which includes the nature and substance of the information and source and names of those who have used the report over the past six months. He or she may also, upon payment of a small fee, see a summary of the file at any time. If the information is inaccurate or unverified, the consumer has a right to have it

FROM THE DESK OF

Laura Lawyer

To: Students

From: Your Lawyer

The FTC Bureau of Consumer Protection suggests that you can find Credit Reporting Agencies under "credit" in the Yellow Pages. It also lists the names and addresses of the three major national credit bureaus:

Equifax, P.O. Box 740241, Atlanta, GA 30374-0241; (800) 685-1111

Experian (formerly TRW), P.O. Box 949, Allen, TX 75013; (888)EXPERIAN (397-3742)

Trans Union, 760 West Sproul Road, P.O. Box 390, Springfield, PA 19064-0390; (800) 916-8800.

removed from the report. If the credit bureau and consumer dispute the information, the consumer is entitled to file a 100-word rebuttal statement to be included in the credit report.

Since consumers are entitled to have correct information in their credit reports, credit agencies are responsible for investigating and correcting a consumer's file if the report is erroneous. As the next case indicates, sometimes this correction does not occur quickly.

STEVENSON V. TRW, INC.

987 F.2d 288 (5th Cir. 1993).

FACTS

In 1989, John Stevenson, a 78-year-old real estate and securities investor, began to receive numerous phone calls from bill collectors. After obtaining a copy of his credit report from TRW, he discovered many errors. Several of the accounts belonged to Mr. Stevenson's estranged son, John Stevenson, Jr. and others belonged to another John Stevenson. In all, Mr. Stevenson disputed 16 accounts, seven inquiries, as well as much of the identifying information. On October 6, 1989, Mr. Stevenson wrote TRW and requested that his report be corrected. On November 1, 1989, TRW asked its subscribers for reverification of the information. TRW did not contact subscribers by telephone; rather it relied only on written responses. On November 11, TRW removed several items in dispute and on February 9, 1990, TRW completed its investigation and claimed that all negative information was removed. After this time, inaccurate information continued to reappear on Mr. Stevenson's account, and TRW did not delete all the negative information. During this time period, Mr. Stevenson had to explain his credit predicament a number of times and was denied credit three times based on the inaccurate report. The district court found in favor of Stevenson. He was awarded $1 for libel, $30,000 in actual damages, $20,700 attorneys' fees, and $100,000 in punitive damages. TRW appealed.

DECISION

Judge Williams wrote the opinion of the court. The question for the Court of Appeals was whether TRW negligently and willfully violated the FCRA by failing to promptly delete inaccurate and incomplete information. The FCRA requires that credit agencies maintain "reasonable procedures" in assuring maximum accuracy in credit reports. The court found that, generally, a reasonable time for resolving these types of disputes is 30 days. In this case, TRW did not complete its investigation until February 9, 1990, over three months after it was notified of the discrepancy and a month after its subscribers were to return their reverification forms. Some of the subscribers did not return their forms, but those debts remained on the credit report. Since the FCRA requires prompt deletion if a debt is inaccurate or unverifiable, the failure to delete the unverified debts was considered negligent. Also, some debts reappeared on the report after they were deleted. This was also found to constitute negligence. Further, since there were a number of disputed debts, the court held that TRW should have made follow-up phone calls to reverify the debts. Not doing so was also negligent. However the court found that the actions were not willful since TRW did not exercise ill will toward Mr. Stevenson. The decision of the trial court was affirmed with regard to actual damages but reversed the punitive damage award.

CASE QUESTIONS

1. Why did the court decide the case the way it did?
2. Do you agree that TRW's actions were not willful?
3. Do you think the actions of TRW were ethical?

Someone who knowingly and willfully obtains information from a credit agency under false pretenses can be subject to one year in jail and a $5,000 fine. A credit bureau will pay civil damages for failure to provide reasonable procedures to gain access to accurate and complete information.

DISCLOSING CREDIT COSTS

Another problem associated with obtaining credit is the determination of its exact cost. For example, Jim may want to buy a television but cannot afford the $800 price. A store may offer to allow Jim to pay $100 a month until the television is "paid off." The store inevitably will charge Jim interest on the $800 debt until the debt is paid in full. Depending on which interest rate is chosen and how it is calculated, Jim may pay well over three or four times the amount of the original $800 price. In order to protect consumers, some states prohibit charging interest over a certain maximum rate. These statutes are known as **usury laws**. Usury laws only apply in a very few states, and exceptions exist even in those states. Usury laws are still important, however, in those states in which they are retained.

usury laws: Laws regulating interest rates.

Other states have abandoned the notion of protecting consumers from themselves and replaced it with a full-disclosure policy. Therefore, in these states most usury laws have been repealed and have been replaced by the **Uniform Consumer Credit Code (UCCC)**. The National Conference of Commissioners on Uniform State Laws drafted the UCCC, and it was approved by the American Bar Association. Ironically, while the UCCC was written to make the laws uniform throughout the states, in fact, states have altered the UCCC provisions and fewer than 20 states have adopted it; in general, the UCCC applies to "all credit offered or extended by a creditor to an individual person primarily for personal, family, or household purposes" under $50,000. Its aim is to require full disclosure of credit terms. It also limits the amount that can be charged on unpaid accounts (**finance charges**). These amounts vary from state to state. Since the UCCC's major goal is disclosure rather than protection, interest rate charges can be very high, unlike usury statutes, which keep interest rates relatively low. Some states adopting the UCCC, however, place a maximum interest rate of 36 percent. The UCCC also allows a person to cancel a contract made at a person's home by door-to-door sales that falls under its provisions within three business days of when the contract is made. This three-day period is known as the **cooling-off period**. We will discuss cooling-off periods in Chapter 18.

Uniform Consumer Credit Code: Uniform law adopted by states governing the amount of interest and charges that can be assessed on consumer loans.

finance charge: Amount of money added to a loan payment when payment is late.

cooling-off period: A period of time to allow further consideration.

SOCIAL/ETHICAL ISSUES

Historically, some religions prohibited making money on money itself. This is one reason why there were prohibitions on the amount of interest that could be charged on debts. Is there any ethical justification for limiting the amount of interest that can be charged? Is there such a thing as a fair price?

TRUTH IN LENDING AND CONSUMER LEASING

Federal legislation aims to provide full disclosure to consumers so they can protect themselves when applying for a loan. In 1968 Congress passed the *Truth in Lending Act*. Like the UCCC, the purpose of Truth in Lending is to give consumers full disclosure of credit terms and to encourage consumers to shop around for credit. Truth in Lending does not limit or fix interest rates on credit. Rather, it requires that all interest rates be stated in terms of an **annual percentage rate (APR)**. The creditor must also disclose all finance charges, direct or indirect, in a dollar amount. If a buyer uses a home as collateral for consumer borrowing, the buyer has a right to cancel the credit within three days of the purchase. This particular rule does not apply to first mortgages on homes.

annual percentage rate (APR): The periodic rate (the monthly effective interest rate) times the number of periods in a year.

The *Truth in Lending Simplification and Reform Act of 1980* made several changes in the Truth in Lending Act. Most of these changes reduced the amount of paperwork a creditor must file. Further, all agricultural transactions were removed from its coverage.

The Consumer Leasing Act applies when a consumer leases personal property for more than four months. Currently, many people enter into long-term leases of cars, furniture, appliances, and computers. The Consumer Leasing Act applies to these transactions. It requires that the consumer receive a written statement about the amount of monthly payments and other costs, like insurance, security deposits, registrations, taxes, and maintenance. Consumers either enter into *open-ended* or *closed-ended* leases. Closed-ended leases generally have higher monthly payments but no **balloon payment** at the end of the lease. Open-ended leases have lower monthly payments, but they may also contain balloon payments based on the value of the leased property when the lease expires. Assume that Clair leases a new automobile for three years at $300 per month. The leasing company assumes that the automobile will be worth $5,000 at the end of three years. At the end of the lease period, the leasing company decides that the car's condition makes it only worth $4,200 and requires that Clair pay an additional $800. This is an open-ended lease with a balloon payment. Clair may think that the car is worth more than $4,200. Under the act she is entitled to have an independent appraisal of the property value of the car, and the balloon must be limited to three times the monthly payment. In this case, if the leased car is appraised at $4,200, she will have to pay the additional $800, since it is less than the $900 allowed under the act.

balloon payment: A large payment due at the end of the contract term.

FAIR CREDIT BILLING ACT

The *Fair Credit Billing Act* (FCBA) became effective in 1975. This Act only applies to **open-ended credit**, which occurs when the parties contemplate repeated transactions; the use of credit cards or an open account at a department store are examples. **Closed-ended credit**, on the other hand, usually involves the sale of a home or automobile. Under the FCBA, if the consumer suspects an error has been made on a billing statement, he or she has 60 days to notify the creditor of the error. The creditor then has 30 days to respond and another 90 days to correct the mistake or to explain why it will not be corrected. During the investigation, the consumer is not responsible for the disputed amount. If the consumer turns out to be wrong, the creditor is entitled to prior finance charges and prompt payment. If the creditor and consumer dis-

open-ended credit: Credit you can use again and again until a certain prearranged borrowing limit is reached.

closed-ended credit: Credit in which there is a set number of payments over a set period of time.

agree, the creditor must notify credit bureaus of the disagreement and notify credit bureaus of any settlement. The FCBA can be very useful when goods are ordered but not delivered or when goods turn out to be defective and the seller refuses to correct the problem.

The act requires the billing agency to notify the consumers concerning the proper procedure for disputing a statement. It also requires that consumers receive a billing statement each billing period. The act also allows a credit card user to refuse to pay for unsatisfactory goods or services that are over $50 if they were purchased in the consumer's home state or within 100 miles of his or her mailing address.

FROM THE DESK OF
Laura Lawyer

To: Students
From: Your Lawyer

Recently, a rash of incidents have occurred in which one person steals another person's credit card number and then charges goods or services to the unsuspecting person's account. When the bill arrives, the victim may have thousands of dollars worth of unordered goods. In such a case, the credit card company should be immediately notified as to the discrepancy, and the account should be immediately closed. Federal law limits the credit card holder's liability to $50 for unauthorized use of the card. If the credit company is notified of the theft or loss of the card before any charges are incurred, the customer has no liability. To prevent such incidents, never give your credit card number over the phone to someone who calls you. Usually, it is safe to give your credit card number over the phone when you have called a reputable firm, like a catalog company, and you know others who have dealt successfully with this firm in the past.

FAIR DEBT COLLECTION PRACTICES ACT

The Fair Debt Collection Practices Act (FDCPA) was passed in 1978. Before FDCPA was passed, bill collectors were allowed to call debtors early in the morning, late at night, and at work. FDCPA's goal was to stop bill collectors from using harassing, intimidating, or abusive methods to obtain payment.

How the law applies to attorneys is the subject of the next case.

GEORGE W. HEINTZ V. DARLENE JENKINS

514 U.S. 291 (1995)

FACTS

Darlene Jenkins had borrowed money from the Gainer Bank to buy a car. She defaulted on that loan and the bank's lawyer, George Heintz, sent a letter to Ms. Jenkins' lawyer "listing the amount she owed under the loan agreement, including $4,173 owed for insurance." Ms. Jenkins claimed that the $4,173 insurance policy was the amount a policy would cost the bank and would insure not only loss and damage to the car but also financial loss in the event Ms. Jenkins defaulted. Under the loan agreement, Ms. Jenkins was only required to keep an insurance policy for loss or damage to the car. She claimed that this letter violated the FDCPA since Mr. Heintz tried to collect an amount "not authorized by the agreement creating the debt," and made a "false representation of . . . the . . . amount . . . of any debt." The district court dismissed the case because it held that attorneys engaging in litigation were not covered by the act. The Seventh Circuit Court of Appeals reversed. The U.S. Supreme Court granted certiorari.

DECISION

Justice Breyer wrote the opinion of the Court. The U.S. Supreme Court held that the act did apply to lawyers engaged in litigation. Lawyers were exempted from the law until 1986. In 1986, the lawyer exemption was specifically repealed, and now the law applies to anyone who "regularly collect[s] or attempt[s] to collect, directly or indirectly, [consumer] debts owed or due or asserted to be owed or due another." According to the Court, this includes lawyers who attempt to collect debts as part of their litigating activities. The decision of the Seventh Circuit was affirmed.

CASE QUESTIONS

1. What do you think will happen on remand? Is the lawyer's statement an attempt to collect a debt not due?
2. Is there an inconsistency in the FDCPA when litigating attorneys are covered, but the act does not allow a collector to contact a consumer after the consumer notifies the collector that an attorney has been retained?
3. Should attorneys be covered by the act?

For the most part, creditors collecting their own debts are exempt. If the consumer, in writing, refuses to pay the debt or has notified the collector that an attorney has been retained or has written a letter requesting freedom from harassment, the collector cannot contact the consumer again except to inform the consumer of action that the collector is taking. Violators of FDCPA are liable for up to $1,000 without any proof of actual damage. Creditors, of course, are entitled to be paid for any legitimate debts. As the article "Nationwide Points to First Data in Record $1 Million Penalty" indicates, violation of the act can result in significant penalties.

Legal Issues: Nationwide Points to First Data in Record $1 Million Penalty

One of the nation's largest collections agencies is behind a record that it wasn't looking to break. Atlanta-based Nationwide Credit Inc. has agreed to pay a $1 million civil penalty as part of a settlement with the Federal Trade Commission to resolve allegations that the company violated the Fair Debt Collection Practices Act.

The case is the latest in a series of alleged violations of debtor rights. In the past year, Sears, Roebuck & Co. and GE Capital Corp. have separately agreed to refund hundreds of millions of dollars to bankrupt consumers who suffered illegal efforts to collect debts.

"The settlement agreement (with Nationwide) reflects a concern about repeated conduct of the company," says Lucy Morris, an attorney with the FTC's Bureau of Consumer Protection. The federal agency says that Nationwide—which counts credit card debt as a significant portion of its business—failed to abide by a 1992 settlement of Fair Debt Collection charges in which the company paid a $100,000 penalty. The latest violations occurred after the previous settlement six years ago, Morris says.

According to the FTC's most recent complaint, Nationwide collectors repeatedly harassed consumers by calling them at work, talking to neighbors, children and other third parties to gather information without the consumers' consent, used obscene language and made false and misleading statements.

However, Nationwide is not sweating the penalty—the largest ever in a debt collection case—saying that the company's former owner, card processing giant First Data Corp., was running the company at the time the alleged practices took place. "It happened on a different watch," says Jerry Kaufman, Nationwide's president, who adds: "There are other ways to collect money, you can do it professionally."

Says a Nationwide spokesperson: "This is good news from our perspective in that it closes out old issues."

First Data, however, is not a willing recipient in shouldering the blame. "The whole issue has to do with their business practices," says a spokesperson who declines to elaborate on the FTC allegations.

Perhaps more importantly, First Data covered the fine in advance, Nationwide says, transferring $1.9 million to Nationwide in late summer to cover the FTC settlement as well as revisions in the amount the U.S. Department of Education had paid Nationwide for debt-collection services.

First Data knew of the FTC investigation when it sold Nationwide for $155 million in cash on Dec. 31, 1997, and originally agreed to pay any fines imposed by the government agency, the First Data spokesperson says. However, an August amendment to the sale agreement shifted the legal responsibility back to Nationwide. "The payment of that penalty is the responsibility of Nationwide Credit, not ours," says the First Data spokesperson, who declines to discuss the actual allegations. "We wired them a certain amount of money, then we agreed as part of that agreement that the liability for payment falls on them."

Responds Nationwide: "First Data Corp. does not have any legal responsibility with respect to the consent decree, that's between us and the government. What First Data Corp. had was an economic responsibility for the fine."

Nationwide's settlement with the FTC includes a consumer resolution program now in place, which both the company and FTC say should set an industry standard for handling consumer complaints.

However, the company may be missing the point, says collections consultant Roger L. Willis of Willis Associates in San Diego. "This is not an issue of having a help line for consumers who have complaints, this is purely, directly and simply an issue of managing the quality of the contact with the consumer." The problem, Willis says, is one shared by other collections agencies. "I can't speak for all the agencies, but I know what we're going to do and what we're doing," says Kaufman, who adds that Nationwide is hiring an independent auditor to monitor the company's progress annually.

Originally, attorneys were exempted from the FDCPA if they were acting as debt collectors. In 1986, however, attorneys lost their exemption and must now comply with the act.

Debt collection is often a difficult process. A creditor usually must receive a judgment, as described in Chapter 2, before the debt can be collected. **Confession of judgment** is a provision in a document permitting the creditor to obtain an entry of judgment by a court. This document is signed by the debtor before any default has even occurred. Confessions of judgment are generally prohibited by state statutes. **Wage assignments** are also prohibited in most states. Wage assignments occur when the debtor signs over a percentage of his or her wage to the creditor.

confession of judgment: Acknowledgment by a debtor of a claim and consent that a judgment may be entered without notice or hearing for the amount of the claim when it is due and unpaid.

wage assignment: An assignment by an employee by which an amount of his or her wages are transferred to a creditor before the wages are paid to the employee.

Also prohibited is **prejudgment garnishment**. Garnishment occurs when a creditor takes a debtor's property to pay for a debt; such garnishment is prejudgment if it occurs before the creditor has received a court judgment that the creditor is owed money on a debt. Historically, some creditors *repossessed* collateral before they received a judgment. In *Fuentes v. Shevin* [407 U.S. 67 (1972)], the U.S. Supreme Court held that this activity violated the due process clause of the U.S. Constitution.

prejudgment garnishment: A remedial device whereby a creditor attaches the property of a debtor to pay the debt owed to the creditor before a court has issued a judgment in the creditor's favor.

AFTER-JUDGMENT REMEDIES

Once a creditor receives a judgment, however, there are several methods that can be used to receive payment. Usually, the debtor will be required to attend a **supplementary proceeding**. The supplementary proceeding allows the creditor to question the debtor about the debtor's sources of income as well as any property he or she may own. This property can be *attached* (taken) and sold. An **execution sale** occurs when the court orders the sale of the debtor's property to satisfy the debts. The sale is conducted by the sheriff, and the money is turned over to the creditor. The debtor will receive any surplus monies. Some items are exempt from execution. For example, most states have a *homestead exemption*, in which the debtor retains some of the equity in a home. Other exemptions can include appliances, furniture, and other household essentials. The exemption lists are very specific as to what can and cannot be sold. All property that is not exempt can be sold at auction to satisfy the debt.

supplementary proceeding: Court proceeding occurring after a judgment has been entered, aimed at determining the extent and whereabouts of the judgment debtor's money and property.

execution sale: A sale carried out to execute a judgment under authority of a judicial officer.

Another method of debt collection is to garnish the debtor's wages. Wage garnishment occurs after the creditor receives a judgment. In order to garnish wages, creditors must file a garnishment request with the court and with the debtor's employer, requesting that the employer pay a percentage of the debtor's wage to the creditor. Most states require that the statement be filed with the creditor every pay period. The FTC's Credit Practice Rules do not allow more money to be garnished than the lesser of 25 percent of take home pay (per pay period) or an amount that exceeds 40 times the federal minimum wage. Most states have similar restrictions.

Creditors are not allowed to engage in *unconscionable practices*. Unconscionable practices are practices that are so unfair to a consumer that a court will refuse to enforce that action. Unconscionable contracts are discussed in Chapter 12.

One of the best ways for a creditor to be protected when a debtor defaults on a loan is to use **collateral** for a loan. If money is given to buy a home or other piece of real property, the creditor almost always uses the real property as collateral. If the debtor then defaults on the debt, the creditor can take the property back and resell it to someone else. In order to use real property as collateral, the creditor must have the debtor sign a *mortgage* or *trust deed*. Some states also allow the use of a *land sales contract*. These devices have been discussed in Chapter 14.

collateral: Property used by the debtor to protect a creditor's interest in case of default.

SECURED TRANSACTIONS

A creditor may also take personal property as collateral for a loan. Personal property is any property that is not real property. (The differences were discussed in detail in Chapter 14.) If a creditor takes personal property as collateral for a loan, in most states the creditor must comply with *Article 9* of the *Uniform Commercial Code* (*UCC*). Taking personal property as collateral is referred to as **secured transactions**.

secured transactions: A credit sale of goods or a secured loan that provides special protection for the creditor in the form of acquiring some legal rights in the goods or property.

In order to use personal property as collateral, a debtor and creditor need to create a *security interest*. The collateral used to create the security interest is divided into two categories, tangible and intangible. Tangible collateral includes items like *consumer goods* (e.g., televisions, stereos), *equipment* (e.g., cash registers), *inventory* (items that will be resold to the consumer), and *farm products* (e.g., milk, chicken, beef). The same item can be categorized differently, depending on the debtor's use of the product. For example, a microwave oven is a consumer good if it is bought by the consumer for personal use. The same microwave oven is inventory if the debtor is a retailer. Further, the same microwave oven becomes equipment if it is used by a restaurant. Intangible collateral are items that cannot be touched but whose value is represented by a paper instrument. Intangible collateral include **accounts receivable**, **chattel paper**, instruments, documents of title, trademarks, and money.

accounts receivable: A balance due a creditor from a debtor on a current account.

chattel paper: A paper that sets out the buyer's obligation to pay and the lender's security interest in the goods.

CREATING THE SECURITY INTEREST

In order to create a security interest, the parties must have a *security agreement*. The security agreement must be in writing and specifically grant a security interest. The agreement must also describe the collateral and be signed by the debtor. The secured party also has to give up something of value. It is not a requirement that the debtor own the collateral, but he or she must have an interest in the collateral. For example, Jane, a debtor, cannot use her neighbor's truck as collateral for a loan if she does not have a legal interest in the truck. Sometimes the security agreement can be oral if the collateral is in the possession of the creditor (referred to as the **secured party**). If a debtor promises to turn an item over to the possession of the secured party, this is called a *pledge*. Some items *must* be in possession of the secured party before a security interest can be created. Items like stock and money are easily transferred, and therefore the secured party must hold possession of the collateral in order to retain the security interest. Written security agreements are required to secure intangible collateral, since there is no way they can be possessed. Once this process occurs, the security interest becomes enforceable against the debtor, or in UCC terminology, it **attaches**, as shown in Figure 17.1.

secured party: A party holding a security interest in another's property.

attach: To create a security interest in property thereby acquiring the right to foreclose on or otherwise deal with property for payment of debt.

One major problem with security interests occurs when several people have a security interest in the same item. For example, assume Don borrows $1,000 from First National Bank to set up a retail store. He gives the bank a

Figure 17.1
Attachment

A Security Interest Attaches When the Debtor Has Rights in the Collateral

AND

- Written security agreement:
- granting a security interest
- describing the collateral
- signed by the debtor

OR

- Oral security agreement:
- granting a security interest and
- secured party possesses the collateral

security interest in all of his equipment, inventory, and accounts receivable. Don then negotiates with Carla's Clothes to provide him with a line of coats to sell in the store. Carla sends the coats to Don and expects payment in 30 days. Carla also takes a security interest in the coats. (She actually obtains a written document indicating that she has a security interest in the coats.) If Don fails to pay both Carla and the bank, who is entitled to recover the coats? This is a question of *perfection* and *priority*.

PERFECTION

Perfected security interests take priority over *unperfected security interests*. The manner in which a creditor perfects a security interest depends on what type of collateral he or she is using. Most security interests are perfected on the date the creditor either takes possession of the collateral or files a *financing statement* with the appropriate state office. Remember, creating a security interest in some items requires that the creditor take possession of the collateral. A financing statement, on the other hand, is a paper document listing the names and addresses of the debtor and the secured party. This statement describes the collateral and is signed by the debtor. Once the financing statement is filed, the security interest is said to be perfected. Filing the financing statement allows other potential creditors the opportunity to check to see if the debtor is using collateral that another party already has secured. Since perfected security interests take preference over junior security interests or interests that are perfected later, those junior interests may turn out to be worthless. All the items necessary to perfect a security interest are shown in Figure 17.2.

One last type of filing is a *fixture filing*. As you will remember from Chapter 14, fixtures are personal property that have become real property. For example, when a furnace is purchased, it is personal property; but when it is installed in a home, it becomes part of the real property. To obtain a perfected security interest in the fixture, the filing must be made in the office where the mortgage on the real property is filed, usually the county recorder's office.

Consumer goods, or goods sold to a consumer for personal or household use on credit (except automobiles), are *automatically perfected*. Thus, the creditor does not need to take possession of the property or file a financing statement to

- Security agreement (written agreement required for intangible collateral)
- Attachment (See Figure 17.1)
- File financing statement (required for intangible collateral)
  - in state office (or required office in the case of fixtures)
  - lists name and address of debtor
  - lists name and address of secured party
  - describes collateral
  - signed by debtor

OR

- Take possession of collateral (required for money and stock)

Figure 17.2
Perfection of Security Interest

obtain the best claim on the collateral. For example, if Ann goes to Don's Store, purchases a coat, and agrees to pay Don $30 a month until the coat is paid off, Don does not need to do anything more to perfect his security interest. If Ann, however, turns around and sells the coat to Steve in a garage sale, Don will not be able to recover the coat from Steve if Ann defaults on the loan and Don has not filed a financing statement. Even though Don's security interest was automatically perfected, because he had not filed a financing statement, that perfection does not apply to other purchasers of the collateral.

Returning to the original scenario in which Don borrowed $1,000 to start a retail store, National Bank has taken a security interest in Don's inventory. In the event of default, if the Bank had filed a financing statement and Carla's Clothes had not, then the bank may recover the coats, and Carla may only sue Don on the underlying debt. Carla would not be able to recover the coats. Since the bank had the only perfected security interest, the bank has the best right to the coats. Assume, though, that Carla had taken a good legal environment course and knew better than to be unperfected. Therefore, she too had filed a financing statement. Now both creditors are perfected. Who wins?

PRIORITY

This is a question of *priority*. If more than one perfected security interest exists, the creditor who perfected the security interest first may repossess the collateral. The creditor who filed second will only collect from the sale of the collateral if the collateral is worth more than the first creditor's debt.

PURCHASE MONEY SECURITY INTEREST

The priority rule seems straightforward except that it does not take into account the **purchase money security interest**. A PMSI is a security interest in which the debtor uses the credit extended by the creditor to purchase the actual collateral being used as security. In other words, a PMSI is created when the creditor gives value for the goods the debtor is financing. To see how a PMSI works, assume Ed goes to Bank 1 and borrows $1,000 for a trip to Europe. Bank 1 takes Ed's boat as collateral for the loan. This transaction does not create a PMSI. On the other hand, if Ed goes to Bank 1 to borrow $1,000

purchase money security interest: A security interest in the collateral specifically financed by the creditor.

for the purchase of a boat, and the bank takes that specific boat as collateral, then, there is a PMSI. A PMSI is *automatically perfected* for 10 days. This means that if Ed obtains the loan on August 1, no other creditor can obtain a higher priority until August 11. Let us assume, then, that Ed goes to Bank 2 and borrows $1,000 to take his trip to Europe and uses his recently purchased boat, which is secured by Bank 1, as collateral. Bank 2 checks the public record on August 3 and determines that no other security interests exist on the boat, loans Ed $1,000 and files a financing statement on August 4. Bank 1 files its financing statement on August 5. If Ed defaults on both loans, who is entitled to repossess the boat? Bank 1 still has priority, because it has a PMSI that was automatically perfected for 10 days. Bank 1 did not need to file a financing statement for 10 days; therefore, it does not matter that Bank 2 checked the records on August 3 and found no financing statement.

What could Bank 2 have done differently? It should have filed a financing statement on August 4 and then waited 10 days before giving Ed any money. After the 10-day period, Bank 2 would have discovered Bank 1's financing statement by checking the public record. If Bank 1 had failed to file its financing statement and no other financing statements secured the boat, Bank 1 could loan the money safely.

INVENTORY FINANCING

Besides those rules governing a PMSI, special rules also exist for inventory financing. A PMSI in inventory takes priority over other secured parties if the PMSI holder notifies, in writing, other secured parties before the inventory is delivered. The PMSI must be perfected *before* delivery. Remember our earlier example in which Don has borrowed $1,000 from National Bank to set up a retail business, and the bank has taken a security interest in all of Don's equipment, inventory, and accounts receivable. Later, Don ordered coats on open account from Carla's Clothes. Carla's, in this case, has a security interest in inventory. In order for Carla to obtain priority over National Bank, Carla will need to send written notification to National Bank that she has taken a purchase money security interest in the coats she is selling on credit. Moreover, she will need to file a financing statement with the appropriate public office before any of the coats are delivered to Don. If Carla does this, she will be able to repossess the coats to satisfy her debt. If she does not follow the proper procedures, National Bank will be able to repossess the coats to satisfy its debt.

Once a security interest is perfected, all later or subsequent buyers of the collateral take subject to the security interest until the debt is paid in full. Thus, subsequent buyers may have to relinquish the collateral to the original secured party or pay the original secured party the price of the collateral if the collateral is no longer in their possession. For example, assume that Don no longer needs his cash register and offers to sell it to Joan. Since National Bank has a security interest in Don's equipment, Joan buys the cash register with the possibility that the Bank can repossess it from her if Don defaults on his loan. Therefore, if Joan buys the cash register, and Don defaults on National Bank's loan, National Bank can repossess the cash register from Joan. Joan's only remedy would be to sue Don.

An exception to this rule occurs if Joan is a *buyer in the ordinary course of business*, a person who buys goods from someone in the business of selling those types of goods. If Joan goes into Don's store and buys a coat, neither

National Bank nor Carla's can repossess the coat from Joan in the event of Don's default, even though (1) they both have perfected security interests in the inventory and (2) Joan may know of the existence of the security interest. The reason for this rule is clear. When shopping in retail stores, consumers do not want to check the public records to ensure that no security interests exist on the goods they buy. To require consumers to do this would thwart the very purpose of retail shopping. The UCC, then, takes this into account and does not make buyers in the ordinary course of business responsible for checking for security interests. Figure 17.3 summarizes the rules for priority in secured transactions.

REPOSSESSION

Of course, none of these rules matter if the debtor pays on time. The problem occurs when the debtor defaults on the loan. A creditor who possesses a security interest has two options if the debtor defaults: first, the creditor may repossess the collateral and sell it; or second, the creditor may repossess the collateral and keep it in full satisfaction of the debt. Private parties are allowed to **repossess** collateral if repossession can be done without breaching the peace (i.e., without causing a fight or breaking the law).

repossess: To take possession of property by judicial process or self-help when a debtor defaults on a debt.

Once collateral is repossessed, the creditor may sell it at a private or public sale. If this is done, the creditor must send written notification of the sale to the debtor and all other secured parties. Also, the sale must be *commercially reasonable*. In other words, the time, place, manner, and terms of the sale must be reasonable. If the collateral is sold for more than the debt plus costs and attorneys' fees, the debtor is entitled to the surplus. If the collateral is sold for less, the debtor is liable for any deficiency.

A secured party may choose to keep the collateral in full satisfaction of the debt. However, the secured party must notify the debtor and other secured parties that this is the intention. The recipient of this notice has a certain number

Figure 17.3 *Priority of Secured Transactions*

The First Party to Perfect the Security Interest Has Priority Unless:

1) The goods are purchased in the ordinary course of business;
2) One party has a purchase money security interest (PMSI) with the following characteristics:
   a) The debtor used the credit extended to purchase the collateral of the security interest; and
   b) A financing statement is filed within ten days (a PMSI is automatically perfected for 10 days).
3) One party has a perfected security interest in inventory with the following characteristics:
   a) The holder has notified the other secured parties;
   b) This notification is in writing; and
   c) This perfection and notification occur before delivery.

of days to object (in most states it is 21 days). If a written objection is received, the secured party must sell the collateral. Most states have special rules for consumer goods. These rules may allow the secured party to keep the goods in full satisfaction of the debt only if less than 60 percent of the debt has been paid. In this case, the creditor must obtain a written statement from the debtor, allowing the creditor to keep the goods. As you can see, perfecting security interests are very important in everyday commercial transactions. They are also very important when a debtor declares bankruptcy.

BANKRUPTCY

bankruptcy debtor: An individual or business that owes money to a creditor.

bankruptcy creditor: An individual or business that has a claim against the debtor before the bankruptcy petition is filed.

Part of the risk associated with a free market economy is the risk of failure. Given the statistics on how many new businesses fail, it is almost surprising that anyone would want to borrow money and start a business. Of course, it is essential for the economy that people continue to start businesses and risk losing their money. Most people would be unwilling to accept this risk if failure meant spending time in debtor's prison or suffering crushing debt from which they would never recover. Thus, the federal bankruptcy laws are intended to strike a balance between **debtor** and **creditor** rights while encouraging people to take financial risks.

Another reason for bankruptcy laws is to give the debtor's creditors a fair way to split what is left of the debtor's property. Without bankruptcy laws, some creditors would receive everything, and other creditors would receive nothing. The bankruptcy rules set up a hierarchy for receiving payment.

The U.S. Constitution gives Congress the power to establish bankruptcy laws. (As a result, no state bankruptcy system exists.) Congress passed the first bankruptcy law in 1800 and repealed it in 1803. Congress then passed and repealed several bankruptcy laws until creating the Bankruptcy Act of 1898. This Act was amended in 1938 and then stayed virtually the same until 1978. In 1978, the bankruptcy courts were completely overhauled with the passage of the *Bankruptcy Reform Act of 1978*. The 1978 Act sets forth several chapters by which individuals or business can file for protection under the bankruptcy statutes. For example, Chapter 7 is known as a *liquidation*, Chapter 11 is known as a *reorganization*, and Chapter 13 applies to persons with a regular income.

In 1982, the U.S. Supreme Court ruled in *Northern Pipeline Co. v. Marathon Pipe Line Co.* [458 U.S. 50 (1982)] that portions of the 1978 Act were unconstitutional. The 1978 Act had given bankruptcy court judges more power than they could constitutionally possess. Congress then amended the act with the *Bankruptcy Amendments Act of 1984*. The Amendments Act clarifies the role of bankruptcy judges. Bankruptcy judges work under federal district court judges and hear everything concerning the bankruptcy laws. This is called the **core proceedings**. State courts also retain jurisdiction over lawsuits involving the debtor, other than the bankruptcy proceedings, like personal injury lawsuits. The 1984 Act also changes the bankruptcy court's jurisdiction and requires that the federal district court enter all final rules unless the parties agree otherwise. In 1994, the Bankruptcy Act was amended again. As shown in the next article, "Congress Is on the Right Track in Acting to Reform Bankruptcy Law," there have been several attempts to reform the current bankruptcy law. As of press time, no reform had been passed.

core proceeding: A proceeding that is integral to the administration of a bankruptcy estate and so falls under the jurisdiction of the bankruptcy court.

Congress Is on the Right Track in Acting to Reform Bankruptcy Law

Even during the unprecedented economic good times of the past year, some 1.39 million individuals and 44,000 businesses have sought protection from creditors in federal bankruptcy courts—more than ever before. The majority of these debtors, faced with medical emergencies or other crisis, had no other choice. Others, however, used the system to escape debts they knowingly built up, costing the average family $550 a year and American companies billions.

That's why it is time to reform the nation's bankruptcy laws and return the concepts of fairness and responsibility to the system. Last year, with elections looming, Congress failed to reach an agreement. This year, however, it looks like Congress will finally act, potentially by a veto-proof margin. The House passed its version of reform in May, and the Senate is scheduled to take up its bill this month. There is bipartisan support among the senators for reform, and compromise with the House is likely to result in new law. That is good news for all of us.

Those supporting reform include retailers, banks and other lenders, as well as many responsible consumers sick of having to pick up the tab for those who default on their debts. Those opposed include some in the bankruptcy bar, who contend the legislation favors big business at the expense of consumers who truly need help, and consumer groups, which blame the ease with which consumers receive credit for increased bankruptcy filings.

Much has been written and said about who is to blame for this "bankruptcy crisis." Consumer groups blame banks, credit card companies and retailers who tempt borrowers to live beyond their means. Indeed most Americans, whether they can afford credit cards or not, know what it's like to open a mailbox filled with applications guaranteeing lines of credit.

"Credit-card issuers are shameless to lobby for personal bankruptcy restrictions while they aggressively market and extend credit," says Stephen Brobeck, the Consumer Federation's executive director.

But access to credit has not been altogether bad. For decades the federal government has encouraged industry to make credit and financial services available to a broader segment of society. As a result, strapped Americans have been able to buy what they need when they need it. It has allowed for emergency purchases and long-term investments. Ultimately it has benefited the American economy.

But the benefits of credit are not free, and that is what Congress has recognized in pushing reform of the bankruptcy system.

Consumers share the blame. Filings are up in part because bankruptcy no longer carries with it a sense of shame, and debtors have failed to act fiscally responsible. Too many of these debtors equate plastic with money-in-hand. They use one credit card to pay off another or play a continuing and sloppy game with balance transfers, all the while watching their debts increase. For them, walking away from the responsibility is an easy answer.

The parallel bills making their way through Congress would make it harder for debtors to escape scot-free. Both encourage personal responsibility by requiring those who are able to pay their debts to do so. At the same time no suggested changes are so drastic as to crush hard-working debtors who have had a run of bad luck.

The most controversial part of the House bill would block most middle- and upper-income debtors from using the bankruptcy courts to walk away from their debts. Those with annual family incomes above $51,000 who have the resources to pay at least 20 percent of what they owe over five years would be prohibited from wiping the slate clean. This means they would have to restructure their debts under Chapter 13 of the bankruptcy code rather than the more lenient Chapter 7, which erases debts.

Significantly, the bill allows bankruptcy judges to take into account a debtor's "extraordinary circumstances," such as a decline in income or unexpected medical expenses, before making the decision to shift a debtor into Chapter 13.

Nevertheless, opponents say the provision is unfair because the debtor has the burden of proving those circumstances exist. In our view that is not unfair: The debtor is the one receiving the benefits of the bankruptcy.

The Senate bill is less stringent and would give greater discretion in the matter to the bankruptcy judge, who would have to consider a debtor's ability to repay his debts. The Senate's version requires only a showing of "special circumstances" for a debtor to avoid a transfer to Chapter 13.

Both bills recognize the obligation of a parent to pay child support. Both make sure a debtor cannot put off collection efforts or delay making child support payments simply by filing for bankruptcy. And child support payments have been made a top priority when determining which debts will be paid first.

Unfortunately, neither bill goes far enough toward closing the loophole that allows debtors unlimited homestead exemptions that protect the wealthiest from having to repay a significant portion of their debt. Last year's Senate bill would have made it impossible for states to let a bankrupt person keep more than $100,000 equity in a home, which would certainly hurt a lot of debtors who headed to Florida to live in their multimillion-dollar mansions.

But the conference committee threw out the provision and instead said simply that states could let a bankrupt person retain any house owned for at least two years before filing, no matter what its value. Both 1999 versions retain this language. We would prefer Congress cap the amount of equity a debtor can retain in a home.

In a consumer-friendly mode, House lawmakers adopted an amendment requiring credit-card companies to clearly disclose their fees for late payments and how long it would take customers to pay off balances when they make only minimum monthly payments. The House would also require companies to clearly reveal the expiration dates of introductory "teaser rates" and the higher interest rates replacing them.

Although we have only mentioned some of the proposed changes, the basic thrust of the legislation in both the House and the Senate is the same—requiring at least some repayment by those who have the ability to pay. The differences in the two measures are not beyond compromise, and either approach would be an improvement over current law.

As we said last year, the goal of the bankruptcy system is to match bankruptcy relief to debtor need. Chapter 13 repayment plans accomplish this objective and restore personal responsibility to the system.

"Congress Is on the Right Track in Acting to Reform Bankruptcy Law," *The Tampa Tribune*, July 6, 1999. Reprinted with permission of *The Tampa Tribune*.

CHAPTER 7 OF THE BANKRUPTCY ACT

trustee: One trusted to administer something.

All parties except railroads, banks, insurance companies, and so on can file a Chapter 7 bankruptcy. If a Chapter 7 bankruptcy is filed, the court appoints a **trustee**. It is the trustee's responsibility to accumulate the assets and pay the debts with whatever funds are available. The trustee will return collateral to secured creditors and will sell the rest of the debtor's nonexempt property. Priority claims, discussed later in the chapter, are then paid and if there is anything left, unsecured creditors will be paid **prorata**. For example, unsecured creditors may receive 10 cents for each dollar they are owed. More often in a Chapter 7 bankruptcy, unsecured creditors do not receive anything.

prorata: In proportion to the calculated debt.

CHAPTER 11 OF THE BANKRUPTCY ACT

Most businesses and some individuals decide that, rather than liquidate, they want to **reorganize** their debts. This is possible with a Chapter 11 bankruptcy. Usually the debtor continues to operate the business and is referred to as the **debtor in possession**. Sometimes the court appoints a trustee to run the business if the court believes that the debtor is unable to continue running the business. The debtor has 120 days from the date the petition is filed to present a reorganization plan. Reorganization plans divide debts into certain *classes*. Each class of debt is then paid differently. For example, Class A debt may be the amount owed to Bank 1, Class B debt is the amount owed to Bank 2, and Class C debt may be the amount owed to unsecured creditors. After the plan is presented, the creditors vote whether to accept or reject the plan. Each class of creditors must accept the plan, to ensure that the creditors themselves believe they are being treated fairly under the circumstances. For a plan to be accepted, the debtor must receive the positive vote of creditors representing two-thirds the total dollar amount and one-half the number of creditors in each class. If secured creditors will receive as much from the plan as they would receive in a Chapter 7 bankruptcy, unsecured creditors can force the secured creditors to accept the plan. This tactic is known as "cram down." A creditors' committee is organized by the Court and includes the seven unsecured creditors with the largest claims that are willing to serve on the committee. Often with the help of its own attorney, the creditors' committee can formulate its own reorganization plan if the debtor fails to get a plan accepted within 120 days. The creditors' committee can seek to have a trustee appointed if it believes the debtor has committed fraud, is dishonest, or is guilty of gross mismanagement. The creditors' committee can also move to dismiss the case or to convert the case to a Chapter 7 bankruptcy. Plans for small businesses, less than $2 million in debt, may proceed without a creditors' committee, and there are simpler procedures for voting on the plan.

reorganization: The rehabilitation of the finances of a business according to a plan approved by a bankruptcy court.

debtor in possession: A debtor who remains in possession of an estate during bankruptcy and has the same duties as a trustee in bankruptcy.

CHAPTER 13 OF THE BANKRUPTCY ACT

Chapter 13 of the Bankruptcy Code can be used by a debtor with a regular source of income (i.e., a regular job). Sole proprietors are also eligible if debt requirements are met. The debtor must have unsecured debt of less than $269,250 and secured debt of less than $807,750. A Chapter 13 bankruptcy includes the following two types of debt: (1) debt that is incurred before bankruptcy was filed (*prepetition debt*) and (2) debt that was incurred after the bankruptcy was filed (*post-petition debt*). Once a Chapter 13 bankruptcy is filed, the bankruptcy court names a trustee who has the responsibility to ensure that all post-petition debt is paid on time. The trustee, with the debtor's help, also proposes a plan to pay the prepetition debt. The plan should pay the prepetition debt in three years, although the court can extend the payment period to five years. The plan is voted on by the creditors. The unsecured creditors must accept the plan if they receive as much as they would have received in a Chapter 7 bankruptcy. Secured creditors must accept the plan if the plan makes a good faith effort to pay the debts.

A Chapter 13 bankruptcy is not a good solution for those whose debts exceed their income; however, it is a good solution for those who have incurred debts as the result of a job layoff or illness and have now recovered and have income that exceeds debts.

DECLARING BANKRUPTCY

A person may declare bankruptcy without being insolvent. Some very large companies have filed for bankruptcy protection before they were insolvent. For example, Johns Manville Corporation, an asbestos manufacturer, and A.H. Robbins, the manufacturer of the Dalkon shield, after losing several product liability lawsuits, used the bankruptcy laws in this manner. Some small gun manufacturers have also recently declared bankruptcy in anticipation of the filing of several gun liability lawsuits.

Before filing a bankruptcy petition, the debtor needs to decide under which chapter to file. If the debtor files under Chapter 7, the debtor is admitting that the situation is hopeless and agrees to liquidate the estate. If a debtor files under Chapter 11, the debtor attempts to reorganize the debts. If the debtor files under Chapter 13, the debtor asks the court to reorganize some debts and pay other debts as they become due. In 1986 Congress passed Chapter 12 to help family farmers restructure their debts. Regardless of the type of bankruptcy the debtor uses, all chapters have some common concepts.

In order to file for bankruptcy relief, a *bankruptcy petition* must be filed with the bankruptcy court. The petition lists the debtor's assets and debts categorized in various *schedules*. The schedules list all of the creditors, the amounts they are owed, and their addresses. Creditors not listed in the schedules are not subject to the final order.

automatic stay: A stay that comes into operation upon the filing of a bankruptcy petition in accordance with bankruptcy law that prevents creditors from attempting to collect from the debtor for debts incurred before the filing.

Once the petition is filed, an **automatic stay** occurs. An automatic stay prohibits all creditors from contacting the debtor; from initiating any collection procedures, including lawsuits; and from continuing lawsuits. Secured creditors are entitled to *adequate protection*, or they can request that their collateral be returned. Adequate protection means the collateral will not depreciate, in effect making the creditor unsecured. For example, in 1995, Bank 1 loaned Francis $50,000, taking a brand new machine worth $60,000 as collateral. Each year, the machine depreciates by 10 percent. By 1996, the machine is worth $50,000, and by 1997 it is worth $40,000. Meanwhile, Francis has paid down the loan to $40,000 before the bankruptcy petition is filed. If Francis declares bankruptcy in 1997 and does not pay on the debt, before very long the machine will be worth much less than the loan amount. In order to prevent this from happening, Bank 1 may ask the bankruptcy court to give it more collateral for its loan or ask that Francis pay an amount equivalent to the amount of depreciation. This is known as providing adequate protection. Once again, it is only available to secured creditors.

If it is the debtor's decision to file a bankruptcy petition, the bankruptcy is said to be *voluntary*. Creditors can also force a debtor into a Chapter 7 or Chapter 11 bankruptcy by filing an *involuntary* petition. Twelve or more creditors can file an involuntary petition if any three or more of those creditors together hold a debt of $10,775. If there are fewer than 12 creditors, anyone holding a debt can file. These amounts are adjusted periodically according to the Consumer Price Index. Creditors may choose to file an involuntary petition for a variety of reasons. One of the most common is the fear that the debtor is preferring some creditors over others and, by filing the involuntary petition, the debtor will have to pay the creditors in the order set out by the Bankruptcy Code. Farmers and charitable corporations cannot be forced into bankruptcy.

FIRST MEETING OF THE CREDITORS

Each creditor listed in the schedules is notified by the bankruptcy court that a petition has been filed. The creditors are then invited to a first meeting of the creditors in which they have the opportunity to question the debtor. The questions usually concern the location of collateral and whether the debtor intends to pay the debt.

PROOF OF CLAIM

Since the petition schedules list all the creditors, each creditor receives a notice of the filing. The notice asks each creditor to file a proof of claim. The proof of claim states the amount of the debt that is due. It also states whether the debt is an unsecured, secured, or a priority. If it is secured, the creditor has to file documentation of the security interest.

PRIORITY DEBTS

Some debts are labeled *priority* debts. These debts are paid before any other debts. The bankruptcy code lists the following order for payment of priority debts: (1) administrative expenses (like court costs); (2) GAP creditors (these are unsecured creditors whose debt arises in the ordinary course of doing business after the involuntary commencement of a petition and before the appointment of a trustee; usually GAP creditors are utility companies, like power, water, and telephone); (3) wages, salaries, and commissions owed to employees up to $4,300 per employee and occurring within 90 days before the petition is filed or cessation of the debtor's business; (4) some payments to benefit plans; (5) money owed to grain producers and fishing professionals up to $4,300; (6) consumer goods that were ordered and paid for but were not delivered, up to $1,950; (7) alimony, maintenance, and child support; and (8) some tax claims. Secured creditors are entitled to a return of their collateral. All other debts are unsecured.

THE BANKRUPTCY ESTATE

The bankruptcy estate includes all of the debtor's assets that exist on the date the petition is filed. It also includes anything the debtor acquires within 180 days after the petition is filed and any item that was in the estate 90 days before the petition was filed. Anything transferred out of the estate within 90 days before the petition is filed is known as a *preferential transfer* and may have to be returned to the estate by the person to whom the transfer was made. Anything transferred to a creditor classified as an insider within one year of filing bankruptcy is also considered preferential and is included in the estate. Fraudulent transfers are also preferential. For example, Sue transfers the title to her house to her daughter, Kay, on August 1 and files a bankruptcy petition on December 1. Since Kay is Sue's daughter, the transfer is preferential, and the house is included in the bankruptcy estate since the transfer occurred within the one-year time frame.

Some transfers are not considered preferential even though they occur within the 90-day period. The first is referred to as *contemporaneous exchange for new value*. For example, on January 2 Jeff goes into Fred's Store and purchases an overcoat for $300. On January 15, Fred's files a bankruptcy petition. Jeff does not need to return the overcoat, since he bought the overcoat and paid for it at the same time. It is assumed that the money paid is now part of the estate. The second exception is for payment of accounts in the ordinary course of business. Fred's paid its light bill 15 days before the petition was filed. The utility company will not have to return the money since the debt was incurred in the ordinary course of business. The third exception is the PMSI discussed previously, as long as it is perfected within 10 days. Perfected security interests for new value, as well as transfers of less than $600 on consumer debts, are also exempted from the preferential transfer rule. A court recently ruled that contributions made to a church (i.e., tithe) within the 90-day period were considered preferential and had to be returned to the estate.

EXEMPTIONS

Several items are exempt from the bankruptcy estate. Federal exemptions exist, or each state can choose to use its own exemptions. A majority of the states have chosen to have their own exemptions, although most are similar to the federal exemption. The federal exemptions include the following:

1. Up to $16,500 of equity in a home (homestead exemption) and burial plot.
2. Up to $2,575 equity in an automobile.
3. Up to $425 for each item of ordinary household furnishings and clothing. The total value cannot exceed $8,625.
4. Up to $1,075 in jewelry.
5. Up to $1,625 in books and tools used in the debtor's trade.
6. Any other property up to $850, plus up to $8,075 of any unused amount in the homestead exception, not including the house.
7. Unmatured life insurance contract owned by debtor.
8. Certain rights in pension, profit sharing, and annuity plans, including Social Security, veterans, disability benefits, and alimony and child support.
9. Up to $16,150 in payments from an award in a personal injury lawsuit.

If an item is exempt from the bankruptcy proceeding, it is not included as part of the bankruptcy estate. Notice, though, that the homestead exemption applies to the equity in the home and not to the actual home itself. Therefore, if the debtor does not have any equity in the home, then the home can be sold. If the debtor does have equity in the home, the home can still be sold, but the debtor is given $16,150 under federal law. The rest of the equity in the home is used to pay the creditors.

DISCHARGE

Once the court issues its final order, the debtor is **discharged** from paying the debts. Discharges are only available to individuals; businesses must liquidate or reorganize. Also, certain debts are not dischargeable. For example, a discharge is not allowed if fraud is present, the debt was incurred because the debtor willfully injured someone (an intentional tort, discussed in Chapter 11), or there has been an earlier discharge within six years. Government-secured student loans cannot be discharged, absent hardship, nor can alimony and child support payments. Certain tax and custom duties cannot be discharged, nor can debts that are not listed with the bankruptcy court. Further, a debtor cannot load up. Loading up occurs when the debtor buys, on credit, luxury goods over $1,075 from one creditor within 40 days of filing the petition or takes over a $1,075 cash advance within 60 days of filing the petition. These debts are also nondischargeable. As the next case suggests, questions about discharging debts continue to arise.

discharged: To release a debtor in bankruptcy from liability for his or her debt.

COHEN V. DE LA CRUZ

1998 U.S. LEXIS 2119.

FACTS

Petitioner Edward Cohen owned several rental properties in New Jersey that were subject to rent control. He violated the rent control provisions and was found liable under New Jersey law for fraudulently obtaining $31,382.50 in rent payments. Under New Jersey law he was also liable for treble damages and attorneys' fees. He subsequently filed for Chapter 7 relief and asked that the debt be discharged. The tenants filed an action in bankruptcy court arguing that the debt payments owed to them were "obtained by actual fraud." The Bankruptcy Court agreed and ruled in the tenants' favor. The court found that Mr. Cohen had committed actual fraud and that his conduct amounted to an "unconscionable commercial practice" under the New Jersey Consumer Fraud Act. The court awarded the tenants treble damages totaling $94,147.50, plus reasonable attorneys' fees and costs. The Third Circuit Court of Appeals agreed. The case was appealed to the United States Supreme Court.

DECISION

Justice O'Connor wrote the opinion for the Court. The question for the Supreme Court was whether treble damage punitive damage awards can be discharged under the bankruptcy law. The Supreme Court held that "§523(a)(2)(A) prevents the discharge of all liability arising from fraud, and that an award of treble damages therefore falls within the scope of the exception." Therefore, under New Jersey law, the debt, which was incurred as the result of fraud, includes treble damages and attorneys' fees and costs; consequently, petitioner's entire debt of $94,147.50 (plus attorneys' fees and costs) is nondischargeable in bankruptcy.

CASE QUESTIONS

1. What logic do you think Cohen used in arguing that the treble damages were dischargeable?
2. Why should some debts be dischargeable and others not dischargeable?
3. Do you agree with the Court in this case?

SUMMARY

As you can see, the process of borrowing and lending money is complicated. The rights of debtors and creditors are the subject of several pieces of legislation both at the state and federal level. Consumers are protected against discrimination in the Equal Credit Opportunity Act. They are protected against unscrupulous business practices with the FCRA, UCCC, FCBA, FDCPA, and Truth in Lending Act.

Creditors who use collateral for their loans are able to repossess the collateral in the event of default using the law of mortgages or the law of secured transactions. Finally, the bankruptcy laws attempt to balance the rights of both creditors and debtors when the debtor gets into financial trouble.

CHAPTER QUESTIONS

1. Door-to-door sales personnel sold two installment contracts to individuals. One contract was for a freezer, and the second contract was for a seven-month supply of frozen food. The sellers told the buyers that the price of the freezer and the price of the food were below what the person was spending on food. The buyers were given a monthly price, which included both contracts. The price of the freezer turned out to be twice the current retail price. How is the UCCC relevant to this case? [See *Vasquez v. Superior Court of San Joaquin County*, 4 Cal.3d 800, 94 Cal. Rptr. 796, 484 P.2d 964 (1971).]
2. A man defaulted on car payments. He drove the car to the dealer where he attempted to negotiate a new payment plan. The dealer blocked his car in the lot and told him to pay the entire loan amount or "walk your ___ home." Is this considered a breach of the peace? What are the legal implications? [See *Deavers v. Standridge*, 242 S.E.2d 331 (Ga. 1978).]
3. Wollenberg agreed to sell his business to Mays. As part of the sale of the business, Wollenberg took a promissory note and security agreement in lieu of full payment. The security agreement gave Wollenberg a security interest in the company's accounts receivable. Mays told Wollenberg that he was going to immediately transfer the business into his corporate entity, Sunrise Security. Wollenberg filed a financing statement naming only Mays as the debtor. Later, Phoenix Leasing agreed to loan Sunrise Security $150,000 and took a security interest in Sunrise Security's accounts receivable. Phoenix checked the state filings and did not find a prior financing statement on Sunrise Security. It was unaware of the security agreement with Wollenberg. Sunrise defaulted on both the Wollenberg and Phoenix Leasing Loans. Who has priority? [See *Wollenberg and Wollenberg v. Phoenix Leasing*, 182 Ariz. 4; 893 P.2d 4; 1994 Ariz. App. LEXIS 180 (1994).]
4. Andy is a guitarist. He buys a guitar from MusicVille on January 10. The cost of the guitar is $1,000. Andy agrees to pay $150 a month. MusicVille receives a security interest and files its financing statement on January 17. Meanwhile, Andy borrows $1,000 from Equity Security on January 11. He gives Equity Security a security interest in the same guitar and Equity Security files a financing statement on January 12. On

January 16, Andy also borrows $1,000 from his friend Beth. Beth receives a security interest in Andy's guitar and takes possession of it on the same day. Andy defaults on every loan. Discuss the legal ramifications.

5. Martha, age 60, and Jay, age 62, are married and want to buy a new home. They want to use a 30-year mortgage to finance the purchase. Both are gainfully employed and can easily afford the monthly payments. Can the lending institution deny the loan?
6. In receiving her monthly credit card bill, Diane noticed a $1,000 charge for airline tickets. Although Diane had been somewhat in a fog during the month, she was sure that she had not taken an airline trip. What is her recourse?
7. Sandra Bossard borrowed money from Beneficial and used her 1978 car as collateral. The loan officer prepared the credit application during a telephone conversation. After receiving a credit report, the loan officer discovered that there were several other unlisted debts. Bossard told the loan officer that some of the debts were satisfied and others were being paid by her estranged husband. The loan was approved anyway and a portion was given to pay another creditor with the remainder going to Bossard. Bossard made one payment and then defaulted on the loan. The car disappeared and Bossard declared bankruptcy. Is the debt dischargeable? [See *In Re Bossard*, 74 B.R. 730 (Bankr. N.D.N.Y. 1987).]
8. Terra Distributing advertised an offer of two free airline tickets with the purchase of a cellular telephone. Gabriel purchased the required cellular telephone for $699 plus tax, paying for the purchase with a check. When Gabriel received the telephone he was told that the airline tickets were not free but would require an additional payment of several hundred dollars. Gabriel refused delivery of the telephone, and sent a letter demanding delivery of the airline tickets. Terra Distributing filed for Chapter 7. What recourse does Gabriel have now? [See *In re: Terra Distributing*, 1992 Bankr. LEXIS 2034.]
9. Many large companies, including Johns-Manville, have filed a Chapter 11 bankruptcy petition without being insolvent. Discuss the ethical implications of such a decision by management.
10. A credit bureau can obtain a great deal of information about a person, depending on the amount of time and energy it chooses to expend. Should credit bureaus be allowed to check a person's school records and contact a person's neighbors, teachers, and acquaintances? Why or why not?

PRACTICAL EXERCISE

Zinna is a new business involved in manufacturing and selling golf clubs to large retail stores as well as to small golf shops. However, Zinna has been having trouble getting customers to pay for its clubs before they are delivered. Most of Zinna's sales are now made on open account, and the customer is given 30 days to pay for the delivered golf clubs. Zinna wants to be able to repossess the golf clubs if its customers fail to pay the account in 30 days.

1. What type of questions can and should Zinna ask on a credit application before it allows customers to use an open account? Draft a credit application that could also be used as a security agreement and still comply with Truth in Lending.

2. What steps can Zinna take in order to ensure that its customers are good credit risks?
3. What steps does Zinna need to take to ensure that it can repossess the golf clubs in the event a customer defaults?
4. Draft additional appropriate documents necessary to create a perfected security interest.
5. Obtain from a local merchant a copy of a security agreement. Interview the manager to determine how important such filings are to the business' sale volume. Summarize the interview.

Your instructor may want you to check your local state law to determine what interest rate you can charge on past due accounts, what finance charges you can use on past due accounts, and what documents are necessary to perfect a security interest in golf clubs in your state.

FURTHER INFORMATION

www.abiworld.org/
www.creditpage.com/
www.pueblo.gsa.gov/money.htm
www.law.cornell.edu/ucc/ucc.table.html

CHAPTER 18

UNFAIR AND DECEPTIVE TRADE PRACTICES AND ADVERTISING

LEARNING OBJECTIVES

After you have read this chapter, you should be able to:

1. Describe how the FTC operates.
2. Identify several types of deceptive trade practices.
3. Explain the difference between federal and common law protections.
4. Discuss the regulations affecting advertising.

CHAPTER OUTLINE

I. Federal Trade Commission
II. Common Law Protections
III. National Advertising Division
IV. Labeling
V. Deceptive Acts and Practices
VI. Advertising to Children
VII. Unfair Trade Practices
VIII. Telephone Solicitations
IX. Consumer Product Safety Commission

Phil wants to open a business to help individuals lose weight. He wants to advertise his "weight loss" plan on the Internet as well as solicit potential customers by telephone. What does Phil need to know about deceptive advertising before he begins?

INTRODUCTION

Consumers are constantly bombarded with marketing ploys aimed at convincing them to purchase one product over another. Marketing means more than simply advertising a product for sale. One need only watch college football bowl games, underwritten by corporate sponsors totally unrelated to collegiate athletics, to understand how multifaceted marketing has become.

In a market economy, marketing is a fact of doing business. It is the process by which consumers are introduced to businesses and their products. Even though marketing has become commonplace, it is not without its critics. Popular opinion polls reflect the fact that the general public does not hold business, especially big business, in high esteem. Much of this perception results from highly publicized events in which some businesses have been less than honest in their advertising. One need only look at the profusion of "cure-alls," "special potions," "magic pills," con artists, and swindlers to understand why consumers may be skeptical. Unfortunately, legitimate businesses have also been known to deceive customers. When consumers are deceived, they often have very little real power as individuals against large business organizations that simply can ignore their complaints.

FEDERAL TRADE COMMISSION

During the Progressive Period (1880–1920) in U.S. history, and at the urging of President Woodrow Wilson, Congress in 1914 passed the *Federal Trade Commission Act*. Its main goal was to shore up the remedies provided under earlier antitrust legislation, most notably the Sherman and Clayton Acts discussed in Chapter 16. Under the Federal Trade Commission Act, Congress established the *Federal Trade Commission (FTC)* in 1915. The FTC is an independent, bipartisan agency with five members called *commissioners*. (Independent agencies are discussed in Chapter 5.) The President appoints the members to the Commission, the Senate confirms them, and each member serves a term of seven years. No more than three members of the commission may be members of the same political party. The Federal Trade Commission Act gives the FTC several powers, including, under §5, the authority to issue rules that define unfair methods of competition, as well as additional authority established by subsequent legislation.

In 1938, the *Wheeler-Lea Act* amended the 1914 Act. Wheeler-Lea prohibited deceptive trade practices as well as unfair methods of competition. In 1973, the *Alaska Pipeline Act* amended the FTC Act by increasing the penalties for violating FTC-issued **cease and desist orders**. A cease and desist order, like an injunction, prohibits a company from continuing a deceptive act or practice. If the FTC finds that a violation has occurred, a cease and desist order requires that the violator completely stop the unlawful activity. The FTC can impose a fine of $25,000 for each day that a cease and desist order is violated. The Act also allows for injunctive relief, and the FTC can impose fines of up to $10,000 per violation. The FTC can require that the violator pay damages to anyone whom the deceptive act has harmed, and the FTC can require that the violator rescind a contract that violates the Act. The *FTC Improvement Act*, another amendment to the FTC Act, was passed in 1975. This Act gives the FTC even more power. For example, it allows the FTC to impose fines for violating trade rules.

cease and desist order: An order from an administrative agency to stop engaging in a particular activity.

The FTC issues *trade practice rules*. These rules are industry-specific guides. They set out, in ordinary language, what acts and practices of a particular industry are deceptive or unfair. For example, in the jewelry industry a specific rule exists for being able to use the term *pearl*. The trade practice rule states:

> It is an unfair trade practice to use the word "pearl" to describe, identify, or refer to a cultured pearl unless it is immediately preceded, with equal conspicuity, by the word "cultured" or by some other word or phrase of like meaning and connotation so as to indicate definitely and clearly that the product is not a pearl. 16 C.F.R. sec. 23.15(b).

The FTC also has the power to issue *trade regulation rules*. Trade regulation rules are promulgated by the FTC pursuant to its rule making authority. These rules define and interpret specific acts the FTC determines to be unfair competition and deceptive trade practices. The difference between trade practice rules and trade regulation rules lies in what burden of proof is necessary to prove a violation. For example, if a company is charged with violating a trade regulation rule, the FTC need only show that the rule was violated. On the other hand, a violation of a trade practice rule requires a showing that the committed act itself was unfair or deceptive. Although the distinction is technical, the result is that it is easier for the FTC to prove violations of trade regulation rules than it is to show violations of trade practice rules.

Under the Federal Trade Comission Act, the FTC has the authority to investigate actions that it believes are violations. The FTC may receive a complaint by a competitor, another government agency, or a consumer. The FTC may or may not decide to investigate the compliant to determine if a violation has occurred. The Federal Trade Comission Act does not allow an individual to bring a private lawsuit against a violator, nor does it require the FTC to independently initiate an investigation. Rather, if someone believes that the Act has been violated, he or she needs to file a complaint with the FTC. The FTC determines an act is deceptive if it has the "potential to **mislead**" the reasonable consumer, and the deception would likely affect the consumer's decision. The fact that a single consumer is deceived may not mean the action is **deceptive**. Rather, the FTC looks at consumer research data and economic analysis to determine whether "reasonable consumers" were deceived. Some states allows a consumer to bring an action in state court if he or she has been deceived.

misleading: Possessing the capacity or tendency to create a mistaken impression.

deceptive: Tending to or having the capacity to cause to accept as true something that is false.

SOCIAL/ETHICAL ISSUES

Since the Federal Trade Comission Act does not allow an injured person, either consumer or creditor, to file a lawsuit against a violator, some have argued that no real penalty exists for running deceptive advertising, especially if the company is small and local. There is little likelihood that the FTC would use its limited resources to go against anyone other than very large businesses. Do you agree with this argument? Should enforcement depend on the size of the company being sued?

One of the FTC's major weapons is the authority to require a violator to run corrective advertising. The FTC can require that a violator spend up to 25 percent of its budget on corrective advertising, although the actual dollar amount imposed varies. As the next case indicates, corrective advertising can be expensive.

WARNER-LAMBERT COMPANY V. FEDERAL TRADE COMMISSION

562 F.2d 749 (D.C.Cir 1977)

FACTS

Warner-Lambert Company manufactures the mouthwash Listerine. Listerine has been marketed since 1879 with no change in its original formula. During all this time, Listerine has been advertised as helping prevent, cure, and alleviate symptoms of the common cold and sore throats. In an extensive hearing, the FTC found that each of these claims was false. First, it found that the ingredients eucalyptol/eucalyptus oil, menthol, and thymol were not found in Listerine in sufficient quantities to be beneficial, nor were there any well-controlled studies to suggest otherwise. Second, gargling does not enable the mouthwash to reach areas in the body where it would be medically significant. Third, even if the medicinal ingredients could reach helpful areas, the mouthwash could not interfere with the virus because the ingredients cannot penetrate tissue cells. Fourth, the clinical study upon which Warner-Lambert relied was not double-blind and was therefore unreliable. Fifth, "while Listerine kills millions of bacteria in the mouth, it also leaves millions. It is impossible to sterilize any area of the mouth, let alone the entire mouth." Further, Listerine kills bacteria; colds, on the other hand, are caused by a virus. Finally, while gargling itself does provide temporary relief of sore throats, "such temporary relief does not 'lessen the severity' of a sore throat any more than expectorating or blowing one's nose 'lessens the severity' of a cold."

With these findings, the FTC ordered Warner-Lambert to cease and desist from making any claims that would contradict the findings, including that Listerine would cure colds or sore throats, prevent colds or sore throats, or lessen the severity of colds and sore throats. It further ordered that the next $10 million of advertising spent on Listerine contain the following conspicuous statement: "Contrary to prior advertising, Listerine will not help prevent colds or sore throats or lessen their severity." Warner-Lambert appealed the FTC decision.

DECISION

Judge Skelly Wright, writing the opinion for the Court of Appeals for the District of Columbia, stated that the first issue concerned whether the FTC has the authority to order corrective advertising and, if so, if corrective advertising was appropriate in this instance. Although the Federal Trade Commission Act itself does not specifically mention corrective advertising as a remedy, neither does the Act prevent it. On several occasions, the FTC had required companies to affirmatively disclose information in order to protect future consumers. This particular order was not substantively different.

The next question concerned whether corrective advertising was appropriate in this case. The FTC has adopted the following standard for determining when to use corrective advertising as a remedy:

If a deceptive advertisement has played a substantial role in creating or reinforcing in the public's mind a false and material belief which lives on after the false advertising ceases, there is clear and continuing injury to competition and to the consuming public as consumers continue to make purchasing decisions based on the false belief. Since this injury cannot be averted by merely requiring [the] respondent to cease disseminating the advertisement, we may appropriately order [the] respondent to take affirmative action designed to terminate the otherwise continuing ill effects of the advertisement. This standard requires the FTC to ask whether the "advertisements play a substantial role in creating or reinforcing in the public's mind a false belief about the product and . . . would this belief linger on after the false advertising ceases."

In this case, the claim was 100 years old. Further, a survey commissioned by Warner-Lambert found that about 70 percent of consumers identified "effective for colds and sore throats" as Listerine's main advertising theme. Therefore, corrective advertising was appropriate in this case. The amount represented a sum equal to Warner-Lambert's average annual advertising budget for a 10-year period. Thus, it was not "an unreasonably long time in which to correct a hundred years of cold claims."

The court did decide that Warner-Lambert did not need to use the words "contrary to prior advertising." Those words may be used in a case of deliberate deception, but the record indicated that Warner-Lambert's claims were made in good faith.

CASE QUESTIONS

1. Warner-Lambert also argued that corrective advertising violated the First Amendment. How should the court respond?
2. Should the FTC have set a time limit on running the ads rather than a dollar amount? Why do you think it chose the dollar amount?
3. Do you think Listerine's claim was deceptive? Why or why not?

Besides federal protection, many states have also passed consumer sales practices acts. These acts are similar to the FTC Act and may provide more consumer protection than federal law.

COMMON LAW PROTECTIONS

Since the FTC does not allow for a private right of action, some injured parties choose to file civil lawsuits in order to collect money damages. Consumers injured by deceptive acts and practices can file lawsuits based on the tort claims of fraud by misrepresentation, using the same *prima facie* case as discussed in Chapter 11. Injured competitors can file common law tort claims based on trade disparagement, trade defamation, and trademark infringement. *Trade disparagement* occurs when untrue statements are made about a product and the competitor suffers financial loss. A competitor claiming *trade defamation* need not show financial loss but does need to show that a statement was made that was damaging to its business reputation in general rather than damaging to one of its products in particular. *Trademark infringement* is also known as *passing* or *palming off*. This occurs when a competitor can show that the consumer is likely to be confused as to who is sponsoring the product. For example, "Enjoy Coca-Cola" was transposed on a poster to read "Enjoy Cocaine." The court held that the poster manufacturer was passing off, since consumers may believe that Coca-Cola was engaged in an advertising gimmick. On the other hand, when the scout motto "Be Prepared" was placed on a picture of a pregnant girl in a girl scout uniform, that court held that the consumer would not be misled into thinking that the "wholesome" Girl Scout organization would sponsor such a poster.

NATIONAL ADVERTISING DIVISION

Another entity addressing deceptive advertising is a self-policing entity known as the *National Advertising Division* (*NAD*), the advertising industry's self-regulatory body. It was formed by the American Association of Advertising

Agencies, American Advertising Federation, Association of National Advertisers, and the Council for Better Business Bureaus. Complaints can be filed with NAD by consumers, competitors, and consumer groups. If an advertiser disagrees with a NAD decision, the advertiser can appeal the decision to the *National Advertising Review Board (NARB)*. If an ad is found to be deceptive, NAD generally requires the ad to be substantiated, modified, or discontinued. Advertisements that are modified or discontinued are reported to the public. NAD's decisions are not legally binding, and a complainant cannot receive financial compensation. However, advertisers participating in NAD investigations tend to abide by the NAD decision.

LABELING

Never before has the need to properly label a product been so important. Early legislation, like the *Wool Products Labeling Act*, the *Textile Fiber Products Identification Act*, the *Fur Products Labeling Act*, and the *Flammable Fabrics Act* required certain products to be properly labeled. The FTC, under the 1966 *Fair Packaging and Labeling Act*, now has the power to issue labeling regulations in all areas. Further, the *Food and Drug Administration (FDA)* and the U.S. Department of Agriculture are charged with overhauling food labeling and promotion under the *1990 Nutrition Labeling and Education Act*. As a result of this act, almost all products are now required to contain nutritional labeling. There is an exemption for fresh meat, which is regulated by the U.S. Department of Agriculture, but cheese, peanut butter, and other foods high in fat must comply. All regulated products must now have nutrition labels that indicate the amount of cholesterol, sodium, and grams of fat contained in each serving size. Further, new labeling guidelines require packages to indicate true serving sizes. For example, is a 12-ounce can of soda really two servings? Is a true serving of potato chips 10 chips? These and other serving claims come under the scrutiny of the FDA. Also, the FDA is looking at the use of terms like "healthy," "cholesterol free," and "lite" as those that might be considered deceptive. Food labeling has also become an international issue. As the next article suggests, the food label is sometimes more confusing than regulators believe.

Attempt at Clarity in Food Labeling Prompts Much Confusion in the U.K.

It seems simple enough: Let consumers know when they're buying bioengineered food by requiring a label. It's an idea being promoted heavily in the U.S. by groups such as Greenpeace and Friends of the Earth, and even by some members of Congress.

But a trip up and down the supermarket aisles of Britain, which has required such labeling since March, shows the new law hasn't exactly made things easier for discerning shoppers. Rather, it has spawned a bewildering array of marketing claims, counterclaims and outright contradictions that only a food scientist possibly could unravel.

Take cheese. One supermarket chain here labels its cheese as being "made using genetic modification," the European catchword for bioengineering. But other supermarket chains, whose cheese is made exactly the same way, haven't changed their labels, saying the cheese itself contains no genetically modified ingredients.

Then there's Birds Eye frozen beef burgers. The label on a box purchased last week states that one ingredient, soya protein, is "produced from genetically modified soya." But a spokesman for maker Unilever PLC insists that the soya isn't genetically modified. The company has reformulated the product, he explains, but has yet to replace the box.

Yes or No?

Confused yet? Then scan over the small print on a Haggen-Dazs chocolate-covered ice-cream bar. No genetically modified ingredients listed there. But consumers who question the company about it are sent a letter stating that the bar's chocolate coatings, in fact, contain soya oil that "may have been derived from genetically modified soya, but it is identical to any other soya oil and therefore does not contain any genetically modified material." The letter adds, "We are, however, investigating whether there are suitable alternative oils."

All of this may seem puzzling to American shoppers, who so far aren't up in arms over whether the food they buy includes ingredients that have been tinkered with in a laboratory. After all, that's already the case with many U.S. products. But European consumers, who have lived through such recent food scares as beef linked to "mad cow" disease, salmonella-contaminated eggs and dioxintainted animal feed, are taking no chances, even if there's no proof that bioengineered foods pose any health risks.

Monster Mash

The result has been a biotech backlash that at times borders on hysteria. In Britain, tabloid newspapers routinely refer to genetically modified products as "Frankenstein food." One prisoner even went on a hunger strike demanding that no genetically modified food be served to inmates.

Critics say bioengineered foods offer consumers no obvious benefit and that despite industry and government assurances, not enough research has been done to assure they are safe. Environmental groups have expressed concern that genetically modified plants could have unintended side effects, including killing beneficial insects and, through the spread of pollen, promoting growth of herbicide-resistant "super weeds" and antibiotic-resistant "super bugs." Others fear genetically modified foods could cause dangerous allergic reactions in some people.

In response to widespread consumer outcry, the European Union last year approved legislation that requires its 15 member countries to begin labeling all foods that contain genetically modified ingredients, namely corn and soybean in which new genes have been added to provide traits such as insect resistance.

American Reverberations

While no such plans have been announced in the U.S., the Food and Drug Administration said last week that it plans hearings around the country this fall to gauge public opinion on the issue. Already, several American health-food companies have begun slapping labels on their products declaring that they contain no genetically modified ingredients.

But before America leaps into mandatory labeling, the government, retailers and consumer groups might want to take a look at the far-reaching impact such a law has had in Britain.

When the European Union introduced its legislation last year, Britain's agriculture minister called it "a triumph for consumer rights to better information." Britain went on to enact the toughest labeling standards in Europe, requiring even restaurants, caterers and bakers to list genetically modified ingredients. Violations are punishable by fines of as much as $8,400, and the government says it intends to conduct surveillance, including independent lab testing.

"This is not a health issue in any way," says J. R. Bell, head of the government's additives and novel-foods division, adding that his ministry believes the latest bioengineered products are safe. "This is a question of choice, of consumer choice."

But, in fact, as a direct result of the labeling law, there's hardly any choice now at all. That's because Britain's new law sparked a mad rush by manufacturers, retailers and restaurant chains to rid their products of any genetically modified ingredients so they wouldn't have to alter their labels and risk losing sales. Even some pet-food manufacturers are claiming their products contain no genetically modified ingredients.

Among the thousands of products sold in Britain that now claim not to contain any genetically modified ingredients are Pillsbury UK Ltd.'s Green Giant vegetables and Old El Paso Mexican food, Kellogg cereals and Unilever's Van den Bergh Foods Beanfeast line. A spokesman for McDonald's Restaurants Ltd., which operates 1,000 restaurants in the United Kingdom, says, "We do not use any genetically modified products or ingredients that contain genetically modified material." He adds, however, that some ingredients, such as soya oil used in hamburger buns, "could have come from a source which itself is genetically modified at some point."

The rush to keep products from being branded as bioengineered is hardly surprising. When J. Sainsbury PLC, a supermarket chain, began selling a bioengineered tomato puree under its own brand in 1996, sales initially exceeded other, more expensive brands by 30%, though the product's label volunteered that it was genetically modified. But as the genetically modified controversy heated up, sales slowed and, by the end of last year, "absolutely fell through the floor," says Alison Austin, Sainsbury's environmental manager. The product has since been taken off the market by its creator and distributor, Zeneca Plant Science, a unit of AstraZeneca PLC.

New Recipes

Having gotten the message that consumers don't want bioengineered foods, Sainsbury's and other supermarket chains, as well as food manufacturers that sell in Britain, launched extensive, monthslong reviews of their product formulations. They began changing recipes to eliminate soya and corn derivatives and ordered their suppliers to find new sources of nonbioengineered raw materials in places such as South America and Asia.

"We poured over something like 5,000 ingredients . . . and made changes to 1,800 recipes as part of this process," says Bob Mitchell, manager of food technical policy at Marks & Spencer PLC, which operates specialty food shops. "It was a colossal task."

Supermarkets soon began declaring in advertising that their own house brands, which in Britain can constitute more than half of all sales, no longer contained genetically modified ingredients.

But a close examination of stores' claims, based on interviews with supermarket executives, shows that one chain's definition of removing genetically modified ingredients isn't necessarily the same as another's.

Sainsbury's, for example, says on its Web site that it is "the first major U.K. supermarket to eliminate genetically modified ingredients from its own-brand products." Does that include food additives, such as sweeteners and flavorings, which may be genetically modified? Alison Austin, the company's environmental manager, replies, "To be honest, we have focused in on major ingredients" such as soya and maize proteins and oils, as well as lecithin, an emulsifier. As for other bioengineered ingredients, she says, "It takes time for the supply chain to provide alternatives."

'We Mean Zero GM'

Tesco PLC, Britain's leading supermarket chain, says it makes no distinction between major and minor genetically modified ingredients. As a result, 150 of its house-brand products are still labeled as containing genetically modified ingredients. "When we say zero GM, we mean zero GM," says Simon Soffe, a Tesco spokesman.

Maybe so, but laboratories that test for genetically modified ingredients say it is almost impossible to guarantee that a product line contains absolutely no genetically modified ingredients. Many growers don't segregate bioengineered and nonbioengineered soybeans and corn. Moreover, genetically modified materials in highly processed additives or oils often can't be detected in testing. "If there's no way to test, then people are going to bend the rules and they're going to bend the truth," says Bruce Ferguson, president of EnviroLogix Inc., an environmental-testing company in Portland, Maine.

Some inconsistencies in supermarket claims can be attributed to the labeling law itself. At the moment, the European Union and British regulations require labeling only if genetically modified material is detectable in DNA or protein. Additives and flavorings are exempt.

Cheese-Making

That has led to some strange labeling dilemmas in items as simple as cheese. Traditionally, cheese was set using an enzyme called rennet, taken from the lining of calves' stomachs. But to appease vegetarians, many European cheese makers in recent years switched to an enzyme called chymosin that is produced from genetically modified bacteria.

There's no evidence that any genetically modified ingredient remains in the cheese after production. Still, one supermarket chain, Co-Op, decided to place labels on its cheese that say "made using genetic modification and so free from animal rennet." "It's a question of whether the retailer is honest or open in labeling it," says a Co-Op spokesman.

Meantime, Iceland, a small but scrappy convenience-store chain whose chairman coined the term "Frankenstein food," says it has switched to making its cheese with another enzyme that doesn't come from animals and isn't produced from genetically modified bacteria. "We've done them one better," says Bill Wadsworth, the chain's technical director.

European Union officials say they are hoping to clear up some of the confusion in the marketplace. Last week, a panel of government representatives voted to extend the labeling law to cover additives and flavorings, a change that is expected to take effect next year and could force many manufacturers and fast-food restaurants to either change recipes, switch suppliers or begin labeling.

Trace Amounts

The EU also decided to address the problem of products "contaminated" with trace amounts of genetically modified material despite the best intentions of manufacturers. In a controversial decision, the panel recommended that products don't require labeling if each of the ingredients contains 1% bioengineered material or less. Consumer groups had argued that the limit should be one-tenth of that.

In the future, the EU may also try to define when a retailer or manufacturer may claim that a product is "GM-free," a phrase that already has sprung up in some advertising and promotional material. Many retailers, such as Marks & Spencer, instead use the term "non-GM," which they insist is different. "We would never call it GM-free because you could never guarantee that," Mr. Mitchell says.

And thornier labeling issues loom. In their competitive frenzy, some British supermarkets have begun introducing raw and frozen chicken that they claim was raised on feed containing no genetically modified ingredients—even though there isn't evidence that bioengineered material ends up in the meat. To accomplish this, Iceland convenience stores say they now buy their chickens in Brazil, instead of Britain. Marks & Spencer says it is about to introduce a new line of free-range, non–genetically modified poultry, egg and pork products.

Sainsbury's has yet to join the non–genetically modified chicken and pork parade, but Mrs. Austin says it's probably "inevitable" and adds it may only be a first step. "We are utterly adamant that if you wish to claim you are GM-free, then you are ultimately going to have to go as far as GM-free veterinary medicines," she says.

DECEPTIVE ACTS AND PRACTICES

Although all deceptive acts and practices are illegal, there are some practices that have been specifically identified as inherently deceptive.

PYRAMID SALES SCHEMES

pyramid sales scheme: An illegal scheme in which participants give money or other valuables in exchange for the opportunity to receive payment for recruiting others to participate in the scheme.

A **pyramid sales scheme** is a type of sales pitch that promises that once a person buys an item, that person gets paid for each additional buyer he or she finds for the company. It is also called multilevel distributorship, chain referral plan, or referral sales plan. The FTC has determined that many forms of pyramid schemes are deceptive acts and practices and are therefore illegal. One of the reasons that such schemes are usually deceptive is that the plan's promoters do not reveal the nature of the plan. Often, the plan is sold as a way to make a lot of money without actually working. In a true pyramid scheme, a person makes money by bringing other individuals into the plan, and that person receives money when those that he or she brought in brings others into the plan. For example, Patty approaches you with a great deal. You pay her $50, and then you recruit two other people into the plan, who each pay you $50. Sounds great! What makes it deceptive, however (besides the question of why pay Patty $50, when you can just ask for $50 from two other unsuspecting "friends"), is that, mathematically, it is impossible for very many people to make money. For example, if there are 7 promoters of the plan and each of the 7 promoters bring in 7 investors, and then those 49 investors each bring in 7 investors, it brings the number of investors to 343. If the pattern continues, eventually the total number exceeds over 2 billion people. By the 12th level you need more people than are alive in the world to continue to make money. The difference between legal and illegal pyramid schemes is sometimes difficult to determine. The key fact is a determination as to what is actually being sold. If it is the "scheme" that is being sold and an individual is rewarded based on the number of recruits brought into the scheme, then the pyramid is illegal. If the individual is rewarded by product sales and the sales goals are not unrealistic, then the pyramid may be legal. This difficulty is discussed in the next FTC case.

FROM THE DESK OF
Laura Lawyer

To: Students
From: Your Lawyer

Multilevel marketing plans are commonly investigated both for deceptiveness and for securities laws violations. The line between what is legal and illegal is often blurred. If you are engaging in a business in which part of your money comes from bringing others into the business, then you should probably seek an attorney's legal advice.

IN THE MATTER OF AMWAY CORPORATION, INC. ET AL.

93 F.T.C. 618 (1979).

FACTS

In 1975, the FTC charged Amway Corporation with violating §5 of the Federal Trade Commission Act. All of the violations involved Amway's distribution network. The Administrative Law Judge (ALJ) found that Amway "had engaged in illegal resale price maintenance but had failed to establish that respondents had committed other violations of §5."

Amway manufactures over 150 products including soaps, detergents, polishes, cleaning supplies, and pharmaceutical preparations. Amway is relatively small when compared with other industry giants. Without large advertising budgets, it is almost impossible to enter this field. "Amway skirted these near-insurmountable barriers and interjected a vigorous new competitive presence into this highly concentrated market by developing what is known as a 'direct selling' distribution network."

Amway sells its products through 360,000 independent distributors, who work through Amway's multilevel distributor system. Under the Amway Plan, a select few distributors, known as direct distributors, purchase products at wholesale directly from Amway and resell the products both at retail to consumers and at wholesale to the distributors they personally "sponsored." Each second-level distributor resells the products both at retail to consumers and at wholesale to the distributors he or she personally sponsored. The third-level distributors perform the same two functions. This multilevel wholesaling network ends with those distributors who have not sponsored any new distributors and who make purchases from their sponsors solely for their own use or for resale to consumers. Distributors earn money by making retail sales themselves and/or by receiving a percentage of their business volume. This computes in the following manner. The direct distributor is paid 25 cents by Amway on each dollar of business volume but only pays 15 cents to second-level distributors on each dollar of the respective business volumes. The direct distributor would net a 25-cent bonus on each dollar of business volume representing retail sales made by him or her to consumers and a 10-cent bonus on each dollar of business volume representing wholesale sales made by the sponsored distributors. Second-level distributors do the same to third-level distributors and so forth down the line. A person can become a direct distributor by being a very high-volume performer. It is alleged that this constitutes an illegal pyramid scheme.

The Commission has defined an illegal pyramid scheme as the "payment of money to the company in return for which they receive (1) the right to sell a product and (2) the right to receive in return for recruiting other participants into the program rewards which are unrelated to sale of the product to ultimate users." "The Amway plan does not contain [these] essential features . . . and therefore, it is not a scheme which is inherently false, misleading, or deceptive."

Amway has several rules that encourage retail sales: (1) a new distributor is required to spend $15.60 for a sales kit, and the purchase price can be refunded if the person decides to leave; (2) a " buy-back" rule requires sponsoring distributors to buy back any unused merchandise from a sponsoring distributor who is leaving the organization; (3) before a distributor receives the performance bonus, the 70-percent rule (requiring distributors to sell at wholesale or retail 70 percent of the products bought during the month) and the 10-customer rule (the distributor must sell products to 10 different customers during the month) must be satisfied. All of these rules make "retail selling an essential part of being a distributor." "Specifically, the Amway Plan is not a plan where participants purchase the right to earn profits by recruiting other participants, who themselves are interested in recruitment fees rather than the sale of products."

Finally, Amway has been charged with making misrepresentations and omissions concerning unrealistic earnings or sales claims. The first category of claims can fall under the heading of "non-earning." These claims consist of "vague references to the achievement of one's dreams, having everything one always wanted, and so on," are phrased in terms of "opportunity," "possibility," or "chance" and are surrounded by warnings that hard work is required. Moreover, these claims are primarily inspirational and motivational, and amount to puffing.

Statements that contain specific references as to how much one is likely to make, however, are deceptive. Recruiting manuals leave the distinct impression that individuals can make $200 per month as an Amway distributor. "[T]he record shows that in 1969–70 the average monthly Business Volume of Amway distributors was about $20, and in 1973–74 it was about $33." Less than 1 percent of Amway distributors make thousands of dollars. "Therefore, these statements constitute illegal misrepresentations under §5."

CASE QUESTIONS

1. What could an Amway distributor say to potential distributors to make the proposition attractive but still comply with the law?
2. What specifically distinguishes Amway's marketing scheme from illegal pyramid schemes?
3. What kinds of statements constitute puffery in this case? What kinds of statements constitute misrepresentations?

LITERAL TRUTH

puffery or puffing: The practice of making exaggerated comments especially for promotional purposes.

As the Amway case suggests, **puffery** is not illegal. Puffery occurs where no reasonable person would believe the statement. For example, if a seller tells a buyer that "this car is the best little car in the world," the statement is obviously puffery.

Misrepresentations, on the other hand, are illegal under §5 of the Federal Trade Commission Act if they have the capacity to deceive. Usually, the difference between puffery and misrepresentation lies in how close to factual the statement sounds. For example, "This car has 100,000 miles on it" is a factual statement. It is either true or false. Absolute truth, however, may not be a defense in some cases. If a statement is literally true but the total impression given by the advertisement is such that the consumer is deceived, there may be a violation, as the following case demonstrates.

KRAFT V. FTC

970 F.2d 311 (7th Cir. 1992)

FACTS

The FTC challenged Kraft's advertising campaign for its Kraft Singles American Pasteurized Process Cheese Food, "Singles." In the 1980s, Kraft began losing market share in the individually wrapped process cheese market. In response, Kraft ran a series of advertisements indicating that Kraft Singles were made with five ounces of milk and implying that the Singles contained the equivalent amount of calcium. The advertisements were focused on growing consumer interest in increasing amounts of calcium in the daily diet. In the individually wrapped process cheese slices market, there are three types of "cheese": process, imitation, and substitute. The FTC requires that products cannot be labeled "process cheese slices," unless they have at least 51 percent natural cheese. Imitation cheese slices, on the other hand, contain little or no cheese and are mostly water, vegetable oil, flavoring, and fortifying agents. Imitation cheese is considered nutritionally inferior to process cheese and must carry the "imitation" label. Substitute cheese falls in between process cheese and imitation cheese.

There are two sets of advertisements at issue. The "Skimp" television advertisements contained the following:

Woman (voice-over): I admit it. I thought of skimping. Could you look into those blue eyes and skimp on her? So I buy Kraft Singles. Imitation slices use hardly any milk. But Kraft has five ounces per slice. Five ounces. So her little bones get calcium they need to grow. No, she doesn't know what that big Kraft means. Good thing I do.

Singers: Kraft Singles. More milk makes 'em . . . more milk makes 'em good.

Woman (voice-over): Skimp on her? No way.

The second television advertisement depicts a group of school children having their class picture taken.

Announcer (voice-over): Can you see what is missing in this picture? Well, a government study says that half the school kids in America don't get all the calcium recommended for growing kids. That's why Kraft Singles are important. Kraft is made from five ounces of milk per slice. So they're concentrated with calcium. Calcium the government recommends for strong bones and healthy teeth!

Photographer: Say Cheese!

Kids: Cheese!

Announcer (voice-over): Say Kraft Singles. 'Cause kids love Kraft Singles, right down to their bones.

In 1987 both advertisements were changed and ran the subscript disclaimer "one 3/4 ounce slice has 70% of the calcium of five ounces of milk."

The Court finds the following facts to be critical: "First, although Kraft does use five ounces of milk in making each Kraft Single, roughly 30% of the calcium contained in the milk is lost during processing. Second, the vast majority of imitation slices sold in the United States contain 15% of the U.S. Recommended Daily Allowance (RDA) of calcium per ounce, roughly the same amount contained in Kraft Singles."

The FTC found that the implied claims in Kraft's advertisements were that a slice of Kraft process cheese had the same amount of calcium as five ounces of milk and that Kraft Singles contained more calcium than imitation cheeses. Since neither of these claims were true, the FTC found that Kraft had violated the Federal Trade Ccommission Act and ordered it to cease and desist. Kraft appealed.

DECISION

Judge Flaum wrote the opinion of the Seventh Circuit Court of Appeals. The decisions of the FTC are entitled to deference since they involve highly technical and complex factual questions. Kraft argued that the FTC was wrong in not requiring proof of actual consumer deception. Since there was no proof of actual deception, the FTC's order chills commercial speech. Further, Kraft claims there is no evidence that the advertisement's claims were material to the consumer.

In order to determine if an advertisement is deceptive, a court first views it. If it cannot be determined whether the advertisement is deceptive after the viewing, then the fact-finding body turns to scientific evidence, like consumer testimony, expert opinion, and copy tests of the advertisement. The Court finds this approach to be appropriate. The FTC can use its subjective judgment and does not need extrinsic evidence to find an advertisement false or deceptive.

Further, the First Amendment protection of commercial speech is not harmed by this approach. Commercial speech is not protected as heavily as other forms of speech, and consumer surveys are not required for proof of deception when the alleged deception is conspicuous even though the deceptive claim is implied. Although Kraft argued that its statements were literally true, literally true statements can be deceptive. The court finds that "the average consumer is not likely to know that much of the calcium in five ounces of milk (30%) is lost in processing, which leaves consumers with a misleading impression about calcium content. The critical fact is not that reasonable consumers might believe that a 3/4 ounce slice of cheese actually contains five ounces of *milk*, but that reasonable consumers might believe that a 3/4 ounce slice actually contains the calcium of five ounces of milk."

In looking at whether the calcium claims were material to the consumer, the court notes that Kraft was warned by ABC television, the California Attorney General, and its own advertising agency in a legal memorandum that the claims were potentially misleading and needed to be substantiated. Instead, a high-level executive argued against altering the advertisement copy, stating, "Singles business is growing for the first time in four years due in large part to the ad copy." This indicates that Kraft thought the claims were material to consumers. Further, the expert who testified at trial and Kraft's own consumer surveys indicated that the calcium content of cheese was important to consumers. The Seventh Circuit agreed with the FTC that the advertisements were deceptive and that the claims made in the advertisements were material to the consumer. The FTC's cease and desist order was upheld.

CASE QUESTIONS

1. Do you find Kraft's advertisements to be deceptive? Why or why not?
2. Does Kraft's disclaimer change your opinion about whether the advertisement is deceptive? Why or why not?
3. Is a cease and desist order an effective remedy against deceptive advertising? Explain.

MISLEADING CLAIMS

Several types of specific claims are also considered to be deceptive. For example, businesses that advertise a "Going Out of Business Sale," or a "Total Liquidation Sale," are engaging in deceptive acts if, in fact, they are not going out of business. Some stores make claims that a product is being sold below its original price or is on sale when, in fact, it is the same price as always. These marketing tactics are considered to be deceptive. Advertising a sales price means that the product must be sold for less than what it actually sold for in the past.

disclaimer: A denial of responsibility or a limitation of a statement or impression.

Other claims that are misleading occur when products are sold together. For example, claims that a consumer will receive three bars of soap for the price of two bars of soap must be read literally. If the consumer can only buy the soap in three-bar packages, then the claim is deceptive. Weight-loss claims must run **disclaimers** that reflect the fact that weight loss rates and amounts vary from individual to individual and are usually the result of exercise and diet rather than the advertised "miracle" device.

MISLEADING PICTORIALS AND DEMONSTRATIONS

Not only can statements be misleading, but the pictures used in advertising can also be deceptive. For example, the makers of Volvo ran a television advertisement that depicted a "monster truck" trying to unsuccessfully crunch a Volvo car. An investigation revealed that the roof of the car used in the advertisement had been reinforced with steel. Volvo agreed to withdraw the promotion and ran corrective advertisements. The corrective advertisement indicated that two of the three cars used in the ad were reinforced. The advertising company that produced the advertisement was fired.

SOCIAL/ETHICAL ISSUES

Many beer commercials show upscale party scenes with young, attractive men and women having a very good time. Some cigarette advertisements have used cartoon characters as the primary focus. These types of advertisements have been attacked for various ethical reasons. What might these reasons be? Should advertisers be allowed to advertise products that are dangerous to people's health? Should they be required to run disclaimers or other types of warnings?

FREE CLAIMS

Everyone likes to receive free items. The claim "Buy One, Get One Free" can be misleading if, in fact, the item is not free. According to FTC regulations, "free" means "free." If the consumer has to pay anything for the product, then the product is not free. Under FTC regulations, the "regular price" of a product is the lowest price at which the product sold during the previous 30 days. Engaging in a pizza promotional campaign and advertising "free pizza delivery," when, in fact, there had not been a charge for pizza delivery over the past 30 days might be construed to be misleading. Also, no free offer should extend for longer than six months. If there are requirements for receiving the free offer, these requirements must be stated clearly and conspicuously in the promotion. If the free offer is not available in all locations, that fact must be stated. To comply with this rule, it is not unusual to see the phrase "subject to local dealer participation" in promotional literature.

BAIT AND SWITCH

Another act that the FTC has deemed deceptive is known as **bait and switch**. Bait and switch occurs when a business advertises a product at a very low price (the bait). When the consumer tries to buy the product, the business either does not have the product available and refuses to order the item, or disparages (says bad things about) the product and tries to convince the consumer to buy a higher-priced product (the switch). For example, Sharon reads in the newspaper that Swindler's Store has a boom box for sale at $69. Sharon goes to Swindler's to buy the $69 boom box. Once in the store the sales clerk

bait and switch: A fraudulent or deceptive sales practice in which a purchaser is attracted by advertisement of a low-priced item but then is encouraged to purchase a higher priced one.

tells Sharon that the $69 boom box is "a piece of junk." But, luckily for Sharon, the store has a $249 boom box that will be perfect. This is classic bait and switch and is considered to be deceptive.

Refusing to demonstrate the advertised product and demonstrating a defective product with the intent to sell the more expensive product are also bait and switch practices. Failure to have enough of the advertised product in inventory can also be a bait and switch practice. Finally, compensating sales clerks in a manner that encourages bait and switch is deceptive.

PRODUCT COMPARISONS

Advertising one's product by comparing it with another product is known as *comparative advertising*. At one time, comparative advertising was rare. Comparative advertising was not used because advertisers feared that the public would feel sorry for the competing product or that the competitor would receive more publicity. In 1972, the FTC began informally to encourage comparative advertising. In 1978, the FTC stated that comparative advertising was not illegal if the advertising was not deceptive. Comparative advertising is encouraged by the FTC but is watched carefully to ensure that the advertising is truthful. Individuals engaged in comparative advertising need to keep records that will substantiate their claims. For example, if it is advertised that four out of five people prefer cola A over cola B, cola A needs records that will detail the research methods that were used to arrive at those numbers. If the claim cannot be substantiated, then the FTC may order the advertisement withdrawn.

Some competitors have not relied on the FTC to bring a lawsuit when they believe that comparative advertising is deceptive. Rather, they have initiated private lawsuits under the federal *Lanham Act of 1946*. The Lanham Act is more commonly known for its protection of trademarks through registration and misuse, as discussed in Chapter 14. However, competitors have used the Act when deceptive and misleading comparative advertising is the issue. Section 43(a) of the Lanham Act states:

> [A]ny person who . . . use[s] in connection with any goods or services, or any containers for goods, a false designation of origin, or any false description or representation, including words or other symbols tending falsely to describe or represent the same, and shall cause such goods or services to enter into commerce . . . shall be liable to civil action by any person . . . who believe[s] that he is or is likely to be damaged by the use of any such false description or representation [15 U.S.C. 1125a].

If a competitor is successful in a Lanham Act lawsuit, the competitor can receive monetary damages, punitive damages (up to three times the amount of monetary damages), and attorneys' fees. In the 1980s, U-Haul was the target of a misleading comparative advertising campaign. U-Haul was granted $20 million in lost profits, $20 million in punitive damages, $13.6 million it spent on advertising to combat the misleading claims, and $2.5 million in attorneys' fees. The trial judge doubled the damages under the Lanham Act. The decision was upheld on appeal. Also, suits filed under the Lanham Act are entitled to preliminary injunctions in appropriate cases.

For example, a series of cases arose between 1978 and 1988 involving the manufacturers of Tylenol, Advil, and Anacin. These manufacturers alleged

FROM THE DESK OF
Laura Lawyer

To: Students
From: Your Lawyer

Comparative advertising can give rise to legal liabilities. Anyone engaging in comparative advertising should be aware that all data supporting the comparison needs to be available for the FTC's scrutiny. These data may also be used in court and attacked for their scientific reliability. Courts also look at how a consumer views the advertisement, not what was intended by the advertiser. This is an important distinction, and comparative advertisements should be made with an eye toward truthfulness.

that each other's nonaspirin pain reliever advertisements were deceptive. For instance, a statement that Maximum Strength Anacin contained "more of the pain reliever doctors recommend most" was held to be misleading because the advertisements seemed to indicate that Maximum Strength Anacin was stronger than Extra-Strength Tylenol. This was untrue. In another interesting case brought by the makers of Advil against the makers of Tylenol, a judge ruled that both Tylenol and Advil's advertising contained misleading statements and issued injunctions on statements made by both companies.

ENDORSEMENTS

Celebrities and experts also sell a variety of products. Picabo Street sells investment companies, Ed MacMahon sells sweepstakes, and Tiger Woods advertises for Nike. Because these implicit and explicit endorsements have the capacity to deceive the public, the FTC has issued rules governing the use of celebrity endorsements. The first of these states that the celebrity must actually use the product. If a gymnast indicates that she wears a certain brand of leotard, then she actually must wear that brand. If the celebrity or expert claims to give an expert opinion, then in fact the person must be qualified to give such an opinion. The celebrity may also be responsible for the opinions of others. In one interesting case, Pat Boone, a popular singer, endorsed an acne product, "Acne-Statin." The commercial for Acne-Statin claimed that using the product would result in skin free of acne blemishes. Further, Pat Boone claimed that his daughters had successfully used the product. These allegations proved to be false. In this case, the FTC held that endorsers must verify claims before the claim appears in advertisements. Further, if the endorser is not an expert, then the endorser must make a reasonable investigation as to the claim's truthfulness. Failure to make an independent evaluation can result in personal liability for the endorser. Some advertisements are also required to make the statement that the endorser is being paid for providing the endorsement.

ADVERTISING TO CHILDREN

Since advertising is a major part of American society, most adults are adept at distinguishing puffery from fact. Children, however, given their age and inexperience, are more likely to be deceived by advertising than adults. In an attempt to protect children, NAD has voluntary guidelines advertisers are asked to follow regarding children's advertising. Further, NAD has a unit, *Children's Advertising Review Unit* (*CARU*), that specifically reviews compliance with the NAD guidelines. Some of those guidelines address advertisements that focus on *premiums*, which are those items used to induce a child to buy a product. The clearest examples are toys that are found in cereal boxes and toys that are given with fast-food purchases. CARU specifically requires the advertisement to emphasize the product rather than the premium. One frequent violation occurs when advertisements focus almost exclusively on the premium rather than on the product. Anyone who has been around small children knows how quickly they know the premium that comes with a special kid's meal at the local fast-food restaurant. Another guideline limits the amount of commercials that can occur during children's programming. New NAD guidelines limit advertising to children during children's programming to 10 1/2 minutes per hour during weekdays and 12 minutes per hour during the weekend. As the next article discusses, marketing to children continues to cause problems.

New FTC rules shield kids online

Moving to protect children from the often sneaky data-gathering tactics of online marketers, the Federal Trade Commission on Wednesday unveiled rules requiring Internet sites that collect such information to first obtain parental permission.

The rules, which take effect April 21, delineate for the first time what the government will require of Internet companies to comply with the Children's Online Privacy Protection Act enacted last year.

The most stringent new rules are aimed at sites that sell or share data collected from children. Youngsters will be required to use signed forms, credit card numbers or other FTC-approved means to verify parental permission before collecting data.

But almost any Web site that caters to children younger than 13 will be affected by the new regulations. Even sites that don't collect marketing data but allow children to enter contests or sign up for newsletters will be required to send parents notice via e-mail.

Companies that violate the rules face civil penalties including fines up to $11,000 per infraction.

Experts said abuses are still bound to occur because of the FTC's limited ability to monitor the millions of daily Internet exchanges.

And despite the new requirements, FTC officials acknowledged companies can't always be sure they are receiving permission from a parent.

"It's not a perfect fix," said Toby Levin, head of the bureau of consumer protection at the FTC. "A child could still take his parent's credit card or dial a toll-free number. But we think these rules go a long way toward giving parents tools to have control over their children's information."

> The rules are the culmination of years of debate over how to protect children from the often sneaky tactics used by online marketers to extract information ranging from birth dates to e-mail addresses to family spending habits.
>
> Source: "New FTC Rules Shield Kids Online" by Greg Miller, *Los Angeles Times* October 21, 1999. Copyright 1999. Los Angeles Times. Reprinted by permission.

The FTC also issues children's advertising rules. The FTC is concerned with premium advertising and considers exclusive premium advertising (advertising the trinket rather than the product) to be an unfair trade practice. Another area of concern for the FTC is advertising that may potentially harm children. For example, a commercial showing a child jumping from a roof with a superhero cape would probably be pulled for fear that children may actually try to imitate the commercial. Advertisers are also prohibited from portraying the use of their products in an unsafe manner. A commercial showing a child using a child's oven around a swimming pool probably would be banned for fear that a child may be electrocuted by using the oven in the same way.

Using hero figures to sell products can create problems for advertisers. Children exhibit a trust relationship with hero figures, and they are used to sell everything from cereal to bedsheets. However, not all products may use hero figures in their advertisements. For example, the FTC has ordered manufacturers of vitamins to stop using hero figures to sell vitamins. There was a fear that children would take too many vitamins and that children would believe that vitamins would help them exhibit "superhero" characteristics. Once again, these regulations are aimed at protecting children who frequently do not have the ability to separate fantasy from reality. Some consumer and parent groups would like the FTC to ban children's advertising altogether.

UNFAIR TRADE PRACTICES

COOLING-OFF PERIODS

Sometimes problems have arisen with door-to-door sales. Many products are sold door to door, including magazines, cosmetics, and vacuums. Once a salesperson is allowed into your home, it may be difficult to get the salesperson to leave, especially if he or she has just poured dirt on your rug and is attempting to vacuum it up. Because of these problems, the FTC has a three-day **cooling-off period** for door-to-door sales. Consumers have three days from the date of the sale or from the date that they are notified of the three-day cooling-off period to cancel the sale. If the transaction was made in Spanish, then the cancellation notice must also be made in Spanish. Many states also have statutes providing for cooling-off periods. If the state statute is more protective for the consumer than the federal provision, then the state statute controls.

cooling-off period: A period of time to allow further consideration for the consumer to change his or her mind.

UNSOLICITED MAIL

Consumers occasionally receive merchandise through the mail that they did not order. When they do not pay for the merchandise, usually they are then sent a series of threatening bills. In 1970, Congress passed the *Postal Reorganization*

FROM THE DESK OF
Laura Lawyer

To: Students:
From: Your Lawyer

Nothing is quite as frustrating as receiving a bill for a product that you did not order. This is especially true when several bills are sent threatening legal action. Often, this occurs when a sample was ordered or when one product in a series was ordered but the recipient never wanted the rest. Usually, writing a letter to the company stating that the product was received but was not ordered, and that all subsequent bills for the product represent dunning, is sufficient to stop any further notices.

Act which included a prohibition against unsolicited mail merchandise and the subsequent threatening bills. This practice is known as *dunning*. Under current law, any unsolicited merchandise that is received through the mail may be kept as a gift. The merchandise need not be returned.

SWEEPSTAKES AND CONTESTS

A *sweepstakes* is a promotion in which consumers win a prize just by being entered in the sweepstakes. On the other hand, *contests* require that a consumer perform some act to win. For example, the consumer may need to provide the winning jingle or guess the number of jelly beans in a jar. The food, retailing, and gasoline industries began using "games of chance" for promotional purposes. The FTC issued special regulations dealing with those contests, but those rules were repealed in 1996. As the article suggests, sweepstakes continue to be regulated by the state, and new federal rules may be enacted soon.

You've Won! . . . or Have You?

Mary Heermance, a 56-year-old personnel director from Jefferson City, Mo., had entered a raffle at her church to win a red Pontiac Grand Am. So when she received a letter saying she'd won a red Pontiac Grand Am and asking her to call a 900 number for details, she scoured the fine print to see where the letter came from. Unable to tell, Heermance decided it was worth the charge of almost $4 a minute to see whether the sweepstakes was the one run by her church. After 10 minutes of listening to taped information, it was clear the church wasn't involved. Out some $40, Heermance hung up in disgust. "Now," she says, "I throw everything away."

Heermance was one of 163,000 Missouri consumers who, within 16 months during 1995 and 1996, racked up $4.5 million in telephone charges calling the letter's sender. Last July, a judge in Missouri handed down a civil verdict of more than $8.5 million against the California-based company that sent the letter, Direct American Marketers Inc. Attorneys for the state of Missouri had alleged that tricking consumers into calling a 900 number violated the state's merchandising-practices law. The company, which has been the target of legal action in other states, filed for bankruptcy after the verdict was announced. "We do not believe we did anything wrong," company president Anthony Brown told us.

January is high season for sweepstakes, and you'll likely receive many offers in this month's mail. Although there's no official estimate of how much sweepstakes mail is sent, it seems safe to say that the big three sweepstakes companies—American Family Publishers, Publishers Clearing House, and Reader's Digest—together send hundreds of millions of letters per year.

Sweepstakes can be fun, and they're a useful way for organizations to market merchandise or solicit donations. In 1996, 69 percent of packaged-goods companies ran sweepstakes, according to a survey by Cox Direct, a Florida-based direct-mail company. (Like many nonprofit groups, Consumers Union runs an annual fundraising sweepstakes—called the Consumer Reports Raffle—which awards a $25,000 grand prize.)

Still, sweepstakes have engendered the largest number of complaints from consumers who have called the National Fraud Information Center since it opened in 1992, and they're one of the top problems reported to the U.S. Postal Service. Before you fill out any entry form, it's important to know the key factors that make a sweepstakes legitimate:

- You don't have to purchase anything to enter. You should be able to use an index card, say, as an entry form.
- You don't have to pay up-front taxes, delivery charges, or judging fees.
- You don't have to call a 900 number before collecting a prize.
- You don't have to divulge your credit-card or bank-account number.

For the record, there are technical differences between a sweepstakes, a skill contest, and a lottery . . . , but people often think of all those "You've won" solicitations as the same animal, and they're generally governed by the same laws. In this report, we'll focus on sweepstakes.

Although there are no statistics for how many consumers have been taken in by illicit sweepstakes or how much money they've lost, a sampling of cases from federal and state agencies suggests that hundreds of thousands of consumers, often elderly, are bilked out of at least tens of millions of dollars a year. In a recent case settled by the Federal Trade Commission, for example, consumers paid $81 million in entry fees in one year to a company that falsely guaranteed they had won a sweepstakes.

Consumers aren't the only victims: Fraudulent operators may actually prey on other sweepstakes companies. Publishers Clearing House—which sells subscriptions to more than 350 magazines, including Consumer Reports—has more than 20,000 listings in its data base of scams, collected mostly from people who contact the company to question the authenticity of promotions using its name. In one scam, a caller pretending to be from Publishers Clearing House told elderly victims they'd won $1 million—but would have to send more than $5000 to cover travel and insurance costs incurred by Dick Clark and Ed McMahon, who, in any event, are associated with American Family Publishers.

Like some other established companies that use sweepstakes to market products or services, Publishers Clearing House itself has occasionally come under scrutiny. In 1994, the company signed a voluntary agreement with 14 state attorneys general. It admitted no wrongdoing but agreed to make clear in its mailings that no purchase is necessary to enter, to use the term "finalist" only for individuals in the last group from which a winner is picked, and to say a sweepstakes is in its final round only during the last 10 percent of the contest.

Who's looking out for you?

Federal and state agencies use various laws to prosecute bad apples. The FTC's Telemarketing Sales Rule requires telemarketers offering a sweepstakes to note that no purchase is necessary to enter and to disclose the odds of receiving a prize. Federal and state deceptive-trade laws prohibit companies from tricking people into making a purchase. And the U.S. Postal Service forbids companies to send mail that appears to be from a government agency.

As of 1990, about a dozen states also had specific prize- and gift-notification statutes. The rash of come-ons in recent years had led additional states to join their ranks: More than half now have such rules. States may, for instance, require that a company's solicitation disclose the odds of winning and the value of prizes. Still, only Florida and New York require companies that run sweepstakes for marketing purposes in their states, and that give away more than $5000, to register with a state agency, post a bond to cover the winnings, and send the state a list of winners. (Rhode Island calls for companies to register sweepstakes offers of more than $500 that involve a store.)

Federal and state authorities occasionally join forces to crack down on prize-promotion operators. Two years ago, 16 states, the FTC, and the Postal Service sued 79 sweepstakes companies and contest promoters in 17 states, accusing many of fraudulently promising consumers valuable prizes to induce them to buy products. Family Publishers Clearing Center and Publishers Award Bureau, for instance, asked consumers to fork over several hundred dollars to be eligible for an award—almost always, the FTC said, a 6724-square-foot "building lot." The lot proved to be nothing more than a license to use land in Baja, California, accessible only by off-road vehicles, without water or electricity. The companies settled without admitting guilt.

And last year, in "Project Mailbox," 3 federal agencies, 25 state attorneys general, and numerous local law-enforcement agencies announced 190 actions against companies that use the mail to con consumers. One target, Suarez Corporation Industries Inc., allegedly promised a free cubic zirconia but left the impression winners should pay $19 for a mounting. As a result of that promotion and others, a court ordered Suarez to reimburse hoodwinked West Virginia consumers. The amount: more than $975,000. The company has appealed.

Another target, Marketing Variations Inc,. allegedly told people they'd won $5000 and would receive a bonus "Commodities Package," worth up to $2000, if they paid $9.97. Consumers who paid claimed they received neither prize nor package.

Despite the crackdowns, problem companies persist. Prosecution is hampered in part because some companies routinely do business under more than a dozen names. Some give only a post-office box as an address. When we tried to contact sweepstakes sponsors by phone, we often had difficulty and occasionally failed completely. Even companies that don't play hide-and-seek may perform all sorts of acrobatics to stay within the letter of the law. . . .

One in a Million or More

Whatever the sweepstakes, your chances of winning big are small. The odds that an individual piece of mail in Reader's Digest's 1998 $1 million "President's Prize" sweepstakes holds the winning number? One in 600 million. It's about as likely that you would be one of 10 people chosen randomly from among every man, women, and child on earth. And what about promotions that say you're a guaranteed winner? Don't plan to retire just yet. One entry, from Guildwood Direct Ltd., said that "in no event will any prize be less than $0.68."

There's a chance the sweepstakes you enter won't even award a winner. Although most companies, including the big three, guarantee they'll award prizes, there's no legal requirement for companies to award a prize by, say, drawing a second number if the person assigned the winning number didn't submit an entry.

Of 100 entry forms we investigated in detail for this report, all but 7 guarantee a winner. If the prize is to be given to the holder of a winning number, and the number is not returned, companies generally say they'll draw from among the numbers that have been returned (which increases each entrant's odds). Grand prizes range from apples, courtesy of the National Arbor Day Foundation, to $11 million, from American Family Publishers.

The Allure

Despite the odds, people keep entering—and some even win. During the 20 years he has been entering sweepstakes, 51-year-old Daniel Rogers has won cameras and T-shirts. But he always wondered whether the big winners shown in television commercials were actors. His outlook changed in 1995, when American Family Publishers awarded him $10 million—at that time, the company's grand prize. (For the record, he didn't make a purchase when he sent in the winning entry.) Rogers retired from his job as a floor supervisor at a casino about a month after he found out he would be getting $333,000 a year for 30 years.

There is a subculture of Americans who enter thousands of prize promotions a year, troll the Internet, read newsletters, and attend conferences in search of information that will help them win prizes. Anita Hodgkins, a New Hampshire resident who publishes a newsletter about sweepstakes, estimates she wins about $35,000 a year in money and prizes.

The rewards come at a cost in stamps and time: Hodgkins enters about 40 sweepstakes a day. Like most avid participants, she concentrates on small ones—those in which participation is likely to be limited because you have to drive to a store to get an official entry form, for example. Although Hodgkins won four cars in one year, she's also won plenty of less glamorous prizes, most notably a year's supply of condoms.

Recommendations

Before you enter any sweepstakes, read the rules carefully. If the directions are confusing—or you can't find the odds, or at least a statement that the odds depend on the number of entries received—don't enter. Make sure there's a guarantee that the prize will be awarded. And never pay taxes directly to a company that gives you a prize.

If you decide to play, stick with sweepstakes run by companies with names you recognize and prizes you want to win, or by organizations you wish to support. If you're suspicious, check the company's reputation with the Better Business Bureau or a local consumer-protection office, listed in the blue pages of the phone book.

If you've been scammed:

- Call the consumer-protection office of your state attorney general.
- Write the Federal Trade Commission, 600 Pennsylvania Ave. N.W., Washington, D.C. 20580.
- Write the Chief Postal Inspector, Mail Fraud Complaints, Washington, D.C. 20260-2100 if you were solicited by mail.

The more complaints these agencies receive, the more likely they are to pursue legal action. You can also:

- Call the National Fraud Information Center, which helps consumers with information, referral services, and assistance in filing complaints, at 800 876-7060, or visit its Web site at www.fraud.org.

Source: "You've Won! . . . or Have You?" © 1998 by Consumers Union of U.S., Inc., Yonkers, NY 10703-1057, a nonprofit organization. Reprinted with permission from the January 1998 issue of *Consumer Reports* for educational purposes only. No commercial use or photocopying permitted. To subscribe, call 1-800-234-1645 or visit us at www.ConsumerReports.org.

Sometimes sweepstakes or contests do not work out as they planned. Kraft had one sweepstakes in which a consumer could win a van if he or she bought a box of macaroni and cheese that contained the proper game piece. Due to a manufacturing mistake, thousands of boxes had the winning game piece. Kraft canceled the sweepstakes as soon as the mistake was discovered, but not before several consumers believed they had won vans. Sometimes individuals figure how to "beat" contests. Also, in many states, games of chance are considered to be **illegal lotteries**, and promoters can be subject to criminal prosecutions. Therefore, promoters need to be very careful when using contests and sweepstakes.

illegal lottery versus sweepstakes: An illegal lottery has three elements: a prize, chance, and consideration. If one of these is missing, it is a sweepstakes.

NEGATIVE OPTION PLANS

Book-of-the-Month, Record-of-the-Month, and Doll-of-the-Month clubs all have something in common. They are usually **negative option plans**. A negative option plan arises where a consumer receives an item (e.g., a book) and agrees to pay for the item unless he or she specifically requests otherwise each time period. Negative option plans are considered unfair and deceptive trade practices unless they are conducted in line with FTC regulations. The FTC requires that all promotional material for the plan conspicuously state the terms and provide for a method whereby the consumer may reject the item. Consumers are entitled to a 10-day period during which they decide whether to accept the item (by doing nothing) or reject the item (by sending a statement indicating rejection). When consumers cancel their memberships in such plans, they will be required to pay for the next item shipped. If items are shipped after the cancellation period, the consumer may keep the items as a gift. It is wise, however, for the consumer to keep records of when the membership was canceled.

negative option plan: A plan where the seller periodically sends the buyer announcements that describe a current selection or new offering. If the buyer wants the selection it will be shipped automatically. If the buyer does not want the selection then a card rejecting the selection needs to be sent to the seller by a certain date.

MAIL ORDER MERCHANDISE

Merchandise can be ordered and purchased through the mail, by fax or on the Internet. In fact, more and more people are using the convenience of the Internet as a replacement for shopping expeditions. Ordering through the mail or on the Internet can be very satisfying, but it can also be frustrating. One problem that can arise is the length of time it takes between ordering the merchandise and shipping the merchandise. In addressing this problem, the FTC has enacted the *Mail and Telephone Order Merchandise Rule*. It applies to all mail, fax or Internet ordering. The rule requires the merchandise to be shipped within 30 days after receiving the order. If a merchant cannot ship within 30 days, the original advertisement must state when the product can be shipped. If for some reason the merchandise cannot be shipped within the specified time-frame, the consumer is required to be notified as to the new shipping date. If the consumer is silent, the new shipping date is assumed to be agreed to. If there are subsequent delays, the consumer must consent. If there is no consent or if the seller wants to cancel the order, the consumer promptly receives a full refund.

TELEPHONE SOLICITATIONS

The most recent consumer protection act was passed in response to the abuses in the telephone solicitation business. This act is the *Telephone Consumer Protection Act of 1991*. This act outlaws autodialing to fax machines, pagers, and cellular phones and prerecorded calls to a residence without the person's consent. The Act is enforced by the *Federal Communications Commission (FCC)*. In 1999, several Texas companies agreed to pay $400,000 to 11 businesses that received unwanted fax advertisements. The FCC also requires telemarketers to keep a list of persons requesting that they not be called and sets calling times from 8 A.M. to 9 P.M. State laws are often more restrictive than the federal law. Some states allow cooling-off periods for products bought during a telephone solicitation. Other states set up a telephone directory containing the names of those who do not wish to be called. In this emerging area of the law, balancing freedom of speech with an individual's right to privacy appears to be difficult.

CONSUMER PRODUCT SAFETY COMMISSION

Besides the FTC, the *Consumer Product Safety Commission (CPSC)*, also governs some consumer issues. The CPSC was formed in 1972 under the *Consumer Product Safety Act (CPSA)*, and is an independent regulatory commission with five commissioners serving seven-year appointments. The CPSC issues safety rules for dangerous or hazardous products. The CPSC also can issue outright bans on products if it finds that there is an "imminent or substantial" hazard, and can recall products. In 1976, Congress passed the *Consumer Product Safety Commission Improvement Act*, which allows consumers to sue the CPSC when it fails to keep a hazardous product off the market. The CPSC is also responsible for implementing the *Refrigerator Safety Act*, aimed at preventing children from getting trapped in refrigerators; the *Poison Prevention Packaging Act,* requiring child-resistant safety caps; the *Flammable Fabrics Act,* requiring flammability standards for fabrics, especially for children's clothes; and the *Federal Hazardous Substances Act*, which looks at children's toys and other hazardous products.

There was a great deal of hope that the CPSC would help make consumer items safer. Its record, however, is mixed. There have been thousands of dangerous products recalled and/or banned. Other dangerous products, however, have been allowed to stay on the market or were only recalled after several consumers were seriously injured.

SUMMARY

Unfair and deceptive trade practices are prohibited by the Federal Trade Commission Act, state deceptive practices acts, and common law torts. Further, self-regulating entities in the advertising community also issue advertising guidelines. The FTC has issued industry-specific regulations prohibiting deceptive practices. It also brings complaints against businesses that are engaged in several types of unfair and deceptive practices. These practices include misleading pictorials and claims, free claims, product comparisons, cooling-off periods, and bait and switch practices. The FTC also regulates labeling as well as endorsements, unsolicited mail, and negative option plans. Telephone solicitation, the Internet, and faxes have recently been more heavily regulated. In some instances consumers or competitors may bring a direct civil action against an unscrupulous business for deceptive practices. In most instances, however, only the FTC has the power to proceed.

The Consumer Product Safety Commission is responsible for ensuring that dangerous and hazardous products are properly labeled or banned.

CHAPTER QUESTIONS

1. Assume that a television advertisement depicts the following: Immediately after shaving cream is spread on sandpaper, a razor easily cuts through the sandpaper, leaving a smooth surface. In reality, the sandpaper must be soaked in the shaving cream for several minutes before it can be easily shaved. Also, the razor actually "shaves" sand off plexiglass. Is this deceptive? Is there any difference between this commercial and a commercial that uses colored mashed potatoes instead of ice cream in an ice cream commercial? [See *F.T.C. v. Colgate-Palmolive Co.*, 380 U.S. 374 (1965).]
2. The FTC's cooling-off period only applies to home solicitation. Do you think it should also include telephone solicitation? Why or why not?
3. Is a claim that a product contains "no aspirin" deceptive if the product does not contain aspirin but does contain the ingredients that are associated with the same side effects that occur with aspirin? [See *Adria Laboratories*, 103 F.T.C. 512 (1984).]
4. 900 numbers now are advertised on almost every television channel; some are aimed at children. Is there anything that prohibits an advertisement encouraging young children to call Santa Claus for a charge of $2 for the first minute and 30 cents for each additional minute after? What if the advertisement tells the child to ask for mom or dad's permission before dialing?
5. You are in a supermarket with your three-year-old niece. She is pestering you to buy a breakfast cereal called "Fruity Fruits." She wants Fruity Fruits because her hero, Fruit-Woman, was in a Fruity Fruit commercial shown during her favorite children's cartoon. Being nutritionally conscious, you know that the advertised cereal contains anywhere between 38 to 50 percent sugar by weight. When you say no, your niece throws herself in the aisle and begins to scream. Everyone in the store stare at you. You are angry at the manufacturer and want to sue! What will you have to show to recover? [See *Committee on Children's Television, Inc., et al. v.*

General Foods Corporation et al., 35 Cal. 3d 197, 673 P.2d 660, 197 Cal. Rptr. 783 (1983) (remanded on procedural grounds).]

6. US Sales Corporation's television and radio advertising used the following copy: "Thinking of buying a red hot car? Did you know that you can find cars and trucks and vans, right now for hot prices . . . as little as . . . $100. That's right . . . red hot cars in good condition, right now for as little as $100. . . . These hot cars were confiscated by drug seizures, used by government agents, or repossessed by banks . . . and they're practically giving them away!" Showroom quality sports cars were shown during the television commercials, and consumers were given a 900 number to call. The advertisement informed consumers that the call was $2. Callers who stayed on the 900 line until the end of the recorded message were charged $24 and were given another toll-free number to call. If consumers called the toll-free number they were solicited to buy a lifetime membership in US Sales for $99.95. Although 40 out of 42 cars sold at auction by the Department of Defense sold for under $500, 41 were deemed unserviceable. In what ways is the advertisement misleading? [See *FTC v. US Sales Corp.*, 1992 U.S. Dist. LEXIS 1078.]
7. Several telephone companies advertise 10-10-XXX numbers for inexpensive long distance. One such advertisement claimed to be selling 20-minute long distance calls for 99 cents. Charlie saw the advertisement and made 20 calls to his children, who lived out-of-state. The children were never home and he only got their answering machines. Even though the calls lasted a few seconds, he was charged the full 99 cents. Does this advertisement violate any laws?
8 Some telemarketers, posing as representatives of major credit card companies, tell consumers they could be liable for unauthorized charges that appear on their credit cards. They then try to sell the consumer additional fraud protection insurance costing between $200 and $400. Federal law already protects consumers from unauthorized charges to their credit cards that exceed $50 and most credit card companies have a zero liability policy if the unauthorized charge is reported immediately. Have the telemarketers violated any laws?
9. A local electronics store advertised a "new" brand-name personal computer, PC, for a very low price. The PC was not assembled by the brand manufacturer, but rather the store reconfigured the PC with a variety of parts. Only the motherboard and computer casing were from the brand-name manufacturer. The same store also heavily advertised low-end computers. When consumers inquired about the advertised computer, the sales staff would try to convince the customer to buy a higher-end computer. Are these actions legal?
10. Given mathematical improbabilities, are multilevel marketing schemes ethical? Why or why not?

PRACTICAL EXERCISE

Phil has just lost 100 pounds by reducing fat in his diet and by exercising. Phil now wants to open a business where customers, for a large fee, would buy prepared food under the label "Phil's Fat-Free Food." Customers would also have access to exercise classes (at the current time, this means a low-impact aerobic class once a day and two stationary bicycles) and "Phil's Famous Counselors" (who at this time includes only Phil himself). Phil has come to you to design a marketing plan that will entice customers to pay for this service in what is a highly competitive market.

Your task is to develop a marketing plan that will comply with both federal and state regulations (use your own state regulations). Your instructor may also want you to compile a list of current advertisements in the weight-loss field and discuss whether they are deceptive.

FURTHER INFORMATION

www.ftc.gov/opa/1996/9602/scam.htm
www.bbb.org/advertising/nadproc.html
www.ama.org/
www.asa.org.uk/

PART 5:
EMPLOYER/EMPLOYEE LEGAL ISSUES

CHAPTER 19

CONTEMPORARY LEGAL ISSUES IN EMPLOYMENT

LEARNING OBJECTIVES

After you have read this chapter, you should be able to:

1. Describe the concept of employment at will and the primary exceptions to it.
2. Discuss guidelines for avoiding defamation of former employees.
3. Discuss and analyze the legal and managerial issues involved with drug testing of employees.
4. Describe the limits of the legal protection for employees' use of e-mail and the Internet on the job.

CHAPTER OUTLINE

I. Employment at Will
II. Defamation of Former Employees
III. Drug Testing of Employees
IV. Other Privacy Issues

An employer concerned that his employees are falsely filing claims for workers' compensation decides to check up on one of those employees. How far can the employer go to investigate the employee? What actions can the employer take against the employee? What claims could the employee bring against the employer because of the investigation?

INTRODUCTION

No area within the legal environment of business is undergoing change faster than the law concerning the employment relationship. Significant social changes in the U.S. workforce, the globalization of business and increasing competitiveness affecting all aspects of business, and heightened public concern for fair treatment of workers have contributed to the creation of new legal rights and responsibilities for employers and employees. Many of these rights are extensions of earlier legal theories and are developing through the common law on a case-by-case basis.

Employee dishonesty and theft, the loss of productivity, and the rising medical and safety expenses caused by drug and alcohol abuse cost U.S. business billions of dollars a year. These concerns have driven many employers to institute drug or alcohol testing of employees, to conduct extensive background checks on prospective employees, to subject employees to increased surveillance on the job, or even to adopt rules prohibiting certain off-the-job conduct, such as dating coworkers. All of these actions have significant legal and ethical implications.

This chapter explores several of the most challenging contemporary issues affecting the employment environment, involving job security, and employee privacy.

EMPLOYMENT AT WILL

The relationship between employer and employee is governed by contract—the contract of employment. The employment contract may be written or implied, and it may be for a definite period of time, or it may be an "at will" contract. Some employees, such as professional athletes and high-level executives, are hired under written contracts for a specified term or period of time. If the employee is discharged, or fired, before that set period is up, then the employee may bring suit for breach of contract; likewise, if the employee leaves before the contract expires, the employer may pursue breach of contract action against the employee. Most employees, however, work under contracts of employment that are not of a specified length. Such contracts are said to be *at will contracts*—either the employer or the employee can terminate the employment relationship at his or her discretion.

This legal principle, originally borrowed from the English law of master and servant, was an extension of agency theory (as discussed in Chapter 8) in that the employment relationship was said to last only as long as the employee and employer both consented that it continue (in other words, had the "will" to continue). Therefore, if either one wanted to end the relationship, he or she could do so merely by saying, "I quit," or "You're fired." The effect of this concept in practice was that an employer could terminate an employee for, as one court said, "any reason or no reason." Similarly, an employee could quit at any time without reason.

Although the rule no longer holds force in England, courts in the United States have continued to follow it. This has tremendous significance for U.S. workers because the majority—perhaps as many as 70 percent—are "employees at will." Subsequent state and federal legislation, however, has narrowed the broad scope of the at will doctrine. For example, the National Labor Relations Act forbids firing employees because they join a union or engage in union activities; Title VII of the Civil Rights Act of 1964 prohibits discharge because of an employee's race, color, sex, religion, or national origin; the Age Discrimination in Employment prohibits discharging older workers because of their age; and the Occupational Safety and Health Act forbids discharging an employee in retaliation for filing a safety complaint. State law may also limit an employer's right to fire—most states forbid firing an employee who has filed a workers' compensation claim for a work-related injury, and a number of states have also adopted "whistle-blower" laws, which prohibit discharging employees who have publicly disclosed employer wrongdoing. Montana has adopted legislation that requires an employer to have "good cause" for firing employees.

The at will rule, and any nonlegislative exceptions to it, are creatures of the common law; that is, they are judicially created. In the United States, common law doctrine is generally a matter of state jurisdiction—thus, the courts of each state determine to what extent the at will rule applies in their state.

Although on its face, the rule appears to treat employers and employees equally, in fact its application is usually harder on employees. When a worker is abruptly fired for no reason by a firm where he or she has worked for many years, the effect on the worker and his or her family is likely to be much more damaging than the effect on the company caused by one worker quitting a job. The company can typically hire someone else or eliminate the position, whereas the employee's family may be without income while he or she searches for another job.

Many commentators have argued that it is unethical and unfair to allow a business firm with numerous workers and considerable financial resources to simply terminate an employee without any good reason, thereby cutting off his or her sole source of income.

As the result of public pressure and numerous lawsuits initiated by fired employees over the past 10–20 years, three major nonstatutory exceptions to the employment at will rule have emerged (described in the following sections). Although no states have totally eliminated the rule, the growth of those exceptions has permitted many employees to challenge successfully their terminations. The cases usually arise when the fired employee brings a tort or contract lawsuit against the former employer under the theory of **wrongful discharge**.

wrongful discharge: Suit in tort or contract seeking damages for wrongfully terminating employment.

VIOLATION OF PUBLIC POLICY

Most of us would be outraged if a friend of ours was fired from a job simply because he or she refused to perform an illegal act. Even though the employee may not have an employment contract for a definite term, this type of termination causes serious ethical concerns. Many would question the wisdom of our legal system if, for example, it permitted or encouraged the firing of a distributor who refused to pay a bribe to a customer, a lab technician who refused to certify false test results in a government safety report, or a salesperson who refused to participate in a price-fixing scheme.

Courts in several states have recognized this position by establishing the *public policy* exception to the employment at will rule. This doctrine generally holds that it is unlawful to terminate an employee for doing something that the official public policy of the state supports or promotes, such as refusing to break the law. It is sometimes difficult to determine exactly what "public policy" is; at the very least, however, this policy is established at the state level by the laws enacted by the legislature, the executive orders of the governor and top officials, and the major court decisions of the state. Some state courts are willing to construe statutory provisions very liberally in order to find a public policy that has been violated by a discharge. Other states are less willing to stretch conceptions of public policy; for example, the California Supreme Court, in *Foley v. Interactive Data Corp.* [47 Cal. 3d 654 (1988)], held that the employee alleging a discharge in violation of public policy must show that the policy or duty involved exists for the benefit of the public at large, not just the particular employer or employee.

EXPRESS OR IMPLIED CONTRACTS OF EMPLOYMENT

Some states have also recognized other exceptions to the at will doctrine. If a company provides its employees with a personnel handbook that says that employees will only be fired for certain enumerated offenses or that the company will follow certain procedures in disciplining employees, some state courts hold that the manual forms part of the contract of employment, binding the employer to follow its terms. Employers can avoid that result by including a disclaimer in the handbook stating that it does not constitute part of the contract or create a binding obligation on the employer to follow its terms.

In other cases, fired employees have been able to convince a court that employers intended employees to rely on certain conduct, promises, or statements made by the employer. Where those actions have created an impression or reasonable belief in the employee's mind that the employing firm will live up to its promises, courts have sometimes held that those promises became part of an "implied contract" with the employee.

In one leading case in this area of the law, Charles Toussaint, a manager for Michigan Blue Cross/Blue Shield, was fired for no stated reason after working there for five years. Blue Cross argued that he was hired for an indefinite time and thus was an employee at will. Mr. Toussaint stated that, when he was hired, he was told that he would be retained as long as he did his job properly. For proof, Mr. Toussaint pointed to the company personnel manual, which stated that the firm would release employees "for just cause only." The Michigan Supreme Court found that even though there was no actual contract, "when the employer chooses, presumably in its own interest, to create an environment in which the employee believes that . . . the personal policies and practices . . . are established and official at any given time, purport to be fair, and are applied consistently and uniformly," the employer is bound to honor that promise as part of the "implied contract" with its employees. [See *Toussaint v. Blue Cross and Blue Shield of Michigan*, 408 Mich. 579 (1980).]

implied covenant of good faith and fair dealing: Obligation, implied by law, that the employer cannot terminate an employee in bad faith.

COVENANT OF GOOD FAITH AND FAIR DEALING

Perhaps the broadest exception to the employment at will rule is the **implied covenant of good faith and fair dealing**. This doctrine, only adopted in approximately 10 states so far, is based on the concepts of ethics and fairness and is enforced through the judicial power of equity—the ability of courts to reform contracts, create implied trusts, and take other actions to avoid an unjust result. The cases recognizing this implied "covenant" (a word often used in connection with religious or ethical concepts) represent instances in which one party, usually a company, has terminated an employee for a reason or in a manner that simply cannot be allowed.

In one example, an employer terminated an employee, after many years of good service, just a few days before the worker would have qualified for a company pension. In another example, a court sided with an employee who had been fired after 25 years without any good cause, apparently so the firm could avoid paying him $46,000 in sales commissions. These covenant of fair dealing cases often involve situations in which the first two exceptions cannot be used, that is, the employee cannot prove the existence of any implied contract term, or he or she cannot show that the firing was due to a refusal to violate a state law.

The following case discusses the exceptions to the employment at will rule.

E.I. DUPONT DE NEMOURS AND COMPANY V. PRESSMAN

679 A.2d 436 (Del. Sup. Ct. 1996)

FACTS

Pressman, a biomedical engineer at DuPont, was hired to develop the company's medical imaging technology. During his time at DuPont, Pressman received raises and positive evaluations from his managers, including Pensak, his immediate supervisor. In January 1988, Pressman met with Pensak to discuss a possible conflict of interest created by Pensak's involvement as a paid technical advisor with a competing medical imaging technology company, Genesis. Pensak had arranged for Pressman to meet with representatives of Genesis to discuss Pressman's knowledge of medical imaging technology. When Pressman told Pensak that the relationship with Genesis was a conflict of interest, Pensak became livid and told Pressman to mind his own business. Shortly thereafter, Pensak ordered Pressman "grounded"—restricting his travel and requiring Pensak's permission to meet with any visitors. Pensak also began to raise questions about Pressman's work performance with company personnel officials. Pensak placed an "anonymous unsigned" negative evaluation in Pressman's file. Pressman's performance rating was lowered to "satisfactory," and then "marginal." Pressman was terminated by Pensak on April 12, 1989. Pressmen sued DuPont and Pensak for wrongful dismissal in breach of an implied contract and for breach of the implied covenant of good faith and fair dealing. The trial jury held that Pensak misrepresented Pressman's responsibilities to make it appear that Pressman did not complete assigned tasks, edited progress reports to superiors to understate Pressman's accomplishments, and failed to pass along reports showing Pressman's significant accomplishments during the time period in which Pressman's termination was decided. For DuPont's breach of the implied covenant of good faith and fair dealing, the trial jury awarded Pressman $422,700 in compensatory damages for lost wages. The jury also awarded Pressman $25,000 for emotional distress and interest, and $75,000 in punitive damages on the breach of the covenant claim. The court held for DuPont on the breach of implied contract claim. DuPont appealed; the appeals court reversed the trial court verdict, holding for DuPont on all claims. Pressman appealed to the Delaware Supreme Court.

DECISION

Where an employee does not have a contract of employment for a specified term, there is a strong legal presumption that the contract for employment is at will. However, courts have recognized exceptions to the at will doctrine in which the employer acts in violation of public policy, in violation of an implied contract, or in bad faith, fraud, or deceit in violation of an implied covenant of good faith and fair dealing.

An employee states a claim for wrongful termination in violation of public policy when the employee's actions that led to the termination were protected by a clearly defined public policy—a public interest recognized or protected by some legislative, administrative, or judicial authority. Examples include *Monge v. Beebe Rubber Co.* [114 N.H. 130, 316 A.2d 549 (N.H. Sup. Ct. 1974)], in which an employee was fired for refusing the sexual demands of her employer, and *Shearin v. E.F. Hutton Group Inc.* [652 A.2d 578 (Del. Chanc. Ct. 1994)], in which a lawyer was fired for refusing to violate her ethical duties. Pressman's claim does not fit within the public policy category since he has not identified a clear statement of public policy that was violated prior to his termination. He alleges that DuPont fired him in retaliation for questioning the propriety of Pensak's business practices. This fact, standing alone, does not rise to the level of a recognized claim under the public policy exception.

Another recognized exception to the at will doctrine involves an implied contract—in which the employee reasonably relies upon employer's promises of job security statements, as created by the employer's actions, promises, or documents such as a handbook. Here Pressman did not establish that there was any promise of secure employment.

Some courts have held that an employee has a claim for wrongful termination in breach of an implied covenant of good faith and fair dealing where the discharge was based on an employer's desire to avoid the payment of benefits already earned by the employee, such as the sales commissions [as in *Fortune v. National Cash Register*, 373 Mass. 96, 364 N.E. 2d 1251 (Mass. Sup. Ct. 1977)] or sick leave benefits [as in *Metcalf v. Intermountain Gas Co.*, 116 Idaho 622, 778 P. 2d 744 (Idaho Sup. Ct. 1989)]. But Pressman has not stated a claim under that line of cases because he has not identified any benefit to which he was entitled, such as earned commissions.

Other courts have held that the implied covenant of good faith and fair dealing allows an employee to sue when an employer or its agent induces another to enter into an employment contract through actions, words, or the withholding of information, which is intentionally deceptive in some material way to the contract, or manufactures materially false grounds to cause an employee's dismissal. In Pressman's case, the application of the implied covenant of good faith and fair dealing relates solely to the acts of the employer manifesting bad faith and unfair dealing through deceit or misrepresentation in falsifying or manipulating Pressman's employment record to create false grounds to terminate him. Because Pressman was an at will employee, he can not sue over the termination itself; rather his legal claim arises from Pensak's creation of false grounds and manufacturing a fictitious record as a basis for termination. The evidence shows that Pensak set out on a campaign to discredit Pressman by creating fictitious negative information about Pressman's work and hiding positive information. Based on the distorted record he created, Pensak went to his superiors and caused Pressman to be terminated. If Pensak did these acts, and did them intentionally, that amounted to a breach of the implied covenant of good faith and fair dealing.

But the trial court erred when it stated that DuPont breached the implied covenant of good faith and fair dealing if it discharged Pressman as a result of hatred, ill will, or intent to injure. Dislike or hatred as the sole basis for termination of an at-will employee does not violate the implied covenant; but fraud, deceit, and misrepresentation, either in the inducement to enter a contract or in intentionally fictionalizing the employee's performance to cause dismissal, may be actionable as a breach of the implied covenant. The legal harm to Pressman, and the breach of the implied covenant of good faith and fair dealing, come from Pensak's creation of false and fraudulent grounds for the discharge; such maliciously employed deceit and subterfuge constitutes bad faith prohibited by the implied covenant. DuPont was made aware of this course of events after the fact and ratified Pensak's actions. Thus, DuPont can be held liable to Pressman on the claim of breach of the implied covenant of good faith and fair dealing.

But even though Pressman has established that he was discharged in breach of the implied covenant, he cannot recover damages for emotional distress or punitive damages; according to *Foley v. Interactive Data Corp.* [47 Cal.3d 654, 254 Cal. Rptr. 211, 765 P. 2d 373, 396 (Cal. Sup. Ct. 1988)], only contractual damages, that is, lost wages and employment benefits, are available as damages for the wrongful termination of an at-will employee in breach of the implied covenant of good faith and fair dealing.

The decision of the court of appeals was reversed and the trial court decision for Pressman on the breach of the implied covenant of good faith and fair dealing was affirmed; the court remanded the case for the calculation of damages in accordance with its opinion.

CASE QUESTIONS

1. Why did the courts state that Pressman's firing was not in violation of public policy? Did Pressman establish that there was an implied contract not to discharge him except for good cause?
2. What does the implied covenant of good faith and fair dealing require of an employer? Could Pressman have been legally fired for refusing to follow his supervisor's orders?
3. Why does the court state that the legal harm to Pressman comes not from his discharge but from the manner in which Pensak caused it? Explain.
4. What remedies are available for an employee discharged in breach of the implied covenant of good faith and fair dealing?

WHISTLE-BLOWERS

Many wrongful discharge cases involve employees who were terminated after they reported to the press or to governmental authorities some illegal or unethical actions that had occurred in the company. These people are often called *whistle-blowers* because they "blew the whistle" (like a referee in a game) on some activity they thought was improper.

Whistle-blowers who are fired because they disclose employer wrongdoing may be able to challenge their discharge under the exceptions to the at will doctrine. Such whistle-blower claims usually raise a claim that the discharge was in violation of public policy, especially where the employee was fired for refusing to violate a law. A number of states have passed whistle-blower laws to protect employees who act to report employer wrongdoing that poses a threat to public safety or health, and federal legislation such as the Occupational Safety and Health Act and Energy Reorganization Act (applying to employees of nuclear facilities) protect employees from retaliation for reporting employer violations of the law. The whistle-blower laws are clear statements of public policy to protect employees who blow the whistle, as required by the courts to establish a claim under the public policy exception to the at will doctrine. However, where the whistle-blower laws provide for specific remedies for employees terminated in violation of such laws, the courts generally require that the fired employee seek the statutory remedies rather that sue under the common law exceptions to the at will doctrine. Where the whistle-blowing employee, for whatever reason, does not come under the coverage of the whistle-blower law, courts may allow the employee to sue under the common law public policy exception and will still look to the whistle-blower law as the expression of public policy, as in *Kulch v. Structural Fibers, Inc.* [78 Ohio St.3d 134, 677 N.E. 2d 208 (Ohio Sup. Ct. 1997)].

DEFAMATION OF FORMER EMPLOYEES

Increasingly, employers who fire employees are facing defamation suits by these former employees. This may occur, for example, when the former employer gives an unfavorable reference regarding the employee to a potential future employer. One recent national study estimated that one-third of all defamation actions filed in recent years were suits brought by former employees. As was discussed in Chapter 11, the tort of defamation can result when one person makes a false statement about another that is "published" (communicated to one or more third parties). The statement must not only be false but also cause harm to the employee—for example, by damaging his or her reputation or hurting his or her future job prospects. The defamation will be called *libel* if it is written and *slander* if it is verbal.

Juries are often sympathetic to the claims of fired employees. During the 1980s employees won 72 percent of employment defamation cases tried in California, with an average award of $582,000.[1] A former employee of Procter & Gamble was awarded $15.6 million by a Texas jury in a defamation case, as the following reading describes.

COMPANIES DISCOVER THAT SOME FIRINGS BACKFIRE INTO COSTLY DEFAMATION SUITS

A company can't be too careful in how it fires an employee. A $15.6 million Texas jury verdict against Procter & Gamble Co. underscores that point. The money was awarded April 23 to Don Hagler, a 41-year veteran of the company, who said P&G fired him after publicly accusing him of stealing a $35 company telephone. Mr. Hagler said that the phone was his property and that P&G libeled him by posting notices accusing him of theft on company bulletin boards. The state-court jury awarded Mr. Hagler $1.6 million in actual damages and $14 million in punitive damages.

P&G says it is reviewing the verdict for a possible appeal. "We're disappointed in the verdict," says a spokeswoman for the Cincinnati-based company.

"I'm not surprised the jury found liability, but the amount of the award is incredible," says Greg Rasin, an employment attorney with Jackson, Lewis, Schnitzler & Krupman in New York.

Defamation Lawsuits

Lawyers say more ex-employees are using defamation lawsuits to fight firings. "Workers are broadening their allegations to include things like defamation, rather than just claiming unlawful termination," says Jay W. Walks, an employment attorney with Kaye, Scholer, Fireman, Hays & Handler in New York City. "It reflects a lack of care by management in expressing the reason why the person's been terminated."

[1] Yulish and Heshizer, "Defamation in the Workplace," *Labor Law Journal* (June 1989), p. 355.

This week, the New Jersey Supreme Court held that a former Bell Laboratories manager fired in 1984 for allegedly misusing $250,000 in company funds can sue the company for defamation. The former employee, Barbara A. Williams, won a $670,000 jury award against Bell Labs, the research arm of American Telephone & Telegraph Co., in Superior Court in Newark in 1983, but the verdict was overturned on appeal. The Supreme Court reversed part of the appeals-court ruling and said Ms. Williams must prove her case at another trial.

Ms. Williams had worked for Bell for 12 years, becoming manager of the company's Aid to Black Colleges program. In 1984, Bell received an anonymous letter claiming she had embezzled or misused company funds. After an internal investigation, Bell fired Ms. Williams and disclosed the results of the probe to the Essex County, N.J., prosecutor's office. However, the prosecutor's office later dropped its investigation of Ms. Williams.

Ms. Williams sued Bell in 1985, alleging, among other things, that Bell defamed her to the prosecutor's office. After an 11-day trial during which Bell argued it had a right to present the results of its investigation to the prosecutor's office, a jury returned a verdict in Ms. Williams's favor on the defamation charge. The verdict was reversed by the appeals court, which cited issues relating to jury instructions and statute-of-limitations. This past Monday, however, the state Supreme Court reversed the statute-of-limitations portion of the appeals court's ruling and remanded the case for trial.

Trial, Re-Trials and Appeals

Another defamation case was filed in federal court in Baltimore by a former Contel Corp. executive, Thomas Hassey, who claimed Contel executives defamed him by blaming him for morale and turnover problems in meetings and speeches before employees, both before and after he was fired in 1987. Contel has since been acquired by GTE Corp.

In 1990, Mr. Hassey was awarded $3.5 million by a jury. In a second trial ordered by the judge, who raised the issue of inadequate jury instructions, Mr. Hassey was awarded $7.1 million by a jury, according to his attorney. That judge, however, ordered a third trial, and both sides have appealed aspects of the order to the U.S. Court of Appeals for the Fourth Circuit.

Also moving through the courts is the case of Willard A. Thompson, a former employee of Public Service Co. of Colorado. Mr. Thompson sued the utility in state court in Colorado, claiming he was defamed by disciplinary notices sent to his union and several bosses after he was suspended in 1983 for allegedly bothering a customer's female employees with personal questions. About a year and half ago, the U.S. Supreme Court refused to consider a Public Service Co. appeal of a Colorado Supreme Court decision setting the case for trial, and it was returned to state court for trial. But a series of snafus involving Mr. Thompson's attorneys have delayed the trial's scheduling.

The firing that led to the P&G case took place on March 4, 1991, six days after security guards at the front gate of the company's detergent plant in Dallas stopped Mr. Hagler at the end of a shift, searched a bag he was toting and found a telephone. Mr. Hagler told superiors he had purchased the phone after a flood damaged a phone on his desk in the plant. He said he hadn't been reimbursed by P&G because he had lost the receipt and his boss had told him he could keep the phone.

P&G fired him after a six-day internal investigation and posted notices on 11 bulletin boards and the plant's electronic mail system saying, in part: "It has been determined that the telephone in question is Procter & Gamble's property and that Don had therefore violated Work Rule #12 . . . concerning theft of company property."

Mr. Hagler filed suit two months later in 101st District Court, Dallas County, Texas, charging that P&G had libeled him. Two years later, witnesses at the trial included a co-worker who had accompanied Mr. Hagler to a mall where he bought the phone with his own cash. Mr. Hagler testified P&G used him as an example to stop a rash of theft at the plant. He said that since his firing, he has applied for more than 100 new jobs, only to be turned down when prospective employers learned why he had been fired by P&G. After a five-day trial, the jury took five hours to deliberate.

Employment attorneys who represent corporate clients say companies can take precautions to avoid being sued when firing workers. Bruce Sanford, a libel lawyer with Baker & Hostetler, says, among other considerations, "You have to be careful about what you write in personnel files" when an employee is fired. He adds: "Write it very factually, and don't include gratuitous opinions."

Says Mr. Rasin, the employment attorney: "You'd better be right if you're planning to make an example of someone. The absolute defense to any defamation act is truth. In a theft situation, unless an employee admits to it, I'd be reluctant to publish it beyond those who need to know. This is a society where people sue when they've been wronged."

Mr. Rasin presents another pointer: juries will sympathize with workers. They're the little person against the big company.

In the Hagler case, the jury foreman told the Dallas Morning News that jurors never questioned whether P&G was guilty and immediately began discussing how much to award Mr. Hagler. The award for actual damages broke down into $1.3 million for damage to Mr. Hagler's character or reputation, $200,000 for mental anguish, and $100,000 for physical injury. (Mr. Hagler's attorney, Neal Manne of the Dallas firm of Gorman Godfrey, said his client became depressed after the firing and was diagnosed with dangerously high blood pressure.)

Mr. Hagler says he has strong feelings about his former employer. "I'm not proud of the fact that I had to sue the company I was dedicated to for 41 years," he says. "I sued because they called me a thief and put it on 11 bulletin boards in the plant. I think P&G's a good company. But I think they've changed. They're not as nice to people as they used to be."

JOB REFERENCES

Most employee/employer defamation cases have resulted from statements made by employers regarding job references for ex-employees. Employment applications typically ask for a list of an applicant's previous employers. If an employee has been terminated for poor performance on the job, the former employer is likely to make negative comments about the worker when contacted by a prospective employer. Of course, in order to be defamatory, the statements made must be false. If the comments are accurate, then there is no defamation. But if the former employer reports, for example, that the employee was fired for theft, habitual lateness, or poor work habits, such information will adversely affect the individual's employment opportunities. If the information is not true, or if the documentation of the poor performance is so incomplete that it is unclear whether the statements are true, the employee may succeed in a defamation lawsuit.

Employers who, in good faith, mistakenly furnish inaccurate information to prospective employers are afforded some protection, however, by the legal principle called **qualified privilege**. This theory holds that if a good reason exists why the employer made the statement, the statement is made in good faith, and it is limited to the response to the inquiry, then the employer is not liable even though the statement made is inaccurate—in other words, the statement is "privileged."

qualified privilege: Protection from liability for good faith actions by employers providing references to prospective employers.

The doctrine of qualified privilege is especially applicable where the ex-employee has asked for a reference—there will be no liability for an innocent misrepresentation. On the other hand, if the former employer intentionally or maliciously gives false information, or if the information is disseminated to a wider circle than necessary, such communication is not covered by the privilege.

In light of these theories, many firms have refused to provide any information on former employees. However, employers who believed that a "no comment" policy would totally protect them have occasionally still been held liable for defamation under the doctrine of **compelled self-publication**. This theory provides that if the employer can "foresee" that an employee will have to repeat to a prospective employer the false reason given for his dismissal, the former employer may be held liable. This developing doctrine has only been adopted in a few states but represents a threatening trend to management.

compelled self-publication: The doctrine holding an employer liable for an employee's reporting of the reason for the employee's dismissal to a prospective employer.

To protect employers against defamation claims arising out of references, several states, such as California, Illinois, Georgia, Oklahoma, and West Virginia, have passed laws that provide immunity for employers providing references. Most such legislation simply restates the common law qualified privilege doctrine as it applies to employers communicating information regarding current or former employee job performance to prospective employers; however, the Oklahoma law also requires that the affected employee consent to the employer's communication to the prospective employer.

DRUG TESTING OF EMPLOYEES

One of society's most difficult problems today is the abuse of drugs by persons at all economic levels. According to one report, 68 percent of drug users are employed. Without doubt, some of this drug use occurs on the job, as well as off. Studies have shown that workers under the influence of drugs have more accidents, contribute disproportionately to other safety problems, have higher rates of absenteeism and turnover, raise health insurance and liability costs, and produce less, at a lower quality level, than other employees. One study put the cost of drug use to U.S. business at $60 billion per year. By 1996, more than 81 percent of U.S. companies had instituted some sort of program to test potential and/or current employees for drugs, and many more test today. Firms have also developed drug awareness, education, and counseling programs. Companies often have decided to begin preemployment drug testing programs, mainly to avoid a rush of drug-using applicants who cannot get jobs elsewhere.

SOME EMPLOYERS RETHINKING DRUG TESTING

Although the American Management Association estimates that approximately 81 percent of U. S. companies require their employees to take a drug test, some employers have discontinued their drug testing programs. Employers facing stiff competition to recruit employees in a tight labor market may feel that drug testing is an impediment; some high-tech Silicon Valley firms, such as Cisco Systems, feel that drug testing of employees displays a lack of trust that does not fit in their corporate culture. An American Management Association study indicates that companies testing all employees spend about $77,000 to find one drug user, and that 80 percent of those companies that do drug testing have never done a cost-effectiveness analysis of their drug testing programs. A report prepared by the American Civil Liberties Union, based on studies done by the National Academy of Sciences and the American Management Association, indicated that drug testing was ineffective in reducing drug use and had no noticeable impact on productivity or reducing absenteeism; another study reported in the January 1999 issue of *Working USA* magazine showed that productivity was 29 percent lower in Silicon Valley firms that used preemployment and random drug testing than productivity in firms that did not test employees for drugs. The American Management Association reports that drug education and drug awareness programs have proven to be more effective than drug testing.

Sources: "Drug Testing Takes a Hit," *The San Francisco Chronicle* (November 5, 1999); "Tight Labor Market Shakes Up Workplace Drug Testing," *Los Angeles Times* (December 15, 1999); "Drug Testing Overpriced, Overused," *The Times-Picayune* (New Orleans) (October 11, 1999); "Worker Drug Tests Usually a Solution Seeking a Problem," *The Atlanta Constitution* (October 10, 1999).

Although surveys have shown that a large majority of the population favors drug testing in connection with employment, technical, ethical, and legal problems abound. Testing procedures normally involve taking a sample of urine or blood from an individual. Nonspecific, "broad spectrum" tests, such as radio immunoassay (RIA) and Enzyme-Multiplied Immunoassay Technique (EMIT), have not proven to be particularly reliable. These tests only identify a broad class of organic chemicals rather than a particular chemical. A person who has eaten a poppyseed bagel, or taken over-the-counter medication like Advil or Nuprin, can produce positive results under these tests.

Other more comprehensive, "narrow spectrum" tests, such as Gas Chromatography (GC) and the Gas Chromatography/Mass Spectrometry Test (GC/MS), are much more accurate—and more expensive. The latter tests cost $200 to $300, compared with $20 to $30 for the broad spectrum tests. Many companies use the cheaper tests first and then follow up with a second narrow spectrum test when the individual's first result is positive. Another technical problem is that the tests cannot show exactly when the person used the drug, only that it is present in the body fluids at the time of the test.

Drug testing can create ethical problems for companies as well, depending on how the tests are conducted. Ethical issues associated with drug testing are discussed in Chapter 7.

On the legal front, the National Labor Relations Board has held that unionized employers must bargain with their respective unions before implementing drug testing programs for employees, since such tests represent a "substantial change in working conditions." Blood and urine tests have been legally challenged as a violation of the right to privacy. A valid urine test requires that an individual urinate into a container in the presence of another person—normally a very private act. The need for actual observation has been demonstrated because some potential employees have actually hidden a bag containing "clean" urine in their clothes when they went for their preemployment drug test.

A number of legal issues concerning the right to perform drug testing in employment apply somewhat differently for public and private employees.

PUBLIC EMPLOYEES

Public employees have greater rights to "privacy" and against illegal search and seizure because the Constitution protects persons against actions *by the government*. The Constitution does not protect individual citizens against acts by other private parties (such as private businesses). Public sector employers are subject to the requirements of the Fourth (for federal employers) and the Fourteenth (for state and local employers) Amendments of the U.S. Constitution, which prohibit unreasonable searches and seizures. Drug testing is considered to be a search; therefore, in order to conduct legal drug tests, government agencies must show that a strong public interest is involved to overcome the individual's rights under the Constitution.

Drug use in the workplace can have devastating consequences. Several well-publicized railroad accidents have occurred in recent years, and some were apparently caused by employees who were acting under the influence of drugs. A particularly tragic accident happened in 1987 when a Conrail engineer, driving a string of locomotives, ran a stopswitch and collided with an oncoming Amtrak passenger train. Sixteen people were killed and 176 injured. The engineer later admitted to smoking a marijuana joint shortly before the crash. The following case involves drug testing requirements in the railroad industry.

SKINNER V. RAILWAY LABOR EXECUTIVES' ASSOCIATION

489 U.S. 602 (1989)

FACTS

The Secretary of Transportation of the United States is authorized by a federal statute to issue rules and regulations addressing railroad safety. Evidence indicates that alcohol and drug abuse by railroad employees has contributed to several train accidents. As a result, the Secretary issued regulations prohibiting crew members and certain other railroad employees from using drugs or alcohol while on duty or while subject to being called for duty. The federal regulations required railroads to perform blood and urine tests on all those employees after accidents, even though there was no indication of previous or current drug use by those persons. Several labor organizations representing employees of private railroads challenged the regulations on the grounds that they violated the Fourth Amendment of the Constitution.

DECISION

In an opinion written by Justice Kennedy, the U.S. Supreme Court noted first that although the drug tests were carried out by privately owned railroad corporations, the actions were required by regulations of the federal government. Although the acts of private businesses are not usually covered by the Constitution, where the private party acts as an instrument or agent of the Government, the protection of the Fourth Amendment was held to apply to the procedure in question.

As to whether the blood and urine tests were considered a "search," the Court stated that "a compelled intrusion into the body for blood to be analyzed for alcohol content" has been recognized, in many previous cases, to be a search. Similarly, the collection and testing of urine intrudes upon an expectation of privacy long recognized by society. Therefore, the Fourth Amendment will apply to these actions to prevent unreasonable searches and seizures.

The Constitution does not prohibit all searches, only those that are not "reasonable" and are not made pursuant to a warrant issued by a judicial officer. The permissibility of the search is determined by balancing "its intrusion on the individual's Fourth Amendment interests against its promotion of legitimate governmental interests." Clearly, the government has a strong interest in regulating the conduct of railroad employees to ensure "the safety of the traveling public and of the employees themselves."

The Court considered whether a warrant, based upon "probable cause," should be required before such a search could be conducted. Finding that the warrant requirement was designed in large part to protect citizens from random or arbitrary searches, the Court noted that the law and regulations at issue here set limits and specify when such a test can be performed. Furthermore, since the evidence of drugs will disappear quickly, any testing must be done soon after the accident to have meaning. The government, therefore, has a strong interest in performing the tests without delay.

Justice Kennedy also pointed out that employees in safety-sensitive railroad positions have a diminished expectation of privacy because they are employed in an industry pervasively regulated by the government. Further, the regulations will promote the public and governmental interest by deterring employees from using drugs or alcohol in the first place. Since they realize that they will be discovered if an accident occurs, employees will be less likely to use drugs and alcohol, and accidents will be prevented.

Overall, the Court found that the concerns for public safety, the limited nature and scope of the tests, and the lessened privacy expectations of the railroad employees, more than balanced their individual privacy rights. Thus, the Court upheld the drug testing program of the Department of Transportation.

CASE QUESTIONS

1. Did the employees to be tested work for the federal government or private business? Why were the testing procedures subject to the requirements of the Fourth Amendment?
2. Are public or private employees given more Constitutional protection related to searches and privacy issues? Why?
3. What are the interests that are balanced by the Supreme Court in reaching its decision? Do you agree with the decision?

As the Supreme Court held in *Skinner*, the government may subject employees to random drug testing when the testing supports an important government interest, such as public safety. In *National Treasury Employees Union v. Von Raab* [489 U.S. 656 (1989)], decided the same day as *Skinner*, the

Supreme Court also upheld drug testing for U.S. Customs Service employees who were involved in combating drug smuggling, who carried guns, or who had access to classified material. In general, such "focused" drug testing requirements are more likely than "blanket" testing programs to pass constitutional requirements, because it is easier to demonstrate that the focused programs promote a compelling government purpose or public interest. However, the Supreme Court did uphold a mandatory drug testing program for all high school varsity athletes in *Vernonia School District v. Acton* [515 U.S. 646 (1995)] and refused to hear an appeal of a U.S. Court of Appeals decision allowing a school district to subject all employees to random testing for drugs and alcohol to promote and protect public safety [*Knox County Education Association v. Knox County Board of Education*, 158 F.3d 361 (6th Cir. 1998), *cert. denied*, 120 S.Ct. 46 (Oct. 4, 1999)]. The Supreme Court did strike down a Georgia law that required all candidates for state political offices to certify that they passed a drug test, because the state officials had not shown that there was a drug problem among public officials, and the political offices did not involve high-risk or safety-sensitive positions [*Chandler v. Miller*, 520 U.S. 305 (1997)].

PRIVATE EMPLOYEES

In 1988, Congress enacted the Drug-Free Workplace Act. This law established a federal policy that federal contractors must maintain a work environment free of illegal drugs. All contractors who receive federal funds must certify that they will abide by this rule and must inform employees of their written policy. Employers doing more that $25,000 of business per year with the federal government must have a written drug-free workplace policy and establish a drug-free awareness program.

In addition to the Drug-Free Workplace Act, other federal regulations require drug testing of employees in particular industries, such as transportation. (Recall that regulations requiring testing of all members of train crews involved in accidents were discussed in the *Skinner v. Railway Labor Executives' Association* case.) Although the U.S. Constitution does not afford protection to employees in the private sector, some state constitutions do extend rights to private sector employees. Several states, such as Alaska, Arizona, California, Illinois, Florida, Louisiana, Hawaii, Massachusetts, Montana, Rhode Island, and South Carolina, have an express right to privacy in their state constitutions. Other states have constitutional provisions that recognize some specific aspects of privacy rights or have established the right to privacy as part of their common law, allowing persons whose privacy is violated to sue in tort. West Virginia courts have held that drug testing, in the absence of reasonable suspicion, is an invasion of privacy (except for employees in safety-sensitive positions or subject to federal testing regulations). Laws in Connecticut and Iowa restrict drug testing of employees to those employees in safety-sensitive positions, to employees subject to federal testing regulations, or when the employer has reasonable grounds to suspect an employee is using drugs. These legal provisions offer private sector employees some protection against unreasonable drug testing—testing that is overly intrusive or that violates the reasonable expectations of privacy of employees.

Although the states are taking some steps to protect employees from unreasonable drug testing requirements, they are also taking steps to discourage

FROM THE DESK OF
Laura Lawyer

To: Students
From: Your Lawyer

An employer should keep in mind certain general principles when thinking about employee drug testing.

1. Drug testing of employees is more likely to be held legally proper if the employer has "probable cause" to suspect drug use on the job—for example, observations of certain employees acting strangely or the presence of drug paraphernalia. The civil rights laws do not protect employees who use illegal drugs, but employees who are participating in supervised drug rehabilitation programs are protected by the Americans with Disabilities Act.
2. Public employees have greater rights to privacy and freedom from unreasonable searches than private employees, due to the U.S. Constitution's restriction on governmental actions.
3. Preemployment drug testing is less likely to be challenged than is testing of current employees. Employees may acquire certain job security rights, under employment contracts or civil service regulations, that prospective employees do not possess.
4. Many cases have held that workers enjoy an "expectation of privacy" in certain actions. Some types of employment carry higher, and some carry lower, expectations of privacy. Jobs that affect public safety and welfare carry lower expectations, because of the public interest involved.
5. When performing the test, an employer should be sensitive to the employee's "reasonable expectation of privacy." The test should attempt to minimize the embarrassment to the employee. If the test involves producing

urine, it should be done in as private a manner as possible. The test results should be kept confidential and should not be disseminated beyond essential personnel. To televise employees giving urine samples or post the results of all employee test results would be to invite liability.

6. Drug testing is more likely to be upheld when the employer has a reasonable basis for individualized suspicion, as opposed to random unannounced testing of all employees.
7. Employers must be familiar with, and follow, all relevant federal and state laws dealing with drug testing.

employees from abusing drugs and to encourage employers to test employees. A number of states have drug-testing laws; such legislation generally sets out procedural requirements to be followed by employers testing their employees or applicants for drugs. Those requirements usually include giving employees and applicants written notice of the employer's drug testing policy, strict requirements for handling and storing of testing samples, confidentiality requirements, and the right of employees who test positive for drug use to demand a confirmatory test at their own expense. In Georgia, employers that establish drug testing programs for employees receive reductions in their insurance premiums for the state's workers' compensation program. Georgia and Tennessee deny unemployment benefits to employees fired for failing, or refusing to take, a drug test, and also deny workers' compensation benefits to employees injured on the job while under the influence of drugs.

OTHER PRIVACY ISSUES IN EMPLOYMENT

HONESTY TESTING

Many other types of tests are used to screen prospective employees today. The federal Employee Polygraph Protection Act of 1988 made polygraph (lie detector) testing by most private sector employers illegal. Polygraph test results are generally not admissible in court cases, because their reliability is questionable. Such tests are effectively measuring the sweat in a person's palm or a rise in blood pressure when someone is subjected to stressful questioning on sensitive matters, but that does not necessarily correlate with the honesty of the answers. These tests normally can be used on employees only when the employer is investigating a theft that has occurred in the workplace. Most states have similar legislative prohibitions. As a result, employers are increasingly turning to psychological tests and exhaustive database searchers.

Paper-and-pencil tests, designed to measure an employee's or applicant's honesty and integrity, have become commonplace since polygraph testing was outlawed. Such tests may include "honesty tests" or psychological profile tests; honesty tests generally seek to measure various counterproductive workplace behaviors such as untruthfulness, perceptions about the pervasiveness of employee theft, illegal drug use, and admissions of theft. The validity of the honesty tests is a matter of controversy—a 1990 study by the federal Office of Technology and Assessment found research on the effectiveness of such tests to be inconclusive, but a 1991 study by the American Psychological Association is much more positive and favorable to honesty testing. Psychological profile tests are generally not intended to be used as an employment screening device, but some employers may use them in the hiring process. Honesty testing is not prohibited by federal polygraph legislation but is restricted in several states. Massachusetts specifically prohibits employers from using honesty tests; Rhode Island bars using honesty tests as the primary basis of employment decisions, and Wisconsin also limits the use of honest tests by employers.

Psychological tests may include questions regarding religious beliefs, sexual behavior, or even bathroom habits—such testing may be viewed by employees (or applicants) as overly intrusive. Using psychological profile tests as an employee selection device may raise issues under the Americans with Disabilities Act or state antidiscrimination legislation; those laws will be discussed in Chapter 21. Employers desiring to use psychological profile tests should have a legitimate, work-related rationale for such testing and should not use psychological tests as a screening device for employment.

ON-THE-JOB SURVEILLANCE

Traditionally, employees have had little legal protection from various forms of spying, eavesdropping, and surveillance by their bosses. Many employers believe that electronically monitoring employee actions provides important data related to product quality and customer satisfaction. In recent years, technological advances have made it possible for companies to monitor workers using computers, cameras, and sophisticated audio and video recording equipment. Companies have installed tiny, fish-eye lenses in walls to watch employees suspected of crimes, as well as computers that can track which airline employees write the most reservations. One even used special chairs to measure employee wiggling ("wigglers aren't working"). In response to this increased use of new technology, employee groups have pushed for creation of additional state and federal statutory and common law protections regarding a right to privacy for employees.

In general, federal and state laws allow employers to intercept phone and electronic communications with a court order or with the consent of at least one party to the call. The employer owns the telephones and can normally give the required consent. Secret tape recording of such phone conversations, particularly those of an employee's personal conversations, and later disclosure of the contents of private conversations, however, are beyond the provisions of the law and may subject the employer to substantial criminal and tort liability.

Employers contend that such methods improve efficiency, honesty, and guarantee that customer calls will be handled quickly and politely. Employee groups argue, however, that the surveillance creates an atmosphere so full of stress and fear that productivity and quality actually decline. They point to a series of studies suggesting that workers who are secretly monitored suffer significantly higher stress levels, including depression, anxiety, and exhaustion.

Some companies are already reducing their use of secret screening procedures in advance of any federal legislation. U.S. West Communications, for example, in 1989 began keeping statistics on blocks of telephone operators rather than just on individuals and also started warning operators of plans to monitor conversations. Bell Canada stopped keeping close tabs on the amount of "working time" each operator spent with callers after numerous employee complaints. Now the company averages the scores of "working time" with callers by entire offices—without any decline in efficiency.[2]

Some workers have turned the tables by secretly recording conversations with their bosses. Federal law allows secret taping, as long as one of the people being recorded knows about it. At least 12 states (including New York) have similar state laws, while about 14 other states (including California) prohibit such secret taping. Maryland law prohibits secret taping of telephone conversations, as Linda Tripp found out when she was prosecuted for taping her telephone conversations with Monica Lewinsky. Whether legal or not, employees who feel they are being set up for termination are increasingly more likely to hide tape recorders in their purses or jackets when they meet with their bosses.

For example, a senior sales consultant won a $500,000 verdict recently after jurors heard a tape of her supervisor telling her openly that she was fired because she had filed a state labor grievance. The employer had consistently maintained before and during the trial that she was terminated for poor performance. The worker stated that she hid a tape recorder in her pocket because "I was very frightened. I was feeling like my job was, obviously, on the line." Most companies confronted by a tape that records officials making statements opposite to what the firm has publicly claimed choose to settle out of court, since juries tend to give great weight to such evidence.[3]

In the modern workplace, many employees are encouraged or told to use e-mail to send messages to fellow workers and other business contacts. Although each employee has a different code that he or she enters to access the appropriate electronic menu, such codes are commonly known and, in fact, increasingly published in directories. Employees are human beings, and there is no doubt that many e-mail messages sent and received on company computers are of a personal nature. The employee may believe that such messages are private and cannot or will not be monitored by other employees of the company, but this is not true.

Business firms that invest substantial sums of money to establish e-mail systems intend that they be used for business purposes. Moreover, it is not difficult to write programs allowing managerial employees to access all e-mail files. There are even some commercial software programs available for purchase to achieve this goal. Hence, many firms monitor employees' messages regularly or occasionally. Employees who are fired as a result of using their systems for personal purposes have sometimes sued their employers for invasion of privacy. Most of these suits have been decided in favor of the companies, on the grounds that they own the systems, and ought to be able to monitor

[2] Allen, "Legislation Could Restrict Bosses From Snooping on Their Workers," *The Wall Street Journal* (September 24, 1991), B1. See also "Is Your Boss Spying on You?" *Business Week* (January 15, 1990), p. 74.

[3] Woo, "Secret Taping of Supervisors Is on the Rise, Lawyers Say," *The Wall Street Journal* (November 3, 1992), B1.

them, similar to telephone calls. However, when an employer goes beyond monitoring to publish and publicly humiliate an employee as the result of some personal message, the employer may be held liable.

EMPLOYERS MONITOR EMPLOYEES' E-MAIL AND WEB SURFING

E-mail and the Internet make it possible for employees to communicate instantaneously with coworkers and clients halfway across the world and let employees access up-to-the-minute news or financial information. Employees can also visit on-line with friends, circulate dirty jokes or chain letters to thousands of people, shop on-line, play the stock market, bid on items for auction, or download hard-core pornography from their desk—instead of working on their employer's business. Employers—both public and private sector—are increasingly becoming concerned about how employees use the company's computer network and are attempting to control that use.

The state of Virginia passed legislation that prohibits state employees from using state-owned or state-leased computers to access sexually explicit materials. [The constitutionality of that law is currently being challenged before the federal courts, *Urofsky v. Allen*, 995 F.Supp. 634 (E.D. Va. 1998), reversed on appeal, but vacated and rehearing *en banc* granted, 167 F.3d 191 (4th Cir., June 3, 1999).] In December, 1999, the *New York Times* announced that it had terminated "more than 20" employees (some sources indicated that up to 53 workers were fired) for sending "inappropriate and offensive" e-mail messages at its Norfolk, Virginia, payroll processing center. Investment firm Edward Jones & Co. terminated 19 employees, and warned an additional 41, for addressing or sending inappropriate material over the company's computer system. Xerox Corp. fired 40 workers for violating its Internet policies during 1999. A 1999 survey of 900 employers conducted for the *Washington Post* by the American Management Association indicated that nearly half of them now monitor employees' Internet usage, and another 12 percent indicate they intend to start such monitoring. The survey also indicated that 11 percent of the employers had fired employees for Internet abuse.

Sources: "Companies Move to Curb Workers' Online Usage," *The Washington Post* (December 20, 1999); "Workers Get Caught in Company's Web," *The Houston Chronicle* (December 5, 1999); "Computer Misuse Concerns Bosses," *The Times-Picayune* (New Orleans) (November 28, 1999); "New York Times Fires 20 People Over E-Mail," *The Washington Post* (December 1, 1999); "More Companies Monitor Employees' E-Mail," *The Wall Street Journal* (December 2, 1999).

IN CONSULTATION

Marvin Manager has a problem. He suspects his subordinate, Ellen Employee, is looking for another job. He has heard rumors that Ellen is sending résumés via her company e-mail and that she may even be sending out confidential company information to her prospective new employers. He wants to monitor secretly her e-mail correspondence. Marvin reviewed all published company policies and the company handbook. Although he found nothing that addresses whether company e-mail can be read, he did find materials that require employees keep company secrets confidential and maintain sufficient productivity. Ellen has never signed anything giving Marvin or anyone else permission to read her e-mail.

Marvin approached his company's in-house corporate counsel, Laura Lawyer. He asked Laura whether he would create legal liability for himself or the company if he secretly read Ellen's e-mail. Here is their conversation:

Marvin:

1. Ellen is using a company computer and a company e-mail system. As the company manager, I should automatically have the right to monitor what she does with our equipment.
2. If Ellen is using the computer during company time, I should be able to monitor her to make sure she is being productive and completing her job assignments.
3. I have to read Ellen's e-mail to ensure that she is not spreading company secrets to our competitors or otherwise creating legal risk for the company.

Laura:

1. That is not necessarily true. Employees may have a reasonable expectation of privacy in the workplace. Ellen may also have free speech protection in her statements made using e-mail.
2. As a manager, you can monitor Ellen's productivity, but not at the expense of her constitutional rights to privacy and free speech.
3. The company does require employees keep proprietary commercial information confidential. Company policy expressly sets out guidelines for the protection of company secrets. Company policy and the company handbook, however, do not address whether e-mail can be monitored in an effort to keep those secrets. **I will review the applicable law to see whether we can monitor Ellen's e-mail and get back to you.**

FROM THE DESK OF

Laura Lawyer

To: Marvin Manager

Re: Implications of Secretly Monitoring Employee E-mail

Dear Marvin:

Technical experts say that in the year 2000, an estimated 40 million users will send 60 billion e-mail messages. E-mail at work, which makes up a large part of total e-mail usage, has revolutionized communication in the workplace. The issue of whether workplace e-mail is private, however, is rather controversial. The courts have been challenged with balancing employee privacy rights with the employer's need to maintain productivity and limit its potential legal liability created by employee communications. To date, the law is tipped in favor of employers' right to monitor employee e-mail. The law addressing e-mail privacy at work breaks down into three areas:

1. The Electronic Communications Privacy Act of 1986[1] (ECPA) directly prohibits accessing or disclosing the contents of e-mail without proper consent. The ECPA is an amendment to Title III of

[1] 18 U.S.C. § 2510 (1998).

the Omnibus Crime Control and Safe Streets Act of 1968, also known as the "wiretap law." The ECPA does not directly address employer rights but offers three exceptions that may allow employers to monitor workplace e-mail. E-mail may be monitored if (a) one party consents, (b) the employer provides the e-mail service, and (c) the monitoring is done in the ordinary course of business. Courts have interpreted the ECPA to allow employers to monitor e-mail if the employee has consented, the employer provides the e-mail service, or if the employer is monitoring e-mail for business content and use.

2. The First Amendment of the Constitution protects speech, even speech via e-mail. Free speech protection is paramount but is not without exception. Commercial speech receives limited protection, and other types of speech such as defamation, obscenity, and fighting words are not fully protected. If Ellen is violating company secrets, her speech is less protected. Even if Ellen is not going so far as to spread company secrets but is merely looking for other employment or just using the e-mail for personal communication, the company can likely monitor her. Companies may restrict employees' speech in the workplace to limit legal liability and also to improve morale and productivity.

3. Employees have a constitutional right to privacy, but their rights at work are limited. Employees have Fourth Amendment protection against unreasonable search and seizure, but this protection does not apply to private employers like our company. The U.S. Constitution does not contain an express provision protecting privacy rights, but several state constitutions do. We should check our state constitution to ensure that there is no conflict. If there is no conflict, there is probably no constitutional protection because Ellen is at work using company-provided equipment and e-mail systems, so she is unlikely to have a reasonable expectation of privacy.

Although the ECPA and the First and Fourth Amendments would currently allow us to monitor Ellen, I have three concerns. First, Congress passed the ECPA in 1986—before the widespread use of e-mail both inside and outside work. As its common name, "wiretap law," late indicates, the ECPA was not intended to cover e-mail; thus, it may not be a reliable source of legal insulation from our liability if we choose to secretly monitor employees. Second, we could create bad morale and actually decrease productivity if our employees feel that we do not trust them and are "snooping" into their private affairs. Third, we should have an express company policy on this issue that every employee signs off on and that posts onto each employee's computer before they can use the system in the first place. By notifying employees that we reserve the right to monitor their e-mail, we reduce, if not eliminate, any expectation of privacy they may have. We are then free both legally and ethically to check for productivity and legal liability risks in our employee's e-mail communications.

With specific regard to Ellen, we should consider the following questions in deciding whether to monitor her e-mail:

1. Even if Marvin is legally entitled to monitor Ellen's e-mail, what are some of the reasons why he should not?
2. What are some alternatives to monitoring Ellen's e-mail that would allow Marvin to investigate his concerns over her productivity and violation of company secrets without "snooping" into her personal affairs?
3. How could Marvin construct a company policy that allows e-mail to operate efficiently in the workplace and balances employers' interest in productivity and legal protection with employees' privacy, morale, and need to communicate?

OFF-THE-JOB ACTIVITIES

Not only do some employers occasionally monitor their employees' actions at work, but others take an interest in what their workers do away from the job. With health care costs rising about 9 percent each year, some companies have instituted programs that charge higher health care premiums to those employees who engage in activities that cause health problems, such as smoking. Some, like Turner Broadcasting, simply will not hire smokers at all. Texas Instruments found, through an in-house study, that smokers' health costs at the company were 50 percent higher than nonsmokers and began charging smokers an additional $10 per month.

Although the negative health implications of smoking are quite well-established, there is concern about the future implications of employer monitoring of off-the-job actions. "When they tell you that you can't smoke on your own time, the next thing you know they'll tell you that you can't have sex but once a week, and if you have sex twice a week you're fired," declared Oklahoma State Senator Carl Franklin. "What about the health implications of the guy who eats fried chicken 20 times a month?" asked one company executive.

A few companies have allowed employees to reduce their health-care premiums if they achieve certain levels of weight loss or cholesterol standards, or if they quit smoking. In response to employer actions against smokers, some 29 states have passed laws prohibiting discrimination against people who smoke off the job. These efforts are often supported by the tobacco companies.

LOVE, SEX, AND DATING: WHAT CAN THE EMPLOYER SAY?

Whenever men and women work together, the potential for dating and workplace romance arises. Office romances raise several concerns for employers. Employers worry that employees' morale and productivity will suffer if and when the romance sours and the employees must work in close proximity. Fellow employees who must work with the lovers may feel resentment and jealously. The prospect for sexual harassment claims resulting from one employee's unrequited attempts to date a coworker are also major concerns for employers. As a result, some employers have adopted work rules prohibiting dating among coworkers. The following case involves a suit by a female employee who was fired because she was involved in a romantic relationship with the manager of a rival firm.

RULON-MILLER V. INTERNATIONAL BUSINESS MACHINE CORP.

162 Cal. App. 3d 241 (1984)

FACTS

Virginia Rulon-Miller worked for IBM at its San Francisco office products division. She had started with IBM as a receptionist in 1967 and had worked her way up to a low-level marketing manager position by 1978. Rulon-Miller met Matt Blum in 1976; Blum was then an account manager for IBM at the San Francisco office. Blum and Rulon-Miler began dating, and their relationship was widely known within the company. In 1977, Blum took a job with a competitor of IBM and transferred to Philadelphia; later in 1978, he returned to the competitor's San Francisco office. Blum and Rulon-Miller again began dating; IBM executives were aware that they had resumed their relationship but did not see that as a problem, even when Rulon-Miller was promoted to marketing manager. Rulon-Miller received good performance ratings as a manager, and in 1979, she was granted a $4,000 merit raise. Shortly after the raise, she was confronted by her supervisor (the same one who had promoted her) and asked whether she was dating Blum. When Rulon-Miller asked why that was relevant, she was told that it was a "conflict of interest"; her supervisor said she could either stop dating Blum or lose her job. The next day the supervisor called her into his office and told her she was removed from the management position; when she protested, he fired her. Rulon-Miller filed suit against IBM for wrongful discharge and for intentional infliction of emotional distress. At trial, a jury held for her and awarded $100,000 in compensatory damages and $200,000 in punitive damages against IBM. IBM appealed to the California Court of Appeal.

DECISION

IBM had adopted a corporate policy of respecting the privacy of employees by stating that off-the-job behavior was only a concern of the employer when it reduced the employee's ability to perform regular job assignments, interfered with the job performance of other employees, or affected the reputation of the company in a major way. IBM also had a policy against "conflicts of interest" by employees, but that policy was concerned with employees involved in activities for personal gain that interfered with IBM's business interests. IBM did not interpret its policy to prohibit romantic relationships, and it did not have any policy against employees socializing with competitors.

The court held that the policy gave IBM the right to terminate an employee because of a conflict of interest; but the question of whether Rulon-Miller's conduct constituted a conflict of interest was a question of fact for the trial jury, which held in her favor. The court noted that Rulon-Miller's job did not give her access to sensitive information that could be useful to competitors, and that there was no evidence that she had given information or help to IBM's competitor. The IBM corporate policies established that the outside activities of employees were of no interest to the company as long as the activities did not interfere with the work of the employee. Whether those policies gave IBM the right to inquire into the personal or romantic relationships of its managers was a question for the jury to decide.

With regard to Rulon-Miller's claim of intentional infliction of emotional distress, the court stated that the issue was whether IBM had acted in an extreme and outrageous manner in terminating her. That question was also a matter for the jury to decide, after considering the corporate policies of IBM and the conduct and comments of Rulon-Miller's supervisor. The jury could reasonably find that the company's invasion of Rulon-Miller's privacy rights constituted extreme and outrageous conduct. Rulon-Miller's supervisor acted in flagrant disregard of the IBM corporate policies and was deceitful in acting as if her relationship with Blum was something new, when the evidence was clear that he had been aware of it well before he promoted her. The supervisor, when first confronting her about the relationship with Blum, said he was giving her "a few days" to think it over, but the very next day he told her, "I'm making the decision for you." The combination of his conduct and statements humiliated and degraded her; his conduct was intended to emphasize that she was powerless to assert her rights as an IBM employee. The court held that the evidence supported the jury's finding of extreme and outrageous conduct and the award of punitive damages. The court affirmed trial court judgment for Rulon-Miller against IBM.

CASE QUESTIONS

1. What was the nature of Rulon-Miller's cause of action here—was she suing in tort, for breach of contract, or some other claim?
2. Did the court uphold IBM's right to terminate an employee who violates its conflict of interest policy?
3. Did Rulon-Miller's conduct interfere with her ability to do her job or with the quality of her job performance? Who was the appropriate person to determine whether Rulon-Miller's conduct was a conflict of interest or interfered with her job performance?

At least six states have passed laws that prohibit firms from discriminating against employees for any off-the-job actions that are legal in that state. This type of law prohibits discriminations against those workers who smoke or drink alcohol or eat fried chicken away from work, but also possibly those employees who date other employees in violation of company policy or commit other violations of company regulations. Note that the determination of just what conduct is protected by such laws is open to judicial interpretation.

Section 201-d of the New York State Labor Law protects employees from discrimination in terms or conditions of employment because of their "legal recreational activities," their political activities, and their "legal use of consumable products" off the job. The courts are split over the question of whether the New York legislation protects an employee from being fired because of a personal relationship: the Appellate Division of the New York Supreme Court held that it did not protect an employee from termination for violation of Wal-Mart's "no fraternization" [*New York v. Wal-Mart Stores, Inc.*, 207 A.D.2d 150 (1995)]; but the U.S. District Court for the Southern District of New York held that an employee could not be fired because she lived with a former employee [*Pasch v. Katz Media Corp.*, 10 I.E.R. Cases 1574, 1995 WL 469710 (Aug. 8, 1995)]. Other courts have also upheld employer "no dating coworkers" policies.[4]

Employers may go beyond forbidding dating by coworkers and adopt policies that prevent spouses from working together; such policies are usually motivated by morale concerns—to avoid coworkers bringing their domestic disputes into the workplace—and to avoid charges of favoritism. In *Harper v. TWA* [525 F.2d 409 (8th Cir. 1975)], the U.S. Court of Appeals upheld a TWA policy that prohibited spouses from working together in the same department; if coworkers married, the employer required that the spouse with less seniority had 30 days to transfer, take a leave, or be terminated. The court held that the

[4] See *Patton v. J.C. Penney Co.* [301 Or. 117, 719 P.2d 854 (1986)] and *Federated Rural Insurance Co. v. Kessler* [131 Wis. 2d 189, 388 N.W. 2d 553 (1986)]. But see *Slohoda v. U.P.S., Inc.* [193 N.J. Super. 586, 475 A.2d 618 (1984)], holding that UPS's policy violated New Jersey law.

policy was neutral on its face and did not have a discriminatory effect on female employees. (TWA subsequently changed the policy to apply only when one spouse supervised the other.)

One of the more controversial issues in society today is the appropriate degree of protection and tolerance the legal system should provide for homosexual behavior. Federal antidiscrimination laws do not include lesbians or homosexuals as a protected class, although several state statutes do. Nevertheless, an employer who terminates or takes disciplinary action against a gay employee is sometimes held to have violated the "right to privacy," as the following reading shows.

GAY EMPLOYEE WINS DAMAGES FOR INVASION OF PRIVACY

In 1985 Dr. Jeffry Collins, an executive at a Shell Oil Co. subsidiary, was fired after company officials found a flyer for a nude sex party he had prepared on his office computer. A secretary found a copy of the flyer near the photocopy machine and showed it to other company managers. Dr. Collins had worked for Shell for 19 years and was then the second ranking executive at Triton Biosciences, Inc. Following his firing, Collins filed a wrongful discharge lawsuit and, in 1991, was awarded $5.3 million by a California court, including $2 million in emotional distress and punitive damages.

An Alameda County judge called the company's behavior "outrageous," finding that Shell violated California law by using information about Collins' personal life as a basis for firing him. Judge Jacqueline Taber held that "the evidence is clear and convincing that [he] was terminated for private homosexual conduct away from his employment . . . and not for unsatisfactory job performance." Furthermore, Judge Taber wrote that the evidence clearly showed that "homosexual group sexual activity was beyond the pale of conduct acceptable to the top management of Shell."

Shell countered by stating that "sexual orientation is not a consideration in our hiring or other employment practices." A Shell lawyer maintained that Collins was fired "for preparing a sexually explicitly memo" at the office, using company equipment, and for leaving it where it could offend other employees."

Judge Taber found that prior to the memo, Dr. Collins had an exemplary employment history with consistently high performance reviews. The judge held that Collins had been fired "solely" because he was an active homosexual, and she also criticized Shell for waiting until Dr. Collins had made a major presentation to Triton's board before firing him, and for telling headhunters about the flyer, thus seriously hurting Collins search for new employment.

The lawyer for Dr. Collins stated that the ruling should cause employers in California to evaluate carefully whether they should terminate any employee for a reason that is not related to job performance, an opinion echoed by other employment specialists. There are no federal laws protecting persons from being discriminated against on the basis of sexual orientation, but a few states and some 100 cities do protect gays against housing and employment discrimination.

Sources: "The Right to Privacy: A $5.3 Million Lesson for Shell?" *Business Week* (August 26, 1991), p. 72; "Homosexual Wins Damages Over Firing," *The Wall Street Journal* (June 18, 1991), p. B5.

FROM THE DESK OF

Laura Lawyer

To: Students

From: Your Lawyer

1. Do not acquire or retain information on employees that the company has no need to know. Why? Someday someone will seek to use this information improperly, and this type of information retention policy can be used against the company in an invasion of privacy suit.
2. Impose disciplinary measures firmly and fairly for work-related conduct, not for outside-the-workplace actions and lifestyle choices.

SUMMARY

Some of the most difficult legal issues in employment law today involve job security, drug testing, and other employee privacy concerns. Employers faced with the pressures of global competition and the need to increase efficiency and make their workers more productive are placing increased demands on employees; some employees resent the pressures and requirements of the workplace that intrude into their personal lives. The social changes in the workforce and the rapid increase in technology have created new tensions and pressures. The courts are called upon to attempt to strike some balance; employers who go too far face extensive liability, and employees who resent such intrusions and pressures too much may lose their jobs. Much of the law in these areas comes through development of older common law principles on a case-by-case basis.

It is crucial that employers and employees understand each other's needs and goals and the principles of law that apply to such situations. The ever-increasing worldwide competition faced by U.S. businesses makes it unlikely that such problems will disappear in the future—if anything, they are likely to intensify. In time, there may be calls for more laws regulating the workplace, although the current antiregulatory mood of the public makes increased government involvement in employment unlikely in the near future. Thus, the courts will need to resolve legal disputes and update common law legal theories as employees bring actions concerning job security, privacy, drug testing, surveillance of workers, and other infringements on their rights both on and off the job. Employment law will necessarily develop to meet the new problems arising from the changing nature of employment in the 21st century.

CHAPTER QUESTIONS

1. An in-house attorney employed full-time by a division of General Dynamics told his supervisor that parts of the company's pay policy appeared to violate federal law and later refused to sign off on a letter approving the policy. He was fired some time later. When he sued for wrongful discharge, the company defended on the ground that a client should always have the right to dismiss his or her attorney, since the relationship is one of trust. The attorney argued that as a full-time employee, he should have the same rights as any other worker. What should the result be? What arguments could you make in support of or in opposition to the decision? [*General Dynamics v. Superior Court*, 876, P.2d 487, 32 Cal. Rptr. 2d 1, 7 Cal. 4th 1164 (1994)]
2. Kramer worked for Rite-Aid in downtown Baltimore. His supervisor became concerned about "inventory shrinkage" that she suspected was caused by employee theft. The supervisor requested that Kramer take a polygraph test, according to company policy. Kramer refused to take the test, and in response, the supervisor cut back Kramer's work hours and arranged to transfer him to a store 50 miles away. The supervisor hoped that such changes would force Kramer to quit; Kramer did quit two weeks later. Maryland state law prohibits employers from requiring employees to take polygraph tests and forbids discharging employees who refuse to take such tests. Kramer files a wrongful discharge against Rite-Aid and the supervisor. What arguments can Kramer make to challenge Rite-Aid's actions? Under which of the exceptions to the at will rule can he base his suit? What defense can Rite-Aid make to those claims? Who is likely to win the suit? Why? Explain. [*Moniodis v. Cook*, 494 A.2d 212, 64 Md. App. 1 (1985)]
3. Catherine Wagenseller, a nurse at an Arizona hospital, went on an eight-day rafting trip with several coworkers. Prior to the trip she had established a superior work record and had a very good relationship with her supervisor, Ms. Smith. During the trip, she became increasingly uncomfortable with certain activities such as nude bathing and heavy drinking. During the trip, members of the group, including her boss, created and performed a skit to the tune "Moon River," which ended with the group "mooning" the audience. After returning from the trip, the group performed the skit twice back at the hospital. Ms. Wagenseller chose not to participate in any of these activities. Upon her return to work, her relationship with her supervisor deteriorated sharply, and she was eventually fired. Although she was an employee at will, she sued for wrongful discharge. Should any of the exceptions apply? What should the result be? [*Wagenseller v. Scottsdale Memorial Hospital*, 710 P.2d 1025 (Ariz. 1985)]
4. Homer Simpson was employed as an instrument panel monitor at a nuclear power plant operated by Giant Electrical Utility Co. of Springfield, Pennsylvania. Giant required all of its power-plant employees to sign a form consenting to random drug testing as a condition of employment; the form stated that refusal to submit to such tests would result in termination of employment. After 10 months on the job, Mr. Simpson was requested to take a drug test; he refused, claiming he did not use drugs and that there was no reasonable basis to suspect him of drug use. Giant

terminated Mr. Simpson, and he filed for unemployment compensation. Giant contested his unemployment compensation claim. What arguments can Mr. Simpson make to support his claim for unemployment compensation? What arguments can Giant make to oppose his claim? What is the likely outcome of the case? Why? Explain. [See *Moore v. Unemployment Compensation Board of Review*, 134 Pa. Cmwlth. 274, 578 A.2d 606 (1990).]

5. Richard Metille was hired as a loan officer by Pine River State Bank; his employment agreement was an oral agreement, and no specific term of employment was specified. After he had completed his probationary period, Metille was given a printed Employee Handbook, which the bank distributed to all of its employees. The handbook contained information on the bank's policies and set out a three-step disciplinary policy. The first step involved an oral warning or reprimand for the employee conduct, and the second step involved a written warning to the employee. The third step called for suspension or discharge but said that discharge would only be imposed when "the employee's conduct does not improve as a result of the previous action taken." When Metille received his annual performance review, he was given a 7 percent raise and a satisfactory rating. He had never received any reprimands or complaints about his performance. The next month, state banking inspectors examined the bank's operations and reported that a number of loans had been made without proper documentation. The bank's president determined that Metille was responsible for a number of the documentation problems; she called him into her office and fired him. The president did not review the violations Metille was suspected of committing, and she did not follow the procedures outlined in the Employee Handbook. Can Metille challenge his discharge, and can he state a claim under one of the exceptions to the at will doctrine? What arguments can the bank make to support the discharge? Is Metille likely to be successful? Explain your answers. [See *Pine River State Bank v. Metille*, 333 N.W. 2d 622 (Minn. 1983).]

6. Mr. and Mrs. Spears owned a package store in Arkansas that had been burglarized. Suspecting that one of their employees was involved, they installed a recording device on the business telephone extension in their mobile home and secretly listened to and recorded 22 hours of the conversations of the employee over the next two months. Much of the conversation involved "sexually provocative" exchanges between the employee and a married man with whom she was having an affair. Later, Mr. and Mrs. Spears told the employee's husband and the other man's wife about the conversations. The employee sued for damages. What should the result be? [*Deal v. Spears*, 980 F.2d 1153 (8th Cir. 1992)]

7. The U.S. Customs Service is the government agency responsible for processing and inspecting people and goods coming into the country. One important role it has is stopping and seizing illegal drugs. In 1986 the Customs Service announced that drug tests would thereafter be given to all persons seeking employment or promotion to positions that have the following responsibilities: (1) deal with drug enforcement, (2) involve the carrying of firearms, and (3) handle "classified" materials. The employees' union filed suit to block the program, claiming that it violated the Fourth Amendment. What should be the result and why? [*National Treasury Employees Union v. Von Raab*, 489 U.S. 656 (1989)]

8. United Parcel Service, Inc., fired a manager in Mississippi who violated the company's "no dating between managers and subordinates" policy. Mississippi has no law prohibiting employers from terminating employees for actions that are not illegal in that state. The manager sued, claiming that the company's regulation of his off-duty actions invaded his privacy. What should be the result? Why? [*Watkins v. United Parcel Service, Inc.*, 979 F.2d 1538 (5th Cir. 1992)]
9. Cort and Pincus had worked for Bristol Meyers Co. as sales representatives in the Boston area for a number of years; they were at will employees. After a period of reduced sales in the region, the company's sales manager sent the sales representatives a lengthy questionnaire containing questions that could be used for making a psychological evaluation of the sales force. Cort and Pincus objected to a number of the questions on the grounds that they were highly personal, offensive, and were not related to job performance in any way. They either left such questions blank or gave frivolous answers to them. They subsequently received poor job performance reviews and were later terminated. They argued that the poor sales performance was due to Bristol Meyer's difficulties in producing one drug and the loss of a customer bid on another drug. When Bristol Myers refused to reinstate them, they sued for wrongful discharge and invasion of privacy. Under which of the exceptions to the at will rule should they sue? Explain. What arguments can they use to support their invasion of privacy claim? What arguments can the employer make to defend against its suit? What is the likely outcome of their suit? Why? Explain. [*Cort v. Bristol Meyers Co.*, 431 N.E. 908 (Ma. 1982)]
10. Manuel, an African American male, was employed by International Harvester Co. as the Director of its Equal Opportunity Programs. His zealous advocacy for improving International Harvester's employment of minorities met with some opposition by company executives. After a year on the job, he was terminated due to a reduction in force. Manuel feels that his discharge was racially motivated. He filed a suit against International Harvester, alleging, among other things, a violation of the state and federal civil rights laws prohibiting employment discrimination. He also included a claim for unjust discharge, in violation of public policy. International Harvester claimed that, because Manuel can pursue statutory remedies under the state and federal civil rights laws, the court should reject the unjust discharge claim. What arguments can be made for allowing Manuel to pursue the unjust discharge claim in addition to the civil rights law claims? What arguments can be made to support Harvester's position that the statutory remedies are sufficient? How should the court rule on this question? Explain. [See *Manuel v. International Harvester Co.*, 502 F.Supp. 45 (N.D. Ill. 1980).]

PRACTICAL EXERCISE

Steven suspects that the employees at his book store are cheating him on workers compensation. He has had 5 of his 25 employees collect workers compensation in the past year for various injuries they allegedly incurred while working. Some claimed back strains from lifting heavy boxes, one broke an arm after slipping on a wet floor, and one claimed stress-related disability. Steven does not agree with the stress claim and thinks some of the injuries were the result of off-time activities. Rather than work on eliminating workplace hazards, Steven has decided to hire a private detective to monitor secretly his employees on and off the job.

Steven's private eye follows one employee, Elyse, who is currently receiving workers compensation for a back injury to her fitness club, and shoots videotape of her sitting in the hot tub, talking with friends, doing aerobics, and swimming with her two-year-old child. The detective then follows Elyse to her home, which she shares with another woman and child. He later places a tap on her phone. After monitoring 25 hours of her private conversations, the investigator learns that she is involved in a romantic relationship with the other woman. He also learns that Elyse really did hurt her back lifting a box at work, and her doctor has urged her to swim on a regular basis to build up her back. Elyse also has talked on the phone about smoking marijuana at least once.

You have just been hired as a consultant for Steven's bookshop. He asks you to meet with his private eye and then prepare a memo to him (Steven) regarding: (1) whether he can fire Elyse—or refuse to reinstate her when she "recovers"—due to her apparent lesbian activity, (2) whether he should confront Elyse with the evidence he has about her personal life, (3) whether he can require her to take a lie detector test or a drug test before returning to work. Also include in your memo a discussion of whether Steven has incurred any liability to Elyse due to his actions.

FURTHER INFORMATION

www.aclu.org/issues/worker/hmwr.html
The American Civil Liberties Union workplace rights page.

www.shrm.org/
The Society for Human Resource Management.

www.epic.org/
The Electronic Privacy Information Center.

www.amanet.org/
The American Management Association.

http://smallbiz.findlaw.com/employmentbook/
"From Hiring to Firing: The Survival Guide For Employers."

CHAPTER 20

EQUAL EMPLOYMENT OPPORTUNITY LAW: TITLE VII

LEARNING OBJECTIVES

After you have read this chapter, you should be able to:

1. Explain the coverage, administration, and enforcement of Title VII of the Civil Rights Act of 1964.
2. Describe the concepts of unintentional and intentional discrimination, disparate treatment and impact, race-norming, and seniority and their applications under Title VII.
3. Discuss the issues raised by the concept of affirmative action.
4. Analyze Title VII's application to sex discrimination issues, including payment concerns, pension benefits, and sexual harassment.
5. Discuss how Title VII applies to discrimination based on religion or national origin.

CHAPTER OUTLINE

You are an employer whose manufacturing business has expanded in the past few years because you were successful in winning government contracts; but as those contracts expire, your business is shrinking. You may have to lay off some employees—whom you had hired to work on the government contracts; a large percentage of those employees are Latinos and African-Americans. If you use inverse seniority ("last hired, first fired") to lay off the employees, the minority employees will lose their jobs. How do you decide which employees to lay off without getting sued for employment discrimination? After studying this chapter, you should be able to decide how to proceed with the layoffs.

INTRODUCTION

Chapters 20 and 21 discuss the law of employment discrimination, usually known as Equal Employment Opportunity (or EEO) law. This chapter focuses on the primary law addressing employment discrimination: Title VII of the Civil Rights Act of 1964 (referred to simply as Title VII). Chapter 21 will discuss other EEO legislation and related employment issues.

Prior to the passage of the Title VII, no legal prohibition existed against race, sex, or other discrimination by private sector employers. (The Equal Protection and Due Process provisions of the U.S. Constitution dealt with discrimination by public sector employers.) The Civil Rights Movement of the late 1950s and early 1960s was the moving force behind the development of Title VII and the Civil Rights Act. In the summer of 1963, Dr. Martin Luther King Jr. led a massive march on Washington to press for passage of civil rights legislation, and President Kennedy made such legislation a priority. When Lyndon Johnson became President after Kennedy was assassinated, he mobilized all of his legislative and persuasive skills to push the law through Congress, despite stiff opposition from Southern legislators. A member of the House of Representatives from Virginia offered an amendment to the bill, extending the prohibition against the forms of employment discrimination covered in the bill to include sex discrimination, hoping that such a change would scuttle the bill. He was wrong—the Civil Rights Act was passed by Congress and signed into law by President Johnson in 1964. Title VII of the Act, which deals with employment discrimination, took effect July 2, 1965.

Title VII was amended in 1968 to modify the procedures for enforcing the law; the 1972 amendments extended the law to cover public sector employers at the state and local level. The Pregnancy Discrimination Act of 1978 amended Title VII to include pregnancy within the definition of sex discrimination. Also, the Civil Rights Act of 1991 made substantial changes to the law. Specifically, the Act provides for jury trials and extends the types of damages available. The 1991 legislation was passed to overturn several decisions by the Supreme Court that were perceived as making it more difficult for plaintiffs to sue under the Title VII.

TITLE VII OF THE CIVIL RIGHTS ACT OF 1964

Title VII of the Civil Rights Act prohibits employment discrimination based on race, color, religion, sex, and national origin. Any discrimination in the terms or conditions of employment, such as the refusal or failure to hire, the discharge of any individual, or the discrimination against any individual with respect to compensation, privileges, or benefits of employment because of that individual's race, color, religion, sex or national origin, is illegal under Title VII.

COVERAGE OF TITLE VII

Title VII applies to employers with at least 15 employees who are engaged in an industry affecting interstate commerce. The Supreme Court decision in *Walters v. Metropolitan Education Enterprises, Inc.* [117 S.Ct. 660 (1997)] upheld the use of the "payroll method" for determining the number of employees—are there at least 15 employees on the payroll for each working day of 20 or more weeks in the current or preceding calendar year? State and local governments are also covered by Title VII; the federal government and wholly owned federal corporations are covered under separate provisions of Title VII. Coverage was extended in 1995 to include the employees of Congress and such bodies as the Government Printing Office, the General Accounting Office, and the Congressional Budget Office. The 1991 amendments also extend Title VII to cover U.S. employers that employ U.S. citizens abroad; however, if compliance with Title VII would force the employer to violate the law of the country in which the workplace is located, then the employer need not comply.

Title VII also applies to employment agencies and to labor unions that either operate a hiring hall or have at least 15 members. Employment agencies are prohibited from discriminating on any of the prohibited grounds (race, color, religion, sex, or national origin) in announcing openings, interviewing candidates, or in referring applicants to employers. Title VII prohibits labor unions from discriminating in employment opportunities or in the status of members or applicants.

ADMINISTRATION AND ENFORCEMENT OF TITLE VII

The *Equal Employment Opportunity Commission* (*EEOC*) administers and enforces Title VII. The EEOC investigates and litigates complaints under the Act. The EEOC also has the power to initiate enforcement actions on its own if it finds a "pattern or practice" of discrimination in employment. The EEOC is empowered to issue binding regulations and nonbinding guidelines for interpreting and complying with the legislation. The regulations under Title VII require employers, unions, and employment agencies to post notices summarizing the act's requirements; failure to display the notice is punishable by a fine of not more than $100 per violation. The Act also requires that employers must maintain payroll records and other records relating to applicants and to employee promotion, demotion, transfer, and discharge.

Enforcement Procedures Section 706(c) of Title VII requires that an individual seeking to file a complaint under the Act must first file with the state or local agency authorized to handle employment discrimination, if one exists. Sixty days after filing with the state or local agency, or upon termination if the state or local agency terminates its proceedings prior to 60 days, the individual may file the complaint with the EEOC. If an individual is required to go to the state or local agency first, the limitations period under Title VII requires that a complaint be filed with the EEOC within 300 days from the alleged act of discrimination. If no state or local agency exists, then the individual must file the complaint with the EEOC within 180 days of the alleged act of discrimination.

When Does a Violation Occur? The time limit for filing a complaint under Title VII makes it important to determine when the alleged act of discrimination took place. In most situations, it will not be difficult to determine the date of the violation. However, some cases present problems in determining when the alleged violation actually occurred. For example, in *Delaware State College v. Ricks* [449 U.S. 250 (1982)], a professor alleged that he was denied tenure because of his race; after he was informed of the college's decision to deny him tenure, he was given a final, one-year contract. At the expiration of the one-year contract, he was terminated; he then filed a complaint with the EEOC, alleging race discrimination. The Supreme Court held that the time limit for a Title VII violation starts on the date that the individual becomes aware of, or should be aware of, the alleged violation (in Ricks' case, the date he learned that he was denied tenure), and not from the date on which the alleged violation begins to have an adverse effect on the individual (the date Ricks was discharged).

Continuing Violations Some violations of Title VII may be continuing violations—actions that are ongoing. In *Bazemore v. Friday* [478 U.S. 385 (1986)], the plaintiffs alleged that the employer paid African-American employees less than white employees. The pay policy had originated prior to the date that Title VII applied to the employer, but the Supreme Court held that the violation was a continuing one—a new violation occurred each time the employees received a paycheck based on the racially discriminatory policy.

Seniority-Related Violations Section 706(e)(2) of the act states that in cases involving claims that a seniority system was adopted for discriminatory reasons, the date on which the violation occurs will be either the date the seniority system was adopted, the date on which the complainant became subject to the system, or the date on which the complainant is injured by the application of the seniority system.

EEOC Procedure for Handling Complaints The EEOC, as noted previously, may file suit on its own initiative when it finds a pattern or practice of discrimination; however, most EEOC actions are initiated by individual complaints. Upon receipt of a complaint, the EEOC serves a notice upon the respondent (the employer, union, or employment agency alleged to have engaged in illegal employment discrimination); the EEOC staff then conducts an investigation to determine whether there is reasonable cause to believe that the allegations of the complaint are true. If the investigation does not reveal any reasonable cause, the complaint is dismissed. If the investigation indicates that there is reasonable cause, the EEOC attempts to settle the complaint through voluntary negotiation. If, within 30 days, the voluntary procedures are not successful in settling the complaint to the satisfaction of the parties involved, the EEOC may then choose to file suit in federal court.

If the complaint is dismissed by the EEOC, or if it decides not to file suit, the EEOC notifies the complainant that he or she may personally file suit. The complainant must file suit within 90 days of receiving the right-to-sue notice. If the EEOC has neither dismissed the complaint nor filed suit within 180 days of its filing, the complainant may request a right-to-sue letter from the EEOC. The complainant then has 90 days from receipt of that letter to file suit. If the EEOC decides to file suit at a later date, the suits are joined and are tried together by the court. Suits under Title VII may be filed in either federal district court or in the appropriate state court, according to the Supreme Court decision in *Yellow Freight System, Inc. v. Donnelly* [494 U.S. 820 (1990)].

Relationship Between State and Federal Courts Because the procedures under Title VII require the complainant to file first with a state or local agency, if one exists, it is possible that the complainant's case may proceed to a trial under the relevant state legislation as well as under Title VII. In *Kremer v. Chemical Construction Co.* [456 U.S. 461 (1982)], the Supreme Court held that a decision by a state court dismissing a suit alleging discrimination in employment is binding on the federal courts; in other words, the complainant may not file suit, based on the same facts, under Title VII in federal court. The holding in *Kremer* is limited only to the effect of state court decisions; a negative determination by a state administrative agency does not affect the complainant's right to sue in federal court, according to *University of Tennessee v. Elliot* [478 U.S. 788 (1986)].

Following the *Elliot* rationale, the courts have held that decisions by other administrative agencies do not affect the ability of the complainant to sue under Title VII. For example, National Labor Relations Board decisions on unfair labor practice complaints involving discrimination do not affect the complainant's right to file suit over the same actions under Title VII. However, if the complainant accepted reinstatement with back pay in settlement of the complaint, the courts have held that the employee then waives his or her right to sue for the same facts under Title VII.

Arbitration and EEO Claims Businesses increasingly are turning to alternative dispute resolution instead of litigation to resolve disputes, and that includes employment disputes. A growing number of employers require employees to agree, as a condition of employment, to arbitrate any dispute growing out of their employment. How does such an agreement to arbitrate affect an employee's right to bring suit under the EEO laws? In *Gilmer v. Interstate/Johnson Lane Corp.* [500 U.S. 20 (1991)], the Supreme Court held that an employee who had signed an agreement to arbitrate all disputes arising from his employment was required to arbitrate, rather than litigate, his age discrimination claim. Subsequent cases applied that *Gilmer* decision to claims under Title VII and other EEO legislation. According to *Brisentine v. Stone & Webster Engineering Corp.* [117 F.3d 519 (11th Cir. 1997)], in order for an arbitration agreement to be enforced, it must meet three requirements: (1) the employee must have individually agreed to the arbitration provision, (2) the arbitration must authorize the arbitrator to resolve the statutory EEO claims, and (3) the agreement must give the employee the right to insist on arbitration if the statutory EEO claim is not resolved to his or her satisfaction in any grievance procedure or dispute resolution process of the employer. As a result, an agreement to arbitrate, knowingly and voluntarily agreed to by an employee, is binding and requires the employee to arbitrate EEO claims instead of taking them to court. Courts will refuse to enforce any arbitration agreement that was not voluntarily agreed to [*Prudential Insurance Co. v. Lai*, 42 F.3d 1299 (9th Cir. 1994)] or that is unfair to the employee [*Kinney v. United Health Care Services, Inc.*, 70 Cal. App.4th 1322, 83 Cal. Rptr.2d 348 (Cal. Ct. App. 1999)]. An agreement to arbitrate signed by an individual employee does not prevent the EEOC from bringing suit against the employer to enforce the EEO laws, according to *EEOC v. Waffle House, Inc.* [193 F.3d 805 (4th Cir. 1999)], *EEOC v. Kidder, Peabody & Co.* [156 F.3d 298 (2d Cir. 1998)], and *EEOC v. Frank's Nursery & Crafts, Inc.* [177 F.3d 448 (6th Cir. 1999)]; but the EEOC may be prevented from seeking individual remedies (such as back pay and reinstatement) for the employee who had signed the arbitration agreement.

DISCRIMINATION UNDER TITLE VII

Discrimination means making a choice—an employer discriminates among the several applicants when choosing which person to hire for the job, and a professor discriminates upon the basis of performance when grading exams. It must be emphasized that not all discrimination is illegal—discriminating in favor of the most qualified applicant is acceptable. Title VII merely prohibits discrimination in terms or conditions of employment that is based on race, color, religion, sex, or national origin.

In certain limited instances, Title VII does allow an employer to select employees on the basis of sex, religion, or national origin when the employer can establish that such a distinction is a **bona fide occupational qualification (BFOQ)**. In order to establish a BFOQ, the employer must demonstrate that business necessity—the safe and efficient operation of the business—requires that employees be of a particular sex, religion, or national origin. Note that race or color can never serve as the basis of a BFOQ under Title VII. (BFOQs will be discussed more fully later in this chapter.)

bona fide occupational qualification [BFOQ]: Requirement, based on business necessity, that only employees of a specific gender, religion, or national origin will be hired.

Intentional Discrimination—Disparate Treatment It should be clear that Title VII prohibits intentional discrimination in employment based on race, color, religion, sex, or national origin. An employer that refuses to hire Hispanic Americans, for example, or that will only hire women for certain limited positions, is in violation of Title VII. Such intentional discrimination is known as **disparate treatment**. (The particular individual is subjected to different treatment because of his or her race, color, religion, sex, or national origin.)

disparate treatment Intentional discrimination based on race, color, religion, sex, or national origin.

In the years immediately following the passage of Title VII, some people believed that the legislation was intended only to protect minority employees. The Supreme Court, however, in the case of *McDonald v. Sante Fe Trail Transportation Co.* [427 U.S. 273 (1976)], held that Title VII applied to employees of all races. In this case, an employer that discharged two white employees for stealing, but only suspended an African-American employee involved in the same incident, was held to be in violation of Title VII—the employer had treated the white employees differently because of their race.

Unintentional Discrimination—Disparate Impact Does Title VII, in addition to forbidding intentional discrimination, also prohibit unintentional discrimination in employment based on the prohibited grounds? An employer may specify certain requirements for a job that effectively disqualify otherwise capable prospective employees. However, what if the requirements in effect disqualify a large proportion of minority applicants? The discriminatory effect of apparently neutral job requirements is known as **disparate impact**.

disparate impact: The discriminatory effect of apparently neutral job requirements.

An employer may frequently use a test for screening job applicants. Although Title VII does permit the use of employment testing, Section 703(h) provides that employers may legally give and act upon the results of any professionally developed ability test only when such tests do not discriminate because of race, color, religion, sex, or national origin.

The following case addressed the legality under Title VII of an employer's use of job requirements that have a disparate impact.

GRIGGS V. DUKE POWER COMPANY

401 U.S. 424 (1971)

FACTS

Prior to the passage of the Civil Rights Act of 1964, Duke Power had openly discriminated in hiring on the basis of race. The workforce was organized into five departments: Labor, Coal Handling, Operations, Maintenance, and Laboratory and Test. African-Americans were employed only in the Labor department, which paid less than any of the other departments. In 1955, the company began to require a high school diploma as a requirement for hiring in any department except Labor. When the Civil Rights Act took effect in 1965, the company abandoned its policy of racial discrimination in hiring and job assignment; the company did require a high school diploma, however, in order to transfer from Labor to any other department. At the same time, white employees hired before the institution of the high school diploma requirement continued to perform satisfactorily and to be promoted in the other departments. The company also required new employees, hired after July 2, 1965, to pass two aptitude tests as well as have a high school diploma in order to be assigned to any department other than Labor. The tests were developed to measure general intelligence and mechanical aptitude; neither was directed or intended to measure the ability to learn to perform a particular job or category of jobs. The scores used for passing the two tests were approximately the national median scores achieved on the tests by high school graduates. Griggs (after going through the required procedures with the EEOC) filed suit alleging that Duke Power violated Title VII by using the high school diploma and testing requirements as a condition of employment when neither requirement was significantly related to successful job performance, and both requirements operated to exclude African-Americans at a substantially higher rate than white applicants.

The trial court found that Duke Power had stopped intentionally discriminating against African-Americans when Title VII took effect and that the company's present requirements did not violate Title VII. The Court of Appeals agreed, holding that there was no intentional discrimination. Griggs appealed to the U.S. Supreme Court on the issue of whether the use of job requirements that are not related to job performance but that have a disparate impact on minority applicants violates Title VII.

DECISION

The Supreme Court held that the objective of Title VII was to achieve equality of employment opportunities and to remove barriers that have operated in the past to favor white applicants over minorities. Under Title VII, "practices, procedures and tests neutral on their face, and even neutral in terms of intent, cannot be maintained if they operate to 'freeze' the status quo of prior discriminatory employment practices." Whites faired far better on the company's requirements than did African Americans; such consequences would appear to be directly traceable to race. Title VII prohibits not only overt or intentional discrimination but also practices that are fair in form but discriminatory in operation. "The touchstone is business necessity," stated the Court. "If an employment practice which operates to exclude Negroes cannot be shown to be related to the job performance, the practice is prohibited." Neither the high school diploma requirement nor the testing requirement was shown to bear a demonstrable relationship to successful performance of the jobs for which they were required. Both requirements were adopted without any meaningful study of their relationship to job performance. "The evidence, however, shows that employees who have not completed high school or taken the tests have continued to perform satisfactorily and make progress in departments for which the high school and test criteria are now used."

The Court held that "good intent or the absence of discriminatory intent does not redeem employment procedures or testing mechanisms that operate as 'built-in headwinds' for minority groups and are unrelated to measuring job capability." Title VII was directed against the consequences of employment practices, not simply the motivation behind the practices; "Congress has placed on the employer the burden of showing that any given requirement must have a manifest relationship to the employment in question. . . . Far from disparaging job qualifications as such, Congress has made such qualifications the controlling factor, so that race, religion, nationality, and sex become irrelevant. What Congress has commanded is that any test used must measure the person for the job and not the person in the abstract." The Supreme Court reversed the Court of Appeals decision.

CASE QUESTIONS

1. What was the effect of the company's high school diploma requirement on African-American employees? What was the effect of the test requirement?
2. When did the employer establish the diploma and testing requirements?
3. Were employees hired prior to the adoption of the requirements less able to perform the job than those hired after the adoption of the requirements? What other evidence indicates that the requirements were not job related?
4. Why does the Court feel that the employer's lack of intent to discriminate is not relevant to whether the requirements violate Title VII?

The job requirements in *Griggs* were both objective criteria—having a high school diploma and attaining a passing score on a particular exam. Can subjective criteria, such as supervisors' post-interview rankings of job applicants, also be challenged under disparate impact analysis? In *Watson v. Fort Worth Bank & Trust* [487 U.S. 977 (1989)], the Supreme Court held that subjective employment selection practices were also subject to disparate impact analysis. In the *Watson* case, the employer promoted employees based on supervisors' recommendations; Watson, an African-American female, was continually passed over for promotions because her white supervisors rated her lower than other employees who were white. The Supreme Court said that disparate impact analysis could be applied to the promotion practices. A second Supreme Court decision, *Wards Cove Packing Co. v. Atonio* [490 U.S. 642 (1989)], held that the plaintiff raising a disparate impact argument must identify a specific employment practice that allegedly caused the disparate impact. Section 703(k), inserted in Title VII by the 1991 amendments, provides that when a plaintiff has demonstrated that an employment practice has a disparate impact, the defendant-employer must then show that the employment practice is job-related.

Showing a Disparate Impact To argue successfully a claim of disparate impact, a plaintiff must prove that a protected group is adversely affected by an employment practice or requirement. Hence, the plaintiff's prima facie case must necessarily involve evidence of a statistical nature. While the Supreme Court has not identified any specific statistical formulation that is required, the courts have allowed several different means of proof to be used. One method involves a simple comparison between the workforce of the employer in question, and another is known as the **four-fifths rule**.

four-fifths rule: A method of showing that an employment practice has a disparate impact.

The workforce comparison method involves a statistical comparison of the representation of the relevant protected group in the employer's workforce with the protected group's representation in the relevant labor market (the area from which the employer draws most of its employees—it may be local or even national, depending on the job in question). What does this comparison prove? When a marked discrepancy exists between the percentage of the protected group in the workforce and the percentage in the relevant labor market, that discrepancy likely is due to the effect of the challenged employment practice or requirement.

If the job in question requires specific skills and training, the population used for the comparison may be limited to available qualified individuals within the relevant labor market, according to the Supreme Court decision in *Wards Cove*. Defining the relevant labor market, however, is a question of fact in each case, and may be a major issue in contention between the parties to the case, as was evident in the Supreme Court decision in *Hazelwood School District v. U.S.* [433 U.S. 299 (1977)].

Four-Fifths Rule A second means of showing a disparate impact is the four-fifths rule set out in the *Uniform Guidelines on Employee Selection Procedures*, a set of regulations adopted by the EEOC and other federal agencies. The four-fifths rule compares the selection rates (the rates at which applicants meet the requirements or pass the selection procedure) for the various groups protected under Title VII. The rule states that a disparate impact will be demonstrated when the proportion of applicants from the protected group with the lowest selection rate is less than 80 percent of the selection rate of the group with the highest selection rate. Stating the rule in equation form, a disparate impact exists when:

$$\frac{\text{Pass rate for group with lowest selection rate}}{\text{Pass rate for group with highest selection rate}} < .80$$

For example, suppose a municipal fire department requires that applicants for firefighter positions be at least five feet, six inches tall and weigh at least 130 pounds. Of the applicants for the positions, 5 of the 25 Hispanic-American applicants meet the requirements, while 30 of 40 of the white applicants meet the requirements. The selection rate for Hispanic-American applicants is 20 percent (5/25), or .20; the selection rate for whites is 75 percent (30/40). To determine whether the requirements have a disparate impact on Hispanic-Americans, we need to divide .20 (the selection rate for Hispanic-Americans) by .75 (the selection rate for whites); if the result is less than .80, a disparate impact exists. Here, $.20/.75 = .266 < .80$; therefore a disparate impact exists, establishing a prima facie case of employment discrimination.

Section 703(k) of Title VII addresses disparate impact claims; it states that the plaintiff has the burden of proof to show that the challenged employment practice causes an impact on one of the bases prohibited by Title VII. Using the example discussed previously, a Hispanic-American challenging the use of the minimum height and weight requirements by the fire department must show that such requirements disproportionately disqualify Hispanic-Americans. If the plaintiff makes such a showing, the employer must then demonstrate that the employment practice is job-related for the position in question; the fire department must convince the court that only persons who meet the height and weight requirements are capable of performing the job satisfactorily. If the employer is able to show that the challenged employment practice does not have a disparate impact, then there is no need to demonstrate that the practice is required by job-related factors.

Even if the employer is able to show the employment practice is job related, if the plaintiff can then demonstrate that an alternative employment practice—one that does not have a disparate impact but serves the same job-related purpose—is available, and the employer refuses to adopt it, the employer is still in violation of the Act. For example, the fire department may try to justify the height and weight requirements on the basis that they indicate upper body strength needed by firefighters. Although height and weight may be related to a person's strength, the plaintiff may be able to demonstrate that an upper body strength test serves the same purpose and does not have a disparate impact on Hispanic-Americans. If the fire department refuses to adopt the strength test and continues to use the height and weight requirements, it is in violation of Title VII.

Section 703(k) also states that work rules that bar the employment of persons using or possessing illegal drugs are exempted from disparate impact analysis; such rules are a violation of Title VII only if they were adopted or applied with the intention to discriminate on grounds prohibited by Title VII.

The employer may continue to use an employment practice that has been shown to be sufficiently job related or required by business necessity, and the plaintiff has not shown that an alternative practice without a disparate impact is available. Nothing in Title VII prohibits an employer from hiring those people best able to do the job. If an employer is intentionally discriminating in employment, the fact that an employment practice may be job related is not a defense to a claim of disparate treatment discrimination under Title VII. For example, it is no defense for an employer who deliberately refuses to hire qualified female accountants to show that CPA certification is necessary for the job and that female CPAs are less common than male CPAs.

PROVING DISCRIMINATION—BURDENS OF PROOF

When a suit under Title VII has been filed, the question of the burden of proof arises—what must a plaintiff demonstrate to establish a valid claim of discrimination, and what must the defendant show to defeat a claim of discrimination?

The Supreme Court has consistently held, in a number of cases, that the plaintiff always has the burden of persuasion; that is, the plaintiff must persuade the judge (or jury, if it is a jury trial) that there has been employment discrimination in violation of Title VII. In order to do this, the plaintiff must establish a **prima facie case** of discrimination—enough evidence to raise a presumption of discrimination. If the plaintiff fails to establish a prima facie case of discrimination, then the case will be dismissed—the plaintiff will lose the suit. The plaintiff may use factual evidence or statistical evidence to establish the prima facie case. The specific elements of a prima facie case, and the means to establish it, will vary depending on whether the complaint involves disparate treatment or disparate impact.

prima facie case: Establishing facts sufficient to raise a presumption of discrimination.

Defendant's Burden After the plaintiff has successfully demonstrated a prima facie case, the defendant must overcome the plaintiff's claims. As the Supreme Court initially noted in *McDonnell Douglas Corp. v. Green* [411 U.S. 792 (1973)] and reemphasized in *Texas Department of Community Affairs v. Burdine* [450 U.S. 248 (1979)], in disparate treatment cases, the defendant is not required to disprove the plaintiff's claims. The defendant is only required to produce some evidence that offers a legitimate, nondiscriminatory reason for its actions, or, in the words of the Court, "to articulate a legitimate justification" for its actions. For example, the employer may demonstrate that the plaintiff was not hired because he or she was not sufficiently qualified for the job in question. In disparate impact cases, as noted previously, once a plaintiff shows that an employment selection practice has a disparate impact, §703(k) requires the employer to prove that the selection practice is job related.

Plaintiff's Burden of Showing Pretext When the defendant has offered a legitimate justification for the challenged conduct, the plaintiff must be afforded the opportunity to show that the offered justification is a mere pretext, a false claim used to cover up the real reason for the actions. This can be shown either directly, by persuading the court that a discriminatory reason probably motivated the defendant, or indirectly, by showing that the justification is not worthy of credence. The Supreme Court, in the decision of *St. Mary's Honor Center v. Hicks* [509 U.S. 502 (1993)], held that the plaintiff has the burden of proof to persuade the court that illegal discrimination has occurred even when the plaintiff can show that the reasons offered by the defendant are false. That is, even when the plaintiff demonstrates that the employer's offered reason for the action is a pretext, the plaintiff, in order to prevail, must also convince the court that the employer's decision was based on an illegal ground of discrimination.

MIXED MOTIVES

The 1991 amendments to Title VII added §703(m) to the act, which states "an unlawful employment practice is established when the complaining party demonstrates that race, color, religion, sex or national origin was a motivating factor for any employment practice, even though other factors also motivated the practice." Thus, an employer violates Title VII when an illegal factor (race, color, religion, sex, or national origin) is considered, even though other factors or reasons may motivate the decision or practice as well. If the employer in such a situation is able to demonstrate that it would have reached the same decision in the absence of the illegal factor, then the employer's liability for remedies for the violation is limited by §706(g)(2)(B), also added in 1991. This section states that the employer is subject to a court order to cease violating Title VII and is liable for the plaintiff's legal fees. However, the employer is not required to pay damages or to reinstate or hire the plaintiff.

THE "BOTTOM LINE" AND DISCRIMINATION

The case of *Connecticut v. Teal* [457 U.S. 440 (1982)] addressed whether promotion of a greater percentage of successful minority applicants than successful white applicants was a sufficient defense to a claim that the test used to qualify for promotion had a disparate impact on African-American applicants. The plaintiffs showed that the test had a disparate impact under the four-fifths rule, and the employer had not validated the test. The Supreme Court held that using the test to determine which applicants were qualified for promotion was in violation of Title VII, despite the fact that a greater percentage of African-Americans than whites who had qualified were promoted. The problem did not concern the actual promotions; rather, the problem concerned the means used to determine who was qualified for promotion—the test really did not measure or select for ability to perform the job in question. Therefore, the actual percentages of the different groups who were promoted (known as the "bottom line") were irrelevant, because potentially qualified African-Americans were screened out by the use of the test. As a result of the *Teal* case, the bottom line is not a viable defense to a claim of discrimination against an individual employee.

RACE-NORMING

Section 703(l), added to Title VII by the 1991 amendments, prohibits the practice of **race-norming**, which is the use of different cutoff or passing scores for different protected groups under Title VII. The same section also prohibits adjusting the scores or altering the results of employment tests on the basis of race, color, religion, sex, or national origin. Prior to the addition of that section, some employers had adjusted scores for minority applicants, or had used different passing scores for different groups, in an effort to avoid any disparate impact that might result from the use of the employment tests. The prohibition of such practices now means that the employer must ensure that any employment tests used are validated under the Uniform Guidelines on Employee Selection.

race-norming: The practice of setting different passing scores for different races or other protected groups; race-norming is prohibited by Title VII.

SENIORITY AND TITLE VII

Seniority, or the length of service on the job, is frequently used to determine entitlement or eligibility for certain job benefits, promotions, transfers, and even job security itself. Seniority systems usually provide that layoffs will be conducted on the basis of inverse seniority—the last employee hired is the first to be laid off.

Seniority may have a discriminatory effect on employees when an employer has, in the past, discriminated against women or minority workers. If the employer had refused to hire women or minorities in the past but now does hire them, those employees will have less seniority than white male employees. In the event of a layoff, the women and minorities will be the first to lose their jobs, whereas the white males retain their jobs. The layoffs by inverse seniority, therefore, have a disparate impact on women and minorities. Does that mean that the seniority system violates Title VII, as in the *Griggs* case?

Section 703(h) of Title VII contains an exemption for bona fide seniority systems; it states, in part, the following:

> Notwithstanding any other provision of this title, it shall not be an unlawful employment practice for an employer to apply different standards of compensation or different terms, conditions, or privileges of employment pursuant to a bona fide seniority or merit system provided that such differences are not the result of an intention to discriminate because of race, color, religion, sex, or national origin.

In the following case, the seniority system had the effect of deterring minority employees from transferring out of their low-paying and inferior jobs. The

Supreme Court needed to decide what effect §703(h) had on the seniority system that perpetuated the effects of prior discrimination.

INTERNATIONAL BROTHERHOOD OF TEAMSTERS V. UNITED STATES

451 U.S. 324 (1977)

FACTS

The U.S. Attorney General brought suit against the Teamsters Union and a trucking company, alleging that the employer had engaged in a pattern or practice of illegal employment discrimination against Hispanics and African Americans by refusing to hire them as over-the-road drivers, and that the union had violated Title VII by agreeing with the employer to create and maintain a seniority system that perpetuated the effects of prior discrimination. The employer would hire minority employees only in maintenance and operations, the lowest paying and least desirable jobs, and thereafter discriminated with respect to transfers and promotions. The seniority system used *bargaining unit seniority*—time an employee was a member of the particular bargaining unit—for determining eligibility for transfer, promotion, or layoffs. The over-the-road drivers were in a bargaining unit separate from the maintenance and operations jobs; any maintenance or operations employee transferring into an over-the-road job would lose all prior seniority and would start at the bottom of the over-the-road seniority list. The United States Attorney General alleged that this system discouraged transfers and "locked in" minority employees in the least desirable jobs.

The trial court held that the employer had violated Title VII by engaging in a plan and practice of discrimination, and that the union violated Title VII by agreeing to a seniority system that operated to "impede the free transfer of minority groups into and within the company." The Court of Appeals affirmed the trial court; the union appealed to the U.S. Supreme Court on the issue of the legality of the seniority system.

DECISION

The union argued that the seniority system was protected by §703(h) as being bona fide, while the United States argued that a system that perpetuates the effects of prior discrimination can never be bona fide. Victims of discrimination can receive remedial seniority as part of the "make whole" relief without attacking the legality of the seniority system. The presence of §703(h) prevents a seniority system such as the present one from being attacked under the disparate impact analysis used in *Griggs v. Duke Power*. Here, because of the employer's prior discrimination, the over-the-road drivers with the greatest seniority were white, and the advantages of the seniority system flow disproportionately to them and away from the minority employees who might have enjoyed those benefits had it not been for the employer's discrimination. The seniority system effectively froze the status quo of the prior discriminatory employment practices. But, despite that effect, the literal terms of §703(h) extend a measure of immunity to seniority systems, as long as they are "bona fide." Any differences in treatment under such a system must not be "the result of an intention to discriminate because of race . . . ." The Court rejected the United States Attorney General's position because of the wording of §703(h), and held that "an otherwise neutral legitimate seniority system does not become unlawful under Title VII simply because it may perpetuate pre-Act discrimination."

The Court held that the seniority system here was bona fide because it applied equally to all races; to the extent that it locked employees into less desirable jobs, it did so for all the employees in those jobs, not just the minority employees. The placing of the over-the-road drivers in a separate bargaining unit is rational and in accord with industry practices. The seniority system did not originate from an intention to discriminate, and it had been negotiated and maintained free from intent to illegally discriminate. Because the seniority system was protected under §703(h) as bona fide, the union's conduct in agreeing to and maintaining the system did not violate Title VII.

CASE QUESTIONS

1. How did the seniority system deter minority workers from transferring to other, more desirable jobs?
2. Did the seniority system have the same deterrent effect on nonminority workers? Why?
3. Was the seniority system intentionally adopted by the union and the employer in order to discriminate against the minority workers?
4. According to the Supreme Court, when is a seniority system a bona fide system under the exemption of §703(h)? Explain.

Subsequent Supreme Court decisions have further interpreted the provisions of §703(h). In *American Tobacco Co. v. Patterson* [456 U.S. 63 (1982)], the Court ruled that §703(h) applies to seniority systems that were adopted after the passage of Title VII as well as those in operation at the time Title VII was adopted. The term "seniority system" in §703(h) should be interpreted broadly, to encompass rules that determine eligibility for various classifications under a seniority system, according to the decision in *California Brewers Association v. Bryant* [444 U.S. 598 (1980)].

As a result of these decisions, together with the *Teamsters* case, a seniority system and its ancillary rules will be bona fide within the meaning of §703(h) if the system is neutral on its face, applies equally to all employees, and is not intentionally used to discriminate. The court will consider whether the system had its origin in discrimination, whether it has been negotiated and maintained free from discriminatory intent, and whether the basis of the seniority system is reasonable in light of industry practice. If a seniority system is bona fide under §703(h), then actions taken pursuant to the seniority system can only be challenged under Title VII if the employer is intentionally discriminating; in other words, disparate impact claims may not be brought against actions based on bona fide seniority systems.

AFFIRMATIVE ACTION AND TITLE VII

As noted previously, Title VII protects all individuals from employment discrimination on the prohibited bases. Affirmative action programs usually involve giving preference in hiring or promotion to qualified female or minority applicants or employees; persons who are not members of the group given preference may be at a disadvantage in hiring or promotion decisions. Does such preferential treatment, pursuant to an affirmative action program, violate Title VII?

Affirmation action continues to be a very controversial issue. California and several other states have ended all state affirmative action programs. A number of court decisions have dealt with the legality of affirmative-action programs. Employers are not required by Title VII to set up affirmative-action programs; the courts have, however, often ordered affirmative action after an employer has been found guilty of violating Title VII. The Supreme Court, in the case of *Local 28, Sheet Metal Workers Int'l. Ass'n. v. EEOC* [478 U.S. 421 (1986)], held that affirmative action may be ordered to remedy "persistent or egregious discrimination" even if the affirmative action has the result of benefiting individuals who were not themselves victims of discrimination. The Supreme Court also held that affirmative action should only be ordered as a last resort and should be tailored "to fit the nature of the violation" the court seeks to correct.

More recently, in *Adarand Constructors, Inc. v. Pena* [515 U.S. 200 (1995)], dealing with the legality of a set-aside program that required that at least 10 percent of federally funded public work projects must be done by minority-owned contractors, the Supreme Court held that government-required racial preferences must be justified under the **strict scrutiny test**. That test requires that the government show a compelling government interest or purpose to justify the program, and that the program must be narrowly tailored to accomplish that purpose. Although the *Adarand* case applies only to public work project set-asides and not employment, it does signal that the Supreme Court will take a very close look at any required racial preference. Although court-ordered, or remedial, affirmative-action programs are acceptable under Title VII, what about voluntary affirmative-action programs—programs adopted voluntarily by employers who have not violated Title VII? In *United Steelworkers of America v. Weber* [443 U.S. 193 (1979)], the Supreme Court held that voluntary affirmative programs were legal under Title VII if (1) the purposes of the plan are consistent with those of Title VII—if the plan was designed to break down old patterns of job segregation, and (2) the plan does not "unnecessarily trammel the interests" of the persons not subject to the preference under the plan—the nonpreferred group is not severely disadvantaged. For example, in the *Weber* case, the employer and union set up an affirmative action program to train more minority employees for skilled jobs because very few minority employees held skilled positions. A white male was not accepted into the training program, while an African American with less seniority was; the white employee was not permanently barred from the program and was eligible to apply for admission to the program the next year. In other cases, laying off employees because of their race, so that white employees lose their jobs while less senior minority employees retain their jobs, was not acceptable because the burden on the nonpreferred white employees was substantial.

strict scrutiny test: A judicial test requiring that the government show that its action is required by a compelling government purpose or interest, and is narrowly tailored to achieve that interest or purpose.

What must an employer seeking to justify an affirmative-action program show to meet the *Weber* criteria? What kind of evidence must an individual seeking to challenge decisions made under an affirmative-action program demonstrate to establish a claim under Title VII? Those issues were addressed by the Supreme Court in *Johnson v. Transportation Agency, Santa Clara County* [480 U.S. 616 (1987)]. The majority in *Johnson* held that an employer may justify a voluntary affirmative-action plan under Title VII by showing that the plan was adopted to remedy the existence of a "manifest imbalance" reflecting the underrepresentation of women or minorities in "traditionally segregated job categories." In determining whether an imbalance exists, the employer should compare the percentage of women or minorities in the employer's workforce with the percentage in the area labor market. Where the jobs require no special expertise, a comparison with the general population is appropriate; but when the jobs require special training or qualifications, the comparison should be to those in the labor force who possess the relevant qualifications. The manifest imbalance need not be such that it would make out a prima facie case that the employer had violated Title VII. The Court also noted in *Johnson* that the person claiming the employer had illegally discriminated has the burden of proving that the voluntary affirmative-action plan is not valid under Title VII.

Several other points regarding affirmative action have been addressed by the Supreme Court and by Congress. In *Local 93, International Ass'n of Firefighters v. Cleveland* [478 U.S. 501 (1986)], the Court held that an employer admitting to discrimination in violation of Title VII may agree to set up an affirmative-action program pursuant to a consent decree.

Also §703(n), added to Title VII by the 1991 amendments, states that affirmative-action programs resulting from judicial decisions or consent decrees may not be challenged later by persons who had notice of such decisions or decrees and had an opportunity to present objections to the plan at the time it was ordered or adopted. The same section also applies to persons whose interests were adequately represented by another person who had previously challenged the decision or decree on the same legal grounds and with a similar factual situation. Section 703(n) does not preclude subsequent challenges to decisions or decrees that were obtained through fraud or collusion, are "transparently invalid," or were entered by a court that lacked proper jurisdiction over the case.

BONA FIDE OCCUPATIONAL QUALIFICATIONS

As mentioned previously, Title VII does allow employers to restrict their hiring for certain positions to members of one sex or of a particular religion or national origin if that trait is a BFOQ for the job. For example, a Baptist church seeking to hire a new pastor would certainly want to restrict the selection to Baptists rather than to Catholics or Buddhists. An employer seeking to justify a BFOQ must show that it is necessary for the safe and efficient operation of the business. The courts have interpreted the business necessity requirement very strictly—customer preference or employer convenience are not sufficient to justify a BFOQ. Section 703(e)(1) defines the BFOQ exception as follows:

> . . . [I]t shall not be an unlawful employment practice for an employer to hire and employ employees, for an employment agency to classify, or refer for employment any individual, for a labor organization to classify its membership or refer for employment any individual . . . on the basis of his religion, sex, or national origin in those certain instances where religion, sex, or national origin in a bona fide occupational qualification reasonably necessary to the normal operation of that particular business or enterprise . . .

The language of §703(e)(1) prohibits using race or color as a BFOQ. What must an employer do to meet the business necessity requirement in order to establish a BFOQ? In *Dothard v. Rawlinson* [433 U.S. 321 (1977)], the Supreme Court upheld Alabama's requirement that guards in maximum security prisons who have direct contact with male prisoners must be male, because the threat of assault on female guards would pose a danger not only to the female guard herself, but also to the basic control and protection of the inmates and other security personnel.

In dealing with claims of BFOQs, the courts have also recognized BFOQs based on sex when community standards of morality or propriety require that employees be of a particular gender, such as only hiring men as fitting room attendants in a men's clothing store or hiring only females as locker room attendants for the women's locker room of an athletic club.

TITLE VII AND SEX DISCRIMINATION

Title VII prohibits any discrimination in terms or conditions of employment because of an employee's sex, unless it is a BFOQ. Title VII prohibits advertising for male or female employees in help-wanted ads (unless the employer demonstrates that it is a BFOQ) and maintaining separate seniority lists for male and female employees. Unions that negotiate separate seniority lists or that discriminate in membership because of sex also violate Title VII. Sex discrimination in employment may take various different forms, as are discussed in the following sections.

STEREOTYPING

It is illegal sex discrimination for an employer to apply different standards for promoting female employees than for male employees when those standards reflect sex stereotyping. In *Price Waterhouse v. Hopkins* [490 U.S. 228 (1989)], the Supreme Court held that a female employee who was considered "difficult, abrasive, and unfeminine" for behavior that was perceived as acceptable if engaged in by a male was the victim of sex discrimination when she was denied a partnership. The employer held her to a different standard than the employer used for male employees, and consequently was in violation of Title VII.

"SEX-PLUS" DISCRIMINATION

Employers who refuse to hire women with preschool-aged children but will hire men with preschool-aged children are guilty of sex discrimination in violation of Title VII. This is the result of the Supreme Court decision in *Phillips v. Martin Marietta Corp*. [400 U.S. 542 (1971)]. In that case, female employees were subjected to an additional requirement (no preschool-aged children) because of their sex. An employer who places additional requirements on employees of one sex, and not the other, violates Title VII. Such discrimination is known as "sex-plus" discrimination.

SEX-BASED PAY DIFFERENTIALS

Both Title VII and the Equal Pay Act of 1963 prohibit sex discrimination in pay (paying different wages to men and women performing the same job in the same location). Both laws allow for exceptions when the pay differentials are due to a bona fide seniority system, a merit pay system, a productivity pay system, or a "factor other than sex." Those four defenses are set out in §703(h) of Title VII and in the Equal Pay Act. The Equal Pay Act applies *only* when the work performed by the male and female employees is *substantially equivalent*, as determined by the required skills, effort, responsibility, and working conditions of the job.

Title VII, rather than the Equal Pay Act, can be used to challenge pay differentials due to intentional sex discrimination *even when the work being performed is not equivalent*, according to the Supreme Court holding in *County of Washington v. Gunther* [452 U.S. 161 (1981)]. In this case, female guards in the Washington County jail guarded female inmates, while the male prisoners were guarded by male guards. The male guards supervised up to 10 times more prisoners than the female guards, who spent much of their time performing clerical duties. Although a job evaluation study rated the female guard positions at 90 percent of the male guard positions, the county paid the female guards only 70 percent of the male guards' pay. The pay differential was allegedly due to intentional sex discrimination on the part of the county. The Supreme Court held that Title VII applied to the situation—it prohibited intentional sex discrimination in pay by the county, even though the jobs involved were not equivalent.

Subsequent to the *Gunther* decision, the U.S. Court of Appeals for the Ninth Circuit held that *Gunther*-type claims are restricted to cases of disparate treatment discrimination; in these cases, plaintiffs need to show that the pay differentials are due to intentional sex discrimination. That court rejected disparate impact claims of sex-based pay discrimination in *Spalding v. University of Washington* [740 F. 2d 686 (1984)], in which the plaintiffs alleged that the university's pay policy discriminated against professors in female-dominated fields such as nursing. The court held that statistical evidence alone was not sufficient to establish intentional discrimination as required by *Gunther*.

The Equal Pay Act The coverage of the Equal Pay Act is greater than that of Title VII; it applies to all employers engaged in interstate commerce and covers all employees of an enterprise engaged in commerce. A plaintiff claiming a violation of the Equal Pay Act must show that an employer paid lower wages to employees of one gender who are performing work substantially equal to the work performed by employees of the opposite gender in the same establishment. Note that the act requires "equal pay for equal work" rather than "equal pay for work of equal value," also known as comparable worth.

The Equal Pay Act is administered by the EEOC, but there is no requirement that plaintiffs suing on their own must first file with the EEOC before filing suit in federal court. If the EEOC files suit, it precludes an individual suit on the same complaint. An individual suit must be filed within two years of the alleged violation; a violation will be held to be continuing for each payday in which unequal pay is received for equal work.

Plaintiffs suing under the Equal Pay Act may recover the unpaid wages due and also may receive an equal amount as liquidated damages; in addition, plaintiffs can recover legal fees and court costs. The trial court has discretion to deny recovery of liquidated damages if it finds that the employer acted in good faith. The back pay awarded to a successful plaintiff can be awarded for the period going back two years prior to the filing of the suit; that period is extended to three years prior to filing the suit if the court finds that the violation was "willful." A violation is willful if the employer was aware of the appreciable possibility that its actions might violate the act. Remedies in suits by the EEOC include injunctions and back pay with interest; the act does not provide for the recovery of liquidated damages in a suit by the government.

COMPARABLE WORTH

comparable worth: The concept that persons performing work of equal value should be paid equally—"equal pay for work of equal value."

Some commentators believe that the decision in *Gunther* was an endorsement of the concept of **comparable worth**, the idea that employees performing work of equal value should receive equal pay. (Note that comparable worth's idea of equal pay for work of equal value differs from the Equal Pay Act requirement of equal pay for equal work.) Comparable worth would require that an employer set pay according to the value of the job to the employer; for example, a school system might be required to pay secretaries and janitors equally if their jobs were evaluated equally under the employer's job evaluation system. The Supreme Court in *Gunther*, however, emphasized that it was not endorsing comparable worth; it was simply prohibiting intentional sex discrimination in pay. The courts have consistently maintained that Title VII does not require comparable worth—where the work at issue is not equivalent, the employer need not pay equally for work of equal value, as long as the pay differentials are not due to intentional sex discrimination. Although federal law does not require comparable worth in pay, a number of states have adopted comparable worth, or pay equity, policies for public sector employees.

SEX-BASED PENSION BENEFITS

Women, on average, live longer than men do; such differences in average life expectancy are used by actuaries in determining premiums and benefit levels for insurance policies and annuities purchased by individuals. Sex-based actuarial tables used to determine premiums and benefits for pensions may require that women pay higher premiums than men of the same age in order to receive the same benefit. When insurance and pension annuities are employment-related benefits, they are subject to Title VII. An employer's use of sex-based actuarial tables in determining pension premiums, requiring women to pay higher monthly premiums for the same pension benefit payments as men, was held by the U.S. Supreme Court in *City of Los Angeles v. Manhart* [435 U.S. 702 (1978)] to be in violation of Title VII's prohibition of sex discrimination. The Court stated that because the actuarial tables used an employee's gender as a predictor of longevity, the basis for differentiating between employees was sex rather than actual longevity and, therefore, the practice constituted sex discrimination in employment benefits. Any benefits offered to employees by an employer must be free from sex discrimination in order to comply with Title VII.

PREGNANCY DISCRIMINATION

The Pregnancy Discrimination Act of 1978 added §701(k) to Title VII. Section 701(k) states that:

> The terms "because of sex" or "on the basis of sex" include, but are not limited to, because of or on the basis of pregnancy, childbirth, or related medical conditions; and women affected by pregnancy, childbirth, or related medical conditions shall be treated the same for all employment-related purposes, including receipt of benefits under fringe benefit programs, as other persons not so affected but similar in their ability or inability to work . . . .

The amendment requires that pregnant employees be treated the same as other employees suffering non–pregnancy-related temporary disabilities. If an employer's benefit plan covers temporary disabilities, it must also cover pregnancy-related leaves. If the employer's medical plan covers 80 percent of hospital costs for conditions other than pregnancy, then it must provide equal coverage for pregnancy-related conditions as well, according to the Supreme Court decision in *Newport News Shipbuilding and Dry Dock Co. v. E.E.O.C.* [462 U.S. 669 (1983)].

An employer may feel that some jobs may expose women to substances or working conditions that may be hazardous to the developing fetus carried by pregnant employees. The employer may seek to avoid such potential health problems by prohibiting women of childbearing age from working in such jobs. Does such a restriction violate Title VII, or can it be justified as a BFOQ? In *U.A.W. v. Johnson Controls* [499 U.S. 187 (1991)], the Supreme Court held that the employer may restrict pregnant women from particular jobs only when the pregnancy actually interferes with the employee's ability to perform the job. The employer cannot use concerns about the health of future children to justify a BFOQ; the Court noted "an employer must direct its concerns about a woman's ability to perform her job safely and efficiently to those aspects of the woman's job-related activities that fall within the 'essence' of the particular business."

SEXUAL HARASSMENT

Employees on the job may be subjected to unwelcome sexual remarks, advances, or requests for sexual favors by coworkers or supervisors. Such conduct is known as *sexual harassment*. Although Title VII does not specifically mention sexual harassment, the guidelines adopted by the EEOC under Title VII provide that sexual harassment constitutes sex discrimination in violation of Title VII. The guidelines were upheld by the U.S. Supreme Court in *Meritor Savings Bank v. Vinson* [477 U.S. 57 (1986)]. The Court agreed that conditioning job status, such as hiring, promotion, or other benefits, on submission to requests for sexual favors (known as **quid pro quo** sexual harassment) was prohibited by Title VII. The Court also held that harassment that creates a hostile environment that interferes with an employee's job performance constitutes sex discrimination, even though job status may not be linked to the harassment. Such harassment, known as **hostile environment** sexual harassment, also violates Title VII. The key to what constitutes sexual harassment is "unwelcome" comments, taunts, requests for sexual favors, and other conduct of a sexual nature; an isolated comment probably does not amount to harassment, but repeated acts or comments, especially after the target of such conduct has indicated that they are unwelcome, is harassment. (In addition to sexual harassment, Title VII also prohibits harassment based on race, color, religion, or national origin.) Title VII's prohibition of sexual harassment includes "same-sex" sexual harassment—that is, harassment of a sexual nature in which the harasser and the victim are of the same sex ("male on male" or "female on female" harassment), according to *Oncale v. Sundowner Offshore Services, Inc.* [523 U.S. 75 (1998)].

quid pro quo: Sexual harassment where job status or benefits are conditioned on submission to requests for sexual favors.

hostile environment: Sexual harassment that has the effect of creating a hostile or offensive work environment.

A plaintiff need not establish that the hostile environment sexual harassment caused her or him psychological trauma; the Supreme Court decision in

Harris v. Forklift Systems, Inc. [510 U.S. 17 (1993)] held that harassment creating an environment that is reasonably perceived, and is perceived, as being hostile or abusive is prohibited by Title VII. Factors to consider when determining whether the harassment creates a hostile environment include the frequency and severity of the harassment, whether it is physically threatening or humiliating, and whether it unreasonably interferes with employees' work performance.

Employers' Liability for Sexual Harassment Employers may be held liable for harassment by supervisors or managerial employees, by coworkers of the victim of the harassment, or even by nonemployees. The employer may be liable for sexual harassment by the victim's coworkers (who are neither managerial nor supervisors) if the employer knew or should have known of such harassment and failed to take effective corrective action. Where the harassment is done by nonemployees (such as clients or visiting salespersons), the employer may be held liable if it had some measure of control or influence over the harasser and if the employer failed to take corrective action when it knew or should have known of the harassment.

The following Supreme Court decision discusses when an employer will be held liable for sexual harassment by supervisors or managerial employees.

FARAGHER V. CITY OF BOCA RATON

524 U.S. 775 (1998)

FACTS

From 1985 to 1990, Beth Ann Faragher worked part-time and summers during college as an ocean lifeguard for the Parks and Recreation Department of the City of Boca Raton, Florida (City). Faragher's immediate supervisors were Bill Terry, David Silverman, and Robert Gordon. In June 1990, Faragher resigned.

The lifeguards and supervisors were stationed at the city beach and had no significant contact with higher city officials. The lifeguards reported to lieutenants and captains, who reported to Terry; Terry was supervised by the Recreation Superintendent, who in turn reported to a Director of Parks and Recreation, answerable to the City Manager.

The City adopted a sexual harassment policy in 1986 and revised it in 1990, but it failed to disseminate its policy among employees of the Marine Safety Section—Terry, Silverman, Gordon, and many lifeguards were unaware of it. Faragher claimed that Terry and Silverman created a sexually hostile atmosphere at the beach by repeatedly subjecting Faragher and other female lifeguards to uninvited and offensive touching, lewd remarks, and by speaking of women in offensive terms. During Faragher's five years as a lifeguard, Silverman and Terry repeatedly touched the bodies of female employees without invitation, and asked female lifeguards to have sex with them. Faragher did not complain to higher management about Terry's or Silverman's conduct. She did speak about it to Gordon, but she regarded these discussions as personal conversations with a colleague rather than formal complaints to a supervisor. Other female lifeguards had similarly informal talks with Gordon, but he did not report these complaints to Terry or to other city officials. Gordon told one lifeguard that "the City just [doesn't] care."

In April 1990, two months before Faragher's resignation, Nancy Ewanchew, a former lifeguard, wrote to the City's Personnel Director, complaining that Terry and Silverman had harassed her and other female lifeguards. The City then investigated the complaint, reprimanded Terry and Silverman and required them to choose between a suspension without pay or the forfeiture of annual leave. Faragher filed a suit under Title VII against Terry, Silverman, and the City in 1992; she claimed that Terry and Silverman, as supervisors, were acting as agents of the City, and that their conduct amounted to discrimination in the "terms, conditions, and privileges" of her employment.

The trial court held that the conduct of Terry and Silverman was discriminatory harassment sufficiently serious to alter the conditions of Faragher's employment and constitute an abusive working environment, and that the City was liable for the harassment by its supervisory employees. The court noted that the harassment was pervasive enough to support an inference that the City knew or should have known of it, and the City was liable because Terry and Silverman were acting as its agents when they committed the harassing acts. Finally, the court observed that Gordon's inaction, given his knowledge of the harassment, was a further basis for holding the City liable. The trial court awarded Faragher nominal damages under Title VII.

On appeal by the City, the Court of Appeals for the Eleventh Circuit reversed the judgment against the City, holding that Terry and Silverman were not acting within the scope of their employment when they engaged in the harassment, that they were not aided in their actions by the agency relationship, and that the City had no constructive knowledge of the harassment by virtue of its pervasiveness or Gordon's actual knowledge. Faragher appealed to the U.S. Supreme Court.

DECISION

The Supreme Court reversed the Court of Appeals decision. Justice Souter, writing the majority opinion, stated that hostile environment sexual harassment by supervisors and coworkers is now recognized as a persistent problem in the workplace. The employer is in the best position to prevent such harassment; therefore, it makes sense, given the rationale of Title VII, to hold the employer liable for harassing conduct of a supervisor when such conduct is possible by the abuse of the supervisor's authority. When a supervisor harasses or discriminates in the terms and conditions of subordinates' employment, his or her actions necessarily draw upon the supervisor's position over the people who report to him or her, or those who work under them—an employee generally cannot avoid a supervisor's abusive conduct the same way that he or she might deal with abuse from a coworker. When a coworker harasses, the victim can walk away or tell the offender where to go, but it may be difficult to offer such responses to a supervisor, who controls the victim's working conditions and may have the power to fire, demote, or reduce pay. The victim may well be reluctant to accept the risks of blowing the whistle on a superior. Employers have a greater opportunity to guard against misconduct by supervisors than by common workers; employers have greater opportunity and incentive to screen supervisors, train them, and monitor their performance.

Although there are good reasons for holding the employer liable for harassment by supervisors, employers are not always automatically liable for all harassing conduct by supervisors. An employer is liable to a victimized employee for sexual harassment by a supervisor of an employee when the harassment causes the employee to suffer some tangible negative employment action—demotion, transfer, pay or benefit reduction, termination, and so on. Where the harassment causes a hostile work environment but the employee does not suffer any negative employment consequences, the employer may raise an affirmative defense by showing that the employer exercised reasonable care to prevent and correct promptly any sexually harassing behavior and that the employee victim unreasonably failed to take advantage of any preventive or corrective opportunities provided by the employer or to avoid harm otherwise. The employer's defense goes both to liability and the amount of damages. Such a defense is not available to the employer when the supervisor's harassment results in some negative employment consequence. In Faragher's case, it is clear that the harassers were her supervisors, the harassment created a hostile work environment, and the City failed to take reasonable steps to prevent sexual harassment. Therefore, the decision of the Court of Appeals was reversed and the trial court's decision was reinstated. Justices Scalia and Thomas dissented.

CASE QUESTIONS

1. Why should an employer be held responsible for the actions of a supervisor?
2. Is an employer always liable for a supervisor's sexual harassment? When can an employer establish a defense to being held liable for sexual harassment by a supervisor?
3. Does Faragher's failure to make a formal complaint about the harassing conduct prevent the City from being held liable for that conduct? Explain.

IN CONSULTATION

Marvin Manager has a problem. Sara Subordinate has accused one of ABC's mid-level managers of sexual harassment. She says that he repeatedly made inappropriate remarks about her private life, her appearance, and her manner of dress. She stated that she asked him to stop, but he never did. Sara was not demoted nor did she suffer any other financial loss as a result of the harassment.

Marvin did not hear of Sara's complaint until after she filed charges with the Equal Employment Opportunity Commission (EEOC). Marvin contacted Sara as part of his internal investigation. She admitted that she never reported her concerns to anyone but the manager whom she accused. She did not report his behavior to the human resources department, another manager, or even Marvin. When asked why she never reported the harassment, she stated that she assumed no one would do anything about it.

Marvin's company, ABC, Inc., has a sexual harassment policy that states, among other things, that the company does not tolerate sexual harassment. The policy provides a procedure for employees to notify and report wrongful behavior. It also provides an investigative procedure with assurances of discretion and confidentiality. Sara was informed of the policy when she was hired, and she reviewed the policy every year during her annual performance evaluation.

Marvin approached his company's in-house corporate counsel, Laura Lawyer, to discuss Sara's complaint. He asked Laura about ABC's potential liability to Sara. Here is their conversation:

Marvin:

1. I know sexual harassment is illegal, and I don't condone it. But how can we be liable if we didn't even know about it?
2. Can what happened to Sara even be sexual harassment if she suffered no tangible job consequences?
3. What is the effect of Sara's failure to follow our sexual harassment policy?

Laura:

1. Knowledge of sexual harassment certainly increases employer liability. A lack of knowledge, however, does not necessarily diminish or remove employer liability. It depends on why the employer didn't know.
2. Yes. An employee can suffer sexual harassment even if they did not lose their job or job benefits.
3. Sara's failure to report her concerns in accordance with our sexual harassment policy may provide us with a defense. The law is supportive of companies who have and enforce sexual harassment policies. **Let me research the applicable law to see whether we have a viable defense, and I'll get back to you.**

FROM THE DESK OF
Laura Lawyer

To: Marvin Manager
Re: Liability for Sexual Harassment

Dear Marvin:

Sexual harassment law has undergone significant changes in the past few years. The Supreme Court recently provided new insight into the standards for proving a sexual harassment case and for defending against one. Two primary revelations the recent case law offers are that (1) an employee does not have to suffer tangible job consequence in order to have a viable sexual harassment claim and (2) employers can create an affirmative defense to a sexual harassment claim by having an effective and enforced sexual harassment policy. An employer's affirmative defense is further bolstered by an employee's unreasonable failure to report the sexual harassment.

With regard to Sara's case, her lack of financial loss does not mean she was not harassed. The mid-level manager she accused may have created a hostile environment for her if the statements she alleges that he made about her private life, appearance, and manner of dress are true. We need to investigate the accuracy of her allegations and do so with the confidentiality and discretion that our policy promises.

In fact, it is our policy that gives us our best chance in defending against Sara's claim. We need to prove that the policy is effective and that we enforce it. Part of that proof may involve the type of punishment that Sara's manager receives if what she alleged is true. The fact that we made Sara aware of the policy at her hiring and at her evaluations supports our position that our policy is taken seriously by the company—especially if we undertook similar steps with all of our other employees. We would like to know what sort of additional training managers and supervisors receive, as they are the parties to whom sexual harassment is reported.

If we can prove that our policy is effective and enforced, then the court will ask why Sara never reported the alleged harassment. If her failure to report the harassment was unreasonable, we retain our affirmative defense against her sexual harassment claim. She stated that she did not report the behavior because she thought nothing would be done in response. A court may not consider that a reasonable basis for failing to report the behavior in accordance with our policy unless she had real justification for her fear. Courts are more supportive of employees who fail to report behavior when those employees are unaware of their ability to do so or have fear of retribution if they make a complaint. Sara should have known of her ability to report, since she was made aware of our policy on a regular basis and she makes no allegation of fear of consequences. Therefore, our affirmative defense may be intact against her sexual harassment charge with the EEOC.

With regard to Sara's sexual harassment charges, consider the following:

1. Why is it unnecessary for Sara to have suffered tangible job consequences like a demotion in order to bring a sexual harassment case?
2. Do you think Marvin or ABC could have done something differently so that Sara could have felt more comfortable reporting her claim?
3. Why do you think the Supreme Court has been so supportive of employers who maintain an effective and enforced sexual harassment policy? What sorts of provisions do you think are necessary in order for a sexual harassment policy to be effective?

Not all unpleasant conduct in the workplace constitutes harassment in violation of Title VII, as the following reading indicates.

DISAGREEABLE WORKERS ARE NO BASIS FOR BIAS CLAIMS, COURTS CONCLUDE

They are repulsive, boorish, and obnoxious—and a fact of life in most job situations.

But the presence of offensive employees does not necessarily establish a cause of action under civil rights laws—either for them or by their coworkers, according to two courts that recently addressed the issue (*Vore v. Indiana Bell Telephone Co.*, CA 7, 93-3706, 8/16/94; *Marquart v. McDonnell Douglas Corp.*, DC EMo, 4:92CV00054, 8/4/94).

"Federal law provides that an employee is to be free from racial discrimination in the workplace, which includes freedom from a racially hostile workplace. It does not guarantee a utopian workplace, or even a pleasant one," wrote Judge William J. Bauer of the U.S. Court of Appeals for the Seventh Circuit. The court dismissed a claim by white workers who were abused by a "vulgar, loudmouth" co-worker, who was the only black employee among them. "In short, personality conflicts between employees are not the business of federal courts," he concluded.

In the second case, a federal judge in St. Louis dismissed a sexual harassment claim by an employee who was terminated from her job at McDonnell Douglas Corp. for refusing to cooperate in obtaining psychiatric treatment for her abnormal behavior at work.

'A Disagreeable Sort'

In the Seventh Circuit case, a group of current and former white employees at an Indiana Bell facility claimed that their employer discriminated against them by permitting a hostile work environment in allowing a difficult co-worker—the only black employee among them—to perform his disruptive antics at their expense.

The employee, a planning engineer, "by all accounts, was a disagreeable sort," the court recounted. His coworkers alleged that, in his negative behavior, the employee "harassed everyone in sight . . . physically threatened his co-workers, engaged in loud, angry tirades (typically directed at his computer terminal), yelled obscenities, stood atop his desk, played his radio at loud and disruptive levels, and used foul and vulgar language, which he often directed at female employees." None of his behavior "indicated any sort of racial animus," according to the white employees.

In response to complaints from co-workers, management downgraded the employee in his performance appraisal, reduced his salary opportunities, and admonished him for his use of foul language, the court said. Other than one grievance, the complaints were verbal and informal and the white employees never dealt with the situation through the company's EEO system.

A federal judge granted the company's motion for summary judgment and the white employees appealed to the Seventh Circuit.

The court rejected the employees' argument that the company demonstrated disparate treatment because it would have dealt more harshly with a white employee who was misbehaving among fellow black workers. The court found no parallel situation where the racial makeup was reversed and not "a shred of evidence" that the company had a policy of favoring blacks over whites.

"[We] are left with an unpleasant working environment in which one lout, who happens to be black, greatly annoys his co-workers, who happen to be white. Without racial animus, there is no Title VII claim," the court concluded. Judges Harlington Wood Jr. and Richard D. Cudahy joined in the decision.

The Seventh Circuit covers Illinois, Indiana, and Wisconsin.

Work Relations: 'Anything But Smooth'

In the Missouri case, Ruth Marquart had been employed as a custodial worker at McDonnell Douglas for 11 years before she was terminated for refusing to cooperate in obtaining psychiatric treatment for her abnormal behavior at work.

She asserted that she had faced a hostile work environment and was terminated in retaliation for her complaints regarding a sexually hostile work environment.

Dismissing the claim, Judge George F. Gunn Jr. with the U.S. District Court for the Eastern District of Missouri said the working relationships between Marquart, her co-workers, and supervisors "was anything but smooth," and that she "exhibited abnormal behavioral tendencies which were bound to irritate those with whom she had working relationships, including fellow employees, union representatives and supervisors—even physicians who treated her for behavioral problems."

The court found that a supervisor had taken immediate remedial action to each complaint of sexual harassment made by the employee, and "gave assiduous attention to each of [her] complaints, although it was obvious that some of them were chimerical."

Evidence submitted by Marquart, the court acknowledged, "does support a finding of hostility directed at plaintiff," and that her co-workers "both male and female did not like her." But the court said, the animus was the result of Marquart's actions against her co-workers.

The court also found no merit in the retaliation claim. Marquart's abnormal behavior at work prompted the company physician to direct additional diagnosis and when she refused to cooperate with a psychiatrist, the court said, the termination for insubordination was "reasonable, legitimate, and non-pretextual."

DISCRIMINATION BASED ON RELIGION OR NATIONAL ORIGIN

RELIGIOUS DISCRIMINATION

What if an employee claims that he or she is unable to work after sundown on Fridays because of religious beliefs, or if an employee insists that religious beliefs require him to wear a turban and a beard: must the employer grant these requests? The Title VII prohibition against employment discrimination based on religion is broad in scope; the EEOC regulations state that "religion" under Title VII includes an individual's personal moral and philosophical beliefs when those beliefs are held with the strength of traditional religious belief. Title VII has also been held to protect atheists from discrimination because of their beliefs.

However, Title VII's prohibition against discrimination in employment based on religion is not absolute. Religion, as with sex or national origin, may be used as a BFOQ when the employer demonstrates that business necessity requires hiring individuals of a particular religion. In addition, §702(a) and §703(e)(2) of Title VII allow religious corporations or educational institutions to give preference to hiring employees who are members of that religion. Section 703(e)(2) allows a Catholic university, such as the University of Notre Dame, to require that the university president be Catholic, or a Hebrew day school to require that its teachers be Jewish. Some religious organizations may carry on activities that are not specifically "religious" in character: Does the §702(a) exemption apply to these activities as well? In *Corporation of Presiding Bishops of the Church of Jesus Christ of Latter-day Saints v. Amos* [483 U.S. 327 (1987)], the Supreme Court held that the §702(a) exemption extends to the not-for-profit activities of religious organizations, not just to the activities that are "religious" in character. The *Amos* case involved a community gymnasium run by the Church of Jesus Christ of Latter-day Saints (known as the Mormons); all employees of the gymnasium were required to be members of that church.

Reasonable Accommodation Even if the employer is not able to establish religion as BFOQ, and if §702(a) does not apply, the prohibition against religious discrimination in employment is still not absolute. Title VII prohibits an employer from discriminating against an employee because of religious belief, practice, or observance unless the employer demonstrates that it is unable to accommodate such belief, practice, or observance without undue hardship on the conduct of the employer's business. An employer must make a reasonable attempt to accommodate the religious beliefs or practices; but if such attempts at accommodation fail or involve undue hardship, then the employer's obligation ends.

In *Trans World Airlines v. Hardison* [432 U.S. 63 (1977)], an employee transferred to a job that required him to work weekends; his religion prohibited working from sundown Friday to sundown Saturday. The employer insisted that the job was too important to leave vacant, and it was too expensive to pay another employee overtime to work for Hardison. Hardison wanted to arrange a swap of jobs with another employee on Friday evenings, but the collective agreement covering the jobs used employee seniority for bidding on jobs. Hardison had too little seniority to transfer into a job that would not require him to work Friday evenings, and the union would not waive the seniority system to let Hardison swap jobs. The employer fired Hardison when he refused to work Friday evenings. Consequently, he filed suit under Title VII. The Supreme Court held that the employer's actions did not violate Title VII; the duty to make reasonable accommodation did not require the regular payment of overtime wages or bearing more than a **de minimis** cost, nor did it require the employer to override the seniority provisions of a collective agreement.

de minimis: Small or minimal, insignificant.

When there are several ways to accommodate an employee's beliefs, Title VII does not require that the employer offer the accommodation preferred by the employee; according to *Ansonia Board of Education v. Philbrook* [479 U.S. 60 (1986)], the court requires only that the accommodation offered to the employee must be reasonable. In *Philbrook*, the Court upheld the employer's practice of allowing the employee to take unpaid leave for religious holidays rather than using paid sick days.

NATIONAL ORIGIN DISCRIMINATION

Title VII protects all individuals, both citizens and noncitizens, from employment discrimination based on national origin. The prohibition against national origin discrimination under Title VII includes discrimination because of a person's ethnic background, membership in groups associated with particular ethnic backgrounds, or a person's accent. Harassment because of a person's national origin is also prohibited. National origin, however, may be used as a BFOQ under §703(e)(1) where required by business necessity.

Examples of national-origin discrimination include the use of English language tests when English language skill is not a requirement for the work to be performed, and the refusal to recognize degrees from foreign universities. One area of controversy has been the use of "English-only" rules—rules that require all employees to speak only English while on the job. The EEOC regulations state that employees who work in public contact positions (such as sales clerks or receptionists) may be required to speak English on the job; however, a "blanket" English-only rule covering all employees during working hours may violate Title VII. However, in *Garcia v. Spun Steak* [998 F. 2d 1480 (9th Cir. 1993), *cert. denied*, 512 U.S. 1228 (1994)], the U.S. Court of Appeals for the Ninth Circuit held that an employer's English-only rule, based on job safety concerns, did not have an adverse impact on bilingual employees—they may have preferred to speak Spanish but were capable of speaking English and were not adversely affected by the English-only rule.

Title VII does not prohibit discrimination on the basis of citizenship, according to the Supreme Court in *Espinosa v. Farah Mfg. Co.* [414 U.S. 86

(1973)]. This case held that an employer may refuse to hire persons who are not U.S. citizens because the Title VII prohibition against national origin discrimination does not prohibit discrimination based on citizenship. The EEOC regulations under Title VII, however, state that using a citizenship requirement with the intent to discriminate on the basis of national origin violates the act.

REMEDIES UNDER TITLE VII

Remedies available under Title VII include the following: court orders requiring hiring or reinstatement of employees; awards of back pay, seniority, and other benefits; injunctions against unlawful employment practices; punitive damages; legal fees; and "such affirmative action as may be appropriate."

The 1991 amendments to Title VII added the right to recover compensatory and punitive damages against defendants, apart from government agencies or other public sector employers, that have engaged in an intentional violation of Title VII. Claims for punitive and compensatory damages are brought under 42 U.S.C. §1981A, which allows for damages in addition to any remedies recoverable under §706(g) of Title VII. The punitive damages available under §198A are limited by the size of the defendant employer, ranging from $50,000 against employers with fewer than 101 employees to $300,000 against employers with more than 500 employees.

In *Kolstad v. American Dental Association* [119 S.Ct. 2118 (1999)], the Supreme Court held that an employer may not be liable for punitive damages because of the conduct of a supervisory or managerial employee if the employer demonstrates that the supervisor or manager acted contrary to the employer's good faith efforts to comply with Title VII. If the employer can demonstrate that its policies clearly prohibited the discriminatory conduct, and that it took prompt and effective corrective action when it became aware of the discriminatory conduct, the employer may escape liability for punitive damages. As with the *Faragher* defense to sexual harassment claims, it is not enough just to have a policy—the employer must make sure employees are aware of the policy and that the policy is enforced. Individual employees are not personally liable under Title VII; only employers, unions, or employment agencies are subject to liability under Title VII. However, individuals may be held personally liable for damages, including punitive damages, under state EEO and tort laws.

Legal fees are available under §706(k), in the court's discretion, to the prevailing party, other than to the United States or the EEOC. Section 706(k) does not require that legal fees be awarded but leaves such an award to the trial court's discretion. In *Christianburg Garment Co. v. EEOC* [434 U.S. 412 (1978)], the Supreme Court held that a prevailing plaintiff should "ordinarily recover an attorney's fees unless special circumstances would render such an award unjust," while a prevailing defendant should recover legal fees only when the plaintiff's claims were held to be "frivolous, unreasonable or groundless. . . ." In *New York Gaslight Club v. Carey* [447 U.S. 54 (1980)], the Supreme Court held that a prevailing plaintiff in a suit under Title VII may also recover legal fees for work done at state or local agency proceedings when the complainant is required to file with that agency by §706(c).

SUMMARY

The purpose of EEO legislation is to eliminate discrimination that prevents capable and qualified individuals from being employed or from performing effectively on the job. The scope of the protection of the EEO laws has been expanding, from Title VII's initial prohibition of discrimination because of race, color, sex, religion, and national origin, to age and disability discrimination. Some state legislation protects against discrimination based on marital status and sexual orientation as well. The U.S. workforce is becoming more diverse, and employees are becoming more aware of the EEO legislation and sensitive to real or perceived discrimination than ever before. More employment discrimination litigation, with potentially greater liability for employers, is one result of these trends. Managers of today and tomorrow, therefore, must understand the EEO laws thoroughly and must practice the principles of equal employment in their workplace.

CHAPTER QUESTIONS

1. Dr. Pronting, an Emergency Room Supervisor at Inner City Hospital, was having an affair with Nurse Harper, who worked in the Emergency Room. When the position of Head Nurse in the Emergency Room became vacant, several nurses, including Harper, applied for the position. The other nurses had more Emergency Room experience, more seniority, and were more qualified than Harper, but Pronting promoted Harper because of her relationship with him. Were the other, more qualified nurses victims of sexual harassment? Explain your answer. [*King v. Palmer*, 778 F. 2d 878 (D.C. Cir. 1985)]
2. McGinnis worked as a clerk for the U.S. Postal Service. The Postal Service distributes the draft registration materials for the Selective Service to young men required to register for the draft. McGinnis had a longtime association with the Society of Friends (Quakers), although she was not formally a member of the Society. Because of her personal religious beliefs, McGinnis refused to distribute the draft registration materials while she was working. The Postal Service fired her. Was her refusal to distribute the draft registration materials protected by Title VII? Explain your answer. [*McGinnis v. U.S. Postal Service*, 24 F.E.P. Cases 999 (N.D.Cal. 1980)]
3. Madeline O'Hara was a professor in the religion and theology department at Aquinas College, a Catholic institution. Half of the 15 members of her department were ordained priests; only one other member of the department was female. O'Hara was denied tenure because of her personal pro-choice views favoring abortion, which were in conflict with the Catholic Church's position strictly opposing all abortions. Was the denial of tenure to O'Hara in violation of Title VII? Explain. [*Maguire v. Marquette University*, 814 F. 2d 1213 (7th Cir. 1987)]
4. Childress was a cook for the Pennsylvania Department of Corrections; she was the only female cook at Walburg Prison. Although she was paid the same wage rate as the male cooks, she earned less money than they did because she was denied the opportunity to work overtime. Childress filed a

complaint under the Equal Pay Act. How should the court rule on her case? Explain. Is there a violation of Title VII here? [*True v. N.Y. Dept. of Correctional Services*, 36 F.E.P. Cases 1048 (W.D. N.Y. 1985)]

5. Ally McBee applied for a job as a prison guard with the Arkansas State Board of Corrections. The Board of Corrections required that applicants for guard positions be at least 5'2" tall and no taller than 6'10", and weigh no less than 120 lbs. and no more than 300 lbs. McBee was only 5'1" and was therefore rejected. She filed suit under Title VII. On what basis should she make her claim? Is her suit likely to be successful? What must the Board of Corrections show to counter her claim? Explain. [*Dothard v. Rawlinson*, 433 U.S. 321 (1977)]

6. Sheila Forsythe worked as a blackjack dealer at the Sphinx Hotel Casino in Atlantic City. The "theme" of the hotel and casino is of an ancient Egyptian temple; most of the employees who work in "public contact" positions—cashiers, croupiers, dealers, attendants, etc.—are female. The female employees are required to wear skimpy "Egyptian slave girl" outfits while on the job. The casino's management constantly exhorted the employees to "keep the customers happy" and reminded the employees that their jobs depend on happy customers who are willing to gamble large amounts of money. Because of her outfit and the fact that alcohol is freely available to customers, Forsythe was frequently subjected to comments of a sexual nature—propositions, comments about her appearance, and comments about specific parts of her anatomy. Customers often attempted to, or actually did, touch, pat, grab, or hug her—conduct that she found offensive and degrading.

   When she resisted such behavior by customers or rebuked customers for comments, the managers warned her not to upset the customers and placed written warnings in her employment file. Forsythe periodically complained to casino management about being subjected to such behavior by customers, but the response of the management was that such behavior is "part of the job" and she must accept it. Finally, Forsythe was told that one more "incident" on her part will result in her discharge. Does Forsythe have grounds under Title VII to sue for sexual discrimination? Explain.

7. Nyugen Ang Mai operates a Vietnamese restaurant in downtown Bakersfield. Mai has restricted hiring for the restaurant to his family and relatives; he now employs 17 people at the restaurant. Smith, an African American, applies for a job at the restaurant; there are waiter and kitchen help positions available. Mai refuses to hire Smith; he says that customers expect Vietnamese, or at least Asian, waiters at a Vietnamese restaurant. Mai also explains that his Vietnamese customers, who constitute a significant portion of his business, would be reluctant to be waited on by an African American, because that might bring up memories of the war in Vietnam. Smith files a claim with the EEOC, alleging race discrimination. Has Mai established a BFOQ, or is Smith likely to prevail? Explain.

8. Michelle Swanson worked as a waitress at the Michigan City Holiday Inn. Fred Lubber, the manager at the Holiday Inn restaurant, was a fundamentalist Christian, as were many of the other restaurant employees. Swanson, who was not married, discovered that she was pregnant; she considered having an abortion and discussed the matter with some of the other employees. She was subsequently fired by Lubber, who claimed that

the other employees became very upset by her discussion of abortion and the resulting uproar was very disruptive to the restaurant's operations. Swanson filed a claim under Title VII, challenging her discharge. To what kind(s) of discrimination has Swanson been subjected here? How should the court rule on her suit? Explain. [*Turic v. Holland Hospitality Inc.* (D.C.W.D. Mich., No. 1:93:CV:379, 1/27/94)]

9. Brown was a store detective at AAFES. Brown reported to manager George Bass. Bass was supervised by William Boyd, Chief of Safety and Security for AAFES' Eastern Region. Boyd was not directly involved with any employment decisions concerning Brown, but Brown believed that Boyd could influence her career and future advancement. In March 1999, Brown met Boyd at a required AAFES conference for loss prevention personnel held at the Ramada Inn in Alexandria, Virginia. Boyd hosted a social gathering in his hotel room for conference attendees. Brown attended this gathering at the urging of Bass. Several other employees were present when Brown arrived, but by 11:30 P.M. only Brown and Boyd were left in the room. The two then discussed Brown's career for approximately half an hour before Brown decided to leave. As she moved toward the door, Boyd grabbed her shoulders, pushed her against the wall, and kissed her face and neck. He told her, "[Y]ou're so beautiful. I can make you feel like no one else can." Brown freed herself and left Boyd's room. Boyd, however, followed her and when she reached the door to her room in the hotel, he kissed her and stated, "You know, baby, I'll always take care of you." Brown then managed to elude Boyd's grasp and entered her own room.

   Brown immediately contacted Bass about the incident, but the next day Brown advised him that she had decided not to file a complaint about Boyd's conduct and Bass did not investigate the matter further. Brown did tell Bass that she would like Boyd to apologize. Brown had no further contact with Boyd until September 21, 1999, when AAFES held another conference at the same hotel in Alexandria, Virginia. Brown was required to attend and to stay at the hotel. Boyd was also present at the conference, and he once again held a social gathering in his room. Brown was reluctant to attend, but Bass stressed the importance to her career of attending the social and assured her that he would be there with her; Brown agreed to go. Upon their arrival, Boyd apologized to Brown for his previous conduct and Brown and Boyd shook hands. Brown was once again the last guest at the gathering. Brown and Boyd again began to discuss Brown's career. Brown and Boyd then left the hotel and walked to a pub, where they each had a beer. While at the pub, they continued to discuss her career; after 20 minutes, approximately at midnight, they returned to the hotel. Upon arriving at the hotel, Boyd asked Brown to come up to his room. Brown agreed after Boyd promised "he would not touch her in any way." Once they were in Boyd's room, he turned off the lights and put on music. Brown tried to leave, but Boyd grabbed her by the arms, got down on his knees, and pulled her on top of him. As Brown tried to free herself, Boyd continually kissed and groped her. Brown finally broke free and returned to her room. Brown did not tell anyone about the incident until after the conference; when she returned to work, Brown informed Bass about the incident. He was not supportive, expressing surprise and dismay that Brown would have allowed herself to be alone with Boyd again. Brown then filed a complaint under the AAFES antiharassment policy; AAFES ordered Boyd to refrain from having any further direct or indirect contact with Brown or with anyone assigned in any capacity to Brown's work location. Brown entered into a voluntary settlement of her complaint with AAFES on November 23, 1993. The settlement agreement provided that (1) the director of loss prevention would issue a formal apology to Brown, (2) Boyd would have no further contact with Brown and no dealings with any employee at her location, and (3) Brown's allegations would be investigated and appropriate corrective action taken upon completion of the investigation. Boyd received a 30-day suspension for his "inappropriate physical contact and advances toward" Brown and several other inappropriate work-related activities.

After the September incident, Brown's job performance began to decline; she quit her job with AAFES and was treated for post-traumatic stress disorder and depression. She then filed a Title VII suit against AAFES, seeking injunctive relief and money damages. Is Brown likely to be successful in her suit? Explain your answer. How does the *Faragher v. City of Boca Raton* case affect Brown's suit? [*Brown v. Perry*, 184 F. 3d 388 (4th Cir. 1999)]

10. Helio Inc., is a company that provides charter helicopter services. Helio signed a contract with the Saudi Arabian government to provide helicopter flights to Muslims who make pilgrimages to Mecca. The flights involved traveling over the sacred shrines and sites of Islam, such as the Kaaba. Islamic law, in effect in Saudi Arabia, forbids non-Muslims from entering such holy sites; the penalty for violating this law is death by beheading. For the Saudi Arabian flights, Helio, Inc., decides to hire only pilots who were Muslims or who were willing to convert to the Islamic faith before starting the flights. Kern, a qualified helicopter pilot, applied for a job with Helio but was refused because he was not a Muslim. Kern claimed that Helio discriminated against him because of his religion; Helio claimed that being a Muslim was a BFOQ for the job. Who is likely to prevail if Kern files suit? Explain your answer. [*Kern v. Dynaelectron Corp.*, 577 F. Supp. 1196 (N.D. Tex., 1983)]

PRACTICAL EXERCISE

Don Franks owns a manufacturing company that makes machine parts for automotive equipment. Business had been slow until the company successfully bid on a large contract to produce tank tread sprockets for the U. S. Army. The three-year contract significantly increased Franks' business. To meet the production demands of the contract, Franks expanded his workforce by 30 percent. Most of the new employees Franks hired for the contract were African Americans and Latinos; prior to the new hiring, the workforce was predominantly made up of white males.

Now that the tank tread contract has expired, Franks' business has slowed down significantly. Unless new orders can be found, he may be forced to lay off a number of production employees. If Franks uses inverse seniority (last hired, first fired) as the basis of the layoff, most of the employees who lose their jobs will be minorities. Franks feels that having a racially balanced workforce may help him to win more government contracts, so he is reluctant to lay off the minority workers. At the same time, Franks is afraid that some of the more senior white workers will file an employment discrimination suit if he lays them off instead of the more junior minority workers.

How should Franks determine which employees should be laid off? You are Franks' Human Resource Manager; he asks you to prepare a memo outlining the various choices and their pros and cons. What arguments can you make for retaining the minority employees? What arguments can you make for using inverse seniority for the layoffs? Which option would you recommend? Would your answer change if the employees are unionized, and the collective agreement covering them requires that employment decisions be based on seniority? Weighing the various options and explaining why you recommend a particular choice, answer these queries in a memo.

FURTHER INFORMATION

www.eeoc.gov/
The Equal Employment Opportunity Commission's Web site.
www.eeac.org/
The Equal Employment Advisory Council's Web site.
www.shrm.org/
The Society for Human Resource Management's Web site.
http://hr.monster.com/
Human resource management and general employment information.

CHAPTER 21

OTHER STATUTORY REGULATION OF EMPLOYMENT

LEARNING OBJECTIVES

After you have read this chapter, you should be able to:

1. Understand the scope of protection that the Family and Medical Leave Act provides for employees.
2. Recognize what legal principles govern age and disability discrimination in the workplace, and suggest legal remedies.
3. Explain how laws such as the Occupational Safety and Health Act protect worker safety.
4. Understand the remedies workers' compensation laws provide for employees once they are ill or injured.
5. Discuss how the Fair Labor Standards Act affects employers and employees.
6. Describe how laws such as the Employment Retirement Income Securities Act regulate company pension funds.

CHAPTER OUTLINE

One of the surgical technicians at your hospital is HIV positive but has no real symptoms of AIDS. The supervisor of the operating room wants you to transfer the technician in order to protect patients and other employees. The technician claims that he can take adequate precautions to avoid accidentally infecting a patient or coworker during surgery. As the employer, what steps can you take to protect patients and coworkers? What are the legal rights of the technician? After studying this chapter, you will be able to decide how to proceed legally.

INTRODUCTION

One of the most significant trends in labor and employment law in the past 25 years has been the shift in emphasis from collective bargaining as a means of regulating conditions in the workplace to regulation by means of expanding statutory and common law definitions of individual legal rights. The percentage of U.S. employees represented by labor unions has dropped from about 33 percent to approximately 15 percent over that time. In place of the union representation, the worker is increasingly being protected by new federal and state laws and the development of new legal principles from older laws.

In addition to Title VII of the Civil Rights Act (as examined in Chapter 20), which prohibits discrimination on the basis of race, color, sex, religion, or national origin in any aspect of employment, a number of other important federal and state laws regulate aspects of employment. The Family and Medical Leave Act allows some employees to take time off for the birth or adoption of a child, or to care for a spouse, child, or parent who has a serious medical condition. Two laws enacted right after the Civil War can be used to redress the victims of race discrimination. Federal laws also prohibit discrimination in employment based on factors such as age or disability. Other laws require workplaces to maintain a certain level of safety for their employees and to compensate workers for injuries and illnesses arising out of employment. Federal statutes establish a minimum wage that employers are required to pay employees, and set hours and safety requirements for the employment of children and youth. Another federal law regulates pension plans established by employers and enacts certain duties on those who set up and maintain such retirement programs. Each of these federal and state laws is discussed in the following sections.

PARENTAL AND FAMILY LEAVE: THE FAMILY AND MEDICAL LEAVE ACT

One of the most striking employment trends over the past 40 years is the huge increase in the number of women who are employed outside the home. As we saw in Chapter 20, Title VII of the Civil Rights Act of 1964 prohibits discrimination in employment based on race, color, sex, religion, or national origin. Title VII's prohibitions against sex discrimination include discrimination based on pregnancy, childbirth, or related condition. In its *U.A.W. v. Johnson Controls* decision, the U.S. Supreme Court held that a woman should not be forced to choose between her right to a job and her right to have a family. But what happens after a female employee has a family—and is torn between the demands of her job and the need to care for her newborn child, or a seriously ill child, spouse, or parent?

For many years, the United States was alone in the industrialized world in having no national legislation requiring companies to grant leave to new parents. Most European countries have laws requiring employers to grant paid leave of several months for childbirth. Several bills were introduced into Congress in the 1980s, but, because of the opposition of the Reagan and Bush Administrations, were not enacted into law. Finally, Congress passed the *Family and Medical Leave Act (FMLA)*, and it was signed into law by President Clinton in early 1993.

eligible employees: Under the FMLA, employees who have been employed for at least 12 months and who worked at least 1,250 hours during the past year.

The FMLA provides that **eligible employees** are entitled to take up to 12 weeks of unpaid leave during any 12-month period *to care for a newborn or newly adopted child* or *a spouse, parent, or child with a serious health problem* or *because of the employee's own serious health condition*. Eligible employees are those who have been employed for at least 12 months and have worked at least 1,250 hours during the preceding year. The FMLA applies to employers with 50 or more employees.

The FMLA requires the employee to provide 30 days' advance notice of the leave to the employer unless such notice is not "practicable." Employers may require employees to use their paid vacation and personal or sick leave as the first part of their 12-week leave, before beginning the unpaid portion. Employers may also require employees to present certification from a health-care provider in a timely manner when requesting leave under the Act. *Key employees* may be denied leave under the FMLA. Key employees are those employees whom it would be necessary for the employer to replace in order to prevent substantial and serious economic injury to the operation of the business; no more than 10 percent of the employees at a worksite can be designated as key employees, and they must be given written notice of their status as key employees when they request a leave.

The employer must restore the employee to *the same or an "equivalent" position* upon expiration of the leave. This provision requires equivalent benefits, pay, and other terms and conditions of employment. The employee cannot be stripped of any employment benefits he or she accrued prior to the leave. Health benefits must be continued throughout the leave period, but the employer can recover the premiums paid for employees who fail to return from leave, unless due to a serious health condition.

Although 11 states had laws and many companies already had policies that required that employees' jobs be held for them when a child or an elderly parent needed care, the majority of U.S. companies did not. The FMLA provides that state laws that afford greater rights to employees are not to be superseded by the Act.

The FMLA covers about 5 percent of all employers in the United States, and only about 40 percent of U.S. employees. The FMLA is intended to create greater peace of mind for those employees who need some time off to care for a newborn or adopted child, or an aging parent, or to deal with their own health difficulties. Of course, implementing the law will require dealing with many complex issues, often through litigation.

The following case involves the question of what constitutes a "serious health condition" under the FMLA and whether a parent was seeking leave to "care for" her child as envisioned by the act.

MARCHISHECK V. SAN MATEO COUNTY

1999 WL 1188978 (9th Cir. Dec. 16, 1999)

FACTS

Fe Castro Marchisheck was employed as a medical technologist by San Mateo County General Hospital. She was a single mother raising a 14-year-old son, Shaun. Marchisheck sought counseling for Shaun because she suspected he was abusing drugs and alcohol, but the counselor concluded that Marchisheck's suspicions were unfounded. In August, 1995, Shaun was beaten by some acquaintances and suffered minor injuries. Marchisheck decided that she would send Shaun to live with his uncle (her brother) in the Philippines. She asked her supervisor for a five-week vacation leave, to begin August 18, 1995. The supervisor denied her request because he would be unable to schedule employees to cover her shifts without paying overtime. Marchisheck asked another supervisor for leave, but was told not to take leave without approval. In the meantime, Marchisheck made travel arrangements and bought airplane tickets to the Philippines. She met again with her supervisors to request the leave, and presented a letter from Shaun's therapist supporting her request. Marchisheck's request for a leave was again denied, but she was offered the options of taking five weeks off at the end of September, or two weeks off starting on Labor Day. She rejected those choices and left for the Philippines with Shaun that evening. Her supervisors sent her a letter on September 7 informing her that she would be terminated on September 20 for insubordination and absence without leave, and offering her an opportunity to respond. She responded to the letter in a meeting held September 21 but was terminated September 22; she filed suit under the FMLA against the County. Marchisheck claimed that she had sought the leave to "care for Shaun, who was suffering from a serious health condition."

The U.S. District Court granted San Mateo County's motion for summary judgment on the grounds that Shaun did not have a serious medical condition that would entitle Marchisheck to the protection of the FMLA. She appealed to the U.S. Court of Appeals for the Ninth Circuit.

DECISION

The Court of Appeals stated that the FMLA allows employees up to 12 weeks' unpaid leave because of the birth or adoption of a child, or to care for a spouse, son, daughter, or parent who has "a serious health condition." The FMLA defines serious health condition as "an illness, injury, impairment or physical or mental condition that involves—(A) inpatient care in a hospital, hospice or residential medical care facility; or (B) continuing treatment by a health care provider."

Shaun did not receive inpatient care in a hospital or other medical facility, so the main issue in Marchisheck's claim was whether Shaun had a condition involving "continuing treatment by a health care provider." The regulations under the FMLA state that "continuing treatment by a health care provider" requires that the patient be incapacitated for at least three consecutive days, that the patient be treated two or more times by a health care provider, or that the patient have a "chronic serious health condition" that results in a period of incapacity. Marchisheck never clearly identified what "serious health condition" prompted her to take Shaun to the Philippines. Neither his injuries from the beating nor his behavioral problems and psychological condition qualifies as a serious health condition under the FMLA definition. But even if either condition would meet the FMLA definition of *serious health condition*, Marchisheck would still not qualify for leave under the FMLA because she was not taking Shaun to the Philippines to "care for" him—she was not seeking treatment or any medical or psychological care for him there. She simply wanted to keep him safe from any further beatings—and although she was motivated by concern for Shaun's safety, that did not amount to "caring for" Shaun under the FMLA definition. The FMLA definition of "caring for" involves some level of participation in the ongoing treatment of the serious health condition. Marchisheck was simply taking Shaun to the Philippines—where he would not receive any treatment—and leaving him there. Although Marchisheck's desire to provide a more wholesome environment for her son was understandable, her conduct here was not protected by the FMLA, and her employer was free to terminate her employment because she was absent without leave.

CASE QUESTIONS

1. What protection does the FMLA provide for employees? When does such protection apply?
2. Why did Marchisheck seek five weeks' leave? Under which provisions of the FMLA did she justify her request?
3. Why did the court reject her claim for FMLA protection? What would she have had to show in order to be covered by the FMLA?

The FMLA only protects about 40 percent of the nation's employees—those who work for small businesses (with less than 50 employees) are not covered by the FMLA, although they may be covered by state legislation. But even if employees are protected under the FMLA, they may be reluctant to take leave to which they are legally entitled because their employer may question their commitment to their job. If they are viewed as less dedicated to their job, they may be passed over for promotions or raises, and their progression through the employer's ranks could be slowed—they could be shunted aside to the "mommy track."

With both parents or the sole parent working, conflicts between the family and work are bound to occur. Obtaining quality childcare at affordable prices is a real challenge for many working parents. Parents may also be unable to attend conferences with their children's teachers or to be present at other school functions or activities. President Clinton proposed expanding the FMLA to grant parents time off for such purposes, but opposition in Congress and by employers make such legislation unlikely. Some employees may already have that right—several states have laws that allow working parents unpaid time off work to attend school functions: California requires employers with 25 or more employees to allow employees unpaid time off, up to 40 hours per year, to participate in school activities; Illinois allows employees up to 8 hours unpaid leave per year to attend school functions; Minnesota allows up to 16 hours unpaid leave in any 12 month period; North Carolina allows up to 4 hours unpaid leave per year; and Nevada simply prohibits employers from discharging employees because of absences to attend school conferences or meetings.

OTHER FEDERAL STATUTES PROHIBITING DISCRIMINATION

Hiring the best possible employees—employees who are able, productive, and honest—is an important matter for any business. Employers may want to hire young, physically fit persons, who are perceived by the employer as being more productive than older applicants. Such policies, however, may raise legal concerns under equal employment laws prohibiting discrimination because of age or against otherwise qualified persons with a disability.

Some laws prohibiting employment discrimination actually predate Title VII. For example, the Civil Rights Acts of 1866 and 1871, passed during the Reconstruction Era after the Civil War, were intended to safeguard the rights of the newly freed slaves. However, they have been interpreted by the courts as applying to employment discrimination as well. The U.S. Constitution may also be used to prohibit employment discrimination by public sector employers. Most equal opportunity employment legislation, though, was passed after Title VII. The Age Discrimination in Employment Act, passed in 1967, prohibits discrimination in terms or conditions of employment based on age against employees over 40 years. The Rehabilitation Act of 1973 and the Americans with Disabilities Act, passed in 1990, both prohibit employment discrimination against otherwise qualified handicapped individuals. Executive Order 11246, promulgated by President Johnson in 1965 and revised under President Nixon in 1969, requires that companies doing business with the federal government must be equal opportunity employers. Lastly, most states have their own equal employment laws, similar to Title VII, that apply to employers operating in those states.

THE CIVIL RIGHTS ACTS OF 1866 AND 1871

Section 1981 of the *Civil Rights Act* of 1866 provides, in part, that "All persons within the jurisdiction of the United States shall have the same right in every State and Territory to make and enforce contracts . . . as is enjoyed by white citizens. . . ." The courts have held that §1981 gives plaintiffs the right to sue for damages for intentional race discrimination in terms or conditions of employment. The Civil Rights Act of 1991 extended the protection of §1981 to the "making, performance, modification, and termination of contracts, and the enjoyment of all benefits, privileges, terms and conditions of the contractual relationship."

The Supreme Court has indicated that "race" will be interpreted broadly. For example, in *Saint Francis College v. Al-Khazraji* [481 U.S. 604 (1987)], the court held that a professor who alleged denial of tenure because he was an Arab could sue under §1981. The Civil Rights Act of 1991 also added §1981A, which gives persons the right to sue for punitive and compensatory damages for intentional violations of Title VII, the Rehabilitation Act, and the Americans with Disabilities Act.

Section 1983 of the Civil Rights Act of 1871 also allows claims for damages against intentional discrimination. Unlike §1981, however, it is not limited to race discrimination. In *Maine v. Thiboutot* [448 U.S. 1(1980)], the Supreme Court held that §1983 encompasses claims based on deprivation of rights granted under the U.S. Constitution and federal statutory law. Consequently, §1983 can be used to challenge intentional discrimination on grounds prohibited by federal law, such as age, sex, religion, national origin, disability, and so forth. The wording of §1983 restricts claims under it to cases in which the alleged discrimination is by someone acting (or claiming to act) under government authority. Thus, courts have interpreted §1983 to mean that it can be used only to challenge discrimination by public sector employers (and private sector employers acting pursuant to state action).

THE AGE DISCRIMINATION IN EMPLOYMENT ACT

The federal *Age Discrimination in Employment Act* (*ADEA*), passed in 1967, prohibits discrimination based on age in any terms or conditions of employment. The Act was intended to protect older workers who were more likely subject to such discrimination; thus, its provisions cover only age discrimination against employees aged 40 years and above. State and local laws may provide greater protection from age discrimination. For example, New York State's Human Rights Law prohibits age discrimination against employees 18 years or older.

The act covers employers engaged in commerce with 20 or more employees, labor unions that either operate a hiring hall or have more than 25 members and represent the employees of an employer covered by the act, and employment agencies. State and local governments are included in the definition of *employers* under the ADEA. However, in *Kimel v. Florida Board of Regents* [120 S.Ct. 631 (2000)], the U.S. Supreme Court held that state governments are immune from suits under the ADEA by reason of the Eleventh Amendment of the U.S. Constitution.

The ADEA prohibits the refusal or failure to hire, the discharge, or any other discrimination in terms, conditions, or privileges of employment because of an individual's age (40 years and over). The mandatory retirement of employees because of their age is also prohibited, but the act does not affect voluntary retirement by employees.

Exceptions and Defenses Under the ADEA The ADEA does provide for some limited exceptions and recognizes that age may be a bona fide occupational requirement (BFOQ) for certain jobs. Age can be a BFOQ when the employer can demonstrate that it is reasonably necessary to the safe and efficient operation of the employer's business to refuse to hire employees over a certain age. For example, the courts have upheld the requirement that New York State Police troopers must retire at age 55 years because of the strenuous nature of their police work. The ADEA was amended in 1996 to allow state and local governments to pass laws setting retirement ages for police or firefighters, provided that the retirement age is at least 55 years.

The ADEA also states that employees who are in executive or high policy-making positions may be retired at age 65 years if they have been in such a position for at least two years and are entitled to retirement benefits of at least $44,000 per year. This provision was inserted into the ADEA to allow employers to ensure that senior executives do not remain in their jobs indefinitely; by providing for turnover in senior jobs, employers can retain talented junior executives by offering them the prospect of advancement into top jobs.

An employer is also permitted to observe the terms of a bona fide seniority system or employee benefit plan (such as a retirement or pension plan) as long as it is not "a subterfuge to evade the purpose" of the act and does not require the involuntary retirement of any individual. That means that an employer may treat employees differently under a benefit plan, as long as the differential is cost justified. For example, the cost of insurance generally increases with the age of the person to be insured. An employer providing life insurance as a benefit to employees can provide reduced coverage for older employees, as long as that reduced coverage costs the same as the insurance coverage provided for younger employees.

In addition, an employer may differentiate between employees as long as the different treatment is based on a factor other than age. For example, an employer may use a productivity-based pay plan even if older employees produce less and earn less than younger employees. In this case, the pay is based on each employee's productivity, a factor other than age. Also note that in *Hazen Paper Co. v. Biggins* [507 U.S. 604 (1993)], the Supreme Court held that discharging an employee because the person would be entitled to a pension was not the same as discharging him because of age. Although such conduct might violate another law, such as the Employment Retirement Income Security Act, the conduct did not violate the ADEA.

The ADEA does not prohibit voluntary retirement, and an employer may offer incentives to employees to get them to participate voluntarily in an early retirement program. Employers may also require employees to sign waivers of possible ADEA claims as a condition of receiving such early retirement incentives, but the waivers must comply with the specific requirements set out in the ADEA, according to the Supreme Court decision in *Oubre v. Entergy Operations, Inc.* [522 U.S. 422 (1998)].

ADEA Procedures The ADEA is enforced and administered by the Equal Employment Opportunity Commission (EEOC), but the act also allows for private suits as well. An individual alleging a violation of the ADEA must file a written complaint with the EEOC and with the state or local EEOC agency if one exists. Unlike under Title VII, the complaint may be filed with the EEOC and state agency simultaneously. The complaint must be filed with the EEOC within 180 days of the alleged violation, if no state or local agency exists, or within 300 days if a state or local agency does exist. After filing with the EEOC and state or local agency, the individual must wait at least 60 days before filing suit in federal court; even though the suit may be filed at least 60 days from filing with the EEOC and state agency, the suit must be filed no later than 90 days from receipt of a right to sue notice from the EEOC. If the EEOC chooses to file suit, the EEOC suit supersedes any ADEA suit filed by the individual or by the state or local agency.

If the individual has agreed to submit any employment disputes to arbitration, she or he can be required to submit an ADEA claim to arbitration rather than sue in court, according to the Supreme Court decision in *Gilmer v. Interstate/Johnson Lane Corp.* [500 U.S. 20 (1991)].

Remedies Under the ADEA The remedies available under the ADEA are similar to those under the Equal Pay Act. Successful plaintiffs can be granted an injunction and may recover any back wages owed, as well as legal fees and court costs. Double damages in the amount equal to any wages owed may be recovered if the employer acted "willfully" (note the difference from the Equal Pay Act). According to the Supreme Court, an employer acts "willfully" under the ADEA when the employer either knows or shows reckless disregard for the matter of whether its conduct is prohibited by the ADEA [see *Trans World Airlines v. Thurston*, 469 U.S. 111 (1985)]. In suits brought by the EEOC, possible remedies include injunctions and back pay. Liquidated damages, however, are not available in such suits.

THE AMERICANS WITH DISABILITIES ACT AND THE REHABILITATION ACT

Two legislative provisions prohibit discrimination because of disability or handicap against otherwise qualified persons in employment. First, the Americans with Disabilities Act, passed in 1990, is a comprehensive law that protects the rights of disabled persons in employment and public accommodations. Second, the Vocational Rehabilitation Act of 1973 applies only to employees of the federal government or activities that receive federal funding.

Title I of the *Americans with Disabilities Act* (*ADA*) addresses employment; it prohibits discrimination in any aspect of employment against an otherwise qualified individual with a disability because of such disability. The ADA defines "**otherwise qualified individual with a disability**" as "an individual with a disability who, with or without reasonable accommodation, can perform the essential functions of the employment position that such individual holds or desires." An employee who has applied for, or received, disability benefits under Social Security or some other disability benefit program is not automatically disqualified from bringing suit under the ADA, according to *Cleveland v. Policy Management Systems Corp.* [119 S.Ct. 1597 (1999)].

otherwise qualified individual with a disability: Individuals who, despite their disability, or with reasonable accommodation to their disability, are capable of performing the essential functions of a particular job.

The *Rehabilitation Act* imposes on employers or organizations or activities that do business with the federal government or receive federal funding an obligation not to discriminate against "otherwise qualified individuals with a disability." Section 503 requires that firms having contracts or subcontracts with the federal government for more than $10,000 must agree not to discriminate in employment against otherwise qualified handicapped individuals. Section 504, which has much broader application than §503, applies to any program, activity, or organization receiving federal funding. There is no minimum level of funding required under §504—any organization, activity, or program receiving federal funding, no matter how small, is subject to §504. Specifically, this section prohibits the denial to a qualified individual with a disability the chance to participate in a program, activity, or organization or receive the benefits of a program, activity, or organization that receives federal funding. *Consolidated Rail Corp. v. Darrone* [465 U.S. 624 (1984)] held that in particular, §504 may be used to challenge discrimination in employment against an otherwise qualified individual with a disability.

In general, both acts define *disability* with respect to an individual broadly. *Disability* means:

(a) a physical or mental impairment that substantially limits one or more of the major life activities of such individual;

(b) a record of such an impairment; or

(c) being regarded as having such an impairment.

When determining whether an employee is disabled within the meaning of the ADA, should an employer consider whether the employee can take corrective or remedial measures? That is the question the Supreme Court considered in the following case.

SUTTON V. UNITED AIR LINES

119 S.Ct. 2139 (1999)

FACTS

Karen Sutton and Kimberley Hinton were twin sisters, each of whom had severe myopia. Their uncorrected eyesight was 20/200 or worse in the right eye and 20/400 or worse in the left eye; but by using corrective lenses, each had vision of 20/20 or better. Both sisters applied for commercial airline pilot jobs with United Air Lines, but were rejected because they failed to meet United's minimum vision requirements of uncorrected vision of 20/100 or better. The sisters then filed suit against United under the ADA, alleging that United had discriminated against them because of their disabilities, or had regarded them as having a disability, in violation of the ADA. The trial court dismissed their suit, holding that because they could fully correct their vision and were not actually substantially limited in any major life activity, they were not disabled under the ADA. Because United did not regard them as being unable to perform a whole range of jobs, but rather simply held that they were unable to satisfy the requirements of a particular job, the court held that United did not regard them as having an impairment that substantially limited the life activity of working. The sisters appealed, and the U.S. Court of Appeals for the 10th Circuit affirmed the trial court decision. The sisters then appealed to the U.S. Supreme Court.

DECISION

The Supreme Court majority, in an opinion written by Justice O'Connor, held that the language of the ADA as a whole indicates that corrective measures are to be considered when determining whether an individual has a condition that substantially impairs a major life activity. The ADA defines disability as a "physical or mental impairment that substantially limits one or more major life activities." The phrase "substantially limits" is in the present indicative verb form, according to the Court, which indicates that the language is read as requiring that the person be presently—not potentially or hypothetically—substantially limited in order to demonstrate a disability. A disability exists only when the impairment substantially limits a major life activity, rather than might, could, or would be substantially limiting if corrective or mitigating measures were not taken. A person whose impairment is corrected by mitigating measures has an impairment, but the corrected impairment does not substantially limit a major life activity.

The ADA requires that the disability be evaluated with respect to the individual and determined based on whether the impairment substantially limits a major life activity of the individual. To attempt to determine the effects of the disability without considering the corrective or mitigating measures would require an employer to speculate about the person's condition based on general information about how the uncorrected impairment usually affects individuals, rather than on the individual's actual condition.

As for the plaintiffs' claim that United regarded them as having a disability that substantially limits a major life activity, there is no dispute that the plaintiffs are physically impaired; the plaintiffs contend that United mistakenly believes that the impairments substantially limit them in the major life activity of working. However, the position of commercial airline pilot is not a class of jobs but only a single position. The ADA does allow employers to prefer certain physical attributes over others and to establish physical criteria; however, the employer violates the ADA when it makes an employment decision based on a physical or mental impairment, real or imagined, that is regarded as substantially limiting a major life activity. But the employer is free to decide that some physical characteristics or medical conditions that do not rise to the level of an impairment are preferable to others; and the employer is free to decide that some limiting, but not substantially limiting, impairments make individuals less than ideally suited for a job. Here the plaintiffs have alleged that United regards their vision as precluding them from holding the position of commercial airline pilot, a single position; but the fact that there are other positions available to the plaintiffs, such as pilot for courier service or commercial copilot, means that the plaintiffs would not be substantially limited in the major life activity of working.

Justice Stevens, joined by Justice Breyer, dissented, noting that eight of the nine U.S. Courts of Appeals that had considered the question had held that the determination of disability should be made without regard to corrective or mitigating conditions. The dissent also argued that the definition of *disability* under the ADA focused on the existence of an impairment—past or present—that substantially limits or did limit the individual before amelioration, rather than whether the person is currently functionally limited in a major life activity. The dissent stated that remedial legislation, such as the ADA, should be construed broadly to effectuate its purposes.

CASE QUESTIONS

1. What must a plaintiff demonstrate in order to be disabled within the meaning of the ADA?
2. What is the effect of corrective measures—such as the sisters wearing corrective lenses—on whether a person is disabled under the ADA?
3. When does a disability substantially limit a person's ability to work? How does the sisters' eyesight affect their employment?
4. Why does the Court state that United does not regard the sisters as having a disability that substantially impairs their ability to work?

On the same day that the Supreme Court decided the *Sutton v. United Air Lines* case, it also decided *Murphy v. United Parcel Service, Inc.* [119 S.Ct. 2133 (1999)] and *Albertsons, Inc. v. Kirkingburg* [119 S.Ct. 2162 (1999)]; both involved similar questions to that in *Sutton*. In *Murphy*, the Court held that UPS can refuse to hire a person with high blood pressure for a commercial truck mechanic position, because the position required driving trucks, and Murphy's high blood pressure prevented him from qualifying for a commercial truck driver's license. *Albertsons* involved a truck driver with sight in only one eye; because of his vision condition, Kirkingburg could not meet federal Department of Transportation requirements for a commercial driver's license. In each case, although the plaintiff could not meet federal standards for commercial drivers, both plaintiffs were capable of performing other mechanic or driver positions. Because of that, the plaintiffs were not "regarded as having a disability that substantially limited" their ability to work.

By court interpretation, the definition of *disability* under both acts also includes contagious diseases such as tuberculosis and AIDS [see *School Board of Nassau County, Florida v. Arline*, 480 U.S. 273 (1987) and *Chalk v. U.S. District Court*, 840 F.2d 701 (9th Cir. 1987)]. Neither act, however, protects individuals whose use of illegal drugs prevents those individuals from performing the duties of their jobs or whose employment would present a direct threat to the property or safety of others. Nothing under either the ADA or the Rehabilitation Act prevents private employers from instituting drug testing programs. The ADA does protect individuals who are former drug users or recovering drug users, individuals enrolled in a supervised rehabilitation program, and individuals who are "erroneously regarded" as using drugs. The act also protects alcoholics who do not use alcohol at work or who are not under the influence of alcohol at the workplace.

Employers are permitted to ask about an individual's ability to perform the functions and requirements of the job in question but are prohibited from asking abut the existence, nature, or severity of a disability. Employers also cannot require a preemployment medical examination of applicants but may require such an exam once a job offer has been extended, provided that the exam is required of all entering employees.

The ADA and the regulations under the Rehabilitation Act impose on employers the duty to make *reasonable accommodation* for qualified individuals with a disability, unless such accommodation would impose undue hardship on the employer. Failure to make reasonable accommodation, or the failure to hire an individual because of the need to make accommodation for that individual, is included in the definition of illegal discrimination prohibited by the ADA. The ADA defines "undue hardship" in a complicated definition that includes a number of factors for consideration, such as the nature and cost of the accommodation needed, the financial resources of the facility involved, the number of persons employed at the facility, the size of the business or the entity involved, and the type of operations of the covered entity. The definition of undue hardship is intended to be flexible and determined on a case-by-case basis.

Employers are not required to create a new position for the disabled applicant, nor are they required to offer the individual the most expensive means of accommodation. Reasonable accommodation includes the minimal realignment or reassignment of job duties or the provision of certain assistance devices. An employer, for example, could reassign certain filing or reception duties from the requirements of a typist job in order to accommodate a person requiring the use of a wheelchair, or telephones could be fitted with amplifiers to accommodate an individual's hearing disability. The regulations state, and the courts have held, that the extent of the accommodation required must be determined on a case-by-case basis; drastic realignments of job requirements or imposition of severe financial costs would be considered unreasonable and would not be required.

Defenses In addition to the "undue hardship" defense, the ADA lists four other possible defenses for employers:

1. Employers may refuse to hire or accommodate an individual when that person's condition poses a direct threat to the safety or health of others in the workplace, such a person with a contagious or infectious disease. The Vocational Rehabilitation Act also provides that a person with a contagious disease or infection who, because of that condition, presents a direct threat to the health or safety of others or is unable to perform the duties of the job, is excluded from the Act's protection.
2. Employers are permitted to hire, select, or promote individuals based on tests, standards, or criteria that are job related or consistent with business necessity; a disabled individual who was unable to meet such standards need not be hired.
3. Employers in the food service industry may refuse to hire individuals who have infectious or communicable diseases that can be transmitted to others through the handling of food, when the risk of infection cannot be eliminated by reasonable accommodation. The ADA directs the Secretary of Health and Human Services to develop a list of diseases that can be transmitted through food handling; only the diseases on that list may be used as a basis for refusing to hire individuals under this defense.
4. Religious corporations, associations, or societies are permitted to give preference to individuals who are members of that particular religion when hiring for positions involved in carrying on the activities of the religious corporation, association, or society.

Enforcement The enforcement of the ADA is assigned to the EEOC; the act provides that the procedures and remedies under Title VII of the Civil Rights

Act shall be used for the ADA. An individual complaining of a violation of the Act must first file a complaint with the appropriate state or local agency, if one exists. After 60 days or the termination of proceedings by the state or local agency, the individual can file with the EEOC; the EEOC, then, or the individual if the EEOC declines to do so, may file suit against the employer. Remedies available under the ADA are the same as under Title VII—injunctions, hiring or reinstatement orders, back pay, and legal fees. Punitive damages under 42 U.S.C. §1981A are available for cases of intentional discrimination violating the ADA.

Section 503 of the Rehabilitation Act is enforced by the Office of Federal Contract Compliance Programs (OFCCP) of the Department of Labor. An individual alleging a violation of §503 must take the complaint to the OFCCP, which will pursue administrative remedies against the employer. There is no individual right to sue under §503.

Enforcement of §504 of the Rehabilitation Act is coordinated by the federal Department of Education, but the particular agency or department administering the federal funding is the primary enforcement agency for complaints against the recipient of such funding. An individual alleging a violation must first file a complaint with the agency administering the funding; that agency may use administrative or judicial proceedings to pursue the complaint. If the agency determines that there is a violation, it may suspend, terminate, or refuse to grant federal assistance to a recipient found in violation of §504. If the agency fails to act on the complaint, the individual can file suit to challenge the alleged violation of §504.

EXECUTIVE ORDER 11246

Firms doing business with the federal government are required to agree not to discriminate in employment on the basis of race, color, religion, sex, or national origin by *Executive Order 11246*. Firms doing at least $10,000 worth of business with the federal government must include a nondiscrimination clause in their contract or subcontract. Firms doing more than $50,000 worth of business and having more than 50 employees are required to develop and maintain written affirmative action plans for the utilization of women and minorities in their workforce. The OFCCP in the U.S. Department of Labor enforces the obligations of E.O.11246; individuals alleging a violation of the requirements must file a written complaint with the OFCCP within 180 days of the alleged violation. The OFCCP may refer the complaint to the EEOC for investigation or may initiate its own administrative enforcement proceedings. There is no individual right to sue under E.O.11246. Firms found to be in violation of E.O.11246 may be subject to injunctions to cease the violation and may be required to hire, with back pay and remedial seniority, affected individuals. The firm in violation may also have its government contracts canceled or suspended and may be declared ineligible for future government contracts.

THE U.S. CONSTITUTION AND EMPLOYMENT DISCRIMINATION

Public sector employees are protected by the requirements of the U.S. Constitution. The main provision of the Constitution addressing discrimination is the equal protection clause, found in the 14th Amendment, which has also been applied to federal employees through the Fifth Amendment's due process requirement. The equal protection clause prohibits intentional discrimination that is not justified by a compelling government purpose (see Chapter 4 for a more thorough discussion of constitutional law issues).

In considering claims of discrimination under the Constitution, the Court will first consider the basis of discrimination. Some bases of discrimination, or "classifications" by public sector employers, will be considered "suspect classes"—that is, there is little or no legitimate reason for the government to subject persons to different treatment because they are members of a particular class. The courts have consistently held that race, color, and religion are suspect classes. For example, racial discrimination involves treating persons differently because of their race or color; such conduct can rarely ever by justified. The court will require that the government employer show that the conduct is required by some compelling government interest and that no less discriminatory alternatives exist. For example, in *U.S. v. Paradise* [480 U.S. 149 (1987)], the Supreme Court upheld an affirmative action plan requiring the Alabama State Police to promote to corporal one African-American trooper for every white trooper promoted until a new promotion policy was instituted. The Court imposed the requirement in order to remedy past "pervasive" discrimination against African-Americans by the State Police. Conversely, in *Wygant v. Jackson Board of Education* [476 U.S.267 (1986)], the Supreme Court held that an affirmative action provision in a collective agreement, requiring that senior white teachers be laid off rather than junior minority teachers in certain situations, violated the 14th Amendment because there were other alternatives available that would not have such a severe effect on the senior teachers. More recently, the federal courts have displayed general hostility to government affirmative action programs. While reaffirming that the constitutionality of any government affirmative action policy must be subject to the "strict scrutiny" test, the Supreme Court held that a federal set-aside program requiring that a certain percentage of contracts under any federally funded highway construction projects be awarded to minority-owned businesses was unconstitutional in *Adarand Constructors, Inc. v. Pena* [515 U.S. 200 (1995)].

STATE EQUAL EMPLOYMENT OPPORTUNITY LAWS

Most states, and a number of cities, have their own equal employment opportunity legislation. Many such laws go beyond the protection of Title VII and other federal legislation; they also apply to smaller employers who may not be covered by Title VII. For example, the New York Human Rights Law prohibits discrimination in employment on the basis of race, color, religion, sex, national origin, disability, marital status, age (18 or older), and criminal record. Connecticut state law prohibits employers from requiring an employee to take drug tests without a "reasonable suspicion" that the employee is using drugs. Some states, such as Minnesota, Connecticut, Wisconsin, Massachusetts, Rhode Island, New Jersey, California, Vermont, Nevada, the District of Columbia, and Hawaii prohibit discrimination because of sexual orientation or sexual preference. The specific procedures and requirements of the law vary from state to state; most of the laws involve some sort of administrative procedure by a state enforcement agency before the individual may file suit in the state courts. Recall that Title VII and the ADA require an individual filing a complaint with the EEOC to first have filed with the appropriate state or local agency, if one exists.

GAYS SEEK PROTECTION IN THE COURTS

Neither Title VII nor other federal EEO legislation prohibits discrimination based on sexual preference or sexual orientation. Ten states (Vermont, Massachusetts, Connecticut, Rhode Island, New Jersey, Wisconsin, Minnesota, Nevada, California and Hawaii) and the District of Columbia have laws that prohibit discrimination against gays or lesbians in employment, housing or public accommodations. But the coverage of, and protection granted by, such laws varies, and is subject to judicial interpretation. The New Jersey Supreme Court held that the Boy Scouts are a public accommodation under the New Jersey Law Against Discrimination [NJLAD], which prohibits the Boy Scouts of America from dismissing a gay Assistant Scoutmaster [*Dale v. Boy Scouts of America*, 160 N.J. 562, 734 A.2d 1196 (1999) *cert. granted*, 120 S.Ct. 865 (Jan 14, 2000)]. The California Supreme Court reached the opposite conclusion, deciding that the Boy Scouts were not subject to California's Unruh Civil Rights Act, and allowing a Boy Scout council to exclude a gay male from serving as a Scoutmaster [*Curran v. Mount Diablo Council of Boy Scouts of America*, 17 Cal. 4th 670, 952 P.2d 218 (1998)].

But even apart from legislation, gays and lesbians have been winning some legal rights through the courts. The Vermont Supreme Court held that the Vermont State Constitution requires the state to give the same benefits and protections to gay or lesbian couples as it provides to heterosexual married couples [*Baker v. State of Vermont*, 1999 WL 1211709, 1999 Vt. LEXIS 406 (Dec. 20, 1999)]. The Vermont Supreme Court stopped short of legally recognizing gay marriages, stating that it was up to the state legislature to decide whether to issue marriage licenses to gay or lesbian couples or to set up a domestic partnership registration system. Vermont is the first state to grant some legal protections to gay couples. When the Hawaiian Supreme Court appeared to give some recognition to gay marriages in a 1993 decision, the state legislature passed an amendment restricting legal marriage to heterosexual couples only; that amendment was ratified by state voters in 1998. The Hawaii Supreme Court upheld the amendment as constitutional in *Baehr v. Miike* [1999 Haw. LEXIS 391 (Dec. 9, 1999)]. On the European front, in November 1999, the government of France approved legislation that sets up a system of registration for homosexual couples ["Pacte de civil solidarite"] granting them most, but not all, legal rights of married heterosexual couples; the inheritance rights of gay partners are limited, and dissolution procedures for registered gay couples are simpler than getting a divorce for married couples.

The U.S. military forces have had the "don't ask, don't tell" policy for gays in the military since 1993; the policy represented a political compromise between the Clinton administration and Congress. Under the policy, gays are not automatically disqualified from serving in the military, but those who participate in homosexual practices, or demonstrate a propensity to engage in such practices, are disqualified. The "don't ask, don't tell" policy has consistently been held to be constitutional by the federal courts [*Thomasson v. Perry*, 80 F.3d 915 (4th Cir. 1996) and *Phillips v. Perry*, 106 F.3d 1420 (9th Cir. 1997)], but the policy has been criticized for failing to protect gays in the military from harassment or physical abuse. In response to such criticism, in December 1999 President Clinton announced a review of the "don't ask, don't tell" policy, which will remain in place during the review.

Sources: "Pacs Gallica," *The Economist* (November 20, 1999); "Vermont Court Backs Gay-Couple Benefits," *The Washington Post* (December 21, 1999); "For Gays, Tolerance Translates to Rights," *The Washington Post* (November 5, 1999); "Gay Rights Advocates Plan to Press Clinton to Undo Policy," *New York Times* (December 25, 1999); "Don't Ask, Don't Tell; President Jumps Ship on Own Policy," *The San Diego Union-Tribune* (December 26, 1999); "Don't Lie: Clinton Admits Don't Ask, Don't Tell Is a Policy Failure," *The Plain Dealer* (Cleveland), (December 20, 1999).

OCCUPATIONAL SAFETY AND HEALTH

Approximately 10,000 American workers are killed each year in job-related accidents; and nearly 2 million workers suffer disabling injuries, and more than 300,000 develop some form of occupational disease. In addition to the human pain and suffering, these workplace accidents cost the nation an estimated $83 billion in 1992, including nearly $52 billion in lost production.

Congress enacted the *Occupational Safety and Health Act* in 1970 to attempt to make American workplaces safer. The purpose of the act was to "assure, so far as possible every working man and woman in the nation safe and healthful working conditions and to preserve our human resources." The law established a new agency, the Occupational Safety and Health Administration, within the Department of Labor. Both the law and the agency are known by the acronym "OSHA." As part of a line agency, the OSHA administrator is appointed by the President and carries the actual title of Assistant Secretary of Labor for Occupational Safety and Health. The agency had 2,221 employees in 1998, and an annual budget of $353 million. Although OSHA has often been controversial, it is a relatively small federal agency. By comparison, in 1998 the Environmental Protection Agency had more than 18,000 employees and a budget in excess of $7 billion.

The OSHA covers virtually all private employees, perhaps as many as 80 million, in the United States. In addition, many public employees are also covered in some way. Federal employees are not directly covered by OSHA, but the federal agencies employing them are required to give them protection equal to the standards set by OSHA. However, only eight agencies have set up such plans, and most of those are inadequate, according to experts. No fines or penalties can be assessed against federal agencies by OSHA.

Workers in mines, railroads, nuclear facilities, and the maritime industry are not covered by OSHA, but they are protected by other laws. Also, the approximately 7 million local and state employees are exempted from the federal OSHA. Many of these workers are covered by occupational safety laws enacted in their states. Together the federal and state programs are responsible for protecting the health and safety of an estimated 100 million workers at almost 6.5 million workplaces.

HEALTH AND SAFETY STANDARDS

specific standards: Regulations setting particular limits for exposing employees to workplace hazards or toxic substances.

general duty clause: The OSHA provision that requires employers to provide a safe workplace for employees.

The law authorizes OSHA to establish **specific standards** for various industries, and standards applicable to all types of employment. Rules and regulations have been promulgated over the past 24 years addressing noise, dust, air, heat, toxic substances, types of protective equipment, ladders, scaffolds, and many other aspects of the workplace.

The OSHA statute also includes the so-called **general duty clause**, which requires employers "to furnish a workplace free from recognized hazards that have caused or are likely to cause death or serious physical harm to employees." This broad language authorizes OSHA to take action against an employer for failing to correct any "recognized hazard," without the need to cite any specific OSHA regulation if none covers the specific dangerous condition.

The OSHA statute began its existence under considerable public pressure to set immediately health and safety standards. As a result, OSHA adopted hundreds of standards established by private industry groups and trade associations. Many of these regulations were originally intended by their organizations as "consensus" standards, which were benchmarks that businesses were to attempt to reach. When OSHA made them regulations—minimum standards that must be met in order to avoid sanctions—it caused a great deal of anger and resistance in the business community. Today, OSHA develops most standards following recommendations of the National Institute for Occupational Safety and Health (NIOSH), a part of the Department of Health and Human Services. These proposed standards are then subject to comment from representatives of both labor and industry, as well as the general public, before they are legally enacted.

The standards adopted by OSHA are rules limiting or prohibiting the exposure of employees to toxic materials or harmful physical agents. The act states that the standards must ensure, to the extent feasible on the basis of the best available evidence, that no employee will suffer material impairment of health or functional capacity because of exposure to the hazard. The feasibility of a standard must be examined from both a technological perspective and a financial perspective. The Secretary of Labor, acting through OSHA, has to establish that the standard is both technologically and economically feasible; but, according to the Supreme Court decision in *American Textile Manufacturers' Institute v. Donovan* [452 U.S. 490 (1981)], the Secretary does not have to show that the benefits of a standard bear a reasonable relationship to its costs.

right to refuse: Right granted to employees by OSHA to refuse to work in a dangerous situation.

Employees under OSHA have the right to a workplace free from recognized hazards and are also protected from any employer discrimination because they have exercised any right granted by the act. Employees are also given the "**right to refuse**," the right to refuse to work in the face of a dangerous condition; employees can exercise that right only if they have reasonable grounds to conclude that they face a real and immediate danger of death or serious injury.

ENFORCEMENT

Once a regulation has come into effect, OSHA has the duty and power to inspect all businesses to determine if the standards are being met. Federal OSHA has only about 1,000 inspectors on its staff (called Compliance Officers [COs]) for the whole country. In 1998 these COs performed over 34,000 inspections. The inspections resulted in the issuance of 76,980 violation notices, of which 50,646 were listed as "serious," 1,756 were "repeat," and 640 were "willful" (that is "intentional," the most serious category). Following these inspections, OSHA proposed penalties in excess of $79 million in 1998. Prior to 1991, the maximum fine was $1,000 for a serious violation and $10,000 for a willful violation.

As part of the Budget Reconciliation Act of 1990, Congress authorized OSHA to increase the maximum fines for a violation sevenfold. OSHA began using the new structure in spring 1991, but did not automatically raise each fine. For example, statistics for fiscal 1992 show that for "serious" violations, the average fine rose from $273 in 1990 to $800 in 1992. In 1992 total OSHA penalties did increase to $116.1 million. Despite the higher fines, in 1992 only about 11.8 percent of the violation notices OSHA issued were contested by the employers, a relatively small increase over the previous year.

At the completion of an inspection, the compliance officer and a representative of the employer sit down and discuss any violations noted. Then OSHA mails a notice informing the employer of violations and proposing penalties of a specific amount. Employers can request informal conferences in the next 15 days to discuss the problems, and many cases are settled during this time. If the employer wants to contest the violation, a notice must be filed by the end of the 15-day period. The case will subsequently be heard by an administrative law judge (ALJ). Following the ALJ's decision, an appeal is possible to the three-member Occupational Safety and Health Review Commission, which is independent from OSHA.

In the late 1980s and early 1990s OSHA began to use a new tactic, called the "egregious case" policy, to deal with particularly serious health and safety situations. Instead of counting numerous violations of one standard as one violation, OSHA decided in some cases to count each violation as a separate illegal act. For example, if an inspection showed that 200 employees in one plant were not wearing hard hats as required or that 200 injuries had not been properly recorded on OSHA forms, the inspector might assess penalties based on 200 violations rather than one. National OSHA officials made the decision on whether to use the "egregious" policy in each case based on a number of factors, including the following: the seriousness of the problems, the amount and extent of deaths and injuries, the company's attitude toward the problem, and the company's previous record for workplace safety and OSHA violations. The use of this policy led to imposition of some of the largest penalties in OSHA history.

Over the years businesspersons have told numerous "horror stories" about OSHA inspectors looking for small, technical, "nitpicky" violations to cite—such as the width of toilet seats or the spacing between ladder steps. Particularly in the early days of OSHA, when the first group of inspectors was hired from the maritime industry, there was probably good reason for businesses' complaints. As OSHA has matured, the inspectors appear to have developed more tact and experience and now focus more attention on serious problems. Complaints have decreased somewhat, though there are still unhappy individuals. After all, having a safety inspector arrive unannounced at your facility to thoroughly look for safety violations will never be one of life's great pleasures.

Search Warrant Requirements The OSHA law specified that the inspections could be done by surprise, without a warrant. Why? The COs may arrive at the inspection site and immediately go through the facility before any hazardous conditions could be altered or cleaned up. However, as we have previously mentioned, the U.S. Supreme Court held in *Marshall v. Barlow's Inc.* that the Fourth Amendment of the Constitution requires OSHA to obtain a search warrant when the owner of the business demands one. Most owners and managers permit an OSHA inspector to enter the premises without a warrant, but some troublesome situations do still arise, as in the following case.

NATIONAL ENGINEERING & CONTRACTING CO. V. OSHA REVIEW COMM.

45 F.3d 476 (D.C. 1995)

FACTS

OSHA chooses to inspect construction sites using a randomly generated list from a computer at the University of Tennessee. The list itself is based on a commercially published list of current construction projects known as the "Dodge Reports." Pursuant to this policy, OSHA chose in April 1992 to inspect a bridge construction site near Cincinnati, on which National Engineering was the general contractor.

Compliance Officer John Collier was assigned to do the inspection. Believing that National had a policy of refusing inspections without a warrant, Collier applied and was granted a warrant by a federal magistrate. In his application, Collier stated that he believed a warrant was necessary because of National's policy. He also attached a copy of OSHA's written policy regarding random inspections of construction sites.

Due to changes in Collier's schedule, CO James Denton actually carried out the inspection a few days later. When he arrived at the site, the National representative refused him entry, then asked him to wait one hour until National's attorneys arrived. After consulting with his supervisor, Denton refused this request, then showed the warrant, and began his inspection. After the inspection, Denton issued several citations for violations of OSHA law and regulations. National contested the violations before an ALJ acting for the Occupational Safety and Health Review Commission. Two of the violations, the first concerning a slight worn place on an electrical extension cord and the other a lack of a ground on a plug on an office fax machine, were held to be "not serious" and no penalty was assessed. The other violation, a line of exposed vertical steel bars (rebar), posed the hazard of impalement to workers who might fall. The ALJ found this violation "serious" and assessed a $400 penalty. National appealed to the District of Columbia Circuit Court of Appeals.

DECISION

National challenged the violations, arguing that the warrant was not sufficient. National claimed that OSHA must include information in its warrant request specifically demonstrating how National was chosen for inspection, and that in the absence of such information, there was a lack of probable cause to support the warrant.

In *Marshall v. Barlow's Inc.* [436 U.S. 307 (1978)], the Supreme Court held that a warrant for an OSHA inspection must be obtained when requested by the business. The Court went on to explain that the showing needed to establish probable cause for a routine regulatory inspection is less than that required for a search warrant in a criminal case. OSHA merely needs to "demonstrate that its inspection program is a neutral one and that, using those criteria, it selected National for inspection."

Since Collier had attested in his request for a warrant that the inspection was to be conducted in accordance with OSHA's written policy (which was attached), the *Barlow's* test was met. National's request for more specific details on the selection process was refused. The court noted one case in which a court required more documentation, but several in which the exact OSHA policy used here was upheld. The court stated that "the absence of an encoded establishment list will only be fatal to a warrant application where the target company can make a factual showing that it was placed on the list for reasons other than the application of specific, neutral criteria." National had not alleged that it was selected on other than neutral criteria, so this test was not met.

Thus the court upheld the citations and the penalty assessed by the ALJ against National Engineering.

CASE QUESTIONS

1. Why do you suppose Congress wrote the law in a way that allowed inspectors to enter businesses without a warrant? Has the law been made ineffective by the cases requiring warrants where the business so demands?
2. What is the standard that OSHA must meet to obtain a warrant? Will OSHA be able to justify every inspection?
3. How might a business show that it was placed on the list for reasons other than the application of specific, neutral criteria?

STATE PROGRAMS

Some 25 states and territories (Puerto Rico, for example) have established their own occupational safety and health programs that operate under approval from OSHA. Two of the states (New York and Connecticut) only cover public sector employees, whereas the others cover both public and private sector employees. In order to "opt out" of the federal OSHA, the state must pass a law and issue regulations to establish standards that are "at least as effective" as federal OSHA and enforce them in an equivalent manner to gain exemption. The federal government monitors these programs and will reimburse the state for up to one-half the costs of the state program. Of course, the state regulations may be more strict than OSHA, but normally the states simply adopt the regulation issued by OSHA. In 1998, state inspectors conducted nearly 56,000 inspections, and found a total of 149,513 violations. Of the violation notices issued, 59,729 were for serious violations, 2,005 were for repeat violations, and 313 were for willful violations; penalties assessed for the violations were in excess of $53 million.

The following reading concerns the effectiveness of state health and safety regulations in North Carolina.

FIRE IN CHICKEN PLANT KILLS 25 WORKERS

In the fall of 1991, the Imperial Food Products plant in Hamlet, North Carolina, employed about 200 people. These employees—mostly black and female—cooked, weighed, and packed fried chicken parts for fast-food restaurants. Although it was a difficult job, with chicken parts moving swiftly down conveyer belts, it was about all there was in the small town of Hamlet.

In September 1991, a leak developed in a hydraulic line carrying chicken parts. Oil spilled onto the floor where it was ignited by the gas burners under the cooking vats. A huge ball of flame was created, accompanied by thick, black smoke. Terrified workers rushed to emergency exits, only to find most of them locked from the outside—apparently to keep the workers from stealing chicken parts. Some were able to break the locks, but 25 employees died in the fire from smoke inhalation.

North Carolina, like some 25 other states and territories, has developed its own occupational safety program, which exempts it from federal OSHA inspections. At the time of the fire, North Carolina had only 27 job safety inspectors to oversee some 163,000 workplaces. Under federal guidelines the state should have had 116 inspectors. Moreover, enforcement was decreasing. The number of inspections performed in 1990 was 35 percent less than the previous year. It was later learned that the Imperial Food Products plant had never been inspected. In addition to the obvious hazard of locked emergency exits, many other unsafe conditions existed at the Imperial plant.

This tragic incident led to a series of civil and criminal cases, a fine of over $800,000, and an overhaul of the North Carolina occupational safety and health program. After federal OSHA threatened to withdraw its approval for North Carolina to operate its own program, substantial additional funding and more inspectors were added to bolster the enforcement effort.

Sources: "Death on the Shop Floor," *Time Magazine* (September 16, 1991), pp. 28–29; "Fire at Chicken Processing Plant Kills 25," *Los Angeles Times* (September 4, 1991), p. 4; "What a Way to Watch Out for Workers," *Business Week* (September 23, 1991), p. 42.

SOCIAL/ETHICAL ISSUES

The Occupational Safety and Health Administration has never been funded at anywhere near the level necessary to inspect more than a fraction of workplaces in the United States. State enforcement varies, but in many cases it is even less vigorous due to low state funding. The chances are very good that a facility that does not engage in construction, meat-packing, logging, mining, or other high-hazard industrial manufacturing will rarely be visited by OSHA and may never be inspected at all.

What is the ethical duty of an employer to provide workers with a safe working environment by improving working conditions (that already meet minimum OSHA legal requirements), at potentially substantial cost, without the likely threat of OSHA penalties?

EMPLOYEE DUTIES AND RIGHTS

The OSHA law, while directing employees to follow all OSHA rules and regulations, contains no penalties for workers; it puts the primary responsibility for meeting the standards (and the penalties) on employers. Why? Apparently employers have the power, without involving the government in enforcement, to discipline workers who refuse to follow job safety rules, just as employers can with respect to any other rule of the workplace.

But what if the employer directs employees to do a job that they have good reason to believe is unsafe and hazardous? The OSHA law itself does not address this problem, but an OSHA regulation does give workers the right to refuse to perform an assignment in very limited situations. The requirements are the following: (1) the employee must reasonably believe that the job poses an imminent risk of death or serious bodily injury and (2) there is not sufficient time to seek redress from the employer or OSHA before the task must be performed. In this limited situation, the worker justifiably can refuse to perform the task. In all other cases, OSHA must be called in to determine whether or not the job is safe.

CRIMINAL PENALTIES

The Occupational Safety and Health Act is primarily enforced by inspections and the issuance of civil monetary penalties. OSHA also provides, in limited situations, the power to refer cases to the Justice Department for the filing of criminal charges. Lying to an OSHA inspector, falsifying records, and the willful (intentional) violation of health and safety regulations that results in the death of a worker are subject to criminal penalties under the act. The administration, however, has only rarely used this power to institute criminal charges, and few people have ever served any jail time for OSHA violations.

Because of the lack of criminal enforcement by federal officials, local prosecutors in cities such as Los Angeles, Chicago, New York, Milwaukee, and Austin, Texas, have filed murder and/or manslaughter charges against companies (and individual managers) when it was apparent that a worker's death was caused by a dangerous condition that the company knew about and could have prevented. The prosecutors were frustrated by the fact that employers were aware that conditions in the workplace put workers at risk of death or serious physical danger but chose to do nothing about it.

Several of these case resulted in convictions of employers and managers, although some of them were reversed for various technical reasons on appeal. In these cases, the prosecution argued that the defendant, although not specifically intending to kill anyone, acted with total reckless disregard for the consequences of his or her dangerous actions. Therefore, because this conduct resulted in the death of another, she or he can be held criminally responsible for that death. This argument resembles that used to charge with negligent homicide a driver who becomes so drunk that she or he does not know or care what she or he is doing and then causes an accident that kills another motorist. Similarly, a manager who knowingly sends workers into an unshored trench, demands that they use defective machinery, or causes them to breathe cyanide fumes continuously without respirators, may be charged with negligent homicide if a worker dies from those avoidable conditions.

The filing and prosecution of these cases received considerable national publicity. In response, OSHA began to refer more cases of willful violations resulting in death to the U.S. Attorney General for possible prosecution. However, the Justice Department brought only a few of them to court. Federal prosecutors were reluctant to ask for more referrals or spend too much time on these cases because the maximum criminal penalty for conviction on this charge is only six months in jail. By 1992, the number of criminal referrals had dropped again. However, commentators hope that the few criminal cases brought on the federal and state level are enough to awaken managers to their responsibilities regarding worker safety, leading companies to increase their efforts to correct workplace safety problems before accidents occur.

WORKERS' COMPENSATION

Although the purpose of OSHA is to make workplaces safer, the law does not provide aid of compensation to those employees who actually suffer work-related injuries. In the early part of this century, workers who were hurt on the job were forced to sue their employers in a tort action to obtain compensation. The burden of proof was on the employee to show that the employer was negligent in a way that directly caused the injury. Remember from our study of negligence that the plaintiff must prove that the defendant was "at fault" in order to prevail. Thus, in an occupational injury case, the worker would have to demonstrate that the employer's conduct fell below the standard of the mythical "reasonable employer," given the particular factual situation, and that this failure directly caused the worker's injury. This burden proved difficult for employees to meet, especially since the courts recognized several defenses that the employer could raise to avoid liability. For example, if the employee was negligent at all in causing the injury, the *contributory negligence* defense allowed the employer to win. If the accident was caused at least in part by the negligence of another worker, the **fellow-servant rule** barred the worker's claim. If the employee knowingly took on a risky job and was injured, sometimes the doctrine of *assumption of risk* barred recovery. The application of these common law theories resulted in the total denial of damages to many employees who suffered serious injuries at work.

fellow-servant rule: A common law defense of the employer that barred an employee from suing an employer for injuries caused by a fellow employee.

The public demanded a better system, and by the 1930s most states had enacted some form of workers' compensation program. These laws, while differing slightly from state to state, have similar basic features and provide that employees who are injured or become ill in the course of their work will be entitled to compensation. The costs of the system are primarily placed on the employers, who may be able to pass at least a portion of them along to their customers as a cost of production and who have a financial incentive to take actions to decrease workplace injuries (and thus lower their costs). All states now have such laws.

COVERAGE AND BENEFITS

Unlike lawsuits, in which a plaintiff can ask a jury for any amount of damages, including a large sum for "pain and suffering," the maximum compensation that may be awarded injured employees under workers' compensation is set forth in and limited by the governing state law.

Generally, employees who are unable to work due to a covered injury will receive the following:

1. Monetary compensation for their wage loss, usually some percentage of the worker's average wage, for the period of time he or she is disabled from working;
2. All reasonable medical and hospital expenses connected with the injury;
3. A fixed sum for a permanent injury or disability, such as the loss of an arm or an eye;
4. In many states, some type of rehabilitation assistance or compensation to help the worker recover physically and mentally so she or he can get back to work (and thus get off workers' compensation); and
5. A death benefit awarded to the family if the worker is killed.

Most employers purchase insurance to cover the expenses of workers' compensation, although some states may allow them to be "self-insured." In all states, there is some administrative agency that administers the program. This agency receives applications for compensation from workers, determines eligibility, and processes payments to workers. Often the employer will contest the worker's claim, arguing that the worker was not injured "in the course of employment" or that the injury does not really disable the person from working. The administrative agency will assign a referee or administrative law judge (ALJ) to hear evidence and make a decision in contested cases. After the case has been heard and appealed within the administrative system, it can be appealed to the regular court system.

ELIGIBILITY

Note that compensation is due to workers whose injuries "*arise out of*" and occur "*in the course of*" employment. Thus, the system is called "no-fault" because coverage does not depend on whether the injured worker (or coworker) was at fault (that is, negligent). As a result, the common law defenses once available to the employer have been basically eliminated. (Some state programs may vary.)

For example, if an automobile factory worker is injured in the plant when his hand is caught in a machine, the determination is simple: The employee is entitled to compensation. However, many workers, such as salespersons or regional managers of a retail business, travel from place to place in connection with their jobs. If the employee is injured in a car accident, 1,000 miles from her home office while driving to lunch, the determination as to whether the injury is covered by workers' compensation is tougher. More difficult still, suppose the worker breaks a leg while dancing at a sales convention in Las Vegas to which he was sent by his employer?

In general, employees are not covered when going to and from their work, but they are covered during lunch and other normal breaks on the job. Court decisions have developed a broad view toward what is "on the job," including some slightly "off task" activities within workers' compensation coverage if the activities are normal types of things that employees do. Some "goofing around" or "horseplay" while on the job is probably a fact of life in most employment situations. For example, an employee who jumped and broke an arm after another employee put a bug down his shirt, and a worker who fell down while swatting a cockroach in the company shower, were both held to be covered by the state workers' compensation system. However, most state workers' compensation laws take a hard line against drug and alcohol abuse—workers who were under the influence of drugs or alcohol at the time they were injured are generally denied benefits.

On the other hand, when it can be said that the employee has really "abandoned the job," or gone on a "frolic," injuries that occur will not be covered. For example, one employee of a steel factory was seriously injured when he was caught in a conveyer belt while he was attempting to cook a pot pie in one of the factory ovens. This act was so unrelated to his job that he was denied compensation. Another employee was refused compensation when she was injured in an auto accident while visiting her sister who lived 50 miles away from the city the employee had traveled to on a business trip.

In order to resolve difficult cases, the courts often look at the following factors: (1) whether the injury occurred during the time of employment and at the place of employment; (2) whether the employee was reasonably performing her or his duties, or at least doing something "incidental to" her or his employment; and (3) whether the activity was of any benefit to the employer or was an activity knowingly allowed by the employer. Courts weigh all these factors in each case and then decide if the injury is covered by workers' compensation.

EXCLUSIVE REMEDY

When an injury or illness is covered by workers' compensation, the worker may not sue the employer for damages—that is, workers' compensation is the *exclusive* remedy the employee has against the employer. However, the employee may still be able to institute a lawsuit against a third party who caused the injury (e.g., a manufacturer of the machine that caused the injury or the driver of the other automobile that caused the crash). If a recovery is obtained against a third party, generally the law requires the employee to reimburse the state workers' compensation system for the benefits previously paid.

CURRENT ISSUES

In recent years the "exclusive remedy" theory has begun to develop some exceptions as employees attempt to "get around" the general rule and sue their employers in court. Several cases around the country have held that a worker may sue an employer in court if the injury resulted from some "intentional" act by the employer.

Similarly, controversy has arisen in many states concerning the amount of workers' compensation benefits. Generally, the amount of the wage loss benefits the worker receives is quite a bit lower than what the worker would have received in actual wages. Many states put the figure at two-thirds of the worker's average weekly wage, but some use a much lower number. A tort lawsuit, for example, would likely result in much higher rewards, including damages for pain and suffering, attorneys' fees, and sometimes a large award of punitive damages. Unions and worker groups argue that since the employee has lost the right to sue the employer through the adoption of workers' compensation, the benefits should be more realistic.

Business associations, on the other hand, have lobbied their state legislatures for other reforms of the workers' compensation system. They complain that the overly broad and generous interpretations regarding what types of injuries are "work-related" (such as swatting a cockroach in the shower) have greatly increased the employer's costs of doing business. Employers also argue that the system makes it difficult to "cut off" malingerers—those workers who are really able to go back to work but would rather stay on workers' compensation. In addition, since each state program is slightly different, multistate employers must deal with a variety of standards, timelines, benefits, and administrative matters, thus adding significant cost to the employer.

UNEMPLOYMENT COMPENSATION

Another type of compensation program for workers is unemployment insurance. This system, created by the federal Social Security law and administered by the states, provides temporary financial support to certain workers who are "ready, willing, and able" to work but cannot find employment.

Employers pay a tax of at least 3 percent of the payroll to support this system, but the employer's percentage will increase if the "experience rating"—that is, the number of ex-employees who collect—is high. Employers who have one or more employees working a total of 20 weeks a year are subject to the law.

In order to qualify for benefits, the person claiming compensation must have been employed for a certain period of time during the preceding 52 weeks, must have earned a specific average wage, and must not have quit the job "without good reason attributable to the employer" or have been fired for serious misconduct. Employees who were fired for failing or refusing to take a drug test are generally denied unemployment benefits. In each state, the claimant must report to the unemployment office on a regular basis and verify that she or he is seeking work and has not turned down suitable employment. The benefits are fairly modest, and usually last for a maximum of 26 weeks, although in times of high unemployment federal legislation sometimes extends this period.

As with workers' compensation, an administrative agency in each state determines eligibility, hears contested cases, and pays benefits. A claimant for unemployment compensation, however, must be able to work and must actively be seeking work.

THE FAIR LABOR STANDARDS ACT

Until the 1930s the federal government was not significantly involved in regulating labor and employment issues. The first wage and hour and child labor laws enacted by Congress were held unconstitutional by the courts. However, in 1938 the *Fair Labor Standards Act* (*FLSA*) was enacted and upheld by the Supreme Court. The act established a minimum wage for covered employees, required that those employees be paid extra for overtime work, and set forth protections for younger employees.

BASIC COVERAGE

The FLSA covers all employers if any aspect of their business affects, or is involved in, interstate commerce, which thus includes most employers. Civilian federal employees and state and local government workers are also covered. A few specific industries, such as fishing, agriculture, and some retail establishments, are not covered. "Executive, professional, and managerial" positions (including salespersons) are not covered if they involve "discretion."

Contrary to what many people believe, the FLSA does not contain provisions addressing lunch hours, break times, vacation or holiday periods, sick leave, or fringe benefits. Those matters are left to state regulation or to the employer and employees to work out.

MINIMUM WAGE AND OVERTIME

When Congress enacted the FLSA in 1938, the *minimum wage* was set at 25 cents an hour. In the years since then, the minimum wage has been raised a number of times; most recently, it was raised in 1997 to $5.15 per hour. Because raising the minimum wage requires legislative action by Congress and must be approved by the President, attempts to raise the minimum wage often become involved in partisan political disputes. (For example, in 1999, Congressional Republicans proposed raising the minimum wage but included large tax breaks for employers as well, which were opposed by President Clinton; as a result, the minimum wage remained at $5.15 per hour.) The 1997 legislation raising the minimum wage also included several special wage provisions: (1) employees under 20 years of age may be paid $4.25 per hour for their first 90 days of employment (this rate rises to $5.15 when they reach 20 or work more than 90 days—whichever comes first); (2) full-time students employed in retail stores, agriculture, or colleges and universities may be paid 85 percent of the minimum wage, and are restricted to working no more than 20 hours per week when school is in session; and (3) workers whose productive capacity is impaired by a physical or mental disability may be paid less than the minimum wage if the employer has been certified by the U.S. Secretary of Labor. Covered employees must be paid at least minimum wage for the first 40 hours of work per week. For additional hours, employees are to receive *overtime pay* at one and one-half times the regular rate, although there are many technical aspects to this standard.

In general, each week of employment is treated separately. For example, if an employee works 50 hours in one week, he or she must receive 50 percent additional pay per hour for the extra 10 hours. The employer cannot average an employee's 30 hours one week with 50 hours the next week to make two 40-hour weeks. A worker who is paid on a commission or piecework basis must still receive at least the minimum wage for whatever hours worked. Employers whose workers regularly receive tips may credit up to 40 percent against the minimum wage if the employees actually receive that much in tips. Food and lodging provided to employees may also count as partial credit against the minimum wage.

CHILD LABOR PROVISIONS

The FLSA includes provisions designed to prohibit the employment of children in hazardous occupations and to prevent their working excessive amounts of time during their schooling years. The requirements of the law apply to those workers under the age of 18 years only. Some of the provisions are as follows:

1. Persons of 14 and 15 years of age may not work during school hours at all and may only work three hours on a school day and eight hours on a non–school day. These persons may not work more than 18 hours in a school week or 40 hours in a non–school week. They may not start work before 7:00 A.M. or end after 7:00 P.M. (9:00 P.M. in the summer). They may not be employed in hazardous jobs (as defined next).

2. Persons 16 and 17 years of age are not covered by the hour restrictions for younger workers. However, they may not work in "hazardous" occupations, such as mining, logging, roofing, excavation, the operation of certain types of power machines, or those involving radioactive substances.

The law, like most laws, provides for some exceptions. Younger workers employed by their parents, who work as actors, in entertainment, or who deliver newspapers are exempt from the child labor requirements of the FLSA.

The following case, decided by an ALJ in the U.S. Department of Labor, concerns the enforcement of the child labor provision of the FLSA.

MARSHALL V. GENERAL MOTORS CORP.

23 Wage & Hours Cases 1134

FACTS

LaVera Palice Holmes applied to a job with the Frigidaire Division of General Motors Corporation on Feb. 25, 1976. She listed her birth date on the application as March 2, 1957; she listed the same birth date on the medical insurance and benefits forms. The employer relied on her statements as to her age and made no efforts to verify her statements. She was hired and started employment March 1, 1976; her work involved the operation of a punch press. On March 9, 1976, she suffered an injury on the job, which resulted in the amputation of her left arm below the elbow. She was hospitalized and underwent surgery because of the injury. She later made an application for benefits under the GM medical insurance plan; on that application she listed her birth date as March 2, 1958. During her hospitalization, her supervisor at Frigidaire began an effort to determine her true age. They contacted her high school to determine if her educational records showed her date of birth. The school replied that its records indicated her birth date as March 2, 1959. The supervisor then contacted the Health Department for Abbeville County, South Carolina, where she was born, to request a copy of her birth certificate. The certificate listed March 2, 1959 as her date of birth.

Upon learning of the accident that injured Holmes, the U.S. Department of Labor cited Frigidaire for violating the regulations under the FLSA that prohibit the employment of minors in dangerous occupations and assessed a penalty of $1,000 for the violation. (The operation of a punch press was one of the hazardous occupations identified in the regulations.)

DECISION

Frigidaire argued that it should not be held in violation of the child labor regulations, or in the alternative that it should not be subject to any penalty for the violation, because Holmes deliberately falsified her birth date and her age. Frigidaire also claimed that Holmes' appearance and her personal history indicated that she was at least 18 at the time she was hired. The ALJ held that Frigidaire had violated the child labor prohibitions of the FLSA by employing Holmes, a minor under the age of 18, in a dangerous occupation. Such conduct, whether intentional or unintentional, was a violation of the FLSA and the child labor regulations under FLSA. In considering whether to impose a penalty, the ALJ considered the employer's size, its past history of any violations, the seriousness of the violation, whether the act was willful, and whether any injury resulted from the violation. In this case, despite the fact that the violation was not willful, the minor (Holmes) suffered a serious injury that resulted in permanent disability. Although the ALJ did not condone Holmes' actions in falsifying her birth date and age, he upheld the penalty of $1,000 assessed against Frigidaire because the employer failed to take any steps to verify Holmes' age.

CASE QUESTIONS

1. Why should Frigidaire be subject to a penalty under FLSA when it was not aware of the fact that Holmes was a minor?
2. Can you think of any reasons why the FLSA prohibitions of child labor apply to both intentional and unintentional violations?
3. What steps, if any, could Frigidaire have taken to verify Holmes' age?

ENFORCEMENT

The FLSA is administered by the Wage and Hour Division of the Department of Labor, with offices in many cities across the country. The act requires employers to keep records and other documentation regarding their workers, ages, and hours worked and make such data available to inspectors. Civil and criminal fines may be assessed for violations of the FLSA, and surprise inspections do sometimes occur. Individual employees may also file suit on their own to recover back wages, overtime pay, and liquidated damages; they can also recover legal fees. Violations of the child labor laws, whether intentional or not, carry a penalty of $1,000 per violation. Employees who feel they may not have been paid the minimum wage or received the correct amount of overtime pay should contact their local Wage and Hour Division office.

PENSIONS AND RETIREMENT

THE EMPLOYEE RETIREMENT INCOME SECURITY ACT

Many, but certainly not all, employees accrue retirement and pension benefits through their employment. The employer often sets up a private retirement plan, and a certain amount of the employee's pay is withheld (often matched by a contribution from the employer) and sent to the pension administrator to hold and invest. When the worker retires, a sum of money, called a pension, will be paid to him or her on an annual or monthly basis, depending on how much is in his or her account. In a large company, these funds hold millions of dollars. The investment and use of this substantial fund of money is a very important and complex task.

In the past years incidents occurred in which these funds were not maintained carefully—the persons or companies controlling them used large amounts of money for their own purposes or abused them in other ways not in the best interests of the employees. Employees who had worked for a company for years were deprived of the pension benefits that they had earned. In 1974, in response to numerous instances of such pension fund mismanagement and abuse, Congress passed the *Employee Retirement Income Security Act* (*ERISA*) to protect the retirement pensions of workers. The act does not require that employers provide pensions for employees, but it does impose standards of conduct for persons having authority or control over pension fund assets. Such persons are known as **fiduciaries**; they must exercise their duties under the pension plan solely in the interests of the participants of the plan and their beneficiaries for the exclusive purpose of providing them with benefits. The fiduciaries are prohibited from dealing with the pension plan assets for their own interests and are prohibited from receiving any consideration or benefit personally from persons who do business with the plan. They are also required to disclose relevant financial information to employees and the Department of Labor. The act also specifies certain standards that pension plans must meet in order to entitle the employer to tax deductions for contributions to the pension plans.

fiduciaries: Persons with control of financial assets owned by others; the law imposes a duty on the fiduciary to act in the interest of the asset owners.

The ERISA standards apply to all employee welfare benefit plans, such as those providing medical coverage, disability benefits, death benefits, vacation pay, or unemployment benefits for employees, but the main focus of the act concerns pensions. ERISA sets minimum requirements for **vesting** of persons—that is, how long a pension plan participant must contribute before being entitled to a nonforfeitable right to payments from the plan. The act requires that pension plans meet one of two vesting schedules based on employees' length of service with the employer: (1) Employees must either become entirely vested after completing five years of service or (2) The company must vest gradually beginning after three years of service and becoming fully vested after seven years. ERISA also sets minimum funding standards, requiring employers to set aside a sufficient amount of funds each year to cover the benefit liabilities that have accrued, or accumulated, under the plan during that year.

vesting: Becoming entitled to a nonforfeitable pension upon retirement.

The act created the Pension Benefit Guarantee Corporation (PBGC) to insure employees against the loss of pension benefits when an employer terminates a **defined-benefit pension plan**—that is, one that ensures participants a specified monthly income upon their retirement. (The other type of pension plan is called a **defined contribution plan**; under such a plan, employees pay a specified amount each month during their employment. Upon retirement, the employees receive the income generated by their contributions. Such plans are not subject to the PBGC insurance provisions because they do not present underfunding problems.) PBGC will pay a monthly benefit to plan participants, up to a maximum monthly amount. It finances this pension insurance program by charging a premium to employers offering defined-benefit pensions. An employer who terminates an insufficiently funded pension plan is liable to the PBGC for 100 percent of the underfunding, subject to a limit of 30 percent of the employer's net worth; this liability is treated as a tax lien against the property of the employer. In one well-publicized example, LTV, a steel company experiencing financial difficulties, terminated an underfunded pension plan. PBGC began to make payments to the affected participants. The steel company subsequently set up a new pension plan for existing employees. The PBGC then ruled that LTV was also liable for all the benefits due to participants under the terminated plan. LTV sued to challenge that ruling. The Supreme Court upheld the PBGC ruling holding LTV liable [*PBGC v. LTV Corp.*, 496 U.S. 633 (1990)].

defined-benefit pension plan: Plan paying employees a specified amount each month upon retirement.

defined contribution pension plan: Pension plan in which employees or the employer pay a specified amount into the employee's pension account.

The reporting and disclosure requirements of ERISA and the duties and obligations of fiduciaries are enforced by the Department of Labor. The Internal Revenue Service enforces the vesting and funding requirements. Individual participants in pension plans may sue to enforce their rights under the act. ERISA also provides for criminal penalties for willful violations of the fiduciary requirements and the reporting and disclosure provisions; persons may be fined up to $5,000 and receive up to one year in jail, and corporations and unions are subject to fines up to $100,000. Suits to enforce ERISA provisions may be brought in federal or state courts, but any state laws that relate to pensions or benefit plans are preempted by §514 of ERISA.

SUMMARY

Federal and state statutes regulate a myriad of elements of employment in U.S. workplaces. Since the 1960s federal law has prohibited discrimination in all aspects of employment based on race, and recent statutes ban any discrimination based on age or disability. From the moment that an employee begins work, the OSHA controls the standards of safety and health protection that must be provided by the employer, and workers' compensation laws establish the compensation and medical benefits to which workers are entitled if they are injured or become sick due to work-related causes. The federal FLSA regulates the minimum wages that must be paid to most employees and imposes restrictions on the number of hours and conditions under which children and youth may work. Pensions and retirement plans offered by employers are regulated by the federal ERISA.

CHAPTER QUESTIONS

1. El Paso Natural Gas Company required that the company pilots who flew the firm's fleet of private jets, upon reaching age 60, either take a nonflying job, if one was available, or retire. El Paso claimed that it was impractical to monitor the health of pilots after age 60 and based its rule on the Federal Aviation Authority requirement that commercial pilots retire at age 60. Does the El Paso Company's rule violate the ADEA? Is it a BFOQ? Explain. [*EEOC v. El Paso National Gas Co.*, 626 F. Supp. 182 (W.D. Tex. 1985)]
2. Lorraine Gargiul was employed as a kindergarten teacher by the Liverpool, New York, Central School District. In November 1994, she took an extended sick leave because of a back problem. In February 1995, she was contacted by the superintendent of schools, Virgil Tompkins, and told to report to Dr. Paul Wadsworth, the school district physician, for a physical examination. Gargiul informed Tompkins that she would be able to return to work on March 17, 1995, and submitted a certificate from her own physician. She also informed Tompkins that she had always gone to a female physician and that it was against her personal beliefs to be examined by a male physician. She refused to report to Dr. Wadsworth but instead offered to make an appointment with any female physician selected by Tompkins. In response, the Liverpool District School Board adopted a resolution requiring that Gargiul be examined by Dr. Wadsworth to determine whether she was physically able to return to work and suspending her without pay until she was examined by Dr. Wadsworth. The School Board again directed Gargiul to report to Dr. Wadsworth for an examination, and she again refused. The School Board then fired her for insubordination. She filed suit to challenge her firing. On what legal provisions can she base her suit? What legal arguments can she make to challenge the firing? Is she likely to win her suit? Explain your answer. [*Gargiul v. Tompkins*, 704 F. 2d 661 (2d Cir. 1983), vacated and remanded on other grounds, 465 U.S. 1016 (1983)]
3. Charlotte Adams was a police officer in North Little Rock, Arkansas. She was assigned to a street patrol position. After nearly two years on the job, she became pregnant. She notified her supervisor of her pregnancy and provided him with a letter from her doctor stating that she should be assigned to light duty work and that she would need six weeks of pregnancy leave at the end of her pregnancy. Her request for a light duty position was denied. She continued to request a light-duty position over the next five months, but all of her requests were refused. During the time Adams was making

her requests, a desk job was available on a "fill-in" basis when the regular person was unavailable; Adams, however, was never given the job even though she specifically requested it. Instead, the job was filled by two other employees who had temporary, non–job-related injuries. Adams was told by her supervisor that she would not get the desk job because her request "didn't fit within our leave policy." Because her requests were refused, Adams was forced to use up all of her vacation time and then to take six months unpaid leave. When she sought to return after her baby was born, she was told her former position was unavailable, and she was assigned to a less desirable position. Adams filed suit against the North Little Rock Police Department over its denial of her request. Under which legal provision(s) should she file her suit? What arguments can she make to support her claim? What arguments can the Police Department make to support its position? How should the court decide her claim? Why? [*Adams v. Nolan*, 962 F.2d 791 (8th Cir., 1992)]

4. An employer at a public works facility in Connecticut allowed workers to purchase a ping pong (table tennis) table and put it in the garage where they gathered before starting work. The employer allowed them to play one-half hour before work and after work and during their lunch hour. One of the employees seriously injured his ankle playing ping pong about five minutes before starting the working day. He was unable to work for a while and incurred medical expenses. Was he covered by workers' compensation? [*McNamara v. Town of Hamden*, 176 Conn.547 (1979)]

5. Global Home Products Enterprise manufactured cookies and candy and sold them through local groups, retail stores, and door-to-door salespeople. Charles Thomas was one of the door-to-door salespeople employed by Global in Charlotte, North Carolina. Thomas would hire children between the ages of 14 to 18 to sell Global products. Thomas then picked up the children at their homes, drove them to a neighborhood, and assigned them streets on which to sell cookies and candy. The children turned over all the proceeds from the sales to Thomas and in return, were paid $0.60 per box sold (out of the $3 purchase price). Thomas then drove the children home. On school nights, Thomas frequently kept the children out after 7 P.M., often returning them after 9 P.M. On weekends, the children often did not return to their homes until 11:30 P.M. or 12 midnight. Parents complained the children returned home tired and hungry; one parent filed a complaint with the Department of Labor. Has Thomas violated the child labor provisions of the FLSA? Has Global? Explain. [*Thomas v. Brock*, 615 F. Supp. 553 (W.D.N.C. 1985)]

6. Whirlpool Corp. manufactures household appliances at a plant in Ohio. Overhead conveyers transport various components throughout the plant. A mesh screen some 20 feet above the floor catches objects that fall off the conveyers. Maintenance workers are assigned to retrieve the objects from time to time. In June 1974, one worker fell through the screen and was killed. Certain repairs were then made to the screen, and workers were told to stand on the steel supports and not the screen. About a week later two other employees were told to retrieve objects from the screen and refused to do so, believing that it was still unsafe. They called OSHA, but no CO was available to come immediately. They were then told to punch out without being paid for the rest of their shift and that letters would be

placed in their files. OSHA filed suit on their behalf to clear their records. Who should win this suit and why? [*Whirlpool Corp. v. Marshall*, 445 U.S. 1 (1980)]

7. Ralph Forrisi was employed as a utility systems repairer and operator by Niagara Electric Utility Co. The job description for his position requires the worker to be able to climb stairs, ladders, and utility poles for emergency repairs and for routine maintenance. Forrisi developed a serious fear of heights (acrophobia) and requested to be transferred to a different job that would not require climbing; Niagara refused to transfer him and subsequently fired him because he was not able to perform the full range of his required job duties. Under what law(s) should Forrisi file suit to challenge his discharge? What legal arguments can he make against his discharge? What legal arguments can Niagara make to support the discharge? Who should win the suit? Explain. [*Forrisi v. Bowen*, 794 F. 2d 931 (4th Cir. 1986)]
8. DialAmerica Marketing, Inc. is a telephone marketing firm. A primary part of its business is the sale or renewal of magazine subscriptions by telephone to persons whose subscriptions are near expiration or have expired. Magazine publishers supply DialAmerica with the names of subscribers, and DialAmerica employees locate telephone numbers for those subscribers and contact them by phone in an effort to sell renewal subscriptions to them. DialAmerica employed "home researchers" to find the telephone numbers of subscribers; the home researchers were given a list of subscriber names and were expected to use telephone books or contact operators to find the telephone numbers of the subscribers. The home researchers would then complete cards with the subscribers' names and telephone numbers on them, filled out according to specific directions from DialAmerica. The completed cards were to be returned to DialAmerica the next week. The subscriber names were grouped in batches of 500, with the home researchers free to take as many batches as they wished. The home researchers were free to decide which weeks they would work and were not required to record the times or hours they worked on the batches. For each completed card, DialAmerica paid the home researchers 10 cents; the home researchers were given checks for their earnings, and DialAmerica did not deduct anything for taxes or for Social Security. The Department of Labor brought a complaint against DialAmerica, alleging that it violated the FLSA by paying its home researchers less than the minimum wage and by failing to keep records of the hours the home researchers worked. Dial America argued that the home researchers were not "employees." What arguments can you make for the Department of Labor's position that the home researchers were employees? What arguments can you make for DialAmerica's position that the home researchers were not employees? Who should win this case? Explain your answer. [*Donovan v. DialAmerica*, 757 F.2d 1376 (3rd Cir.), cert. denied, 474 U.S. 919 (1985)]
9. Robert E. McCrocklin was employed as an engineering writer by Butler Service Group. He worked in an unventilated room containing numerous partially enclosed cubicles; each cubicle was six feet wide and five feet deep and open at the top. Three of the nine people in the work area where McCrocklin worked were smokers; the smoke they produced entered McCrocklin's cubicle. McCrocklin was not allergic to smoke, but he found it

unpleasant and offensive; he objected to the carcinogenic effect of breathing smoke produced by other people in an enclosed room. McCrocklin made complaints about the smoke and ventilation problems in his workspace soon after he was hired. He was promised that conditions would be improved by the installation of an air circulation system, ceiling partitions, and doors on the cubicles. Despite the promises, the situation remained unchanged. McCrocklin tried to use portable fans to avoid the smoke, but it did not alleviate the problem. McCrocklin requested to be able to work at his home, but his request was denied. After four years, McCrocklin quit his job. His application to the California Employment Department (CED) for unemployment compensation was denied because CED held that he had quit his job voluntarily, without good cause. McCrocklin filed suit to challenge the denial of benefits. What arguments can McCrocklin make to support his position that he should receive unemployment benefits? What arguments can the CED make to support its position that McCrocklin quit without good cause? How should the court decide the case? Explain your answer. [*McCrocklin v. Employment Development Dept.* (*Butler Service Group, Inc.*), 156 Cal. App. 3d 1067 (Cal Ct. of App., 3rd Dist., 1984)]

10. The State of Wyoming had a series of laws requiring all law enforcement officers to retire at the age of 55 years. The laws apply even to Game Wardens, who enforce the state's hunting and fishing laws and regulations. The state justified the laws on the basis that by nature law enforcement jobs require possible strenuous physical exertion, and the physical conditioning of individuals starts to decline around age 55. Wyoming also argued that it is too difficult to screen all individuals to determine their level of fitness and conditioning, and therefore, a blanket retirement age is appropriate. Posby was a Game Warden who just reached his 55th birthday. He felt that the retirement law was in violation of the federal ADEA. Can he successfully file and win an ADEA complaint? Explain. [*EEOC v. Wyoming*, 460 U.S. 226 (1983)]

PRACTICAL EXERCISE

Adam Bradley is a surgical technician—he assists surgeons during operations—at the Harrington Cancer Clinic in Dallas. During an interview with a local paper, Bradley admitted that he is HIV positive—he is infected with the virus that causes AIDS. Upon learning that he is HIV positive, the operating room supervisor asks the clinic's chief administrator to transfer Bradley from the surgical technician position to a clerical position. The supervisor claims that Bradley poses a risk of accidentally infecting a patient during an operation. Although the possibility of such an incident may be slight, the consequences of such an incident would be catastrophic. The supervisor argues that the clinic should not take any chances that such an incident may occur. Bradley claims that the risk of infecting patients is very small and can be prevented by taking reasonable precautions during surgery. You are the executive assistant for the clinic's chief administrator. She has asked you to advise her regarding the decision of whether to transfer Bradley. What factors should be considered in making the decision? What recourse would Bradley have to challenge the transfer? Under what legislation could he bring suit? What would be the legal and ethical consequences of a patient being infected while undergoing surgery? What defenses could the clinic demonstrate?

Prepare a memorandum outlining your recommended decision, addressing and discussing all of these questions. See *Bradley v. University of Texas*, 510 U.S. 1119 (1994).

FURTHER INFORMATION

www.9to5.org/
9 to 5 National Association of Working Women.
www.worknwoman.com/
Women in the World of Work.
www.eeoc.gov/
The Equal Employment Opportunity Commission.
www.eeac.org/
The Equal Employment Advisory Council.
www.osha.gov/
The Occupational Safety and Health Administration.
www.dol.gov/elaws/flsa.htm
The U.S. Department of Labor Wage and Hour Division FLSA Advisor.

CHAPTER 22

LABOR–MANAGEMENT LAW AND REGULATION

LEARNING OBJECTIVES

After you have read this chapter, you should be able to:

1. Chronicle the development of labor relations law.
2. Describe the organization and procedures of the National Labor Relations Board and other provisions of the National Labor Relations Act.
3. List several unfair labor practices set out by the NLRA.
4. Discuss bargaining procedures and the administration and enforcement of collective arguments.
5. Compare labor relations in the public and private sectors.

CHAPTER OUTLINE

I. The Development of Labor Relations Law
II. Coverage of the NLRA
III. Provisions of the NLRA
IV. Unfair Labor Practices
V. Public Sector Employees

This chapter discusses labor management relations—the laws under which employees organize and join unions, and bargain collectively with their employers to determine wages and conditions of their employment. Are graduate students who teach classes considered employees of the university? Should they be able to organize in a union and bargain with the university over their working conditions? Should they have the right to strike? What about medical students who are working at hospitals as part of their internship or residency requirements? Should it matter whether the university is public or private? After reading this chapter, you should be able to answer those questions.

INTRODUCTION

Although the percentage of U.S. employees who are union members has been steadily declining over the past 40 years, the importance of labor relations and employment-related legal issues has been increasing (as noted in Chapter 21). Labor relations law remains a significant aspect of U.S. employment policy—the relevant legislation defines rights and duties for employers, whether their employees are unionized or not, and for employees whether they are or are not members of a union.

Workers join unions in order to have a voice in determining the terms and conditions of their employment. Collective bargaining between a union and employer is the primary means for such involvement. The rights of employees to join or organize unions and to bargain collectively with their employer are guaranteed under the *National Labor Relations Act* (*NLRA*). This chapter focuses on the NLRA, and the rights, duties, and obligations that it creates for both employees and employers.

THE DEVELOPMENT OF LABOR RELATIONS LAW

The rationale behind the at will doctrine (discussed in Chapter 19) is that the employer and employee are free to negotiate for a contract for a specific term if they so desire. However, in reality, most employees have very little bargaining power in relation to the employer. The employer's position in negotiating for a job is generally "take it or leave it." By acting jointly, however, employees can counter the employer's advantage. That is why employees join unions—there is strength in numbers, and their joint action creates bargaining power for the employees.

The first unions were craft guilds—groups of skilled employees who agreed to work under certain terms and conditions and for certain wages. All the members of the guild were bound by its rules and agreed not to work for employers who paid less than the specified wage. Employers were forced to pay the going wage or to face boycotts by the skilled workers.

Employers argued that the guilds' actions were conspiracies to increase wages and to interfere with the freedom of workers to contract with employers. Most courts in the early- to mid-19th century agreed with the employers' position; hence, unions were held to be criminal conspiracies. It was not until the 1842 case of *Commonwealth of Mass. v. Hunt* [45 Mass. (4 Met.) 111], that the Massachusetts Supreme Court held that unions were not per se illegal conspiracies; the court's opinion reflected an awareness of the growing public support of unions.

Although the years following the *Hunt* case were marked by a grudging tolerance on the part of the courts toward unions, employers still had several legal weapons to use against unions: the injunction, yellow dog contracts, and the antitrust laws.

Injunctions are court orders directing persons either to refrain from certain activity or, occasionally, to perform certain activity. Employers facing strikes or union boycotts would ask courts for injunctions against the union's activity; the courts, moreover, did not require the employer to show that the strike or boycott actually harmed its business. Often the injunctions were issued ***ex parte***, that is, with only the employer appearing before the court—the union would not have a chance to present its side to the court. Once an injunction was issued, it would be enforced by officers of the court. Union members who resisted were subject to fines and jail terms for contempt of court. The injunction effectively stopped the strike but failed to address the problem that caused the strike. The injunction prevented the union from taking any action against the employer, and the employer was free to continue the conduct that provoked the union.

injunctions: Court orders directing persons either to refrain from or perform certain activity.

***ex parte*:** A court proceeding in which only the party asking for the court action is present.

Yellow dog contracts were contracts of employment that required the employee to agree not to join a union. Because the contract made the promise not to join a union a condition of employment, the employer could legally fire any worker who joined a union for breach of his or her employment contract. The Supreme Court upheld the legality of yellow dog contracts in *Hitchman Coal Co. v. Mitchell* [254 U.S. 229 (1917)].

yellow dog contracts: Contracts requiring employees to agree not to join unions.

The antitrust laws (discussed in Chapter 16) also provided employers with another means to attack unions. In several celebrated cases, the courts held that union boycotts of employers' products were "combinations or conspiracies in restraint of trade" in violation of the Sherman Act. In *Loewe v. Lawlor* [208 U.S. 274 (1908)], the Supreme Court upheld a decision finding individual members of the United Hatters' Union liable for $240,000 in damages for a boycott of the products of D.E. Loewe Co. In response to the *Loewe* case, Congress amended the Clayton Act to provide that ". . . the labor of a human being is not a commodity or article of commerce . . ." and that labor unions and their members shall not be held to be "combinations or conspiracies in restraint of trade." Despite Congress's intention to exempt union activities from the antitrust laws, the Supreme Court held that there was no general grant of immunity for union activities and upheld, in *Duplex Printing Press Co. v. Deering* [254 U.S. 443 (1921)], an injunction against a union for organizing a national boycott of an employer's products.

LABOR LEGISLATION

Not until the Great Depression of the 1930s did Congress legislatively endorse the activities of labor unions. Part of Roosevelt's New Deal included recognition of unions and collective bargaining as a means to improve the economic lot of workers.

The first piece of labor legislation was the *Norris-LaGuardia Act*, passed in 1932. The Norris-LaGuardia Act limited the ability of federal courts to issue injunctions in labor disputes: Injunctions could only be issued after both parties appeared before the court and only if the court was convinced that irreparable harm to property was likely to occur and the police were unwilling or unable to protect the property. The act also made yellow dog contracts unenforceable in any federal court. The Norris-LaGuardia Act had the effect of ensuring that the federal judiciary played a neutral role in any labor dispute. Although the act only applied to federal courts, a number of states passed similar laws (known as "little Norris-LaGuardia acts") applying the same restrictions to their state courts.

The second major piece of labor legislation was the *NLRA*, also known as the *Wagner Act*, passed in 1935. The Wagner Act establishes a legislative framework for industrial relations; specifically, it provides for legal recognition of unions and imposes on employers a duty to bargain with the unions representing their employees. The most important provision of the act concerns the right of employees to join unions and to engage in collective bargaining and other concerted activity for mutual aid and protection. Employer actions that interfere with or restrain those rights are **unfair labor practices**. (Although the Wagner Act only defined unfair labor practices by employers, later legislation added a list of unfair union labor practices.) The Act created the National Labor Relations Board (NLRB), an administrative agency to enforce and administer the act's provisions.

unfair labor practices: Actions that violate the rights granted under the labor regulations legislation.

Under the protection of the Wagner Act, unions flourished; many commentators, however, criticized the act and the NLRB as being too pro-union. Public and Congressional concern over union power led to the passage of the *Labor Management Relations Act*, also known as the *Taft-Hartley Act*, in 1947. Taft-Hartley amended the NLRA by creating a list of union activities that are unfair labor practices and also providing that employees also have the right to refrain from joining unions or engaging in concerted activities. The act outlawed the **closed shop**, a contract provision that requires the employer to hire only union members. Lastly, the act also empowered the President to forestall strikes that threaten the national health or safety.

closed shop agreements: Contract provisions requiring the employer to hire only employees who are already union members.

The third major piece of labor legislation was the *Labor-Management Reporting and Disclosure Act*, or the *Landrum-Griffin Act*, passed in 1959. Landrum-Griffin was passed in response to concerns about union racketeering and abusive practices aimed at union members. The act establishes specific rights for individual union members against the union and prohibits financial abuses, manipulation of union election procedures, and racketeering by union officials.

These laws provide the legislative framework for private sector labor relations in the United States.

NATIONAL LABOR RELATIONS BOARD

The NLRB is the administrative agency that administers and enforces the provisions of the National Labor Relations Act.[1] The NLRB is really made up of two independent authorities within the same administrative structure: the five-member National Labor Relations Board and the Office of the General Counsel. The General Counsel is the chief administrative officer in charge of the day-to-day operation of the agency and is appointed by the President, subject to confirmation by the Senate. The General Counsel also oversees the prosecutorial efforts of the agency to enforce the provisions of the act. The NLRB has 33 regional offices, headed up by regional directors, who report to the General Counsel.

[1] For the purposes of this chapter, we will refer to the legislation resulting from the Wagner Act and the Taft-Hartley Act as the National Labor Relations Act (NLRA). Scholars and labor lawyers differ in whether the legislation should be referred to as the NLRA or the Labor Management Relations Act, or both.

The five-member National Labor Relations Board is the judicial branch of the agency and acts as a specialized court of appeals. Its members are appointed by the President and must be confirmed by the Senate. They hear appeals from decisions by the agency's administrative law judges (ALJs), who act as the agency's trial judges. The ALJs are independent of both the General Counsel and the Board; they decide unfair labor practice complaints filed under the NLRA. The ALJs' decisions involve both findings of fact and of law together with a recommended remedial order; the decisions are subject to review by the Board, which can affirm, amend, reverse, or vary an ALJs' decision.

Procedures The NLRB handles two kinds of cases: those involving allegations of unfair labor practices and those involving **representation questions**. The NLRB does not initiate proceedings; rather, it responds to complaints of unfair labor practices and to petitions for elections. Unfair labor practice cases are initiated by the filing of a complaint within six months of the alleged violation, with the regional director of an NLRB regional office. The regional director and office staff investigate the complaint and may dismiss it if it lacks merit. If the complaint is valid, the regional office will attempt to settle the dispute; failing that, the regional director will issue a formal complaint. The complaint is served on the alleged violator, and a formal hearing on the complaint is held before an ALJ. After the ALJ issues a decision, either party has 20 days to file exceptions to the decision. If there are no exceptions, the decision becomes final; if there are exceptions, they are reviewed by the Board, which then issues its decision and remedial order.

representation questions: Cases dealing with employees seeking to join unions or unions seeking to represent employees.

Remedies for unfair labor practices under the Act usually involve a cease and desist order, directing the wrongdoer to stop the illegal act and to refrain from it in the future. The remedy may also include reinstatement or hiring of employees illegally fired or refused a job, payment of compensation for lost wages and benefits, remedial seniority, and payment of legal fees. The NLRB does not have the power to award punitive damages—only compensation for actual losses can be awarded.

The Board's orders are subject to judicial review by the federal courts of appeals; any party to the case may seek review, and the Board may seek enforcement of its order before the courts of appeals. The Board may also seek injunctions in federal courts to prohibit conduct violating the NLRA. Upon review, the court examines whether the NLRB was acting within its jurisdiction under the Act and whether the NLRB's decision is supported by substantial evidence on the record as a whole. (See Chapter 5 for a discussion of judicial review.) After the court of appeals issues its decision, any affected party may seek a further appeal by petitioning the U.S. Supreme Court to review the decision. The Supreme Court generally grants review only to cases involving novel issues of law or when the courts of appeals are divided on the issue; hence, only a very small percentage of cases reach this final step.

Representation cases involve employees choosing whether to be represented by a union as their exclusive bargaining agent. A union or group of employees may petition a regional office of the NLRB to hold an election to determine whether the employees of an employer wish to be represented by a union. The NLRB also considers **decertification petitions** filed by employees who no longer wish to be represented by a union. The petitions must be supported by evidence that at least 30 percent of the employees in the appropriate group support the union (or the decertification effort). The regional office staff

decertification petitions: Petitions by employees seeking to revoke a union's right to represent them.

investigates the petition to determine if the employer and employees are subject to the NLRA and whether an election can be held—an election cannot be held if a valid election took place within the past 12 months or if a valid collective bargaining agreement covering the employees exists. If an election is appropriate, the regional director will hold a hearing to determine the appropriate **bargaining unit**—the particular group of employees seeking union representation, the eligibility of employees to vote in the election, and the administrative details of holding the election (the date for the vote, the location of ballot boxes, and so on).

bargaining unit: The group of employees that is represented by a union—the basic unit of constituency for labor relations.

The employer and the union campaign to influence how the employees should vote during the period prior to the actual election. The purpose of the election is to determine the employees' choice; conduct that coerces, intimidates, or threatens the employees will invalidate the election results. Because the employees are dependent on the employer for their economic livelihood, the NLRB takes the position that they will be susceptible to employer threats, either explicit or implicit, of dire consequences such as firings, plant closing, or relocation if the union wins the election. Unfair labor practices committed by either party during the campaign may also invalidate the election. When such conduct occurs, the other party can file an objection to such conduct with the NLRB. Objections must be filed no later than five days after the election.

The election is by secret ballot, and the employees vote on whether they wish to be represented by a union. There may also be two or more unions seeking representation rights; voters must choose among the unions or choose for no union representation. The choice receiving a majority of votes cast is declared the winner; if no choice receives a majority, then a runoff election is held between the top two choices. After the votes are counted, the results are certified by the regional director. If a union wins, it becomes the exclusive bargaining agent for that group of employees; if employees choose no union representation, the employer is free from another election for at least 12 months.

If either party has filed objections, the regional office's staff will investigate the objections and hold a hearing on them. If the objections are upheld, the election results will be set aside; if the objections are rejected by the regional director, the election results will be certified.

COVERAGE OF THE NLRA

The NLRA gives the NLRB authority to deal with labor disputes "in or affecting commerce"; the NLRB has adopted jurisdictional guidelines that require a firm or operation to involve commerce (sales or purchases of goods) of at least $50,000 yearly to ensure that a firm has at least a minimal effect on commerce. The Act also excludes certain employers and employees from its coverage. Section 2(2) of the NLRA excludes all public section employers (federal, state, or local) and railroads and airlines (which are both subject to the Railway Labor Act instead). Section 2(3) of the NLRA excludes the following employees: agricultural laborers, persons employed as domestic servants within another person's home, persons employed by their parent or spouse, supervisors (who have the power to hire, fire, direct, or discipline other employees), independent contractors, and persons working for employers covered by the Railway Labor Act. In addition to the statutory exceptions to NLRA coverage, the courts have created other exceptions. The courts have held that parochial schools and employers closely identified with, or operated by, foreign governments are outside the NLRB's jurisdiction, and that persons who are managerial employees—those who formulate or carry out management policies—and confidential employees—those whose jobs give them access to confidential labor relations information of the employer—are excluded from the act's definition of employee.

The Supreme Court, in *NLRB v. Town & Country Electric, Inc.* [516 U.S. 85 (1995)] held that union organizers hired by construction contractors but also being paid by a union to help unionize the contractor's workers are employees under §2(3) and enjoy the protections of the NLRA. The following case involves that question in the context of the legality of an employer's refusal to hire persons who are also in the union. The NLRB, reversing previous decisions that held medical students working in hospitals as residents or interns as a requirement of their medical education were students and not employees under the NLRA, recently decided that medical interns and residents are employees within the definition of §2(3) [*Boston Medical Center*, 330 NLRB No. 30 (Nov. 26, 1999)].

The following case involves the question of whether certain nurses, who direct other nursing personnel as part of their work to care for patients, were supervisors as defined in Section 2(11) of the NLRA.

NLRB V. HEALTH CARE & RETIREMENT CORPORATION OF AMERICA

511 U.S. 571 (1994)

FACTS

The NLRB held that Health Care & Retirement Corp. (HCRC), which operated the Heartland Nursing Home, committed unfair labor practices in disciplining four staff nurses. The staff nurses, who are the senior ranking employees on duty after 5 P.M. during the week and at all times on weekends, are responsible to ensure adequate staffing, make daily work assignments, monitor and discipline aides (who directly provide patient care) to ensure proper performance, resolve aides' problems and grievances, and evaluate aides' performances. HCRC argued that the four nurses involved in this case were supervisors and were therefore excluded from the protection of the NLRA. The ALJ concluded that the nurses were not supervisors, because their supervisory work did not "equate to responsibly directing the aides in the interest of the employer," noting that "the nurses' focus is on the well-being of the residents rather than of the employer." The NLRB affirmed the ALJ's decision, holding that the nurses' direction of less-skilled employees, in the exercise of the nurses' professional judgment for the treatment of patients, is not authority exercised "in the interest of the employer." The NLRB takes that position because professional employees, especially registered nurses, would otherwise be generally excluded from the right to organize and bargain under the NLRA. The attorneys for HCRC argued that the NLRB position contradicts the plain language of §2(11).

Section 2(11) defines a supervisor as: "[a]ny individual having authority, in the interest of the employer, to hire, transfer, suspend, lay off, recall, promote, discharge, assign, reward, or discipline other employees, or responsibly to direct them, or to adjust their grievances, or effectively to recommend such action, if in connection with the foregoing the exercise of such authority is not of a merely routine or clerical nature, but requires the use of independent judgment."

The attorneys for HCRC sought judicial review of the NLRB's decision, and the U.S. Court of Appeals for the Sixth Circuit reversed, holding that the four licensed practical nurses involved in this case were supervisors. The

NLRB then appealed to the U.S. Supreme Court.

DECISION

Because the NLRA does not grant the rights to organize unions and bargain collectively to supervisory employees, the statutory definition of supervisor is essential in determining which employees enjoy those rights.

The Supreme Court stated that deciding whether a worker is a supervisor under §2(11) requires the resolution of three questions, which must each be answered in the affirmative if an employee is to be deemed a supervisor. First, does the employee have authority to engage in one of the 12 listed activities? Second, does the exercise of that authority require "the use of independent judgement"? Third, does the employee hold and exercise that authority "in the interest of the employer"?

This case concerns only the third question: Do the charge nurses exercise their authority to direct other employees "in the interest of the employer"? The NLRB's position sets up a false split between acts taken in connection with patient care and acts taken in the interest of the employer. That split, or dichotomy, makes no sense. Patient care is the business of a nursing home, and it follows that attending to the needs of the nursing home patients, who are the employer's customers, is in the interest of the employer. There is no basis for the NLRB's blanket assertion that supervisory authority exercised in connection with patient care is somehow not in the interest of the employer. The NLRB's test is inconsistent with the ordinary meaning of the phrase "in the interest of the employer," and would render portions of the statutory definition in §2(11) meaningless. The NLRA is to be enforced according to its own terms, not by creating legal categories inconsistent with its meaning, as the NLRB has done in nurse cases. The Court held that the Court of Appeals was correct in deciding that the NLRB's position was inconsistent with the language of the statute.

Justices Ginsburg, Blackmun, Stevens, and Souter dissented, arguing that the NLRB position was necessary to ensure that professional employees are able to exercise the right to join unions and to bargain collectively under the NLRA.

CASE QUESTIONS

1. What is the test to determine whether an employee is a supervisor under the NLRA?
2. Why does the NLRB take the position that the staff nurses exercise their duties in the interest of the residents' health care rather than in the employer's interest? What is the basis of the NLRB's position? Explain.
3. What is the significance of the determination that the staff nurses are supervisors under the NLRA? What implications does this case have for other professional employees such as doctors and lawyers? Explain.

PROVISIONS OF THE NLRA

The basic provision of the NLRA is contained in §7, which states:

> Employees shall have the right to self-organization, to form, join or assist labor organizations, to bargain collectively through representatives of their own choosing, and to engage in other concerted activities for the purpose of collective bargaining or other mutual aid or protection, and shall also have the right to refrain from any and all such activities . . .

SECTION 7 RIGHTS

Section 7 gives rights to all employees under the NLRA; employees need not be members of labor unions in order to enjoy such rights. Section 7 requires that the conduct of employees be "concerted" for the purpose of collective bargaining or other mutual aid or protection, in order to be protected. The effect of §7 protection means that the employees cannot be disciplined or discharged for their conduct. Such protected conduct includes discussing the need for a union or the need to improve working conditions with other employees, and attempts to get fellow employees to join a union. But the protection of §7 extends to other conduct as well—in one case, a group of non-union employees who walked off the job to protest the extremely cold temperatures inside the shop were protected under §7, as was an employee who circulated a petition about the management of the company's credit union.

There are limits to the protection under §7. Employees acting individually, without the support or authorization of fellow employees or for purposes unrelated to collective bargaining, mutual aid, or protection, may not be protected. The following case involves the question of whether an employee, acting alone to exercise a right under the collective agreement, is within the protection of §7.

NLRB V. CITY DISPOSAL SYSTEMS

465 U.S. 822 (1984)

FACTS

James Brown was employed as a truck driver by City Disposal Systems, a trash-hauling and disposal firm. The employees of City Disposal were members of Local 247 of the International Brotherhood of Teamsters Union. The collective agreement covering the employees provided that the employer would not require employees to operate any vehicle or equipment that was not in safe operating condition; employees were given the right to refuse to operate unsafe equipment. When the truck he usually drove needed repairs, Brown was ordered to drive a truck that had had brake problems the previous day. Brown refused to drive that truck, stating that there was something wrong with its brakes; Brown did not specifically refer to the collective agreement for his refusal. His supervisor again directed Brown to drive the truck, and when Brown again refused, he angrily directed Brown to go home. Later that day, Brown was notified that he had been fired; he immediately returned to work to seek reinstatement but was unsuccessful.

Brown filed an unfair labor practice complaint with the NLRB against City Disposal, challenging his discharge. The ALJ hearing the complaint held that the discharge violated Brown's rights under §7 of the NLRB and that Brown's refusal to drive the unsafe truck was concerted action under the language of §7. The NLRB affirmed the ALJ's decision and ordered that Brown be reinstated with back pay. City Disposal sought judicial review of the NLRB decision by the Court of Appeals; the Court of Appeals held that Brown's action was not concerted activity because he acted solely on his own behalf. The NLRB appealed to the U.S. Supreme Court on the issue of whether an individual employee's actions could be "concerted" within the meaning of §7.

DECISION

The Supreme Court referred to the language of §7 of the NLRA, which grants employees the right to ". . . form, join or assist labor organizations, to bargain collectively through representatives of their own choosing, and to engage in other concerted activities for the purpose of collective bargaining or other mutual aid or protection. . . ." The Court then looked to the NLRB ruling in the *Interboro Contractors, Inc.* case, which held that an individual employee's assertion of a right granted under a collective bargaining agreement is recognized as concerted activity and is protected under §7. The board's rationale for the *Interboro* doctrine was that exercising a right granted under a collective agreement is an extension of the concerted process of collective bargaining that produced the agreement and that the exercise of a right under a collective agreement affects the rights of all employees covered by that agreement. The Court agreed that the assertion of a right granted under a collective agreement was "unquestionably an integral part of the process that gave rise to the agreement. . . . Moreover, when an employee invokes a right grounded in the collective bargaining agreement, he does not stand alone. Instead, he brings to bear on his employer the power and resolve of all his fellow employees." The Court held that the NLRB's *Interboro* doctrine preserved the integrity of the entire collective bargaining process, which includes the invoking of rights under the agreement by individual employees. "As long as the employee's actions are based on a reasonable and honest belief that he is being, or has been, asked to perform a task that he is not required to perform under his collective bargaining agreement, and the statement or action is directed toward the enforcement of a collectively bargained right, there is no justification for overturning the Board's judgment that the employee is engaged in concerted activity. . . ." The Court therefore reversed the decision of the Court of Appeals and upheld the NLRB determination that Brown had been engaged in concerted activity protected under §7.

CASE QUESTIONS

1. What right was Brown attempting to exercise? What was the source of that right?
2. How is seeking to enforce a collective agreement perceived to be "an extension of the bargaining process"?
3. Would an individual employee who was not a union member be protected by §7 in acting alone to enforce a right to a safe workplace?

UNFAIR LABOR PRACTICES

The NLRA sets out a list of actions by employers and unions that interfere with employees' rights under the act; these unfair labor practices are prohibited by the act. Section 8(a) lists unfair labor practices by employers, and §8(b) lists unfair labor practices by unions. Section 8(e) also prohibits certain conduct by unions. The following discussion of unfair labor practices focuses on the conduct, whether by union or employer, prohibited by §8.

SECTIONS 8(A)(1) AND 8(B)(1): INTERFERENCE WITH §7 RIGHTS

Sections 8(a)(1) and 8(b)(1) prohibit any conduct that interferes with, coerces, or restrains employees in the exercise of their rights under §7 of the NLRA. The NLRB has held that any conduct that has the natural tendency to restrain or coerce employees in the exercise of the §7 rights is prohibited. Actual coercion or restraint of employees need not be shown for a violation, nor is intention to coerce or restrain employees required. Employer threats to fire employees who join unions, threats to close the plant if the employees vote for a union, employer or union threats of violence, interrogation of employees as to their union sympathies, union attempts to force employees to join, and actual violence directed against employees are all examples of conduct that violate §8(a)(1) or §8(b)(1). Such conduct often occurs during union organizing campaigns. Unreasonable restrictions on employees' organizing activities also violate §8(a)(1) and §8(b)(1). Employers may restrict such efforts by employees to nonworking times (such as lunch break or coffee breaks) and to nonworking areas (e.g., washrooms, locker rooms, cafeteria, parking lots); total prohibitions on employees' organizing activities on the employer's property violate §8(a)(1). Under some circumstances, the employer may also be required to allow union organizers who are not employees onto the property to contact employees. The following Supreme Court decision discusses that requirement.

LECHMERE, INC. V. NLRB

112 S. Ct. 841 (1992)

FACTS

Lechmere operated a retail store located at a shopping plaza in Newington, Connecticut. Lechmere owns the property on which the store is located, along with the parking lot adjacent to the store. A grassy strip of land separates the parking lot from an adjacent highway; the grassy strip is public property. Lechmere company policy prohibited solicitation or distribution of handbills or leaflets of any kind on its property; the policy was posted in all entrances to the store and was consistently enforced against all groups, including the Girl Scouts and the Salvation Army.

Local 919 of the United Food and Commercial Workers Union sought to unionize the employees of Lechmere. After a full-page newspaper ad by the union drew little response, union organizers entered Lechmere's parking lot and placed handbills on the windshields of the cars parked in the corner of the lot used by employees. Lechmere's manager confronted the organizers, informed them of the company policy, and ordered them to leave; Lechmere employees removed the handbills. The union organizers attempted to distribute handbills several other times but each time were asked by store officials to leave, and the handbills were removed. The union later attempted to distribute handbills from the grassy strip of land and picketed there as well. The union then filed an unfair labor practice complaint with the NLRB, alleging that Lechmere had violated §8(a)(1) by barring the organizers from company property. The ALJ upheld the union complaint; the NLRB affirmed and ordered Lechmere to cease and desist from barring the organizers from the parking lot. The U.S. Court of Appeals for the First Circuit enforced the NLRB decision, and Lechmere appealed to the U.S. Supreme Court.

DECISION

The Court referred to the language of §7 of the NLRA, which, it held, granted rights only to employees, not to unions or to nonemployee union organizers. In some instances, the Court held, an employer may be required to allow the nonemployee organizers onto its property when it is necessary to allow employees to exercise their §7 right to organize or to join unions.

The Court then looked to its decision in *NLRB v. Babcock & Wilcox Co.*, which considered the circumstances in which the employer is required to allow organizers access to its property. *Babcock & Wilcox* held that, as a rule, an employer is not required to allow nonemployee organizers to distribute union literature on its property; however, when "the location of a plant and the living quarters of the employees place the employees beyond the reach of reasonable union efforts to communicate with them," the employer may be required to allow the organizers access to "permit communication of information on the right to organize . . . ."

The court stated that its prior cases determined that the employer was required to allow access to the nonemployee organizers when "unique obstacles" prevented other means of communication with the employees. The NLRB, in deciding in favor of the union against Lechmere, considered the availability of "reasonably effective alternative means of communication with the employees." The Court held that the NLRB had erred by focusing on whether other available means of communication were reasonably *effective*; *Babcock & Wilcox* required focus on whether other means of communication were reasonably *available*—did the "inaccessibility of the employees make ineffective the reasonable attempts by nonemployees to communicate with them through the usual channels?" Where reasonable alternative means of access to the employees exist, the employer is not required to allow nonemployee organizers onto its property. Classic examples of when an employer will be required to allow access to the organizers include, according to the court, cases in which employees work in logging camps, mining camps, or resort hotels, where employees are isolated from the reach of usual means of communication.

Because Lechmere's employees did not reside on company property, the court held that they were not beyond the reach of usual means of communication; the employees were not "inaccessible" in the sense required by *Babcock & Wilcox*. The Court emphasized that "*access* to employees, not success in winning them over, is the critical issue" [emphasis added]; because the union failed to establish that there were unique obstacles frustrating its access to the Lechmere employees, the NLRB erred in finding that Lechmere had committed an unfair labor practice by denying the union organizers access to its property. The Court reversed the Court of Appeals decision and refused enforcement of the NLRB's order.

CASE QUESTIONS

1. Why would the employer want to prohibit all solicitation and distribution of literature by nonemployees?
2. Why would the union want to solicit employees at their workplace? What other means might be available to the union to reach the employees?
3. Under what circumstances must an employer allow nonemployee organizers on the employer's property? Give some examples of such situations.
4. Was Lechmere required to allow the organizers to solicit on its property? Explain.

SECTION 8(A)(2): EMPLOYER DOMINATION OF UNIONS

In order for employees to exercise their right to organize or join a union, the union must be free to represent those employees effectively. For that reason, employer interference, support, domination, or assistance of a labor organization is prohibited. An employer who helps a union to solicit membership or who agrees to recognize a union that does not have the support of a majority of employees also violates §8(a)(2). The union agreeing to such an unlawful recognition violates §8(b)(1). Employers who organize employee work groups may run afoul of §8(a)(2) if the work group discusses wages or working conditions with the employer. Remedies for violations of §8(a)(2) involve directing the employer to cease recognizing or supporting the union and canceling any agreement that may have resulted from it.

Section 8(a)(2) was originally aimed at "company unions"—unions organized and controlled by the employer; such company unions were common in the first years of the NLRA. More recent issues arising under §8(a)(2) have involved employee participation programs and innovative workplace arrangements. In *Electromation, Inc.* [309 N.L.R.B. No. 163, 142 L.R.R.M. 1001 (1992)], affirmed by the U.S. Court of Appeals for the Seventh Circuit [35 F.3d 1148 (7th Cir.1994)], the employer set up a series of action committees, comprised of employees and management representatives, to handle matters such as absenteeism, bonuses, pay progression, and a no-smoking policy. The committee members could propose new policies, but management had final authority to adopt any recommendations. The NLRB held that the committees were labor organizations because they acted in a representative capacity and dealt with the employer regarding terms and conditions of employment. Because the committees were established and controlled by the employer, the employer was held to have violated §8(a)(2).

The NLRB addressed the same issue in *E.I. DuPont de Nemours & Co.* [311 N.L.R.B. No. 88 (1993)]. The company created several union–management safety and fitness committees to discuss matters and submit recommendations to management. The NLRB held that the committees were labor organizations under the NLRA because they dealt with the employer on terms and conditions of employment. DuPont decided which employee volunteers served on the committees, reserved the right to abolish any committee, and in some cases sought to use the committees to avoid dealing with the union on the same issues; DuPont therefore was held to have violated §8(a)(2).

IS §8(A)(2) A RELIC FROM AN EARLIER TIME?

A number of commentators criticized the NLRB decisions in *Electromation* and *E.I. DuPont* as reflecting an old, adversarial era of labor relations and not being in touch with the changed nature of today's workplace. They argue that today's (and tomorrow's) workforce is more educated, includes more women and minorities, and is increasingly part-time, in contrast with the workforce of the 1950s, when union strength was at its height. As well, the critics claim, staying competitive in today's business world demands cooperation between managers and employees, rather than the "labor versus management" attitudes reflected by the NLRA. In response to those criticisms, President Clinton appointed the Commission on the Future of Worker–Management Relations, chaired by John T. Dunlop, a Harvard professor and a former Secretary of Labor. The commission heard testimony from 354 witnesses and issued a report in 1994; most employer witnesses recommended that the NLRA be amended to accommodate employee–management committees such as those outlawed in *Electromation*. The commission report noted that between one-fifth and one-third of the workforce is involved in some sort of employee participation in decision making in the workplace but did not recommend any major changes to the labor relations laws.

The Clinton administration took the position that amending the law was not necessary, because the NLRA already allows for labor–management cooperation. Congress, over the opposition of President Clinton, passed the Teamwork for Employees and Managers Act of 1995 (known as the TEAM Act), which would have amended §8(a)(2) to allow management-initiated employee–management cooperative efforts. Sponsors of the TEAM Act argued that such a change was needed to bring labor law into harmony with the realities of the workplace in the next century. President Clinton, Congressional Democrats, and unions charged that the TEAM Act would allow for employer-dominated unions and undermine employee rights to bargain collectively through unions of their own choosing. President Clinton vetoed the TEAM Act on July 31, 1996, and that was the end of such proposed legislation. Since then neither political party has raised the issue of changing the labor laws to reflect the needs of the 21st century.

SECTIONS 8(A)(3) AND 8(B)(2)

Section 8(a)(3) prohibits employers from discriminating with regard to any terms or conditions of employment in order to encourage or discourage union membership. Section 8(b)(2) prohibits unions from causing or attempting to cause an employer to discriminate against an employee in violation of §8(a)(3). The purpose of the sections is to ensure that an employee does not suffer economically because of the employee's decision to join, or not to join, a union. If employees are to have the free choice, under §7, to join or refrain from joining a union, then they must be protected from being fired, laid off, or refused a job because of their choice. Violations of §§8(a)(3) or 8(b)(2) have two elements: Discrimination must occur against an employee in terms or conditions of employment, and the discrimination must be for the purpose of encouraging or discouraging union membership. Firing employees who have joined a union is a clear violation of §8(a)(3); moreover, a union that seeks to have an employee fired for joining a rival union violates §8(b)(2). An employer who closes a plant because the workers have voted to be represented by a union violates §8(a)(3), according to the Supreme Court decision in *Textile Workers Union v. Darlington Mfg. Co.* [380 U.S. 263 (1965)].

FROM THE DESK OF *Laura Lawyer*

To: Students

From: Your Lawyer

Because of the NLRB decisions in the *Electromation* and *DuPont* cases, employers who wish to set up employee-participation programs must be careful not to run afoul of §8(a)(2). However, it is possible to set up such programs and avoid problems under the NLRA. Employers whose employees are unionized must negotiate participation programs with the union before implementing them; failure to do so will be an unfair labor practice—failing to bargain in good faith in violation of §8(a)(5).

Employers whose employees are not unionized can unilaterally create such programs, but employers must emphasize that any employees participating on committees are not representing their coworkers. Employee membership on committees should be rotated periodically to avoid any semblance of representation. As well, the employer should avoid "dealing with" or negotiating with the employees through the committees; rather, the committees should make suggestions or recommendations to management, with no formal response or negotiation by management required.

Union Security Agreements Several specific issues arising under these sections deserve more detailed discussion. The first issue involves **union security agreements**. Union security agreements are contract provisions between a union and employer that require an employee, in order to remain employed, to either join the union or at least pay union dues. Union security agreements clearly have the effect of encouraging union membership. *Closed shop agreements*, which require the employer to hire only union members—that is, in order to be hired, an employee must already be a member of the union—are illegal. However, **union shop agreements**, which require that the employee join the union after completing a probationary period of at least 30 days, or an **agency shop agreement**, which requires that the employee pay union dues and fees but need not actually join the union, are permissible under the sections. Such agreements are possible because of a specific exception contained in §§8(a)(3) and 8(b)(2).

union security agreements: Contract provisions that require an employee to join, or at least pay dues to, a union.

union shop agreements: Contract provisions that require employees to join a union after completing a probationary period.

agency shop agreements: Contract provisions requiring employees to pay union dues and fees.

Where a union security agreement is in effect, the employer must fire, upon the union's request, an employee who is denied union membership or expelled from the union for failing to pay the required union dues or fees. If an employee is expelled from the union or refused union membership for any reason other than failing to pay required dues or fees, then the employer is not required to fire that employee. This protects employees from union discrimination.

Right to Work Laws Section 14(b) of the NLRA permits states to pass **right to work laws** that prohibit union security agreements. In states that have such laws, union shop and agency shop agreements are illegal. A number of states, mainly in the South and West, have passed such laws.

right to work laws: State laws that prohibit union security agreements.

The Right to Strike The second issue that arises under these sections concerns the right to strike. Employees enjoy the right to strike under §7. (A *strike* is the essence of concerted action for purposes of collective bargaining or mutual aid and protection.) Strikes under the NLRA are classified as either economic strikes—strikes arising out of negotiations over wages or conditions of employment—or unfair labor practice strikes—strikes to protest illegal action by the employer. Employers are forbidden to fire employees for going on either unfair labor practice strikes or economic strikes; however, in the event of an economic strike, the employer is free to hire permanent replacements for the workers who went on strike. After the strike is over, the striking workers are not guaranteed to get their jobs back if those jobs have been filled by replacement workers and no other positions are available. As long as the former strikers indicate their intent to return to their jobs, the employer is required to rehire them when positions become available. Recent proposed legislation attempted to outlaw the permanent replacement of workers on economic strikes, but Congress failed to pass it. In an unfair labor practice strike, employers are not permitted to permanently replace strikers—to do so would allow the employer to provoke the workers by illegal action and then capitalize upon that wrongdoing by getting rid of the unionized workers.

In recent years, unionized employees have seemed less willing to go on strike and to risk permanent replacement. The percentage of the workforce that is unionized has been decreasing since the 1950s, and employers are more likely during the strike to hire permanent replacements. For these reasons, unions have been developing alternative tactics to striking; these alternatives include consumer boycotts, publicity campaigns, and shareholder resolutions.

hiring halls: Arrangements where a union refers employees to an employer.

Hiring Halls In some industries, employers do not maintain a permanent workforce but rather hire employees as needed for a particular project or period. In those situations, the employer may rely on the union to refer prospective employees. Such arrangements are known as **hiring halls**. Sections 8(a)(3) and 8(b)(2) require that hiring halls must not discriminate on the grounds of union membership in referring prospective employees and that employers have the right to refuse any applicant the union refers. It is legal for the union to set specific skill requirements necessary for being referred, such as having completed an apprenticeship program. Hiring halls are common in the construction, shipping, and longshore industries.

SECTIONS 8(D), 8(A)(5), AND 8(B)(3): THE DUTY TO BARGAIN IN GOOD FAITH

When a union has the support of a majority of employees in a bargaining unit, it becomes the exclusive bargaining agent for those employees. (The usual method for demonstrating such majority support is by winning a representation election, but that is not the only way—the NLRA requires that an employer with knowledge of the union's majority support, independent of the union's claim of such support, must recognize and bargain with the union.) Thus, the employer must recognize and bargain, in good faith, with the union with regard to wages, hours, terms, and conditions of employment for those employees. The union is also under a duty to bargain in good faith with the employer. Bargaining in good faith does not require the parties to reach an agreement; rather, they are only required to meet and negotiate.

Bargaining in Good Faith Section 8(d) defines the duty to bargain in good faith as:

> [T]he performance of the mutual obligation of the employer and the representative of the employees to meet at reasonable times and confer in good faith with respect to wages, hours, and other terms and conditions of employment, or the negotiation of an agreement or any question arising thereunder . . .

Once a union has the support of a majority of employees in a bargaining unit, the employer may no longer negotiate with individual employees (unless the collective agreement so allows); the union is now the exclusive bargaining agent of all the employees in the bargaining unit, and matters relating to the wages, hours, terms, and conditions of employment of those employees must be negotiated with the union. Section 9(a) of the NLRA does allow the employer to address individual grievances of the employees, as long as it is done in a manner consistent with the collective agreement and the union has been given notice of such matters.

Bargaining Procedures A union or employer seeking to bargain with the other party must give notice to that party at least 60 days prior to the expiration of an existing collective agreement; if no agreement presently exists, then the notice is to be given at least 60 days prior to the date it proposes the agreement to go into effect. Section 8(d) requires that any current agreement must be continued in effect from the date of the notice to bargain, for 60 days or until the agreement expires, whichever comes later. During that 60-day-period, the union is prohibited from going on strike, and the employer is forbidden to lock out the employees. When the employer is a health care institution, the notice period is 90 days, and the ban on strikes or lockouts is extended to 90 days. If a union seeks to strike or picket at a health care institution, it must give the employer at least 10 days notice prior to taking such action to give the institution time to make arrangements to ensure that patient care is not disrupted.

Nature of the Duty The duty of the parties to bargain in good faith is enforced by §§8(a)(5) and 8(b)(3), which make it an unfair labor practice for an employer or union to refuse to bargain in good faith. Section 8(d) also states that the obligation to bargain "does not compel either party to agree to a proposal or require the making of a concession. . . ." In other words, neither party has an obligation to reach an agreement, only the obligation to bargain in good faith. The NLRB regulates the process of collective bargaining but not the results of the process. Hard bargaining is not illegal; but a position of "take it or leave it," with no willingness to bargain, is bargaining in bad faith.

Bargaining Subjects Although the NLRB does not regulate the results of collective bargaining, it does exert some control over the subject bargained over. Why? This control helps to prevent the parties from making a charade of the process by holding to arbitrary or frivolous positions. The NLRB distinguishes between mandatory bargaining subjects, permissive subjects, and illegal subjects.

Mandatory bargaining subjects are those that relate to wages, hours, terms, and conditions of employment of the employees in the bargaining unit. In the case of *Allied Chemical & Alkali Workers v. PPG* [404 U.S. 157 (1971)], the Supreme Court held that mandatory subjects are those matters "that vitally affect the terms and conditions of employment" of the bargaining unit. The NLRB and the courts broadly interpret the matters subject to mandatory bargaining. "Wages," for example, have been held to include all forms of employee compensation and fringe benefits, including stock options, employee discounts, pensions, and incentive plans. "Hours and other terms and conditions" of employment have received similar broadening. Why label an item a mandatory bargaining subject? To do so ensures that the parties must negotiate over it when the issue is raised by either party. Remember, however, they still need not reach an agreement. Parties, when the negotiations are deadlocked, may insist on a mandatory subject to the point of impasse; the parties may strike or lock out over mandatory subjects. Either party can only make a unilateral change in a mandatory subject after first bargaining in good faith to an impasse. For example, once an existing collective agreement expires, an employer may not unilaterally make changes in wages until it has negotiated to impasse with the union over this issue. Making a unilateral change in mandatory subjects without bargaining to impasse is a violation of §8(a)(5) or §8(b)(3).

mandatory bargaining subjects: Matters relating to wages, hours, terms, and conditions of employment of the members of the bargaining unit, and over which the parties are required to bargain by the NLRA.

Permissive bargaining subjects are those matters that are neither mandatory subjects nor illegal subjects—they are matters not directly related to wages, hours, terms, and conditions of employment of the bargaining unit. Examples of such matters are union and management participation in social or charitable activities and industry promotion activities. Either party is free to raise such matters at the bargaining table but cannot insist on them to the

permissive subjects: Those matters that are neither mandatory nor illegal; the parties may, but are not required to, bargain over them.

point of impasse. If the other party refuses to accept the permissive matter proposal, then it must be dropped. Insisting on permissive subjects to the point of impasse or conditioning agreement on mandatory subjects upon agreement to permissive matters violates §8(a)(5) or §8(b)(3).

illegal bargaining subjects: Matters that would violate the NLRA or other laws; any attempt to bargain over such matters is a violation of the duty to bargain in good faith under the NLRA.

Illegal bargaining subjects are those proposals that involve matters that would violate the NLRA or other laws. For example, a union attempt to negotiate a closed shop agreement would be an illegal bargaining subject. Other examples include negotiating separate wage scales for men and women or agreeing to exclude minorities from certain jobs. Any attempt to bargain over illegal subjects violates §8(a)(5) or §8(b)(3), and any agreement reached on such matters is null and void. Illegal subjects may not be insisted upon to the point of impasse.

The following case discusses whether an employer must bargain with the union over a decision to close a plant (i.e., is this a mandatory bargaining subject?).

FIRST NATIONAL MAINTENANCE CORP. V. NLRB

452 U.S. 666 (1981)

FACTS

First National Maintenance (FNM) performed the maintenance and housekeeping work at Greenpark Care Center, a nursing home in Brooklyn, and employed approximately 35 employees at Greenpark. It became aware that it was losing money at the Greenpark location and informed Greenpark that it wished to increase its weekly fee to $500 per week; FNM then informed Greenpark that it would cease its operations at Greenpark on August 1, 1977, if the increase was not granted. On 25 July 1977, FNM gave Greenpark final notice of termination of its services.

While FNM was experiencing difficulties with Greenpark, District 1199, National Union of Hospital and Health Care Employees (Dist. 1199), was conducting an organizing campaign among the FNM workers at Greenpark. The FNM employees selected Dist. 1199 as their bargaining agent and representative in a representation election held March 31, 1977. Dist. 1199 gave notice to FNM, but FNM did not respond to, or consult with, the union. On July 28, 1977, FNM notified its employees at Greenpark that they would be discharged on August 1. The company only engaged in perfunctory discussions with the union and shut down its Greenpark operations on July 31; the employees were discharged. District 1199 then filed an unfair labor practice complaint, alleging that FNM had violated §§8(a)(1) and (5) by refusing to bargain over the decision to cease operations at Greenpark. The ALJ held in the union's favor, and the NLRB adopted the ALJ's decision ordering FNM to bargain in good faith with the union. The U.S. Court of Appeals for the Second Circuit enforced the NLRB's order, and FNM appealed to the U.S. Supreme Court.

DECISION

The Court noted that the Courts of Appeals had taken different positions on the duty of an employer to bargain with a union over decisions involving "a major commitment of capital investment" or a "basic operational change" in the scope or direction of the enterprise. Although the parties (employer and union) are free to bargain about any legal subject, the NLRA only mandates bargaining over "wages, hours, and other terms and conditions of employment"; Congress, noted the Court, had no intention that the union representing employees of an enterprise would become an equal partner in the running of that enterprise. Some management decisions, such as advertising and promotion strategy, have only an indirect effect on the employment relationship, whereas other management decisions, such as layoffs and recall and work rules, are clearly an aspect of the employment relationship. The decision to cease operations, noted the Court, involved a third type of management decision—one that had a direct effect on the employment relationship, but one that focused on the profitability of the contract with Greenpark, a concern "wholly apart form the employment relationship." Although the decision to cease operations touched on the continued employment of the employees, a matter of central concern to the union, it involved a change in the scope and direction of the enterprise.

The purpose of labeling a matter as a mandatory bargaining subject is to "promote the fundamental purpose" of the NLRA by bringing labor and management together "within the framework established by Congress as most conducive to industrial peace." The rationale behind mandatory bargaining is that the process will result in decisions that are better for both labor and management. "This will be true, however, only if the subject proposed for discussion is amenable to resolution through the bargaining process. Management must be free from the constraints of the bargaining process to the extent essential for the running of a profitable business." The Court concluded that, "in view of an employer's need for unencumbered decision making, bargaining over management decisions that have a substantial impact on the continued availability of employment should be required only if the benefit, for labor–management relations and for the collective bargaining process, outweighs the burden placed on the conduct of the business." If labor costs are an important factor in a failing operation and the decision to close, management will have an incentive to bargain with the union to seek concessions that may make continuing the business profitable. The Court concluded that "the harm likely to be done to an employer's need to operate freely in deciding whether to shut down part of its business purely for economic reasons outweighs the incremental benefit that might be gained through the union's participation in making the decision." Therefore, the Court held that the decision to cease operations was not a mandatory bargaining subject.

Even if a decision is not a mandatory bargaining subject, it is clear that the employer is required by §8(a)(5) to bargain with the union over the effects of that decision on the employees in the bargaining unit; examples include severance pay, retraining allowances, transfer rights, and preferential hiring at other locations.

CASE QUESTIONS

1. Why was FNM planning to cease operations at the Greenpark Care Center?
2. How could the union have affected FNM's decision to cease operations at Greenpark?
3. What test does the Supreme Court set out for determining when a management decision, such as a plant closing, is a mandatory bargaining subject?

Plant Closing Legislation The Worker Adjustment and Retraining Act (WARN), passed by Congress in 1988, requires employers with 100 or more employees to give at least 60 days notice prior to any plant closing or "mass layoffs." The employer must give advance written notice to the employees or their representative (union), to the state economic development officials, and to the chief elected local government official. Two exceptions to the notice requirement exist: (1) the "failing firm" exception—when giving the required notice would prevent the firm from obtaining capital or business necessary to maintain the operation of the firm and (2) when the work loss is due to "unforeseen circumstances"—such as when the plant is damaged by fire or disaster. The WARN notice requirements do not include the obligation to bargain over the decision to close; the duty to bargain is governed by the *First National Maintenance* decision.

The Duty to Furnish Information The duty to bargain in good faith also includes the duty of the employer to furnish information to the union in certain situations. When the employer pleads inability to pay in response to union demands, the employer must provide financial information that supports this claim. The information must be requested by the union, and though it need not be in the form requested by the union, the information must be in a reasonably accessible and usable form. Note that the duty to furnish information is not a "truth in bargaining" requirement; it relates only to claims of financial inability to meet union demands.

The employer also has a continuing obligation to provide the union with information relating to the administration and enforcement of the collective agreement that is necessary for the union to perform its role as exclusive bargaining representative for the bargaining unit. Such information includes wage scales, factors entering into compensation, job classifications, and a list of names and addresses of the employees in the bargaining unit.

Remedies for the Duty to Bargain When the violation of the duty to bargain involves specific practices, such as the refusal to provide information, the NLRB orders the offending party to comply; when a party has made illegal unilateral changes to mandatory subjects, the NLRB requires that the prior conditions be restored. However, when the violation involves the refusal to recognize or to negotiate seriously with the other party, the NLRB is limited to a **cease and desist order** and a **bargaining order** directing, respectively, the offending party to stop the illegal conduct and to negotiate in good faith. The NLRB cannot require either party to reach an agreement or to offer concessions. Such orders only require the parties to return to the bargaining table and make a serious effort to explore the basis for an agreement.

cease and desist order: An order directing a party to stop the illegal conduct and to refrain from such conduct in the future.

bargaining order: NLRB order directing a party to bargain in good faith.

SECTIONS 8(B)(4) AND 8(E): SECONDARY ACTIVITY

Union picketing directed against parties other than the employer with whom it has a dispute may be an unfair labor practice. When a union directs a strike or picket line against a neutral employer, such conduct is called **secondary picketing**. Because the neutral party is not involved in the labor dispute, it is entitled to be free from economic pressure; a union targeting a neutral employer with a strike or picketing violates §8(b)(4). Picketing at a neutral location that is merely intended to inform consumers of the existence of a labor dispute, however, is not a violation. Union picketing against an employer who is an ally of the employer against whom the union is striking is also not a violation. An ally relationship arises when the other employer is performing the work usually done by the striking employees.

secondary picketing: Picketing directed against an employer that is not a party to the labor dispute.

The NLRB is required to seek a court injunction against conduct that violates §8(b)(4) when such a complaint is filed with it; the injunction is to prevent the illegal conduct while the NLRB holds a hearing on the alleged unfair labor practice. If the NLRB determines that the conduct is in violation of the act, it will issue a cease and desist order against it. Unions engaging in illegal secondary activity are also subject to damage suits under §303 of the act—employers injured by such conduct can sue the union for damages and legal fees.

Contract provisions that purport to allow a union to engage in secondary conduct are known as **hot cargo clauses**. Section 8(e) prohibits a union from negotiating or attempting to negotiate such clauses. Any agreement containing

hot cargo clauses: Contract provisions that would purport to allow unions to engage in secondary picketing; they are illegal under the NLRA.

a hot cargo clause is null and void. [Note, too, that a union attempting to negotiate a hot cargo clause also violates §8(b)(3).]

Not all union activity directed at neutral, or secondary, employers is illegal. An exception to §8(b)(4), known as the *publicity proviso*, states that the union does have the right to engage in "publicity picketing"—picketing done peacefully that is intended to advise the public that the products of the employer against whom the union is striking (the primary employer) are being sold or distributed by the secondary employer. In addition, union conduct that is outside the publicity proviso may also be protected under the First Amendment's guarantee of free speech. In *Edward J. Debartolo Corp. v. Florida Gulf Coast Building Trades Council* [485 U.S. 568 (1988)], the Supreme Court held that a union's peaceful distribution of handbills calling upon consumers to boycott the stores in a mall, because of a labor dispute with one of the stores, was not picketing; such conduct was therefore not subject to §8(b)(4) and was protected by the First Amendment.

OTHER UNFAIR LABOR PRACTICE PROVISIONS

Reprisals Section 8(a)(4) prohibits an employer from discharging or otherwise discriminating against an employee who has filed charges or has given testimony in proceedings under the NLRA. This section is intended to protect employees exercising their rights under the act from any employer reprisals for such protected action. Reprisals by a union would violate §8(b)(1).

Excessive Union Dues or Fees Section 8(b)(5) prohibits a union from requiring excessive dues or membership fees of employees covered by a union security agreement. This section is intended to protect employees from union abuse or exploitation. In deciding whether dues or fees are excessive, the NLRB is directed to consider "the practices and customs of labor organizations in the particular industry, and the wages currently paid to the employees affected."

Featherbedding It is an unfair labor practice under §8(b)(6) to cause an employer to pay for services that are not actually performed. The practice of getting paid for services not actually performed is called **featherbedding**. For example, if the local musicians' union requires an employer to pay wages for a minimum of three musicians, even if only two actually perform, that is featherbedding. When the work is actually performed, although not really needed by the employer (e.g., the employer agrees to hire three musicians even though only two were desired), it is not featherbedding. Featherbedding at one time was a common occurrence where unions had great power in an industry; now that unionized firms face stiff economic competition from nonunion firms and because of labor-saving technology, featherbedding complaints are relatively rare today.

featherbedding: The union practice that requires an employer to pay for work that is not actually performed.

ADMINISTRATION AND ENFORCEMENT OF COLLECTIVE AGREEMENTS

During the term of a collective agreement, disputes over the interpretation or administration of a collective agreement occasionally may arise. The disputes may involve questions of a worker's entitlement to several hours of overtime, the employer's liability for cost of living adjustments, or the employer's right to change job requirements. The parties to the agreement have several options for resolving the dispute. The union may choose to strike, or the employer may choose to lock out the employees to try to force the other party to accept its position. Alternatively, either party may choose to sue in court for breach of contract; §301 of the NLRA allows court suits to enforce agreements between unions and employers. Lastly, the parties may choose to pursue arbitration of their dispute; that is, they submit the dispute to a neutral adjudicator (in effect, a private judge) chosen by the parties. For a number of reasons, arbitration is the usual method chosen. Arbitration of the type discussed here is known as **rights arbitration**, because it deals with the rights of the parties under the collective agreement—the arbitrator interprets and applies the agreement. (You may be familiar with another type of arbitration, in which the arbitrator actually defines the terms of the agreement—usually the wages or salary provisions. That type of arbitration is known as **interest arbitration** and is used to resolve salary disputes of professional baseball players and public sector employees who are forbidden to strike.)

rights arbitration: Arbitration used to resolve disputes over the rights and duties of the parties to a collective agreement.

interest arbitration: Arbitration used to determine rates of pay and other terms of a collective agreement.

grievance procedure: Process set out in a collective agreement for resolving disputes under the agreement.

no-strike clause: A contract provision by which the parties agree not to engage in a strike or lockout during the term of the collective agreement.

Employees are reluctant to go on strike, and suffer a resulting loss of wages and risk of permanent replacement, over relatively minor matters; employers, likewise, are not usually willing to lock out and lose the profits from production over such disputes. Lawsuits are relatively expensive and may take a long time to resolve; the parties are not likely to sue unless there is an extremely important matter—or a lot of money—at stake. Thus, arbitration is a wise solution. Arbitration is not required by law, but more than 90 percent of all collective agreements contain rights arbitration provisions.

Arbitration is popular because it is created by the parties to the agreement, and they are free to tailor the arbitration process to fit their particular situation or desires. Arbitration provisions are usually included in an agreement as part of a **grievance procedure** (a method for dealing with grievances or complaints that a party has violated the agreement). The first steps of the grievance procedure usually involve conferences between union and management officers. If the parties are unable to negotiate a settlement, either side may submit the grievance to arbitration.

Arbitration provisions in collective agreements also usually contain **no-strike clauses** (in which the parties agree not to strike or lock out over a matter that is subject to arbitration). When an agreement contains an arbitration provision, and either party refuses to submit to arbitration a dispute that is within the scope of that provision, the other party can bring a court action under §301 seeking a court order forcing the reluctant party to arbitrate. Similarly, when a union strikes or an employer locks out over an issue subject to arbitration, the other party can use §301 to seek a court order stopping the strike or lockout. If the strike or lockout does not involve a matter subject to arbitration, the courts will not order an end to it. (The Norris-LaGuardia Act prohibits federal courts from enjoining such labor disputes.)

When a party files a breach of contract suit over a matter that is subject to arbitration, the courts will defer to arbitration rather than hear the suit itself. In *United Steelworkers of America v. Warrior & Gulf Navigation Co.* [363 U.S. 574 (1960)], the Supreme Court held that if the parties have agreed to an arbitration clause, they have agreed to let the arbitrator, and not the court, decide the dispute. The court, by ordering arbitration, is simply giving the parties that to which they have already agreed. The court, therefore, is not to rule on the merits of the dispute, but rather simply to determine if the subject of the dispute is within the scope of the arbitration provision; if so, then the dispute must be sent to arbitration. After the arbitrator has decided the dispute, either party may also file an action under §301 to force the other party to abide by that decision. A court being asked to enforce the arbitrator's decision is not to substitute its own judgment for that of the arbitrator; rather, the court is simply to consider whether the arbitrator acted within the scope of authority granted under the collective agreement. If so, then the court is to enforce the decision. The court should refuse to enforce the arbitrator's decision only when the arbitrator has exceeded his or her authority granted under the agreement or when the decision conflicts with a "clearly defined" public policy, that is, a policy defined by "reference to the laws and legal precedents," according to the Supreme Court decision in *Paperworkers v. Misco, Inc.* [484 U.S. 29 (1987)].

As with the courts, the NLRB also defers its unfair labor practice procedures to arbitration between the parties when the dispute is subject to arbitration and does not involve antiunion motives. Examples include complaints alleging that an employer made a unilateral change to a collective agreement. In these cases, the union could allege that the unilateral change violated §8(a)(5) in addition to seeking arbitration over the alleged breach of the agreement. Some recent courts of appeals decisions have criticized the NLRB's policy of deferring to arbitration; in *Hammondtree v. NLRB* [894 F.2d 438 (D.C.Cir., 1990)], the court held that the deferral policy improperly forces complaining employees to give up rights under the NLRA simply because the employer and union have established contractual procedures for resolving similar disputes.

PUBLIC SECTOR EMPLOYEES

Although there are a few significant differences, labor relations in the public sector—whether federal or state, local or municipal—are similar in many respects to private sector labor relations under the NLRA. The U.S. Constitution and the various state constitutions regulate the relationship of government and its citizens. Actions by government employers may raise constitutional issues because public sector employees are also citizens and retain their rights under the constitutions.

A major difference involves the idea of government sovereignty. The government is under specific legal obligations to provide certain services and perform certain functions, and government officials are authorized by law to take certain actions and to make certain decisions. Collective bargaining involves shared decision making between the employer and the union. For public employers, collective bargaining may involve delegating to the union the authority relating to the employer's statutory obligations, or it may affect the employer's financial condition, requiring tax increases or cutbacks in services provided. Because of these concerns, public sector labor relations statutes may narrowly define the matters that are subject to collective bargaining; some state public sector labor relations statutes do not provide for collective bargaining but rather simply require consultation or "meeting and conferring" on working conditions.

A second major difference between public and private sector labor relations involves the right to strike. The federal courts have held that no constitutional right to strike exists; such a right may be created by statute, as §7 of the NLRA does for private sector employees. But in the public sector, most statutes prohibit strikes by public employees; impasses in negotiations over wages or working conditions are resolved by interest arbitration instead. Federal employees who strike are subject to losing their jobs, and unions calling such strikes are subject to losing their right to represent federal employees. The federal air traffic controllers went on strike in 1981, in violation of the Federal Service Labor–Management Relations Act, and consequently lost their jobs. Moreover, the representative union was decertified. Some state statutes only prohibit strikes by employees directly involved in public safety and health—such as police officers, prison guards, and firefighters—while allowing other public workers, such as teachers, to strike. Workers who cannot legally strike sometimes engage in nonstrike pressure tactics such as "working to rule" (doing only what is specifically required by their contracts and job descriptions), "blue flu" (whole groups of police officers or firefighters calling in sick), or work slowdowns (reducing the amount of work actually performed), in order to force the employer to address their concerns.

DOCTORS SEEK TO UNIONIZE TO COUNTER POWER OF HMOS

Although the percentage of American workers represented by unions has been steadily declining over the past 40 years, at least one group of workers is actively seeking to join unions. Doctors, increasingly frustrated by the increasing control of Health Maintenance Organizations (HMOs) over the practice of medicine, see unions as a possible solution. At its 1999 national meeting, the American Medical Association (AMA) voted to seek legislative changes that would allow independent medical practitioners to form a union to provide doctors with bargaining power to negotiate collectively reimbursement rates and steps to ensure quality care for patients in the face of HMO cost-cutting measures. The AMA vote was in response to the NLRB dismissal of a petition filed by the United Food and Commercial Workers Union, Local 56, seeking to represent a group of independent physicians who contract with AmeriHealth, an HMO, to accept set fees as payment for medical services rendered to patients who are enrolled in AmeriHealth's medical plan.

The NLRB, in its decision in *AmeriHealth and United Food and Commercial Workers Union, Local 56* [329 NLRB No. 76 (Oct. 18, 1999)], held that the doctors were not employees of AmeriHealth but were independent contractors, and thus were not within the definition of employee under §2(3) of the National Labor Relations Act [NLRA]. AmeriHealth did not control the manner in which the doctors provided patient care, did not control the doctors' hours of work, and did not have any economic interest in the doctors' practices. The doctors engaged in the occupation of the practice of medicine separate and distinct from AmeriHealth, supplied their own tools of the trade, and worked at their own offices without supervision from AmeriHealth. AmeriHealth paid the doctors a set fee per the type of patient care provided, and the doctors were responsible for covering the various expenses of their business, including wages and benefits, from the fees. AmeriHealth had no control over the doctors' expenses, and the doctors retained wide entrepreneurial control over how they ran their practices and made profits. Therefore the doctors operate as separate business entities, or independent contractors, who contract with AmeriHealth on a fee-for-service basis and are not employees within the definition under the NLRA.

Although doctors in private practice, such as the doctors in the AmeriHealth case, are considered to be independent contractors and denied the protections of right to unionize under the NLRA, doctors who are employees—those who are on hospital staff, some emergency room doctors, and doctors on the payroll of corporations—fall within the coverage of §2(3) of the NLRA and are entitled to form unions and bargain collectively. Approximately 5 percent of physicians in the United States are union members.

In addition to their status as independent contractors, private practice physicians face another legal obstacle in their attempts to unionize. Because the independent practice doctors are separately engaged in business, any attempt by them to act collectively could be considered a combination or conspiracy in restraint of trade and would be illegal under the antitrust laws (see Chapter 16). The Supreme Court decision in *Arizona v. Maricopa County Medical Society* [457 U.S. (1982)] held that an agreement among competing doctors to set maximum (or minimum) fees for particular services was a violation of Section 1 of the Sherman Act.

Sources: "Labor Official Says No to Union for Doctors," *The Cincinnati Post* (May 26,1999); "Union Rethinks Tactics in Attempt to Organize Private-practice Doctors," *The Seattle Times* (May 25, 1999); "Doctors See Unions as Cure for Their Woes," *The Patriot Ledger* (Quincy, Mass.) (September 7, 1999).

SUMMARY

The percentage of the U.S. private sector workforce that is unionized is presently around 15 percent; that figure has been declining steadily since the early 1950s. Some commentators attribute this decline to the failure of organized labor to adapt to the changing attitudes of U.S. workers and to the country's change from a manufacturing-based economy to one based on service and information industries. Although the importance and influence of unions have been declining as membership declines, labor law remains an important concern for both employers and employees. Employees will continue to seek a role in determining the conditions of their employment; for many employees, unions will continue to provide that role through collective bargaining. For employees who choose not to join unions, labor law is still essential to protect their rights in the workplace. All employees and employers should have an awareness of the provisions of the NLRA and an understanding of their rights and obligations under it.

CHAPTER QUESTIONS

1. Burman was a production supervisor employed by Vincow, Inc. He was fired because his brother and cousin led a union organizing campaign among the employees at Vincow, Inc. Burman filed an unfair labor practice charge with the NLRB, alleging that his discharge violated §§8(a)(1) and 8(a)(3). What arguments should the employer make to support the discharge? What arguments should Burman make to convince the NLRB that the discharge was an unfair labor practice? How should the NLRB rule on

his complaint? Why? [*Kenrich Petrochemicals v. NLRB*, 893 F.2d 1468 (3rd Cir. 1990)]

2. Potter Manufacturing Co. laid off 15 employees, claiming there was a lack of work due to economic conditions. The union representing the employees at Potter subsequently discovered that the employer laid off the employees it believed were most likely to honor a picket line in the event of a strike. The union filed an unfair labor practice charge with the NLRB. On which sections of the NLRA should the union base its charge? Why? What arguments can Potter make to support the layoffs? How is the NLRB likely to rule on the charge? Explain. [*National Fabricators*, 295 N.L.R.B. No. 126, 131 LRRM 1761 (1989)]
3. The employer had established a recreation fund to provide the employees with recreational opportunities; the employer had administered the fund for the benefit of the employees. The union sought to bargain over the allocation of funds from the recreation fund, but the employer refused; the employer claimed that it had total control over the fund, so there was no obligation to bargain over it. The union filed a §8(a)(5) complaint with the NLRB. Was the refusal to bargain over the recreation fund a violation of the NLRA? Explain your answer. [*Getty Ref. & Mktg. Co.*, 279 N.L.R.B. No. 126, 122 L.R.R.M. 1150 (1986)]
4. The Teamsters Union, Local 572, went on strike against Silver Linen Supply, an industrial laundry supply company. During the strike, the customers normally supplied by Silver were supplied by Puritan Laundry Service. The union also began to picket at the Puritan plant, attempting to stop the Puritan trucks from making deliveries. After several days of the picketing, Puritan stopped supplying the customers of Silver but did not inform the union that they had stopped supplying the Silver customers. The union continued to picket at Puritan, and Puritan filed a §8(b)(4) complaint with the NLRB. Was the union picketing at Puritan an unfair labor practice, both before and after Puritan stopped supplying the Silver customers? Explain your answers. [*Laundry Workers Int., Local No. 259*, 164 NLRB 426 (1967)]
5. Mahon, an employee of Alpha Beta Corp., was fired for refusing to follow a supervisor's order. Mahon claimed that the order violated the work rules set out in the collective agreement. The union filed a grievance over the discharge, and Mahon also filed a complaint alleging a violation of §§8(a)(1) and (3). During discussions pursuant to the grievance procedure, the union and employer agreed to a settlement reinstating Mahon, subject to a two-week suspension. Mahon asked the NLRB to reinstate him with full back pay; the employer argued that the NLRB should defer to the grievance settlement like it defers to an arbitration award. What arguments should Mahon make to urge the NLRB to decide his complaint? What arguments should the employer make to urge the NLRB to defer to the grievance settlement? Should the NLRB hear the complaint, or should it defer to the settlement? Why? [*Alpha Beta Corp.*, 273 N.L.R.B. No. 194, 118 L.R.R.M. 1202 (1985), *aff'd sub nom Mahon v. NLRB*, 808 F.2d 1342 (9th Cir. 1987)]
6. In a bargaining unit of 100 employees, only 65 voted in a representation election, and the union won the election by a vote of 45 to 20. The employer

objected to the results of the election, claiming that the number of voters was not substantial in light of the overall number of employees in the unit. Should the election be set aside because of the relatively low voter turnout? Explain your answer. [*Lemco Construction, Inc.*, 283 N.L.R.B. No. 68, 124 L.R.R.M. 1329 (1987)]

7. Callaghan was employed by Smiths Transportation until he became one of the leaders of an effort to unionize Smiths' employees. On January 15, 1999, when his supervisor discovered Callaghan's involvement, Callaghan was fired. On July 29, 1999, Callaghan filed a complaint with the NLRB, alleging that his discharge violated §§8(a)(1) and 8(a)(3) of the NLRA. How should the NLRB rule on Callaghan's complaint? Explain. [*United States Postal Service*, 271 N.L.R.B. No. 61, 116 LRRM 1417 (1984)]

8. While negotiating with Mercy Hospital for renewing a collective bargaining agreement, the union representing the hospital employees proposed that the hospital open the hospital cafeteria for all employees during the hours of 6 A.M.–8 P.M. and 2 A.M.–4 A.M. There were approximately 175 workers on the overnight shift, and many of them used the cafeteria for their lunch break. The hospital had operated the cafeteria during those hours for the past 10 years but was now considering closing the cafeteria overnight because it was losing money during the overnight hours. One week after the union made its proposal, the hospital closed the cafeteria overnight and installed some vending machines, a toaster, and a microwave oven for use by the employees. The union filed an unfair labor practice complaint with the NLRB over the hospital's actions. Has the hospital violated the NLRA? Why? Is the decision to close the cafeteria overnight a mandatory bargaining subject under the NLRA? Explain. [*Mercy Hospital of Buffalo*, 311 NLRB 869 (1993)]

9. Burkes, a meter reader for Consolidated Power, was assaulted by a customer while attempting to read the electric meter in the customer's house. Burkes informed Trumane, a coworker, of the assault, and both of them decided to discuss the need for protection of meter readers with their supervisor, Rolle. Burkes had raised the matter earlier during a meeting between employees and their supervisors. As the two employees waited outside Rolle's office, Burkes decided not to discuss the matter. Trumane, however, confronts Rolle and demands that the company provide more protection for meter readers. Rolle fires Trumane. Has the employer committed an unfair labor practice? [*Consumers Power Co.*, 282 N.L.R.B. No. 24, 123 L.R.R.M. 1001 (1986)]

10. Franklin was employed as a dental technician. During a staff meeting, Dr. Trufner, her employer, discussed some work-related problems with the office staff. Franklin and a coworker were reprimanded during the meeting several times for giggling and for disagreeing with Dr. Trufner's comments. On the following Monday morning, Franklin presented Dr. Trufner with a list of complaints from the staff, after having discussed such matters with the other office staff, Franklin was immediately fired by Dr. Trufner. Was the firing of Franklin an unfair labor practice? Why? What factors would the NLRB consider in determining the legality of Dr. Trufner's action? [*Joseph DeRario, DMD, P.A.*, 283 N.L.R.B. No. 86, 125 L.R.R.M. 1024 (1987)]

PRACTICAL EXERCISE

Graduate students who are teaching assistants and research assistants in the School of Management of Farber University (a private university) are concerned over what they regard as excessive workloads and inadequate pay. They approached the dean of the Management School with their concerns, but the dean refused to take any action. As a result, the graduate students have decided to explore the possibility of forming a union in order to force the School of Management to bargain with them over workloads and pay scales.

The dean of the School of Management argues that the students are not covered by the NLRA and legally are not able to unionize. The graduate students insist that they are covered by the NLRA and are free to unionize.

Write position papers that do the following:

1. Argue the case that the graduate students who work as teaching assistants or research assistants should be considered employees under the NLRA.
2. Argue the case of the dean, that the graduate students should not be considered employees.
3. Discuss what steps the graduate students need to take to get the NLRB to decide this question.
4. Discuss how the NLRB is likely to rule on this issue.
5. Discuss how your answer to #4 would be different if Farber University were a state school rather than a private one. Explain all your answers.

FURTHER INFORMATION

www.nlrb.gov/
The National Labor Relations Board Web site.

www.aflcio.org/home.htm
The American Federation of Labor Web site.

www.shrm.org/
The Society for Human Resource Management Web site.

http://hr.monster.com/
Human Resource Management Information (and job listings).

APPENDIX A
THE CONSTITUTION OF THE UNITED STATES

We the people of the United States, in order to form a more perfect union, establish justice, insure domestic tranquility, provide for the common defense, promote the general welfare, and secure the blessings of liberty to ourselves and our posterity, do ordain and establish this Constitution for the United States of America.

ARTICLE I

Section 1. All legislative powers herein granted shall be vested in a Congress of the United States, which shall consist of a Senate and a House of Representatives.

Section 2.1. The House of Representatives shall be composed of members chosen every second year by the people of the several States, and the electors in each State shall have the qualifications requisite for electors of the most numerous branch of the State legislature.

2. No person shall be a representative who shall not have attained the age of twenty-five years, and been seven years a citizen of the United States, and who shall not, when elected, be an inhabitant of that State in which he shall be chosen.

3. Representatives and direct taxes shall be apportioned among the several States which may be included within this Union, according to their respective numbers, which shall be determined by adding to the whole number of free persons, including those bound to service for a term of years, and excluding Indians not taxed, three fifths of all other persons.[1] The actual enumeration shall be made within three years after the first meeting of the Congress of the United States, and within every subsequent term of ten years, in such manner as they shall by law direct. The number of representatives shall not exceed one for every thirty thousand, but each State shall have at least one representative; and until such enumeration shall be made, the State of New Hampshire shall be entitled to choose three, Massachusetts eight, Rhode Island and Providence Plantations one, Connecticut five, New York six, New Jersey four, Pennsylvania eight, Delaware one, Maryland six, Virginia ten, North Carolina five, South Carolina five, and Georgia three.

4. When vacancies happen in the representation from any State, the executive authority thereof shall issue writs of election to fill such vacancies.

5. The House of Representatives shall choose their speaker and other officers; and shall have the sole power of impeachment.

Section 3.1. The Senate of the United States shall be composed of two senators from each State, chosen by the legislature thereof, for six years; and each senator shall have one vote.

1. See the 14th Amendment.

2. Immediately after they shall be assembled in consequence of the first election, they shall be divided as equally as may be into three classes. The seats of the senators of the first class shall be vacated at the expiration of the second year, of the second class at the expiration of the fourth year, and of the third class at the expiration of the sixth year, so that one third may be chosen every second year; and if vacancies happen by resignation, or otherwise, during the recess of the legislature of any State, the executive thereof may make temporary appointments until the next meeting of the legislature, which shall then fill such vacancies.[2]

3. No person shall be a senator who shall not have attained to the age of thirty years, and been nine years a citizen of the United States, and who shall not, when elected, be an inhabitant of that State for which he shall be chosen.

4. The Vice President of the United States shall be President of the Senate, but shall have no vote, unless they be equally divided.

5. The Senate shall choose their other officers, and also a president pro tempore, in the absence of the Vice President, or when he shall exercise the office of the President of the United States.

6. The Senate shall have the sole power to try all impeachments. When sitting for that purpose, they shall be on oath or affirmation. When the President of the United States is tried, the chief justice shall preside: and no person shall be convicted without the concurrence of two thirds of the members present.

7. Judgment in cases of impeachment shall not extend further than to removal from office, and disqualifications to hold and enjoy any office of honor, trust or profit under the United States: but the party convicted shall nevertheless be liable and subject to indictment, trial, judgment and punishment, according to law.

Section 4.1. The times, places, and manner of holding elections for senators and representatives, shall be prescribed in each State by the legislature thereof; but the Congress may at any time by law make or alter such regulations, except as to the places of choosing senators.

2. The Congress shall assemble at least once in every year, and such meeting shall be on the first Monday in December, unless they shall by law appoint a different day.

Section 5.1. Each House shall be the judge of the elections, returns and qualifications of its own members, and a majority of each shall constitute a quorum to do business; but a smaller number may adjourn from day to day, and may be authorized to compel the attendance of absent members, in such manner, and under such penalties as each House may provide.

2. Each House may determine the rules of its proceedings, punish its members for disorderly behavior, and, with the concurrence of two thirds, expel a member.

3. Each House shall keep a journal of its proceedings, and from time to time publish the same, excepting such parts as may in their judgment require secrecy; and the yeas and nays of the members of either House on any question shall, at the desire of one fifth of those present, be entered on the journal.

4. Neither House, during the session of Congress, shall, without the consent of the other, adjourn for more than three days, nor to any other place than that in which the two Houses shall be sitting.

Section 6.1. The senators and representatives shall receive a compensation for their services, to be ascertained by law, and paid out of the Treasury of the United States. They shall in all cases, except treason, felony, and breach of the peace, be privileged from arrest during their attendance at the session of their respective Houses, and in going to and returning from the same; and for any speech or debate in either House, they shall not be questioned in any other place.

2. No senator or representative shall, during the time for which he was elected, be appointed to any civil office under the authority of the United States, which shall have

2. See the 17th Amendment.

been created, or the emoluments whereof shall have been increased during such time; and no person holding any office under the United States shall be a member of either House during his continuance in office.

Section 7.1. All bills for raising revenue shall originate in the House of Representatives; but the Senate may propose or concur with amendments as on other bills.

2. Every bill which shall have passed the House of Representatives and the Senate, shall, before it becomes a law, be presented to the President of the United States; if he approves he shall sign it, but if not he shall return it, with his objections to that House in which it shall have originated, who shall enter the objections at large on their journal, and proceed to reconsider it. If after such reconsiderations two thirds of that House shall agree to pass the bill, it shall be sent, together with the objections, to the other House, by which it shall likewise be reconsidered, and if approved by two thirds of that House, it shall become a law. But in all such cases the votes of both Houses shall be determined by yeas and nays, and the names of the persons voting for and against the bill shall be entered on the journal of each House respectively. If any bill shall not be returned by the President within ten days (Sundays excepted) after it shall have been presented to him, the same shall be a law, in like manner as if he had signed it, unless the Congress by their adjournment prevent its return, in which case, it shall not be a law.

3. Every order, resolution, or vote to which the concurrence of the Senate and the House of Representatives may be necessary (except on a question of adjournment) shall be presented to the President of the United States; and before the same shall take effect, shall be approved by him, or being disapproved by him, shall be repassed by two thirds of the Senate and House of Representatives, according to the rules and limitations prescribed in the case of a bill.

Section 8. The Congress shall have the power

1. To lay and collect taxes, duties, imposts, and excises, to pay the debts and provide for the common defense and general welfare of the United States; but all duties, imposts, and excises shall be uniform throughout the United States;

2. To borrow money on the credit of the United States;

3. To regulate commerce with foreign nations, and among the several States, and with the Indian tribes;

4. To establish a uniform rule of naturalization, and uniform laws on the subject of bankruptcies throughout the United States;

5. To coin money, regulate the value thereof, and of foreign coin, and fix the standard of weights and measures;

6. To provide for the punishment of counterfeiting the securities and current coin of the United States;

7. To establish post offices and post roads;

8. To promote the progress of science and useful arts, by securing for limited times to authors and inventors the exclusive rights to their respective writings and discoveries;

9. To constitute tribunals inferior to the Supreme Court;

10. To define and punish piracies and felonies committed on the high seas, and offenses against the law of nations;

11. To declare war, grant letters of marque and reprisal, and make rules concerning captures on land and water;

12. To raise and support armies, but no appropriation of money to that use shall be for a longer term than two years;

13. To provide and maintain a navy;

14. To make rules for the government and regulation of the land and naval forces;

15. To provide for calling forth the militia to execute the laws of the Union, suppress insurrections and repel invasions;

16. To provide for organizing, arming, and disciplining the militia, and for governing such part of them as may be employed in the service of the United States, reserving

to the States respectively, the appointment of the officers, and the authority of training the militia according to the discipline prescribed by Congress;

17. To exercise exclusive legislation in all cases whatsoever, over such district (not exceeding ten miles square) as may, by cession of particular States, and the acceptance of Congress, become the seat of the government of the United States, and to exercise like authority over all places purchased by the consent of the legislature of the State in which the same shall be, for the erection of forts, magazines, arsenals, dockyards, and other needful buildings; and

18. To make all laws which shall be necessary and proper for carrying into execution the foregoing powers, and all other powers vested by this Constitution in the government of the United States, or in any department or officer thereof.

Section 9.1. The migration or importation of such persons as any of the States now existing shall think proper to admit, shall not be prohibited by the Congress prior to the year one thousand eight hundred and eight, but a tax or duty may be imposed on such importation, not exceeding ten dollars for each person.

2. The privilege of the writ of habeas corpus shall not be suspended, unless when in cases of rebellion or invasion the public safety may require it.

3. No bill of attainder or ex post facto law shall be passed.

4. No capitation, or other direct, tax shall be laid, unless in proportion to the census or enumeration hereinbefore directed to be taken.[3]

5. No tax or duty shall be laid on articles exported from any State.

6. No preference shall be given by any regulation of commerce or revenue to the ports of one State over those of another: nor shall vessels bound to, or from, one State be obliged to enter, clear, or pay duties in another.

7. No money shall be drawn from the treasury, but in consequence of appropriations made by law; and a regular statement and account of the receipts and expenditures of all public money shall be published from time to time.

8. No title of nobility shall be granted by the United States: and no person holding any office of profit or trust under them, shall, without the consent of the Congress, accept of any present, emolument, office, or title, of any kind whatever, from any king, prince, or foreign State.

Section 10.1. No State shall enter into any treaty, alliance, or confederation; grant letters of marque and reprisal; coin money; emit bills of credit; make anything but gold and silver coin a tender in payment of debts; pass any bill of attainder, ex post facto law, or law impairing the obligation of contracts, or grant any title of nobility.

2. No state shall, without the consent of the Congress, lay any imposts or duties on imports or exports, except what may be absolutely necessary for executing its inspection laws: and the net produce of all duties and imposts laid by any State on imports or exports, shall be for the use of the treasury of the United States; and all such laws shall be subject to the revision and control of the Congress.

3. No State shall, without the consent of the Congress, lay any duty of tonnage, keep troops, or ships of war in time of peace, enter into any agreement or compact with another State, or with a foreign power, or engage in war, unless actually invaded, or in such imminent danger as will not admit of delay.

ARTICLE II

Section 1.1. The executive power shall be vested in a President of the United States of America. He shall hold his office during the term of four years, and, together with the Vice President, chosen for the same term, be elected as follows:

3. See the 16th Amendment.

2. Each State shall appoint, in such manner as the legislature thereof may direct, a number of electors, equal to the whole number of senators and representatives to which the State may be entitled in the Congress: but no senator or representative, or person holding an office of trust or profit under the United States, shall be appointed an elector.

The electors shall meet in their respective States, and vote by ballot for two persons, of whom one at least shall not be an inhabitant of the same State with themselves. And they shall make a list of all the persons voted for, and of the number of votes for each; which list they shall sign and certify, and transmit sealed to the seat of the government of the United States, directed to the president of the Senate. The president of the Senate shall, in the presence of the Senate and House of Representatives, open all the certificates, and the votes shall then be counted. The person having the greatest number of votes shall be the president, if such number be a majority of the whole number of electors appointed; and if there be more than one who have such majority, and have an equal number of votes, then the House of Representatives shall immediately choose by ballot one of them for President; and if no person have a majority, then from the five highest on the list the said House shall in like manner choose the President. But in choosing the President, the votes shall be taken by States, the representation from each State having one vote; a quorum for this purpose shall consist of a member or members from two thirds of the States, and a majority of all the states shall be necessary to a choice. In every case, after the choice of the President, the person having the greatest number of votes of the electors shall be the Vice President. But if there should remain two or more who have equal votes, the Senate shall choose from them by ballot the Vice President.[4]

3. The Congress may determine the time of choosing the electors, and the day on which they shall give their votes; which day shall be the same throughout the United States.

4. No person except a natural born citizen, or a citizen of the United States, at the time of the adoption of this Constitution, shall be eligible to the office of President; neither shall any person be eligible to that office who shall not have attained to the age of thirty-five years, and been fourteen years a resident within the United States.

5. In the case of removal of the President from office, or of his death, resignation, or inability to discharge the powers and duties of the said office, the same shall devolve on the Vice President, and the Congress may by law provide for the case of removal, death, resignation, or inability, both of the President and Vice President, declaring what officer shall then act as President, and such officer shall act accordingly, until the disability be removed, or a President shall be elected.

6. The President shall, at stated times, receive for his services a compensation, which shall neither be increased nor diminished during the period for which he shall have been elected, and he shall not receive within that period any other emolument from the United States, or any of them.

7. Before he enter on the execution of his office, he shall take the following oath or affirmation:—"I do solemnly swear (or affirm) that I will faithfully execute the office of the President of the United States, and will to the best of my ability, preserve, protect and defend the Constitution of the United States."

Section 2.1. The President shall be commander in chief of the army and navy of the United States, and of the militia of the several States, when called into the actual service of the United States; he may require the opinion, in writing, of the principal officer in each of the executive departments, upon any subject relating to the duties of their respective office, and he shall have power to grant reprieves and pardons for offenses against the United States, except in cases of impeachment.

4. Superseded by the 12th Amendment.

2. He shall have power, by and with the advice and consent of the Senate, to make treaties, provided two thirds of the senators present concur; and he shall nominate, and by and with the advice and consent of the Senate, shall appoint ambassadors, other public ministers and consuls, judges of the Supreme Court, and all other officers of the United States, whose appointments are not herein otherwise provided for, and which shall be established by law: but the Congress may by law vest the appointment of such inferior officers, as they think proper, in the President alone, in the courts of law, or in the heads of departments.

3. The President shall have power to fill up all vacancies that may happen during the recess of the Senate, by granting commissions which shall expire at the end of their next session.

Section 3. He shall from time to time give to the Congress information of the state of the Union, and recommend to their consideration such measures as he shall judge necessary and expedient; he may, on extraordinary occasions, convene both Houses, or either of them, and in case of disagreement between them with respect to the time of adjournment, he may adjourn them to such time as he shall think proper; he shall receive ambassadors and other public ministers; he shall take care that the laws be faithfully executed, and shall commission all of the officers of the United States.

Section 4. The President, Vice President, and all civil officers of the United States, shall be removed from office on impeachment for, and conviction of, treason, bribery, or other high crimes and misdemeanors.

ARTICLE III

Section 1. The judicial power of the United States shall be vested in one Supreme Court, and in such inferior courts as the Congress may from time to time ordain and establish. The judges, both of the Supreme and inferior courts, shall hold their offices during good behavior, and shall, at stated times, receive for their services, a compensation, which shall not be diminished during their continuance in office.

Section 2.1. The judicial power shall extend to all cases, in law and equity, arising under this Constitution, the laws of the United States, and treaties made, or which shall be made, under their authority;—to all cases affecting ambassadors, other public ministers and consuls;—to all cases of admiralty and maritime jurisdiction;—to controversies to which the United States may be a party;—to controversies between two or more States; between a State and citizens of another State;[5]—between citizens of different States;—between citizens of the same State claiming lands under grants of different States, and between a State, or the citizens thereof, and foreign States' citizens or subjects.

2. In all cases affecting ambassadors, other public ministers and consuls, and those in which a State shall be party, the Supreme Court shall have original jurisdiction. In all the other cases before mentioned, the Supreme Court shall have appellate jurisdiction, both as to law and to fact, with such exceptions, and under such regulations as the Congress shall make.

3. The trial of all crimes, except in cases of impeachment, shall be by jury; and such trial shall be held in the State where the said crimes shall have been committed; but when not committed within any State, the trial shall be at such place or places as the Congress may by law have directed.

Section 3.1. Treason against the United States shall consist only in levying war against them, or in adhering to their enemies, giving them aid and comfort. No person shall be

5. See the 11th Amendment.

convicted of treason unless on the testimony of two witnesses to the same overt act, or on confession in open court.

2. The Congress shall have power to declare the punishment of treason, but no attainder of treason shall work corruption of blood, or forfeiture except during the life of the person attainted.

ARTICLE IV

Section 1. Full faith and credit shall be given in each State to the public acts, records, and judicial proceedings of every other State. And the Congress may by general laws prescribe the manner in which such acts, records and proceedings shall be proved, and the effect thereof.

Section 2.1. The citizens of each State shall be entitled to all privileges and immunities of citizens in the several States.[6]

2. A person charged in any State with treason, felony, or other crime, who shall flee from justice, and be found in another State, shall on demand of the executive authority of the State from which he fled, be delivered up to be removed to the State having jurisdiction of the crime.

3. No person held to service or labor in one State under the laws thereof, escaping into another, shall in consequence of any law or regulation therein, be discharged from such service or labor, but shall be delivered up on claim of the party to whom such service or labor may be due.[7]

Section 3.1. New States may be admitted by the Congress to this Union; but no new State shall be formed or erected within the jurisdiction of any other State, nor any State be formed by the junction of two or more States, or parts of States, without the consent of the legislatures of the States concerned as well as of the Congress.

2. The Congress shall have power to dispose of and make all needful rules and regulations respecting the territory or other property belonging to the United States; and nothing in this Constitution shall be so construed as to prejudice any claims of the United States, or of any particular State.

Section 4. The United States shall guarantee to every State in this Union a republican form of government, and shall protect each of them against invasion; and on application of the legislature, or of the executive (when the legislature cannot be convened) against domestic violence.

ARTICLE V

The Congress, whenever two thirds of both Houses shall deem it necessary, shall propose amendments to this Constitution, or, on the application of the legislature of two thirds of the several States, shall call a convention for proposing amendments, which in either case, shall be valid to all intents and purposes, as part of this Constitution when ratified by the legislatures of three fourths of the several States, or by conventions in three fourths thereof, as the one or the other mode of ratification may be proposed by the Congress; provided that no amendment which may be made prior to the year one thousand eight hundred and eight shall in any manner affect the first and fourth clauses in the ninth section of the first article; and that no State, without its consent, shall be deprived of its equal suffrage in the Senate.

6. See the 14th Amendment, Sec. 1.

7. See the 13th Amendment.

ARTICLE VI

1. All debts contracted and engagements entered into, before the adoption of this Constitution, shall be as valid against the United States under this Constitution, as under the Confederation.[8]

2. This Constitution, and the laws of the United States which shall be made in pursuance thereof; and all treaties made, or which shall be made, under the authority of the United States, shall be the supreme law of the land; and the Judges in every state shall be bound thereby, anything in the Constitution or laws of any State to the contrary notwithstanding.

3. The senators and representatives before mentioned, and the members of the several State legislatures, and all executive and judicial officers, both of the United States and of the several States, shall be bound by oath or affirmation to support this Constitution; but no religious test shall ever be required as a qualification to any office or public trust under the United States.

ARTICLE VII

The ratification of the conventions of nine States shall be sufficient for the establishment of this Constitution between the States so ratifying the same.

Done in Convention by the unanimous consent of the States present the seventeenth day of September in the year of our Lord one thousand seven hundred and eighty-seven, and of the independence of the United States of America the twelfth. In witness whereof we have hereunto subscribed our names.

AMENDMENTS

First Ten Amendments passed by Congress September 25, 1789.
Ratified by three-fourths of the States December 15, 1791.

AMENDMENT I

Congress shall make no law respecting an establishment of religion, or prohibiting the free exercise thereof; or abridging the freedom of speech, or of the press; or the right of the people peaceably to assemble, and to petition the government for a redress of grievances.

AMENDMENT II

A well regulated militia, being necessary to the security of a free State, the right of the people to keep and bear arms, shall not be infringed.

AMENDMENT III

No soldier shall, in time of peace be quartered in any house, without the consent of the owner, nor in time of war, but in a manner prescribed by law.

AMENDMENT IV

The right of the people to be secure in their persons, houses, papers, and effects, against unreasonable searches and seizures, shall not be violated, and no warrants shall issue,

8. See the 14th Amendment, Sec. 4.

but upon probable cause, supported by oath or affirmation, and particularly describing the place to be searched, and the person or things to be seized.

AMENDMENT V

No person shall be held to answer for a capital, or otherwise infamous crime, unless on a presentment or indictment of a grand jury, except in cases arising in the land or naval forces, or in the militia, when in actual service in time of war or public danger; nor shall any person be subject for the same offense to be twice put in jeopardy of life or limb; nor shall be compelled in any criminal case to be a witness against himself, nor be deprived of life, liberty, or property, without due process of law; nor shall private property be taken for public use without just compensation.

AMENDMENT VI

In all criminal prosecutions, the accused shall enjoy the right to a speedy and public trial, by an impartial jury of the State and district wherein the crime shall have been committed, which district shall have been previously ascertained by law, and to be informed of the nature and cause of the accusation; to be confronted with the witnesses against him; to have compulsory process for obtaining witnesses in his favor, and to have the assistance of counsel for his defense.

AMENDMENT VII

In suits at common law, where the value in controversy shall exceed twenty dollars, the right of trial by jury shall be preserved, and no fact tried by a jury shall be preserved, and no fact tried by a jury shall be otherwise reexamined in any court of the United States, then according to the rules of the common law.

AMENDMENT VIII

Excessive bail shall not be required, nor excessive fines imposed, nor cruel and unusual punishments inflicted.

AMENDMENT IX

The enumeration in the Constitution of certain rights shall not be construed to deny or disparage others retained by the people.

AMENDMENT X

The powers not delegated to the United States by the Constitution, nor prohibited by it to the States, are reserved to the States respectively, or to the people.

AMENDMENT XI

Passed by Congress March 5, 1794. Ratified January 8, 1798.

The judicial power of the United States shall not be construed to extend to any suit in law or equity, commenced or prosecuted against one of the United States by citizens of another State, or by citizens or subjects of any foreign State.

AMENDMENT XII

Passed by Congress December 12, 1803. Ratified September 25, 1804.

The electors shall meet in their respective States, and vote by ballot for President and Vice President, one of whom, at least, shall not be an inhabitant of the same State with themselves; they shall name in their ballots the person voted for as President, and in distinct ballots, the person voted for as Vice President, and they shall make distinct lists of all persons voted for as President and of all persons voted for as Vice President, and of the number of votes for each, which lists they shall sign and certify, and transmit sealed to the seat of the government of the United States, directed to the President of the Senate;—the President of the Senate shall, in the presence of the Senate and House of Representatives, open all the certificates and the votes shall then be counted;—the person having the greatest number of votes for President, shall be the President, if such number be a majority of the whole number of electors appointed; and if no person have such majority, then from the persons having the highest numbers not exceeding three on the list of those voted for as President, the House of Representatives shall choose immediately, by ballot, the President. But in choosing the President, the vote shall be taken by the States, the representation from each State having one vote; a quorum for this purpose shall consist of a member or members from two thirds of the States, and a majority of all the States shall be necessary to a choice. And if the House of Representatives shall not choose a President whenever the right of choice shall devolve upon them, before the fourth day of March next following, then the Vice President shall act as President, as in the case of the death or other constitutional disability of the President. The person having the greatest number of votes as Vice President shall be the Vice President, if such number be a majority of the whole number of electors appointed, and if no person have a majority, then from the two highest numbers on the list, the Senate shall choose the Vice President; a quorum for the purpose shall consist of two thirds of the whole number of Senators, and a majority of the whole number shall be necessary to a choice. But no person constitutionally ineligible to the office of President shall be eligible to that of Vice President of the United States.

AMENDMENT XIII

Passed by Congress February 1, 1865. Ratified December 18, 1865.
Section 1. Neither slavery nor involuntary servitude, except as punishment for crime whereof the party shall have been duly convicted, shall exist within the United States, or any place subject to their jurisdiction.
Section 2. Congress shall have power to enforce this article by appropriate legislation.

AMENDMENT XIV

Passed by Congress June 16, 1866. Ratified July 23, 1868.
Section 1. All persons born or naturalized in the United States, and subject to the jurisdiction thereof, are citizens of the United States and of the State wherein they reside. No State shall make or enforce any law which shall abridge the privileges or immunities of citizens of the United States; nor shall any State deprive any person of life, liberty, or property, without due process of law; nor deny to any person within its jurisdiction the equal protection of the laws.
Section 2. Representatives shall be apportioned among the several States according to their respective numbers, counting the whole number of persons in each State, excluding Indians not taxed. But when the right to vote at any election for the choice of electors for President and Vice President of the United States, representatives in Congress, the executive and judicial officers of a State, or the members of the legislature thereof, is denied to any of the male inhabitants of such State, being twenty-one years of age, and citizens of the United States, or in any way abridged, except for participation in rebellion, or other crime, the basis of representation therein shall be reduced in the proportion which the number of such male citizens shall bear to the whole number of male citizens twenty-one years of age in such State.
Section 3. No person shall be a senator or representative in Congress, or elector of President and Vice President, or hold any office, civil or military, under the United

States, or under any State, who having previously taken an oath, as a member of Congress, or as an officer of the United States, or as a member of any State legislature, or as an executive or judicial officer of any State, to support the Constitution of the United States, shall have engaged in insurrection or rebellion against the same, or given aid or comfort to the enemies thereof. But Congress may by a vote of two thirds of each House, remove such disability.

Section 4. The validity of the public debt of the United States, authorized by law, including debts incurred for payment of pensions and bounties for services in suppressing insurrection or rebellion, shall not be questioned. But neither the United States nor any State shall assume or pay any debt or obligation incurred in aid of insurrection or rebellion against the United States, or any claim for the loss or emancipation of any slave; but all such debts, obligations, and claims shall be held illegal and void.

Section 5. The Congress shall have power to enforce, by appropriate legislation, the provisions of this article.

AMENDMENT XV

Passed by Congress February 27, 1869. Ratified March 30, 1870.

Section 1. The right of citizens of the United States to vote shall not be denied or abridged by the United States or by any State on account of race, color, or previous condition of servitude.

Section 2. The Congress shall have power to enforce this article by appropriate legislation.

AMENDMENT XVI

Passed by Congress July 12, 1909. Ratified February 25, 1913.

The Congress shall have power to lay and collect taxes on incomes, from whatever source derived, without apportionment among the several States, and without regard to any census or enumeration.

AMENDMENT XVII

Passed by Congress May 16, 1912. Ratified May 31, 1913.

The Senate of the United States shall be composed of two senators from each State, elected by the people thereof, for six years; and each senator shall have one vote. The electors in each State shall have the qualifications requisite for electors of the most numerous branch of the State legislature.

When vacancies happen in the representation of any State in the Senate, the executive authority of such State shall issue writs of election to fill such vacancies: Provided, That the legislature of any State may empower the executive thereof to make temporary appointments until the people fill the vacancies by election as the legislature may direct.

This amendment shall not be construed as to affect the election or term of any senator chosen before it becomes valid as part of the Constitution.

AMENDMENT XVIII

Passed by Congress December 17, 1917. Ratified January 29, 1919.

After one year from the ratification of this article, the manufacture, sale, or transportation of intoxicating liquors within, the importation thereof into, or the exportation thereof from the United States and all territory subject to the jurisdiction thereof for beverage purposes is hereby prohibited.

The Congress and the several States shall have concurrent power to enforce this article by appropriate legislation.

This article shall be inoperative unless it shall have been ratified as an amendment to the Constitution by the legislatures of the several States, as provided in the Constitution, within seven years from the date of the submission hereof to the States by Congress.

AMENDMENT XIX

Passed by Congress June 5, 1919. Ratified August 26, 1920.

The right of citizens of the United States to vote shall not be denied or abridged by the United States or by any State on account of sex.

The Congress shall have power by appropriate legislation to enforce the provisions of this article.

AMENDMENT XX

Passed by Congress March 3, 1932. Ratified January 23, 1933.

Section 1. The terms of the President and Vice President shall end at noon on the 20th day of January, and the terms of Senators and Representatives at noon on the 3d day of January, of the years in which such terms would have ended if this article had not been ratified; and the terms of their successors shall then begin.

Section 2. The Congress shall assemble at least once in every year, and such meeting shall begin at noon on the 3d day of January, unless they shall by law appoint a different day.

Section 3. If, at the time fixed for the beginning of the term of the President, the President-elect shall have died, the Vice President-elect shall become President. If a President shall not have been chosen before the time fixed for the beginning of his term, or if the President-elect shall have failed to qualify, then the Vice President-elect shall act as President until a President shall have qualified; and the Congress may by law provide for the case wherein neither a President-elect nor a Vice President-elect shall have qualified, declaring who shall then act as President, or the manner in which one who is to act shall be selected, and such person shall act accordingly until a President or Vice President shall have qualified.

Section 4. The Congress may by law provide for the case of the death of any of the persons from whom the House of Representatives may choose a President whenever the right of choice shall have devolved upon them, and for the case of the death of any of the persons from whom the Senate may choose a Vice President whenever the right of choice shall have devolved upon them.

Section 5. Sections 1 and 2 shall take effect on the 15th day of October following the ratification of this article.

Section 6. This article shall be inoperative unless it shall have been ratified as an amendment to the Constitution by the legislatures of three-fourths of the several States within seven years from the date of its submission.

AMENDMENT XXI

Passed by Congress February 20, 1933. Ratified December 5, 1933.

Section 1. The Eighteenth Article of amendment to the Constitution of the United States is hereby repealed.

Section 2. The transportation or importation into any State, Territory, or possession of the United States for delivery or use therein of intoxicating liquors in violation thereof, is hereby prohibited.

Section 3. This article shall be inoperative unless it shall have been ratified as an amendment to the Constitution by conventions in the several States, as provided in the Constitution, within seven years from the date of the submission thereof to the States by Congress.

AMENDMENT XXII

Passed by Congress March 24, 1947. Ratified February 26, 1951.

Section 1. No person shall be elected to the office of the President more than twice, and no person who has held the office of President, or acted as President, for more than two years of a term to which some other person was elected shall be elected to the office of the President more than once. But this article shall not apply to any person holding the office of President when this article was proposed by the Congress, and shall not prevent any person who may be holding the office of President, or acting as President, during the term within which this article becomes operative from holding the office of President or acting as President during the remainder of such term.

Section 2. This article shall be inoperative unless it shall have been ratified as an amendment to the Constitution by the legislatures of three-fourths of the several States within seven years from the date of its submission to the States by the Congress.

AMENDMENT XXIII

Passed by Congress June 16, 1960. Ratified April 3, 1961.

Section 1. The District constituting the seat of Government of the United States shall appoint in such manner as the Congress may direct:

A number of electors of President and Vice President equal to the whole number of Senators and Representatives in Congress to which the District would be entitled if it were a State, but in no event more than the least populous State; they shall be in addition to those appointed by the States, but they shall be considered, for the purposes of the election of the President and Vice President, to be electors appointed by a State; and they shall meet in the District and perform such duties as provided by the twelfth article of amendment.

Section 2. The Congress shall have power to enforce this article by appropriate legislation.

AMENDMENT XXIV

Passed by Congress August 27, 1962. Ratified February 4, 1964.

Section 1. The right of citizens of the United States to vote in any primary or other election for President or Vice President, for electors for President or Vice President, or for Senator or Representative in Congress, shall not be denied or abridged by the United States or any State by reason of failure to pay any poll tax or other tax.

Section 2. The Congress shall have power to enforce this article by appropriate legislation.

AMENDMENT XXV

Passed by Congress July 6, 1965. Ratified February 23, 1967.

Section 1. In case of the removal of the President from office or of his death or resignation, the Vice President shall become President.

Section 2. Whenever there is a vacancy in the office of Vice President, the President shall nominate a Vice President who shall take office upon confirmation by a majority vote of both Houses of Congress.

Section 3. Whenever the President transmits to the President pro tempore of the Senate and the Speaker of the House of Representatives his written declaration that he is unable to discharge the powers and duties of his office, and until he transmits to them a written declaration to the contrary, such powers and duties shall be discharged by the Vice President as Acting President.

Section 4. Whenever the Vice President and a majority of either the principal officers of the executive departments or of such other body as Congress may by law provide, transmit to the President pro tempore of the Senate and the Speaker of the House of Representatives their written declaration that the President is unable to discharge the powers and duties of his office, the Vice President shall immediately assume the powers and duties of the office as Acting President.

Thereafter, when the President transmits to the President pro tempore of the Senate and the Speaker of the House of Representatives his written declaration that no inability exists, he shall resume the powers and duties of his office unless the Vice President and a majority of either the principal officers of the executive department or of such other body as Congress may by law provide, transmit within four days to the President pro tempore of the Senate and the Speaker of the House of Representatives their written declaration that the President is unable to discharge the powers and duties of his office. Thereupon Congress shall decide the issue, assembling within forty-eight hours for that purpose if not in session. If the Congress, within twenty-one days after receipt of the latter written declaration, or, if Congress is not in session, within twenty-one days after Congress is required to assemble, determines by two-thirds vote of both Houses that the President is unable to discharge the powers and duties of his office, the Vice President shall continue to discharge the same as Acting President; otherwise, the President shall resume the powers and duties of his office.

AMENDMENT XXVI

Passed by Congress March 23, 1971. Ratified July 5, 1971.
Section 1. The right of citizens of the United States, who are eighteen years of age or older, to vote shall not be denied or abridged by the United States or by any State on account of age.

AMENDMENT XXVII

Originally passed by Congress September 25, 1789. Ratified May 18, 1992. (Really, it took 200 years!)

No law, varying the compensation of services of the Senators and Representatives, shall take effect, until an election of Representatives shall have intervened.

APPENDIX B

UNIFORM COMMERCIAL CODE (EXCERPTS) SECTIONS 2-205, 207, 312, 313, 314, 315

§2-205. FIRM OFFERS

An offer by a merchant to buy or sell goods in a signed writing which by its terms gives assurance that it will be held open is not revocable, for lack of consideration, during the time stated or if no time is stated for a reasonable time, but in no event may such period of irrevocability exceed three months; but any such term of assurance on a form supplies [supplied] by the offeree must be separately signed by the offeror.

§2-207. ADDITIONAL TERMS IN ACCEPTANCE OR CONFIRMATION

(1) A definite and seasonable expression of acceptance or a written confirmation which is sent within a reasonable time operates as an acceptance even though it states terms additional to or different from those offered or agreed upon, unless acceptance is expressly made conditional on assent to the additional or different terms.

(2) The additional terms are to be construed as proposals for addition to the contract. Between merchants such terms become part of the contract unless:

(a) the offer expressly limits acceptance to the terms of the offer;
(b) they materially alter it; or
(c) notification of objection to them has already been given or is given within a reasonable time after notice of them is received.

(3) Conduct by both parties which recognizes the existence of a contract is sufficient to establish a contract for sale although the writings of the parties do not otherwise establish a contract. In such case the terms of the particular contract consist of those terms on which the writings of the parties agree, together with any supplementary terms incorporated under any other provisions of this act.

§2-312. WARRANTY OF TITLE AND AGAINST INFRINGEMENT; BUYERS' OBLIGATION AGAINST INFRINGEMENT

(1) Subject to subsection (2), there is in a contract for sale a warranty by the seller that

(a) the title conveyed shall be good, and its transfer rightful; and
(b) the goods shall be delivered free from any security interest or other lien or encumbrance of which the buyer at the time of contracting has no knowledge.

(2) A warranty under subsection (1) will be excluded or modified only by specific language or by circumstances which give the buyer reason to know that the person selling does not claim title in himself or that he is purporting to sell only such right or title as he or a third person may have.

(3) Unless otherwise agreed a seller who is a merchant regularly dealing in goods of the kind warrants that the goods shall be delivered free of the rightful claim of any third person by way of infringement or the like but a buyer who furnishes specifications to the seller must hold the seller harmless against any such claim which arises out of compliance with the specifications.

§2-313. EXPRESS WARRANTIES BY AFFIRMATION, PROMISE, DESCRIPTION, SAMPLE

(1) Express warranties by the seller are created as follows:

(a) Any affirmation of fact or promise made by the seller to the buyer which relates to the goods and becomes part of the basis of the bargain creates an express warranty that the goods shall conform to the affirmation or promise.

(b) Any description of the goods which is made part of the basis or the bargain creates an express warranty that the goods shall conform to the description.

(c) Any sample or model which is made part of the basis of the bargain creates an express warranty that the whole of the goods shall conform to the sample or model.

(2) It is not necessary to the creation of an express warranty that the seller use formal words such as *warrant* or *guarantee* or that he have a specific intention to make a warranty, but an affirmation merely of the value of the goods or a statement purporting to be merely the seller's opinion or commendation of the goods does not create a warranty.

§2-314. IMPLIED WARRANTY; MERCHANTABILITY; USAGE OF TRADE

(1) Unless excluded or modified (Section 2-316), a warranty that the goods shall be merchantable is implied in a contract for their sale if the seller is a merchant with respect to goods of that kind. Under this section, the serving for value of food or drink to be consumed either on the premises or elsewhere is a sale.

(2) Goods to be merchantable must be at least such as

(a) pass without objection in the trade under the contract description; and

(b) in the case of fungible goods, are of fair average quality within the description; and

(c) are fit for the ordinary purposes for which such goods are used; and

(d) run, within the variations permitted by the agreement, of even kind, quality and quantity within each unit and among all units involved; and

(e) are adequately contained, packaged and labeled as the agreement may require; and

(f) conform to the promises or affirmations of fact made on the container or label, if any.

(3) Unless excluded or modified (Section 2-316), other implied warranties may arise from course of dealing or usage of trade.

§2-315. IMPLIED WARRANTY: FITNESS FOR PARTICULAR PURPOSE

Where the seller at the time of contracting has reason to know any particular purpose for which the goods are required and that the buyer is relying on the seller's skill or judgment to select or furnish suitable goods, there is unless excluded or modified under the next section an implied warranty that the goods shall be fit for such purpose.

APPENDIX C
UNIFORM PARTNERSHIP ACT

PART I

PRELIMINARY PROVISIONS

§1. Name of Act
This act may be cited as Uniform Partnership Act.

§2. Definition of Terms

In this act, "Court" includes every court and judge having jurisdiction in the case.

"Business" includes every trade, occupation, or profession.

"Person" includes individuals, partnerships, corporations, and other associations.

"Bankrupt" includes bankrupt under the Federal Bankruptcy Act or insolvent under any state insolvent act.

"Conveyance" includes every assignment, lease, mortgage, or encumbrance.

"Real property" includes land and any interest or estate in land.

§3. Interpretation of Knowledge and Notice

(1) A person has "knowledge" of a fact within the meaning of this act not only when he has actual knowledge thereof, but also when he has knowledge of such other facts as in the circumstances shows bad faith.

(2) A person has "notice" of a fact within the meaning of this act when the person who claims the benefit of the notice

(a) States the fact to such person, or

(b) Delivers through the mail, or by other means of communication, a written statement of the fact to such person or to a proper person at his place of business or residence.

§4. Rules of Construction

(1) The rule that statutes in derogation of the common law are to be strictly construed shall have no application to this act.

(2) The law of estoppel shall apply under this act.

(3) The law of agency shall apply under this act.

(4) This act shall be so interpreted and construed as to effect its general purpose to make uniform the law of those states which enact it.

(5) This act shall not be construed so as to impair the obligations of any contract existing when the act goes into effect, nor to affect any action or proceedings begun or right accrued before this act takes effect.

§5. Rules for Cases Not Provided for in this Act

In any case not provided for in this act the rules of law and equity, including the law merchant, shall govern.

PART II

NATURE OF PARTNERSHIP

§6. Partnership Defined

(1) A partnership is an association of two or more persons to carry on as co-owners of a business for profit.

(2) But any association formed under any other statute of this state, or any statute adopted by authority, other than the authority of this state, is not a partnership under this act, unless such association would have been a partnership in this state prior to the adoption of this act; but this act shall apply to limited partnerships except in so far as the statutes relating to such partnerships are inconsistent herewith.

§7. Rules for Determining the Existence of a Partnership

In determining whether a partnership exists, these rules shall apply:

(1) Except as provided by Section 16 persons who are not partners as to each other are not partners as to third persons.

(2) Joint tenancy, tenancy in common, tenancy by the entireties, joint property, common property, or part ownership does not of itself establish a partnership, whether such co-owners do or do not share any profits made by the use of the property.

(3) The sharing of gross returns does not of itself establish a partnership, whether or not the persons sharing them have a joint or common right or interest in any property from which the returns are derived.

(4) The receipt by a person of a share of the profits of a business is prima facie evidence that he is a partner in the business, but no such inference shall be drawn if such profits were received in payment:

(a) As a debt by installments or otherwise,
(b) As wages of an employee or rent to a landlord,
(c) As an annuity to a widow or representative of a deceased partner,
(d) As interest on a loan, though the amount of payment vary with the profits of the business,
(e) As the consideration for the sale of a goodwill of a business or other property by installments or otherwise.

§8. Partnership Property

(1) All property originally brought into the partnership stock or subsequently acquired by purchase or otherwise, on account of the partnership, is partnership property.

(2) Unless the contrary intention appears, property acquired with partnership funds is partnership property.

(3) Any estate in real property may be acquired in the partnership name. Title so acquired can be conveyed only in the partnership name.

(4) A conveyance to a partnership in the partnership name, though without words of inheritance, passes the entire estate of the grantor unless a contrary intent appears.

PART III

RELATIONS OF PARTNERS TO PERSONS DEALING WITH THE PARTNERSHIP

§9. Partner Agent of Partnership as to Partnership Business

(1) Every partner is an agent of the partnership for the purpose of its business, and the act of every partner, including the execution of the partnership name of any instrument, for apparently carrying on in the usual way the business of the partnership of which he is a member binds the partnership, unless the partner so acting has in fact no authority to act for the partnership in the particular matter, and the person with whom he is dealing has knowledge of the fact that he has no such authority.

(2) An act of a partner which is not apparently for the carrying on of the business of the partnership in the usual way does not bind the partnership unless authorized by the other partners.

(3) Unless authorized by the other partners or unless they have abandoned the business, one or more but less than all the partners have no authority to:

(a) Assign the partnership property in trust for creditors or on the assignee's promise to pay the debts of the partnership,
(b) Dispose of the goodwill of the business,
(c) Do any other act which would make it impossible to carry on the ordinary business of a partnership,
(d) Confess a judgment,
(e) Submit a partnership claim or liability to arbitration or reference.

(4) No act of a partner in contravention of a restriction on authority shall bind the partnership to persons having knowledge of the restriction.

§10. Conveyance of Real Property of the Partnership

(1) Where title to real property is in the partnership name, any partner may convey title to such property by a conveyance executed in the partnership name; but the partnership may recover such property unless the partner's act binds the partnership under the provisions of paragraph (1) of section 9 or unless such property has been conveyed by the grantee or a person claiming through such grantee to a holder for value without knowledge that the partner, in making the conveyance, has exceeded his authority.

(2) Where title to real property is in the name of the partnership, a conveyance executed by a partner, in his own name, passes the equitable interest of the partnership, provided the act is one within the authority of the partner under the provisions of paragraph (1) of section 9.

(3) Where title to real property is in the name of one or more but not all the partners, and the record does not disclose the right of the partnership, the partners in whose name the title stands may convey title to such property, but the partnership may recover such property if the partners' act does not bind the partnership under the provisions of paragraph (1) of section 9, unless the purchaser, or his assignee, is a holder for value, without knowledge.

(4) Where the title to real property is in the name of one or more or all the partners, or in a third person in trust for the partnership, a conveyance executed by a partner in the partnership name, or in his own name, passes the equitable interest of the partnership, provided the act is one within the authority of the partner under the provisions of paragraph (1) of section 9.

(5) Where the title to real property is in the names of all the partners a conveyance executed by all the partners passes all their rights in such property.

§11. Partnership Bound by Admission of Partner

An admission or representation made by any partner concerning partnership affairs within the scope of his authority as conferred by this act is evidence against the partnership.

§12. Partnership Charged with Knowledge of or Notice to Partner

Notice to any partner of any matter relating to partnership affairs, and the knowledge of the partner acting in the particular matter, acquired while a partner or then present to his mind, and the knowledge of any other partner who reasonably could and should have communicated it to the acting partner, operate as notice to or knowledge of the partnership, except in the case of a fraud on the partnership committed by or with the consent of that partner.

§13. Partnership Bound by Partner's Wrongful Act

Where, by any wrongful act or omission of any partner acting in the ordinary course of the business of the partnership or with the authority of his co-partners, loss or injury is caused to any person, not being a partner in the partnership, or any penalty is incurred, the partnership is liable therefor to the same extent as the partner so acting or omitting to act.

§14. Partnership Bound by Partner's Breach of Trust

The partnership is bound to make good the loss:

(a) Where one partner acting within the scope of his apparent authority receives money or property of a third person and misapplies it; and

(b) Where the partnership in the course of its business receives money or property of a third person and the money or property so receive is misapplied by any partner while it is in the custody of the partnership.

§15. Nature of Partner's Liability

All partners are liable

(a) Jointly and severally for everything chargeable to the partnership under sections 13 and 14.

(b) Jointly for all other debts and obligations of the partnership; but any partner may enter into a separate obligation to perform a partnership contract.

§16. Partner by Estoppel

(1) When a person, by words spoken or written or by conduct, represents himself, or consents to another representing him to any one, as a partner in an existing partnership or with one or more persons not actual partners, he is liable to any such person to whom such representation has been made, who has, on the faith of such representation, given credit to the actual or apparent partnership, and if he has made such representation or consented to its being made in a public manner he is liable to such person, whether the representation has or has not been made or communicated to such person so giving credit by or with the knowledge of the apparent partner making the representation or consenting to its being made.

(a) When a partnership liability results, he is liable as though he were an actual member of the partnership.

(b) When no partnership liability results, he is liable jointly with the other persons, if any, so consenting to the contract or representation as to incur liability, otherwise separately.

(2) When a person has been thus represented to be a partner in an existing partnership, or with one or more persons not actual partners, he is an agent of the persons consenting to such representation to bind them to the same extent and in the same manner as though he were a partner in fact, with respect to persons who rely upon the representation. Where all the members of the existing partnership consent to the representation, a partnership act or obligation results; but in all other cases it is the joint act or obligation of the person acting and the persons consenting to the representation.

§17. Liability of Incoming Partner

A person admitted as a partner into an existing partnership is liable for all the obligations of the partnership arising before his admission as though he had been a partner when such obligations were incurred, except that this liability shall be satisfied only out of partnership property.

PART IV

RELATIONS OF PARTNERS TO ONE ANOTHER

§18. Rules Determining Rights and Duties of Partners

The rights and duties of the partners in relation to the partnership shall be determined, subject to any agreement between them, by the following rules:

(a) Each partner shall be repaid his contributions, whether by way of capital or advances to the partnership property and share equally in the profits and surplus remaining after all liabilities, including those to partners, are satisfied; and must contribute toward the losses, whether of capital or otherwise, sustained by the partnership according to his share in the profits.

(b) The partnership must indemnify every partner in respect of payments made and personal liabilities reasonably incurred by him in the ordinary and proper conduct of its business, or for the preservation of its business or property.

(c) A partner, who in aid of the partnership makes any payment or advance beyond the amount of capital which he agreed to contribute, shall be paid interest from the date of the payment or advance.

(d) A partner shall receive interest on the capital contributed by him only from the date when repayment should be made.

(e) All partners have equal rights in the management and conduct of the partnership business.

(f) No partner is entitled to remuneration for acting in the partnership business, except that a surviving partner is entitled to reasonable compensation for his services in winding up the partnership affairs.

(g) No person can become a member of a partnership without the consent of all the partners.

(h) Any difference arising as to ordinary matters connected with the partnership business may be decided by a majority of the partners; but no act in contravention of any agreement between the partners may be done rightfully without the consent of all the partners.

§19. Partnership Books

The partnership books shall be kept, subject to any agreement between the partners, at the principal place of business of the partnership, and every partner shall at all times have access to and may inspect and copy any of them.

§20. Duty of Partners to Render Information

Partners shall render on demand true and full information of all things affecting the partnership to any partner or the legal representative of any deceased partner or partner under legal disability.

§21. Partner Accountable as a Fiduciary

(1) Every partner must account to the partnership for any benefit, and hold as trustee for it any profits derived by him without the consent of the other partners from any transaction connected with the formation, conduct, or liquidation of the partnership or from any use by him of its property.

(2) This section applies also to the representatives of a deceased partner engaged in the liquidation of the affairs of the partnership as the personal representatives of the last surviving partner.

§22. Right to an Account

Any partner shall have the right to a formal account as to partnership affairs:

(a) If he is wrongfully excluded from the partnership business or possession of its property by his co-partners,

(b) If the right exists under the terms of agreement,

(c) As provided by Section 21,

(d) Whenever other circumstances render it just and reasonable.

§23. Continuation of Partnership Beyond Fixed Term

(1) When a partnership for a fixed term or particular undertaking is continued after the termination of such term or particular undertaking without any express agreement, the rights and duties of the partners remain the same as they were at such termination, so far as is consistent with a partnership at will.

(2) A continuation of the business by the partners or such of them as habitually acted therein during the term, without any settlement or liquidation of the partnership affairs, is prima facie evidence of a continuation of the partnership.

PART V

PROPERTY RIGHTS OF A PARTNER

§24. Extent of Property Rights of a Partner
The property rights of a partner are (1) his rights in specific partnership property, (2) his interest in the partnership, and (3) his right to participate in the management.

§25. Nature of a Partner's Right in Specific Partnership Property
(1) A partner is co-owner with his partners of specific partnership property holding as a tenant in partnership.
(2) The incidents of this tenancy are such that:
(a) A partner, subject to the provisions of this act and to any agreement between the partners, has an equal right with his partners to possess specific partnership property for partnership purposes; but he has no right to possess such property, for any other purpose without the consent of his partners.
(b) A partner's right in specific partnership property is not assignable except in connection with the assignment of rights of all the partners in the same property.
(c) A partner's right in specific partnership property is not subject to attachment or execution, except on a claim against the partnership. When partnership property is attached for a partnership debt the partners, or any of them, or the representatives of a deceased partner, cannot claim any right under the homestead or exemption laws.
(d) On the death of a partner his right in specific partnership property vests in the surviving partner or partners, except where the deceased was the last surviving partner or partners, or the legal representative of the last surviving partner, has no right to possess the partnership property for any but a partnership purpose.
(e) A partner's right in specific partnership property is not subject to dower, courtesy, or allowances to widows, heirs, or next of kin.

§26. Nature of Partner's Interest in the Partnership
A partner's interest in the partnership is his share of the profits and surplus, and the same is personal property.

§27. Assignment of Partner's Interest
(1) A conveyance by a partner of his interest in the partnership does not of itself dissolve the partnership, nor, as against the other partners in the absence of agreement, entitle the assignee, during the continuance of the partnership to interfere in the management or administration of the partnership business or affairs, or to require an information or account of partnership transactions, or to inspect the partnership books; but it merely entitles the assignee to receive in accordance with his contract the profits to which the assigning partner would otherwise be entitled.
(2) In case of a dissolution of the partnership, the assignee is entitled to receive his assignor's interest and may require an account from the date only of the last account agreed to by all the partners.

§28. Partner's Interest Subject to Charging Order
(1) On due application to a competent court by any judgment creditor of a partner, the court which entered the judgment, order, or decree, or any other court, may charge the interest of the debtor partner with payment of the unsatisfied amount of such judgment debt with interest thereon; and may then or later appoint a receiver of his share of the profits, and of any other money due or to fall due to him in respect of the partnership, and make all other orders, directions, accounts and inquiries which the debtor partner might have made, or which the circumstances of the case may require.

(2) The interest charged may be redeemed at any time before foreclosure, or in case of a sale being directed by the court may be purchased without thereby causing a dissolution:

(a) With separate property, by any one or more of the partners, or

(b) With partnership property, by any one or more of the partners with the consent of all the partners whose interests are not so charged or sold.

(3) Nothing in this act shall be held to deprive a partner of his right, if any, under the exemption laws, as regards his interest in the partnership.

PART VI

DISSOLUTION AND WINDING UP

§29. Dissolution Defined

The dissolution of a partnership is the change in the relation of the partners caused by any partner ceasing to be associated in the carrying on as distinguished from the winding up of the business.

§30. Partnership Not Terminated by Dissolution

On dissolution the partnership is not terminated, but continues until the winding up of partnership affairs is completed.

§31. Causes of Dissolution

Dissolution is caused: (1) Without violation of the agreement between the partners,

(a) By the termination of the definite term or particular undertaking specified in the agreement,

(b) By the express will of any partner when no definite term or particular undertaking is specified,

(c) By the express will of all the partners who have not assigned their interest or suffered them to be charged for their separate debts, either before or after the termination of any specified term or particular undertaking,

(d) By the expulsion of any partner from the business bona fide in accordance with such a power conferred by the agreement between the partners;

(2) In contravention of the agreement between the partners, where the circumstances do not permit a dissolution under any other provision of this section, by the express will of any partner at any time;

(3) By any event which makes it unlawful for the business of the partnership to be carried on or for the members to carry it on in partnership;

(4) By the death of any partner;

(5) By the bankruptcy of any partner or the partnership;

(6) By decree of court under Section 32.

§32. Dissolution by Decree of Court

(1) On application by or for a partner the court shall decree a dissolution whenever:

(a) A partner has been declared a lunatic in any judicial proceeding or is shown to be of unsound mind,

(b) A partner becomes in any other way incapable of performing his part of the partnership contract,

(c) A partner has been guilty of such conduct as tends to affect prejudicially the carrying on of the business,

(d) A partner willfully or persistently commits a breach of the partnership agreement, or otherwise so conducts himself in matters relating to the partnership business that it is not reasonably practicable to carry on the business partnership with him,

(e) The business of the partnership can only be carried on at a loss,

(f) Other circumstances render a dissolution equitable.

(2) On the application of the purchaser of a partner's interest under Sections 27 or 28:
(a) After the termination of the specified term or particular undertaking,
(b) At any time if the partnership was a partnership at will when the interest was assigned or when the charging order was issued.

§33. General Effect of Dissolution on Authority of Partner
Except so far as may be necessary to wind up partnership affairs or to complete transactions begun but not then finished, dissolution terminates all authority of any partner to act for the partnership,
(1) With respect to the partners,
(a) When the dissolution is not by the act, bankruptcy or death of a partner, or
(b) When the dissolution is by such act, bankruptcy or death of a partner, in cases where Section 34 so requires.
(2) With respect to persons not partners, as declared in Section 35.

§34. Right of Partner to Contribution from Copartners After Dissolution
Where the dissolution is caused by the act, death or bankruptcy of a partner, each partner is liable to his co-partners for his share of any liability created by any partner acting for the partnership as if the partnership had not been dissolved unless
(a) The dissolution being by act of any partner, the partner acting for the partnership had knowledge of the dissolution, or
(b) The dissolution being by the death or bankruptcy of a partner, the partner acting for the partnership had knowledge or notice of the death or bankruptcy.

§35. Power of Partner to Bind Partnership to Third Persons After Dissolution
(1) After dissolution a partner can bind the partnership except as provided in Paragraph (3)
(a) By any act appropriate for winding up partnership affairs or completing transactions unfinished by dissolution;
(b) By any transaction which would bind the partnership if dissolution had not taken place, provided the other party to the transaction
(I) Had extended credit to the partnership prior to dissolution and had no knowledge or notice of the dissolution; or
(II) Though he had not so extended credit, had nevertheless known of the partnership prior to dissolution, and, having no knowledge or notice of dissolution, the fact of dissolution had not been advertised in a newspaper of general circulation in the place (or in each place if more than one) at which the partnership business was regularly carried on.

(2) The liability of a partner under paragraph (b) shall be satisfied out of partnership assets alone when such partner had been prior to dissolution.
(a) Unknown as a partner to the person with whom the contract is made; and
(b) So far unknown and inactive in partnership affairs that the business reputation of the partnership could not be said to have been in any degree due to his connection with it.
(3) The partnership is in no case bound by any act of a partner after dissolution.
(a) Where the partnership is dissolved because it is unlawful to carry on the business, unless the act is appropriate for winding up partnership affairs; or
(b) Where the partner has become bankrupt; or
(c) Where the partner has no authority to wind up partnership affairs; except by a transaction with one who
(I) Had extended credit to the partnership prior to dissolution and had no knowledge or notice of his want of authority; or
(II) Had not extended credit to the partnership prior to dissolution, and, having no knowledge or notice of his want of authority, the fact of his

want of authority has not been advertised in the manner provided for advertising the fact of dissolution in paragraph (1bII).

(4) Nothing in this section shall affect the liability under section 16 of any person who after dissolution represents himself or consents to another representing him as a partner in a partnership engaged in carrying on business.

§36. Effect of Dissolution on Partner's Existing Liability

(1) The dissolution of the partnership does not of itself discharge the existing liability of any partner.

(2) A partner is discharged from any existing liability upon dissolution of the partnership by an agreement to that effect between himself, the partnership creditor and the person or partnership continuing the business; and such agreement may be inferred from the course of dealing between the creditor having knowledge of the dissolution and the person or partnership continuing the business.

(3) Where a person agrees to assume the existing obligations of a dissolved partnership, the partners whose obligations have been assumed shall be discharged from any liability to any creditor of the partnership who, knowing of the agreement, consents to a material alteration in the nature or time of payment of such obligations.

(4) The individual property of a deceased partner shall be liable for all obligations of the partnership incurred while he was a partner but subject to the prior payment of his separate debts.

§37. Right to Wind Up

Unless otherwise agreed the partners who have not wrongfully dissolved the partnership or the legal representative of the last surviving partner, not bankrupt, has the right to wind up the partnership affairs; provided, however, that any partner, his legal representative or his assignee, upon cause shown, may obtain winding up by the court.

§38. Rights of Partners to Application of Partnership Property

(1) When dissolution is caused in any way, except in contravention of the partnership agreement, each partner as against his co-partners and all persons claiming through them in respect of their interests in the partnership, unless otherwise agreed, may have the partnership property applied to discharge its liabilities, and the surplus applied to pay in cash the net amount owing to the respective partner. But if dissolution is caused by expulsion of a partner, bona fide under the partnership agreement and if the expelled partner is discharged from all partnership liabilities, either by payment or agreement under Section 36(2), he shall receive in cash only the net amount due him from the partnership.

(2) When dissolution is caused in contravention of the partnership agreement the rights of the partners shall be as follows:

- (a) Each partner who has not caused dissolution wrongfully shall have
  - (I) All the rights specified in paragraph (1) of this section, and
  - (II) The right, as against each partner who has caused the dissolution wrongfully, to damages for breach of the agreement.
- (b) The partners who have not caused the dissolution wrongfully, if they all desire to continue the business in the same name, either by themselves or jointly with others, may do so, during the agreed term for the partnership and for that purpose may possess the partnership property, provided they secure the payment by bond approved by the court, or pay to any partner who has caused the dissolution wrongfully, the value of his interest in the partnership at the dissolution, less any damages recoverable under clause (2aII) of the section, and in like manner indemnify him against all present or future partnership liabilities.
- (c) A partner who has caused the dissolution wrongfully shall have:
  - (I) If the business is not continued under the provisions of paragraph (2b) all the rights of a partner under paragraph (1), subject to clause (2aII), of this section,

(II) If the business is continued under paragraph (2b) of this section the right as against his co-partners and all claiming through them in respect of their interest in the partnership, less any damages caused to his co-partners by the dissolution, ascertained and paid to him in the case, or the payment secured by bond approved by the court, and to be released from all existing liabilities of the partnership; but in ascertaining the value of the partner's interest the value of the good-will of the business shall not be considered.

§39. Rights Where Partnership Is Dissolved for Fraud or Misrepresentation
Where a partnership contract is rescinded on the ground of the fraud or misrepresentation of one of the parties thereto, the party entitled to rescind is, without prejudice to any other right, entitled

(a) To a lien on, or right of retention of, the surplus of the partnership property after satisfying the partnership liabilities to third persons for any sum of money paid by him for the purchase of an interest in the partnership and for any capital or advances contributed by him; and
(b) To stand, after all liabilities to third persons have been satisfied, in the place of the creditors of the partnership for any payments made by him in respect of the partnership liabilities; and
(c) To be indemnified by the person guilty of the fraud or making the representation against all debts and liabilities of the partnership.

§40. Rules for Distribution
In settling accounts between partners after dissolution, the following rules shall be observed, subject to any agreement to the contrary:

(a) The assets of the partnership are:
  (I) The partnership property,
  (II) The contributions of the partners necessary for the payment of all the liabilities specified in clause (b) of this paragraph.
(b) The liabilities of the partnership shall rank in order of payment, as follows:
  (I) Those owing to creditors other than partners,
  (II) Those owing to partners other than for capital and profits,
  (III) Those owing to partners in respect of capital,
  (IV) Those owing to partners in respect of profits.
(c) The assets shall be applied in the order of their declaration in clause (a) of this paragraph to the satisfaction of the liabilities.
(d) The partners shall contribute, as provided by Section 18(a) the amount necessary to satisfy the liabilities; but if any, but not all, of the partners are insolvent, or, not being subject to process, refuse to contribute, the other parties shall contribute their share of the liabilities, and, in the relative proportions in which they share the profits, the additional amount necessary to pay the liabilities.
(e) An assignee for the benefit of creditors or any person appointed by the court shall have the right to enforce the contributions specified in clause (d) of this paragraph.
(f) Any partner or his legal representative shall have the right to enforce the contributions specified in clause (d) of this paragraph, to the extent of the amount which he has paid in excess of his share of the liability.
(g) The individual property of a deceased partner shall be liable for the contributions specified in clause (d) of this paragraph.
(h) When partnership property and the individual properties of the partners are in possession of a court for distribution, partnership creditors shall have priority on partnership property and separate creditors on individual property, saving the rights of lien or secured creditors as heretofore.

(i) Where a partner has become bankrupt or his estate is insolvent the claims against his separate property shall rank in the following order:
(I) Those owing to separate creditors,
(II) Those owing to partnership creditors,
(III) Those owing to partners by way of contribution.

§41. Liability of Persons Continuing the Business in Certain Cases
(1) When any new partner is admitted into an existing partnership, or when any partner retires and assigns (or the representative of the deceased partner assigns) his rights in partnership property to two or more of the partners, or to one or more of the partners and one or more third persons, if the business is continued without liquidation of the partnership affairs, creditors of the first or dissolved partnership are also creditors of the partnership so continuing the business.

(2) When all but one partner retire and assign (or the representative of a deceased partner assigns) their rights in partnership property to the remaining partner, who continues the business without liquidation of partnership affairs, either alone or with others, creditors of the dissolved partnership are also creditors of the person or partnership so continuing the business.

(3) When any partner retires or dies and the business of the dissolved partnership is continued as set forth in paragraphs (1) and (2) of this section, with the consent of the retired partners or the representative of the deceased partner, but without any assignment of his right in partnership property, rights of creditors of the dissolved partnership and of the creditors of the person or partnership continuing the business shall be as if such assignment had been made.

(4) When all the partners or their representatives assign their rights in partnership property to one or more third persons who promise to pay the debts and who continue the business of the dissolved partnership, creditors of the dissolved partnership are also creditors of the person or partnership continuing the business.

(5) When any partner wrongfully causes a dissolution and the remaining partners continue the business under the provisions of Section 38(2b), either alone or with others, and without liquidation of the partnership affairs, creditors of the dissolved partnership are also creditors of the person or partnership continuing the business.

(6) When a partner is expelled and the remaining partners continue the business either alone or with others, without liquidation of the partnership affairs, creditors of the dissolved partnership are also creditors of the person or partnership continuing the business.

(7) The liability of a third person becoming a partner in the partnership continuing the business, under this section, to the creditors of the dissolved partnership shall be satisfied out of partnership property only.

(8) When the business of a partnership after dissolution is continued under any conditions set forth in this section the creditors of the dissolved partnership, as against the separate creditors of the retiring or deceased partner or the representative of the deceased partner, have a prior right to any claim of the retired partner or the representative of the deceased partner against the person or partnership continuing the business, on account of the retired partner or the representative of the deceased partner against the person or partnership continuing the business, on account of the retired or deceased partner's interest in the dissolved partnership or on account of any consideration promised for such interest or for his right in partnership property.

(9) Nothing in this section shall be held to modify any right of creditors to set aside any assignment on the ground of fraud.

(10) The use by the person or partnership continuing the business of the partnership name, or the name of a deceased partner as part thereof, shall not of itself make the individual property of the deceased partner liable for any debts contracted by such person or partnership.

§42. Rights of Retiring or Estate of Deceased Partner When the Business Is Continued
When any partner retires or dies, and the business is continued under any of the conditions set forth in Section 41 (1, 2, 3, 5, 6), or Section 38(2b), without any settlement of accounts as between him or his estate and the person or partnership continuing the business, unless otherwise agreed, he or his legal representative as against such persons or partnership may have the value of his interest at the date of dissolution ascertained, and shall receive as an ordinary creditor an amount equal to the value of his interest in the dissolved partnership with interest, or, at his option or at the option of his legal representative, in lieu of interest, the profits attributable to the use of his right in the property of the dissolved partnership as against the separate creditors, or the representative of the retired or deceased partner, shall have priority on any claim arising under this section, as provided by Section 41(8) of this act.

§43. Accrual of Actions
The right to an account of his interest shall accrue to any partner, or his legal representative, as against the winding up partners or the surviving partners or the person or partnership continuing the business, at the date of dissolution, in the absence of any agreement to the contrary.

PART VII

MISCELLANEOUS PROVISIONS

§44. When Act Takes Effect
This act shall take effect [when properly adopted by the state].

§45. Legislation Repealed
All acts or parts of acts inconsistent with this act are hereby repealed.

APPENDIX D

REVISED MODEL BUSINESS CORPORATION ACT AS AMENDED IN 1986 AND 1987 (EXCERPTS)

§1.20. FILING REQUIREMENTS

(a) A document must satisfy the requirements of this section, and of any other section that adds to or varies from these requirements, to be entitled to filing by the secretary of state.

(b) This Act must require or permit filing the document in the office of the secretary of state.

(c) The document must contain the information required by this Act. It may contain other information as well.

(d) The document must be typewritten or printed.

(e) The document must be in the English language. A corporate name need not be in English if written in English letters or Arabic or Roman numerals, and the certificate of existence required of foreign corporations need not be in English if accompanied by a reasonably authenticated English translation.

(f) The document must be executed:

(1) by the chairman of the board of directors of a domestic or foreign corporation, by its president, or by another of its officers;

(2) if directors have not been selected or the corporation has not been formed, by an incorporator; or

(3) if the corporation is in the hands of a receiver, trustee, or other court-appointed fiduciary, by that fiduciary.

(g) The person executing the document shall sign it and state beneath or opposite his signature his name and the capacity in which he signs. The document may but need not contain:

(1) the corporate seal,

(2) an attestation by the secretary or an assistant secretary,

(3) an acknowledgement, verification, or proof.

(h) If the secretary of state has prescribed a mandatory form for the document under section 1.21, the document must also be in or on the prescribed form.

(i) The document must be delivered to the office of the secretary of state for filing and must be accompanied by one exact or conformed copy (except as provided in sections 5.03 and 15.09), the correct filing fee, and any franchise tax, license fee, or penalty required by this Act or other law.

§1.21. FORMS

(a) The secretary of state may prescribe and furnish on request forms for:

(1) an application for a certificate of existence,

(2) a foreign corporation's application for a certificate of authority to transact business in this state,
(3) a foreign corporation's application for a certificate of withdrawal, and
(4) the annual report. If the secretary of state so requires, use of these forms is mandatory.

(b) The secretary of state may prescribe and furnish on request forms for other documents required or permitted to be filed by this Act, but their use is not mandatory.

§1.23. EFFECTIVE TIME AND DATE OF DOCUMENT

(a) Except as provided in subsection (b) and section 1.2d(c), a document accepted for filing is effective:
(1) at the time of filing on the date it is filed, as evidenced by the secretary of state's date and time endorsement on the original document; or
(2) at the time specified in the document as its effective time on the date it is filed.

(b) A document may specify a delayed effective time and date, and if it does so the document becomes effective at the time and date specified. If a delayed effective date but no time is specified, the document is effective at the close of business on that date. A delayed effective date for a document may not be later than the 90th day after the date it is filed.

§1.25. FILING DUTY OF SECRETARY OF STATE

(a) If a document delivered to the office of the secretary of state for filing satisfies the requirements of section 1.20, the secretary of state shall file it.

(b) The secretary of state files a document by stamping or otherwise endorsing "Filed," together with his name and official title and the date and time of receipt, on both the original and the document copy and on the receipt for the filing fee. After filing a document, except as provided in sections 5.03 and 15.10, the secretary of state shall deliver the document copy, with the filing fee receipt (or acknowledgment of receipt if no fee is required) attached, to the domestic or foreign corporation or its representative.

(c) If the secretary of state refuses to file a document, he shall return it to the domestic or foreign corporation or its representative within five days after the document was delivered, together with a brief, written explanation of the reason for his refusal.

(d) The secretary of state's duty to file documents under this section is ministerial. His filing or refusing to file a document does not:
(1) affect the validity or invalidity of the document in whole or part;
(2) relate to the correctness or incorrectness of information contained in the document;
(3) create a presumption that the document is valid or invalid or that information contained in the document is correct or incorrect.

§1.40. ACT DEFINITIONS

In this Act:

(1) "Articles of incorporation" include amended and restated articles of incorporation and the articles of merger.

(2) "Authorized shares" means the shares of all classes a domestic or foreign corporation is authorized to issue.

(3) "Conspicuous" means so written that a reasonable person against whom the writing is to operate should have noticed it. For example, printing in italics or boldface or contrasting color, or typing in capitals or underlined, is conspicuous.

(4) "Corporation" or "domestic corporation" means a corporation for profit, which is not a foreign corporation, incorporated under or subject to the provisions of this Act.

(5) "Deliver" includes mail.

(6) "Distribution" means a direct or indirect transfer of money or other property (except its own shares) or incurrence of indebtedness by a corporation to or for the benefit of its shareholders in respect of any of its shares. A distribution may be in the form of a declaration or payment of a dividend; a purchase, redemption, or other acquisition of shares; a distribution of indebtedness; or otherwise.

(7) "Effective date of notice" is defined in section 1.41.

(8) "Employee" includes an officer but not a director. A director may accept duties that make him also an employee.

(9) "Entity" includes corporation and foreign corporation; not-for-profit corporation; profit and not-for-profit unincorporated association; business trust, estate, partnership, trust, and two or more persons having a joint or common economic interest; and state, United States, and foreign government.

(10) "Foreign corporation" means a corporation for profit incorporated under a law other than the law of this state.

(11) "Governmental subdivision" includes authority, county, district, and municipality.

(12) "Includes" denotes a partial definition.

(13) "Individual" includes the estate of an incompetent or deceased individual.

(14) "Means" denotes an exhaustive definition.

(15) "Notice" is defined in section 1.41.

(16) "Person" includes individual and entity.

(17) "Principal office" means the office (in or out of this state) so designated in the annual report where the principal executive offices of a domestic or foreign corporation are located.

(18) "Proceeding" includes civil suit and criminal, administrative, and investigatory action.

(19) "Record date" means the date established under chapter 6 or 7 on which a corporation determines the identity of its shareholders and their shareholdings for purposes of this Act. The determinations shall be made as of the close of business on the record date unless another time for doing so is specified when the record date is fixed.

(20) "Secretary" means the corporate officer to whom the board of directors has delegated responsibility under section 8.40(c) for custody of the minutes of the meetings of the board of directors and the shareholders and for authenticating records of the corporation.

(21) "Shares" means the units into which the proprietary interests in a corporation are divided.

(22) "Shareholder" means the person in whose name shares are registered in the records of a corporation or the beneficial owner of shares to the extent of the rights granted by a nominee certificate on file with a corporation.

(23) "State," when referring to a part of the United States, includes a state and commonwealth (and their agencies and governmental subdivisions) and a territory and insular possession (and their agencies and governmental subdivisions) of the United States.

(24) "Subscriber" means a person who subscribes for shares in a corporation, whether before or after incorporation.

(25) "United States" includes district, authority, bureau, commission, department, and any other agency of the United States.

(26) "Voting group" means all shares of one or more classes or series that under the articles of incorporation or this Act are entitled to vote and be counted together collectively on a matter at a meeting of shareholders. All shares entitled by the articles of incorporation of this Act to vote generally on the matter are for that purpose a single voting group.

§1.41. NOTICE

(a) Notice under this Act must be in writing unless oral notice is reasonable under the circumstances.

(b) Notice may be communicated in person; by telephone, telegraph, teletype, or other form of wire or wireless communication; or by mail or private carrier. If these forms of personal notice are impracticable, notice may be communicated by a newspaper of general circulation in the area where published; or by radio, television, or other form of public broadcast communication.

(c) Written notice by a domestic or foreign corporation to its shareholder, if in a comprehensive form, is effective when mailed, if mailed postpaid and correctly addressed to the shareholder's address shown in the corporation's current record of shareholders.

(d) Written notice to a domestic or foreign corporation (authorized to transact business in this state) may be addressed to its registered agent at its registered office or to the corporation or its secretary at its principal office shown in its most recent annual report or, in the case of a foreign corporation that has not yet delivered an annual report, in its application for a certificate of authority.

(e) Except as provided in subsection (c), written notice, if in a comprehensible form, is effective at the earliest of the following:

(1) when received;

(2) five days after its deposit in the United States Mail, as evidenced by the postmark, if mailed postpaid and correctly addressed;

(3) on the date shown on the return receipt, if sent by registered or certified mail, return receipt requested, and the receipt is signed by or on behalf of the addressee.

(f) Oral notice is effective when communicated if communicated in a comprehensible manner.

(g) If this Act prescribes notice requirements for particular circumstances, those requirements govern. If articles of incorporation or bylaws prescribe notice requirements, not inconsistent with this section or other provisions of this Act, those requirements govern.

§1.42. NUMBER OF SHAREHOLDERS

(a) For purposes of this Act, the following identified as a shareholder in a corporation's current record of shareholders constitutes one shareholder:

(1) three or fewer co-owners;

(2) a corporation, partnership, trust, estate, or other entity;

(3) the trustees, guardians, custodians, or other fiduciaries of a single trust, estate, or account.

(b) For purposes of this Act, shareholdings registered in substantially similar names constitute one shareholder if it is reasonable to believe that the names represent the same person.

§2.01. INCORPORATIONS

One or more persons may act as the incorporator or incorporators of a corporation by delivering articles of incorporation to the secretary of state for filing.

§2.02. ARTICLES OF INCORPORATION

(a) The articles of incorporation must set forth:

(1) a corporate name for the corporation that satisfies the requirements of section 4.01;
(2) the number of shares the corporation is authorized to issue;
(3) the street address of the corporation's initial registered office and the name of its initial registered agent at that office; and
(4) the name and address of each incorporator.

(b) The articles of incorporation may set forth:
(1) the names and addresses of the individuals who are to serve as the initial directors;
(2) provisions not inconsistent with law regarding:
(i) the purpose or purposes for which the corporation is organized;
(ii) managing the business and regulating the affairs of the corporation;
(iii) defining, limiting, and regulating the powers of the corporation, its board of directors, and shareholders;
(iv) a par value for authorized shares or classes of shares;
(v) the imposition of personal liability on shareholders for the debts of the corporation to a specified extent and upon specified conditions; and
(3) any provision that under this Act is required or permitted to be set forth in the bylaws.

(c) The articles of incorporation need not set forth any of the corporate powers enumerated in this Act.

§2.03. INCORPORATION

(a) Unless a delayed effective date is specified, the corporate existence begins when the articles of incorporation are filed.

(b) The secretary of state's filing of the articles of incorporation is conclusive proof that the incorporators satisfied all conditions precedent to incorporation except in a proceeding by the state to cancel or revoke the incorporation or involuntarily dissolve the corporation.

§2.04. LIABILITY FOR PREINCORPORATION TRANSACTIONS

All persons purporting to act as or on behalf of a corporation, knowing there was no incorporation under this Act, are jointly and severally liable for all liabilities created while so acting.

§2.05. ORGANIZATION OF CORPORATION

(a) After incorporation:
(1) if initial directors are named in the articles of incorporation, the initial directors shall hold an organizational meeting, at the call of a majority of the directors, to complete the organization of the corporation by appointing officers, adopting bylaws, and carrying on any other business brought before the meeting;
(2) if initial directors are not named in the articles, the incorporator or incorporators shall hold an organizational meeting at the call of a majority of the incorporators:
(i) to elect directors and complete the organization of the corporation; or
(ii) to elect a board of directors who shall complete the organization of the corporation.

(b) Action required or permitted by this Act to be taken by incorporators at an organizational meeting may be taken without a meeting if the action taken is evidenced by one or more written consents describing the action taken and signed by each incorporator.

(c) An organizational meeting may be held in or out of this state.

§2.06. BYLAWS

(a) The incorporators or board of directors of a corporation shall adopt initial bylaws for the corporation.

(b) The bylaws of a corporation may contain any provision for managing the business and regulating the affairs of the corporation that is not inconsistent with law or the articles of incorporation.

§2.07. EMERGENCY BYLAWS

(a) Unless the articles of incorporation provide otherwise, the board of directors of a corporation may adopt bylaws to be effective only in an emergency defined in subsection (d). The emergency bylaws, which are subject to amendment or repeal by the shareholders, may make all provisions necessary for managing the corporation during the emergency, including:

(1) procedures for calling a meeting of the board of directors;
(2) quorum requirements for the meeting; and
(3) designation of additional or substitute directors.

(b) All provisions of the regular bylaws consistent with the emergency bylaws remain effective during the emergency. The emergency bylaws are not effective after the emergency ends.

(c) Corporate action taken in good faith in accordance with the emergency bylaws:

(1) binds the corporation; and
(2) may not be used to impose liability on a corporate director, officer, employee, or agent.

(d) An emergency exists for purposes of this section if a quorum of the corporation's directors cannot readily be assembled because of some catastrophic event.

§3.01 PURPOSES

(a) Every corporation incorporated under this Act has the purpose of engaging in any lawful business unless a more limited purpose is set forth in the articles of incorporation.

(b) A corporation engaging in a business that is subject to regulation under another statute of this state may incorporate under this Act only if permitted by, and subject to all limitations of, the other statute.

§3.02. GENERAL POWERS

Unless its articles of incorporation provide otherwise, every corporation has perpetual duration and succession in its corporate name and has the same powers as an individual to do all things necessary or convenient to carry out its business and affairs, including without limitation power:

(1) to sue and be sued, complain and defend in its corporate name;

(2) to have a corporate seal, which may be altered at will, and to use it, or a facsimile of it, by impressing or affixing it or in any other manner reproducing it;

(3) to make and amend bylaws, not inconsistent with its articles of incorporation or with the laws of this state, for managing the business and regulating the affairs of the corporation;

(4) to purchase, receive, lease, or otherwise acquire, and own, hold, improve, use, and otherwise deal with, real or personal property, or any legal or equitable interest in property, wherever located;

(5) to sell, convey, mortgage, pledge, lease, exchange, and otherwise dispose of all or any part of its property;

(6) to purchase, receive, subscribe for, or otherwise acquire; own, hold, vote, use, sell, mortgage, lend, pledge, or otherwise dispose of; and deal in and with shares or other interests in, or obligations of, any other entity;

(7) to make contracts and guarantees, incur liabilities, borrow money, issue its notes, bonds, and other obligations (which may be convertible into or include the option to purchase other securities of the corporation), and secure any of its obligations by mortgage or pledge of any of its property, franchises, or income;

(8) to lend money, invest and reinvest its funds, and receive and hold real and personal property as security for repayment;

(9) to be a promoter, partner, member, associate, or manager of any partnership, joint venture, trust, or other entity;

(10) to conduct its business, locate offices, and exercise the powers granted by this Act within or without this state;

(11) to elect directors and appoint officers, employees, and agents of the corporation, define their duties, fix their compensation, and lend them money and credit;

(12) to pay pensions and establish pension plans, pension trusts, profit sharing plans, share bonus plans, share option plans, and benefit or incentive plans for any or all of its current or former directors, officers, employees, and agents;

(13) to make donations for the public welfare or for charitable, scientific, or educational purposes;

(14) to transact any lawful business that will aid governmental policy;

(15) to make payments or donations, or do any other act, not inconsistent with law, that furthers the business and affairs of the corporation.

§3.03. EMERGENCY POWERS

(a) In anticipation of or during an emergency defined in subsection (d), the board of directors of a corporation may:

(1) modify lines of succession to accommodate the incapacity of any director, officer, employee, or agent; and

(2) relocate the principal office, designate alternative principal offices or regional offices, or authorize the officers to do so.

(b) During an emergency defined in subsection (d), unless emergency bylaws provide otherwise:

(1) notice of a meeting of the board of directors need be given only to those directors whom it is practicable to reach and may be given in any practicable manner, including by publication and radio; and

(2) one or more officers of the corporation present at a meeting of the board of directors may be deemed to be directors for the meeting, in order of rank and within the same rank in order of seniority, as necessary to achieve a quorum.

(c) Corporate action taken in good faith during an emergency under this section to further the ordinary business affairs of the corporation:

(1) binds the corporation; and

(2) may not be used to impose liability on a corporate director, officer, employee, or agent.

(d) An emergency exists for purposes of this section if a quorum of the corporation's directors cannot readily be assembled because of some catastrophic event.

§3.04. ULTRA VIRES

(a) Except as provided in subsection (b), the validity of corporate action may not be challenged on the ground that the corporation lacks or lacked power to act.

(b) A corporation's power to act may be challenged:

(1) in a proceeding by a shareholder against the corporation to enjoin the act;

(2) in a proceeding by the corporation, directly, derivatively, or through a receiver, trustee, or other legal representative, against an incumbent or former director, officer, employee, or agent of the corporation; or

(3) in a proceeding by the Attorney General under section 14.30.

(c) In a shareholder's proceeding under subsection (b)(1) to enjoin an unauthorized corporate act, the court may enjoin or set aside the act, if equitable and if all affected persons are parties to the proceeding, and may award damages for loss (other than anticipated profits) suffered by the corporation or another party because of enjoining the unauthorized act.

§4.01. CORPORATE NAME

(a) A corporate name:

(1) must contain the word "corporation," "incorporated," "company," or "limited," or the abbreviation "corp.," "inc.," "co.," or "ltd.," or words or abbreviations of like import in another language; and

(2) may not contain language stating or implying that the corporation is organized for a purpose other than that permitted by section 3.01 and its articles of incorporation.

(b) Except as authorized by subsections (c) and (d), a corporate name must be distinguishable upon the records of the secretary of state from:

(1) the corporate name of a corporation incorporated or authorized to transact business in this state;

(2) a corporate name reserved or registered under section 4.02 or 4.03;

(3) the fictitious name adopted by a foreign corporation authorized to transact business in this state because its real name is unavailable; and

(4) the corporate name of a not-for-profit corporation incorporated or authorized to transact business in this state.

(c) A corporation may apply to the secretary of state for authorization to use a name that is not distinguishable upon his records from one or more of the names described in subsection (b). The secretary of state shall authorize use of the name applied for if:

(1) the other corporation consents to the use in writing and submits an undertaking in form satisfactory to the secretary of state to change its name to a name that is distinguishable upon the records of the secretary of state from the name of the applying corporation; or

(2) the applicant delivers to the secretary of state a certified copy of the final judgment of a court of competent jurisdiction establishing the applicant's right to use the name applied for in this state.

(d) A corporation may use the name (including the fictitious name) of another domestic or foreign corporation that is used in this state if the other corporation is incorporated or authorized to transact business in this state and the proposed user corporation:

(1) has merged with the other corporation;
(2) has been formed by reorganization of the other corporation; or
(3) has acquired all or substantially all of the assets, including the corporate name, of the other corporation.

(e) This Act does not control the use of fictitious names.

§5.01. REGISTERED OFFICE AND REGISTERED AGENT

Each corporation must continuously maintain in this state:

(1) a registered office that may be the same as any of its places of business; and
(2) a registered agent, who may be:
  (i) an individual who resides in this state and whose business office is identical with the registered office;
  (ii) a domestic corporation or not-for-profit domestic corporation whose business office is identical with the registered office; or
  (iii) a foreign corporation or not-for-profit foreign corporation authorized to transact business in this state whose business office is identical with the registered office.

§6.03. ISSUED AND OUTSTANDING SHARES

(a) A corporation may issue the number of shares of each class or series authorized by the articles of incorporation. Shares that are issued are outstanding shares until they are reacquired, redeemed, converted, or canceled.

(b) The reacquisition, redemption, or conversion of outstanding shares is subject to the limitations of subsection (c) of this section and to section 6.40.

(c) At all times that shares of the corporation are outstanding, one or more shares that together have unlimited voting rights and one or more shares that together are entitled to receive the net assets of the corporation upon dissolution must be outstanding.

§6.20. SUBSCRIPTION FOR SHARES BEFORE INCORPORATION

(a) A subscription for shares entered into before incorporation is irrevocable for six months unless the subscription agreement provides a longer or shorter period or all the subscribers agree to revocation.

(b) The board of directors may determine the payment of terms of subscriptions for shares that were entered into before incorporation, unless the subscription agreement specifies them. A call for payment by the board of directors must be uniform so far as practicable as to all shares of the same class or series, unless the subscription agreement specifies otherwise.

(c) Shares issued pursuant to subscriptions entered into before incorporation are fully paid and nonassessable when the corporation receives the consideration specified in the subscription agreement.

(d) If a subscriber defaults on payment of money or property under a subscription agreement entered into before incorporation, the corporation may collect the amount owed as any other debt. Alternatively, unless the subscription agreement provides otherwise, the corporation may rescind the agreement and may sell the shares if the debt remains unpaid more than 20 days after the corporation sends written demand for payment to the subscriber.

(e) A subscription agreement entered into after incorporation is a contract between the subscriber and the corporation subject to section 6.21.

§6.22. LIABILITY OF SHAREHOLDERS

(a) A purchaser from a corporation of its own shares is not liable to the corporation or its creditors with respect to the shares except to pay the consideration for which the shares were authorized to be issued (section 6.21) or specified in the subscription agreement (section 6.20).

(b) Unless otherwise provided in the articles of incorporation, a shareholder of a corporation is not personally liable for the acts or debts of the corporation except that he may become personally liable by reason of his own acts or conduct.

§7.01. ANNUAL MEETING

(a) A corporation shall hold a meeting of shareholders annually at a time stated in or fixed in accordance with the bylaws.

(b) Annual shareholders' meetings may be held in or out of this state at the place stated in or fixed in accordance with the bylaws. If no place is stated in or fixed in accordance with the bylaws, annual meetings shall be held at the corporation's principal office.

(c) The failure to hold an annual meeting at the time stated in or fixed in accordance with a corporation's bylaws does not affect the validity of any corporate action.

§7.04. ACTION WITHOUT MEETING

(a) Action required or permitted by this Act to be taken at a shareholders' meeting may be taken without a meeting if the action is taken by all the shareholders entitled to vote on the action. The action must be evidenced by one or more written consents describing the action taken, signed by all the shareholders entitled to vote on the action, and delivered to the corporation for inclusion in the minutes or filing with the corporate records.

(b) If not otherwise fixed under section 7.03 or 7.07, the record date for determining shareholders entitled to take action without a meeting is the date the first shareholder signs the consent under subsection (a).

(c) A consent signed under this section has the effect of a meeting vote and may be described as such in any document.

(d) If this Act requires that notice of proposed action be given to nonvoting shareholders and the action is to be taken by unanimous consent of the voting shareholders, the corporation must give its nonvoting shareholders written notice of the proposed action at least 10 days before the action is taken. The notice must contain or be accompanied by the same material that, under this Act, would have been required to be sent to nonvoting shareholders in a notice of meeting at which the proposed action would have been submitted to the shareholders for action.

§7.05. NOTICE OF MEETING

(a) A corporation shall notify shareholders of the date, time, and place of each annual and special shareholders' meeting no fewer than 10 nor more than 60 days before the meeting date. Unless this Act or the articles of incorporation require otherwise, the corporation is required to give notice only to shareholders entitled to vote at the meeting.

(b) Unless this Act or the articles of incorporation require otherwise, notice of an annual meeting need not include a description of the purpose or purposes for which the meeting is called.

(c) Notice of a special meeting must include a description of the purpose or purposes for which the meeting is called.

(d) If not otherwise fixed under section 7.03 or 7.07, the record date for determining shareholders entitled to notice of and to vote at an annual or special shareholders' meeting is the day before the first notice is delivered to shareholders.

(e) Unless the bylaws require otherwise, if an annual or special shareholders' meeting is adjourned to a different date, time, or place, notice need not be given of the new date, time, or place if the new date, time, or place is announced at the meeting before adjournment. If a new record date for the adjourned meeting is or must be fixed under section 7.07, however, notice of the adjourned meeting must be given under this section to persons who are shareholders as of the new record date.

§7.06. WAIVER OF NOTICE

(a) A shareholder may waive any notice required by this Act, the articles of incorporation, or bylaws before or after the date and time stated in the notice. The waiver must be in writing, be signed by the shareholder entitled to the notice, and be delivered to the corporation for inclusion in the minutes or filing with the corporate records.

(b) A shareholder's attendance at a meeting:

(1) waives objection to lack of notice or defective notice of the meeting, unless the shareholder at the beginning of the meeting objects to holding the meeting or transacting business at the meeting;

(2) waives objection to consideration of a particular matter at the meeting that is not within the purpose or purposes described in the meeting notice, unless the shareholder objects to considering the matter when it is presented.

§7.07. RECORD DATE

(a) The bylaws may fix or provide the manner of fixing the record date for one or more voting groups in order to determine the shareholders entitled to notice of a shareholders' meeting, to demand a special meeting, to vote, or to take any other action. If the bylaws do not fix or provide for fixing a record date, the board of directors of the corporation may fix a future date as the record date.

(b) A record date fixed under this section may not be more than 70 days before the meeting or action requiring a determination of shareholders.

(c) A determination of shareholders entitled to notice of or to vote at a shareholders' meeting is effective for any adjournment of the meeting unless the board of directors fixes a new record date, which it must do if the meeting is adjourned to a date more than 120 days after the date fixed for the original meeting.

(d) If a court orders a meeting adjourned to a date more than 120 days after the date fixed for the original meeting, it may provide that the original record date continues in effect or it may fix a new record date.

§7.21. VOTING ENTITLEMENT OF SHARES

(a) Except as provided in subsections (b) and (c) or unless the articles of incorporation provide otherwise, each outstanding share, regardless of class, is entitled to one vote on each matter voted on at a shareholders' meeting. Only shares are entitled to vote.

(b) Absent special circumstances, the shares of a corporation are not entitled to vote if they are owned, directly or indirectly, by a second corporation, domestic or foreign, and the first corporation owns, directly or indirectly, a majority of the shares entitled to vote for directors of the second corporation.

(c) Subsection (b) does not limit the power of a corporation to vote any shares, including its own shares, held by it in a fiduciary capacity.

(d) Redeemable shares are not entitled to vote after notice of redemption is mailed to the holders and a sum sufficient to redeem the shares has been deposited with a bank, trust company, or other financial institution under an irrevocable obligation to pay the holders the redemption price on surrender of the shares.

§7.22. PROXIES

(a) A shareholder may vote his shares in person or by proxy.

(b) A shareholder may appoint a proxy to vote or otherwise act for him by signing an appointment form, either personally or by his attorney-in-fact.

(c) An appointment of a proxy is effective when received by the secretary or other officer or agent authorized to tabulate votes. An appointment is valid for 11 months unless a longer period is expressly provided in the appointment form.

(d) An appointment of a proxy is revocable by the shareholder unless the appointment form conspicuously states that it is irrevocable and the appointment is coupled with an interest. Appointments coupled with an interest include the appointment of:

(1) a pledgee;

(2) a person who purchased or agreed to purchase the shares;

(3) a creditor of the corporation who extended it credit under terms requiring the appointment;

(4) an employee of the corporation whose employment contract requires the appointment; or

(5) a party to a voting agreement created under section 7.31.

(e) The death or incapacity of the shareholder appointing a proxy does not affect the right of the corporation to accept the proxy's authority unless notice of the death or incapacity is received by the secretary or other officer or agent authorized to tabulate votes before the proxy exercises his authority under the appointment.

(f) An appointment made irrevocable under subsection (d) is revoked when the interest with which it is coupled is extinguished.

(g) A transferee for value of shares subject to an irrevocable appointment may revoke the appointment if he did not know of its existence when he acquired the shares and the existence of the irrevocable appointment was not noted conspicuously on the certificate representing the shares or on the information statement for shares without certificates.

(h) Subject to section 7.24 and to any express limitation on the proxy's authority appearing on the face of the appointment form, a corporation is entitled to accept the proxy's vote or other action as that of the shareholder making the appointment.

§8.01. REQUIREMENT FOR AND DUTIES OF BOARD OF DIRECTORS

(a) Except as provided in subsection (c), each corporation must have a board of directors.

(b) All corporate powers shall be exercised by or under authority of, and the business and affairs of the corporation managed under the direction of, its board of directors, subject to any limitation set forth in the articles of incorporation.

(c) A corporation having 50 or fewer shareholders may dispense with or limit the authority of a board of directors by describing in its articles of incorporation who will perform some or all of the duties of a board of directors.

§8.03. NUMBER AND ELECTION OF DIRECTORS

(a) A board of directors must consist of one or more individuals, with the number specified in or fixed in accordance with the articles of incorporation or bylaws.

(b) If a board of directors has power to fix or change the number of directors, the board may increase or decrease by 30 percent or less the number of directors last approved by the shareholders, but only the shareholders may increase or decrease by more than 30 percent the number of directors last approved by the shareholders.

(c) The articles of incorporation or bylaws may establish a variable range for the size of the board of directors by fixing a minimum and maximum number of directors. If a variable range is established, the number of directors may be fixed or changed from time to time, within the minimum and maximum, by the shareholders or the board of directors. After shares are issued, only the shareholders may change the range for the size of the board or change from a fixed to a variable-range size board or vice versa.

(d) Directors are elected at the first annual shareholders' meeting and at each annual meeting thereafter unless their terms are staggered under section 8.06.

§8.04. ELECTION OF DIRECTORS BY CERTAIN CLASSES OF SHAREHOLDERS

If the articles of incorporation authorize dividing the shares into classes, the articles may also authorize the election of all or a specified number of directors by the holders of one or more authorized classes of shares. A class (or classes) of shares entitled to elect one or more directors is a separate voting group for purposes of the election of directors.

§8.05. TERMS OF DIRECTORS GENERALLY

(a) The terms of the initial directors of a corporation expire at the first shareholders' meeting at which directors are elected.

(b) The terms of all other directors expire at the next annual shareholders' meeting following their election unless their terms are staggered under section 8.06.

(c) A decrease in the number of directors does not shorten an incumbent director's term.

(d) The term of a director elected to fill a vacancy expires at the next shareholders' meeting at which directors are elected.

(e) Despite the expiration of a director's term, he continues to serve until his successor is elected and qualifies or until there is a decrease in the number of directors.

§8.06. STAGGERED TERMS FOR DIRECTORS

If there are nine or more directors, the articles of incorporation may provide for staggering their terms by dividing the total number of directors into two or three groups, with each group containing one-half or one-third of the total, as near as may be. In that event, the terms of directors in the first group expire at the first annual shareholders' meeting after their election, the terms of the second group expire at the second annual shareholders' meeting after their election, and the terms of the third group, if any, expire at the third annual shareholders' meeting after their election. At each annual shareholders' meeting held thereafter, directors shall be chosen for a term of two years or three years, as the case may be, to succeed those whose terms expire.

§8.08. REMOVAL OF DIRECTORS BY SHAREHOLDERS

(a) The shareholders may remove one or more directors with or without cause unless the articles of incorporation provide that directors may be removed only for cause.

(b) If a director is elected by a voting group of shareholders, only the shareholders of that voting group may participate in the vote to remove him.

(c) If cumulative voting is authorized, a director may not be removed if the number of votes sufficient to elect him under cumulative voting is voted against his removal. If cumulative voting is not authorized, a director may be removed only if the number of votes cast to remove him exceeds the number of votes cast not to remove him.

(d) A director may be removed by the shareholders only at a meeting called for the purpose of removing him and the meeting notice must state that the purpose, or one of the purposes, of the meeting is removal of the director.

§8.20. MEETINGS

(a) The board of directors may hold regular or special meetings in or out of state.

(b) Unless the articles of incorporation or bylaws provide otherwise, the board of directors may permit any or all directors to participate in a regular or special meeting by, or conduct the meeting through the use of, any means of communication by which all directors participating may simultaneously hear each other during the meeting. A director participating in a meeting by this means is deemed to be present in person at the meeting.

§8.30. GENERAL STANDARDS FOR DIRECTORS

(a) A director shall discharge his duties as a director, including his duties as a member on a committee:

(1) in good faith;

(2) with the care an ordinarily prudent person in a like position would exercise under similar circumstances; and

(3) in a manner he reasonably believes to be in the best interest of the corporation.

(b) In discharging his duties a director is entitled to rely on information, opinions, reports, or statements, including financial statements and other financial data, if prepared or presented by:

(1) one or more officers or employees of the corporation whom the director reasonably believes to be reliable and competent in the matters presented;

(2) legal counsel, public accountants, or other persons as to matters the director reasonably believes are within the person's professional or expert competence; or

(3) a committee of the board of directors of which he is not a member if the director reasonably believes the committee merits confidence.

(c) A director is not acting in good faith if he has knowledge concerning the matter in question that makes reliance otherwise permitted by subsection (b) unwarranted.

(d) A director is not liable for any action taken as a director, or any failure to take any action, if he performed the duties of his office in compliance with this section.

§8.31. DIRECTOR CONFLICT OF INTEREST

(a) A conflict of interest transaction is a transaction with the corporation in which a director of the corporation has a direct or indirect interest. A conflict of interest transaction is not voidable by the corporation solely because of the director's interest in the transaction if any one of the following is true:

(1) The material facts of the transaction and the director's interest were disclosed or known to the board of directors or a committee of the board of direc-

tors and the board of directors or committee authorized, approved, or ratified the transaction;

(2) The material facts of the transaction and the director's interest were disclosed or known to the shareholders entitled to vote and they authorized, approved, or ratified the transaction; or

(3) The transaction was fair to the corporation.

(b) For the purposes of this section, a director of the corporation has an indirect interest in a transaction if

(1) another entity in which he has a material financial interest or in which he is a general partner is a party to the transaction or

(2) another entity of which he is a director, officer, or trustee is a party to the transaction and the transaction is or should be considered by the board of directors of the corporation.

(c) For purposes of subsection (a)(1), a conflict of interest transaction is authorized, approved, or ratified if it receives the affirmative vote of a majority of the directors on the board of directors (or on the committee) who have no direct or indirect interest in the transaction, but a transaction may not be authorized, approved, or ratified under this section by a single director. If a majority of the directors who have no direct or indirect interest in the transaction vote to authorize, approve, or ratify the transaction, a quorum is present for the purpose of taking action under this section. The presence of, or a vote cast by, a director with a direct or indirect interest in the transaction does not affect the validity of any action taken under subsection (a)(1) if the transaction is otherwise authorized, approved, or ratified as provided in that subsection.

(d) For purposes of subsection (a)(2), a conflict of interest transaction is authorized, approved, or ratified if it receives the vote of a majority of the shares entitled to be counted under this subsection. Shares owned by or voted under the control of a director who has a direct or indirect interest in the transaction, and shares owned by or voted under control of an entity described in subsection (b)(1), may not be counted in a vote of shareholders to determine whether to authorized, approve, or ratify a conflict of interest transaction under subsection (a)(2). The vote of those shares, however, is counted in determining whether the transaction is approved under other sections of this Act. A majority of the shares, whether or not present, that are entitled to be counted in a vote on the transaction under this subsection constituted a quorum for the purpose of taking action under this section.

§8.33. LIABILITY FOR UNLAWFUL DISTRIBUTIONS

(a) A director who votes for or assents to a distribution made in violation of section 6.40 or the articles of incorporation is personally liable to the corporation for the amount of the distribution that exceeds what could have been distributed without violating section 6.40 or the articles or incorporation if it is established that he did not perform his duties in compliance with section 8.30. In any proceeding commenced under this section, a director has all of the defenses ordinarily available to a director.

(b) A director held liable under subsection (a) for an unlawful distribution is entitled to contribution:

(1) from every other director who could be held liable under subsection (a) for the unlawful distribution; and

(2) from each shareholder for the amount the shareholder accepted knowing the distribution was made in violation of section 6.40 or the articles of incorporation.

(c) A proceeding under this section is barred unless it is commenced within two years after the date on which the effect of the distribution was measured under section 6.40(e) or (g).

§8.40. REQUIRED OFFICERS

(a) A corporation has the officers described in its bylaws or appointed by the board of directors in accordance with the bylaws.

(b) A duly appointed officer may appoint one or more officers or assistant officers if authorized by the bylaws or the board of directors.

(c) The bylaws or the board of directors shall delegate to one of the officers responsibility for preparing minutes of the directors' and shareholders' meetings and for authenticating records of the corporation.

(d) The same individual may simultaneously hold more than one office in a corporation.

§8.41. DUTIES OF OFFICERS

Each officer has the authority and shall perform the duties set forth in the bylaws or, to the extent consistent with the bylaws, the duties prescribed by the board of directors or by direction of an officer authorized by the board of directors to prescribe the duties of other officers.

§8.42. STANDARDS OF CONDUCT FOR OFFICERS

(a) An officer with discretionary authority shall discharge his duties under that authority:

- (1) in good faith;
- (2) with the care an ordinarily prudent person in a like position would exercise under similar circumstances; and
- (3) in a manner he reasonably believes to be in the best interests of the corporation.

(b) In discharging his duties an officer is entitled to rely on information, opinions, reports, or statements, including financial statements and other financial data, if prepared or presented by:

- (1) one or more officers or employees of the corporation whom the officer reasonably believes to be reliable and competent in the matters presented; or
- (2) legal counsel, public accountants, or other persons as to matters the officer reasonably believes are within the person's professional or expert competence.

(c) An officer is not acting in good faith if he has knowledge concerning the matter in question that makes reliance otherwise permitted by subsection (b) unwarranted.

(d) An officer is not liable for an action taken as an officer, or any failure to take any action, if he performed the duties of his office in compliance with this section.

§11.01. MERGER

(a) One or more corporations may merge into another corporation if the board of directors of each corporation adopts and its shareholders (if required by section 11.03) approve a plan of merger.

(b) The plan of merger must set forth:

- (1) the name of each corporation planning to merge and the name of the surviving corporation into which each other corporation plans to merge;
- (2) the terms and conditions of the merger; and
- (3) the manner and basis of converting the shares of each corporation into shares, obligations, or other securities of the surviving or any other corporation or into cash or other property in whole or part.

(c) The plan of merger may set forth:
   (1) amendments to the articles of incorporation of the surviving corporation; and
   (2) other provisions relating to the merger.

§13.02. RIGHT TO DISSENT

(a) A shareholder is entitled to dissent from and obtain payment of the fair value of his shares in the event of, any of the following corporate actions:
   (1) consummation of a plan of merger to which the corporation is a party (i) if shareholder approval is required for the merger by section 11.03 or the articles of incorporation and the shareholder is entitled to vote on the merger or (ii) if the corporation is a subsidiary that is merged with its parent under section 11.04;
   (2) consummation of a plan of share exchange to which the corporation is a party as the corporation whose shares will be acquired, if the shareholder is entitled to vote on the plan;
   (3) consummation of a sale or exchange of all, or substantially all, of the property of the corporation other than in the usual and regular course of business, if the shareholder is entitled to vote on the sale or exchange, including a sale in dissolution, but not including a sale pursuant to court order or a sale for cash pursuant to a plan by which all or substantially all of the net proceeds of the sale will be distributed to the shareholders within one year after the date of sale;
   (4) an amendment of the articles of incorporation that materially and adversely affects rights in respect of a dissenter's shares because it:
      (i) alters or abolishes a preferential right of the shares;
      (ii) creates, alters, or abolishes a right in respect of redemption, including a provision respecting a sinking fund for the redemption or repurchase, of the shares;
      (iii) alters or abolishes a preemptive right of the holder of the shares to acquire shares or other securities;
      (iv) excludes or limits the right of the shares to vote on any matter, or to cumulate votes, other than a limitation by dilution through issuance of shares or other securities with similar voting rights; or
      (v) reduces the number of shares owned by the shareholder to a fraction of a share if the fractional share so created is to be acquired for cash under section 6.04; or
   (5) any corporate action taken pursuant to a shareholder vote to the extent the articles of incorporation, bylaws, or a resolution of the board of directors provides that voting or nonvoting shareholders are entitled to dissent and obtain payment for their shares.

(b) A shareholder entitled to dissent and obtain payment for his shares under this chapter may not challenge the corporate action creating his entitlement unless the action is unlawful or fraudulent with respect to the shareholder or the corporation.

§13.28. PROCEDURE IF SHAREHOLDER IS DISSATISFIED WITH PAYMENT OR OFFER

(a) A dissenter may notify the corporation in writing of his own estimate of the fair value of his shares and amount of interest due, and demand payment of his estimate (less any payment under section 13.25), or reject the corporation's offer under section 13.27 and demand payment of the fair value of his shares and interest due, if:

(1) the dissenter believes that the amount paid under section 13.25 or offered under section 13.27 is less than the fair value of his shares or that the interest due is incorrectly calculated;

(2) the corporation fails to make payment under section 13.25 within 60 days after the date set for demanding payment; or

(3) the corporation, having failed to take the proposed action, does not return the deposited certificates or release the transfer restrictions imposed on uncertified shares within 60 days after the date set for demanding payment.

(b) A dissenter waives his right to demand payment under this section unless he notifies the corporation of his demand in writing under subsection (a) within 30 days after the corporation made or offered payment for his shares.

SUBCHAPTER C. JUDICIAL APPRAISAL OF SHARES

§13.30 COURT ACTION

(a) If a demand for payment under section 13.28 remains unsettled, the corporation shall commence a proceeding within 60 days after receiving the payment demand and petition the court to determine the fair value of the shares and accrued interest. If the corporation does not commence the proceeding within the 60-day period, it shall pay each dissenter whose demand remains unsettled the amount demanded.

(b) The corporation shall commence the proceeding in the [name or describe] court of the county where a corporation's principal office (or, if none in this state, its registered office) is located. If the corporation is a foreign corporation without a registered office in this state, it shall commence the proceeding in the county in this state where the registered office of the domestic corporation merged with or whose shares were acquired by the foreign corporations was located.

(c) The corporation shall make all dissenters (whether or not residents of this state) whose demands remain unsettled parties to the proceeding as in an action against their shares and all parties must be served with a copy of the petition. Nonresidents may be served by registered or certified mail or by publication as provided by law.

(d) The jurisdiction of the court in which the proceeding is commenced under subsection (b) is plenary and exclusive. The court may appoint one or more persons as appraisers to receive evidence and recommended decision on the question of fair value. The appraisers have the powers described in the order appointing them, or in any amendment to it. The dissenters are entitled to the same discovery rights as parties in other civil proceedings.

(e) Each dissenter made a party to the proceeding is entitled to judgment (1) for the amount, if any, by which the court finds the fair value of his shares, plus interest, exceeds the amount paid by the corporation, or (2) for the fair value, plus accrued interest, of his after-acquired shares for which the corporation elected to withhold payment under section 13.27.

§13.31. COURT COSTS AND COUNSEL FEES

(a) The court in an appraisal proceeding commenced under section 13.30 shall determine all costs of the proceeding, including the reasonable compensation and expenses of appraisers appointed by the court. The court shall assess the costs against the corporation, except that the court may assess costs against all or some of the dissenters, in amounts the court finds equitable, to the extent the court finds dissenters acted arbitrarily, vexatiously, or not in good faith in demanding payment under section 13.28.

(b) The court may also assess the fees and expenses of counsel and experts for the respective parties, in amounts the court finds equitable:

(1) against the corporation and in favor of any or all dissenters if the court finds the corporation did not substantially comply with the requirements of sections 13.20 through 13.28; or

(2) against either the corporation or a dissenter, in favor of any other party, if the court finds that the party against whom the fees and expenses are assessed acted arbitrarily, vexatiously, or not in good faith with respect to the rights provided by this chapter.

(c) If the court finds that the services of counsel for any dissenter were of substantial benefit to other dissenters similarly situated, and that the fees for those services should not be assessed against the corporation, the court may award to these counsel reasonable fees to be paid out of the amounts awarded the dissenters who were benefitted.

§16.01. CORPORATE RECORDS

(a) A corporation shall keep as permanent records minutes of all meetings of its shareholders and board of directors, a record of all actions taken by the shareholders or board of directors without a meeting, and a record of all actions taken by a committee of the board of directors in place of the board of directors on behalf of the corporation.

(b) A corporation shall maintain appropriate accounting records.

(c) A corporation or its agent shall maintain a record of its shareholders, in a form that permits preparation of a list of the names and addresses of all shareholders, in alphabetical order by class of shares showing the number and class of shares held by each.

(d) A corporation shall maintain its records in written form or in another form capable of conversion into written form within a reasonable time.

(e) A corporation shall keep a copy of the following records at its principal office:

(1) its articles or restated articles of incorporation and all amendments to them currently in effect;

(2) its bylaws or restated bylaws and all amendments to them currently in effect;

(3) resolutions adopted by its board of directors creating one or more classes or series of shares, and fixing their relative rights, preferences, and limitations, if shares issued pursuant to those resolutions are outstanding;

(4) the minutes of all shareholders' meetings, and records of all action taken by shareholders without a meeting, for the past three years;

(5) all written communications to shareholders generally within the past three years, including the financial statements furnished for the past three years under section 16.20;

(6) a list of the names and business addresses of its current directors and officers; and

(7) its most recent annual report delivered to the secretary of state under section 16.22.

§16.02. INSPECTION OF RECORDS BY SHAREHOLDERS

(a) A shareholder of a corporation is entitled to inspect and copy, during regular business hours at the corporation's principal office, any of the records of the corporation described in section 16.01(e) if he gives the corporation written notice of his demand at least five business days before the date on which he wishes to inspect and copy.

(b) A shareholder of a corporation is entitled to inspect and copy during regular business hours at a reasonable location specified by the corporation, any of the following records of the corporation if the shareholder meets the requirements of subsection

(c) and gives the corporation written notice of his demand at least five business days before the date on which he wishes to inspect and copy:

(1) excerpts from minutes of any meeting of the board of directors, records of any action of a committee of the board of directors while acting in place of the board of directors on behalf of the corporation, minutes of any meeting of the shareholders, and records of action taken by the shareholders or board of directors without a meeting, to the extent not subject to inspection under section 16.02(a);

(2) accounting records of the corporation; and

(3) the record of shareholders.

(c) A shareholder may inspect and copy the records described in subsection (b) only if:

(1) his demand is made in good faith and for a proper purpose;

(2) he describes with reasonable particularity his purpose and the records he desires to inspect; and

(3) the records are directly connected with his purpose.

(d) The right of inspection granted by this section may not be abolished or limited by a corporation's articles of incorporation or bylaws.

(e) This section does not affect:

(1) the right of a shareholder to inspect records under section 7.20 or, if the shareholder is in litigation with the corporation, to the same extent as any other litigant;

(2) the power of a court, independently of this Act, to compel the production of corporate records for examination.

(f) For purposes of this section, "shareholder" includes a beneficial owner whose shares are held in a voting trust or by a nominee on his behalf.

§16.20. FINANCIAL STATEMENTS FOR SHAREHOLDERS

(a) A corporation shall furnish its shareholders annual financial statements, which may be consolidated or combined statements of the corporation and one or more of its subsidiaries, as appropriate, that include a balance sheet as of the end of the fiscal year, an income statement for that year, and a statement of changes in shareholder's equity for the year unless that information appears elsewhere in the financial statements. If financial statements are prepared for the corporation on the basis of generally accepted accounting principles, the annual financial statements must also be prepared on that basis.

(b) If the annual financial statements are reported upon by a public accountant, his report must accompany them. If not, the statements must be accompanied by a statement of the president or the person responsible for the corporation's accounting records:

(1) stating his reasonable belief whether the statements were prepared on the basis of generally accepted accounting principles and, if not, describing the basis of preparation; and

(2) describing any respects in which the statements were not prepared on a basis of accounting consistent with the statements prepared for the preceding year.

(c) A corporation shall mail the annual financial statements to each shareholder within 120 days after the close of each fiscal year. Thereafter, on written request from a shareholder who was not mailed the statements, the corporation shall mail him the latest financial statements.

APPENDIX E
THE CLAYTON ACT, AS AMENDED BY THE ROBINSON-PATMAN ACT (EXCERPT)

§2 DISCRIMINATION IN PRICE, SERVICES, OR FACILITIES

(a) Price; selection of customers

It shall be unlawful for any person engaged in commerce, in the course of such commerce, either directly or indirectly, to discriminate in price between different purchasers of commodities of like grade and quality, whether either or any of the purchases involved in such discrimination are in commerce, where such commodities are sold for use, consumption, or resale within the United States or any Territory thereof or the District of Columbia or any insular possession or other place under the jurisdiction of the United States, and where the effect of such discrimination may be substantially to lessen competition or tend to create a monopoly in any line of commerce, or to injure, destroy, or prevent competition with any person who either grants or knowingly receives the benefit of such discrimination, or with customers of either of them: Provided, That nothing herein contained shall prevent differentials which make only due allowance for differences in the cost of manufacture, sale, or delivery resulting from the differing methods or quantities in which such commodities are to such purchasers sold or delivered:

Provided, however, that the Federal Trade Commission may, after due investigation and hearing to all interested parties, fix and establish quantity limits, and revise the same as it finds necessary, as to particular commodities or classes of commodities, where it finds that available purchasers in greater quantities are so few as to render differentials on account thereof unjustly discriminatory or promotive of monopoly in any line of commerce; and the foregoing shall then not be construed to permit differentials based on differences in quantities greater than those so fixed and established; And provided further, That nothing herein contained shall prevent persons engaged in selling goods, wares, or merchandise in commerce from selecting their own customers in bona fide transactions and not in restraint of trade; And provided further, That nothing herein contained shall prevent price changes from time to time where in response to changing conditions affecting the market for or the marketability of the goods concerned, such as but not limited to actual or imminent deterioration of perishable goods, obsolescence of seasonal goods, distress sales under court process, or sales in good faith in discontinuance of business in the goods concerned.

(b) Burden of rebutting prima-facie case of discrimination

Upon proof being made, at any hearing on a complaint under this section, that there has been discrimination in price or services or facilities furnished, the burden of rebutting the prima-facie case thus made by showing justification shall be upon the person charged with a violation of this section, and unless justification shall be affirmatively shown, the Commission is authorized to issue an order terminating the discrimination; Provided, however, That nothing herein contained shall prevent a seller rebutting the prima-facie case thus made by showing that his lower price or the furnishing of services or facilities to any purchaser or purchasers was made in good faith to meet an equally low price of a competitor, or the services or facilities furnished by a competitor.

(c) Payment or acceptance of commission, brokerage or other compensation

It shall be unlawful for any person engaged in commerce, in the course of such commerce, to pay or grant or to receive or accept, anything of value as a commission, brokerage, or other compensation, or any allowance or discount in lieu thereof, except for services rendered in connection with the sale or purchase of goods, wares, or merchandise, either to the other party to such transaction or an agent, representative, or other intermediary therein where such intermediary is acting in fact or in behalf, or is subject to the direct or indirect control, of any party to such transaction other than the person by whom such compensation is so granted or paid.

(d) Payment for services or facilities for processing or sale

It shall be unlawful for any person engaged in commerce to pay or contract for the payment of anything of value to or for the benefit of a customer of such person in the course of such commerce as compensation or in consideration for any services or facilities furnished by or through such customer in connection with the processing, handling, sale or offering for sale of any products or commodities manufactured, sold, or offered for sale by such person, unless such payment or consideration is available on proportionally equal terms to all other customers competing in the distribution of such products or commodities.

(e) Furnishing services or facilities from processing, handling, etc.

It shall be unlawful for any person to discriminate in favor of one purchaser against another purchaser or purchasers of a commodity bought for resale, with or without processing, by contracting to furnish or furnishing, or by contributing to the furnishing of, any services or facilities connected with the processing, handling, sale or offering for sale of such commodity so purchased upon terms not accorded to all purchasers on proportionally equal terms.

(f) Knowingly inducing or receiving discriminatory price

It shall be unlawful for any person engaged in commerce, in the course of such commerce, knowingly to induce or receive a discrimination in price which is prohibited by this section.

SECTION 3

It shall be unlawful for any person engaged in commerce, in the course of such commerce, to lease or make a sale or contract for sale of goods, wares, merchandise, machinery, supplies, or other commodities, whether patented or unpatented, for use, consumption, or resale within the United States or any Territory thereof or the District of Columbia or any insular possession or other place under the jurisdiction of the United States, or fix a price charged therefor, or discount from or rebate upon, such price, on the condition, agreement, or understanding that the lessee or purchaser thereof shall not use or deal in the goods, wares, merchandise, machinery, supplies, or other commodities of a competitor or competitors of the lessor or seller, where the effect of such lease, sale, or contract for sale or such condition, agreement, or understanding may be to substantially lessen competition or tend to create a monopoly in any line of commerce.

SECTION 7

No person engaged in commerce or in any activity affecting commerce shall acquire, directly or indirectly, the whole or any part of the stock or other share capital and no person subject to the jurisdiction of the Federal Trade Commission shall acquire the whole or any part of the assets of another person engaged also in commerce or in any activity affecting commerce, where in any line of commerce in any section of the country, the effect of such acquisition may be substantially to lessen competition, or to tend to create a monopoly.

No person shall acquire, directly or indirectly, the whole or any part of the stock or other share capital and no person subject to the jurisdiction of the Federal Trade Commission shall acquire the whole or any part of the assets of one or more persons engaged in commerce or in any activity affecting commerce, where in any line of commerce in any section of the country, the effect of such acquisition, of such stocks or assets, or of the use of such stock by the voting or granting of proxies or otherwise, may be substantially to lessen competition, or to tend to create a monopoly.

This section shall not apply to persons purchasing such stock solely for investment and not using the same by voting or otherwise to bring about, or in attempting to bring about, the substantial lessening of competition. . . .

APPENDIX F
THE SHERMAN ACT (EXCERPTS)

SECTION 1. TRUSTS, ETC., IN RESTRAINT OF TRADE ILLEGAL; PENALTY

Every contract, combination in the form of trust or otherwise, or conspiracy, in restraint of trade or commerce among the several States, or with foreign nations, is declared to be illegal. Every person who shall make any contract or engage in any combination or conspiracy hereby declared to be illegal shall be deemed guilty of a felony, and, on conviction thereof, shall be punished by fine not exceeding one million dollars if a corporation, or, if any other person, one hundred thousand dollars or by imprisonment not exceeding three years, or by both said punishments, in the discretion of the court.

SECTION 2. MONOPOLIZATION; PENALTY

Every person who shall monopolize, or attempt to monopolize, or combine or conspire with any other person or persons, to monopolize any part of the trade or commerce among the several States, or with foreign nations, shall be deemed guilty of a felony, and, on conviction thereof, shall be punished by fine not exceeding $10,000,000 if a corporation, or, if any other person, $350,000 or by imprisonment not exceeding three years, or by both said punishments, in the discretion of the court.

APPENDIX G
TEXT OF THE CIVIL RIGHTS ACT OF 1964

42 U.S.C. SECTION 2000E, AS AMENDED BY THE CIVIL RIGHTS ACT OF 1991, P.L. 102–116.

TITLE VII—NONDISCRIMINATION IN EMPLOYMENT

DEFINITIONS

Section 701. For the purposes of this subchapter—

(a) The term "person" includes one or more individuals, governments, governmental agencies, political subdivisions, labor unions, partnerships, associations, corporations, legal representatives, mutual companies, joint-stock companies, trusts, unincorporated organizations, trustees, trustees in cases under Title 11, or receivers.

(b) The term "employer" means a person engaged in an industry affecting commerce who has fifteen or more employees for each working day in each of twenty or more calendar weeks in the current or preceding calendar year, and any agent of such a person, but such term does not include (1) the United States, a corporation wholly owned by the Government of the United States, an Indian tribe, or any department or agency of the District of Columbia subject by statute to procedures of the competitive service (as defined in Section 2102 of Title 5) or (2) a bona fide private membership club (other than a labor organization) which is exempt from taxation under section 501(c) of Title 26, except that during the first year after March 24, 1972, persons having fewer than twenty-five employees (and their agents) shall not be considered employers.

(c) The term "employment agency" means any person regularly undertaking with or without compensation to procure employees for an employer or to procure for employees opportunities to work for an employer and includes an agent of such a person.

(d) The term "labor organization" means a labor organization engaged in an industry affecting commerce, and any agent of such an organization, and includes any organization of any kind, any agency, or employee representation committee, group, association, or plan so engaged in which employees participate and which exists for the purpose, in whole or in part, of dealing with employers concerning grievances, labor disputes, wages, rates of pay, hours, or other terms or conditions of employment, and any conference, general committee, joint or system board, or joint council so engaged which is subordinate to a national or international labor organization.

(e) A labor organization shall be deemed to be engaged in any industry affecting commerce if (1) it maintains or operates a hiring hall or hiring office which procures employees for an employer or procures for employees opportunities to work for an employer, or (2) the number of its members (or, where it is a labor organization composed of other labor organizations or their representatives, if the aggregate number of the members of such other labor organization) is (A) twenty-five or more during the first year after March 24, 1972, or (B) fifteen or more thereafter, and such labor organization—

(1) is the certified representative of employees under the provisions of the National Labor Relations Act, as amended, or the Railway Labor Act, as amended;

(2) although not certified, is a national or international labor organization or a local labor organization recognized or acting as the representative of employees of an employer or employers engaged in an industry affecting commerce; or

(3) has chartered a local labor organization or subsidiary body which is representing or actively seeking to represent employees of employers within the meaning of paragraph (1) or (2); or

(4) has been chartered by a labor organization representing or actively seeking to represent employees within the meaning of paragraph (1) or (2) has the local or subordinate body through which such employees may enjoy membership or become affiliated with such labor organization; or

(5) is a conference, general committee, joint or system board, or joint council subordinate to a national or international labor organization which includes a labor organization engaged in an industry affecting commerce within the meaning of any of the preceding paragraphs of this subsection.

(f) the term "employee" means an individual employed by an employer except that the term "employee" shall not include any person elected to public office in any State or political subdivision of any State by the qualified voters thereof or any person chosen by such officer to be on such officer's personal staff, or an appointee on the policy making level or an immediate adviser with respect to the exercise of the constitutional or legal powers of the office. The exemption set forth in the preceding sentence shall not include employees subject to the civil service laws of a State government, governmental agency or political subdivision.

With respect to employment in a foreign country such term includes an individual who is a citizen of the United States.

(g) The term "commerce" means trade, traffic, commerce, transportation, transmission, or communication among the several States; or between a State and any place outside thereof; or within the District of Columbia, or a possession of the United States; or between points in the same State but through a point outside thereof.

(h) The term "industry affecting commerce" means any activity, business, or industry in commerce or in which a labor dispute would hinder or obstruct commerce or the free flow of commerce and includes any activity or industry "affecting commerce" within the meaning of the Labor-Management Reporting and Disclosure Act of 1959, and further includes any governmental industry, business, or activity.

(i) The term "State" includes a State of the United States, the District of Columbia, Puerto Rico, the Virgin Islands, American Samoa, Guam, Wake Island, the Canal Zone, and Outer Continental Shelf lands defined in the Outer Continental Shelf Lands Act.

(j) The term "religion" includes all aspects of religious observance and practice as well as belief unless an employer demonstrates that he is unable to reasonably accommodate to an employee's or prospective employee's religious observance or practice without undue hardship on the conduct of the employer's business.

(k) The terms "because of sex" or "on the basis of sex" include, but are not limited to, because of or on the basis of pregnancy, childbirth, or related medical conditions; and women affected by pregnancy, childbirth, or related medical conditions shall be treated the same for all employment-related purposes, including receipt of benefits under fringe benefit programs, as other persons not so affected but similar in their ability or inability to work and nothing in section 2000e-2(h) of this title shall be interpreted to permit otherwise. This subsection shall not require an employer to pay for health insurance benefits for abortion, except where the life of the mother would be endangered if the fetus were carried to term, or except where medical complications have arisen from an abortion: Provided, That nothing herein shall preclude an employer from providing abortion benefits or otherwise affect bargaining agreements in regard to abortion.

(l) The term "complaining party" means the Commission, the Attorney General, or a person who may bring an action or proceeding under this title.

(m) The term "demonstrates" means meets the burdens of production and persuasion.

(n) The term "respondent" means an employer, employment agency, labor organization, joint labor-management committee controlling apprenticeship or other training or retraining program, including an on-the-job training program, or Federal entity subject to section 717.

SUBCHAPTER NOT APPLICABLE TO EMPLOYMENT OF ALIENS OUTSIDE STATE AND INDIVIDUALS FOR PERFORMANCE OF ACTIVITIES OF RELIGIOUS CORPORATIONS, ASSOCIATIONS, EDUCATIONAL INSTITUTIONS, OR SOCIETIES

Section 702.

(a) This subchapter shall not apply to an employer with respect to the employment of aliens outside any State, or to a religious corporation, association, educational institution, or society with respect to the employment of individuals of a particular religion to perform work connected with the carrying on by such corporation, association, educational institution, or society of its activities.

(b) It shall not be unlawful under section 703 or 704 for an employer (or a corporation controlled by an employer), labor organization, employment agency, or joint management committee controlling apprenticeship or other training or retraining (including on-the-job training programs) to take any action otherwise prohibited by such section, with respect to an employee in a workplace in a foreign country if compliance with such section would cause such employer (or corporation), such organization, such agency, or such committee to violate the law of the foreign country in which such workplace is located.

(c) (1) If an employer controls a corporation whose place of incorporation is a foreign country, any practice prohibited by section 703 or 704 engaged in by such corporation shall be presumed to be engaged in by such employer.

(2) Sections 703 and 704 shall not apply with respect to the foreign operations of an employer that is a foreign person not controlled by an American employer.

(3) For purposes of this subsection, the determination of whether an employer controls a corporation shall be based on—

(A) the interrelation of operations;

(B) the common management;

(C) the centralized control of labor relations; and

(D) the common ownership or financial control, of the employer and the corporation.

UNLAWFUL EMPLOYMENT PRACTICES

Section 703.

(a) It shall be an unlawful employment practice for an employer—

(1) to fail or refuse to hire or to discharge any individual, or otherwise to discriminate against any individual with respect to his compensation, terms, conditions, or privileges of employment, because of such individual's race, color, religion, sex, or national origin; or

(2) limit, segregate, or classify his employees or applicants for employment in any way which would deprive or tend to deprive any individual of employment opportunities or otherwise adversely affect his status as an employee, because of such individual's race, color, religion, sex, or national origin.

(b) It shall be an unlawful employment practice for an employment agency to fail or refuse to refer for employment, or otherwise to discriminate against, any individual because of his race, color, religion, sex, or national origin, or to classify or refer for employment any individual on the basis of his race, color, religion, sex, or national origin.

(c) It shall be an unlawful employment practice for a labor organization—

(1) to exclude or to expel from its membership, or otherwise to discriminate against, any individual because of his race, color, religion, sex, or national origin;

(2) to limit, segregate, or classify its membership or applicants for membership or to classify or fail or refuse to refer for employment any individual, in any way which would deprive or tend to deprive any individual of employment opportunities, or would limit such employment opportunities or otherwise adversely affect his status as an employee or as an applicant for employment, because of such individual's race, color, religion, sex, or national origin; or

(3) to cause or attempt to cause an employer to discriminate against an individual in violation of this section.

(d) It shall be an unlawful employment practice for any employer, labor organization, or joint labor–management committee controlling apprenticeship or other training or retraining, including on-the-job training programs to discriminate against any individual because of his race, color, religion, sex, or national origin in admission to, or employment in, any program established to provide apprenticeship or other training.

(e) Notwithstanding any other provision of this subchapter, (1) it shall not be an unlawful employment practice for an employer to hire and employ employees, for an employment agency to classify, or refer for employment any individual, for a labor organization to classify its membership or to classify or refer for employment any individual, or for an employer, labor organization, or joint labor–management committee controlling apprenticeship or other training or retraining programs to admit or employ any individual in any such program, on the basis of his religion, sex, or national origin in those certain instances where religion, sex, or national origin is a bona fide occupational qualification reasonably necessary to the normal operation of that particular business or enterprise, and (2) it shall not be an unlawful employment practice for a school, college, university, or other educational institution or institution of learning to hire and employ employees of a particular religion if such school, college, university, or other educational institution or institution of learning is, in the whole or in substantial part, owned, supported, controlled, or managed by a particular religion or by a particular religious corporation, association, or society, or if the curriculum of such school, college, university, or other educational institution or institution of learning is directed toward the propagation of a particular religion.

(f) As used in this subchapter, the phrase "unlawful employment practice" shall not be deemed to include any action or measure taken by an employer, labor organization, joint labor–management committee, or employment agency with respect to an individual who is a member of the Communist Party of the United States or of any other organization required to register as a Communist-action or Communist-front organization by final order of the Subversive Activities Control Board pursuant to the Subversive Activities Control Act of 1950.

(g) Notwithstanding any other provision of this title, it shall not be an unlawful employment practice for an employer to fail or refuse to hire and employ an individual for any position, for an employer to discharge an individual from any position, or for an employment agency to fail or refuse to refer any individual for employment in any position, or for a labor organization to fail or refuse to refer any individual for employment in any position, if—

(1) the occupancy of such position, or access to the premises in or upon which any part of the duties of such position is performed or is to be performed, is

subject to any requirement imposed in the interest of the national security of the United States under any security program in effect pursuant to or administered under any statute of the United States or any Executive order of the President; and

(2) such individual has not fulfilled or has ceased to fulfill that requirement.

(h) Notwithstanding any other provision of this subchapter, it shall not be an unlawful employment practice for an employer to apply different standards of compensation, or different terms, conditions, or privileges of employment pursuant to a bona fide seniority or merit system, or a system which measures earnings by quantity or quality of production or to employees who work in different locations, provided that such differences are not the result of an intention to discriminate because of race, color, religion, sex, or national origin; nor shall it be an unlawful employment practice for an employer to give and to act upon the results of any professionally developed ability test provided that such test, its administration or action upon the results is not designed, intended or used to discriminate because of race, color, religion, sex or national origin. It shall not be an unlawful employment practice under this subchapter for any employer to differentiate upon the basis of sex in determining the amount of the wages or compensation paid or to be paid to employees of such employer if such differentiation is authorized by the provisions of section 206 (d) of Title 29.

(i) Nothing contained in this subchapter shall apply to any business or enterprise on or near an Indian reservation with respect to any publicly announced employment practice of such business or enterprise under which a preferential treatment is given to any individual because he is an Indian living on or near a reservation.

(j) Nothing contained in this subchapter shall be interpreted to require any employer, employment agency, labor organization, or joint labor–management committee subject to this subchapter to grant preferential treatment to any individual or to any group because of the race, color, religion, sex, or national origin of such individual or group on account of an imbalance which may exist with respect to the total number of percentage of persons of any race, color, religion, sex, or national origin employed by an employer, referred or classified for employment by any employment agency or labor organization, admitted to membership or classified by any labor organization, or admitted to, or employed in, any apprenticeship or other training program, in comparison with the total number or percentage of persons of such race, color, religion, sex, or national origin in any community, State, section, or other area, or in the available work force in any community, State, section, or other area.

(k) (1) (A) An unlawful employment practice based on disparate impact is established under this title only if—

(i) a complaining party demonstrates that a respondent uses a particular employment practice that causes a disparate impact on the basis of race, color, religion, sex, or national origin and the respondent fails to demonstrate that the challenged practice is job related for the position in question and consistent with business necessity; or

(ii) the complaining party makes the demonstration described in subparagraph (C) with respect to an alternative employment practice and the respondent refuses to adopt such alternative employment practice.

(B) (i) With respect to demonstrating that a particular employment practice causes a disparate impact as described in subparagraph (A) (I), the complaining party shall demonstrate that each particular challenged employment practice causes a disparate impact, except that if the complaining party can demonstrate to the court that the elements of a respondent's decisionmaking process are not capable of separation for analysis, the decisionmaking process may be analyzed as one employment practice.

(ii) If the respondent demonstrates that a specific employment practice does not cause the disparate impact, the respondent shall not be required to demonstrate that such practice is required by business necessity.

(C) The demonstration referred to by subparagraph (A) (ii) shall be in accordance with the law as it existed on June 4, 1989, with respect to the concept of 'alternative employment practice.'

(2) A demonstration that an employment practice is required by business necessity may not be used as a defense against a claim of intentional discrimination under this title.

(3) Notwithstanding any other provision of this title, a rule barring the employment of an individual who currently and knowingly uses or possess a controlled substance, as defined in schedules I and II of section 102(6) of the Controlled Substances Act (21 U.S.C. 802(6)), other than the use or possession of a drug taken under the supervision of a licensed health care professional, or any other use or possession authorized by the Controlled Substances Act or any other provision of Federal law, shall be considered an unlawful employment practice under this title only if such rule is adopted or applied with an intent to discriminate because of race, color, religion, sex, or national origin.

(l) It shall be an unlawful employment practice for a respondent, in connection with the selection or referral of applicants or candidates for employment or promotion, to adjust the scores of, use different cutoff scores for, or otherwise alter the results of, employment related tests on the basis of race, color, religion, sex, or national origin.

(m) Except as otherwise provided in this title, an unlawful employment practice is established when the complaining party demonstrates that race, color, religion, sex, or national origin was a motivating factor for any employment practice, even though other factors also motivated the practice.

(n) (I) (A) Notwithstanding any other provision of law, and except as provided in paragraph (2), an employment practice that implements and is within the scope of a litigated or consent judgment or order that resolves a claim of employment discrimination under the Constitution or Federal civil rights laws may not be challenged under the circumstances described in subparagraph (B).

(B) A practice described in subparagraph (A) may not be challenged in a claim under the Constitution or Federal civil rights laws—

(i) by a person who, prior to the entry of the judgment or order described in subparagraph (A), had—

(I) actual notice of the proposed judgment or order sufficient to apprise such person that such judgment or order might adversely affect the interests and legal rights of such person and that an opportunity was available to present objections to such judgment or order by a future date certain;

(II) a reasonable opportunity to present objections to such judgment or order; or

(ii) by a person whose interests were adequately represented by another person who had previously challenged the judgment or order on the same legal grounds and with a similar factual situation unless there has been an intervening change in law or fact.

(2) Nothing in this subsection shall be construed to—

(A) alter the standards for intervention under rule 24 of the Federal Rules of Civil Procedure or apply to the rights of parties who have successfully intervened pursuant to such rule in the proceeding in which the parties intervened;

(B) apply to the rights of parties to the action in which a litigated or consent judgment or order was entered, or of members of a class represented or sought to be represented in such action, or of members of a group on whose behalf relief was sought in such action by the Federal Government;

(C) prevent challenges to a litigated or consent judgment or order on the ground that such judgment or order was obtained through collusion or fraud, or is transparently invalid or was entered by a court lacking subject matter jurisdiction; or

(D) authorize or permit the denial to any person of the due process of law required by the Constitution.

(3) Any action not precluded under this subsection that challenges an employment consent judgment or order described in paragraph (1) shall be brought in the court, and if possible before the judge, that entered such judgment or order. Nothing in this subsection shall preclude a transfer of such action pursuant to section 1404 of Title 28, United States Code.

OTHER UNLAWFUL EMPLOYMENT PRACTICES

Section 704.

(a) It shall be an unlawful employment practice for an employer to discriminate against any of his employees or applicants for employment, for an employment agency, or joint labor–management committee controlling apprenticeship or other training or retraining, including on-the-job training programs, to discriminate against any individual or for a labor organization to discriminate against any member thereof or applicant for membership, because he has opposed any practice made an unlawful employment practice by this subchapter, or because he has made a charge, testified, assisted, or participated in any manner in an investigation, proceeding, or hearing under this subchapter.

(b) It shall be an unlawful employment practice for an employer, labor organization, employment agency, or joint labor–management committee controlling apprenticeship or other training or retraining, including on-the-job training programs, to print or publish or cause to be printed or published any notice or advertisement relating to employment by such an employer or membership in or any classification or referral for employment by such a labor organization, or relating to any classification or referral for employment by such an employment agency, or relating to admission to, or employment in, any program established to provide apprenticeship or other training by such a joint labor–management committee, indicating any preference, limitation, specification, or discrimination, based on race, color, religion, sex, or national origin, except that such a notice or advertisement may indicate a preference, limitation, specification, or discrimination based on religion, sex, or national origin when religion, sex, or national origin is a bona fide occupational qualification for employment.

APPENDIX H
TEXT OF THE NATIONAL LABOR RELATIONS ACT (EXCERPTS)

RIGHTS OF EMPLOYEES

Sec. 7. Employees shall have the right to self-organization, to form, join, or assist labor organizations, to bargain collectively through representatives of their own choosing, and to engage in other concerted activities for the purpose of collective bargaining or other mutual aid or protection, and shall also have the right to refrain from any or all such activities except to the extent that such right may be affected by an agreement requiring membership in a labor organization as a condition of employment as authorized in section 8(a)(3).

Sec. 8.

(a) It shall be an unfair labor practice for an employer—,

(1) to interfere with, restrain, or coerce employees in the exercise of the rights guaranteed in section 7;

(2) to dominate or interfere with the formation or administration of any labor organization or contribute financial or other support to it: Provided, That subject to rules and regulations made and published by the Board, pursuant to section 6, an employer shall not be prohibited from permitting employees to confer with him during working hours without loss of time or pay.

(3) by discrimination in regard to hire or tenure of employment or any term or condition of employment to encourage or discourage membership in any labor organization: Provided, That nothing in this Act, or in any other statute of the United States, shall preclude an employer from making an agreement with a labor organization (not established, maintained, or assisted by any action defined in section 8(a) of this Act as an unfair labor practice) to require as a condition of employment membership therein on or after the thirtieth day following the beginning of such employment or the effective date of such agreement, whichever is the later, (i) if such labor organization is the representative of the employees as provided in section 9(a), in the appropriate collective-bargaining unit covered by such agreement when made, and (ii) unless following an election held as provided in section 9(3) within one year preceding the effective date of such agreement, the Board shall have certified that at least a majority of the employees eligible to vote in such election have voted to rescind the authority of such labor organization to make such an agreement: Provided further, That no employer shall justify any discrimination against any employee for nonmembership in a labor organization (A) if he has reasonable grounds for believing that such membership was not available to the employee on the same terms and conditions generally applicable to other members, or (B) if he has reasonable grounds for believing that membership was denied or terminated for rea-

sons other than the failure of the employee to tender the periodic dues and the initiation fees uniformly required as a condition of acquiring or retaining membership;

(4) to discharge or otherwise discriminate against an employee because he has filed charges or given testimony under this Act;

(5) to refuse to bargain collectively with the representatives of his employees, subject to the provisions of section 9(a).

(b) It shall be an unfair labor practice for a labor organization or its agents—

(1) to restrain or coerce (A) employees in the exercise of the rights guaranteed in section 7: Provided, That this paragraph shall not impair the right of a labor organization to prescribe its own rules with respect to the acquisition or retention of membership therein; or (B) an employer in the selection of his representatives for the purpose of collective bargaining or the adjustment of grievances;

(2) to cause or attempt to cause an employer to discriminate against an employee in violation of subsection (A)(3) or to discriminate against an employee with respect to whom membership in such organization has been denied or terminated on some ground other than his failure to tender the periodic dues and the initiation fees uniformly required as a condition of acquiring or retaining membership;

(3) to refuse to bargain collectively with an employer, provided it is the representative of his employees subject to the provisions of section 9(a);

(i) to engage in, or to induce or encourage any individual employed by any person engaged in commerce or in an industry affecting commerce to engage in, a strike or a refusal in the course of his employment to use, manufacture, process, transport, or otherwise handle or work on any goods, articles, materials, or commodities or to perform any services; or (ii) to threaten, coerce, or restrain any person engaged in commerce or in an industry affecting commerce, where in either case an object thereof is:

(A) forcing or requiring any employer or self-employed person to join any labor or employer organization or to enter into any agreement which is prohibited by section 8(e);

(B) forcing or requiring any person to cease using, selling, handling, transporting, or otherwise dealing in the products of any other producer, processor, or manufacturer, or to cease doing business with any other person, or forcing or requiring any other employer to recognize or bargain with a labor organization as the representative of his employees unless such labor organization has been certified as the representative of such employees under the provisions of section 9: Provided, That nothing contained in this clause (B) shall be construed to make unlawful, where not otherwise unlawful, any primary strike or primary picketing;

(C) forcing or requiring any employer to recognize or bargain with a particular labor organization as the representative of his employees if another labor organization has been certified as the representative of such employees under the provisions of section 9;

(D) forcing or requiring any employer to assign particular work to employees in a particular labor organization or in a particular trade, craft, or class rather than to employees in another labor organization or in another trade, craft, or class, unless such employer is failing to conform to an order or certification of the Board determining the bargaining representative for employees performing such work:

Provided, That nothing contained in this subsection (b) shall be construed to make unlawful a refusal by any person to enter upon the premises of any employer (other than his own employer), if the employees of such employer are engaged in a strike ratified or approved by a representative of such employees whom such employer is required to recognize under this Act: Provided further, That for the purposes of this paragraph (4) only, nothing contained in such paragraph shall be construed to prohibit publicity, other than picketing, for the purpose of truthfully advising the public, including consumers and members of a labor organization, that a product or products are produced by an employer with whom the labor organization has a primary dispute and are distributed by another employer, as long as such publicity does not have an effect of inducing any individual employed by any person other than the primary employer in the course of his employment to refuse to pick up, deliver, or transport any goods, or not to perform any services, at the establishment of the employer engaged in such distribution;

(5) to require of employees covered by an agreement authorized under subsection (a)(3) the payment, as a condition precedent to becoming a member of such organization, of a fee in an amount which the Board finds excessive or discriminatory under all the circumstances. In making such a finding, the Board shall consider, among other relevant factors, the practices and customs of labor organizations in the particular industry, and the wages currently paid to the employees affected;

(6) to cause or attempt to cause an employer to pay or deliver or agree to pay or deliver any money or other thing of value, in the nature of an exaction for services which are not performed or not to be performed; and

(7) to picket or cause to be picketed, or threaten to picket or cause to be picketed, any employer where an object thereof is forcing or requiring an employer to recognize or bargain with a labor organization as the representative of his employees, or forcing or requiring the employees of an employer to accept or select such labor organization as their collective bargaining representative, unless such labor organization is currently certified as the representative of such employees:

   (A) where the employer has lawfully recognized in accordance with this Act any other labor organization and a question concerning representation may not appropriately be raised under section 9(c) of this Act,

   (B) where within the preceding twelve months a valid election under section 9(c) of this Act has been conducted, or

   (C) where such picketing has been conducted without a petition under section 9(c) being filed within a reasonable period of time not to exceed thirty days from the commencement of such picketing: Provided, That when such a petition has been filed the Board shall forthwith, without regard to the provision I section 9(c)(1) or the absence of a showing of a substantial interest on the part of the labor organization, direct an election in such unit as the Board finds to be appropriate and shall certify the results thereof: Provided further; That nothing in this subparagraph (C) shall be construed to prohibit any picketing or other publicity for the purpose of truthfully advising the public (including consumers) that an employer does not employ members of, or have a contract with, a labor organization, unless an effect of such picketing is to induce any individual employed by any other person in the course of his employment, not to pick up, deliver or transport any goods or not to perform any services.

Nothing in this paragraph (7) shall be construed to permit any act which would otherwise be an unfair labor practice under this section 8(b).

(c) The expressing of any views, argument, or opinion, or the dissemination thereof, whether in written, printed, graphic, or visual form, shall not constitute or be evidence of an unfair labor practice under any of the provisions of this Act, if such expression contains no threat of reprisal or force or promise of benefit.

(d) For the purposes of this section, to bargain collectively is the performance of the mutual obligation of the employer and the representative of the employees to meet at reasonable times and confer in good faith with respect to wages, hours, and other terms and conditions of employment, or the negotiation of an agreement or any question arising thereunder, and the execution of a written contract incorporating any agreement reached if requested by either party, but such obligation does not compel either party to agree to a proposal or require the making of a concession: Provided, That where there is in effect a collective-bargaining contract covering employees in an industry affecting commerce, the duty to bargain collectively shall also mean that no party to such contract shall terminate or modify such contract, unless the party desiring such termination or modification—

(1) serves a written notice upon the party to the contract of the proposed termination or modification sixty days prior to the expiration date thereof, or in the event such contract contains no expiration date, sixty days prior to the time it is proposed to make such termination or modification;
(2) offers to meet and confer with the other party for the purpose of negotiating a new contract or a contract containing the proposed modifications;
(3) notifies the Federal Mediation and Conciliation Service within thirty days after such notice of the existence of a dispute, and simultaneously therewith notifies any State or Territorial agency established to mediate and conciliate disputes within the State or Territory where the dispute occurred, provided no agreement has been reached by that time; and
(4) continues in full force and effect, without resorting to strike or lockout, all the terms and conditions of the existing contract for a period of sixty days after such notice is given or until the expiration date of such contract, whichever occurs later.

The duties imposed upon employers, employees, and labor organizations by paragraphs (2), (3), and (4) shall become inapplicable upon an intervening certification of the Board, under which the labor organization or individual, which is a party to the contract, has been superseded as or ceased to be the representative of the employees subject to the provisions of section 9(a), and the duties so imposed shall not be construed as requiring either party to discuss or agree to any modification of the terms and conditions contained in a contract for a fixed period, if such modification is to become effective before such terms and conditions can be reopened under the provisions of the contract. Any employee who engages in a strike within any notice period specified in this subsection, or who engages in any strike with the appropriate period specified in subsection (g) of this section, shall lose his status as an employee of the employer engaged in the particular labor dispute, for the purposes of sections 8, 9, and 10 of this Act, as amended, but such loss of status for such employee shall terminate if and when he is reemployed by such employer. Whenever the collective bargaining involves employees of a health care institution, the provisions of this section 8(d) shall be modified as follows:

(A) The notice of section 8(d)(1) shall be ninety days; the notice of section 8(d)(3) shall be sixty days; and the contract period of section 8(d)(4) shall be ninety days.

(B) Where the bargaining is for an initial agreement following certification or recognition, at least thirty days' notice of the existence of a dispute shall be given by the labor organization to the agencies set forth in section 8(d)(3).

(C) After notice is given to the Federal Mediation and Conciliation Service under either clause (A) or (B) of this sentence, the Service shall promptly communicate with the parties and use its best efforts, by mediation and conciliation, to bring them to agreement. The parties shall participate fully and promptly in such meetings as may be undertaken by the Service for the purpose of aiding in a settlement of the dispute.

(e) It shall be an unfair labor practice for any labor organization and any employer to enter into any contract or agreement, express or implied, whereby such employer ceases or refrains or agrees to cease or refrain from handling, using, selling, transporting or otherwise dealing in any of the products of any other employer, or to cease doing business with any other person, and any contract or agreement entered into heretofore or hereafter containing such an agreement shall be to such extent unenforceable and void: Provided, That nothing in this subsection (e) shall apply to an agreement between a labor organization and an employer in the construction industry relating to the contracting or subcontracting of work to be done at the site of the construction, alteration, painting, or repair of a building, structure, or other work: Provided further, That for the purposes of this subsection (e) and section 8(b)(4)(B) the terms "any employer," "any person engaged in commerce or industry affecting commerce," and "any person" when used in relation to the terms "any other producer, processor, or manufacturer," "any other employer," or "any other person" shall not include persons in the relation of a jobber, manufacturer, contractor, or subcontractor working on the goods or premises of the jobber or manufacturer or performing parts of an integrated process of production in the apparel and clothing industry: Provided further, That nothing in this Act shall prohibit the enforcement of any agreement which is within the foregoing exception.

(f) It shall not be an unfair labor practice under subsections (a) and (b) of this section for an employer engaged primarily in the building and construction industry to make an agreement covering employees engaged (or who, upon their employment, will be engaged) in the building and construction industry with a labor organization of which building and construction employees are members (not established, maintained, or assisted by any action defined in Section 8(a) of this Act as an unfair labor practice) because (1) the majority status of such labor organization has not been established under the provisions of section 9 of this Act prior to the making of such agreement, or (2) such agreement requires as a condition of employment, membership in such labor organization after the seventh day following the beginning of such employment, or the effective date of the agreement, whichever is later, or (3) such agreement requires the employer to notify such labor organization of opportunities for employment with such employer, or gives such labor organization an opportunity to refer qualified applicants for such employment, or (4) such agreement specifies minimum training or experience qualifications for employment or provides for priority in opportunities for employment based upon length of service with such employer, in the industry or in the particular geographical area: Provided, That nothing in this subsection shall set aside the final proviso to section 8(a)(3) of this Act: Provided further, That any agreement which would be invalid, but for clause (1) of this subsection, shall not be a bar to a petition filed pursuant to section 9(c) or 9(e).

(g) A labor organization before engaging in any strike, picketing, or other concerted refusal to work at any health care institution shall, not less than ten days prior to such action, notify the institution in writing and the Federal Mediation and Conciliation Service of that intention, except that in the case of bargaining for an initial agreement following certification or recognition the notice required by this subsection shall not be given the expiration of the period specified in clause (B) of the last sentence of section 8(d) of this Act. The notice shall state the date and time that such action will commence. The notice, once given, may be extended by the written agreement of both parties.

REPRESENTATIVES AND ELECTIONS

Sec. 9.

(a) Representatives designated or selected for the purposes of collective bargaining by the majority of the employees in a unit appropriate for such purposes, shall be the exclusive representatives of all the employees in such unit for the purposes of collective bargaining in respect to rates of pay, wages, hours or employment, or other conditions of employment:

Provided, That any individual employee or a group of employees shall have the right at any time to present grievances to their employer and to have such grievances adjusted, without the intervention of the bargaining representative, as long as the adjustment is not inconsistent with the terms of a collective-bargaining contract or agreement then in effect: Provided further, That the bargaining representative has been given opportunity to be present at such adjustment.

(b) The Board shall decide in each case whether, in order to assure to employees the fullest freedom in exercising the rights guaranteed by this Act, the unit appropriate for the purposes of collective bargaining shall be the employer unit, craft unit, plant unit, or subdivision thereof: Provided, That the Board shall not (1) decide that any unit is appropriate for such purposes if such unit includes both professional employees and employees who are not professional employees unless a majority of such professional employees vote for inclusion in such unit; or (2) decide that any craft unit is inappropriate for such purposes on the ground that a different unit has been established by a prior Board determination, unless a majority of the employees in the proposed craft unit votes against separate representation; or (3) decide that any unit is appropriate for such purposes if it includes, together with other employees, any individual employed as a guard to enforce against employees and other persons rules to protect property of the employer or to protect the safety of persons in the employer's premises; but no labor organization shall be certified as the representative of employees in a bargaining unit of guards if such organization admits to membership, or is affiliated directly or indirectly with an organization which admits to membership, employees other than guards.

(c)(1) Wherever a petition shall have been filed, in accordance with such regulations as may be prescribed by the Board—

(A) by an employee or group of employees or any individual or labor organization acting in their behalf alleging that a substantial number of employees (i) wish to be represented for collective bargaining and that their employer declines to recognize their representative as the representative defined in section 9(a), or (ii) assert that the individual or labor organization, which has been certified or is being recognized by their employer as the bargaining representative, is no longer a representative as defined in section 9(a); or

(B) by an employer, alleging that one or more individuals or labor organizations have presented to him a claim to be recognized as the representative defined in section 9(a):

the Board shall investigate such petition and if it has reasonable cause to believe that a question of representation affecting commerce exists shall provide for an appropriate hearing upon due notice. Such hearing may be conducted by an officer or employee of the regional office, who shall not make any recommendations with respect thereto. If the Board finds upon the record of such hearing that such a question of representation exists, it shall direct an election by secret ballot and shall certify the results thereof.

(2) In determining whether or not a question of representation affecting commerce exists, the same regulations and rules of decision shall apply irrespective of the identity of the person filing the petition or the kind of relief sought and in no case shall the Board deny a labor organization a place on the ballot by reason of an order with respect to such labor organization or its predecessor not issued in conformity with section 10(c).

(3) No election shall be directed in any bargaining unit or any subdivision within which, in the preceding twelve-month period, a valid election shall have been held. Employees engaged in an economic strike who are not entitled to reinstatement shall be eligible to vote under such regulations as the Board shall find are consistent with the purposes and provisions of this Act in any election conducted within twelve months after the commencement of the strike. In any election where none of the choices on the ballot receives a majority, a run-off shall be conducted, the ballot providing for a selection between the two choices receiving the largest and second largest number of valid votes cast in the election.

(4) Nothing in this section shall be construed to prohibit the waiving of hearings by stipulation for the purpose of a consent election in conformity with regulations and rules of the decision of the Board.

(5) In determining whether a unit is appropriate for the purposes specified in subsection (b) the extent to which the employees have organized shall not be controlling.

(d) Whenever an order of the Board made pursuant to section 10(c) is based in whole or in part upon facts certified following an investigation pursuant to subsection (c) of this section and there is a petition for the enforcement or review of such order, such certification and the record of such investigation shall be included in the transcript of the entire record required to be filed under section 10(e) or 10(f), and thereupon the decree of the court enforcing, modifying, or setting aside in whole or in part the order of the Board shall be made and entered upon the pleadings, testimony, and proceedings set forth in such transcript.

(e) (1) Upon the filing with the Board, by 30 per centum or more of the employees in a bargaining unit covered by an agreement between their employer and a labor organization made pursuant to section 8(a)(3), of a petition alleging they desire that such authority be rescinded, the Board shall take a secret ballot of the employees in such unit and certify the results thereof to such labor organization and to the employer.

(2) No election shall be conducted pursuant to this subsection in any bargaining unit or any subdivision within which, in the preceding twelve-month period, a valid election shall have been held.

GLOSSARY

absolute privilege: Protection from liability for slander or libel given under certain circumstances regardless of the fact that the statements are false or maliciously made.

abuse of discretion: When an agency has not properly followed the APA rules or has acted in an "arbitrary or capricious" manner.

accounting: A detailed statement of all income, expenses, and assets of the partnership.

accounts receivable: A balance due a creditor from a debtor on a current account.

acid rain: Pollution caused by certain gases mixed with rain, which then becomes acidic and causes damage to plants and animals.

Act of State Doctrine: A principle of law that holds that the courts of one nation will not judge the legality of the actions of other nations' governments.

actions at law: Civil cases in which the plaintiff seeks money damages.

actions in equity: Civil cases in which the plaintiff seeks to have the court order the defendant to do something or to not do something.

actual authority: An agent's actions that are within the power given by the principal. The principal is bound to contracts made by the agent within the agent's actual authority.

actual notice: Directly telling the other party about a legal matter either in person or by a letter.

adhesion contracts: Standardized contract forms offered to consumers of goods and services on a "take-it-or-leave it" basis.

administrative law judge: An impartial government official who hears and decides administrative cases, involving federal rules and regulations.

adverse possession: One person obtains title to real property by actually "possessing" a portion of the property, for a number of years, without the permission of the owner.

affirm: When an appellate court upholds a lower court decision.

agency coupled with an interest: An unusual type of agency in which the agent has a legal interest in the property of the agency. Such an agent cannot be terminated "at will," unlike a normal agency.

agency shop agreements: Contract provisions requiring employees to pay union dues and fees.

agent: One who performs some action on behalf of another person or firm, called the principal.

aggregate: A business firm whose existence is tied in with a certain group of owners.

The American rule: Each party in a lawsuit normally pays his or her own lawyer, whether the case is won or lost.

annual percentage rate (APR): The periodic rate (the monthly effective interest rate) times the number of periods in a year.

answer: The defendant's point by point response to the complaint.

anticipatory breach: The repudiation by a promisor of the contract prior to the time that the performance is required when such repudiation is accepted by the promisee as a breach of the contract.

apparent authority: A situation where an agent acting without authority can sometimes enter contracts binding on the principal. This theory requires that some action *of the principal* leads the third party to believe that the agent has the authority he or she claims to have.

appellant: The party who appeals a case to a higher court, after a trial court decision.

appellee: The party who is defending the lower court decision in an appellate court.

arbitration: Using a neutral party to hear arguments from the two disputing parties. The arbitrator then makes a decision in the matter.

arraignment: A court hearing at which the defendant is asked to respond to the criminal charge by stating "guilty" or "not guilty."

articles of incorporation: A written document prepared by founders (incorporators) of a corporation, which sets out its name, purposes, number of authorized shares, official address, and other information.

articles of partnership: A written document containing the names of the partnership and the partners, which sets forth the agreements of the partners, including such items as the organizational structure, purposes, ownership percentages, capital contributions, sharing of profits and losses, and other agreements.

assault: A condition that occurs when one person's actions put another in fear of bodily harm.

assignment: A present transfer of property or rights.

associate: A lawyer who is a salaried member of the firm but not yet a partner.

assumption of risk: A defense to negligence that asserts that the plaintiff knowingly accepted the risks of the activity causing the injury.

attach: To create a security interest in property thereby acquiring the right to foreclose on or otherwise deal with property for payment of debt.

attorney–client privilege: An attorney may not disclose to anyone confidential statements made to him or her by the client.

automatic stay: A stay that comes into operation upon the filing of a bankruptcy petition in accordance with bankruptcy law that prevents creditors from attempting to collect from the debtor for debts incurred before the filing.

bait and switch: A fraudulent or deceptive sales practice in which a purchaser is attracted by advertisement of a low-priced item but then is encouraged to purchase a higher priced one.

balloon payment: A large payment due at the end of the contract term.

bankruptcy creditor: An individual or business that has a claim against the debtor before the bankruptcy petition is filed.

bankruptcy debtor: An individual or business that owes money to a creditor.

bar association: An organization of attorneys—may be a local, statewide, or national group.

bargaining order: NLRB order directing a party to bargain in good faith.

bargaining unit: The group of employees that is represented by a union—the basic unit of constituency for labor relations.

BAT standard: The best available technology—that is, control and treatment—that now exists or is capable of being achieved.

battery: Unauthorized touching of another's body.

beneficial owner: A person for whose benefit brokerage firms hold securities in their (the brokerage's) name.

beyond all reasonable doubt: The standard of proof in a criminal case, which requires the prosecutor to prove each essential element to the point where no member of the jury has any reasonable doubt as to its existence.

bilateral contract: A contract in which each party makes a promise to the other.

bill of lading: A shipping document that carefully describes the goods shipped and indicates the person who has the right to possession of the goods.

blue sky laws: State statutes designed to protect the public from the sale of worthless stocks and bonds.

board of directors: This group of people, elected by the shareholders, has the legal duty of managing the corporation.

bona fide occupational qualification [BFOQ]: Requirement, based on business necessity, that only employees of a specific gender, religion, or national origin will be hired.

bondholder: The person or company that holds a certificate of debt issued by a company or government and payable on a specified date.

BPT standard: Best practicable control technology currently available; the average of the best existing technology of industrial plants of various sizes.

brief: A written document containing the party's legal arguments.

broker: Buys securities from underwriter for accounts of others.

bubble policy: An EPA rule that allows a company to expand and emit more pollution from one source of the plant, if it reduces pollution from another source. The plant is said to be under an imaginary "bubble."

the business judgment rule: If the directors have made a decision after careful consideration, they will not be liable to the shareholders even if the decision has bad consequences for the company.

capital: Accumulated assets (as money) invested or available for investment.

case citation: The heading of a court case, which contains the name of the parties, the volume and page of the set of books where it can be found, the court, and year of the decision.

cease and desist order: An order issued by an administrative agency directing a person or firm to stop engaging in a particular activity.

CEQ: A three-member agency which advises the President on environmental matters.

certiorari: The request to the U.S. Supreme Court to hear a particular case.

challenge for cause: One attorney asks the judge to remove a juror from the jury because of some possible bias. The judge decides.

charging order: A court order allowing creditors of a partner to "attach" and receive the proceeds of the partner's share of a partnership.

charter: Another name for the articles of incorporation, establishing a corporation.

chattel paper: A paper that sets out the buyer's obligation to pay and the lender's security interest in the goods.

choice of law clause: A provision in a contract specifying which nation's laws will apply in case of contract disputes.

civil law: The body of law that allows one person or firm to sue a second person or firm for physical or economic damages caused by the second party.

class action: A type of lawsuit in which a few plaintiffs act to represent a much larger group, who have suffered the same type of injury.

close corporations: Corporations with a small number of shareholders, often family members.

closed-ended credit: Credit in which there is a set number of payments over a set period of time.

closed shop agreements: Contract provisions requiring the employer to hire only employees who are already union members; such agreements are illegal under labor relations law.

codicil: An amendment to an existing will.

collateral: Property used by the debtor to protect a creditor's interest in case of default.

Commerce Clause: The power given to Congress "to regulate commerce with foreign nations and among the several states." It has been interpreted to allow Congress to enact laws in any area that "affects interstate commerce."

commercial speech: A type of speech engaged in for business and commercial purposes.

common law: Legal theories that arise from precedents established by court decisions, not legislative statutes.

common stock: The most typical type of equity (stock) ownership by shareholders in a corporation.

community property: A type of property ownership for married couples recognized in nine states.

comparable worth: The concept that persons performing work of equal value should be paid equally—"equal pay for work of equal value."

comparative negligence: A defense to negligence that calls for the jury to assess ("compare") the negligence of the plaintiff and the defendant, and adjust the damages to reflect the percentage of negligence of the plaintiff.

compelled self-publication: The doctrine holding an employer liable for an employee's reporting of the reason for the employee's dismissal to a prospective employer.

compensatory damages: Actual damages.

complaint: The plaintiff's version of the events that led to the suit, and request for damages or other relief.

Comprehensive Environmental Response, Compensation, and Liability Act (CERCLA) ("Superfund") Law: A federal law that provides funding for the cleaning up of contaminated areas and imposes strict liability on "owners or operators."

concerted activity: Firms or individuals acting together, or collectively.

concurrent jurisdiction: A type of case in which either the state or federal courts would have jurisdiction.

condition precedent: A condition that must be fulfilled before performance under a contract can become due, an estate can vest, or a right can become effective.

condition subsequent: A condition whose fulfillment defeats or modifies an estate or right already in effect or vested or discharges an already existing duty under a contract.

confession of judgment: Acknowledgment by a debtor of a claim and consent that a judgment may be entered without notice or hearing for the amount of the claim when it is due and unpaid.

conflict of interest: A situation that occurs when an attorney attempts to act for both his client and for one whose interest is adverse to that of his client.

conglomerate mergers: Mergers that are neither horizontal nor vertical.

conscious parallelism: Firms acting independently, but similarly to their rivals.

consent decrees or consent orders: Settlement agreements allowing firms to cease allegedly anticompetitive conduct without admitting to a violation of the law.

consequential or special damages: Damages awarded in an amount deemed to compensate for losses that arise not as a natural result of an injury but because of some particular circumstance of the injured party.

consideration: The promise or performance that the promisor demands as the price of the promise in a contract.

constructive notice: An indirect type of notice, such as putting a notice in the newspaper.

contingent fee: When the lawyer's fee is a certain percentage of the total money obtained by the client, at trial or by settlement.

contributory negligence: A defense to negligence that asserts that the plaintiff was also negligent. If applied, this defense results in dismissal of the case.

cooling-off period: A period of time to allow further consideration, such as a period of time for consumers to reconsider and possibly change their minds.

copyright: The legal right of an author, composer, or artist to prevent others from copying or reproducing his or her work.

core proceeding: A proceeding that is integral to the administration of a bankruptcy estate and so falls under the jurisdiction of the bankruptcy court.

corporate compliance program: A program undertaken by the management of a corporation to ensure that all relevant laws are being followed.

corporate counsel or "in-house" counsel: Lawyers who work full-time, at a salary, for a corporation.

corporate opportunity rule: If a director learns of a business opportunity that the corporation might want to pursue, he or she must bring the idea to the board for consideration, before taking advantage of it personally.

counterclaim: The defendant in a civil case files a counter action, alleging that the plaintiff has caused some injury to the defendant.

countervailing duty: A tax or tariff added to certain imported goods to counteract a subsidy given to the goods by the government of the nation where they were made.

covenant not to compete: An agreement by an employee or owner of one business, promising not to open a competing business.

cover: The buyer's right to purchase substitute goods if the seller fails to deliver the correct goods.

crashworthiness: The duty of vehicle manufacturers to build cars, trucks, and motorcycles that do not enhance or worsen the injuries of persons when involved in accidents.

credit bureau: A private business that compiles information on consumers' creditworthiness and provides this information to lenders.

creditor beneficiary: A direct beneficiary whom the party paying for the other party's performance intends to benefit as payment for a debt or obligation.

criminal law: Violation of a specific statute, enacted by the legislature to protect society, which carries penalties such as a fine or imprisonment.

Critical Legal Studies Movement: The theory that laws, particularly those which represent a positivist view, are rules established by those who are currently in power.

cross-examination: Questions asked by an attorney of a witness called by the opposing side.

cumulative voting: When the shareholders are allowed to vote their shares multiplied by the number of directors to be elected. A shareholder can cast all of these votes for one person.

cure: The seller who delivers nonconforming goods to the buyer can correct the deficiency if the contract time limit has not expired.

de facto corporation: A corporation which has been properly established except for minor details, which the incorporators intend to promptly correct.

de jure corporation: A corporation which has been properly established and has met all incorporation requirements in its state of incorporation.

de minimis: Small or minimal, insignificant.

dealer: Buys securities from underwriter to resell to general public or for its own account.

debt securities: A loan made to the corporation, such as a bond, that does not carry an ownership interest.

debtor in possession: A debtor who remains in possession of an estate during bankruptcy and has the same duties as a trustee in bankruptcy.

deceptive: Tending to or having the capacity to cause to accept as true something that is false.

decertification petitions: Petitions by employees seeking to revoke a union's right to represent them.

decisions: EU legislation directed at one specific person or nation.

deed: A written document used to transfer ownership in real property.

defamation: The communication of damaging, false information about a person to at least one other person.

default judgment: The court enters judgment for the plaintiff when the defendant fails to answer the complaint.

defendant: The person against whom a civil or criminal lawsuit is brought.

defined benefit pension plan: Plan paying employees a specified amount each month upon retirement.

defined contribution pension plan: Pension plan in which employees or the employer pay a specified amount into the employee's pension account.

delegation of power: Congress transfers part of its legislative power to an administrative agency, by giving it the power to enact rules and regulations to implement a statute.

deontology: A group of ethical theories that examine the nature of the action itself, without regard to its consequences, to determine whether it is ethical.

deposition: An out-of-court procedure where the attorney for one side can ask direct questions of the opposing party.

derivative lawsuit: A lawsuit brought by one or more shareholders on behalf of a corporation, where the board of directors has refused to act.

detour: When an employee deviates slightly from the scope of employment. The employer-principal is still liable (along with the employee) for torts committed on a detour.

direct effects doctrine: European Court of Justice doctrine that provides that when an EU law or treaty provision is very clear, it becomes immediately effective as law in all EU nations.

direct examination: The series of questions asked by an attorney of a witness called by that attorney.

directed verdict: When the judge enters a verdict, after the evidence has been presented, because one side has failed to prove some essential element of the case.

directive: A type of European Union law that establishes an EU standard but allows each member to enact a law in its own nation to implement the law.

Directorates General: The 23 cabinet subdivisions of the EU Commission, each one having a particular area of responsibility.

disaffirm: A decision not to be bound to a contract.

discharge: To release from an obligation; such as to release a debtor in bankruptcy from liability for his or her debt.

disclaimer: A denial of responsibility or a limitation of a statement or impression; such as a statement in a warranty that limits or eliminates implied warranties.

disclosed principal: Where the agent clearly informs the third party whom he/she is working for.

disgorge: To give up illegally gained profits by court order to prevent unjust enrichment.

disgruntled shareholders: Those shareholders who disagree with the current management of the company.

disparagement: Defamation of a business or product.

disparate impact: The discriminatory effect of apparently neutral job requirements.

disparate treatment: Intentional discrimination based on race, color, religion, sex, or national origin.

dissent: The right of a shareholder to object to a merger and to be paid the fair market value for the shares owned.

dissolution: The termination of the existence of a corporation or partnership, such as when a partnership entity comes to an end upon the death or withdrawal of one partner.

dissolution orders: Court orders requiring a monopolist firm to split up into several firms.

diversity jurisdiction: Federal jurisdiction based on the fact that the parties live in different states, and the case involves $75,000 or more.

divestiture orders: Court orders requiring firms to separate—to "undo" the merger.

donee beneficiary: A direct beneficiary whom the party paying for the other party's performance intends to benefit as a gift or donation.

The Due Process Clause: The constitutional provision that requires some type of fair hearing (process) before the government can take away anyone's life, liberty, or property.

dumping: The sale of a product in a foreign country for a lower price than that charged in the home country, or below the cost of production.

duress: The threat of physical intimidation or coercion aimed at forcing individuals to enter into contracts against their will.

easement: A legal right to use a portion of real property owned by someone else for a specific purpose.

effluent: Liquid substances discharged into waterways.

eligible employees: Under the FMLA, employees who have been employed for at least 12 months and who worked at least 1,250 hours during the past year.

eminent domain: The power of government to take title to private property for a "public use," upon payment of just (fair) compensation.

emission allowances: The amount of reduction in emissions of a polluting substance, which results in a "credit" granted by the EPA.

employee or servant: An agent whose actions are under the control of the principal/employer. The employee is usually paid by the hour or week, uses the tools of the employer, is directly supervised by the employer, and may work for several different principals at the same time.

enabling law: A statute passed by Congress or a state legislature, which creates an administrative agency, or which gives specific powers to an agency.

Endangered Species Act: A federal law enacted to protect plant and animal species from extinction.

entity: A business firm whose existence is separate from its owners.

enumerated powers: Those powers specifically given to the federal government in the Constitution.

Environmental Impact Statement (EIS): A thorough study of the environmental effects that may be caused by a proposed federal project or license, along with alternatives that were considered.

equity: The ownership interests of shareholders in a company.

equity securities: Shares of stock representing ownership interests in a corporation.

The Establishment Clause: The part of the First Amendment that prohibits the government from promoting or "establishing" any religion.

EU Court of Justice (ECJ): The highest court in the European Union, which makes final decisions concerning EU laws and regulations.

European Council: A meeting, held every six months, attended by the head of state of each EU nation.

ex parte: A court proceeding in which only the party asking for the court action is present.

exchange: Any organization, association, or group of persons that constitutes, maintains, or provides a marketplace for facilities for bringing together purchasers and sellers of securities.

exclusionary rule: A court-made rule that prohibits evidence which was illegally seized from being used in court by the prosecutor.

exclusive dealing arrangement: Agreement prohibiting a firm from dealing with other suppliers of a particular product.

execution sale: A sale carried out to execute a judgment under authority of a judicial officer.

executive branch agencies: Federal agencies which are part of the executive branch of the government, under the control of the President.

executor: The person named in the will to carry out the decedent's requests and pay bills and expenses.

exhaustion of administrative remedies: A person must use all possible methods of appeal within an administrative agency before a court will hear the case.

Export Administration Act of 1979: A U.S. law that allows the government to prohibit exports of certain goods from the U.S.

express warranty: A warranty that is expressed in written or verbal form, or by use of a sample or model.

"fair use" doctrine: A legal principle, an exception to a copyright owner's exclusive rights, that allows another to make some limited ("fair") use of the copyrighted work without permission.

featherbedding: The union practice that requires an employer to pay for work that is not actually performed.

Federal Privacy Act: A federal law designed to keep certain information held by agencies private.

federal question jurisdiction: Federal jurisdiction based on the fact that the case involves an issue of federal law.

federalism: The sharing of power between the federal and state governments.

fee simple absolute: The most complete ownership of real property.

fee simple determinable: A fee simple ownership that may be lost if the property is used in certain ways.

fellow-servant rule: A common law defense of the employer that barred an employee from suing an employer for injuries caused by a fellow employee.

feminist jurisprudence: The theory that law has been dominated by males and needs to adjust to more accurately include female views and experiences.

fiduciary: A person in a financial relationship that creates a duty to exercise a high degree of care and an obligation to avoid conflicts of interest; persons with control of financial assets owned by others are under a fiduciary duty to act in the interests of the owners of the assets.

fiduciary duty: The duty owed by the agent to the principal, which includes trust, honesty, loyalty, obedience, and full disclosure of relevant facts.

Fifth Amendment: The Amendment to the Constitution that provides that no person will be compelled to be a witness against him- or herself; that no person shall be deprived of life, liberty, or property without due process of law; and that property will not be taken for public use without just compensation.

finance charge: Amount of money added to a loan payment when payment is late.

firm offer: An offer that cannot be revoked, withdrawn, or amended for the time stated.

fitness for a particular purpose: The implied warranty given when the buyer needs the item for some particular (not regular) purpose and relies on the seller to furnish such an item.

foreclosure: The process by which the holder of the mortgage exercises the legal right to force the sale of the property.

formal rulemaking: An agency develops and issues regulations after holding at least one public hearing.

forum non conveniens: A legal principle that attempts to determine the nation in which the trial would be "most convenient" or appropriate.

four-fifths rule: A method of showing that an employment practice has a disparate impact.

Fourth Amendment: The Amendment to the U.S. Constitution that guarantees people the right to be secure in their homes and property against unreasonable searches and seizures and provides that no warrants shall issue except upon probable cause.

The Free Exercise Clause: The part of the First Amendment which prohibits the government from interfering with a person's right to "exercise" his/her religion.

Free Trade Area of America (FTAA): A proposed free trade area that would include all 34 democratic nations of South, Central, and North America.

Freedom of Information Act: A federal law allowing members of the public access to information filed with administrative agencies, with some exceptions.

freehold estate: An ownership interest lasting at least for one's life.

frolic: When an employee deviates significantly from the scope of employment.

future interest: A legal right in real property, which will or may become full ownership in the future.

garnishment: An order from a court to an employer or other party who owes money to a defendant in a case who has not paid a judgment. The order tells the employer to pay part of the wages owed to the court.

general agent: An agent who has authority to do a wide range of actions for the principal.

general duty clause: The OSHA provision that requires employers to provide a safe workplace for employees.

general partner: The managing partner in a limited partnership who has unlimited personal liability.

generic term: A word or phrase that is synonymous with a whole class of products and cannot receive trademark protection.

geographic market: The area of the country in which a firm exercises market power.

golden parachute: The nickname for a generous severance package provided to a corporate executive terminated in a takeover.

grievance procedure: Process set out in a collective agreement for resolving disputes under the agreement.

harmonization: The process of making the laws of the 15 EU nations more similar to one another.

hazardous waste: Solid waste that poses a substantial hazard to human health.

hiring halls: Arrangements where a union refers employees to an employer.

historical jurisprudence: The theory that law is produced and shaped by important historical facts and developments.

horizontal mergers: Mergers among firms that compete with each other.

hostile environment: Sexual harassment that has the effect of creating a hostile or offensive work environment.

hostile takeover: A takeover in which an outside investor attempts to purchase all or a majority of stock in a company against the wishes of corporate management.

hot cargo clauses: Contract provisions that would purport to allow unions to engage in secondary picketing; they are illegal under the NLRA.

hourly fee: Where the lawyer charges the client a specified rate for each hour spent on the client's legal matters.

illegal bargaining subjects: Matters that would violate the NLRA or other laws; any attempt to bargain over such matters is a violation of the duty to bargain in good faith under the NLRA.

illegal lottery versus sweepstakes: An illegal lottery has three elements: a prize, chance, and consideration. If one of these is missing, it is a sweepstakes.

implied covenant of good faith and fair dealing: Obligation, implied by law, that the employer cannot terminate an employee in bad faith.

implied in law contract: A contract expressed by conduct or implied or deduced from the facts.

implied powers: Laws and actions taken by the federal government that are "necessary and proper" to carry out enumerated powers.

incidental beneficiary: A third-party beneficiary to a contract whom the parties to the contract did not intend to benefit.

incidental damages: Damages recoverable under section 2-715 of the Uniform Commercial Code in breach of contract cases for losses that include expenses incurred in handling and caring for goods which were the subject of the contract, reasonable expenses incurred in obtaining cover, and any other reasonable expenses resulting from the breach that do not fall into any other category.

independent contractor: A type of special agent, hired to do one type of job for the principal. The independent contractor usually is paid by the job, uses his or her own equipment, and often operates his or her own business.

Independent Regulatory Commissions: Agencies established by Congress, which act independently of Congress and the President, to some degree.

informal rulemaking: An agency develops a proposed federal regulation and then publishes it in the *Federal Register,* so interested persons may offer comments before the regulation is final.

infringement: Unauthorized use of copyrighted or patented material.

injunctions: An equitable order from a court directing persons either to refrain from, or perform a certain activity.

innocent landowner: One who carefully researches the history of a property prior to purchase and has no knowledge of any improper disposal of hazardous wastes.

inside directors: Members of the board of directors who are also officers and/or employees of the corporation.

integrated: The contract contains all of each party's understanding.

intellectual property: The legal rights covering such topics as patents, copyrights, trademarks, and trade secrets.

interbrand competition: Competition among all the dealers of a product—such as competition among all the coffee shops.

interest arbitration: Arbitration used to determine rates of pay and other terms of a collective agreement.

interference with contracts: One person intentionally interferes with a contract between two other people (or businesses).

interrogatories: A set of written questions sent by one side to the opposing party.

intestate: When a person dies without leaving a will, the property is distributed according to state law.

intrabrand competition: Competition among the dealers of a particular brand of a product—such as all the Starbucks Coffee Shops.

inverse condemnation: When a significant portion of the value of one's private property is "taken" by government-imposed restrictions.

issuer: Controlling person, individual, or business offering to sell its own securities.

joint and several liability: When two or more defendants are found liable, the plaintiff can collect the entire award from any one defendant.

joint tenancy: Ownership of property by two or more persons. When one dies, his or her share is automatically distributed to the co-owners who survive. Joint tenants cannot leave their share to their heirs. Shares must be equal.

Judgment N.O.V.: The judge enters a judgment different from the jury verdict.

judicial review: The power of the judicial branch to review the actions of the executive and legislative branches to determine if their actions are Constitutional.

jurisdiction: The power of a particular court to hear and decide a case.

jurisprudence: The philosophy of the law.

jury instructions: The judge gives the jury instructions on legal issues they must decide and rules they should apply to the case before them.

law and economics movement: The theory that law is the set of rules which express the choices of people in a free market system.

legal entity: A corporation has an existence separate from, and independent of, any individual shareholder or director.

legal realists: Those who hold that law is simply the body of rules enforced by the courts and society.

letter of credit: A promise or guarantee of payment by a bank.

libel: Written defamation.

life estate: A type of ownership that lasts only for the life of the owner and cannot be extended.

limited liability: When investors, such as limited partners, only risk losing their investment in the business, not their personal assets.

limited liability company: A type of unincorporated business entity which provides limited liability to the owners.

limited liability partnership: A relatively new form of business entity, which permits the partners to take an active role in management, while protecting them from personal liability.

limited partner: The partner in a limited partnership who does not have any personal liability for partnership debts.

liquidated damages: Damages whose amount is agreed upon by the parties to a contract as adequately compensating for loss in the event of a breach.

liquidated debt: A debt not in dispute.

long-arm statute: A law giving the courts of one state jurisdiction over a non-resident defendant.

look and feel cases: Where someone has created a computer program or user interface that "looks" and acts ("feels") like another copyrighted program, but the second author did not copy the actual code of the first program.

Maastricht Treaty: An important EU treaty signed in 1991 which brought the EU closer to social, economic, and political union.

Magnuson-Moss Warranty Act: A federal law that requires certain disclosures and provides certain rights to consumers, where written warranties are provided.

mailbox rule: Making an offer or acceptance valid when it is deposited in the mail.

mandatory bargaining subjects: Matters relating to wages, hours, terms, and conditions of employment of the members of the bargaining unit, and over which the parties are required to bargain by the NLRA.

manifest system: A series of documents designed to track hazardous waste.

mediation: Use of a neutral party to help the two sides reach an agreement.

merchant: Person who deals with goods of the kind sold in his or her business.

merchantability: The implied warranty given to a purchaser by a merchant—that the item is fit for its ordinary use.

Mercosur: The "Common Market of the South" is an organization aimed at reducing trade barriers and tariffs. Members are Brazil, Argentina, Paraguay, and Uruguay.

merger clause: A clause in a contract stating that the contract is a complete statement of the agreement and supersedes any prior terms, representations, or agreements whether made orally or in writing.

minitrial: An out-of-court hearing before a neutral advisor, attended by key officers of each side.

minor: An individual under the legal age to contract.

The Miranda rule: The rule, issued in a famous Supreme Court case, that police officers must tell a suspect in custody, of his or her right to remain silent.

mirror image rule: A rule that states that in order for an acceptance to exist, the response must be a mirror image of the offer and cannot add new terms.

misappropriation: The wrongful taking of a non-public business secret or asset from one firm and its use by another firm.

misleading: Possessing the capacity or tendency to create a mistaken impression.

misuse: When someone uses a product in a way that the manufacturer could not have reasonably foreseen.

Model Business Corporation Act (MBCA): A model state law dealing with corporations, drafted by an organization of business lawyers, which has been enacted by many states.

monopoly: A single firm that is the sole supplier of a product; a firm that has power over price and output.

mortgage: An agreement to give a lender a legal right in real property owned by another person.

most favored nation (MFN): The term used to describe the rule that if one nation gives a good tariff rate to certain goods from one WTO member, it must give the same rate to all WTO members.

motion to dismiss: A request by the defendant that the case be dismissed because no valid legal claim has been made.

National Ambient Air Quality Standards (NAAQS): Maximum allowable amounts of seven types of pollutants.

National Pollutant Discharge Elimination System (NPDES): The system by which those who discharge (from a point source) effluent into streams or lakes are to obtain a state or federal permit.

national treatment: The GATT/WTO principle that once goods are legally imported into a nation, they must be treated the same as goods produced in that nation.

natural law: The theory that law is the basic system of moral principles developed through the power of reasoning, analysis, religion, and philosophy.

negative option plan: A plan where the seller periodically sends the buyer announcements that describe a current selection or new offering. If the buyer wants the selection it will be shipped automatically. If the buyer does not want the selection then a card rejecting the selection needs to be sent to the seller by a certain date.

negligence: The most common type of tort, involving an injury to a person caused by another person's failure to act with reasonable care.

negligence per se: A category of negligence in which the defendant has violated a statute intended to protect the public from such conduct.

nominal damages: Very small damages ("in name only") to a winning plaintiff.

nonfreehold estate: A legal right to possession, but not ownership, of real property, such as a lease.

nonprofit corporations: Corporations formed under another state law, which are not established to earn a profit, but rather to provide a service. There are no shareholders and no dividends.

nontariff barriers: Laws and regulations of one nation that tend to restrict the free flow of products into that country from other nations.

North American Free Trade Agreement (NAFTA): An agreement between Canada, Mexico, and the United States that will eliminate tariffs on goods traded between the three nations over a 15-year period.

no-strike clause: A contract provision by which the parties agree not to engage in a strike or lockout during the term of the collective agreement.

nuisance: A common law theory that allows one owner a right to sue a neighbor if that person's use of his or her land interferes with the first owner's use and enjoyment of his or her property.

oligopoly: Industry dominated by a few large firms.

open-ended credit: Credit you can use again and again until a certain prearranged borrowing limit is reached.

opening statement: At the beginning of a trial, each lawyer has an opportunity to tell the jury what the case is about.

option contract: A preliminary contract in which value is given to the offeror in exchange for keeping the offer open for a specified time.

ordinance: A law enacted by a city or town council.

otherwise qualified individual with a disability: Individuals who, despite their disability, or with reasonable accommodation to their disability, are capable of performing the essential functions of a particular job.

outside directors: Members of the board who are not officers or employees of the corporation.

oversight hearings: Hearings held by a Congressional Committee to review the performance of an agency.

paralegals: Nonlawyers who work for a law firm under the supervision of a lawyer.

parol evidence: Oral testimony in court about the terms of a written contract.

partially disclosed principal: Where the agent indicates that he/she is representing a principal, but does not disclose the identity.

partnership: An association of two or more persons, as co-owners, to carry on a business for profit.

partnership interest: Each partner's percentage share of the total net assets of the partnership.

partnership property: Property owned by the partnership. No partner has exclusive rights to such property.

patent: A legal right of the creator or inventor of a product, process, or invention. The patent holder has the exclusive right to use, develop, and license the subject of the patent for 20 years.

per se rule: Judicial approach to antitrust law that holds certain conduct to be illegal regardless of its actual effect on competition.

peremptory challenge: Each side in a case is allowed to excuse a few potential jurors without giving a reason.

periodic tenancy: A tenancy lasting for a certain time.

permissive subjects: Those matters that are neither mandatory nor illegal; the parties may, but are not required to, bargain over them.

piercing the corporate veil: The normal rule that shareholders do not have personal liability for debts of the corporation may be overcome where a dominant shareholder has disregarded the corporate form and operated the firm like it was a sole proprietorship, or a mere "alter ego" of that person.

piracy: The manufacture and sale, without permission, of goods copyrighted or trademarked by another firm.

plaintiff: The person who files a civil lawsuit against another.

plea-bargain: The settlement of a criminal case, whereby the prosecutor dismisses one charge if the defendant pleads guilty to another charge.

point source: An identifiable point where liquid waste is discharged.

poison pill plan: A defensive tactic used by a company facing an unwanted takeover bid that makes the purchase of its stock very costly.

police power: The right of states to enact a wide range of laws to protect the health, safety, and welfare of their citizens.

positivism: The theory that law is the set of rules adopted by the lawful authority which governs that nation.

precedents: Judicial decisions used to establish standards for subsequent similar cases.

preemption doctrine: The doctrine or theory that when a federal law and a state law govern the same subject and are in conflict, the federal law prevails over the state law.

preemptive rights: The right of shareholders to purchase the same percentage of new shares, as they hold in existing shares.

preferred stock: A type of equity (stock) ownership which provides the owners certain preferences over common stockholders.

prejudgment garnishment: A remedial device whereby a creditor attaches the property of a debtor to pay the debt owed to the creditor before a court has issued a judgment in the creditor's favor.

preliminary hearing: A court hearing in a criminal case, at which the prosecutor must produce sufficient evidence to show that a crime has been committed and that there is good cause to believe that the defendant committed it.

preliminary ruling: When a case in a national court of an EU member involves an issue of EU law, the case can be sent to the ECJ for a ruling on the EU law question, and then the case returns to the national court.

preponderance of the evidence: Evidence which is of greater weight or more convincing than the evidence which is offered in opposition to it; the standard of proof in a civil case.

pre-trial conference: A meeting between the judge and the lawyers, prior to the trial, to discuss the issues in the case and set the date for the trial.

price discrimination: Charging different customers different prices for the same product.

prima facie case: Establishing facts sufficient to raise a presumption of discrimination.

principal: A person who hires another to act as an agent.

prior restraint: Court restrictions preventing a person from making a particular statement.

privity: When two parties have contract with each other. This concept is no longer very important in warranty cases.

procedural law: The legal rules governing court processes and procedures.

product market: All the reasonably interchangeable products that may be substituted for a particular product.

promissory estoppel: A situation in which one party's reliance on a promise prevents the promisor from denying the existence of a contract.

promoters: The people who organize and start the corporation. They may be liable for contracts they make before the corporation is incorporated.

promulgating: The correct process for developing and issuing a regulation.

prorata: In proportion to the calculated debt.

proximate cause: One of the key elements of a negligence case is that the defendant's lack of care must be the direct cause of the injury to the plaintiff, and that the injury was a "foreseeable" result of such negligence.

proxy: A written document by which one shareholder authorizes someone else (often management) to vote his or her shares at the annual meeting.

puffery or puffing: Bragging or making exaggerated comments, especially for promotional purposes, about an item; comments not specific enough to create an express warranty.

punitive damages: Damages, in excess of those required to compensate the plaintiff for the wrong done, that are imposed in order to punish the defendant because of the particularly wanton or willful character of the wrongdoing.

purchase money security interest: A security interest in the collateral specifically financed by the creditor.

pyramid sales scheme: An illegal scheme in which participants give money or other valuables in exchange for the opportunity to receive payment for recruiting others to participate in the scheme.

qualified privilege: Protection from liability for otherwise defamatory statements, where the statements are made without actual malice and with a legitimate reason for disclosure, such as an employee providing a reference to a prospective employer.

quantum meruit: "As much as he deserved."

quasi contract: An obligation that is not created by a contract but is imposed by law to prevent unjust enrichment of one party from the acts of another party.

quid pro quo: Sexual harassment where job status or benefits are conditioned on submission to requests for sexual favors.

quitclaim deed: A deed that merely conveys what ownership the grantor has without any warranties.

race-norming: The practice of setting different passing scores for different races or other protected groups; race-norming is prohibited by Title VII.

Racketeer Influenced and Corrupt Organization Act (RICO): A federal law allowing a prosecutor to charge a business firm with racketeering if the firm has engaged in two or more prohibited acts within a 10-year period. The law contains very serious penalties and can also be used in civil suits.

ratification: When a principal who would not be bound to a contract made by an agent (beyond authority) nevertheless accepts the benefits of the contract, then the principal may be bound to honor it.

ratify: To adopt the act even if it was not approved beforehand; to agree to be bound to a contract.

recording: Filing a deed or mortgage in a public records office to give notice to others of the legal interests in the real property.

redemption period: A period of time during which a foreclosed owner can re-acquire the property.

regulations: A type of EU law that is directly effective in all member nations, as though it were a national law.

rejection: The buyer inspects the goods and says, "These are not the correct items."

remand: The appellate court sends the case back to the lower court for more hearings or a new trial.

remedy: Money or performance awarded by a court.

"rent-a-judge" process: The parties employ a retired judge to hear the dispute in private.

reorganization: The rehabilitation of the finances of a business according to a plan approved by a bankruptcy court.

repossess: To take possession of property by judicial process or self-help when a debtor defaults on a debt.

representation questions: Cases dealing with employees seeking to join unions or unions seeking to represent employees.

res ipsa loquitur: A situation in which the injury-causing incident could not have happened without negligence, and the defendant was in control of the event or premises where the accident occurred.

rescind: To take back and make void.

rescission: A court order cancelling a contract.

resell: If the buyer wrongfully refuses to accept the goods, the seller can sell the goods and then sue the buyer for any loss.

Resource Conservation and Recovery Act (RCRA): A federal law requiring that certain hazardous wastes be documented and tracked from the time they come into existence until proper disposal.

respondeat superior: The legal theory that holds that an employer/principal can be held liable for torts committed by employees within the scope of employment.

Restatement of Contracts: One of several volumes produced by American Law Institute and authored by legal scholars that sets forth statements on the law of contracts. It is widely referred to but not binding.

restrictive covenant: A restriction on the use of real property, contained in a deed. Such covenants are common in subdivision developments.

retainer: An advance payment to secure the services of a lawyer.

reverse: The appellate court changes the ruling of the lower court.

revocation: Withdrawing an offer before it is accepted or mutual agreement to cancel contract.

right to refuse: Right granted to employees by OSHA to refuse to work in a dangerous situation.

right to work laws: State laws that prohibit union security agreements.

rights arbitration: Arbitration used to resolve disputes over the rights and duties of the parties to a collective agreement.

ripeness: A court will not hear a case challenging an agency action until the action or decision is "final."

rule of reason: Judicial approach to antitrust law that holds certain conduct illegal only if it unreasonably restricts competition.

S corporation: A type of corporation in which the shareholders have limited liability.

secondary picketing: Picketing directed against an employer that is not a party to the labor dispute.

Section 201: A U.S. law which allows the temporary imposition of quotas or tariffs on certain imports, where a U.S. producer is seriously harmed.

Section 337: A U.S. law which permits sanctions against imports, where unfair trade acts are shown.

secured party: A party holding a security interest in another's property.

secured transactions: A credit sale of goods or a secured loan that provides special protection for the creditor in the form of acquiring some legal rights in the goods or property.

securities: Term applied to a wide variety of investment vehicles.

security interest: The legal interest in property owned by another that allows a creditor to repossess and resell collateral and to apply the proceeds to pay off the owner's loan.

selective incorporation: Although the Bill of Rights technically applies only to the federal government, many of the important protections have been "selectively" applied to state actions by court decisions.

separation of powers: The division of federal power into three separate branches of the government.

service of process: Delivery of the complaint and summons to the defendant.

set fee: When a lawyer charges a fixed fee for a specific service.

short swing profits: Profits made by an insider through sale or disposition of the corporate stock within six months after purchase.

Single European Act (SEA): An EU treaty that led to the removal of many trade barriers.

slander: Oral or verbal defamation.

sociological jurisprudence: The theory that law is the product of social forces and social movements involving different segments of the population.

sole proprietorship: A business owned by one person, who has full control and full responsibility.

sovereignty: Each nation's right to decide and determine issues within its borders without interference or control from other nations.

special agent: An agent who is hired to do only one task for the principal.

specific performance: A remedy in equity, by which a court orders someone to perform fully their contractual obligations; for example, a court may direct a seller to perform the contract as agreed to with the buyer.

specific standards: Regulations setting particular limits for exposing employees to workplace hazards or toxic substances.

stakeholder: Groups or individuals who can affect or are affected by the actions of a business.

standard of due care: Board members owe to the shareholders the duty to act with care and to diligently carry out their responsibilities in a non-negligent manner.

standing: The requirement that one or more of the plaintiffs in a case show that they have actually suffered some direct effect or loss due to the defendant's actions.

stare decisis: The legal principle that decisions of a higher court in previous cases establishing legal theories must be followed by lower courts in that jurisdiction.

state action: The requirement that there be some action by the government in order to invoke the protections of, or rights guaranteed by, the constitution.

state action doctrine: An exemption from the antitrust laws when government regulation requires the conduct in question.

state of the art defense: A defense to liability recognized in some states, if the product was made using the best methods then available.

state corporation law: Corporations are formed by following the law of the state where they choose to be incorporated.

State Implementation Plan (SIP): Each state may develop its own plan for meeting the federal standards.

statute: A law enacted by the U.S. Congress or by a state legislature.

Statute of Frauds: A state law modeled on the English Statute of Frauds dealing with the enforcement and requirements of agreements in particular circumstances.

statute of limitations: A law that specifies how many years after an event a person has in which to bring a lawsuit.

statute of repose: An outer limit on how many years after a product was manufactured that the maker could be held liable for a defect.

statutory interpretation: The power of courts to interpret laws enacted by legislatures.

strict liability: Liability without proof of negligence or fault.

strict scrutiny test: A judicial test requiring that the government show that its action is required by a compelling government purpose or interest, and is narrowly tailored to achieve that interest or purpose.

strict product liability: A legal theory that allows a person injured by a defective product to win a lawsuit against the manufacturer without proving "fault" or lack of due care.

substantial evidence rule: A rule followed by courts in reviewing agency decisions. The court will follow the factual findings made by the ALJ and agency as long as there is "substantial evidence" to support the findings.

substantive law: The legal principles that define one's rights in specific subject areas.

summary judgment: The court enters a judgment in favor of one side, without a trial, when there are no "fact issues" in dispute, only legal questions.

summons: A document issued by the court when a civil case is filed. It notifies the defendant of the suit and tells him/her when an answer must be filed.

supplementary proceeding: Court proceeding occurring after a judgment has been entered, aimed at determining the extent and whereabouts of the judgment debtor's money and property.

Supremacy Clause: The clause in the U.S. Constitution that establishes the Constitution as the final authority in the land, superior to conflicting state laws.

surrogacy: An activity in which a woman agrees to give birth to a baby of a mother unable to carry the child.

taking: When some government action deprives an owner of significant property rights without compensation.

tangible personal property: Property, other than real estate, that has a physical existence.

tariff: A tax assessed on goods as they are imported into a country.

teleology: A group of ethical theories that judge actions by their consequences.

temporary restraining order: A short-term injunction used to preserve the status quo until the court can schedule a full hearing.

tenancy in common: Ownership of property by two or more persons. Each can sell his or her share or leave to heirs. Shares do not have to be equal.

tenancy by the entireties: A type of joint tenancy for married couples.

tender offer: A public offer to purchase stock at a specified price per share; for example, an attempt by an investor to take control of a corporation by offering to buy a majority of the shares from existing shareholders.

third party: Someone with whom the agent interacts, on behalf of the principal.

third-party beneficiary: A person or entity that is not a party to but has rights under a contract made by two other parties.

tort: A wrongful action done by one person which causes damage or injury to another.

Toxic Substances Control Act (TSCA): A federal law that requires the notification to, and approval of, the EPA before chemicals can be made or imported.

trade secrets: Intellectual property assets of a business, such as a formula or a customer list, which are kept secret.

trademark: A word, phrase, or symbol that identifies and distinguishes a product.

treasury stock: Shares of stock that have been issued and sold by a corporation, and then later repurchased by the corporation.

Treaty of Rome: An important agreement among six nations in 1957 that created the European Economic Community (EEC), which has grown into the European Union.

trust: A legal mechanism by which one person transfers ownership of property to a trustee, who holds, uses, or invests the property for the benefit of another person (the beneficiary).

trustee: One trusted to administer something.

tying arrangement: Vertical restriction that conditions the sale of one product upon the sale of a different product.

ultrahazardous activity: One which is inherently dangerous.

unconscionable contract: A contract so unfair that no reasonable person would enter into it.

underwriter: Purchases or participates in original offering of securities.

undisclosed principal: A type of agency in which neither the existence nor the identity of the agent is disclosed to the third party.

undue influence: A situation in which a dominant person, or a person in a position of trust and confidence, takes advantage of another person.

unenforceable contract: A contract for which the law gives no court remedy.

unfair labor practices: Actions that violate the rights granted under the labor relations legislation.

uniform commercial code (UCC): A model law dealing with the sale of goods, adopted by 49 states, that specifies contract rights and remedies of buyers and sellers (and other issues).

Uniform Consumer Credit Code: Uniform law adopted by states governing the amount of interest and charges that can be assessed on consumer loans.

uniform limited partnership act (ULPA): A model statute setting forth principles governing limited partnerships, which has been adopted by many states.

unilateral contract: A contract in which one party makes a promise offering some benefit if another party performs a specified act (rather than making a return promise).

union security agreements: Contract provisions that require an employee to join, or at least pay dues to, a union.

union shop agreements: Contract provisions that require employees to join a union after completing a probationary period.

universal: Applicable to everyone.

unjust enrichment: A benefit received by chance, mistake or at someone else's expense.

unliquidated debt: A debt that is disputed.

usury laws: Laws regulating interest rates.

utilitarianism: The theory that an act is good which produces the greatest good for the greatest number of people.

variance: Permission from a zoning board to use land in a way not allowed by the zoning classification.

venue: The particular court location within a specific court system, where a case should be heard.

vertical mergers: Mergers involving firms that are suppliers or customers of each other.

vertical restrictions: Restrictions imposed by a manufacturer or supplier on firms that distribute the product.

vesting: Becoming entitled to a nonforfeitable pension upon retirement.

voidable contract: A contract in which one party has the option to disaffirm the bargain or back out.

voir dire: The process of asking questions to potential jurors, to make sure they can be fair and impartial.

voting trust: Legal device by which a few persons could control leading firms in an industry through voting rights of the firms' stock.

wage assignment: An assignment by an employee by which an amount of his or her wages are transferred to a creditor before the wages are paid to the employee.

warranty: A promise that the goods are of the quality indicated.

warranty deed: A deed that "warrants" that the buyer is receiving good, clear title to the property.

wetlands: Areas saturated or inundated by surface or groundwater.

whistle-blower: One who reveals something covert or informs authorities about some illegal or unethical business actions.

will: A document that states how a person wishes his or her property distributed after death.

The World Court: An international court located in the Netherlands, which hears legal disputes between nations.

wrongful discharge: Suit in tort or contract seeking damages for wrongfully terminating employment.

yellow dog contracts: Contracts requiring employees to agree not to join unions.

zoning: A plan developed by a city or county that regulates the uses of land in different "zones" of the city or county.

SUBJECT INDEX

CASE INDEX